INTERNATIONAL BUSINESS TRANSACTIONS:
A PROBLEM–ORIENTED COURSEBOOK

Eleventh Edition
■ ■ ■

By

Ralph H. Folsom
Professor of Law
University of San Diego

Michael Wallace Gordon
John H. and Mary Lou Dasburg Professor of Law
University of Florida

John A. Spanogle, Jr.
William Wallace Kirkpatrick Professor of Law
The George Washington University

Peter L. Fitzgerald
Professor of Law
Stetson University College of Law

Michael P. Van Alstine
Professor of Law
University of Maryland
Francis King Carey School of Law

AMERICAN CASEBOOK SERIES®

WEST®
A Thomson Reuters business

Mat #41121468

COPYRIGHT © 1987, 1989, 1991, 1995, WEST PUBLISHING CO.
© West, a Thomson business, 1999, 2002–2006
© 2009 Thomson Reuters
© 2012 Thomson Reuters
   610 Opperman Drive
   St. Paul, MN 55123
   1–800–313–9378
Printed in the United States of America

ISBN: 978–0–314–27446–5

We Dedicate This Book to:

Pixie

———————

Elsbeth Wallace and Huntly Milne Gordon

———————

Pamela

———————

Susan

———————

Lisa

PREFACE TO THE ELEVENTH EDITION

Few lawyers engaged in commercial or corporate law, even those located in the most remote corners of the United States, are likely to pass their careers without confronting one or more issues of international business. A farm client in Iowa learns that the President has imposed export controls on grain, or that the European Union has established a substantial levy on grain imports for the year because of unexpectedly high European farm production. A Texas manufacturer of tennis racquets discovers the market is flooded with a patent-infringing copy made in the Far East. A New Hampshire grocery store chain, which wants to purchase a new line of chocolates directly from Belgium, is introduced to letters of credit in the international context. A North Carolina fast food franchisor is asked by a group of Canadians for the franchise rights for Canada. The list could go on.

Of particular importance is that clients may never be directly engaged in international commerce, but nevertheless may have a serious international business problem. The tennis racquet manufacturer was satisfied with the United States market. But it now confronts the pirating of its patents and must consider whether imports of those tennis racquets may be stopped, and if any action might be taken in the foreign nation where the racquets are being illegally made. A manufacturer of dictating machines discovers the market flooded with machines from abroad at a price which must be well below cost. Was that government subsidizing the production or was the company dumping its products in the United States?

After a brief introduction to the conduct of business in the world community, the book uses 36 hypothetical problems to present what we believe are some of the most important issues in international business transactions. There is an Appendix which introduces the European Union Legal System. Except for a few areas, such as documentary sales, letters of credit, sovereign immunity, act of state, and the litigation problems, there is a modest amount of case law which is useful in discussing these issues. Extracted materials thus come from a wide variety of sources, including treaties, conventions, statutes and regulations. The hypothetical problems provide comparatively brief situations which are intended to make the purpose and relevance of the readings clear. Our choice of problems will not be agreed to by all. But we hope that it will promote a useful teaching method and, with other assigned readings, fulfill many interests.

There is a Documents Supplement prepared especially for use with the book. References are made in each problem to those parts of the Documents Supplement which are necessary to an analysis of the problem. The Documents Supplement includes the principal United States trade acts, with successive amendments integrated to earlier acts. There are also numerous other United States statutes governing exports, sovereign immunity, foreign corrupt practices, the Caribbean Basin and the enforcement of foreign judgments. International treaties, such as the Convention on Contracts for the International Sale of Goods (CISG), as well as excerpts from numerous World Trade Organization agreements are included. Several regional documents are presented, including parts of the North American Free Trade Agreement. Portions of other laws and rules are included in the text, such as parts of the IMF rules, UCC, Incoterms, UCP, Restatements, CFR and the laws of Canada, Mexico, the United Kingdom and the European Union. It is essential that students use the Documents Supplement in many of the problems.

None of us has ever completely covered all of the book in a single semester. The book provides ample material for a single broad survey course, or separate offerings such as a "Contracting Across Borders" focusing primarily upon sales, letters of credit and dispute settlement, an "International Trade and Economic Relations" course centered on governmental regulation of trade and and technology, or a "Foreign Investment" course. These three approaches also are reproduced in separate break-out volumes published by and available from West.

By design there are many other course variations that can be taught from this book. We expect some professors may wish to expand upon Part One, which is a very condensed introduction, and then allocate one class session per problem. Most of the problems could easily be extended to additional class sessions, and many have been divided into two (or more) parts which may help such allocation. This should permit faculty to omit problems which they feel are less relevant to their goals in teaching the course, and to enhance those problems which they feel are most important with other readings.

This coursebook has been used in well over 130 schools. We have received comments from faculty using prior editions suggesting ways to improve the book. Many are incorporated and we are very thankful for these comments. We hope more suggestions will be forthcoming with this edition. The Teacher's Manual will help faculty using this edition for the first time, and should assist previous users by comments in the initial paragraphs to each problem which explain changes made in each specific problem, hopefully helping in the preparation of new class notes where they are needed. Professors can obtain a looseleaf edition of this coursebook, which facilitates the transfer of teaching notes, from West Group.

This coursebook is designed to introduce law students to a wide range of problems that are sequenced in Parts: International Sales and Letters of Credit, Trade Regulation, Technology Transfers, Foreign Investment and Dispute Settlement. We explore those problems in developed, developing, nonmarket and transition economies. Our focus is on lawyers, public and private, as problem solvers. None of us was interested in undertaking this project for the sake of producing a "casebook". We believed rather that a problem-oriented approach and the sequence of our Parts would offer a different perspective for law faculty teaching in this area. Professors of international business law often have extremely diverse concepts of what the course should include. We hope that we have been sufficiently diverse to satisfy many of those views.

With this Eleventh Edition, we welcome a new co-author, Professor Michael Van Alstine of the University of Maryland School of Law. We also announce the retirement of Professors Spanogle and Fitzgerald, neither of whom participated in the preparation of this edition, but whose past contributions resonate throughout. Thank you Andy and Peter!

RALPH H. FOLSOM
rfolsom@sandiego.edu

MICHAEL W. GORDON
gordon@law.ufl.edu

JOHN A. SPANOGLE
aspanogle@law.gwu.edu

PETER L. FITZGERALD
fitz@law.stetson.edu

MICHAEL P. VAN ALSTINE
mvanalstine@law.umaryland.edu

March 2012

ACKNOWLEDGMENTS

We wish to acknowledge that in writing this book we have been aided by numerous colleagues and students. Special appreciation is due several persons who have thoughtfully commented on individual problems. They are Amy Boss of Temple University, Andrzej Burzynski of Warsaw, James Byrne of George Mason University Law School, Richard Cummins of George Washington University, E. Allan Farnsworth of Columbia University, Roger Goebel of the Fordham Law School, Ignacio Gomez-Palacio of Mexico, Trevor Hartley of the London School of Economics, Hellen Hartnell of Golden Gate Law School, John O. Honnold of the University of Pennsylvania, Elmer Leroy Hunt, Robert B. Moberly and Jeffrey Davis of the University of Florida, Herbert I. Lazerow and Michael Ramsey of the University of San Diego, Peter Lichtenbaum of Steptoe and Johnson, Osvaldo Marzorati of Buenos Aires, Robin Morse of King's College, University of London, Professor Pierre Mousseron of the Faculte de Droit, Montpellier, Robert S. Rendell of Rogers & Wells, New York City, Keith S. Rosenn of the University of Miami and Peter Winship of Southern Methodist University. We also give particular thanks to the many foreign colleagues abroad with whom we have worked over the years and who by adding to our knowledge in international business transactions have helped make this volume possible.

SUMMARY OF CONTENTS

PART 5. FOREIGN INVESTMENT

PART 6. DISPUTE SETTLEMENT

TABLE OF CONTENTS

PART 4. TRANSFERS OF TECHNOLOGY

Chapter 9. Licensing, Theft and Protection of Intellectual Property

TABLE OF CASES

The principal cases are in bold type. Cases cited or discussed in the text are in roman type. References are to pages. Cases cited in principal cases and within other quoted materials are not included.

INTERNATIONAL BUSINESS TRANSACTIONS:
A PROBLEM–ORIENTED COURSEBOOK

Eleventh Edition

PART 1

THE CONDUCT OF BUSINESS IN THE WORLD COMMUNITY

■ ■ ■

CHAPTER 1

COMMERCE OR ISOLATION: THE DECISION TO TRADE, TRANSFER TECHNOLOGY AND INVEST ABROAD

■ ■ ■

International Business Transactions is taught at most law schools in many nations. It has not been so for very long. For many years law schools offered a single course on international law issues, entitled Public International Law, or merely International Law. As international commerce increased, especially after World War II, law school courses devoted to international business followed. In some nations, including most of Europe, the division became Public International Law and Private International Law. Many of the issues taught abroad as Private International Law are what we call in the United States Conflict of Laws. But a Conflict of Laws course in a U.S. law school often ignored conflicts arising in cross border situations where the border was between nations rather than states. Slowly Conflict of Laws courses added international issues, especially when the professor teaching the basic conflicts course had a strong interest in international issues. Slowly, separate courses were developed covering various aspects of trade and investment.

As recently as the 1970s, there were few casebooks available for teaching international business. Some International Law casebooks included nominal attention to trade agreements (e.g., European Union, the GATT), and to issues arising under Friendship, Commerce and Navigation treaties. Expropriation issues in casebooks that were principally focused on *public* international law were often considered as part of state responsibility, rather than being viewed from the perspective of a foreign investor's rights, such as contract or concession breach. This casebook was introduced in 1987 as the first single volume to cover international contracts (including letters of credit), import and export issues, international intellectual property, foreign investment and international dispute settlement (plus an appendix on the European Union). Very few of the problems have remained the same over the past 25 years and 11 editions. The GATT was largely absorbed into the WTO. Services, intellectual property and foreign investment, absent in the GATT, were added in the WTO. When the first edition was published free trade agreements essentially meant the European Union. Currently, numerous FTAs exist, such as the NAFTA, the foundation for trade among Canada, Mexico and the United States. The EU is vastly different in 2011, both as to the membership composition and scope of governance, than three decades ago. The adoption of a common currency—the Euro—by most of the EU nations was a signal achievement.

While the contours of modern international business rise largely from the ashes of World War II, trading goods between the most primitive tribal groups in prehistoric times may be the earliest form of commodity exchange. Land trade by caravan over deserts and mountains evolved between diverse peoples. For 1,000 years sea based trade was the hallmark of the Phoenicians in the ancient world. Traders founded Mediterranean cities such as Carthage in north Africa and Tarshish in southern Spain. As the Roman Empire flourished so did trade and investment, through such trading cities as Alexandria. When Rome collapsed in 476, its successors in European domination were traders. The Crusades increased trade among Muslims and Christians.

Stagnation marked the millennium from the 5th to the 15th centuries—the Middle Ages. China's sent out a vast fleet, but soon retreated unto itself, rejecting overseas exploration and economic interaction. But there were exceptions, Venice in the 11th century traded with Constantinople, and other cities tried to emulate its success, including Florence and Genoa. Enhancing trade was the development of banking and accounting methods. Trade came more slowly to the feudal northern European states, but grew with the knowledge brought by returning Crusaders and stories of Marco Polo's travels to the Orient. Northern European trading centers developed in such cities as Amsterdam, Antwerp, Hamburg and London. Exploration after 1400, thanks to the development of the astrolabe and compass, enhanced trading opportunities, as did the conquest of the Ottoman Turks who had blocked trade routes. Trade became the basis of enormous wealth of nations like the Netherlands and England by the operation of their trading "companies," such as the Dutch East India Company and the Hudson's Bay Company.

England's industrial revolution made the country a world workshop and allowed it to become the strongest power. The development of new power, electricity and steam, that ran machinery and locomotives, vehicles and ships, allowed an industrialization that made Great Britain and Germany (later France) in Europe and the United States (and later Japan) great powers. In the early 20th century, the depression caused nations to contract their international business relations (the United States enacted the Smoot–Hawley act that imposed large increases on import tariffs), and such contractions further deepened the depression. Germany and Japan, in hindsight unreasonably punished after World War I, retaliated with World War II. It is with the end of that war in 1945 that we look more closely at decade-by-decade developments in international business to the beginning of the current young 21st century.

The ending of World War II brought about the formation of the United Nations. And it brought about the creation of some entities intended to assist economic development. From discussions at Breton Woods, the World Bank was established as an instrument of lending to help restore war sustained damage, and to help developing nations. The International Monetary Fund (IMF) was created to try to stabilize monetary fluctuations, providing loans to nations in debt. Finally, the import-focused General Agreement on Tariffs and Trade (GATT) was created to begin a long process of reducing tariffs and other barriers to trade. A singular failure of Bretton Woods was the attempt to create a world trade organization because the United States decided it would not be in its own best interests.

World War II left the United States the dominant economic power. Great Britain and France were war damaged, Germany and Japan even more so, compounded by the burdens of being the defeated nations. The USSR and China received considerable war damage, but were additionally isolated by preference, and the incapacity of a communist nation to compete on world markets. Through the remainder of the 1940s, and throughout the 1950s into the 1960s, the United States was the supplier of consumer and industrial products to the world. But as Japan and European nations recovered, they began to export large quantities of products to the United States. Not only small consumer goods, in the 1960s Japanese cars began to be seen on American roads in rapidly increasing numbers, and European producers restored their prior abilities to tap the huge U.S. market.

There were rumblings from some different quarters in the 1960s. Less developed nations long dominated by foreign presence asserted authority previously untested. Indonesia expropriated Dutch property; Cuba confiscated all foreign property. Expropriations tended to follow political revolutions. The USSR had slowly squeezed Eastern Europe into the Soviet sphere after the war; by 1960 there was little foreign owned property, and far less domestic owned business, in the vast dominions of the Soviets. Despite the Cold War, and the annoyances of small countries such as Cuba, the United States was the unquestioned major economic player.

The 1970s brought a new look to the world. Colonialism was quickly diminishing as independence was given or taken. The United Nations expanded rapidly by membership granted to newly independent nations. An intense debate began between the lesser developed and the developed, referred to as the North–South Dialogue. The South claimed that they were poor because the North was rich. Their frustrations were shown less by the expropriations that typified the earlier decades, than by the adoption of strict foreign investment laws mandating local ownership and control, the use of local inputs in the manufacturing process, mandatory levels of exports and the transfer of technology. Nations as disparate as India, Nigeria and Mexico enacted such laws, the consequence of which was the discouragement of new foreign investment and achievement of few of the intended goals.

As the 1970s ended with the North remaining far more affluent than the South, two decades of borrowing by many nations of the South ultimately caused severe defaults in the early 1980s. Mexico and Argentina, and many others, defaulted on their international debts. The North partially bailed out the failed nations, extracting promises by the debtor nations to look more at home to solve their problems than to blame them on the North. Mexico, which had rejected participation in the GATT, reversed its position and joined, preparing it for NAFTA.

If the 1960s witnessed expropriations and the 1970s the adoption of restrictive investment and technology laws, the 1980s debt crises brought a reversal of thinking about what causes a nation to develop. The 1990s would witness a different process. It was privatization, selling state owned industries to the private sector. When the Soviet Union collapsed and the disassembled nations were left to their own, most began some process of privatization, or de-nationalization. China as well unilaterally dismantled much of the communist economic apparatus, pursuing a "socialist market economy" while preserving a communist government, if it can currently be called communist.

Part of the privatization process, which brought to many nations familiar foreign businesses and the term McDonaldization, caused concerns that local culture would be adversely impacted. Nations remain divided whether a nation may limit or regulate foreign investment for reasons related to a perceived loss of local culture. Culture remains a contested issue, as illustrated by the Questions and Comments to follow.

The first decade after the turn of the century cannot be labeled as one of expropriation, restrictive rules or privatization. It witnessed the rise in economic strength of two of the world's largest nations—China and India. Further development of free trade areas has slowed and the idea of a Free Trade Agreement of the Americas was effectively dead. Indeed, several nations of Latin America had returned to an earlier failed policy of increased state participation in the economy and seemed well on the road to again attempt some form of socialism. Nicaragua was already in that group, but added were Venezuela, Bolivia and Ecuador. Where the world was headed during the first part of the 21st century remained unclear at the end of the first decade.

For the United States, international terrorism and unpopular wars in Iraq and Afghanistan were the main focus. Trade policy was unclear in a time of severe economic downturn and the consequent unemployment. Moving more jobs abroad was increasingly challenged and further trade agreements were stifled. At least half of the next decade—2010 to 2020—seemed likely to be focused on recovery. Many questions faced the world's nations, including how to contour the economic recovery in the United States and Europe; whether the Euro zone will survive with such members as Greece and Portugal, and perhaps even Spain and Italy; whether Russia can cure extreme corruption; whether China will act as a world leader or as a single nation asserting the economic power of the world's biggest producer; whether drug cartels can be brought under control; and other issues too numerous to mention that are explored in this course-book. One theme remains constant: The decision to trade, transfer technology and invest abroad remains critical to the future of this world.

QUESTIONS AND COMMENTS

1. Jeffrey Garten, Under–Secretary of Commerce for International Trade in the first Clinton Administration, commented on the impact of culture by exporting nations affecting the capital and goods receiving nations. See Business Week, Nov. 30, 1998, at pg. 26. Noting that superpowers have always spread their culture, whether Italian Renaissance by Lorenzo De Medici or Disney images by Michael Eisner, he stated:

> Americans should not have difficulty empathizing with foreign fears of cultural invasion. Recall U.S. anxieties a decade ago when Sony Corp. bought Columbia Pictures and Mitsubishi Corp. purchased New York's Rockefeller Center. Now reaction against American "cultural imperialism" is building. Just a few years ago, France almost torpedoed the Uruguay Round of global trade negotiations because it wanted to limit the activities of U.S. entertainment companies. Last spring, a multilateral treaty on investment rules was derailed in part because of a spat between Brussels and Washington over protection of Europe's cultural industries. In August, Canada called together 19 other governments to plot ways to ensure their cultural independence from America. Mexico is considering legislation requiring that a certain percentage of its media programming remain in the hands of its citizens.

Suggesting that the United States ought to pay some attention to these warnings, he further commented:

> The U.S. should ... recognize that strong cultures abroad are in American's self-interest. Amid the disorientation that comes with globalization, countries need cohesive national communities grounded in history and tradition. Only with these in place can they unite in the tough decisions necessary to building modern societies. If societies feel under assault, insecurities will be magnified, leading to policy paralysis, strident nationalism, and anti-Americanism.

Garten suggests the United States might allow some quotas and subsidies abroad when nations wish to protect their cultures, such as TV and film. He worries that the protection of national culture might become a defensive "rallying point" for developing nations overwhelmed by the process of globalization, and that a more sensitive approach might help U.S. exports in the long run.

This spread of U.S. culture is sometimes referred to generically as McDonaldization. How do you view the increasingly protective responses from abroad—more as trade barriers, or as a justified reaction to seriously threatened culture? Garten's comments address the issue of the impact of a nation's culture abroad. In the next chapter we will see the issue of culture return, but this time addressing how we need to understand foreign culture (which may not be the same as respecting it) in order to successfully engage in international business.

CHAPTER 2

THE ACTORS: THE NATIONS AND INSTITUTIONS OF INTERNATIONAL BUSINESS

■ ■ ■

SECTION 2.1 WHO ARE THE FOREIGN TRADERS?

International business affects almost every person. The consumer purchasing a Japanese camera or a German automobile constitutes the last of a series of links in a foreign trading relationship. But their roles were indirect, they undoubtedly bought the camera or car from a U.S. retailer. The *individual* was not directly engaging in international trade. The Japanese or German seller of the camera or the car may have been, although it is quite possible that they also were indirect links, selling first to a distributor who exported the camera or car. At some point, however, an entity in the United States ordered these goods from abroad. Or the foreign manufacturers may have established subsidiaries in the United States to undertake the distribution. In that case, the purchasers from the distributors were dealing with a foreign direct investment, an equity investment in the U.S. by foreign capital. It is likely that international banking concerns provided the financing and issued letters of credit. International shipping companies transported the goods across the oceans. Insurance companies protected the parties from loss while the goods were in transit on the ocean crossing. Numerous international trade actors played a role in the movement of the camera and automobile from their place of manufacture in Japan and Germany to the ultimate purchaser in Missouri or Indiana.

The trading of goods across borders may be done by individuals, or by very large institutions, or many variations in between. A New York lawyer orders an old print for his office from an English antique dealer in London. The oboist in the Cleveland Symphony Orchestra sends for special cane from France to carve reeds. An orchid hobbyist sends for new hybrids from a dealer in Thailand. Each of these trades involves characteristics which differ from similar purchases completed entirely within the United States. Each of the orders has been placed in a country with a

7

different currency. Should one send dollars? The lawyer in New York may have little difficulty in obtaining English pounds to buy the print, but the orchid hobbyist in Baton Rouge may find it hard to locate Thai bahts. The problem may be solved if the dealer accepts, or indeed requests, dollars. The Thai government may welcome them, it may be short of hard currency. The English antiques dealer selling the print will want UK Sterling, and may state the price in that currency placing the obligation on the New York lawyer to undertake the currency exchange.

These have been individual purchases, but they have involved international trade. The purchasers of those same items in the United States could well be commercial dealers. They may be a New York gallery that sells foreign prints, a Cleveland musical instrument company which imports reeds, or a Baton Rouge commercial orchid grower which imports these exotic flowers from many nations of the tropic zone. These dealers may be individuals or partnerships or incorporated business organizations. They are our smaller traders. Most of our very largest corporations engage in extensive international trade. Their foreign trade and investment activities are usually sufficiently extensive to give them the label "multinational" or "transnational" corporations.

A multinational corporation is not easily defined. Is it a corporation chartered in one nation which has branches or affiliates or subsidiaries in many other nations? No one would deny that IBM is a multinational corporation. But what about the company with extensive activities in the United States and one small subsidiary across the border in Canada? We might have no hesitation in calling it a multinational were it to have more extensive activities in Canada, but we seem reluctant to do so where its interests abroad are extremely modest. Defining multinationals by considering how widely spread are the activities of their business in other areas of the world is only one method. We may prefer to use some other criterion. What about the company located in the United States which has no ownership interests in any enterprises abroad, but which sells 80 percent of its products outside of the United States through foreign distributors? The tendency is not to call the company a multinational, however, but to label it a domestic company engaged extensively in foreign trade. Still another way of labeling companies as multinationals is by the nationality of ownership of the shares of the company. Is a Delaware chartered enterprise with all of its production and sales facilities located in Pennsylvania a multinational if ten percent of its stock is owned by a German corporation? What if 51 percent of the stock is owned by the German entity, thus making the Delaware corporation a majority owned subsidiary of the German enterprise? Or what if 80 percent of the stock of the enterprise is owned by individuals scattered widely throughout the world, but the company is effectively controlled by a self perpetuating board of directors in the United States? How should we define these often illusive corporate creatures? The answers have more than academic appeal. They may be important when attempting to identify the nationality of a corporation for purposes of jurisdiction or appropriate forum.

We have noted above how goods frequently cross borders, and how enterprises may have foreign linkages. People also cross borders while engaged in international business. A company may wish to send workers abroad to a subsidiary. Will they be allowed into the country to work? Will they be allowed in at all? Once there, will they be treated the same as local employees for purposes of pay? Will they be subject solely to the labor laws of the host nation? Is a female employee of an American multinational's subsidiary located in a developing nation able to benefit from anti-sex discrimination laws of the United States? Persons moving across borders introduce new issues not present in the domestic setting.

Nations *as nations* also participate in trading and investment activities. Governments order goods from abroad. The German military buys new tanks from England. The Brazilian government purchases Japanese turbines for a hydroelectric project. Governments *sell* products as well. The United States acquires surplus dairy products from its farmers and sells them to Egypt and Jamaica. Paraguay sells hydroelectric power to its neighbor Brazil. Governments not only trade goods and services; they also participate in owning equity in multinational enterprises. The Mexican government becomes a part owner of an automobile company with Peugeot of France. The Omani government wholly owns an airline serving domestic and foreign centers.

The extent of government ownership of the nation's total means of production and distribution varies from comparatively little such ownership, as in the case of Australia or the United States, to virtually total such ownership in some of the few remaining nonmarket economies, such as North Korea. In between, most nations have some degree of a mixed economy, with direct government participation in ownership of the means of production and distribution in different industries. The recent pattern of privatization of state industries has diminished state ownership. The extent to which a government participates in such ownership is an important characteristic for foreign actors dealing with such enterprises. If the government is the owner of a commercial activity will it be able to hide behind a defense of sovereign immunity? If a U.S. company engages in a joint venture abroad with a government as a participant, to what greater degree might social policy of the government play a role in board decisions than where the equity is held by private persons? If the government is your client's partner abroad, will your client be more apt to have access to hard currency to repatriate profits, to obtain government permission to import goods or to have greater ease in penetrating the maze of bureaucracy surrounding many business activities?

Government is also an actor in trade and investment in a different sense. It is as a third party establishing and regulating the framework within which trade and investment transpires. Trade may be sufficiently important to have a minister of trade with cabinet status. The U.S. Trade Representative has considerable status, and is likely to have increased powers in the years to come. Many Departments have special trade interests, such as Agriculture, Commerce, Defense and Treasury—and of course the Department of State.

Government participation in trade is extensive. It is the government which creates or reduces tariffs. Goods passing through a border may be subjected to these costs of entry, the collection of which is assigned to the nation's customs service. Customs also will have to classify entering goods (as to their nature and country of origin), and determine their valuation, opening many possibilities for establishing nontariff barriers. It is also the government which grants subsidies to encourage exports, such as low interest credit to foreign purchasers, subsidized shipbuilding or tax exemptions or deferrals for foreign sales. Further, it is the government which throws up a screen of nontariff barriers preventing foreign products from competing with local industry. It is also the government which sometimes mandates government equity participation in investment activities in the nation. And it is the government which reaches outward with laws imposing extraterritorial application. Such laws have not been well received abroad and have generated retaliatory legislation, even (if not almost exclusively) by our best friends.

Governments tend to act principally in their own best interests, but they also play an important role in assisting the stabilization of worldwide economic activities. As trade actors the developed nations may agree to provide special treatment to the products entering from developing nations. And as actors they gather to collectively lower tariffs, create areas of economic integration or debate whether there should be a reallocation of worldwide resources through a revised international economic order. One cannot avoid and indeed one must not ignore that if the government does not play a direct role on stage, it is ever present in the wings and ready to raise or drop the curtain on the activities of private traders, licensors and investors.

The principal way in which governments act to regulate trade is through legislation and administrative regulations. The United States has numerous statutes directed specifically to aspects of international trade, and many more with major implications for that trade. Congress has delegated considerable authority to the President to reach agreements with other nations on trade issues. There is often tension between the executive and the Congress regarding trade agreement authority. In other cases the Congress has set very clear rules regarding aspects of trade. This nation has sometimes deferred to rules evolving from international organizations and agreements, for example the World Trade Organization, although one needs many fingers to count the breaches of these multi-nation established rules. Resolution of the issues raised in the problems will often take us to legislation, which should illustrate the diversity of sources of law governing international business transactions.

SECTION 2.2 NONMARKET ECONOMIES AND STATE TRADING ORGANIZATIONS

In no sector of the world has there been greater change in process than in those nonmarket economies which have chosen to diminish their dependency on strict central planning of all production, state ownership of the means of production and distribution, and general adherence to Marxist–Leninist economic theory. Since the late 1980s, the formerly nonmarket economy nations of Eastern Europe, and what was the USSR, have been in a state of transition. They have rejected socialism and are in various stages of transition towards market economies and elected, democratic governments. China has also moved toward a market economy, but retaining its socialist government. Much debate exists about whether a true market economy nation must have a democratic government. These nations are often referred to as "nations in transition". A few dedicated socialist nonmarket economies survive, notably North Korea and Cuba. And some developing nations in Latin America seem determined to once again adopt nonmarket characteristics thought long discredited, such as Bolivia, Ecuador and Venezuela. But the general world directions are certainly encouraging to trade and investment.

SECTION 2.3 INTERNATIONAL ECONOMIC ORGANIZATIONS

There is another identifiable group of actors in international trade and investment—international organizations. There are far too many to enumerate in an introductory chapter, but we are more interested in what they do. We accept that they play a positive role. They have been created to assume a supportive role in international business and economic relations. Some, however, in their capacity to regulate international trade, often appear to unduly restrict it. Whether or not such restrictions are positive is usually subject to considerable dispute.

Some international organizations have assumed nearly the status of nations, and indeed an importance far greater than many nations. Who would deny that the United Nations (as an economic institution) is more important to the United States than many of its mini-state members? Or the European Union? Or the World Trade Organization? The United Nations enjoys a special status. Representatives of considerable stature are accredited to it. The U.S. delegate may have cabinet rank, a position not accorded to any delegate to any individual nation. The International Court of Justice of the U.N. has considerable respect as the judicial body expected to establish norms of international law. But the court is not very active for many reasons, and the work of the General Assembly has tried to fill the gap. The U.N. has several structures important to international trade and investment. Under the Economic and Social Council economic commissions have been created to promote sectoral development. The

U.N. Conference on Trade and Development (UNCTAD) promotes world trade and seeks multilateral trade agreements and the harmonization of trade and development policies. The U.N. Commission on International Trade Law (UNCITRAL) has played an important role in the past two decades, and has achieved notable success, especially the drafting of the Convention on the International Sale of Goods (CISG). The U.N. Commission on Transnational Corporations has sought to establish international norms for the conduct of multinational enterprises, but has been less enthusiastic about developing standards of state responsibility towards these corporations. The U.N. Industrial Development Organization (UNIDO), provides advisory and technical aid to industries in low income countries. Regrettably, the usefulness of the United Nations in resolving many of these problems has been diminished by political factionalism and a use of the U.N.'s economic institutions by many of the members to serve short term political ends rather than long term economic development goals. However disappointing the United Nations has been in resolving many problems of trade and investment, it has achieved notable successes and it remains one of the most important international organizations for developing rules and policies of trade and investment.

As noted in Chapter 1, different but no less useful forms of international organization evolved from the Bretton Woods Conference at the expiration of World War II. They were the International Monetary Fund (IMF), the General Agreement on Tariffs and Trade (GATT) and the World Bank. The world economy had been subject to a decade and a half of disruption. A world-wide depression (with excessive use of tariffs) was followed by a devastating war. Bretton Woods was intended to correct economic imbalances of the previous two decades. The International Monetary Fund would urge alterations in government policies where there were severe balance of payments dislocations. Restrictions were placed on what governments could do with respect to foreign exchange controls. When imbalances occurred, members could draw on various lines of credit. Those credit lines have been increased and the IMF has assumed a major role as a lender of last resort to numerous developing nations unable to service their foreign debts. Lending has been in the form of conditional loans with mandates for internal political and economic changes to adjust the economy so as to enable the nation to reduce its debtor status. The measures imposed on developing economies, often referred to as austerity measures, have been difficult for developing countries to live with. They include numerous conditions designed to reduce severe inflation, such as the reduction of indexing (automatic increases in wages as inflation rises), reduction in government spending and the boosting of exports. The IMF has become in the view of some a world economic policeman, and the final source of loans before debtor nations turned to the potentially disastrous ultimate step, a default on international obligations.

A second part of the structures evolving from Bretton Woods was the World Bank. While the IMF was created to deal with exchange issues, the World Bank was formed as a lending agency. Organized in three sections, the International Bank for Reconstruction and Development (IBRD) was to make loans principally for major infrastructure projects in developing nations (to some degree the IBRD and the IMF have overlapped in their actual functions), the International Finance Corporation (IFC) to provide loans to private investors for projects in the developing world, and the International Development Association (IDA) to provide the lowest interest loans for the poorest of the world's communities. Later developments of the World Bank include the creation of the International Center for Settlement of Investment Disputes (ICSID), which provides panels of experts for arbitration or conciliation, and the Multilateral Investment Guaranty Agency (MIGA), which offers various forms of insurance for trade and investment.

Another organization was planned to evolve from Bretton Woods, the International Trade Organization (ITO). A number of circumstances, mostly the opposition of the United States Senate, prevented its formation, to the detriment of the world economy today since it was intended to create standards which would govern many of the issues of trade and foreign investment which have created so many conflicts in the last four decades. The work it was to do has since been the focus of a number of the United Nation's organizations, but with only limited success. The organizations created from the Bretton Woods Conference are basically open to all nations, with some requirements of membership in one (*i.e.*, IBRD), to be a member of another (*i.e.*, IFC, IDA or ICSID).

A final major achievement of Bretton Woods was the establishment of the General Agreement on Tariffs and Trade. The GATT had fewer participants than the IMF. It was created to address the issue of world tariff barriers, but over the decades, as a significant reduction of tariffs has been achieved, the GATT turned its attention to negotiating the elimination of nontariff barriers. They are more difficult to identify and resolve than tariff distortions, but they include quotas, "buy local" policies, some customs valuation methods, and even such trade diminishing devices as unjustified safety labeling and packaging requirements. Through various "rounds" (*e.g.*, the Kennedy Round and the Tokyo Round), the approximately ninety members of the GATT sought to keep the discussion of international trade barriers on a multi-nation level, rather than having world trade arrangements be the result of an aggregate of bilateral agreements. Thus, the GATT incorporated "most favored nation treatment," the policy that trade barrier reductions when adopted should apply to all trading members rather than only to a single or few limited trading partners.

The GATT became a major source of international trade law, probably more important for the major trading nations than all of the organizations of the United Nations. But it remained to a large degree an organization within which the United States, Japan and the European Union discussed their most important trading concerns. Only in the Uruguay Round, which created the World Trade Organization (WTO), did the advanced developing nations have an important part in the negotiations. Many developing nations were reluctant to join the GATT, for fear that while the focus of GATT remained on resolving issues among the major trading nations, the developing nations had more to lose in opening their nations to the GATT requirements of membership, than they had to gain in benefits from that membership. If the IMF tended to concentrate on issues involving the developing world, the GATT tended to concentrate on resolving disputes among the major economic powers.

Unlike the United Nations, the GATT did not have a court to which parties could take their disputes. Its regulatory role was accomplished rather through the expected adherence by members to the rules in the General Agreement and in other developed "Codes", often referred to as "side agreements." When nations were alleged to violate the rules of the GATT, working panels were established and a GATT ruling would hopefully have sufficient persuasive force to cause the curtailment of abuses. Dispute resolution was significantly altered in the WTO.

The long negotiations which constituted the GATT Uruguay Round finally ended. This most ambitious round to date commenced in the mid–1980s. The round was completed in late 1993, with the GATT/WTO entering into force in January, 1995. The favorable U.S. vote, crucial to the success of the round and the creation of the WTO, came at the "eleventh hour" in late 1994. The Uruguay Round made important advances towards freer trade, not only in the traditional areas of lower tariffs and fewer nontariff barriers, but in addressing problems of trade in services, intellectual property, foreign investment and agriculture. It further created new methods of dispute resolution of trade agreements, making the process more like a judicial than an arbitral proceeding, and reducing opportunities of parties to block proceedings. Unlike the U.S. Senate's rejection of a world trade organization nearly a half century ago, the Senate and House approved implementing legislation for the WTO by large majorities.

There are other international organizations which are of considerable importance to world or regional trade, but with far more limited membership. They include the organizations which have been created for the purpose of economic integration, and those which have evolved with a participation of member nations with similar levels of development and attitudes toward what should be the governing international law norms.

Economic integration associations have been notable successes, and notable failures. Called free trade agreements, free trade areas, customs unions or common markets, usually without consistent meaning, they have focused on regional development of nations with common interests. The starting point in any consideration of successful economic integration is the European Economic Community (EEC or EC), now referred to as the European Union (EU). Originally six nations, the "inner six" in contrast to the "outer seven" European nations which comprised the less ambitious European Free Trade Association (EFTA), the EU had grown to 27 by early 2009.

The United States began a major step towards economic integration with the enactment of the Canada–United States Free Trade Agreement in 1989. This was followed by the North American Free Trade Agreement in 1994, which joined Canada, Mexico and the United States in a new trade area in this hemisphere of somewhat similar size to the EU. The EU and the NAFTA suggest that economic development will depend as much on regional trade agreements as on the worldwide WTO. Both the EU and the NAFTA appear likely to expand. The EU has begun to admit some of the former nonmarket economy nations of Eastern Europe, as well as other European nations. The Western Hemisphere nations unsuccessfully debated the creation of a Free Trade Agreement of the Americas (FTAA), which would expectedly draw ideas significantly from the NAFTA, and to some extent from the MERCOSUR. But as the first decade of the new century ended, several Latin American nations seemed determined to reject free trade and renewed experiments with expropriation and non-market economy characteristics.

Similar economic integration has occurred in other parts of the world. In Latin America integration has been attempted by the Central American Common Market (CACM), the Latin American Free Trade Association (LAFTA), the Andean Common Market, and most recently MERCOSUR. The Caribbean has the Caribbean Common Market (CARICOM). Similar groups have been organized in Africa and Asia, especially the Asia–Pacific Economic Cooperation (APEC) group, and the Association of Southeast Asian Nations (ASEAN). Attempts at integration in the developing nations have never been very successful, the most promising hope may be by having developing nations added to developed nation areas. Although attempts at integration among developing nations have not always been successful, they have in some cases generated many improvements in trade among the members.

A final class of organization includes those created by nations with mutual trade and investment interests. The most prominent is the Organization for Economic Cooperation and Development (OECD). Composed almost exclusively of developed nations, the OECD is a free trade advocate which also has in the past two decades addressed many of the obstacles to development, for example by attempting to establish some guidelines for the conduct of corporations, and the adoption of an antibribery convention.

International economic institutions are often an important source of the development of international legal rules. In other cases, where these institution's pronouncements have not achieved such status, portions of these pronouncements have been adopted as domestic law of some nations. They serve at least as an indication of the aspirations of much of the world community. One ought not ignore the role of international organizations in international trade and investment. As actors they effect even the most basic trading transactions.

SECTION 2.4   THE ROLE OF COUNSEL IN INTERNATIONAL BUSINESS

Private traders and nations, and also international organizations, rarely function efficiently in international business transactions without the advice of those skilled in the knowledge and implementation of the rules of international trade and investment. These needed actors are the lawyers engaged in planning, negotiating and implementing international business transactions, as well as those who assume more policy oriented roles in establishing local, national and international legal rules which govern those transactions. In some nations, such as many Asian cultures, the work of the practicing lawyers may be limited to documenting transactions planned and negotiated by business executives. But in others the lawyer may enter at a far earlier stage and be part of the negotiating and planning of a client's international business. International business has become increasingly complex. Predictability is important and all the more difficult because of the maze of rules governing international trade and investment. Thus the role of lawyers in international business has become more pervasive.

Any of the actors above may and likely will use the skills of a lawyer. Those skills may well have to go beyond what a law student may imagine the role of the international business lawyer to be. Possessing a knowledge of international legal rules is understood to be a prerequisite. But one also must know something about foreign law. The client may be sued in a foreign court. Foreign counsel will have to be retained, although the American lawyer may wish to participate very closely in the proceedings abroad. Will the American lawyer be allowed to play any role in the proceedings in the foreign court? What evidence will be admissible in the foreign court? What substantive rules will apply? What rules of professional responsibility apply? Perhaps a client may wish to establish a subsidiary in Europe and the lawyer will need to explain the different nature of the company in a civil law setting. Thus some understanding of the civil law, and how the common law may vary in other systems than the American, may be invaluable. But the lawyer's advice may go far beyond the knowledge of legal systems and substantive rules. The successful international lawyer will likely possess a knowledge of other languages and other cultures. And of considerable importance, a basic understanding of international economics. What are trade imbalances and balance of payments problems? How do changes in the value of the currencies of two different countries affect trade? Do such changes offset tariffs? Will the lawyer be prepared to respond when the client asks, "If we establish a foreign direct investment in Nigeria, what is likely to be the Nigerian government's attitude toward foreign investment over the next decade or two?" No one can answer that question, obviously, but the lawyer with a sound background in economics and an awareness of differences in political systems may be able to provide a useful perspective of the various alternatives that may face the company, and the consequences of different choices which the nation may make.

Who is an international business lawyer? We certainly apply that label to the lawyer in the international law department of a large multinational enterprise who is involved in drafting licensing agreements for foreign joint ventures or negotiating the sale of products with foreign governments. Many lawyers with large private law firms also work exclusively in international business law, while others only occasionally undertake a matter properly labeled as international. But it is perhaps this latter group that most need to be aware of the dimensions involved in many international trade problems. The lawyer in the small rural community whose practice appears to be limited exclusively to local issues may suddenly have need for knowledge of some element of international business law. A client on a two week tour of Europe ordered a set of china from an Amsterdam store and the goods have not arrived. The rural attorney has thus become engaged in an international business transaction. Although the attorney may seek additional advice, what is important is to be aware that there are significant problems that may mandate that additional advice. The various problems in this book should illustrate the diversity of roles played by the international business lawyer. The following comments of the late Professor Wilson of a typical office day for an international counsel to a multinational corporation emphasize that diversity.

By way of hypothetical illustration, a typical office day, for corporate counsel to a MNC, might include work on problems such as: Senegal has served notice that MNC revenues worldwide will be taxed unitarily irrespective of the MNC's tax posture in other countries; MNC use of its trade name in western Canada is impeded by a "prior use" problem in Saskatoon; a Uruguayan appeals court has held that the MNC trade name is generic and thus not subject to legal protection in Uruguay; a line management employee of the MNC's Austrian subsidiary company needs an "L" visa to spend some time at the MNC headquarters offices in the United States; new advertising from the MNC advertising department has possible legal implications if placed in newspapers throughout Europe; reports of resale price maintenance agreements being made by certain companies in Transylvania and Neverland need to be checked in light of antitrust implications under United States law and "Article 85–86" implications within the European Common Market; MNC products stolen in Hamburg must be traced through INTERPOL; ways must be explored to get blocked currencies from New Country to MNC headquarters in the United States, testimony needs to be prepared for presentation to an environmental control authority in Germany, and a presentation must be made to the transportation commissioner of the Province of Ontario to secure permits to increase haulage capacity of the MNC subsidiary company in Canada; charges of employee discrimination in the Far Islands need to be answered; sale-leaseback agreements need to be negotiated in Sydney; a company needs to be formed for trade name protection in the Unusual Islands; an expropriation in Libya requires attention; the Philippine and Saudi Arabian Governments want to increase their equity participation in existing MNC joint ventures in each country; certain inquiries by the United States Federal Trade Commission need to be answered; someone from the American Bar Association wants counsel to serve on an international trade committee; all standard form contracts used by the MNC and its subsidiary companies are due for another review; line management in one subsidiary company has served notice that the company's local counsel is unenthusiastic about servicing the legal needs of the subsidiary and should be replaced quickly; and some MNC line management people are interested in hearing ideas about ways to avoid legal problems in connection with their proposals for new MNC activity.[a]

We should also point out that there are many attorneys employed by government and international economic institutions. Many departments of the U.S. government employ attorneys who work on international issues. Many issues before the State Department involve international business, as well as matters of public international law. The two frequently overlap. The International Trade Commission and Court of International Trade use legal specialists. The role of counsel as an actor on the government's side in international business transactions will be apparent in a number of the problems included in this book.

American law firms have often followed their multinational clients abroad, as have other service activities including advertising, banking and accounting. Although they may initially go abroad to serve American multinationals, law firms will over time establish a more diversified practice in their foreign location. But they may be restricted in what legal services they may render in the foreign nation. Some nations will admit no foreign attorneys, other severely limit their activities to representation exclusively of American corporate clients located in the nation. But many law firms have established offices in the major capital cities of the world, including Moscow and Beijing, despite obstacles, and some law firm letterheads read like a global encyclopedia. The era of the "multinational law firm" has clearly arrived. Without international regulations, multinational law firms have encountered numerous domestic regulatory impediments to the development of their international legal practices. Near preclusion (Japan) or reciprocity (France) confront lawyers providing services on an international basis. Many states permit certified "foreign legal consultants" to give advice on foreign law applicable to international business transactions, partly in response to reciprocal legal practice rules encountered by U.S. lawyers operating abroad.

What lawyers going abroad are permitted to do illustrates the diversity of what lawyers may wish to do. Few would object to a lawyer for a

---

a. Donald Wilson, *International Business Transactions In A Nutshell* 13 (2nd ed. 1984). Reprinted with permission of the West Publishing Co.

multinational company going abroad to spend a few days or even a few weeks working on special problems in the multinational's foreign office. But what if the company wishes to have a branch law department in its foreign facility? As long as the lawyer remains within the company the work is not likely to be challenged. But when the lawyer acts in a negotiating capacity with other persons or entities, then local lawyers may find their turf challenged. But the clearer obstacle arises when a lawyer wishes to go into a foreign court. They are rarely permitted to do so even in the most liberal of jurisdictions. But they may be permitted to appear along with local counsel and to speak on issues under the guidance of that counsel. What constitutes most international law practice is not litigation in foreign courts, but rather centers on advice, counseling and drafting of documents. Staying "in house" tends to draw little criticism and indeed may even be protected by treaties of Friendship, Commerce, and Navigation.

Where foreign law firms are permitted to exist, they may be subjected to less criticism when they employ local lawyers. It is indeed unlikely that a firm would not employ local attorneys to assist in understanding and handling local issues in areas of expertise not possessed by the foreign lawyers. The mixture of attorneys from different nations may result in a truly "multinational legal practice." Of particular interest is European Union law facilitating a European legal practice by EU nationals. Through an extensive body of treaty, regulatory and case law it is possible for EU attorneys to move more freely than before within the EU in establishing law firms and providing legal services. But no blanket permission has been established to represent clients and appear in courts of all member nations.

The growth in international legal practice has to some degree supplanted traditional law firm ties based (in part) on reciprocal referrals of business. This network, nevertheless, continues to be employed by smaller firms and may also be used by multinationals in selecting local counsel. Choosing local counsel is indeed one of the difficult aspects of international business and obviously involves some careful selection. And it involves some luck. If a lawyer in Texas needs to obtain the services of a lawyer abroad, assumptions should not be made that it is only a little more difficult than obtaining distant services for a transaction in Maine or Oregon. In some foreign nations there is a divided profession, some lawyers limiting their practice to advocacy in courts and others to office practice. In other nations lawyers are only admitted to practice before certain courts. If the nation has a federal system, like the United States, a lawyer licensed in one state or province may be allowed to practice in another, unlike the rule in the United States. Costs become an important consideration. Work may be done in some areas by hourly rates not dissimilar to the practice in the United States, but in others the fee may be established by national legislation depending on the value of the subject matter, or for litigation, the type of court appearance. Thus, the costs of legal services should be discussed in advance.

CHAPTER 3

FORMS OF INTERNATIONAL BUSINESS

■ ■ ■

SECTION 3.1 TRADING GOODS ACROSS BORDERS: EXPORTS AND IMPORTS

Having noted who the international lawyers are, and made some comments on how they vary from nation-to-nation, we now move to consider some of the forms of international business in which these actors will be engaged.**

Those simple initial transactions between parties in different nations based on comparative advantage have over the centuries developed into what is today a massive movement of goods and services across borders. A manufacturer of goods in the United States may intentionally sell abroad, or its goods may find their way across national boundaries without the knowledge of the manufacturer. They may be sold to distributors who in turn sell them both domestically and abroad. The trading of goods across boundaries, the import and export of goods, is the initial stage of international business. The actors engaged in trading need not cross those boundaries themselves. There is no need for any equity capital to move across those borders. A U.S. producer of pharmaceutical products may have no interest in establishing productive facilities outside of the United States. But if there is a market abroad that company may wish to sell its goods there. Trading of goods across borders is likely to be a major part of international business activities handled by U.S. lawyers. A hypothetical should illustrate many of the characteristics of this level of trade.

An Ohio Machine Tool Company (MTC) has a fair share of the machine tool market industry in the Eastern part of the United States. MTC may decide that it should expand its market to Canada or Europe. It thus begins international trade by design. Or it may be content with its sales in the United States, but after having shown its products at a trade fair in Cleveland, receive orders from a German purchaser. It has no reason not to sell to the German buyer, but it does wonder what different problems may be raised with such sales. The movement into international trade was not by planned activity, but by external demand. No longer can

---

** Important developments in international business law are included in the annual International Legal Developments in Review in the ABA's International Lawyer.

20

the company send the machine tools by one of its trucks to a neighboring city, or place them into the hands of a domestic trucking or railway delivery service. But there are many international transportation services ready to take the goods from MTC and deliver them to the German buyer. The distance may not be much greater than sending them to California, but the cost may be more if they travel by various means of transportation and face greater risk of loss. MTC may be familiar with payment by letters of credit. Whether the buyer is in Germany or Arizona, MTC does not wish to have the goods arrive only to have the buyer say, "I don't like them and I won't pay for them."

A letter of credit, whether in international commerce or domestic commerce, will allow MTC to be paid when the goods have been delivered to the carrier, so that neither the buyer nor the seller has both the goods and the payment funds at the same time. But when the letter of credit is part of an international sale, its use may mean something different to the German buyer than it does to MTC. Legal rules governing letters of credit in Ohio and Arizona are likely to be quite similar. But they may be very different in Germany. If a dispute arises what law *will* apply? Will it be that of Ohio? Or that of Germany? Or will there be some international rules which might be applied by a court, whether or not adopted by the parties? It is not only rules regarding the letter of credit that may differ, but those affecting other aspects of the transaction as well. And it is not only choice of law issues which may be more complex than in a domestic transaction, but choice of forum issues as well. Will issues be tried in the courts in Germany or in the courts of Ohio? Should international arbitration be used? Would some other court accept jurisdiction, such as the courts in England, which have long been sought to resolve international commercial disputes?

A further question involves the currency to be used. While the Ohio company may not be concerned with its ability to convert Euros into dollars, it may be worried that the value of the Euro vis-à-vis the dollar will change between the time of the contract and the time of receiving payment. MTC will be even more concerned if the goods are being sold to a country where the currency is "soft." The currency of many third world nations would not be accepted by a U.S. bank for conversion into dollars. Or the goods may be sold to a nonmarket economy which precludes the removal of its currency. That country may suggest that in exchange for the machine tools, MTC accept goods rather than currency.

Many of these problems will be present also when a U.S. company imports goods. MTC may discover that Brazilian steel is cheaper than U.S. steel. Some of the same issues will arise that were involved with its own exports. It is not solely the buyer and seller who are interested in these commercial transactions. The governments of the participating nations regulate trade, often placing limitations on imports and sometimes on exports. MTC's former steel suppliers will be disturbed that Brazilian steel may replace their market and they may seek to prevent the importation of such steel into the United States. They may claim that the

Brazilian government subsidizes the steel production, or that the Brazilian steel company is dumping steel on the U.S. market, or that simply the steel industry is being seriously injured by this foreign competition. The United States may already have tariffs against the importation of steel, or it may have quotas. There further may be nontariff barriers which affect MTC's purchase of Brazilian steel. Or trade with Brazil may be helped by the United States. The steel may qualify under special preferences given to Brazil as a developing nation. Regarding MTC's products being sold to Germany, the company may face some of the same attitudes on the part of the German government toward imports. And there may be U.S. restrictions on the sale of goods abroad. If the machine tools possess particularly sophisticated computer technology, the United States may be fearful that their destination might be a nation with which the United States does not trade, such as North Korea. A special export license may be mandated. These are only a few of the new issues which will confront the company when it decides to sell or purchase goods in international trade. Without even considering the manufacture of its products abroad, MTC has had to think about a number of problems different than or in addition to those involved in domestic trade.

SECTION 3.2   LICENSING PRODUCTION ABROAD

MTC may decide that it cannot sell its goods in other countries because labor rates in the United States make the goods too costly. But MTC may have little interest in setting up a productive facility (a foreign direct investment) in Germany, even though the German market and other markets within Europe might make such a facility a success. The company may have no previous experience with equity investments abroad. MTC may not feel that it wants to expend the time and funds necessary to set-up abroad. Or the directors may express some antipathy regarding "going foreign" in any substantial form. MTC, however, may be willing to license the production of its machine tools to an already existing German company. A number of new issues arise. If the market is throughout Europe and not limited to Germany, in what nation would a licensing arrangement be most appropriate? This may not be as complex a decision as deciding in which country to locate a direct investment, but there may be business and legal benefits to licensing in a certain nation. For example, does the government regulate licensing? Probably not in a developed European country, but many developing nations become essentially a third party when there is a licensing arrangement between a foreign licensor and a local licensee. But even assuming the choice of a German licensee is made, there are more questions. How will MTC assure that the quality of the machine tools manufactured by the German licensee will be equal to the quality of those manufactured in Ohio? Because of the reputation of German products for quality (perhaps undeserved in your client's product area, however), MTC may be much less concerned than were they to be licensing their manufacture in a developing or nonmarket economy nation where no reputation for quality control exists.

Once licensing begins, MTC is going to be sending valuable property to the foreign licensee. It will not have the same control over that technology that it would have were the licensee to be its own subsidiary. MTC will not want to lose valuable new technology. Will MTC be willing to transfer its latest machine tool technology? If it does not send its best technology will the products be competitive? Whatever technology it does license, it will do whatever it can to protect that technology. Does Germany recognize MTC's right to the machine tool designs? Should the design patent be registered in Germany? In other European nations? In the European Union? How should MTC be paid? Should it be a percentage of sales or a royalty per item produced? What if the German company during the production of the machine discovers new and better design elements for the product? May MTC mandate that the German licensee grant back to MTC the exclusive rights to all such new ideas? How can MTC restrict the sales of the German licensee to Germany and certain other countries, but preclude it from selling in, for example, England, where MTC products are already sold through distributorship arrangements? Will there be any EU rules which will affect such territorial restrictions? Nor does MTC want the German licensee to sell the products in the United States in competition with those which MTC produces here. If the licensee begins to sell in the United States will the U.S. laws help block such sales?

If the licensing were to a licensee in a developing nation, additional problems will be present. The licensing agreement may have to be registered with a national commission. The process may involve more than mere registration. The agreement may be subjected to a very careful evaluation. Every provision may be questioned. Many may have to be modified to comply with transfer of technology laws. The amount agreed as a royalty may be too high according to the national commission. The nation may have a balance of payments problem and thus try to lower all royalty outflow. Nationalist sentiment may limit choice of law and choice of forum clauses in the agreement, stipulating the choice of *local* law and *local* forums. The nation may reject provisions which restrict exports; developing nations currently view exports as critical to earning hard currency to pay extensive foreign debts. They may view grant back provisions as unfair, and require some sharing of use. It is to licensees in developing nations that much less than the latest technology has often been transferred. The multinational may decide to produce an earlier generation item because it will sell for less in a market where the consumers have less to spend. If that is thought laudable, the local government may not agree, but instead charge that the technology is obsolete and should not be compensated. Thus, a licensing agreement may be of interest not only to MTC as the licensor and the third world licensee, but to the government of the licensee as well. It may in some instances be of interest to the government of the licensor also, in this case the United States. U.S. government imposed limitations on the transfer of certain technologies may preclude MTC from licensing its production abroad.

The WTO includes an Agreement on Trade–Related Aspects of Intellectual Property (TRIPs). While this does not directly offer a private client any rights to challenge the intellectual property laws of other nations, it provides a basis for the United States to urge other nations to adopt adequate protection, and to comply with the TRIPs mandates. TRIPs creates standards and obligates WTO members to follow some of the concepts in several international conventions which safeguard intellectual property.

MTC has gone beyond the trading of its goods across borders. It has established an arrangement by which its own designs are manufactured in other countries. It has lost some of the control over the production of those goods, and has had to delegate much of the responsibility for their production to the licensee. But its products may now be sold in larger quantities and in new areas. The reputation of MTC machine tools has spread. If the demand increases significantly, MTC may decide to take an even further step—it may decide to itself produce its machine tools abroad, rather than to continue their manufacture under a licensing agreement.

SECTION 3.3   FOREIGN INVESTMENT

MTC has now decided not to continue to license its production in Germany but to own a facility in Germany which manufactures its machine tools. Thus it will have much greater control over the manufacturing process and over where the goods are marketed. It will be engaged in what is called a foreign direct investment. Many new choices confront the company. Where to locate becomes even more important than where to license; the company will be spending a great deal of money to open a new facility. It could opt to buy an existing plant, rather than commence a new entity. But that may raise antitrust issues, or issues of nationalism if many local businesses are bought-out with foreign money. Once the decision to establish a company is made, and where to locate it, MTC must decide what form of business it should or must choose. Are the forms in Germany similar to those in the United States, such as partnerships and corporations? Is there a European Union incorporation process? If MTC chooses a corporation is there more than one form of incorporated business? Are there important variations in how a German company is managed in contrast to the United States? Does labor play a more active role than in the United States? Will the company be able to own 100 percent of the equity? Is the MTC industry one of those sensitive industries which in some countries is drawn into state ownership?

Were MTC considering a developing or nonmarket economy nation other issues would arise. Although investment laws in these nations are becoming increasingly less restrictive, joint venture legislation may require the company to find local partners to own a majority of the company. Would MTC be willing to give up majority equity participation, or would such restriction cause the company to prefer to remain as a licensor? By deciding on a foreign direct investment the company has not escaped issues of licensing and trading goods. Its foreign productive facility may be a separate legal entity wholly owned by MTC, but that subsidiary will still have to contract with the parent MTC to produce the goods. But this essentially intra-multinational enterprise agreement will be easier to conclude than where the German entity is a locally owned licensee. The company undoubtedly will have to bring goods across borders, even though they are intra-company transactions. All the components for the manufacture of the machine tools may not be available in the nation where the subsidiary is located. If the subsidiary is in a developing country, the government may urge the subsidiary to reduce imports by finding "adequate" local substitutes. They may not appear very adequate to MTC, but they may have to be used. There may be no choice. The WTO Agreement on Trade–Related Investment Measures (TRIMs) may help reduce some restrictions in foreign nations which MTC may face. It is a positive step.

Since MTC now has a subsidiary which it wholly owns, it probably will have a larger share of the profits than where it has licensed the production. If that seems to be a good situation to be in, it may not be if the nation later imposes severe exchange controls. Then how will the company repatriate its profits? It may not be able to do so. It may have to reinvest the profits in the company or in other local ventures. But that may only compound the problem if there is little expectancy of a repeal of the exchange restrictions, and an adequate supply of foreign currency.

A few scattered sales of machine tools to foreign customers has, over the years, led MTC to manufacture them abroad. MTC has confronted many new issues not present at all or in the same form as at home. These introductory chapters should illustrate that moving from domestic trade and investment across borders raises new and often complex legal issues, and requires lawyers to expand their knowledge of other cultures and economies if they are to serve effectively as actors in international trade. We should now be ready to turn to the specific problems, each of which fits somewhere into the above matrix of international business transactions.

PART 2

INTERNATIONAL TRADING OF GOODS

■ ■ ■

CHAPTER 4

AGREEMENTS FOR THE INTERNATIONAL TRADING OF GOODS

■ ■ ■

INTRODUCTION 4.0 THE BASIC TRANSACTION—TOYS TO GREECE

Chapters 4 and 5, and Problems 4.1–5.3, arise out of a basic form of international sales of goods transaction called a documentary sale. The purpose of these problems is to go through a step-by-step consideration of some of the legal difficulties that arise in such transactions. However, before beginning to consider the legal problems involved, an understanding of the transaction itself is necessary. The purpose of this material is to introduce the documentary transaction, to illustrate not only what is being done, but also why it is being done in a particular manner. In order to accomplish this, the materials proceed, step-by-step, through a documentary sale which the parties perform correctly according to traditional practices, and in which no legal problems arise. In other words, the transaction in this illustration is "done right."

General reference to R. Folsom, M. Gordon and J.A. Spanogle, *Principles of International Business Transactions* (2nd ed., 2010) Chapters 1–8, is recommended.

PART A. FACTORS TO CONSIDER—HOW IS AN INTERNATIONAL COMMERCIAL TRANSACTION DIFFERENT FROM A DOMESTIC ONE?

Many of the aspects of international transactions are different only in degree from some domestic transactions (*e.g.*, a sale of goods from New York to California), but others are novel and have no counterpart in any domestic transaction. These factors are illuminated by examining the risks arising out of such a transaction, and whether these risks are heightened by the fact that the transaction is international. Once a transaction is identified as international, it will usually involve distance between the parties, and therefore require transportation of the goods. It will also involve more than one legal system, and could involve different currencies. In addition, it is more likely that buyer and seller do not know each other, and do not wish to trust each other or to rely upon litigation (especially in a foreign legal system) for protection.

The primary risk to seller is of not being paid after shipping the goods. Thus seller wants some assurance of payment, as long as the goods are shipped, and that payment will be made in seller's home country. Buyer, on the other hand, will have several different worries. First, buyer will not want to pay unless assured that the goods have arrived, or at least have been shipped. Second, buyer will worry about whether the goods meet the quantity and quality requirements of the contract. For this reason, buyer prefers to pay only after inspecting the goods. However, where buyer and seller are at a distance from each other, and the goods must be transported, it is impossible both to have seller be paid upon shipment and to allow buyer to delay payment until after inspection after arrival of the goods. Intermediaries must be enlisted.

Payment also causes problems. Currencies fluctuate in value relative to each other. In addition, seller usually wants the funds to be available in its home country and in its currency, for its costs are more likely to be incurred in that currency; buyer, on the other hand, may not be able to pay in any currency but its own. Thus, the sales contract must specify the currency to be used for payment and assign the risk of currency fluctuations to one of the parties. In addition, when dealing with a buyer from a "soft currency" nation, seller must carefully ascertain whether buyer is authorized to pay in a "hard currency" or not. A simple declaration from buyer may not be sufficient, and much extra paper-work may be required even when such payment is authorized. Finally, if seller relies upon foreign sources for payment, unforeseen events can always interrupt the expected orderly flow of funds—as recent events in the Middle East have demonstrated. Thus, seller prefers someone "on the hook" to pay that is located within its jurisdiction and subject to its legal system.

In this day of "long-arm jurisdiction," both buyer and seller must worry about the cultural and legal system of the other party. It may be difficult to determine what law governs the contract—the domestic law of seller's state, the domestic law of buyer's state, or perhaps even an international treaty. Regardless of what law is applicable, extra regulations may be imposed upon international contracts—*e.g.,* license requirements on exports, customs duties or even quotas on imports. In addition, different rules may be provided for international contracts than for domestic ones. For example, in the United States, instead of consulting Article 7 of the UCC on Documents of Title (including bills of lading), the appropriate statute for regulation of bills of lading will be the Federal Bill of Lading Act, 49 U.S.C. §§ 80101–16, and for regulation of contracts with carriers will be the Carriage of Goods by Sea Act (COGSA, 46 U.S.C. § 30701 note). The Convention on International Sales of Goods (CISG) may govern the sales contract itself, rather than UCC Article 2, unless expressly excluded. If foreign law is applicable to the transaction, the substance of such law may be very difficult to ascertain in a variety of senses, including that it may be in a foreign language, that it may be difficult to find in available law libraries, and also that the available materials may be insufficiently detailed to answer detailed questions. Further, your training is as a common law attorney, and not as a civil law attorney.

The international trading community has formulated two principal responses to these risks. First, it has sought to assign the foreseeable risks of the transaction as clearly as possible in the contracts involved. To do this it has developed a special language of commercial terms such as FAS, CIF, FOB vessel, non-negotiable bill of lading, negotiable draft (or bill of exchange), confirmed and irrevocable letter of credit. Many of these commercial terms of art are defined in several publications of the International Chamber of Commerce, in INCOTERMS (2010 edition) and Uniform Customs and Practice for Documentary Credits (2007 edition) and others.

Second, it has sought to avoid large and uncertain risks by creating devices that break them down into many small and measurable risks. That is what the documentary transaction is all about. For example, the letter of credit is a device to assure that seller will be paid upon shipment of the goods. However, there are interrelationships which must be understood. Thus, use of a documentary transaction to assure payment upon shipment may deprive the buyer of its ability to inspect the goods before payment— but a third-party Inspection Certificate may protect buyer's position.

How is a documentary sale set up by the parties? To explain this process, the remainder of this introduction will trace such a sale of toys between the Santa Claus Company of East Aurora, New York, and Alpha Company of Athens, Greece.[1] The documentary sale transaction illustrated below is made up of several different interrelated contracts. The three most important of these contracts will be used to organize our discussion: (1) the sale contract between buyer and seller, (2) the letter of credit contract between buyer's bank and seller, and (3) the bill of lading contract between seller and the carrier.

PART B.   THE SALES CONTRACT

Forms 1–3 will be used by the parties to form the sales contract, and to define its terms. The initial contact is Form 1, a letter sent by Alpha, the buyer, to Santa Claus, the seller, requesting a price quotation. Alpha could send a simple letter asking for quotations from Santa Claus' price catalog; but, since this is a specialized sale, it will request a "proforma invoice" which should state the price of each of the components of the international sale. In addition, Alpha's request can indicate sale terms which it prefers—*e.g.*, payment and shipping terms, including the preferred method of handling insurance during transit.

---

1. Many of the forms accompanying this text have been provided through the courtesy of Dorothy Dervay of the Fisher Price Company.

Santa Claus' response is a Proforma Invoice, Form 2. That form gives multiple price options to Alpha. If Alpha wishes to purchase the goods "FOB Santa Claus' Plant," it need pay Santa Claus only the list price of the toys, including the cost of crating them. Alpha would then be responsible for the costs and risks of transportation from Santa Claus' factory. Alternatively Alpha could purchase the goods "FAS Port of New York City." The price would then include not only the price of the goods FOB Santa Claus' plant, but also the costs of transportation within the United States from Santa Claus' factory to the port facilities in New York City.

Two other prices are quoted by Santa Claus in its Proforma Invoice— "CIF" and "CFR." The "CIF" price is the price of the goods delivered in Athens, the destination point. This price includes all of the factors included in "FAS Port of New York City," and in addition the cost of ocean freight, handling fees of various types, and insurance covering the goods during the ocean voyage. "CFR" would be the price term used if Alpha did not want Santa Claus to purchase insurance coverage during that voyage. Under a contract using a CIF or CFR price term, Santa Claus must bear the cost of the freight charges (and, for CIF, insurance as well). In addition, Santa Claus must also bear the risk of fluctuations in freight costs (and, for CIF, insurance also) until the goods arrive at their destination port. Thus, there are advantages to Santa Claus to quote prices "FOB Santa Claus Plant." On the other hand, a sales contract bearing a CIF term requires buyer to pay when presented with documents—such as bills of lading—usually before the goods arrive, so there are also advantages to Santa Claus to sell on a CIF basis.

After receipt of the Proforma Invoice, and comparison shopping, Alpha decides to purchase Santa Claus' toys. It therefore sends a Purchase Order (Form 3) which duplicates the pricing in the Proforma Invoice. The Purchase Order Form may or may not have a large amount of small print clauses set forth on the reverse side. If it does, a "Battle of the Forms" can arise. Alpha considers its Purchase Order to be an offer, but could others consider the Purchase Order to be an acceptance of an offer contained in the Proforma Invoice? Santa Claus' normal practice, in any event, is to acknowledge all purchase orders with an Order Acknowledgement Form, which repeats the essential "business" terms of the Purchase Order. The Order Acknowledgement Form may or may not have large amounts of small print clauses on the reverse side. If it does, another round of the "Battle of the Forms" ensues. We will address in detail the special issues of contract formation that arise in international sales transactions in Problem 4.1 below.

FORM 1. LETTER FROM BUYER REQUESTING PROFORMA INVOICE

ALPHA COMPANY

ATHENS

GREECE

April 1, 2012

Santa Claus Company
Main Street
East Aurora, New York 14052

Gentlemen:

We have visited your booth at the Nürnburg Toy Fair and now wish to give you our order. We require a Proforma Invoice, four copies, for the following:

Item 930—	Play Family Garage	252 Pieces
Item 942—	Play Family Lift & Load	252 Pieces
Item 300—	Scoop Loader	360 Pieces
Item 313—	Roller Grader	360 Pieces
Item 307—	Adventure People & Their Wilderness Patrol	360 Pieces
Item 936—	Medical Kit	360 Pieces
Item 993—	Play Family Castle	225 Pieces

Please indicate your best price and delivery, including export packing, FAS New York, CFR, CIF Athens, Greece. Prices and terms should be quoted firm for a period of 90 days.

Yours very truly,
ALPHA COMPANY

Alexandros Pappas

FORM 2.   PROFORMA INVOICE

SANTA CLAUS COMPANY

EAST AURORA, NEW YORK

Alpha Company
Athens, Greece

April 13, 2012

PROFORMA INVOICE NO. G–12

Your Ref. No.:   Your letter of April 1, 2012
Price: Net, including export packing, CIF Athens, Greece
Payment Terms: Confirmed Irrevocable Letter of Credit confirmed by U.S.
                        bank and calling for payment against documents in New
                        York City in U.S. funds.
Shipment: Approximately 15 days after receipt of your order and
                        Confirmed Irrevocable Letter of Credit.
Estimated Total Weight: 9,633 Lbs.   4369.576 Kgs.
Estimated Measurement: 2102.4 Cu. Ft.   59.53 M3

QUANTITY	DESCRIPTION	UNIT PRICE U.S. $	AMOUNT U.S. $
252 Pcs.	930 Play Family Garage	$10.95	$ 2,759.40
252 Pcs.	942 Play Family Lift & Load	10.95	2,759.40
360 Pcs.	300 Scoop Loader	5.25	1,890.00
360 Pcs.	313 Roller Grader	4.25	1,530.00
360 Pcs.	307 Adventure People & Their Wilderness Patrol	8.75	3,150.00
360 Pcs.	936 Medical Kit	6.65	2,394.00
225 Pcs.	993 Play Family Castle	12.95	2,913.75

TOTAL PRICE FOB EAST AURORA, NEW
YORK $17,396.55
INLAND FREIGHT TO NEW YORK CITY $ 500.00
TOTAL PRICE FAS N.Y.C. $17,896.55
OCEAN FREIGHT N.Y.C. TO
ATHENS, GREECE $ 2,044.00
FORWARDING FEES $ 45.00
TOTAL PRICE CFR ATHENS, GREECE $19,985.55
INSURANCE $ 87.00
TOTAL PRICE CIF ATHENS, GREECE $20,072.55

THE PRICES QUOTED ABOVE ARE FIRM
FOR 90 DAYS AFTER THE DATE OF THIS
PROFORMA INVOICE

SANTA CLAUS COMPANY

RACHEL SMITH
EXPORT MANAGER

FORM 3.   PURCHASE ORDER

ALPHA COMPANY

ATHENS, GREECE

April 26, 2012

Santa Claus Company
East Aurora
New York

Re: Our Purchase Order 1234
Your G–12

Gentlemen:

Please supply in accordance with your Proforma Invoice No. G–12 the following:

252 Pcs.	930	Play Family Garage	@ $10.95 each
252 Pcs.	942	Play Family Lift & Load	@ $10.95 each
360 Pcs.	300	Scoop Loader	@ $ 5.25 each
360 Pcs.	313	Roller Grader	@ $ 4.25 each
360 Pcs.	307	Adventure People & Wilderness Patrol	@ $ 8.75 each
360 Pcs.	936	Medical Kit	@ $ 6.65 each
225 Pcs.	993	Play Family Castle	@ $12.95 each

Total Price FAS New York $17,896.55

CIF Athens, Greece $20,072.55

Delivery required prior to July 1, 2012
Insurance to be covered by yourselves at 110% CIF value
Import License No. 143210

MARKS:

ALPHA CO.

ATHENS, GREECE

ORDER NO. 1234

MADE IN U.S.A.

NOS. 1/UP

We have instructed our bank, COMMERCIAL BANK OF GREECE, in Athens to open the Letter of Credit per your Proforma Invoice through the Marine Midland Bank Western in Buffalo.

We would appreciate receiving your order acknowledgement by early mail.

Very truly yours,
Alpha Company

Alexandria Pappas

PART C.   THE LETTER OF CREDIT

Both the Proforma Invoice (Form 2) and the Purchase Order (Form 3) state as the payment term "Letter of Credit." Payment through the letter of credit device assures Santa Claus of payment as long as it can demonstrate to a bank through appropriate documents that it has shipped the goods. Thus, Santa Claus will not risk rejection of the goods after they arrive in Greece, where it will be expensive and inconvenient either to reship or to resell.

A letter of credit is simply another contract—a promise by Buyer's Bank which runs directly to Seller that Buyer's Bank will pay the sales contract amount to Seller, if Seller produces the documents required by the sales contract which evidence that Seller has shipped the goods required by the sales contract (*e.g.,* a negotiable bill of lading). Letters of credit may be revocable or irrevocable, but in a documentary sales transaction it is customarily understood that an irrevocable one is required. Letters of credit may also be either confirmed or not. A confirmed letter of credit includes a promise from Seller's Bank to Seller that Seller's Bank will pay the contract amount to Seller if Seller produces the required documents evidencing shipment of the goods. Thus, under a confirmed letter of credit, Seller has a promise from a local bank, before shipment of the goods, of payment if the goods are shipped.

To obtain a letter of credit, Alpha goes to its bank, The Commercial Bank of Greece, and requests it to issue a letter of credit in favor of Santa Claus. Alpha has done business with this bank for many years, and it knows Alpha's financial position, so no additional bank investigation is needed. However, if Alpha were a stranger to the issuing bank, the bank would investigate Alpha's credit standing, or even require it to provide sufficient funds or other collateral to cover the amount of the letter of credit. Alpha will also provide the Commercial Bank of Greece with a copy of its Purchase Order or the Proforma Invoice, so that the bank will know the essential terms of and documents required by the sales contract. Commercial Bank of Greece then contacts its New York correspondent bank, Marine Midland Bank, advising the latter that it has opened a letter of credit in Santa Claus' favor, and stating all the details of the letter of credit contract.

FORM 4. LETTER OF CREDIT—CONFIRMED, IRREVOCABLE

Marine Midland Bank—Western
    Buffalo, New York
To: Santa Claus Company
    East Aurora, New York

Letter of Credit # 34576
Issued on May 1, 2012
From: Alpha Company
    Athens, Greece

Gentlemen:

We are instructed by Commercial Bank of Greece, Athens, Greece, to inform you that they have opened their irrevocable credit in your favor for account of Alpha Company, Athens, Greece, for the sum in U.S. dollars not exceeding a total of about $21,000.00 (Twenty One Thousand and $^{00}/_{100}$ Dollars), available by your drafts on the Commercial Bank of Greece, to be accompanied by:

1. Full Set On Board Negotiable Ocean Bills of Lading, stating: "Freight Prepaid," and made out to the order of Commercial Bank of Greece.

2. Insurance Policy or Certificate, covering Marine and War Risk.

3. Packing List.

4. Commercial Invoice in triplicate:
   Covering 252 Pcs. 930 Play Family Garage
              252 Pcs. 942 Play Family Lift & Load
              360 Pcs. 300 Scoop Loader
              360 Pcs. 313 Roller Grader
              360 Pcs. 307 Adventure People & Their Wilderness Patrol
              360 Pcs. 839 Medical Kit
              225 Pcs. 993 Play Family Castle
   Total Value $20,072.55 CIF Athens, Greece

   Import Lic. No. 143210, Expires July 13, 2012.

5. Certificate of Origin
   Partial Shipment Permitted. Transshipment Not Permitted.
   Merchandise must be shipped on SS Livorno.

All documents must indicate Letter of Credit No. 34576, Import License No. 143210, expires July 13, 2012.

All drafts must be marked "Drawn under Letter of Credit No. 34576, confirmed by Marine Midland Bank-Western". Drafts must be presented to this company not later than July 1, 2012.

This credit is subject to the Uniform Customs and Practices for Documentary Credits (2007 edition) International Chamber of Commerce Publication No. 600.

We confirm the credit and thereby undertake to purchase all drafts drawn as above specified and accompanied by the required documents.

                 By:

                 International Credit Department

Marine Midland Bank then contacts Santa Claus. If the letter of credit is not to be confirmed, then Marine Midland Bank will send Santa Claus an "Advice of Credit", which merely notifies Santa Claus of the action taken by Commercial Bank of Greece. However, in this transaction Marine Midland Bank sends Santa Claus a Confirmed Irrevocable Letter of Credit (Form 4). As with many modern day forms, the bank produces it by computer, rather than a printed form. Note the detail with which Santa Claus' performance is specified—the types of documents, originals or copies, the specific vessel, import license numbers, etc. However, if Santa Claus meets these detailed requirements, it will be paid in dollars in the United States as soon as it ships the goods. The last two lines indicate Marine Midland Bank's contractual obligation. The three preceding lines incorporate by reference the International Chamber of Commerce Uniform Customs and Practices for Documentary Credits—in derogation of Article 5 of the UCC.

What has this letter of credit accomplished? Without this device, Santa Claus and Alpha, neither of which knows anything about the trustworthiness or credit standing of the other, are in a situation which seems to demand that one of them trust or extend credit to the other. Either Santa Claus must ship, and then await payment; or Alpha must pay, and then await shipment and delivery of the goods.

After issuance of the letter of credit, Commercial Bank of Greece has promised to pay Santa Claus when presented with the required documents, and that bank has the risk of Alpha's financial failure or refusal to perform the contract. However, Commercial Bank of Greece has a unique ability to evaluate Alpha's credit standing, and can enforce contract obligations locally. Marine Midland Bank has also promised to pay Santa Claus against the required documents, and it has the risk of the financial failure, or refusal to perform, of Commercial Bank of Greece. However, Marine Midland Bank can obtain information on the financial standing of Commercial Bank of Greece with relative ease, and can enforce contract obligations through banking channels. Santa Claus now can ship the goods without having received any prior payment, but is at risk only if Marine Midland, Commercial Bank of Greece *and* Alpha fail financially or refuse to perform. Any refusal to perform by Marine Midland Bank is subject to enforcement through courts in the United States.

PART D. SELLER SHIPS THE GOODS

After receipt of the letter of credit, it is Santa Claus' duty to manufacture, crate, and ship the goods. The actual details of arranging the shipment will usually be handled by a "freight forwarder." (Note the "Forwarder's Fee" in Form 2.) However, Santa Claus must give detailed instructions to the forwarder. It will send to the forwarder a Letter of Instructions (Form 5), and some required documents, such as the Commercial Invoice (Form 6) and a Packing List (Form 7). It will also provide the forwarder with other information and documents required by the government, even if not specifically mentioned in the letter of credit. This includes information necessary to complete an "Electronic Export Information" form (Form 8), which the U.S. government now requires through its "Automated Export System" for nearly all exports, as well as a Certificate of Origin (Form 9).

FORM 5. SHIPPER'S LETTER OF INSTRUCTIONS

CONTAINER INSTRUCTION SHEET

TO: ALPHA COMPANY
        C/O F. W. MYERS
        EMPIRE STATE BUILDING
        350 FIFTH AVE.
        NEW YORK, NEW YORK 10118

FOR: ALPHA COMPANY
        ATHENS, GREECE

PO#   1234

VIA: EXPORT MOTOR FREIGHT

MANIFEST REQUIRED NO

NOTE ON BILL OF LADING:

(1) ACCOUNT & PO#

(2) DOCK RECEIPTS LODGED AT PIER

(3) BOOKING # _____

(4) NOTIFY J. EMMA 432–0670 UPON AR

(5) PRE–PAY TO New York, New York

(6) CONTAINER #   XTRU 423890

(7) CARRIER PLEASE TYPE ORDER # ON ALL FR BILLS.

(8) SPECIAL MARKS

DATE:

CARTONS:

WEIGHT:

SEALS: Santa Claus:
       Santa Claus:

. . . .

SPECIAL NOTES

FORM 6. COMMERCIAL INVOICE

SANTA CLAUS COMPANY
EAST AURORA, NEW YORK 14052

SANTA CLAUS COMPANY
EAST AURORA, NEW YORK 14052

INVOICE

D-U-N-S 00-210-1863

SOLD TO

ALPHA COMPANY
ATHENS
GREECE

Ship Date	Invoice No
May 9, 2012	A-10

CONTAINER NO: XTRU #423890
LETTER OF CREDIT NO: 34576

SHIP TO

SAME

SHIPPING TERMS ARE C. I. F. FOREIGN
PORT OF ENTRY. TITLE TO THE GOODS

Your Order No./Dept. No. 1234	Store No.	Terms	PASSES TO BUYER UPON DELIVERY OF THE GOODS TO BUYER AT THE PORT OF SHIPMENT. Conf Irrev L/C U.S. Funds	Shipped Via EXPORT MOTOR NEW YORK S.S. Livorno	FRT. TO to Athens

Our Order No 61245	Ship to Cust. 0425	Bill to Cust 0426	Slsm

Item	Description	Pcs Ordered	Price Per Piece	Pieces Back Ord	Pcs Shipped	Amount	
930	Play Family Garage	252	10 95		252	$2,759	00
942	Play Family Lift & Load	252	10 95		252	2,759	00
300	Scoop Loader	360	5 25		360	1,890	00
313	Roller Grader	360	4 25		360	1,530	00
936	Medical Kit	360	6 25		360	2,394	00
993	Play Family Castle	225	12 95		225	2,913	75
307	Adventure People & their Wilderness Patrol	360	8 75		360	3,150	00

IMPORT LICENSE NO. 143210

THESE COMMODITIES LICENSED BY
U.S.A. FOR ULTIMATE DESTINATION
GREECE. DIVERSION OR RE-EXPORT
CONTRARY TO U.S. LAW PROHIBITED.

CERTIFIED TRUE AND CORRECT AND
OF U.S. MANUFACTURE

SANTA CLAUS COMPANY
EAST AURORA, N.Y.

Rachel Smith
RACHEL SMITH
EXPORT MANAGER

TOTAL PRICE FOB EAST AURORA, NY	17,396	55
INLAND FREIGHT TO N.Y.C.	500	00
TOTAL PRICE FAS NEW YORK CITY	17,896	55
OCEAN FREIGHT – N.Y.C. TO ATHENS, GREECE	2,044	00
FORWARDING FEES	45	00
TOTAL PRICE CFR ATHENS, GREECE	19,985	55
INSURANCE	87	00
TOTAL CIF ATHENS, GREECE	20,072	55

File All Claims For Damage or Shortage with Delivering Carrier	Cartons 513	Pounds 9633	2102.4 CuF$	20,072	55

[D4663]

FORM 7. PACKING LIST

SANTA CLAUS COMPANY PACKING LIST

Exporter/Shipper Santa Claus Company East Aurora, NY 14052		Shipping marks		
Importer/Consignee Alpha Company Athens, Greece		Buyer (if other than consignee)		
Invoice No. & Date A-10—May 9, 2012	Buyer's Order No. 1234—April 26, 2012	BOL/Air waybill A-10		References
Port of loading New York City	Port of discharge Athens, Greece	Vessel/flight SS Livorno		Final Dest. Athens
Country of origin of goods United States of America		Country of final destination Greece		

Packages and Numbers	Description	Quantity	Dimensions (hxlxd cms.)	Weight
82 Ctns—Nos. 1-82	Play Family Garage	252 pcs.	66x49x33	
70 Ctns—Nos. 83-152	Play Family Lift & Load	252 pcs.	66x49x33	Total
55 Ctns—Nos. 153-207	Scoop Loader	360 pcs.	66x49x33	9633
60 Ctns—Nos. 208-267	Roller Grader	360 pcs.	66x49x33	lbs.
50 Ctns—Nos. 268-317	Medical Kit	360 pcs.	66x49x33	
80 Ctns—Nos. 318-397	Play Family Castle	225 pcs.	66x49x33	
116 Ctns—Nos. 398-513	Adventure People and Wilderness Patrol	360 pcs.	66x49x33	
513 Total Cartons				
Signature:	Date: May 9, 2012	Remarks:		

FORM 8. ONLINE ELECTRONIC EXPORT INFORMATION (EEI) FORM

AESDirect: Shipment Editor: EEI: Shipment Information

Shipment Information	AES*Direct* Assistant
USPPI	
Ultimate Consignee	• To return to the Shipment Viewer, click 'View Shipment'
Freight Forwarder	• To edit another section, select the section in the scrollbox, and click 'Edit Shipment'
Equipment Details	• To delete this section, click 'Clear Section', and then return to the Shipment Viewer, or Edit another section
Add Commodity Line	• Label Colors: ◆ Mandatory, ▪ *Conditional*, ▪ Optional
Commodity Line 1	

EEI – Shipment Information

Edit	▪ E-Mail Response Address — ramith@santaclaus.com
Clear	▪ AESDirect VPN e-Response? — N
View EEI	◆ Shipment Reference Number — 1234
Options	▪ *Transportation Reference Number* — 12-3456789

Main Menu:
Logout of AESDirect

Shipments:
Create
Retrieve
Reporting
Delete

Profiles:
USPPIs
Consignees
Forwarders

Templates:
Delete

EDI Upload:
Upload

Archive:
Retrieve
Reporting

Links:
AESDirect
AES Codes
Privacy Policy

◆ Origin State	NEW YORK
▪ *Foreign Trade Zone*	48452
◆ Port of Export	1001
◆ Country of Destination	GR
▪ *Port of Unloading*	N/A
◆ Departure Date [Format: MM/DD/YY]	05/14/12
◆ Shipment Reference Number	NEW YORK
▪ *Carrier SCAC/IATA*	9876
▪ *Conveyance Name*	SS LIVORNO
▪ Vessel Flag	GR

◆ Is this shipment a Routed Transaction?
    ○ Yes
    ● No
◆ Are USPPI and Ultimate Consignee related companies?
    ○ Yes
    ● No
◆ Is any commodity on this shipment hazardous?
    ○ Yes
    ● No

Other Information Required by EEI Form

PAGE 2
U.S. Principal Party in Interest (USPPI)

Company Information

◆ Company Name — The Santa Clause Company

◆ ID Number — 987654321

Contact Information

◆ First Name — Rachel

◆ Last Name — Smith

◆ Phone Number — 7155551111

Cargo Origin

◆ Address — 1 Main Street

◆ City — East Aurora

◆ State — New York

◆ Postal Code — 14052

PAGE 3
Ultimate Consignee

◆ Company Name — Alpha Company

◆ Address — 100 Pirou Avenue

◆ City — Athens

◆ Country — Greece

PAGE 4
Commodity Line

◆ Commodity Description — Children's Toys

◆ Value in US Dollars — 20,072

◆ Weight in Kilograms — 4388

◆ Export Code — D3: General Exports

◆ License Type — C33: NLR (No License Required)

◆ Is this Commodity a Used Vehicle? — NO

FORM 9. CERTIFICATE OF ORIGIN

CERTIFICATE OF ORIGIN

The undersigned....... Agent ....
....
(Owner or Agent, or &c)

for..... Santa Claus Company, East Aurora, New York 14052 ....declares
(Name and Address of Shipper)

that the following mentioned goods shipped on S/S... Livorno ....
(Name of Ship)

on the date of.... May 14, 2012 ....consigned to.... Order of Shipper ....

....are the product of the United States of America.

| MARKS AND NUMBERS | NO. OF PKGS. BOXES OR CASES | WEIGHT IN KILOS | | DESCRIPTION |
		GROSS	NET	
K Alpha Co. Athens, Greece Order No. 1234 Made in U.S.A. Nos. 1-513	513			Ctns. Childrens Toys

Sworn to before me

this.... 25th ....day of........ April 2012

Dated at. Buffalo, N.Y. .....on the.. 25th day of.... April 2012

.... Agent ....
(Signature of Owner or Agent)

The... Buffalo Area Chamber of Commerce ...., a recognized Chamber of Commerce under the laws of the State of

.... has examined the manufacturer's invoice or shipper's affidavit concerning the origin of the merchandise and, according to the best of its knowledge and belief, finds that the products named originated in the United States of North America.

Secretary..
(Signature)

FORM 10. DOCK RECEIPT

	BOOKING NO	D/R NO

DOCK RECEIPT — NON-NEGOTIABLE
INFORMATION HEREON IS FOR SHIPPER'S MEMORANDA—NOT PART OF BILL OF LADING

SHIPPER/EXPORTER
SANTA CLAUS COMPANY
EAST AURORA, NEW YORK 14052

DOCUMENT NO.
A-10

EXPORT REFERENCES

FORWARDING AGENT - REFERENCES
F.W. MYERS (ATLANTIC) & CO., INC.   FMC 1397
EMPIRE STATE BUILDING
NEW YORK, NEW YORK 10118

POINT AND COUNTRY OF ORIGIN
EAST AURORA, NEW YORK

DOMESTIC ROUTING EXPORT INSTRUCTIONS

Notify on arrival in New York City
Mr. J. Emma Phone 432-0670 for pier
delivery instructions.

EXPORT MOTOR FREIGHT TO DELIVER TO PIER
DOCK RECEIPTS LODGED AT PIER.

PIER
Pier 29 Black Ball Terminal

ONWARD INLAND ROUTING

VESSEL   VOYAGE NO   FLAG   PORT OF LOADING
S.S. Livorno   NEW YORK

PORT OF DISCHARGE   FOR TRANSSHIPMENT TO
ATHENS

PARTICULARS FURNISHED BY SHIPPER

MARKS AND NUMBERS	NO. OF PKGS	DESCRIPTION OF PACKAGES AND GOODS	GROSS WEIGHT (IN POUNDS)	MEASUREMENT (CUBIC FEET)
◇K◇ ALPHA CO. ATHENS, GREECE ORDER NO. 1234 MADE IN U.S.A. NOS. 1-513	1	Container XTRU STC: 513 Ctns Childrens Toys IMPORT LICENSE #143210 Letter of Credit #34576 CLEAN ON BOARD G-DEST	9633 lbs.	2102.4 C.F

Those Commodities Licensed by the U.S. for Ultimate Destination GREECE
Diversion Contrary to U.S. Law Prohibited.

DELIVERED BY:

TRUCK
LIGHTER
CAR

ARRIVED— DATE TIME

UNLOADED— DATE TIME

CHECKED By

PLACED IN SHIP ON DOCK LOCATION

SL 1159 12-71

Received the above described merchandise in apparent good order and condition, except as noted to be held and transported subject to all the terms and conditions contained in the regular form of bill of lading of the carrier which are incorporated herein and shall be considered a part hereof with the same force and effect as if set forth herein in full. The goods are received subject to delay or carrier's inability to carry due to accumulation of good, lack of conveyances, space or facilities of any sort, labor disturbances, strikes, lockouts, riots, war, government authority or any condition whatsoever beyond the control of the carrier. Any valuation in excess of $500. per package or customary shipping unit as provided for in the carrier's regular form of bill of lading shall be declared in writing by the shipper upon delivery to the carrier and inserted herein, as well as in the bill of lading, and extra freight paid if required. Nothing in this dock receipt shall operate to limit or deprive the carrier of any statutory protection or exemption of limitation of liability.

SEA-LAND SERVICE, INC.

By
    Receiving Clerk

Date

150M N.J. 12 '73
'04667'

Once the forwarder has made arrangements, Santa Claus can have the goods transported to Carrier's pier. Carrier's clerk will then issue a Dock Receipt (Form 10) which covers the goods until the named vessel arrives. When the vessel arrives, the goods are loaded on board, and carrier then issues a "bill of lading" (Form 11) covering them. The forwarder prepares the bill of lading by filling in the blanks on a standard form created by Carrier. Forwarder fills out the form stating the description of the goods and the description, markings and weight of the crates or containers as directed by Shipper's Letter of Instructions (Form 5), so that the bill of lading conforms to the requirements of the letter of credit. Carrier prepares the basic, printed language of the bill of lading, for it is also the contract between Carrier and Santa Claus.

Carrier promises to take the goods to a named destination, and Santa Claus promises that carrier's fee will be paid. If the freight is "prepaid," Santa Claus has paid it before shipment; if it is "collect," buyer is to pay it before receiving delivery. The bill of lading is to state which arrangement is made, and the sale contract should state which arrangement is to be made. If the bill of lading is "non-negotiable," Carrier promises to deliver the goods only to the person named as recipient ("consignee") in the bill of lading, or to a person named by the consignee. If the bill of lading is "negotiable," Carrier promises to deliver the goods only to the person who is in possession of the bill of lading, properly indorsed. Thus, with a negotiable bill of lading, control of the bill itself is the equivalent of control of the goods—for the Carrier may not deliver the goods without first obtaining the surrender of the bill of lading. Because the issuing bank will want this kind of control over the goods after it has paid seller, it is understood that a letter of credit transaction typically requires a negotiable bill of lading.

Note that the bill of lading may be stamped "Clean On Board." Carriers can also issue "Received for Shipment" bills of lading, but they do not evidence that the named vessel has arrived at the time that the bill of lading is issued, or that the goods have survived the risk of being loaded on board the vessel. The sales contract or letter of credit will often call for "Clean On Board" bills of lading.

If the sales contract is CIF, Santa Claus must also procure, at its expense, insurance covering the goods during their transportation. In such a case, the letter of credit will require, as one of the necessary documents, an Insurance Certificate (Form 12) which states that all premiums are prepaid. The insurance company will limit its risks to a stated value, a named vessel, and transportation between designated places. Even if the sales contract is FOB seller's plant, seller may still procure insurance to cover the goods during transportation (to protect buyer), but it is clear that seller may add the cost of any insurance to the price of the goods if it is prepaid. In any documentary transaction, the banks will usually insist on inclusion of any insurance certificate, to assure themselves that *their* security in the goods is protected from the perils during transportation.

FORM 11. BILL OF LADING

INTERNATIONAL BILL OF LADING
NOT NEGOTIABLE UNLESS CONSIGNED "TO ORDER"

(2) SHIPPER/EXPORTER (COMPLETE NAME AND ADDRESS) SANTA CLAUS COMPANY EAST AURORA, NEW YORK 14052	(5) BOOKING NO (5A) BILL OF LADING NO A-10 (6) EXPORT REFERENCES
(3) CONSIGNEE (COMPLETE NAME AND ADDRESS) TO ORDER OF SHIPPER	(7) FORWARDING AGENT F M C NO F.W. MYERS (ATLANTIC) & CO., INC. Empire State Building New York, New York 10118 (212) 432-0670
	(8) POINT AND COUNTRY OF ORIGIN EAST AURORA, NEW YORK FMC 1397
(4) NOTIFY PARTY (COMPLETE NAME AND ADDRESS) ALPHA COMPANY ATHENS GREECE	(9) ALSO NOTIFY - ROUTING & INSTRUCTIONS notify on arrival in NYC Mr. J. Emma Phone 432-0670 for pier delivery instructions EXPORT MOTOR FREIGHT TO DELIVER TO PIER DOCK RECEIPTS LODGE AT PIER

(12) PRE-CARRIAGE BY ★ EXPORT MOTOR FREIGHT	(13) PLACE OF RECEIPT BY PRE-CARRIER ★ EAST AURORA, NY	
(14) VESSEL VOY FLAG SS LIVORNO	(15) PORT OF LOADING NEW YORK	(10) LOADING PIER/TERMINAL Pier 29, Black Ball Terminal (10A) ORIGINAL(S) TO BE RELEASED AT
(16) PORT OF DISCHARGE ATHENS	(17) PLACE OF DELIVERY BY ON-CARRIER ★	(11) TYPE OF MOVE (IF MIXED, USE BLOCK 20 AS APPROPRIATE)

PARTICULARS FURNISHED BY SHIPPER

MKS & NOS. / CONTAINER NOS. (18)	NO. OF PKGS (19)	HM	DESCRIPTION OF PACKAGES AND GOODS (20)	GROSS WEIGHT (21)	MEASUREMENT (22)
K ALPHA CO. ATHENS, GREECE ORDER NO. 1234 Made in U.S.A. NOS. 1-513			CONTAINER XTRU STC: 513 Cartons Childrens Toys IMPORT LICENSE #143210 Letter of Credit #34576 CLEAN ON BOARD G-DEST	9633 lbs.	2102.4 C.F.

These Commodities Licensed by the U.S. for Ultimate Destination GREECE
Diversion Contrary to U.S. Law Prohibited.

23) Declared Value $ If shipper enters a value, carriers package limitation of liability does not apply and the ad valorem rate will be charged				(23A) RATE OF EXCHANGE	(24) FREIGHT PAYABLE AT/BY
TB	RATED AS	PER	RATE	PREPAID	COLLECT	LOCAL CURRENCY

☐ If this box is checked, goods have been loaded, stowed and counted by Shipper. Carrier has NOT done so and is not responsible for accuracy of count, condition or nature of goods described in PARTICULARS FURNISHED BY SHIPPER.

THE RECEIPT, CUSTODY, CARRIAGE AND DELIVERY OF THE GOODS ARE SUBJECT TO THE TERMS APPEARING ON THE FACE AND BACK HEREOF AND TO CARRIER'S APPLICABLE TARIFF.

In witness whereof three (3) original bills of lading all of the same tenor and date, one of which being accomplished the others to stand void, have been issued by the originating carrier for and on behalf of itself, other participating carriers, the vessel and her master and owners or charterers.

(Date) ....

At ....

....(Originating Carrier)

By ....

TOTAL CHARGES

★ APPLICABLE ONLY WHEN USED FOR MULTIMODAL TRANSPORTATION

BILL OF LADING NO ....   DATE ....

COMBINED TRANSPORT BILL OF LADING.

1. DEFINITIONS

"Carrier"	means the Owners or Charterer of the ocean vessel on whose behalf this Bill of Lading has been issued.
"Goods"	means the cargo accepted from the Shipper and includes any Container not supplied by or on behalf of the Carrier.
"Container"	includes any Container (including an open top Container) flat rack, platform, trailer, transportable tank, pallet or any other device used for the transportation of Goods.
"Merchant"	includes the Consignor, Shipper, Holder, Consignee, the receiver of the Goods, any person including any Corporation, Company or other legal entity owning or entitled to the possession of the Goods or this Bill of Lading and anyone acting on behalf of any such persons.
"Holder"	means any person for the time being in possession of this Bill of Lading to whom the property in the Goods has passed on or by reason of the consignment of the Goods or the endorsement of this Bill of Lading or otherwise.

"The Internal Law of a State" shall be deemed to exclude all principles of private international law applied by such State.

2. CARRIER'S TARIFF

The terms of the Carrier's applicable Tariff are incorporated herein. Copies of the relevant provisions of the applicable Tariff are obtainable from the Carrier upon request. In the case of inconsistency between this Bill of Lading and the applicable Tariff, this Bill of Lading shall prevail.

3. SUB-CONTRACTING

(1) The Carrier shall be entitled to sub-contract on any terms the whole or any part of the carriage, loading, unloading, storing, warehousing, handling and any and all duties whatsoever undertaken by the Carrier in relation to the Goods.

(2) The Merchant undertakes that no claim or allegation shall be made against any servant, agent, stevedore or sub-contractor of the Carrier which imposes or attempts to impose upon any of them or any vessel owned or chartered by any of them any liability whatsoever in connection with the Goods, and, if any such claim or allegation should nevertheless be made to indemnify the Carrier against all consequences thereof. Without prejudice to the foregoing, every such servant, agent, stevedore and sub-contractor shall have the benefit of all provisions herein benefiting the Carrier as if such provisions were expressly for their benefit, and all limitations of and exonerations from liability provided to the Carrier by law and by the terms hereof shall be available to them, and, in entering into this contract the Carrier, to the extent of those provisions, does so not only on its own behalf, but also as agent and trustee for such servants, agents, stevedores and sub-contractors.

(3) The expression "sub-contractor" in this clause shall include direct and indirect sub-contractors and their respective servants and agents.

4. DELIVERY OF CARGO BEYOND PORT OF DISCHARGE OR PLACE OF DELIVERY

In the event that Consignees/Receivers of cargo require the Carrier to deliver cargo at a port or place beyond the place of delivery originally designated in this Bill of Lading and the Carrier in its absolute discretion agrees to such further carriage, such further carriage will be undertaken on the basis that the Bill of Lading terms and conditions are to apply to such carriage as if the ultimate destination agreed with Consignees/Receivers had been included in the description of the transport on the reverse side of this Bill of Lading.

5. CARRIER'S RESPONSIBILITY

The Carrier undertakes responsibility from the place of receipt if named herein or from the port of loading to the port of discharge or the place of delivery if named herein as follows:

(1) If it can be proved that the loss or damage occurred while the Goods were in the custody of an inland carrier the liability of the Carrier and the limitation thereof shall be determined in accordance with the inland carrier's contracts of carriage and tariffs, or in the absence of such contracts or tariffs, in accordance with the internal law of the state where the loss or damage occurred.

(2) Where loss or damage has occurred between the time of receipt of the Goods by the Carrier at the port of loading and the time of delivery by the Carrier at the port of discharge, or during any prior or subsequent period of carriage by water, the liability of the Carrier shall be determined as follows:

(a) If the carriage is to or from the United States of America, the "Carriage of Goods by Sea Act 1936" (COGSA) of the United States of America, shall apply.

(b) For carriage in all other trades, the "International Convention for Unification of certain Rules relating to Bills of Lading", dated Brussels, August 25, 1924 (The Hague Rules, excluding Article IX), shall apply except when the "Hague Visby Rules" (dated Brussels, February 23, 1968) are compulsorily applicable at the port of loading in which case the "Hague Visby Rules" shall apply.

(3) Where it cannot be established where the loss or damage occurred the liability of the Carrier shall be determined in accordance with sub-paragraph 2 above.

In no event shall the liability of the Carrier exceed the amount of compensation payable under Clause. 6.

The Carrier shall be entitled to the full benefit of and right to all limitations of or exemptions from liability authorized by any provision of Section 4281 to 4289 of the Revised Statutes of the United States of America and amendments thereto and of any other provisions of the laws of the United States or of any other country whose laws shall apply.

Nothing in this Bill of Lading, expressed or implied, shall be deemed to waive or operate to deprive the Carrier of or lessen the benefits of any such rights, immunities, limitations or exemptions.

6. THE AMOUNT OF COMPENSATION

(1) For shipment to or from ports in the United States of America neither the Carrier nor the Ship shall in any event be or become liable for any loss or damage to or in connection with the transportation of Goods in an amount exceeding $500.00 per package lawful money of the United States of America, or in case of Goods not shipped in packages, per customary freight unit, or the equivalent of that sum in other currency, unless the nature and value of such Goods have been declared by the shipper before shipment and inserted on the face of this Bill of Lading and extra freight paid.

13. LIEN

The Carrier shall have a lien on the Goods and any documents relating thereto for all sums payable to the Carrier under this contract and/or any other contract and for general average contributions to whomsoever due and for the cost of recovering the same, and for that purpose shall have the right to sell the Goods by Public Auction or private treaty without notice to the Merchant. If on sale of the Goods the proceeds fail to cover the amount due and the cost incurred, the Carrier shall be entitled to recover the deficit from the Merchant.

14. OPTIONAL STOWAGE, DECK CARGO AND LIVESTOCK

(1) The Goods may be stowed by the Carrier in Containers or similar articles of transport used to consolidate Goods.

(2) Goods whether stowed in Containers or not, may be carried on deck or under deck without notice to the Merchant unless on the face hereof it is specifically stipulated that the Containers or Goods will be carried under deck, and if carried on deck, the Carrier shall not be required to note, mark or stamp on the Bill of Lading any statement of such on deck carriage. Such Goods (other than livestock) whether carried on deck or under deck and whether or not stated to be carried on deck shall participate in general average and shall be deemed to be within the definition of Goods for the purpose of the "Carriage of Goods by Sea Act 1936" (COGSA) of the United States of America or similar provisions of any other Act which may be applicable.

(3) Goods (not being Goods stowed in Containers other than flats or pallets) which are stated herein to be carried on deck and livestock, whether or not carried on deck, are carried without responsibility on the part of the Carrier for loss or damage of whatsoever nature arising during carriage by sea whether caused by unseaworthiness or negligence or any other cause whatsoever.

15. METHODS AND ROUTES OF TRANSPORTATION

(1) The Carrier may at any time and without notice to the Merchant:

(a) use any means of transport or storage whatsoever;

(b) transfer the Goods from one conveyance to another including trans-shipping or carrying the same on another vessel than the vessel named overleaf or on any other means of transport whatsoever and even though transhipment or forwarding of the Goods may not have been contemplated or provided for herein;

(c) sail without pilots, proceed via any route, proceed to, return to and stay at any port or place whatsoever (including the port of loading herein provided) in any order in or out of the route or in a contrary direction to or beyond the port of discharge once or more often for bunkering or loading or discharging cargo or embarking or disembarking any person(s) whether in connection with the present a prior or subsequent voyage or any other purpose whatsoever, and before giving delivery of the Goods at the port of discharge or the place of delivery herein provided and with liberties as aforesaid leave and then return to and discharge the Goods at such port, tow or be towed, make trial trips, adjust compasses, or repair or dry-dock, with or without cargo onboard;

(d) load and unload the Goods at any port or place (whether or not any such port is named overleaf as the Port of Loading or Port of Discharge) and store the Goods at any such port or place;

(e) comply with any orders or recommendations given by any government or authority or any person or body or purporting to act as or on behalf of such government or authority or having under the terms of the insurance on the conveyance employed by the Carrier the right to give orders or directions.

(2) Anything done or not done in accordance with sub-clause (1) or any delay arising therefrom shall be deemed to be within the contractual carriage and shall not be a deviation.

16. MATTERS AFFECTING PERFORMANCE

(1) If at any time the performance of the contract evidenced by this Bill of Lading is or is likely to be affected by any hindrance, risk, delay, difficulty or disadvantage of whatsoever kind which cannot be avoided by the exercise of reasonable endeavours, the Carrier (whether or not the transport has commenced) may without notice to the Merchant treat the performance of this contract as terminated and place the Goods or any part of them at the Merchant's disposal at any port or place whatsoever which the Carrier or Master may consider safe and advisable in the circumstances, whereupon the responsibility of the Carrier in respect of such Goods shall cease. The Carrier shall nevertheless be entitled to full freight and charges on Goods received for transportation, and the Merchant shall pay any additional costs of carriage to and delivery and storage at such port or place.

(2) The circumstances referred to in sub-clause (1) above shall include, but shall not be limited to, those caused by the existence or apprehension of war declared or undeclared, hostilities, warlike or belligerent acts or operations, riots, civil commotions or other disturbances, closure of, obstacles in or danger to any canal; blockade of port or place or interdict or prohibition of or restriction on commerce or trading; quarantine, sanitary or other similar regulations or restrictions; strikes, lockouts or other labour troubles whether partial or general and whether or not involving employees of the Carrier or his sub-contractors; congestion of port, wharf, sea terminal or any other place; shortage, absence or obstacles of labour or facilities for loading, discharge, delivery or other handling of the Goods; epidemics or diseases; bad weather, shallow water, ice, landslide or other obstacle in navigation or haulage.

17. PERISHABLE CARGO

Goods of a perishable nature shall be carried in ordinary Containers without special protection, services or other measures unless there is noted on the reverse side of this Bill of Lading that the Goods will be carried in a refrigerated, heated, electrically ventilated or otherwise specially equipped Container or are to receive special attention in any way.

The Merchant undertakes not to tender for transportation any Goods which require refrigeration without giving written notice of their nature and the required temperature setting of the thermostatic controls before receipt of the Goods by the Carrier. In case of refrigerated Container(s) packed by or on behalf of the Merchant, the Merchant undertakes that the Goods have been properly stowed in the Container and that the thermostatic controls have been adequately set by him before receipt of the Goods by the Carrier.

The Merchant's attention is drawn to the fact that refrigerated Containers are not designed to freeze down cargo which has not been presented for stuffing at or below its designated carrying temperature and the Carrier shall not be responsible for the consequences of cargo presented at a higher temperature than that required for the transportation.

If the above requirements are not complied with, the Carrier shall not be liable for any loss of or damage to the Goods howsoever arising.

(2) In all other trades where the Hague Rules apply the Carrier's maximum liability shall in no event exceed £100.00 lawful money of the United Kingdom per package or unit, unless the nature and value of such Goods have been declared by the shipper before shipment and inserted on the face of this Bill of Lading and extra freight paid.

7. GENERAL

(1) The Carrier does not undertake that the Goods shall arrive at the port of discharge or the place of delivery at any particular time or to meet any particular market or use and save as is provided in clause 4 the Carrier shall in no circumstances be liable for any direct, indirect or consequential loss or damage caused by delay. If the Carrier should nevertheless be held legally liable for any such direct or indirect or consequential loss or damage caused by delay, such liability shall in no event exceed the freight paid for the transport covered by this Bill of Lading.

(2) Save as is otherwise provided herein, the Carrier shall in no circumstances be liable for direct or indirect or consequential loss or damage arising from any other cause.

(3) The terms of this bill of Lading shall govern the responsibility of the Carrier in connection with or arising out of the supplying of a Container to the Merchant whether before or after the Goods are received by the Carrier for transportation or delivered to the Merchant.

8. NOTICE OF LOSS, TIME BAR

Unless notice of loss or damage and the general nature of such loss or damage be given in writing to the Carrier or his agents at the port of discharge or the place of delivery as the case may be before or at the time of removal of the Goods into the custody of the Merchant such removal shall be prima facie evidence of the delivery by the Carrier of the Goods as described in this Bill of Lading. If the loss or damage is not apparent, then notice must be given within three days of the delivery. In any event, the Carrier shall be discharged from any liability unless suit is brought within one year after delivery of the Goods or the date when the Goods should have been delivered.

9. SHIPPER-PACKED CONTAINERS

(1) If a Container has not been stuffed by the Carrier, this Bill of Lading shall be a receipt only for the Container(s) and the Carrier shall not be liable for loss of or damage to the contents and the Merchant shall indemnify the Carrier against any injury, loss, damage, liability or expense incurred by the Carrier if such injury, loss, damage, liability or expense has been caused by:

(a) The manner in which the Container has been filled, packed, stuffed or loaded: or

(b) the unsuitability of the contents for carriage in Containers; or

(c) the unsuitability or defective condition of the Container which would have been apparent upon reasonable inspection by the Merchant at or prior to the time the Container was filled, packed, stuffed or loaded.

(2) The Shipper shall inspect Containers before stuffing them and the use of the Containers shall be prima facie evidence of their being sound and suitable for use.

10. INSPECTION OF GOODS

The Carrier shall be entitled, but under no obligation, to open any Package or Container at any time and to inspect the contents. If it thereupon appears that the contents or any part thereof cannot safely or properly be carried or carried further, either at all or without incurring any additional expense or taking any measures in relation to such Package or Container or its contents or any part thereof, the Carrier may abandon the transportation thereof and/or take any measures and/or incur any reasonable additional expense to carry or to continue the carriage or to store the same ashore or afloat under cover or in the open, at any place, which storage shall be deemed to constitute due delivery under this Bill of Lading. The Merchant shall indemnify the Carrier against any reasonable additional expense so incurred.

The Carrier in exercising the liberties contained in this clause shall not be under any obligation to take any particular measures and the Carrier shall not be liable for any loss, damage or delay howsoever arising from any action or lack of action under this clause.

11. SHIPPER'S RESPONSIBLITY

(1) The Shipper warrants to the Carrier that the particulars relating to the Goods as set out overleaf have been checked by the Shipper on receipt of this Bill of Lading and that such particulars and any other particulars furnished by or on behalf of the Shipper are correct,

(2) The Shipper shall indemnify the Carrier against all loss, damage or expenses arising or resulting from inaccuracies or inadequacy of such particulars.

12. FREIGHT AND CHARGES

(1) Full freight hereunder shall be due and payable by the Shipper in cash without deduction on receipt of the Goods or part thereof by the Carrier for shipment and shall be deemed to have been fully earned upon such receipt of Goods. All charges due hereunder together with freight shall be due from and payable by the Shipper, Consignee, Owner of the Goods or Holder of this Bill of Lading (who shall be jointly and severally liable to the Carrier therefore) on demand at such port or place as the Carrier may require, vessel or other means of transportation of cargo lost or not lost from any cause whatsoever.

(2) The freight stated herein to be paid or payable has been calculated and based on the particulars of the Goods furnished by the Shipper to the Carrier. The Carrier shall be entitled at any time to open and re-classify or re-weigh or re-measure or re-value any Goods, and freight shall be paid on the proper classification or the excess weight or measurement or value.

(3) The Merchant's attention is drawn to the stipulations concerning currency in which the freight and charges are to be paid, rate of exchange, devaluation and other contingencies relative to freight and charges in the applicable Tariff.

(4) The freight has been calculated on the basis of particulars furnished by or on behalf of the Shipper. The Carrier may at any time open any Container or other Package or Unit in order to re-weigh, re-measure, re-classify or re-value the contents, and if the particulars furnished by or on behalf of the Shipper are incorrect, it is agreed that a sum equal to the difference between the correct freight and the freight charged shall be payable by the Merchant to the Carrier.

18. DANGEROUS GOODS

(1) The Merchant undertakes not to tender for transportation any Goods which are of a dangerous, inflammable, radioactive or damaging nature without previously giving written notice of their nature to the Carrier and marking the Goods and the Container or other covering on the outside as required by any laws or regulations which may be applicable during the carriage. The Carrier or the Master may however, in their absolute discretion reject any such cargo.

(2) If the requirements of sub-clause (1) are not complied with or if the Goods which were tendered in compliance with sub-clause (1) shall become a danger to the vessel, cargo or any other property or person, such Goods may be unloaded, destroyed or rendered harmless without compensation and the Merchant shall indemnify the Carrier against all loss, damage or expense which the Carrier could not avoid by the exercise of reasonable diligence by incurred as a result of the carriage of such Goods.

19. REGULATIONS RELATING TO GOODS

The Merchant shall comply with all regulations or requirements of Customs, port and other authorities, and shall bear and pay all duties, taxes, fines, imposts, expenses or losses incurred or suffered by reason thereof or by reason of any illegal, incorrect or insufficient marking, numbering or addressing of the Goods, and indemnify the Carrier in respect thereof.

20. NOTIFICATION AND DELIVERY

(1) Any mention in this Bill of Lading of parties to be notified of the arrival of the Goods is solely for information of the Carrier, and failure to give such notification shall not involve the Carrier in any liability nor relieve the Merchant of any obligation hereunder.

(2) The Merchant shall take delivery of the Goods within the time provided for in the Carrier's applicable Tariff.

(3) If the Merchant fails to take delivery of the Goods or part of them in accordance with this Bill of Lading, the Carrier may without notice unstow the Goods or that part thereof and/or store the Goods or that part thereof ashore, afloat, in the open or under cover. Such storage shall constitute due delivery hereunder, and thereupon all liability whatsoever of the Carrier in respect of the Goods or that part thereof shall cease.

(4) The Merchant's attention is drawn to the stipulations concerning free storage time and demurrage contained in the Carrier's applicable Tariff, which is incorporated in this Bill of Lading.

(5) The Carrier may in his absolute discretion receive the Goods as Full Container Load and deliver them as less than Full Container Load and/or as break bulk cargo and/or delivery of the Goods to more than one receiver. In such event the Carrier shall not be liable for any shortage, loss, damage or discrepancies of the Goods, which are found upon unpacking of the Container.

(6) If the Goods are unclaimed during a reasonable time, or whenever in the Carrier's opinion the Goods will become deteriorated, decayed or worthless, the Carrier may, at his discretion and subject to his lien and without any responsibility attaching to him, sell, abandon or otherwise dispose of the Goods at the sole risk and expense of the Merchant.

21. BOTH-TO-BLAME COLLISION CLAUSE

If the carrying ship comes into collision with another ship as a result of negligence of the other ship and any act, neglect or default in the navigation or the management of the carrying ship, the Merchant undertakes to pay the Carrier, or, where the Carrier is not the owner and in possesison of the carrying ship, to pay to the Carrier as trustee for the owner and/or demise charterer of the carrying ship, a sum sufficient to indemnify the Carrier and/or the owner and/or demise charterer of the carrying ship against all loss or liability to the other or non-carrying ship or her owners insofar as such loss or liability represents loss of or damage to, or any claim whatsoever of the Merchant, paid or payable by the other or non-carrying ship or her owners to the Merchant and set off, recouped or recovered by the other or non-carrying ship or her owners as part of their claim agaany shipsinst the carrying ship or her owner or demise charterer or the Carrier. The foregoing provisions shall also apply where the owners, operators, or those in charge or any ship or ships or objects, other than, or in addition to, the colliding ships or objects, are at fault in respect to a collision, contact, stranding or other accident.

22. GENERAL AVERAGE

(1) General average shall be adjusted at any port or place in the option of the Carrier in accordance with the York-Antwerp Rules 1974.

(2) If the Carrier delivers the Goods without obtaining security for general average contributions, the Merchant, by taking delivery of the Goods, undertakes personal responsibility to pay such contributions and to provide a cash deposit or other security for the estimated amount of such contribution as the Carrier shall reasonably require.

23. NEW JASON CLAUSE

(1) In the event of accident, danger, damage or disaster before or after the commencement of the voyage, resulting from any cause whatsoever, whether due to negligence or not, for which or for the consequence of which the Carrier is not responsible, by statute, contract or otherwise, the Goods and the Merchant shall jointly and severally contribute with the Carrier in general average to the payment of any sacrifices, losses or expenses of a general average nature that may be made or incurred and shall pay salvage and special charges incurred in respect of the Goods.

(2) If a salving ship is owned or operated by the Carrier, salvage shall be paid for as fully as if the said salvage ship belonged to strangers.

24. VARIATION OF THE CONTRACT ETC.

No servant or agent of the Carrier shall have power to waive or vary any terms of this Bill of Lading unless such waiver or variation is in writing and is specifically authorized or ratified in writing by the Carrier.

25. LAW AND JURISDICTION

Whenever the "Carriage of Goods by Sea Act of 1936" (COGSA) of the United States of America applies by virtue of clause 5.2(a) above this contract is to be governed by United States law and the United States Federal Court Southern District of New York is to have exclusive jurisdiction to hear all disputes hereunder.

In all other cases this Bill of Lading is subject to English law and jurisdiction.

[G4115]

FORM 12. INSURANCE CERTIFICATE

The Prudential Assurance Co., Ltd.

MARINE DEPARTMENT

4 FENCHURCH AVENUE, LONDON, FC3M 5BX
Telephone: 01–626–9176 Cable: **PRUMARIN**

INSURANCE CERTIFICATE No. 23456 . . . .

This Certificate acknowledges the receipt of a Declaration under an
OPEN POLICY issued by the Company's Agents

in GLASGOW (Stenhouse) to F. W. Myers & Co. Inc.

Name of Assured: Santa Claus Co., East Aurora, N.Y.

Vessel/Conveyance: SS Livorno

Voyage: Voyage 21 E New York to Athens

Interest & Marks: 513 Cases Childrens Toys in Cont # XTRU
432890

Insured Value: $22,079.81

Against all risks as per Institute Cargo Clauses (All Risks).

Including War, Strikes, Riots and Civil
Commotions as per Institute Clauses
current at date of this Certificate.

Claims payable at .Athens . . . .

In case of Claim apply to   Prudential Assurance Co. Ltd.
. . . .
Athens, Greece

. . . .

Examined . . . .

DATE . . . .

Buffalo, N.Y.

UNDERWRITER

PART E. SELLER OBTAINS PAYMENT; BUYER OBTAINS THE GOODS

Once the seller has obtained a negotiable bill of lading to his own order, how does he obtain payment? The letter of credit (Form 4) does not actually say that anyone will "pay" Santa Claus. Instead, it states that Marine Midland Bank "undertake[s] to purchase all drafts drawn as above specified." The text of the letter of credit also states that funds are "available by your drafts on the Commercial Bank of Greece, to be accompanied by:" and then lists the required documents.

What is a draft? See Form 13. Form 13 resembles a check form, with which you are familiar. In one of your checks, you (the Drawer) draw a check on your bank (the Drawee), ordering it to pay a person you designate (the Payee) from funds in your own account. In the Form 13 draft (or bill of exchange, as it is also known), Seller (Drawer) draws on Buyer's Bank (the Drawee), ordering Buyer's Bank to pay Seller itself (Payee) from the "credit" created at Buyer's request and for Buyer's account. The contract between Buyer and Buyer's Bank will allow Buyer's bank to do this. The draft could have been drawn on Seller's Bank or Buyer's Bank. In this case, it is drawn on Commercial Bank of Greece (Buyer's Bank) because of the language in the letter of credit ("drafts on Commercial Bank of Greece"). Most letters of credit list a draft as one of the documents Seller is required to submit in order to be paid, together with the invoice, bill of lading, etc., and the terms of the draft will be specified in the letter of credit. The draft in Form 13 is drawn for the amount due under the letter of credit and the sales contract, and is payable "to the order of" Seller, which makes the draft negotiable.

FORM 13.   SIGHT DRAFT

U.S. $20,072.55   May 16, 2012
To: Commercial Bank of Greece, Athens, Greece
Pay to the Order of Santa Claus Co., East Aurora, New York, Twenty thousand seventy two and $^{55}/_{100}$ United States Dollars, for Value received.
Santa Claus Co.
Rachel Smith   Export Manager
Drawn under Letter of Credit No. 34576, confirmed by Marine Midland Bank–Western
Import Lic. No. 143210

A draft is a negotiable instrument that is used in most cases as the legal vehicle for payment under the letter of credit. While the letter of credit is a contract by which an issuing bank promises to pay if certain stated conditions are met, it is not itself a payment device. The letter of credit creates the right to payment; the seller then uses a negotiable instrument (the draft) to "draw on" that credit (just as you might use a check to withdraw money from your own bank account).

The draft can be payable either immediately ("on demand," or "at sight") or at a time subsequent to the "presentment" of the draft ("30 days after sight"), depending upon the letter of credit terms. In the latter case, by using a "time draft" the parties have arranged for a credit transaction. The drawee (in our case, the issuing bank) need not pay upon presentment, but it must "accept" the time draft at presentment, which creates a promise by the drawee to pay at the later time stated in the draft. This promise through "acceptance of the draft" also deprives the acceptor of most potential defenses against payment. Thus, if Commercial Bank of Greece accepts a time draft and Buyer later becomes insolvent, Commercial Bank must still pay the holder of the draft at presentment.

Once Santa Claus has drawn a draft on Commercial Bank of Greece, how does it obtain payment? It uses the banking system as a collection agent. It takes the draft, together with all required documents (Forms 6, 7, 9, 11, 12), to Marine Midland Bank. There, it indorses both the draft and the negotiable bill of lading to the bank and presents all the documents to the bank. In the letter of credit, the bank said it would "purchase" such drafts, and it does so by paying Santa Claus—usually by crediting Santa Claus' bank account, either with Marine Midland Bank or with some other bank with which Santa Claus already has an account.

Marine Midland Bank will then indorse the draft and forward that draft, with the required documents attached, to Commercial Bank of Greece in Athens. As the issuing bank, Commercial Bank of Greece must in turn pay Marine Midland (the confirming bank) upon the presentation of the draft and the other documents required by the letter of credit. Since there is already a correspondent bank relationship between the two banks, Commercial Bank of Greece will credit Marine Midland's account with the payment. Commercial Bank of Greece will then advise Alpha that the documents have arrived, and that payment is due under the letter of credit contract. Since Alpha and Commercial Bank of Greece have an established relationship, the usual course of events will be for the bank to be authorized to charge the amount of the draft to Alpha's bank account, and to forward the documents to Alpha. If Alpha has arranged for credit (*i.e.*, a loan) from Commercial Bank of Greece, the credit will be advanced when the draft and documents arrive. If there was not an established relationship between Buyer and its bank, Buyer would be required to pay (or to arrange sufficient credit for) the draft before the documents were released to it. As the draft and documents are forwarded from Santa Claus to Marine Midland to Commercial Bank of Greece, each of these parties will indorse the bill of lading (Form 11) to the next party. To better understand this transaction pattern, consult the diagram on the next page.

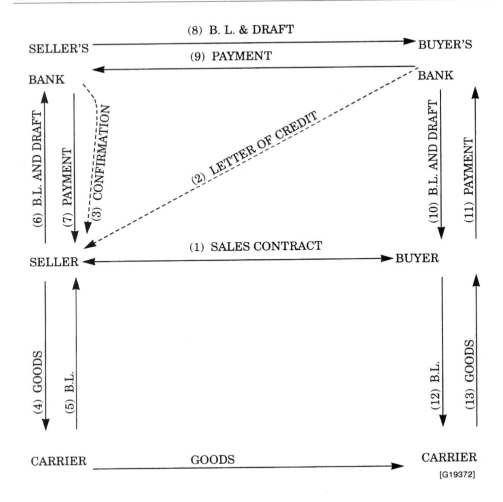

When the goods arrive, Alpha uses the negotiable bill of lading, properly indorsed to it, to obtain the goods from Carrier. Note that Alpha has effectively paid for the goods while they were at sea, long before their arrival. In fact, Alpha was bound to pay for the goods as soon as the draft and required documents were presented to Marine Midland Bank. If the goods failed to arrive, Alpha must look to its Insurance Certificate for protection and reimbursement. When the goods arrive, Carrier may not release them to Alpha unless it is in possession of the negotiable bill of lading, properly indorsed *to* Alpha. Further, the terms of the bill of lading will prohibit Alpha from even inspecting the goods unless it has obtained physical possession of the bill of lading. Thus, until Commercial Bank of Greece is satisfied that it will be paid by Alpha, it can control the goods by controlling the bill of lading.

QUESTIONS AND COMMENTS

1. This description of the international documentary sale transaction has been brief and, in the interest of readability, has eliminated the legal connotations of several aspects of this transaction. The purpose of these comments is to explore three of these aspects in more detail: commercial terms, the bill of lading, and how the structure of the transaction addresses the risks to each party.

2. The role of "commercial terms" is to create a stable set of background rules for the obligations of buyers and sellers relating to the transportation of the goods. Several are discussed in the Basic Transaction: FOB (Free on Board), FAS (Free Alongside Ship), CFR (Cost and Freight) ("C & F" under the UCC), and CIF (Cost, Insurance, and Freight). The sales contract expressly negotiated by the parties is of course the starting point for defining their respective rights and obligations. Problem 4.1 below will address the special problems in the formation of sales contracts in international transactions. (Of particular significance there will be an international treaty, the Convention on Contracts for the International Sale of Goods (CISG)). Problem 4.4 then analyzes the same subject within the context of the growing significance of electronic commerce.

3. Even a relatively simple domestic sale of goods contract, however, must address a number of essential questions, *e.g.*, price, payment, quality and quantity, delivery, risk of loss, and passing of title. But even these basic matters can become more complex in international transactions. We have noted that issues of business culture, language, applicable law, and currency, among myriad others, may make simple negotiations more difficult. These issues may become even more challenging if transportation of the goods is required, and especially if intermediaries (carriers, banks) are involved.

First, there are "price term" issues: Does the quoted price include freight? Insurance? Loading charges? Storage?

Second, there are transportation issues: When does "title" to the goods pass? At what point must seller take responsibility for paying property taxes? Import or export fees? Excise taxes? At what point is it too late for buyer to refuse to take and pay for the goods? At what point is it too late for seller to stop delivery because buyer's credit is shaky, or a revolution has broken out at the place of delivery—or the International Monetary Fund has imposed austerity measures on the State of the place of delivery, and repatriation of the sales price in dollars may not be possible?

The commercial terms used by merchants are short-hand references to sets of rules which answer some or all of the questions above, without stating each issue and each risk allocation separately. Where can statements of these sets of rules be found? For a domestic transaction the UCC would probably be applicable, and UCC §§ 2–319, 2–320 contain relevant definitions. For an international transaction, the Convention on the International Sale of Goods (CISG), if applicable, may provide some general background rules. But it is also more likely that the parties themselves will incorporate by reference a specialized set of contractual rules, the I.C.C. Incoterms (2010 edition). The role and substance of these Incoterms is the subject of analysis in Problem 4.2 below.

Perhaps the best illustration of the effect of these commercial terms on the price of the goods appears in Form 2, the Proforma Invoice, where the additional duties and costs of the seller are detailed for each commercial term. The difference in duties has other effects, however. In Toys for Greece, under an "FOB Seller's Plant" term, Santa Claus would have had no further duties after the carrier has taken the goods away, if a proper transportation contract had been arranged. However, under an "FAS NYC" term, Santa Claus' duties would have continued during transportation within the United States until the goods were "alongside" the SS Livorno. CFR and CIF prolong seller's duties and responsibilities until delivery of the goods at their stated destination.

In FAS, CFR, and CIF contracts, buyer is expected to make payment against documents, but this is not required of buyer under the ordinary FOB place of shipment contract, unless the contract also states "payment against documents." So what? Well, usually buyer has a right to inspect the goods before accepting or paying for them, unless the sales contract requires (expressly or implicitly) payment against documents. Thus, Alpha's specification of a "CIF" term in its Purchase Order Form (Form 3) implicitly proposed a contract in which Alpha could not inspect the goods before paying for them (*i.e.*, before paying "against the documents" under the letter of credit).

4. An integral part of the Basic Transaction is the negotiable bill of lading (Form 11), for when Alpha pays "against the documents," and before inspection of the goods, this bill of lading is both its proof of shipment of the goods and the method of obtaining possession of the goods from the carrier after the arrival of the SS Livorno. The bill of lading must, therefore: (1) control ownership of the goods themselves, and (2) conform to the sales contract, especially in its description of the goods.

There are two different types of bills of lading—a "straight," or non-negotiable, bill of lading, and an "order," or negotiable, bill of lading. (These are also known in the trade as "white" and "yellow" for the different colors of paper on which they are often printed.) Each usually represents the shipper's contract with the carrier, and expressly or implicitly will set forth the terms of that contract.

In the cash transaction, in theory, seller has control of the goods until payment is in hand, and buyer has control of the goods as soon as they are paid for. In reality, these measures of control are available only in the face-to-face exchange of goods between buyer and seller. In a documentary exchange, the only method available to seller to obtain equivalent control of the goods is, first, for seller to maintain control of the bill of lading until the goods are paid for, and second, for possession of the bill of lading to control the goods themselves. If a straight bill of lading is used, the carrier must deliver the goods to the person named as consignee on the bill of lading, and possession of the straight bill of lading does not control the goods. Thus, straight bills of lading are not appropriate for a documentary transaction, and the case reporters are full of litigation where an attorney tried a short-cut using a straight bill of lading with a "Surrender Clause" as the "easy" way to do this transaction. *See, e.g., C-Art, Ltd. v. Hong Kong Islands Line America, S.A.,* 940 F.2d 530 (9th Cir.1991); *Porky Products, Inc. v. Nippon Exp. U.S.A. (Illinois), Inc.,* 1 F. Supp. 2d 227 (S.D.N.Y. 1997)(describing "centuries of clearly established principles" on the point), *aff'd,* 152 F.3d 920 (2nd Cir. 1998).

On the other hand, the order, or negotiable, bill of lading requires the carrier to deliver the goods to the holder of the document. Thus, the seller can maintain control of the goods by obtaining a negotiable bill of lading to his own order, and then maintaining control over the document. By controlling the document, and thereby keeping control over the goods, seller can maintain an interest in the goods until buyer has "paid against the document." Problem 4.5 below explores in more detail the rights and obligations arising out of bills of lading in international transactions.

Other specific attributes of bills of lading may be required by specific terms in the sale contract. For example, "FOB vessel" in the sales contract requires, unless otherwise agreed, that seller obtain an "on board" bill of lading, stating that the goods have actually been loaded. On the other hand, "CIF" or "CFR" in the sales contract is satisfied, unless otherwise agreed, by a "received for shipment" bill of lading, which does not state that the goods have been loaded.

5. To understand the collection transaction by the banking system, consult the flow chart on page 52. With a letter of credit, the seller's bank typically will serve either as a "confirming bank" or as an "advising bank." The Basic Transaction illustrates the use of a confirming bank. An advising bank, in contrast, merely informs the seller that the issuing bank has established a letter of credit it seller's favor.

Even without a letter of credit, a seller may utilize banking channels to forward documents to the buyer. Seller's bank may agree take the draft and accompanying documents "for collection" only (although it may decide to "discount," or buy, the documents outright and become the owner). If it Seller's Bank takes the documents "for collection only," it is required to send them for presentation to the buyer, typically through "customary banking channels." Seller's Bank deals with "for collection" items individually, without assuming that they will be honored, and therefore without giving the seller a provisional credit in the seller's account until the buyer pays the draft.

The draft, with its attached documents, will finally pass through "customary banking channels" to Buyer's Bank, which will notify the buyer of the arrival of the documents. Buyer's Bank will demand that the buyer pay the amount of draft. The buyer may require the bank to "exhibit" the documents to it to allow the buyer to determine whether they conform to the contract. The buyer has three banking days after the notice was sent to decide whether to pay, if mere notice is sent. However, if the documents are exhibited directly to the buyer, the buyer must decide whether to pay or not by the close of business on that same day, unless there are extenuating circumstances.

6. Note the risks to each party. If the seller ships goods to a foreign buyer without setting up a full documentary transaction, including a letter of credit, it has shipped goods for which it has not yet been paid. Even if the

contract provides for "payment against documents," and the seller obtains a bill of lading and forwards it to the buyer with a sight draft attached, the buyer might refuse to pay the sight draft, with documents attached, when it arrives. This would give the seller a cause of action, but often it is usable only in the buyer's jurisdiction, which means bringing a suit abroad with its extra expense, delay and uncertainty. In particular, a plaintiff could feel that it will be the target of discrimination in the courts of another nation.

The seller would still have control of the goods, because after dishonor of the draft the bill of lading will be returned to the seller. However, the goods would now be at a foreign destination—one at which the seller may have no agents, and no particular prospects for resale. In addition, if the seller wished to bring the goods back to its base of operations (and normal sales territory), it would have to pay a second transportation charge, and this may be substantial in relation to the value of the goods.

Thus, the dishonor of the draft and rejection of the goods by the buyer can create economic circumstances where seller's only rational option is a distress sale in buyer's nation. It is to protect against that possibility that the letter of credit is used. Despite its fancy name, the letter of credit is just another contract—this time between Buyer's Bank and the seller. In this contract, Buyer's Bank promises to pay drafts accompanied by stated documents. The bank's promise is issued directly to the seller, and therefore is a direct obligation of that bank to the seller, regardless of what action the buyer may or may not take. Naturally, the bank will also have a contract with the buyer, to ensure that the buyer reimburses Buyer's Bank. The letter of credit can be revocable, but usually it is irrevocable (a "firm credit") because an irrevocable credit is more useful in calming the seller's fears concerning a wrongful rejection of the goods by the buyer.

The requirement that the buyer provide a letter of credit is a term of the sales contract that must be separately bargained for and stated. If the sales of goods contract merely states "payment against documents," that does not establish a requirement for a letter of credit; that merely obligates buyer, not a bank, to honor the draft which accompanies the bill of lading. As pointed out above, the letter of credit term should specify not only the bank, but also precisely what documents are required for payment.

In many instances, the seller does not trust Buyer's Bank any more than the buyer. Buyer's Bank may be a foreign, state-owned bank, or a foreign, private bank, or simply a bank with which seller is not familiar. The seller wants the promise of a United States bank, preferably a known bank. In fact, the seller wants the promise of its bank that, if a presentation of certain documents is made, payment *will* be made. Seller can get such a promise by including a term in the sale of goods contract requiring a "confirmed" letter of credit, and specifying its bank as the "confirming bank." If Seller's Bank merely writes "confirmed" and its signature on Buyer's Bank's letter of credit, that constitutes Seller's Bank's direct obligation to the seller that it will pay the seller against the described documents. The seller will now have three independent promises to pay: (1) from buyer (sales contract), (2) from Buyer's Bank (letter of credit), and (3) from Seller's Bank (confirmation of letter of credit).

7. Now, note how the risks of this international transaction between two people who know nothing about each other have been broken down and distributed to those parties that have the ability to evaluate them with some degree of accuracy.

A. If the buyer cannot pay (becomes insolvent) or will not pay (wrongfully rejects the goods), Buyer's Bank must still pay the seller against conforming documents. What protects Buyer's Bank? First, it is in a particularly good position to investigate and to evaluate the risk of the buyer's insolvency, and to either obtain funds from the buyer when issuing the letter of credit or sue the buyer for breach of contract if there is a wrongful refusal to pay. In addition, it has protection from the bill of lading. Because a negotiable bill of lading controls the goods themselves, Buyer's Bank may resell them to cover at least part of its losses.

B. If Buyer's Bank cannot pay (in a confirmed letter of credit transaction), Seller's Bank has the credit risk concerning solvency of Buyer's Bank, which it can evaluate better than either the buyer or the seller. It also has a risk that Buyer's Bank will not pay. However, it will have a legally enforceable claim for payment and, since it has multiple level relationships with Buyer's Bank, it is in a better position to induce compliance than the other parties. Thus, when the seller ships and procures conforming documents, there is a risk of nonpayment only if both Buyer's Bank and Seller's Bank fail.

C. And, if Seller's Bank refuses to pay, the seller can deal with its personnel directly in resolving the dispute, or bring an action against it in United States courts.

One large risk has been reduced to several smaller ones, and each smaller risk placed on a party that can fairly evaluate it. The lack of substantial risk in the vast bulk of these transactions can best be seen by looking at the usual bank charges for this service (in developed countries, commonly under 1% of the letter of credit amount). Problems 5.0, 5.1, and 5.2 below explore in more detail the rights and obligations arising out of international letter of credit transactions.

8. Under the foregoing analysis, the seller seems to have extensive protection: under a confirmed letter of credit, the seller has the separate promises of a local bank, a foreign bank, and the buyer that each will pay seller upon presentation of the required documents. The buyer has some protection, in that it need not pay until presentation of the documents—and the documents purport to evidence the shipment of the goods described in them. But, how well is the buyer protected? What could possibly go wrong? There are *at least* six problems which could arise from the buyer's point of view:

(a) The goods could be lost or stolen.

(b) The carrier could stow the goods or operate so negligently that they are damaged in transit.

(c) The goods shipped could be non-conforming to the contract. The non-conformity could range from (1) the seller shipping scrap paper to (2) the labelling on the packaging being incorrect (which can cause problems with customs agents in both countries).

(d) The bill of lading could be forged—and no goods were ever shipped.

(e) The bill of lading and attached draft could be stolen and presented to buyer by a thief—with any necessary indorsements having been forged.

(f) A transmitting bank could become insolvent while in possession of the bill of lading, before it reaches the buyer, and before the draft is paid.

Note that some of these problems are recognized and dealt with in the standard handling of the documentary transaction. For example, insuring the goods against loss or theft is standard practice (*see* Form 12), but problems can still arise (*see* Problems 4.2, 4.5, and 5.2 below).

9. Other problems, such as payment before inspection, make buyers feel unprotected, and they have searched for devices within the transaction which can afford them more protection. Such a device, in common use in modern transactions, is the Inspection Certificate. The purpose of such a document is to provide a certification by an independent third-party at the time of shipment (*i.e.*, before the seller is able to obtain payment on the letter of credit) that the goods conform to the description in the sales contract. However, as one might expect, many legal issues can arise concerning the use and effect of Inspection Certificates. When does the absence of such a certificate allow the buyer to reject the documents and the goods? If the seller provides an Inspection Certificate, may the buyer reject the goods? If the seller provides an Inspection Certificate which conforms to the contract, but the goods do not in fact conform to either the certificate or the contract, is the buyer precluded by the certificate from bringing a successful action for the nonconformity?

PROBLEM 4.1 FORMATION OF AN INTERNATIONAL TRANSACTION: INSULATION TO GERMANY

SECTION I. THE SETTING

PART A.

(Basic Fact Pattern) Officers of Universal Pipe, Inc., a small Kansas manufacturer of pipe insulation, attend an international trade fair in New York, where they meet an agent of Eurobuilders, Ltd. (Euro), a builder of industrial facilities whose headquarters are in London, England. Euro is interested in Universal's insulation for use in a refinery Euro is building in Darmstadt, Germany, which fact Euro explains to Universal. Universal's representative gives Euro's agent a price list which states that Universal's "Standard Pipe Insulation Product A" is priced at $200 per 100 lb., F.O.B. Plant, Kansas City.

One month later, Euro faxes Universal a signed Purchase Order Form stating, "We order today 5,000 lb. Universal Standard Pipe Insulation Product A for $10,000 F.O.B. Kansas City for immediate delivery to Darmstadt, Federal Republic of Germany. This contract shall be governed by the laws of England (U.K.). Euro."

That same day Universal responded by faxing a signed Order Acknowledgement Form to Euro's headquarters. That form stated: "We accept your order to buy 5,000 lb. Universal Standard Pipe Insulation Product A for $10,000 F.O.B. Kansas City. Goods sold as is and with all faults (see UCC 2–316). This contract is governed by the laws of Kansas."

(Expanded Fact Pattern) All of the events described above occur, and in addition within a week Universal ships the goods and bills Euro. Euro accepts the goods and pays for them.

Euro uses the insulation in constructing the refinery. The insulation corrodes the metal of the refinery piping, which piping is governmentally mandated and customarily used in all such facilities in Europe. Universal has sold its product throughout the United States and Canada, and has never encountered a similar problem before. However, the type of piping used in North America contains different critical alloys.

Euro incurs a $1 million loss due to corrosion of the refinery piping. There is some question as to whether the standard commercial insurance of either Euro or Universal covers the loss, because the insulation may not necessarily be "defective," but might instead be considered only "unsuitable." Thus, any damages *might not* arise out of product liability (tort) concepts, which are more likely to be covered by such insurance; but they might arise out of breach of contract concepts, which are less likely to be covered by such insurance.

PART B.

For Part B below, assume, *instead*, that Euro has its headquarters in Darmstadt, Germany (*not* in London, England) and that its Purchase Order states that the contract shall be governed by "the laws of the Federal Republic of Germany" (*not* the laws of England). All other facts in Basic and Expanded Fact Patterns above remain the same.

SECTION II. FOCUS OF CONSIDERATION

Most first year courses in Contract Law explore the issues relating to "the Battle of the Forms." This problem is "the Battle of the Forms" revisited, but with a couple of new twists and variations. The most important of these is that the parties are transacting across national borders. This raises the fundamental issue of what law governs the contract formation process in the first place. In addition, the parties (as many merchants seem to do) were not overly concerned with the differences between their communications. They shipped and accepted the goods as though they had a contract. But, now a problem has arisen, involving significant damages, and each party claims that the terms of its communication control the terms of the contract as to the choice of governing law and whether warranties are available or are effectively disclaimed.

A growing body of international law now regulates commercial relations across borders, especially the United Nations Convention on Contracts for the International Sale of Goods (CISG). However, the United Kingdom has not ratified this treaty. What then? That is, which national law then governs the contract formation process—that of the United Kingdom (or more specifically of England, a distinct legal system within the U.K.) or that of the State of Kansas? The answer to this question in turn can have direct consequences for the parties' contractual rights and obligations, if any, under both the Basic and Expanded Fact Patterns. We will explore this subject in Part A below. [If, contrary to all expectations, the United Kingdom were to ratify the CISG, assume that the parties validly agreed on an express exclusion of the CISG through corresponding clauses in their respective forms.]

In Part B, the same basic issues arise, but the change in Euro's headquarters from the United Kingdom to Germany creates a different legal context. Both Germany and the United States have ratified the CISG. As a result, this body of international legal rules is also the domestic law of both countries, and where applicable it displaces otherwise-applicable sale of goods laws such as the UCC. We will explore the substance and effect of the CISG in our revised Euro–Universal transaction in Part B below.

Most significantly, Part C of this Problem asks how you can advise your clients to act during the contract formation process so as to prevent this problem from arising.

Web sources for further study include:

(1) Pace Law School CISG database *http://www.cisg.law.pace.edu/*

(2) UNCITRAL Digest of Case Law on the CISG, *http://www.uncitral. org/uncitral/en/case_law/digests/cisg.html* and

(3) UNIDROIT Principles of Int'l Commercial Contracts webpage *http://www.unidroit.org/english/principles/contracts/main.htm*

SECTION III.   READINGS, QUESTIONS AND COMMENTS

PART A.   THE TRADITIONAL ANALYSIS—CONFLICTS OF LAW

We will first analyze the competing arguments for using English or United States law to govern the formation and interpretation of the contract. You may conclude, as the authors do, that there really is no certain resolution of these issues.

Because the UCC may govern the Universal–Euro transaction, a reading of UCC §§ 1–105 (Rev. 1–301), 2–207, 2–314, 2–315 and 2–316 is essential to analysis of this Problem. Those sections can be found in the Documents Supplement to this book.

NAFZIGER, THE LOUISIANA AND OREGON CODIFICATIONS OF CHOICE–OF–LAW RULES IN CONTEXT

58 Am. J. Comp. L. 165, 169–170, Supp. 1 (2010).*

By far the most significant set of statutory choice-of-law rules * * * is embedded in the Uniform Commercial Code (UCC). This legislation has been adopted with minor variations by every state as well as the District of Columbia and Puerto Rico. The importance of the UCC merits a closer look at it.

Historically, Section 1–105 of the UCC established the overall choice-of-law framework. This framework is significant to the extent of variations among the states in their respective versions of the UCC and to the extent that state choice-of-law rules may differ in their receptivity to the application of the law of a foreign country. It has allowed parties to a commercial transaction to exercise autonomy in selecting the law to govern their respective rights and duties related to or arising out of the transaction so long as that law bears a "reasonable relation" to the "state or nation" whose law is selected. Failing such agreement, the UCC "applies to transactions bearing an appropriate relation" to a state. The definition of "an appropriate relation" has been unclear, having been identified with both a "minimum contacts" theory borrowed from constitutional analysis of adjudicative jurisdiction and the "most significant relationship" test of the Second Restatement.

* * *

The frequent litigation concerning the terms and criteria for choice of law in the UCC indicates a substantial ambiguity and lack of uniformity in application[.] * * * Section 1–105 is potentially troublesome insofar as it better enables states to apply their own choice-of-law variations and thereby indirectly threaten the national uniformity of what, after all, is intended to be a uniform law throughout the country.

BRAND, THE EUROPEAN MAGNET AND THE U.S. CENTRIFUGE: TEN SELECTED PRIVATE INTERNATIONAL LAW DEVELOPMENTS OF 2008

15 ILSA J. Int'l & Comp. L. 367, 371–372 (2009).**

Regulation (EC) No 593/2008 of the European Parliament and of the Council of 17 June 2008 on the law applicable to contractual obligations (Rome I) was issued on June 17, 2008, and appl[ies] to contracts concluded after December 17, 2009. This Regulation completes the package of basic private international law instruments through internal Community legislation, with the Brussels I and II Regulations providing rules for jurisdic-

---

* Copyright © 2010, and reprinted with permission.

** Copyright © 2009, and reprinted with permission.

tion and for the recognition and enforcement of judgments, and the Rome I and II Regulations providing rules of applicable law for contractual obligations and non-contractual obligations, respectively.

The fundamental rule of Article 3 of the Rome I Regulation provides for party autonomy, stating that "[a] contract shall be governed by the law chosen by the parties." This rule gives way, however, to mandatory rules of a country other than the country of the chosen law, when "all other elements relevant to the situation at the time of the choice are located" in that other country. It also is preempted by mandatory rules of Community law when the parties have chosen the law of a non–Member State and the forum is a court in a Member State. If no law is chosen by the parties, then Article 4 provides that, in the most common situations:

> 1) A contract for the sale of goods shall be governed by the law of the country where the seller has his habitual residence; and

> 2) A contract for the provision of services shall be governed by the law of the country where the service provider has his habitual residence.

[T]he Rome I Regulation contains special rules for consumer, employment, and insurance contracts, designed to protect the party commonly considered to have the lesser bargaining power in the relationship. This follows the more paternalistic approach of civil law systems, generally, and departs from the more economic-oriented approach for similar rules in the United States and some other common law countries.

JUENGER, THE E.E.C CONVENTION ON THE LAW APPLICABLE TO CONTRACTUAL OBLIGATIONS: AN AMERICAN ASSESSMENT

P. North, Contract Conflicts, Ch. 13, p. 299 (1982).*

Let us now discuss the problem of the law applicable in the absence of a contractual choice. * * *

How well have American * * * conflicts experts coped with the difficult and frustrating problem of selecting a law for the parties? Not too well, I am afraid. The Second Restatement imposes a formidable task on the judiciary. The first paragraph of its section 188 requires a separate choice-of-law analysis for each contracts issue presented. The key term of this provision, the "most significant relationship", has an appealing ring. But what sounds simple and straightforward becomes quite complex if one attempts to apply the qualifying proviso, which requires recourse to the choice-influencing considerations the Restatement enumerates in section 6. That section contains a shopping list of desiderata, all of which are very plausible, except that they conflict with one another. How, for instance, is it possible to pursue, at the same time, the goals of certainty, predictability and uniformity of result mentioned in letter (f) of Section 6, second

---

paragraph, and the protection of forum policies specified in letter (b)? Nor does it simplify matters if paragraph 2 of section 188 lists numerous contacts, and then ordains that they should be evaluated in the light of their relative importance to the particular issue presented. The permutations of any number of issues, six choice-of-law factors and five contacts, combined with the need to evaluate the contacts in the light of each particular issue, would stymie a computer.

Everyone might agree that the search for the proper law should not be a mechanical process of counting contacts. But even a juggler, not to mention a trial judge, can only cope with a finite number of balls in the air. The Second Restatement, of course, recognizes this difficulty. To alleviate it the last paragraph of section 188 diffidently offers a near-rule, which provides that if the place of negotiation coincides with the place of performance, the law of that jurisdiction should "usually" be applied, whatever that may mean. Sections 189–197 try to offer some further guidance by stating tentative rules for a number of specific contracts. However, these rules in turn are subject to an escape clause that permits application of whatever law has a more significant relationship to the specific issue. Nor are the black-letter statements of sections 198–207 (which deal with various specific contract issues, such as form requirements and capacity) of much help, for most of them simply refer back to the general provisions of sections 187–188.

RESTATEMENT, CONFLICTS OF LAW (SECOND) (1971)*

§ 6. Choice-of-Law Principles

(1) A court, subject to constitutional restrictions, will follow a statutory directive of its own state on choice of law.

(2) When there is no such directive, the factors relevant to the choice of the applicable rule of law include

(a) the needs of the interstate and international systems,

(b) the relevant policies of the forum,

(c) the relevant policies of other interested states and the relative interests of those states in the determination of the particular issue,

(d) the protection of justified expectations,

(e) the basic policies underlying the particular field of law,

(f) certainty, predictability and uniformity of result, and

(g) ease in the determination and application of the law to be applied.

§ 188. Law Governing in Absence of Effective Choice by the Parties

(1) The rights and duties of the parties with respect to an issue in contract are determined by the local law of the state which, with respect

---

to that issue, has the most significant relationship to the transaction and the parties under the principles stated in § 6.

(2) In the absence of an effective choice of law by the parties (see § 187), the contacts to be taken into account in applying the principles of § 6 to determine the law applicable to an issue include:

(a) the place of contracting,

(b) the place of negotiation of the contract,

(c) the place of performance,

(d) the location of the subject matter of the contract, and

(e) the domicil, residence, nationality, place of incorporation and place of business of the parties.

These contacts are to be evaluated according to their relative importance with respect to the particular issue.

(3) If the place of negotiating the contract and the place of performance are in the same state, the local law of this state will usually be applied, except as otherwise provided in §§ 189–199 and 203.

J. WHITE AND R. SUMMERS, UNIFORM COMMERCIAL CODE

37–49, 53–54 (6th ed., 2010).*

§ 2–3   Battle of the Forms and the Like Under Existing Section 2–207

Many sales contracts are not fully bargained, not carefully drafted, and not understandingly signed or otherwise acknowledged by both parties. Often, here is what happens: underlings of seller and buyer each sit in their offices with a telephone and a stack of form contracts. Today the "stack of forms" is more likely on the party's hard drive and it may be transmitted from there digitally to the other party. Seller's lawyer has drafted seller's forms to give seller advantage. Buyer's lawyer has drafted buyer's forms to give buyer advantage. The two sets of forms naturally diverge. They may diverge not only in substantive terms but also in permissible methods of contract formation.

The process of "contracting" begins with an underling telephoning another underling or with the dispatch of a form. When the process ends, there will usually be two forms involved, seller's and buyer's. The documents will usually have the same bargained terms such as price, quality, quantity and delivery terms. But on other terms the forms will diverge in important respects. Frequently this will pose no problem, for the deal will go forward without breakdown. But sometimes the parties will fall into dispute even before the occasion for performance. More often, one or both will perform or start to perform and a dispute will break out. In all these cases the parties will haul out their forms and read them—perhaps for the

---

first time—and they will find that their forms diverge. Is there a contract? If so, what are its terms?

Unfortunately the section [UCC 2–207] is like an amphibious tank that was originally designed to fight in the swamps, but was sent to fight in the desert. The original drafter of 2–207 designed it mostly to keep the welsher in the contract. * * *

But it is a mistake to think of 2–207 as a law dealing principally with contract formation. Parties to sales much more often call on courts to use 2–207 to decide the terms of their contract after they exchange documents, perform, or start to perform and then fall into dispute. Here the courts are not deciding whether there is a contract. They are answering a different question: what are its terms? This is not only a different but also a more difficult problem for the law than that of keeping the welsher in.

* * *

In our discussion of these cases, a central problem will be this: how may 2–207 be interpreted so as not to give an unearned and unfair advantage to the contracting party who by pure happenstance sends the first or in other cases the second form? When the parties send their forms blindly and blindly file the forms they receive, it makes little sense to give one an advantage over the other with respect to unbargained terms *simply* because one mailed the first form. Yet avoiding favoritism because of timing is a difficult task under 2–207.

1. Express Term in Second Form Different from Terms in First

Assume that buyer sends a purchase order which provides that any dispute will be governed by arbitration. Seller responds with an acknowledgement which provides that any dispute will not be resolved by arbitration. At least if the *bargained* terms on the purchase order and acknowledgement agree, we would find that the seller's document is a definite and seasonable expression of acceptance under 2–207 and that a contract has been formed by the exchange of the documents. We would thus bind any party who seeks to get out of the contract before either performs.

Assume that the seller ships the goods, the buyer receives and pays for them, and the parties fall into dispute about their quality. Does the contract call for arbitration or does it not? Buyer will argue that buyer's document was the offer (and it appears to us that buyer's document was the offer since it was sent first) and that seller's document operated as an acceptance of all of the terms on buyer's form. Furthermore, buyer will correctly point out that seller's term (no arbitration) was not an additional term which could come into their contract under 2–207(2) but was a "different" term and therefore could not become part of the contract under 2–207(2). Section 2–207(1) applies to an *acceptance* that "states terms additional to or different from those offered." But the text of 2–207(2) only refers to "additional" terms, and the drafters could easily have inserted "or different" if they had so intended. Yet it would be more than a little difficult to view a different term in an acceptance as a proposal for addition to the contract where the offer already includes a contrary term. It is not possible to have different terms on the same subject as "a part" of the same contract.

First, the seller offeree might respond that his "no arbitration" document differed from the buyer's ("arbitration") so substantially that it did not constitute an "acceptance" under 2–207(1). But in our view, it is clear that a document may be an acceptance under 2–207(1) and yet differ substantially from the offer. The wording of 2–207(2)(b) supports this, too, for it presupposes that a contract can be formed under 2–207(1) even though the acceptance includes an additional term that "materially alters" the offer.

But how much can an acceptance differ? Certainly there is some limit. We think that in the usual purchase order-acknowledgement context the forms do not approach this limit at least if the forms do not diverge as to price, quality, quantity, or delivery terms, but only as to the usual unbargained terms on the reverse side concerning remedies, arbitration, and the like.

* * *

[T]he seller may [also] argue that seller's acceptance is only an acceptance of the terms on which the two documents agree, and they did not agree on arbitration, nor do Code gap fillers provide for arbitration. This argument finds no explicit support in 2–207, but one of us (White) thinks part of Comment 6 supports it.

* * *

Most of the decisions agree with White. * * *

Consider this further problem. Assume for example that the offer contains an otherwise valid disclaimer of warranties and that the acceptance contains a conflicting express warranty. According to White, neither become part of the contract under 2–207(1) despite the fact that a contract is formed. Likewise neither enters the contract through 2–207(2) because the term in the acceptance is a different, not an additional term. Moreover by its terms 2–207(3) does not apply to this case but applies only to the case where "the writings of the parties do not otherwise establish a contract." Is it possible, nonetheless, that an *implied* warranty enters the contract directly as a gap filler without reference to 2–207(3)? White believes that it does and that indeed most of the gap fillers do not depend upon 2–207 to enter the contract. He says there are many contracts adequately formed by an offer and an acceptance which a gap filler dealing with price or warranty or terms of delivery would enter without any reference to 2–207. On White's view, that seems the proper result. * * *

Summers believes White misreads 2–207, both in text and in spirit. Summers would, in the foregoing further hypothetical case, uphold the offeror's otherwise valid disclaimer as to both express and implied warranties. The offeree's term is a different term and falls out.

* * *

3. Term in Second but not in First Form

This is the problem of the *Roto-Lith* case. In that case the buyer sent an offer—a purchase order—to seller. Though the offer was silent as to warranties, Code gap-fillers (e.g., 2–314) might supply them. Subsequently seller returned an acknowledgment that contained a disclaimer. The court ultimately found that the seller's document was "expressly conditional" and therefore not an acceptance but a counteroffer, accepted by the buyer's performance in receiving and using the goods. Under that case the seller got all of his terms, disclaimer included.

On the facts, we would find the second document to be an acceptance and would reject the *Roto-Lith* assumption that it was expressly conditional and therefore a counteroffer. Of course, the offeror could specify in the offer that acceptance must be in the exact terms of the offer, with the result that any additional or different terms would constitute a counteroffer. Similarly under 2–207(1), an acceptor could explicitly make acceptance "expressly conditional" on the offeror's assent to additional or different terms, and thus also a counteroffer. Because neither is true in our hypothetical, we would find that a contract was formed upon the exchange of documents without reference to the subsequent performance. * * * [T]he additional (not "different") term in the acceptance that did not appear in the offer must pass through subsection (2) of 2–207 to become part of the contract. * * * Doubtless the parties in our case are merchants, but in the absence of a contrary course of dealing or usage of trade, a disclaimer "materially alters" the contract, and the disclaimer would not become part of the contract.

* * *

5. At Least One Form Insists on All Its Terms and Expressly Prohibits a Contract on Any Other Terms

Assume that no contract exists under 2–207(1) yet the parties perform. A court can find a contract in one of two ways. First, a court can take the common law, *Roto-Lith,* approach and find that the second document is a counteroffer and hold that subsequent performance by the party who sent the first document constitutes acceptance. This gives one party (who fortuitously sent the second document) all of its terms. In our view, Code drafters rejected this approach, and the drafters sent us to section 2–207(3). * * *

After this problem flowered in *Roto-Lith,* the Code's Permanent Editorial Board added a new Comment 7 to 2–207, which reads in full as follows:

In many cases, as where goods are shipped, accepted and paid for before any dispute arises, there is no question whether a contract has been made. In such cases, where the writings of the parties do not establish a contract, it is not necessary to determine which act or document constituted the offer and which the acceptance. See Section 2–204. The only question is what terms are included in the contract, and subsection (3) furnishes the governing rule.

* * *

CONCLUSION

Under the present state of the law we believe that there is no language that a lawyer can put on a form that will always assure the client of forming a contract on the client's own terms. * * * If one must have a term, that party should bargain with the other party for that term; a client should not get it by a lawyer's sleight of hand. If a seller must have the term to reduce its liability but cannot strike a bargain for it, the only answer may be to raise the price, buy insurance, or—as a last resort—have an extra martini every evening and do not capitalize the corporation too heavily.

[**Authors' Note**: In 2003, the American Law Institute (ALI) and the National Council of Commissioners on Uniform State Laws (NCCUSL)— the folks who brought us the original UCC—proposed a Revised UCC Article 2. For battle of the forms situations, this Revised Article included a complete rewrite of UCC § 2–207 in favor of a general "knock-out" rule. However, no state has enacted this revised Article 2 (nor is any likely to) and in 2011 even the ALI withdrew its support. As a consequence, as Professors White and Summers have concluded, "Amended Article 2 is dead."]

RÜHL, THE BATTLE OF THE FORMS: COMPARATIVE AND ECONOMIC OBSERVATIONS

24 U. Pa. J. Int'l Econ. L. 189, 191–193 (2003).*

Although by now most common law countries have abandoned or at least dramatically limited the scope of the last-shot rule, it is still the prevailing solution to the battle of the forms problem under English law. * * *

The application of the last-shot rule under English law is due to the fact that English courts tackle battle of the forms cases through the general rules of offer and acceptance. Therefore, a contract comes into existence only if the terms of the acceptance correspond exactly to the terms of the offer. An acceptance that is not in conformity with the terms of the offer is considered a rejection of the offer and usually treated as a counteroffer. Of course, there are a few exceptions to this rule[.] * * * However, as the terms that are generally in question in battle of the forms cases usually do not fall into one of these categories, formation of the contract requires one party to accept the terms of the other party, including the general conditions.

Acceptance of an offer under English law may be expressed either explicitly by words of acceptance or implicitly by conduct. In battle of the forms cases, this rule will usually result in formation of the contract through conduct: The buyer makes an offer that is rejected by the seller because he refers to his own general conditions. Subsequently, he delivers the goods. Acceptance of the goods by the buyer amounts to acceptance of the seller's counteroffer by conduct. Because the buyer accepted the seller's offer, the seller's terms, as the party who "fired the last shot," govern the contract. The general principles of offer and acceptance under English law, thus, naturally lead to application of the last-shot rule.

QUESTIONS AND COMMENTS

1.   If only the facts stated in the Basic Fact Pattern have occurred, is there a binding contract between the parties? The answer to that question will depend upon your analysis of two issues: First, would the issues be governed by the law of England or the law of Kansas? Second, what are the substantive contract formation rules in "the Battle of the Forms" situation under that governing law? Note that the analysis of these two issues is likely to be interdependent.

2.   As to applicable law, this is not a course in conflicts of law. However, some relevant readings on the subject from both European Union and American sources have been included in the Readings—enough to give you a flavor of the difficulties involved in any analysis.

Note that the choice of law rules applicable throughout the European Union are different from the American choice of law rules. Thus, two questions are posed: 1) Which "choice of law" rules will be used? and 2) What substantive law is chosen by the applicable rules?

As to the first question, an English court will use English choice of law rules, and an American court will use American choice of law rules. Thus, at the beginning there is a basic division as to the applicable principles which depends upon where the lawsuit is filed—and that cannot be predicted at the time of contract formation.

3.   If a lawsuit is filed in England, the court will apply the E.U. Rome I Regulation on the Law Applicable to Contractual Obligations (2008)(*see* the Documents Supplement). That Regulation transformed a free-standing treaty, the so-called "Rome Convention," into binding law throughout the European Union. If, in contrast, the lawsuit is filed in Kansas, a court there will turn first to the UCC because this sale of goods transaction falls within its broad scope. *See* UCC §§ 2–102, 2–105(1). As noted in the Nafziger excerpt, the UCC has its own general choice of law rule, UCC § 1–105 (Revised § 1–301, *see* below).

4.   The fundamental principle of both the Rome I Regulation and the UCC § 1–105(1) is "party autonomy," that is, the power of the parties to

choose the governing law for their contracts (subject to certain limits). *See* the Brand and Nafziger excerpts. Issues relating to "Choice of Law" clauses will be discussed in detail in Problem 11.2; but note in our Problem here that Euro sought to include such a clause in the contract through a choice of English law in its Purchase Order form and that Universal tried to do the same through the choice of Kansas law in its Order Acknowledgement form. The question, therefore, is whether the par*ties* have agreed on either choice of law. This would require you to find, first, that the parties formed a contract and, second, that one of those clauses is part of that contract. But note that both of these questions are substantive law issues and thus will depend what law governs contract formation issues in the first place.

Is there any way for a party to put a choice of law clause in its standard business terms and be assured *in advance* that the clause will be effective? In absence of a formally negotiated contract document, how would the par*ties* choose the law that would govern the formation of their (proposed) contract in any event?

5. Now it is time for you to determine what law applies to contract formation issues in the Euro–Universal transaction in Part A. Note, again, that the answer may well turn on where the lawsuit is filed. In E.U. countries, the Rome I Regulation opts for a bright-line approach in sale of goods transactions. *See* the Brand excerpt. Under this bright-line rule, which jurisdiction's laws would an English court apply to our contract formation problem?

6. UCC § 1–105 takes an entirely different approach, allowing a court in any UCC state to use its own law if the transaction "bears an appropriate relation" to the state. This so-called "Imperial Clause" was expressly used as a method of encouraging forum shopping as a means of pressuring non-UCC states into adopting the UCC. For that purpose it was successful, but it has never been regarded as a serious attempt at reconciling the competing interests involved in typical choice of law rules, especially by courts abroad.

There is now a Revised UCC Article 1, and original UCC § 1–105 has been replaced by Revised § 1–301. *See* the Documents Supplement. To date, 40 states have enacted Revised UCC Article 1, but all of them have refused to enact Revised § 1–301. Instead, they have enacted the language of original UCC § 1–105 and simply renumbered that provision as § 1–301. Thus the approach of original § 1–105 seems destined to continue.

7. But what does "appropriate relation" mean? A court's natural tendency will be to apply its home state UCC for a lawsuit filed there (although Official Comment 2 to § 1–105 makes clear that this fact alone is not enough). Failing more explicit guidance, courts have generally retreated to general common law notions, especially the "most significant relationship" test of the Restatement (Second) of Conflicts of Law. *See e.g. Butler v. Ford Motor Co., 724 F.Supp.2d 575, 584 (D.S.C. 2010); In re General Motors Corp. Dex–Cool Products Liability Litigation, 241 F.R.D. 305, 317 (S.D. Ill. 2007).*

The reference to the Second Restatement's "most significant relationship" test makes matters more complicated. *See* the critical analysis in the Juenger excerpt. Where is the "place of negotiation" when the parties do not negotiate in person, but exchange communications from points distant?

Where is the "place of performance"? Of its nature, an international transaction also is likely to involve differing places of incorporation and places of business. If you were a Kansas judge, would you find that the transaction bears an "appropriate relation" to Kansas when the only contact is that Universal happens to be located there? Would you instead find that "most significant relationship" is with England? (Or perhaps even Germany?)

Finally, with the relative clarity of the Rome I Regulation for sale of goods transactions as compared to the fact-specific analysis of the UCC/Restatement are there incentives for forum-shopping?

8. If it is difficult to decide whether Kansas law or English law will apply to resolve this contract formation problem, does it matter which one is used? What is the result under each set of substantive rules?

(a) First, as to American law, the applicable statute would be the Kansas version of the Uniform Commercial Code (UCC). Before the UCC, application of common law principles to this fact pattern would have meant that, under the "mirror image" rule, any variation between Euro's order and Universal's response would result in the response being a counteroffer and not an acceptance. Universal's disclaimer of warranty and reference to the "laws of Kansas" are such variations. UCC § 2–207 sought to ameliorate this Common Law rule, but did it extinguish the principle completely? Read the excerpts from White & Summers.

If only the facts in the Basic Fact Pattern have occurred (*i.e.*, the parties have not yet performed), have the parties formed a contract under UCC § 2–207? What does § 2–207(1) require for a response to "operate[] as an acceptance"? Note that Universal's form agreed with Euro's order on the essential terms of price, goods, and delivery time, but did not agree in other respects. What is the effect of such a response under UCC § 2–207(1)?

(b) As to English law, read the excerpt from Rühl. Again, if *only* the facts in the Basic Fact Pattern have occurred, have the parties formed a contract under English contract formation rules? Could a contract be formed by Universal's reply and Euro's subsequent silence?

9. Now consider the legal situation under the Expanded Fact Pattern. If all the facts stated in the Expanded Fact Pattern have occurred, the nature of the legal analysis changes. It is relatively clear under both English and American law that a contract was formed when goods were delivered, accepted and paid for. Now the issue becomes one of determining the terms of that contract—but those terms, in turn, will depend upon *how* the contract was formed.

(a) Consider, first, the analysis under Kansas law. Universal could have delayed contract formation by making its purported acceptance "expressly conditional" on Euro's subsequent assent to all of the terms in the Order Acknowledgement as provided in the final clause of UCC § 2–207(1). *See* White and Summers, Case No. 5. But courts have set very high standards for such clause—and the mere fact of a new or different term in the reply, even a material one, clearly is not enough (the contrary approach of the *Roto-Lith* case having been expressly overruled and also uniformly rejected by other courts). So this argument is not a viable one here.

What, then, is the effect of the actual conflict between Euro's choice of English law and Universal's choice of Kansas law? On this point, note the disagreement between White and Summers. Under White's view, what would be the result in the case of a conflict between such non-essential terms in an offer and an acceptance under UCC § 2–207? What would be the result under Summers' view?

The warranty disclaimer clause in Universal's Order Acknowledgement requires separate analysis. Note that this clause does not conflict with any express term in Euro's offer. *See* White and Summers, Case No. 3. For such an "additional term" in a reply document, as White and Summers note, the proper analysis is found solely in UCC § 2–207(2). Universal's warranty disclaimer is very likely a proposal for a material alteration under § 2–207(2)(b) and no indication of assent was received from Euro. As a result, the clause would not become part of the contract.

(b) Now consider the analysis under English law. If all of the facts in the Expanded Fact Pattern have occurred, what is the effect of the parties' subsequent performance of the transaction without further discussion? Read the Rühl excerpt. Which party, then, would most likely want to have English contract formation rules apply to this transaction?

10. Finally, if all of the facts in the Expanded Fact Pattern have occurred, what is the result with respect to Universal's warranty obligations?

(a) If Kansas substantive law applies and Universal's warranty disclaimer did not become part of the contract, the UCC provides implied warranties in §§ 2–314 and 2–315, but does not provide implied disclaimers under § 2–316. Thus, Universal probably would have to proceed to trial on the merits. Was this insulation not fit for "ordinary use" under UCC § 2–314, or was it only unfit for the special use with the particular metal in European refinery piping? Note the special conditions for creating liability under UCC § 2–315. Between buyer and seller, who has—or should have—the burden of seeking information about whether there are specialized circumstances involved in the proposed use?

If, in contrast, Universal's warranty disclaimer were to become part of the contract under applicable contract formation rules, its use of the express language of UCC § 2–316(3)(a) would seem to function as an effective disclaimer of liability for the implied warranties of §§ 2–314 and 2–315.

(b) If English substantive law were to apply, the same basic issues arise. Under a formal statute, the Sale of Goods Act (SGA) of 1979, a seller is deemed to extend implied warranties of "satisfactory quality" and of "fitness for all the purposes for which goods of the kind in question are commonly supplied." *See* SGA, Article 14. But what is "satisfactory" quality for the insulation supplied by Universal? And what is the proper frame to measure the purposes for which such goods are "commonly" supplied (Europe or the United States)? Finally, although one commentator has observed with reference to this Act that "the parties are permitted to opt-out of the statutory implied terms by mere agreement," he also notes that "English case law concerning international sales transactions rarely refers to the [Act], and at times makes marked departures from [its] express provisions." *See* Markel, *American, English and Japanese Warranty Law Compared: Should the U.S.*

Reconsider Her Article 95 Declaration to the CISG?, 21 Pace Int'l L. Rev. 163, 175, 182 (2009).

PART B.   ENTER INTERNATIONAL LAW (HEREIN OF CISG)

The change of Euro's place of business from the United Kingdom to Germany in the revised facts for Part B has a significant effect on the legal analysis. Both Germany and the United States have ratified the Convention on International Sale of Goods (CISG). We thus must analyze issues concerning contract formation and interpretation as they would arise under that Convention. The issues may appear clearer under the Convention, but they are certainly still elusive.

Part A raised, inter alia, two major new and different problems: First, what law is applicable—English or Kansas? Second, if English law is applicable, what is the content of that law on the issues presented? The first of these problems is not easily resolved for the simple reason that we cannot even determine in advance what choice of law rules will apply, because we do not know where the lawsuit will be filed. Moreover, many of the involved issues leave substantial room for play in the analysis.

The second of these problems is even more difficult, for it involves research into foreign legal materials that often are not available in the ordinary law library. Even if available online, the risk is great that a U.S. lawyer may not understand the conceptual structure of and appropriate analytical methods for the foreign legal system. These challenges are compounded if the foreign country follows a civil law system and speaks an unfamiliar language.

However, these problems are obviated when one does not have to rely on the domestic law of a foreign country or the United States. One method of accomplishing that goal is to create a treaty—an agreement between the United States and the foreign country to use a specific law of sales of goods to govern all transnational sales transactions between the two nations. Such a treaty would create international law on the subject and, under the Supremacy Clause of Article VI of the Constitution, supercede the Kansas UCC.

Because international commerce is not simple, a single transaction often involves entities with contacts relating to more than two nations. Thus, for reasonable efficiency, a practical treaty would not be merely bilateral, but would be multilateral, and would involve as many nations as possible. Such a treaty has been drafted by UNCITRAL—the United Nations Commission on International Trade Law—and adopted by a diplomatic conference in Vienna in 1980. It is the Convention on International Sale of Goods (CISG), set forth in the Documentary Supplement. As of March, 2012, seventy-seven countries, including the United States and Germany, have become contracting States. Thus, CISG is federal law governing all covered contracts, unless the parties have effectively excluded its application (see below).

However, both the United States and Germany made statements about the applicability of the Convention when their instruments of ratification were deposited with the United Nations. The United States made a "declaration," as permitted under CISG Article 95, that it "will not be bound by subparagraph (1)(b) of Article 1."

The German government, on the other hand, made the following statement:

> The Government of the Federal Republic of Germany holds the view that Parties to the Convention that have made a declaration under article 95 of the Convention are not considered Contracting States within the meaning of subparagraph (1)(b) of article 1 of the Convention. Accordingly, there is no obligation to apply—and the Federal Republic of Germany assumes no obligation to apply—this provision when the rules of private international law lead to the application of the law of a Party that has made a declaration to the effect that it will not be bound by subparagraph (1)(b) of article 1 of the Convention. Subject to this observation the Government of the Federal Republic of Germany makes no declaration under article 95 of the Convention.

Because the CISG may govern the Universal–Euro transaction under Part B, a reading of CISG Articles 1, 6, 7, 8, 10, 14, 18, 19, 35 and 36 is essential to analysis of this problem.

HANWHA CORPORATION v. CEDAR PETROCHEMICALS, INC.

United States District Court, S.D. New York, 2011.
760 F. Supp. 2d 426.

[After preliminary negotiations over a sale of goods, Cedar (a New York-based seller) and Hanwha (a South Korea-based buyer) exchanged standard business forms. Cedar's form designated New York law as the governing law, but Hanwha's form chose Singapore law. When a dispute arose over whether the parties had formed a contract, the court first had to confront the fact that both the United States and the Republic of Korea have ratified the CISG. Some citations have been omitted—*the Authors.*]

* * *

Before deciding whether the parties formed a contract, I must establish which law governs the analysis. Here, both parties are [located in] CISG signatory nations, but they have attempted to opt out of the CISG's substantive terms by designating other choices of substantive law. The question therefore arises whether the CISG, some other law, or both, governs the question of contract formation.

* * *

The CISG is a self-executing treaty, binding on all signatory nations, that creates a private right of action in federal court under federal law. As a treaty, the CISG is a source of federal law. * * *

* * *

The intent to opt out of the CISG must be set forth in the contract clearly and unequivocally. Absent a clear choice of law, "the Convention governs *all* contracts between parties with places of business in different nations, so long as both nations are signatories to the Convention." *Filanto, S.p.A. v. Chilewich Intern. Corp.*, 789 F. Supp. 1229, 1237 (S.D.N.Y.1992) (emphasis in original).

In this case, the parties each attempted to opt out of the CISG, but could not agree on the law to displace it, Cedar preferring New York law and the UCC, and Hanwha preferring Singapore law. * * * Here, the parties never agreed to a substantive law to displace the CISG, and their competing choices must fall away, leaving the CISG to fill the void by its own self-executing force.

Accordingly, * * * I apply the terms of the CISG without regard to the law either party attempted to select when bargaining over the terms of the [proposed] contract.

DIMATTEO, DHOOGE, GREENE, MAURER AND PAGNATTARO, THE INTERPRETIVE TURN IN INTERNATIONAL SALES LAW: AN ANALYSIS OF FIFTEEN YEARS OF CISG JURISPRUDENCE

24 Nw. J. Int'l Law & Bus. 299, 349–357 (2004).*

C. Battle of the Forms

Article 19 raises the difficult issue of an acceptance with modification or the exchange of forms containing additional or conflicting terms. Negotiated terms, essential to the contract, may appear on the front of a form while additional terms and general conditions appear on the reverse side. Buyers' and sellers' forms undoubtedly contain provisions that favor their respective positions. The boilerplate terms are routinely ignored until a dispute arises. Forms are exchanged in what one author termed *"une conversation des sourds"* (a conversation of the deaf). Two questions arise when there is dispute. First, was a valid contract formed despite the existence of conflicting, non-dickered terms? Second, if a valid contract was concluded, what are the terms of the contract? Article 19(1) provides that an offer that "contains additions, limitations or other modifications is a rejection of the offer and constitutes a counter-offer." If the additional terms do not materially alter the offer, however, a valid contract is formed and the additional terms enter the contract[,] unless the receiving party promptly objects * * *.

Article 19(3) sets a broad materiality standard by listing "price, payment, quality and quantity of the goods, place and time of delivery, extent of one party's liability to the other or the settlement of disputes" as terms that would materially alter the offer. The breadth of these categories of material terms is susceptible to even further extension by the open-endedness of the introductory phase "among other things." Article 19 is essentially an adoption of the now-discarded common law mirror image rule with the exception that minor differences do not defeat an otherwise valid acceptance. The breadth of Article 19(3) severely limits the scope of the minor term.

A battle of the forms arises when parties exchange forms that have inconsistent terms. * * * Courts seem willing to find a valid contract where there is an exchange of forms and a general intent to enter into a binding agreement. The more difficult issue to predict is the courts' determinations of what terms enter into the contract. * * * [T]he existence of conflicting terms creates a gap that the court can fill by recourse to Article 7(1)'s principle of good faith ("knock out rule"). [Another] solution that has been offered is that the terms provided in the acceptance controls (the "second shot rule"). * * *

Two cases decided by the German courts applied the knock out rule. In a case involving the sale of knitwear by an Italian seller to a German buyer, the parties had agreed on the *essential terms* of the contract and had performed. When a dispute arose about whether the goods conformed to the contract, the parties disagreed on whether certain general terms were part of the contract. The German buyer had included in its general terms a forum selection clause that was additional to the terms in the seller's form. Under Article 19, it could be argued that no contract was formed because the forum selection clause was a material alteration to the offer. Article 19(3) identifies differing terms regarding "the settlement of disputes" as material. Because the parties had performed based on the essential terms of the agreement, the court found that there was a valid contract and that the parties had either "waived their claim to the application of their respective standard business terms or derogated from Article 19 in exercise of their party autonomy under Article 6." The court held that neither party's general conditions became part of the contract.

The Federal Supreme Court of Germany confirmed the knock out rule approach to cases where the parties have agreed on the essential terms of the contract for the sale and have performed. Professor Schlechtriem has asserted that the German Supreme Court's message was that "[c]onflicting standard forms [terms] are entirely invalid and are replaced by CISG provisions, while the contract as such remains valid." In that case, a dispute arose when customers of a buyer complained that the powdered milk delivered by the seller had a sour taste. The standard terms exchanged by the parties contained conflicting terms regarding the extent of the seller's liability. The court found that the contradiction in terms "did not prevent the existence of the sales contracts because the parties did not view this contradiction as an obstacle to the execution of the contracts."

The seller argued that the CISG was derogated by a clause in its standard forms and that under the applicable German Civil Code, no damages could be claimed. In concluding that neither the buyer's nor the seller's standard forms were included in the contractual arrangement, the court refused to single out some clauses which might be beneficial to one side or the other.

The *Cour de Cassation* in France also applied the knock out rule regarding conflicting jurisdiction clauses. Recognizing that jurisdiction provisions are material terms according to Article 19(3), the court, instead of invalidating the contract, applied traditional conflict of law rules to determine jurisdiction. * * *

Some national courts have used the last shot doctrine to resolve cases involving the battle of the forms. According to this approach, courts interpret an action or performance by one of the parties as an indication of assent to additional terms. The last shot doctrine can be seen as evolving from rules of offer and acceptance, with each new offer being a counter-offer until the last one is accepted when one party indicates assent by performance or other conduct. Therefore, if a party fails to object to an additional or modified term, performs, or partially performs, then he has accepted the additional or modified term. Whereas the knock out rule would ignore conflicting terms, the last shot approach incorporates the terms of last communication. Some commentators maintain that the last shot rule is out of touch with commercial reality and encourages parties to act in bad faith by producing numerous forms with standard terms in hopes of controlling the contract through the last shot. Others consider the last shot rule to be the best approach to a difficult situation because it provides "certainty and legal security."

A German court held that an 8-day notice of defects provision in a confirmation letter was enforceable at the time the buyer took delivery of the goods. The notification terms contained in the seller's confirmation letter were additional material terms that amounted to a counter-offer under Article [19(1)], but the court found that the buyer accepted those terms by accepting delivery. Another German court found that a buyer of cashmere sweaters accepted the seller's additional terms which incorporated the "Standard Conditions of the German Textile Industry" by performing under the contract. The court merely cited Articles 18 and 19 without comment. Similarly, another German court held that acceptance of delivery indicated assent to a material modification. When the buyer claimed to have ordered a certain quantity of shoes and the seller delivered a different quantity, the court interpreted the delivery of a different quantity as a material alteration under Article 19(3). The court held, however, that the delivery was a counter-offer which the buyer accepted by taking the goods. * * *

If a party continues to perform, or fails to object in a timely manner, to additional terms, she runs the risk that her conduct, silence, or act of performance will be interpreted by a court as an acceptance of the disputed term. This was the issue in *Filanto v. Chilewich*, where the court found that a manufacturer accepted an arbitration provision as part of the agreement, because he failed to object in a timely manner and commenced performance by opening a letter of credit. This was despite the fact that it repeatedly objected during negotiations to the incorporation of an arbitration clause and that such a clause is a material term under Article 19(3). In *Magellan Int'l Corp. v. Salzgitter Handel GmbH*, the court found that a contract was formed when a distributor indicated assent by opening a letter of credit. The court held that the terms of the contract were those agreed on at the time the letter of credit was opened.

* * *

It is important to understand the reach of Article 19. It is limited to issues of contract formation and not to modifications of contract. Thus, it is universally accepted that where a contract has been validly concluded, one party may not change a material term in the contract without the acceptance of the other party. The court in *Chateau des Charmes Wines Ltd. v. Sabate USA Inc.* found that where an oral agreement did not contain a forum selection clause, one party's attempt to include such a provision in subsequent invoices did not alter the contract. Because the contract had already been concluded, any new terms were merely offers which required express assent and did not create an obligation to reject the term. The court noted that the mere performance of obligations under the oral contract did not indicate assent to what would be additional material terms under Article 19(3).

BRAND, PROFESSIONAL RESPONSIBILITY IN A TRANSNATIONAL TRANSACTIONS PRACTICE

17 J. of Law & Commerce 301, 335–6 (1998).*

A. MUST A LAWYER INVOLVED IN NEGOTIATION OR LITIGATION OF A CONTRACT MATTER BE AWARE OF THE SALES CONVENTION?

This question is not a difficult one. The duty of competence set forth in Model Rule 1.1 clearly requires of a lawyer "the legal knowledge, skill, thoroughness and preparation reasonably necessary for the representation." Any lawyer involved in the negotiation or litigation of a contract for which the parties have their places of business in different countries has a duty to determine (1) whether two or more countries involved are contracting states to the Sales Convention, and (2) if one country is a party to the Sales Convention, whether that country has filed an Article 95 reservation to Article I(1)(b). If, as a result of either of these inquiries, the lawyer determines that the Sales Convention applies to the transaction, he or she then has a duty to understand fully the rules of the Convention and the application of those rules to the transaction in question. If the representation is in the context of negotiations, the lawyer is also responsible for determining and advising the client whether exercising the Article 6 possibility of "opting out" of the Convention rules would be to the benefit of the client. If the representation is in the context of litigation, the lawyer clearly has an obligation to know (1) whether the Convention applies to the transaction in question, and (2) if it does, the impact on his or her client of application of the Convention rules. The failure to understand and properly apply the Convention in regard to any of these obligations clearly constitutes a violation of Rule 1.1.

PERILLO, UNIDROIT PRINCIPLES OF INTERNATIONAL COMMERCIAL CONTRACTS: THE BLACK LETTER TEXT AND A REVIEW

63 Fordham L. Rev. 281 (1994).*

To an extent, Principles is modelled on CISG. But in three significant ways it departs from CISG. First, it is far broader in scope. CISG is limited to contracts for the sale of goods and furthermore eschews many issues relevant to sales contracts. For example, CISG avoids the question of contractual validity. On the other hand, Principles deals not only with the broad range of commercial contracts, but also with some questions of validity. A second departure from CISG is that, to the extent that the two documents cover the same ground, Principles is a better, more mature product. For example, it deals with the "Battle of the Forms" in an innovative way, which presents a considerable improvement over the wretched draftsmanship of Uniform Commercial Code section 2–207 and the timorous Article 19 of CISG. The third departure is that Principles is not intended for adoption as a treaty or as a uniform law; rather, the document is in the nature of a restatement of the commercial contract law of the world.

I.   The Function of Principles

One could ask what might be the function of such a restatement. The Preamble lists a number of practical uses the statement of principles might have for the judge, arbitrator or practicing lawyer. If the parties negotiating a contract have difficulty in agreeing on a choice of law clause, the choice of Principles could avoid deadlock. If the principles had been in existence at the relevant time, it would have been an ideal choice of legal principles for contracts dealing with the construction of the "Chunnel" connecting England and France. Feelings of national dignity precluded each side from acceding to the choice of the other's law. Similarly, if the contract declares that it is governed by "general principles of law" or the like, Principles can be a primary source for the adjudication of any dispute that may arise from the contract. In addition, Principles could be employed as a supplement for decisions under other international agreements, such as CISG. Moreover, if the rules of conflict of laws point to a

State whose law is obscure, undeveloped or merely difficult to ascertain, the judges or arbitrators have a neutral resource to apply. This last function of Principles should not be underestimated, as this is one of the primary functions of a restatement in the United States.

There is, I believe, another dimension to Principles that the Preamble does not state. Comparative law is a humanistic discipline. A comparison of legal systems expands the mind. Provisions within Principles regarding issues on which the common law and civil law systems have different conceptual frameworks (e.g., specific performance and penalty clauses) show that the drafters were able to break out of their respective conceptual straitjackets to reach common ground. This only could have happened by a process of mutual education and the expansion of understanding.

* * *

IV. BATTLE OF THE FORMS

The "battle of the forms" receives innovative and generally sound treatment in Principles. What the U.C.C. deals with in one section, the newer document addresses in three sections. The first deals with additional or different terms in a "custom-made" acceptance, and the second governs the use of a pre-printed standard form as an acceptance of the other party's standard form. The third deals with written confirmations. The custom-made acceptance receives basically the same treatment as in CISG. The battle of the forms, however, is solved by a "knock-out" principle. A term on a printed form will be part of the contract only to the extent that both party's forms agree to the substance of the term. Either party can, in advance, or, without undue delay, after the exchange of forms, declare to the other party that it does not intend to be bound by a contract formed under the knock-out rule. The commentary indicates that the inclusion of such a declaration in a standard-form offer or acceptance would not ordinarily be a sufficient declaration of intent not to be bound. If a written confirmation of a contract previously made is sent by one party to the other, an additional or different term becomes part of the contract unless it materially alters the contract or the recipient of the confirmation objects to the term.

* * *

UNIDROIT took precisely the bold step that was necessary by separating its provision on the battle of the forms from its rules governing offer and acceptance and inserted its solution as the last of four Articles dealing with standard forms. The first of these is a provision defining what is meant by the words "standard terms" and providing that, in general, "standard terms," whether on a printed form or incorporated by reference, [may be] binding on the parties. The second of these provides that a "surprising" standard term is ineffective unless it is expressly accepted by the party adhering to the term. This in essence replicates one aspect of the U.C.C.'s approach to unconscionability that is designed for "the prevention of oppression and unfair surprise." The other provision with respect to standard terms is the obvious rule that if there is a conflict between a standard term and an individually agreed term the latter prevails.

* * *

On a pragmatic note, Principles will have a limited impact unless its implementation is made available to merchants and their attorneys. The implementation of CISG by court decisions and scholarly discussion of its provisions is reported in an ingenious piece of software known as UNI-LEX. Unless a comparable aid to research is provided with respect to Principles, uniformity of application is unlikely to occur, diffusion of knowledge of its implementation will be erratic, and its effect limited.

APPENDIX

UNIDROIT PRINCIPLES OF INTERNATIONAL COMMERCIAL CONTRACTS

* * *

Article 2.19 (Contracting under standard terms)

(1) Where one party or both parties use standard terms in concluding a contract, the general rules on formation apply, subject to Articles 2.20–2.22.

(2) Standard terms are provisions which are prepared in advance for general and repeated use by one party and which are actually used without negotiation with the other party.

Article 2.20 (Surprising terms)

(1) No term contained in standard terms which is of such a character that the other party could not reasonably have expected it, is effective unless it has been expressly accepted by that party.

(2) In determining whether a term is of such a character regard is to be had to its content, language and presentation.

Article 2.21 (Conflict between standard terms and non-standard terms)

In case of conflict between a standard term and a term which is not a standard term the latter prevails.

Article 2.22 (Battle of forms)

Where both parties use standard terms and reach agreement except on those terms, a contract is concluded on the basis of the agreed terms and of any standard terms which are common in substance unless one party clearly indicates in advance, or later and without undue delay informs the other party, that it does not intend to be bound by such a contract.

[**Authors' Note:** In 2010, UNIDROIT issued a revision of the Principles of International Commercial Contracts. However, the wording of the

Articles quoted above did not change, although the inclusion of an unrelated new provision changed the numbering format to 2.1.19, etc.]

BONELL, THE CISG, EUROPEAN CONTRACT LAW AND THE DEVELOPMENT OF A WORLD CONTRACT LAW

56 Am. J. Comp. L. 1, 22–25 (2008).*

It still remains to be seen whether and to what extent the relevant rules of private international law permit the parties to choose a soft law instrument such as the UNIDROIT Principles as the law governing their contract in lieu of a particular domestic law. In the context of international commercial arbitration, the answer is currently definitely in the affirmative. As far as court proceedings are concerned, however, the traditional and still prevailing view is that the parties' freedom of choice is limited to a particular domestic law, with the result that a reference to the UNIDROIT Principles will be considered as a mere agreement to incorporate them into the contract. As such, the UNIDROIT Principles can bind the parties only to the extent that they do not affect the mandatory provisions of the lex contractus. Things may change, however, in the near future, and it is fair to say that the appearance of the UNIDROIT Principles has considerably contributed to such new prospects.

* * *

Let us look at some figures. As of October 2007, 150 decisions referencing to the UNIDROIT Principles were reported in the UNILEX database * * *. Moreover, while 106 of those decisions were arbitral awards, 44 were court decisions, which contradicts the widespread belief that in view of their non-binding nature, the UNIDROIT Principles can only be relevant in the context of arbitration. Finally, the truly universal application of the UNIDROIT Principles is confirmed by the fact that in more than two-thirds of the cases, at least one of the parties was non-European. In fact, in almost one-third of the cases, all parties involved were from outside Europe, representing some thirty-five countries worldwide.

As to content, the decisions may be divided into three categories, depending on the way in which the UNIDROIT Principles are used.

First, there are decisions—clearly the most important ones and all of them arbitral awards—in which the UNIDROIT Principles were applied as the law governing the substance of the dispute. Sometimes this was expressly requested by the parties, either in the contract itself or at the beginning of the arbitration proceedings. More often however, the contracts merely referred to "general principles of law," "principles of international law," "lex mercatoria" or the like, and the arbitrators applied the UNIDROIT Principles on the assumption that they represented a particu-

---

larly authoritative expression of supra-national or transnational principles and rules of law. Recently there have been an increasing number of cases in which arbitral tribunals have gone even further and applied the UNIDROIT Principles—either alone or in conjunction with the otherwise applicable law—even in the absence of any choice of law clause in the contract. In doing so, the arbitrators relied on the relevant statutory provisions or arbitration rules according to which they may—to quote the language used in Article 17 of the ICC Rules of Arbitration—"apply the rules of law which [they] determine to be appropriate" and "in all cases [. . .] shall take account of [. . .] the relevant trade usages."

In a second group of decisions—which include court opinions—the UNIDROIT Principles have been used to interpret or supplement international uniform law instruments. For obvious reasons, most of these decisions concerned Article 7 CISG, which states that the Convention should be interpreted by taking into account its international character and the need to promote uniformity and that gaps should be filled whenever possible by the general principles underlying it. Yet, occasionally the UNIDROIT Principles have also been used to interpret other international instruments.

In a third category of decisions—which represents almost half of the reported cases and again includes a number of court decisions—the UNIDROIT Principles have been referred to in applying a particular domestic law. * * *

R. FOLSOM, M. GORDON AND J. A. SPANOGLE, INTERNATIONAL BUSINESS TRANSACTIONS IN A NUTSHELL

53–54 (8th ed. 2009).*

Can seller exclude these obligations concerning the quality of the goods by terms in the contract—and, if so, how? CISG Article 6 states that the parties may, by agreement, derogate from any provision of the Convention, and Article 35(2) supports that ability to limit obligations concerning the quality of the goods. However, it is also clear that the standard formulation in domestic contracts—disclaiming implied warranties—will be inapposite, since the CISG obligations are neither "warranties" nor "implied." New verbal formulations must be found, which deal directly with the description of the goods and their expected use.

The major unresolved issue is the extent to which local law regulating disclaimers will impact on the international contracts governed by CISG. Such local law covers a spectrum from prohibitions on disclaimers in printed standard terms to the "how to do it manual" set out in UCC 2–316. There seems to be agreement that the former raises a question of "validity," and therefore governs contracts arising under CISG; and that the UCC provisions do not raise questions of "validity," and therefore do not govern CISG contracts. The distinction drawn seems to depend upon whether the local public policy prohibits the conduct completely, or allows it but only within certain conditions.

QUESTIONS AND COMMENTS

1. Does CISG govern this German–American transaction under the revised facts of Part B? Both countries are "Contracting States", *i.e.*, those that have ratified or acceded to the Convention, even if with reservations. (Note that "State" refers to independent sovereigns, not to individual states within the United States.) Further, the determinative "place" under CISG Article 1 is the "place of business" of each party, not the parties' formal nationality, where the goods are, or whether the goods themselves move in international commerce. *See* CISG, Articles 1(1) and 1(3).

Under Article 1(1)(b), if only one Contracting State is involved, then the analysis of the issues becomes similar to that of Part A. One must determine whether applicable domestic choice of law concepts—so-called "rules of private international law"—lead to the application of the law of a Contracting State. If so, then CISG is applicable; if not, the domestic commercial law of the chosen noncontracting state is applicable. But, remember that United States courts are not bound by Article 1(1)(b).

2. It may still be possible to get different answers from different court systems. An American court would approach the issue only under subparagraph (1)(a) of CISG Article 1, since it is not bound by subparagraph (1)(b) of Article 1. It would find a transaction between parties in two different Contracting States, and hold the Convention to be governing law, unless the parties' contract expressly excludes its application.

Analysis by German courts might be more complicated. The "observation" presented by the German government indicates that German courts will not consider the United States to be a Contracting State for purposes of Article 1(1)(b), due to the U.S. declaration under CISG Article 95. Does that mean that we must again go through the traditional choice of law analysis raised in Part A of this Problem? If German choice of law principles are more likely to select American law, then there are at least two possible sources of such law: CISG and the UCC. Does the German observation make clear which of these will be selected?

An alternative analysis for the German courts is to make CISG govern the transaction under Article 1(1)(a). Under that analysis, the restrictions in the "observation" are limited to analysis under Article 1(1)(b), and do not affect analysis under Article 1(1)(a). Such an analytical approach does leave open one question however: If the German observation does not apply to this transaction, under what circumstances could it *ever* apply?

3. Even when the parties have their respective places of business in different Contracting States, CISG Article 6 permits the parties to exclude its application (to "opt-out" of the CISG). But similar to the general rule on choice of law clauses discussed in Part A above, Article 6 requires an agreement of the parties. The *Hanwha Corporation* case makes clear how

difficult this is to achieve through standard business terms, at least as to the contract formation rules in the CISG.

In the revised fact pattern for Part B, Euro's form chose German law and Universal's form chose Kansas law. Even if the parties actually agreed on one of the choices, would such a simple statement suffice to exclude application of the CISG? *See Travelers Property Casualty Co. v. Saint-Gobain Tech. Fabrics Canada Ltd.*, 474 F.Supp.2d 1075, 1082 (D. Minn. 2007)("[A]bsent an express statement that the CISG does not apply, merely referring to a particular state's law does not opt out of CISG. As the Fifth Circuit stated, '[a]n affirmative opt-out requirement promotes uniformity and the observance of good faith in international trade, two principles that guide interpretation of the CISG.' ")(*quoting BP Oil Int'l, Ltd. v. Empresa Estatal Petroleos*, 332 F.3d 333, 337 (5th Cir. 2003)).

4.   What is the effect of the CISG's contract formation rules as applied to the Euro–Universal transaction in Part B? Note, first, that the CISG follows the basic offer-acceptance scheme. *See* Articles 14 and 18. But what are the "battle of the forms" rules under Article 19? For non-material alterations in the reply, Article 19(2) seems to water down the strict mirror image rule of Article 19(1); but—unlike UCC § 2–207(2)—if an offeror timely objects to such non-material terms, no contract is formed at all under the CISG. Does Universal's Order Acknowledgement Form contain terms that "materially alter" the terms of the offer? Comment 4 to UCC 2–207 indicates that a warranty disclaimer likely would be a material alteration. Is a United States court likely to follow the same reasoning in interpreting CISG? Is it even permitted to do so for an international treaty?

Now focus on the broad list in CISG Article 19(3). If the parties have *only* exchanged forms (*i.e.*, have not yet performed at all), what then is the result under CISG Article 19 for our German–American transaction in Part B?

5.   Now assume the parties in Part B have performed as in the Expanded Fact Pattern. If they did not establish a contract through their forms under Article 19, they probably did so through their conduct after delivery and acceptance of the goods. Is this a type of situation for which Article 18(1) is designed? If so, does the seller's shipment of the goods constitute conduct accepting the buyer's offer—and its terms, without modification; or is the buyer's acceptance of the goods in Germany conduct accepting the seller's counteroffer in the Order Acknowledgement Form—and its terms, without modification? Reread Article 18(3). Is it biased in favor of sellers, since they most often send the second form? Or is it biased against sellers, since their shipment ("dispatch of the goods") usually occurs before payment?

6.   On the other hand, Universal's Order Acknowledgement Form seems to be a rejection of Euro's offer. Under CISG Article 17, when such a rejection reaches Euro, Euro's offer is "terminated." Perhaps then Euro's offer may not be available to be accepted by Universal when it ships the goods. Such an analysis would argue that Euro accepted Universal's terms when it accepted and paid for the goods.

7.   This standard analysis in Comments 4–6 above has been challenged by case decisions and articles. The courts should be expected to balk at following the traditional approach, when most modern legal systems have

constructed a way around the "mirror image rule." For the CISG, the German Supreme Federal Court observed, in the so-called "powdered milk case" noted by DiMatteo, *et al.*, that the "knock-out" rule is "probably the prevailing view" for battle of forms situations. But as DiMatteo, *et al.* also note, German courts have used both the "knock out" rule and the "last shot" rule in different cases, without attempting to harmonize the results. The U.S. courts are in similar disarray, including holding silence to be acceptance when the parties had been exchanging counter-offers for a long time. All this should alert the practitioner to a basic desire of many courts to avoid the "mirror image" and "last shot" rules suggested by Articles 19(1) and 18(3), and to arrive at a doctrine that adopts the "knock out" rule. What would be the terms of the Euro-Universal contract under a knock out rule?

8.   Professor Brand suggests that an attorney violates the Model Rules of Professional Responsibility if he or she *negotiates* an international contract without understanding the CISG. Simply "opting out" automatically, because you know it exists, but do not know how it works, could be malpractice. The CISG may of course favor your clients, especially if they are sellers or exporters. Could this be a problem for the practicing bar?

Professor Peter Fitzgerald recently surveyed the legal communities on this subject across the spectrum of states (Florida, New York, California, Hawaii, and Montana) and reported the results in *The International Contracting Practices Survey Project*, 27 J.L. & Com. 1 (2008). This survey revealed that only 30% of practitioners were "thoroughly" or "moderately" familiar with the CISG, results that tracked almost exactly those of a similar survey of the Florida Bar by Professor Michael Gordon ten years earlier. The results for judges were even starker, with 82% reporting that they were "not at all familiar" with the CISG.

What are the implications of only 30% of international practitioners believing they have a reasonable knowledge of CISG? What are the implications of over 80% of judges being unfamiliar with an international treaty, which constitutes "the supreme Law of the Land" and thereby trumps the UCC?

9.   A new entry into the effort to harmonize international contract law is the Principles of International Commercial Contracts, drafted and published by UNIDROIT (The Rome Institute) in 1994 and revised in 2004 and again in 2010. Their rules on standard terms and the "battle of the forms" are reprinted as an Appendix to Professor Perillo's article. The UNIDROIT Principles function as an international Restatement of the Law, but are more equivalent to a Restatement of the Best Practices in International Practice. Because they are not a treaty, domestic courts are not likely to use the Principles, unless the parties to a contract incorporate them by reference. They may, however, be much more widely used by arbitrators as a *de facto* international law merchant, just as Restatements are used domestically.

The Principles take a different analytical approach than either UCC § 2–207 or the traditional "last shot" doctrine. Can the Principles be used to aid those courts that want to interpret the CISG so as to avoid the "mirror image" and "last shot" rules? *See* CISG Article 7 and the Bonell excerpt.

10. Professor Fitzgerald's survey, cited in Comment 8., found even less knowledge of the UNIDROIT Principles than of CISG. Roughly half as many international practitioners know about the Principles as know of CISG, and barely 10% of judges knew about them. The one bright spot—on both the CISG and the UNIDROIT Principles—was law faculty, who reported significantly increased knowledge as well as coverage in law school courses as compared to ten years earlier.

11. Finally, what about disclaimers of warranty? *See* CISG Articles 35 and 36. Article 35(2) allows the parties to "agree otherwise," which is the standard statutory euphemism for permitting disclaimers. What must the contract say in order to "agree otherwise" effectively? Must some formalism be met which states a concept contrary to each of the ideas expressed in Article 35(2)(a)–(d) (*e.g.*, "The parties agree that the goods may not be fit for the purposes for which goods of the same description would ordinarily be used.")—or, is "as is" sufficient to exclude all expected properties of the goods—or, is there some usable middle ground?

In addition, there are the issues relating to the degree of "unfitness" required to show a breach of any of the CISG warranties.

12. Would it matter if Euro and Universal had sent their respective forms electronically or otherwise had conducted all of their communications orally? We will analyze "electronic commerce" in much more detail in Problem 4.4 below. But for now, is there a general "statute of frauds" for CISG transactions? *See* CISG Article 11. *But see also* CISG Articles 12 and 96.

13. Is it always clear when CISG would be applied to sales transactions entered into by multinational corporations? For example, suppose in the German–American transaction in Part B that Universal (our Kansas-based seller) owns a subsidiary warehousing corporation in England, and the goods are shipped out of stock in the English warehouse directly to Germany. Recall, moreover, that as of now the United Kingdom has not ratified the CISG. CISG Article 1(1)(a) makes the Convention applicable to contracts "between parties whose places of business are in different States," when both states are "Contracting States," unless its application is expressly excluded in the contract. If Universal's "place of business" is in Kansas, the conditions of Article 1(1)(a) can be met. However, if Universal's "place of business" is in England, they cannot be met. CISG Article 10(a) provides that

> if a party has more than one place of business, the place of business is that which has the closest relationship to the contract and its performance, having regard to the circumstances known to or contemplated by the parties at any time before or at the conclusion of the contract.

Which Universal office would have "the closest relationship to the contract *and* its performance"? (emphasis added) Would it now become important to know whether Euro knew of the English warehouse? Would it be relevant that Universal's representative had said during negotiations, "We ship all of our products from England, on European orders"? *See also* CISG Article 1(2).

14. In addition to the CISG, a series of further international treaties have been negotiated and opened for ratification. The most significant of

these is the 1974 Convention on the Limitation Period in the International Sale of Goods (as amended by Protocol in 1980). *See* 19 I.L.M. 696 (1980). This Convention, which has been ratified by the United States and two dozen other countries, provides special rules for what American lawyers would call the "statute of limitations" for international sale of goods transactions.

The other noteworthy Conventions provide analogues—as does the CISG for UCC Article 2—to UCC Articles 2A, 3, and 9. They include: The United Nations Convention on International Bills of Exchange and International Promissory Notes, (UNCITRAL, 1988) *reprinted in* 28 Int'l Legal Materials 176 (1988); The Convention on International Financial Leasing (UNIDROIT, 1988) *reprinted in* 27 Int'l Legal Materials 931 (1988); and The Convention on International Factoring (UNIDROIT, 1988) *reprinted in* 27 Int'l Legal Materials 943 (1988). UNCITRAL also has prepared "model laws" for consideration by individual countries as domestic legislation, the most significant of which for our purposes are the 1996 Model Law on Electronic Commerce and the 1992 Model Law on International Credit Transfers.

PART C.   HOW CAN CLIENTS AVOID THIS PROBLEM?

We finally turn to how you should counsel your client to act—if you are able to give advice *before* the first communication arrives. In view of the uncertainties, is it wise to seek to win a "tactical victory" in the battle of the forms? If not, what conduct should your client undertake to protect its interests?

Suppose that after its representative had visited the trade fair, but before it received Euro's Purchase Order, Universal consults you. It wants you to advise its sales department on how to handle incoming foreign orders—whatever the form of the "offer to buy," whether it comes by telephone, telegraph, letter, email, or printed form. What is your advice?

Would you find this counseling to be easier or more difficult if Universal's likely customers are located in countries that also have ratified the CISG?

One *fact* that should be clear from all of the uncertainties involved in analyzing this Problem is that the lawyer who thinks primarily in terms of litigation would not find any of these uncertainties very appealing for either party in any jurisdiction. The uncertainties of both sides are very high and so will be the costs of litigation. Most such cases will be settled by negotiation, with each attorney carefully appraising the client's and the opponent's position.

A more important service to the client is counselling—how to prevent this problem from arising.

QUESTIONS AND COMMENTS

1.   By now, you should be aware that courts have a wide latitude in deciding issues that arise out of such fact situations. We saw in Part A that choice of law issues may leave substantial uncertainty about what contract formation rules will apply to an international sales transaction. Moreover,

even if we knew that, for example, Kansas substantive law would apply, we have seen that two of the most learned commentators (White and Summers) disagree on at least one core issue of contract formation under the UCC. Read again the excerpt from their "Conclusion."

The choice of law rule seems more predictable if the law of a European Union member state applies. Nonetheless, and notwithstanding substantial efforts to bring harmony, each of these states still has its own substantive contract formation rules. And even if we had some confidence that the law of one particular state would apply, it may not be possible, with the available research tools and resources, to determine what ambiguities may exist in that law, much less how to resolve them. And what if Universal receives an order from India or Indonesia? Or Mali? How much do you know (or, can you even find out) about any of these legal systems?

If the CISG governs, some ambiguities will still exist. But, in comparison to the law of any particular foreign system, many more aids to interpretation in English are available for the CISG. One of the most valuable of these is the UNCITRAL Digest of Case Law on the CISG, which contains analyses and abstracts on CISG court decisions organized by specific Articles. Beyond this, a rich variety of legal commentaries and treatises should make the CISG more easily accessible (both practically and conceptually) for an American lawyer. Nonetheless, as we have seen in the analysis of Part B above, substantial disagreement exists about the proper resolution of the "battle of the forms" under the CISG as well.

2. With this degree of uncertainty, would you seek to rely upon terms inserted in an Order Acknowledgement Form to win a "tactical victory" in "the Battle of the Forms"? If not, what advice can you give to your client? What positive steps can the client take to prevent misunderstandings, and when should they be taken?

3. If your client communicates with the other party, what should be the content of the communication? If the warranty term of the contract is at issue, should the client communicate to the buyer that "we don't stand behind our goods at all"—before the contract is binding? The Sales Department might object to that approach.

4. What is it about this possible fact situation that scares Universal? Universal has pride in its product and has had few complaints with its sales within the United States. The price of the goods is not a significant loss or risk in an effort to open up a new sales territory, if the goods fail to perform due to some new operating conditions. However, one million dollars in "consequential damages" is a significant loss or risk for Universal. The rules for damages under the CISG are found in Articles 74–77. (Fortunately or not for Universal, the CISG does not apply to personal injury claims. *See* CSIG Article 5.) Under the UCC, damages rules in §§ 2–714, 2–715 both invoke "foreseeability," and visions of *Hadley v. Baxendale,* 156 Eng.Rep. 145 (1854). However, under both, the stated provisions may be varied by agreement of the parties. CISG Article 6, UCC §§ 2–718, 2–719. With these concepts in mind, what should the client do to obtain protection without overreaching?

5. Does your client, Universal, have any duty to investigate the context in which its product will be used in foreign markets before it ships to those

markets? This Problem is a remarkable demonstration of ignorance by all parties. Who has the burden of initiating investigation? Who should have that burden? One clear counselling point is that a party should discuss the matter with the other party if it has not investigated the commercial and legal environment in a foreign country.

PROBLEM 4.2 COMMERCIAL TERMS, BILLS OF LADING AND INSURANCE—BOOKS TO BATH

SECTION I. THE SETTING

Your client, Sam Silver, of Savannah, Georgia, wishes to consult with you about a sale of goods he has just negotiated with a couple of buyers in England. Sam is a publisher of "romance novels," and his latest publication is "Desire Under the Thornbush." Bill Bones is a book distributor in Bath who wants "two dozen gross" of this latest publication. Howard Hunt is a competing book distributor, also in Bath. Not to be outdone, Howard ordered "three dozen gross" of "Desire Under the Thornbush."

Sam has never sold goods outside the United States before, but he is very proud of his ability to write a "lawyer-like contract." Thus, when Sam comes to consult you, he has a piece of paper signed by both Bill and himself and labelled "Contract," containing all the necessary items for a contract, such as price, description, quantity, and quality of the goods. The contract does not state whether the sale is for cash or on credit, but it does have two terms which catch your eye: "Price: F.O.B. Savannah;" and "This Contract shall be governed by I.C.C. INCOTERMS (2010 Edition)." Sam also has a second piece of paper signed by both Howard and himself and labelled "Contract." It also contains all necessary terms, including: "Price: C.I.F., Bath, United Kingdom," and "This Contract shall be governed by I.C.C. INCOTERMS, 2010 Edition."

Sam explains that Howard was very insistent on the CIF term, and would not purchase under any different arrangement, and so Sam now has these two contracts with different terms. Sam is well aware of the different components in the price of the two different contracts, and tells you that the problem is "already taken care of." But Sam does want to know "just a couple of things" about how to set up the transportation of the goods. In particular, he needs your advice on:

1. Is Sam supposed to arrange for the transportation of the books to Bill or Howard, or is that their responsibility?

2. If Sam does arrange the transportation for Bill (as a favor or otherwise), and Bill is supposed to pay the freight charges, how can Sam assure himself that Bill will do so?

3. Is Sam supposed to arrange for insurance on the books to Bill during transit, or is that Bill's responsibility?

4. Sam also wants to know whether to get negotiable or non-negotiable bills of lading. See the Basic Transaction in the Introduction to this Chapter. Should they be issued "to bearer" or "to order"? If the latter, to *whose* order?

5. After discussing the problem with Sam for a few minutes, it becomes clear that what Sam *really* wants to do—for his own ease and convenience—is load all the books for both Bill and Howard into one container, obtain one bill of lading to cover them, and ship them off to Bill and Howard jointly. Can Sam do this? If not, please explain to him why it would not be possible.

6. Will either Bill or Howard have a right to inspect the goods before accepting or paying for them?

7. Does anyone need to obtain insurance on any of the books sent to Bill? After all, if these books are damaged, it will be due to negligence of the carrier, so carrier would be liable for any loss or damage. Thus, Sam wants you to assure him that insurance is an unnecessary expense.

8. Several days later, at 4 p.m. on a Friday afternoon, Sam calls you from the Carrier's office. He has delivered 30 boxes of books in cardboard cartons to the carrier. Sam filled out two Commercial Invoices, one each for Bill and Howard, stating that they covered 12 and 18 cartons respectively "each carton containing two gross books: 'Desire Under the Thornbush.'" The carrier's clerk waited until the cartons were loaded, then stamped the bills of lading "On Board," "Shipper's Load, Weight & Count," and "Contents Unknown." Sam protested, but the carrier's clerk said he stamps all bills of lading that way, on orders of his supervisor, "so we never have to get involved with disputes between the parties over the quality or quantity of the goods." Sam is worried and frustrated. He wants to know whether he can safely accept the bills of lading so stamped, and allow the goods and these documents to go forward, or whether the documents will cause problems when they arrive in Bath. What is your advice? (Incidentally, he does not want you to research the matter and call him on Monday.)

SECTION II.   FOCUS OF CONSIDERATION

It is possible to have a cash sale international transaction that does not involve a letter of credit. Such a transaction uses the negotiable bill of lading and a series of collecting banks to require the buyer to pay before it can obtain physical possession of the bill of lading, and therefore control of the goods. These principles are at the heart of the CIF transaction. "CIF", as a term of a contract, is typically not just a price term (as is shown in Introduction 4.0), but is also a payment term (payment is due against tender of documents) and a delivery term (at shipment). The CIF transaction can be diagramed in exactly the same way as the transaction in Introduction 4.0, but deleting the letter of credit. (See diagram on page 52, supra.)

Most international sales contracts are not cash transactions, however. Instead they are sales on open credit between buyers and sellers who deal with each other on a long-term basis, or who are subsidiaries of the same parent company. For such sales, the complexities of a CIF contract are not necessary, and the use of FOB place of shipment is more typical. "FOB place of shipment," as a contract term, is typically both a price term (as is shown in Introduction 4.0) and a delivery term (at shipment), but is not a payment term. Thus, it does not require the formalities of payment against documents, unless otherwise agreed.

The first Part of this problem compares and contrasts the FOB shipment and CIF contracts to explore the fundamental differences between them and the fundamental difference in their uses. To analyze these issues one must consider not only local laws, but also international customs, of which the predominant one in U.S.–European trade is Incoterms.

In the second Part of this problem, we begin our analysis of the regulation of international bills of lading. What does it mean when a piece of paper is a "document of title" (such as a bill of lading)? In specific, what are the obligations of a carrier when it issues such a document covering the international transportation of goods? Problem 4.5 below will examine in detail the grounds for the carrier's potential liability arising out of bills of lading, and in particular where a bill misdescribes the goods in the first place or the carrier delivers them contrary to the bill's terms.

In this Problem 4.2, we begin with the carrier's basic responsibility for loss of, or damage to, the goods in transit (*i.e.*, after they have been entrusted to the carrier's care). But the special focus here will also be on attempts by carriers to limit the *amount* of their liability, and on the domestic and international regulatory responses to those efforts.

The regulation of the terms of the bill of lading, *i.e.*, the relationship of the carrier and its customers, is the subject of three international conventions and three United States federal statutes. The three conventions—the Hague Rules, the Hague/Visby Rules, and the Hamburg Rules, respectively—all cover the same subject matter, but are progressively more customer-oriented. (As noted in the Comments below, a compromise fourth convention, the Rotterdam Rules, is also now available.) The United States has enacted the Hague Rules into its domestic law as the Carriage of Goods by Sea Act (COGSA), but also has in force nonconforming pre-COGSA legislation (the Harter Act) as well as a special Federal Bill of Lading Act (the so-called Pomerene Act). English law is based on the Hague/Visby Rules.

A final issue raised by this problem is the differences between the 1) mandatory laws of a state which are binding on the parties and may not be set aside by contractual clauses, 2) optional laws of a state which may be subject to contrary contractual agreement by the parties, and 3) trade customs and usages which arise out of contractual terms and not out of the law of a state. Examples of the first are COGSA and the Pomerene

Act. Examples of the second are most provisions of the UCC and the Common Law of contract. An example of the third is the I.C.C.'s Incoterms. The practical importance of the provisions of each of these sources of rules does not depend upon its place in the legal hierarchy, however.

Web sources for further study include the International Chamber of Commerce web page *http://www.iccwbo.org/incoterms/id3045/index.html/*

If the UCC is applicable to this transaction, then a reading of UCC §§ 1–302(a), 2–319, 2–320 is essential to an analysis of the Problem. For Part B below, please also read the Carriage of Goods by Sea Act (COGSA)(*see* the Document Supplement).

SECTION III. READINGS, QUESTIONS AND COMMENTS

PART A. THE ROLE OF COMMERCIAL TERMS

SCHMITTHOFF'S EXPORT TRADE: THE LAW AND PRACTICE OF INTERNATIONAL TRADE

¶ 2–006, 07 (Murray, Holloway, Timson–Hunt, eds., 11th ed., 2007).*

AMERICAN PRACTICE

In the United Kingdom and the Commonwealth "f.o.b." is understood as meaning "f.o.b. vessel." In the American practice "f.o.b." has become a general delivery term which, if used in the form "f.o.b. place of destination" even denotes free delivery at that place. The equivalent to the English meaning of "f.o.b." is the American term "f.o.b. vessel." The American regulation can be gathered from the following provisions of the Uniform Commercial Code [UCC 2–319]:

Unless otherwise agreed the term f.o.b. (which means "free on board") at a named place, even though used only in connection with the stated price, is a delivery term under which

(a) when the term is f.o.b. the place of shipment, the seller must at that place ship the goods * * * and bear the expense and risk of putting them into the possession of the carrier; or

(b) when the term is f.o.b. the place of destination, the seller must at his own expense and risk transport the goods to that place and there tender delivery of them * * *;

(c) where under either (a) or (b) the term is also f.o.b. vessel, car or other vehicle, the seller must in addition at his own expense and risk load the goods on board. If the term is f.o.b. vessel the buyer must name the vessel and in an appropriate case the seller must comply with the provisions of this Article on the form of bill of lading * * *.

TYPES OF F.O.B. CLAUSES

The term f.o.b. may be used by an exporter who buys from a manufacturer or merchant in the United Kingdom and who intends to resell the goods abroad; this transaction may be concluded f.o.b. UK Port. Further, an exporter may sell or resell goods to an overseas buyer f.o.b. UK Port; in this case the f.o.b. term is used in the export transaction. The exporter should be aware of the fact that the f.o.b. term when used in the supply transaction may carry different incidental obligations from such a term when used in the export transaction. This point was made clear by Singleton L.J. in *M.W. Hardy & Co., Inc. v. A.V. Pound & Co. Ltd.*, who explained that this difference might be material for the decision whether an export licence has to be obtained by the seller or the buyer.

A further distinction of considerable practical importance is that between three types of f.o.b. contract, and, here again, it depends on the intention of the parties which of these types is used.

The first type is the *strict or classic f.o.b. contract.* Under this arrangement the buyer has to nominate a suitable ship. When it arrives in the port of shipment, the seller places the goods on board under a contract of carriage by sea which he has made with the carrier, but this contract is made for the account of the buyer. The seller receives the bill of lading which normally shows him as consignor and is to his order, and he transfers it to the buyer. Marine insurance is normally arranged by the buyer directly, if he wishes to insure, but he may also ask the seller to arrange marine insurance for his—the buyer's—account.

The second type is the *f.o.b. contract with additional services.* Under this arrangement the shipping and insurance arrangements are made by the seller, but this is done for the account of the buyer. In this type of f.o.b. contract the buyer is not under an obligation to nominate a suitable ship but the nomination is done by the seller. Again, as in contracts of the first type, the seller enters into a contract with the carrier by sea, places the goods on board ship and transfers the bill of lading to the buyer.

The third type may be described as the *f.o.b. contract (buyer contracting with carrier).* Here the buyer himself enters into a contract of carriage by sea directly or through an agent, *e.g.* a forwarder. Naturally the buyer has nominated the ship, and when it calls on the port of shipment, the seller puts the goods on board. The bill of lading goes directly to the buyer, usually through an agent of the buyer in the port of shipment, such as a freight forwarder, and does not pass through the seller's hands.

Considerable legal differences exist between these three types of f.o.b. contract. They indicate the flexible nature of this arrangement. Indeed, variations and combinations of these types of f.o.b. contract are met in practice. In f.o.b. contracts of the first and third type the duty to nominate the ship falls on the buyer, but in those of the second type it falls on the seller. In contracts of the first and second type the seller is in contractual relationship with the sea carrier, and for this reason the second type has been described as a variant of the first type. In a contract of the third type, on the other hand, the contract of carriage by sea is made directly with the buyer and the seller is not a party to it.

The three different types of f.o.b. contract are described by Devlin J. in *Pyrene Co. Ltd. v. Scindia Navigation Co. Ltd.* as follows:

> The f.o.b. contract has become a flexible instrument. In ... the classic type ... for example, in *Wimble, Sons & Co. Ltd. v. Rosenberg & Sons,* the buyer's duty is to nominate the ship, and the seller's to put the goods on board for account of the buyer and procure a bill of lading in terms usual in the trade. In such a case the seller is directly a party to the contract of carriage at least until he takes out the bill of lading in the buyer's name. Probably the classic type is based on the assumption that the ship nominated will be willing to load any goods brought down to the berth or at least those of which she is notified. Under present conditions, when space often has to be booked well in advance, the contract of carriage comes into existence at an earlier point of time. Sometimes the seller is asked to make the necessary arrangements; and the contract may then provide for his taking the bill of lading in his own name and obtaining payment against the transfer, as in a c.i.f. contract. Sometimes the buyer engages his own forwarding agent at the port of loading to book space and to procure the bill of lading; if freight has to be paid in advance this method may be most convenient. In such a case the seller discharges his duty by putting the goods on board, getting the mate's receipt and handing it to the forwarding agent to enable him to obtain the bill of lading.

R. FOLSOM, M. GORDON, J. A. SPANOGLE, PRINCIPLES OF INTERNATIONAL BUSINESS TRANSACTIONS

§§ 2.3, 2.8, 2.9 (2nd ed., 2010).*

Incoterms as Trade Usage

* * *

Although the UCC has definitions for some commercial terms (e.g., F.O.B., F.A.S., C.I.F.), these definitions are expressly subject to "agreement otherwise." Thus, an express reference to Incoterms will supercede the UCC provisions, and United States courts have so held.

* * *

The Free on Board (FOB) Term

Under the Incoterms Free on Board (FOB) commercial term, the seller is obligated to deliver the goods on board a ship arranged for and named by the buyer at a named port of shipment. Thus, this term is also appropriate only for water-borne transportation, and seller must bear the costs and risks of inland transportation to the named port of shipment,

---

* Copyright © 2010 and reproduced with permission from Thomson Reuters.

and also of loading the goods on the ship. * * * Seller has no obligation to arrange transportation or insurance, but does have a duty to notify buyer "that the goods *have been delivered* on board" the ship. The risks of loss will transfer to the buyer also at the time the goods [are "on board the vessel"]. The seller must provide a commercial invoice, or its equivalent electronic message, and necessary export license, and usually a transport document that will allow buyer to take delivery—or an equivalent electronic [record]. The seller must also provide an export license, and clear the goods for export from the place of delivery. The seller must therefore pay any costs of customs formalities and export taxes.

In addition, the seller must provide all customary packaging and working, and pay for checking operations. The latter include measuring, weighing, counting, and checking of the goods considered necessary to accomplish delivery. [*Authors' Note: The new 2010 edition of the Incoterms provides that seller also must bear the cost of any pre-shipment inspection required by authorities in the export country.*]

The Cost, Insurance and Freight (CIF) Term

Under the Incoterms Cost, Insurance and Freight (CIF) commercial term, the seller is obligated to arrange for both transportation and insurance to a named destination port and then to deliver the goods on board the ship arranged for by the seller. Thus, the term is appropriate only for water-borne transportation. Seller must arrange the transportation, and pay the freight costs to the *destination port*, but has completed its delivery obligations when the goods are "on board the vessel at the port of shipment." The seller must pay the freight and unloading costs of the carrier at the destination port under the CIF term, but the buyer must pay all other costs, including unloading costs not collected by the carrier. However, demurrage charges for the cost of docking the ship longer than agreed are to be borne by the party causing the delay.

* * *

The seller must arrange and pay for insurance during transportation to the *port of destination*, but the risk of loss transfers to the buyer at the time the goods [are "on board the vessel"] at the *port of shipment*. Thus, the risk of damage to the goods due to improper loading or stowing on board the vessel is on the buyer. The buyer bears the risk of damages that occur to the goods during transit, even though the seller has a duty to procure insurance against such risks. Seller must notify buyer "that the goods have been delivered on board" the ship to enable buyer to receive the goods. Seller must provide a commercial invoice, or its equivalent electronic message, any necessary export license, and "the usual transport documents" for the destination port.

The transportation document "must ... enable the buyer to sell the goods in transit by the transfer of the document to a subsequent buyer ... or by notification to the carrier," unless otherwise agreed. The traditional manner of enabling buyer to do this, in either the "payment against documents" transaction or the letter of credit transaction, is for seller to obtain a negotiable bill of lading from the carrier and to tender that negotiable document to buyer through a series of banks. The banks allow buyer to obtain possession of the document (and control of the goods) only after buyer pays for goods. Thus, buyer "pays against documents," while the goods are at sea, and pays for them before any post-shipment inspection of the goods is possible.

COMMENTS

1. The leading case concerning buyer's (lack of a) right of inspection under a CIF contract (or any other contract that requires "payment against documents") is *Biddell Bros. v. E. Clemens Horst Co.*, [1912] A.C. 18 (House of Lords), which construed both the commercial usage and the British Sales of Goods Act. Earl Loreburn, L.C. summed up the issues in the following language:

> This is a contract usually called a c.i.f. contract, under which the seller is to ship a cargo of hops and is to contract for freight and to effect insurance; and he is to receive 90s. per 112 lbs. of hops. The buyer is to pay cash. But when is he to pay cash? The contract does not say. The buyer says that he is to pay cash against physical delivery and acceptance of the goods when they have come to England.

> Now § 28 of the Sale of Goods Act says in effect that payment is to be against delivery. Accordingly we have supplied by the general law an answer to the question when this cash is to be paid. But when is there delivery of goods which are on board ship? That may be quite a different thing from delivery of goods on shore. The answer is that delivery of the bill of lading when the goods are at sea can be treated as delivery of the goods themselves, this law being so old that I think it is quite unnecessary to refer to authority for it.

> Now in this contract there is no time fixed at which the seller is entitled to tender the bill of lading. He therefore may do so at any reasonable time; and it is wrong to say that he must defer the tender of the bill of lading until the ship has arrived; and it is still more wrong to say that he must defer the tender of the bill of lading until after the goods have been landed, inspected and accepted.

2. To the extent that one regards commercial practices (and law) as dynamic—involving a continuous jostling by different parties for a more advantageous position—there are two more items of interest. All of the foregoing doctrines can seem to favor seller, leaving an aggrieved buyer with little protection, even if buyer proceeds to sue the seller in the seller's home jurisdiction. The attack by buyers on this problem has been the specification in the sales contract that the seller provide an Inspection Certificate by a trusted and financially responsible third party. The Certificate, if properly arranged, allows the buyer to rely upon the credit and stability of the third party, as was discussed in Problem 4.0.

3. However, as one might expect, sellers have developed a method of parrying the effect of Inspection Certificates—by specifying in the sales

contract that the representations in any Certificate shall be final and binding on the buyer. Thus, where a contract specifies that a certificate of quality is final, and a seller then ships wheat which does not conform to the contract, but the certificate describes the wheat as conforming, the buyer is bound by the description in the certificate; and any later inspection is irrelevant. *Toepfer v. Continental Grain Co.,* [1974] 1 Lloyd's Rep. 11 (C.A.); *Gill & Duffus S.A. v. Berger & Co.,* [1984] 1 All E.R. 438 (House of Lords).

ZWILLING-PINNA, UPDATE OF IMPORTANT COMMERCIAL TERMS: REVISION OF THE INCOTERMS AS OF 2011

Der Betriebs–Berater, v. 65, pp. 2980–2981 (2010).*

[Translation from German by the Authors]

* * *

The Legal Nature of Incoterms 2010

The Incoterms were not designed to supplant domestic law, but rather to bridge the conflicts that arise for the parties from the contract law rules of the different domestic legal systems. The Incoterms do not apply as formal law of their own force * * *, but rather have the character of recommended contract terms. A specific Incoterm rule may become part of a contract through an agreement of the parties. But the Incoterms also may apply as a usage of trade if they are referred to as a whole either in the contract of the parties or in standard business terms accepted by them. Within the scope of the CISG, which recognizes binding trade usages, this result obtains through a party agreement on a trade usage under CISG Art. 9(1) or through the recognition of the Incoterms as a widely known trade usage under CISG Art. 9(2).

Each term in the Incoterms, with ten specific rights and duties of seller and buyer for their sales contract, theoretically represents a complete and integrated system within the background of the domestic law otherwise applicable to the contract. The parties that incorporate the Incoterms nonetheless may agree on different rules for specific issues. To avoid conflicts, however, such agreements should be expressly and clearly defined.

Authors' Note on Incoterms 2010

In September, 2010, the International Chamber of Commerce, following an extensive period of consultation, adopted a new edition of the Incoterms. These "Incoterms 2010", which formally entered into effect on January 1, 2011, are designed to respond to general developments in trade and transport practices and otherwise to simplify and clarify uncertain aspects of Incoterms 2000.

Two Broad Categories. The result was, first, a distillation and organization of the defined commercial terms into two general categories: those limited to sea and inland waterway transport, and those allowed for any mode of transport. The former category includes the most frequently used terms in large international transactions, CIF and FOB, as well as their less common cousins CFR (Cost and Freight) and FAS (Free Alongside Ship). The latter category covers a number of detailed terms also used in water transport, but which are more prevalent for air, land, and rail transportation: CIP (Carriage and Insurance Paid), CPT (Carriage Paid To), DAP (Delivered At Place), DAT (Delivered At Terminal), DDP (Delivered Duty Paid), EXW (Ex Works), and FCA (Free Carrier). One might also align these eleven different terms along a spectrum according to the relative responsibilities of seller and buyer. At one end of the spectrum would be EXW (Ex Works), under which seller must merely make the goods available at its own place of business (or other named place); at the other end would be DDP (Delivered Duty Paid), which obligates seller to place the goods at buyer's disposal at the destination location and to assume the responsibility and cost of both export and import customs clearance.

Electronic Commerce. In more practical terms, the principal purpose for the 2010 revisions of Incoterms was to address specific legal and factual developments relating to the transportation of goods. Perhaps most significant, the new rules expressly endorse the substitution of paper communications with an "equivalent electronic record or procedure." The previous edition allowed the agreed use of electronic data interchange (EDI) messages, the most prominent early form of which was the rules for electronic bills of lading developed by the Comité Maritime International (CMI). At the core of this system was a unique "private key" issued by the carrier to the shipper upon receipt of the goods. The shipper (the "holder" of the private key) could then transfer rights over the goods by notification to the carrier. If the transferee agreed with this electronic system, the carrier would cancel the original private key and issue a new one to the transferee as the new "holder" of the electronic bill of lading.

Incoterms 2010, however, now broadly embrace both electronic communications and electronic records where either the parties so agree or such is "customary" in the trade. This reference to trade custom is significant because it will increasingly authorize buyers and sellers to fulfill communication and documentation requirements with electronic equivalents. Moreover, the new Incoterms intentionally adopted an open-ended definition of "electronic records" to permit the rules to adapt to new technologies as they arise in the future. (We will examine the subject of electronic bills of lading in more detail in Problem 4.5 below.)

Use in International and Domestic Trade. Incoterms 2010 also expressly recognize that they may be used in "both domestic and international trade." The goal of this language was to facilitate the use of Incoterms in customs-free trade zones such as the European Union (where international borders are less significant) as well as in large domestic legal systems (such as in the place of the UCC in the United States).

INCOTERMS® 2010

International Chamber of Commerce pub. no. 715.*

FREE ON BOARD

FOB (insert named port of shipment) Incoterms® 2010

This rule is to be used only for sea or inland waterway transport.

* * *

A THE SELLER'S OBLIGATIONS

A1 General obligations of the seller

The seller must provide the goods and the commercial invoice in conformity with the contract of sale and any other evidence of conformity that may be required by the contract.

Any document referred to in A1–A10 may be an equivalent electronic record or procedure if agreed between the parties or customary.

A2 Licenses, authorizations, security clearances and other formalities

Where applicable, the seller must obtain, at its own risk and expense, any export license or other official authorization and carry out all customs formalities necessary for the export of the goods.

A3 Contracts of carriage and insurance

a) Contract of carriage

The seller has no obligation to the buyer to make a contract of carriage. However, if requested by the buyer or if it is commercial practice and the buyer does not give an instruction to the contrary in due time, the seller may contract for carriage on usual terms at the buyer's risk and expense. In either case, the seller may decline to make the contract of carriage and, if it does, shall promptly notify the buyer.

b) Contract of insurance

The seller has no obligation to the buyer to make a contract of insurance. However, the seller must provide the buyer, at the buyer's request, risk, and expense (if any), with information that the buyer needs for obtaining insurance.

A4 Delivery

The seller must deliver the goods either by placing them on board the vessel nominated by the buyer at the loading point, if any, indicated by the buyer at the named port of shipment or by procuring the goods so delivered. In either case, the seller must deliver the goods on the agreed date or within the agreed period and in the manner customary at the port.

If no specific loading point has been indicated by the buyer, the seller may select the point within the named port of shipment that best suits its purpose.

A5 Transfer of risks

The seller bears all risks of loss of or damage to the goods until they have been delivered in accordance with A4 with the exception of loss or damage in the circumstances described in B5.

A6 Allocation of Costs

The seller must pay

a) all costs relating to the goods until they have been delivered in accordance with A4, other than those payable by the buyer as envisaged in B6; and

b) where applicable, the costs of customs formalities necessary for export, as well as all duties, taxes and other charges payable upon export.

A7 Notices to the buyer

The seller must, at the buyer's risk and expense, give the buyer sufficient notice either that the goods have been delivered in accordance with A4 or that the vessel has failed to take the goods within the time agreed.

A8 Delivery document

The seller must provide the buyer, at the seller's expense, with the usual proof that the goods have been delivered in accordance with A4.

Unless such proof is a transport document, the seller must provide assistance to the buyer, at the buyer's request, risk and expense, in obtaining a transport document.

A9 Checking–packaging–marking

The seller must pay the costs of those checking operations (such as checking quality, measuring, weighing, counting) that are necessary for the purpose of delivering the goods in accordance with A4, as well as the costs of any pre-shipment inspection mandated by the authority of the country of export.

The seller must, at its own expense, package the goods, unless it is usual for the particular trade to transport the type of goods sold unpackaged. The seller may package the goods in the manner appropriate for their transport, unless the buyer has notified the seller of specific packaging requirements before the contract of sale is concluded. Packaging is to be marked appropriately.

A10 Assistance with information and related costs

The seller must, where applicable, in a timely manner, provide to or render assistance in obtaining for the buyer, at the buyer's request, risk and expense, any documents and information, including security-related information, that the buyer needs for the import of the goods and/or for their transport to the final destination.

The seller must reimburse the buyer for all costs and charges incurred by the buyer in providing or rendering assistance in obtaining documents and information as envisaged in B10.

B THE BUYER'S OBLIGATIONS

B1 General obligations of the buyer

The buyer must pay the price of the goods as provided in the contract of sale.

Any document referred to in B1–B10 may be an equivalent electronic record or procedure if agreed between the parties or customary.

B2 Licenses, authorizations, security clearances and other formalities

Where applicable, it is up to the buyer to obtain, at its own risk and expense, any import license or other official authorization and carry out all customs formalities for the import of the goods and for their transport through any country.

B3 Contracts of carriage and insurance

a) Contract of carriage

The buyer must contract, at its own expense for the carriage of the goods from the named port of shipment, except where the contract of carriage is made by the seller as provided in A3 a).

b) Contract of insurance

The buyer has no obligation to the seller to make a contract of insurance.

B4 Taking delivery

The buyer must take delivery of the goods when they have been delivered as envisaged in A4.

B5 Transfer of Risks

The buyer bears all risks of loss of or damage to the goods from the time they have been delivered as envisaged in A4.

If

a) the buyer fails to notify the nomination of a vessel in accordance with B7; or

b) the vessel nominated by the buyer fails to arrive on time to enable the seller to comply with A4, is unable to take the goods, or closes for cargo earlier than the time notified in accordance with B7;

then, the buyer bears all risks of loss or damage to the goods:

(i) from the agreed date, or in the absence of an agreed date,

(ii) from the date notified by the seller under A7 within the agreed period, or, if no such date has been notified,

(iii) from the expiry date of any agreed period for delivery,

provided that the goods have been clearly identified as the contract goods.

B6 Allocation of costs

The buyer must pay

a) all costs relating to the goods from the time they have been delivered as envisaged in A4, except, where applicable, the costs of customs formalities necessary for export, as well as all duties, taxes and other charges payable upon export as referred to in A6 b);

b) any additional costs incurred, either because:

(i) the buyer has failed to give appropriate notice in accordance with B7, or

(ii) the vessel nominated by the buyer fails to arrive on time, is unable to take the goods, or closes for cargo earlier than the time notified in accordance with B7,

provided that the goods have been clearly identified as the contract goods; and

c) where applicable, all duties, taxes and other charges, as well as the costs of carrying out customs formalities payable upon import of the goods and the costs for their transport through any country.

B7 Notices to the seller

The buyer must give the seller sufficient notice of the vessel name, loading point and, where necessary, the selected delivery time within the agreed period.

B8 Proof of delivery

The buyer must accept the proof of delivery provided as envisaged in A8.

B9 Inspection of goods

The buyer must pay the costs of any mandatory pre-shipment inspection, except when such inspection is mandated by the authorities of the country of export.

B10 Assistance with information and related costs

The buyer must, in a timely manner, advise the seller of any security information requirements so that the seller may comply with A10.

The buyer must reimburse the seller for all costs and charges incurred by the seller in providing or rendering assistance in obtaining documents and information as envisaged in A10.

The buyer must, where applicable, in a timely manner, provide to or render assistance in obtaining for the seller, at the seller's request, risk and expense, any documents and information, including security-related information, that the seller needs for the transport and export of the goods and for their transport through any country.

COST, INSURANCE AND FREIGHT

CIF (insert named port of destination) Incoterms® 2010

This rule is to be used only for sea or inland waterway transport.

* * *

A THE SELLER'S OBLIGATIONS

A1 General obligations of the seller

The seller must provide the goods and the commercial invoice in conformity with the contract of sale and any other evidence of conformity that may be required by the contract.

Any document referred to in A1–A10 may be an equivalent electronic record or procedure if agreed between the parties or customary.

A2 Licenses, authorizations, security clearances and other formalities

[Same as FOB A2]

A3 Contracts of carriage and insurance

a) Contract of carriage

The seller must contract or procure a contract for the carriage of the goods from the agreed point of delivery, if any, at the place of delivery to the named port of destination or, if agreed, any point at that port. The contract of carriage must be made on usual terms at the seller's expense and provide for carriage by the usual route in a vessel of the type normally used for the transport of the type of goods sold.

b) Contract of insurance

The seller must obtain, at its own expense, cargo insurance complying at least with the minimum cover provided by Clauses (C) of the Institute Cargo Clauses (LMA/IUA) or any similar clauses. The insurance shall be contracted with underwriters or an insurance company of good repute and entitle the buyer, or any other person having an insurable interest in the goods, to claim directly from the insurer.

When required by the buyer, the seller shall, subject to the buyer providing any necessary information requested by the seller, provide at the buyer's expense any additional cover, if procurable, such as cover provided by Clauses (A) or (B) of the Institute Cargo Clauses (LMA/IUA) or any similar clauses and/or cover complying with the Institute War Clauses and/or Institute Strikes Clauses (LMA/IUA) or any similar clauses.

The insurance shall cover, at a minimum, the price provided in the contract plus 10% (i.e., 110%) and shall be in the currency of the contract.

The insurance shall cover the goods from the point of delivery set out in A4 and A5 to at least the named port of destination.

The seller must provide the buyer with the insurance policy or other evidence of insurance cover.

Moreover, the seller must provide the buyer, at the buyer's request, risk, and expense (if any), with information that the buyer needs to procure any additional insurance.

A4 Delivery

The seller must deliver the goods either by placing them on board the vessel or by procuring the goods so delivered. In either case, the seller must deliver the goods on the agreed date or within the agreed period and in the manner customary at the port.

A5 Transfer of risks

The seller bears all risks of loss of or damage to the goods until they have been delivered in accordance with A4, with the exception of loss or damage in the circumstances described in B5.

A6 Allocation of Costs

The seller must pay

a) all costs relating to the goods until they have been delivered in accordance with A4, other than those payable by the buyer as envisaged in B6;

b) the freight and other costs resulting from A3 a), including the costs of loading the goods on board and any charges for unloading at the agreed port of discharge that were for the seller's account under the contract of carriage;

c) the costs of insurance resulting from A3 b); and

d) where applicable, the costs of customs formalities necessary for export, as well as all duties, taxes and other charges payable upon export, and the costs for their transport through any country that were for the seller's account under the contract of carriage.

A7 Notices to the buyer

The seller must give the buyer any notice needed in order to allow the buyer to take the measures that are normally necessary to enable the buyer to take the goods.

A8 Delivery document

The seller must, at its own expense, provide the buyer without delay with the usual transport document for the agreed port of destination.

This transport document must cover the contract goods, be dated within the period agreed for shipment, enable the buyer to claim the goods from the carrier at the port of destination and, unless otherwise agreed, enable the buyer to sell the goods in transit by the transfer of the document to a subsequent buyer or by notification to the carrier.

When such a transport document is issued in negotiable form and in several originals, a full set of originals must be presented to the buyer.

A9 Checking–packaging–marking

[Same as FOB A9.]

A10 Assistance with information and related costs

[Same as FOB A10.]

B THE BUYER'S OBLIGATIONS

B1 General obligations of the buyer

The buyer must pay the price of the goods as provided in the contract of sale.

Any document referred to in B1–B10 may be an equivalent electronic record or procedure if agreed between the parties or customary.

B2 Licenses, authorizations, security clearances and other formalities

[Same as FOB B2]

B3 Contracts of carriage and insurance

a) Contract of carriage

The buyer has no obligation to the seller to make a contract of carriage.

b) Contract of insurance

The buyer has no obligation to the seller to make a contract of insurance. However, the buyer must provide the seller, upon request, with any information necessary for the seller to procure any additional insurance requested by the buyer as envisaged in A3 b).

B4 Taking delivery

The buyer must take delivery of the goods when they have been delivered as envisaged in A4 and receive them from the carrier at the named port of destination.

B5 Transfer of Risks

The buyer bears all risks of loss of or damage to the goods from the time they have been delivered as envisaged in A4.

If the buyer fails to give notice in accordance with B7, then it bears all risks of loss of or damage to the goods from the agreed date or the expiry date of the agreed period for shipment, provided that the goods have been clearly identified as the contract goods.

B6 Allocation of costs

The buyer must, subject to the provisions of A3 a), pay

a) all costs relating to the goods from the time they have been delivered as envisaged in A4, except, where applicable, the costs of customs formalities necessary for export, as well as all duties, taxes and other charges payable upon export as referred to in A6 d);

b) all costs and charges relating to the goods while in transit until their arrival at the port of destination, unless such costs and charges were for the seller's account under the contract of carriage;

c) unloading costs including lighterage and wharfage charges, unless such costs and charges were for the seller's account under the contract of carriage;

d) any additional costs incurred if it fails to give notice in accordance with B7, from the agreed date or the expiry date of the agreed period for shipment, provided that the goods have been clearly identified as the contract goods;

e) where applicable, all duties, taxes and other charges, as well as the costs of carrying out customs formalities payable upon import of the goods and the costs of their transport through any country, unless included within the cost of the contract of carriage; and

f) the costs of any additional insurance procured at buyer's request under A3 b) and B3 b).

B7 Notices to the seller

The buyer must, whenever it is entitled to determine the time for shipping the goods and/or the point of receiving the goods within the named port of destination, give the seller sufficient notice thereof.

B8 Proof of delivery

The buyer must accept the transport document as envisaged in A8 if it is in conformity with the contract.

B9 Inspection of goods

[Same as FOB B9.]

B10 Assistance with information and related costs

[Same as FOB B10].

INTERNATIONAL CHAMBER OF COMMERCE, INCOTERMS IN PRACTICE

14, 21, 32 (C. Debattista, ed., 1995).*

For the seller to perform his duty to tender a "usual" contract of carriage, the contract tendered must provide the buyer with continuous documentary cover against the carrier. This means two things: first, the seller must provide the buyer with a document which gives the buyer a contract enforceable by him against the carrier. The document tendered must give the buyer legal *locus standi* against the carrier. Secondly, the cover afforded to the buyer by the contract of carriage must contain no gaps. Thus, for example, where a seller tendered a bill of lading covering only the second leg of a voyage during which goods were transhipped, the seller was held to be in breach of his obligations under a c.i.f. contract.

The duty to provide the buyer with continuous documentary cover may cause difficulties where the goods are carried in containers, difficulties which illustrate the importance of choosing the right incoterm for the mode of transport envisaged.

* * *

[CIF clause] A8 goes directly to the nature of the document tendered as a key to the warehouse and raises the issue as to what type of transport document can be tendered by the seller to the buyer.

The article identifies two separate aspects of the "key" tendered by the seller to the buyer: it must allow the buyer access to the goods and it must, unless otherwise agreed, allow the buyer to transfer that right of access through the transfer of the document. Clearly a bill of lading would satisfy both requirements of article A8 if it is made out to the shipper's or the consignee's order, appropriately endorsed in full or in blank to the ultimate buyer if the goods have been sold while in transit.

However, difficulties arise where the document tendered by the seller provides the buyer with the right of access to the goods but not with the power of transfer. Thus, for example, what if the seller tenders a sea waybill, a bill of lading made out to the buyer without it being "to order", or a ship's delivery order acknowledging the buyer's right to delivery on discharge. All these documents clearly give the party for the time named as consignee a right of access to the goods; none of them grant the buyer the power of transferring that right through transfer of the document. The upshot is that tender of such documents under the CIF incoterm would put the seller in breach "unless otherwise agreed." Where sellers expect to tender such a document, the documents clause in the contract of sale needs to be appropriately drafted, making it clear that the seller performs his documentary duties through tender of a bill of lading **or** a sea waybill **or** a ship's delivery order. A failure to do so may catch the seller unawares where a buyer who is no longer interested in the goods, or in the goods at the contract price, puts the seller in breach and threatens to cancel the contract.

* * *

The **Multimodal Transport bill of lading** differs from the ocean bill of lading in the kind of carriage the carrier has agreed upon.

The Multimodal Transport bill of lading evidences the contract between shipper and carrier, here called the Multimodal Transport Operator (MTO), for the carriage of goods involving at least two different modes of transport. The MTO issuing a Multimodal Transport bill of lading is responsible for the goods from the time he receives them until the time he delivers them at destination.

There is considerable doubt as to whether the Multimodal Transport Document is a document of title. While there is no doubt that such a document is acceptable to the banks in the circumstances envisaged by article 26 of the Uniform Customs and Practice for Documentary Credits, the better view seems to be that it cannot transfer control of the goods while in transit through the simple endorsement of the document.

RAMBERG: ICC GUIDE TO INCOTERMS® 2010
71–74 (2010).*

[T]he seller's duty to provide proof of delivery and the transport document

All terms except EXW require the seller to submit to the buyer formal proof that he has fulfilled his delivery obligation (A8).

Under [CFR and CIF], when the seller has to arrange and pay for the carriage, the transport document becomes very important, since it must show not only that the goods have been handed over to the carrier by the date agreed, but also that the buyer has an independent right to claim the goods from the carrier at destination.

* * *

Surrender of original bill of lading essential

In some trades, there is a further problem connected with the use of bills of lading. This is caused by the need to present and surrender one original document to the carrier in order to obtain delivery of the goods. Ships frequently arrive at destination before an original bill of lading is available there. In such cases, the goods are often delivered to the buyer against a bill of lading guarantee issued by a bank. This is to protect the carrier if some person other than the person to whom the goods were delivered is the rightful holder of the original bill of lading.

This practice—or rather malpractice—defeats the whole bill of lading system, which depends for its validity on the firm principle that under no circumstances should the goods be delivered except in return for an original bill of lading. If that principle is not strictly followed, one can no longer say that the "bill of lading represents the goods".

Non-negotiable transport documents

In recent years, transport documents other than bills of lading for carriage of goods by sea have been increasingly used. These documents in the "waybill system" are similar to those used for modes of transport other than carriage by sea and when no original document is required to obtain the goods from the carrier at destination. It is sufficient that the consignee be named and that he can properly identify himself, as in the widespread use of air waybills (AWBs) and waybills for international road and rail carriage.

Such documents cannot be used, however, for transferring rights to the goods by the transfer of the document; they are therefore called non-negotiable. They bear various names such as "liner waybills", "ocean waybills", "data freight receipts", "cargo quay receipts" or "sea waybills". Although in such transport documents a buyer or a bank has been named as consignee, the seller and the seller alone enters into a contractual relationship with the carrier when the seller has contracted for carriage. The carrier takes instructions from his contracting party—the seller—and from no one else.

Payment against sea waybills requires caution

If the buyer has paid for the goods in advance, or a bank wishes to use the goods as security for a loan extended to the buyer, it is not sufficient that the buyer or the bank be named as consignee in a non-negotiable document. This is the case because the seller, by new instructions to the carrier, could replace the named consignee with someone else. To protect the buyer or the bank it is therefore necessary that the original instructions from the seller to the carrier to deliver the goods to the named consignee be irrevocable.

It follows that * * * the buyer should not pay for the goods, and the bank should not rely on security in the goods, merely by accepting transport documents naming the buyer and the bank respectively as consignees, unless such instructions to the carrier are made irrevocable.

The problems of replacing bills of lading by EDI

Apart from the need to agree on a method for using EDI and adopting international message standards, there should be no particular problems when replacing transport documents by electronic messages. However, it is difficult to replace the bill of lading because it is not only proof of the delivery of the goods to the carrier but also a legal symbol often expressed by the principle that "the bill of lading represents the goods".

* * *

The Incoterms rules CFR and CIF and EDI

The Incoterms 1990 rules, in the trade terms CFR and CIF, section A8, already took the development of EDI into consideration. They did this first by maintaining the traditional principle that, unless otherwise agreed, the transport document must enable the buyer to sell the goods in transit by the transfer of the document to a subsequent buyer. But they also indicated that the transfer could be made by notification to the carrier. In the former case, the negotiable bill of lading is expressly referred to. In the latter, reference is made to a system of notification. In any event, a mere notification to the carrier is not sufficient to replace a bill of lading.

Authors' Note on UCC Revisions

As noted in Problem 4.1 above, in 2003 the Uniform Commissioners and the ALI, the folks responsible for the UCC, proposed substantial amendments to UCC Article 2. These amendments would have deleted all the detailed statutory definitions of commercial terms (FOB, CIF, etc.). No state has adopted the proposed revision of UCC Article 2, however, and none is likely to do so in the future. For domestic transactions, therefore, we are left with the uncomfortable relationship between UCC Article 2's definitions of commercial terms and those of the Incoterms. Nonetheless, as noted above, the new 2010 edition of the Incoterms now expressly permits the use of these uniform international commercial terms in "both domestic and international trade."

QUESTIONS AND COMMENTS

1. The excerpt from Schmitthoff indicates that there are different interpretations in the United States and the United Kingdom of the term "FOB," including differences as to arranging for freight and insurance, shifting of risk

of loss, and even duty to procure an export license. The United States rules on FOB are found in UCC § 2–319 in the Documents Supplement.

2.   Under the classic form of FOB place of shipment, the seller may have risks, and need insurance protection, after the goods have left seller's premises but before they have been loaded on the vessel at the port of shipment. However, more modern approaches under domestic law shift risks to the buyer under an FOB place of shipment contract after the goods are delivered to the first carrier, regardless of whether they are then placed on a ship or not.

3.   With such large variations on fundamental aspects, how can an attorney determine the specific meaning of "FOB shipment" or "CIF destination"? The goal of Incoterms, a product of the International Chamber of Commerce, is to solve the problem of conflicting domestic law approaches by providing a uniform set of definitions for such common commercial terms.

What is the *legal* nature of Incoterms? *See* the excerpt from Zwilling–Pinna.

The Incoterms definitions of "FOB shipment" and "CIF destination" are set out in the Readings, as are excerpts from several books which explain their use and critique them. These definitions should allow you to analyze many of Sam's questions.

4.   Both American and English law allow contracting parties to specify most of the terms of a contract, and Sam, Bill and Howard have chosen to do so through the reference to Incoterms. As noted in the excerpt from Zwilling–Pinna, such detailed terms can be expressed in the contract, incorporated by reference, or implied by commercial usage and custom. However, although they are useful for the types of disputes that arise in Problem 4.2, note that they would not be useful in resolving the type of dispute that arose in Problem 4.1. If Sam and Bill later have a dispute about whether a contract between them was formed or not, that dispute would be determined by the substantive contract law of Georgia or England. Incoterms, in contrast, address only the allocation of rights, obligations, risks, and costs as between buyer and seller on the specific subject of the delivery and transportation of the goods.

5.   The excerpts from Folsom *et al.* describe the legal consequences of the incorporation of an FOB term as compared to a CIF term. Sam's contract with Bill uses the FOB term, whereas the one with Howard uses CIF. Now analyze the initial questions Sam posed to you at the beginning of this Problem with reference to the specific clauses in Incoterms.

(a) What are Sam's obligations to Bill regarding the transportation of the goods and who bears the associated risks and costs? If Sam does not have this obligation, but does so anyway, does it have a right to recover the costs from Bill?

(b) What are Sam's obligations to Howard on the same subjects?

(c) The CIF term in Howard's contract specifically obligates Sam to procure insurance. But is Sam similarly obligated to arrange insurance covering the books to Bill while in transit?

6. Now turn to Sam's question about bills of lading. What type of "transport document" may or must Sam obtain for the CIF shipment to Howard? *See* the Debattista and Ramberg excerpts. Why would Howard care whether Sam obtained a negotiable or a non-negotiable bill of lading? Also, if a negotiable bill of lading is required, would you recommend that Sam arrange for an "order" or a "bearer" bill (if Sam wants to be on the safe side in this regard)?

Debattista and Ramberg also discuss "sea waybills" and similar non-negotiable transport documents. Note that, unless otherwise agreed, these documents would not comply with an Incoterm CIF term, because the buyer cannot sell the goods in transit by transferring the document alone.

A second issue discussed by Debattista is the problem created by the use of multiple carriers in most individual transactions. A trucker may take the goods to a railroad yard, a railroad may then take them to a shipment port, where a ship will take them to a destination port for further transfer by rail and truck. Multimodal transport is involved, and a multimodal transport bill of lading may be more efficient. Note, however, that it may not be useable to control the goods in the letter of credit transaction in Problem 4.0. For that, you may still need a negotiable bill of lading.

7. One of the most pressing demands in modern transportation practice is for a uniform and secure legal framework for the use of electronic bills of lading. As noted in the Ramberg excerpt, electronic versions of this essential document as of yet have not been able to fulfill all of the characteristics of the traditional paper form, with the result that they have proved unsuitable for documentary sale transactions, and especially those with letters of credit. An early effort at creating the needed legal framework for electronic commerce in this field was the 1996 UNCITRAL Model Law for Electronic Commerce.

A recently concluded treaty, the United Nations Convention on Contracts for the International Carriage of Goods Wholly or Partly by Sea, provides even more hope for the future of electronic bills of lading. These so-called "Rotterdam Rules," which were opened for signature in 2009, create an explicit legal framework to support the recognition of "negotiable electronic transport records" as reliable systems develop in the future. Although only one country has ratified the Rotterdam Rules as of 2012, twenty-three have signed it, including the United States.

8. One functional method of comparing and contrasting the two types of contracts is to analyze whether Sam can put both orders in one container and ship it off. A starting point for such an analysis is the documents normal to each transaction. Note that the bill of lading is fundamental to a CIF transaction, and must pass an inspection of the buyer which is independent of any inspection of the goods. The bill of lading in an FOB shipment contract is somewhat more incidental, however, since the buyer is not normally expected to pay against the document. In the Incoterms definitions, compare clauses A.8 under each definition. In light of this requirement of a negotiable bill of lading for a CIF transaction, may Sam properly send Howard's books in a container covered by a bill of lading made out to Howard and Bill jointly?

9. Another starting point for such analysis is the buyer's right of inspection. The Incoterms rules say nothing about inspection, so that the

answer to that issue depends upon local law, either Georgia or England. As Folsom *et al.* state, inspection is usually allowed before payment, as in an FOB shipment contract. UCC § 2–513(1) and CISG Article 58(3) agree.

What about a CIF contract such as that with Howard? From the nature of a CIF contract, does Howard have a legal right to demand inspection of the *goods* before he is obligated to pay Sam? *Compare* UCC § 2–320(4) and the *Biddle Bros.* case noted in the first set of Comments above.

10. Note when the risk of loss passes from seller to buyer under Incoterms. Compare clauses A.5 and B.5 in each definition. As noted in Question 2. above, the classic approach on this issue has transferred the risk from seller to buyer at a highly specific point—when the goods "pass the ship's rail" at the port of shipment. The new Incoterms 2010 have a revised rule. Under this new rule, when does the seller fulfill its delivery obligation and when does the risk of loss pass to the buyer? *Compare* clauses A.4/B.4 and A.5/B.5 in both FOB and CIF. Note also here that the risk of loss passes at this time for a CIF contract as well, even though the seller is obligated to procure insurance. *See* CIF clauses A.3(b), and A.5.

11. Finally, what is the effect of the "shipper's load, weight and count" clause that the carrier's clerk stamped on the bills of lading? We will see more about such clauses concerning the liability of the carrier in Problem 4.5 below. But for now, we need to clarify that such a clause does not cause problems for Sam. The 1980 edition of Incoterms (in a provision equivalent to CIF clause A.8) required seller to provide a "clean" bill of lading. A related note stated, however, that clauses "disclaim[ing] on the part of the carrier knowledge of the contents" of packages were not a problem. Note that Incoterms 2010, CIF clause A8, now has no limiting language about such descriptions on the transport document that seller must provide to buyer (other than the obvious requirement that it "cover the contract goods").

PART B.   THE BASICS OF CARRIER LIABILITY

TETLEY, MARINE CARGO CLAIMS

Vol. 1, 5–6, 9, 39, 652, 2157–2158, 2182–2186 (4th ed., 2008).*

The Hague Rules[1] were adopted in 1924, the Hague/Visby Rules[2] in 1968 * * * and the Hamburg Rules[4] in 1978. Each international convention in turn attempted to broaden its application in order to avoid lacunae, to encompass all contracts of carriage as well as bills of lading, and to

---

* Copyright © 2008 and reproduced by permission of the publisher Les Editions Yvon Blais, Inc.

1. *International Convention for the Unification of Certain Rules of Law Relating to Bills of Lading* signed at Brussels, August 25, 1924 and entered into force June 2, 1931, better known as the "Hague Rules." * * *

2. The term "Hague/Visby Rules 1968" refers to the Hague Rules 1924, as amended by the "Protocol to Amend the International Convention for the Unification of Certain Rules of Law Relating to Bills of Lading", adopted at Brussels, February 23, 1968, which Protocol entered into force June 23, 1977, and is often referred to as the "Visby Rules". * * *

4. United Nations Convention on the Carriage of Goods by Sea, signed at Hamburg on March 31, 1978, and entered into force November 1, 1992.

permit incorporation by reference. This chapter deals with the application of the three sets of rules.

While the Hamburg Rules are in force in about thirty-two countries, the Hague Rules or the Hague/Visby Rules are presently in force in most of the world's shipping nations. Some nations such as France have two international regimes. They apply the Hague Rules to shipments from a Hague Rules nation and the Hague/Visby Rules to all outbound shipments. Belgium applies the Hague/Visby Rules inbound and outbound and the United States applies COGSA (the "Hague Rules")[6] in the same way. Some nations have a national local law for internal shipments which is similar but not identical, to the Hague Rules or the Hague/Visby Rules. Finally some nations such as the United States have a local law for inland traffic * * * which is unique to them.[9]

* * *

Art. 10 of the Hague Rules states: "The provisions of this Convention shall apply to all bills of lading issued in any of the contracting States."

Most national laws invoking the Hague Rules stipulate that the bill of lading shall contain a paramount clause. Sect. 13, para. sixth, of COGSA states:

[[E]very bill of lading or similar document of title which is evidence of a contract for the carriage of goods by sea from ports of the United States, in foreign trade, shall contain a statement that it shall have effect subject to the provisions of this [Act]].

Even if the bill of lading does not contain a paramount clause, the Rules still apply. * * *

If the bill of lading does not contain a paramount clause and does not invoke the Hague Rules but invokes some other law, the Hague Rules still apply. * * *

COGSA and the Harter Act apply *outwards* from U.S. ports, as well as *inwards*, unlike [the Hague Rules] which apply outwards only * * *. The inwards application of COGSA to bill of lading contracts made outside the United States for carriage to the United States is unfortunate and chauvinistic. * * * The consequences are even more incongruous now that most shipping nations have adopted the Visby Rules. Shipments to the U.S. from a Hague/Visby nation may be subject to two compulsory regimes: the Hague/Visby Rules and COGSA. One district court has characterized this situation as a "legal Gordian Knot," and has seemingly approved of this chauvinistic legislation, stating: "* * * United States courts must apply COGSA, when its terms so require, regardless where bills of lading were issued or when carriage began."

* * *

---

6. The American *Carriage of Goods by Sea Act*, * * * 46 U.S. Code Appx. 1300–1315, is commonly referred to by the acronym "COGSA". * * *

9. The Harter Act, Act of February 13, 1893, * * * 46 U.S. Code 30701–30707. * * *

The condition of the goods at shipment is usually proven by the bill of lading which describes the goods as received on board.

A bill of lading is important for the three different roles it plays. First, although not the contract of carriage itself, it is the best evidence of the contract. Secondly, it serves as a receipt for the goods. Finally, it is a document of title to property, which can be endorsed and negotiated.

* * *

Because the carrier is obliged to state the marks and the number or the quantity or the weight of the goods and in every case their apparent order and condition on the bill of lading, it is clear that the carrier must inspect the goods upon receiving them.

The inspection, nevertheless, of the carrier, master or agent is only a reasonable inspection. The master need not be an expert nor need he employ experts.

On the other hand, the carrier cannot contradict the clean bill of lading which he gave by relying on the laxity with which the cargo was examined on the ship's behalf.

* * *

The Hague Rules at art. 3(4) stipulate that a clean bill of lading only creates a *prima facie* presumption that the goods are as described on the bill of lading. Nevertheless, the principle of estoppel has prevented a carrier from proving that the goods were other than as described against a third party holder of the bill of lading for value who is acting in good faith. The principle is codified in the last sentence of art. 3(4) of the Hague/Visby Rules and in art. 16(3) of the Hamburg Rules.

* * *

In order to avoid being bound by the description of the goods on the bill of lading, the carrier will often add qualifying clauses such as "shipper load and count" or "particulars furnished by the shipper". The carrier's dilemma, particularly if he cannot verify the description of the goods, is to avoid being bound by that description, and yet not to issue a bill of lading which is "unclean"; such a bill of lading is unacceptable to the carrier's client, the shipper, and to the shipper's client, the consignee, because its negotiability, and therefore its commercial value, is jeopardized.

* * *

Ocean carriers for over 100 years have attempted to avoid their heavy responsibility as common carriers by inserting non-responsibility clauses into bills of lading. Neither the U.S. *Harter Act* 1893 nor the other national legislation modelled upon it * * * contained a package or unit limitation but all contained stipulations voiding non-responsibility clauses. * * * The Hague Rules of 1924 were a compromise whereby nonresponsibility clauses were disallowed by art. 3(8) but, on the other hand, the carrier was not to be responsible for more than £100 sterling per package or unit as stipulated in art. 4(5). [The COGSA package limit is $500.]

* * *

The shipper may avoid the package or kilo limitation by making a declaration as to "the nature and value" of the goods "before shipment and inserted in the bill of lading." A statement by the shipper that he wanted to insure his goods for a certain amount was held to be a sufficient declaration. * * * Art. 4(5) of the Hague Rules and art. 4(5)(a) of the Visby Rules indicate that the obligation to declare the higher value is on the shipper.

2) Opportunity to declare a higher value

As the package limitation has decreased with inflation (the $500.00 U.S. package limitation in 1936 when COGSA was adopted had the buying power of about $7,400 in U.S. in 2007 money), American courts have become increasingly reluctant to impose the package limitation. One method whereby the courts avoid the limitation has been to insist that the shipper be given a clear opportunity to declare the true value of the goods when it is higher than the package limitation.

The requirement of a fair opportunity to declare the true value was first raised in U.S. sea carriage in 1953 and in subsequent years the requirement became a standard practice as the COGSA $500 package limitation became more and more devalued and obsolete. * * *

3) What is a "fair opportunity"?

* * *

It has generally been accepted by American courts that a blank square on the face of the bill of lading in which to declare a higher value is a fair opportunity, although the courts have quite properly recognized that providing such a blank space on the bill's face is not required by COGSA. Even a reference to COGSA in the general clauses of the bill of lading was understood to be a fair opportunity or a "constructive notice" to declare a higher value. Similarly a published tariff which gave the shipper a choice of valuations was sufficient, as were the tariff terms incorporated in the bill of lading, although the Ninth Circuit disagreed.

More recently, the Ninth Circuit has clarified its position by holding that a clear reference to the COGSA limitation * * * suffices to afford the shipper a fair opportunity to declare a higher value. * * *

In other circuits, incorporation of COGSA by reference in the bill of lading, by way of a clause paramount, has been held sufficient to constitute fair opportunity * * *.

* * *

N. HORN & C. SCHMITTHOFF, THE TRANSNATIONAL LAW OF INTERNATIONAL COMMERCIAL TRANSACTIONS

11, 20 (1982).*

Contracts for international commercial transactions are normally governed by the national law of a given country (the *lex contractus*), according to national conflict of laws rules concerning contracts (sometimes also termed *lex contractus*) and often under express choice of law clauses. It is still a widely accepted rule that each contract with a private (non-sovereign) party is necessarily governed by a national law, and that there are no "homeless" contracts or obligations in international commerce. On the other hand, with respect to the aforementioned practice of purposely omitting an express choice of law, one could argue that the parties can, at least under certain circumstances, entirely disconnect their contract from any national law. This may be the case in contracts with an international institution such as the World Bank, or in multi-party contracts involving governmental agencies and private parties of various states. It seems that today the 'no homeless contract' rule is not without exceptions.

Both in the normal case of a private contract under an applicable national contract law and in the still rather exceptional and debated case of a 'homeless' contract, the private parties make use of their party autonomy as conferred and recognised by the national laws in question. They make use of this autonomy not only in the choice of applicable law, but also in the precise regulation of the substance of their contractual obligations; thus they substitute the (non-mandatory) rules of applicable law with their own freely agreed arrangements, their private *lex contractus*. If we look for uniformity in international commercial contracts, we have to inspect not only the applicable contract laws, but also the substance of the contractual arrangements, the freely agreed *"lex contractus"*.

* * * [T]he various systems of national law * * * essentially consist of two types of legal rules. Some of them are mandatory in character, others are optional. The mandatory rules have to be accepted by the persons affected by them, whether they like them or not. The optional rules may be accepted by the parties or not; they may be modified or adapted to suit their convenience. Ultimately it is the interest of the state which determines whether a particular rule shall be mandatory or optional. Speaking generally, branches of law such as criminal law, family law, property law or tax law are dominated by mandatory rules. On the other hand, a wide area of contract law is optional. It is governed by the principle of the autonomy of the parties' will, in the common law countries called the principle of freedom of contract. * * * Of course, there exist

---

also mandatory rules in the law of contract and their impact should not be minimised. * * * In the domestic sphere of civil and commercial contracts there exists, in fact, a growing tendency to impose mandatory restrictions on the freedom of the parties to contract as they like. * * * They serve, *e.g.,* the protection of the consumer or the prevention of the abuse of dominant economic power or the maintenance of fair competitive conditions in the free market economies.

BERISFORD METALS CORP. v. S/S SALVADOR

United States Court of Appeals, Second Circuit, 1985.
779 F.2d 841.

MANSFIELD, CIRCUIT JUDGE.

Berisford Metals Corporation (Berisford), plaintiff in this cargo-loss action, appeals from an order and judgment of the Southern District of New York, Gerard L. Goettel, Judge, granting its motion for summary judgment against the ship S/S Salvador and A/S Ivarans Rederi (Ivarans), its owner and operator, for loss of 70 bundles of tin ingots valued at $483,214.90 but applying the limitation of liability provision of § 4(5) of the Carriage of Goods by Sea Act,[1] (COGSA), to limit the defendants' liability to $500 per bundle, or a total of $35,000. Defendants cross-appeal from the district court's denial of their motion for dismissal of the action. We reverse the judgment to the extent that it limits defendants' liability to $500 per bundle and remand the case with directions to enter judgment in Berisford's favor for the full value of the lost cargo. We affirm the district court's denial of defendants' motion to dismiss the complaint.

The material facts are not in dispute. On June 23, 1983, Berisford contracted to purchase from Paranapanema International Ltd. (Paranapanema), located in Sao Paolo, Brazil, 50 metric tons of grade A tin ingots in bundles at a price of $13,140 per metric ton (a price later changed by the parties [to] $13,300 per metric ton). The terms were F.O.B. vessel at Santos, Brazil, for shipment to New York in January 1984.[2] Payment was to be made net cash 45 days after ocean bill of lading date against presentation of a "full set of shipping documents," which, in conjunction with the F.O.B. vessel term, was understood by the parties as requiring a clean on board bill of lading.

---

1. Section 4(5) of COGSA, * * * provides:

"Neither the carrier nor the ship shall in any event be or become liable for any loss or damage to or in connection with the transportation of goods in an amount exceeding $500 per package lawful money of the United States, or in case of goods not shipped in packages, per customary freight unit, or the equivalent of that sum in other currency, unless the nature and value of such goods have been declared by the shipper before shipment and inserted in the bill of lading. This declaration, if embodied in the bill of lading, shall be prima facie evidence, but shall not be conclusive on the carrier."

2. F.O.B. or Free on Board "means that title to property passes from the seller to buyer at the designated FOB point." 10 *Williston on Contracts,* § 1079A, at 94 n. 6 (3d ed. 1967). Since the vessel was designated as the FOB point in this case title to the goods was to pass when the goods were loaded on board the ship. *See id.,* § 1080A, at 109–10 (Standard American Foreign Trade Definitions).

Pursuant to the contract Paranapanema delivered 100 bundles, each containing 30 tin ingots and steel-strapped onto wooden pallets, to Ivarans' agent at Santos, Agencia de Vapores Grieg, S.A. (Grieg), which maintains a terminal located about 5 kilometers from the dock where cargo would be loaded onto Ivarans' ship. Grieg acknowledged receipt of the bundles on December 29, 1983. Grieg stuffed the 100 bundles into four 20-foot containers at its terminal, * * *. Clause 6 of the bill of lading later issued by Ivarans authorized the carrier to stow goods "as received or, at Carrier's option, by means of containers or similar articles of transport used to consolidate goods".

After stuffing of each container its doors were closed, locked and sealed. On January 3, 1984, the containers were transported by Grieg to a Brazilian government-controlled storage yard located near the loading dock. Upon delivery of the containers to that yard they appeared, from the sound and handling of the trucks used to transport them, to be loaded, not empty. The government storage yard issued receipts indicating weights approximately equaling those listed on the shipping documents. At that point the seals and locks appeared unchanged.

On January 4, 1984, the containers were removed from the yard and loaded by stevedores aboard the vessel. On the same date Grieg, acting on behalf of Ivarans and the Master of the S/S Salvador, issued a clean on board bill of lading stating that the ship had received "100 bundles steel strapped on wooden skids containing 3000 refined tin ingots, 'Mamore' brand, with a minimum purity of 99.9%". The gross weight was stated on the bill to be "50,647" kilos and the net weight as "49,845" kilos. Par. 3 of the conditions on the back side of the bill of lading provided that the provisions of COGSA would apply throughout "the entire time the goods [would be] in the carrier's custody, including the period of carrier's custody before loading on and after discharge from the ship". The bill further stated that unless a higher value had been declared in writing prior to delivery and inserted in the bill, the $500 limit per package specified by COGSA would govern the carrier's liability.

Upon the loading of the four containers aboard the ship, neither Ivarans nor its agent Grieg verified the contents or made a tally of the 100 bundles represented by the bill of lading to be in the containers. After being loaded aboard the ship, the containers were not shifted from their place of stowage until the ship arrived in New York on January 19, 1984, at the Red Hook Terminal in Brooklyn. There the four containers were discharged on January 20, 1984, and placed on the ground outside Pier 11 to await stripping. On January 24, 1984, Universal Maritime Services, Ivarans' stevedore, opened the four containers by using a bolt cutter or pliers to cut the seals and found that two of them supposed to contain 70 bundles were empty. Before being broken the seals of the containers appeared to be intact, with no evidence of tampering; in fact, the seals were pitted and rusted. Neither the floors of the two containers nor the snow-covered ground around them near Pier 11 revealed any evidence of recent removal of any cargo from the containers. Each bundle would have weighed approximately 1100 lbs.

* * *

In the meantime the Mellon Bank in New York, representing Paranapanema, the seller and shipper of the tin ingots, presented to Berisford in accordance with the purchase contract a full set of shipping documents with respect to the 100 bundles of tin ingots purchased by Berisford, including three original on board bills of lading issued by the carrier (Ivarans), Paranapanema's invoice, weight and analysis certificates, and a draft in the amount of $662,938.50, payable 45 days after the bill of lading date. Since the papers were in order and complied with the parties' purchase contract Berisford accepted the draft and on February 17, 1984, paid the full amount of the purchase price to the Mellon Bank as collection agent for Paranapanema. In addition, Berisford paid Ivarans' freight charges amounting to $10,101.67.

On August 31, 1984, Berisford commenced the present action, seeking $525,000 damages for the missing cargo. Defendants' answer admitted receipt of the shipment of bundles of tin ingots but denied liability, asserting its rights under COGSA and its bill of lading with respect to the shipment, including COGSA's $500 per package limitation on its liability, and alleging that it acted without any fault or neglect. * * *

In an oral bench opinion Judge Goettel concluded that an evidentiary hearing was unnecessary since the existing evidence demonstrated that the loss had occurred while the cargo was in the possession of the Brazilian government's stevedores in Santos. He rejected Ivarans' argument that it was not responsible for a loss occurring while the cargo was in the possession of the Brazilian Government. However, he also rejected Berisford's contention that Ivarans' issuance of a false on board bill of lading constituted a "quasi deviation" negating the availability of the COGSA per package limitation on liability. Instead, he held that a carrier is estopped from denying that the goods were loaded only upon a showing that it knew that they had not been loaded. He accordingly granted plaintiff's motion to the extent of awarding it judgment in the sum of $35,000, from which both parties appeal.

DISCUSSION

The central question raised by this appeal is whether a carrier that issues a clean on board bill of lading erroneously stating that certain goods have been received on board when they have not been so loaded should be precluded from limiting its liability pursuant to an agreement binding the parties to the terms of § 4(5) of COGSA * * *

* * * [A] negotiable or order bill of lading is a fundamental and vital pillar of international trade and commerce, indispensable to the conduct and financing of business involving the sale and transportation of goods between parties located at a distance from one another. It constitutes an acknowledgement by a carrier that it has received the described goods for shipment. It is also a contract of carriage. As a document of title it controls the possession of the goods themselves. It has been said that the bill and the goods become one and the same, with the goods being "locked up in the bill." * * * The necessity for maintaining the integrity of and confidence in bills of lading has been recognized by us in a line of cases beginning before and continuing after the 1936 enactment of COGSA. In *Higgins v. Anglo–Algerian Steamship Co.,* for instance, after reviewing decisions of English courts on the question we held that a carrier which issued a clean bill of lading falsely representing that it received goods in apparent good order and condition when it knew they were damaged may not take advantage of exceptions and limitations in the bill for its own benefit.

* * *

* * * [W]e have steadfastly adhered to * * * the proposition that the $500 per package limitation of liability may not be invoked by a carrier that has issued an on board bill of lading erroneously representing that goods were loaded aboard its ship, regardless whether or not the carrier acted fraudulently. * * *

* * * Whether one likens the carrier's issuance of a false bill of lading with respect to its loading of cargo to a "deviation," a "breach of warranty" or a representation which it must be "estopped" to deny, its adverse impact on trade and on reliance on bills as an essential method of facilitating trade is serious. Title to the goods usually passes from the seller to the buyer when the seller delivers the goods to the carrier and the carrier or its agent issues a bill. In the past, on board bills, signifying that the goods had been loaded on board the ship, were generally required. More recently, "received for shipment" bills, which indicate merely that the carrier has received the goods, are sometimes used. In this case, an on board bill was clearly required by the parties. When the proper bill issues, the seller then ceases to assume any risk of loss or damage. The carrier, by issuing the bill, enables the seller to collect full payment of the purchase price from the buyer since presentation of the bill to the buyer assures it that the seller has fulfilled its commitment to ship the goods and obligates the buyer to pay for them. Presentation of an on board bill also serves to satisfy the buyer that the goods have not been stolen or lost while in the custody of the carrier prior to loading, an interval during which the seller bears the risk of any loss in any transaction requiring such a bill. If, instead, the buyer were free to question the accuracy of the bill upon presentation, the entire structure would be weakened as a method of carrying out commercial transactions.

In support of their contention that a carrier may be held liable for a misstatement in its bill of lading only if it acted intentionally or fraudulently, defendants direct our attention to decisions holding that when a carrier issues a bill of lading to the effect that it has received goods in apparent good condition it may not be held liable beyond a per package limitation for damaged goods contained in the bill of lading or COGSA unless it had actual knowledge of the damaged condition at the time of loading or the damage was readily apparent at that time. These "conditions" cases are readily distinguishable * * *. The "conditions" cases raise the issue of the extent to which a carrier must inspect the condition of goods made, sold and bought by others. Since the imposition of a duty to make a detailed inspection of the condition of the contents of every package received from others would be excessive, the carrier may be held liable only if it knew or could readily see that the packages were not in good condition. A carrier is not required to open every package received from a shipper and inspect the contents before issuing a bill to the effect that they appear to be in good condition.

When a carrier, on the other hand, makes a representation in a bill of lading with respect to *its own conduct* it is properly held to a higher standard since it is reasonably expected to be aware of *its own actions,* including whether or not it has loaded cargo, or has loaded the cargo below or above decks. * * *

Applying the foregoing principles to the present case, we conclude that the defendants must be held responsible for the full value of the lost cargo at the time of shipment in Santos and cannot invoke the $500 per package limitation of liability provision of § 4(5) of COGSA. The carrier here, having received 100 bundles of tin ingots from the shipper in Santos, issued a false F.O.B. bill of lading with respect to its own conduct, warranting that on January 4, 1984, it had loaded 100 bundles on its ship when in fact it had loaded only 30. The bill of lading, whether or not intentionally false, enabled the shipper to collect from Berisford, the buyer, the full purchase price for 100 bundles. If the carrier had disclosed that 70 bundles had not been loaded, Berisford would have been entitled to refuse payment and the loss would have fallen on the seller of the goods as required by the conditions of the sales contract. The carrier's misrepresentation therefore amounted to a fundamental breach going to the very essence of its contract and precluding it from invoking those provisions extending the limitation of liability terms of § 4(5) of COGSA to the period when the goods were on shore.

Defendants cannot escape responsibility on the ground that the four containers into which it claims that it had placed the bundles after receipt from the shipper were locked and sealed at the time when the containers were loaded aboard its ship, the S.S. Salvador. It is undisputed that the defendant received from the shipper the 100 separate bundles and that for its own convenience it placed them in the four containers. It was thereafter responsible for verifying the contents before loading the containers and issuing a clean on board bill of lading. The weight of the missing 70 bundles of tin ingots was approximately 78,885 lbs. Even if opening of the containers posed difficulties, at the very least the carrier owed a duty to verify the weight of the containers at shipside before they were placed aboard its ship and before it stated that they contained 100 bundles of tin ingots weighing the equivalent of 50,647 kilos or 111,656 lbs., which would have been 78,885 lbs. in excess of the weight of the containers actually loaded.

* * *

Our holding leaves intact the principle that, once goods are aboard the ship as represented, a carrier may be responsible for misdescription of the apparent condition of the goods loaded by it only upon proof of knowledge or intent. We hold simply that when a carrier misrepresents its own conduct in loading goods aboard ship it is responsible for the misrepresentation and may not invoke contract provisions incorporating COGSA's limitations on liability.

The order and judgment of the district court are reversed and the case is remanded to the district court with directions to enter judgment in favor of Berisford in the sum of its full damages, plus that portion of freight and handling charges attributable to the lost bundles, and costs and interest from January 20, 1984.

QUESTIONS AND COMMENTS

1. Should the goods be insured against loss or damage in transit—or will the liability of the carrier fully protect parties such as Sam, Bill, and Howard? As Tetley notes, the Hague Rules create a presumption that the carrier received the goods as described in the bill of lading, with the result that it generally should be liable for loss or damage in transit. *See also* COGSA, § 3(4)("[A] bill of lading shall be prima facie evidence of the receipt by the carrier of the goods as therein described[.]''). Nonetheless, there are many factors which affect the carrier's liability under COGSA, and many limitations on its liability. The $500 per package limit is the best known, but others include limitations on the types of harm for which a carrier can be held liable. Thus, reliance on carrier liability may be misplaced, and insurance advisable.

2. We will see much more about the grounds for the carrier's potential liability arising out of the bill of lading in Problem 4.5 below. One issue of special importance there will be the effect of so-called "Shipper's Load and Count" (SLC) clauses. But as a general matter for now, recall that the carrier's agent stamped such a clause on Sam's bills of lading. If Sam misdescribed the goods, does such a clause relieve the carrier of *all* obligations regarding the nature of the goods received from Sam? Would your answer change if the carrier could have discovered the discrepancy only by opening sealed cartons? Or if the discrepancy instead was apparent from the markings on the outside of the cartons? The fundamental point is that the carrier must, as Tetley points out, make only a "reasonable" inspection of the goods. And note also that, if the shipper provides a description of the condition of the goods, COGSA § 3(3)(c) permits the carrier to exclude from the bill of lading any information that it "has had no reasonable means of checking."

3. Our special focus here is also on rules that set monetary limits on the *amount* of carrier liability. The goal of the Hague Rules, on which COGSA is based, was to bring international uniformity on this and other issues relating to the obligations of carriers. The Hague Rules were at one time widely

adopted and uniform, but developments in commercial practice have led to amendments (the Hague–Visby Rules) and further amendments (the Hamburg Rules). Since not all nations have adopted either set of amendments, the earlier uniformity has disintegrated.

However, the newly concluded Rotterdam Rules, noted above, provide hope for greater international uniformity. The product of two decades of negotiation and drafting by interested parties from a broad range of perspectives, this proposed treaty—which the United States has not ratified as of 2012—may well be acceptable to a noteworthy majority of maritime states, whether principally supportive of buyers, sellers, or carriers. The Rotterdam Rules also contain detailed provisions on limitations of carrier liability. *See* Articles 59–61.

4. The Hague Rules, and therefore COGSA, were an attempt to introduce more balance into the shipper-carrier relationship. Before those rules, the carrier drafted the clauses in bills of lading and so the contract clauses were thought to favor the carrier too much. Thus, the Hague Rules were designed to overcome the carrier's contract clauses, and were designed to govern the carrier-shipper relationship *despite* what the carrier-written contract might say. In other words, they were designed to be "mandatory law."

Horn and Schmitthoff discuss the distinction between "optional" and "mandatory" rules, and use COGSA as an example of the latter. Its application is mandatory, *inter alia*, on all contracts for carriage of goods by sea from the United States to a foreign port. Thus, it will govern relations between Sam and the carrier, and that application cannot be disturbed by clauses in the bill of lading.

Are Sam's shipments at all subject to the $500 per package limitation? What are Sam's options for providing full protection to his customers against harm to the goods during transit?

5. As Tetley notes, COGSA's limitation of liability to $500 "per package"—which is itself a complicated issue—has eroded in value substantially over the decades. Some courts have responded to this development with the "fair opportunity" doctrine described by Tetley. One court of appeals, however, recently rejected this entire doctrine as contrary to the plain language of COGSA. *See Ferrostaal, Inc. v. M/V Sea Phoenix*, 447 F.3d 212, 228–229 (3rd Cir. 2006).

The *Berisford Metals Corp.* case describes another court-created exception to COGSA's limit on carrier liability. The decisive fact for the removal of the limitation there was that the goods clearly disappeared after delivery to the carrier and before it issued the false bill of lading. But is this the full extent of the exception? Assume, for example, the following slight changes to the *Berisford Metals Corp.* facts: (a) the shipper was responsible for loading, counting, and weighing the goods, but it in fact loaded only worthless junk, and (b) in reliance on information from the shipper, the carrier stamped on the bill of lading an SLC clause and "said to contain 100 bundles of tin ingots." With these new facts, could the carrier be certain that COGSA's $500 per package limitation would apply under the court's reasoning in *Berisford Metals Corp.*? *See also St. Paul Travelers Ins. Co. v. M/V Madame Butterfly*, 700 F. Supp. 2d 496, 506 (S.D.N.Y. 2010)("Courts have limited the false bill of lading exception to the COGSA package limitation 'to misrepresentations concerning the physical condition or location of the goods at the time the bill of lading was issued.' ")(*quoting* an earlier case), *aff'd*, 2011 WL 1901738 (2nd Cir. 2011).

PROBLEM 4.3 WARS AND OTHER FRUSTRATIONS: OIL FROM ARABY

SECTION I. THE SETTING

Your client, Jean Val Jean, is a heating oil broker in Boston. He was able to obtain a contract to sell a huge amount of heating oil at a respectable profit to Javert in Marseilles, France, this winter—and he thought that this "deal" would make his financial fortune. He made a covering contract to buy heating oil from Gulf Refinery, an oil refining company located in Araby, and made another contract with Constant Carrier to have the oil shipped from Araby to Marseilles. Araby is a small nation located on the Persian Gulf.

The contract between Jean and Gulf Refinery in Araby contains several clauses of interest: One states that Refinery will deliver 100,000 tons of heating oil to Jean in Araby on November 1. Another states a price per bbl. of heating oil. The price is stated to be FOB Refinery in Araby, and is payable in United States dollars. The other clause is a *force majeure* clause, as follows:

> If the performance of any part of this contract by the seller is prevented, hindered, delayed or otherwise made impracticable by reason of any strike, flood, riot, fire, explosion, war or any other casualty or cause beyond the control of seller, and which cannot be overcome by reasonable diligence and without unusual expense, seller shall be excused from such performance to the extent that it is necessarily prevented, hindered or delayed thereby, during the continuance of any such happening or event and for so long as such event shall continue to prevent, hinder or delay such performance. This contract shall be deemed suspended so long as and to the extent that any such cause shall operate to prevent, hinder or delay the performance by seller of its obligations.

The contract with Constant Carrier provides for carriage charges that are dependent upon the time and distance sailed by the vessel used and any tolls paid by the vessel. It also contains an estimate of the charges involved, calculated from the Persian Gulf to Marseilles via the Suez Canal, and including the Suez Canal toll charge. The charges are to be paid in United States dollars. The contract also contains the following "Liberties Clause" (which is identical to the corresponding clause in the Bill of Lading reproduced as Form 11 in Problem 4.0 above):

(1) If at any time the performance of the contract evidenced by this Bill of Lading is or is likely to be affected by any hindrance, risk, delay, difficulty or disadvantage of whatsoever kind which cannot be avoided by the exercise of reasonable endeavors, the Carrier (whether or not the transport has commenced) may without notice to the Merchant treat the performance of this contract as terminated and place the Goods or any part of them at the Merchant's disposal at any port or place whatsoever which the Carrier or Master may consider safe and advisable in the circumstances, whereupon the responsibility of the Carrier in respect of such goods shall cease. The Carrier shall nevertheless be entitled to full freight and charges on Goods received for transportation, and the Merchant shall pay any additional costs of carriage to and delivery and storage at such port or place.

(2) The circumstances referred to in sub-clause (1) shall include, but shall not be limited to, those caused by the existence or apprehension of war declared or undeclared, hostilities, warlike or belligerent acts or operations, riots, civil commotion or other disturbances, closure of, obstacles in or danger to any canal; blockage of port or place or interdict or prohibition of or restriction on commerce or trading; quarantine, sanitary or other similar regulations or restrictions; strikes, lockouts or other labour troubles whether partial or general and whether or not involving employees of the Carrier or his sub-contractors; congestion of port, wharf, sea terminal or any other place; shortage, absence or obstacles of labour or facilities for loading, discharge, delivery or other handling of the Goods; epidemics or diseases; bad weather, shallow water, ice, landslide or other obstacle in navigation or haulage.

The contract between Jean and Javert obligates Jean to provide 100,000 tons of a specified grade of heating oil "c.i.f. Marseilles, France," on or before February 1. The price is fixed and stated in the contract, and there is no "escalator clause". The contract also contains the following "excuse" clause (which Javert found in an old form contract):

Any circumstance beyond the control of the parties, which a diligent party could not have avoided and the consequences of which he could not have prevented, shall be considered a case of relief where it intervenes after the formation of the contract and prevents its fulfillment whether wholly or partially.

Soon after the contracts were all signed, things began to go wrong. First, there was a very bad fire at the Refinery in Araby. Its production capacity was almost destroyed, but is in the process of being repaired and brought back to normal. The Refinery has informed Jean that, due to the fire, there will be a three month delay in delivering his 100,000 tons of heating oil. Jean informs you that the wholesale market for heating oil in Europe ends on or about March 1 each year, because the heavy heating season ends about April 1, and distribution to retailers (and then to consumers) takes about a month.

When Jean informed Constant Carrier of the delay, Constant threatened to cancel the contract due to the scheduling difficulties which the delay would create. Since then, relations between Jean and Constant have gone downhill. During November, another Iraq-Iran war started and both sides began sinking ships of third parties in the Persian Gulf. Three ships loaded at the Gulf Refinery in Araby were sunk. In December, someone (unknown) started placing very powerful mines in the Red Sea, which so far have sunk ten ships which had passed through, or were en route to, the Suez Canal. Minesweeping efforts have not yet been successful. Constant Carrier categorically refuses to traverse the Suez Canal, but is willing to consider taking the heating oil around the Cape of Good Hope. That voyage will take 40 days instead of ten days, and involve traveling an 80 percent greater distance, so that Constant wants a 25 percent greater fee for performing the carriage of the goods. In addition, war risk insurance has become customary for all Persian Gulf voyages, and the war risk insurance premium has risen from 0.5 to 1.5 percent of the value of any insured items.

The reduction of the oil supply due to the Gulf Refinery fire, the sinking of ships in the Persian Gulf, and the Red Sea mines has caused the price of oil on the Rotterdam "spot" market to increase to its present price of $150 per bbl. from its price of $100 per bbl. at the time Jean signed his contract.

Having expounded this litany of woes, Jean seeks your advice. Javert has stated categorically that deliveries of heating oil will not be accepted after March 1, and that damages will result if delivery occurs after February 1. The Araby oil contracted for cannot arrive in Marseilles before March 10—and it will involve greatly increased freight and insurance charges—and Jean will lose money on the contract. Jean can "cover" (buy substitute oil) on the Rotterdam spot market, but the price on that market is so high that Jean is likely to be unable to pay for the oil, and would have to file a petition in bankruptcy.

Jean sees three possible courses of action and seeks your advice concerning the best course of action—or, whether there are others:

1. Cancel the contracts with Gulf Refinery, Constant Carrier and Javert, each on the grounds of "impossibility," "frustration," or "commercial impracticability." This would lead to no profit, but also no loss to Jean, if successful—but only if failure to perform *each* contract were excused through some legal doctrine.

2. Perform the contract to deliver the oil as soon as possible (March 10) and require Javert to accept the oil, even though delivered late, on the grounds of "impossibility," or "frustration," or "commercial impracticability." This would lead to a loss on the contract (but a bearable loss), if successful—but only if Javert can be compelled to accept the late delivery.

3. Cancel the contracts with Gulf Refinery and Constant Carrier, but buy substitute oil on the Rotterdam spot market and deliver the substitute on February 1, as per the contract. Jean would then face bankruptcy, so this alternative should be recommended only if there is no other feasible course of action.

Jean nonetheless recognizes that he must pursue one of these options—that is, unless Gulf Refinery is not excused from timely performing due to the fire, and is already in breach for failure to deliver on November 1, and is liable to Jean for sufficient damages to cover the losses created by purchasing on the Rotterdam spot market.

If either of the sales transactions is governed by the UCC, it is essential to read UCC § 2–615. If either is governed by CISG, please read CISG art. 79.

SECTION II. FOCUS OF CONSIDERATION

Once a "deal" is made, it is unlikely that everything will go right and remain as the status quo. Thus, the occurrence of unexpected events should be expected, especially in international transactions. The traditional "impossibility" doctrines have not been useful in the commercial context, and have been superceded by doctrines concerning "frustration of contract" and "commercial impracticability." These doctrines are usually used to "excuse" a failure of a condition of the contract or a failure of performance by one of the parties. Thus, the doctrines can be used either as a shield or as a sword. However, as the cases indicate, the courts allow resort to these doctrines very sparingly—they are not to be used to get out of an obligation merely because it has become an unprofitable bargain. What then are the criteria?

This problem attempts to create a number of different events, each of which arguably raises the possibility of using these doctrines in the international setting. The problem also presents the arguments in several different contexts. Some must be considered individually, but can others be considered cumulatively? Do the circumstances create complete or only partial excuses from performance? Jean is attempting to create a shield by claiming to be excused from performing obligations owed. On the other hand, Jean must also worry about whether the other parties to the contracts (especially Refinery and Carrier) are also excused from performing their obligations to him.

And, above all else, will the applications of the doctrines and the determinations of excuse create consistent results? Jean is reasonably well protected if all parties are excused from performing; and is also somewhat protected if no one is excused from performing (the latter protection effectively depending upon both an ability to recover against Gulf Refinery *and* measurement of damages problems). *And,* in each circumstance protection of Jean is also dependent upon your advice being based upon correct analysis before the disputes go to negotiation, arbitration or litigation. However, if Refinery's performance is excused, but Jean's is not, then Jean is in great trouble.

Web sources for further study include the UNCITRAL Digest of Case Law on the CISG, *http://www.uncitral.org/uncitral/en/case_law/digests/cisg.html.*

SECTION III. READINGS, QUESTIONS AND COMMENTS

PART A.   PICKING UP THE PIECES

1.   The readings provide four different elaborations of the concepts involved. *The Eugenia* sets the context with a typical "commercial impracticability" case in which an English court reasons out the doctrine from basic contract principles. The White and Summers excerpt adds an American view, and problems related to changes in governmental regulations, as well as an indication that the UCC provides no great new strides in the criteria for use of "commercial impracticability" as an excuse. (It does provide strides concerning the mechanisms to be used after an excuse, partial or complete, is determined to be available.)

The Schwenzer excerpt introduces an international perspective, including the use of more European terminology ("force majeure," "hardship") for the same basic concepts. The Honnold and Spivak excerpts then examine the CISG's approach to this issue of unexpected "impediments." After Baker guides you through a practical example under the UCC, the French *Code Civil*, and the CISG, Perillo examines "force majeure" and "hardship" under the UNIDROIT Principles.

2.   Each of the commercial impracticability cases in this section involves a different *force majeure* clause and each is different. The drafting is often done by a trade association, and reflects that association's allocation of risks known to have occurred in past transactions, *i.e.,* foreseen risks. However, note that it is likely that only one party is a member of the trade association—and the views of the other party are not represented in the clause.

3.   If the goods are not delivered, and the seller is not excused by commercial impracticability or otherwise, the aggrieved buyer has a cause of action for damages. As the Note on Measuring Damages indicates, this requires a careful analysis of the proper date for setting the damages available to the buyer (once that date has passed, the risk of any rise in the market price of the goods will be on the buyer if substitute goods are purchased).

Modern approaches to this issue permit the buyer to return to the market to replace the non-delivered goods with substitute goods, and then to measure its damages against this "cover" purchase. But these modern approaches, although different in nuance, also require reasonably prompt action to prevent the buyer from "speculating" on future market prices at the seller's expense. That is sensible if the seller's failure to perform on time is a breach of contract—but what if the seller claims excuse by "impossibility," "frustration," "hardship," or "commercial impracticability"? Then, the backdrop of the damage measurement rules still seem to put pressure on the buyer to act promptly, even though the buyer may not be certain whether it is aggrieved or not.

4. However, one of the buyer's great concerns continues to be whether it is allowed to purchase substitute goods and hold the seller liable for any damages. This, in turn, depends upon the certainty of application of the doctrines of "frustration" and "commercial impracticability."

OCEAN TRAMP TANKERS CORP. v. V/O SOVFRACHT (THE EUGENIA)

Court of Appeal, 1963.
[1964] 1 All E.R. 161.

LORD DENNING, M.R.: On July 26, 1956, the Government of Egypt nationalised the Suez Canal. Soon afterwards the United Kingdom and France began to build up military forces in Cyprus. It was obvious to all mercantile men that English and French forces might be sent to seize the canal, and that this might lead to it becoming impassable to traffic. It was in this atmosphere that negotiations took place for the chartering of the vessel Eugenia. She flew the Liberian flag. The proposal was to charter her to a Russian State Trading Corporation, called V/O Sovfracht. The Russians wanted her to carry iron and steel from the Black Sea to India. The negotiations took place in London between the agents of the parties from Aug. 29 to Sept. 9, 1956. The agents of both sides realised that there was a risk that the Suez Canal might be closed, and each agent suggested terms to meet the possibility. But they came to no agreement. And, in the end, they concluded the bargain on the terms of the Baltime Charter without any express clause to deal with the matter. That meant that, if the canal were to be closed, they would "leave it to the lawyers to sort out". The charterparty was concluded on Sept. 9, 1956, but was dated Sept. 8, 1956. The vessel was then at Genoa. By the charterparty, she was let to the charterers for a "trip out to India via Black Sea". It was a time-charter in this sense, that the charterers had to pay hire for the vessel at a fixed rate per month from the time of the vessel's delivery until her re-delivery. The charterers had, however, no wide limits at their disposal. They could not direct her anywhere they wished, but only within the following limits "Genoa via Black Sea thence to India". The charter included the printed war clause without modification. It was in these terms:

> 21(A) The vessel unless the consent of the owners be first obtained not to be ordered nor continue to any place or on any voyage nor be used on any service which will bring her within a zone which is dangerous as the result of any actual or threatened act of war, war, hostilities, warlike operations * * * (B) Should the vessel approach or be brought or ordered within such zone * * * (i) the owners to be entitled from time to time to insure their interests in the vessel * * * on such terms as they shall think fit, the charterers to make a refund to the owners of the premium on demand; and (ii) * * * hire to be paid for all time lost * * *

The Eugenia was delivered at Genoa on Sept. 20, 1956. The charterers ordered her to proceed first to Novorossik and then to Odessa (both on the Black Sea) to load. A few days later the charterers sub-chartered her to two other Russian State Trading Corporations who agreed to pay, by way of freight, whatever the charterers had to pay the owners, plus five per cent. The two sub-charterers loaded her with iron and steel goods (joists, girders, etc.). The master signed bills of lading. These made the cargo deliverable to shipper's order at Vizagapatam and Madras (both on the East Coast of India), freight pre-paid. On Oct. 25, 1956, the Eugenia sailed from Odessa. The customary route at this time to India was still by the Suez Canal. The charterers told the master to cable their agent in Port Said when he was within twenty-four hours' sailing of Port Said. He did so. The Eugenia arrived off Port Said at 11.00 a.m. on Oct. 30, 1956, and entered port at 4.30 p.m. At that time Egyptian anti-aircraft guns were in action against hostile reconnaissance planes. It was quite apparent that Port Said and the Suez Canal were zones which were "dangerous" within this war clause. Indeed, on the morning of Oct. 30, the owners' London agent called on the charterers' London agent to take action under the war clause to ensure that the ship should not enter Port Said or the Suez Canal. The charterers' agent in London, however, took no action. He let things be. But at Port Said the charterers' agent had taken action. He boarded the vessel and stated that he had made arrangements for the vessel to enter the canal the next morning. In consequence, the vessel entered the canal at 9.35 a.m. on Oct. 31 and proceeded in convoy fifty-eight kilometres south. Then the convoy tied up to allow a northbound convoy to pass. Soon afterwards English and French aircraft began to drop bombs on Egyptian targets. That evening the Egyptian Government blocked the canal by sinking ships at Port Said and Suez and in the canal and by blowing up bridges. So the Eugenia was trapped where she was. On Nov. 7, 1956, there was a cease-fire. Early in January, 1957, a passage was cleared northwards. But there was no hope of southward passage for a long time. So the Eugenia started to move north. She anchored in Port Said Roads on Jan. 8, 1957. On Jan. 11, 1957, she went to Alexandria and arrived there on Jan. 12, 1957.

Meanwhile, however, the charterers, on Jan. 4, 1957, claimed that the charterparty had been frustrated by the blocking of the canal. The owners denied that it had been frustrated and treated the charterers' conduct as a repudiation. So on either view the charter was at an end. On Jan. 15, 1957, the owners entered into a new charterparty direct with the original sub-charterers. This new charter was an ordinary Gencon voyage charter by which the owners agreed to carry the cargo already on board via the Cape of Good Hope to India. The freight was very high, for the freight market had risen rapidly; so much so, that the owners did well out of the new charter. Indeed, they might not have suffered any loss were it not for the long spell during which the ship was trapped in the canal. The owners wish to claim hire so as to cover the period in the canal, but the charterers dispute it. Hence their claim that the charter was frustrated. On Jan. 20,

1957, under this new charterparty, the Eugenia left Alexandria and went round the Cape. She arrived at Vizagapatam about Apr. 5, 1957, unloaded part of her cargo there, then went to Madras and unloaded the rest there, and finished discharging on May 22, 1957. The southern exit from the canal was not cleared until April, 1957. So the Eugenia arrived at her destination earlier by going northward out of the canal than if she had waited to get out by the southern exit.

Such being the facts, the first question is whether the charterers, by allowing the Eugenia to go into the canal on Oct. 31, 1956, were in breach of the war clause. Both the arbitrator and the judge held that they were in breach. * * * I find myself in complete agreement with the arbitrator and the judge on these points.

The second question is whether the charterparty was frustrated by what took place. The arbitrator has held that it was not. The judge has held that it was. Which is right? One thing that is obvious is that the charterers cannot rely on the fact that the Eugenia was trapped in the canal; for that was their own fault. They were in breach of the war clause in entering it. They cannot rely on a self-induced frustration. But they seek to rely on the fact that the canal itself was blocked. They assert that, even if the Eugenia had never gone into the canal but had stayed outside (in which case she would not have been in breach of the war clause), nevertheless she would still have had to go round by the Cape; and that, they say, brings about a frustration, for it makes the venture fundamentally different from what they contracted for. The judge has accepted this view. He has held that, on Nov. 16, 1956, the charterparty was frustrated. The reason for his taking Nov. 16, 1956, was this: Prior to Nov. 16, 1956, mercantile men (even if she had stayed outside) would not have formed any conclusion whether the obstructions in the canal were other than temporary. There was insufficient information available to form a judgment. On Nov. 16, 1956, mercantile men would conclude that the blockage of the southern end would last till March or April, 1957; so that, by that time, it would be clear that the only thing to do (if the ship had never entered the canal) would be to go round the Cape. The judge said:

> I hold that the adventure, involving a voyage round the Cape, is basically or fundamentally different from the adventure involving a voyage via the Suez Canal.

So he held that the contract was frustrated. He was comforted to find that, in *Société Franco Tunisienne D'Armement* v. *Sidermar S.P.A.,* PEARSON, J., came to a similar conclusion. I must confess that I find it difficult to apply the doctrine of frustration to a hypothetical situation, that is, to treat this vessel as if she had never entered the canal and then ask whether the charter was frustrated. The doctrine should be applied to the facts as they really are. But I will swallow this difficulty and ask myself what would be the position if the vessel had never entered the canal but stayed at Port Said. Would the contract be frustrated? This means that, once again, we have had to consider the authorities on this vexed topic of frustration. But I think that the position is now reasonably clear. It is simply this: If it should happen, in the course of carrying out a contract, that a fundamentally different situation arises for which the parties made no provision—so much so that it would not be just in the new situation to hold them bound to its terms—then the contract is at an end.

It was originally said that the doctrine of frustration was based on an implied term. In short, that the parties, if they had foreseen the new situation, would have said to one another: "If that happens, of course, it is all over between us". But the theory of an implied term has now been discarded by everyone, or nearly everyone, for the simple reason that it does not represent the truth. The parties would not have said: "It is all over between us". They would have differed about what was to happen. Each would have sought to insert reservations or qualifications of one kind or another. Take this very case. The parties realised that the canal might become impassable. They tried to agree on a clause to provide for the contingency. But they failed to agree. So there is no room for an implied term.

It has frequently been said that the doctrine of frustration only applies when the new situation is "unforeseen" or "unexpected" or "uncontemplated", as if that were an essential feature. But it is not so. It is not so much that it is "unexpected", but rather that the parties have made no provision for it in their contract. The point about it, however, is this: If the parties did not foresee anything of the kind happening, you can readily infer that they have made no provision for it. Whereas, if they did foresee it, you would expect them to make provision for it. But cases have occurred where the parties have foreseen the danger ahead, and yet made no provision for it in the contract. Such was the case in the Spanish Civil War when a ship was let on charter to the Republican Government. The purpose was to evacuate refugees. The parties foresaw that she might be seized by the Nationalists. But they made no provision for it in their contract. Yet, when she was seized, the contract was frustrated. So, here, the parties foresaw that the canal might become impassable. It was the very thing that they feared. But they made no provision for it. So the doctrine may still apply, if it be a proper case for it.

We are thus left with the simple test that a situation must arise which renders performance of the contract "a thing radically different from that which was undertaken by the contract". To see if the doctrine applies, you have first to construe the contract and see whether the parties have themselves provided for the situation that has arisen. If they have provided for it, the contract must govern. There is no frustration. If they have not provided for it, then you have to compare the new situation with the old situation for which they did provide. Then you must see how different it is. The fact that it has become more onerous or more expensive for one party than he thought is not sufficient to bring about a frustration. It must be more than merely more onerous or more expensive. It must be positively unjust to hold the parties bound. It is often difficult to draw the line. But it must be done, and it is for the courts to do it as a matter of law.

Applying these principles to this case, I have come to the conclusion that the blockage of the canal did not bring about a "fundamentally different situation" such as to frustrate the venture. My reasons are these: (i) The venture was the *whole* trip from delivery at Genoa, out to the Black Sea, there load cargo, thence to India, unload cargo, and re-delivery. The time for this vessel from Odessa to Vizagapatam via the Suez Canal would be twenty-six days, and via the Cape fifty-six days. But that is not the right comparison. You have to take the whole venture from delivery at Genoa to re-delivery at Madras. We were told that the time for the whole venture via the Suez Canal would be 108 days, and via the Cape 138 days. The difference over the whole voyage is not so radical as to produce a frustration. (ii) The cargo was iron and steel goods which would not be adversely affected by the longer voyage, and there was no special reason for early arrival. The vessel and crew were at all times fit and sufficient to proceed via the Cape. (iii) The cargo was loaded on board at the time of the blockage of the canal. If the contract was frustrated, it would mean, I suppose, that the ship could throw up the charter and unload the cargo wherever she was, without any breach of contract. (iv) The voyage round the Cape made no great difference except that it took a good deal longer and was more expensive for the charterers than a voyage through the canal.

J. WHITE AND R. SUMMERS, UNIFORM COMMERCIAL CODE

§ 4.10 (6th ed., 2010).*

Students who have concluded a first year contracts course in confusion about the doctrine of impossibility and have since had difficulty mastering 2–615 or have found that the cases somehow slip through their fingers when they try to apply them to new situations, may take some comfort in knowing that they are in good company.

* * *

If performance is rendered impracticable by a governmental regulation or order, the seller is freed from his obligation without reference to the language of 2–615 concerning contingency and basic assumption. Of course it is still necessary that the regulation itself and not the seller's fault cause the impracticability. If, for example, the seller could have escaped the effect of a government regulation, it will not be freed. * * *

* * * One court has summarized the statute as follows:

> Three elements must be proven before excuse or adjustment becomes available under § 2–615: (1) the seller must not have assumed the risk of some unknown contingency; (2) the nonoccurrence

---

* Copyright © 2010, and reprinted with permission of Thomson Reuters.

of the contingency must have been a basic assumption underlying the contract; and (3) the occurrence of that contingency must have made performance commercially impracticable.

Of course determining whether the seller has "assumed the risk" is often very much like trying to determine whether or not the occurrence was foreseeable. Obviously if a seller has explicitly assumed the risk, it has foreseen it. * * *

[T]he rub comes in determining which "nonoccurrences" were "basic" assumptions and which were not. In some cases this interpretative difficulty is compounded by the necessity of also deciding whether the performance has been made "impracticable" or not. Assume for example that seller has entered into a long-term contract to deliver fuel oil of a specified grade to buyer. The seller argues that his performance has been made impracticable because his cost of oil has gone out of sight. The language of the Code does not carry one far in determining whether this seller's performance has been made "impracticable", and if so, whether the "basic assumptions" of the parties extended to the nonoccurrence of the Arab Oil Embargo, the Iranian revolution and attendant general market disruptions.

To assist in answering such questions, it may be helpful to follow an analysis suggested by Professor Farnsworth. In his view, impracticability cases are really cases where the parties have failed adequately to state their intentions. If in our foregoing case the seller had agreed that it would provide the oil or pay damages notwithstanding war, embargo or any other disruption, there would be no impracticability problem. The seller would be liable for breach. Our problem arises because the parties did not foresee the eventuality or if they foresaw it, did not incorporate a governing clause. Professor Farnsworth suggests that a court faced with our problem should first attempt to determine whether the contingency was one that was in fact foreseen by the parties. If it was foreseen by them, he suggests that the courts should then attempt to determine the parties' actual expectations. Their expectations might be revealed by the course of the negotiations, including the various proposals that the seller may have made concerning different prices based upon different contingencies, or by trade usage. If any of these sources adequately reveals the parties' expectations, it should govern.

More commonly, however, the contingency will be one not foreseen by the parties and about which they had no expectations. In that case it would be fictional to purport to carry out their expectations. Here the court is not called upon to interpret the contract; its job is to direct a just and reasonable result. In light of the terms on which the parties did agree, what would reasonable persons have further agreed if they had contemplated this contingency?

Perhaps the most significant factor in this analysis is the foreseeability of the contingency that actually occurred. If it was foreseeable that soybeans would be in short supply because of bad summer weather, that the Suez Canal would be closed because it had been closed once ten years earlier when the Arabs and Israelis were at war, or that copper would be hard to buy because of continuous political unrest in Peru and Chile, the parties should be held to have foreseen those contingencies and to have made their contract with the expectation that such contingencies might occur. In that case it is usually appropriate to hold the seller liable notwithstanding the occurrence. [Put] in Code terms, if the parties made the contract with the understanding that the Peruvian mines might well be closed, the closing of the mines is not a "contingency the nonoccurrence of which was a basic assumption * * * " thus 2–615 does not apply, and the seller is liable in damages notwithstanding its inability to deliver Peruvian copper. Put another way, the seller's agreement to a fixed quantity, fixed price contract allocates the risk of shortages to the seller.

* * *

The most persistent problem under 2–615 in the last forty years has been the question whether a radical rise in a seller's costs frees seller from its obligation to perform. This was the issue with respect to uranium in the famous *Westinghouse* case; it was raised by Gulf Oil in Eastern Air Lines, Inc. v. Gulf Oil Corp. concerning aviation fuel; by Atlas Corporation in Iowa Electric Light and Power Co. v. Atlas Corp.; by Alcoa in Aluminum Co. of America v. Essex Group, Inc. and by others in similar circumstances. Many of these cases were somehow related to the radical increase in the price of crude oil that has occurred since 1972. With rare exceptions the courts have rejected the sellers' 2–615 arguments. For example, in the Sabine case, the court held a two-fold increase in cost of performance no excuse.

* * *

As commerce grows more sophisticated and multinational it becomes more vulnerable to disruption from embargoes, wars, revolutions, and terrorism in countries producing natural resources. It is paradoxical that with each disruption, subsequent disruptions become more foreseeable and therefore less likely to provide a basis for escape from a contract under 2–615. No one remotely related to the petroleum or uranium industry will be able to argue persuasively for the foreseeable future that it should be freed from its contract obligation because of an unforeseen rise in price or cost. If anything is certain and foreseeable, it is that prices in those markets will experience periodic radical changes.

We would not argue that a seller should never be excused from its obligations because of cost increases, however we agree with the thrust of the cases discussed above. In our judgment an increase in price, even a radical increase in price, is the thing that contracts are designed to protect against. * * *

SCHWENZER: FORCE MAJEURE AND HARDSHIP IN INTERNATIONAL SALES CONTRACTS

39 Vict. U. Wellington L. Rev. 709, 709–712 (2009).*

Unforeseeable changed circumstances are probably one of the major problems parties—especially those who are party to a long or longer term complex contract—may face in international trade. Indeed, with globalisation these problems are increased as the involvement of more and more countries in production and procurement entails even greater imponderables. Natural disasters or changes of political and economic factors may considerably affect the very basis of the bargain. There may be an earthquake, a flood or a civil war in one of the production countries, forcing the producer to resort to countries with much higher production costs; import or export bans may hinder the envisaged flow of goods; or price fluctuations that were not foreseeable at the time of the conclusion of the contract make the performance by the seller unduly burdensome or devaluate the contract performance for the buyer.

The paradigm of *pacta sunt servanda* or sanctity of contract simply places the burden of such a change of circumstances upon the party on which it falls. However, since the old Roman days the principle of *impossibilium nulla est obligatio*, or there is no obligation to perform impossible things, has been recognised. * * * Furthermore, under the doctrine of *rebus sic stantibus* developed by the Roman *praetor*, an unforeseeable and extraordinary change of circumstances rendering a contractual obligation extremely burdensome could be recognised. Since these days, impossibility, *force majeure* or the like have become grounds for exemption in every legal system. * * *

II. SOME DOMESTIC SOLUTIONS

The position of French law represents one extreme and it is well documented. Whereas the rule for *force majeure* is laid down in Article 1148 of the Code Civil (CC), neither general civil law nor commercial law has been favourable to the concept of hardship. The famous theory of *imprévision* that allows a contract to be modified in case of a change of circumstances has been applied to administrative contracts only. However, the Cour de Cassation has apparently moved away slightly from the strict *pacta sunt servanda* principle; it appears to be heading in the direction of eventually recognising some kind of hardship.

Many continental legal systems, however, accept the theory of hardship, among them Germany, The Netherlands, Italy, Greece, Portugal, Austria as well as the Scandinavian countries. The most recent acknowledgement by statute can be found in Germany. The Statute on the Modernisation of the Law of Obligations in 2001 finally codified the right to have the contract adapted to the changed circumstances in section 313

---

of the *Bürgerliches Gesetzbuch* [German Civil Code; the doctrine is known in German as *Wegfall der Geschäftsgrundlage—the Authors*].

English law seems to reject any notion of relief for changed circumstances that do not amount to impossibility. However, in case of frustration of contract–that means where the contract is rendered useless by the change of circumstances–an exception is granted to this general rule. In the United States, the Uniform Commercial Code has enacted the general doctrine of impracticability.

III. *INTERNATIONAL APPROACHES*

The Principles on International Commercial Contracts (PICC 2004), the Principles on European Contract Law (PECL 1999) as well as the Draft of a Common Frame of Reference (DCFR 2008) expressly provide for rules in case of a change of circumstances. In 2003, the International Chamber of Commerce (ICC) published model clauses on *force majeure* and hardship.

The Convention on the International Sale of Goods (CISG), however, does not contain a special provision dealing with questions of hardship. It does not mention either *force majeure* or hardship. Article 79 of the CISG relieves a party from paying damages only if the breach of contract was due to an impediment beyond its control. The drafting history of this provision is not quite clear. During the preparations of the CISG, the question of whether economic difficulties should give rise to an exemption was a highly controversial one. * * *

Today, however, it is more or less unanimously accepted in court and arbitral decisions, as well as in scholarly writing, that Article 79 does indeed cover issues relating to hardship. Accordingly, first and foremost, there is no room to resort to domestic concepts of hardship as there is no gap in the CISG regarding the debtor's invocation of economic impossibility and the adaptation of the contract to changed circumstances. If one were to hold otherwise, unification of the law of sales would be undermined in a very important area. Domestic concepts such as frustration of purpose, *rebus sic stantibus*, fundamental mistake or *Wegfall der Geschäftsgrundlage* would all have to be considered.

HONNOLD, UNIFORM LAW FOR INTERNATIONAL SALES UNDER THE 1980 UNITED NATIONS CONVENTION

616, 623, 627–630 (H. Flechtner ed., 4th ed. 2009).*

Article 79 of the Convention follows the approach of important civil law systems in extending the rules on excuse to all aspects of a party's performance. Under paragraph (1) *either party* may be excused from liability "for a failure to perform *any* of his obligations." On the other hand, UCC 2–615 provides excuse *only for the seller*, and then only with respect to *two aspects* of performance—"delay in delivery" and "non-delivery."

(a) Defective Goods. The differing scope of the provisions on exemption in the Convention and in the UCC leads to this question: May a nonnegligent seller be excused from liability when he delivers defective goods? Under the UCC, the answer is No, since the situation involves neither "delay" nor "non-delivery." Under the Convention the answer is not so obvious, since exemption may apply to a party's failure to perform *any* of his obligations.

* * *

Attention has been drawn * * * to the danger that local tribunals may unconsciously read the patterns of their domestic law into the general language of the Convention—an approach that would be inconsistent with the Convention's basic goal of international unification (Article 7(1)). And deliberate recourse to the exemption rules of a single domestic system would flagrantly violate the Convention. As we have seen, Article 7(2) permits recourse to "the law applicable by virtue of the rules of private international law" only as a last resort—that is, when questions are "not expressly settled" by the Convention and cannot be "settled in conformity with the general principles on which it is based." The fact that a provision of the Convention presents problems of application does not authorize recourse to some one system of domestic law since this would undermine the Convention's objective "to promote uniformity in its application" (Article 7(1)). However, no such difficulty arises from a comparative law approach that seeks guidance from the prevailing patterns and trends of modern domestic law.

* * * However, the language of Article 79(1) seems to leave room for exemptions based on economic dislocations that provide an "impediment" to performance comparable to non-economic barriers that excuse failure of performance. From this view, which is widely but not universally shared, the standard for exemption is not strict impossibility, but rather such extreme difficulty in performance as amounts to impossibility from a practical (although not technical) viewpoint.

Assume that the supply of a material needed for performance of a contract unexpectedly becomes so reduced in quantity and inflated in price that only a minority of producers that need this material can continue in production. This situation clearly constitutes an "impediment" rendering performance impossible for most producers whose contracts to sell the goods overlap the onset of the shortage; requiring production by only one (or a minority) unfairly prejudices some in favor of their competitors.
* * *

The question whether something less than literal impossibility of performance (such as in extreme increase in the cost of performance) can satisfy the requirements of Article 79 raises the question of the applicability of "hardship" doctrine in transactions governed by the CISG. Civil law hardship doctrine requires the parties to negotiate an adjustment to a contract—and, if they fail to reach a negotiated adjustment, permits a court to end the contract or even impose a judge-made adjustment—when the contract's economic balance is severely disrupted by unforeseen developments. * * * Proposals to include a hardship-like doctrine aimed at adapted performance of an economically disrupted contract were rejected during the drafting of Article 79. Thus such doctrines * * * should have no application in contracts governed by the CISG. Extreme price and (especially) currency dislocations may be sufficiently widespread to lead to laws or administrative regulations that require contract adjustment. Although the Convention does not displace domestic rules of "validity" unless it has "expressly provided" for an issue (Article 4(a)), Article 79 comprehensively regulates the impact of changed circumstances on the parties' obligations and should be read to pre-empt domestic rules on this question.

SPIVACK, OF SHRINKING SWEATSUITS AND POISON VINE WAX: A COMPARISON OF BASIS FOR EXCUSE UNDER UCC § 2–615 AND CISG ARTICLE 79

27 U. Pa. J. Int'l Econ L. 757, 759–60, 789–91 (2006).*

This article compares CISG and U.C.C. jurisprudence on excuse for nonperformance and argues for an application of the CISG in excuse cases which is stricter than the U.C.C. and, I suggest, is more consistent with the drafters' intent and the goals of the Treaty. As I will discuss, the CISG's Article 79 seems to set out much narrower grounds for excuse than does U.C.C. § 2–615 (2005). In practice, however, cases in the two jurisdictions diverge less than the wording of the two statutes might lead one to expect, evincing comparable reluctance to excuse nonperformance. There are two reasons for this similarity: first, U.S. courts construe U.C.C. § 2–615 more narrowly than its language might predict; second, tribunals applying the CISG hear more bases for excuse than Article 79, based on its drafters' intentions, probably allows. In other words, U.S. courts construe U.C.C. § 2–615 more narrowly than its wording seems to allow, while tribunals applying the CISG apply Article 79 more broadly than its wording seems to justify. The result is that Article 79 tribunals hear cases for excuse that would seem to be acceptable only under the U.C.C., while cases actually decided under the U.C.C. do not show any tendency to excuse nonperformance more often than the CISG.

* * *

International business deals tend to consist of what are called "relational contracts": they extend over many years; involve series of transactions rather than single isolated deals; and rest upon a strong relationship between the parties involved. First of all, because they are long-term, such

---

contracts face a high risk of being disrupted by a vast array of changing political and economic factors. To enter into such long-term agreements, parties on both sides need some assurances of stability despite this risk. Article 79, if applied consistently with its wording, renders most of the political and economic vicissitudes attendant on transborder sales unavailable as excuses for nonperformance—in fact, it would deny them a forum to be heard. As a consequence, Article 79 gives parties to a contract incentive to write into the agreement details about what changes in circumstance will permit renegotiation or modification, and the requirement that such modification be negotiated between the parties rather than in litigation. Renegotiation during the life of a contract is the norm in international business transactions and the more the parties can anticipate and provide for it, the less painful and disruptive it need be. The CISG language may also move parties to include some kind of renegotiation clause, which would allow for the contractual relationship to continue rather than falter—clearly promoting the CISG's goals. Knowing that the CISG offers no recourse in times of change, the parties, who are in a much better position to do so than a tribunal brought in after the fact, will work to anticipate possible events which might change the nature of the deal and write provisions for dealing with them into the contract.

* * *

For cases decided under the CISG, I turn to European arbitration tribunals, which so far have far outstripped U.S. courts in deciding cases under the Treaty. So far, tribunals in Bulgaria, France, Germany, and Russia, as well as at the International Chamber of Commerce, have refused to excuse performance due to changed market conditions. This makes perfect sense—even more so than under the U.C.C.—based on the wording of the treaty and in the context of trans-border sales. First, it is unlikely that a mere market change could impose the kind of physical impossibility that the wording of Article 79 seems to require. Second, in the context of trans-border sales, parties need to be assured that the fluctuations of national markets will not put their contracts at risk. Only a strict policy in this regard would further the CISG's stated goal of promoting international sales: a seller or buyer who had to worry about every shift within a country's borders would endanger the contract would be unwilling to take the risk.

Tribunals applying the CISG have so far looked upon market failure defenses unsympathetically but have allowed them to be heard, despite indications that Article 79 was not meant to cover this defense at all. CISG commentators have suggested that increased costs of one hundred percent may offer a basis for excuse, and that even less than that might be considered under certain circumstances. On the other hand, there is a consensus that fluctuations of up to fifty percent are insufficient. Moreover, as mentioned supra, some commentators argue that the word "impediment" was chosen to limit the application of the section to cases when a physical hindrance literally makes performance impossible, and that economic hardship is not covered by the section at all. The ultimate goal of the CISG in this regard is to force parties to negotiate into their contracts hardship clauses specifically designed to reflect and allocate the risks attendant upon the particular enterprise, rather than using a "one size of economic risk fits all" approach.

BAKER, "A HARD RAIN'S A-GONNA FALL"—TERRORISM AND EXCUSED CONTRACTUAL PERFORMANCE INA POST SEPTEMBER 11TH WORLD

17 Transnat'l Law 1 (2004).*

III. A HYPOTHETICAL

In the pre-September 11th World Trade Center, resides Tech Chef Co., an American software company. Tech Chef Co. has developed a prototype of a highly specialized cooking software, with the intent to distribute the software in the U.S. and abroad. This software product, The Tech ChefTM, creates a new kitchen management system that allows orders to be transmitted to and from the kitchen more efficiently, thus increasing restaurant profitability. At this juncture, the product is virtually complete; however it is necessary to have optimizing algorithms imbedded by its inventor Bob Smith, the CTO of Tech Chef Co. It is widely known that French chefs are among the best in the world, however, they lack the business acumen to produce food efficiently. Due to these factors, Tech Chef Co. feels that their new software is a perfect fit for French kitchens. Franco Tex S.A., a public corporation based in Vichy, France, has contracted with Tech Chef Co. to distribute the new software in France. As a distributor, Franco Tex S.A. will order, pay for, and take title of the goods it distributes. As the news of the new software quickly spread, Franco Tex S.A. has already taken 800 orders for The Tech ChefTM. These orders, along with arrangements for payment, have been passed along to Tech Chef Co. to be filled and shipped by September 20, 2001.

The day is September 11, 2001. An unexpected terrorist attack is launched against the United States. [In the attack on] the World Trade Center towers, Tech Chef Co.'s offices are destroyed along with its entire inventory. * * * The software will have to be completely rebuilt, along with the rest of the company. In the late afternoon of September 11th, while * * * watching CNN worldwide, Mr. Piastra, CEO of Franco Tex S.A., is horrified by the unfolding events. [After the shock slowly wears off,] he becomes aware of the effect the attack could have on his business and his customers. The next day, Mr. Piastra e-mails Tech Chef Co. hoping to get answers regarding their functionability. A week later, Mr. Piastra receives the following response:

Sept. 19, 2001

My Dear Monsieur Piastra,

Please excuse my delay in responding to your e-mail dated September 12, 2001. As you are aware, the tragic events of September 11th have caused great turmoil for this company and this country. I am sorry to report we lost approximately half of our staff and most of our hardware and software in the attack. Bob Smith, our CTO whom you have worked with for the last eight months, was one of the victims. On the business front, I regret to report that our product has been completely wiped out and therefore none of the goods that you have ordered for the September 20th delivery can be shipped. In fact, as we assess our losses, it is apparent that we may have to recreate The Tech ChefTM software from scratch. I have, as you can understand, virtually no idea how long this will take, and therefore would not speculate as to a future delivery date. I know this will affect your company and your customers greatly, especially since The Tech ChefTM software is the only product that can fulfill the needs of you clientele. I sincerely wish that I could reimburse your company for any financial losses caused by our inability to deliver, but unfortunately, the disaster has crippled Tech Chef Co. not only emotionally and physically, but also financially. Truthfully Sir, I am at a complete loss and await your reply.

Mr. Hamilton Berger, CEO Chef Tech Co.

The legal questions which are posed herein are cogent and worthy of inquiry. What are the rights and responsibilities of parties when an unanticipated terrorist attack occurs which prevents performance? More specifically, what will happen if Franco Tex S.A. sues Tech Chef Co. for breach of contract? What are the legal consequences under principles of common law, the American Uniform Commercial Code and International Law?

* * *

V.　THE UNIFORM COMMERCIAL CODE

The doctrine of impossibility has been expanded over the years to include a broader spectrum of intervening circumstances that could give rise to contractual discharge. One expansion of the doctrine includes commercial impracticability which first came into existence in 1916. Governing bodies have set out statutory guidelines concerning such cases that codify and expand on existing common law, and provide tests for the validity of impossibility-like defenses.

As our hypothetical contract involves the sale of goods, the Uniform Commercial Code ("UCC") may apply. * * *

Courts have said that "[t]hree conditions must be present before a seller is excused from performance under the UCC: (1) a contingency must occur, (2) performance must thereby be made 'impracticable' and (3) the nonoccurrence of the contingency must have been a basic assumption on which the contract was made." A party asserting an impracticability defense has the burden of proof on these three requirements. However, the UCC does not provide a comprehensive list of contingencies that would warrant excuse due to commercial impracticability. Instead, a court should look to the specific circumstances surrounding the frustrating occurrence in each case.

The text of the UCC sets out two requirements that must be fulfilled in order to assert an impracticability defense pursuant to section 2–615. First, the defaulting party must not have assumed any greater obligation than imposed by section 2–615 which would allocate the risk of the contingency's occurrence to her. To determine whether a party assumed obligations additional to those in section 2–615, a court will look to both the language of the contract, and the circumstances surrounding contractual negotiations. * * *

Courts may also look at a seller's conduct that implies a greater obligation has been assumed. In United States v. Wegematic Corp., an electronics manufacturer contracted with the government to create a general computing system. In winning the bid for the contract, Wegematic advertised their system as "a truly revolutionary system utilizing all of the latest technical advances." Wegematic delayed the nine-month delivery deadline twice before finally communicating to the government that engineering difficulties had made it impracticable to create and deliver the computing system. The court ruled that there was "no basis for thinking that when an electronics system is promoted by its manufacturer as a revolutionary breakthrough, the risk of the revolution's occurrence falls on the purchaser; the reasonable supposition is that it has already occurred or, at least, that the manufacturer is assuring the purchaser that it will be found to have when the machine is assembled." The court went on to say that ruling for the seller would make a manufacturer "free to express what are only aspirations and gamble on mere probabilities of fulfillment without any risk of liability."

The second requirement included in the text of section 2–615 is a condition that the seller must seasonably notify the buyer if there will be a delay of, or failure to, deliver. Seasonable notification has been construed differently on the basis of the specific facts of each case. "Whether a seller's communication to a buyer constitutes seasonable notification will depend upon various factors, including whether the buyer had actual notice, the specific content of the transmission, and whether notice was delivered in a timely fashion allowing the buyer opportunity to make other arrangements."

As described above, section 2–615 does not include an exhaustive list of contingencies that would bring about a commercial impracticability defense. A commonality of contingencies that has given rise to a section 2–615 defense is their relative unforeseeability at the time the contractual negotiations took place. If the contingency was foreseeable, parties may provide for it in the contract. Thus, if a party agrees to perform despite this contingency, impracticability may not be used as a defense for nonperformance. However, a strict requirement of unforeseeability to support a commercial impracticability defense would serve to nullify the doctrine as anything and everything could conceivably be foreseen. As stated succinctly by the Second Circuit, to require absolute unforeseeability would:

> practically destroy the doctrine of supervening impossibility, notwithstanding its present wide and apparently growing popularity. Certainly, the death of a promisor, the burning of a ship, the requisitioning of a merchant marine on the outbreak of a war could and perhaps should, be foreseen. In fact, the more common expression of the rule appears to be in terms which tend to state the burden the other way, e.g., that "the duty of the promisor is discharged, unless a contrary intention has been manifested" or "in the absence of circumstances showing either a contrary intention or contributing fault on the part of the person subject to the duty."

Returning to our hypothetical, given the text of UCC section 2–615, and the surrounding case law, it appears that if decided under U.S. law Tech Chef Co. should be excused from its contractual obligations to Franco Tex S.A. The three conditions for a section 2–615 commercial impracticability defense are present. First, a contingency has occurred with the attack on the World Trade Center. Second, performance of the contract has been made impracticable due to the contingency because Tech Chef Co. has lost half of its workforce including its CTO, its principle place of business, all equipment, and virtually all existing inventory, including the software on which the contract was based. Third, the nonoccurrence of the contingency was a basic assumption on which the contract was made because presumably, neither Tech Chef Co., nor Franco Tex S.A. would have entered the contract if they assumed otherwise.

Additionally, Tech Chef Co. has met the two textual requirements of section 2–615. Tech Chef Co. has not expressly or impliedly taken on any additional obligations not imposed by section 2–615. Based on the severity of the attack, and the relatively prompt response which arrived prior to the agreed upon delivery date, Tech Chef Co. has probably given Franco Tex S.A. seasonable notification of its non-delivery. As to the foreseeability of the attack, an area to which many courts look, Tech Chef Co. might fail a strict requirement of unforeseeability. In a world in which terrorist threats have become a global and real threat to governments, businesses, and individuals alike, one might say that contracting parties could very easily foresee the possibility of a terrorist attack affecting their infrastructure, employees suppliers, and means of delivery. However, as noted above, a strict requirement of unforeseeability would drive a stake through the heart of the doctrine of commercial impracticability. Although terrorist attacks have become increasingly commonplace, their frequency and predictability have not risen to a level at which they could be reasonably and accurately foreseen. It is arguably unreasonable to impose hardship on contracting parties who have not expressly or impliedly negotiated on the subject of terrorist attacks.

VI. THE FRENCH SYSTEM AND THE CODE CIVIL

The French system interprets the concept of impossibility narrowly. If the impossibility is total, the debtor is relieved of all contractual duties and any damages resulting from non-performance. This system is in line with the common law of England and most of the United States in holding that an accidental destruction of a thing, caused by something other than the fault of the obligor, excuses the obligation to convey that thing in an executory contract. Anything less than total impossibility however, does not excuse the debtor from the contract. The parties are expected to perform their duties under the contract even when performance would be ruinous to them. The French system refuses to give the judge any power to alter the contract upon equitable consideration. If the hypothetical were to be based on French law, the Code Civil would apply.

The applicable articles of the Code Civil are articles 1147 and 1148 which provide:

Article 1147: The debtor is liable, where appropriate, to pay damages, either because he has not performed an obligation or he was late in performing, in all cases in which cannot prove the non-performance resulted from a cause étrangère for which he was not responsible and also that there is no bad faith on his part.

Article 1148: There will be no damages when as a result of force majeure or cas fortuit the debtor has been prevented from delivering or doing that which he was obliged to deliver or do or has done that which is forbidden.

For an event to constitute force majeure in France, case law has traditionally required it to be irresistible, unforeseeable, and external to the party seeking excuse from the contract. The foreseeability of a contingency is not a substantive requirement, but instead becomes a condition of admissibility. An event cannot be avoided if it was not foreseen. However, some foreseeable events may constitute force majeure if the event is inevitable or impossible to resist. If a party foresees an inevitable event, he must take precautions "necessitated by its foreseeability."

In the hypothetical, Franco Tex S.A. may have a stronger claim in France than in the United States. First, since the software is not completely destroyed, Franco Tex S.A. may argue that it is not impossible for Tech Chef Co. to replace it. While forcing the company to rebuild the software from scratch may be ruinous for a small company, this would not excuse performance under French law. Second, Franco Tex S.A. may be able to argue that the terrorist event was foreseeable and therefore, cannot constitute force majeure. Again, we are confronted with the foreseeability question. Was a terrorist attack on the World Trade Center foreseeable to this small company? One would most probably find such foreseeability doubtful. Even if Tech Chef Co. cannot prove that the event was unforeseeable, it can try to show that the attack was inevitable. In this scenario, Franco Tex S.A. may be able to assert that while Tech Chef Co. could not have taken precautions to avoid terrorism, the company could have taken precautions to guard against the destruction of the software. In response, Tech Chef Co. can show that the terrorist attack was not resistible by showing that the attack was unavoidable by the ordinary person exercising reasonable care. A normal person in Tech Chef Co.'s position would not be able to resist a terrorist attack. Tech Chef Co. can also show that the attack was external because it had not control over the attack.

Franco Tex S.A. would have a stronger case under the first approach, rather than the second; by showing a court that, while the terrorist attack may have resulted in problematical performance for Tech Chef Co., it is still less than total impossibility. The French system has rejected the theory of imprévision in civil law. As a result, the terrorist attack would not constitute an event excusing Tech Chef Co. from delivering the software.

VII.   INTERNATIONAL LAW, EUROPEAN LAW, AND THE UNITED NATIONS CONVENTION ON CONTRACTS FOR THE INTERNATIONAL SALE OF GOODS

* * *

Perhaps the most universally followed doctrine of contractual impossibility emanates from the United Nations. The United Nations Convention on Contracts for the International Sale of Goods ("CISG") was adopted at a 1980 United Nations Diplomatic Conference in Vienna. Over fifty countries, including the United States, have adopted the CISG since the time of its creation. The CISG is a multilateral treaty that governs international contractual obligations, and it seems to constitute the international equivalent to the UCC. The CISG will apply to a contract, in the absence of a choice of law provision, when both principle places of business for the contracting parties are in different nations and those nations have adopted the convention. The CISG also provides conflict of law regulations, which would also allow it to apply to some contracts when only one of the contracting parties is from an adopting CISG nation. The United States has taken exception to the conflict of law regulations. Contractual impossibility is addressed in Section IV of CISG article 79.
* * *

It is worth noting that the UCC section 2–615 and CISG article 79 differ in several important respects. Most notably, article 79 provides an excuse for impossibility while the UCC has adopted the less stringent test of commercial impracticability. The degree of this difference is very much dependent upon the court's interpretation of impracticability. If, for example, a court defines impracticability objectively, where no one would be able to perform the contract, then the degree of difference is minimal. However, if a court defines impracticability as the occurrence of a contingency, the non-occurrence of which is a basic assumption of the contract, more events will fit into the definition, excusing performance in more contracts. The second difference is to whom the defense applies. The CISG applies to both parties whereas the language of section 2–615 would indicate that it is only applicable to sellers of goods. Third, the instances that could give rise to a CISG article 79 defense are much broader than those of the UCC. The CISG applies to all aspects impeding contractual performance, while the UCC limits its defense to situations involving delay, or non-delivery. Also, importantly, the CISG allows excuse for "impediments beyond [the contracting party's] control." This seems to be a much more lenient standard than section 2–615's requirement that the "non-occurrence of the event that occurs be a basic assumption on which the contract is based to excuse performance."

To assert an impossibility defense under the CISG, a party must show three things: (1) failure was due to an external impediment beyond the party's control; (2) the impediment was not reasonably foreseeable at the time the contract was made; and (3) both the impediment and its effects were unavoidable. Further, a party seeking a CISG discharge must also have notified the non-breaching party within a reasonable time after learning of the impediment.

* * *

Returning to the hypothetical, CISG article 79 would apply to the case, as the contract in question is a sale of goods between parties whose principle places of business are in different states which are parties to the Convention. It will probably render the same result as that under UCC section 2–615. The three showings required by the convention are present in Tech Chef Co.'s case. The terrorist attack on the World Trade Center will most definitely be considered an external impediment to Tech Chef Co.'s performance as it has completely devastated the company. Furthermore, it would be very difficult for a court to find that Tech Chef Co., a small software company, could have had any control over the occurrence or non-occurrence of the attack. With regard to the foreseeability requirement, it is arguable that Tech Chef Co. could have foreseen the possibility of the attack, but it would not be reasonable to assume that such a small company should have foreseen the possibility of the attack. Indeed, for Tech Chef Co. to forgo entering the contract with Franco Tex S.A. due to the remote possibility of a terrorist attack would be thought to be unreasonable. Finally, there is nothing that Tech Chef Co. could do to avoid the attack or its consequences. It would be irrational to think that a small software company could avoid this terrorist attack when the United States' and world's intelligence community was unable to prevent it. Tech Chef Co. was also left with no way to avoid breaching its contract as its place of business was destroyed, it had lost key employees, and the goods it contracted to sell were destroyed and not easily replaceable. Further, Tech Chef Co. notified Franco Tex S.A. within seven days of the attack; a very reasonable amount of time given the severity of the damage caused. As Tech Chef Co.'s predicament meets the three requirements for discharge, and the company seasonally notified Franco Tex S.A. of its inability to perform, Tech Chef Co. arguably should be discharged from its contractual duties under CISG article 79.

Notwithstanding the arguments presented above, it is important to note that a court may not find this situation to constitute one of total impossibility. Franco Tex S.A. may argue that while the terrorist attack was external, it was not an impediment making performance totally impossible. Mr. Berger has stated that Tech Chef Co. may have to rebuild the product from scratch and that he does not know how long this will take. He has not said that it would be impossible to rebuild the product. Surely, in time a substitute product can be created. This may be seen as a temporary impediment, excusing performance for the duration of the impediment, or it may be seen as hardship. If a court finds the latter, Tech Chef Co. would be required to perform the contract regardless of how impracticable. As mentioned above, Tech Chef Co. may have much difficulty in replacing the software or finding a company who can, but this difficulty is less than total impossibility. If a court finds the impediment to be temporary the company's performance is excused the length of time to rebuild the software, but ultimately Tech Chef Co. must still deliver the product.

PERILLO, FORCE MAJEURE AND HARDSHIP UNDER THE UNIDROIT PRINCIPLES OF INTERNATIONAL COMMERCIAL CONTRACTS

5 Tul. J. Int'l & Comp. L. 5 (1997).*

The UNIDROIT Principles deal with force majeure in the chapter on nonperformance. Hardship is dealt with in the chapter on performance. The logic of this divided treatment is clear. If performance is impossible it will not be performed; whether the nonperformance is excused or will be the basis for a money judgment for damages or restitution is a question dealt with under nonperformance. If performance is burdensome, the consequences of the burden are dealt with as an aspect of performance.

The provisions on force majeure are rigid. Nothing less than total impossibility will suffice as a predicate for an excuse. There must have been an "impediment beyond [the party's] control" and the party "could not reasonably be expected to have taken the impediment into account at the time of the conclusion of the contract or to have avoided or overcome it or its consequences." * * *

* * *

In Canadian Industries Alcohol Co. v. Dunbar Molasses Co., OFN., apparently involving international commerce, a middleman promised delivery to the buyer of one-and-a-half million gallons of blackstrap molasses from a specific sugar refinery. The seller failed to deliver and, in defense of a breach of contract action, argued impossibility, proving that the specified refinery did not produce a sufficient quantity to fulfill the contract. The defense was unsuccessful as the seller failed to show what efforts it had made to attempt to secure a contract for the production and delivery of sufficient molasses from the operator of the refinery.

What if the impediment is caused by the party's financial embarrassment? Neither Article 7.1.7, nor the commentary to it, refers to this kind of impediment. Under American law, it is quite clear that financial impediments provide no excuse; these are regarded as "subjective" rather than "objective" impossibility and there is unanimity in the case law and in doctrine that subjective impossibility provides no excuse, whether or not it was the result of conditions outside the control of the obligor. It is generally believed that the risk of financial ability to perform is such a basic assumption underlying all contracts that it cannot be excused, except by a decree in a bankruptcy proceeding. It is hard to believe that this general belief is suspended in international trade.

* * *

D. HARDSHIP

The provisions on "hardship" contained in the chapter on performance should be compared with the provision on "force majeure," contained in the chapter on nonperformance. The rule of force majeure is draconian and unforgiving. Nothing short of total impossibility will excuse nonperformance or partial nonperformance. Impracticability will not suffice as an excuse. Rather, impracticability as well as hardship far short of impracticability must be tested under the hardship articles. Hardship alone never forgives nonperformance. It instead compels renegotiation and authorizes courts to "adapt" (revise) the contract to take the hardship into account. Nonetheless, the hardship provision starts with the caption: "Contract[s] to be observed." Article 6.2.1 provides that "[w]here the performance of a contract becomes more onerous for one of the parties, that party is nevertheless bound to perform its obligations subject to he following provisions on hardship."

Hardship: The Factual Predicate

The definition of hardship, which appears in Article 6.2.2, is complex, because it not only defines the nature of the burden, but also other factors that must coexist with the burden to make it legally relevant. As a predicate to legally relevant hardship there must have been "the occurrence of events fundamentally alter[ing] the equilibrium of the contract either because the cost of a party's performance has increased or because the value of the performance a party receives has diminished...." When is the equilibrium of a contract fundamentally altered? * * * [O]ne illustration involves a ten-year contract for the sale of uranium at fixed prices in U.S. dollars payable in New York. The currency in the buyer's country declines to 1% of the value that it had at the time of contracting. The buyer cannot invoke force majeure. Similarly, if the price is increased tenfold because some Texans have almost cornered the market, force majeure is not present. Nonetheless, the buyer may have redress under the hardship provisions. In addition, it must be shown that the events could not reasonably have been taken into account, are not within the party's control, and the risk was not assumed.

* * *

"The events are beyond the control of the disadvantaged party...."

The Principles give no illustration of this subdivision. I will construct a hypothetical. A middleman contracts to deliver goods in the future that he does not have and has no contract with a supplier for the acquisition of them. He could immediately contract for the goods from a manufacturer at a price that would make the resale profitable. Instead, speculating that the manufacturer will lower its price, the middleman takes no action to secure the goods. Because of changing market conditions, the manufacturer raise[s] its prices dramatically. The middleman can only fulfill its contract at a considerable loss. Hardship cannot be invoked, because the reseller could have avoided the loss by promptly entering into a contract with the manufacturer.

"The risk of the events was not assumed by the disadvantaged party."

The contract may expressly allocate the risk of supervening hardship, in which case the contract itself supersedes the rules of hardship in the Principles. However, it is clear from the nature of the hardship doctrine, that, unlike American law, the mere fact that the contract contains a fixed price does not allocate that risk.

[Authors' Note: In 2004 and 2010, UNIDROIT issued a revision of the Principles of International Commercial Contracts. However, the revisions made no changes to the text of the provisions discussed by Perillo.]

COMMENT ON MEASURING DAMAGES FOR NON-DELIVERY

1.   In order to appreciate the full complexity of a contractual relationship (potentially) influenced by unforeseen circumstances, we must also consider the situation of the party whose performance is *not* directly affected. Consider, for example, the position of a buyer where the seller asserts that an unforeseen event establishes an excuse based on frustration or commercial impracticability. How is the buyer to know whether such a claim is well-founded or instead represents a breach of contract by seller? And in order to decide on a course of action, the buyer also will need to know what its rights are—especially the amount of recoverable damages—in the event of a wrongful non-delivery of the goods by the seller.

When a seller fails to deliver on the contract date, the standard remedy at common law is an award of damages. (Although it is commonly said that the standard remedy is specific performance in civil law countries such as Germany and France, in practice damages for breach of contract are "by far the dominant form of relief" there as well. *See* Lando and Rose, *On the Enforcement of Specific Performance in Civil Law Countries*, 24 Int'l Rev. L. & Econ.

473, 478 (2004)). The damage award is intended to allow the buyer to use the marketplace to replace the non-delivered goods without economic loss. The traditional damage calculation is the difference between the contract price and the market price at the time and place for delivery under the contract.

2. The United Kingdom's Sale of Goods Act, art. 51(3), thus provides that damages are measured as of the time the goods "ought to have been delivered" under the contract. In the case of a documentary sale, the traditional common law view in England refined this rule to require measurement of the damages as of the time when the seller should have delivered the shipping documents covering the goods. *See* C. Sharpe & Co., Ltd. v. Nasawa & Co., [1917] 2 K.B. 814.

3. The UCC in the United States, however, introduced more flexibility for an aggrieved buyer in the event a seller fails to deliver. Of special importance, it permits the buyer, as an alternative, to measure damages according to the actual cost of purchasing replacement goods. *See* UCC §§ 2–711, 2–712. Under the UCC, after the seller's "breach," the buyer may "without unreasonable delay" purchase substitute goods and recover the difference between the contract price and the "cost of cover." Thus, if the aggrieved buyer does purchase cover, the UCC allows it to obtain sufficient damages to cover its economic loss.

Even in cases where the buyer does not purchase cover, UCC § 2–713 provides a different rule for measuring damages. Under that section the proper measure is the difference between the contract price and the market price "at the time when the buyer *learned of* the breach" (emphasis added). This change of the date for measurement is part of a larger UCC effort to reduce the effect of "title" concepts on unrelated, and separable, rules. The result is that the buyer has no risk of a rising market in the price of the goods until it *learns of* the breach, but thereafter is not allowed to speculate at the seller's risk (unless cover is timely purchased under § 2–713).

4. The CISG follows a similar approach. CISG Article 75 also permits damages to be measured by the difference between the contract price and the "price in the substitute transaction," if the buyer purchases substitute goods "within a reasonable time after avoidance."

CISG Article 76 applies in cases where the buyer does not purchase substitute goods "under Article 75." Article 76(1) specifies use, for measuring damages, of the market price "at the time of avoidance" of the contract. This rule is well adapted to anticipatory repudiation by the seller or to rightful rejection of delivered goods by the buyer. *See Honnold, Uniform Law for International Sales Under the 1980 United Nations Convention 587–589* (H. Flechtner ed., 4th ed. 2009).

5. Under both the UCC and the CISG, however, the buyer's right to measure damages as against the cost of cover is limited by a general requirement of reasonably prompt action. *See* UCC § 2–712; CISG Arts. 75 and 77. *See also* UCC § 2–610 (requiring in the event of an anticipatory repudiation that buyer decide on its contract remedies within "a commercially reasonable time"); on the CISG *see* Fountoulakis, art. 72, para. 37, in Schechtriem and Schwenzer, *Commentary on the UN Convention on the International Sale of Goods (CISG)* (3rd ed., 2010) (stating that a declaration of avoidance for

anticipatory breach "must be made without delay" in order to prevent "speculation . . . at the expense of the party in breach").

This poses special challenges for a buyer when the price of the relevant goods is rising. Simply stated, if the buyer waits too long to cover in a rising market, it runs the risk that the damages will be measured against an earlier, and thus lower, market price. On the other hand, this approach also protects the seller against strategic speculation by the buyer, who otherwise might base its cover decision solely on future changes in the market price.

The counseling point should be clear, however. The buyer can, and usually should, protect itself by purchasing substitute goods reasonably promptly after seller's breach becomes clear. This seems to be the only method under CISG which measures damages in such a way as to give the buyer complete protection in a rising market.

QUESTIONS AND COMMENTS

1. *The Governing Law.* What law governs the two sales transactions? Both France and the U.S. have ratified CISG, but Araby's status is not known. If Araby also has ratified the CISG, things are somewhat clearer for Jean, at least with respect to the governing law. Recall (from Problem 4.1) that under the basic rule of CSIG Article 1(1)(a), the CISG applies to contracts "between parties whose places of business are in different states" if both of those states are CISG "Contracting States." Why does this rule mean that the CISG should then apply to both the Jean–Gulf Refinery contract and the Jean–Javert contract?

(a) If Araby is not a CISG Contracting State, however, determination of the governing law may depend on where the lawsuit is filed. For Jean's sales contract with Javert, the CISG should still govern under Article 1(1)(a), as long as the related lawsuit is filed in either France or the U.S. But please explain why this is so, under Article 1(1)(a), even though Gulf Refinery (in Araby) is the "ultimate" supplier of the oil.

(b) Now turn to Jean's contract to purchase oil from Gulf Refinery. In the unlikely event that a lawsuit were allowed in France, the French court should apply the domestic law of Araby. This is so because, as we saw in Problem 4.1, the E.U. Rome I Regulation (2008) selects the law of the "habitual residence" of the seller of goods. *See* Art. 4.1(a). Here, Gulf Refinery—the seller to Jean—is located in Araby (and Araby is not a CISG Contracting State).

But what if the lawsuit were filed in the United States? Could a court in Massachusetts conclude that the Jean–Gulf Refinery transaction bears an "appropriate relation" to Massachusetts under UCC § 1–105 (Rev. § 1–301) and thus apply the UCC? Or could it instead find that the "most significant relationship" is with Araby? Or France? As to the latter possibility, recall that, although France is a CISG Contracting State, CISG Article 1(1)(b) does not apply for courts in the United States. (Again, see Problem 4.1.)

Finally, you likely have no way of even knowing what law an Araby court would apply if a lawsuit were filed there.

This all leads to the essential question: Why does it matter to Jean that different substantive law might govern its contract with Javert as compared to the one with Gulf Refinery?

2. This legal uncertainty is highlighted when we focus on the category of related doctrines known by the various names impracticability, frustration, *force majeure*, and hardship. In order to advise Jean about his legal situation regarding the three separate contracts, you may need to analyze (as applicable) some or all of the following rules discussed in the Readings: (1) the general approach as reflected in *The Eugenia*, (2) the UCC rule in the United States, (3) the approach of French courts under the *Code Civil*; and (4) the rule under the CISG.

But first, identify the specific test for excuse under each of these bodies of law. The basic tests for the UCC (*see* White and Summers) and for the CISG and French law (*see* Baker) are set forth in the Readings. For the CISG, the Schwenzer excerpt makes clear that the concept of an "impediment" under Article 79 extends to the substantive notion of an economic "hardship" for performance. But the same author also notes in an influential treatise that even price fluctuations "amounting to over 100 per cent do not yet constitute a ground for exemption" and that in speculative transactions "a party may have to accept even a tripled market price." Schwenzer, art. 79, para. 30, in Schechtriem and Schwenzer, *Commentary on the UN Convention on the International Sale of Goods (CISG)* (3rd ed., 2010).

The Eugenia reflects a traditional common law approach to the doctrine of "frustration." What test does it ultimately employ? In specific, must a party demonstrate *only* that a "fundamentally different situation" arose in order to be excused from its contractual obligations?

3. *The Jean–Gulf Refinery Contract.* Now turn to the first link in the Jean's chain of contracts. Will the various doctrines discussed above provide a valid excuse for Gulf Refinery for not delivering the oil on the contract date? In specific, note that timely delivery may not be technically "impossible," because this contract is for generic heating oil and Gulf Refinery could purchase substitute oil on the Rotterdam "spot" market. Does that option alone preclude Gulf Refinery from asserting a valid impracticability or frustration excuse? How certain are you of your answer?

On the other hand, Gulf Refinery is not seeking a complete excuse, but only a right to delay delivery beyond the contract date. Note that UCC § 2–615 expressly extends to a "delay in delivery" and that CISG Article 79(1) refers to a failure to perform "any" obligation. Is the threshold for excuse lower if a party only wishes to delay performance?

Finally, what is the role of the *force majeure* clause in the Jean–Gulf Refinery contract? That clause expressly addresses the possibility of a "fire" and provides an excuse, including a temporary one, if the event cannot be overcome "without unusual expense." The relationship between such contractual clauses and the general legal doctrines discussed above is a recurrent issue in excuse cases. The specific question you must resolve is this: Which has priority? In specific, would Gulf Refinery merely have to prove that its expenses have become "unusual" as opposed to the seemingly higher thresholds of the general legal doctrines?

4. *The Jean–Constant Carrier Contract*. Now analyze whether Constant Carrier may have an excuse for the carriage contract with Jean because of the events in the Middle East. Neither the UCC nor the CISG will apply to this service contract, so you must resort to general contract doctrines as reflected in *The Eugenia*, the French *Code Civil* and U.S. common law. (The general law in the United States similarly requires an "extreme and unreasonable" hardship or expense; *see American Trading & Production Corp. v. Shell Intern. Marine Ltd.*, 453 F.2d 939, 943–944 (2nd Cir. 1972)). Based on those general doctrines, would Constant Carrier have a right either to take a longer route or raise its rate (or both)? Note that, for Jean's purposes, the delay caused by the longer voyage, if permitted, may be more important than the extra freight charges.

But again, the most important question is likely to be the effect of the contract's "Liberties Clause," which is simply another form of a *force majeure* clause. The broad, one-sided language of this clause is common in carriage contracts. Constant Carrier certainly will argue that the various events in the Middle East reflect a "hindrance, risk, delay, difficulty or disadvantage of whatsoever kind" that cannot be avoided "by the exercise of reasonable endeavors." As Jean's attorney, how would you respond to this argument? Even under this clause, does Carrier have a legal right to hold Jean to the contract and assess additional freight charges if it unilaterally chooses to take the longer route?

5. *The Jean–Javert Contract* (for which, as noted above, the CISG should govern). If either Gulf Refinery or Constant Carrier has a strong excuse argument, will Jean in turn have a valid excuse for his inability to deliver the oil to Javert in Marseilles on time?

The place to begin, again, is the effect of the *force majeure* clause in the contract between Jean and Javert. This is a much more balanced clause (and in fact comes from a form contract drafted by a UN agency some time ago). But how effectively does it consider, define, and allocate the likely risks of future events that may affect contracts for the sale and delivery of oil? In Jean's case, are the various events in the Middle East "circumstances" that "prevent" fulfillment of the contract with Javert "whether wholly or partially"?

6. Jean may seek, however, not a complete excuse from the obligation to deliver oil, but only an excuse to delay delivery beyond the contract date—a delay which is coextensive with the delay allowed to Refinery or Constant. *See* CISG Art. 79(3). Can you be certain whether the obligation to deliver by the contract date is excused?

In any of the above authorities, is an excuse of performance by one party expressly linked to an excuse of performance by another party? Should it be?

Consider again the language of the "excuse clause" in Jean's sales contract with Javert. Does that clause expressly link excuse of performance by one party to an excuse of performance by another party?

7. If Jean has a valid excuse for delivering the oil after March 1, what would be the legal consequence? In response, Javert will claim that he has no use for the oil after the winter heating season and that, therefore, such a late

delivery would substantially deprive him of what he was entitled to receive under the contract in the first place. The claims by Jean and Javert would obviously lead to a conflict. The CISG addresses such conflicts directly in Article 79(5), which provides that even a valid excuse only relieves a party from liability for damages. (As the Honnold excerpt notes, the civil law remedy of a required adjustment of the contract in impediment cases was rejected in the drafting of the CISG.)

Thus, for example, if the desired late delivery by Jean would otherwise amount to a fundamental breach, Javert retains his right to avoid the entire contract. *See also* CISG Articles 25 and 49. The UCC in contrast suggests that a court may have the right to "adjust" a contract in furtherance of "commercial standards and good faith," *see* UCC § 2–615, comment 6; but to put it mildly, courts have been very reluctant to do so. Even with this further information, how certain can you be of your advice to Jean regarding performance of the contract with Javert?

8. Now read the second paragraph of CISG Article 79. This provision seems to address the modern phenomenon of a series of interrelated contracts. But read the provision carefully. Does it apply in a situation such as Jean's, where a seller under one contract purchases goods from an upstream supplier? Has Jean "engaged [Gulf Refinery] to perform" Jean's contract with Javert?

9. Finally, to step back a bit, what is the essence of the related group of excuses we have been discussing here? After surveying a variety of different jurisdictions, one scholar some time ago offered the following summary: "[I]t seems that, despite the differences, the following general characteristics can be traced in all jurisdictions: (a) occurrence of an event after the making of the contract; (b) exceptionality and unforeseeability of the event; (c) alteration of the contract in an intolerable degree; and (d) no fault on the obligor's part." Rapsomanikis, *Frustration of Contract in International Trade Law and Comparative Law*, 18 Duq. L. Rev. 551 (1980).

But also read again the White and Summers excerpt. Their analysis concentrates on the practical aspects of a transaction: A court should first seek to determine whether the parties consciously allocated between them the risk of the event that ultimately occurred—in practical terms, whether at the time the parties made their contract the adversely affected party consciously assumed the risk. If so, the court should enforce the parties' expectations and not recognize an excuse. If not, the court should decide which party should bear the unforeseen risk not merely by looking at the words of the contract, but also at the entire contextual background of the transaction. That all sounds pragmatic, but also highly subjective. Does it lead to unpredictable results?

10. If this case goes to arbitration, UNIDROIT's Principles of International Commercial Contracts may be consulted. The examination of "force majeure" under the Principles will be similar to the doctrines already discussed. However, the doctrine of "hardship" is different and requires a separate analysis. An original comment (since deleted) to Principle 6.2.2 suggested that a price or cost change "amounting to 50% or more" is "likely" to amount to a "fundamental alteration." But even with that perspective, the

prices on the Rotterdam "spot market" may be fluctuating wildly, sometimes below and sometimes well above this possible "limit of sacrifice." What is your advice to Jean about the likelihood of success on this element? (Note that the comment to 6.2.2. now states simply that "[w]hether an alteration is 'fundamental' in a given case will of course depend on the circumstances.") Also, was this risk assumed by Jean or not? Note that we are again back to concepts analyzed earlier. The primary concept to grasp from the Principles, however, is that the aggrieved party is not excused from the performance by hardship, but only has a right to "request renegotiation" of the contract.

In such a renegotiation concerning the Gulf Refinery–Jean contract, must the refinery purchase oil on the Rotterdam "spot market"? Must it negotiate with Jean about whether, when and how much of such oil to purchase? Although the fire may be "beyond the control of" the Refinery, any purchases on the spot market are not. Was the risk of fire "not assumed" by Refinery? Was the risk also "not assumed" by Jean? There is a clause in the contract. What is its effect on the concepts in the UNIDROIT Principles?

PART B.   COUNSELLING DURING CONTRACT DRAFTING

Suppose Jean had consulted you before any of the contracts were signed. What changes could you have made in the overall pattern of this transaction which would have protected Jean when the present problems arose?

QUESTIONS AND COMMENTS

1.   The primary objective of Jean should be to avoid having one *force majeure* clause excuse his obligor, while his obligations are not excused under another such clause.

2.   One method of attempting to accomplish this objective is to try to draft all the *force majeure* clauses in each of the contracts to be identical. However, some of these clauses are established by trade groups, and it will be almost impossible to negotiate a change. Thus, to succeed in this method, one might have to allow the draftsmanship of one trade group to prevail over other contracts. A further problem with this approach would be that the formula adopted by one trade group (*e.g.,* carriers) might not be useful when applied to other contracts, such as contracts for the sale of goods.

One possible solution comes from the International Chamber of Commerce, which has published a model ICC Force Majeure Clause 2003 and a model ICC Hardship Clause 2003. Like the Incoterms from Problem 4.2, parties may adopt these detailed terms through a mere general reference in their contract.

3.   Another approach would be to include in *force majeure* clauses an express reference to other contracts upon which Jean's performance is dependent, thus expressly creating an excuse for Jean if one of his suppliers is excused. Does this create problems of its own? If you were Javert's attorney, would you agree to such a clause in the contract? Under what conditions?

4.   Would the introduction of the "hardship" concepts from the UNIDROIT Principles be helpful here, and especially the concept of renegotiation?

Into which contract(s) would you want them included? What is the likelihood of their inclusion in any contract? In any event, remember that business persons are interested in transactions, not lawsuits. Thus, as Spivak notes, "renegotiation during the life of a contract is the norm in international business transactions."

5. Another standard lawyer's approach is to obtain insurance against the perceived risk. The problem with this approach is that insurance companies do not seem to issue policies to cover the types of risks that concern your client, Jean. For example, if Jean tries to insure Gulf's refinery against loss due to fire, an insurance company is likely to reject the application, since Jean does not own the refinery.

6. Are there mechanisms to compensate Jean for this type of loss which are not called "insurance"?

PROBLEM 4.4 ELECTRONIC COMMERCE: OUTBOUND ORGANICS COMPANY AND DIGITAL PRODUCTS LTD.

SECTION I. FACTS

The Outbound Organics Company is a family partnership run from a farm in Maryland that grows and sells organic produce. Outbound Organics' produce acquired an excellent reputation over time, and its products are now in great demand. One of the partners decided to take advantage of the company's growing reputation, and to further expand sales by designing a website to take orders "online" that runs on a personal computer at the family farm. A list of available products is posted on the website. Customers place orders by simply clicking on an icon for the products they wish to purchase, and then filling in their credit card and shipping information on an automatically generated online form which includes the pricing information for the selected products. Other than a notice that shipment of the goods is "subject to availability" and that "all sales are final" which appear on the online order form, no other "contractual" terms and conditions appear. With the new popularity of their produce, the family also started selling their own special recipes in the *Outbound Organics Family Cookbook*—either in a hardcopy signed by each of the family members, or in an electronic version that can be downloaded directly and automatically from their website. Soon after the website and ordering system went online, Outbound Organics was surprised—and pleased—to see that they were receiving substantial orders for their products from France.

The new computerized ordering system also provided a convenient excuse to buy a very large high-end flat panel display monitor. The new display monitor is used to help with Outbound Organics online business operations, but is also part of the home entertainment system in the family room at the farm. The best computer or video monitor on the market is the Sony "Super Screen High Definition Display" which has a wide format active matrix liquid crystal screen with a variety of inputs, and can display standard computer generated signals as well as five different video signals. It initially appeared that the best price for the "SSHDD" monitor was offered by Digital Products Ltd, an online retailer in the United Kingdom. The family owners of Outbound Organics thus ordered the monitor on the retailer's website for $1500 and clicked the "Accept" button when the website generated an electronic invoice. However, three days after receiving the monitor, the same product was advertised at the local Best Buy in Maryland for several hundred dollars less. While Outbound Organics would like to return the monitor to Digital Products it also knows that it would refuse a return from any of its own online customers, so it wonders what it can do under the circumstances?

SECTION II.   FOCUS OF CONSIDERATION

This Problem surveys several issues that arise when international transactions are conducted electronically. It touches upon some of the changes occurring as private contractual legal rules are adapted to electronic commerce transactions.

The Zaremba excerpt provides an overview of the various basic laws applicable to online transactions in the United States and the European Union, and provides the basic framework for the discussion of the private contractual issues. The Rustad and Onufrio excerpt then surveys the various directives of the European Union that provide special consumer protections in distance and electronic commerce. The Cordera excerpt builds upon this framework to compare the approach taken to consumer protection in each system, an area which often poses difficult issues because of the presence of strong local policies that often override basic contractual rules. Next, the Andrews excerpt examines some of the strengths and weaknesses of the European Union's highly regulatory approach to addressing online transactions through a series of detailed Directives aimed at harmonizing the laws in all of the various member states of the EU.

Excerpts from the CISG, the UNCITRAL Convention on the Use of Electronic Communications in International Contracts, the Uniform Commercial Code, the Electronic Records and Signatures in Commerce (E–SIGN) Act, the Uniform Electronic Transactions Act, UCITA, and the EU Electronic Commerce Directive and the Unfair Commercial Practices Directive are all included in the Documents Supplement and are essential to this Problem.

Web Resources for further study include the UNCITRAL E–Commerce web page (http://www.uncitral.org/uncitral/en/uncitral_texts/electronic_commerce.html), and the European Union Information Society web pages http://europa.eu/pol/infso/index_en.htm.

SECTION III. READINGS, QUESTIONS AND COMMENTS

ZAREMBA, INTERNATIONAL ELECTRONIC TRANSACTION CONTRACTS BETWEEN U.S. AND EU COMPANIES AND CUSTOMERS

18 Conn. J. Int'l L. 479 (2003).*

I. INTRODUCTION

* * *

Electronic transaction contracts raise several questions: What is the applicable law? What is the governing jurisdiction? Where and when was the electronic contract concluded? Does the electronic contract constitute writing? Is an electronic signature legally recognized and enforceable? And what constitutes an offer or an acceptance when utilizing the Internet?

* * *

II. APPLICABLE LAW

The first and most important issue with respect to the outcome of disputes resulting from international electronic contracts is the question of what body of law governs the contract. Only when the applicable law is determined can the remaining questions be answered. At first glance this problem is easily overcome by including a choice of law clause in the contract. However, in a large number of contracts, parties do not choose the governing jurisdiction or law. The Internet promotes this carelessness since people who are not experienced in business matters can easily use the Internet as a means to sell their [products]. There are three possibilities as to applicable law: international law, the law of the seller's country, or the law of the purchaser's country.[8]

A. *International Law*

There are three sources of international law that might play a role in an international electronic transaction contract. First, the United Nations Convention on Contracts for International Sale of Goods (CISG). This is the most important body of law on the international level. Second, the UNCITRAL Model Law on Electronic Commerce, and third, the UNIDROIT Principles.

1. *The United Nations Convention on Contracts for the International Sale of Goods (CISG)*

The United Nations Convention on Contracts for the International Sale of Goods (CISG) is the princip[al] body of international contract law.

---

* Copyright 2003, reprinted with permission of the Connecticut Journal of International Law.

8. Actually there is a fourth possibility. The contractors can choose the law of a third country. This may happen if the parties cannot agree on which country's law should apply.

It is also the only body of international contract law that has been formally adopted by the international community. * * *

a. *Applicability*

The CISG applies to international sales contracts between parties that are located within states which signed the CISG. The Convention also applies when the rules of international private law lead to the application of the law of one of the contracting states. In these cases the CISG applies even if the parties did not contemplate or refer to CISG in their contract. However, the parties can exclude the application of the CISG, derogate from or vary the effect of any of its provisions.[16]

The CISG covers the sale of goods.[17] Excluded are goods bought for personal, family or household use.[18] The CISG is silent on the issue and extent to which it applies to electronic transaction contracts because in 1980, when the CISG was drafted, no one foresaw the impact of software and the Internet. Therefore, the question becomes whether computer software can be subsumed under the term "goods" according to Article 1(1) of the CISG.

Goods under the CISG are essentially movable and identifiable separate objects. Based on this definition the general view is that software on a disk meets this criteria because the disk can be transferred to a different location, even though the software itself is intangible. When software arrives to the customer by a wire, the transaction involves only encoded information carried electronically. Therefore, this reasoning is not applicable to this type of software. However, the mere means of transmission must not be relevant with respect to the applicable law. This would entail uncertainty. * * * Thus, the CISG should be applicable to electronically transmitted software. The few judgments that have yet been reported concerning the applicability of the CISG to computer software tend to favor this point of view. However, it has to be noted that tangible data carriers were involved in all of these decisions. Despite the tendencies towards the applicability of the CISG, it remains to be seen whether courts will consider the presence of a tangible data carrier determinative. Even though the applicability of the CISG to international electronic transaction contracts is likely, there are certain limitations that effectively limit its ability to be the unifying body of international contract law for electronic software. Courts and commentators have acknowledged [for example,] that software that is custom designed according to specifications does not fall under the CISG, because such contracts are not sales contracts.

Part II of the CISG describes the formation of a contract. These provisions are not unusual compared with United States and European

---

16. CISG at Art. 6. *[Cross-references here and below omitted—the Authors.]*

17. CISG at Art. 1(1).

18. CISG at Art. 2(a).

contract law. * * * Under the CISG, a contract need not be concluded in writing.

* * *

2. *UNCITRAL Model Law on Electronic Commerce*

In 1996 the United Nations Commission on International Trade Law (UNCITRAL) promulgated a Model Law on Electronic Commerce. Since the Model Law on Electronic Commerce is neither a convention nor a treaty, it is not directly applicable to electronic contracts. The Model Law lays down principles for e-commerce in order to remove a number of legal obstacles and to create a more secure environment for electronic commerce. The basic principle is that information must not be denied legal effect, validity or enforceability solely because it is in the form of a data message. To some extent these principles of Model Law on Electronic Commerce can be found in all of the United States and European Union legislation dealing with electronic commerce that has been enacted recently. However, there are still differences between these laws. * * *

3. *UNIDROIT Principles*

The third source of international law rules is the UNIDROIT Principles of International Commercial Contracts. The UNIDROIT Principles were drafted in 1994 by a special group composed of representatives of all the major legal systems of the world. Unlike the UNCITRAL Model Law the seven chapters of the UNIDROIT Principles provide a complete set of contract rules, including general provisions, formation, validity, interpretation, content, performance, and non-performance of a contract. Although the UNIDROIT Principles are not applicable directly to electronic contracts, they apply when the parties have agreed that their contract be governed by them, and they might apply when the parties have agreed that their contract be governed by general principles of law. This could be an interesting option if the parties cannot agree as to which national body of contract law should govern their contract. The parties need to be careful, though, because the UNIDROIT Principles can by no means preempt mandatory national or supranational rules, which are applicable in accordance with the relevant rules of private international law.

B. *National Laws*

If none of the mentioned international bodies of contract law apply, conflict of laws—also known as private international law—determines which law governs international contract cases. Private international law itself does not provide the law that governs the dispute, but provides how to determine the applicable law. * * *

1. *EU Law*

a. *EU Law for Electronic Contracts*

In April 1997, the European Commission promulgated * * * a common European position with respect to electronic commerce to encourage the growth of electronic commerce in Europe. This initiative has been followed by several directives. These directives are not self-executing, but need to be transferred into the legal system of the * * * EU member states by adopting new laws or by changing existing legislation according to the terms of the directive. * * * However, the benefit of directives especially for U.S. businesses seeking to contract with EU businesses and customers from different European countries is that they have the certainty that none of the EU members' legislations will be inconsistent with the particular directive. There are three important directives that deal with international electronic contracts: the Electronic Commerce Directive, the Distance Contracts Directive, and the Electronic [Signatures] Directive. Together they represent a coherent scheme of rules to govern electronic commerce within the European Union. However, U.S. businesses must note that these three directives do not provide substantive contract law. Substantive contract rules can only be found in the national laws of the * * * EU member countries.

i.   Electronic Commerce Directive

The Electronic Commerce Directive * * * was issued on June 8, 2000, to facilitate electronic commerce in the European Union. The Electronic Commerce Directive states in Article 1 that the "Directive seeks to contribute to the proper functioning of the internal market by ensuring the free movement of information society services between the Member States." Information society services are services normally provided for remuneration at a distance by electronic means and individual request of a recipient of services, which include the online sale of goods and services and the license of information.[82]

The Directive required the member states to remove legal obstacles to the use of electronic contracts. The Electronic Commerce Directive provides that: "Member States shall ensure that their legal system allows contracts to be concluded by electronic means. Member States shall in particular ensure that the legal requirements applicable to the contractual process neither create obstacles for the use of electronic contracts nor result in such contracts being deprived of legal effectiveness and validity on account of their having been made by electronic means."[84] * * *

ii.   Electronic Signature Directive

On December 13, 1999, the European Parliament and the European Council adopted the Directive 1999/93/EC on a Community framework for electronic signatures (Electronic Signature Directive). The Directive seeks to facilitate the use of electronic signatures and to contribute to their legal recognition. In order to achieve this objective the Directive establishes a legal framework for electronic signatures and certification-services. The Directive does not cover any other aspects related to the conclusion or validity of contracts.

* * *

---

82.   Electronic Commerce Directive at Art. 2(a) and Recital (17).

84.   Electronic Commerce Directive at Art. 9(1).

2. *U.S. Law*

a. *U.S. Laws for Electronic Contracts*

There are five important U.S. bodies of law to consider when it comes to the conclusion of contracts over the Internet: Electronic Signatures in Global and National Commerce Act (E–Sign), Uniform Electronic Transaction Act (UETA), Uniform Computer Information Transactions Act (UCITA), the Uniform Commercial Code (U.C.C.), and the common law. They differ in applicability and scope.

i. E–Sign

On the federal level, the Electronic Signatures in Global and National Commerce Act (E–Sign) plays an important role with regard to electronic contracts. E–Sign became effective on October 1, 2000. It was enacted not to provide substantive contract law, but to promote and facilitate the use of electronic records and signatures in interstate and foreign commerce on a federal level. E–Sign's core provision states that electronic signatures, records, or contracts cannot be denied effect solely because they are in electronic form.[112] E–Sign does not apply to all records and signatures, but only to those that relate to a transaction. According to E–Sign, a transaction is "an action or set of actions relating to the conduct of business, consumer, or commercial affairs between two or more persons."[114] However, there are specific exceptions. E–Sign does not apply to [the] transaction to the extent it is governed by other laws or rules. These include laws and rules governing the creation and execution of wills, codicils, or testamentary trusts; adoption, divorce, or other matter of family law; court orders or notices and official court documents, such as briefs or pleadings, required to be executed; any notice of the cancellation of utility services; any notice of default or foreclosure under a credit agreement secured by a primary residence of an individual, or a rental agreement for such a residence; any notice of the termination of health insurance or benefits; any notice of recall of a product, or material failure of a product, that could endanger health or safety; and any document required to accompany the transportation or handling of hazardous materials. Finally, E–Sign is excluded to the extent the transaction is governed by the U.C.C. other than sections 1–107 and 1–206 and Articles 2 and 2A.[123]

ii. UETA

Like E–Sign, the Uniform Electronic Transaction Act (UETA) does not create new substantive contract law rules, but intends to validate the use of electronic media. In order to achieve this objective, UETA provides that "a record or signature may not be denied legal effect or enforceability solely because it is in electronic form" and that "a contract may not be denied legal effect or enforceability solely because an electronic record was

---

112. E–Sign at § 101(a).

114. E–Sign at § 106(13).

123. E–Sign at § 103.

used in its formation."[126] UETA only applies to records and signatures that relate to a transaction.[127] It defines transaction as "an action or set of actions occurring between two or more persons relating to the conduct of business, commercial or governmental affairs."[128] However, the following areas are explicitly excluded from the coverage of the UETA: (1) wills, codicils, and testamentary trusts; (2) transactions covered by the Uniform Commercial Code, except the sections 1–107 and 1–206, and Articles 2 and 2A [to which UETA still applies]; (3) transactions covered by the Uniform Computer Information Transaction Act (UCITA); and (4) other laws identified by each State.[129] These are fewer exceptions compared with E–Sign. Therefore, UETA has a broader applicability.

The relationship between E–Sign and UETA requires some explanation. Even though UETA was enacted prior to E–Sign, UETA is merely a model law that may be adopted by the states, whereas E–Sign is an enacted federal law, which is applicable in the states without transfer. Generally, E–Sign preempts state laws and regulations. However, E–Sign can be superseded by the states if they adopt the original UETA version.[132] In this case UETA, and not E–Sign, controls the transaction. If a state has adopted a modified UETA version or some legislation on electronic contracting other than UETA, such legislation is valid if it does not demand a certain type of technology, is consistent with the principles of E–Sign, and makes specific reference to E–Sign. * * *

iii. UCITA

Many people felt that Article 2 of the Uniform Commercial Code (U.C.C.) did not adequately cover transactions involving software because, in contrast to contracts involving ordinary goods, software contracts transfer intangible goods and often entail a license of right to use rather than a sale. In order to resolve this problem the Electronic Contracting Rules of the Uniform Computer Information Transactions Act (UCITA) was enacted. UCITA provides substantive contract law and establishes a legal framework for computer information transactions similar to U.C.C. Article 2 for the sale of goods.[137] Additionally, UCITA states that electronic records and signatures must be equivalent to paper records and written signatures. * * * UCITA's scope is limited to computer information transactions such as contracts to license or purchase computer software. A

---

126. UETA at § 7.

127. UETA at § 3(a).

128. UETA at § 2(16).

129. UETA at § 3(b).

132. E–Sign at § 102 (a)(1).

137. From 1995 to 1999, UCITA was known as U.C.C. Article 2B and was drafted in order to be included into the U.C.C. See Ed Foster, What is UCITA, available at http:// www.infoworld. com/articles/ uc/xml/02/01/03/ 020103ucwhatis.xml (last visited Nov. 18, 2002). However, due to a great amount of criticism, the status of the proposed U.C.C. Article 2B was shifted from a prestigious U.C.C. article to the separate uniform act. See ALI & NCCUSL, NCCUSL to Promulgate Freestanding Uniform Computer Information Transaction Act—ALI and NCCUSL Announce the Legal Rules for Computer Information Will Not Be Part of U.C.C., April 7, 1999, available at http://www.2bguide.com/ docs/040799pr.html (last visited Jan. 17, 2003).

computer information transaction is an agreement and the subsequent performance of that agreement to create, modify, transfer, or license computer information or informational rights in computer information. Computer information is defined as information in electronic form that is obtained through the use of a computer or capable of being processed by a computer. However, unless otherwise agreed by the parties, UCITA expressly states that it does not apply to audio or visual programming that is provided by broadcast, satellite, or cable; financial service transactions; motion pictures, sound recordings, or musical works; compulsory licenses; employment contracts; contracts that do not require that information be furnished as computer information, or contracts in which the form of the information as computer information is otherwise insignificant with respect to the primary subject matter of the transaction; and transactions within the scope of Article 3, 4, 4A, 5, 6, 7, or 8 of the U.C.C. On the other hand, it is important to note that UCITA precludes UETA.

Like the provisions of U.C.C. Article 2, most of the UCITA rules only apply if the parties have not agreed otherwise.

* * *

iv. U.C.C.

The Uniform Commercial Code (U.C.C.) was developed in the 1940s and 1950s to standardize commercial transaction laws, and Article 2 of the U.C.C. governs the sale of goods. The U.C.C. provides substantive contract law rules. Those U.S. states that have not already enacted UCITA might apply U.C.C. [Article] 2 or 2A to computer information transactions. The problem is that the U.C.C. Article 2 has been established to govern the sale of goods. Again the question arises whether software, which itself is intangible, can be considered a goods in the meaning of U.C.C. Article 2. In recent decisions U.S. courts have subsumed software under goods. However, since tangible data carriers were involved in all in these decisions, the courts did not focus on the intangibility of the computer software. As is true on the international level with respect to the applicability of CISG, it remains uncertain, although likely, that courts would apply Article 2 [to] electronically transmitted software.

[Zaremba here discusses the proposed revision of UCC Article 2 noted in Problem 4.1 above. This reform effort also proposed provisions that parallel UETA, including an express validation of electronic records, contracts, and signatures. However, as noted in Problem 4.1 above, no state has enacted revised Article 2 and in 2011 even the ALI withdrew its support. Accordingly, references to the proposed revision to Article 2 have been deleted below—The Authors.]

v. Common Law

In those states where UCITA has not yet been adopted, the states' common law applies if a court is of the opinion that the U.C.C. is not applicable. The common law also applies if gaps in the U.C.C. have to be supplemented. Since common law varies widely among the states it provides the least predictable source of contract law. Even though the Restatement (Second) of Contracts is available everywhere, it is not consistently followed.

* * *

b. U.S. Conflict of Laws

In the United States, conflict of laws rules regarding contracts are found in UCITA,[171] the U.C.C.,[172] the Restatement (Second) of Conflict of Laws (1971),[173] the Restatement (First) of Conflict of Laws (1934), and the common law. All these sources of law are applicable to interstate and international cases.

UCITA provides a straightforward rule. In the absence of a choice of law agreement, UCITA section 109(b)(1) states that an Internet transaction for the electronic transfer of information is governed by the law where the licensor is located. UCITA section 109(c) does, however, provide an exception if the jurisdiction whose law governs is outside of the United States. In this case, the foreign law governs only if it allows for substantially similar protection and rights to a party not located in that jurisdiction as are provided under UCITA. Otherwise, the law of the state that has the most significant relationship to the transaction governs. Since foreign law can only govern if the licensor is located outside the United States, this clause inherently protects U.S. customers and licensees. In all other cases, UCITA adopts the rule of the Restatement (Second) of Conflict of Laws. In absence of effective choice by the parties, U.C.C. section [1–]105(1) describes how to determine the applicable law. U.C.C. section [1–]105(1) directs the forum to apply its own law if the transaction bears "an appropriate relation to this state." In the same situation section 188(1) of the Restatement (Second) of Conflict of Laws requires that "[t]he rights and duties of the parties with respect to an issue in contract are determined by the local law of the state which, with respect to that issue, has the most significant relationship to the transaction and the parties."[179] Over 24 states are using the Restatement (Second) rules.

Since the seller performs the characteristic performance of an international transaction contract, usually the state in which the seller is located has the most significant relationship to the transaction and the parties. Likewise, due to the seller's characteristic performance, an international electronic transaction bears an appropriate relation to the seller's state. Therefore, generally under UCITA, the U.C.C. and the Restatement (Second) of Conflict of Laws, in international electronic transactions the

---

171. UCITA at § 109.

172. U.C.C. at § 1–105(1).

173. Restatement (Second) of Conflict of Laws §§ 6, 10, 188 (1971).

179. Restatement (Second) of Conflict of Laws § 188(1) (1971) (emphasis added). § 188(1) also states that the choice-of-law principles stated in sec. 6 of the Restatement have to be considered. § 188(2) provides lists of certain types of contacts that have to be taken into account to determine the most significant relationship, e.g., place of contracting, place of performance, place of business of the parties, etc.

law of the country where the seller is located applies. The outcome is less predictable if UCITA applies and a U.S. customer wants to sue a foreign seller in the United States.

The situation becomes more complicated when the Restatement (First) of Conflict of Laws applies. The Restatement (First) distinguishes between contract validity and contract performance issues. If the validity of a contract is in dispute, the law applies where the contract was made.[182] This is, in the case of a formal contract, the place of delivery,[183] and in the case of a bilateral contract, the place of the offeree's promise.[184] As a result, the buyer country's law controls a dispute that refers to the validity of an electronic transaction contract. If the performance of a contract is in dispute, the law of the country where the performance occurs rules.[185] It is likely that in the case of an electronic contract the choice would focus on where the buyer receives the information to form the contract. The Restatement (First) of Conflict of Laws is still important, since it remains applicable in a few states.

* * *

IV.   FORMATION AND VALIDITY

To apply the conventional rules of formation and validity of contracts to electronic contracts can be challenging because some of the applicable laws did not contemplate this new type of contract when they were enacted. Even though hundreds of thousands of contracts have already been executed over the Internet without legal challenge, remarkably legal certainty in contract law is and has always been one of the most important prerequisites for economic growth. As in the case of paper contracts, it must be determined, what constitutes an offer and an acceptance, when such a declaration is dispatched or received, how assent can be manifested, and how writing or signature requirements can be fulfilled in an electronic environment. The answers to these questions derive from the applicable jurisdiction's laws.

A.   Formation of a Contract

With respect to certainty and predictability it is important to know how contracts are formed when the Internet is used. The demonstration of the willingness on a web page to sell a certain product is usually not an offer but an invitation to make an offer. In these cases the click on the purchase icon constitutes an offer. Often, this offer is then accepted by a program run on behalf of the offeree, which either accepts the offer explicitly or by conduct. In electronic transaction cases acceptance by conduct would be to let the offeror download the computer program. The peculiar thing with respect to such automated Internet contracts is that

---

182.   Restatement (First) of Conflict of Laws § 332 (1934).

183.   Id. at § 312.

184.   Id. at § 325.

185.   Id. at § 358.

since the seller uses a computer program, which accepts the offers, the seller usually does not act himself but receives the contracts after they have already been concluded.

1. U.S. Law

UCITA [and] U.C.C. Article 2 * * * deal with the formation of contracts. This distinguishes them from E–Sign and UETA. UCITA's formation rules can be found in Sections 202 through 206 [and] the U.C.C.'s formation rules can be found in its Sections 2–204 through 2–210 * * *. According to UCITA [and] the U.C.C. * * * a contract may be formed in any manner sufficient to show agreement. UCITA * * * even clarif[ies] that sufficient manner includes electronic means.

a. Offer and Acceptance

UCITA [and] the current U.C.C. Article 2 * * * state that an offer invites an acceptance in any reasonable manner and by any reasonable medium, and that shipment or the promise to ship is a proper means of acceptance unless the offer provides otherwise.[228] According to UCITA section 203(4) * * * a contract is formed when the electronic acceptance is received. If the response consists of beginning performance, full performance, or giving access to information, then UCITA states a contract is formed when the performance is received, or access is enabled and materials are received.

b. Acceptance With Varying Terms

According to UCITA, a definite and seasonable acceptance operates as an acceptance even if it contains terms which are different from the offer, unless it materially alters the offer. UCITA, further, provides that if an acceptance materially alters an offer, a contract is not formed unless a party agrees to the other party's offer or acceptance, or all other circumstances including the parties' conduct establish a contract.[232] Under * * * U.C.C. Article 2, a definite and seasonable acceptance operates as an acceptance even though it states terms additional to or different from the offer.[233] These provisions reject the "mirror image" rule and require that additional or different terms should not make a rejection out of an acceptance.

* * *

d. Electronic Agents

Unlike the current U.C.C., UCITA * * * deals with electronic agents. An electronic agent is "a computer program, or electronic or other automated means, used by a person to initiate an action, or to respond to electronic messages or performances, on the person's behalf without review or action by an individual at the time of the action or response to

---

228. UCITA at § 203(1) and (2); U.C.C. at § 2–206(1).

232. UCITA § 204.

233. U.C.C. § 2–207(1).

the message or performance." UCITA * * * state[s] that contracts may be formed by the interaction of electronic agents.[239] * * * UCITA * * * also assert[s] that "[a] contract may be formed by the interaction of electronic agents [and] an individual[,] acting on the individual's own behalf or for another person." In these cases, a contract is formed if the individual takes action that the individual is free to refuse to take or makes a statement that the individual has reason to know will either (1) cause the electronic agent to perform, or (2) indicate acceptance, regardless of other actions or expressions by the individual to which the electronic agent is unable to react. UCITA [is] * * * clear with respect to the use of an electronic agent. Although the use of an electronic agent should be regarded as a manner sufficient to show acceptance of an offer, the current U.C.C. Section 2–204(1) leaves Internet purchasers with uncertainty.

2. EU Law

Unlike UCITA * * *, the EU Directives do not address the specific issues that refer to offer and acceptance of an electronic contract. Article 9(1) of the Electronic Commerce Directive requires the EU member states to "ensure that their legal systems allow electronic contracts to be concluded by electronic means." Therefore, offer and acceptance of electronic contracts in the EU are addressed by the different national legal systems.

* * *

B. Writing Requirements

Statutes of Frauds and similar laws traditionally require certain contracts to be memorialized in writing in order to be enforceable.[244] When records or contracts are formed electronically the question becomes, whether this is sufficient to fulfill the writing requirement.

1. U.S. Law

a. Electronic Records

E–Sign, UETA, [and] UCITA * * * have replaced "writing" with the term "record."[245] Since record is defined as "information that is inscribed on a tangible medium or that is stored in an electronic or other medium and is retrievable in perceivable form,"[246] it includes both written and electronic records. "The term 'electronic record' means a contract or other record created, generated, sent, communicated, received, or stored by electronic means."[247]

---

239. UCITA at § 206.

244. See, e.g., U.C.C. § 2–201 (1998); § 655b(1) BGB (German Civil Code).

245. E–Sign at § 101(a)(1); UETA at § 7(a); UCITA at § 107(a); [revised] U.C.C. § 2–211(1).

246. UCITA at § 102(a)(54).

247. E–Sign at § 106(4).

According to E–Sign the legal effect, validity, or enforceability of a contract or a record shall not be denied solely because it is in electronic form, and that the legal effect, validity, or enforceability of a contract shall not be denied solely because an electronic record was used in its formation.[248] UETA provides that "a record ... may not be denied legal effect or enforceability solely because it is in electronic form" and that "a contract may not be denied legal effect or enforceability solely because an electronic record was used in its formation."[250] Similarly, UCITA asserts that "[a] record ... may not be denied legal effect or enforceability solely because it is in electronic form."[251] * * * Thus, in cases in which a certain law requires the contract to be in writing, the contract will [not] be invalid due to its electronic form, if either E–Sign, UETA, [or] UCITA applies.

There is one major difference between E–Sign [and] UCITA, * * * on the one side, and UETA on the other side. UETA requires, in contrast to E–Sign [and] UCITA * * *, that both parties have agreed to use electronic means. Without such an agreement UETA does not apply. UETA does not require an explicit agreement, but the agreement may be determined from the context, the surrounding circumstances, and the parties' conduct.[255] It is not clear to what extent the agreement requirement actually restricts UETA's application. The Official Comment to UETA section 5 acknowledges that section 5(b) limits the applicability of UETA to transactions which parties have agreed to conduct electronically. At the same time, however, the Official Comment to section 5 argues that a "[b]road interpretation of the term agreement is necessary to assure that this Act has the widest possible application consistent with its purpose of removing barriers to electronic commerce." Even though the Official Comment lists examples of circumstances from which an agreement to conduct transactions electronically may be found, and examples of circumstances that may demonstrate the absence of such an agreement, the breadth of the interpretation is still unclear. If somebody uses the Internet to purchase and download a computer program, his agreement to use electronics appears to be the only possible inference. However, * * * [a] cautious * * * business should ask potential customers on their web page whether they agree to use electronics, before they allow them to download programs or purchase products. This could be realized by implementing an additional icon, and related terms, that has to be clicked to get to the order icon. In the cases in which the precondition of an agreement to use electronics present is met, under UETA the legal effect of a contract or record will not be denied because of its electronic form.

b. Retainability Requirement

In electronic contracts the writing requirement must be viewed in combination with the requirement of retainability. E–Sign section 101(e)

---

248.   E–Sign at § 101(a).

250.   UETA at § 7.

251.   UCITA at § 107.

255.   UETA at § 5(b).

asserts "if a statute, regulation, or other rule of law requires that a contract or other record ... be in writing, the legal effect, validity, or enforceability of an electronic record of such contract or other record may be denied if such electronic record is not in a form that is capable of being retained and accurately reproduced for later reference by all parties or persons who are entitled to retain the contract or other record." E–Sign leaves it open to the states how they interpret their own writing requirements. Therefore, the states can either conclude that some or all of their laws requiring a writing demand retainability and reproducibility in the case of electronic records or that they do not. This is a factor of uncertainty. * * *

E–Sign refers to "all parties or persons who are entitled to retain the contract or other record."[260] With this language E–Sign considers that some laws only require that a written disclosure be shown to a party, or be available for review by a party. UETA is stricter when it states that if "a law requires a person to provide, send, or deliver information in writing to another person, the requirement is satisfied if the information is provided, sent, or delivered ... in an electronic record capable of retention by the recipient."[262]

E–Sign contains another factor of uncertainty. It is unclear as to when and how long the electronic record needs to be capable of being retained and reproduced. At first glance, UETA appears to be clearer on this point. According to UETA section 8(a), the capability of retention must be present "at the time of the receipt." However, the official comment to UETA section 8(a) states that "the recipient of an electronic record ... must be able to get to the electronic record and read it, and must have the ability to get back to the information in some way at a later date." Courts might interpret the Official Comment's emphasis on the recipient's ability to subsequently refer to the information contained in the electronic record to suggest that the sender has to preserve and provide the information for an unlimited time. However, this would carry the protection of the other contractor too far. It would be inconsistent with commercial practice and too expensive, and it would require too much administration. A reasonable interpretation would be that the electronic record must be retainable and reproducible at least at the time when the transaction occurs. Nevertheless, businesses should be aware of this uncertainty.

In contrast to E–Sign, UETA clarifies that "[a]n electronic record is not capable of retention by the recipient if the sender or its information processing system inhibits the ability of the recipient to print or store the electronic record." UETA further provides that "[i]f a sender inhibits the ability of a recipient to store or print an electronic record, the electronic record is not enforceable against the recipient."[268] Since the latter rule is

---

260. E–Sign at § 101(e).

262. UETA at § 8(a).

268. UETA at § 8.

not restricted to situations where the underlying laws require a writing, it is unclear whether it also applies to cases in which the laws do not require a writing. E–Sign does not contain a comparable rule.

2. EU Law

None of the Directives explicitly deal with writing requirements of electronic records or contracts. Again, the general rule of Article 9(1) of the Electronic Commerce Directive applies, which requires the member states to change their legislation in order to allow contracts to be concluded by electronic means. Article 9(1) of the Directive further provides that the Member States' laws must not create obstacles for the use of electronic contracts and that such contracts must not be deprived of legal effectiveness and validity on account of their formation by electronic means. This rule forbids any formal contract requirement that cannot be satisfied by electronic means. With regard to the writing requirement the consequence is that EU Member States' laws cannot require the retainability of electronic records or contracts, since this would be an additional obstacle compared with paper records or contracts. Furthermore, it is not necessary that both parties have agreed to use electronics. Thus, the EU writing requirement rules are more liberal and more e-commerce friendly than their U.S. equivalents.

* * *

C. Signature Requirements

National contract laws worldwide traditionally require the parties to affix their signatures to certain agreements.[270] The online version of the traditional signature is the electronic signature. An electronic signature is defined as "any letters, characters, or symbols manifested by electronic or similar means and executed or adopted by a party with the intent to authenticate a writing," or as "data in electronic form which are attached to or logically associated with other electronic data and which serve as a method of authentication."[272] * * * One of the core issues with regard to electronic signatures is whether electronic commerce legislation should give legal effect to all electronic signatures or only to those that fulfil certain security standards such as digital signatures. * * *

* * *

1. U.S. Law

* * * UCITA replaced the term "signature" by the term "authentication,"[282] demonstrating that an electronic process or symbol are equivalents to written signatures. According to UCITA "authentication" means "to sign; or with the intent to sign a record, otherwise to execute or adopt an electronic symbol, sound, message, or process referring to, attached to,

---

270. See, e.g., U.C.C. §§ 2–201, 2–209 (1998); § 655b(1) BGB (German Civil Code).

272. Electronic Signature Directive Art. 2(1).

282. UCITA at § 107(a).

included in, or logically associated or linked with, that record."[283] Under E–Sign, "electronic signature" is defined as "an electronic sound, symbol, or process, attached to or logically associated with a contract or other record and executed or adopted by a person with the intent to sign the record."[284] UETA contains an almost identical definition.[285] The two elements that make these technologies signatures are the intent of the person to sign the record, and the logical association of the signature with the record.

According to E–Sign the legal effect, validity, or enforceability of a signature shall not be denied solely because it is in electronic form, and that the legal effect, validity, or enforceability of a contract shall not be denied solely because an electronic signature was used in its formation.[286] UETA states that a signature cannot be denied legal effect or enforceability solely because it is in electronic form.[287] UCITA provides that the legal effect or enforceability of an authentication may not be denied solely because it is in electronic form.[288] * * * Thus, in cases in which a certain law requires the contract to contain a signature, under U.S. law an electronic signature is sufficient.

2. EU Law

In the European Union the Electronic Signature Directive is supposed to establish a legal framework for electronic signatures. The EU approach is different from the U.S. approach. Article 5 of the Electronic Signature Directive distinguishes between two different types of electronic signatures.

Article 5(1) of the Electronic Signature Directive deals with "advanced electronic signatures." An advanced electronic signature is an electronic signature which is (1) uniquely linked to the signatory;[291] (2) capable of identifying the signatory; (3) created by using means that the signatory can maintain under his sole control; and (4) linked to the data to which it relates in such a manner that any subsequent changes are detectable.[292] However, Article 5(1) does not stop here. The security standard is even higher. Article 5(1) refers only to those advanced electronic signatures "which are based on a qualified certificate and which are created by a secure-signature-creation device."

* * *

---

283. UCITA at § 102(a)(6).

284. E–Sign at § 106(5).

285. UETA § 2(8).

286. E–Sign at § 101(a).

287. UETA at § 7(a).

288. UCITA at § 107(a).

291. A signatory is a person who holds configured software or hardware used to implement the unique data which are used to create an electronic signature. Electronic Signature Directive at Art. 2(3), (4), and (5).

292. Electronic Signature Directive at Art. 2(2).

Article 5(2) of the Directive requires member states to ensure that electronic signatures are not denied legal effect, validity, or enforceability solely on the grounds that the signature is in electronic form, not based upon a qualified certificate, or not created by a secure signature-creation device. * * *

* * *

D. Manifestation of Assent

Both in the United States and in Europe it is acknowledged that the manifestation of assent may be made in any manner sufficient to show agreement. Contractors that negotiate and finally conclude a contract via e-mail or similar means do not face new legal problems. These means resemble the traditional written form. However, if contracts are concluded merely by clicking on icons, it is questionable whether this automatically demonstrates assent. A consumer might underestimate the legal consequences of a simple click on an icon, or misinterpret the meaning of the click. Two fundamental questions arise. First, what conduct will suffice to demonstrate assent? Second, can the use of an electronic agent without the knowledge of its operator create a contract binding on its operator?

1. U.S. Law

According to UCITA, a person manifests assent to a record or term if the person (1) authenticates the record or term with the intent to adopt or accept it, or (2) intentionally engages in conduct or makes statements from which the other party or its electronic agent might reasonably infer the person's assent. UCITA also states that an electronic agent manifests assent to a record or term if the electronic agent (1) authenticates the record or term, or (2) engages in operations that indicate acceptance. According to UCITA, a person can only manifest assent if he acted with knowledge of or after having an opportunity to review the record or term, and an electronic agent can manifest assent only after having an opportunity to review the record or term. UCITA describes what opportunity to review means: a person has an opportunity to review the record or term only if the record or term is made available in a manner that would call the attention of a reasonable person and in fact permits review;[308] an electronic agent has an opportunity to review the record or term only if the record or term is made available in a manner that would enable a reasonably configured electronic agent to respond. UCITA also states that in those cases in which the record or term can be reviewed only after a person becomes obligated or begins to perform, availability for review means that the person must have the right to a return if it rejects the record or term.

---

308. UCITA at § 112. It must be presented in a way that reasonably permits review. A record promptly accessible through an electronic link usually qualifies. However, it is insufficient if the review of the record is so time-consuming or cumbersome, or the presentation is so obscure or oblique that it is difficult to review. Official Comment 8b to UCITA at § 112.

Neither E–Sign nor UETA address[es] the issue of manifestation of assent. Their focus is on equalization of written contracts and signatures on the one hand and electronic contracts and signatures on the other hand. * * * [The] U.C.C. contains [no] provisions dealing explicitly with the manifestation of assent. Therefore, [its] general rule, which says that a contract may be made in any manner sufficient to show agreement, including conduct that recognizes the existence of a contract and the interaction of an electronic record, applies.

2. EU Law

None of the EU directives provide specific provisions as to what constitutes manifestation of assent. However, the lack of guidance through the Electronic Commerce Directive will hardly cause problems. All * * * EU countries have functional contract laws, even though they do not exactly contain the notion of manifestation of assent. All * * * EU countries' contract laws contain a rule which is similar to the United States U.C.C. and common law, which state that a contract may be made in any manner sufficient to show agreement. If obstacles should nevertheless become apparent, the Electronic Commerce Directive requires the member states to remove them.[314]

Like UCITA, the EU Electronic Commerce Directive contains a provision, which deals with the seasonable opportunity to review the record.[315] The Electronic Commerce Directive provides that the Member States have to ensure that the service provider makes available to the user appropriate and effective means of allowing him to identify and correct input errors, prior to the placing of the order.[316]

[As suggested by Zaremba, UCITA's goal to create uniform national law on electronic computer transactions has met only very limited success, principally because of concerns that it unfairly favored licensors over licensees (and especially consumers). Only Maryland and Virginia have adopted UCITA, and at least four states—Iowa, West Virginia, North Carolina, and Vermont—have even passed "bomb shelter" statutes that prohibit application of UCITA against their residents—The Authors.]

CISG ADVISORY COUNCIL OPINION NO. 1 ELECTRONIC COMMUNICATIONS UNDER CISG

(15 August 2003).

OPINION

A contract may be concluded or evidenced by electronic communications.

---

314. Electronic Commerce Directive at Art. 9(1).

315. Electronic Commerce Directive at Art. 10(3).

316. Electronic Commerce Directive at Art. 11(2).

COMMENT

11.1. The purpose of CISG Art. 11 is to ensure that there are no form requirements of writing connected to the formation of contracts. The issue of electronic communications beyond telegram and telex was not considered during the drafting of the CISG in the 1970s. By not prescribing any form in this article, CISG enables the parties to conclude contracts electronically.

RUSTAD AND ONUFRIO, THE EXPORTABILITY OF THE PRINCIPLES OF SOFTWARE: LOST IN TRANSLATION?

2 Hastings Sci. & Tech. L.J. 25, 55–68 (2010).*

* * *

2. Rome I Regulation for Choice of Law

Choice of law in Europe is a branch of private international law that governs the principles courts use in determining which law to apply in a cross-border transaction. The Rome I Regulation on the law applicable to contractual obligations ("Rome I") governs the choice of law in European cross-border transactions. * * * The Rome I Regulation establishes mandatory rules to determine which law applies to contracts with connections in more than one European Union Member State.

3. Courts' Choice of Law

Rome I gives the parties in business-to-business commercial transactions the power to make their own choice as to the governing law. If the parties do not choose the law, the court will apply the Rome I by default, which is the "close connection" test. Article 4 of the Rome I Regulation mandates the law determined partially by substantive field of law as follows shall govern the contract. For a * * * sale [of goods], for example, the contract "shall be governed by the law of the country in which the seller has his habitual residence." In service contracts, for example, the law is "governed by the law of the country in which the party who is required to perform the service characterizing the contract has his habitual residence at the time of the conclusion of the contract." * * *

4. Mandatory Consumer Rule

In Europe, a party's choice of law clause is ineffective in divesting the consumer of the protection of mandatory rules. * * * The Rome I Regulation adopts the consumer's home court rule, which means the governing law of the place where a consumer has her "habitual residence." The special consumer rules apply only to natural persons who have their place of residence in European Union Member States. Article 6 of the Regulation applies to natural persons for a purpose which can be regarded as being outside his trade or profession (the consumer). If a consumer * * * contracts with a business, the contract is governed by the law of the country where the consumer has her habitual residence. If an American software company licenses software to an Italian consumer, the Italian consumer will have an absolute right to have the decision decided by Italian rather than U.S. law because of Article 6's mandatory choice of law provisions. This consumer rule binds U.S. companies if they "pursue[s] . . . commercial or professional activities in the country where the consumer has his habitual residence." Similarly, any software vendor directing activities to a Member State will be bound by the Rome Regulation's mandatory consumer rules.

Article 7 of the Unfair Contract Directives requires "Member States . . . [to take] the necessary measures to ensure that the consumer does not lose the protection granted by the Directive by virtue of the choice of the law of a non-Member country." As a result, America Online, for example, cannot require European consumers to litigate disputes according to Virginia law.

* * *

A. Distance Selling Directive

The European legislature enacted the Distance Selling Directive to guarantee that all consumers in the twenty-seven Member States of the European Union have the same rights whether they purchase goods in person or through distance communications. The European Legislature defines "Distance Selling" as "the conclusion of a contract regarding goods or services whereby the contract between the consumer and the supplier takes place by means of technology for communication at a distance." The Directive applies to any distance contract made under the law of an EU Member State. The purpose of the Directive is to guarantee fundamental legal rights for consumers in contracts arising out of direct marketing, including mail order, telephone sales, television sales, newspapers, and magazines.

The Distance Selling Directive is presumably applicable to all remote software website sales as well as digital information contracts. While the Distance Selling Directive does not expressly address Internet-related transfers of software, scholars argue that the Directive applies equally well to cyberspace and any other digital transfers of information. The legislative purpose of the Distance Selling Directive is to promote cross-border contracts by providing consumers with mandatory consumer protection no matter where they reside or whether they complete the contract by telephone, online, or in person at a bricks-and-mortar retail establishment.

Article 4 of the Directive requires all distance sellers to provide consumers with minimum disclosures about key terms in a durable medium prior to the conclusion of the contract. This information includes the name and address of the supplier; a description of the goods or services sold or supplied; the price of those goods or services (including all taxes); delivery costs (if any), payment arrangements, delivery and performance; and the period for which the offer remains valid, as well as the minimum duration of the contract. The seller must make these disclosures "in writing, or in another durable medium which is available and accessible to the consumer." The supplier must make these disclosures to the consumer prior to the conclusion of the contract or at the latest at the time of delivery.

The EU requires all Member States to enact legislation to guarantee consumers a seven-day-minimum cooling off period or right of withdrawal. * * * Article 6 of the Distance Seller's Directive gives consumers an unconditional right to cancel the contract within seven working days starting from the day of the receipt of the goods or from the day of the conclusion of the contract. The cooling-off period will be extended by a further three months if the supplier fails to provide the necessary information in writing or in another durable medium. The right of withdrawal begins tolling from the date on which the supplier provides the information. The supplier is obliged to reimburse the sums paid by the consumer without charges other than the direct cost of returning the goods. American software licensors, like their European counterparts, may not penalize European consumers for canceling a distance contract and may only assess the cost of returning the item. This European-wide cooling-off period gives consumers an opportunity to inspect goods and reject them just as if they were in a brick and mortar shop. Consumers may also cancel the contract if the seller cannot deliver the goods or services within thirty days.

The consumers' right of withdrawal does not apply to software contracts if the product is unsealed by the consumer. This means that the Directive's right of withdrawal is inapplicable also to click-wrap agreements where the consumer downloads the software from the Internet. By contrast, the right of withdrawal can be exercised if a consumer places a telephone order and the sealed software arrives in a durable medium at home.

* * *

Under the Distance Seller's Directive, sellers must not only make pre-contract disclosures but confirmatory disclosures [of Article 4 information noted above] at the latest when the computer hardware or software is delivered to a European consumer where there is a distance contract. * * *

B. Unfair Commercial Practices

The European Union adopted The Unfair Commercial Practices Directive ("UCP") on 11 May 2005. * * * The UCP Directive prohibits advertising distorting economic behavior. This includes misleading actions (Article 6), misleading omissions (Article 7), and aggressive commercial practices (Article 8) on the advertiser's behalf. Article 6 of the UCP defines commercial practices as misleading if it contains false information or otherwise deceives the consumer. Article 6 covers misleading practices that shape economic behavior, in particular the existence and nature of the product, its main characteristics, and other qualities. Software vendors that advertise the capabilities of their product and then proceed to disclaim them will likely violate the misleading advertising directive.

Article 7 treats commercial practices as misleading if it omits material information that the average consumer needs in order to take an informed transactional decision. Finally, Article 8 provides that an unfair practice includes any aggressive commercial practice which significantly impairs the average consumer's freedom of choice and therefore causes to take him a transactional decision that he would not have taken otherwise. * * * This Directive is a touchstone for identifying consumer protection standards for software transactions, digital media transactions, and Internet-related licensing in the European electronic marketplace.

C.   E–Commerce Directive

European Member States are required to develop national legislation implementing the E–Commerce Directive. The E–Commerce Directive governs the activities of information society service providers ("ISSPs"). The European Union Electronic Commerce Directive took effect on January 6, 2002. The E–Commerce Directive creates a legal infrastructure for online service providers, commercial communications, electronic contracts, and establishes the liability of intermediary service providers for posted content. The Directive also covers topics such as the unsolicited commercial email and the prohibition of Internet-related surveillance unrelated to software contracts.

The E–Commerce Directive states an ISSP established within one European Member State needs only comply with the laws of that state, even if the activities of the ISSP affect individuals from other Member States. If an ISSP complies with the law of the country in which it is established, it is free to engage in electronic commerce throughout the European Union. The "country of origin principle," is the cornerstone of the E–Commerce Directive. The applicable law is the country of origin where the seller performed services. The country of origin principle is inapplicable to consumer transactions because mandatory rules apply to business to consumer relationships. * * * Article 9 of the E–Commerce Directive validates electronic or computer-to-computer contracts except for designated exceptions like real estate transfers or family law.

The E–Commerce Directive requires seller to give consumers disclosures before electronic contracting on how to conclude online contracts, as well as the means of correcting errors. Similarly, users must be able to store and retrieve contracts or they are unenforceable. * * *

D.   The Directive on Unfair Contract Terms

Software licenses are broadly classifiable as contracts and are therefore subject to the EU's Directive on Unfair Contract Terms. The Unfair Contract Terms Directive requires the twenty-seven EU Member States to harmonize rules consumer specific contract laws governing unfair terms. The Directive reflects mandatory rules that supplement regulatory provisions in each European Member State. Unfair terms in software licensing agreements are not binding for consumers. The Directive requires all courts to construe ambiguous provisions in software contracts in favor of consumers.

1. Application to Software Contracts

American software companies licensing content or code to the European consumer market must ensure that unfair terms are not included in their license agreements. The Council Directive on Unfair Terms in Consumer Contracts ("Unfair Contract Terms Directive") applies only to non-negotiated consumer software licenses not to business-to-business license agreements. The European legislature defines a consumer as a natural person "who is acting for purposes which are outside his trade, business or profession." The Unfair Contract Terms Directive applies only to contracts of adhesion offered on a "take it or leave it basis" as opposed to negotiated contracts.

This means that any U.S software company that licenses its product using standard form contracts must comply with the Directive. An Annex to the Unfair Contract Terms Directive is a non-exclusive list of terms considered suspect under Article 3(3). If a given term in a license agreement is not addressed in the Annex of suspect terms, the court may turn to a more general test of unfairness.

* * *

2. Formation of Software Contracts: U.S. vs. Europe

The European Union's Unfair Contract Directive gives, in effect, all European consumers a fundamental right to read, review, and understand standard terms before concluding a contract. The Directive is viewed by the Commission as the chief tool to achieve a fair result and to prevent unfair surprise and oppression. The Directive's purpose is free consumers from distortions of competition which impede cross-border contracts.

* * *

The Annex to the Unfair Contract Terms Directive makes it clear that the consumer is "not bound by terms which he had no real opportunity of becoming acquainted before the conclusion of the contract." * * *

The Unfair Contract Terms Directive is a tool for striking down "rolling contracts" with imbalanced substantive terms even if the vendor satisfies the consumer's procedural rights of having an opportunity to review the terms before concluding the contract. The Unfair Contract Terms Directive calls for rules-based policing of contractual terms giving the courts greater powers to strike down unfair clauses than the American doctrine of unconscionability. In fact, in Europe "if a contract term is drafted in advance and the consumer has no influence over the substance of the term, then it is always considered not to be individually negotiated, and hence subject to review based on substantive fairness." Article 3 of the Unfair Contract Terms Directive considers non-negotiated terms to be unfair if, "contrary to the requirement of good faith, it causes a significant imbalance in the parties' rights and obligations under the contract, to the detriment of consumers."

CORDERA, E–CONSUMER PROTECTION: A COMPARATIVE ANALYSIS OF EU AND US CONSUMER PROTECTION ON THE INTERNET

27 Rutgers Computer & Technology Law Journal 231 (2001).*

* * *

III.   CURRENT E–CONSUMER PROTECTION

[T]here is a substantial amount of consumer regulation within the EU that prevents suppliers from taking advantage of consumers in other countries. The * * * degree of e-consumer protection in the EU is much more advanced than it is in the United States. * * *

A.   *U.S. Consumer Protection*

The United States, in contrast to the European Union, has not enacted a great deal of new legislation to protect consumers who contract or buy goods via the Internet. Rather, the Federal Trade Commission ("FTC") and various state agencies apply traditional laws to the Internet. The FTC has implemented a three pronged strategy aimed at protecting e-consumers: aggressive enforcement of existing regulations, consumer education, and business education. Thus far, this strategy is aimed at traditional fraud conducted in the cyber context. While the effectiveness of this policy in protecting consumers is debatable, it certainly has engendered a growth environment for the Internet.

1.   *Advertising Regulation*

The FTC has the power granted by statute[125] to prohibit unfair methods of competition, unfair acts or practices, deceptive acts or practices, and false advertising. Unfair acts or advertising are those which: 1) cause or are likely to cause substantial consumer injury; 2) are not reasonably avoidable by consumers themselves; and 3) are not outweighed by countervailing benefits to consumers or competition. An act or advertisement is deceptive if: "1) it contains a misrepresentation or omission, 2) that is likely to mislead consumers acting reasonably under the circumstances, and 3) the representation or omission is material" An advertisement is false if it misleads in a material sense.[132] However, the false advertising prohibition only applies to food, drugs, cosmetics, and medical devices.

2.   *Uniform Codes, State and Federal Laws*

* * *

---

125.   15 U.S.C. § 45.

132.   15 U.S.C. § 52(a)(1).

The U.C.C. recognizes both express warranties and implied warranties of merchantability.[140] The remedies for both include rejection, revocation, refund and damages. In addition, under the Magnuson–Moss Consumer Warranty Act, certain aspects of consumer warranties must be disclosed.

The U.C.C. specifies that any "affirmation, promise, description, or sample" may create an express warranty. To be enforceable, the warranty must be more than the seller's opinion or "puffery," but rather, part of the "basis for the bargain." A good faith belief as to the veracity of a statement is not a defense for the seller. An implied warranty of merchantability means that the goods must at least be "fit for the ordinary purpose for which they are to be used." In essence, a seller who is in the business of supplying the particular goods is guaranteeing that they be free of defects regardless of good faith.

In addition to the U.C.C., the Magnuson–Moss Federal Trade Commission Improvement Act[148] authorizes the FTC to promulgate rules concerning the terms and disclosure of implied and express warranties. For consumer goods over $15, the Act requires that any warranties be available before purchase on request.[149] The Act also covers informal dispute resolution processes and the limitation that such clauses cannot be binding on consumers.

In addition to these federal regulations, "many States have initiated law enforcement actions concerning online fraud." They do not, however, diverge from federal regulations. Instead, most state laws broadly prohibit unfair and deceptive trade practices, and further define some of the terms used in federal acts. Though subtle differences in states' approaches to the enforcement of these prohibitions exist, they are largely consistent with FTC in the cyber context because of the aggressive stance the Federal Government has taken in enforcing existing anti-fraud legislation.

Because of the state and federal regulations, the Federal Government has not found it necessary to significantly alter current legislation. As will be shown below, the current state of European consumer regulation affords more protection than that available to U.S. consumers. Therefore, the proposed changes to the Brussels Convention are unwarranted.

B. EU Consumer Protection

As stated previously, there are a number of EU regulations and proposals aimed at protecting consumers. When considered in unison, these directives and proposals offer a substantial amount of consumer protection. * * *

[Cordera here first addresses the various EU Directives analyzed by Rustad and Onufrio above and then turns to certain substantive EU consumer protection rules—The Authors.]

---

140. U.C.C. §§ 2–313 to 2–314.

148. 15 U.S.C. §§ 2301–312.

149. 15 U.S.C. §§ 2301–312.

4. Payment

Currently, there is no specific consumer protection legislation concerning payment for electronic transactions. However, there are relevant provisions in existing legislation. The Distance Directive provides that if a consumer's credit card has been used fraudulently, he should be able to cancel payment or have the sums returned.[181] The European Commission also recommended that when a loss or theft of an electronic payment occurs, a consumer's liability should be limited * * * unless the consumer acted negligently or fraudulently.

5. Guarantees

The EU [also issued a directive aimed at] harmonizing national legislation concerning the rights of consumers with respect to the quality of goods purchased in the "electronic marketplace." The * * * Directive on the Sale of Consumer Goods and Associated Guarantees[184] ("Consumer Goods Directive") is a parallel to the Directive on Unfair Terms. While the latter has been characterized as dealing with the "small print," the former "regulates the 'substance' of the consumer contracts." In essence, the seller must ensure that the goods or services are in conformity with the contract: they must (1) "comply with the description given by the seller; (2) [be] fit for the purpose the consumer made known to the seller;" and (3) be of equal quality to similar goods, taking into account any statements the purchaser made in advertising or labeling.[188] If the goods fail to conform to the specifications contained in the contract, the seller will be liable to the consumer.[189]

At a minimum, under the Consumer Goods Directive, contractual guarantees are legally enforceable under the national legislation of each Member State, and must be set out in "plain intelligible language." However, guarantees cannot provide fewer rights than the national legislation. In case of non-conformity, a consumer may request rescission, repair, reduction in price, or replacement.

6. Dispute Settlement

Because of the relatively high costs of court proceedings in relation to the economic value of a typical consumer dispute, the Commission claims to place an emphasis on alternative forms of dispute resolution, such as arbitration. * * * [T]he basic principles of any kind of dispute resolution system are set forth in the Commission Recommendation on the Principles Applicable to the Bodies Responsible for Out of Court Settlement of Consumer Disputes.[194] Suffice to say they require dispute resolution bodies to operate effectively and without bias towards any party.

---

181. Distance Directive Art. 8.

184. [Council Directive 1999/44/EC of 25 May 1999 on Certain Aspects of the Sale of Consumer Goods and Associated Guarantees (Consumer Goods Directive), 1999, 1999 O.J. (L 171/12).]

188. [Consumer Goods Directive, Art.2]

189. [Consumer Goods Directive, Art.4]

194. 1998 O.J. (L 115) 31, 31–34.

In cases where a supplier in another Member State infringes consumers' rights, consumer interest groups may resort to the Directive on Injunctions for the Protection of Consumers' Interests.[196] This Directive's purpose is to harmonize national consumer protection legislation by codifying the specific instances in which qualified advocacy groups may bring forth cross-border injunction actions. In addition, the Directive helps individual consumers overcome the legal and financial obstacles they face before the courts of other Member States.

Thus, citizens of the EU have a comprehensive set of regulations that protect their rights. Though some differences in standards remain, the EU, as evidenced by the preceding proposals, is working toward the unification of certain consumer guarantees. * * * The goal of the EU is to achieve a level of integration among Member States' laws that is comparable to that of state and federal law in the United States.

* * *

ANDREWS, ELECTRONIC COMMERCE: LESSONS LEARNED FROM THE EUROPEAN LEGAL MODEL

9 Intellectual Property Law Bulletin 81 (2005).*

* * *

III. CRITICISMS OF THE EUROPEAN LEGISLATIVE MODEL

A. *Harmonization*

The European Union has not fully harmonized the laws applicable to electronic commerce. In particular, the European Union has failed to provide a coherent framework for the application of contract law in cyberspace. For instance, no directive specifically states what constitutes a manifestation of assent in the online environment. The result is likely to be a sense of confusion amongst e-businesses about the applicable law, and largely dissimilar laws amongst member states on these issues.

Similarly, although the country of origin principle in the E–Commerce Directive harmonizes many key areas of e-commerce law, there are some important exceptions to the country of origin principle.[71] Most notably, the country of origin rule does not apply to consumer protection issues. As with contract law, e-businesses must therefore continue to comply with consumer protection laws of other Member states. Since member states' laws significantly diverge in this area, the costs of ensuring compliance can be prohibitive. As noted by the European Commission, for example, diverging contract laws force contracting parties to expend money obtaining legal advice on the interpretation and application of foreign law. Although there have been moves within Europe to harmonize consumer

---

196. Parliament and Council Directive 98/27, 1998 O.J. (L 166) 51.

* Copyright 2005, reprinted with permission.

71. Council Directive 00/31/EC, at Article 3(4) and Annex.

protection law, these measures have stalled. It seems likely, therefore, that European e-businesses will potentially be subject to the laws of all member states in this area for some time to come.

In addition, the measures taken by the European Union to harmonize e-commerce are in the form of directives. Unlike regulations, directives do not immediately become law in European member states. Instead, each state must implement the directive through domestic legislation. The implementation process allows each member state to interpret the European directive in question, and as a result, member states have the opportunity to dilute or strengthen the rules set out in the directive. The United Kingdom, for example, received criticism for allowing too many exceptions to the country of origin principle when it implemented the E–Commerce Directive in the form of the Electronic Commerce (EC Directive) Regulations 2003. It was argued that if the United Kingdom allowed too many exceptions to the country of origin principle, then "the aims of the measure would shatter and prove ineffective." Again, this clearly suggests that European e-commerce is not as harmonized as it would seem.

Finally, one must remember that the European legislative model only harmonizes European law. European e-businesses are therefore still potentially subject to the laws of non-European countries.

* * *

C. Comparison to the approach of the United States

Some have argued that the European legislative model suffers in comparison to the U.S. legislative approach to e-commerce, particularly the Uniform Computer Information Transactions Act ("UCITA") * * * Some argue that many of the consumer protection provisions in the European directives create unnecessary burdens for e-businesses, particularly in comparison to similar U.S. legislation. They criticize the "cooling off" period in the Distance Selling Directive on the ground that it imposes significant costs on businesses. Comparing this requirement with the provisions set out in UCITA, which allows consumers to return goods only if the terms of the contract were not made available to the consumer before payment is made,[91] some commentators favor this latter provision. [Others argue] that Article 11 of the E–Commerce Directive (which requires ISSPs to electronically acknowledge receipt of the recipient's order "without undue delay") is another example of an unnecessary administrative burden, and is "not suited to the instantaneous nature of electronic commerce."

The E–Signatures Directive has similarly received criticism. * * * In particular, one critic argues that the E–Signatures Directive is not technologically neutral, because it favors electronic signatures over all other signatures, including written ones. Another similarly argues that the

---

91. Uniform Computer Information Transactions Act, Sec. 112(e)(3)–(4) * * *.

model "locks in" certain technologies. This critic prefers the U.S. approach to electronic signatures in the form of the revisions to the Uniform Commercial Code, UCITA and the Uniform Electronic Transactions Act, because it "recognize[s] the legal equivalency of electronic records and traditional writing without favoring any particular technology."

Finally, it has also been argued that the U.S. model law is superior, because it more clearly establishes how contract law applies online. For example, UCITA states that assent is manifested if a record or term is authenticated, or if an individual intentionally acts or makes statements and knows that the other party will infer assent from those acts or statements. According to UCITA, authentication can occur by adopting a symbol or by processing the record with the intent to authenticate it. * * * These provisions of UCITA [and other provisions of US law] therefore establish that contractual acceptance can occur simply by clicking an icon on a website. The European directives, on the other hand, neither expressly nor implicitly state that contractual acceptance can occur in this manner. Unlike the European directives, [recent US law] also establishes that a contract may be formed between an individual and an electronic agent, or between two electronic agents.

IV.　Analysis of the Criticisms and Lessons for the Future

A.　Analysis of the criticisms

* * *

The most positive element of the European model is the country of origin principle in the E–Commerce Directive. As a consequence of the country of origin principle, e-businesses must generally only comply with the law of their own member state, rather than the laws of other countries within the European Union, even if their customers are based in those other countries. As noted by the UK's Advertising Association, "studying, understanding and respecting the various different laws [of other member states] would place highly restrictive burdens upon legally established businesses." The country of origin principle therefore significantly reduces legal risks and costs for European e-businesses. Admittedly, legal risks and costs to e-businesses would decrease even further if consumer protection law fell within the country of origin principle, or alternatively if the European Union enacted a directive that harmonized consumer protection law throughout Europe. In reality, however, there is a strong reluctance amongst nations to cede control over consumer protection issues that affect their citizens. By allowing each nation to retain responsibility for consumer protection issues that affect its citizens, the country of origin principle therefore represents an acceptable compromise between the desire for harmonization and the reluctance of nations to cede sovereignty.

In addition, the European model fosters consumer confidence by providing consumers with numerous protections, and by ensuring that e-commerce is simple. * * * According to the Commission, consumers were reluctant to engage in e-commerce because they felt that they were "in an unclear and vague situation with few guarantees as to the level of protection afforded." The European legislature responded to this frustration by ensuring that consumers are made fully aware who they are buying from, precisely what they are buying, and the transaction costs involved.[111] Consumer confidence is bolstered by the obligation in the E–Commerce Directive to provide consumers with information concerning the steps needed to conclude the contract and the method by which errors can be corrected.[112] These measures ensure that consumers are neither frustrated nor confused by the experience of purchasing online. Finally, the cooling off period in the Distance Selling Directive aims to make the experience of purchasing online equivalent to purchasing in a shop by allowing consumers the right to return their goods after they have inspected them.[113] The rationale behind this rule is to ensure that consumers are not disadvantaged by choosing to purchase online.

While the European directives create administrative burdens for e-businesses, they are not overly burdensome to e-businesses. For instance, e-businesses can comply with the information requirements set out in the Distance Selling Directive simply by including all of the relevant "prior information" in a set of terms and conditions on their website. To comply with the "written information" requirement in the Distance Selling Directive, the consumer should then be advised to print this page.

Similarly, while the measures taken by Europe to increase consumer confidence will never remove the risk of unscrupulous e-businesses, it is nevertheless important to provide consumers with a minimum level of protection. * * * These consumer protection initiatives are therefore fundamental to the success of e-commerce in Europe.

Perhaps the only real flaw of the directives, therefore, is their failure to address certain key principles of contract law. It can only be hoped that the European Union will remedy this failure in the near future.

* * *

CONCLUSIONS

It is certainly true that the European Union's directives governing e-commerce are flawed in numerous ways. Perhaps the greatest flaw of the directives is their failure to harmonize consumer protection law and contract law. As a result, European e-businesses are potentially obliged to comply with the laws of other member states in these key areas. Nevertheless, the directives bring profound benefits to European e-businesses and consumers. For example, European consumers are provided with significant protections, making the European online environment a relatively safe and easy place for European consumers to visit. In addition, the E–Commerce Directive significantly reduces legal burdens for e-businesses

---

111.   Council Directive 00/31/EC at Article 5.

112.   Id. at Article 10.

113.   Council Directive 97/7/EC at Article 6.

by ensuring that in general, e-businesses must only comply with the laws of their own member states. Using this system as a model provides instructive lessons for proponents of an international convention on e-commerce, such as the U.S. Government and the European Union. In particular, the European experience shows that it will be difficult, if not impossible, to reach international consensus on consumer protection and contractual issues that arise in cyberspace. It also shows that it is nevertheless worthwhile to enact a convention, even if key areas of law are excluded from its ambit.

QUESTIONS AND COMMENTS

1. What is it about electronic communication that creates challenges for the traditional rules of contract law? Separately, what is it about the ability to download electronic content directly from computer to computer that creates problems for the application of, for example, UCC Article 2?

2. Assume that a wholesaler from France places an order on Outbound Organics' website for 1000 watermelons for overnight delivery to France and enters the required credit card information.

(a) What law would govern this transaction and why?

(b) If the CISG governs, could this electronic interaction form a contract? *See* Advisory Opinion No. 1 of the "CISG Advisory Council" (a private project of prominent scholars designed to address important interpretive issues under the CISG). *See also* CISG Articles 14 and 18.

(c) Must the contract be in "writing"? *See* CISG Article 11. Note that, although Articles 12 and 96 permit a Contracting State to opt out of Article 11, only a very few have (and none of those involved in this Problem).

3. Now focus on the purchase by Outbound Organics of the SSHDD monitor from the online retailer in the United Kingdom for $1500. Recall also (from Problem 4.1) that the United Kingdom has not ratified the CISG.

(a) Which jurisdiction's law would apply to questions of contract formation if a lawsuit were filed in a Maryland court? *See* UCC §§ 2–102, 2–105(1), and (especially) 1–105. What if the lawsuit were instead filed in a court in the U.K.? *See* the Rustad and Onufrio excerpt. (Do you also recall the analysis of these issues from Problem 4.1?)

(b) Assume that Maryland contract formation rules would govern the transaction. Could Outbound Organics' online order form a contract? In specific, would there be any questions about a valid manifestation of assent or a valid "signature"? (Note that, like nearly all of the states, Maryland has adopted UETA.)

(c) Would the electronic invoice generated by the retailer's website satisfy any applicable writing requirement under Maryland law?

(d) Given that Maryland has adopted UETA, what is the effect of the federal "E–Sign" act? *See* the Zaremba excerpt.

4. Assume, instead, that Outbound Organics' purchase of the SSHDD monitor is governed by U.K. law and also that the U.K. has implemented into domestic law all relevant EU Directives.

(a) Could the electronic interaction in this transaction create a contract under U.K. law? In specific, would there be any questions about a valid manifestation of assent or a valid "signature"?

(b) Would the electronic invoice generated by the retailer's website satisfy any applicable writing requirement?

5. Assume that a chain of "American style" restaurants in France orders 50 copies of the electronic version of the *Family Cookbook* and, after paying by credit card, has its chefs download the cookbooks directly to their IPads for use at its various restaurants. For a variety of reasons, Outbound Organics has now filed a lawsuit against the French restaurant chain in Maryland for breach of contract.

(a) Would the CISG govern this transaction? *See* CISG Article 1.

(b) Assuming that it does not, what specific law would the Maryland court apply to the transaction?

(c) Could the electronic interaction between the parties form a contract and must such a contract be in "writing"?

6. Assume that an individual in France, Francois, places an order on Outbound Organics' website for a hardcopy of the *Family Cookbook* for use in his home and enters the required credit card information. Would the CISG govern this transaction? *See* CISG Article 2(a).

7. Assume that the *Family Cookbook* has become a big hit in France and that Outbound Organics now is receiving numerous orders on its website for hardcopy versions from fine folks like Francois from Question 6. Reread the excerpts from Rustad and Onufrio and from Cordera and assume that France has implemented into domestic law all of the relevant EU Directives. What special risks arise for Outbound Organics in such transactions with consumers in France? Which aspects of the various EU consumer protection directives are most likely to be of concern for Outbound Organics?

8. Now return to Outbound Organics' purchase of the SSHDD monitor from the online retailer in the United Kingdom and assume that the family members who run Outbound Organics bought it principally for use as a home entertainment system. Do you expect that the family members would enjoy the benefits of the various EU consumer protection directives? *See* the Rustad and Onufrio excerpt.

9. Because of all of its success, Outbound Organics now has decided that it needs a "lawyerly" set of "terms and conditions" for its online sales and has come to you for advice. It has the following specific questions:

(a) Hoping for success with its electronic book sales, it originally moved its headquarters to Maryland on the advice of a local lawyer who said that UCITA was much more favorable for such purposes. Can Outbound Organics be assured that UCITA will apply for transactions with French consumers? For transactions with residents of other American states? Could it ensure success on this point by putting a new clause on its webpage that expressly chooses Maryland law as the governing law (maybe even by requiring assent through a special "click here if you agree" box)?

(b) Outbound Organics wants to have "bold and exciting" advertising of its products on its homepage, but also wants protection against lawsuits by consumers on any basis other than allowed by its express terms and conditions. What is your advice on this? Would your advice be different regarding buyers from Europe as opposed to buyers from the United States? Would your advice be different regarding commercial buyers as opposed to consumer buyers?

(c) In your answers to the questions above, you advised Outbound Organics on electronic contract formation issues in both Europe and the United States. Beyond such initial issues of assent and writing requirements, what else should it do to ensure, as a matter of electronic contracting, that its new terms and conditions will apply, especially in transactions with consumers?

10. Outbound Organics is aware that some produce buyers have set up computer programs to search the internet nightly for the freshest vegetables at the lowest prices (or otherwise to order goods automatically at specified times or prices). If such programs place orders on its Outbound Organics' website, could such purely computer-to-computer interactions form a contract?

11. Not surprisingly, the growth of electronic commerce has spurred efforts toward creating legal uniformity at an international level as well. The most noteworthy measure in this regard is the 2005 United Nations Convention on the Use of Electronic Communications in International Contracts. This treaty may be found in the Documents Supplement and on the UNCITRAL website (*www.uncitral.org*). Like E–SIGN, UETA, UCITA, and the EU Directives discussed above, the goal of this treaty is to ensure the legal validity and enforceability of electronic communications and electronic contracts, including through the interaction of "automated message systems." *See* Articles 8–13. As of 2012, however, only two countries have ratified this treaty (and not the United States). Separately, the International Chamber of Commerce has published a set of optional contract terms (the "ICC eTerms 2004") that parties may use to govern their electronic communications.

PROBLEM 4.5 THE BILL OF LADING: COMPUTERS TO CARACAS

SECTION I. THE SETTING

Sancho and Alfonso (S & A) is a partnership in Toledo, Ohio. It is a broker for various lines of computers. Its specialty is arranging sales of very high quality computers outside the United States. Campeador Computer, S.A., is a Venezuela corporation that buys computers from the United States for resale within Venezuela. Campeador had need of 100 computers to fill an order. S & A persuaded Campeador that the best computer to fill its customer's needs was the "El Cid" model by Vivar, which cost $10,000 each at wholesale. Campeador contracted to buy 100 such "El Cid" computers from S & A. The computers could be shipped in one or several lots. The contract terms were "CIF" and "payment against documents," and the contract price was $1,025,000. The documents, however, were to include an Inspection Certificate signed by Ms. Jimena, a person known to and trusted by Campeador. The contract also stated that Saragossa Sea Shipping Lines was the carrier to be used.

S & A decided to ship some conforming and some non-conforming goods. First, they bought only ten El Cids for Campeador. Second, they bought 20 cheap computers for $1,000 each, and repackaged them in "El Cid" cartons. Third, they produced three "Certificates of Inspection," attesting that Ms. Jimena had inspected the goods and stating that they were "Vivar Computers, El Cid Models," and they forged Ms. Jimena's signature to each one. Then, S & A took the ten cartons containing El Cids to Saragossa Sea Shipping Lines, where the shipping clerk took out a bill of lading form, which had "Saragossa Sea Shipping Lines" printed at the top, and filled it out describing the goods (in reliance on a "Certificate of Inspection") as "10 cartons said to contain Vivar Computers, El Cid Model." The shipping clerk signed the bill of lading, and stamped it "Shipper's Load, Weight, and Count." The bill of lading was issued to "Sancho & Alfonso or order." The goods were actually loaded by Saragossa personnel.

The next day S & A took the 20 cartons of cheap, repackaged computers to Saragossa. The shipping clerk described the goods as "20 cartons containing Vivar Computers, El Cid Model," but this time he forgot to stamp it "Shipper's Load, Weight, and Count."

While S & A was in the shipping clerk's office, they also procured several of the blank bill of lading forms used by Saragossa. Next, S & A took one of the blank bill of lading forms and filled it out with the description "70 cartons marked Vivar Computers, El Cid Model." S & A also forged the shipping clerk's signature—and it was an almost perfect forgery.

Finally, S & A attached a "Certificate of Inspection" and a draft to each bill of lading—one for $102,500, a second for $205,000, and a third one for $717,500—and took them to Citibank for collection. S & A had used Citibank for all its overseas transactions, and had maintained an account there for almost two years. The Citibank officer informed S & A that Citibank accepted the drafts for collection only, and that no funds would be made available until after Campeador had paid the drafts. S & A agreed to that, but also asked Citibank to inform them the moment that funds were available. S & A indorsed the bills of lading to Citibank.

Citibank sent the drafts, and the attached documents, to the Bank of Valencia in Caracas, and indorsed the bills of lading to that bank. Somewhere in the process one of the bills of lading—the one covering the ten cartons of actual El Cids—became separated from the others. It somehow wound up in the hands of Garcia Ordonez who obtained it without paying for it. Garcia forged the indorsement of the Bank of Valencia and used the bill of lading to obtain the ten cartons of computers from Saragossa. Garcia has disappeared.

The Bank of Valencia indorsed the two remaining bills of lading and forwarded them, along with the other two drafts and the attached documents, to Campeador. Campeador examined the documents, was satisfied that the "Inspection Certificates" were included, and "paid" the drafts by authorizing the Bank of Valencia to charge $922,500 against the Campeador account with that bank. Valencia then notified Citibank of the payment and made an interbank transfer to it in the same amount, and Citibank both credited the S & A account and notified S & A of the credit. S & A withdrew all of its funds, and neither of the partners can be found.

In the meantime, the 20 cartons containing the cheap computers arrived and were obtained by Campeador. All of the above facts have now become known. Campeador realizes that it cannot find, or retrieve funds from, S & A or Garcia. However, it wants to know from you whether it has a successful cause of action against either Citibank or Saragossa.

SECTION II. FOCUS OF CONSIDERATION

It is possible to have a cash sale international transaction that does not involve a letter of credit. Such a transaction uses the negotiable bill of lading and a series of collecting banks to require the buyer to pay before it can obtain physical possession of the bill of lading, and therefore control of the goods. This bill of lading transaction can be diagramed in exactly the same way as the transaction in Introduction 4.0, but omitting steps number 2 and 3 concerning the letter of credit.

This problem explores the statutory framework that surrounds and regulates the international bill of lading. What does it mean to call a piece of paper a "document of title," and what can go wrong in the handling of that piece of paper? We consider three different problems. (a) The loss of the bill of lading, followed by the forgery of a necessary indorsement and the possibility of carrier's misdelivery (delivery of the goods to the wrong person under a bill of lading). (b) The misdescription of the goods by the shipper and in the bill of lading followed by carrier's delivery of goods that do not conform to the description in the bill of lading. (c) The forgery of a complete bill of lading by shipper without carrier's knowledge.

Article 7 of the UCC regulates legal relationships arising out of bills of lading, but in this field federal law preempts the UCC for most international transactions. The Federal Bill of Lading Act (also called the Pomerene Act) governs all bills of lading for interstate or outbound international shipments. Other countries of course have their own statutes on the subject, including the United Kingdom Carriage of Goods by Sea Act of 1992. With this multiplicity of statutes governing the terms of the bill of lading and its use, conflicting concepts from overlapping statutes should be expected.

Web sources for further study include the BOLERO web page *http://www.bolero.net* and the UNCITRAL webpage for the new "Rotterdam Rules," http://www.uncitral.org/uncitral/en/uncitral_texts/transport_goods/2008rotterdam_rules.html

SECTION III. READINGS, QUESTIONS AND COMMENTS

PART A. FORGED INDORSEMENTS AND MISDELIVERY

SCHMITTHOFF'S EXPORT TRADE

§§ 15–020, –024, –039 (Murray, Holloway, Timson–Hunt, eds., 11th ed., 2007).*

THE INTERNATIONAL RULES RELATING TO BILLS OF LADING

Although the clauses contained in a duly tendered and signed bill of lading represent in law the terms of agreement between the shipper and the carrier, the shipper has little discretion in the negotiation of these terms. The terms of the contract which he concludes are fixed in advance, and his position is not unlike that of a railway passenger who, when buying a ticket, concludes an elaborate standard contract with the railway authority for the carriage of his person from one locality to another. The shipper, like the railway passenger, is protected by Act of Parliament against abuse of the greater bargaining power of the other party. As far as the shipper is concerned, this protection is contained in the Carriage of Goods by Sea Act 1971, which implements the Hague–Visby Rules. The legislative intention is, in the words of Lord Sumner, to "replace a conventional contract, in which it was constantly attempted, often with much success, to relieve the carrier from every kind of liability, by a legislative bargain, under which ... his position was to be one of restricted exemption."

* * *

Bills of lading can perform their principal function of enabling a person to dispose of goods which are not in his possession only if they are, at least to some extent, negotiable. * * *

Bills of lading, like bills of exchange, may be made out to bearer, or to a particular person or his order. If made out to bearer, they are transferred by delivery while, if made out to order, they are transferred by indorsement and delivery of the bill. In practice, bills of lading made out to bearer are rarely used, as the bill of lading is a document of title which is a symbol of the goods represented by the bill. A transfer of the bill of lading passes such rights in the goods as the parties wish to pass, e.g. the property if the goods are sold and the parties intend to pass the property on delivery of the bill, or a charge if the goods are pledged. It is the quality of the bill of lading as a document of title which, though logically distinct from its mode of transfer, confers great practical significance on the latter: by making the bill of lading "negotiable" the cargo is, in fact, made negotiable. * * *

[One] respect in which the negotiability of bills of lading varies from that of bills of exchange is that a holder of a bill of lading, unlike the holder in due course of a bill of exchange, cannot acquire a better title than that of his predecessor. He does not take "free of equities." This is a significant difference; it means that, where a negotiable bill of lading is obtained by fraud and indorsed to a bona fide indorsee for value, the latter does not acquire a title to the goods represented by the bill. If the same happens in case of a bill of exchange which is regular on its face, and not overdue or dishonoured, the indorsee is entitled to all rights arising under the bill of exchange.

* * *

It has been seen that the principal purpose of the bill of lading is to enable the person entitled to the goods represented by the bill to dispose of the goods while they are in transit. By mercantile custom, possession of the bill is in many respects equivalent to possession of the goods and the transfer of the bill of lading has normally the same effect as the delivery of the goods themselves. The bill of lading is thus a symbol of, or a key to, the goods themselves. This is why it is referred to as a document of title.

* * * The carrier is protected if he delivers the goods to the holder of the first original bill presented to him—even if it is only one in a set—and need not inquire into the title of the holder of the bill or the whereabouts of the other parts of the bill. The bill of lading retains its character of document of title until the contract of carriage by sea is discharged by delivery of the goods against the bill, and the carrier is not responsible for wrongful delivery of the goods against the bill unless he knows of the defect in the title of the holder. If the carrier (or his agent) delivers the goods to a person who is not the holder of the bill of lading, he does so at his peril. If that person is not the true owner, the carrier is liable to the latter for conversion of the goods. In practice, carriers normally rigorously insist on the production of a bill of lading, but, where the bill is produced and the identity of the consignee is in doubt or in other exceptional cases, they sometimes deliver the goods against letters of indemnity which, in some instances, have to be provided by a bank.

* * *

On the other hand, even the true owner of the goods cannot claim the goods if unable to produce a bill of lading. In one case a Canadian company bought six trucks and certain spare parts from a seller in England. The seller shipped the goods from Southampton to Montreal and paid the freight but the carriers refused to deliver the bills of lading (which were duly drawn up and signed) to the seller until he paid them certain shipping charges incurred in respect of previous shipments. The carriers, who alleged to have a general lien on the bills of lading, forwarded them to their agents at Montreal with instructions to hold them until they sanctioned their release. The Canadian company claimed to be the owners of the goods and applied to the English court for an interim injunction ordering the carriers to deliver the goods to them without production of a bill of lading. The Court of Appeal refused to make such an order. Denning L.J. said: "Whether the property has passed or not, in my opinion, they [the buyers] ought to produce the bills of lading duly endorsed in order to make a good title at this stage," and Lloyd–Jacob J. observed: "A decision affirming title at this stage may create grave injustice to some person or persons acquiring a title through the bills of lading in ignorance of the circumstances with which this action is concerned."

Logically, the function of the bill of lading as a document of title is distinct from its negotiable quality. Even a bill of lading which is not made negotiable operates as a document of title, because the consignee named therein can only claim delivery of the goods from the shipowner if able to produce the bill of lading. However, the great practical value of the bill of lading as a means of making goods in transit rapidly transferable is due to the customary combination of the two features of the bill, *viz.* its quasi-negotiability and its function as a document of title.

SCHOENBAUM, ADMIRALTY AND MARITIME LAW

Vol. 1, 820–821 (5th ed., 2011).*

STRAIGHT BILLS AND ORDER BILLS

An order bill of lading is negotiable by endorsement of the order party and delivery of the bill. The endorsement may be in blank (converting the bill to a bearer instrument transferable by delivery alone) or special to a named person.

The negotiability feature of the order bill of lading means that it functions as a *document of title*. The goods are merged with the instrument, and the owner (holder) of the bill of lading has title to the goods. The seller thus can retain control of goods in transit by requiring the payment of the purchase price before the bill is delivered to the buyer. An intermediary bank that extends credit is fully protected by becoming a consignee or by retaining possession of the bill. The goods can be transferred or resold by negotiation of the bill. The carrier satisfies its duty to deliver by delivery of the goods against the bill. If the carrier delivers goods without taking up and canceling the order bill of lading, it remains liable to anyone who has purchased the bill for value and in good faith before or after the delivery of the goods. In addition, the carrier, the issuer of the bill of lading, is responsible for releasing the cargo only to the party who presents the original bill of lading. If the carrier delivers the goods to someone other than the authorized holder of the bill of lading, the carrier is liable for misdelivery.

A straight bill of lading, on the other hand, is not negotiable. A straight bill must contain the words "non-negotiable" or "not negotiable," on its face.[21] The duty of a carrier under a straight bill is to deliver the goods to the named consignee * * *.

The carrier is not required to take up and cancel a straight bill of lading at the time of delivery of the goods,[24] but it is prudent to do so.

WAYBILLS

The requirements of intermodal carriage, shipment of goods in containers, and other technological advances have produced new types of shipping documents with different functions than traditional ocean bills of lading. An increasingly popular and useful alternative is to ship goods under a non-negotiable receipt known as a liner (sea) waybill. This is a contract for the shipment of goods (including loading and delivery by the carrier) by which the carrier undertakes to deliver the goods to the consignee named in the document. Accordingly, in contrast to the traditional bill of lading, the liner waybill is non-negotiable. The goods may be delivered to the consignee who identifies himself as such. The waybill is not a document of title, but merely conveys information. Since the physical document is no longer necessary to the transaction, the liner waybill may be transmitted electronically or telexed between the parties. As a non-negotiable bill of lading, the liner waybill is subject to the Pomerene Act and the Hague Act under American law. The Hague (or Hague/Visby) Rules are generally incorporated by a standard clause on the face of the waybill.

HUAL AS v. EXPERT CONCRETE, INC.

2002 A.M.C. 741 New York Supreme Court, Second Department 2001.
45 UCC Rep. Serv. 2d 882.

[Jeill Enterprises, a Korean company, contracted to sell four pumps to Expert Concrete (acting through an agent, Donald McHenry). Expert paid for three of the pumps via a letter of credit, but it could not arrange financing for the fourth, Pump D705011. Upon shipment, the carrier, Haul AS, issued a separate order bill of lading for Pump D705011, which Jeill retained pending full payment by Expert. Upon arrival of the goods at a terminal in New Jersey ("North East"), Expert presented to Haul's local representative various documentation, but not the order bill of lading for Pump D705011. Haul's representative nonetheless released all four pumps to Expert. Jeill then obtained a judgment in Korea against Haul for

---

21. 49 U.S.C. § 80103(b)(2). The legal status of a straight bill that omits this legend is unclear. It would not seem to be an order bill. The prudent carrier should investigate before delivery of the goods.

24. In Gold Medal Trading Corp. v. Atlantic Overseas Corp., the carrier delivered the goods shipped under a straight bill of lading to the named consignees, disregarding the instructions of the shipper to deliver them only against the presentation of the original bill of lading. The court held the carrier liable to the shipper for misdelivery of the goods on the basis of 46 U.S.C. § 80111(a), which was interpreted to mean that the carrier was bound to follow the shipper's instructions.

misdelivery of Pump D705011. After paying the judgment, Haul and its local representative (the "Haul Plaintiffs") obtained possession of the order bill of lading from Jeill and then brought this action against Expert.—*The Authors*]

In addressing the Hual plaintiffs motion in Action No. 1, the court notes that the rights and liabilities of parties to bills of lading are found in article 7 of the Uniform Commercial Code, the Federal Bills of Lading Act (49 USC §§ 80101–80116), the Carmack Amendment to the Interstate Commerce Act (49 USC § 11707), and the Carriage of Goods by Sea Act (46 USC § 1300). Under both Federal law and UCC article 7, where misdelivery occurs when the carrier is to deliver goods to a purchaser who presents a negotiable bill of lading and the carrier delivers the goods without requiring the purchaser of such goods to hand over the negotiable bill, the carrier is absolutely liable.

"As a document of title [the bill of lading] controls [the] possession of the goods" (Berisford Metals Corp. v. S/S Salvador). "A negotiable bill of lading calls for the freight to be delivered to the bearer of the bill; one who has possession of a negotiable bill of lading is deemed to have title to the shipped goods." Absent presentation of the original negotiable bill of lading, a buyer is not entitled to possession of the goods. Since Jeill has recovered a judgment as against the Hual plaintiffs and the Hual plaintiffs currently hold the bill of lading and, thus, are subrogated to the rights and stand in the shoes of Jeill, they may assert Jeill's rights with respect to misdelivery and proceed as against defendants.

It is undisputed that Expert never presented the bill of lading for Pump D705011 and never paid the balance due for such pump. Indeed, Donald McHenry testified at his deposition that it was his understanding that Jeill would maintain the shipping documents until Expert had made full payment on Pump D705011, that the balance due on Pump D705011 was never paid, that when he arrived at North East it was his impression that he would be picking up only three pumps, and that Jeill never told him that he could remove Pump D705011 from North East. Expert, thus, never lawfully obtained title to Pump D705011 and was never entitled to possession of it.

Expert's argument * * * that the bill of sale, the canceled Korean registration, and a letter dated February 9, 1999 stating that Jeill has not placed a lien and has no security interest on Pump D705011 show that Jeill admitted that Expert was the rightful owner of the pump, is rejected. As noted above, the bill of sale and canceled Korean registration were given to Expert by Jeill at Donald McHenry's request and based upon his representation to Jeill that this would enable Expert to obtain financing * * * to pay off the balance due it. Donald McHenry also specifically testified at his deposition that the February 9, 1999 letter was created at Expert's request for the sole purpose of enabling Expert to obtain financing; its purpose was not to acknowledge to Expert that it had transferred any title to it prior to its payment of the balance due. Jeill, in providing this letter and the other documents, relied upon its continued possession of the bill of lading to insure that Pump D705011 would not be relinquished until it had received payment.

* * *

Accordingly, the Hual plaintiff[s'] motion for summary judgment in their favor as against defendants Expert, Donald McHenry, Howard and Norman Baker Co., and the Bakers for replevin of Pump D705011 is granted. * * *

EDELWEISS (USA), INC. v. VENGROFF WILLIAMS & ASSOCIATES, INC.

Supreme Court, Appellate Division, New York, 2009.
59 A.D.3d 588, 873 N.Y.S.2d 714.

[A client brought a malpractice action against a lawyer for failing to file a lawsuit against a carrier within the statute of limitations. To prevail on that claim, the client, a shipper of goods, had to demonstrate that it had a valid cause of action against the carrier in the first place. The underlying claim was that the carrier had wrongfully delivered the goods to the purchasers merely because they were the consignees named in the bills of lading at issue—*The Authors.*]

The plaintiff sold frozen poultry to a purchaser in Russia, and arranged to have the poultry transported by boat, in three shipments, from the United States to Russia. It hired Orient Overseas Container Line Limited (hereinafter OOCLL) to ship the poultry. Upon the plaintiff's delivery of the poultry to OOCLL's ships in the United States, OOCLL tendered the plaintiff an original bill of lading, in triplicate, for each of the three shipments.

The plaintiff never received payment for the poultry from the purchasers, and consequently did not tender a bill of lading to them with respect to any of the shipments. Nevertheless, without receiving bills of lading from the Russian purchasers, OOCLL released the three shipments to them.

* * *

We held [in an earlier appeal] that, if the bills of lading were nonnegotiable, OOCLL was obligated, under the Pomerene Bills of Lading Act (49 USC § 80101 et seq.), to release the poultry to the purchasers notwithstanding their failure to tender the bills of lading. In that event, OOCLL could not be liable to the plaintiff for having released the poultry, and the plaintiff could not have prevailed in the underlying action against OOCLL.

[Upon remand] the parties conducted further discovery and it was developed that two of the bills of lading, dated January 10, 2001, and January 31, 2001, were non-negotiable, while the bill of lading dated January 24, 2001, was negotiable.

* * *

Inasmuch as there are no longer issues of fact as to whether the bill of lading dated January 24, 2001, was negotiable and therefore whether the plaintiff would have prevailed in the underlying action against OOCLL with respect to the shipment evidenced by that bill of lading, the plaintiff was entitled to summary judgment as to liability for the failure of Vengroff to timely commence so much of the underlying action as sought to recover damages for misdelivery of that shipment. However, with respect to * * * the non-negotiable bills of lading, dated January 10, 2001, and January 31, 2001, Vengroff established its entitlement to judgment as a matter of law on the ground that the plaintiff could not have prevailed on those claims.

AUTHORS' NOTE ON *UCC* REVISED ARTICLE 7

The Uniform Commissioners revised UCC Article 7 in 2003 to modernize it and make it compatible with electronic bills of lading and other documents of title. Forty states have enacted Revised Article 7, and more are likely to do so. However, there are no changes in the substantive law in the revisions of the sections dealt with in Problem 4.5. Thus, the changes in UCC §§ 7–501, 7–507, 7–508 are all stylistic. Those sections of Revised UCC Article 7 are set forth in the Documents Supplement.

ADEL PRECISION PRODUCTS CORP. v. GRAND TRUNK WESTERN R. CO.

Supreme Court of Michigan, 1952.
332 Mich. 519, 51 N.W.2d 922.

REID, JUSTICE * * *

Plaintiff in July, 1948, sold a carload of farm machinery to Hickman, which machinery was for the most part manufactured by Newkirk Manufacturing Company (hereinafter called Newkirk) at Anaheim, California. The manner of the shipment was directed on the part of plaintiff from plaintiff's home office at Burbank, California. The shipment was by plaintiffs' direction made by Newkirk from Anaheim, California, direct to order of plaintiff in Lansing, Michigan.

The questions involved are stated by defendant in its brief as follows:

1. Was the defendant justified as a matter of law under the Federal bill of lading act in delivering the merchandise to Hickman upon the surrendering [by Hickman] to the defendant of possession of the bill of lading? * * *

[The evidence before the court showed that the carrier issued a "uniform order bill of lading" for the machinery to the order of "Adel Prec. Prod. Corp.," and sent the original (by mistake) to Hickman. One copy went to Newkirk and another was retained by the railroad. The railroad delivered the goods to Hickman when it produced the bill of lading with "Adel Prec. Prod. Corp." typed on the back. The evidence, however, showed that this typing was not authorized by

Adel, and was therefore a forgery. Adel sued the carrier, but not Hickman.]

Under its claim that the delivery was justified, defendant cites provisions of § 8 of the Federal Bill of Lading Act, Title 49 U.S.C.A. § 88 [These provisions now appear as 49 U.S.C.A. § 80110ᵃ.] as follows:

A carrier, in the absence of some lawful excuse, is bound to deliver goods upon a demand made either by the consignee named in the bill for the goods or, if the bill is an order bill, by the holder thereof, if such a demand is accompanied by—

a) An offer in good faith to satisfy the carrier's lawful lien upon the goods;

b) Possession of the bill of lading and an offer in good faith to surrender, *properly indorsed*, the bill which was issued for the goods, if the bill is an order bill; and

c) A readiness and willingness to sign, when the goods are delivered, an acknowledgment that they have been delivered, if such signature is requested by the carrier. (Italics supplied.)

Also, § 9 of the act, Title 49 U.S.C.A. § 89:

(a) A person lawfully entitled to the possession of the goods, or

(b) The consignee named in a straight bill for the goods, or

(c) A person in possession of an order bill for the goods, by the terms of which the *goods are delivered to his order;* or which has been indorsed to him, or in blank by the consignee, or by the mediate or immediate indorsee of the consignee. (Italics supplied.)

Under the order bill of lading in the instant case, exhibit No. 7, the goods were consigned to the order of *plaintiff* at Lansing.

---

a. § 80110. Duty to deliver goods

(a) General rules.—Except to the extent a common carrier establishes an excuse provided by law, the carrier must deliver goods covered by a bill of lading on demand of the consignee named in a nonnegotiable bill or the holder of a negotiable bill for the goods when the consignee or holder—

(1) offers in good faith to satisfy the lien of the carrier on the goods;

(2) has possession of the bill and, if a negotiable bill, offers to indorse and give the bill to the carrier; and

(3) agrees to sign, on delivery of the goods, a receipt for delivery if requested by the carrier.

(b) Persons to whom goods may be delivered.—Subject to section 80111 of this title, a common carrier may deliver the goods covered by a bill of lading to—

(1) a person entitled to their possession;

(2) the consignee named in a nonnegotiable bill; or

(3) a person in possession of a negotiable bill if—

(A) the goods are deliverable to the order of that person; or

(B) the bill has been indorsed to that person or in blank by the consignee or another indorsee.

There was no proper endorsement on the order bill of lading, according to undisputed testimony, because the typewritten endorsement is clearly shown to have been unauthorized.

Defendant cites Pere Marquette R. Co. v. J.F. French & Company, 254 U.S. 538, and particularly seems to rely upon the words, "The real cause of the loss was the wrongful surrender of the bill of lading by the Indianapolis bank to Marshall & Kelsey by means of which the car was taken to Camp Taylor and the shipper deprived of the Louisville market", but defendant overlooks the following words, "Concluding, therefore, that there was a delivery, that it was made to a person in possession of the bill of lading *properly indorsed* and that it was made in good faith, the important question remains: Does such a delivery exonerate the carrier upon suit by the shipper when it failed to require surrender of the bill of lading as provided in that instrument?" (Italics supplied.)

* * *

Exhibit No. 7 is on a blank form, "uniform order bill of lading," and contains the statement, "The surrender of this original order bill of lading *properly indorsed* shall be required before the delivery of the property." (Italics supplied.)

The opinion of the trial court upon the motion of defendant for judgment notwithstanding the verdict indicates that there had been submitted to the jury (among other things) the questions of whether there was misdelivery and the question whether the original bill of lading was properly endorsed, both of which questions were evidently resolved by the jury in favor of the plaintiff, as to which questions we find there was a sufficient foundation in the testimony for the verdict. We overrule defendant's contention that in those last recited particulars there was reversible error as a matter of law.

The Federal Bill of Lading Act did not authorize defendant, under the circumstances of this case, to deliver to Hickman the goods in question.

* * *

Judgment for plaintiff affirmed. Costs to plaintiff.

BEECHER, CAN THE ELECTRONIC BILL OF LADING GO PAPERLESS?
40 Int'l Law. 627, 635–638 (2006).*

[I]n light of the increasingly relaxed attitude that many cargo owners have about the role of the bill of lading, industry specialists and legal professionals are considering a variety of electronic alternatives as possible solutions, none of which have taken root in a meaningful way.

A recurring component of these various proposals is dependence upon a reliable intermediary. The substitution of electronic documents for paper

* * *

ones has been explored in a variety of contexts, whether the document in question is a bill of lading, chattel paper or electronic transfer of funds, and users seem repeatedly to have the same concerns. First, electronic data can be lost in the event of a hardware or software failure. Second, when information is in digital form, it is possible to generate perfect copies, indistinguishable from the originals.

1. *Legal Foundations for the Electronic Alternative*

Federal law requires that the carrier provide "a bill of lading" or "shipping document," but the statutes do not require that the bill of lading be on paper. COGSA only requires that "[a]fter receiving the goods into his charge the carrier, or the master or agent of the carrier, shall, on demand of the shipper, issue to the shipper a bill of lading." Statutes regarding bills of lading are silent as to whether the document may be electronic in form, and it does not appear that the Supreme Court has specifically addressed this question. Electronic bills of lading have been specifically recognized by the Ninth Circuit, and by at least one district court in the Second Circuit. The Ninth Circuit has also expressly ruled that "documents" in general may be electronic. While there is nothing on point for bills of lading, many federal statutes specify that "documents" include electronic documents, and many Supreme Court cases seem to assume, without arguing, that electronic documents are included in the definition of "documents." The ICC Incoterms are not legally binding, but they do form the foundation of a large percentage of international transactions. Beginning in 1990, Incoterms made specific accommodation for the use of electronic documentation. * * *

Every indication is that an electronic instrument that accomplishes the functions of a bill of lading can qualify as a bill of lading, even if never reduced to paper.

2. *Early Efforts—Third Parties*

International bodies such as Comité Maritime International (CMI) have prepared model rules for EDI transactions, and entities such as BOLERO have offered their services as third-party intermediaries for electronic transactions. These well-intended efforts have not been warmly embraced, for reasons that are still debated. At the same time, changes are slowly appearing in industry practices, and the industry seems to be groping for a solution of its own invention. Steamship lines have had profitable years from 2002 to the present, and appear to be plowing a significant part of their profits into software and technology development. Buyers and sellers are now frequently opting for alternative documents, such as cargo receipts and waybills.

CMI created rules for electronic transactions in 1990. These rules presumed that: (1) transactions would be conducted using the Electronic Data Interchange (EDI) technology, which was developed in the 1970's; (2) the carrier would act as the custodian of the electronic document; and (3) the parties involved would negotiate the document through the use of an electronic signature based on the use of cryptographic keys. This electronic key would be reissued to the new owner when the previous owner of title to the cargo was prepared to relinquish her property interest. This system depends upon access to and competence with the EDI technology. Many cargo owners and also many NVOCCs do not, however, have access to this capability.

BOLERO has presented itself as an alternative, a third-party intermediary, supported by a consortium of carriers, shippers, banks, insurers, and telecommunications companies. It began operations in 1995, but has not managed to gain a foothold. GT Nexus, a representative example of the many commercial entities in the field, professes to offer a neutral platform "to unite suppliers [and] service providers [and to] create and manage digital documents . . . ." to enable users to create a "digital 'document pouch' that travels [on] its own electronic highway." However, the service simply enables transmission of a digital image of the required paper documents. If the exporter wants a negotiable bill of lading, he must still rely on the paper document printed from the service. As [the] Director of Corporate Communications for GT Nexus conceded, "[b]ills of lading are managed electronically until final, then a copy is printed out by the shipper to accompany the cargo. I do not anticipate that the bill of lading would be retired any time soon."

3. *Early Efforts: Carriers*

Steamship lines also are individually offering "electronic bills of lading," most of which are non-negotiable electronic waybills. Shippers provide shipment information through the carrier's website, from which the shipper or consignee prints out the non-negotiable document at either origin or destination. Because a waybill is used, no document need be surrendered for release of goods. A few carriers, however, offer negotiable electronic bills of lading. American President Lines, for example, offers a document that could more properly be called "U–Print" bills of lading. After the exporter completes the application and screening process, the carrier provides it with a supply of APL bill of lading stock; shippers then enter their cargo data at the APL website and print their bills in their own offices. Australia New Zealand Direct Line offers negotiable electronic bills of lading printed from a web-based program on plain paper, rather than on bill of lading stock. The resulting "original" looks like a photocopy and, of course, has no manual signature. The potential for fraud is stunning.

Courts have not had much opportunity to review these electronic waybills, but the Federal District Court for the Southern District of New York in *Delphi-Delco Elec. Sys. v. M/V Nedlloyd Europa* found that, because the bill of lading terms were at the website and otherwise available to the shipper, these documents constituted evidence of a contract between the shipper and the carrier to transport the goods. This ruling was based on an earlier Ninth Circuit ruling to the same effect. Neither of these courts had opportunity to address the question of whether these electronic documents were evidence of affreightment. Finally, because most of the electronic bills offered are waybills and are therefore non-negotiable even in their paper form, title to the goods is not embodied in the document because the document cannot be used to enable the shipper to control when title will be released to the consignee, and it does not enable any interest to be passed to third parties. It is suitable only for shipments for which no change of ownership is contemplated. When the electronic bill of lading is negotiable, it must be printed before it can be used as a negotiable document. The new wine of the electronic bill keeps getting poured back into the old wine skin of paper transmission.

4.   *Innovation from the Legal Community*

The legal community has proposed solving the control problem through requirements that are outlined in section 16 of the Uniform Electronic Transactions Act. The E–SIGN (Electronic Signatures in Global and National Commerce) law adopted these solutions, and the Uniform Commercial Code (UCC) has applied them specifically to bills of lading in [revised] article 7. The method of document control proposed in UETA provides exceptional security, but involves a level of technology that may place it beyond the reach of many carriers and cargo owners. In consideration of the vulnerability of the current bill of lading system, whether relying on paper or on carrier-specific electronic systems now in use, the international shipping community may be better served by a system that does not reach this gold standard, but which can be made quickly and cheaply available to most participants in the market.

5.   *Alternate Approaches—What to Look For*

To meet the requirements of the law, the electronic bill of lading must address evidence of affreightment, contract of carriage, and control of title. To meet the requirements of the marketplace, the digital bill of lading must be reasonably inexpensive and must be secure from tampering. What is more difficult, it must be easy for authorized users to access and must be understood, recognized and accepted widely, though not necessarily universally. To satisfy the banking industry and other more legally sophisticated participants, the electronic bill of lading should provide a level of security as nearly comparable to UCC section 7–106(b) [on *"Control of Electronic Documents of Title"—the Authors*].

QUESTIONS AND COMMENTS

1.   The transaction involving the bill of lading for the ten real El Cid computers raises issues concerning misdelivery. First, under this bill of lading, to whom should Saragossa have delivered the goods? Second, if the goods were not delivered properly, who has a cause of action—and against whom?

2.   What does it mean to call a piece of paper a "document of title"? This question is the principal subject of the Schmitthoff excerpt. As a first, fundamental step in the analysis of our Problem here, what does Schmitthoff tell us about the legal relationship between a document of title (such as a bill of lading) and the underlying asset (such as shipped goods)? An understanding

of this basic relationship is a necessary foundation for analyzing to whom the carrier must deliver the goods (and, therefore, whether it has "misdelivered" them) when it issues a bill of lading.

3. Schmitthoff gives basic rules concerning negotiable bills of lading, and also indicates the types of sources for the governing law concerning such rules. For shipments governed by the law of the United Kingdom, statutes that parallel COGSA and the Federal Bill of Lading Act provide the applicable rules. Note that bills of lading have their own statute, and thus negotiable bills of lading may be subject to rules different from those for negotiable drafts (bills of exchange). Schmitthoff discusses some of the differences between bills of lading and drafts (bills of exchange).

4. Schmitthoff also illustrates—following a theme with which you should now be familiar—that the law applicable to a bill of lading in an international transaction may well depend on where the relevant lawsuit is filed. Courts in the United Kingdom will follow U.K. statutes; United States courts will begin with our own statutes; presumably, Venezuelan courts likewise would follow domestic statutes in that country.

The United States statute applicable to international bills of lading is often not the UCC, even though Article 7 of that state statute does deal with bills of lading, but instead is the Pomerene Act (Federal Bill of Lading Act), 49 U.S.C. §§ 80101–16. (*See* the Documents Supplement.) The federal statute is applicable to any bill of lading issued by any common carrier for the transportation of goods in either interstate commerce or international commerce from the U.S. to another country. 49 U.S.C. § 80102. This is the statute which, along with COGSA, is the foundation of the United States decisions in the Readings.

As reflected in the *Haul* opinion, however, the Federal Bill of Lading Act does not preempt UCC Article 7 for "inbound" shipments from a foreign port to the United States. *See also* 49 U.S.C. § 80102. Finally, note (again) that the law of other countries, such as addressed by Schmitthoff, may be different in various particulars, even though the basic transaction pattern is roughly the same for international bill of lading transactions.

5. *Haul* and *Edelweiss* set forth the carrier's basic delivery obligation under a negotiable bill of lading: Delivery should be against surrender of the bill of lading itself. Although *Haul* applies UCC Article 7 (for an "inbound" shipment) and *Edelweiss* applies the Federal Bill of Lading Act (for an "outbound" shipment), the result under both is the same. *See* 49 U.S.C. § 80110 and UCC § 7–403.

How are things different under a non-negotiable bill of lading? That is, can you explain why in *Edelweiss* the carrier was not liable for misdelivery regarding the two non-negotiable bills of lading at issue there?

6. Some shippers have sought to avoid the complexities of negotiable bills of lading, and of indorsements, by using straight (non-negotiable) bills of lading with a "surrender clause," which typically states: "Cargo to be released only against submission of duly endorsed bill of lading." The authorities are in agreement that, absent such a clause, the consignee of a straight bill of lading would not need to produce an original bill to receive the goods.

However, with the clause, even though there is no cause of action under the Pomerene Act, shipper has a breach of contract action against the carrier. *See Lite–On Peripherals, Inc. v. Burlington Aire Express, Inc.*, 255 F.3d 1189 (9th Cir. 2001); and the principal early case on this subject, *Pere Marquette Ry. Co. v. J.F. French and Co.*, 254 U.S. 538 (1921).

7. Under United States law, if the bill of lading is stolen and Garcia forges a necessary indorsement and claims the goods from the carrier, is that a delivery or a misdelivery by the carrier?

The Schmitthoff excerpt discusses carrier's duty of delivery—to deliver the goods only to the "holder" of an order bill of lading. The negotiable bills of lading in this Problem are order bills of lading, but who is a "holder"? The term connotes possession of the paper, but also requires something more— otherwise Hickman would have been such a "holder" in *Adel Precision Products* and would have been entitled to delivery. What more does that case suggest is necessary?

UCC § 7–501(a)(1) requires "indorsement *and* delivery" for the document to be "negotiated," and UCC § 1-201(21) then defines the indorsee as a "holder." (*See* Documents Supplement). The Federal Bill of Lading Act has similar provisions on "negotiation" in 49 U.S.C. § 80104, but its definition of "holder" in 49 U.S.C. § 80101 is less precise. Nonetheless, its rule on to whom the carrier may deliver under a negotiable bill of lading provides clarity on the point. *See* 49 U.S.C. § 80110(b)(3).

8. If the carrier does not deliver the goods to the proper person, who has a cause of action against it? Read 49 U.S.C. § 80110(b). In our case, Saragossa delivered the goods neither to the consignee named in a non-negotiable bill of lading nor to a person in possession of a properly indorsed negotiable bill of lading. But it also already took (from Ordenez) the order bill of lading that covered the 10 real El Cids (and then likely cancelled the bill as part of its standard practice). As a result, no one is likely to get possession, and thus become a holder, of this negotiable bill of lading (unlike in the *Haul* case).

Now read 49 U.S.C. § 80111(a) on "Liability for delivery of goods." In the typical case, which party likely will have "title to, or right to possession of," the goods when a carrier misdelivers them? The choice generally will be between the seller/shipper and the buyer. In the typical case, what fact do you think will determine whether seller or buyer ultimately will have title to the goods?

9. The Schoenbaum excerpt notes the increasingly common use of non-negotiable "sea waybills." *See also* the CMI Uniform Rules for Sea Waybills (1990), which reflect standard contract terms drafted by an influential non-governmental body, the Comite Maritime International. The Beecher excerpt also alerts you to the next step in the development of this commercial transaction—the paperless, electronic bill of lading. The payment part of a commercial transaction can now be accomplished without paper-based mechanisms, and the other parts of the transaction are not far behind—and especially electronic bills of lading transmitted by electronic mail. Such speed is necessary when the goods are to be delivered by air freight. However, the security mechanisms attached to the electronic bill of lading are still less than the protection afforded by requiring signatures on paper-based bills of lading.

And, banks are not yet convinced that they control the cargo through their contractual rights in electronic bills of lading.

As noted in Problem 4.2, however, a recently concluded treaty, the 2009 United Nations Convention on Contracts for the International Carriage of Goods Wholly or Partly by Sea, provides hope for the future of electronic bills of lading. These so-called "Rotterdam Rules" create an explicit legal framework for the creation, transfer, and enforcement of "negotiable electronic transport records." Deliberately medium and technology neutral, these rules should both accommodate and foster future technological innovations. Although only one country has ratified the Rotterdam Rules as of 2012, there are positive indications that many countries will do so (including the United States).

PART B. MISDESCRIPTION AND DISCLAIMERS OF DESCRIPTION

TETLEY, MARINE CARGO CLAIMS

654–655, 670–672, 692, 1545, 1552–1556, 1561–1563 (4th ed., 2008).*

Because the carrier is obliged to state the marks and the number or the quantity or the weight of the goods and in every case their apparent order and condition on the bill of lading, it is clear that the carrier must inspect the goods upon receiving them.

The inspection, nevertheless, of the carrier, master or agent is only a reasonable inspection. The master need not be an expert nor need he employ experts.

On the other hand, the carrier cannot contradict the clean bill of lading which he gave by relying on the laxity with which the cargo was examined on the ship's behalf.

* * *

The Hague Rules at art. 3(4) stipulate that a clean bill of lading only creates a *prima facie* presumption that the goods are as described on the bill of lading. Nevertheless, the principle of estoppel has prevented a carrier from proving that the goods were other than as described against a third party holder of the bill of lading for value who is acting in good faith.
* * *

The United Kingdom *Carriage of Goods by Sea Act 1992* at sect. 4, like the Canadian *Bills of Lading Act* at sect. 4, provides a rule of estoppel in respect to the *quantity* of the goods shipped on board. The estoppel is against the carrier in the United Kingdom, but in Canada is against only the master or "other person signing the bill of lading." In both countries, the estoppel is in favour of the consignee or endorsee for valuable consideration.

* * *

The *Pomerene Bills of Lading Act*, 1916/1994 at sect. 80113(a) provides a similar estoppel, but (i) it is against the "carrier," (ii) is not merely for quantity, but for the description in the bill of lading (i.e. marks, quantity and condition), and (iii) the date of shipment, and (iv) is in favour of the owner of the goods under a non-negotiable bill of lading or the holder of an order bill for value in good faith who relied on the description or the date of shipment as shown on the bill. The *Pomerene Act*, in this and many other provisions, is a very superior statute.

* * *

Where the bill of lading is issued in the United States for the carriage of goods by sea from a U.S. port in foreign trade, both COGSA and the Pomerene Act 1916/1994 apply. In that case, the rules of COGSA on the bill of lading as prima facie evidence of the receipt by the carrier of the goods "as therein described" are subject to the rules on that same matter in the *Pomerene Act.* * * *

The United States *Pomerene Act* [49 U.S.C.] § 80113(b) permits the carrier to qualify a bill of lading, covering either packaged goods or bulk cargo which have been loaded on board by the shipper, by inserting terms such as "contents or condition of contents of packages unknown", "said to contain", "shipper's weight, load, and count", or "words of the same meaning".

* * *

When the shipper has loaded and sealed the container, the bill of lading is usually marked "shipper's load and count" and yet at times, the bill of lading also lists the number of packages. In such a case, a "package" for limitation purposes is each of the packages listed on the bill of lading. Because of the clausing "shipper's load and count" the shipper is obliged to prove that each package listed on the bill of lading was actually stowed in the container. Nor is the limitation for a container global. For example, if there are ten cartons in a container and they are so declared on the bill of lading but only one carton worth $5000 is damaged, the carrier may limit its responsibility to $500.

* * *

If the carrier wishes the container to be the "package", the shipment should be described on the bill of lading as "one container". A clause in the general clauses of the bill of lading defining the container as a package is null and void as being contrary to art. 3(8) [of COGSA]. Even when the container is packed by the shipper such a clause is invalid.

* * *

The carrier must of course inspect the condition of the container itself, if only the outward condition, should the container have been packed and sealed by the shipper. In a through carriage case it was held that the fact that the rail carrier did not inspect the roof of the container before giving a clean receipt to the ocean carrier, prevented the rail carrier from proving that the container had been received in a damaged condition.

* * *

The carrier who packs a container is bound by the description on the bill of lading of the number of packages in the container or their weight. Where the carrier receives a container packed and sealed by the shipper, there arises only a rebuttable presumption (*prima facie* evidence) that the goods as described on the bill of lading (including the number of packages or weight mentioned there) were received by the carrier. The presumption becomes irrebuttable, however, when the bill is transferred to a third party holder in good faith.

The carrier should attempt to protect itself from third parties by adding a notation such as "shipper load and count", "said to contain" and even better to add as well "container sealed by shipper". * * * Such provisions overcome the *prima facie* evidentiary effect of stating the weight or quantity of the shipment on the bills of lading * * *.

[49 U.S.C. § 80113(b)(2)(B)] properly protects a carrier who receives a container packed by the shipper. The carrier need only clause the bill of lading "shipper's weight, load and count" or other words of like purport in order to avoid liability for non-receipt or misdescription of the goods.

* * *

The practice of sealing containers with a special identifiable numbered seal is a useful tool in allocating losses. The number is noted on the bill of lading, waybill or other shipping document. That the seal is broken at the time of delivery is evidence that the shortage happened in the hands of the carrier. * * * That the seal is unbroken at delivery raises a presumption that the loss happened before shipment or after delivery rather than during the carrier's period of responsibility.

* * *

If the carrier is unable to inspect the contents of a container before shipment, he should note this fact on the bill of lading by such words as "shipper's load and count, container sealed by shipper." This properly notifies third parties.

JAIN IRRIGATION SYSTEM, LTD. v. CHEMCOLIT, INC.

United States District Court, Southern District of Texas, 2000.
2000 WL 1802069.

WERLEIN, J.

Pending is Ocean Knight Shipping, Inc.'s Motion for Summary Judgment. After having reviewed the motion, response, reply, and applicable law, the Court concludes that the motion should be GRANTED.

In this admiralty case Plaintiffs seek to recover for a misdescription of the goods that they purchased. Plaintiffs Jain Irrigation System, Ltd. and

Texchemie ("Jain" collectively) purchased 700 metric tons of S–PVC Resin from Defendant Chemcolit, Inc. Chemcolit contracted with Defendant Ocean Knight Shipping, Inc. ("Ocean Knight") to transport the resin from Houston, Texas, to Mumbai, India. The uncontroverted summary evidence is that Chemcolit stuffed, sealed, and locked the containers, presumably with resin. Ocean Knight issued to Chemcolit bills of lading which recited that the containers were "said to contain . . .," followed by descriptions that were provided to Ocean Knight by Chemcolit. The bills of lading identified Chemcolit as shipper/exporter. The cargo was carried over land from Houston to Long Beach, California, and then loaded onto vessels bound for India. The containers arrived in India sealed, but when they were opened, the contents were neither what Jain had purchased nor what was represented on the bills of lading. Instead, the containers contained 700 metric tons of soil, lumps of chemicals, and other waste material. Jain rejected the containers.

Jain alleges that Ocean Knight is liable for its damages resulting from the misdescription of goods on the bills of lading. Based on the bills of lading, Jain variously alleges that Ocean Knight warranted the goods and breached the warranty, violated the Texas Deceptive Trade Practices Act, and negligently misrepresented the goods. Ocean Knight moves for summary judgment contending that it is not liable because the bills of lading used the phrase "said to contain" and, as a common carrier, it is not liable for the misdescribed goods under federal law.

* * *

The Pomerene Act, 49 U.S.C. §§ 80101–80116, applies to all bills of lading issued by a common carrier for the transportation of goods from a place in the United States. The Pomerene Act "allows the carrier to place on the shipper the burden of proving the actual number, weight, or type of goods loaded onto a vessel since bulk packaging prevents the carrier from inspecting the goods and noting these exceptions on the bill of lading." A common carrier that issues a bill of lading is not liable for the misdescription of goods when (1) the goods are loaded by the shipper, (2) the bill of lading is qualified by the phrase "said to contain," and (3) the carrier does not know whether any part of the goods was received or conform to the description. *See* 49 U.S.C. § 80113(b).

A non-vessel-operating common carrier ("NVOCC"), such as Ocean Knight, is a "common carrier that does not operate the vessels by which the ocean transportation is provided." In other words, "[a]n NVOCC is an intermediary between the shipper of goods and the operator of the vessel that will carry the goods." An NVOCC can be considered both a shipper and a carrier depending on the relationship created in a bill of lading. With respect to its relationship with an ocean common carrier, an NVOCC may be a shipper. With respect to its relationship with a shipper, an NVOCC is a common carrier. In determining whether an NVOCC is a shipper or a carrier, the court looks to the relationship between the parties under the specific bill of lading at issue in the case.

The bills of lading (which form the basis of this case) were issued by Ocean Knight to Chemcolit and clearly identify Chemcolit as the "shipper" and Ocean Knight as the "carrier." Chemcolit, as the shipper, stuffed, sealed, locked, and loaded the containers. The bills of lading describing the containers' contents each contained the phrase "said to contain," and set forth descriptions provided by Chemcolit. Ocean Knight had no knowledge of the containers' contents except for Chemcolit's descriptions on the bills of lading. Therefore, under the Pomerene Act, Ocean Knight is not liable for the misdescription of goods. Defendant's Motion for Summary Judgment is GRANTED.

INDUSTRIA NACIONAL DEL PAPEL, CA. v. M/V ALBERT F

United States Court of Appeals, Eleventh Circuit, 1984.
730 F.2d 622.

HATCHETT, CIRCUIT JUDGE:

In this action, we must determine whether a vessel may be held liable in rem for non-delivery of its cargo described in a clean on board bill of lading. We affirm the district court which held the vessel liable in rem because it was estopped from impeaching the bill of lading.

On January 9, 1979, the appellee, Industria Nacional Del Papel (Induspapel), ordered 1,500 metric tons of soft wood kraft pulp from Sanca Steel Corporation (Sanca), costing $569,790. In February, 1979, the cargo was loaded aboard the appellant vessel, the M/V ALBERT F, in southern Florida, and the vessel sailed for the Dominican Republic. On the same date, Induspapel paid Sanca.

The M/V ALBERT F arrived in Port Haina, Dominican Republic, on February 19, 1979, without the cargo specified in the bill of lading. Instead, it outturned 505 bales of wastepaper. Induspapel received practically worthless cargo, and sued the vessel and its claimant owner, Fairwind Container Express (Fairwind) to recover the amount it paid.

Claiming to be acting on behalf of Induspapel, Sanca originally arrested the M/V "ALBERT F." Subsequently, the vessel was released upon Fairwind's posting of $344,500 as security, and Induspapel was substituted for Sanca as the proper plaintiff. The district court ruled for Induspapel holding that the vessel was estopped from impeaching the clean bill of lading, and therefore, was liable in rem for the non-delivery of the cargo specified in the bill of lading. The M/V ALBERT F contends the district court erred in holding that it was estopped from impeaching the bill of lading and in finding it liable in rem. * * *

The Pomerene Act applies to all "[b]ills of lading issued by any common carrier for the transportation of goods ... from a place in a State to a place in a foreign country...." * * * Since the vessel was a common carrier transporting cargo from the United States to a foreign country, the Pomerene Act applies to this case.

[49 U.S.C.A. § 80113(a)] of the Pomerene Act provides that a carrier issuing a bill of lading will be liable "[to] the holder of an order bill, who has given value in good faith, relying upon the description therein of the goods, . . . for damages caused by the nonreceipt by the carrier of all or part of the goods upon or prior to the date therein shown, or their failure to correspond to their description thereof in the bill at the time of its issue." This provision codified the estoppel princip[le] which held "carriers liable to consignees and good faith assignees for value for misrepresentations in their bill of lading."

Title 49 U.S.C.A. § [80113(a)] holds the carrier liable for goods receipted for by him but not actually received. The M/V ALBERT F received certain goods and issued a bill of lading describing 854 tons of soft wood kraft pulp, but the goods received did not conform to the goods described in the bill of lading. The vessel, therefore, is liable for the non-delivery of the goods pursuant to 49 U.S.C.A. § [80113(a)].[2]

The M/V ALBERT F contends, however, that the exculpatory provision of the Pomerene Act, 49 U.S.C.A. § [80113(b)], exempts it from liability. The vessel claims that certain words contained in the bill of lading free them from liability. The bill of lading declares that "particulars [are] furnished by shipper;" the bill also states

> the shipper, consignee and owner of the goods and the holder of this bill of lading agree to be bound by all the stipulations, exceptions, and conditions stated herein whether written, printed, stamped, or incorporated on the front or reverse side hereof, as fully as if they were all signed by such shipper, consignee, owner, or holder.

These statements are insufficient to escape liability under 49 U.S.C.A. § § [80113(b)]. The words "particulars furnished by shipper" fail to relieve the carrier of liability under COGSA, and therefore, they do not exempt the M/V ALBERT F from liability under the Pomerene Act. Since COGSA and the Pomerene Act protect the holder in due course from misleading bills of lading, statements insufficient to avoid liability under COGSA should not be permitted to avoid liability under the Pomerene Act. Moreover, the words "particulars furnished by shipper" fail to indicate that the shipper loaded the cargo, because COGSA presumes the shipper will furnish the particulars placed in the bill of lading by the carrier.

The preprinted paragraph in the bill of lading also fails to satisfy the standard in 49 U.S.C.A. § [80113(b)]. The paragraph does not indicate that the shipper loaded the cargo, and therefore, such an attempted disclaimer of liability is ineffective.

* * *

The judgment of the district court is affirmed.

---

2. A holder in due course cannot recover from a carrier under 49 U.S.C.A. § [80113(a)], unless he has relied on the bill of lading. Induspapel relied on the bill of lading. Only after receiving the bill of lading did it pay Sanca.

DISTRIBUIDORA INTERNACIONAL ALIMENTOS
v. AMCAR FORWARDING, INC.

United States District Court, S.D. Florida, 2011.
2011 WL 902093.

In or about April 2009, Plaintiff hired Amcar to load and transport merchandise from Miami, Florida to Guatemala City, Guatemala. In accordance with the Parties' agreement, Amcar issued a bill of lading that detailed the amount of merchandise in the shipment, loaded the merchandise into a shipping container and arranged for the merchandise to be transported to Guatemala. Plaintiff alleges that the bill of lading contained inaccurate information, in violation of the Federal Bill of Lading Act, 46 U.S.C. § 80101, et al. As a result of the bill of lading's misdescription, the merchandise was seized by Guatemalan customs and delivery of the merchandise was delayed for several months.

* * *

Amar argues that dismissal is proper because Plaintiff had the burden to ensure that the merchandise was properly loaded and counted. Specifically, Amcar claims that the descriptive language of "Shipper's Load and Count" on the face of the bill of lading precludes a finding of liability under the Federal Bill of Lading Act. I disagree. Pursuant to the Federal Bill of Lading Act, a common carrier is liable for damages to the shipper when the goods fail to correspond to the description contained in the bill of lading issued by the carrier. 49 U.S.C. § 80113(a). A carrier is not liable when the bill contains the language "shipper's weight, load, and count," the shipper loads the goods, and the carrier does not know whether the goods conformed to the description in the bill of lading. 49 U.S.C. § 80113(b). Ultimately, "a bill of lading containing the recital 'shipper's load and count' places the burden of proof and correct loading on the shipper" who then accepts responsibility for the description and count of the goods. Amcar, however, cannot escape liability by merely inserting the words "shipper's load and count" in the bill of lading. When goods are loaded by a common carrier, as is the case here, the carrier is responsible for verifying that the quantity of the goods described on the bill of lading matches what is actually loaded for transit.

QUESTIONS AND COMMENTS

1. The transaction involving the bill of lading covering 20 cartons of cheap computers, but describing the goods as "20 cartons containing Vivar Computers, El Cid Model," raises issues concerning misdescription. Here, Campeador—which is in possession of the bill properly indorsed over to it—is clearly a holder, and the carrier and banks are running for cover.

2. *Industria Nacional, Jain Irrigation* and *Distribuidora Internacional* explain the approach of the Pomerene Act and COGSA in this area. An independent cause of action under the Pomerene Act was asserted in all three cases. Can you explain why it succeeds or fails in all three cases?

3. The primary fact of concern to Saragossa is that the clerk forgot to write "said to contain" and to stamp "Shipper's Load, Weight, and Count" ("SLC") on this bill of lading. How much difference in the analysis of the problem does this actually create? In other words, what is the extent of Saragossa's obligation under this description?

Test your analysis in each of the following situations by determining whether Saragossa should be liable for misdescription of the goods delivered if the bill of lading refers to 20 cartons of Vivar Computers, El Cid Model, and:

(a) Saragossa delivers 20 cartons of new El Cid computers, but none of them are operational at the time of delivery (no "said to contain" and no "SLC");

(b) Saragossa delivers 20 cartons of new El Cid computers, and all are operational at the time of delivery but five of them become inoperative during the first week (month?) (year?) (no "said to contain" and no "SLC");

(c) Saragossa delivers 15 cartons of new El Cid computers, all are operational and continue to be so (no "said to contain" and no "SLC");

(d) Same as (c), but Saragossa describes the goods as "cartons said to contain" and stamps "Shipper's Load, Weight, and Count" on the bill of lading;

(e) Same as (d), but Saragossa actually does the loading;

(f) Saragossa delivers 20 cartons of cheap "Mickey Mouse" computers in clearly marked "Mickey Mouse" cartons, and Saragossa describes the goods as "cartons said to contain" and stamps "Shipper's Load, Weight, and Count" on the bill of lading;

(g) Same as (f), but Saragossa actually does the loading.

Is Campeador entitled to rely upon those connotations of a description that relate to reliability, or operability, of electronic goods covered by a bill of lading? Or, the contents within a sealed carton or container?

Note that the "contract" represented by a bill of lading is a form, drafted and printed by the carrier, which carrier's clerk is not authorized to amend, full of fine-print clauses in 2–point photoreduced type. Form 11 from Problem 4.0 gives you the idea.

4. If a shipper misdescribes the goods to a carrier, which then issues a bill of lading that misdescribes the goods, why should the carrier be liable at all? In other words, whom is the law trying to protect in such a case?

On the other hand, is the carrier *absolutely* immune from liability if it stamps the bill of lading with an SLC clause? Two challenging situations present themselves in such a case:

(a) What if, notwithstanding the SLC clause, a shipper were able to *prove* that the goods actually were lost or damaged *after* delivery to the carrier? What, then, is the legal effect of a valid SLC clause?

(b) What if it had been readily apparent to the carrier at the time it issued the bill of lading that the bill contained a misdescription of the goods?

Compare the "Mickey Mouse" computers example in Question 3(f) above. Reread the requirements for a valid SLC clause in § 80113(b). On this point about the level of the carrier's knowledge, how much of an inspection of the goods must it undertake? Must it open sealed cartons or containers? Consult the Tetley excerpt.

PART C. FORGED BILLS OF LADING

POWLES AND HAZLEWOOD, MARITIME FRAUD—I*

1984 J.Bus.Law 31.

BILL OF LADING FRAUDS

The bill of lading, with its three functions of receipt for the goods, document of title to the goods and evidence of contract of carriage, may well be described as the lynchpin of international trade. The long standing recognition that it may pass both title in the goods and all rights of suit under the contract of carriage has made it a vital document both in the contract of sale, especially the c.i.f. contract and the documentary credit.

* * *

(i) Non–Shipment of the goods

One of the most simple frauds to commit against the gullible is to sell goods represented by a bill of lading which is either forged on the standard form of a known shipping company or concocted for the occasion using imaginary names for the carrier, ship, master, *etc.* Such "bills" have even been known to emanate from fictitious shipping companies whose only address was a P.O. Box in Switzerland! In such cases clearly the carrying vessel named in the bill may not exist and even if it does, it may well not be involved in the voyage in question. The bill of lading, therefore, is used in such a case purely as a vehicle for documentary fraud.

In such a case, the position of the "shipper" as named in the bill, requires little erudition. He is clearly liable to the person to whom he "sells" the non-existent goods to return the full purchase price. The buyer's major problems [are] finding the trickster and bringing an action against him in a jurisdiction where the court has *locus standi* to hear the action, * * *.

Such a bill of lading may, however, be used, in all innocence by the consignee or other holder, to effect a subsequent sale of the goods. In such a case, the position between the innocent seller and the equally innocent buyer requires consideration.

Where the contract of sale is on c.i.f. terms, the position was made clear in *Hindley & Co. v. East Indian Produce Co. Ltd.* and reflects the basic nature of a c.i.f. contract, namely that the seller has to ship goods of the contractual description and tender the sales, shipping and insurance documents to the buyer. That done, the seller is not concerned with the safe arrival of the goods and their subsequent delivery to the buyer. This led Kerr J. to remark in the above case, "If no goods have in fact been shipped the sellers have not performed their obligation." The fact that the seller is not privy to the nonshipment is clearly irrelevant in considering his liability to the buyer.

Clearly where the sale is on "classic" f.o.b. terms, the problem would not arise as the buyer books the shipping space and takes the bill of lading in his own name. Where the sale is on such terms as "f.o.b. with services" or similar, so that the seller does take the bill of lading in his own name, the same problem could arise as in a c.i.f. contract. There seems, however, no reason why the same rule should not apply, as the seller is in breach of the same duty broken in the c.i.f. contract, *i.e.* to ship to the goods.

In either case, where the bill of lading is a forgery, the carrier in whose name it is issued will clearly not be bound by it.

(ii) Short Shipment of goods

The above comments would appear to apply, *mutatis mutandis,* where a false bill of lading is delivered showing incorrectly the quantity shipped. Where the bill of lading is delivered signed with proper authority, however, be it by the master, ship's agent, charterer's agent, etc., and the person signing is deceived in doing so, problems may arise for several parties. As between buyer and seller who rely on the bill of lading, the arguments in the *Hindley* case would appear to apply, in that the seller has contracted to put a certain quantity of goods on board or that a certain quantity has been put on board and is, therefore, liable if that quantity is not delivered to the buyer.

The carrier may also be liable to the consignee or indorsee of the bill of lading. Faced with the bill of lading, the carrier is not estopped at common law from showing that the reference to quantity is incorrect. The bill of lading is, however, prima facie evidence that the amount referred to has been shipped and the onus is clearly on the carrier to show that the amount recorded has not in fact been shipped. This will require "very satisfactory evidence," and, indeed, proof of extreme probability of any removal of goods during transit was held by the House of Lords in *Hain S.S. Co. v. Herdman & MacDougall* to be insufficient. Only by inserting the term "weight unknown" into the bill of lading can the carrier protect himself.

Where the contract of carriage is subject to the Hague or Hague–Visby Rules, however, statements as to the number of packages or pieces, or the quantity or weight may not be later disproved after the bill of lading has been transferred to a third party acting in good faith. In such cases, the right of the carrier to insert a "weight unknown" clause is limited to cases where he has reasonable grounds to believe that an amount which he has been asked to insert does not truly represent the amount shipped, or he has no reasonable means of checking. Where a carrier is thus made liable for delivering a short quantity he has a right of action against the shipper for an indemnity, as the shipper is deemed to guarantee the accuracy of, *inter alia,* statements as to quantity. Such a right arises, however, only where the bill is signed "by or on behalf of" the carrier, not the master. Even where the right can be pursued, the carrier may face an impossible task in finding the shipper and bringing an action in a jurisdiction to which the shipper is subject.

G. GILMORE AND C. BLACK, THE LAW OF ADMIRALTY

99 (2d ed., 1975).*

* * * Unlike the general indorser of a negotiable instrument, who engages that if the bill is not paid on due presentment he will pay it, the indorser of a bill does not engage to take back the bill if the carrier fails to make delivery. The indorser warrants only the genuineness of the bill and, in substance, his own good faith and authority to transfer both bill and goods; if the indorser is a seller of goods, but not if he is a bank to which the bill has been pledged, he also makes the standard sales warranties with respect to the quality and condition of the goods. * * *

T.C. ZIRAAT BANKASI v. STANDARD CHARTERED BANK

Court of Appeals of New York, 1994.
84 N.Y.2d 480, 619 N.Y.S.2d 690, 644 N.E.2d 272.

KAYE, Chief Judge.

UCC 7–507 provides that the transferor of a document of title warrants the genuineness of the document except as provided in UCC 7–508, which exempts from this duty a mere "intermediary." Defendant bank, which unknowingly accepted a fraudulent bill of lading as security for a loan and, upon satisfaction of the loan, transferred the document to plaintiff bank, claims that it was entitled to the exemption provided by UCC 7–508. We agree with the Appellate Division that, in the transaction at issue, defendant was an intermediary entitled to the UCC 7–508 exemption and therefore affirm dismissal of the complaint.

In September 1991, defendant Standard Chartered Bank established a $5 million line of credit in favor of its customer, Red Rock Commodities, Ltd., for use in purchasing steel billets for export to Israel. At Red Rock's request, on December 19, 1991, Standard issued an irrevocable letter of credit in the amount of $2,107,000 against Red Rock's account in favor of Narahami, Inc., a Swiss steel merchant, for purchase of the billets.

To obtain payment under the terms of the letter of credit, on January 6, 1992 Narahami presented Standard with a negotiable bill of lading issued December 21, 1991 for the shipment of 10,520.4 metric tons of steel billets "clean on board" the motor vessel *Szombierki* in Szczecin, Poland, bound for Ashdod, Israel. Standard made payment to Narahami and debited Red Rock's account $2,261,886 apparently intending to hold the bill of lading until redeemed by the purchaser, Ram Metals and Building Industries, Inc., by payment in full upon arrival of the shipment in Israel.

When several months later Ram Metals had not made payment to Standard, Red Rock sought to free its line of credit. At Red Rock's urging, Ram Metals borrowed $2.5 million from the Park Avenue Bank, N.A. to pay the debt owed to Standard, in exchange for a promissory note payable February 26, 1993. That loan was backed by a standby letter of credit in the amount of $2.5 million issued by plaintiff T.C. Ziraat Bankasi (Ziraat) in favor of Park Avenue Bank. By its terms, the standby letter of credit was payable on or after March 6, 1993 upon presentation of a sight draft drawn on Ziraat accompanied by a statement by Park Avenue Bank that Ram Metals had defaulted on the promissory note. On June 30, 1992, Park Avenue Bank transferred the proceeds of the loan to Standard in satisfaction of Red Rock's debt.

The next day, at Red Rock's request, Standard endorsed and transferred the bill of lading to Ziraat to collateralize the standby letter of credit. Standard and Ziraat had a total of three communications. The first was a brief telephone conversation between the banks' vice-presidents on June 24 regarding Red Rock's need for credit. The other two were by letter—one dated June 30, 1992 reciting in language suggested by Red Rock that "We undertake that upon receipt of these funds from Park Avenue Bank, we will endorse the original Bills of Lading to T.C. Ziraat Bankasi and deliver said Bills of Lading to your Bank," and the other actually transmitting the bill on July 1.

By December 1992, Red Rock had disclosed to Ziraat that the bill of lading was fraudulent—the steel billets never existed, and the *Szombierki* was not even in port at Szczecin on the date of the bill's issuance. Standard was apparently unaware of the fraud. In January 1993, Ram Metals was placed in liquidation in Israel.

Ziraat commenced this action against Standard for breach of warranty in transferring the fraudulent bill of lading, and Standard asserted as a defense that it was a mere intermediary, not responsible for the genuineness of the document. Supreme Court granted Standard summary judgment dismissing the complaint, the Appellate Division affirmed for the reasons stated in the comprehensive opinion of Justice Myriam Altman, and we granted leave to appeal.

I.

Lacking a definition of "intermediary" in the Uniform Commercial Code, we look to the rationale underlying UCC 7–507 and 7–508, in which the term appears. UCC 7–507 provides:

"Where a person negotiates or transfers a document of title for value otherwise than as a mere intermediary under the next following section, then unless otherwise agreed he warrants to his immediate purchaser only in addition to any warranty made in selling the goods

"(a) that the document is genuine; and

"(b) that he has no knowledge of any fact which would impair its validity or worth; and

"(c) that his negotiation or transfer is rightful and fully effective with respect to the title to the document and the goods it represents."

A "mere intermediary" warrants only its own good faith and authority to transfer the document, as set forth in UCC 7–508:

"A collecting bank or other intermediary known to be entrusted with documents on behalf of another or with collection of a draft or other claim against delivery of documents warrants by such delivery of the documents only its own good faith and authority. This rule applies even though the intermediary has purchased or made advances against the claim or draft to be collected."

A collecting bank—which Standard concedes it was not—is "any bank handling the item for collection except the payor bank," in other words, a bank that transfers an item between principals. An "other intermediary" is necessarily broader but still, like a collecting bank, is essentially a go-between with no real stake in the underlying transaction, which is the common understanding of the common word "intermediary."

UCC 7–507 warranties are owed to the "immediate *purchaser* only" of the document of title, signaling that the section contemplates a transaction in the nature of a sale. Indeed, the section goes on to provide that the warranties as to the document are in addition to "any warranty made in selling the goods." The drafters noted that the warranties described in UCC 7–507 "derive from the contract of sale and not from the transfer of the documents". The section 7–508 exemption, by contrast, applies to "delivery of documents" entrusted to the transferor "on behalf of another."

Thus, the purpose underlying UCC 7–508's exemption appears to be protection of the reasonable commercial expectation of a transferor who merely forwards—and does not itself sell—a document of title. While a seller may be held accountable for the quality of what it sells, one who merely transfers on behalf of another—an intermediary—is generally not expected to know or represent its quality. The UCC 7–507 warranty is therefore properly imposed in transactions more in the nature of a sale than transfer of documents on behalf of another.

This reading is supported as well by the history of the sections, which may be traced back to the Personal Property Law and the common law before it. Personal Property Law former § 221, with which UCC 7–507 is "generally in accord", imposed a warranty of genuineness only upon *sale* of a bill of lading. Personal Property Law former § 223—the predecessor of UCC 7–508—exempted transactions in which the pledgee of the bill of lading transferred the bill upon payment of the underlying debt. Applying those provisions to facts similar to this case, the Appellate Division concluded in *Archibald & Lewis Co. v. Banque Internationale de Commerce*, that endorsement and transfer of a fraudulent bill of lading upon satisfaction of a debt was not a sale subject to the warranty of genuineness (*see also, Springs v. Hanover Natl. Bank*, [transferor of fraudulent bill of lading for collection of accompanying draft not liable to transferee at common law]).

* * *

Finally, we find significant that our holding is consistent with the express provisions of the Federal Bills of Lading Act (FBLA) (49 U.S.C. § 80101 *et seq.*), a statute that would have controlled here had the bill of lading not reflected shipment of goods entirely outside the United States (*see*, 49 U.S.C. § 80102; UCC 7–103).

Like UCC 7–507, the FBLA imposes a warranty of genuineness on the transferor of a bill of lading. However, "[a] person holding a bill of lading as security for a debt and in good faith demanding or receiving payment of the debt from another person does not warrant by the demand or receipt—(1) the genuineness of the bill; or (2) the quantity or quality of the goods described in the bill" (49 U.S.C. § 80107[b]). But for the fortuity of the situs of the shipment, Standard—a holder of the bill of lading as security for a debt—would under the Federal statute have been exempt from warranting the genuineness of the document. Uniformity of the law among the various jurisdictions is of course among the objectives of the Uniform Commercial Code.

As Ziraat does not dispute that Standard satisfied its warranties of good faith and authority as an intermediary under UCC 7–508, the complaint for breach of warranty was properly dismissed.

QUESTIONS AND COMMENTS

1. Powles and Hazelwood outline two of the three basic types of conduct which create problems, and the resolution of rights and liabilities between buyer and seller. That, of course, is not our concern in this Problem, since seller (S & A) is long gone. However, it is necessary background for analyzing the rights and duties of other parties to the transactions.

2. The transaction involving the forged bill of lading covering 70 cartons raises issues concerning liability for forgery. Certainly the forger (S & A) is liable, if found—but that may not be possible, so Campeador will seek other sources of liability.

Saragossa did not issue the bill of lading, and it did not authorize it. The Federal Bill of Lading Act (FBLA) creates liability for "nonreceipt" of goods by carriers only in connection with bills of lading that they "issue." *See* 49 U.S.C. § 80113(a). Therefore, it will be difficult to place liability on Saragossa (in absence of some clever claim that it was culpably negligent for permitting access to its blank bill of lading forms—but carriers routinely give such access to brokers, freight forwarders, shippers and their agents for them to fill out at their loading facilities).

As to the forged "Inspection Certificates," there is no evidence of any complicity, or even negligence, by Ms. Jimena, so this option is likely foreclosed for Compeador as well.

3. If Campeador is not likely to recover from Saragossa, does it have any causes of action against the banks that handled the forged paper? Here, it is important to focus on which piece of paper was, in fact, forged upon issuance. The bill of lading is forged; the draft is not. Moreover, a broad consensus holds that the specific liability rules for forged drafts do not apply to forged bills of lading.

Even if the general rules governing drafts (as one form of "negotiable instruments") were to be relevant, an action by Compeador on that basis would face a variety of complicated issues: First—following our common theme in international business transactions—, what is the governing law?; and second, what are the substantive rules concerning causes of actions on drafts? United States law (UCC Articles 3 and 4) is most likely to be the applicable law concerning the draft, if it was issued by S & A in the United States. The fact that it was payable in Venezuela might undermine that assertion, however, and make Venezuelan law arguably applicable.

If U.S. law applies, Compeador likely has no claim against the banks on the draft. UCC § 3–418 would make payment by Compeador final as against a person who in good faith acted in reliance on the payment, and it certainly appears that both Bank of Valenzia and Citibank satisfy that test. Moreover, it is likely that neither breached any of the warranties under UCC § 3–417, because the draft here in fact was not forged. More generally, a bank's basic obligations when handling a documentary draft for its customer clearly do not extend to the goods in the underlying transaction. *See* UCC § 4–503 (stating that, other than following its customer's instructions, such a bank "is under no obligation with the respect to the goods represented by the documents").

4. Compeador of course also may be able to pursue an action in Venezuela; and in fact wide differences exist in negotiable instruments law throughout the world. These differences led the United Nations Commission on International Trade Law some time ago to draft a Convention on International Bills of Exchange and Promissory Notes in an effort to bring cross-jurisdictional uniformity. *See* 28 I.L.M. 176 (1988). Only five countries have ratified this treaty, however, and none of those potentially involved in our transaction.

5. The bill of lading was the piece of paper that was, in fact, forged. Compeador now has a bill of lading that confers no rights against Saragossa, but Compeador already authorized the Bank of Valencia to debit its account. Campeador would like to rescind that transaction due to mistake of fact, or to proceed against the bank on the grounds that it impliedly warranted the genuineness of the bill of lading.

6. As noted above, if Compeador were to file suit in the U.S. over the forged bill of lading for the 70 cartons of computers, the FBLA will govern, because the bill covers a shipment from the U.S. to a foreign country. 49 U.S.C. § 80102. Regarding the possible liability of transferors of bills of lading, the relevant provision is 49 U.S.C. § 80107 (see the Document Supplement). Gilmore and Black state the traditional view on the warranties made

by transferors of bills of lading. Unfortunately, however, the authority on § 80107 is extremely limited.

Ziraat Bankasi addressed the legal situation of intermediary banks; but because the shipment there was entirely outside of the United States, the court applied UCC Article 7, not the FBLA. The court notes that under UCC Article 7 a "mere intermediary" warrants only good faith and its own authority to transfer. This provision raises a few difficult questions, however: First, how does one define the term "intermediary" (a matter that vexed the court in *Ziraat Bankasi*)? In addition, must a bank indicate in some way that it is acting as a mere intermediary in order to enjoy the protection in UCC § 7–508? If not, how do other parties in a transaction know whether a bank is an intermediary or not? As an illustration, what did all of this mean for the innocent transferee of the forged bill of lading in *Ziraat Bankasi*? Does this rule make any policy sense? Any commercial sense? What might be done to distribute the loss among innocent parties more efficiently in such a case?

7. *Ziraat Bankasi* indicates in dicta that the result would have been the same under the FBLA. But note, first, that the factual position of the transferor bank in that case is different from that of Citibank in our Problem. Moreover, the FBLA has no express exception for "mere intermediaries."

Nonetheless, § 80107(a) states that a transferor of a bill of lading is not liable for the substantive transfer warranties set forth there if "a contrary intention appears." We are focusing here on banks that transfer bills of lading for their customers. What in your view would be the minimum factual circumstance necessary for such a "contrary intention" to "appear" and thus relieve a transferor bank from liability? If such a contrary intention is indicated, who bears the loss for forged bills of lading under the FBLA?

8. Finally, the FBLA's protection of transferors that express a "contrary intention" in bills of lading also is consistent with the basic principles discussed in Part B above regarding the misdescription of goods in a bill of lading. (Recall the analysis of "SLC" clauses in Part B). In addition, as we will see in more detail in Problem 5.1 below, the uniform rules for letters of credit (the "UCP") also firmly separate the bank (and its responsibilities in handling letter of credit documents such as bills of lading) from the underlying sales transaction. *See* UCP Article 5 ("Banks deal with documents and not with goods, services or performance to which the documents may relate.").

CHAPTER 5

FINANCING THE INTERNATIONAL SALE OF GOODS

■ ■ ■

INTRODUCTION 5.0   LETTERS OF CREDIT

The cases arising out of letters of credit read like a survey of modern diplomatic and economic history. The start of every war, many revolutions, and realignments of a government of a country can cause disruptions serious enough to lead to letter of credit litigation—although in peaceful times, the amount is substantially reduced. Thus, a reading of modern letter of credit cases is a review of Middle East wars and revolutions, Indian subcontinent wars, World War II (if you go back far enough), and high-profile international bankruptcies (such as Enron Corp.).

The buyer who has arranged the issuance of a letter of credit has at least four different categories of potential problems. First, there is the possibility that the buyer's bank will pay when the documents are not those specified by the letter of credit. Second, there is the possibility that the buyer's bank may refuse to pay when the documents do conform to the letter of credit. Third, and more likely than either of the above, is that the parties may get into an argument about whether the documents conform or not. Finally, the buyer's bank may "know" (or, at least, be told) that the seller has breached the sales contract by shipping nonconforming goods (under conforming documents) before it pays against the documents.

As to the first three problems, the legal rules—at least when stated in the abstract—are very clear: The bank must pay before the goods arrive, so it has only the documents to rely upon. There is no room in documentary transactions for the doctrine of substantial performance. All of the obligations of all of the parties must be measured by the documents tendered, and must not encompass anything outside "the four corners" of the documents. And, the documents tendered must be "perfect" and strictly comply with the letter of credit, as issued. All that sounds nice and predictable. But, do you really believe that failure to dot an "i" or to cross a "t" or a misspelling will send a $1,000,000 deal down the drain?

Remember that these are contracts, and thus are subject to interpretation from time to time.

Many terms have been used and construed enough to become terms of art and have a settled meaning: A "clean credit" is one which requires no bill of lading; a "documentary credit" does require a bill of lading. A "clean bill of lading" requirement cannot be met by a "foul bill of lading," in which the carrier has noted that there is patent damage to the cartons shipped. An "on board bill of lading" requirement is not satisfied by a "carrier's receipt;" but a requirement for a "bill of lading" is usually met by a carrier's receipt. The description in the bill of lading may be vague, but the goods must be described in the invoice, even when no inspection certificate is required—"11 cartons of unknown stuff" usually will not do. (Customs personnel get upset about that.)

FOLSOM, GORDON AND SPANOGLE, INTERNATIONAL BUSINESS TRANSACTIONS IN A NUTSHELL

163–167 (8th ed., 2009).*

Although the irrevocable documentary letter of credit is used most often in international commercial transactions, documentary letters may be also "revocable," giving the beneficiary a right to payment "unless previously canceled" by the account party. * * * Letters of credit may be "sight" (payable on demand) or "time" (such as, six months following presentation of documents). * * * A "general" letter of credit does not restrict the beneficiary's right to transfer its rights thereunder, while a "special" letter of credit limits permissible transferees, usually to one or more banks. A letter of credit is "fixed" if it can become "exhausted" either when drafts for payment have been drawn by beneficiary for the full amount of the letter or when the time period for drawing upon the letter has expired.

Brokers of goods have a problem because they often have two transactions in the same goods. They will sell the goods to a buyer in one transaction and then buy them from a supplier in a separate transaction. If both sales transactions involve payment by letters of credit, the broker will be the beneficiary (seller) of the letter of credit in the first transaction and the account party (buyer) in the second. If the documents required by each letter of credit are *identical,* the broker can assign its rights in the first credit to the issuing bank of the second credit. Such arrangements are facilitated if the credits specify the use of time drafts (e.g., "pay 30 days after sight"). This arrangement is a "back to back credit" and allows broker to finance its purchase of the goods from supplier with the credit of its buyer. Such arrangements work more easily using general letters of credit, although special credits can be used by giving an issuing bank a security interest in its proceeds.

---

* Copyright © 2009 and reprinted with permission of Thomson Reuters.

However, back to back credits can also become unworkable if one of the credits is amended, and no similar amendment is made to the other credit. Thus, most banks prefer not to use the back to back letter of credit transaction. Instead, they recommend that sellers and brokers obtain financing through a "transferable letter of credit" or an "assignment of proceeds" from a letter of credit.

A transferable letter of credit is one that expressly states that it can be transferred by the original beneficiary to third parties, who become new and substitute beneficiaries. * * * Thus, a broker who is the beneficiary of a transferable letter of credit can use its rights under that credit to finance the purchase of the goods from suppliers by transferring part of the broker's rights under the credit to the suppliers. Partial transfers are allowed, so the broker can use this device to finance purchases from several suppliers. However, although substitute commercial invoices and drafts may be used, all other necessary documents must be presented to the original account party, which will reveal the identity of the substitute beneficiary. That may compromise commercially sensitive information, and so brokers tend to avoid use of such credits.

The beneficiary of a letter of credit may irrevocably assign a portion of the credit's proceeds to a third party. If the proceeds are assigned, the advising bank notifies the assignee of the assignment. Thus, a broker who is the beneficiary of a letter of credit that permits assignment of proceeds can use its rights under that credit to finance the purchase of the goods from a supplier by assigning a part of the broker's rights under the credit to the supplier. The assignment of proceeds does not change the parties to a letter of credit. The original account party is obligated to pay only if it receives documents which conform to the credit, so the assignee will not be paid unless it ships the goods using conforming documents. The assignee is not a party to the original credit, it may not know what the terms of the credit are, and must trust the broker (the original beneficiary) to fulfill those terms. The assignment is not governed by the UCP, but by the applicable law of contract.

Rapid expansion of turn-key construction contracts (e.g., for building a complete steel mill or cement plant needing someone only to "turn a key" to begin plant operation) has expanded use of "revolving" letters of credit as a vehicle for ensuring that contractors are given progress payments promptly as initial construction phases are completed and to permit further construction phases to occur. Revolving letters of credit are usually clean (no documents required), sight letters which work in the same way and are subject to the same legal rules for fixed letters of credit. But there are differences—first, the importer (often a third world host government) pays, by way of a letter of credit, to import services (building skills) and raw materials rather than finished goods, and second the importer (account party) restores the amount of the letter (by payment to issuer) to an agreed level of further payment to beneficiary (the foreign construction company) following each time that beneficiary has drawn upon the letter for payment. Revolving letters may be documentary (requiring presentation of a certificate of construction phase completion), but "red tape" in obtaining such interim certifications prompts many contractors to seek less formal arrangements, requiring the account party to trust the contractor not to draw upon the letter before such action is appropriate. As a result, the payment ceiling (amount) of the revolving letter will usually be a modest fraction of the total value of the construction contract.

PROBLEM 5.1   THE LETTER OF CREDIT AND ELECTRONIC COMMUNICATION: GOLD WATCH PENS FOR FRANCE

SECTION I.   THE SETTING

On September 4, 2012, the Banque Nationalisee de Paris (BNP) opened a documentary credit in favor of the beneficiary, Shady Lane Enterprises (Shady) in Jersey City, by sending an inter-bank message via the SWIFT system to Metrobank (Metro) in New York. The message also requested that Metro both advise the beneficiary and confirm the credit. The SWIFT message (using appropriate SWIFT codes* and the international date system DD–MM–YYYY) read as follows:

––––––––––Message Header––––––––––

SWIFT output delivery status: 700 Issue of Documentary Credit

Sent by: BNPFFR33PPX–Banque Nationalisee de Paris, France

Sent to: Metrobank, NA, New York, NY USA

Message output Reference: 120904BNPFFR33PPX883948726

––––––––––Message Text 04 09 2012––––––––––

20:	Documentary credit number: 16567
31C:	Date of Issue: September 04, 2012
31D:	Date and place of expiry: September 25, 2012/New York, NY USA
32B:	Currency code amount Forty Nine Thousand Seven Hundred Fifty U.S. Dollars (USD 49,750.00), Partial Payments Not Permitted
40A:	Form of documentary credit Irrevocable
40E:	Applicable Rules UCP (2007 Revision), No. 600
41D:	Available with ... by ... Draft(s) drawn on Banque Nationalisee de Paris
42C:	Drafts at At Sight for Full Invoice Value
42D:	Drawee—Name and Address

* Society for Worldwide Interbank Financial Telecommunication, available at www.swift.com

Banque Nationalisee de Paris, Paris France

43P: Partial shipments
Not Permitted

43T: Transhipments
Not Permitted

44A: On board/disp/taking charge at/from
Northeast USA Airport

44B: For transportation to
De Gaulle Airport, Paris, France

45A: Description of goods and services
-11,000 Gold LCD Watch Pens with Box at USD 4.00/unit, CIF De Gaulle Airport
-700 LCD Lighters with Clock and Box (Model Cartier) at USD 5.75/unit, CIF De Gaulle Airport
-300 LCD Lighters with Clock and Box, in Colours White, Blue and Red, 100 Units of Each Colour at USD 5.75/unit, CIF De Gaulle Airport
-All Boxes to be Marked: U.G. Printed in USA, of Hong Kong Origin
-All goods shall be in proper working order

46A: Documents required
-Air Consignment Notes or Air Waybills Made Out in Our Name Marked "Air–Freight Pre–Paid", showing documentary credit number; Notify: Applicant
-Signed commercial invoice, in six (6) copies, marked CIF De Gaulle Airport, and made out in the name of Applicant
-Insurance Policy or Certificate for 110% CIF value covering All Risks from Warehouse to Warehouse, evidencing that claims are payable in Import Country
-Copy of Packing List
-A Draft Marked: "Drawn under Documentary Credit No. 16567 of Banque Nationalisee de Paris"

47A: Additional conditions
This credit is subject to the Uniform Customs and Practice for Documentary Credits, 2007 Revision, I.C.C. Publication No. 600

48: Period of presentation
Documents Must be Presented for Payment Within 3 (Three) Days of Date of Shipment

49: Confirmation instructions
Add Your Confirmation in Letter to Beneficiary

50: Applicant
Galleries Rochambeau, Paris, France

52A: Issuing bank
Banque Nationalisee de Paris, Main Office, Paris, France

57D: Advise through bank
Metrobank to Advise Beneficiary and Acknowledge Receipt to Issuer

59: Beneficiary
Shady Lane Enterprises, Inc., P.O. Box 6341 JSQ. Station, Jersey City, New Jersey, USA

72: Sender to receiver information
This is operative instrument, no further letters to be sent

78: Instruction to pay/accept/negot. bank
Documents to be Promptly Forwarded to Us

– – – – – – – – – Message End – – – – – – – – –

That same day, Metro confirmed this credit in a hardcopy letter to Shady that in all relevant respects was identical to the electronic SWIFT message it had received from BNP.

On September 25, 2012 (within three days of the shipment of the goods), Shady appeared at Metro's headquarters and presented all of the documents required by the letter of credit. Unfortunately, however, the documents described the goods as "ICD" (not "*L*CD"). (It seems that a new Shady manager simply misread the letter of credit as referring to *I*CD and his staff then replicated the error in preparing the relevant documents.) Moreover, all of the six required commercial invoices had a stamped signature along with the words "original" and "pro forma." Nonetheless, thinking that these were not matters for concern, a Metro manager honored the presentation a few days later by accepting the documents and paying Shady the full amount stated in the letter of credit.

Metro then promptly sent an electronic notice to BNP that the credit had been used and that it had charged BNP's account at Metro in the same amount. Problems arose, however, when BNP received the hardcopy documents from Metro on October 3. First, BNP noticed the ICD vs. LCD issue. Moreover, in the meantime the goods arrived and—although they are in fact LCD pens and lighters—Galleries believes that the quality is substantially below accepted standards for LCD products. This set off a series of meetings between BNP and Galleries over what BNP should do, a process that ran through the weekend and until October 9. On that day, Metro received the following electronic notice from BNP:

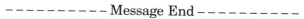

– – – – – – – – – Message Text 09 10 2012 – – – – – – – – –

With reference to your presentation on our L/C 16567, we note the following discrepancies: (1) Our credit requires goods of "LCD" description and the documents describe goods as "ICD"; (2) the goods are not in "proper working order" as stated in the credit; (3) among the presentation documents was a copy of the original offer from Galleries, which is not required by the credit and has unnecessary additional information; and (4) no "original" commercial invoice presented.

We thus refuse to accept the documents and hold them at your disposal. Please recredit our account with yourselves in full amount.

– – – – – – – – – Message End – – – – – – – – –

The next day (October 10), Metro received another electronic notice from BNP stating as follows:

– – – – – – – – – Message Text 10 10 2012 – – – – – – – – –

In addition to discrepancies stated in our notice to you of 9 October 2012, we note the following discrepancy in your presentation on our L/C 16567: (5) and all invoices were marked "pro forma."

We thus refuse to accept the documents and hold them at your disposal. Please recredit our account with yourselves in full amount.

–––––––––– Message End ––––––––––

Metro has come to you for advice. Because of the relatively small amount involved, the parties will not investigate the facts further, but also are not likely to litigate. Metro thus instead wants advice on its legal situation for its negotiations with BNP. In specific, it wants to know whether it was entitled to payment from BNP (that is, to debit BNP's account) on the basis of the documents it received from Shady and then presented to BNP.

SECTION II.   FOCUS OF CONSIDERATION

If BNP is to pay against documents, the documents must be specified in the letter of credit. They will usually include at least bills of lading, commercial invoices, and insurance certificates, all to be accompanied by a draft, as in the ordinary bill of lading transaction. They are also likely to include customs documents and inspection certificates, because Galleries will take extra precautions to ensure that the goods are conforming, since BNP will pay against documents. The documents listed in the letter of credit should be the same as those required by the contract for the sales of goods. However, parties have been known to take short-cuts in describing documents—and descriptions of documents are sometimes negotiated after the sale of goods has been contracted for.

Since Galleries and BNP are paying against documents, it should be clear that the documents offered by Shady must conform strictly to the letter of credit contract. This is not a proper setting for substantial performance, and BNP should be expected to be cautious, to insist on strict compliance. If the documents comply strictly, BNP is protected even if the agreement between Galleries and Shady to sell goods falls apart. If they do not comply strictly, BNP has at least brought a lawsuit, and at worst it may have paid out its own funds to buy worthless goods. As you might suspect, the concept of "strict compliance" is open to interpretation.

However, if Shady (or carrier) fails to dot an "i" or to cross a "t", does that excuse payment? Is there no recognition of commercial custom, trade practice, or simple typographical errors? Note that we have already seen some interpretation in this area of the law ("shipper's load, weight, and count" vs. "clean bills of lading"—Problem 4.2). One purpose of this problem is to explore further these interpretative concepts.

If there was no strict compliance in these documents, a second issue arises: Who bears the loss due to the discrepancies? How are losses allocated under the contract, or under the law applicable to this transaction?

Web sources for further study include the International Chamber of Commerce "Banking Technique and Practice" web page *http://www.*

iccwbo.org/policy/banking and the SWIFT (Society for Worldwide Interbank Financial Telecommunication) webpage, http://www.swift.com.

If this transaction is governed by the UCC, it is essential to read UCC §§ 5–107, 5–108 and 5–116, set forth in the Documents Supplement.

SECTION III. READINGS, QUESTIONS AND COMMENTS

What laws can apply? Article 5 of the UCC was clearly designed to apply to letters of credit. There is an alternative set of "rules," but they have not been enacted by a nation or state. This is the Uniform Customs and Practice for Documentary Credits (UCP), published first in 1933 by the International Chamber of Commerce (I.C.C.), and regularly updated thereafter. The current version is Publication No. 600 (2007 Revision). The UCP constitutes a rather detailed manual of operations, but they are a restatement of "custom" in the industry, and they do not purport to be law. However, as you can see from the cases, banks ordinarily specify that their letters of credit are "subject to" the UCP. Revised UCC § 5–116(c) also expressly validates such incorporations of the UCP in letters of credit.

A body of decisions is developing under the UCP. Some of these are decisions of courts in many different nations, but the I.C.C. also has a Banking Commission which renders advisory opinions on queries related to the UCP. These opinions include: 1) a commercial invoice describing the goods as "secondhand," when no such term appeared in the credit, would be non-conforming and unacceptable, and 2) a commercial invoice stating the brand name of the goods, when the brand name was not stated in the credit, would be considered conforming and acceptable. In the latter case, the Commission observed that banks should not act like robots, but should check each case individually, and use their judgment. In recent decisions on new provisions in UCP 600, the Commission also has opined that (1) although a bank generally must disregard documents not required by a credit, a discrepancy would arise if a beneficiary presented such a document and it contained data that directly conflicted with required data in the letter of credit, and (2) a simple misquoting of one number of a letter of credit in a bill of lading did not justify dishonor where the documents were presented to the correct bank and otherwise referred to the correct letter of credit.

UCC § 5–116(b) provides that issuing banks and confirming banks are each governed by the law of the jurisdiction in which they are located, thus providing different rules for different parties to the same transaction. There are no choice of law provisions for applicants or beneficiaries.

PIETRZAK, SLOPING IN THE RIGHT DIRECTION: A FIRST LOOK AT THE UCP 600 AND THE NEW STANDARDS AS APPLIED TO VOEST-ALPINE

7 Asper Rev. Int'l Bus. & Trade L. 179 (2007).*

INTRODUCTION

International business has grown substantially in the past decade and continues to grow in importance globally. As a business engaged in an international transaction must consider translation risks, political turmoil, exchange rate fluctuations, and buyer or seller insolvency, the financial strength of a company affects its ability to buy and sell products in the global marketplace. The capacity of businesses to engage in such transactions is of great importance, as the majority of global business transactions involve the export and import of goods. In these transactions, it is usually the case that the buyer locates a product that it wishes to purchase from a foreign country and the seller arranges to ship the goods requested. Although the transaction itself may seem simplistic, different mercantile laws, payment structures, and changes in currency evaluation play a major role in the execution of the sale.

For example, a seller in Germany may want to sell automobile parts to a buyer in the U.S. The parties have never transacted before and both have concerns regarding the sale. The buyer is concerned with the quality of the parts, whether they conform to contract specifications, and, if advance payment is required, that the seller will even ship the goods. If the German seller pays for the packaging and shipment of the goods and the buyer becomes insolvent, or refuses to pay for the goods, he risks the further expense of litigation in an unfamiliar jurisdiction or the expense of finding another American buyer. Therefore, the seller wants assurances that the buyer is financially secure and is able to make payment once the parts ship. To minimize the concerns of both parties, they may agree to use a financial instrument known as a letter of credit, a common and accepted method of guaranteeing and obtaining payment in international sales contracts.

* * *

I. BACKGROUND

The letter of credit is a creation of the business and finance industries whereby a neutral party, such as a bank, substitutes its creditworthiness for that of the buyer and simultaneously assures timely payment of any amount owed under the contract for the seller.

The standard letter of credit contains the party names, payment amount, expiration date, and description of the merchandise, and specifies the documents, special conditions, and instructions that it requires for payment. A letter of credit is either a commercial letter of credit or standby letter of credit, and typically involves at least three parties and three independent contracts. [T]he commercial letter of credit ... is a payment mechanism, rather than the standby letter of credit, which serves as a guarantee. Presently, the two major sources of law governing commercial letters of credit are Article 5 of the Uniform Commercial Code ("UCC") and the Uniform Customs and Practice for Documentary Credits ("UCP").

A. The Basics of the Commercial Letter of Credit

Today, commercial letters of credit play an important role in international commerce. The commercial letter of credit is a payment instrument used for international sales of goods, and has a high degree of commercial utility because it benefits all parties concerned. There are typically three parties involved in the formation of a letter of credit. Using the example above, the German seller is the "beneficiary," the American buyer is the "applicant" or the "customer," and the bank issuing the letter of credit on behalf of the buyer is the "issuer" or "issuing bank."

There are also three separate transactions that create a letter of credit: (1) the underlying contract between the buyer and seller for the purchase and sale of goods; (2) the agreement between the issuer and its customer; and (3) the bank's obligation to pay the seller under the letter of credit itself. These transactions are independent of each other and do not occur simultaneously.

1. The First Transaction: The Buyer and the Seller

The underlying transaction is the contract between the buyer and the seller. Traditional contract law governs this transaction. The contract must stipulate that the buyer will make payment using a letter of credit and must indicate the law to govern the letter of credit transactions, which in most instances is the UCP.

2. The Second Transaction: The Buyer and the Bank

The buyer and the bank form the second transaction, whereby the bank issues the letter of credit in favor of the seller, and the buyer reimburses the bank when payment is made. Typically, the bank has a relationship with the buyer and secures a partial payment and a commission before drafting the letter of credit. A copy of the letter of credit document is sent to the beneficiary directly or to the beneficiary's bank— the "intermediary bank" or the "advising bank."

3. The Third Transaction: The Bank and the Seller

The third transaction occurs between the bank and the seller, and involves the letter of credit itself. Commentators believe that document presentation is the most important stage of the letter of credit transaction because current jurisprudence requires banks to adhere to a strict compliance standard when checking documents. Additionally, if a bank determines that documentary discrepancies exist, the bank may elect to dishonour the letter of credit or ask the applicant for a waiver of the documentary requirements.

B. The Fundamental Principles of Letters of Credit

At the core of the letter of credit are the principles of independence and strict compliance. First, the principle of independence establishes that each contract is completely independent of the next. Therefore, a letter of credit is independent of the underlying sales contract, and both the banks and the parties must construe and perform the letter of credit in accordance with their own terms, without reference to any other agreement or transaction. The independence principle is codified in Article 5 of the UCC and has been acknowledged in American courts.

Second, the princip[le] of compliance dictates that documents presented to the bank must comply with the letter of credit requirements. Document examination and rejection is therefore one of the most important topics concerning letters of credit, especially as empirical studies have shown that document discrepancies are the rule and perfect tenders are the exception.

C. The Laws Governing the Commercial Letter of Credit

* * *

1. Domestic Law: UCC Article 5

The U.S. is the only country with an extensive specific regulation for letters of credit. Article 5 of the UCC is a uniform statutory scheme governing letters of credit. International practice, as reflected in the UCP, heavily influenced the 1995 revision of UCC Article 5.

2. International Law: UCP

The UCP, created by the International Chamber of Commerce ("ICC"), is a set of rules based on internationally accepted banking practices regulating the issuance and use of letters of credit. The * * * ICC approved a new, sixth version of the rules, known as the UCP 600, [which became effective] in July 2007. Although the UCP is neither an international convention nor the law of any one country, U.S. courts and arbitration tribunals recognize and enforce the UCP where it is specifically incorporated into the letter of credit. When incorporated, the UCP is binding on all parties unless expressly modified or excluded by the credit. Despite the existence of Article 5 of the UCC, the UCP has great authority in the U.S., especially because Article 5 of the UCC governs only a limited part of the letter of credit transaction.

JH RAYNER AND COMPANY, LTD.
v. HAMBROS BANK LTD.

Court of Appeal.
[1943] K.B. 37.

APPEAL FROM ATKINSON, J.

On March 29, 1940, the defendants, Hambro's Bank, Ltd., received a cable from correspondents in Denmark, which was not then in enemy occupation, requesting them to open an irrevocable sight credit expiring June 1, 1940, in favour of J.H. Rayner & Co., the plaintiffs. The material words of the mandate contained in this cable were: "account Aarhus Oliefabrik for about 16,975*l.* against invoice full set straight clean bills of lading to Aarhus Oliefabrik dated Madras during April, 1940, covering about 1400 tons Coromandel groundnuts in bags at 12*l.* 2*s.* 6*d.* per ton f.o.b. Madras shipment motorship *Stensby* to Aarhus." On April 1, the defendants issued a letter of credit to the plaintiffs in these terms: "Confirmed credit No. 14597. We beg to inform you that a confirmed credit has been opened with us in favour of yourselves for an amount of up to about 16,975*l.* account of Aarhus Oliefabrik available by drafts on this bank at sight to be accompanied by the following documents—invoice, clean on board bills of lading in complete set issued to order Aarhus Oliefabrik, dated Madras during April, 1940, covering a shipment of about 1400 tons Coromandel groundnuts in bags at 12*l.* 2*s.* 6*d.* per ton f.o.b. Madras per m.s. *Stensby* to Aarhus. This credit is valid until June 1, 1940. All drafts drawn hereagainst must contain the clause 'Drawn under confirmed credit No. 14597.' We undertake to honour drafts on presentation, if drawn in conformity with the terms of this credit." On April 15, the plaintiffs presented to the defendant bank a draft, accompanied by an invoice of the same date for "17,724 bags Coromandel groundnuts. Bill of lading dated 2.4.40" and three bills of lading, differing only as to the number of bags, which totalled 17,724, in each of which the goods were described in these terms: In the margin were the marks "O.T.C. C.R.S. Aarhus," and in the body of the bill "* * * bags machine-shelled groundnut kernels, each bag said to weigh 177 lb. nett. Country of origin, British India. Country of final destination, Denmark. Goods are Danish property." Those documents having been presented to the defendants, they refused to accept the draft, on the ground that the terms of the letter of credit called for an invoice and bill of lading both covering a shipment of "Coromandel groundnuts" whereas the bills of lading presented described the goods as "machine-shelled groundnut kernels. Country of origin, British India." The plaintiffs thereupon brought this action, alleging that the defendants' refusal to honour their draft was wrongful, and a breach of the undertaking in the letter of credit. At the trial before Atkinson J. evidence was given and accepted by him that "machine-shelled groundnut kernels" were the same commodity as "Coromandel groundnuts" and would be universally understood to be so in the trade in London, and, further, that the marginal mark "C.R.S." was short for "Coros" or

"Coromandels" and would be so understood in the trade. Atkinson J. gave judgment for the plaintiffs, and the defendants appealed.

MacKINNON L.J. The legal result of a banker issuing a letter of credit has been considered in various cases to which I do not think it is necessary to refer, but two passages which have been mentioned by Goddard L.J., seem to me to sum up the position in general terms with the greatest accuracy. In *English, Scottish and Australian Bank, Ltd. v. Bank of South Africa (I)*, Bailhache J. said: "It is elementary to say that a person who ships in reliance on a letter of credit must do so in exact compliance with its terms. It is also elementary to say that a bank is not bound or indeed entitled to honour drafts presented to it under a letter of credit unless those drafts with the accompanying documents are in strict accord with the credit as opened." And Lord Sumner in *Equitable Trust Co. of New York v. Dawson Partners, Ltd.* (2) said: "It is both common ground and common sense that in such a transaction the accepting bank can only claim indemnity if the conditions on which it is authorized to accept are in the matter of the accompanying documents strictly observed. There is no room for documents which are almost the same, or which will do just as well. Business could not proceed securely on any other lines. The bank's branch abroad, which knows nothing officially of the details of the transaction thus financed, cannot take upon itself to decide what will do well enough and what will not. If it does as it is told, it is safe; if it declines to do anything else, it is safe; if it departs from the conditions laid down, it acts at its own risk." The defendant bank were told by their Danish principals to issue a letter of credit under which they were to accept documents—an invoice and bills of lading—covering "Coromandel groundnuts in bags." They were offered bills of lading covering "machine-shelled groundnut kernels." The country of origin was stated to be British India. The words in that bill of lading clearly are not the same as those required by the letter of credit. The whole case of the plaintiffs is, in the words of Lord Sumner, that "they are almost the same, or they will do just as well." The bank, if they had accepted that proposition, would have done so at their own risk. I think on pure principle that the bank were entitled to refuse to accept this sight draft on the ground that the documents tendered, the bill of lading in particular, did not comply precisely with the terms of the letter of credit which they had issued.

Atkinson J., however, in his judgment says: "A sale of Coromandel groundnuts is universely understood to be a sale of machine-shelled kernels, that is, dry decorticated, and there is a standard form of contract, No. 37, used in the trade. The marking C.R.S. is short for 'Coros,' which is itself an abbreviation for 'Coromandels.' If a bag of kernels is marked 'C.R.S.,' it means that it is a bag of Coromandel groundnuts." That is stating the effect of evidence given by persons who deal in groundnuts in Mincing Lane, and when Atkinson J. says that it is "universally understood," he means that these gentlemen from Mincing Lane have told him: "We dealers in Mincing Lane all understand these things. We understand that 'Coromandel groundnuts' are machine-shelled groundnut kernels,

and we understand when we see 'C.R.S.' that that means 'Coromandels.' "
It is suggested that as a consequence the bank, when this bill of lading for
machine-shelled groundnut kernels with C.R.S. in the margin was brought
to them, ought to be affected with this special knowledge of those
witnesses who deal in these things on contracts in Mincing Lane. I think
that is a perfectly impossible suggestion. To begin with, this case does not
concern any transaction in Mincing Lane. It is a transaction with Denmark, and for aught I know, and for aught the evidence proved, the people
in Denmark know nothing about this business usage of Mincing Lane.
Moreover, quite apart from that special application of the relevant considerations, it is quite impossible to suggest that a banker is to be affected
with knowledge of the customs and customary terms of every one of the
thousands of trades for whose dealings he may issue letters of credit.
* * *

For these reasons, I think that this appeal succeeds, that the judgment in favour of the plaintiffs must be set aside, and judgment entered
for the defendants with costs, here and below.

GODDARD L.J. I agree. It seems to me that Atkinson J. has based his
judgment on the consideration that the bank was affected in some way by
this custom of the trade, and, secondly, that he has considered whether
what the bank required was reasonable or unreasonable. I protest against
the view that a bank is to be deemed affected by knowledge of the trade of
its various customers, but, quite apart from that, even if the bank did
know of this trade practice by which "Coromandel groundnuts" can be
described as "machine-shelled groundnut kernels," I do not think that
would be conclusive of the case. In my opinion, in this case, whether the
bank knew or did not know that there was this trade practice to treat
"Coromandel groundnuts" and "machine-shelled groundnut kernels" as
interchangeable terms, is nothing to the point. They were told to establish
a credit, and to pay against a bill of lading describing particular goods, and
the beneficiary under that credit presented a bill of lading which was not
what they had promised to pay against. Therefore, it seems to me,
whether it is reasonable or unreasonable for their principals to say that
they want a bill of lading for "Coromandel groundnuts," or whether the
bank had or had not knowledge of some of the trade practices which are
referred to, is not the question. The question is "What was the promise
which the bank made to the beneficiary under the credit, and did the
beneficiary avail himself of that promise?"

ADODO, CONFORMITY OF PRESENTATION DOCUMENTS AND A REJECTION NOTICE IN LETTERS OF CREDIT LITIGATION: A TALE OF TWO DOCTRINES

36 Hong Kong L.J. 309 (2006).*

Introduction

In the field of letter of credit, one of the most fundamental principles is that the bank to which a presentation is designated to be made under a credit transaction must honour the beneficiary's demand for payment if the presentation complies with the requirements of the credit; otherwise it may dishonour. Thus, in advising the terms and conditions of the credit to the beneficiary, the bank is usually taken to have impliedly promised that, provided the conforming documents are tendered, payment is not only assured but will also be made promptly. Unfortunately, in modern practice, the marvellous character of this promise has increasingly been plagued by the alarming frequency of rejection of first time presentations under a credit on account of discrepancies either between the terms of the letter of credit and the tendered documents or among the documents. * * * The result is that the bank's promise of quick and assured payment is rendered illusory and, in consequence, the reliability and efficacy of the letter of credit as a means of payment in international trade suffers.

Not infrequently, though, the exporter/beneficiary may be unable to procure a waiver from the importer/account party or effect a cure. In such a case, if he still desires payment under the credit, he may have to fall back on the question of whether, in advising its refusal to pay, the bank strictly complied with its obligation to give a valid rejection notice. If the bank did not, it might be in a serious difficulty: it might forfeit the right to adduce the documentary discrepancies to justify its refusal to make payment and, faced with a falling market, the importer/buyer might fasten on the discrepancies to repudiate his reimbursement obligation under the credit contract. In the event, the ultimate fate of the letter of credit transaction will, on the one hand, turn on the legality of the bank's refusal to pay by reason of the failure of the presentation documents to comply strictly with the terms of the credit, and the beneficiary's claim of an invalid rejection on the other hand.

* * *

The Nature of Strict Compliance

* * *

Conceptually, though, the obligation of the account party to furnish explicit, unambiguous mandate to the issuing bank is matched with the obligation of the beneficiary, if he desires to draw down on the credit, to

---

present documents which strictly answer to the requirements of the letter of credit. The earlier part of the twentieth century witnessed the evolution of the principle that if presentation documents do not *strictly* comply with the stipulations in a letter of credit, the bank is not obligated to make payment, and if it pays, cannot claim reimbursement from the account party. In *English, Scottish and Australia Bank Ltd v Bank of South Africa*, Bailhache J captured the rule precluding payment against nonconforming presentation documents as follows:

> "It is elementary to say that a person who ships in reliance on a letter of credit must do so in *exact compliance* with its terms. It is also elementary to say that a bank is not bound or indeed entitled to honour drafts presented to it under a letter of credit unless those drafts with the accompanying documents are in *strict accord* with the credit as opened."

This view was echoed four years later in *Equitable Trust Co. of New York v Dawson Partners Ltd*. There, in an oft-quoted passage, Viscount Sumner said:

> "It is both common ground and common sense that in [letter of credit] transaction the accepting bank can only claim indemnity if the conditions on which it is authorized to accept are in the matter of the accompanying documents *strictly* observed. There is no room for documents which are almost the same, or which will do just as well... The bank's branch abroad, which knows nothing officially of the details of the transaction thus financed, cannot take upon itself to decide what will do well enough and what will not. If it does as it is told, it is safe; if it declines to do anything else, it is safe; if it departs from the conditions laid down, it acts at its own risk."

In a number of cases, the court took the view that Bailhache J's statement together with Viscount Sumner's dictum did not require literal compliance with the terms of credit, so that a presentation could not be rejected on the ground of an obvious misspelling. But in several others, a different approach was taken: the beneficiary could not exact payment unless the tendered documents conveyed a *mirror image* of the credit. Thus, a plea that dishonour was wrongful because the alleged discrepancy was committed bona fide was unavailing. Nor did it matter that the dishonour was motivated by bad faith, or that the defect is a mere technicality.

In contrast to the common law position, Article 13(a) of the UCP 500—usually incorporated into letters of credit transactions made in nearly all the jurisdictions in the world—provides that banks must examine all presentation documents to determine whether they conform, *ex facie*, to the requirements of the credit; the criterion for determining conformity is "international standard banking practice as reflected in [the UCP provisions]." The UCP compliance test just quoted was the butt of a stream of considerable criticisms. * * *

[A]lthough banking practice and opinions of experts tend to vary in their finer details from place to place and even from bank to bank, by adopting the words "international banking standard," the UCP *implicitly* prescribe the standard of a reasonably knowledgeable and diligent bank documents checker. Consistent with this standard is the exercise of commercial common sense, on a case-by-case basis, such that a minor deviation of a clerical, typographical nature will, generally, not justify dishonour.[26]

Notably, there are two classes of case where the *character* of a discrepancy may not matter. One instance is where the information required in the letter of credit is omitted in the presentation documents. In this regard, one view is that "[w]here it can be shown that [a] supposed discrepancy results from a patent error or obvious typographical mistake, it is unrealistic to treat the ... tender as invalid by reason only of a technical slip or mistake." Further support for this view is that many of the documents tendered under a documentary credit are prepared not by the beneficiary but by a third party, such as a shipping agent, surveyor or carrier. The beneficiary has no control over the clerks of such a party. Even where the documents are authored by the beneficiary's own staff, such persons cannot be expected to be infallible.

* * *

Another instance of documentary discrepancies that may not displace literal adherence to the terms of a letter of credit arises where the tendered documents are discordant with the terms of the credit on the ground that the requisite designation of a party, name of a person or place, or number has been mis-transcribed in the presentation documents *and* the mis-transcription is such as would invite a reasonable bank document checker to make inquiry beyond the tendered documentations, mislead the bank, necessitate the solicitation of legal advice, or raise the likelihood of non-performance or fraud by the beneficiary. For example, in *Bank of Cochin Ltd v Manufacturers Hanover Trust Co.*, the issuing bank disclaimed its reimbursement obligation against a set of documents bearing "St. Lucia Enterprises" instead of "St. Lucia Enterprises *Ltd*", and insurance cover note number *"4291"* rather than *"429711."* The Southern District Court of New York held that the discrepancy relating to the

---

26. See, generally, Flagship Cruises Ltd. v. New England Merchants, 569 F 2d 699 (1st Cir, CA) (1977), where the credit required all drafts to be marked "Drawn under NEMNB Credit No 18506" is satisfied by a draft marked "No 18506"; Tosco Corp. v. FDIC, 723 F.2d 1242 (6st Cir., CA) (1983), legend on a presentment draft showed "Drawn under Bank of Clarksville, Clarksville, Tennessee letter of Credit NO 105" rather than "Drawn under Bank of Clarksville Letter of Credit Number 105". Three discrepancies were alleged: (i) change of "L" in "Letter" to "I"; (ii) the use of "NO" as opposed to "Number"; and (iii) the addition of the words "Clarksville, Tennessee". All these were held to be nitpicking; First National Bank of Atlanta v Wynne 149 Ga. App. 811 (CA, Ga.) (1979), a certificate and a draft were required to indicate "credit NO S-3753." It was held that notwithstanding the omission of this information, beneficiary's covering letter adequately identified the draft; New Braunfels National Bank v. Odiorne, 780 S.W.2d 313 (1989), legend on a presentment draft stated "Number 86–122–5" instead of "Number 86–122–S" was held conforming; First Bank v Paris Savings & Loan Association, 756 S.W.2d 329 (Tex. App.) (1988), where it was held that the tendered documents were conforming since they contained the requisite legend irrespective of the addition of the words "dated June, 12, 1986, i/a/o $250,000"; American Airlines Inc v. FDIC, 610 F Supp 199 (1985), the incorrectly stated legend in the draft was not misleading to the bank because the accompanying cover letter correctly contained the requisite number.

beneficiary's name could only possibly be evidence of forgery. Further, the failure to provide the correct insurance cover note "was not inconsequential" as the mistake could have resulted in the Insurance Company's justifiable refusal to honour the account party's insurance policy. The Second Circuit affirmed. Similarly, in *United Bank Ltd. v. Banque Nationale de Paris*, the High Court of Singapore held that presentation documents bearing the beneficiary's name as "Pan Associated *Pte* Ltd." as opposed to "Pan Associated Ltd" in the letter of credit justified dishonour notwithstanding that the Registrar of Companies would not, *except* with the consent of the Minister, register two companies with such similarity in names, a fact that naturally invited the bank document checker to make inquiries outside the tendered documentations.

In any event, in letters of credit transaction, matters of names, numbers, and designation of a requisite party will continue to constitute a matter of critical importance. If a misspelling of such appellation would ostensibly create doubt in the issuing bank's mind, then the paying bank is entitled to reject the document(s) in which the error is contained. However, the question whether a misspelling or misprint is unmistakably a typographical error is determined by having regard to the place or country of the issuing bank. The much maligned decision in *Beyene & Hanson v. Irving Trust Co.* is explicable on this basis. There, the misspelling of "So*f*an" as "So*r*an" was held by the United States Second Circuit to be a material discrepancy because it was established in evidence that in the Middle East such misspelling would not be recognised as an inadvertent misspelling.

Notwithstanding the foregoing, it is important to bear in mind that strict documentary compliance principle does not require rigid, literal, mirror image replication of the terms of the credit; in certain cases some margin is permitted. Otherwise, the wider attributes of integrity and efficiency of letter of credit will be defeated.

* * *

From the foregoing, the conclusion is inevitable that the decision in *Equitable Trust*, besides reaffirming the pre-existing common law standard of strict compliance, stands for the proposition that commercial reality and reasonableness should be brought to bear on the process of determining whether a tendered document is or is not conforming to the terms of a letter of credit. In a sense, the essence of *functional equivalent standard* is rooted in the need to give effect to the commercial intent of a credit in so far as such intent can reasonably be gathered from the letter of credit itself. This approach is consistent with the well-established presumption in law that the object of a contract is intended to be realised by the parties thereunder, and a construction that will sustain that object is preferable to the one that will defeat it. * * *

Often, after a painstaking and thorough review of the credit, the beneficiary may not spot in the letter of credit advised to him any error or typographical mistake through no fault of his or his staff. In such a case, the problem is determining whether or not the beneficiary should be paid. This question was addressed in the American case of *Tradax Petroleum American Inc. v Coral Petroleum Inc.* The facts were that the credit simultaneously called for documentation evidencing shipment of "sweet oil" and "sour oil." The court held that the contradictory requirements in the credit, rendering performance impossible, did not excuse strict compliance and it was not open to the court to reform the credit because the terms at issue were free of ambiguity. The emerging solution seems to be that once the credit has been advised and a presentation made, absent ambiguity in the credit, the beneficiary must live with the terms of the credit as notified.

This may appear rather harsh on the beneficiary. But then, hard cases do not make good law: the unenviable circumstance of the beneficiary is the natural consequence of his omitting, recklessly or innocently, to catch the mistake in the credit. Otherwise, it will be necessary to ascertain the shoulders more deserving of bearing the effect of the mistake in the credit, a task that is evidently fraught with considerable difficulties. What cannot be denied, however, is that the concept of strict compliance makes the beneficiary to be acutely aware well in advance of making a request for payment, of the kind or nature of the documents he is expected to tender, and to bear in mind that there would be no payment if the documents he wishes to present are non-conforming.

In *Hanil Bank v PT Bank Negara Indonesia*, a buyer instructed an issuing bank to open a letter of credit in favour of "Sun *Jun* Electronics Co., Ltd." But the issuing bank advised the beneficiary of the opening of the credit for "Sun *Jin* Electronic Co., Ltd." The plaintiff bank negotiated documents bearing "Sun *Jun* Electronics Co., Ltd." The Southern District Court of New York held that the beneficiary who negotiated the credit to the plaintiff bank was in a position to examine the credit for possible errors, but failed or neglected to do so.

On the basis of commercial reality, however, our sympathy for the beneficiary in *Hanil Bank* must necessarily be guarded. Although it may be argued that in determining whether the presentation conform to the credit, the issuing bank ought to consider the account party's application letter which correctly conveyed the beneficiary's name, the fact of the matter is that the variance between the words "Jin" and "Jun" would not be recognised in Korea, where the issuing bank and the account party carried on business, as obvious typographical error; the alphabetical difference would almost certainly provoke some inquiry about whether "Sung *Jin* Electronics Co., Ltd" is one and the same with "Sung *Jun* Electronics Co., Ltd." In this regard, the documents affected by the defect could occasion difficulties for the account party in clearing the goods from the customs department due to local regulatory enactments regarding clients claiming to be entitled to clear certain merchandise; there might also be difficulties in negotiating such discrepant documents to another buyer. The decision in *Hanil Bank* is on this basis unassailable.

VOEST-ALPINE TRADING USA CORP. v. BANK OF CHINA

United States District Court, S.D. Texas.
167 F.Supp.2d 940 (2000).

FINDINGS OF FACT AND CONCLUSIONS OF LAW

GILMORE, DISTRICT JUDGE.

* * *

On June 23, 1995, Plaintiff Voest–Alpine Trading USA Corporation ("Voest–Alpine") entered into a contract with Jiangyin Foreign Trade Corporation ("JFTC") to sell JFTC 1,000 metric tons of styrene monomer at a total price of $1.2 million. To finance the transaction, JFTC applied for a letter of credit through Defendant Bank of China. . . . The letter of credit was issued by the Bank of China on July 6, 1995. . . . In addition to numerous other typographical errors, Voest–Alpine's name was listed as "Voest–Alpine USA Trading Corp." instead of "Voest–Alpine Trading USA Corp" with the "Trading USA" portion inverted. The destination port was also misspelled in one place as "Zhangjiagng," missing the third "a". The letter of credit did indicate, however, that the transaction would be subject to the 1993 Uniform Customs and Practice, International Chamber of Commerce Publication Number 500 ("UCP 500").

By the time the product was ready to ship, the market price of styrene monomer had dropped significantly from the original contract price between Voest–Alpine and JFTC. Although JFTC asked for a price concession in light of the decrease in market price, Voest–Alpine declined and, through its agents, shipped the styrene monomer on July 18, 1995. All required inspection and documentation was completed. On August 1, 1995, Voest–Alpine presented the documents specified in the letter of credit to Texas Commerce Bank, the presenting bank. Texas Commerce Bank found discrepancies between the presentation documents and the letter of credit which it related to Voest–Alpine. Because Voest–Alpine did not believe that any of the noted discrepancies would warrant refusal to pay, it instructed Texas Commerce Bank to forward the presentation documents to the Bank of China.

* * *

On August 11, 1995, the Bank of China sent a telex to Texas Commerce Bank, informing them of seven alleged discrepancies between the letter of credit and the documents Voest–Alpine presented, six of which are the subject of this action. The Bank of China claimed that 1) the beneficiary's name differed from the name listed in the letter of credit, as noted by the presenting bank; 2) Voest–Alpine had submitted bills of lading marked "duplicate" and "triplicate" instead of "original"; 3) the invoice, packing list and the certificate of origin were not marked "original"; 4) the date of the survey report was later than that of the bill of lading; 5) the letter of credit number in the beneficiary's certified copy of the fax was incorrect, as noted by the presenting bank; and 6) the destination was not listed correctly in the certificate of origin and the beneficiary's certificate, as noted by the presenting bank. The telex further stated. "We are contacting the applicant of the relative discrepancy [sic]. Holding documents at your risks and disposal."

On August 15, Texas Commerce Bank faxed the Bank of China, stating that the discrepancies were not an adequate basis to refuse to pay the letter of credit and requested that the bank honor the letter of credit and pay Voest–Alpine accordingly. The telex identified Voest–Alpine as the beneficiary in the transaction. Voest–Alpine also contacted JFTC directly in an effort to secure a waiver of the discrepancies but was unsuccessful.

On August 19, 1995, the Bank of China sent another telex to Texas Commerce Bank further explaining what it believed to be discrepancies between the letter of credit and the documentation presented by Voest–Alpine according to the UCP 500. In relevant part, the telex provided:

You cannot say [the discrepancies] are of no consequence. The fact is that our bank must examine all documents stipulated in the credit with reasonable care, to ascertain whether or not they appear, on their face, to be incompliance [sic] with the terms and conditions of the credit. According to Article 13 of UCP 500. An irrevocable credit constitutes a definite undertaking of the issuing bank, providing that the stipulated documents are complied with the terms and conditions of the credit according to Article UCP 500. Now the discrepant documents may have us refuse to take up the documents according to article 14(B) of UCP 500.

The Bank of China returned the documents to Voest–Alpine and did not honor the letter of credit.

I

* * *

The current statutory law requires an issuer to honor a presentation that, as determined by standard practice of financial institutions that regularly issue letters of credit, "appears on its face strictly to comply with the terms and conditions of the letter of credit." Tex. Bus. & Comm.Code Ann. § 5.108(a), (e) (Vernon's 2000). Determination of what constitutes standard practice of financial institutions is a "matter of interpretation for the court." Tex. Bus. & Comm.Code Ann. § 5.108(e) (Vernon's 2000).

The Uniform Customs and Practices for Documentary Credits, first issued in 1930 by the International Chamber of Commerce and revised approximately once every ten years since, is a compilation of internationally accepted commercial practices which may be incorporated into the private law of a contract between parties. *Banco General Runinahui, S.A. v. Citibank Int'l*, 97 F.3d 480, 482 (11th Cir.1996)(citing Alaska Textile Co., Inc. v. Chase Manhattan Bank, N.A., *Alaska Textile*, 982 F.2d at 816).

In this case, the parties expressly adopted the UCP 500 as the governing authority in the letter of credit. Where parties explicitly refer to the UCP 500 in their contracts, the UCP has been interpreted to apply to the transaction. Accordingly, the Court will look to the UCP for guidance in analyzing whether the actions of the Bank of China were in conformity with "standard practice" of financial institutions.

* * *

II

Voest–Alpine claims that the six remaining discrepancies cited by the Bank of China are mere technicalities and typographical errors that do not warrant the rejection of the documents. Voest–Alpine argues for a "functional standard" of compliance, contending that if the whole of the documents obviously relate to the transaction covered by the credit, the issuing bank must honor the letter of credit. The Bank of China argues that the discrepancies were significant and that if the documents contain discrepancies on their face, it is justified in rejecting them and is not required to look beyond the papers themselves.

Section 13(a) of the UCP 500 provides:

Banks must examine all documents stipulated in the Credit with reasonable care, to ascertain whether or not they appear, on their face, to be in compliance with the terms and conditions of the Credit. Compliance of the stipulated documents on their face with the terms and conditions of the Credit shall be determined by international standard banking practice as reflected in these Articles. Documents which appear on their face to be inconsistent with one another will be considered as not appearing on their face to be in compliance with the terms and conditions of the Credit.

INTERNATIONAL CHAMBER OF COMMERCE, ICC UNIFORM CUSTOMS AND PRACTICE FOR DOCUMENTARY CREDITS, ICC PUBLICATION NO. 500 19 (1993).

The UCP 500 does not provide guidance on what inconsistencies would justify a conclusion on the part of a bank that the documents are not in compliance with the terms and conditions of the letter of credit or what discrepancies are not a reasonable basis for such a conclusion. The UCP 500 does not mandate that the documents be a mirror image of the requirements or use the term "strict compliance."

The Court notes the wide range of interpretations on what standard banks should employ in examining letter of credit document presentations for compliance. Even where courts claim to uphold strict compliance, the standard is hardly uniform. The first and most restrictive approach is to require that the presentation documents be a mirror image of the requirements. *See Banco General Runinahui, S.A. v. Citibank Int'l*, 97 F.3d 480, 483 (11th Cir.1996)("This Court has recognized and applied the 'strict compliance' standard to requests for payment under commercial letters of credit ... [T]he fact that a defect is a mere technicality' does not matter.")(quoting *Kerr-McGee Chem. Corp. v. FDIC,* 872 F.2d 971, 973 (11th Cir.1989)); *Alaska Textile Co. v. Chase Manhattan Bank,* 982 F.2d 813, 816 (2d Cir.1992)(Noting that documents that are nearly the same as those required by the letter of credit are unacceptable for presentation in a letter of credit transaction).

Second, there are also cases claiming to follow the strict compliance standard but support rejection only where the discrepancies are such that would create risks for the issuer if the bank were to accept the presentation documents. *See Flagship Cruises Ltd., v. New England Merchants Nat'l Bank of Boston,* 569 F.2d 699, 705 (1st Cir.1978) ("We do not see these rulings as retreats from rigorous insistence on compliance with letter of credit requirements. They merely recognize that variance between documents specified and documents submitted is not fatal if there is no possibility that the documents could mislead the paying bank to its detriment") * * *

A third standard, without much support in case law, is to analyze the documents for risk to the applicant. * * *

The mirror image approach is problematic because it absolves the bank reviewing the documents of any responsibility to use common sense to determine if the documents, on their face, are related to the transaction or even to review an entire document in the context of the others presented to the bank. On the other hand, the second and third approaches employ a determination-of-harm standard that is too unwieldy. Such an analysis would improperly require the bank to evaluate risks that it might suffer or that might be suffered by the applicant and could undermine the independence of the three contracts that underlie the letter of credit payment scheme by forcing the bank to look beyond the face of the presentation documents.

The Court finds that a moderate, more appropriate standard lies within the UCP 500 itself and the opinions issued by the International Chamber of Commerce ("ICC") Banking Commission. One of the Banking Commission opinions defined the term "consistency" between the letter of credit and the documents presented to the issuing bank as used in Article 13(a) of the UCP to mean that "the whole of the documents must obviously relate to the same transaction, that is to say, that each should bear a relation (link) with the others on its face ... "INT'L CHAMBER OF COMMERCE, BANKING COMM'N, PUBLICATION NO. 371, DECISIONS (1975–1979) OF THE ICC BANKING COMMISSION R. 12 (1980). The Banking Commission rejected the notion that "all of the documents should be *exactly* consistent in their wording." *Id.* (emphasis in original).

A common sense, case-by-case approach would permit minor deviations of a typographical nature because such a letter-for-letter correspondence between the letter of credit and the presentation documents is virtually impossible. *See* INT'L CHAMBER OF COMMERCE, COMM'N ON BANKING TECHNIQUE AND PRACTICE, PUBLICATION NO. 511,

UCP 500 & 400 COMPARED 39 (Charles del Busto ed.1994)(noting the difficulty in attaining mirror-image compliance). While the end result of such an analysis may bear a strong resemblance to the relaxed strict compliance standard, the actual calculus used by the issuing bank is not the risk it or the applicant faces but rather, whether the documents bear a rational link to one another. In this way, the issuing bank is required to examine a particular document in light of all documents presented and use common sense but is not required to evaluate risks or go beyond the face of the documents. The Court finds that in this case the Bank of China's listed discrepancies should be analyzed under this standard by determining whether the whole of the documents obviously relate to the transaction on their face.

First, the Bank of China claimed that the beneficiary's name in the presentation documents, Voest–Alpine *Trading USA*, differed from the letter of credit, which listed the beneficiary as Voest–Alpine *USA Trading*. While it is true that the letter of credit inverted Voest–Alpine's geographic locator, all the documents Voest–Alpine presented that obviously related to this transaction placed the geographic locator behind "Trading", not in front of it. Furthermore, the addresses corresponded to that listed in the letter of credit and Texas Commerce Bank's cover letter to the Bank of China identified Voest–Alpine Trading USA as the beneficiary in the transaction with JFTC. The letter of credit with the inverted name bore obvious links to the documents presented by Voest–Alpine Trading USA. This is in contrast to a misspelling or outright omission. *See Beyene v. Irving Trust Co.*, 762 F.2d 4 (2d Cir.1985)(listing beneficiary as "Soran" rather than "Sofan" was sufficient basis for refusal); *Bank of Cochin, Ltd. v. Manufacturers Hanover Trust Co.*, 612 F.Supp. 1533 (S.D.N.Y.1985)(omitting "Ltd." from corporate name justified rejection). In contrast with these cases, the inversion of the geographic locator here does not signify a different corporate entity. * * *

Second, the Bank of China pointed out that the set of originals of the bill of lading should have all been stamped "original" rather than "original," "duplicate" and "triplicate." It should be noted that neither the letter of credit nor any provision in the UCP 500 requires such stamping. In fact, the ICC Banking Commission expressly ruled that "duplicate" and "triplicate" bills of lading did not need to be marked "original" and that failure to label them as originals did not justify refusal of the documents. INT'L CHAMBER OF COMMERCE, BANKING COMM'N, PUBLICATION NO. 565, OPINIONS OF THE ICC BANKING COMM'N 1995–1996 38 (Gary Collyer ed.1997). While it is true that this clarification by the ICC came after the transaction at issue in this case, it is clear from the face of the documents that these documents are three originals rather than one original and two copies. The documents have signatures in blue ink vary slightly, bear original stamps oriented differently on each page and clearly state on their face that the preparer made three original bills. Further, one possible definition of duplicate is "[t]o make or execute again" and one definition of triplicate is "[o]ne of a set of three identical things." WEBSTER'S II NEW RIVERSIDE UNIVERSITY DICTIONARY 410, 1237 (1994). While the "duplicate" and "triplicate" stamps may have been confusing, stamps do not make obviously original documents into copies.

Third, the Bank of China claimed that the failure to stamp the packing list documents as "original" was a discrepancy. Again, these documents are clearly originals on their face as they have three slightly differing signatures in blue ink. There was no requirement in the letter of credit or the UCP 500 that original documents be marked as such. The ICC's policy statement on the issue provides that, "banks treat as original any document that appears to be hand signed by the issuer of the document." (Int'l Chamber of Commerce, Comm'n on Banking Technique and Practice, *The determination of an "Original" document in the context of UCP 500 sub-Article 20(b)* July 12, 1999).<*http://www.iccwbo.org/home/ statements rules/statements /1999/the_ determination_of_an_original_docu ment.asp*>. The failure to mark obvious originals is not a discrepancy.

Fourth, the Bank of China argues that the date of the survey report is after the bill of lading and is therefore discrepant. A careful examination of the survey report reveals that the survey took place "immediately before/after loading" and that the sample of cargo "to be loaded" was taken. The plain language of the report reveals that the report may have been issued after the bill of lading but the survey itself was conducted before the ship departed. The date does not pose a discrepancy.

Fifth, the Bank of China claims that the letter of credit number listed in the beneficiary's certified copy of fax is wrong. The letter of credit number was listed as "LC95231033/95" on the copy of fax instead of "LC9521033/95" as in the letter of credit itself, adding an extra "3" after "LC952." However, adding the letter of credit number to this document was gratuitous and in the numerous other places in the documents that the letter of credit was referenced by number, it was incorrect only in one place. Moreover, the seven other pieces of information contained in the document were correct. The document checker could have easily looked to any other document to verify the letter of credit number, or looked to the balance of the information within the document and found that the document as a whole bears an obvious relationship to the transaction. Madame Gao, the document checker who reviewed Voest–Alpine's presentation documents for the Bank of China, testified that she did not look beyond the face of this particular document in assessing the discrepancy. The cover letter from Texas Commerce Bank, for example, had the correct number.

Finally, the Bank of China claims that the wrong destination is listed in the certificate of origin and the beneficiary's certificate. The certificate of origin spelled Zhangjiagang as "Zhangjiagng" missing an "a" as it is misspelled once in the letter of credit, making it consistent. The beneficiary's certificate, however, spelled it "Zhanjiagng," missing a "g" in addition to the "a", a third spelling that did not appear in the letter of credit.

Madame Gao first considered the discrepancy a "misspelling" rather than an indication of the wrong port, according to her notes. There is no port in China called "Zhangjiagng" or "Zhanjiagng." "Gng" is a combination of letters not found in Romanized Chinese, whereas "gang" means "port" in Chinese. The other information contained in the document was correct, such as the letter of credit number and the contract number, and even contained the distinctive phrase "by courie lukdt within 3 days after shipment", presumably meaning by courier within three days after shipment, as in the letter of credit. The document as a whole bears an obvious relationship with the transaction. The misspelling of the destination is not a basis for dishonor of the letter of credit where the rest of the document has demonstrated linkage to the transaction on its face.

Based on the foregoing, the Court finds in favor of the plaintiff, Voest–Alpine.

UNIFORM CUSTOMS AND PRACTICE FOR DOCUMENTARY CREDITS (2007 REVISION)

International Chamber of Commerce, Pub. No. 600.*

Article 1

Application of UCP

The Uniform Customs and Practice for Documentary Credits, 2007 Revision, ICC Publication no. 600 ("UCP") are rules that apply to any documentary credit ("credit") (including, to the extent to which they may be applicable, any standby letter of credit) when the text of the credit expressly indicates that it is subject to these rules. They are binding on all parties thereto unless expressly modified or excluded by the credit.

Article 2

Definitions

For the purpose of these rules:

Advising bank means the bank that advises the credit at the request of the issuing bank.

Applicant means the party on whose request the credit is issued.

Banking day means a day on which a bank is regularly open at the place at which an act subject to these rules is to be performed.

Beneficiary means the party in whose favour a credit is issued.

Complying presentation means a presentation that is in accordance with the terms and conditions of the credit, the applicable provisions of these rules and international standard banking practice.

Confirmation means a definite undertaking of the confirming bank, in addition to that of the issuing bank, to honour or negotiate a complying presentation.

Confirming bank means the bank that adds its confirmation to a credit upon the issuing bank's authorization or request.

Credit means any arrangement, however named or described, that is irrevocable and thereby constitutes a definite undertaking of the issuing bank to honour a complying presentation.

Honour means:

a. to pay at sight if the credit is available by sight payment.

b. to incur a deferred payment undertaking and pay at maturity if the credit is available by deferred payment.

c. to accept a bill of exchange ("draft") drawn by the beneficiary and pay at maturity if the credit is available by acceptance.

Issuing bank means the bank that issues a credit at the request of an applicant or on its own behalf.

Negotiation means the purchase by the nominated bank of drafts (drawn on a bank other than the nominated bank) and/or documents under a complying presentation, by advancing or agreeing to advance funds to the beneficiary on or before the banking day on which reimbursement is due to the nominated bank.

Nominated Bank means the bank with which the credit is available or any bank in the case of a credit available with any bank.

Presentation means either the delivery of documents under a credit to the issuing bank or nominated bank or the documents so delivered.

Presenter means a beneficiary, bank or other party that makes a presentation.

Article 4

Credits v. Contracts

a. A credit by its nature is a separate transaction from the sale or other contract on which it may be based. Banks are in no way concerned with or bound by such contract, even if any reference whatsoever to it is included in the credit. Consequently, the undertaking of a bank to honour, to negotiate or to fulfil any other obligation under the credit is not subject to claims or defences by the applicant resulting from its relationships with the issuing bank or the beneficiary. A beneficiary can in no case avail itself of the contractual relationships existing between banks or between the applicant and the issuing bank.

b. An issuing bank should discourage any attempt by the applicant to include, as an integral part of the credit, copies of the underlying contract, proforma invoice and the like.

Article 5

Documents v. Goods, Services or Performance

Banks deal with documents and not with goods, services or performance to which the documents may relate.

Article 7

Issuing Bank Undertaking

a. Provided that the stipulated documents are presented to the nominated bank or to the issuing bank and that they constitute a complying presentation, the issuing bank must honour if the credit is available by:

i. sight payment, deferred payment or acceptance with the issuing bank;

ii. sight payment with a nominated bank and that nominated bank does not pay;

iii. deferred payment with a nominated bank and that nominated bank does not incur its deferred payment undertaking or, having incurred its deferred payment undertaking, does not pay at maturity;

iv. acceptance with a nominated bank and that nominated bank does not accept a draft drawn on it or, having accepted a draft drawn on it, does not pay at maturity;

v. negotiation with a nominated bank and that nominated bank does not negotiate.

b. An issuing bank is irrevocably bound to honour as of the time it issues the credit.

c. An issuing bank undertakes to reimburse a nominated bank that has honoured or negotiated a complying presentation and forwarded the documents to the issuing bank. Reimbursement for the amount of a complying presentation under a credit available by acceptance or deferred payment is due at maturity, whether or not the nominated bank prepaid or purchased before maturity. An issuing bank's undertaking to reimburse a nominated bank is independent of the issuing bank's undertaking to the beneficiary.

Article 8

Confirming Bank Undertaking

a. Provided that the stipulated documents are presented to the confirming bank or to any other nominated bank and that they constitute a complying presentation, the confirming bank must:

i. honour, if the credit is available by

    a. sight payment, deferred payment or acceptance with the confirming bank;

    b. sight payment with another nominated bank and that nominated bank does not pay;

    c. deferred payment with another nominated bank and that nominated bank does not incur its deferred payment undertaking or, having incurred its deferred payment undertaking, does not pay at maturity;

    d.   acceptance with another nominated bank and that nominated bank does not accept a draft drawn on it or, having accepted a draft drawn on it, does not pay at maturity;

    e.   negotiation with another nominated bank and that nominated bank does not negotiate.

  ii. negotiate, without recourse, if the credit is available by negotiation with the confirming bank.

    b. A confirming bank is irrevocably bound to honour or negotiate as of the time it adds its confirmation to the credit.

    c. A confirming bank undertakes to reimburse another nominated bank that has honoured or negotiated a complying presentation and forwarded the documents to the confirming bank. Reimbursement for the amount of a complying presentation under a credit available by acceptance or deferred payment is due at maturity, whether or not another nominated bank prepaid or purchased before maturity. A confirming bank's undertaking to reimburse another nominated bank is independent of the confirming bank's undertaking to the beneficiary.

    d. If a bank is authorized or requested by the issuing bank to confirm a credit but is not prepared to do so, it must inform the issuing bank without delay and may advise the credit without confirmation.

Article 11

Teletransmitted and Pre-Advised Credits and Amendments

    a. An authenticated teletransmission of a credit or amendment will be deemed to be the operative credit or amendment, and any subsequent mail confirmation shall be disregarded. If a teletransmission states "full details to follow" (or words of similar effect), or states that the mail confirmation is to be the operative credit or amendment, then the teletransmission will not be deemed to be the operative credit or amendment. The issuing bank must then issue the operative credit or amendment without delay in terms not inconsistent with the teletransmission.

    b. A preliminary advice of the issuance of a credit or amendment ("pre-advice") shall only be sent if the issuing bank is prepared to issue the operative credit or amendment. An issuing bank that sends a preadvice is irrevocably committed to issue the operative credit or amendment, without delay, in terms not inconsistent with the pre-advice.

Article 14

Standard for Examination of Documents

    a. A nominated bank acting on its nomination, a confirming bank, if any, and the issuing bank must examine a presentation to determine, on the basis of the documents alone, whether or not the documents appear on their face to constitute a complying presentation.

b.   A nominated bank acting on its nomination, a confirming bank, if any, and the issuing bank shall each have a maximum of five banking days following the day of presentation to determine if a presentation is complying. This period is not curtailed or otherwise affected by the occurrence on or after the date of presentation of any expiry date or last day for presentation.

c.   A presentation including one or more original transport documents subject to articles 19, 20, 21, 22, 23, 24 or 25 must be made by or on behalf of the beneficiary not later than 21 calendar days after the date of shipment as described in these rules, but in any event not later than the expiry date of the credit.

d.   Data in a document, when read in context with the credit, the document itself and international standard banking practice, need not be identical to, but must not conflict with, data in that document, any other stipulated document or the credit.

e.   In documents other than the commercial invoice, the description of the goods, services or performance, if stated, may be in general terms not conflicting with their description in the credit.

f.   If a credit requires presentation of a document other than a transport document, insurance document or commercial invoice, without stipulating by whom the document is to be issued or its data content, banks will accept the document as presented if its content appears to fulfil the function of the required document and otherwise complies with sub-article 14 (d).

g.   A document presented but not required by the credit will be disregarded and may be returned to the presenter.

h.   If a credit contains a condition without stipulating the document to indicate compliance with the condition, banks will deem such condition as not stated and will disregard it.

i.   A document may be dated prior to the issuance date of the credit, but must not be dated later than its date of presentation.

j.   When the addresses of the beneficiary and the applicant appear in any stipulated document, they need not be the same as those stated in the credit or in any other stipulated document, but must be within the same country as the respective addresses mentioned in the credit. Contact details (telefax, telephone, email and the like) stated as part of the beneficiary's and the applicant's address will be disregarded. However, when the address and contact details of the applicant appear as part of the consignee or notify party details on a transport document subject to articles 19, 20, 21, 22, 23, 24 or 25, they must be as stated in the credit.

k.   The shipper or consignor of the goods indicated on any document need not be the beneficiary of the credit.

l.   A transport document may be issued by any party other than a carrier, owner, master or charterer provided that the transport document meets the requirements of articles 19, 20, 21, 22, 23 or 24 of these rules.

Article 15

Complying Presentation

a.   When an issuing bank determines that a presentation is complying, it must honour.

b.   When a confirming bank determines that a presentation is complying, it must honour or negotiate and forward the documents to the issuing bank.

c.   When a nominated bank determines that a presentation is complying and honours or negotiates, it must forward the documents to the confirming bank or issuing bank.

Article 16

Discrepant Documents, Waiver and Notice

a.   When a nominated bank acting on its nomination, a confirming bank, if any, or the issuing bank determines that a presentation does not comply, it may refuse to honour or negotiate.

b.   When an issuing bank determines that a presentation does not comply, it may in its sole judgement approach the applicant for a waiver of the discrepancies. This does not, however, extend the period mentioned in sub-article 14 (b).

c.   When a nominated bank acting on its nomination, a confirming bank, if any, or the issuing bank decides to refuse to honour or negotiate, it must give a single notice to that effect to the presenter. The notice must state:

i.   that the bank is refusing to honour or negotiate; and

ii.   each discrepancy in respect of which the bank refuses to honour or negotiate; and

iii. a) that the bank is holding the documents pending further instructions from the presenter; or

 b) that the issuing bank is holding the documents until it receives a waiver from the applicant and agrees to accept it, or receives further instructions from the presenter prior to agreeing to accept a waiver; or

 c) that the bank is returning the documents; or

 d) that the bank is acting in accordance with instructions previously received from the presenter.

d.   The notice required in sub-article 16 (c) must be given by telecommunication or, if that is not possible, by other expeditious means no later than the close of the fifth banking day following the day of presentation.

e.   A nominated bank acting on its nomination, a confirming bank, if any, or the issuing bank may, after providing notice required by sub-article 16 (c) (iii) (a) or (b), return the documents to the presenter at any time.

f.   If an issuing bank or a confirming bank fails to act in accordance with the provisions of this article, it shall be precluded from claiming that the documents do not constitute a complying presentation.

g.   When an issuing bank refuses to honour or a confirming bank refuses to honour or negotiate and has given notice to that effect in accordance with this article, it shall then be entitled to claim a refund, with interest, of any reimbursement made.

Article 17
Original Documents and Copies

a. At least one original of each document stipulated in the credit must be presented.

b. A bank shall treat as an original any document bearing an apparently original signature, mark, stamp, or label of the issuer of the document, unless the document itself indicates that it is not an original.

c. Unless a document indicates otherwise, a bank will also accept a document as original if it:

    i. appears to be written, typed, perforated or stamped by the document issuer's hand; or

    ii. appears to be on the document issuer's original stationery; or

    iii. states that it is original, unless the statement appears not to apply to the document presented.

d. If a credit requires presentation of copies of documents, presentation of either originals or copies is permitted.

e. If a credit requires presentation of multiple documents by using terms such as "in duplicate", "in two fold" or "in two copies", this will be satisfied by the presentation of at least one original and the remaining number in copies, except when the document itself indicates otherwise.

Article 18
Commercial Invoice

a. A commercial invoice

    i. must appear to have been issued by the beneficiary (except as provided in Article 38);

    ii. must be made out in the name of the applicant (except as provide in sub-article 38(g));

    iii. must be made out in the same currency as the credit; and

    iv. need not be signed.

* * *

c. The description of the goods, services or performance in a commercial invoice must correspond with that appearing in the credit.

Article 30
Tolerance in Credit Amount, Quantity and Unit Prices

a. The words "about" or "approximately" used in connection with the amount of the credit or the quantity or the unit price stated in the credit are to be construed as allowing a tolerance not to exceed 10% more or 10% less than the amount, the quantity or the unit price to which they refer.

b.   A tolerance not to exceed 5% more or 5% less than the quantity of the goods is allowed, provided the credit does not state the quantity in terms of a stipulated number of packing units or individual items and the total amount of the drawings does not exceed the amount of the credit.

c.   Even when partial shipments are not allowed, a tolerance not to exceed 5% less than the amount of the credit is allowed, provided that the quantity of the goods, if stated in the credit, is shipped in full and a unit price, if stated in the credit, is not reduced or that sub-article 30 (b) is not applicable. This tolerance does not apply when the credit stipulates a specific tolerance or uses the expressions referred to in sub-article 30 (a).

Article 35

Disclaimer on Transmission and Translation

A bank assumes no liability or responsibility for the consequences arising out of delay, loss in transit, mutilation or other errors arising in the transmission of any messages or delivery of letters or documents, when such messages, letters or documents are transmitted or sent according to the requirements stated in the credit, or when the bank may have taken the initiative in the choice of the delivery service in the absence of such instructions in the credit.

If a nominated bank determines that a presentation is complying and forwards the documents to the issuing bank or confirming bank, whether or not the nominated bank has honoured or negotiated, an issuing bank or confirming bank must honour or negotiate, or reimburse that nominated bank, even when the documents have been lost in transit between the nominated bank and the issuing bank or confirming bank, or between the confirming bank and the issuing bank.

A bank assumes no liability or responsibility for errors in translation or interpretation of technical terms and may transmit credit terms without translating them.

Article 36

Force Majeure

A bank assumes no liability or responsibility for the consequences arising out of the interruption of its business by Acts of God, riots, civil commotions, insurrections, wars, acts of terrorism, or by any strikes or lockouts or any other causes beyond its control.

A bank will not, upon resumption of its business, honour or negotiate under a credit that expired during such interruption of its business.

Article 37

Disclaimer for Acts of an Instructed Party

a.   A bank utilizing the services of another bank for the purpose of giving effect to the instructions of the applicant does so for the account and at the risk of the applicant.

b.   An issuing bank or advising bank assumes no liability or responsibility should the instructions it transmits to another bank not be carried out, even if it has taken the initiative in the choice of that other bank.

c.   A bank instructing another bank to perform services is liable for any commissions, fees, costs or expenses ("charges") incurred by that bank in connection with its instructions.

If a credit states that charges are for the account of the beneficiary and charges cannot be collected or deducted from proceeds, the issuing bank remains liable for payment of charges.

A credit or amendment should not stipulate that the advising to a beneficiary is conditional upon the receipt by the advising bank or second advising bank of its charges.

d.   The applicant shall be bound by and liable to indemnify a bank against all obligations and responsibilities imposed by foreign laws and usages.

BERGAMI, WHAT CAN UCP 600 DO FOR YOU?

11 VJ 1 (2007).*

* * *

3   THE CHANGES TO THE RULES

The UCP 600 has 39 articles, whereas the UCP500 has 49. It is beyond the scope of this paper to analyse all of the changes that were made between the UCP 500 and the UCP 600, but rather to concentrate on the most important aspects of change and the likely results of the implementation of the new rules. It is worth noting that, notwithstanding the fact that the UCP 600 has been issued, there is still a degree of confusion and concern over its interpretation and implementation. * * *

3.1   DEFINITIONS

This is a new helpful addition to the rules. Interestingly, the definition of 'Complying Presentation' alters the current notion of compliant documents. The UCP 600 defines such a presentation as one that 'is in accordance with the terms and conditions of the credit, the applicable provisions of these rules and international standard banking practice'. This definition does not specifically refer to the International Standard Banking Practice published by the ICC or any published standard for that matter. This issue has possibly been the most contentious of the UCP 500 and is further discussed below at Art. 13.

3.2   ARTICLE 4 UCP 500 v. ARTICLE 4 UCP 600

The independence principle has been retained in the new rules. The letter of credit is separate from, and not subject to the contract of sale, insofar as banking operations are concerned.

Given that typically banks are not party to the contract of sale, this separation seems logical. To highlight the need for this separation, the UCP 600 has sought to reinforce this principle by the addition of sub-article (b):

> An issuing bank should discourage any attempt by the applicant to include, as an integral part of the credit, copies of the underlying contract, proforma invoice and the like.

The wording chosen for this article does [not] place an absolute ban on the practice of including extraneous material and it may be impossible for the issuing bank to effectively prevent this. Counsel should advise the client to ensure that a 'workable' letter of credit is received, that is, one that does not have overly onerous and extremely detailed requirements, as this is likely to lead to an unnecessary documentary burden and increase the risk of non-compliance and therefore payment delays or bad debts. If a letter of credit is received that incorporates such extraneous material, counsel should advise the client to seek the removal of the requirements imposed by such extraneous material through an amendment to the original letter of credit by the buyer, and this must be done prior to the dispatch of the goods.

3.3   ARTICLE 5 UCP 500 v ARTICLE 5 UCP 600

The words 'in credit operations all parties concerned' has been substituted by the word 'banks'. This is a clearer definition and reinforcement of the role of banks in the transaction—they will only deal with documents.

3.4   ARTICLE 13 UCP 500 v ARTICLE 14 UCP 600

Sub-article (a) retains the words 'on their face'. This is even though its meaning in English is unclear and it cannot be translated into some languages. The reason for the retention of this expression is certainly unclear, as it appears that the Consulting Group deemed this expression superfluous and decided to remove it on an 18–5 vote, but apparently that vote was ignored in the final version. This does not change current banking practices, but fails to clarify exactly the meaning of the expression 'on its face' and questions this in the light of international standard banking practice as discussed below.

Sub-article (b) allows banks less time to check documents for compliance—five days instead of the current seven days. This is good news for exporters, as it potentially lessens delays in payments, particularly when letters of credit are drawn at sight and payable at the counters of the issuing bank.

Sub-article (d) refers to international standard banking practice when checking data on documents. This is a fundamental issue that is linked to the issue of the UCP 500. When the UCP 500 was issued in 1993, Art. 13 (in part) read 'compliance [. . .] shall be determined by international standard banking practice as reflected in these articles'. The problem was that no such reference actually existed. The world had to wait until 2003 for the ICC to publish the International Standard Banking Practice (ISBP).

In a curious twist, the ICC deemed the ISBP voluntary and therefore banks could adopt it if they so desired. To make the ISBP even less authoritative, it was given guideline status. In checking documents, banks could use the ISBP for clarification, but decisions as to compliance or non-compliance still must be made in accordance with the UCP alone. * * *

Counsel should advise a client to seek information from the banks in relation to the standards being applied to determine documentary compliance. Sub-article (d) makes attempts to water down the practice of inventing discrepancies mentioned earlier in the paper. In some parts of the world, this is indeed common practice and this was openly disclosed at an ICC meeting in 2005 where there were 'a number of very frank admissions from some banks in Asia that re-examination of documents represented a very significant source of income'. The wording used in the UCP 600 appears to take less of a strict compliance approach, but that is entirely dependent on the 'standard' the document checker applies. There are still ample opportunities for 'mischievous checking' practice to develop. * * *

Sub-article (j) indicates that the addresses of the seller and buyer need not be the same as in the letter of credit, provided they are in the same respective country. Furthermore, contact details—such as telephone numbers, fax numbers, email addresses and the like—will not be checked unless they form part of either the consignee, or notify party detail on a transport document in which case they must be as stated in the letter of credit. Although this may seem a small issue, a discrepancy on transport document data is a common problem for exporters. Counsel advising the client should highlight the importance of the accuracy of transport document data to avoid non-compliance.

3.5 ARTICLE 14 UCP 500 v ARTICLE 16 UCP 600

This article prescribes the path banks must follow in the light of discrepant documents. The [old] rules (Art. 14 UCP 500) place complete control of the process in the hands of the issuing bank when discrepant documents have been presented. Essentially, the issuing bank at its discretion [was entitled to] approach the buyer to seek a written waiver of the discrepancies—in other words, a formal written acceptance that payment may be released notwithstanding errors in the documentation. * * * The letter of credit having been applied for and having been issued [would] require the applicant to pay/reimburse the bank against documents presented. If those documents are non-compliant, the bank [was] not * * * able to demand the funds from the applicant because the documents would be in breach of the requirements on the initial letter of credit application. Therefore, the issuing bank [needed] 'permission' to accept the documents from the applicant and pay against them.

Article [16] UCP 600 introduces a new option without disturbing the existing framework. It does so by allowing the exporter an opportunity to provide prior instructions to the bank in case of discrepant documents. The exporter may now request that the issuing bank consult with them prior to approaching the importer for a waiver of the discrepancies. This is an important consideration for the exporter, because the price of the goods sold may have appreciated between the date of shipment and arrival of the documents at the counters of the issuing bank. The exporter under such circumstances has an opportunity to gain additional revenue. Counsel advising the client should ensure that the option provided under Art. 16 UCP 600 is invoked against every letter of credit transaction to provide for an opportunity to increase revenue where possible. It does not seem that there are any disadvantages in invoking such action.

3.6   ARTICLE 37 UCP 500 v ARTICLE 14 UCP 600

The UCP 500 adopted the doctrine of strict compliance insofar as the description of the goods on the commercial invoice was concerned. The UCP 600 appears to have diluted this requirement. Article 37 UCP 500 states (in part) 'the description of the goods on the commercial invoice must correspond with the description in the credit'. The UCP 600 does not carry such a statement and therefore there is a presumption that the document checker will adopt a more flexible approach in determining documentary compliance. This should hopefully result in fewer discrepancies and be to the benefit of the exporter.

PIETRZAK, SLOPING IN THE RIGHT DIRECTION: A FIRST LOOK AT THE UCP 600 AND THE NEW STANDARDS AS APPLIED TO VOEST–ALPINE

7 Asper Rev. Int'l Bus. & Trade L. 179 (2007).*

* * *

II.   ANALYSIS

Although letters of credit fuel international sales by reducing the risks of unknown creditworthiness and offering secure payment for buyers and sellers, standards for determining compliance remain inconsistent among courts and this can eliminate many benefits that letters of credit can provide. The second princip[le] of letter of credit law is compliance, where the documents presented to the bank by the beneficiary must comply with the documents required in the letter of credit. Therefore, document examination and rejection is one of the most important topics concerning letters of credit. In the absence of a clear standard by which to accept or reject documents, banks have not only failed to honour letters of credit for the wrong reasons, but have also been unclear about how to effectively notify the seller of the decision to reject payment.

Fortunately for buyers, sellers, and banks, the UCP 600 coupled with the recent U.S. court decision in Voest–Alpine, has made significant strides to end the uncertainty and has clarified many unresolved issues stemming from the UCP 500. Under the UCP 600, the standard of compliance is not "strict" compliance. This approach is consistent with recent court decisions such as Voest–Alpine, which reject the strict compliance standard. Finally, the UCP 600 also clarifies effective refusal both in terms of waiver and notice.

The UCP 600 Rejects the Strict Compliance Test and Supports Compliance under a Rational Link Test as Applied in Voest–Alpine * * *

Because the UCP 500 does not provide guidance on what the standard of compliance should be, courts in the U.S. and courts abroad began to create new standards of compliance that varied across districts. At least four standards of compliance have developed among courts: (1) strict compliance; (2) flexible strict compliance; (3) substantial compliance; and (4) reasonable compliance. Recognizing that courts have failed to agree on a uniform approach to compliance, the writers of the UCP 600 sought to relieve uncertainty by revamping the law. Consequently, the UCP 600 provides the much needed guidance to find the optimum standard. The UCP 600 rejects the strict compliance test and supports compliance under a rational link test as applied by the District Court for the Southern District of Texas in Voest–Alpine. * * *

The UCP 600 embraces the case-by-case approach, permitting minor deviations and adopting the position taken by the court in Voest–Alpine * * *, as the UCP 600 states that banks can read data in a document in context with the letter of credit. Furthermore, the UCP 600 expressly refutes any claim that a document needs to be identical to all other information in that document, any other stipulated document, or the credit. Therefore, the District Court in Voest–Alpine * * * was correct to examine "whether the whole of the documents obviously relate to the transaction on their face" and whether the documents "bore obvious links," and their decision would be upheld under the UCP 600.

The holding of Voest–Alpine * * * and the UCP 600 effectively prohibit the courts from utilizing the standard of strict compliance in future letter of credit cases. Letter of credit industry experts have gone as far as to define the practice-oriented approach taken in Voest–Alpine * * * as "refreshing." Arguably, however, the adoption of the common-sense approach taken in Voest–Alpine * * * will require courts to distinguish between obvious typographical errors and documents that are distinctly different from those required by the letter of credit. Some commentators suggest that this judicial scrutiny does not satisfy the needs of bankers.

The view that judicial scrutiny is contrary to the needs of the letter of credit community is valid and does not contradict the holding of Voest–Alpine. * * * Prior courts interpreted strict compliance to mean unwavering adherence and thereby failed to consider parties' motives, expectations, and reasoning for accepting or rejecting a document that merely had a typographical error. It is true that courts applying strict compliance did not judicially interpret the actions of the banks. However, they also did not give deference to reasonable banking practices. By nullifying the strict compliance standard, the UCP 600 and Voest–Alpine...are not asking courts to impose their own judicial interpretations of what constitutes a material discrepancy; rather courts are to apply a reasonable document checker standard. Under this standard, if a bank determines that a discrepancy is material, a court will uphold that decision if international banking standards imply that the same is true. Likewise, a court will reject that decision if it is not supported by international banking standards. Commentators have made various recommendations on how to establish such a standard. * * *

The UCP 600 Clarifies the Rules Governing Dishonour * * *

In addition to their concerns regarding the proper standard of compliance, bankers are also unsure as to how much time they have to notify a beneficiary of a decision to dishonour a letter of credit, whether they must always seek an applicant waiver when faced with document discrepancies, and how to effectuate proper notice of rejection. * * *

The UCP 600 provides clarity in a number of ways. Firstly, UCP 600 Article 14(b) will permit a bank a maximum of five, rather than seven, banking days following the day of presentation to determine if a presentation is complying. Secondly, * * * the words "reasonable time" and "not to exceed" have been entirely eliminated from the UCP 600 article. Finally, UCP 600 Article 16(b) makes it clear that when a bank determines that a presentation does not comply and requests a waiver from the applicant, this does not extend the period mentioned in Article 14(b). Therefore, UCP 600 put an end to courts determining what qualifies as "reasonable time" and will succeed in providing a bright line rule to banks and businessmen where the UCP 500 failed.

2. Waiver and Notice of Dishonour Rules are Clear and Unambiguous under UCP 600

Understanding that banks have a full five days to review documents, seek waiver, and inform the beneficiary of acceptance or rejection is just the beginning. They must also understand how and when to seek waiver and how to properly dishonour the credit in order to avoid future liabilities. * * *

* * * Acknowledging that the UCP 500 lacked clarity with regard to the rejection of documents, the writers of the UCP 600 rewrote UCP 500 Article 14(B) in UCP 600 Article 16(c) and provided the much needed instruction.

The new article states that when a bank decides to refuse to honour or negotiate, it must give a single notice to the presenter. The UCP 600 is clearer than the UCP 500 because it provides that the notice must expressly state that the bank is refusing to honour or negotiate and must include each discrepancy upon which the bank made its decision to refuse payment. The UCP 600 goes even further and directs that the notice must also state either: (a) that the bank is holding the documents pending instructions from the applicant, (b) that the bank is holding the documents until it receives a waiver from the applicant and agrees to accept it, (c) that the bank is returning the documents, or (d) that the bank is acting in accordance with instructions previously received from the applicant.

Regardless of which option the bank chooses, it is clear that banks are required to expressly state their rejection of the documents. Accordingly, whether or not the beneficiary fully understands the refusal notice becomes a non-issue, as the UCP 600 clearly mandates a requirement of an express rejection of documents. This is just one example of how the UCP 600 will alleviate potential litigation on the issue of refusal language in the aftermath of Voest–Alpine * * *

FOLSOM, GORDON AND SPANOGLE, INTERNATIONAL BUSINESS TRANSACTIONS IN A NUTSHELL

143–150 (8th ed., 2009).*

Electronic communication has taken over some aspects of letters of credit practice, but not others. They dominate the issuance process in bank-to-bank communications, and are sometimes used by applicants to stimulate the issuance process. However, at this time they have not been able to create an entirely paperless transaction pattern for many reasons. First, the beneficiary still wants a piece of paper committing the banks to pay upon specified conditions. Second, electronic bills of lading still are not accepted in most trades as transferable documents of title * * *. Thus, in the collection of the letter of credit, physical documents will be forwarded, while funds settlement may be electronic.

About three quarters of letter of credit communication between banks, for other banks' issuance, advice, confirmation or negotiation of letters of credit is paperless; and the communication is electronic. While bank-to-bank communication is electronic, bank-to-beneficiary (Seller) communication is still paper-based. Letter of credit issuers can now communicate directly with beneficiaries' computers, however, and use of this practice should be expected to increase. The UCP rules are now written in terms of "teletransmissions," rather than paper-based terminology, which facilitates the use of electronic practices.

Most bank-to-bank communication concerning letters of credit are routed through the dedicated lines of SWIFT (the Society for Worldwide Interstate Financial Telecommunications). SWIFT is a Belgian not-for-profit organization owned by banks as a cooperative venture for the transmission of financial transaction messages. It requires all such messages to be structured in a uniform format, and uses standardized elements for allocating message space and for message text. Thus, messages can be communicated on a computer-to-computer basis without being re-keyed.

* * *

On the other end of the electronic communications, the beneficiary (Seller, in the documentary sale), who must be induced to part with value on the basis of the bank's promises, wants a "hard copy", a written letter of credit in the traditional form. The receiving bank therefore will convert the SWIFT electronic message into such a written, paper credit. However, the SWIFT message has been designed for bank-to-bank use, and not necessarily for use by beneficiaries, which creates some problems. First, it does not bear a signature in the traditional sense, even though it has been thoroughly authenticated within the computer-based transmission mechanisms. Thus, the beneficiary is entitled to doubt whether the sending bank is bound to the beneficiary to perform by the written credit derived from the SWIFT electronic message.

The issue if usually framed as: "Is the SWIFT message to be considered to be *the* operative credit instrument as far as the beneficiary is concerned?" The issue is of importance to beneficiaries not only in the original issuance of the credit, but also in the myriad of amendments to the credit which may follow. Under SWIFT rules, SWIFT users treat the electronic message as a binding obligation, and treat the authentication as the functional equivalent of a signature. However, the beneficiary is not a SWIFT user, and banking practice has been that a beneficiary can rely on an electronic message only after it has been issued in a paper-based format, properly signed or otherwise authenticated. The Revised UCC states that a letter of credit "may be issued in any form," including an electronic format, but that provision does not necessarily answer the question as to whether the unsigned, paper-based transcription of a SWIFT message, generated by the recipient of that message, is the operative credit instrument and binds the issuing bank.

Under the UCP, whether an electronic message is the operative credit instrument or not depends upon the terminology in the message itself. The UCP provides that, if the electronic message states "full details to follow," or states that a mail confirmation will be the operative credit instrument, then the electronic message is not that instrument, and the subsequent message is. However, another provision of the UCP states that other authenticated electronic messages to advise or amend credits *are* the operative credit instrument. In the latter transactions, mail confirmations should not be sent, and are to have no effect if sent.

However, there is some doubt as to whether SWIFT–generated transcriptions are subject to the UCP. SWIFT internal rules provide that credits issued through its system are subject to the UCP, but the transcription into a hard copy may bear no reference to the UCP. The UCP states that the UCP provisions govern "where they are incorporated into the text of the credit." That language is deemed, in some parts of the world, to require an express reference to the UCP in the message to the beneficiary.

QUESTIONS AND COMMENTS

A.　*Strict Compliance of the Documents to the Letter of Credit*:

1.　It is certainly accurate to say that *Rayner* indicates the common law "strict compliance" requirement at its most rigorous echoing Viscount Sumner's comments in *Equitable Trust v. Dawson*. As such, it raises some troubling questions:

If a bank should not be expected to know "a whole variety of foreign law," what, if anything, *should* it be expected to know? *Rayner* seems to suggest that it need not know trade terms, even one "universally understood," such as the equivalence between "Coromandel groundnuts" and "machine-shelled kernels." However, the "universe" of understanding in *Rayner* may, in fact, be very small—encompassing only Mincing Lane. How broad a universe of understanding is needed before bankers may be expected to comprehend it? For example, are "electronic computer parts having two gigabites of dynamic random access memory" the same as "2 GG DRAM chips"? In particular, is "LCD," when it is used with watches, a trade term cognizable only within a limited universe, or a term used in common parlance?

2.　The *Rayner* facts can also raise a separate issue concerning whether a bank should be required to investigate certain points. If the bills of lading in *Rayner* had described the goods only as "bags C.R.S., each bag said to weigh 177 lb. net," could the bank safely reject these documents? Would there be a duty on the bank, if it did not know what "C.R.S." meant, to inquire of someone what it meant? The alternative may be to allow bankers who know there is a problem willfully to remain ignorant. How does the *Rayner* decision advise bankers to act?

In the Problem facts, would you have advised Metro to make further inquiries when it found a term ("ICD") that it did not recognize? What would be the consequences of requiring banks to make inquiries in such circumstances? If, out of an abundance of caution, you would advise further investigation, to whom should Metro address its inquiries?

3.　If courts do not demand mirror-image conformity to meet a "strict compliance" standard, how far from a mirror image can the documents be, and still "constitute a complying presentation" under UCP art. 14?

4.　Under U.S. law, the Comments to UCC § 5–108 indicate that "slavish conformity" is not required for strict compliance, which suggests that typographical errors will be excused. The Adodo excerpt cites several such cases in footnote 26. But it also notes in the text the *Bank of Cochin*, *BNP*, *Beyene*, *Hanil Bank*, and *Tradax* decisions to the contrary. Is the error in Problem 5.1 more or less "material" than the errors in these cases?

5.　Leading figures in the U.S. letter of credit community would prefer a looser standard. Should the courts adopt whatever standard is customary in the banking community, or should they create their own standard, based on their reading of the UCC text?

6. Adodo and Pietrzak both refer to "the reasonable document checker" standard. Does such a standard give too much power to the bank, at a cost to the applicant-buyer? If all that the applicant receives for its payment are documents, should the applicant have the right to insist on either mirror-image quality or an actual waiver of any defects, even "typographical errors"? In other words, should the banks, through the UCP—a rather one-sided instrument—be able to control both the terms of the contract and its interpretation? Whatever happened to the concept of interpreting a contract against the drafter of the contract?

7. Careful wording changes in UCP 600 have sparked a debate about whether it has created a more flexible compliance standard. Like its predecessor, it refers to "international standard banking practice;" but it also expressly states that data in a document "need not be identical to" the requirements of the credit. *See* UCP 600, Article 14d. The 2007 edition of the ICC's "International Standard Banking Practice" (ISBP) manual similarly explains that "a misspelling or typographical error that does not affect the meaning of a word or the sentence in which it occurs does not make a document discrepant." It cites as an example a description of goods as "fountan pen" instead of "fountain pen." *See* ICC Publ. 681E, p. 22 (2007).

Is this binding upon the courts? Would you expect the new wording in UCP 600 and the ISBP explanation to solve all "strict compliance" issues? Also, how does a court identify what "international standard banking practice" is?

8. According to Pietrzak, UCP 600 has substantially changed the standard for examining documents. Bergami is more skeptical. Which of the two approaches do you find more persuasive? Note also that Professors White and Summers observe in their influential treatise that UCP 600 "still does not express a choice in explicit terms, although Articles 2 and 14d refer to compliance with international banking standards, which arguably constitutes strict compliance in today's world." *See* White and Summers, *Uniform Commercial Code* 1096 (6th ed., 2010).

9. In light of the phrasing in UCP 600 Article 14, the case law described in the excerpts, and all of the scholarly analysis, what, ultimately, is your advice to Metro on the "ICD vs. LCD" issue? Does this discrepancy mean that Shady's (and thus Metro's) documents do not reflect a "complying presentation"? What are the arguments for and against?

10. Now assume that "ICD" in fact is an accepted alternate acronym for "LCD" in the lighters and pens business. What effect would that have on whether BNP may properly refuse to accept Metro's presentation of "ICD" documents?

B. BNP's Other Grounds for Rejecting Metro's Presentation

1. What is the basic legal relationship between BNP and Metro? Could BNP, for example, simply refuse to pay Metro under any circumstances and instead tell it to seek reimbursement from Galleries Rochambeau (the applicant on the letter of credit)? *See* UCP Article 7. *Compare* UCC § 5–107(a).

2. (i) Was BNP's October 9 message to Metro timely? *See* UCP Articles 14b, 16d. (ii) Note also that the UCP time limit is different from that in the UCC. *Compare* § 5–108(b). Which takes priority? *See* UCC §§ 5–116(c), 5–103(c), and Rev. § 1–302. (iii) Finally, do BNP's consultations with Galleries have any effect on the timeliness of its response? *See* UCP Article 16a, b.

3. BNP's first notice raised the objection that—at least as claimed by Galleries—Shady's goods were not in "proper working order" as required by the letter of credit (*see* SWIFT Code 45A). Is that a valid ground for dishonor under the UCP? *See* Article 14. *See also* UCC § 5–108(g).

4. BNP raised as an additional discrepancy that Metro presented (from Shady) a copy of the original offer from Galleries, reasoning that this document was not required by the letter of credit. Is that a valid ground for dishonor under the UCP? *See* Article 14.

5. Is BNP's objection concerning an "original" commercial invoice a valid one, given that all six of Shady's invoices were stamped "original"? *See* UCP Article 17.

6. What is the effect of BNP's second notice (on October 10)? First, recall (from Problem 4.0) that there may be a noteworthy difference between a "pro forma" invoice and a final "commercial invoice." But what is the effect of BNP raising this issue in a second notice? *See* UCP Article 16c-f. *See also* UCC § 5–108(c).

7. Finally, note that issuing banks commonly require a "reimbursement agreement" when an applicant requests a letter of credit. These agreements often include a variety of waivers and consents by the applicant as well as additional rights and protections for the issuer (such as an ability to disregard minor discrepancies). UCC Article 5 generally permits such agreements, provided that they do not excuse liability or limit remedies for the issuer's failure to perform, or otherwise remove general obligations of good faith and reasonableness. *See* UCC § 5–103(c) and Rev. § 1–302.

C. *Errors in Communication and Transmission*

1. With all of the messages, letters, and presentations, international letter of credit transactions carry noteworthy risks of errors in communication and transmission. Consider in this regard two twists on the facts for this Problem:

2. Assume that Shady sent conforming documents to Metro for presentation, but that they were lost or damaged in the mail. Although Shady kept copies, the expiry date for the letter of credit has now passed. What result? *See* UCP Article 35.

3. Assume, _instead_, that, due to a printer malfunction in Metro's offices, the "LCD" references in Code 45A of BNP's SWIFT message actually looked like "ICD" when a Metro manager read the automatic printout the next morning. As a result, *Metro* used "ICD" to describe the goods in its confirmation letter to Shady. Shady then used that term in all of its documents to ensure a presentation that complied with Metro's "confirmation" of the letter of credit—although Shady had no idea what "ICD" might mean.

a. After Metro honored and in turn presented Shady's documents to BNP, BNP raised the discrepancy (as against the SWIFT message that it originally sent) and refused to pay. The Adodo excerpt notes that courts have not been sympathetic to beneficiaries where an error occurred in the letter of credit itself. But here, Shady saw the error and made a complying (though senseless) presentation. Did Shady have any duty to highlight the obvious error?

b. What about the relationship between Metro and BNP? UCP Article 35 generally relieves banks of liability for transmission errors. But this is not particularly helpful when, as here, the dispute is between two banks. Metro will argue that it acted entirely in good faith in confirming the letter of credit and thus in honoring Shady's presentation. Could it validly rely on "international standard banking practice" (*see* UCP Article 14d) to argue that it should not bear the loss for the "transmission" error? If this rule formally does not apply, may Metro turn to the UCC as a gap-filler? *See* UCC § 5–108(e), (f)(referring to "standard practice of financial institutions") and Rev. § 1–304 (generally imposing a duty of good faith).

4. Finally, to avoid the risks and costs of paper documents, numerous groups have attempted to develop an entirely electronic letter of credit transaction, and especially an electronic bill of lading. As noted in Problems 4.2 and 4.5 above, however, these efforts thus far have not met widespread success, although the new "Rotterdam Rules" may provide hope for the future. For its part, the I.C.C. in 2002 and again in 2007 issued a set of UCP supplementary rules designed to "accommodate presentation of electronic records alone or in combination with paper documents." This "eUCP" applies, however, only if a letter of credit specifically refers to it, not merely to the general UCP.

PROBLEM 5.2   ENJOINING PAYMENT OF LETTERS OF CREDIT FOR FRAUD: TABLETS FROM CHINA

SECTION I.   THE SETTING

Your client, John Little, has signed a contract to buy 1000 "computer tablets in working condition, with standard manufacturer's warranty" from Robbin Hood, who is based in Shanghai, People's Republic of China. Hood is shipping the tablets CIF San Francisco. The contract requires payment by irrevocable letter of credit. At Little's request, Nottingham Bank has issued an appropriate letter of credit on Little's behalf, promising to honor a draft accompanied by an invoice and clean, on board bill of lading for "1000 new computer tablets, accompanied by standard manufacturer's warranty." Little now has been told by Scarlet, a "friend in the business" and a competitor of Hood, that although Hood obtained actual bills of lading describing the goods as "1000 cartons said to be new computer tablets, in working condition, and accompanied by a standard manufacturer's warranty; Shipper's load, weight and count," in fact the tablets shipped are all used and inoperable—junk. Little wants to know what he can do.

Would it make a difference if Hood were known to be very shaky financially, and likely to file a petition in bankruptcy at any time?

Would it make a difference if Hood's Bank had confirmed the letter of credit and had already paid over the amount of the draft to Hood, before you learned about the alleged defective shipment?

SECTION II. FOCUS OF CONSIDERATION

The "fraud exception" for letters of credit started, as many other legal concepts have, with a Cardozo dissent. "I dissent from the view that, if [the issuing bank] chooses to investigate and discovers thereby that the merchandise tendered is not in truth the merchandise which the documents describe, it may be forced by the delinquent seller to make payment of the price irrespective of its knowledge." *Maurice O'Meara Co. v. National Park Bank*, 239 N.Y. 386, 146 N.E. 636 (1925). The Cardozo concept was in direct contravention of the general rule that a breach of the sales contract did not create a breach of the letter of credit contract, as long as the documents in fact conformed. Cardozo's concept was later used in *Sztejn v. J. Henry Schroder Banking Corp.*, 177 Misc. 719, 31 N.Y.S.2d 631 (1941), to permit issuance of an injunction against payment against documents under a letter of credit, or presentment of the draft and accompanying documents under the letter of credit, where the buyer alleged, not merely a breach of warranty, but intentional fraud (the boxes allegedly had rubbish in them), *and* the party presenting the draft was also a party to the fraud.

Sztejn left a very narrow avenue for buyer to seek and obtain judicial intervention through injunctive relief in the letter of credit transaction. To sellers, the concept creates great uncertainty about prompt payment, because they know nothing about the judicial system and fear the worst. To buyers, the concept creates a theoretical argument; but buyers have succeeded on this argument in very few reported cases. The *Sztejn* opinion limits itself in several ways: (1) The issuer (Buyer's Bank) allegedly knew that the documents were "forged or false," even though they conformed on their face to the letter of credit; and (2) allegedly, no one other than the fraudulent party (seller) had relied upon the letter of credit—*i.e.*, Seller's Bank had paid over no funds to seller. Apparently, if Seller's Bank had relied, the court would have rejected the petition for an injunction.

Web sources for further study include the ICC web page on the UCP *http://www.iccwbo.org/policy/banking/id2434/index.html*

If this transaction is governed by the UCC, it is essential to read UCC § 5–109, set forth in the Documents Supplement.

SECTION III. READINGS, QUESTIONS AND COMMENTS

MID-AMERICA TIRE, INC. v. PTZ TRADING LTD.

Supreme Court of Ohio, 2002.
95 Ohio St.3d 367, 768 N.E.2d 619.

ALICE ROBIE RESNICK, J.

* * *

PARTIES AND PARTICIPANTS

Given the multilateral nature of the negotiations and arrangements in this case, it is beneficial to provide a working list of the various parties and key participants and their relationships to one another and the transactions at hand.

The American parties and participants are as follows:

(1) Plaintiff-appellant and cross-appellee, Mid-America Tire, Inc. ("Mid-America"), is an Ohio corporation doing business as a tire wholesaler. Mid-America provided the financing for the purchase of the tires in this case and was the named applicant by whose order and for whose account the LC was issued.

(2) Arthur Hine is the president of Mid-America and signatory to the LC application.

(3) Plaintiff-appellant and cross-appellee, Jenco Marketing, Inc. ("Jenco"), is a Tennessee corporation doing business as a tire wholesaler. Jenco formed a joint venture with Mid-America to purchase the tires at issue.

(4) Fred Alvin "F.A." Jenkins is the owner of Jenco and also acted as Mid-America's agent in the underlying negotiations.

(5) Paul Chappell is an independent tire broker who resides in Irvine, California. Chappell works as an independent contractor for Tire Network, Inc., a company owned by his wife, and acted throughout most of the negotiations as an agent for Jenco.

(6) First National Bank of Chicago ("First National"), on behalf of NBD Bank Michigan, is the issuer of the LC in this case. First National was a defendant below, but is not a party to this appeal.

The European parties and participants are as follows:

(1) Defendant-appellee and cross-appellant, PTZ Trading Ltd. ("PTZ"), is an offshore import and export company established in Guernsey, Channel Islands. PTZ is the seller in the underlying transaction and the beneficiary under the LC.

(2) Gary Corby is an independent tire broker operating as Corby International, a trading name of Corby Tyres (Wholesale) Ltd., in Wales, United Kingdom. Corby was the initiator of the underlying negotiations.
* * *

(3) John Evans is the owner of Transcontinental Tyre Company located in Wolverhampton, England, and PTZ's admitted agent in the underlying negotiations.

(4) Aloysius Sievers is a German tire broker to whom PTZ owed money from a previous transaction unconnected to this case. Sievers, also an admitted agent for PTZ, procured and shipped the subject tires on behalf of PTZ, and signed and presented the draft for payment under the LC.

(5) Patrick Doumerc is the son of the proprietor of Doumerc SA, a French company that is authorized to sell Michelin overstock or surplus tires worldwide. Doumerc is the person from whom Sievers procured the mud and snow tires for sale to Jenco and Mid-America.

(6) Barclays Bank PLC in St. Peter Port, Guernsey, is the bank to which Sievers presented the invoice and shipping documents for payment under the supporting LC. Barclays Bank was a defendant below, but is not a party to this appeal.

EVENTS LEADING TO THE ISSUANCE OF THE LC

In October 1998, Corby approached Evans about obtaining large quantities of Michelin winter tires. Evans contacted Sievers, to whom PTZ owed money. Evans knew that Sievers had a relationship with a sole distributor of Michelin surplus tires out of France. Eventually, an arrangement was worked out under which Sievers would buy the tires from Doumerc's warehouse in France and Evans would sell them on behalf of PTZ through Corby to an American purchaser.

Meanwhile, Corby contacted Chappell in California and asked whether he was interested in importing Michelin tires on the gray market for sale in the United States. "Gray imports" are tires that are imported without the knowledge or approval of a manufacturer into a market that the manufacturer serves, at a greatly reduced price. Corby told Chappell that he had a large client who negotiated an arrangement directly with Michelin to handle all of its overstock blem tires from France and who could offer 50,000 to 70,000 Michelin tires per quarter at 40 to 60 percent below the United States market price on an exclusive and ongoing basis. Chappell contacted Jenkins in Tennessee, who called Hine in Ohio, and it was arranged that Jenco and Mid-America would pursue the deal through Chappell.

On October 28, 1998, Corby faxed Chappell a list of Michelin mud and snow tires that were immediately available for shipment and Chappell forwarded the list to Jenkins. The list was arranged in columns for quantity, size, pattern, and other designations applicable to the European market with which Chappell and Jenkins were unfamiliar. In particular, many of the tires on the list bore the designation "DA/2C." Chappell and Jenkins understood that DA meant "defective appearance," a European marking for a blem, but they were not familiar with the "/2C" portion of the designation. When they asked for clarification, Corby told Chappell that "DA/2C" means the same thing as "DA," but since all of the listed tires are not warehoused at a single location, "/2C" is used merely to indicate that those blemished tires are located in a different warehouse.

Chappell also asked Corby whether he could procure and offer summer or "highway" tires, along with the winter tires. Chappell, Jenkins, and Hine had no interest in purchasing strictly snow tires, as it was already too late in the season to market them profitably. However, they would have an interest in buying both winter and highway tires and marketing them together as a package deal.

Corby told Chappell that 50,000 to 70,000 highway tires would be made available on a quarterly basis at 40 to 60 percent below the United States market price. However, when Chappell received another list of available tires from Corby on November 11, 1998, he complained to Corby that this list contained no summer tires and nowhere near 50,000 units. Corby responded that Michelin was anxious to get rid of these tires first, as the market for snow tires in Europe was coming to a close, that a list of summer highway tires would be made available over the next few weeks, and that Chappell and appellants would not have an opportunity to procure the highway tires unless they first agreed to purchase the snow tires. Corby explained that Michelin does not list available summer tires in the mid-month of a quarter. Instead, it waits for these tires to accumulate in a warehouse and then puts out the list at the end of the month. Thus, a list of summer tires would be available over the next few weeks.

In a transmission dated November 13, 1998, Corby wrote to Chappell:

"The situation is as I explained yesterday, there are no summer tyres available at all but, if, and a very big if, this deal goes ahead we will get all surplus stocks at the end [of] each qu[arter] from now on, but if this deal does not go, then I know we can kiss any future offers good buy [sic]."

On November 20, 1998, Corby faxed Chappell a list of summer tires available for immediate shipment, but the listed units were not priced, were composed of many small "odd ball sizes" unmarketable in the United States, and did not approach the 50- to 70,000-range in aggregate quantity. In his cover letter, Corby assured Chappell that "I have of course been in contact with Michelin regarding the list of summer tyres" and "they have confirmed that in the next three/four weeks we have exclusive to us the new list of Michelin summer tyres, quantity unknown as yet, but they believe to be anything from 50,000/70,000 tyres, which would not be too bad for Jan sales." The letter also stated that Michelin was offering the tires at "the price of $1.50 per tyre more than the M & S tyres * * * based on taking the whole lot."

* * *

"Just to confirm once again, I have been assured by PTZ Trading who are acting on behalf of the factory that we will have exclusivity to all tyres that come available from now on."

* * *

Effective February 1, 1999, and expiring in Guernsey, Channel Islands, on April 2, 1999, First National issued an irrevocable credit at Hine's request in favor of PTZ and for the account of Mid-America in the amount of $517,260.33. The LC provided, among other things:

"COVERING SHIPMENT OF:

"14,851 MICHELIN TYPES AT USD 34.83 PER TIRE IN ACCORDANCE WITH SELLER'S PROFORMA INVOICE 927–98 DATED 11–19–98

"SHIPPING TERMS: EXWORKS ANY EUROPEAN LOCATION

"* * *

"THE CREDIT IS SUBJECT TO THE UNIFORM CUSTOMS AND PRACTICE FOR DOCUMENTARY CREDITS (1993 REVISION), INTERNATIONAL CHAMBER OF COMMERCE–PUBLICATION 500."

* * *

On March 1, 1999, Jenkins wrote to Evans, "We are with drawing [sic] our offer effective immediately to purchase the snow package, as PTZ has failed to meet their agreed commitment on the Michelin summer tire offer." (Emphasis deleted.) Jenkins stated that the listed prices for the tires are "not competitive" and "TOTALLY UNACCEPTABLE," and that "[w]e have gone from a reported 50,000 tires to a total offer of about 12,000 tires of which approximately 2,500 of those are TRX tires not sold in this country."

Between March 1 and March 5, 1999, Chappell and Jenkins discovered that it was Doumerc, not PTZ, who all along had the direct and exclusive relationship with Michelin to sell all of its overstock and blem tires. They also discovered that Corby had misrepresented the "DA/2C" designation, which attached to many of the tires on the summer lists as well as on the original winter list. Rather than indicating the warehousing location for those tires, "/2C" actually meant that the Department of Transportation serial numbers had been buffed off those units, rendering them illegal for import or sale in the United States.

During this time, Jenkins informed Evans that he would notify the United States Customs Service if the DA/2C tires were shipped, and Evans confirmed that he would not ship those tires to the United States. Also, Chappell informed Doumerc of the entire course of events, and Doumerc agreed not to ship the tires until Chappell and Jenkins had the opportunity to come to France, inspect the tires, and resolve the situation.

Chappell and Jenkins made arrangements to fly to France, but when they called Doumerc on March 11, Sievers answered the phone. They explained the entire matter to Sievers and offered to extend the LC expiration date in order to allow for a peaceful resolution. Sievers rejected the offer, however, stating that the winter tires belonged to him, not Doumerc, that he did not care what Doumerc had agreed to, and that "I have a letter of credit and I am shipping the tires."

The following day, Mid-America instituted the present action to enjoin payment under the LC. The complaint was later amended to add Jenco as a plaintiff. The trial court granted a temporary restraining order on March 16, 1999, and a preliminary injunction on April 8, 1999.

[After the trial court granted a permanent injunction, the court of appeals reversed, reasoning that a court may enjoin payment under a letter of credit only based on a beneficiary's presentation of forged or fraudulent documents, not on fraud solely in the underlying sales transaction. This appeal followed—the Authors.]

II. Issues for Review

* * *

1. Is the absence of an adequate legal remedy one of the prerequisites for injunctive relief under R.C. 1305.08(B) [Revised UCC § 5–109(b)]?

2. With regard to the availability and scope of a fraud exception to the independence principle, is the LC in this case governed by the UCP or R.C. 1305.08(B)?

3. Under the governing law, is there any fraud exception to the independence principle beyond the situation involving the beneficiary's presentation of forged or fraudulent documents? In particular, does the governing law recognize an exception for fraud in the inducement of the underlying contract and the supporting LC?

4. Are the trial court's factual findings sufficient to support the application of a recognized exception to the independence principle?

* * *

INADEQUATE LEGAL REMEDY

PTZ argues, and the court of appeals held, that appellants should be denied injunctive relief under R.C. 1305.08(B) because they have an adequate remedy at law. * * *

We hold, therefore, that in order for a court of competent jurisdiction to enjoin the issuer of a letter of credit from honoring a presentation under R.C. 1305.08(B), the court must find that the applicant has no adequate remedy at law.

In actions to enjoin honor on the basis of fraud, courts usually find that the applicant has an adequate remedy at law where the alleged injury is capable of being measured in pecuniary terms. While there is some authority to the contrary, most courts find that the availability of a monetary damage award for fraud in the underlying contract constitutes an adequate legal remedy, even if the applicant must travel overseas and submit to the uncertainties of foreign litigation in order to obtain it. On the other hand, the availability of a damage award is usually held to be inadequate where resort to foreign courts would be futile or meaningless, where the beneficiary is insolvent or may abscond with the money drawn, where honoring a draft would likely force the applicant into bankruptcy, or where the determination of damages would be difficult or speculative.

* * *

In Ohio, "courts of equity are more insistent that the legal remedy shall be in all respects adequate to justify the refusal of the injunction upon that ground." In order to be considered adequate, the legal remedy must "be of such a nature that full indemnity may be recovered without a multiplicity of suits." " 'It is not enough that there is a remedy at law; it must be plain, adequate and complete; or in other words, as practical, and as efficient to the ends of justice and its prompt administration, as the remedy in equity.' " Thus, in determining the propriety of injunctive relief, adequate remedy at law "means that the legal remedy must be as efficient as the indicated equitable remedy would be; that such legal remedy must be presently available in a single action; and that such remedy must be certain and complete."

* * *

In the present case, an action to recover damages for fraud would not be an adequate legal remedy because it would not be as prompt, efficient, and practical as the injunction issued by the trial court, and would not provide appellants with certain and complete relief in a single action. The pursuit of such a remedy would likely entail a multiplicity of suits against a number of defendants in several jurisdictions. The damages that appellants might seek to recover in an action for fraud would be difficult to estimate because of the near impossibility of determining the quantity of winter and summer tires that could or would have been seasonably marketed together and separately, the quantity of the "DA/2C" and other tires not marketable in the United States that could have been sold overseas, and the appropriate market conditions, cost/price differential, and quantity of offered or promised units. While it may be true, as PTZ argues, that appellants accepted some risk of pursuing damages in another nation's courts, it cannot be found that appellants assumed the risk of having to pursue an inadequate legal remedy.

* * *

GOVERNING LAW

R.C. Chapter 1305 is Ohio's version of Article 5 of the Uniform Commercial Code ("UCC"). It was enacted in its current form, effective

July 1, 1998, to reflect the 1995 revision of Article 5, and is applicable to any LC that is issued on or after its effective date.

* * *

The parties in this case have specifically adopted the UCP as applicable to the present undertaking. In fact, "[m]any letters of credit, domestic and international, state that they shall be governed by the UCP." "When rules of custom and practice are incorporated by reference, they are considered to be explicit terms of the agreement or undertaking." UCC 5–103, Official Comment 2.

* * *

The court of appeals, * * * found essentially that the UCP's silence on the issue of fraud precludes the applicant from obtaining relief under R.C. 1305.08(B). We disagree.

In adopting the UCP, "the International Chamber of Commerce undertook to fill in operational details for documentary letter of credit transactions by stating a consensus view of the customs and practice for documentary credits." Because "the UCP 'is by definition a recording of practice rather than a statement of legal rules,' [it] does not purport to offer rules which govern the issuance of an injunction against honor of a draft." Thus, the UCP's silence on the issue of fraud "should not be construed as *preventing* relief under the 'fraud in the transaction' doctrine, where applicable law permits it."

In fact, the overwhelming weight of authority is to the effect that Article 5's fraud exception continues to apply in credit transactions made subject to the UCP. These courts hold, in one form or another, that the UCP's failure to include a rule governing injunctive relief for fraud does not prevent the applicant from obtaining such relief under Article 5. Stated variously, these courts recognize that there is no inherent conflict between the UCP's statement of the independence principle and Article 5's remedy against honor where fraud is charged. Instead, this is merely a situation where Article 5 covers a subject not covered by the UCP.

PTZ concedes that these cases were correctly decided under former UCP Publication No. 400 (1983), which was silent on the issue of fraud. According to PTZ, however, "UCP 500 art. 3,* which controls this action, is no longer silent on the fraud exception." * * *

The UCP has been amended approximately every ten years since 1962. If the current version had finally broken the UCP's longstanding

---

* Authors' Note: The corresponding provision of UCP 600 is Article 4a, which states:

A credit by its nature is a separate transaction from the sale or other contract on which it may be based. Banks are in no way concerned with our bound by such contract, even if any reference whatsoever to it is included in the credit. Consequently, the undertaking of a bank to honour, to negotiate or to fulfill any other obligation under the credit is not subject to claims or defenses by the applicant resulting from its relationship with the issuing bank or the beneficiary. A beneficiary can in no case avail itself of the contractual relationship existing between banks or between the applicant and the issuing bank.

silence on the issue of fraud, one would expect at least a mention of that fact somewhere in the amendatory text or commentary. * * *

We hold, therefore, that when a letter of credit expressly incorporates the terms of the UCP, but the UCP does not contain any rule covering the issue in controversy, the UCP will not replace the relevant provisions of R.C. Chapter 1305. Since the UCP does not contain any rule addressing the issue of injunctive relief where fraud occurs in either the credit documents or the underlying transaction, R.C. 1305.08(B) remains applicable in credit transactions made subject to the UCP.

Accordingly, the rights and obligations of the parties in this case are governed by R.C. 1305.08(B), and the judgment of the court of appeals is reversed as to this issue.

ESTABLISHING FRAUD UNDER R.C. 1305.08(B)

Having determined the applicability of R.C. 1305.08(B), we must now consider its boundaries. In this regard, we have been asked to decide whether an issuer may be enjoined from honoring a presentation on the basis of beneficiary's fraud in the underlying transaction and to characterize the fraudulent activity justifying such relief.

FRAUD IN THE UNDERLYING TRANSACTION

May the issuer be enjoined from honoring a presentation under R.C. 1305.08(B) on the basis of the beneficiary's fraudulent activity in the underlying transaction? The short answer is yes, since R.C. 1305.08(B) authorizes injunctive relief where "honor of the presentation would facilitate a material fraud by the beneficiary on the * * * applicant." To fully appreciate the import of this language, however, it is necessary to review some of the history leading to its adoption.

Before the independence principle was ever codified, its parameters were set in the seminal case of *Sztejn v. J. Henry Schroder Banking Corp.* In that case, the applicant-buyer contracted to purchase a quantity of bristles from the beneficiary-seller, but the seller shipped 50 crates of cow hair and other rubbish. The court concluded that these facts, if established, could support an injunction against honor. In so doing, the court explained that the independence principle applies "in cases concerning alleged breaches of warranty," but does not extend to a case "involving an intentional fraud on the part of the seller." In other words, the fraud defense actually " 'marks the limit of the generally accepted principle that a letter of credit is independent of whatever obligation it secures.' "

As originally drafted in 1955, UCC 5–114 provided that a court of appropriate jurisdiction may enjoin honor only if there was forgery or fraud in a required document.

In 1957, the drafters added language providing that the court may enjoin such honor where "a required document * * * is forged or fraudulent *or there is fraud in the transaction.*" (Emphasis added.) UCC 5–114(2). This rule represents a codification of the *Sztejn* case.

One of the major disputes surrounding former UCC 5–114(2) centered on whether the "transaction" meant only the credit transaction per se or encompassed the underlying transaction as well. * * *

R.C. 1305.08(B) (UCC 5–109[b]) now provides that a court of competent jurisdiction may grant injunctive relief where "honor of the presentation would facilitate a material fraud by the beneficiary on the issuer or applicant." In so doing, R.C. 1305.08(B) refocuses the court's attention away from the particular transaction in which the fraud occurred and toward the level of fraud committed. It clarifies that the beneficiary's fraud in either transaction will suffice to enjoin the issuer from honoring a presentation, provided the fraud is material.

* * *

We hold, therefore, that material fraud committed by the beneficiary in either the letter of credit transaction or the underlying sales transaction is sufficient to warrant injunctive relief under R.C. 1305.08(B). Accordingly, the judgment of the court of appeals is reversed as to this issue.

MEASURE OF FRAUD

Another controversy that surrounded the "fraud in the transaction" language of UCC 5–114(2) involved the degree or quantity of fraud necessary to warrant injunctive relief. As noted in *Cromwell*, "There is more than one measure of 'fraud' in the various jurisdictions in the United States." In fact, manifold tests were devised for establishing fraud under UCC 5–114(2).

However, UCC 5–109(b) (R.C. 1305.08[B]) clarifies that only "material fraud" by the beneficiary will justify an injunction against honor. * * *

As another court adhering to this standard explained, the applicant must show that the letter of credit was, in fact, being used by the beneficiary "as a vehicle for fraud," or in other words, that the beneficiary's conduct, if rewarded by payment, "would deprive the [applicant] of any benefit of the underlying contract and * * * transform the letter of credit * * * into a means for perpetrating fraud."

Thus, we hold that "material fraud" under R.C. 1305.08(B) means fraud that has so vitiated the entire transaction that the legitimate purposes of the independence of the issuer's obligation can no longer be served.

The court of appeals actually did rely on *Sztejn, Intraworld Indus.,* and *Roman Ceramics Corp.*, to establish its so-called "vitiation exception," but construed the exception so narrowly as to preclude relief where the beneficiary's fraudulent conduct occurs solely in the underlying transaction. Thus, the court of appeals relied on the right cases for the wrong reasons. As a consequence, the court of appeals declined to address the issues of agency and fraud in the underlying contract, holding instead that the trial court should not even have taken evidence on these issues.

Accordingly, the judgment of the court of appeals is reversed on this issue as well.

PTZ'S ACTIONS

The trial court found the following facts to have been established by clear and convincing evidence:

"6. Gary Corby represented to F.A. Jenkins that PTZ Trading, Ltd. was in fact the sole distributor for surplus Michelin tires and that there was a direct relationship between PTZ Trading, Ltd. [a]nd Michelin. Corby further represented to Jenkins that there would be 50,000 to 70,000 summer tires available to Jenco per quarter at a price 40 to 60 percent below the U.S. market price within weeks of Jenco showing good faith by purchasing in excess of five hundred thousand dollars worth of mud and snow tires currently offered by PTZ Trading, Ltd.

"7. The Court further finds that John Evans, as agent for PTZ Trading, Ltd., was aware that Corby was making such representations to Jenco and that such representations were false. Mr. John Evans, as an agent for PTZ, knew that Jenco considered the purchase of the summer tires to be necessary in order to make the winter snow and mud tires saleable in the U.S. market. Mr. Evans did nothing to correct Mr. Corby's misrepresentations. Mr. Evans affirmed the misrepresentations and attempted to buttress them in correspondence with Jenco.

"8. Mr. Evans conveyed this information to Mr. Sievers who also acknowledged that he understood that the purchase of the summer tires by Jenco was critical to the conclusion of the sale of the mud and snow tires and without which the winter tire sale would not occur.

"9. John Evans and Aloysius Sievers also knew that a large portion of the mud and snow tires they were attempting to sell were not capable of being imported into the United States or sol[d] here because the United States Department of Transportation identification number had been 'buffed' off of such tires. Both Sievers and Evans knew that Jenco and Mid America Tire intended to sell the snow tires in the United States, but neither advised Jenco or Mid America Tire of the existence of the 'buffed' tires.

"10. Prior to the issuance of the letter of credit, John Evans knew Mid America Tire, Inc. and Jenco were operating under intentionally false and inaccurate representations made by Corby and reinforced by John Evans.

"* * *

"12. The Court finds, specifically, that the representation that PTZ had a direct relationship with Michelin Tire, the representation that PTZ was the exclusive distributor for surplus Michelin Tires, the representation that a substantial quantity of between fifty and seventy thousand tires would be available quarterly on an exclusive basis to Jenco and Mid

America Tire, Inc. at 40 to 60 percent of the U.S. market price were all material statements inducing Plaintiffs to issue the underlying letter of credit and were in fact false and made with knowledge of their falsity."

Given these facts, we are compelled to conclude that PTZ's actions in this case are sufficiently egregious to warrant injunctive relief under the "material fraud" standard of R.C. 1305.08(B). The trial court's findings demonstrate that PTZ sought to unload a large quantity of surplus winter tires on appellants by promising a large number of bargain-priced summer tires, without which the winter tires would be virtually worthless to appellants. Keenly aware that appellants would not agree to purchase the winter tires without the summer tires, PTZ made, participated in, and/or failed to correct a series of materially fraudulent promises and representations regarding the more lucrative summer tires in order to induce appellants to commit to purchasing the winter tires and to open an LC in PTZ's favor to secure payment. Dangling the prospect of the summer tires just beyond appellants' reach, PTZ sought first the issuance of the LC, and then shipping instructions, in an effort to cash in on the winter deal before appellants could discover the truth about the "DA/2C" tires and PTZ's lack of ability and intention ever to provide summer tires at the price and quantity represented. Indeed, when appellants learned of PTZ's fraud after opening the LC, and PTZ was no longer able to stall for shipping instructions with nonconforming lists of summer tires, Sievers proclaimed, "I have a letter of credit and I am shipping the tires."

Under these facts, it can truly be said that the LC in this case was being used by PTZ as a vehicle for fraud and that PTZ's actions effectively deprived appellants of any benefit in the underlying arrangement. In this sense, PTZ's conduct is comparable to the shipment of cow hair in *Sztejn*, the shipment of old, ripped, and mildewed boxing gloves in *Cambridge Sporting Goods*, and the failure to disclose nonconforming performance specifications for the stereo receives in *NMC Ent., Inc.*

PTZ's demand for payment under these circumstances has absolutely no basis in fact, and it would be pointless and unjust to permit PTZ to draw the money. PTZ's conduct has so vitiated the entire transaction that the only purpose served by invoking the independence principle in this case would be to transform the LC into a fraudulent seller's Holy Grail, which once obtained would provide cover for fraudulent business practices in the name of commercial expedience. Accordingly, we reverse the court of appeals' judgment as it bears on this issue.

* * *

Judgment reversed.

DOLAN, TETHERING THE FRAUD INQUIRY IN LETTER OF CREDIT LAW

21 Bank. & Fin. L.R. 479–480, 485–490 (2006).*

1. Introduction

The party (the applicant) that before the fact has caused its bank to issue a letter of credit or other independent obligation and that must reimburse the bank in the event it honours that obligation may prefer after the fact to prevent the bank from honouring it. Generally, independent obligation law forbids banks from dishonouring the request of the obligation's beneficiary for payment and forbids courts from stopping the payment by injunction or otherwise. There is, however, a critical exception to that general pro-payment principle. The exception applies when there is fraud. This article deals with recent developments pertaining to the fraud inquiry and especially with cases that evince absence of a desire to protect independent obligations by limiting the fraud exception.

It is axiomatic that courts and legislatures must tether the fraud inquiry in independent obligations law, for untethered, the inquiry destroys these independent commercial devices, which are crucial to international trade and domestic commerce. Unrestrained, the fraud inquiry transmutes these devices into secondary obligations, and while secondary obligations serve useful commercial purposes, they differ from the critical features of independent obligations—low cost and prompt payment. Both law and commerce generally treat independent obligations as "pay now, argue later" devices and dependent obligations as "argue now, pay later" devices. Wide-ranging inquiry for fraud corrodes that distinction.

* * *

3. The Fraud Exception to the Independence Principle

In common law states engaging in international trade and commerce, courts generally support the independence principle but have fashioned an important exception to it. That exception is the fraud exception * * * Applied broadly, the fraud exception destroys the independence of the bank guarantee and the letter of credit rendering them secondary obligations. * * *

In order to prevent wholesale use of fraud claims to effect that commercially unacceptable result, common law courts have attached to the fraud exception a number of rules narrowing it to the point that it is not destructive of the guarantee's and the letter of credit's independence. U.K. courts have held, for example, that in order to justify stopping payment under a credit, the party seeking to stop payment, the contractor in the foregoing illustration, must "establish" fraud, that is, must make a case of irrefutable fraud. A mere claim of fraud is not sufficient under this rule. U.K. and other courts have tethered the fraud rule further by limiting it to cases in which the beneficiary of the credit and not some third party has practised the fraud. Thus, loading certificates backdated by brokers would not support a fraud exception when the beneficiary of a letter of credit was unaware of the backdating. U.S. courts have traditionally added a high threshold in defining the fraud that will support an injunction stopping payment under a credit. Professor Ellinger characterizes the American rule as one of stopping payment only if the beneficiary that seeks payment "acts without any shred of honest belief in his rights." Canadian authority generally accepts that characterization of the fraud necessary for relief. U.S. jurisdictions to some extent have codified that feature of the fraud definition in the Uniform Commercial Code (hereafter "UCC") by defining letter of credit fraud as fraud that is "material." The UCC limits the fraud application further through the law of equity. The chief resort of the applicant for the credit (the contractor in the illustration) for stopping payment under a letter of credit in virtue of fraud is to ask a court to enjoin the payment. The UCC makes it clear that all conditions for that relief must be satisfied. Generally, that rule invokes equity's prerequisites for an injunction, prerequisites that render injunctions improper if the applicant (the contractor) has an adequate remedy at law. * * *

There has been one further effort to cabin the fraud rule so that it does not destroy independent obligations, an effort that Canadian law and U.S. law have rejected rather emphatically. This was an effort to confine the fraud investigation to the letter of credit transaction and to close the underlying transaction to the fraud inquiry.

4. The Locus of Fraud and Its Relationship to the Underlying Transaction

Common law courts recognize *Sztejn v. J. Henry Schroder Banking Corp.* as playing a central role in the fraud rule. There, the court took pains to limit inquiry into the underlying transaction, for it recognized that enmeshing the courts in that underlying contract and in cognate agreements would corrode the commercial viability of independent obligations. * * *

Given this state of the law, a number of commentators, among them * * * the author of this article, took the position that courts should confine their investigation of fraud to the letter of credit transaction. These commentators justified their position on the ground that opening the inquiry would yield decisions corrosive of independent obligations.

The efforts of the commentators have been largely unsuccessful. Two authoritative sources explicitly permit fraud investigation in the underlying transaction. The Supreme Court of Canada's judgment in *Angelica-Whitewear Ltd. v. Bank of Nova Scotia*, a virtual monograph on independent obligation law of Canada and other common law and civil law jurisdictions, makes it clear that the underlying transaction is open to the fraud inquiry. That ruling is persuasive authority for the position that fraud in the underlying transaction justifies stopping payment on a letter of credit. In the United States, the UCC makes it quite clear that the fraud inquiry may proceed into the underlying transaction.[24] In short, in light of legislative action and court decision, the commentators' position is now untenable in both Canada and the United States.

Nonetheless, the problem evident in the two views remains. * * * [M]any courts, perhaps most, refuse to engage in deep underlying contract inquiry. Those courts recognize the importance of limiting that inquiry in order to protect the independence of the commercial undertakings. Some courts, however, use the invitation to look for fraud in the underlying transaction, delve deeply into the underlying contract dispute, and range widely in the underlying and related transactions. These courts corrode the independent obligation as efficient commercial devices. Three cases, one recent judgment from the British Columbia Court of Appeal; one from the Supreme Court of Victoria, Australia; and one from the U.S. Court of Appeals for the Ninth Circuit, illustrate the confusion and the ease with which courts succumb to underlying transaction facts without proper regard for the independence of letters of credit and independent bank guarantees. These cases illustrate the fragility of the fraud tether. They demonstrate without any doubt that in cases to which the tether should apply, courts may ignore it. Thus, this article concludes, the key ingredient for tethering the fraud rule rest on precarious footings: the court's inclination to tether it. Absent that inclination, an absence that is evident in these three cases and others like them, the fraud inquiry corrodes the independence of the letter of credit and bank guarantee to the point that they become ineffective commercial devices.

MONTROD LTD v. GRUNDKÖTTER FLEISCHVERTRIEBS GmbH

Court of Appeal (Civil Division), 2002.
[2002] 1 W.L.R. 1975.

Thorpe, Potter LJJ and Sir Martin Nourse

The various appeals and applications for permission to appeal before us arise from orders made by [the lower court] in relation to the liability of the various parties arising from payment made by Standard Chartered Bank ("SCB") in London pursuant to a documentary credit issued by SCB in favour of Grundkötter Fleischvertriebs GmbH ("GK"), a German company named as beneficiary, through the advice of its German bank, Commerzbank. That credit had been issued at the request of Fibi Bank (UK) plc ("Fibi") acting on the instructions of Montrod Ltd ("Montrod"), the claimants in the action, who were named as applicants in the credit. The underlying contract was a contract of sale made between GK as sellers and Ballaris, a Russian entity [aligned with Montrod] as buyers of a

---

24. "The courts must examine the underlying transaction when there is an allegation of material fraud, for only by examining that transaction can one determine whether a document is fraudulent or the beneficiary has committed fraud and, if so, whether the fraud was material." UCC § 5–109 (Official comment 1, 2d para., 8th sentence).

consignment of 400 mt of frozen pork sides sold cif Moscow. The credit called inter alia for the presentation of certificates of inspection signed by Montrod.

* * *

The credit was expressed to be subject to the Uniform Customs and Practice for Documentary Credits, International Chamber of Commerce Publications 500 ("UCP 500"). * * * GK presented to SCB documents, including an inspection certificate apparently signed by Montrod, which on their face complied with the terms of the credit. SCB paid the credit in the face of an assertion by Montrod that the inspection certificate which GK presented had not been signed or authorised by Montrod and that the document was fraudulently created. The judge found that the inspection certificate had indeed been signed without the authority of Montrod but that GK was not fraudulent and was entitled to payment by SCB, which was entitled to payment from Fibi, which was in turn entitled to reimbursement by Montrod. [The trial] judge rejected Montrod's alternative argument that SCB was entitled to refuse payment on the grounds that, even if GK was not fraudulent, SCB and GK had prior to payment been made aware that the inspection certificate had not been signed or authorised by Montrod and as such was a "nullity" and/or a non-conforming document.

* * *

Neither as a matter of general principle, nor under UCP 500, is an issuing bank obliged to question or investigate the genuineness of documents which appear on their face to be documents the nature and content of which comply with the requirements of the credit. * * *

Not only is the necessity to examine the documents presented by the beneficiary limited to an examination of the documents alone (article 14(b)) but, under article 15, the bank assumes no liability or responsibility for the genuineness or legal effect of any such document. Finally, it is clear that there is a timetable laid down * * * in which the issuing bank must examine the documents and indicate to the party submitting them whether it accepts or refuses them: see article 14(b) * * *

As already made clear, Montrod's original allegation of fraud on the part of GK as beneficiary has not been pursued before us. There is no issue between the parties that, so far as the state of the authorities is concerned, no English court has yet held an issuing bank entitled to withhold payment under a letter of credit, against documents which on their face conform with the requirements of the credit, save on the ground of fraud of the beneficiary himself, or the person seeking payment. Nor is it in dispute that in England the fraud exception is part of the common law and that it is apt to apply despite the fact that UCP 500 makes no reference to, nor makes allowance for, such an exception. * * *

The argument for Montrod that, where fraud on the part of the beneficiary cannot be established, there should none the less be room for a nullity exception in the case of a document which is worthless in the sense that it is not genuine and has no commercial value, whether as a security for the goods or otherwise, involves an undoubted extension of the fraud exception as hitherto propounded in the English authorities. If the basis of a fraud exception is that the court will only intervene in breach of the autonomy principle for the purpose of preventing or discouraging the perpetration of fraud on the part of the beneficiary or other presenting party, it is a clear extension to hold that presentation of a document which is itself a nullity for reasons which are *not* known to the beneficiary or issuing bank at the time of presentation, are none the less to be similarly treated.

The fraud exception to the autonomy principle recognised in English law has hitherto been restricted to, and it is in my view desirable that it should remain based upon, the fraud or knowledge of fraud on the part of the beneficiary or other party seeking payment under and in accordance with the terms of the letter of credit. It should not be avoided or extended by the argument that a document presented, which conforms on its face with the terms of the letter of the credit, is none the less of a character which disentitles the person making the demand to payment because it is fraudulent *in itself*, independently of the knowledge and bona fides of the demanding party. * * *

In my view there are sound policy reasons for not extending the law by creation of a general nullity exception. Most documentary credits issued in the United Kingdom incorporate the UCP by reference. Various revisions of the UCP have been widely adopted in the USA and by United Kingdom and Commonwealth banks. They are intended to embody inter-national banking practice and to create certainty in an area of law where the need for precision and certainty are paramount. The creation of a general nullity exception, the formulation of which does not seem to me susceptible of precision, involves making undesirable inroads into the principles of autonomy and negotiability universally recognised in relation to letter of credit transactions. In the context of the fraud exception, the courts have made clear how difficult it is to invoke the exception and have been at pains to point out that banks deal in documents and questions of apparent conformity. In that context they have made clear that it is not for a bank to make its own inquiries about allegations of fraud brought to its notice; if a party wishes to establish that a demand is fraudulent it must place before the bank evidence of clear and obvious fraud[.] If a general nullity exception were to be introduced as part of English law it would place banks in a further dilemma as to the necessity to investigate facts which they are not competent to do and from which UCP 500 is plainly concerned to exempt them. Further such an exception would be likely to act unfairly upon beneficiaries participating in a chain of con-tracts in cases where their good faith is not in question. Such a develop-ment would thus undermine the system of financing international trade by means of documentary credits. * * *

BANCO SANTANDER SA v. BANQUE PARIBAS

Court of Appeal (Civil Division), 2000.
2000 WL 191098.

WALLER LJ: * * *

[Banque] Paribas issued a deferred payment letter of credit [one not requiring the use of negotiable drafts] on 5 June 1999 in favour of Bayfern Limited (Bayfern) requiring presentation of documents at the counters of Banco Santander (Santander) (the claimants) in London at any time until 15 September 1999; the deferred payment was promised at 180 days from Bill of Lading; the letter of credit was subject to The Uniform Customs and Practice for Documentary Credits (UCP) (1993 Revision); it expressly provided that Paribas undertook "at maturity... to cover Santander in accordance with their instructions".

Bayfern were advised of the letter of credit by Santander by advice dated 8 June 1999. Santander had been asked by Paribas to add their confirmation to the letter of credit and did so by the same advice. That advice also offered the possibility of discounting, and by letter dated 9 June 1998 Bayfern requested Santander to discount the full value at the rate offered by Santander.

By 15 June 1999 Bayfern had presented documents at the counters of Santander in London. Those documents were found on their face to comply with the terms of the letter of credit, and for the purpose of the preliminary issues it is to be assumed they were entitled so to find. That thus crystallised an obligation on the part of Paribas and Santander to pay Bayfern US\$ 20,315,796.30 on 27 November 1998 pursuant to the letter of credit i.e. the date 180 days after the date of the Bills of Lading.

On 16 June Santander confirmed to Bayfern that they had discounted "amount of documents and credited the sum of USD 19,667,238.84 value 17th June 1998 into your account with Royal Bank of Scotland...". They also asked for a letter from Bayfern "requesting discount and assignment of proceeds under the above mentioned Letter of Credit." Bayfern on 16 June produced that letter and requested the discounting of "your deferred payment/acceptance undertaking to us....", and confirmed that "In consideration we hereby irrevocably and unconditionally assign to you our rights under this letter of credit".

No notice of the assignment was given to Paribas. But in the meanwhile the documents had been passed by Santander to Paribas.

On 24 June 1998 Paribas informed Santander that the documents presented and accepted by Santander included false or forged documents. It is to be assumed for the purpose of the preliminary issues that Bayfern had been guilty of fraud, that one or more documents were forged, and that thus prior to 27 November 1998 both Santander and Paribas had notice of "established fraud".

* * *

As is by now apparent, the real issue between the parties is whether Paribas was entitled to refuse payment to Santander because fraud on the part of Bayfern could be established prior to 27 November 1998.

The resolution of that issue depends in my view on seeking answers to the following questions.

(1) Was the claim that Santander made as at 27 November 1998 made as assignee of Bayfern? If so, is there any reason why Paribas do not have the same defence to that claim as they would have had against Bayfern?;

and/or

(2) Was the claim made by Santander made as confirming bank for "cover" (as per the express terms of the letter of credit) or "reimbursement" under one or other of the articles of the UCP? It is not suggested by either side that the word "cover" in the letter of credit as opposed to "reimbursement" has any significance, and thus it is the terms of the UCP which are relevant. If it is a claim under the UCP, is Paribas entitled to say you had no obligation to pay Bayfern until 27 November 1998, by that date you would have had a defence to making any payment, and you thus have no right to reimbursement?

* * *

It is convenient to deal with the assignee point first.

Were Santander assignees?

The documents produced as between Santander and Bayfern at the instigation of Santander, certainly envisaged that Santander would be assignees of Bayfern's "rights under the letter of credit". Those are the express words used, and although it is probably immaterial as an aid to construction, it accorded with the instructions in Santander's Operational Procedures Manual (see page 74 para 6). What is more, it seems to me that Santander did intend to keep the rights available to the beneficiary under the letter of credit alive. The most obvious reason why they so intended is that whereas they had paid out a figure of $ 19,667,238.84 on 17 June 1998, they wished to be reimbursed not for that figure at that time or at all, but for $ 20,315,796.30 on 27 November so that they could earn their charge for the discounting. Mr Hapgood [for Banco Santander] argued that because the "assignment" involved Santander purchasing Bayfern's rights against Santander, it was plainly intended to extinguish all Bayfern's rights under the letter of credit against both banks. Thus, he argued, Bayfern had nothing to assign. I do not think it is plain at all that it was intended to extinguish all rights for the reasons I have given. I accept that there may be situations in which if a creditor unconditionally assigns the benefit of a debt to a debtor, he will thereby extinguish the debt. Mr Hapgood gets support for that proposition from the judgment of Millett J in In re Charge Card Services Limited where he says that "a charge in favour of a debtor of his own indebtedness to the chargor is conceptually impossible". I also accept that if there is joint and several liability under a contract performance by one discharges all. I further accept that the liability of Santander and Paribas under the letter of credit was joint and several. But it does not follow where as in the instant case there is a joint and several liability, and it is the intention of the parties to the assignment to keep alive the obligation which is joint and several, that that cannot be achieved by an assignment by the obligee (in this case Bayfern) to one of the joint and several contractors, of his rights against both joint and several contractors.

In my view the judge was right in concluding that Bayfern assigned its rights under the letter of credit.

Although before the judge the matter may have developed rather differently, on analysis it seems to me that the above conclusion leads to the following further conclusions.

1. Santander could not on 27 November 1998 be claiming as against Paribas as a confirming Bank which has paid, until it, as assignee of Bayfern, has notionally made the claim against itself at maturity date.

2. In so far as any claim were made by Santander as assignee from Bayfern, against Santander as Confirming Bank, the same question arises as arises in relation to the claim that Santander makes as assignee directly against Paribas.

In other words, unless Santander can make good its claim as assignee of Bayfern, the terms of the UCP are irrelevant and cannot assist Santander.

Are defences which would have been available against Bayfern available as against the assignee Santander?

I do not think that Stoddart v. Union Trust Ltd 1912 1 KB 181 assists Mr Hapgood. That authority has been the subject of criticism * * *. At best from Mr Hapgood's point of view, all that can be said of the case is that it recognises that there may be circumstances where there would have been no defence available as against an assignor but simply a personal counterclaim, where the court does not allow the counterclaim to be raised against the assignee. That does not deal with the situation where there would have been a defence available as against the assignor. In the present case, if Bayfern had sought payment under the letter of credit as at 27 November 1998, Santander and Paribas would have had a complete defence. This, I do not think was disputed by Mr Hapgood, since it follows from Lord Diplock's formulation of the fraud exception in United City Merchants v. Royal Bank of Canada of the former report in the following terms:-

> "To this general statement of principle as to the contractual obligations of the confirming bank to the seller, there is one established exception: that is, where the seller, for the purpose of drawing on the credit, fraudulently presents to the confirming bank documents that contain, expressly or by implication, material representations of fact that to his knowledge are untrue. Although there does not appear among the English authorities any case in which this exception has

been applied, it is well established in the American cases of which the leading or "landmark" case is Sztejn v. J. Henry Schroder Banking Corporation. This judgment of the New York Court of Appeals was referred to with approval by the English Court of Appeal in Edward Owen Engineering Ltd. v. Barclays Bank International Ltd., though this was actually a case about a performance bond under which a bank assumes obligations to a buyer analogous to those assumed by a confirming bank to the seller under a documentary credit. The exception for fraud on the part of the beneficiary seeking to avail himself of the credit is a clear application of the maxim ex turpi causa non oritur actio or, if plain English is to be preferred, "fraud unravels all." The courts will not allow their process to be used by a dishonest person to carry out a fraud."

* * *

GAO, THE FRAUD RULE IN LAW OF LETTERS OF CREDIT IN THE P.R.C.

41 Int'l Law. 1067 (2007).*

I. *Introduction*

... The People's Republic of China (P.R.C.) is currently one of the largest users of letters of credit in the world. Its exports and imports in 2006 exceeded U.S. $1.76 trillion. It is estimated that around 30 percent of the P.R.C.'s exports and imports are settled through letters of credit, which means that the dollar value was close to U.S.$600 billion in 2006. The widespread use of letters of credit in international trade with the P.R.C. means that this practice affects not only the interests of the parties at home but also those of its trading partners abroad.

The raison d'etre of letters of credit is to provide an assurance of payment to the beneficiary when complying documents are presented. The fraud rule in the law of letters of credit allows payment of a letter of credit to be stopped when fraud is involved even though the documents presented are in strict compliance with the terms and conditions of the letter of credit. The fraud rule, therefore, is in direct conflict with the fundamental purpose of the letter of credit and becomes "the most controversial and confused area" in the law governing letters of credit.

The practice of letters of credit, in particular the application of the fraud rule, in the P.R.C., has been a target for criticism over the years. It has been often alleged that the Chinese applicants, banks, and courts have used the fraud rule to avoid payment of letters of credit. Therefore, the application of the fraud rule in the P.R.C. is a hot issue in the use of letters of credit with respect to P.R.C. trade. This is partly because there was no suitable law in the area in the P.R.C. until late 2005, and the practice of the Chinese courts was not consistent.

---

* Copyright © 2007 and reprinted with permission of the author.

To fill the legal gap, streamline the judicial and banking practice of letters of credit in the P.R.C., and facilitate the P.R.C.'s international trade, the Supreme People's Court (SPC) promulgated The Rules of the Supreme People's Court Concerning Several Issues in Hearing Letter of Credit Cases (the "2005 Rules")[6] on November 14, 2005. The fraud rule is the major focus of the 2005 Rules, although they cover other areas of the law of letters of credit.

* * *

II. The Mechanism of the Letter of Credit and the Development of the Fraud Rule

* * *

Because of the principle of independence, the beneficiary requiring payment does not have to show the issuer that it has properly performed its duties under the underlying transaction. It needs only to produce documents that conform to the terms and conditions of the letter of credit. This leaves a loophole for unscrupulous beneficiaries to abuse the system and defraud the other parties involved. * * *

To prevent this unfairness, the fraud rule has been developed to balance the "commercial utility of letters of credit against the desire to prevent the inequitable results that flow from fraudulent misrepresentations in individual cases." The fraud rule in the law of letters of credit is recognized as the exception to the principle of independence, allowing the issuer or the court to view the facts behind the face of conforming documents and disrupting payment of a letter of credit. Under the fraud rule, although documents presented are on their face in strict compliance with the terms and conditions of the letter of credit, payment may be stopped if fraud is found to have been committed in the transaction before payment is made, provided the presenter does not belong to a protected class, such as a holder in due course. The fraud rule is necessary to prevent fraudsters from abusing the letter of credit system, but its scope of application has to be carefully circumscribed so as to maintain the commercial utility of the letter of credit.

---

6. Zuigao Renmin Fayuan Guanyu Shenli Xinyongzhen Jiaofeng Anjian Ruogan Wenti De Guiding [The Rules of the Supreme People's Court Concerning Several Issues in Hearing Letter of Credit Cases] (promulgated by the Adjudication Comm. of the Supreme People's Court, Oct. 24, 2005, effective Jan. 1, 2006), translated at [http://www.icc-china.org/New_Folder/home.htm] [hereinafter 2005 Rules]. The 2005 Rules are a set of judicial interpretations. Judicial interpretations are made by the SPC to provide practical guidance to all levels of courts in the P.R.C. for the application of law with respect to a particular issue, a specific statute, or an area of law if no statute exists therein. They are detailed and problem-solving oriented. Although they are not formally called law, they are law in the practical sense because they are cited in court decisions and legally binding. That is, if there is no statute in an area and a judicial interpretation has been made, that judicial interpretation has in fact become the only law in that area.

III.   The Development of the Fraud Rule in the P.R.C.

A.   Background

The P.R.C. had a highly centralized, planned economy, treated trade as a capitalist vestige, and maintained only marginal contact with the outside world before it embarked on its modernization drive and economic reform in late 1970s. Before it opened up to the world, there was little room for commercial instruments such as letters of credit to be widely utilized. As a result, there were no court cases of letters of credit in the P.R.C. at that time.

The first known letter of credit case in the P.R.C. is *Yuegang Agricultural Resources Development Co. v. Japanese Technology & Science Co.*, which was heard by Zhuhai Intermediate People's Court in 1986. There, the plaintiff, Yuegang Agricultural Resources Development, sued the defendant, Japanese Technology and Science, claiming that the feedstuff machinery delivered was not up to the quality provided in the underlying contract. When filing the action, the plaintiff applied to the court to freeze the payment of [Yen] 216 million under the letter of credit as a measure of property preservation. The Court allowed the application and the payment of the letter of credit was stopped.

To letter of credit experts, the result of the case is stunning and disappointing, as fraud was never mentioned in the case. The dispute was about the quality of goods, which should never trigger the application of the fraud rule. But, this is a true story and a genuine reflection of the approach of a court towards a letter of credit in the P.R.C. at that time.

* * *

D.   Drafting of the 2005 Rules

In order to meet demands on further economic reform and challenges brought by the P.R.C.'s accession to the WTO, a special division, No. 4 Civil Division (the "Division"), was formed by the SPC in August 2000 to deal with foreign-related commercial and maritime matters. One priority of the Division is to make necessary rules to provide guidance for courts of the country dealing with foreign-related commercial and maritime cases. A survey in early 2001 found that 25 percent of the foreign-related commercial cases heard by the Division were related to letters of credit. Following the survey, it was decided that a judicial interpretation concerning letters of credit was to be formulated. After more than four years of drafting and extensive consultation, the document was finally promulgated on October 24, 2005.

IV.   The Fraud Rule Under the 2005 Rule

The fraud rule in the law of letters of credit in the P.R.C. provided under the 2005 rules is detailed and comprehensive. It covers both substantive and procedural matters of the law, including the standard of fraud, parties who can be immune from the application of the fraud rule, parties who can bring an action to the court for the application of the rule, and other detailed court procedures.

A. Standard of Fraud

The fraud rule is developed to prevent fraudsters from using letters of credit to unjustly enrich themselves. It is applied when fraud is found in the transaction, so the first and foremost important question for formulators of the fraud rule and courts hearing letter of credit fraud cases to decide is what is fraud under the law of letters of credit or what kind of fraud can invoke the fraud rule in the law of letters of credit. * * * The divergent views expressed with respect to the kind of fraud that can invoke the fraud rule reflect the tension between two different policy considerations: "the importance to international commerce of maintaining the principle of the autonomy of documentary credits . . . and the importance of discouraging or suppressing fraud in the letter of credit transaction."

On the one hand, if fraud is defined too widely or the standard of fraud is set too low, the fraud rule may be abused by the applicant who does not want the issuer to pay simply because it will not profit from the underlying transaction. If obstruction of payment of a letter of credit is repeated too often, business confidence in letters of credit as effective performance assurances will be destroyed. On the other hand, if fraud is defined too narrowly or the standard of fraud is set too high and the fraud rule cannot be applied in cases where it should be applied, the effectiveness of the fraud rule will be compromised, which may encourage the growth of fraudulent conduct by beneficiaries, discourage the use of letters of credit by applicants, and ultimately harm the commercial utility of letters of credit. Therefore, it was always one of the major tasks in the minds of the drafters of the 2005 Rules to set up a proper standard of fraud to balance the competing interests in a letter of credit transaction.

In the P.R.C., fraud is defined under Article 68 of the Interim Opinions of the Supreme People's Court Concerning the Implementation of the General Principles of the Civil Law of the P.R.C. (IOGPCL) as "one party intentionally telling the other party a lie or concealing the truth of a fact in order to induce the other party to come to a decision that it otherwise would not come to." This is the test generally used in civil and commercial cases to determine if fraud is involved in the P.R.C. Having learned from the experience of other jurisdictions with respect to the issue and, more importantly, taking into consideration the special nature of letters of credit and the practice of the Chinese courts in the past twenty years, the drafters of the 2005 Rules have not taken the easy step of merely adopting the provision of Article 68 of the IOGPCL but have taken another route by enumerating the circumstances that can cause the fraud rule to apply in Article 8 [of the 2005 Rules], saying:

Any of the following shall be considered as letter of credit fraud:

(i) The beneficiary has forged documents or presented documents containing fraudulent information;

(ii) The beneficiary has intentionally failed to deliver goods or delivered goods with no value;

(iii) The beneficiary has conspired with the applicant or a third party and presented fraudulent documents whereas there is no actual underlying transaction; or

(iv) Other circumstances that constitute letter of credit fraud.

* * * Moreover, the 2005 Rules have introduced the concept of "letter of credit fraud" to indicate that the fraud in the law of letters of credit is not entirely the same as that in general civil and commercial cases. The standard of fraud provided here has clearly limited the types of fraud that can invoke the fraud rule in the law of letters of credit in the P.R.C. to the following circumstances:

(1) Documents presented by the beneficiary are forged or fraudulent. This covers two types of situations: one is that the document does not exist at all but is simply forged by the beneficiary; the other is that the document exists but the information contained therein is fraudulent. Presentation of either of types of documents will be considered as fraud under the 2005 Rules. There was a debate over situations such as whether the predating of a bill of lading should be treated as fraud in the drafting process. Some took the view that presenting a set of predated bill of lading might not cause substantive damages to other parties involved in the transaction, therefore mere predating of a bill of lading should not be treated as fraud that could invoke the fraud rule. But others took the view that a letter of credit was a documentary transaction and that any fraud in the documents should be covered under the fraud rule. The current provision has adopted the second view. Therefore, any fraud in the documents can now invoke the fraud rule in the P.R.C.

(2) Goods have not been delivered or delivered but without any value. There is an overlap between subsection (i) and subsection (ii), as the documents presented will be either forged or fraudulent if goods have not been delivered or have been delivered but without any value. Subsection (ii) has simply addressed the fraud problem from another perspective and offered the defrauded party another set of arguments in court. It also has its own practical bearing. It sends a message to parties of letters of credit, lawyers, and courts involved in a letter of credit fraud action that the standard of fraud invoking the fraud rule in the P.R.C. is very high: only non-delivery of goods or goods delivered with no value will be treated as fraud; other situations, such as goods delivered of low quality or short of some quantity, cannot be treated as letter of credit fraud under Chinese law. In other words, disputes over quality or quantity of goods cannot invoke the fraud rule at all in the P.R.C., and cases like *Yuegang Agricultural Re-*

sources Development will never happen again in the P.R.C. under the 2005 Rules.

(3) No genuine underlying transaction. From time to time, cases are reported in the P.R.C. that the beneficiary and the applicant are in collusion to defraud state-owned banks or to avoid the rules of foreign exchange control by making false contracts. Subsection (iii) is drafted to address this particular problem. . . . It clearly tells those who are using or may want to use the letter of credit system to avoid the law of foreign exchange control or to cheat the banks for funds that otherwise cannot be obtained that payment will be stopped by courts if their true intention is discovered.

Concerned that some types of fraudulent conduct may not be covered by subsections (i), (ii), and (iii), subsection (iv) was added to serve as a catch-all clause. The advantage of this clause is that it can serve as a safety valve to prevent any fraudulent acts from leaking through the net. There is, however, a danger that this provision may be used by some parties to interrupt the normal operation of a letter of credit given the history of the development of the fraud rule in the P.R.C. The real effect of this subsection remains to be seen.

B. *Parties Immune from the Fraud Rule*

As mentioned, the fraud rule is not always applied when fraud is found in a letter of credit transaction. It cannot be applied when the party seeking payment belongs to a protected class such as a holder in due course.

The rationale for some parties being immune from the fraud rule is to maintain the commercial utility of the letter of credit. The widespread use of the letter of credit is due to its commercial functions. One of the functions of letters of credit is to raise credit for the applicant and the beneficiary, which is partly achieved by allowing third parties, normally intermediary banks, to participate in the payment process of a letter of credit. These third parties may negotiate, purchase, or discount the beneficiary's drafts or demands for payment under a letter of credit or arrange other means to finance the underlying transaction such as making loans to the beneficiary by taking the right to the proceeds of the letter of credit as security, relying on the undertaking and creditworthiness of the issuing bank. When a letter of credit transaction is tainted with fraud and recourse for fraudster often turns out to be ineffective, the loss caused by the fraud tends to be borne by the innocent parties, including the issuer as well as the applicant and the third party. To protect the commercial interests of the innocent third parties, it has been well recognized that some presenters should be immune from the application of the fraud rule. This has been provided in Article 10 of the 2005 Rules as follows:

A people's court shall make a ruling to suspend the payment or a judgement to permanently stop the payment under a letter of credit when fraud is established, unless one of the following has happened:

(i) The nominated person or the person authorised by the issuing bank has paid in good faith in accordance with the instructions of the issuing bank;

(ii) The issuing bank or its nominated or authorized person has accepted the draft under the letter of credit in good faith;

(iii) The confirming bank has paid in good faith; or

(iv) The negotiation bank has negotiated in good faith.

* * *

Under Article 10 of the 2005 Rules, anyone immune from the fraud rule must act in "good faith." Under Chinese law, good faith denotes that the person acquiring an item of personal property is not aware of the transferor's defective title in that property. In the context of a case of letter of credit fraud, the term good faith should be interpreted as "without notice of the fraud." In other words, in accordance with Article 10 of the 2005 Rules, a person who may be immune from the application of the fraud rule must accept the draft or pay the beneficiary without notice of the fraud involved. Accordingly, if fraud is alleged and the negotiation bank has been notified of the fraud before it negotiates but subsequently negotiates the draft of the beneficiary, the negotiation bank should not be protected, as it has negotiated the presentation with notice of the fraud involved in the transaction.

* * *

C. Court Remedies

Article 9 of the 2005 Rules provides that "[t]he applicant, the issuing bank or any other interested party may apply to a competent people's court for a ruling to suspend the payment under the letter of credit if they have found out that the circumstances [of fraud] set out in Article 8 ... have happened and will cause them irreparable damage."

* * *

In summary, two forms of remedies are available in cases of letter of credit fraud under the 2005 Rules: (1) a ruling to suspend the payment; and (2) a judgement to permanently stop the payment. The former is an interim measure used before initiating the proceedings or during the course of the proceedings; the latter is a permanent measure used when fraud is established after a full trial of the case.

* * *

F. Conditions for the Remedies

Article 11 of the 2005 Rules provides:

A people's court shall accept the application by a party for a ruling to suspend the payment of a letter of credit prior to the filing of the action when the following conditions are met:

(i) The people's court receiving the application has the competent jurisdiction over the case;

(ii) The evidence rendered by the applicant has established the existence of the circumstances set out in Article 8 hereinbefore;

(iii) The applicant will suffer irreparable damage if a ruling to suspend the payment is not issued;

(iv) The applicant has provided effective and adequate security; and

(v) The circumstances set out in Article 10 hereinbefore do not exist.

* * * Five conditions should be met for the granting of the remedies to stop the payment under a letter of credit * * * [T]he discussion here will be focused on those listed in subsections (ii), (iii) and (iv).

Article 11(ii) provides that the applicant applying for the application of the fraud rule must provide the court with sufficient evidence to establish that the fraud listed in Article 8 of the 2005 Rules has occurred. This normally requires the presentation of written evidence, such as a letter from an independent third party showing that the ship has never turned up to the loading port or its arrival at the port is certain days later than claimed in the documents presented. It will be very difficult for a Chinese court to accept a mere oral allegation in order to apply the fraud rule.

Article 11(iii) provides that the fraud rule can only be applied when the applicant will suffer irreparable damages caused by the fraud involved in the transaction. Due to the special nature of the letter of credit, the application of the fraud rule or stopping payment of a letter of credit should be the last resort. The fraud rule should only be applied when no other choices are available. For example, if the defendant is a multi-national corporation or a person with assets in the jurisdiction sufficient for the measure of property preservation to be taken, the Chinese court should not apply the fraud rule to interrupt the payment of a letter of credit.

Article 11(iv) of the 2005 Rules provides that the applicant claiming the application of the fraud rule must provide the court with effective and adequate security.

* * *

When the 2005 Rules were drafted, there were two kinds of views with respect to the issue. One was to follow the position of the Opinions of the Supreme People's Court on the Application of the Civil Procedure Law of the People's Republic of China (OACPL) and require the applicant to furnish a security equal to the amount of payment that was requested to be stopped under the letter of credit. The other was that, given the special features of cases of letters of credit, in particular when the damage might not be as big as the amount of the payment to be stopped, the value of the security provided was not necessarily to be as large as the payment to be suspended or stopped. The security that should be provided was to ensure that the damages caused by the action to other parties were properly compensated if the action was wrongly taken. The 2005 Rules have adopted the latter view and require the security provided to be effective and adequate.

V. *Conclusion*

The P.R.C. is an old country with a young modern legal system that began its development in the late 1970s when it started opening up to the world. The law of letters of credit in the P.R.C. was almost blank, let alone the fraud rule, when it started its economic reform and modernization drive. But along with the overall rapid development of its economy and modern legal system and after almost twenty years of good efforts, the P.R.C. published the 2005 Rules containing the fraud rule in the law of letters of credit in late 2005.

The current fraud rule in the law of letters of credit in the P.R.C. provided under the 2005 Rules is comprehensive and unique. It is comprehensive because it covers almost all the aspects of the law with respect to the application of the fraud rule, whether substantively or procedurally, including the standard of fraud, parties who can be immune from the application of the fraud rule, parties who can bring an action to the court for the application of the rule and other detailed court procedures. Parties and courts dealing with letter of credit fraud can find almost all the provisions for such a case in one place.

The P.R.C. fraud rule is unique because it is different from any of the existing rules. In terms of procedural matters, for instance, under the CPL, a party applying for a ruling for property preservation in a general civil or commercial case can only ask the court to freeze the assets of the defendant and cannot apply for remedies such as restraining orders or injunctions to stop the defendant from doing things that may harm its interests. Under the fraud rule provided under the 2005 Rules, however, it can apply for a ruling to suspend or stop the payment under a letter of credit. In terms of substantive issues, for example, the standard of fraud provided under the 2005 Rules is different from the general standard of fraud set out in Article 68 of the IOGPCL in the P.R.C. or the standard of fraud in the law of letter of credit in other jurisdictions, such as that under Article 5 of the Uniform Commercial Code (U.C.C.) in the United States. By so providing, it has not only introduced the unique concept of "letter of credit fraud" into the law of letters of credit but, more importantly, made the job of courts, lawyers, or other parties dealing with these cases much easier. It is clear and certain for those involved to know what kind of acts can invoke the fraud rule in the P.R.C. They do not have to worry about the interpretation of the generic standard of fraud in individual cases, which can be challenging in many instances.

In summary, in the words of Professor Byrne, one of the leading experts in the law of letters of credit, "[t]he new Chinese LC Rules are a significant contribution to letter of credit jurisprudence." The P.R.C. "LC Rules" cannot be discussed without mentioning the fraud rule embodied in them.

QUESTIONS AND COMMENTS

1. It is very tempting to the law student to read an allegation of fraud, then read UCC § 5–109 (as revised in 1995), and either the five day time limit in UCP 600 Art. 14, or the seven day time limit in UCC § 5–108(b), and decide that the obvious course to follow is to rush to the first available court with a complaint which seeks an injunction—and to do this immediately so as to "beat" the time limit. However, there are a few practical problems which you may wish to consider before taking such action:

Do you have sufficient information upon which to act? What can you do to confirm the allegations you have received?

Is litigation the most efficient way to act? Are there other avenues of action available to you?

Do the facts alleged by Scarlet indicate anything more than a breach of contract by Hood—the very risk Little assumed by signing a sales contract with a clause requiring payment by letter of credit? How will you define "fraud" if you seek to prove that Hood's conduct is fraudulent? And, if you seek to enjoin payment by Nottingham under the letter of credit, how do you plan to prove the necessary requisites for a preliminary injunction—"irreparable injury," etc.?

2. The best source of information on whether the bills of lading had actually been issued or were forged is the Carrier. However, the present allegations by Hood would seem to create different informational problems. The Carrier has, in fact, issued the bills of lading—they are not forgeries. The Carrier does not know whether the computer tablets are new or operable or not—and may not wish to know, so that it will not be caught in an argument between Hood and Little. It has deliberately limited its description of the goods, so as to avoid the misdescription liabilities discussed in Problem 4.5. Is there any way to obtain accurate information without using "James Bond"-type espionage methods (*e.g.,* a mid-ocean, clandestine meeting with the ship carrying the goods, followed by a breaking into the cartons and testing of the goods)? If not, in your analysis concerning possible lines of action on Little's behalf, you must pay strict attention to the level of proof of Hood's culpability required for successful pursuit of any particular line of action. Do you believe that the fraud exception and injunctions against payment are likely to be available without Little having an information leak from an (identified) "insider" in Hood's organization? How often does that occur?

3. Would you prefer to litigate or have Nottingham Bank simply refuse to pay? Do you think Nottingham Bank would prefer to litigate or simply pay? If you have solid evidence of fraud, what is the bank's attitude most likely to be? Remember that their fees for this are very small and will not cover litigation expenses, so they also will not want to be caught in an argument between Little and Hood. They may prefer to retain Little's business and goodwill on a long-term basis, but UCC § 5-109(a) requires them to honor the

draft under many circumstances, even when they are aware of forgery, fraud, or fraud in the transaction.

Moreover, § 5–109(a)(2) states that an issuer in good faith *may* honor a presentation, even after notice. Finally, to avoid an almost inevitable action for wrongful dishonor brought by the beneficiary, the bank most likely will prefer a formal injunction by a court, but § 5–109(b) imposes significant requirements for such an option.

If you don't have solid evidence, a court is not likely to be sympathetic. If you don't have solid evidence *yet,* but think you could get it in a hurry (*e.g.,* less than three days) it may be possible to persuade the bank to delay payment for that amount of time while you obtain any necessary evidence.

4. The UCP has no express provision that addresses fraud or forgery at all. The English court in *Montrod Ltd.* nonetheless notes a well established exception to the core duty of an issuing bank to honor a complying presentation? On what legal basis have English courts recognized such an exception?

The American court in *Mid-America Tire* addresses the same issue. How does this court analyze the potential conflict between the UCP and the UCC on this score?

5. *Sztejn* remained a solitary beacon until the UCC provisions allowed a court to enjoin payment against documents where both no third party would be damaged. UCC Article 5 does not, however, attempt to provide a formal definition of "fraud." As can be seen from the cases in the Readings the courts have construed the concept of "fraud" narrowly, and will usually refuse to intervene in a documentary transaction, even under considerable temptation.

6. As the legal advisor for Little, you must analyze a variety of inter-related issues in order to obtain an injunction to prevent Nottingham Bank from honoring Hood's presentation: (1) What is the standard for "fraud" in this context?; (2) must the relevant nefarious acts occur in the letter of credit transaction itself, and must the beneficiary be involved?; (3) what if anything changes if an intermediary bank has already honored a conforming presentation; and, finally, (4) what are the general requirements for obtaining injunctive relief in any event? The Questions and Comments below will explore these issues in detail.

7. As in most international business transactions, the first question you must resolve is what law applies to the issue of "fraud." The law in all states of the United States is UCC § 5–109. But compare the Chinese approach to letter of credit fraud under the 2005 Rules as outlined in the excerpt from Gao. Which concept of fraud should apply in this case? *See* UCC § 5–116(b).

8. In the United States, fraud concepts have expanded enormously since 1952, and conduct which would not have been actionable during the first half of the 20th Century is now routinely within current caselaw concepts. The conceptual growth in this area of the law is part of the growth of judicial and legislative consumer protection—should it also be applied to commercial transactions?

9. What concept of "fraud" should the courts then apply in deciding whether to enjoin payment under letters of credit and what is the required

quantum of proof? Review the opinion in *Mid-American Tire*. What does it say about the relevant standard, and how does it apply that standard to the facts of that case? Please also review the Dolan excerpt as well as Official Comment 1 to § 5–109, both of which explore this issue in more detail.

10. In our Problem, the special challenge you will face as Little's lawyer is to demonstrate how Hood's conduct differs from an ordinary breach of contract. What more must you show? As you review the cases and commentaries in the Readings, attempt to identify the criteria used to differentiate the kind of fraud that would justify an injunction against payment under a letter of credit as compared a garden-variety case of breach of contract.

11. Professor Dolan regards almost any uncertainty in the execution of international letter of credit transactions as unacceptable. In his view, the value of letters of credit as independent, efficient commercial financing devices is corroded by fraud inquiries beyond the letter of credit transaction itself. He thus is critical of recent cases—from Australia, Canada, and the United States—in which the courts have granted injunctions against payment solely because of claims of fraud in the underlying transaction. From a policy perspective, do you find this argument convincing?

In fact, injunctions against payment are relatively rare in documentary letter of credit cases. In contrast, the fraud doctrine is asserted with some frequency in cases arising out of *standby* letter of credits, as we will explore in more detail in Problem 5.3 below.

12. Who must be involved in the fraud or forgery in order to justify judicial intervention and where must be its "locus"? *Montrod Ltd* describes the approach of English law on this issue. In another famous case, *The American Accord*, a unanimous House of Lords held that a bill of lading fraudulently completed by the carrier, but without the knowledge of the beneficiary, did not justify non-payment by the issuer under a letter of credit. The Dolan excerpt also explores this issue under English, Canadian, and U.S. law.

How does UCC § 5–109(a) differ from the approach of English law? Read that section carefully. Would that provision permit a court to issue an injunction against payment if:

(a) A third party, without the knowledge of the beneficiary, creates a forged or materially fraudulent document that is then presented to the issuer?

(b) The facts are the same as in (a)—including the beneficiary's lack of knowledge—except that the forged or materially fraudulent document is used *only* in the underlying sales transaction; or

(c) The seller/beneficiary commits fraud in the underlying sales transaction, but presents genuine documents to, and otherwise deals honestly with, the issuer of the letter of credit?

13. What role does the knowledge of the bank play? The question of "knowledge" of course tends to be quite ephemeral in most situations. Does Nottingham Bank have knowledge of Hood's alleged fraud if Little insists that there is fraud? Is knowledge by the issuer bank even enough? Read § 5–109(a)(2). What does that provision mean with the language that an issuing or

confirming bank, "acting in good faith, may honor" (subject to certain exceptions explored below) with regard to any rights of the applicant?

In specific, does this provision mean that Nottingham Bank in our Problem may simply fail to investigate and rely on the "clean heart and empty head" test? *See also* § 5–102(a)(7)(defining "good faith"). On the other hand, note that banks in letter of credit transactions are not paid to investigate, or to take affirmative actions to ensure that the wheels of commercial justice turn more smoothly.

14. How does the analysis change if a confirming bank has already honored a conforming presentation by the time Little is able to file a claim to enjoin payment by Nottingham Bank? Read UCC § 5–109(a)(1) and § 5–109(b)(4). *See also*, again, § 5–102(a)(7). (*Banco Santander* highlights the risks for a bank under general law if it buys ("discounts") a beneficiary's letter of credits rights and must rely solely on its rights as an assignee.) The critical distinction you must explore is between the "shall honor" language of § 5–109(a)(1) and the "may honor" language of § 5–109(a)(2).

15. Chinese law, as described by Gao, is equally protective of confirming banks (and more so of nominated or negotiating banks). Assume that a Chinese confirming bank is involved in our Problem, but that it has not yet honored a presentation by Hood in China. Where should Little then seek his injunction—China or the U.S.? If time is short and Little is only able to file in a U.S. court, what law should the court apply to the confirming bank? *See* § 5–116(b). Finally, if Chinese law applies to the Chinese bank, how would that affect the rules governing the issuance of an injunction under § 5–109(b) and associated general equitable principles?

16. What are the criteria for obtaining a preliminary injunction? Note that the federal courts of appeal seem to diverge somewhat when listing the criteria, but that irreparable injury seems to be a common element in all lists.

Is an action for damages an "inadequate remedy" if the seller, the person ultimately liable, is located in an inconvenient forum? Note the two approaches taken by the *Mid-America Tire* decision. Where injury is only monetary, there is presumptively an "adequate remedy at law." This is true even if that remedy is available only through foreign courts. The presumption is rebutted where litigation would be futile, damages are speculative, or bankruptcy is "likely." On the other hand, the remedy at law must be "as prompt, efficient and practical" as the remedy in equity. How does the court get from the first set of criteria to the second? Under the latter, will anyone ever have to litigate in a foreign court rather that obtain an injunction? (Problem 5.3 will have more to say on this subject immediately below.)

PROBLEM 5.3 STANDBY LETTERS OF CREDIT: ELECTRONICS TO ISRAEL

SECTION I. THE SETTING

In July, Israel and SpaceCom International Trade, Inc. (SpaceCom) executed a contract requiring SpaceCom, over a forty month period, to carry out the design and construction of a modern ground-to-air communication system for the Israeli Air Force. Under the contract, SpaceCom was required to send an irrevocable letter of credit in Israel's favor which gave Israel the right to draw on this letter of credit upon presentation of a sight draft and Israel's own "certification that it is entitled to the amount covered by such draft by reason of a clear and substantial breach" of the contract. In August, Citibank in New York opened such an irrevocable letter of credit in Israel's favor for $15,008,098.

The contract also provided that all contract disputes that could not be resolved by negotiation were to be submitted to arbitration in New York in accordance with the rules of the American Arbitration Association (Association) governed by the substantive laws of the State of New York.

By the summer of the next year, it was clear that the project was not proceeding according to the parties' expectation, and on August 3, pursuant to the contract, SpaceCom served on Israel and filed with the Association a Demand for Arbitration, seeking a declaration that Israel had breached its contractual obligations, and demanding damages of approximately $10,000,000. SpaceCom claimed that Israel had failed to provide certain equipment, structures, facilities, documentation, information, and services to SpaceCom as required by the contract, and that Israel had repeatedly insisted upon patently irrational interpretations of the parties' respective contractual rights and obligations. Israel denied SpaceCom's allegations and asserted eleven counterclaims, alleging nonperformance of the contract by SpaceCom.

At a conference on October 7, SpaceCom and Israeli representatives reached a substantial resolution of their disputes, and established a schedule of firm dates for deliveries and co-operation. The parties had, however, exchanged such harsh words that neither was certain of the other's performance. Thus, SpaceCom did not withdraw its Demand for Arbitration, and Israel stated that any breach would lead it to draw funds under the letter of credit.

The new schedule required SpaceCom to deliver a complete communication system to Etzion base in the Negev Desert by November 1. SpaceCom had previously delivered and installed an identical communications system to Ramat David in the Galilean area. This latter system had never performed well, despite numerous attempts to "trouble-shoot" its problems; and by November 2 its performance was so poor that Israel formally demanded that SpaceCom replace it. SpaceCom stated that it would take the Israeli "request" under advisement.

SpaceCom was a little slow in its delivery of the communications system for the Negev installation. In fact, that system was not delivered until November 5. When it arrived, the Israeli Air Force decided that it had a much more pressing need for an operational communications system in Galilee, and so the new system was routed there. It is now November 10, and no communications system has been delivered to the Negev.

Israeli authorities have now presented to Citibank a sight draft for $15 million, attached to a "Certification" which states that "SpaceCom is in clear and substantial breach of the Contract, because it has not delivered the goods required by the Contract to the Israeli Air Force base in the Negev Desert by the date required by the Contract."

SpaceCom consults you. It is a large corporation, has net profits of $15 million per year, and is in no danger of insolvency. But right now it has a cash flow problem. It must make large investments of resources before its obligors begin to make payments to it. It has borrowed to the limit of its credit lines with financers, and if $15 million is paid out on this letter of credit, some of these other loans may be called. Also, if the $15 million is paid out, it is not certain where it will find the funds to meet next week's payroll.

Can it obtain an injunction to prohibit Israel from drawing on the letter of credit, alleging fraud on the underlying transaction?

Alternatively, is there some way to force or convince Citibank to refuse to pay Israel even though the documents, on their face, comply with the letter of credit? Spacecom wants to know from you, in other words, what Citibank's legal situation is now that Spacecom suspects fraud.

For the future, what revisions should SpaceCom make in the terms of standby letters of credit issued to guarantee its performance? Would these have solved SpaceCom's problems with Israel, or merely have sent the dispute into different channels?

SECTION II. FOCUS OF CONSIDERATION

This action raises two types of considerations: one concerns the differences between fraud and breach of contract; the other concerns the procedural requirements and various equitable remedies and defenses. The letter of credit under consideration in this Problem is a "standby" letter of credit.

The previous Problems concerned the "documentary" letter of credit, which arises out of a "documentary" transaction, and which requires the issuer (usually the buyer's bank) to pay against "documents of title"—*e.g.*, bills of lading. However, there is a second type of letter of credit transaction, illustrated by this Problem. It involves a letter of credit that is issued by the seller's bank and runs in favor of the buyer—truly a backwards arrangement—and is payable against a writing certifying that the seller has not performed its promises. Such a standby letter of credit is not for the purpose of ensuring payment to the seller for goods shipped. Instead, this standby letter of credit is used as a guarantee, or a performance bond, or as insurance of the seller's performance. Banks do not issue guarantees or performance bonds or insurance policies because federal law seems to prohibit such transactions by banks under 12 U.S.C. § 24 (Seventh). However, the use of standby letters of credit can accomplish the same results, and has not been prohibited by bank regulatory agencies. The result has been a wealth of both bank activity and litigation.

While the concept of enjoining payment due to fraud has not been widely used in the documentary transaction letter of credit, it has been widely sought in the standby letter of credit transaction. Some limiting concepts in the documentary letter of credit transaction, such as attention to the documents, may become meaningless when the "document" contains a mere allegation by one party that the other party failed to perform properly under the contract. When the limitations which give structure to the transaction become meaningless, the transaction can become a breeding ground for fraud.

Web sources for further study include the ICC's web pages on 1) the ISP *www.iccwbo.org/policy/banking/id3053/index.html/* and 2), the URDG *www.iccwbo.org/policy/banking/id2437/index.html.*

If this transaction may be governed by the UCC, then a reading of UCC § 5–109, set forth in the Documents Supplement, is essential to analysis of the Problem.

If the transaction may be governed by the United Nations Convention on Independent Guarantees and Stand–By Letters of Credit, it is essential to read and analyze Articles 19 and 20 of that Convention.

SECTION III. READINGS, QUESTIONS AND COMMENTS

What law is applicable? There are now five different legal regimes competing to govern the rights and obligations created by standby letters of credit. Two are laws: one an international treaty, the other a U.S. uniform state law. The other three are all publications of the International Chamber of Commerce (I.C.C.). The five legal regimes are:

(1) Article of 5 of the Uniform Commercial Code (UCC) (see the Documents Supplement),

(2) The Uniform Customs and Practices for Documentary Credits (UCP 600) (I.C.C. Pub. No. 600, 2007) (see Problem 5.1),

(3) The Uniform Rules for Demand Guarantees (URDG) (I.C.C. Pub. No. 758, 2010),

(4) The International Standby Practices (ISP98) (I.C.C. Pub. No. 590, 1998), and

(5) The United Nations Convention on Independent Guarantees and Standby Letters of Credit (see the Documents Supplement).

UCC Article 5 has been introduced in Problem 5.1 and 5.2, and its provisions on injunctive relief for fraud were the core of Problem 5.2. The UCP was also introduced in Problem 5.1 and 5.2. UCP Article 1 expressly allows application of the UCP to standby letters of credit, if it is incorporated into the credit. They are binding on all parties thereto, unless otherwise expressly stipulated in the Credit. This application was permitted even though the UCP has no provisions on fraud, but that fact did not preclude the English or Commonwealth courts from acting against fraud in the cases surveyed in Problem 5.2.

The Readings for this Problem survey the domestic and international legal regimes relevant to standby letters of credit. Blau and Jedzig first introduce us to a civil law analog, the independent (or "demand") guarantee. Goode then examines the differences between documentary letters of credit and demand guarantees. The two Turner articles review the background and scope of the two principal international legal regimes, the UN Convention on Standby Letters of Credit and the ICC's "International Standby Practices." Kelly–Louw then provides an overview of the treatment of the fraud doctrine in these and other international instruments in this field. Following a couple of case law examples, Kimball and Sanders finally highlight the special risks that arise from the use of standby letters of credit.

BLAU AND JEDZIG, BANK GUARANTEES TO PAY UPON FIRST WRITTEN DEMAND IN GERMAN COURTS

23 Int.Law. 725 (1989).*

By their legal nature, Guarantees to pay upon first written demand are abstract promissory notes of a bank to pay within a very short period of time, say forty-eight hours, if certain formalized conditions are fulfilled. Typically, such conditions are the first written demand of the beneficiary of a Guarantee. Sometimes an additional written statement by the beneficiary has to be attached if so stipulated. In this respect, a Guarantee is similar to a documentary letter of credit, except that, in the case of a documentary letter of credit, the bank has the duty to examine documents relating to the basic transaction, whereas in the case of a Guarantee the documents are replaced by a unilateral statement of the beneficiary.

The purpose of such unilateral statement may be explained by the following example: A quite common type of Guarantee is a Guarantee under which a bank obligates itself to pay in the event a beneficiary requests payment, stating that the work performed by the contractor was delayed. In the case of such a unilateral allegation of delay, the bank will pay and will not examine the truth of this unilateral contention. It is to no avail that the contractor informs the bank that in his opinion the statement made by the beneficiary is incorrect. The bank will pay all the same, because otherwise the bank's international standing would be jeopardized. The contractor will be forced to hold the bank harmless. He has to reimburse the amount paid by the bank even if the statement made by the beneficiary to the bank concerning a delay was incorrect, and the payment to the beneficiary was not justified because there was no valid claim against the contractor. If the beneficiary's call of the Guarantee was not justified according to the purpose of the Guarantee, the contractor's only choice is to try to be reimbursed by the beneficiary. Since the beneficiary's place of business is usually in a foreign country, it may be rather difficult to sue him for reimbursement and to execute a judgment. In some cases, the amount of the Guarantee may be lost forever.

* * *

Needless to say, it would be in conflict with the Guarantee's purpose if the contractor could easily obtain a preliminary injunction and thereby stop the beneficiary from calling the Guarantee. Where the existence of the claim of the beneficiary secured by the Guarantee is only questionable, as opposed to certain, there is no basis for intervention by a contractor. Otherwise, the purpose of the Guarantee would be frustrated. If, for instance, there is disagreement between beneficiary and contractor as to whether there has been a delay of the contractor's work, the beneficiary's statement prevails and a preliminary injunction is excluded. Especially in such doubtful cases it is the intention of the Guarantee—"pay first, litigate later"—to secure the payment "on demand." The question of whether or not the claim exists will be addressed in subsequent litigation.

A.   AN EVIDENT ABUSE AS PREREQUISITE OF AN INJUNCTION

Legal remedies are acceptable only if it is quite certain that the claims made by the beneficiary and secured by the Guarantee do not exist. Preliminary injunctions might be acceptable, for instance, in cases where it is obvious that the work was performed within the time limit of the contract, so that the call of the Guarantee on the basis of a delay is clearly abusive.

For these reasons, German courts refuse to issue preliminary injunctions in cases where the call of the Guarantee is only "unjustified." Apart from these cases, they are prepared to grant injunctive relief only in the rare cases of a "manifest abuse," which in practice seems to be very similar to the concept of "fraud." Such a manifest abuse is established only if the absence of any entitlement on the basis of the underlying contract is irrefutably proven. There is never a manifest abuse if such proof could be made only on the basis of an interpretation of the contract.

In this connection the following problem arises: In view of the short deadlines for payment under the Guarantee, a contractor most often has only one or two days left for blocking the payment by means of a court order. Thus, as a practical matter, the court is required to make its decision within hours. Therefore, it is impossible to obtain any comments from the beneficiary, let alone to schedule an oral hearing prior to the decision. The proceedings thus are necessarily ex parte as defined in article 936/921 of the German Civil Procedure Code (ZPO). In this case the nonparticipation of the other party is for the benefit of the contractor. A contractor who alleges a manifest abuse of the Guarantee, however, cannot file affidavits to make a prima facie showing of such abuse even though affidavits usually would be sufficient under the German rules of civil procedure in cases of provisional remedies. In the case of a Guarantee, German courts do not accept this procedure, since they are afraid that it could easily lead to an abuse of the injunctive relief. Therefore, German courts demand that the contractor make a clear showing of a manifest abuse and it is not accepted in such cases to submit less evidence than in proceedings on the merits. Contrary to the procedural requirements for cases on the merits, proof has to be furnished by documentary evidence, rather than by affidavits or the testimony of witnesses who are deemed to be unreliable. As a result, injunctive relief is limited to the rare cases of clear showing by documents that the call of the Guarantee is evidently abusive. For instance, if the beneficiary calls the Guarantee, stating that the contractor's work was delayed, an abuse might be proven by filing a certificate of completion signed by the beneficiary that confirms that the contract was performed in time.

There is disagreement as to whether or not, as a second prerequisite, a preliminary injunction should be issued only if for legal or factual reasons ultimate reimbursement by the beneficiary to the contractor is in jeopardy. Those arguing in favor of this approach say that without such prerequisite the principle "pay first, litigate later" would be violated. It can be argued, however, that, in cases of a manifest abuse, this principle should no longer be applicable and therefore, the contractor should be entitled to block the payment caused by such abuse, irrespective of his chances to be reimbursed at a later point of time.

GOODE, ABSTRACT PAYMENT UNDERTAKINGS IN INTERNATIONAL TRANSACTIONS

22 Brook. J. Int'l L. 1 (1996).*

All jurisdictions admit of certain exceptions to the autonomy principle. In particular, fraud on the part of the beneficiary or his agent in relation to documents tendered under the credit disentitles the beneficiary to payment. In England, other defences have been admitted, such as illegality affecting the letter of credit transaction, set-off between beneficiary and issuing bank, and rescission of the letter of credit transaction on the ground that it was induced by misrepresentation. In the United States it is not necessary that the fraud should relate to the documents; fraud in the underlying transaction suffices. In many jurisdictions the ambit of the exceptions to the autonomy principle has been a matter of considerable debate and controversy. Is there conduct short of fraud which nevertheless makes a claim on the credit abusive? Is fraud on the part of a third party for whose acts the beneficiary is not legally responsible a defence? Suppose that such fraud consists in the forgery of a document presented under the credit. Can the beneficiary say that he is innocent of the fraud and entitled to payment, or can the bank plead that while it is entitled to pay against a forged document which appears on its face to be genuine it is not obliged to do so, since a forged document is not a document that conforms to the credit? What is meant by fraud in the underlying transaction (for example, does it cover fraud not reflected in the documents at all, such as a fraudulent misrepresentation by the seller inducing the buyer to enter into the contract of sale) and how far is this a defence? There is a divergence of views not only between different law systems, but even within the same law system both on what constitutes a defence to a claim on a credit and on the approach to be taken by the court on an application for interim injunctive relief. It is therefore helpful that the UNCITRAL Convention on Independent Guarantees and Standby Letters of Credit has addressed these issues. Indeed, it is this part of the Convention which is one of the most likely to be of practical utility.

III.   DEMAND GUARANTEES AND STANDBY CREDITS

A.   *Demand Guarantees and Documentary Credits: Comparisons and Contrasts*

I now turn to demand guarantees. As noted earlier, the documentary credit is designed to ensure the discharge of a payment obligation. By contrast, the demand guarantee is used almost exclusively to secure the performance of a non-monetary obligation—typically the execution of construction works or the delivery of conforming goods under a contract of sale—and is conceived as a default mechanism. It is the principal (the equivalent of the applicant for the credit in a documentary credit transaction) who is primarily responsible for the performance to which the demand guarantee relates, and the agreement between principal and beneficiary requires, expressly or by implication, that the beneficiary resort to the bank only if the principal defaults. So whereas a bank pays a documentary credit only if things go right, in the case of a demand guarantee it is intended that the bank will be called upon to pay only if things go wrong. But the agreement as to the default nature of the demand guarantee is internal to the principal-beneficiary relationship and does not concern the bank, whose duty is to pay against a written demand and such other documents, if any, as the guarantee may specify. Thus the demand guarantee shares with the documentary credit the characteristic that it is an abstract payment undertaking, insulated from the underlying trade transaction, but differs from the documentary credit in that it is improper for the beneficiary to call the guarantee if he does not honestly believe that the principal has committed a breach of the underlying contract. Accordingly, the problem of unfair or abusive calls is peculiar to demand guarantees and cannot arise in relation to documentary credits, where it is agreed from the outset that the bank, not the principal, is to be the first port of call for payment.

Three further differences between documentary credits and demand guarantees may be noted. First, the former usually involve the presentation of a substantial volume of documents, and more often than not these fail to conform to the credit on first presentation, whereas the documentation required for a claim on a demand guarantee is skeletal in the extreme, entailing in most cases presentation of no more than the written demand itself. Second, the making of "extend or pay" demands is a particular feature of demand guarantee practice for which the URDG (though not the UNCITRAL Convention) made special provision. Third, in a four-party demand guarantee transaction [where a primary guarantee is backed by a "counter-guarantee"] the position of the parties to the counter-guarantee has to be covered.

* * *

It is not uncommon for a beneficiary to present an "extend or pay" demand requiring the period of the guarantee to be extended, failing which payment is to be made forthwith. Demands of this kind are not necessarily improper, for there may have been, or the beneficiary may honestly though mistakenly believe that there has been, a breach of the underlying contract but may be willing to allow time for this to be rectified if the guarantee is extended. * * * Upon receiving the extend or pay demand the guarantor must, without delay, inform the party who gave him his instructions and must suspend payment for as long as is reasonable to permit the principal and the beneficiary to reach agreement on the granting of the extension and to enable the principal to arrange for such extension to be issued. There are various possible outcomes. The principal may agree to the extension, wholly or in part, in which case it takes effect when issued by the guarantor. The guarantor is not obliged to issue it, and even if he has agreed with the principal to do so, that is not an agreement of which the beneficiary can take advantage. Alternatively, the principal may refuse the extension, in which case the guarantor must pay in the absence of fraud by the beneficiary or some other vitiating factor. A third possibility is that the beneficiary withdraws the demand, which thereupon lapses. Finally, negotiations may still be in progress when a reasonable time has elapsed, in which event the guarantor must pay, even if by then the guarantee has expired.

TURNER, THE UNITED NATIONS CONVENTION ON INTERNATIONAL STANDBY LETTERS OF CREDIT: HOW WOULD IT CHANGE EXISTING LETTER OF CREDIT LAW IN THE UNITED STATES?

114 Banking L.J. 790 (1997).*

Under Article 1(1) of the Convention, the Convention is applicable only to an "international undertaking." Under Article 4(1), a letter of credit is "international" if the place of business of any two of the following parties to the credit transaction are in different countries:

- The issuer

- The beneficiary

- The applicant

- An "instructing party" (a bank or other institution or person that applies for the credit on behalf of the applicant)

- A confirmer

* * *

* * * [T]he issuer and beneficiary have complete autonomy under Article 21 to choose the applicable law. If they do not exercise that autonomy, the void is filled by Article 22, which designates the law of the jurisdiction in which the credit was issued. The certainty of these conflict of law rules is an important and beneficent feature of the Convention. The provision in Article 21 that chooses the law that is "demonstrated by the terms and conditions of the undertaking" is unclear, however, and may detract from that certainty.

The parties also have autonomy to "opt out" of the Convention, that is, to make the letter of credit rules of the Convention inapplicable to the credit. Under Article 1(1), the Convention does not apply to a letter of credit if "the undertaking excludes the application of the Convention." Under Article 1(3), however, the conflict of law provisions of Articles 21 and 22 apply "independently" of Article 1(1). * * *

* * *

Independent Applicability of Choice of Law Rules of Convention. Under Article 1(3) of the Convention, the conflict of law rules of Articles 21 and 22 apply to international standby letters of credit "independently" of Article 1(1). That means that Articles 21 and 22 constitute the choice of law rules in the Contracting State for international standby letters of credit, and those rules apply to the credit even though the Convention is otherwise inapplicable to the credit.

* * *

A great many rules of the Convention are the same or substantially similar to the rules of UCC Article 5, and the application of these rules of the Convention would yield the same result as the application of the corresponding rule under Article 5. However, the result would or could be different

- When there is a clear conflict between an Article 5 and a Convention rule, * * *

- When a provision of Article 5 and no provision of the Convention applies, or

- When provisions both of the Convention and of Article 5 apply and the provisions do not clearly conflict but are worded very differently.

Examples of clear conflicts may be seen in the provisions that apply when no expiry date is stated, when the credit states that it is transferable, and when it states that the proceeds of the credit are not assignable. These conflicts are relatively insignificant * * *.

* * *

When a Rule of UCC Article 5 Applies and No Rule of the Convention Applies. The Convention leaves many aspects of letters of credit to the jurisdictional law. The Convention does not, for example, require the issuer to dishonor a noncomplying presentation of documents or require the applicant to reimburse the issuer for the issuer's honor of a complying presentation. Indeed, the Convention hardly applies at all to the relationship between the issuer and the applicant, and it does not apply at all to advisers. The Convention contains no statute of limitations or provisions limiting the capacity to issue letters of credit or regarding general disclaimers, legal remedies, choice of forum, subrogation, or successor beneficiaries. The UCC Article 5 rules supplement the Convention and will govern with respect to matters not covered by the Convention when United States law is the jurisdictional law under the Convention.

The Convention contemplates that the parties may also wish to supplement the Convention with rules of custom and practice, such as the UCP and the Uniform Rules for Demand Guarantees, both of which are issued by the International Chamber of Commerce, and other rules such as the Draft International Standby Practices 1997 recently distributed by the Institute of International Banking Law and Practice, Inc. Article 13(1) of the Convention provides that the rights and obligations of the issuer and the beneficiary under a standby letter of credit are determined by "any rules, general conditions or usages specifically referred to therein."

The UCP are often incorporated by reference in letters of credit. The Convention does not resolve whether a conflicting rule of custom or practice incorporated in the credit would prevail over a conflicting rule of the Convention. A court could, by analogy to Section 5-116(c) of UCC Article 5 or the emphasis in the Convention on flexibility, hold that the incorporated rule prevails.

* * *

Fraud. The Convention's provisions on fraud are contained in Articles 19 and 20. They apply when (a) a document is not genuine or has been falsified, (b) no payment is due "on the basis asserted," or (c) the demand "has no conceivable basis." The Convention thus, in effect, defines fraud as the occurrence of one of these events. Section 5–109 of Article 5, by contrast, uses the terms "fraudulent" and "forged" but does not define them. Whether the conduct has been fraudulent under UCC Article 5 is for the courts to determine under state law.

In their goals, the fraud provisions of the Convention seem very similar to those of Section 5–109 of Article 5. In their wording, however, they bear no resemblance to Section 5–109. Both provisions are imprecise, and applying either of them would require a degree of subjectivity. Thus it seems quite possible that the application of one of them could yield a different result than the application of the other to the same facts.

The revised UCC Article 5 clarifies a number of issues that are not clear under the old Article 5. The concept of materiality, for example, and the rule that all of the conditions for the application of equitable remedies must be satisfied, are written into the revised Section 5–109. It is now clear under the Article 5 provisions that relief is available when the fraud is in the underlying transaction and not merely in the presentation of documents and that relief is available when someone other than the beneficiary is the perpetrator of the fraud. These and other issues relating to fraud are addressed in the revised Section 5–109 and the Comments to that Section and not addressed in the Convention.

This writer does not believe that Articles 19 and 20 of the Convention are intended to or should replace the existing jurisdictional law on fraud and on injunctive relief from fraud in letter of credit cases. In this writer's view, the courts should continue to apply the provisions of UCC Article 5 just as they have in the past, provided, of course, that they interpret those provisions in a manner that is consistent with the wording of Articles 19 and 20 of the Convention.

TURNER, NEW RULES FOR STANDBY LETTERS OF CREDIT: THE INTERNATIONAL STANDBY PRACTICES

14 Banking & Fin.L.R. 457 (1999).*

The International Standby Practices (ISP98 or ISP) are rules for standby letters of credit. They were adopted in 1998 by the ISP sponsors and published in late 1998 by the International Chamber of Commerce (ICC). The ISP rules became effective on January 1, 1999.

By their terms, the ISP rules apply to a letter of credit that incorporates them by reference, such as "This letter of credit is subject to ISP98". The ISP are intended to apply to standby letters of credit and not to commercial letters of credit. When used in standby credits, the ISP would replace the ICC's Uniform Customs and Practice for Documentary Credits (UCP).

The ICC intends that the UCP will continue to be the regime for commercial letters of credit, and also that the ICC's Uniform Rules for Demand Guarantees will continue to be used by banks that issue independent demand guarantees. Thus to the extent that issuers incorporate these rules of practice, the three separate sets of ICC rules would govern the three principal forms of primary-obligor independent issuer undertakings in current use.

The UCP were originally written for use only in commercial and not standby letters of credit, and the principal focus of the UCP drafters has always been on commercial credits. The distinction between commercial and standby credits is sometimes difficult to draw, but a commercial credit typically supports the applicant's obligation as a purchaser in a sale of goods, while a standby credit commonly supports the applicant's obligation to pay a loan or similar monetary obligation, or to perform services. The commercial credit is a payment mechanism in which the issuer is expected to pay the beneficiary for the goods purchased by the applicant. In the standby credit, by contrast, the issuer is not expected to pay the beneficiary unless the applicant defaults in the underlying obligation to the beneficiary.

Many of the provisions of the UCP are either inapplicable or inappropriate in a standby credit context. UCP Articles [19] through [27], relating to transport and insurance documents, would normally not be applicable to a standby credit. The UCP rules relating to installment obligations, "stale" shipping documents, and force majeure would typically be not only inappropriate but potentially harmful to the beneficiary in a standby context.

* * *

The ISP eliminate the need to exclude the inappropriate UCP provisions. In addition, the ISP address issues that the UCP have not sought to address because they arise primarily in the standby and not in the commercial credit context.

* * *

While the ISP drafting project benefited from the widespread support and participation of the banking community in the United States and internationally, the users of standby letters of credit, applicants and beneficiaries, were not directly involved in the drafting project. It may have been the failure of the ISP sponsors to seek knowledgeable user participation that resulted in a small number of rules that seem unfair to users. Certainly these rules, some of which will be meaningful to the users, are less favourable to the users than the apposite rules of the UCP.

* * *

Exclusions from Coverage of ISP

Rule 1.05 states that questions of capacity (who may issue a standby credit), formal requirements (such as whether the issuer's undertaking must be contained in a written document), and the issue of fraud are left to the applicable jurisdictional law. These questions are thus beyond the scope of the ISP.

The exclusion of beneficiary fraud from the scope of the ISP is especially welcome. Fraud has been addressed in different ways in different countries. To have included provisions on fraud in the ISP would probably have created needless complications in countries such as the United States, where the issue of fraud has been dealt with by the courts and legislators in detail over a long period of time.

* * *

ISP Rule 4.02 appropriately states that an issuer or nominated person "is required to examine documents for inconsistency with each other only to the extent provided in the standby".

The UCP do not directly address the problem of how to measure the compliance of the presented documents with the requirements of the credit. Instead, UCP Article 13(a) instructs the examining bank to determine whether the documents comply by applying "international standard banking practice as reflected in these Articles".

Under "international standard banking practice", the great majority of courts have held that the documents must "strictly comply" with the terms and conditions of the credit. An English court famously declared that "[t]here is no room for documents which are almost the same, or which will do just as well". Strict compliance, however, as measured by "standard banking practice", is not the equivalent of "mirror image" compliance. The courts have exercised common sense in applying the strict compliance standard. Typographical and spelling errors and other obviously trivial differences between the wording in the credit and the wording in the presented document have been held not to render the presentation noncompliant under the strict compliance standard measured by standard practice.

KELLY-LOUW: INTERNATIONAL MEASURES TO PROHIBIT FRAUDULENT CALLS ON DEMAND GUARANTEES AND STANDBY LETTERS OF CREDIT

1 Geo. Mason J. Int'l Com. L. 74, 75–76, 80–116 (2010).*

The International Chamber of Commerce (ICC) and the United Nations Commission on International Trade Law (UNCITRAL) have both been active in seeking a solution to the problems caused by unfair or fraudulent calls on demand guarantees and standby letters of credit. Four instruments that are particularly relevant are (1) the ICC Uniform Rules for Contract Guarantees (URCG); (2) the ICC Uniform Rules for Demand Guarantees (URDG458); (3) the International Standby Practices (ISP98); and (4) the United Nations Convention on Independent Guarantees and the Stand-by Letters of Credit (the Convention). The first three instruments of the ICC are, in effect, standard-term contract rules available for incorporation into demand guarantees and standby letters of credit by the parties if they so choose. The adoption of the Convention by a state has the effect of making it law in that state.

* * *

Uniform Customs and Practice for Documentary Credits

UCP600 contains no provisions that attempt to prevent unfair or fraudulent calls on commercial or standby letters of credit. * * * There-

---

* Copyright © 2010 and reprinted with permission.

fore, national laws should deal with any injunctive relief on the grounds of fraud by the beneficiary. * * *

* * *

Uniform Rules for Demand Guarantees

[T]he drafters of URDG458 decided to adopt an approach similar to the one taken in the UCP on the issue of fraud in relation to demand guarantees, by simply remaining silent and leaving it to the courts of the various jurisdictions to deal with. * * *

URDG458 attempts to affect a compromise between the interests of the beneficiaries to obtain speedy payment and that of the principals to avoid the risk of unfair calling by the beneficiaries. From all this, in order to prevent the beneficiary's outright unfair calling, a few fundamental articles, in particular Articles 9, 17, 20 and 21, were incorporated into URDG458. However, as will be seen below, Article 20 implicitly goes a small way towards restricting the beneficiary's right of payment.

* * *

Article 20 of URDG458 contains a very distinctive rule requiring the beneficiary to present with his demand a statement that the principal is in breach and the respect in which he is in breach. * * * Therefore, Article 20 requires the beneficiary, when demanding payment, to stipulate in writing both that there is some kind of breach of the underlying contract and what type of breach is involved, therefore giving the other party or parties some form of protection by providing a ground for a claim of fraud. This places a certain obligation on the beneficiary to show his hand. The aim of this provision is to give some measure of protection against the unfair calling of the guarantee without interfering with the documentary character of the guarantee and the need of the beneficiary to have speedy recourse in the event of a perceived breach. * * *

Although the word "fraud" is not used in the URDG, the prevention of fraud is central to URDG458. The demand for payment must stipulate the reasons for calling on the guarantee in order to meet the URDG458's clear preference for reasoned demand guarantees. * * *

Furthermore, the ICC has incorporated Article 21 into the URDG in an attempt to prevent unfair calls. Article 21 provides that "[t]he Guarantor shall without delay transmit the Beneficiary's demand and any related documents to the Principal or, where applicable, to the Instructing Party for transmission to the Principal."

The purpose of Article 21 is to give the principal the chance to challenge an unfair call before payment is made under it[,] * * * but it does not require a bank to hold payment until the principal has received the demand and the documents. * * *

* * *

International Standby Practices (ISP98)

ISP98 does not attempt to regulate fraud or abusive drawing, taking a similar approach to the UCP. In Rule 1.05(c), ISP98 expressly leave the issue of fraudulent or abusive demands for payment (drawings) or "defenses to honour based on fraud, abuse or similar matters" to be determined by the applicable jurisdictional law[.] * * *

Although there is no rule dealing with fraudulent or abusive demands, there are a few rules that are relevant[.] * * * ISP98 Rule 4.08 provides that even if a standby letter of credit does not specify any required document, it will still be deemed to require a documentary demand for payment. * * * The effect of this rule is that if the issuer leaves out the requirement for the demand, the beneficiary who does not present one will have made a non-complying presentation and may lose the entire benefit of the standby.

* * *

[Under ISP98] * * *, a demand for payment under a standby letter of credit is not required to indicate a default or other event in the underlying contract, if that is not required under the terms and conditions of the standby letter of credit. This is a step back from the position of the URDG, where the beneficiary is required to state that there is a breach of the underlying contract and what type of breach is involved.

Furthermore, the issuer under Rule 3.10 of the ISP98, unlike Article 17 of the URDG, is not required to notify the applicant (the principal in the case of a demand guarantee) of receipt of a demand for payment under the standby letter of credit.

The Convention

From 1988 to 1995 UNCITRAL worked on a Uniform Law on International Guaranty. This eventually resulted in the drafting of the Convention. UNCITRAL adopted this Convention and opened it for signature by the General Assembly by its resolution 50/48 of 11 December 1995. * * *

* * *

Fraud and the Convention

The Convention * * * recognises exceptions to the absolute and independent nature of demand guarantees and standby letters of credit. Article 19, under the heading "Exception to Payment Obligation," stipulates the circumstances under which the issuer/guarantor may dishonour the beneficiary's demand for payment. Article 19(1) reads as follows:

If it is manifest and clear that:

   (a) Any document is not genuine or has been falsified;

   (b) No payment is due on the basis asserted in the demand and the supporting documents; or

(c) Judging by the type and purpose of the undertaking, the demand has no conceivable basis,

the guarantor/issuer, acting in good faith, has a right, as against the beneficiary, to withhold payment.

Paragraph (2) of Article 19 explains what the term "no conceivable basis" referred to in subparagraph (c) of paragraph (1) means. * * *

Article 19 deliberately avoids the terms "bad faith," "abuse," and "fraud," since they have confusing and inconsistent meanings in the different legal systems and are often influenced by criminal law notions of malicious intent, which are not suitable in relation to guarantees. Therefore, Article 19(1) of the Convention has instead employed the general formula of a demand for payment that "has no conceivable basis," while paragraph (2) of Article 19 also shows that the impropriety of the demand may relate, or could be determined by reference to, the underlying transaction. As far as the degree of proof is concerned, fraud must be "manifest and clear" and "immediately available." * * *

However, two aspects of Article 19 depart quite clearly from the principle of autonomy. First, in determining whether a call is justified, Article 19(1)(b) and (c) and 19(2)(a), (b), (c) and (d) all require the guarantor/issuer of the demand guarantee/standby letter of credit to look to the underlying contract for good cause to pay. Second, by constantly insisting on the exercise of good faith, Article 15(3), the tailpiece of Article 19(1) and Article 19(2)(e) put both the beneficiary and the guarantor/issuer of the guarantee/letter of credit on notice that payment needs to be justifiable by good cause.

* * *

Article 19 not only provides the guarantor/issuer with some basis for refusing payment, but also enables the principal to take court measures against a fraudulent beneficiary. Paragraph (3) of Article 19 states that "in the circumstances set out in subparagraphs (a), (b) and (c) of paragraph (1) of this article, the principal/applicant is entitled to provisional court measures in accordance with Article 20." * * *

Article 20 of the Convention makes provision both for measures similar to an injunction * * * preventing payment and for attachment * * * to be available to the court where there is a "high probability" shown by "immediately available strong evidence".

AUTHORS' COMMENT ON URDG 758 (2010)

Effective July 1, 2010, the I.C.C. issued a new version of the URDG, the so-called "URDG 758." This new version was designed principally to align the URDG with the terminology and core elements of the UCP 600 (*see* Problem 5.1 above), especially on the requirements of a complying presentation and on the bank's obligation to provide a timely and complete notice for non-complying presentations. *See* URDG 758 Articles 19–23. But the new version also carries forward the moderate approach of its predecessor on the subject of fraud as outlined by Kelly–Louw above. *See* URDG 758, Article 15 (regarding the required statement by the beneficiary on why the applicant is in breach); Article 16 (requiring notice to the applicant when a demand is made under the guarantee).

AMERICAN BELL INT'L., INC. v. ISLAMIC REPUBLIC OF IRAN

United States District Court, Southern District of New York, 1979.
474 F.Supp. 420.

MacMahon, District Judge.

Plaintiff American Bell International Inc. ("Bell") moves for a preliminary injunction enjoining defendant Manufacturers Hanover Trust Company ("Manufacturers") from making any payment under its Letter of Credit No. SC 170027 to defendants the Islamic Republic of Iran or Bank Iranshahr or their agents, instrumentalities, successors, employees and assigns. We held an evidentiary hearing and heard oral argument on August 3, 1979. The following facts appear from the evidence presented:

The action arises from the recent revolution in Iran and its impact upon contracts made with the ousted Imperial Government of Iran and upon banking arrangements incident to such contracts. Bell, a wholly-owned subsidiary of American Telephone & Telegraph Co. ("AT & T"), made a contract on July 23, 1978 (the "Contract") with the Imperial Government of Iran—Ministry of War ("Imperial Government") to provide consulting services and equipment to the Imperial Government as part of a program to improve Iran's international communications system.

The Contract provides a complex mechanism for payment to Bell totalling approximately $280,000,000, including a down payment of $38,800,000. The Imperial Government had the right to demand return of the down payment at any time. The amount so callable, however, was to be reduced by 20% of the amounts invoiced by Bell to which the Imperial Government did not object. Bell's liability for return of the down payment was reduced by application of this mechanism as the Contract was performed, with the result that approximately $30,200,000 of the down payment now remains callable.

In order to secure the return of the down payment on demand, Bell was required to establish an unconditional and irrevocable Letter of Guaranty, to be issued by Bank Iranshahr in the amount of $38,800,000 in favor of the Imperial Government. The Contract provides that it is to be governed by the laws of Iran and that all disputes arising under it are to be resolved by the Iranian courts.

Bell obtained a Letter of Guaranty from Bank Iranshahr. In turn, as required by Bank Iranshahr, Bell obtained a standby Letter of Credit, No. SC 170027, issued by Manufacturers in favor of Bank Iranshahr in the amount of $38,800,000 to secure reimbursement to Bank Iranshahr should it be required to pay the Imperial Government under its Letter of Guaranty.

The standby Letter of Credit provided for payment by Manufacturers to Bank Iranshahr upon receipt of:

> Your [Bank Iranshahr's] dated statement purportedly signed by an officer indicating name and title or your Tested Telex Reading: (A) Referring Manufacturers Hanover Trust Co. Credit No. SC170027, the amount of our claim $ represents funds due us as we have received a written request from the Imperial Government of Iran Ministry of War to pay them the sum of under our Guarantee No. issued for the account of American Bell International Inc. covering advance payment under Contract No. 138 dated July 23, 1978 and such payment has been made by us * * *.

In the application for the Letter of Credit, Bell agreed—guaranteed by AT & T—immediately to reimburse Manufacturers for all amounts paid by Manufacturers to Bank Iranshahr pursuant to the Letter of Credit.

Bell commenced performance of its Contract with the Imperial Government. It provided certain services and equipment to update Iran's communications system and submitted a number of invoices, some of which were paid.

In late 1978 and early 1979, Iran was wreaked with revolutionary turmoil culminating in the overthrow of the Iranian government and its replacement by the Islamic Republic. In the wake of this upheaval, Bell was left with substantial unpaid invoices and claims under the Contract and ceased its performance in January 1979. Bell claims that the Contract was breached by the Imperial Government, as well as repudiated by the Islamic Republic, in that it is owed substantial sums for services rendered under the Contract and its termination provisions.

* * *

On July 25 and 29, 1979, Manufacturers received demands by Tested Telex from Bank Iranshahr for payment of $30,220,724 under the Letter of Credit, the remaining balance of the down payment. Asserting that the demand did not conform with the Letter of Credit, Manufacturers declined payment and so informed Bank Iranshahr. Informed of this, Bell responded by filing this action and an application by way of order to show cause for a temporary restraining order bringing on this motion for a preliminary injunction. Following argument, we granted a temporary restraining order on July 29 enjoining Manufacturers from making any payment to Bank Iranshahr until forty-eight hours after Manufacturers notified Bell of the receipt of a conforming demand, and this order has been extended pending decision of this motion.

On August 1, 1979, Manufacturers notified Bell that it had received a conforming demand from Bank Iranshahr. At the request of the parties, the court held an evidentiary hearing on August 3 on this motion for a preliminary injunction.

CRITERIA FOR PRELIMINARY INJUNCTIONS

The current criteria in this circuit for determining whether to grant the extraordinary remedy of a preliminary injunction are set forth in *Caulfield v. Board of Education*, 583 F.2d 605, 610 (2d Cir.1978):

> [T]here must be a showing of possible irreparable injury *and* either (1) probable success on the merits *or* (2) sufficiently serious questions going to the merits to make them a fair ground for litigation *and* a balance of hardships tipping decidedly toward the party requesting the preliminary relief.

We are not persuaded that the plaintiff has met the criteria and therefore deny the motion.

A. *Irreparable Injury*

Plaintiff has failed to show that irreparable injury may possibly ensue if a preliminary injunction is denied. Bell does not even claim, much less show, that it lacks an adequate remedy at law if Manufacturers makes a payment to Bank Iranshahr in violation of the Letter of Credit. It is too clear for argument that a suit for money damages could be based on any such violation, and surely Manufacturers would be able to pay any money judgment against it.

Bell falls back on a contention that it is without any effective remedy unless it can restrain payment. This contention is based on the fact that it agreed to be bound by the laws of Iran and to submit resolution of any disputes under the Contract to the courts of Iran. Bell claims that it now has no meaningful access to those courts.

There is credible evidence that the Islamic Republic is xenophobic and anti-American and that it has no regard for consulting service contracts such as the one here. Although Bell has made no effort to invoke the aid of the Iranian courts, we think the current situation in Iran, as shown by the evidence, warrants the conclusion that an attempt by Bell to resort to those courts would be futile. * * * However, Bell has not demonstrated that it is without adequate remedy in this court against the Iranian defendants under the Sovereign Immunity Act which it invokes in this very case.

Accordingly, we conclude that Bell has failed to demonstrate irreparable injury.

B. *Probable Success on the Merits*

Even assuming that plaintiff has shown possible irreparable injury, it has failed to show probable success on the merits. * * *

* * * [B]oth the Uniform Commercial Code of New York, which the parties concede governs here, and the courts state that payment is enjoinable where a germane document is forged or fraudulent or there is "fraud in the transaction." N.Y.U.C.C. [§ 5–109(a)]. Bell does not contend

that any documents are fraudulent by virtue of misstatements or omissions. Instead, it argues there is "fraud in the transaction."

The parties disagree over the scope to be given as a matter of law to the term "transaction." Manufacturers, citing voluminous authorities, argues that the term refers only to the Letter of Credit transaction, not to the underlying commercial transaction or to the totality of dealings among the banks, the Iranian government and Bell. On this view of the law, Bell must fail to establish a probability of success, for it does not claim that the Imperial Government or Bank Iranshahr induced Manufacturers to extend the Letter by lies or half-truths, that the Letter contained any false representations by the Imperial Government or Bank Iranshahr, or that they intended misdeeds with it. Nor does Bell claim that the demand contains any misstatements.

Bell argues, citing equally voluminous authorities, that the term "transaction" refers to the totality of circumstances. On this view, Bell has some chance of success on the merits, for a court can consider Bell's allegations that the Government of Iran's behavior in connection with the consulting contract suffices to make its demand on the Letter of Guaranty fraudulent and that the ensuing demand on the Letter of Credit by Bank Iranshahr is tainted with the fraud.

There is some question whether these divergent understandings of the law are wholly incompatible since it would seem impossible to keep the Letter of Credit transaction conceptually distinct. A demand which facially conforms to the Letter of Credit and which contains no misstatements may, nevertheless, be considered fraudulent if made with the goal of mulcting the party who caused the Letter of Credit to be issued. Be that as it may, we need not decide this thorny issue of law. For, even on the construction most favorable to Bell, we find that success on the merits is not probable. Many of the facts alleged, even if proven, would not constitute fraud. As to others, the proof is insufficient to indicate a probability of success on the merits.

* * * Bell asserts that (1) both the old and new Governments failed to approve invoices for services fully performed; (2) both failed to fund contracted-for independent Letters of Credit in Bell's favor; (3) the new Government has taken steps to renounce altogether its obligations under the Contract; (4) the new Government has made it impossible to assert contract rights in Iranian courts; and (5) the new Government has caused Bank Iranshahr to demand payment on the Manufacturers Letter of Credit, thus asserting rights in a transaction it has otherwise repudiated. * * *

As to contention (4), it is not immediately apparent how denial of Bell's opportunity to assert rights under the Contract makes a demand on an independent letter of credit fraudulent.

Contentions (1), (2), (3) and the latter part of (5) all state essentially the same proposition—that the Government of Iran is currently repudiating all its contractual obligations with American companies, including those with Bell. Again, the evidence on this point is uncompelling.

Bell points to (1) an intragovernmental order of July 2, 1979 ordering the termination of Iran's contract with Bell, and (2) hearsay discussions between Bell's president and Iranian officials to the effect that Iran would not pay on the Contract until it had determined whether the services under it had benefited the country. * * * Manufacturers, for its part, points to a public statement in the Wall Street Journal of July 16, 1979, under the name of the present Iranian Government, to the effect that Iran intends to honor all legitimate contracts. * * * Taken together, this evidence does not suggest that Iran has finally and irrevocably decided to repudiate the Bell contract. It suggests equally that Iran is still considering the question whether to perform that contract.

Even if we accept the proposition that the evidence does show repudiation, plaintiff is still far from demonstrating the kind of evil intent necessary to support a claim of fraud. Surely, plaintiff cannot contend that every party who breaches or repudiates his contract is for that reason culpable of fraud. The law of contract damages is adequate to repay the economic harm caused by repudiation, and the law presumes that one who repudiates has done so because of a calculation that such damages are cheaper than performance. Absent any showing that Iran would refuse to pay damages upon a contract action here or in Iran, much less a showing that Bell has even attempted to obtain such a remedy, the evidence is ambivalent as to whether the purported repudiation results from non-fraudulent economic calculation or from fraudulent intent to mulct Bell.

Plaintiff's argument requires us to presume bad faith on the part of the Iranian government. It requires us further to hold that that government may not rely on the plain terms of the consulting contract and the Letter of Credit arrangements with Bank Iranshahr and Manufacturers providing for immediate repayment of the down payment upon demand, without regard to cause. On the evidence before us, fraud is no more inferable than an economically rational decision by the government to recoup its down payment, as it is entitled to do under the consulting contract and still dispute its liabilities under that Contract.

While fraud in the transaction is doubtless a possibility, plaintiff has not shown it to be a probability and thus fails to satisfy this branch of the *Caulfield* test.

C. *Serious Questions and Balance of Hardships*

If plaintiff fails to demonstrate probable success, he may still obtain relief by showing, in addition to the possibility of irreparable injury, both (1) sufficiently serious questions going to the merits to make them a fair ground for litigation, and (2) a balance of hardships tipping decidedly toward plaintiff. * * * Both Bell and Manufacturers appear to concede the existence of serious questions, and the complexity and novelty of this matter lead us to find they exist. Nevertheless, we hold that plaintiff is not entitled to relief under this branch of the *Caulfield* test because the balance of hardships does not tip *decidedly* toward Bell, if indeed it tips that way at all.

To be sure, Bell faces substantial hardships upon denial of its motion. Should Manufacturers pay the demand, Bell will immediately become liable to Manufacturers for $30.2 million, with no assurance of recouping those funds from Iran for the services performed. While counsel represented in graphic detail the other losses Bell faces at the hands of the current Iranian government, these would flow regardless of whether we ordered the relief sought. The hardship imposed from a denial of relief is limited to the admittedly substantial sum of $30.2 million.

But Manufacturers would face at least as great a loss, and perhaps a greater one, were we to grant relief. Upon Manufacturers' failure to pay, Bank Iranshahr could initiate a suit on the Letter of Credit and attach $30.2 million of Manufacturers' assets in Iran. In addition, it could seek to hold Manufacturers liable for consequential damages beyond that sum resulting from the failure to make timely payment. Finally, there is no guarantee that Bank Iranshahr or the government, in retaliation for Manufacturers' recalcitrance, will not nationalize additional Manufacturers' assets in Iran in amounts which counsel, at oral argument, represented to be far in excess of the amount in controversy here.

Apart from a greater monetary exposure flowing from an adverse decision, Manufacturers faces a loss of credibility in the international banking community that could result from its failure to make good on a letter of credit.

CONCLUSION

Finally, apart from questions of relative hardship and the specific criteria of the *Caulfield* test, general considerations of equity counsel us to deny the motion for injunctive relief. Bell, a sophisticated multinational enterprise well advised by competent counsel, entered into these arrangements with its corporate eyes open. It knowingly and voluntarily signed a contract allowing the Iranian government to recoup its down payment on demand, without regard to cause. It caused Manufacturers to enter into an arrangement whereby Manufacturers became obligated to pay Bank Iranshahr the unamortized down payment balance upon receipt of conforming documents, again without regard to cause.

Both of these arrangements redounded tangibly to the benefit of Bell.
* * *

One who reaps the rewards of commercial arrangements must also accept their burdens. One such burden in this case, voluntarily accepted by Bell, was the risk that demand might be made without cause on the funds constituting the down payment. To be sure, the sequence of events that led up to that demand may well have been unforeseeable when the contracts were signed. To this extent, both Bell and Manufacturers have been made the unwitting and innocent victims of tumultuous events beyond their control. But, as between two innocents, the party who undertakes by contract the risk of political uncertainty and governmental caprice must bear the consequences when the risk comes home to roost.

Accordingly, plaintiff's motion for a preliminary injunction, pursuant to Rule 65(a), Fed.R.Civ.P., is denied.

ARCHER DANIELS MIDLAND CO. v. JP MORGAN CHASE BANK, N.A.

United States District Court, Southern District of New York, 2011.
2011 WL 855936.

Jed S. Rakoff, District Judge.

On February 14, 2011, the Court granted the request of plaintiffs, Archer Daniels Midland Co. and ADM Rice, Inc. (collectively "ADM"), for an order temporarily restraining defendant JP Morgan Chase Bank, N.A. ("Chase") from honoring a payment request by the Trade Bank of Iraq ("TBI") under a standby letter of credit ("the Letter of Credit") in the amount of $6,926,850. * * * By Order dated February 28, 2011, the Court directed that the temporary restraining order remain in effect until today, March 7, 2011, pending the Court's ruling on ADM's motion for a preliminary injunction. Having carefully considered the parties' submissions, the Court, for the reasons specified below, hereby grants the motion and preliminary enjoins Chase from honoring TBI's request for payment under the Letter of Credit.

[T]he pertinent facts are as follows. ADM Rice, a wholly-owned subsidiary of Archer Daniels Midland Co., purchases rice and wheat, and exports these commodities to various countries around the world, including Iraq. Since 2005, ADM Rice has sold extensive amounts of rice and wheat to Iraq-in shipments totaling approximately 4.4 millions tons-through the Grain Board of Iraq ("GBI"), an entity under the supervision of the Iraqi Government's Ministry of Trade. As a condition of its transactions with GBI, ADM Rice agrees to post a performance bond which guarantees the quality of the rice or wheat. Until the events that precipitated the instant motion, however, GBI had never demanded payment under any of these performance bonds. * * *

On August 25, 2010, GBI accepted ADM Rice's offer to sell it 120,000 metric tons of rice at a rate of $549.75 per metric ton, for a contract price of roughly $69 million. In typical fashion, the contract required ADM Rice to arrange for a performance bond through an Iraqi bank equivalent to 10% of the contract price. The next day, on August 26, 2010, ADM applied for a letter of credit in the sum of $6,926,850 with defendant Chase. Issuance of the Letter of Credit was contingent on the issuance by TBI—which, like GBI, is an Iraqi governmental entity—of a performance bond to GBI guaranteeing ADM's performance of the contract (the "Performance Bond").

On August 27, 2010, Chase issued the Letter of Credit, with ADM Rice as the account holder and TBI as the beneficiary. The Letter of Credit further states that TBI may draw funds as follows:

> [Funds are] ... available against your authenticated Swift/Tested Telex that you have duly issued your Performance Bond as requested by ourselves and that you have received a claim in accordance with the terms of the performance bond.

The Letter of Credit also expressly incorporates the terms of the Performance Bond itself, which was issued by TBI on or about September 2, 2010. The Performance Bond states, in relevant part, that:

> All claims made under this performance bond must be accompanied by an SGS original laboratory report specifically certifying that the quality of the purchased commodity does not meet the contractual specifications.

SGS, formerly Societe Generale de Surveillance, is an international quality inspection company. However, the Letter of Credit does not require that TBI submit a copy of the SGS report for Chase's review in order to request payment under its terms, but merely that GBI provide TBI with that report.

On September 6, 2010, the sales transaction between GBI and ADM Rice was memorialized in a written contract (the "Contract"). As directed in that contract, ADM Rice shipped 120,000 tons of rice (the "Cargo") from the United States to Iraq on three vessels. The first vessel, the CAPTAIN HARRY, loaded its cargo of 40,000 tons of rice in Darrow, Louisiana between November 19 and November 23, 2010. * * *

Before the Cargo left the United States, the quality of the rice was certified by both SGS and the U.S. Department of Agriculture. * * * After its loadport inspection, which included laboratory analysis of rice samples taken from the cargo, SGS issued a Certificate specifically certifying that the rice was in accordance with contractual specifications regarding its quality. Further, on January 5–6, 2011, * * * the CAPTAIN HARRY stopped in Fujairah, U.A.E., prior to its discharge in Iraq, for additional inspection and sampling of its rice cargo. * * * After an analysis of the sampled cargo, as well as a visual inspection, the SGS inspectors concluded that the "[c]argo [on the CAPTAIN HARRY] was ... in good condition."

The CAPTAIN HARRY then proceeded to Umm Qasr, Iraq, where it arrived on January 8, 2011. Upon arrival, "[r]esampling [of the cargo] was performed at anchorage at Umm–Qasr pilot station area * * *." After the inspection was complete, under the supervision of SGS inspectors, the rice was discharged over a period of eleven days, ending on February 14, 2011. The SGS inspection report issued the following day, February 15, 2011, contains no indication that the condition of the rice cargo on the CAPTAIN HARRY was any different at Umm Qasr than it had been upon loading in Louisiana or upon inspection and sampling in Fujairah.

Nonetheless, on February 10, 2011, Chase received an authenticated Swift notice from TBI stating that it had received a claim from GBI in accordance with the terms of the Performance Bond and seeking to draw down the entire amount of the Letter of Credit. On Friday, February 11, 2011, Chase notified ADM that it had received what was, in Chase's view, "an in compliance drawing" under the Letter of Credit, and, accordingly, that Chase intended to honor the request. Because ADM was not aware of any issues regarding the quality of the Cargo, Christian Bonnesen, President of ADM Rice, immediately contacted Danny Kim, a Vice–President of Chase's Global Trade Division, and communicated ADM Rice's position that the demand was "wrongful and not in compliance with the terms of the Performance Bond." The next day, on February 12, 2011, ADM Rice, through its employee Ashish Mathur, contacted the Iraqi Branch of SGS by e-mail and asked:

> Can you please advise me urgently whether or not SGS have issued a laboratory report in relation to [the] cargo certifying that the quality of the purchased rice does not meet the contractual specifications.

In an e-mail response that same day, Amjad Majdoubeh, the Branch Manager of SGS in Iraq, simply stated "We never issued such report." * * * [H]e then contacted SGS's technical governance office in Geneva, Switzerland, which confirmed that SGS had not issued any adverse quality reports in connection with the Cargo. Finally, he spoke with Majdoubeh, whose approval is required for any quality certificate to be issued by SGS personnel in Iraq. Majdoubeh confirmed that no adverse quality reports had been issued with respect to the Cargo, nor were any forthcoming.

On February 14, 2011, James Alonzo, an Assistant Vice President at Chase, reiterated Chase's position to ADM that—despite the foregoing— because TBI's request for payment facially complied with the terms of the Letter of Credit, Chase felt obliged to honor the request. That same day, ADM filed the instant action seeking to preliminary enjoin Chase from so doing.

To obtain a preliminary injunction in the Second Circuit, the movant must show (1) that it will suffer irreparable harm absent the injunction and (2) either (a) that it is likely to succeed on the merits or (b) that the motion presents sufficiently serious questions going to the merits to make them a fair ground for litigation and a balance of hardships tipping decidedly toward the party requesting the preliminary relief. Accordingly, the Court first turns to whether ADM would suffer irreparable harm absent an injunction. In the instant circumstances, because neither TBI nor GBI have any known presence in the United States, this inquiry requires the Court to ascertain the relative prospects of ADM fairly litigating its claims against TBI and GBI in an Iraqi Court. *See* Rockwell Int'l Systems, Inc. v. Citibank, N.A., 719 F.2d 583, 586 (2d Cir. 1983)(holding that irreparable injury hinges on whether an account holder has an adequate alternate forum to protect its rights under a letter of credit). ADM contends that, as an American company, it stands little chance of receiving a fair adjudication of its claims against TBI and GBI, which are both Iraqi governmental entities, in Iraq. In support, ADM submits a declaration from Sabah Al–Mukhtar, an Iraqi lawyer who states that he is familiar with conditions in the country's judicial system. In his declaration, Al–Mukhtar describes the "almost total collapse of the judicial system" in Iraq because of the lack of sufficiently trained judges, over-whelming caseloads, and "unprecedented corruption." Further, noting the "[l]ack of independence" in the Iraqi judiciary, Al–Mukhtar concludes that "it is my considered opinion that ADM Rice Inc. will not be able to get a fair hearing in an Iraqi court because . . . it is fighting the TBI and/or GBI and [because] it is 'foreign.'"

On the basis of the unrebutted assertions made in the Al–Mukhtar declaration,[1] the Court concludes that ADM has no adequate alternative forum in which it could reasonably pursue its claims against TBI and GBI. Moreover, given the legal hurdles (discussed *infra*) that ADM would confront in pursuing post-payment remedies against Chase, the issuer of the Letter of Credit, which in these circumstances is effectively just a stakeholder, it seems almost certain that, absent an injunction, ADM would be left with no legal recourse whatsoever. Accordingly, the Court concludes that ADM would suffer irreparable harm in the absence of its requested injunction.

As to ADM's likelihood of success on the merits, it is true that New York law (which here governs) requires strict compliance with facially valid requests for payment under a letter of credit. This is because New York courts follow the "independence principle," pursuant to which an issuing bank's obligations under a letter of credit are separate from, and independent of, the rights and obligations of the parties to the underlying commercial transaction. Therefore, under New York law, a bank that issues a letter of credit is not required to look beyond the payment documents presented by the beneficiary in order to ascertain whether the parties to the underlying transaction have complied with their respective duties and obligations.

Here, TBI complied with the express terms under which payment is available under the Letter of Credit by sending Chase an authenticated, facially valid Swift Notice stating that it had received a claim in accor-dance with the terms of the performance bond. Accordingly, Chase was under no obligation to independently verify that the conditions in the Performance Bond had been met before rendering payment to TBI under the Letter of Credit.

Notwithstanding the above, "fraud in the transaction" constitutes a "well established exception to the rule that banks must pay a beneficiary under a letter of credit when documents conforming on their face to the terms of the letter of credit are presented." This exception has been

---

1. The Court, via contacts with TBI and GBI available to the parties here, conveyed through the parties' counsel its willingness to receive input from these entities or from the Iraqi government, but no response was received.

codified in the New York Uniform Commercial Code, which provides that an issuing bank may refuse to honor documents which "appear on [their] face strictly to comply with the terms and conditions of the letter of credit" but which are "forged or materially fraudulent," or if "honor of the presentation would facilitate a material fraud by the beneficiary on the issuer or applicant." N.Y. U.C.C. § 5–109(a).

However, because the smooth operation of international commerce requires that requests for payment under letters of credit not be routinely obstructed by pre-payment litigation, the fraud exception to the independence principle "is a narrow one" that is only available on a showing of "outright" and "intentional fraud." As a consequence, Courts in this Circuit enjoin payment under letters of credit "only rarely" and only upon a strong showing that the request for payment was fraudulently made.

Here, however, just such a strong showing has been made. Indeed, ADM has adduced an array of unrebutted evidence that, taken collectively, strongly supports an inference that the rice aboard the CAPTAIN HARRY was in full compliance with the Contract's quality specifications. As this evidence (detailed above) demonstrates, TBI's representation to Chase that SGS had issued a laboratory report certifying problems with the Cargo's quality is almost certainly false. As Mr. Legemaate testified, and the documents corroborate, no record of an adverse quality report could be located in SGS's electronic records or by SGS's technical governance office, and the Branch Manager of SGS in Iraq confirmed that his office had not issued, nor was it planning to issue, such a report.

Further, absent an adverse SGS quality report, it is difficult to perceive a set of circumstances by which GBI or TBI could have otherwise determined that the Cargo did not meet the Contract's quality specifications, thereby warranting their demand for payment under the Letter of Credit. At the time TBI made its request, on February 10, 2011, two-thirds of the Cargo had not even reached Iraqi shores, and the portion of the Cargo that had arrived, aboard the CAPTAIN HARRY, was still in the process of being unloaded. Moreover * * * SGS sampled, analyzed, and inspected the Cargo several times, and issued at least three reports certifying its quality. None of the several SGS reports issued with regard to the Cargo indicates any problem with the rice's quality, let alone a problem that would justify a full draw down on the Letter of Credit.

Based on the foregoing, the Court fails to perceive a "plausible or colorable basis under the contract" for TBI's request for payment under the Letter of Credit, and therefore concludes that the most reasonable interpretation of the relevant circumstances is that TBI's request was made in an attempt to effectuate a fraud.

For the foregoing reasons, the Court concludes that ADM will be irreparably harmed absent an injunction, and is likely to succeed on the merits of its claims. Accordingly, the Court hereby grants ADM's motion for a preliminary injunction and enjoins Chase from rendering any payment to TBI under the Letter of Credit.

KIMBALL AND SANDERS, PREVENTING WRONGFUL PAYMENT OF GUARANTY LETTERS OF CREDIT—LESSONS FROM IRAN

39 Bus. Lawyer 417 (1984).*

Events in Iran illustrate the dangers of standby credits, particularly suicide credits payable upon unilateral demands. The account party's exposure may be enormous, and the legal protections against arbitrary demands are limited to the fraud exception. While it now seems reasonably clear that fraud in the transaction encompasses more than just the letter of credit, the doctrine's protection remains narrow. However, the cases suggest that a well-drafted credit can both reduce the account party's exposure to fraudulent demands and, if need be, lay the groundwork for legal action. In suggesting that one or another protection be included in a credit we have no illusions that in all cases an account party necessarily has the leverage to dictate terms. Yet in many cases the bargaining power does exist, and, in any case, some of the following suggestions will appear innocuous and readily acceptable, whatever the parties' relative bargaining power. Above all, recent experience in Iran demonstrates that guaranty letters of credit should not be casually extended.

Account parties should avoid the bare suicide credit, payable upon a simple demand in the form of a draft, and insist instead upon detailed documentary requirements and conditions. Detailed documentary requirements help prevent improper payments and, if necessary, lay the foundation for a lawsuit.

Ideally, a letter of credit would require submission of a certificate from the account party acknowledging that the funds are owed. This may be an unrealistic request since it affords a beneficiary no protection against an account party's bad faith refusal to furnish such a certificate.

Alternatively, the credit could require independent confirmation of the account party's default through submission of an auditor's report, independent test report, court judgment, or arbitrator's ruling as a condition of payment. Such clauses are often attainable and afford excellent protection against arbitrary or wrongful demands for payment. The beneficiary's willingness to accept such terms may be conditioned upon the account party's commitment to extend the term of the credit until any proceedings are complete.

If the beneficiary wants a letter of credit to secure an ultimate arbitral award or judgment rather than performance (which ends with cancellation), the account party may insist that payment be conditioned upon presentation of a final judgment or arbitral award. The International Chamber of Commerce's Uniform Rules for Contract Guarantees take this approach:

---

* Copyright © 1984 and reprinted here and below with permission from The Business Lawyer.

If a guarantee does not specify the documentation to be produced in support of a claim or merely specifies only a statement of claim by the beneficiary, the beneficiary must submit * * * either a court decision or an arbitral award justifying the claim, or the approval of the principal in writing to the claim and the amount to be paid.

At a minimum, if a beneficiary is unwilling to agree to independent documentation, account parties should require specific factual representations by a responsible officer of the beneficiary, identified in the credit, that the account party has failed to perform its obligations under specific provisions of the underlying contract. Recital of the factual basis for the demand (for example, failure to deliver) is important. If payment should later be demanded on the basis of demonstrably false representations, the account party may establish fraud from invoices, shipping records, and similar records of performance. While the issuing bank will not investigate the truth of such a certificate, falsehoods permit the account party to establish not only fraud in the transaction, but fraud in the documents.

Whatever documents are specified, the requirements in the credit should be as detailed and extensive as possible. Each additional certificate or document raises an additional opportunity for submission of a nonconforming document. Under the strict conformity doctrine, even a minor or inadvertent defect will justify dishonor, and payments against nonconforming documents are the issuer's responsibility. Often, attempts to draw occur on the eve of the credit's expiration, so defects in the documents are, as a practical matter, incurable. Innocent formalities are therefore useful. For example, all requirements for certifications should either name or identify by title the person to give the certification. It may be well to add requirements for protocolization, notarization, and certificates of incumbency. These formalities are often routine outside the United States. The credit could also prescribe specific wording for required certifications, and so create further opportunities for error.

* * *

To minimize the account party's exposure, a well-drafted letter of credit established to secure prepayments should permit unilateral reduction by the account party upon submission by the account party of invoices or other appropriate evidence of performance. In this way, as goods are delivered or services rendered, the account party's potential liability is progressively reduced, and when the work is complete, the remaining balance will be zero.

Itek and *Touche Ross* suggest that a contract should provide for release of guaranty credits or other performance guaranties upon cancellation of the contract for any reason. In both cases, courts enjoined payment even though the credits themselves did not include the release terms of the underlying contract. Despite that result, both the contract and the credits should—in view of the independence principle—include express language terminating the credits upon termination of the underlying contract. If the beneficiary seeks security for a possible arbitral award or judgment and insists that the credit should survive termination, the account party may fairly require that submission of an award or judgment be a condition of payment.

* * *

Detailed requirements of the kind suggested may not always be possible since many bankers are reluctant to alter their forms and security arrangements are rarely decisive issues when major contracts are negotiated. However, banks will often respect the wishes of major customers transacting business abroad, and after their experience with Iran, some banks may well prefer clear, detailed instructions that prevent disputes of the kind that embroiled so many banks in letter-of-credit litigation.

QUESTIONS AND COMMENTS

1. The necessary foundation to any analysis of this problem is first to understand the transaction pattern of the standby letter of credit. In particular, the parties to a standby transaction are the mirror image of the parties to a documentary letter of credit transaction. Further, the document that the beneficiary of a standby is required to produce has no intrinsic value, which is in sharp contrast to the document required (the negotiable bill of lading) in the documentary letter of credit transaction. The bill of lading controls the goods, and therefore has a value in its own right.

2. At least five types of actions can arise out of fraud in the letter of credit transaction: 1) The applicant (customer) can sue the issuing bank to enjoin payment under the letter of credit. 2) The issuing bank can refuse to pay and be sued by the beneficiary for wrongful dishonor. 3) The issuing bank can pay and then be sued by the applicant for wrongful payment. 4) The issuing bank can pay and then sue the beneficiary for fraud. And, the most obvious but often least productive, 5) the issuing bank can pay and charge the applicant's account, and the applicant then sues the beneficiary. *American Bell* and *Archer Daniels Midland* exemplify the first type of action.

3. If you sought to persuade Citibank to refuse to pay, and defend an action for wrongful dishonor, what documents and affidavits would you need to obtain in order to give them sufficient evidence?

If you are able to persuade Citibank to dishonor—and thus likely trigger a lawsuit by the beneficiary—, the burden of proof on the issue of fraud will be on the bank, although of course the ultimate party in interest will be the bank's customer (your client). Merely proving that its customer made assertions is not sufficient. It must prove facts, both as to conduct of the parties on the underlying contract *and also* as to the knowledge or intent of the beneficiary at the time of presentment of the document. What facts can you present about the Israeli statements that could persuade a court of any malicious intent or knowledge?

4. How does one characterize the conduct of SpaceCom—in conformity with the underlying contract or in breach of the underlying contract? If SpaceCom is in breach, some aspects of Israel's performance under the

contract may be excused. But is SpaceCom complaining about the Israeli failure to perform?

On the other hand, how does one characterize the conduct of Israel—in conformity with the underlying contract, in breach of the underlying contract, or as "fraud in the transaction"? How do you distinguish breach of contract from fraud? Does Israel have any basis for seeking payment under the letter of credit? Does Israel have a better claim to such payment under the basis stated in the "Certification," or under some other facts? What is the purpose of requiring such a "Certification" anyway?

5. In Problem 5.1, we examined the consequences of an issuer not giving complete and timely notice of discrepancies in a presentation. But must the issuer also raise a possible fraud or forgery in its first notice of dishonor? Recall that the UCP has no rules on fraud, so that we must fall back on U.C.C. Article 5 (where it otherwise applies). What does U.C.C. Article 5 say about this question? *See* § 5–108(c), (d).

6. As the article by Blau and Jedzig shows, Western Europe had developed a device which is functionally analogous to the standby letter of credit, called a "Bank Guarantee on First Demand." In such a guarantee, a bank undertakes to pay to the beneficiary on the latter's first demand and a simple statement that the obligor on the guarantee is in default, without investigating whether the obligor is actually in default. The interesting comparison is that the European civil law systems went through the same development of principles to deal with the same types of problems as Common Law judges in dealing with fraud and standby letters of credit. At first, the European courts looked only at principles of suretyship and guarantee. Since the bank's guarantee was independent of the obligor' promise, the bank was required to pay. However, the European courts soon became aware of "abusive demands," and began to develop principles which allow injunctive or other relief, usually arising out of fraud concepts. Thus, there was a parallel development of constraining rules, although the resulting rules were stated in a quite different manner. As can be seen in the readings, whether the results in actual cases are different is the subject of significant debate.

7. The first serious attempt to harmonize these developments concerning demand guarantees was the I.C.C.'s publication of the Uniform Rules for Demand Guarantees (URDG). The effort did not expressly include standby letters of credit, but it did attempt to establish by *contractual provisions* some mechanisms for protecting against "abusive demands" under demand guarantees.

As noted in the Kelly–Louw excerpt, the key innovation of the URDG is a requirement that the beneficiary present a statement "indicating in what respect the applicant is in breach of its obligations" (unless expressly excluded in the credit). *See* URDG 758, Article 15 (Article 20 in URDG 458). This requirement should have the most significant impact with so-called "suicide credits." In this form of a standby letter of credit the bank's obligation is unconditional, save for a simple demand by the beneficiary. In this case as well, however, the URDG requires a statement describing the breach by the applicant that justifies the demand.

For our Problem, assume that, instead of a standby letter of credit, Spacecom had arranged for a demand guarantee that incorporated the URDG. Would the concepts in the URDG have materially changed the situation for Citibank in its decision on whether to honor Israel's demand to pay? In specific, how (if at all) would the requirement of a statement by Israel (the beneficiary) assist Spacecom with its effort to avoid payment by Citibank based on an allegation of fraud?

8. The UNCITRAL Convention on Independent Guarantees and Standby Letters of Credit was an attempt to harmonize the differing rules established for independent guarantees and for standby letters of credit. The Convention is set forth in the Documents Supplement. To what transactions does the Convention apply? *See* the first Turner excerpt and Convention Article 1(1). By what mechanisms and standards does the Convention seek to protect against fraudulent demands for payment in those transactions? *See* the Kelly–Louw excerpt.

(a) Now compare this approach with the URDG and with UCC § 5–109. To which of these is the Convention closer in structure and content? Turner asserts that, although the Convention is worded differently from the UCC, the results in actual cases would be the same. Do you agree?

(b) The Convention could have an impact on this SpaceCom—Israeli dispute in the future. It has entered into force, but has not yet been ratified by either the U.S. or Israel. Under Article 1, since neither country is a Contracting State, the Convention would not apply to this credit. Assume nonetheless that the Convention applies to this credit. What do you think the likely outcome would be if Spacecom sought a preliminary injunction to preclude Citibank from honoring Israel's demand under the Convention? *See* (in the Documents Supplement) Article 19 and in particular 19(2)'s list of the "types of situations in which a demand has no conceivable basis." *See also* Article 20 (for the requirements for "provisional court measures").

9. Ultimately, U.S. bankers decided that the UCP was the sufficiently inhospitable to the standby such that there was a need for a separate regime. By the time they acknowledged that need, the URDG, with no mention of standby and no incorporation of standby locution, was in place.

The I.C.C. also realized that the UCP was not well adapted to standby letter of credit practices. So, in 1998, it issued the International Standby Practices (ISP98) (I.C.C. Publication No. 590). Like the URDG, ISP98 applies when incorporated by reference, but the available evidence is that in fact this is now a widespread practice for international standby letters of credit. Nonetheless, even if applicable, would ISP98 have an impact on the Spacecom's substantive dispute with the Israeli government here? Read the Kelly–Louw excerpt. If ISP98 provides insufficient guidance on issues of fraud, what law would then apply if Spacecom sought an injunction here in the U.S. to bar Citibank from honoring Israel's demand for payment?

10. As the *American Bell* and *Archer Daniels Midland* cases indicate, the same basic fraud rules from U.C.C. § 5–109 that we addressed in Problem 5.2 apply to standby letters of credit. Both cases thus apply the same substantive law and the same standards for an injunction. But in the former case, the court found that American Bell (the applicant) had assumed the risk of even "governmental caprice" and thus had to "bear the consequences when

the risk comes home to roost." In the latter case, Archer Daniels Midland likewise entered into contracts with a governmental agency in the Middle East, but the court nonetheless enjoined payment. What facts, if any, justify the different outcome in these two cases?

11. The usual remedy for breach of contract is an award of monetary damages, not equitable relief (such as specific performance or some other court order or injunction). Thus, beyond a "likelihood of success on the merits," a party seeking an injunction must satisfy certain general equitable criteria. The *American Bell* and *Archer Daniels Midland* opinions discuss in detail these criteria in the context of letter of credit fraud disputes. But note that, again, the two cases reach opposite conclusions. Again, what circumstances, if any, justify the different outcomes in the application of the same general equitable criteria for the issuance of an injunction?

12. As the two cases also discuss, a principal equitable requirement for an injunction is that the claimant will suffer irreparable harm (not "mere" monetary loss). Courts generally have been very skeptical of "irreparable harm" arguments in letter of credit cases. In our Problem, what facts do you have to demonstrate that Spacecom nonetheless will suffer irreparable harm if a court does not enjoin payment by Citibank to Israel? Do the arguments raised by Spacecom meet the standards as described in *American Bell* and *Archer Daniels Midland*?

13. As to the other requirements for an injunction, do you have sufficient facts to convince a court? What other facts might be helpful?

14. *American Bell* is but one example of a number of similar letter of credit cases that arose out of tumultuous events in Iran in the late 1970s. Like *American Bell*, courts in the early cases generally followed the spirit of the independence principle and refused to grant injunctions against payment in the face of fraud claims. The tide turned in later cases, however. *See, e.g., Harris Corp. v. National Iranian Radio and Television*, 691 F.2d 1344 (2nd Cir. 1982)(upholding an injunction that precluded payment to a government controlled bank under a standby letter of credit). What had happened in the interim was a significant change in the broader political-legal context, in specific the end of nearly all diplomatic, commercial, and legal relations between the U.S. and Iran because of a hostage crisis. How might these broader changes affect the analysis of a request for an injunction in an international letter of credit case?

15. Consider now the position of Citibank. It *could* file a lawsuit seeking an injunction against its own honor, but why would it do so? For one thing, it simply could refuse to honor and await a lawsuit by Israel. As a more fundamental point, however, we saw in Problem 5.2 that, as long as it acts in good faith, all of the incentives run in favor of an issuing bank honoring a presentation (*see* UCC § 5–109(a)(2)), and then letting the applicant and beneficiary litigate among themselves.

16. This all highlights the importance of counseling clients to avoid the risks of standby letters of credit at the planning stage. If a client has no choice but to arrange a standby letter of credit for an important transaction, what terms would you recommend for the credit to reduce the risk of fraud, and thus to protect your client's position as best you can? Consult the Kimball and Sanders excerpt for guidance.

PART 3

REGULATION OF INTERNATIONAL TRADE

■ ■ ■

TRADE REGULATION DONE RIGHT

When is international trade regulation "done right?" From a trader's perspective, one of the first concerns is simply knowing what the regulations are. Internationally, this concern is often referred to as the issue of "transparency." U.S. law students and lawyers often forget that many jurisdictions remain undigitized, indeed in some cases even unpaperized. In a nation like China, for example, unwritten law (neibu) has a long tradition, especially so in the regulatory field. Thus one of China's most important commitments upon entry in 2001 to the World Trade Organization (WTO) was greater, if not complete, trade law transparency.

Even in a world of perfect transparency, there can be great variations on the theme of international trade regulation. With roughly 200 nation states, plus the law of distinct "customs territories" like Hong Kong, the multiplicity of jurisdictions that regulate trade is demanding. Add to that the numerous nations with "sub-central" jurisdictions, such as the states and municipalities of the United States, and you have an intimidating mosaic of international trade regulation. Mix in the rapidly growing body of regional and bilateral trade agreements, for example the EU and NAFTA, and the mosaic turns into a labyrinth. The opportunity for "regulatory arbitrage" among all these jurisdictions is significant.

"Done right" one can hope or require that the world's various federal governments will reign in the trade impact of their sub-central units, though (as procurement law illustrates) this does not always happen. "Done right" one can work towards unification of international and regional trade regulation, through the World Trade Organization particularly. Imagine, however, the enormity of the task given the diversity of policy perspectives regulating tariffs and taxation, health and safety, the environment, product standards, service licenses and other parameters of international trade. Remember, also, that politics matters when analyzing trade regulation (contrast U.S. approaches to trading with Cuba versus Israel). Clearly, when it comes to regulation of international trade, "done right" is a monumental undertaking.

Once a trader (or more likely its lawyer) knows the regulations governing specific international transactions, issues of interpretation and dispute may arise. When international trade regulation is "done right,"

335

there will be sound and expeditious procedures to resolve such issues. Of course, like economies, not all of the world's legal systems are "developed" to the point that both traders and government authorities will have reasonable confidence in administrative outcomes. Once again China provides an excellent example. Huge investments of time, talent and energy have been made in modernizing China's legal infrastructure to meet the WTO rule of law.

From a governmental perspective, regulation "done right" results in trader compliance with the law. Millions of international trades occur daily, and compliance is the norm. Lawyers functioning as risk managers seeking to minimize potential legal liabilities contribute significantly to this result. Truth be told, however, not all traders are interested in compliance. Smugglers, for example, are doing their best world-wide not to comply at all. And the smuggling of legal and illegal goods, services, money and people is accelerating. Some traders are marginally compliant, pushing to the limits of the law or beyond. In this respect, for example, payments to regulatory officials are a cutting edge issue. The line between "greasing the wheels," bribery and extortion is often fine. All governments, even the most powerful, may struggle with regulatory compliance for international trade.

From the trader's perspective, regulation "done right" involves a minimum of costly "red tape." All jurisdictions suffer from bureaucratic malaise, but some more than others. France, for example, has a decidedly bureaucratic culture, as does China. The higher the cost of regulatory compliance, the less international trade will occur. Trade regulation, either by content or its administration, can become a significant "nontariff trade barrier." Changing legal rules to mandate transparency, due process and compliance is easier than changing bureaucratic mindsets.

Our coverage of international trade regulation is problem-focused. We commence with tariff and nontariff import barriers in Chapter 6, followed by domestic producer remedies against import competition in Chapter 7, and finally the regulation of exports in Chapter 8. In total, there are 12 problems, each carefully selected as representative of what international traders and their lawyers frequently encounter. We hope you enjoy them.

CHAPTER 6

TARIFF AND NONTARIFF IMPORT BARRIERS

■ ■ ■

INTRODUCTION 6.0   AN OVERVIEW

We shift in this Part of the coursebook to regulation of imports. Much of the regulation of international trade is found in national laws, but the content of such regulation is determined principally by international, regional and bilateral agreements, for example the numerous 1994 World Trade Organization agreements, the treaties governing the European common market, NAFTA and hundreds of bilateral free trade agreements. How effectively such agreements are administered thus becomes a central concern.

Problem 6.1 focuses on global trade law and dispute settlement in the World Trade Organization. The core principle of most-favored-nation (MFN) trading and the Dispute Settlement Understanding (DSU) are highlighted. China's compliance with the terms of its 2001 admission to WTO are explored. What nations must do to gain WTO entry, and whether their governments and people are willing to undertake massive changes, are critical issues for global trade and its regulation.

Problem 6.2 continues the theme of world-wide trade law. Its focus is on three essential areas of customs law; product classification, valuation and origin. The classification of goods for purposes of assessing tariffs is widely governed by the Convention on the Harmonized Commodity Description and Coding System. Valuing goods for customs purposes has been harmonized via the WTO Customs Valuation Code. Uniform international rules of origin for goods are still in the process of being negotiated within the WTO. Meanwhile, we look at prevailing U.S. law on product origin, known as the "substantial transformation" doctrine.

Problem 6.3 moves beyond tariffs and customs to the pervasive problem of nontariff trade barriers (NTBs). Here there are a number of mandatory WTO Codes that seek to reduce the trade negating impact of national health, safety and product standard laws. We review the WTO Sanitary and Phyto–Sanitary (SPS) Code as it applies to trade in food products and the two WTO *Beef Hormones* decisions. Secondly, while not designed to govern environmental or conservation issues, the GATT agreement has nevertheless provided a means to successfully challenge the

United States Sea Turtle Conservation Act. This DSU Appellate Body decision harkens back to the *Tuna–Dolphin* dispute surrounding the U.S. Marine Mammal Protection Act. With these decisions, the interface between world trade law and national environmental concerns has moved into largely unchartered waters.

Problem 6.4 introduces regional economic organizations as a powerful force in the regulation of international trade. While nominally controlled by the WTO, regional groups and bilateral free trade agreements have proliferated in nearly every area of the world. They bring with them a host of discriminatory trading rules that benefit their participants and challenge global MFN principles. Problem 6.4 selectively contrasts two successful regional entities, the European Union (a "customs union") and NAFTA (a "free trade area"). Their differences cause us to revisit rules of origin and nontariff trade barriers in the context of fundamentally different regional dispute settlement systems. We also ponder a critical question. Where do Japan and China fit in the regionalization of trade puzzle?

Problem 6.5 examines tariff laws as they apply to the exports of developing nations. Preferential market access (often duty free) is granted through Generalized Systems of Tariff Preferences (GSP) and discriminatory trade laws. As with free trade areas and customs unions, once again it is global MFN principles that are subordinated. This is evident in the Caribbean Basin and Andean Trade Preference schemes of the United States. Such regimes result in more than most-favored-nations. Problem 6.5 also considers U.S. tariff law promoting the assembly outside of the country of U.S. components, parts and material. This occurs mostly in third world "maquiladoras," a deeply controversial practice as a matter of trade policy.

Lastly, Problem 6.6 explores a nontariff trade barrier for which there is, as yet, only a partial WTO solution ... government procurement preferences for local producers. The Buy American Act, as well as state and local procurement rules, are evaluated in light of the optional 1994 WTO Procurement Code and U.S. constitutional law. NAFTA's procurement preferences and Japan's procurement regime also receive scrutiny. With huge amounts of taxpayer moneys at stake, it is perhaps not surprising that procurement rules remain major international trade barriers.

PROBLEM 6.1   THE WORLD TRADE ORGANIZATION: OXICORP TRADES WITH NONMARKET AND TRANSITION ECONOMIES

SECTION I.   THE SETTING

OXICORP, Inc. is a medium-size United States corporation that traditionally specialized in trade with countries possessing nonmarket economies (NME). Since free market principles are increasingly being recognized and adopted around the world, clearcut NME nations are getting hard to find. OXICORP has therefore had to adapt to what are known as "transition economies" (TE) in countries seeking to shed their NME status. For example, many of the former Soviet Union states and much of Central Europe are in differing degrees of transition to a market economy. China, also, is progressing rapidly along the market economy learning curve. This is especially important to OXICORP since over half its business is with the People's Republic and it has been involved in a lot of tariff and trade disputes with the PRC.

All of this change has been rewarding to John Oxman, the founder of OXICORP, who has long believed that the best policy for the United States is to trade with all countries so that they ultimately recognize that the market system is better able to improve quality of life. Oxman also believes that economic interdependence is the key to world peace.

OXICORP understands that the United States, principally through its obligations under the General Agreement on Tariffs and Trade (GATT), has extended most favored nation (MFN) tariff status to over 150 nations. MFN tariff status is more accurately referred to as 'normal trade relations.' As a result of a series of GATT negotiations since the late 1940s, the average MFN tariff rate (Column 1 tariffs) on dutiable manufactured imports into the United States has been reduced to below 4 percent. This is a remarkably low level when measured against the tariffs applicable to goods imported into the U.S. from some NMEs. Such goods can be subject to the Smoot–Hawley Tariff Act of 1930 (Column 2 tariffs), the source of some of the highest tariffs in United States history.

Managing legal risks is an essential task of business lawyers, especially corporate counsel. Yet little in U.S. legal education trains attorneys in "risk management." The General Counsel to OXICORP is anxious about the level of risk the company faces in continuing to trade heavily in goods from NME and TE countries. The General Counsel has asked you, a junior staff attorney, to prepare a memorandum of law detailing what U.S. tariff levels apply to which goods from which NMEs and TEs and why. The General Counsel also wants to know what are the prospects and conditions for changes in U.S. tariffs as applied to goods from these countries, and in particular whether the emergence of the World Trade Organization (WTO) in 1995 will make a difference in tariff and other trade disputes like the ones it has experienced with China.

SECTION II. FOCUS OF CONSIDERATION

The meaning and significance of most favored nation tariff status is a fundamental concept of international trade. Every nation or customs territory has several levels of tariffs for imported goods. The goods of some nations may not be allowed as imports, or the tariffs are set so high so as to effectively cause the same result. Not to trade with another nation is a political decision. At the other end of the spectrum, some goods or the goods from some nations may be admitted without any tariff, called duty free. This special treatment may be accorded certain countries because they are part of a free trade agreement or customs union, or because they are goods from less developed nations with special relationships. But for most trade, the tariff level set for particular products is the same for almost all other nations—this is what we call most favored nation treatment. That sounds as though we single out some very special trading partners for "most favored" treatment. But that is not the case. Most favored nation treatment is really, or at least ideally, the norm.

One issue is the extent to which the GATT addresses problems of nonmarket and transition economies. Some nations such as China (admitted in 2001) and Vietnam (admitted in 2007) are already GATT signatories and World Trade Organization (WTO) members while others such as Russia is expected to join in 2012 and Iran wishes to join. Determining the terms and conditions for membership is not easy. At the time of the drafting of the GATT agreement, the uniqueness of trading with NMEs was not extensively considered. And little in the 1994 WTO agreements addresses transition economies.

Membership in the WTO matters on a wide range of trade law fronts. MFN tariffs negotiated within the WTO determine most national tariff levels, including U.S. normal or MFN tariffs. With only a few exceptions, WTO membership is a "package deal," binding each country to roughly 30 distinct trade agreements. For example, the WTO package includes agreements on agriculture, textiles, services, intellectual property and government subsidies. All of the WTO agreements are linked to the Dispute Settlement Understanding (DSU). Sorting out the WTO dispute settlement process is a major focus of this problem.

Articles I, III, XI and XVII of the GATT agreement, and the WTO Dispute Settlement Understanding are essential to analysis of this problem. They appear in the Documents Supplement. Web resources for further study include *www.wto.org.*

SECTION III. READINGS, QUESTIONS AND COMMENTS

DEMERET, THE METAMORPHOSES OF THE GATT: FROM THE HAVANA CHARTER TO THE WORLD TRADE ORGANIZATION

34 Columbia J. Transnat'l L. 123 (1995).*

FROM THE HAVANA CHARTER TO THE KENNEDY ROUND

The General Agreement on Tariffs and Trade signed at Geneva in 1947 was not itself intended to remain in force nor to give rise to an international organization. The GATT was a provisional agreement designed to cover the period prior to the entry into force of the Havana

Charter. The former agreement codified the results of an initial negotiation on the reduction of tariffs. To avoid the possibility of tariff concessions being indirectly undermined, it reproduced the content of Chapter IV of the Havana Charter relating to trade policy. The General Agreement is based on the most favored nation principle. It is, however, permissible to derogate from this principle in order to establish a custom union or a free trade area. In addition, the Agreement provides that importations should enjoy the benefit of national treatment as far as internal taxes and trade regulations are concerned. It defines the conditions under which imported products may be subject to antidumping and countervailing duties. It prohibits, in principle, quantitative restrictions, with the exception of measures which are justified in order to protect the balance-of-payments or trade safeguard measures. The General Agreement also contains a provision relating to subsidies. The terms of this provision in relation to production subsidies is vague and quite imprecise in relation to export subsidies, while the provisions relating to the export of manufactured products are more binding.

The Havana Charter was an agreement of much broader scope which provided for the establishment of the International Trade Organization and an elaborate dispute settlement procedure. On a substantive level, the Havana Charter comprised, in addition to the provisions which are reproduced in the General Agreement, chapters relating to employment and economic activity, economic development and reconstruction, restrictive trade practices, as well as agreements on primary products.

Due to the United States' failure to ratify the Havana Charter, the Charter never entered into force, and the General Agreement, by force of circumstances, remained in force. The GATT was the forum for many multilateral rounds of tariff negotiation during the 1950s and 1960s. The most important of these, the Kennedy Round, resulted in the reduction of the customs duties of the contracting parties by an average of 35%. The tariff negotiations succeeded in reducing the effect of both customs duties and tariff reductions on trade. In any case, in the 1970s, trade was even more influenced by the fluctuations in exchange rates than by tariff concessions.

THE TOKYO ROUND AND THE GATT "À LA CARTE"

The Tokyo Round negotiations took place from 1974 to 1979 and, like the Kennedy Round negotiations, were the result of an American initiative. The Tokyo Round had as its principal objective the reduction of nontariff barriers to trade and resulted in the conclusion of different specific agreements, known under the name of "codes." The most important of these agreements relate respectively to the liberalization of certain governments procurements, subsidies and countervailing duties, antidumping duties, technical barriers to trade, and the definition of customs value. It was also at the end of the Tokyo Round that the possibility of granting to developing countries preferential trade treatment, in derogation of the most favored nation clause, was definitively recognized.

The above-mentioned agreements interpreted, defined or completed the relevant provisions of the General Agreement, which was often drafted using terminology both imprecise and of little binding force. In addition, these "codes" served to reduce the effective scope of the "grandfather clause," designed to allow the United States, even after the signature of the GATT, to enforce legislation incompatible with the General Agreement to its foreign trade where such legislation pre-dated the General Agreement.

The technique of using "codes" which was adopted during the Tokyo Round entailed, however, one major inconvenience: it established a GATT "à la carte," thereby leading to what one commentator has called the Agreement's balkanization. Each agreement was subject to its own dispute settlement procedure, even though each was also based on the general procedure that had been developed within the framework of the General Agreement. In addition, national participation in each agreement varied. Although the major industrialized countries and the European Community are members of these specific agreements, such is not the case of many other contracting parties of the General Agreement. The level of obligation falling on the different states which are party to the GATT therefore varies to a considerable extent. * * *

The "Single Package" System

* * *

A state which wishes to become a member of the World Trade Organization must agree to all of the multilateral agreements negotiated within the framework of the Uruguay Round.

In guaranteeing a certain degree of global reciprocity, the formula of "all or nothing" enabled the divergence of interests which divided certain countries to be overcome. Thus, countries which were mainly interested in the development of trade in textile products or agricultural products, but less interested or scarcely interested in the reinforcement of the protection of intellectual property rights or the liberalization of trade in services, were able to accept the multilateral agreements relating to these matters, and vice versa.

The Uruguay Round puts an end to the GATT "à la carte" which resulted from the Tokyo Round. The multilateral system thereby gains coherence. This coherence should be aided by the establishment of a single dispute settlement procedure for the different fields which fall within the competence of the World Trade Organization. The existence of an appeals body, the composition of which enjoys a certain degree of stability, should facilitate the emergence of a real system of jurisprudence and a systematic interpretation of the substantive rules contained in the different agreements.

The system described above does, however, contain one exception. There are four so-called plurilateral agreements annexed to the agreement setting up the WTO. These agreements relate respectively to government procurement, trade in civil aircraft, the dairy sector, and the bovine meat sector. These agreements do not bind all the members of the WTO, but only those who accept them. * * * This system is a derogation from the most favored nation clause and is explained by the fear of "free riders" which was referred to above. The new dispute settlement procedure will, however, be applicable to relations between the parties who have accepted these plurilateral agreements.

WORLD TRADE ORGANIZATION AGREEMENTS

AGREEMENT ESTABLISHING THE MULTILATERAL [WORLD] TRADE ORGANIZATION

ANNEX 1A: AGREEMENTS ON TRADE IN GOODS

     1   General Agreement on Tariffs and Trade 1994

         (a)   Understanding on the Interpretation of Article II:1(b)

         (b)   Understanding on the Interpretation of Article XVII

         (c)   Understanding on Balance-of-Payments Provisions

         (d)   Understanding on the Interpretation of Article XXIV

         (e)   Understanding on the Interpretation of Article XXV

         (f)   Understanding on the Interpretation of Article XXXIII

         (g)   Understanding on the Interpretation of Article XXXV

     2   Uruguay Round Protocol GATT 1994

     3   Agreement on Agriculture

     4   Agreement on Sanitary and Phytosanitary Measures

     5   Agreement on Textiles and Clothing

     6   Agreement on Technical Barriers to Trade

     7   Agreement on Trade–Related Investment Measures

     8   Agreement on Implementation of Article VI

     9   Agreement on Implementation of Article VII

    10   Agreement on Preshipment Inspection

    11   Agreement on Rules of Origin

    12   Agreement on Import Licensing Procedures

    13   Agreement on Subsidies and Countervailing Measures

    14   Agreement on Safeguards

ANNEX 1B: General Agreement on Trade in Services and Annexes

ANNEX 1C: Agreement on Trade–Related Aspects of Intellectual Property Rights, Including Trade in Counterfeit Goods

ANNEX 2:   Understanding on Rules and Procedures Governing the Settlement of Disputes

ANNEX 3:   Trade Policy Review Mechanism

ANNEX 4:   Plurilateral Trade Agreements

     ANNEX 4(a)   Agreement on Trade in Civil Aircraft

     ANNEX 4(b)   Agreement on Government Procurement

     ANNEX 4(c)   International Dairy Arrangement

     ANNEX 4(d)   Arrangement Regarding Bovine Meat

HARDERS–CHEN, CHINA MFN: A REAFFIRMATION OF TRADITION OR REGULATORY REFORM?

5 Minn.J. Global Trade 381 (1996).*

In 1980, China began its bid to reenter the General Agreement on Tariffs and Trade (GATT) and the World Trade Organization (WTO). China then promulgated many new trade regulations in an attempt to meet GATT criticisms concerning the lack of transparency in its trade laws. On May 12, 1994 China enacted its most notable response to GATT criticism: the Foreign Trade Law.

China's Foreign Trade Law sets forth general principles of trade. Article 6 grants most-favored-nation (MFN) treatment to certain foreign nations. The most-favored-nation principle of non-discrimination in trade is the cornerstone of the GATT. By adopting a most-favored-nation clause during its bid to enter the GATT, China appears to demonstrate the compliance required for successful reentry.

The MFN principle adopted by China, however, does not simply reflect the GATT understanding of non-discrimination. China's interpretation of MFN must be examined in the context of the history of MFN in China, the recent debate between the United States and China over China's MFN status, and the changing role of law in Chinese economic reforms. China's interpretation of MFN will affect the enforcement of GATT principles if China becomes a member of the WTO.

* * *

CHINA'S NEW MFN CLAUSE REFLECTS REGULATORY REFORM WITHIN THE HISTORICAL CONTEXT

China's history of trade illustrates the difficulties China may have in adapting to the GATT/WTO. The tribute system [1362–1912] used a bilateral contract-like relationship with its trading powers. While the unequal treaty system [1843–1923] was unilateral, it still consisted of two parties, the European nations as one trading power achieving concessions unilaterally through MFN, and China. Communist China similarly perceived itself as a representative of communism which should avoid any trade with capitalist economies. Today, the multilateral trading system of the GATT presents new challenges of economic integration for both China and the WTO.

CHINA'S MFN CLAUSE REFLECTS HISTORICAL CONCERN FOR RECIPROCITY

The unequal treaty system of the nineteenth century illustrates China's historical concern over achieving reciprocity in trade relations. The unequal treaty system changed China psychologically and materially. China specifically objected to the lack of reciprocity in the treaty negotiations.

This recurrent Chinese concern over reciprocity appears explicitly in China's MFN clause. Article 5 of the Foreign Trade Law describes the principle by which China engages in foreign trade. "The People's Republic of China promotes and develops trade relations with other countries and regions *on the basis of the principles of equality and mutual benefit.*" Hence, China sets forth the principle of mutual benefit or reciprocity as the overriding purpose of foreign trade.

The language of Article 6 similarly defines MFN as a function of reciprocity and mutual benefit. "The Peoples' Republic of China grants Most Favored Nation treatment or national treatment in the field of foreign trade to concluding or acceding parties in accordance with international treaties or agreements concluded or acceded to, *or on the basis of the principles of mutual benefit and reciprocity.*" In basing MFN on reciprocity and mutual benefit, the text of Articles 5 and 6 imply that MFN should be limited to the extent it may impinge on principles of reciprocity. This is consistent with the historical tribute system of China and China's treaties granting MFN in the 1950's and 1960's to its allies. China MFN also addresses concerns of maintaining equal and reciprocal relationships arising from the historical experience of China under the unequal treaties.

* * *

CHINA'S MFN CLAUSE EMBODIES CHINA'S POLITICAL TRADITIONS

China has never differentiated the regulation of trade from politics. The tribute system allowed trade as a consequence of paying tribute under a political relationship. The unequal treaties came into being as a result of military concessions. MFN was similarly inextricably linked to politics by the KMT and Communist China. Though China currently desires the benefits offered by the GATT and especially covets unconditional MFN status in the United States, China may have particular difficulties differentiating regulatory trade from politics.

China MFN is inextricably linked to politics as China attempts to achieve WTO membership. By employing protectionism in its new Foreign Trade Law and maintaining some of its bureaucratic controls, China has not fully complied with standards necessary to enter the WTO. The United States has used China's desire to enter the WTO as a bargaining chip to encourage changes in Chinese trade regulation. China appears, however, to have become impatient with its outsider status and while desiring the benefits of WTO membership, China downplays its importance. In fact, recent Chinese policies have moved away from WTO norms. If China downplays the importance of WTO membership, then U.S. incentives for supporting Chinese membership may lose their force. China MFN is therefore dependent upon the political importance attributed to WTO membership.

Article 7 of the Foreign Trade Law links China MFN to current politics by allowing China to retaliate for failures of other contracting parties to abide by MFN. This calls into question the full effect of Article 6 granting MFN treatment. The ability of China to take unilateral, retaliatory action allows it to avoid the guarantee of MFN in the GATT. This is not a problem unique to China. U.S. policies under Section 301 have been similarly criticized. Many other countries also implement retaliatory actions against other nations for failing to abide by non-discrimination principles in trade. Widespread usage of domestic retaliatory actions outside the WTO may undermine the effectiveness of the GATT.

What differentiates China's use of retaliation under MFN from Western nations is that China has never historically regulated trade as a distinct entity apart from politics. China continues to assert it will retaliate immediately. By threatening withdrawal of MFN status for China based on human rights, the United States bolsters the conceptual connection of MFN to politics. China believes the U.S. position violates proper notions of reciprocity and mutual benefit. Once China becomes a member of the GATT/WTO, it seems unlikely that Chinese foreign policy will abide by unconditional, automatic MFN when it becomes politically expedient to achieve other goals.

BHALA, ENTER THE DRAGON: AN ESSAY ON CHINA'S WTO ACCESSION SAGA

15 Am. U. Int'l L. Rev. 1469 (2000).*

Conceptually, and in practice, accession is a two-step process. First, the applicant must negotiate bilateral concession agreements with each WTO member that asks for one. Collectively, the members requesting bilateral agreements are referred to as an "accession Working Party." The bilateral deals embody the applicant's promises to individual members about opening its market on a government-to-government basis. They should not be confused with previously negotiated deals that the applicant may have made with particular members. Brand new agreements, or at the least, revisions to existing agreements are at issue here. These new agreements are the price of admission into the GATT–WTO system.

The need for this first step is not apparent from the language of GATT Article XXXIII, which, after all, speaks to the joint action of the CONTRACTING PARTIES. Still, the process of forming bilateral concession agreements has become indispensable. What members will ask for such agreements? Those that have a keen export interest in the applicant's market. Therefore, the first step can be a tedious process. For commercially and politically significant applicants like the PRC and Taiwan, many members are sure to request bilateral negotiations. Roughly forty WTO members asked the PRC for bilateral concession agreements (including Australia, Brazil, Canada, Chile, the EU, Hungary, India, Japan, New Zealand, Norway, Switzerland, and the United States), and approximately twenty-six members (including Hong Kong and the United States) asked Taiwan for such deals. The accession of Saudi Arabia, Iran, and Russia are

---

* Reproduced with permission of American University International Law Review.

other examples demonstrating that many existing members will seek bilateral agreements. These agreements need not be identical—indeed, it is unlikely they will be. The members have some common, and some different, export interests. For example, in August 1998, Taiwan completed its bilateral agreement with the United States. Taiwan offered greater market-opening concessions to American agricultural products (specifically, beef and pork innards, and chicken) than it agreed to in its deals with the European Union ("EU") and Japan.

The second step is the negotiation of a protocol of accession with all WTO members, *i.e.*, with the WTO as a whole. Technically, the protocol is not the same thing as the decision of the CONTRACTING PARTIES referred to in GATT Article XXXIII. The decision is taken, and a separate protocol is drafted and approved. Thus, it could be said that accession actually involves three steps: bilateral concession agreements, the decision, and the protocol.

Obviously, the member states will not agree upon a protocol unless the first step is accomplished. When the demands of several members for bilateral concession agreements remain unsatisfied, those members will not support accession. To be sure, if only a few members remain unsatisfied, then they could invoke the non-application provisions of the GATT and WTO Agreements. At the same time, successful completion of the first step does not guarantee an easy negotiation for protocol of accession. To make matters even more complicated, the two steps may overlap.

The protocol represents the terms of entry into the WTO. It is, in effect, a contract between the acceding party and the members in their joint capacity (the CONTRACTING PARTIES, in the language of GATT Article XXXIII). By implication, the members in their joint capacity are a separate legal entity under international law. Many of the arrangements made in the bilateral concession agreements become multilateral through the protocol. In fact, the bilateral agreements are incorporated into a schedule of commitments that is sent with the protocol, along with a report from the Working Party, to the WTO General Council for approval.

In addition, the protocol outlines the applicant's current trade laws and policies, while noting the differences between that regime and the minimum GATT–WTO requirements. The protocol explains how—and when—the applicant intends to correct these differences. Thus, for example, there might be a gap between the applicant's sanitary rules and the SPS Agreement, or its copyright laws and the Trade–Related Aspects of Intellectual Property Rights ("TRIPS") Agreement. The protocol identifies these problem areas and sets out the agreed plan of action for addressing them.

Finally, some applicants may want the protocol to indicate their status as a developing—or least developed—country so as to take advantage of the special and differential ("S&D") treatment afforded by many Uruguay Round agreements for such countries. The PRC, for example, argued vociferously for developing country status. Many WTO members may see this as a ruse to avoid trade obligations for as long as possible. Indeed, as intimated, aside from the problem of status, the question of "when?" often is crucial. Applicants may want to defer the reduction and elimination of tariff and non-tariff barriers for as long as possible. Extant members are sure to pursue the opposite goal in the protocol negotiations.

A sense of urgency often pervades these negotiations, particularly on the part of the applicant. The longer the negotiations drag on, the more likely the terms of entry will become more onerous. This is because the WTO members will agree among themselves to new trade liberalizing initiatives. For example, suppose a new trade negotiating round commences and results in a major market-opening deal on agriculture. A country that acceded before the new round had the opportunity to shape the terms of the deal, and in particular, the opportunity to make sure it can live with the terms. A country seeking accession after the round will be stuck with a deal negotiated by others. Moreover, to use a track-and-field metaphor, "the bar will get raised." Many of the pre-round concessions the applicant made in bilateral negotiations during the first step of the accession process may, after the round, be deemed inadequate. After all, if the new round leads to greater liberalization among the members, then more will be expected of the applicant.

* * *

2010 Report to Congress
On China's WTO Compliance

United States Trade Representative
December 2010.

Summary Analysis of China's WTO Compliance Efforts

TRADING RIGHTS

China appears to be in compliance with its trading rights commitments in most areas. One significant concern involves restrictions on the right to import copyright-intensive products such as books, newspapers, journals, theatrical films, DVDs and music, which China still reserves for state trading; China has agreed to remove these restrictions in 2011 in order to comply with the rulings in a WTO case brought by the United States.

DISTRIBUTION SERVICES

China has made substantial progress in implementing its distribution services commitments, although significant concerns remain in some areas.

Wholesaling Services

China has issued regulations generally implementing its commitments in the area of wholesaling and commission agents' services. China continues to maintain significant restrictions on the distribution of copyright-intensive products such as books, newspapers, journals, theatrical films, DVDs and music; China has agreed to remove these restrictions in 2011 in order to comply with the rulings in a WTO case brought by the United States. U.S. companies also have concerns about continuing restrictions on the distribution of other products, such as pharmaceuticals, crude oil and processed oil.

Retailing Services

China has issued regulations generally implementing its commitments in the area of retailing services, although some concerns remain with regard to licensing discrimination. China continues to maintain restrictions on the retailing of processed oil.

Franchising Services

China has issued regulations generally implementing its commitments in the area of franchising services.

Direct Selling Services

China has issued regulations generally implementing its commitments in the area of direct selling services, although significant regulatory restrictions imposed on the operations of direct sellers continue to generate concern.

IMPORT REGULATION

Tariffs

China has timely implemented its tariff commitments for industrial goods each year.

Customs and Trade Administration

Customs Valuation

China has issued measures that bring its legal regime for making customs valuation determinations into compliance with WTO rules, but implementation of these measures has been inconsistent from port to port, both in terms of customs clearance procedures and valuation determinations.

Rules of Origin

China has issued measures that bring its legal regime for making rules of origin determinations into compliance with WTO rules.

Import Licensing

China has issued measures that bring its legal regime for import licenses into compliance with WTO rules, although a variety of specific compliance issues continue to arise, as in the case of China's import licensing procedures for iron ore imports.

Non-tariff Measures

China has adhered to the agreed schedule for eliminating non-tariff measures.

Tariff-rate Quotas on Industrial Products

Concerns about transparency and administrative guidance have plagued China's tariff-rate quota system for industrial products, particularly fertilizer, since China's accession to the WTO.

Other Import Regulation

Antidumping

China has issued laws and regulations bringing its legal regime in the AD area largely into compliance with WTO rules, although China still needs to issue additional procedural guidance such as rules governing expiry reviews. It appears that China also needs to improve its commitment to the transparency and procedural fairness requirements embodied in WTO rules. In addition, China has begun to invoke AD and CVD remedies under troubling circumstances; the United States is currently challenging China's determinations in one set of AD and CVD investigations in a WTO case alleging multiple violations of WTO rules.

Other Import Regulation (cont'd)

Countervailing Duties

China has issued laws and regulations bringing its legal regime in the CVD area largely into compliance with WTO rules, although China still needs to issue additional procedural guidance such as rules governing expiry reviews. It appears that China also needs to improve its commitment to the transparency, procedural fairness and methodological requirements embodied in WTO rules. In addition, China has begun to invoke AD and CVD remedies under troubling circumstances; the United States is currently challenging China's determinations in one set of AD and CVD investigations in a WTO case alleging multiple violations of WTO rules.

Safeguards

China has issued measures bringing its legal regime in the safeguards area largely into compliance with WTO rules, although concerns about potential inconsistencies with WTO rules continue to exist.

EXPORT REGULATION

China maintains numerous export restraints that raise serious concerns under WTO rules, including specific commitments that China made in its Protocol of Accession to the WTO.

INTERNAL POLICIES AFFECTING TRADE

Non-discrimination

While China has revised many laws, regulations and other measures to make them consistent with WTO rules relating to MFN and national treatment, concerns about compliance with these rules still arise in some areas.

Taxation

China has used its taxation system to discriminate against imports in certain sectors, raising concerns under WTO rules relating to national treatment.

Subsidies

China continues to provide injurious subsidies to its domestic industries, and some of these subsidies appear to be prohibited under WTO rules. China has also failed to file annual WTO subsidy notifications since 2006, and its 2006 notification was incomplete.

Price Controls

China has progressed slowly in reducing the number of products and services subject to price control or government guidance pricing.

Standards, Technical Regulations and Conformity Assessment Procedures

China continues to take actions that generate WTO compliance concerns in the areas of standards, technical regulations and conformity assessment procedures, particularly with regard to transparency, national treatment, the pursuit of unique Chinese national standards, and duplicative testing and certification requirements.

Restructuring of Regulators

China has restructured its regulators for standards, technical regulations and conformity assessment procedures in order to eliminate discriminatory treatment of imports, although in practice China's regulators sometimes do not appear to enforce regulatory requirements as strictly against domestic products as compared to imports.

Standards and Technical Regulations

China continues to pursue the development of unique Chinese national standards, despite the existence of well-established international standards, apparently as a means for protecting domestic companies from competing foreign technologies and standards.

Conformity Assessment Procedures

China appears to be turning more and more to in-country testing for a broader range of products, which does not conform with international practices that generally accept foreign test results and conformity assessment certifications.

Transparency

China has made progress but still does not appear to notify all new or revised standards, technical regulations and conformity assessment procedures as required by WTO rules.

Other Industrial Policies

State-owned and State-invested Enterprises

The Chinese government has heavily intervened in the investment decisions made by state-owned and state-invested enterprises in certain sectors.

State Trading Enterprises

It is difficult to assess the activities of China's state-trading enterprises, given inadequate transparency.

Other Industrial Policies (cont'd)

Government Procurement

While China is moving slowly toward fulfilling its commitment to accede to the GPA, it is maintaining and adopting government procurement measures that give domestic preferences.

INVESTMENT

China has revised many laws and regulations on foreign-invested enterprises to eliminate WTO-inconsistent requirements relating to export performance, local content, foreign exchange balancing and technology transfer, although some of the revised measures continue to "encourage" one or more of those requirements. China has also issued industrial policies covering the auto and steel sectors that include guidelines that appear to conflict with its WTO obligations. In addition, China has added a variety of restrictions on investment that appear designed to shield inefficient or monopolistic Chinese enterprises from foreign competition.

AGRICULTURE

While China has timely implemented its tariff commitments for agricultural goods, a variety of non-tariff barriers continue to impede market access, particularly in the areas of SPS measures and inspection-related requirements.

Tariffs

China has timely implemented its tariff commitments for agricultural goods each year.

Tariff-rate Quotas on Bulk Agricultural Commodities

China's administration of TRQs on bulk agricultural commodities still does not seem to be functioning entirely as envisioned in China's WTO accession agreement, as it continues to be impaired by inadequate transparency.

China's Biotechnology Regulations

Despite continuing problems with China's biotechnology approval process, major trade disruptions have been avoided.

Sanitary and Phytosanitary Issues

In 2010, China's regulatory authorities imposed non-transparent SPS measures that appear to lack scientific bases, including BSE-related bans on beef and some low-risk bovine products, pathogen standards and residue standards for raw meat and poultry products, and Avian Influenza bans on poultry. Meanwhile, China has made progress but still does not appear to have notified all proposed SPS measures as required by WTO rules.

Inspection-related Requirements

China's regulatory authorities continue to administer inspection-related requirements in a seemingly arbitrary manner.

Export Subsidies

It is difficult to determine whether China maintains export subsidies on agricultural goods, in part because China has not notified all of its subsidies to the WTO.

INTELLECTUAL PROPERTY RIGHTS

China is in the process of revising its legal regime and updating a comprehensive set of laws and regulations aimed at protecting the intellectual property rights of domestic and foreign entities in China, but some key improvements in China's legal framework are still needed, and China has continued to demonstrate little success in actually enforcing its laws and regulations in the face of the challenges created by widespread counterfeiting, piracy and other forms of infringement.

Legal Framework

China has established a framework of laws, regulations and departmental rules that largely satisfies its WTO commitment. However, reforms are needed in a few key areas, such as further improvement of China's measures for copyright protection on the Internet following China's accession to the WIPO Internet treaties and changes to address a number of continuing deficiencies in China's criminal IPR enforcement measures.

Enforcement

Effective IPR enforcement has not been achieved, and IPR infringement remains a serious problem throughout China. IPR enforcement is hampered by lack of coordination among Chinese government ministries and agencies, lack of training, resource constraints, lack of transparency in the enforcement process and its outcomes, and local protectionism and corruption.

SERVICES

While China has implemented most of its services commitments, it appears that China has not implemented or has only partially implemented its commitments in some service sectors. In addition, challenges still remain in ensuring the benefits of many of the commitments that China has nominally implemented are available in practice, as China has continued to maintain or erect restrictive or cumbersome terms of entry in some sectors. These entry barriers prevent or discourage foreign suppliers from gaining market access through informal bans on new entry, high capital requirements, branching restrictions or restrictions taking away previously acquired market access rights. In addition, the licensing process in some sectors has generated national treatment concerns or inordinate delays.

Financial Services

Banking

China has taken a number of steps to implement its banking services commitments, although these efforts have generated concerns, and there are some instances in which China still does not seem to have fully implemented particular commitments, such as with regard to Chinese-foreign joint banks and bank branches.

Motor Vehicle Financing

China has implemented its commitments with regard to motor vehicle financing.

Insurance

China has issued measures implementing most of its insurance commitments, but these measures have also created problems in the areas of licensing, branching and transparency.

Financial Information

In response to a WTO case brought by the United States, China has established an independent regulator for the financial information sector and has removed restrictions that had placed foreign suppliers at a serious competitive disadvantage.

Electronic Payment Processing

It appears that China has not yet implemented electronic payment processing commitments that should have been phased in no later than December 11, 2006.

Legal Services

China has issued measures intended to implement its legal services commitments, although these measures give rise to WTO compliance concerns because they impose an economic needs test, restrictions on the types of legal services that can be provided and lengthy delays for the establishment of new offices.

Telecommunications

It appears that China has nominally kept to the agreed schedule for phasing in its WTO commitments in the telecommunications sector, but restrictions maintained by China, such as informal bans on new entry, a requirement that foreign suppliers can only enter into joint ventures with state-owned enterprises and exceedingly high capital requirements for basic services as well as the reclassification of some value-added services as basic services, have created serious barriers to market entry.

Construction and Related Engineering Services

China has issued measures intended to implement its construction and related engineering services commitments, although these measures are problematic because they also impose high capital requirements and other requirements that limit market access.

Express Delivery Services

China has continued to allow foreign express delivery companies to operate in the express delivery sector and has implemented its commitment to allow wholly foreign-owned subsidiaries by December 11, 2004, but China has issued a new law that undermines market access for foreign companies in the domestic express delivery sector and raises questions in light of China's WTO obligations.

Aviation Services

China has provided significant additional market access to U.S. providers of air transport services through a bilateral agreement with the United States.

Maritime Services

Even though China made only limited WTO commitments relating to its maritime services sector, it has increased market access for U.S. service providers through a bilateral agreement.

Other Services

The United States has not identified significant concerns related to China's implementation of commitments made in other service sectors.

LEGAL FRAMEWORK

Transparency

<u>Official Journal</u>

China has re-committed to use a single official journal for the publication of all trade-related laws, regulations and other measures. While it appears that most government entities regularly publish their trade-related measures in this journal, it is not yet clear whether all types of trade-related measures are being published.

<u>Public Comment</u>

China has adopted notice-and-comment procedures for proposed laws and committed to use notice-and-comment procedures for proposed trade- and economic-related regulations and departmental rules, subject to specified exceptions.

<u>Enquiry Points</u>

China has complied with its obligation to establish enquiry points.

Uniform Application of Laws

Some problems with the uniform application of China's laws and regulations persist.

Judicial Review

China has established courts to review administrative actions related to trade matters, but few U.S. or other foreign companies have had experience with these courts.

R. FOLSOM, PRACTITIONER TREATISE ON INTERNATIONAL BUSINESS TRANSACTIONS

§ 9.6 (2011–12).

WTO dispute settlement/U.S. disputes

WTO provides a unified system for settling international trade disputes through the Dispute Settlement Understanding (DSU) and using the Dispute Settlement Body (DSB). The DSB is a special assembly of the WTO General Council, and includes all WTO Members. There are five stages in the resolution of disputes under WTO: 1) Consultation; 2) Panel establishment, investigation and report; 3) Appellate review of the panel report; 4) Adoption of the panel and appellate decision; and 5) Implementation of the decision adopted. There is also a parallel process for binding arbitration, if both parties agree to submit this dispute to arbitration, rather than to a DSB panel. In addition, during the implementation phase (5), the party subject to an adverse decision may seek arbitration as a matter of right on issues of compliance and authorized retaliation.

Although the DSU offers a unified dispute resolution system that is applicable across all sectors and all WTO Covered Agreements, there are many specialized rules for disputes which arise under them. Such specialized rules appear in the Agreements on Textiles, Antidumping, Subsidies and Countervailing Measures, Technical Barriers to Trade, Sanitary and Phytosanitary Measures, Customs Valuation, General Agreement on Trade in Services, Financial Services and Air Transport Services. The special provisions in these individual Covered Agreements govern, where applicable, and prevail in any conflict with the general provisions of the DSU.

Under WTO, unlike under GATT 1947, the DSU practically assures that panels will be established upon request by a Member. Further, under WTO, unlike under GATT 1947, the DSU virtually ensures the adoption of unmodified panel and appellate body decisions. It accomplishes this by requiring the DSB to adopt panel reports and appellate body decisions automatically and without amendment unless they are rejected by a consensus of all Members. This "inverted consensus" requires that all Members of the DSB, including the Member who prevailed in the dispute, decide to reject the dispute resolution decision; and that no Member formally favor that decision. Such an outcome seems unlikely. This inverted consensus requirement is imposed on both the adoption of panel reports or appellate body decisions and also on the decision to establish a panel.

The potential resolutions of a dispute under DSU range from a "mutually satisfactory solution" agreed to by the parties under the first, or consultation phase, to authorized retaliation under the last, or implementation, phase. The preferred solution is always any resolution that is mutually satisfactory to the parties. After a panel decision, there are three types of remedies available to the prevailing party, if a mutually satisfactory solution cannot be obtained. One is for the respondent to bring the measure found to violate a Covered Agreement into conformity with the Agreement. A second is for the prevailing Member to receive compensation from the respondent which both parties agree is sufficient to compensate for any injury caused by the measure found to violate a Covered Agreement. Finally, if no such agreement can be reached, a prevailing party can be authorized to suspend some of its concessions under the Covered Agreements to the respondent. These suspended concessions, called "retaliation," can be authorized within the same trade sector and agreement; or, if that will not create sufficient compensation, can be authorized across trade sectors and agreements.

Phase 1: Consultation. Any WTO Member who believes that the Measures of another Member are not in conformity with the Covered Agreements may call for consultations on those measures. The respondent has ten days to reply to the call for consultations and must agree to enter into consultation within 30 days. If the respondent does not enter into consultations within the 30 day period, the party seeking consultations can immediately request the establishment of a panel under DSU, which puts the dispute into Phase 2.

Once consultations begin, the parties have 60 days to achieve a settlement. The goal is to seek a positive solution to the dispute, and the preferred resolution is to reach whatever solution is mutually satisfactory to the parties. If such a settlement cannot be obtained after 60 days of consultations, the party seeking consultations may request the establishment of a panel under DSU, which moves the dispute into Phase 2.

Third parties with an interest in the subject-matter of the consultations may seek to be included in them. If such inclusion is rejected, they may seek their own consultations with the other Member. Alternatives to consultations may be provided through the use of conciliation, mediation or good offices, where all parties agree to use the alternative process. Any party can terminate the use of conciliation, mediation or good offices and then seek the establishment of a panel under DSU, which will move the dispute into Phase 2.

Phase 2: Panel establishment, investigation and report. If consultations between the parties fail, the party seeking the consultations (the complainant) may request the DSB to establish a panel to investigate, report and resolve the dispute. The DSB must establish such a panel upon request, unless the DSB expressly decides by consensus not to establish the panel. Since an "inverted consensus" is required to reject the establishment of the panel and the complainant Member must be part of that consensus, it is very likely that a panel will be established. Roughly 100 panels were established in the first five years of operation of the DSU.

The WTO Secretariat is to maintain a list of well-qualified persons who are available to serve as panelists. The panels are usually composed of three individuals from that list who are not citizens of either party. If the parties agree, a panel can be composed of five such individuals. The parties can also agree to appoint citizens of a party to a panel. Panelists may be either nongovernmental individuals or governmental officials, but they are to be selected so as to ensure their independence. Thus, there is a bias towards independent individuals who are not citizens of any party. If a citizen of a party is appointed, his government may not instruct that citizen how to vote, for the panelist must be independent. By the same reasoning, a governmental official of a non-party Member who is subject to instructions from his government would not seem to fit the profile of an independent panelist.

The WTO Secretariat proposes nominations of the panelists. Parties may not normally oppose the nominations, except for "compelling reasons." The parties are given twenty days to agree on the panelists and the composition of the panel. If such agreement is not forthcoming, the WTO Director-General is authorized to appoint the panelists, in consultation with other persons in the Secretariat.

Complaints brought to DSB panels can involve either violations of Covered Agreements or nonviolation nullification and impairment of benefits under the Covered Agreements. A prima facie case of nullification impairment arises when one Member infringes upon the "obligations assumed under a Covered Agreement." Such infringement creates a presumption against the infringing Member, but the presumption can be rebutted by a showing that the complaining Member has suffered no adverse effect from the infringement.

The panels receive pleadings and rebuttals and hear oral arguments. Panels can also engage in fact development from sources outside those presented by the parties. Thus, the procedure has aspects familiar to civil law courts. A panel can, on its own initiative, request information from any body, including experts selected by the panel. It can also obtain confidential information in some circumstances from an administrative body which is part of the government of a Member, without any prior consent from that Member. A panel can establish its own group of experts to provide reports to it on factual or scientific issues. In a series of rulings commencing with the *Shrimp-Turtles* decision in 1998, the WTO Appellate Body has affirmed the right of panels and itself to elect to receive unsolicited informational and argumentative briefs or letters from non-governmental organizations (NGOs), business groups and law firms.

A panel is obligated to produce two written reports—an interim and a final report. A panel is supposed to submit a final written report to the DSB within six months of its establishment. The report will contain its findings of fact, findings of law, decision and the rationale for its decision. Before the final report is issued, the panel is supposed to provide an interim report to the parties. The purpose of this interim report is to apprize the parties of the panel's current analysis of the issues and to permit the parties to comment on that analysis. The final report of the panel need not change any of the findings or conclusions in its interim report unless it is persuaded to do so by a party's comments. However, if it is not so persuaded, it is obligated to explain in its final report why it is not so persuaded.

The decisions in panel reports are final as to issues of fact. The decisions in panel reports are not necessarily final as to issues of law. Panel decisions on issues of law are subject to review by the Appellate Body, which is Phase 3, and explained below. Any party can appeal a panel report, and as is explained below it is expected that appeals will usually be taken.

Phase 3: Appellate review of the panel report. Appellate review of panel reports is available at the request of any party, unless the DSB rejects that request by an "inverted consensus." There is no threshold requirement for an appellant to present a substantial substantive legal issue. Thus, most panel decisions are appealed as a matter of course. However, the Appellate Body can only review the panel reports on questions of law or legal interpretation.

The Appellate Body is a new institution in the international trade organization and its process. GATT 1947 had nothing comparable to it. The Appellate Body is composed of seven members (or judges) who are appointed by the DSB to four year terms. Each judge may be reappointed, but only once, to a second four year term. Each judge is to be a recognized authority on international trade law and the Covered Agreements. To date, Appellate Body members have been drawn mostly from the academe and retired justices. They have come from Germany, Japan, Egypt, India, New Zealand, the Philippines, Argentina and the United States. The review of any panel decision is performed by three judges out of the seven. The parties do not, however, have any influence on which judges are selected to review a particular panel report. There is a schedule, created by the Appellate Body itself, for the rotation for sitting of each of the judges. Thus, a party might try to appear before a favored judge by timing the start of the dispute settlement process to arrive at the Appellate Body at the right moment on the rotation schedule, but even this limited approach has difficulties.

The Appellate Body receives written submissions from the parties and has 60, or in some cases 90, days in which to render its decision. The Appellate Body review is limited to issues of law and legal interpretation. The panel decision may be upheld, modified, or reversed by the Appellate Body decision. Appellate Body decisions will be anonymous, and ex parte communications are not permitted, which will make judge-shopping by parties more than usually difficult.

Phase 4: Adoption of the panel or Appellate Body decision. Appellate Body determinations are submitted to the DSB. Panel decisions which are not appealed are also submitted to the DSB. Once either type of decision is submitted to the DSB, the DSB must automatically adopt them without modification or amendment at its next meeting unless the decision is rejected by all Members of the DSB through the form of "inverted consensus" discussed previously.

An alternative to Phases 2 through 4 is arbitration, if both parties agree. The arbitration must be binding on the parties, and there is no appeal from the arbitral tribunal's decision to the DSB Appellate Body.

Phase 5: Implementation of the decision adopted; Compensation; Retaliation. Once a panel or Appellate Body decision is adopted by the DSB, implementation is a three-step process. In the first step, the Member found to have a measure which violates its WTO obligations has "a reasonable time" (usually 15 months) to bring those measures into conformity with the WTO obligations. That remedy is the preferred one, and this form of implementation is the principal goal of the WTO implementation system. To date, most disputes have resulted in compliance in this manner. If the adequacy of compliance is disputed, such disputes typically return to the WTO panel that rendered decision on the merits which also determines, acting as an arbitrator, the amount (if any) of authorized retaliation. The retaliation process is discussed below.

If the violating measures are not brought into conformity within a reasonable time, the parties proceed to the second step. In that second step, the parties negotiate to reach an agreement upon a form of compensation which will be granted by the party in violation to the injured party. Such compensation will usually comprise trade concessions by the violating party to the injured party, which are over and above those already available under the WTO and Covered Agreements. The nature, scope, amount and duration of these additional concessions is at the negotiating parties' discretion, but each side must agree that the final compensation package is fair and is properly related to the injury caused by the violating measures. Presumably, any such concessions need not be extended under MFN principles to all WTO members.

If the parties cannot agree on an appropriate amount of compensation within twenty days, the complainant may proceed to the third step. In the third step, the party injured by the violating measures seeks authority from the DSB to retaliate against the party whose measures violated its WTO obligations. Thus complainant seeks authority to suspend some of its WTO obligations in regard to the respondent. The retaliation must ordinarily be within the same sector and agreement as the violating measure. "Sector" is sometimes broadly defined, as all trade in goods, and sometimes narrowly defined, as in individual services in the Services Sectoral Classification List. "Agreement" is also broadly defined. All the agreements listed in Annex IA to the WTO Agreement are considered a single agreement. If retaliation within the sector and agreement of the violating measure is considered insufficient compensation, the complainant may seek suspension of its obligations across sectors and agreements.

The DSB must grant the complainant's request to retaliate within 30 days unless all WTO members reject it through an "inverted consensus." (Article 22.6, D.S.U.) However, the respondent may object to the level or scope of the retaliation. The issues raised by the objection will be examined by either the Appellate Body or by an arbitrator. The respondent has a right, even if arbitration was not used in Phases 2 through 4, to have an arbitrator review in Phase 5 the appropriateness of the complainant's proposed level and scope of retaliation. The arbitrator will also examine whether the proper procedures and criteria to establish retaliation have been followed. The Phase 5 arbitration is final and binding and the arbitrator's decision is not subject to DSB review.

In addition to objecting to the level of authorized retaliation, the responding WTO member may simultaneously challenge the assertion of noncompliance (Article 21.5, D.S.U.). This challenge will ordinarily be heard by the original panel and must be resolved within 90 days. Thus the request for authorized retaliation and objections thereto could conceivably be accomplished before noncompliance is formally determined. In practice, WTO dispute settlement has melded these conflicting procedures such that compliance and retaliation issues are decided together, typically by the original panel.

Retaliation has rarely been authorized, even less rarely applied. The amount of a U.S. retaliation permitted against the EU after the WTO *Bananas* and *Beef Hormones* decisions were not implemented by the EU was contested. The arbitration tribunals for this issue were the original WTO panels, which did not allow the entire amount of the almost $700 million in retaliatory tariffs proposed by the United States. The U.S. was authorized and levied retaliatory tariffs amounting to about $300 million against European goods because of the EU failure to implement those WTO decisions. Since 2000, Congress has authorized rotating these tariffs in "carousel" fashion upon different European goods. The threat of carousel retaliation contributed to an April 2001 settlement of the *Bananas* dispute and a 2009 settlement of the *Beef Hormones* dispute.

In a landmark ruling, a WTO panel acting as an arbitrator has authorized Ecuador to remove protection of intellectual property rights regarding geographical indicators, copyrights and industrial designs on European Union goods for sale in Ecuador. This authorization is part of Ecuador's $200 million compensation in the *Bananas* dispute. The WTO panel acknowledged that Ecuador imports mostly capital goods and raw materials from the European Union and that imposing retaliatory tariffs on them would adversely harm its manufacturing industries. This risk supported "cross-retaliation" under Article 22.3 of the DSU outside the sector of the EU trade violation.

Both "compensation" in the second step and "retaliation" in the third step of implementation provide only for indirect enforcement of DSB decisions. There is no mechanism for direct enforcement by the WTO of its decisions through WTO orders to suspend trade obligations. Some commentators believe that retaliation will be an effective implementation device; others believe that it will prove ineffective. The division represented by these conflicting views represents two different approaches to the nature of both international law and international trade law. One approach seeks a rule-oriented use of the "rule of law"; the other seeks a power-oriented use of diplomacy. The United States and less developed countries have traditionally sought to develop a rule-oriented approach to international trade disputes. The European Union and Japan have traditionally sought to use the GATT/WTO primarily as a forum for diplomatic negotiations.

U.S. Involvement in WTO Dispute Resolution. The WTO dispute resolution process has been invoked more frequently than many expected. The United States has been a complainant or a respondent in about 200 disputes. It lost a dispute initiated by Venezuela and Brazil (WT/DS 2 and 4) concerning U.S. standards for reformulated and conventional gasoline. The offending U.S. law was amended to conform to the WTO ruling. It won on a complaint initiated jointly with Canada and the European Union (WT/DS 8, 10 and 11) regarding Japanese taxes on alcoholic beverages. Japan subsequently changed its law. When Costa Rica complained about U.S. restraints on imports of underwear (WT/DS 24), the U.S. let the restraints expire prior to any formal DSB ruling at the WTO. Similar results were reached when India complained of U.S. restraints on wool shirts and blouses (WT/DS 23). The United States won a major dispute with Canada concerning trade and subsidies for periodicals (WT/DS 31). This celebrated *Sports Illustrated* dispute proved that WTO remedies can be used to avoid Canada's cultural industries exclusion under NAFTA.

In the longstanding *Bananas* dispute (WT/DS 27) noted above, the United States joined Ecuador, Guatemala, Honduras and Mexico in successfully challenging EU import restraints against so-called "dollar bananas." The EU failed to comply with the Appellate Body's ruling, and retaliatory measures were authorized and imposed. In April 2001, the *Bananas* dispute was settled on terms that convert EU quotas to tariffs by 2006. A patent law complaint by the U.S. against India (WT/DS 50) prevailed in the DSB and ultimately brought changes in Indian law regarding pharmaceuticals and agricultural chemicals. In *Beef Hormones* (WT/DS 26 and 48), also noted above, the European Union once again lost before the Appellate Body. It refused to alter its import restraints and presently faces retaliatory tariffs on selected exports to Canada and the United States.

The United States prevailed against Argentina regarding tariffs and taxes on footwear, textiles and apparel (WT/DS 56). It lost a challenge (strongly supported by Kodak) to Japan's distribution rules regarding photo film and paper (WT/DS 44). In this dispute the U.S. elected *not* to appeal the adverse WTO panel ruling to the Appellate Body. In contrast, the European Union took an appeal which reversed an adverse panel ruling on its customs classification of computer equipment (WT/DS 62, 67 and 68). The U.S. had commenced this proceeding. Opponents in many disputes, Japan, the United States and the European Union united to complain in WT/DS 54, 55, 59 and 64 that Indonesia's National Car Programme was discriminatory and in breach of several WTO agreements. They prevailed and Indonesia altered its program.

India, Malaysia, Pakistan and Thailand teamed up to challenge U.S. shrimp import restraints enacted to protect endangered sea turtles (WT/DS 58). The WTO Appellate Body generally upheld their complaint and the U.S. has moved to comply. The adequacy of U.S. compliance is being challenged by Malaysia. The European Union and the United States jointly opposed Korea's discriminatory taxes on alcoholic beverages (WT/DS 75 and 84). This challenge was successful and Korea now imposes flat non-discriminatory taxes. The United States also complained of Japan's quarantine, testing and other agricultural import rules (WT/DS 76/1). The U.S. won at the WTO and Japan has changed its procedures.

In a semiconductor dumping dispute, Korea successfully argued that the U.S. was not in compliance with the WTO Antidumping Agreement (WT/DS 99/1). The United States amended its law, but Korea has instituted further proceedings alleging that these amendments are inadequate. The United States did likewise after Australia lost a subsidies dispute relating to auto leather exports (WT/DS 126/1). The reconvened WTO panel ruled that Australia had indeed failed to conform to the original adverse DSB decision. A U.S. challenge concerning India's quotas on imports of agricultural, textile and industrial products was upheld (WT/DS 90/1). India and the United States subsequently reached agreement on a timeline for removal of these restraints.

Closer to home, New Zealand and the United States complained of Canada's import/export rules regarding milk (WT/DS 103/1). Losing at the WTO, Canada agreed to a phased removal of the offending measures. The United States also won against Mexico in an antidumping dispute involving corn syrup (WT/DS 132/1), but lost a "big one" when the DSB determined that export tax preferences granted to "Foreign Sales Corporations" of U.S. companies were illegal (WT/DS 108/1). It has been estimated that unless the U.S. complies with this ruling the European Union will be authorized to retaliate up to $4 billion annually. The United States has expanded the FSC regime by removing the requirement that eligible goods be manufactured in the U.S. It claims that this change makes the FSC program not contingent upon exports, and thus WTO-legal. The European Union is challenging this assertion of compliance before the WTO.

Another "big one" went in favor of the United States. The European Union challenged the validity under the DSU of unilateral retaliation under Section 301 of the Trade Act of 1974 (WT/DS 152/1). Section 301 has been something of a bete noire in U.S. trade law, but the WTO panel affirmed its legality in light of Presidential undertakings to administer it in accordance with U.S. obligations to adhere to multilateral WTO dispute settlement.

U.S. involvement in WTO dispute settlement continues to be extensive. The Appellate Body ruled that U.S. countervailing duties against British steel based upon pre-privitization subsidies were unlawful (WT/DS 138/1). The European Union prevailed before a WTO panel in its challenge of the U.S. Antidumping Act of 1916 (WT/DS 136). U.S. complaints against Korean beef import restraints and procurement practices were upheld (WT/DS 161/1, 163/1). Canada's patent protection term was also invalidated by the WTO under a U.S. complaint (WT/DS 170/1). European Union complaints concerning U.S. wheat gluten quotas (WT/DS 166/1) and the royalty free small business provisions of the Fairness in Music Licensing Act of 1998 (WT/DS 160/1) have been sustained. The *Wheat Gluten* dispute questions the legality of U.S. "causation" rules in escape clause proceedings under Section 201 of the Trade Act of 1974.

The WTO Appellate Body ruled against the United States regarding the legality of the royalty free provisions of the 1998 Fairness in Music Licensing Act. The Appellate Body also ruled against Section 211 of the Omnibus Appropriations Act of 1998 denying trademark protection in connection with confiscated assets (the "HAVANA CLUB" dispute). U.S. compliance with these rulings has been slow in forthcoming.

A WTO Panel ruled in 2002 that the Byrd Amendment violates the WTO antidumping and subsidy codes. The Byrd Amendment (Continued Dumping and Subsidy Act of 2000) authorizes the Customs Service to forward AD and CVD duties to affected domestic producers for qualified expenses. Eleven WTO members including the EU, Canada and Mexico challenged the Amendment. This ruling was affirmed by the WTO Appellate Body. Retaliation was authorized and applied in 2005 by the European Union and others. Late in 2005, the U.S. repealed the Byrd Amendment, subject to a contested two-year phase-out.

The United States and other complainants prevailed in a 2002 WTO proceeding against Indian local content and trade balancing requirements for foreign auto manufacturers. These requirements violated the TRIMs agreement. The arbitration panel for the FSC (extraterritorial income tax exclusion) dispute ruled in 2002 that the European Union is entitled to retaliate in the unprecedented amount of $4 billion. The EU indicated it would move slowly before imposing tariffs on U.S. exports under this authorization. Because the United States had not repealed the Antidumping Act of 1916 as required by the WTO, the EU asked permission to retaliate by adopting mirror-image legislation. This request was denied, leaving the EU to retaliate only when and if its producers suffer injury under the rarely invoked 1916 Act. Late in 2004, the United States repealed the Antidumping Act of 1916 (Public Law 108–429).

In March of 2004, the European Union commenced raising tariffs against U.S. goods under the WTO retaliation authorized out of the FSC/export tax subsidy dispute. Monthly increments were planned until either the U.S. complied or the EU reached the maximum of roughly $4 billion annually it is authorized to retaliate. In the fall of 2004, the United States repealed the extraterritorial income exclusions. See Public Law No. 108–357. In 2004, also, Antigua-Barbuda won a 2004 WTO panel ruling under the GATS against U.S. Internet gambling restraints. The Appellate Body affirmed in part, reversed in part. WT/DS285/AB/R(2005). Retaliation has been authorized. The U.S. won a decision against Mexico's exorbitant telecom interconnection rates, but lost cotton subsidy challenge by Brazil. WT/DS267/AB/R(2005) (retaliation authorized in 2008). It also lost a second dispute with the EU about pre-privatization countervailable subsidies, in particular the legality of the U.S. "same person" methodology. WT/DS212/AB/R(2004).

Perhaps most importantly, the U.S. safeguard tariffs against steel were invalidated in 2003 by the Appellate Body (WT/DS248/AB/R et al.). The U.S. won an SPS dispute against Japanese quarantine of U.S. apples (WT/DS245/AB/R), while losing an important softwood lumber "zeroing" methodology complaint brought by Canada WT/DS 257/AB/R.

In 2006, the Mexico-United States "sugar war" came to a head before the Appellate Body. WT/DS 308/AB/R. Mexico's 20% soft drink tax on beverages not using cane sugar, its 20% distribution tax on those beverages, and related bookkeeping requirements were found to violate GATT Article III and not exempt under Article XX(d). Subsequently, the two countries settled their dispute by agreeing, effective in 2008, to free trade in sugar and high fructose corn syrup. Further in 2006, the U.S. failed to persuade the Appellate Body to require the European Union under GATT Article X (3) to undertake a major overhaul of its customs law system targeting inconsistencies therein among the 27 member states. WT/DS 315/AB/R. Lastly in 2006, the United States lost another "zeroing" dispute under its antidumping law. WT/DS 294/AB/R.

In October of 2008, the WTO Appellate Body, for the second time, ruled against the EU *Beef Hormones* ban. U.S. retaliatory tariff sanctions remained in place. In 2009, a settlement was reached. The U.S. effectively gets a higher quota to export hormone-free beef to the EU, in return for phasing out over four years its retaliatory tariffs on EU goods. The U.S.

threat of carousel sanctions, i.e. rotating goods subject to tariff retaliation, was instrumental to this settlement.

The United States continues to lose WTO disputes about its zeroing methodology in antidumping proceedings. See WT/DS 350/AB/R (Feb. 4, 2009). Despite 12 decisions against zeroing, the U.S. remains unwilling to alter its rules to comply with WTO rulings. As the U.S. winds down its "Byrd Amendment" (repealed, 2006) distributions of prior antidumping and countervailing duty revenues to U.S. industries, Japan and the EU continue retaliatory tariffs that correspond in amount to those distributions, $8 million and $95 million in 2010 respectively.

In 2010, the United States agreed to pay $147 million annually to provide technical assistance to Brazilian cotton farmers. In return, Brazil has suspended retaliatory tariffs and cross-sector IP sanctions authorized by the WTO because of U.S. cotton subsidy violations. In 2009, a WTO panel ruled that Airbus had received $20 billion in illegal EU "launch" subsidies. By 2010, that same panel found Boeing the recipient of $5 billion in federal research contract subsidies that violated the WTO Subsidies Code.

The United States has also settled a number of disputes prior to WTO panel decisions, and remains in consultation on other disputes that may be decided by a WTO panel. For the latest summary of all WTO disputes, including many not involving the United States, see www.wto.org.

NOTE ON CHINA AND *WTO* DISPUTES

Canada, the European Union and the United States complained against Chinese duties on imported auto parts (10 percent) that rose to those on complete autos (25 percent) if the imported parts exceeded a fixed percentage of the final vehicle content or price, or if specific combinations of imported auto parts were used in the final vehicle. In addition, extensive record keeping, reporting and verification requirements were imposed when Chinese auto companies used imported parts. In July of 2008, a WTO panel ruled that these "internal charges" violated Articles III(2) and III(4) of the GATT, reproduced in the Documents Supplement to this coursebook. The core Panel ruling found China's auto parts measures discriminatory in favor of domestic producers, a violation of the national treatment standard for taxes and regulations. This ruling marked the first time since China's admission to the WTO in 2001 that China has been held in breach of its WTO commitments and obligations. See WT/DS 339, 340, 342/R (July 18, 2008) (Affirmed by the Appellate Body Oct. 16, 2008).

Less than one month after losing this dispute, China enacted a clever "green tax" on gas-guzzling autos, most of which just happen to be imported. The sales tax on cars with engine capacities over 4.1 litres has been doubled to 40%. Autos with engines between 3 and 4.1 litres are taxed at 25%, up from 15%. Most Chinese-made cars have engines with 2.5 litres or less. Autos with engines between 1 and 3 litres remain taxed at 8% and 10%. The smallest cars with engines below 1 litre have their sales tax reduced from 3 to 1 percent.

Might this green tax achieve protective results similar to China's Auto Parts tariff structure? Is it legal? See GATT Article III, discussed in the nontariff trade barrier and procurement problems found in this chapter.

Other disputes challenging China's compliance with WTO law are pending. They concern China's value-added tax on integrated circuits, discriminatory tax refunds, reductions and exemptions, protection and enforcement of intellectual property rights (2009 WTO panel ruled in part against China), trade and distribution of publications and audiovisual entertainment products (2009 WTO panel ruled completely against China), commodity export tariffs and restrictions (2011 WTO panel ruled against China), and treatment of foreign financial information suppliers. The United States is a complaining party to all of these disputes. China, in turn, has challenged U.S. safeguard measures applied to Chinese steel exports (2010 WTO panel rejected challenge) and tires (2011 WTO panel rejected challenge), and U.S. antidumping and countervailing duties on paper and steel products from China (2011 WTO panel ruled against U.S. dual assessment of AD and CVD duties). It has also applied AD duties to U.S. exports, e.g. chicken.

BHALA, ASSESSING THE MODERN ERA OF INTERNATIONAL TRADE (BOOK REVIEW)

21 Fordham Int'l L.J. 1647 (1998).*

It is not easy to assess the modern era of international trade law and policy in one slender volume. An author must explain the geopolitical and economic context in which the General Agreements on Tariffs and Trade ("GATT") was born in 1947, develop a view as to the nature, evolution, and purpose of the GATT system, and provide a road map of the legal intricacies associated with prominent features of the system-like antidumping law and seemingly arcane features like textile quotas. Sylvia Ostry, the Director of the Center for International Studies at the University of Toronto and the former Canadian Ambassador to the Uruguay Round trade negotiations, does an admirable job of discussing the modern era in *The Post–Cold War Trading System*.

* * *

THE MAJESTIC SCOPE OF THE POST-COLD WAR TRADING SYSTEM

Unintended Results

The Post–Cold War Trading System observes that for Americans, the development of the trading system since World War II has had two unintended and unwelcome results. First, The United States's early post-War economic policy, particularly the willingness to transfer manufacturing technology, allowed the European and Japanese economies ravaged by the War to recover and, by the 1970s, boast a standard of living comparable to that in the United States. The catalyst for this policy was the U.S.

Cold War containment strategy. Accordingly, the Truman Administration enthusiastically sponsored the Marshall Plan to help re-build Europe, and both the Roosevelt and Truman Administrations strongly encouraged the development of the Bretton Woods institutions for the benefit of the world economy. Through foreign direct investment ("FDI") in Europe, technology was transferred that enabled European companies to develop their manufacturing prowess. While the Japanese market was not too open to FDI, and U.S. firms lacked interest in this market, these firms eagerly signed technology transfer license agreements with Japanese companies, thereby enabling the locals to gain manufacturing expertise. The unintended, unwelcome result of American generosity was the convergence of the European and Japanese economies with the U.S. economy by the 1970s. * * *

The second developmental result neither intended nor welcomed by Americans was the emergence of forms of market economies in Europe and Japan that differed from the U.S. model. The European model was marked by greater state planning and ownership of productive resources, and copious welfare benefits. The Japanese model featured a public-private partnership, high concentration (*e.g.,* the notorious *keiretsu*), and lifetime job security for workers in major and mid-level firms. In other words, neither European nor Japanese capitalism tracked the U.S. model in which (1) state intervention had to be justified by market failure, (2) companies behaved in the neoclassical economic manner as short-term profit maximizers rather than long-term market-share maximizers, and (3) a social safety net existed only for the truly dispossessed, not the able-bodied.

System Friction

This diversity in economic systems would, by the 1970s, force an expansion in the trade negotiating agenda. The United States insisted that greater state intervention and industrial concentration reduced market-access opportunities for U.S. exporters and investors. The result, to borrow the catchy term from *The Post–Cold War Trading System,* was greater "system friction," because U.S. trade negotiators demanded reforms in areas previously viewed as the sovereign province of domestic governmental policy. After all, the United States thought it was creating a bulwark against communism that was a replica of itself. When it found out differently, Americans exclaimed "unfair!" * * * In sum, with the end of the Cold War, both the means and ends of trade negotiations became highly contentious and convoluted.

The successes of the Uruguay Round do not alter this central fact. Indeed, *The Post-Cold War Trading System* indicates that the experience of the Uruguay Round is a harbinger of still more system friction to come. The unfinished agenda includes better protections for FDI that are found in the Agreement on Trade Related Investment Measures, labor issues (the United States was not able to persuade the WTO to place trade and labor issues on the agenda at the December 1996 Ministerial meeting in

Singapore), and possibly environmental matters. Likewise, the United States's five trade initiatives with Japan are harbingers of future system friction. Bilateral trade deficits with Japan persist; indeed, given the strong dollar in the wake of the 1997–98 Asian currency crisis, these deficits are certain to increase. U.S. businesses in key sectors, including autos, still complain of market access difficulties. Most importantly, as *The Post–Cold War Trading System* ably presents, the "domain of trade policy has extended inside the border," which means the perceived threat to sovereignty among the enemies of trade liberalization is greater than ever before.

The book's solution, to use the Uruguay Round *Understanding on the Rules and Procedures Governing the Settlement of Disputes* ("*DSU*"), along with the nullification and impairment clause of GATT Article XXIII:1(b) as a way of bringing about incremental adaptation and change, is a constructive one. However, such change is by definition slow. More seriously, it implies a theoretical view of the GATT–WTO system as a dynamic, growing organism, not a static set of rules, and presumes a willingness among WTO Members to allow WTO panels and the Appellate Body to be judicial activists. Such activism creates deep philosophical and political schisms in a domestic legal context. Given the sovereignty howls of protectionists, and even of some more enlightened observers, surely it would be no less controversial in the international context. * * *

* * * At least three theses could have been developed in *The Post–Cold War Trading System* that would have flowed naturally from the existing exposition and suggested a grand vision.

There is No Such Thing As Free Trade At Law

First, an important possible thesis *The Post–Cold War Trading System* might have developed concerns the essential compromise of GATT, or more generally the practical irrelevance of free trade theory. As a matter of law, it can be argued that there is no such thing as free trade. Free trade exists only in the minds and on the graphs of neoclassical economists. If the economic law of comparative advantage were translated fully and faithfully by trade negotiators into "real" law, then surely trade-liberalizing deals like the Uruguay Round agreements or the North American Free Trade Agreement ("NAFTA") need only be one page. Article I of the deal would state that "all tariff and non-tariff barriers are hereby abolished." Article II would define broadly, with no exceptions, the terms "tariff barrier" and "non-tariff barrier." Thereafter would follow the signatures of the parties. It is the myriad exceptions to trade-liberalizing provisions, and the concern with "fair" trade and remedies to "unfair" trade practices, that help explain why so-called free trade agreements are so long and complex. Put slightly differently, it can be argued that as a matter of law, all trade is managed trade, because a careful read of any trade agreement reveals more than mere remnants of trade barriers. It reveals, *inter alia*, express carve-outs for certain preferred sectors, intricate and protective rules of origin, lengthy phase-in periods for trade-liberalizing obligations, and lengthy phase-out periods for trade barriers. The discussion in *The Post–Cold War Trading System* of the five Reagan-Bush-Clinton Administration initiatives regarding Japan, particularly those initiatives establishing foreign market share goals or seeking at least to monitor foreign market share, illustrate this argument. Yet, the book does not make this point, much less highlight the free trade-managed trade distinction implicit in these initiatives.

Developing Countries

A second thesis *The Post–Cold War Trading System* might have advanced concerns developing countries. Except for a chapter on the growth of East Asia, less developed countries ("LDCs") are not given extensive treatment. Yet, it could be argued that the most significant fissure in the world trading system is between LDCs and developed countries ("DCs"). If Hamish McRae's prognostication in *The World in 2020* is accepted, then by 2020 there will be three dominant economic regions: North America, western Europe, and the Far East. Few countries in Latin America, central and eastern Europe, South Asia, and Africa will have achieved sustained economic growth rates by 2020 so as to propel themselves into the ranks of DCs.

Consequently, they may demand wealth redistribution from the DCs, and their demands may in some instances be backed by terrorism. The world in 2020, then, may be a more dangerous place than it is now. *The Post–Cold War Trading System* might have identified the special and differential treatment accorded by the Uruguay Round agreements to LDCs, which principally takes the form of longer phase-in periods during which to meet certain obligations, and relief from other obligations. The book might have characterized this treatment—rightly—as paltry, and thereby concluded that the Uruguay Round was a watershed in DC–LDC relations. History may record that in this Round, the radical demands made by some LDCs since the 1960s for a "new international economic order" in which the world trading system would be restructured to allow for wealth redistribution from DCs to LDCs were finally defeated. Put crudely (and perhaps too simply), all the LDCs got was a little more time to live up to the agreements, and they were forced to make agreements on matters of greatest importance to DCs, namely, services and intellectual property.

Had *The Post–Cold War Trading System* made this observation, the book could have then proceeded along one of two lines of argument. A conservative argument could have been fashioned based on the economic development views of Lord Bauer, namely, that LDCs have largely themselves to blame for much of their plight (*e.g.,* for reasons of corruption and mismanagement), and that most mainstream economic thought about development problems is erroneous. There is, for example, no such thing as a vicious cycle of poverty (*i.e.,* the notion that an LDC cannot escape poverty because incomes are too low to accumulate savings, which in turn are needed for investment in productive assets that raise incomes). After all, Bauer observes, "[t]o have money is the result of economic achievement, not its precondition." Millions of poor Third World farmers have made sizeable investments in agriculture and moved from subsistence to cash crop farming. Thereafter, low-value added manufacturing sectors have evolved. This happy growth process also occurred in what is now the developed world. Most importantly, the process does not, and need not, involve external donations, such as radical wealth redistribution through a restructuring of the trading system. Thus, *The Post–Cold War Trading System* could have argued that the Uruguay Round watershed is to be celebrated, because it represents the triumph of Bauer-type thinking about development problems over radical left demands.

A second and ideologically antipodal argument that the book might have advanced is that the Uruguay Round watershed is to be bemoaned, because it signals the widening and deepening gap between DCs and LDCs. The lack of meaningful special and differential treatment shows LDCs are powerless in multilateral trade negotiations, and underscores that the WTO is not a development agency. To the contrary, it is a system of rules written to ensure market access for products from DCs. This second argument could insist the system become more responsive to LDC needs, and suggest a commitment to a particular conception of justice as a vehicle for greater responsiveness. One possible applicable theory of justice could be distributive justice theory. In very general and no doubt overly-simplistic terms, distributive justice theory begins by positing that "[e]ach person possesses an inviolability founded on justice that even the welfare of society as a whole cannot override." If the polity is reconceived not as individuals in a society, but as countries in a global economy, then it might be re-posited that each country possesses an inviolability that cannot be compromised even for a broader utilitarian good. That inviolability, it could be argued, consists of the right to compete on an equal basis in the global market, and the right to receive assistance designed to ensure equality of competitive opportunity in a broad sense. The assistance ought to include better special and differential treatment than now exists in the Uruguay Round agreements. This non-utilitarian, distributive justice-based logic could be reinforced by a utilitarian point. As long as LDCs cannot compete effectively and are not integrated into the world trading system, global peace and security is at risk. Poor countries with little stake in the system are, after all, susceptible to leaders and movements seeking to disrupt the system. In sum, *The Post–Cold War Trading System* might have bemoaned the shabby treatment of LDCs in the Uruguay Round, and argued from distributive justice theory, utilitarian theory, or both for a new trade order.

Persistent Doubts About Free Trade

Why are free trade theory and empirical evidence on the benefits of trade liberalization not universally persuasive? This issue is not addressed directly in *The Post–Cold War Trading System*, but it is a paradox in international trade law and policy, and it is a third possible basis for the development of a thesis in the book. The compelling nature of Adam Smith's and David Ricardo's static demonstration of comparative advantage, as well as more recent dynamic models of international trade, cannot be doubted. Doubters like India and Argentina that pursued protectionist, import-substitution policies for most of the post-World War II period are reversing course. The resolution to the paradox may lie in the treatment of losers from trade liberalization. As Ravi Batra argues forcefully in *The Myth of Free Trade*, there are workers in certain sectors of the United States whose real wages or jobs are threatened (though as Lester Thurow counters in *The Future of Capitalism*, the threat may come from an inability to develop prized skills and adapt to new technologies). These workers are certain to oppose trade liberalization, and if the sectors they represent are politically dominant in their countries, official policy may be geared against market-opening ventures with other countries. Thus, until international trade law and policy treats the losers better, the paradox is sure to persist.

In terms of economic theory, the way to express this point is that U.S. trade policy has yet to deal with the consequences of the Stopler–Samuelson theorem. This theorem states that "[f]ree international trade benefits the abundant factor and harms the scarce factor." The intuitive argument behind this theorem requires reference to two closely related theorems, the factor price equalization and Heckscher–Ohlin theorems. Assume (as is true) that relative to China, the United States is a capital-abundant and labor-scarce country. Before trade occurs between the two countries, each country produces the capital-and labor-intensive product and consumes each product itself. When trade begins between the two countries, the Stopler–Samuelson theorem predicts returns to capital in the United States (rents) will rise, and the returns to labor (wages) will fall. The converse phenomenon will occur in China. These two outcomes, taken together, represent factor price equalization. The factor price equalization theorem holds that international trade will lead to the international equalization of individual factor prices, assuming there are no trade barriers and factors have equal access to identical technology. Accordingly, capital rents rise in the United States and fall in China to a rough parity, and wage rates fall in the United States and rise in China to a rough parity.

Capital rents rise, and wage rates fall, in the United States because, according to the Heckscher–Ohlin theorem, with international trade the United States specializes in the production of the factor with which it is relatively well endowed, namely capital. That is, the United States exports a capital-intensive product to China, and China exports a labor-intensive product to the United States. Consequently, production of the labor-intensive good in the United States diminishes, and labor is idled, as the Chinese labor-intensive product enters the U.S. market. (Again, the converse phenomenon occurs the in China.) American workers no longer can exploit their relative scarcity and command high wage rates. In contrast, production of the capital-intensive good in the United States rises to meet export demand. Correspondingly the demand for capital increases, and thus so too does the return to capital. Yet, the demand for capital cannot be met entirely by the transfer of capital from the contracting labor-intensive industry. Precisely because the contracting industry is labor-intensive, its capital stock is not sufficiently large to meet the demand. Thus, the Stopler–Samuelson theorem: the abundant factor in the United States, capital, benefits from trade liberalization (*i.e.*, rents rise), while the scarce factor, labor, loses (*i.e.*, wages fall).

QUESTIONS AND COMMENTS

1. What tariff levels apply to manufactured products imported into the United States which do not qualify for MFN tariff treatment? How do these levels compare with MFN tariffs?

2. Russia is expected to join the WTO in 2012. Iran, among others, wishes to join the WTO and subscribe to the GATT. What will these nations have to agree to do in order to become members? How has "reciprocity" been achieved in the past when granting MFN status to new members? See the USTR Report on China's WTO Compliance.

3. Review the five phases of WTO dispute settlement outlined by Folsom. Has the WTO Appellate Body become the "Supreme Court" for world trade? How has the U.S. fared in WTO dispute settlement? Will it reduce or exacerbate what Bhala calls "system friction"?

Does it matter whether a member is accorded "developing country" status? See the provocative comments by Bhala assessing the modern era of international trade.

4. Would adherence to the Dispute Settlement Understanding (DSU) be a plus to OXICORP? To China? To the United States? In this regard, what does the Note on the China Auto Parts dispute suggest? Are DSU panel or Appellate Body reports "binding"? Are they enforceable?

5. China enjoyed MFN tariff status for many years under the "Jackson–Vanik amendment." See 19 U.S.C.A. §§ 2431 et seq. Obtaining this status involved extensive U.S. scrutiny of China's emigration and, sometimes, human rights policies. From China's perspective, Jackson–Vanik is one of many examples of unilateral United States trade policies that it wants to escape. Does WTO membership provide a back door around Jackson–Vanik? See Article I of the GATT and Article XVI.4 of the WTO Agreement in the Documents Supplement. The WTO applicants noted above will be interested in your response.

What does MFN treatment mean in the context of the GATT tariff arrangements? What does it mean to China now that it has joined the WTO? See the insightful historical analysis by Harders–Chen. How is OXICORP's trade with various nonmarket and transition nations affected by MFN tariff treatment?

6. Does the MFN rule of Article I apply only to tariff concessions negotiated and bound under the GATT? Does Article I apply if OXICORP trades in services?

7. Inevitably an unconditional MFN policy allows some nations to receive trade benefits without offering benefits in return. How can this be economically or politically justified? Is there any international legal norm calling for economic nondiscrimination and thus mandating MFN treatment?

8. In what sense is membership in the WTO a "package deal" as Demeret asserts? To what agreements might a member opt out?

9. Negotiations on China's WTO membership lasted for about fifteen years. Note the level of detail in China's commitments and related compliance issues summarized in the USTR Report on China's WTO Compliance. How will China's commitments be enforced?

10. Membership in the WTO will render Article III of the GATT, the "national treatment" standard, applicable to China. This standard is one of the most important obligations of membership. What does Article III prohibit? How was it applied in the China Auto Parts dispute?

Review Article XI of the GATT. What does it prohibit? This provision is likewise an important membership obligation.

11. Bhala argues that there is no such thing as free trade at law. In other words, all trade is managed trade. If he is correct, a question to bear in mind throughout this chapter, are managed economies like China's easy to admit?

12. What do you think of Bhala's application of the Stopler–Samuelson theorem to free trade between China and the United States? Does this theorem help explain why all trade might be managed trade? Does it help explain opposition in the United States to China's membership in the WTO? And China's enthusiasm for joining?

13. In 1999, an attempt at launching a new round of WTO negotiations failed amidst extensive protests on the streets of Seattle. Late in 2001, the Doha Round of WTO negotiations was successfully launched. Agriculture, services, intellectual property, antidumping duties, tariffs, export subsidies, market access, implementation, electronic commerce, dispute settlement, trade and the environment, trade, debt and finance, and special and differential treatment and assistance for developing countries are on the agenda. Developed WTO countries are particularly pushing the so-called "Singapore" issues of investment, competition policy, transparency in procurement and trade facilitation. At Cancun in 2003, the WTO developing nations rejected these issues while focusing on agricultural protection trade restraints. It has been an interesting and difficult Round, scheduled for completion by 2005, but languishing in 2011. Many commentators believe that failure of the Doha Round will increase the number of WTO disputes.

PROBLEM 6.2 CUSTOMS CLASSIFICATION AND VALUATION: PEANUT BUTTER AND JELLY SWIRL FROM CHINA

SECTION I. THE SETTING

Fast Food, Inc., produces lines of foods that can be spread on bread for meals which are "quick, easy and nutritious." One of its "spreadables" is "PB & J," a combination of peanut butter and grape jelly which is "swirled" together in a jar for instant "spreadability." PB & J Swirl allows the customer to avoid spreading its constituent elements separately, and also allows easy use of the combination with a single piece of bread. It costs Fast Food about $0.55 to produce a kilogram (kg.) of PB & J.

Double Happiness is a Chinese company which produces peanut butter and jelly swirl in China for export. Double Happiness has proposed that it seeks to sell the peanut butter and jelly combination to Fast Food, for resale in the U.S. market. For small amounts of the combination, Double Happiness' price would be $0.50 per kg.; but, for orders over 250 metric tons, Double Happiness' special price for large orders would be $0.40 per kg. This price would be for delivery C.I.F. Fast Food's plant on the U.S. west coast, but exclusive of any import duties.

Alternatively, Double Happiness' price would be $0.40 per kg. F.O.B. Hong Kong, for small orders; and its special price for large orders would be $0.30 per kg. F.O.B. Hong Kong. Freight and insurance costs from Hong Kong to the U.S. are estimated to be $0.10 per kg. As a third alternative, Double Happiness would be willing to establish a sales office in the United States, and would sell from that office to Fast Food for $0.50 (or $0.40) per kg., plus any import duties assessed by U.S. Customs.

The executives at Fast Food are interested in obtaining supplies at less than the $0.55 per kg. that it costs to produce PB & J in the United States. A reduction to $0.50 or $0.55 per kg. would be useful, but a reduction to $0.40 per kg. would be spectacular. They have asked you to research whether there are any applicable import duties, or any import laws, which would cause problems with purchases from Double Happiness. Your client wants to know what the amount of the tariff duty will be on such goods before signing a purchase contract, rather than after the goods have arrived in the U.S. What is your advice, counselor?

Incidently, there is a rumor that the peanuts in the Double Happiness product originates in the Philippines. The rumor is ambiguous as to whether China imports just the peanuts from the Philippines, or whether it imports the processed peanut butter. Would these rumored facts make any difference?

SECTION II. FOCUS OF CONSIDERATION

To calculate an import duty, you must first determine the classification, country of origin, and customs valuation of the goods. In other words, what is it, where is it from, and what is its customs value?

The inquiry by Fast Food raises several different issues: (1) classification of the product category of the peanut butter and jelly swirled together, (2) identification of the place of origin of the product shipped from China, and (3) valuation of the peanut butter and jelly in regard to both freight and other charges. Although these issues are interrelated insofar as your advice to Fast Food is concerned, they initially require separate analysis.

The basic tool needed for this analysis is the Harmonized Tariff Schedule of the United States (HTS). The HTS was enacted by Congress as part of the Omnibus Trade and Competitiveness Act of 1988, and became fully effective in 1989, repealing the older Tariff Schedules of the United States. The HTS provides a hierarchical structure or "nomenclature" used to describe the goods, rates of duty, and statistical reporting requirements for imports into the United States and is maintained by the International Trade Commission. However, the Bureau of Customs and Border Protection of the Department of Homeland Security is responsible for interpreting and enforcing the HTS.

The issue for the lawyer is what sources of information will be persuasive to customs collectors (or, if necessary, to the courts), in determining the classification of the goods. Under HTS, any fact pattern you must analyze is likely to be a case of first impression. Thus, there probably will be no precedent directly on point. Further, dictionary meanings are not likely to be determinative—nor is any linguistic approach to interpretation. If the above approaches are not likely to be helpful, then what interpretative approaches *do* the Customs Office and courts use to resolve problems created by ambiguous or overlapping classifications?

The problems of place of origin classification arise when raw materials or partially finished products from one nation are processed or completed in another nation. The issues are especially troublesome when a multinational enterprise is operating subsidiaries in several nations, and each subsidiary performs part of the manufacturing process.

The problems of valuation concern the different components of an invoice price to the United States buyer, and what components may be separated out for valuation purposes. For example, it would make little sense to charge different amounts of duty on two sets of identical imported goods because one set was invoiced "F.O.B. Hong Kong" and the other set was invoiced "C.I.F. United States." But, are freight charges to be included or excluded? And, there are also issues concerning sales commissions.

Web sources for further study include U.S. International Trade Commission "Trade Information Center" web page http://usitc.gov/tata/index. html/ and the U.S. Customs and Border Protection "Trade" web page http:// www.customs.gov/xp/cgov/trade/.

SECTION III. READINGS, QUESTIONS AND COMMENTS

PART A. PRODUCT CLASSIFICATION (WHAT IS IT?)

The initial product and origin classification of the imported goods is made by the importer, consignee, or broker. 19 C.F.R. § 141.90. But this classification is subject to disapproval by the Port Director. If an improper classification is found, the Port Director notifies the importer of the proposed change of rate and amount of tariff duty. 19 C.F.R. § 152.2. The importer then normally has 20 days to pay the increase in the duty or seek further administrative review. If the importer seeks a review of the Customs classification, the importer bears the burden of proof that Customs is wrong. The importer's protest will be reviewed first by the Port Director, and then may be reviewed by the Commissioner of Customs, especially in cases of first impression. 19 C.F.R. §§ 173, 174. If Customs denies the protest, the importer may seek judicial review in the Court of International Trade. 19 C.F.R. § 175.

The HTS nomenclature structure is in turn based upon an international system formally called the Harmonized Commodity Description and Coding System ("the Harmonized System" or "HS"), established under the International Convention on the Simplification and Harmonization of Customs Procedures (Kyoto Convention), and administered by the World Customs Organization (WCO) in Brussels. The WCO was established in established in 1952, as the Customs Co-operation Council, and is an independent intergovernmental body whose mission is to enhance the effectiveness and efficiency of Customs administrations.

The WCO's international HS provides roughly 5,000 article descriptions that appear as headings and subheadings, arranged in 97 chapters grouped in 21 sections, and accompanied by legal rules and notes. Sections of the HS group together articles from branches of industry and commerce (for example, animals and animal products, or textiles and textile articles) or by their functions or use (for example, footwear, arms and ammunition) The HS was established to facilitate trade by means of a standardized tariff nomenclature for the description, classification and coding of goods, as well as a common system for collecting, comparing, and analyzing international trade statistics. Under the terms of Article 3 of the HS convention, contracting parties are required to follow, without change, all of the 4– and 6–digit categories of the HS, as numbered, and the accompanying legal notes.

The United States acceded to the Convention as of January 1, 1989, and implemented its obligations by adopting the HTS. Accordingly, the

HTS is based upon the HS 6–digit nomenclature, but the HS product categories are further subdivided into 8–digit unique U.S. rate lines and 10–digit non-legal statistical reporting categories within the HTS. Classification of goods under the HTS must also be done in accordance with the General and Additional U.S. Rules of Interpretation.

Most problems of product classification arise when it is possible to classify the imported goods under more than one heading. Inventive new products, like PB & J Swirl, often do so. In this Problem, for example, is the product "peanut butter" (see HTS Heading 2008)? Or, is the product "fruit jelly" (see HTS Heading 2007)? This will depend upon interpretation of the HTS Schedules.

The statute which enacted the Harmonized Tariff Schedule (HTS), provided that the HTS "consists of

(A) the General Notes;

(B) the General Rules of Interpretation

(C) the Additional U.S. Rules of Interpretation

(D) sections I to XXII, inclusive (encompassing chapters 1 to 99, and including all section and chapter notes, article provisions, and tariff and other treatment accorded thereto); and

(E) the Chemical Appendix to the Harmonized Tariff Schedule; * * *."

The relevant General Note is found in the Readings, below, as are the relevant provisions of chapters 1 to 99, including chapter notes. The General Rules of Interpretation (GRI) and Additional U.S. Rules of Interpretation are found in the Documents Supplement as part of the Omnibus Trade and Competitiveness Act of 1988 (19 U.S.C. § 3003). What happens when these two sets of Rules conflict? Review of the GRIs and General Note 3(f) is necessary for an analysis of this Part of the Problem.

HARMONIZED TARIFF SCHEDULE OF THE UNITED STATES

(2011).

CHAPTER 20

PREPARATIONS OF VEGETABLES, FRUIT, NUTS OR OTHER PARTS OF PLANTS

Notes

1.   This chapter does not cover:

(a) Vegetables, fruit or nuts, prepared or preserved by the processes specified in chapter 7, 8 or 11;

* * *

2.   Headings 2007 and 2008 do not apply to fruit jellies, fruit pastes, sugar-coated almonds or the like in the form of sugar confectionery (heading 1704) or chocolate confectionery (heading 1806).

* * *

SUBHEADING NOTES

* * *

2. For the purposes of subheading 2007.10, the expression *"homogenized preparations"* means preparations of fruit, finely homogenized, put up for retail sale as infant food or for dietetic purposes, in containers of a net weight content not exceeding 250 g. For the application of this definition no account is to be taken of small quantities of any ingredients which may have been added to the preparation for seasoning, preservation or other purposes. These preparations may contain a small quantity of visible pieces of fruit. Subheading 2007.10 takes precedence over all other subheadings of heading 2007.

Additional U.S. Notes

* * *

5. The aggregate quantity of peanut butter and paste entered under subheading 2008.11.05 in any calendar year shall not exceed the quantities specified in this note (articles the product of Mexico shall not be permitted or included under the aforementioned quantitative limitation and no such articles shall be classifiable therein).

	Quantity (metric tons)
Canada	14,500
Argentina	3,650
Countries or territories identified in additional U.S. note 6 to this chapter combined (aggregate)	1,600
Other countries or areas	250

Imports of peanut butter and paste under this note are subject to regulations as may be issued by the United States Trade Representative or other designated agency.

[**Author's Note:** Additional U.S. Note 6 contains a long list of many countries. The list includes the Philippines, but does not include China or Hong Kong.]

HARMONIZED TARIFF SCHEDULE of the United States (2011)

Heading/ Subheading	Stat. Suffix	Article Description	Units of Quantity	Rates of Duty		
				1		2
				General*	Special*	**
2007		Jams, fruit jellies, marmalades, fruit or nut pureé and fruit or nut pastes, obtained by cooking, whether or not containing added sugar or other sweetening matter:				
2007.10.00	00	Homogenized preparations	kg......	12%	Free (A+, BH, CA, D, E, IL, J, JO, MX, P, PE, SG) 4.8% (MA) 4.8% (OM) 7.2% (AU) See 9911.96.71–9911.96.75 (CL)	35%
		* * *				
		Fruit jellies:				
2007.99.70	00	Currant and berry	kg......	1.4%	Free (A+, AU, BH, CA, CL, D, E, IL, J, JO, MA, MX, OM, P, PE, SG)	35%
2007.99.75	00	Other	kg......	3.2%	Free (A, AU, BH, CA, CL, E, IL, J, JO, MA, MX, OM, P, PE, SG)	35%
2008		Fruit, nuts and other edible parts of plants, otherwise prepared or preserved, whether or not containing added sugar or other sweetening matter or spirit, not elsewhere specified or included:				
		Nuts, peanuts (ground-nuts) and other seeds, whether or not mixed together:				
2008.11		Peanuts (ground-nuts):				
		Peanut butter and paste:				
2008.11.02	00	Described in general note 15 of the tariff schedule and entered pursuant to its provisions	kg......	Free		15¢/kg
2008.11.05	00	Described in additional U.S. note 5 to this chapter and entered pursuant to its provisions	kg......	Free		15¢/kg
2008.11.15	00	Other	kg......	131.8%	Free (JO, MX) 43.9% (CL) 79% (P) 105.4% (PE) See 9910.12.05, 9910.12.20 (SG) See 9912.12.05, 9912.12.20 (MA) See 9913.12.05, 9913.12.20 (AU) See 9914.12.05, 9914.12.20 (BH) See 9915.20.05–9915.20.20 (P+) See 9916.12.05, 9916.12.20 (OM)	155%

* Column 1 **General** Tariffs are "normal" or "MFN" tariffs as negotiated in the GATT/WTO. See the prior problem in this chapter.

* Column 1 **Special** Tariffs refer primarily to preferential or duty free trade agreements and programs of the United States. See the Free Trade problem, and the Tariff Preferences problem, following in this chapter.

** Column 2 Tariffs date principally from the Smoot Hawley Tariff Act of 1930. At this point, they apply only to Cuba and North Korea.

GENERAL NOTES

* * *

3.(f) <u>Commingling of Goods</u>.

(i) Whenever goods subject to different rates of duty are so packed together or mingled that the quantity or value of each class of goods cannot be readily ascertained by customs officers (without physical segregation of the shipment or the contents of any entire package thereof), by one or more of the following means:

(A) sampling,

(B) verification of packing lists or other documents filed at the time of entry, or

(C) evidence showing performance of commercial settlement tests generally accepted in the trade and filed in such time and manner as may be prescribed by regulations of the Secretary of the Treasury,

the commingled goods shall be subject to the highest rate of duty applicable to any part thereof unless the consignee or his agent segregates the goods pursuant to subdivision (f)(ii) hereof.

(ii) Every segregation of goods made pursuant to subdivision (f) of this note shall be accomplished by the consignee or his agent at the risk and expense of the consignee within 30 days (unless the Secretary authorizes in writing a longer time) after the date of personal delivery or mailing, by such employee as the Secretary of the Treasury shall designate, of written notice to the consignee that the goods are commingled and that the quantity or value of each class of goods cannot be readily ascertained by customs officers. Every such segregation shall be accomplished under customs supervision, and the compensation and expenses of the supervising customs officers shall be reimbursed to the Government by the consignee under such regulations as the Secretary of the Treasury may prescribe.

(iii) The foregoing provisions of subdivision (f) of this note do not apply with respect to any part of a shipment if the consignee or his agent furnishes, in such time and manner as may be prescribed by regulations of the Secretary of the Treasury, satisfactory proof—

(A) that such part (1) is commercially negligible, (2) is not capable of segregation without excessive cost and (3) will not be segregated prior to its use in a manufacturing process or otherwise, and

(B) that the commingling was not intended to avoid the payment of lawful duties.

Any goods with respect to which such proof is furnished shall be considered for all customs purposes as a part of the goods, subject to the next lower rate of duty, with which they are commingled.

* * *

(v) The provisions of subdivision (f) of this note shall apply only in cases where the tariff schedule does not expressly provide a particular tariff treatment for commingled goods.

KELLY, REMNANTS OF RECENT CUSTOMS LITIGATION: JURISDICTION AND STATUTORY INTERPRETATION

26 Brook. J. Int'l L. 861, 878–888 (2001).*

A. AN OVERVIEW OF INTERPRETIVE TOOLS

To interpret tariff terms, the CIT first resorts to a host of sources to divine the meaning of the term at the time of enactment, independent of the Customs Service's view. As with all statutory interpretation cases, finding the meaning of the terms begins with the statute. Customs law involves several statutes, but the most prominent of these is the Harmonized Tariff Schedule of the United States (HTSUS). The HTSUS has a number of component parts. The text of the HTSUS, i.e., the statute, consists of the General Rules of Interpretation; the Additional U.S. Rules of Interpretation; the General Notes; Sections I through XXII, inclusive (encompassing chapters 1–99, and including all Section and Chapter notes, heading/subheading numbers through the 8-digit level, article descriptions and tariff and other treatment accorded thereto) * * *. Thus, in any cases where the statute in question involves a tariff term from the HTSUS, the court necessarily will consult the plain meaning of the HTSUS itself, as enlightened by the General Rules of Interpretation (GRI), the Section Notes and Chapter Notes set forth at the beginning of each of the eleven sections and ninety-nine chapters respectively, and any relevant appendices.

Rule 1 of the GRI of the HTSUS is the starting point for an analysis of classification under the HTSUS. It provides:

The . . . titles of sections, chapters and sub-chapters are provided for ease of reference only; for legal purposes, classification shall be determined according to the terms of the headings and any relative section or chapter notes and, provided such headings or notes do not otherwise require, according to the following provisions [indicating GRI 1, 2, 3, et seq.].

GRI 1 states "classification shall be determined according to the terms of the headings and any relative section or chapter notes."

After considering the statute itself, the CIT regularly consults the legislative history of the term. Although the resort to legislative history in Chevron analysis has been challenged by Justice Scalia, it is considered in step one of Chevron by many courts. The CIT has often held that absent contrary legislative intent, HTSUS terms are to be "construed [according] to their common and popular meaning." Thus, the CIT refers to the

---

* Copyright © 2005 and reprinted with permission from the Brooklyn Journal of International Law.

legislative history of tariff statutes to ascertain Congress' precise meaning. In classification cases, the legislative history is found in the Explanatory Notes and in the International Trade Committee's Report and Conversion Tables, documenting the transition from the Tariff Schedule of the United States ("TSUS") to the HTSUS. The Explanatory Notes are non-binding interpretations of the HTSUS developed by the World Customs Organization. The conversion tables provide a reference between the HTSUS and its predecessor, the Tariff Schedule of the United States. Where the statutory language of the HTSUS is clear, resort to the TSUS is not necessary.

The CIT also may inquire into the common and popular meaning of a tariff term absent contrary legislative intent. Where the meaning of a tariff term cannot be ascertained from the term itself or the legislative history, the court will ascribe meaning by looking at the common commercial understanding of the term. Thus, the common and commercial meaning doctrine is often encountered if a resort to GRI 1 and legislative history fails to supply guidance. "To assist it in ascertaining the common meaning of a tariff term, the court may rely upon its own understanding of the terms used, and it may consult lexicographic and scientific authorities, dictionaries, and other reliable information sources." In classification cases, customs tribunals have employed an endless litany of dictionaries, technical manuals, experts, and scientific authorities to extract an understanding of a term. Additionally, some specific tariff terms are subject to a "use" test such that an article will be classified according to its use. Where "use" provisions are concerned, the meaning of the tariff term is in part defined by the principle use or actual use of the object at issue. Beyond the above tools, the court, as a specialized court, frequently reviews its own history of interpretation and can adapt judicial interpretations and aids in statutory construction.

Lastly, the CIT employs more traditional methods of statutory construction including the canons of construction and the general interpretive principles. * * *. Some have commented that it would be odd for the canons of construction to provide Congress' precise intention on a point. Rather, canons of construction are seen as rules which should be generally followed and will allow the court to impute the answer to a particular question.

* * *

B. The HTSUS and its Interpretative Components

The application of the HTSUS, GRIs, and section and chapter notes works in a relatively straightforward, even mechanical, way. For example, in Baxter Healthcare Corp. v. United States, an importer challenged Customs' classification of "capillary membrane" under "synthetic monofilament," sub-heading, 5404.10.8080, HTSUS or as part of an "artificial respiration apparatus" in subheading 9019.20.000, HTSUS, because it was a part of a larger machine, or as part of yet a larger machine, an "electro-medical apparatus" subheading 9018.90.7080, HTSUS.

Thus, the threshold issue was the meaning of the various tariff terms. According to the GRIs, the merchandise would be classified in the most specific alternative. Typically, in customs classification cases, at issue are the meanings of at least two tariff terms. Usually, Customs claims that one provision best describes the article, while the importer claims that a (several) different provision best describes the article. Thus, the CIT had to ascribe a specific contextual meaning to an arguably ambiguous term to ascertain whether a particular product fell within that term's definition. The plaintiff argued that the government's preferred choice, the "synthetic monofilament," required a product to be both "synthetic" and a "monofilament." The plaintiff argued that the merchandise was neither "synthetic" nor a "monofilament."

Despite the plaintiff's attractive argument that the term "synthetic monofilament," requires a product that was both "synthetic" and "monofilament," the government argued the CIT should use the Chapter Notes to the HTSUS to interpret the terms. Note 1 of Chapter 54 provided a definition of synthetics. Thus, as a threshold matter the chapter notes indicated that the membrane should be included in the definition of synthetic in Chapter 54. Resort to the GRIs bolstered this view. GRI 2(b) provides: "Any reference in a heading to a material or substance shall be taken to include a reference to mixtures or combinations of that material or substance with other materials or substances. Any reference to goods of a given material or substance shall be taken to include a reference to goods consisting wholly or partly of such material or substance ...." Thus, the court could conclude in accordance with GRI 2(b) and the Notes to Chapter 54, that (1) the membrane was synthetic within meaning of HTSUS classification; and, (2) the membrane was properly classified as a material, rather than a part. Further, the government claimed that according to the HTSUS and the Explanatory Notes, the merchandise at issue was not part of another article but "is simply a material."

C. EXPLANATORY NOTES AND THE LEGISLATIVE HISTORY OF TARIFF TERMS

In Baxter, the court also considered the Explanatory Notes' description of "monofilament." As previously explained, the Explanatory Notes are non-binding interpretations of the HTSUS developed by the World Customs Organization. As the CIT noted "[t]he General Explanatory Notes to heading 5404 help provide a definition of the term monofilament." The Explanatory Notes provides:

This heading covers: ... (1) Synthetic monofilament. These are filaments extruded as single filaments. They are classified here only if they measure 67 decitex or more and do not exceed 1 mm in any cross-sectional dimension. Monofilament of this heading may be of any cross-sectional configuration and may be obtained not only by extrusion but by lamination or fusion .... All these products are generally in long lengths, but remain classified here even if cut into short lengths and whether or not put up for retail sale. They are used according to their different characteristics in the manufacture of brushes, sports rackets, fishing lines, surgical sutures, upholstery fabrics, belts, millinery, braids, etc.

Thus, in Baxter the CIT noted the HTSUS does not define the term "monofilament" and uses the Explanatory Notes, as well as the common and commercial meaning doctrine, to define the term. Once the term was defined, the CIT had no problem in finding it "clear . . . that Customs correctly classified the merchandise as a synthetic monofilament." The Explanatory Notes will not always be able to provide a definitive definition of a term, however, they are frequently helpful.

D.   THE COMMON AND COMMERCIAL MEANING OF THE TARIFF TERM

In determining the common and commercial meaning of a tariff term, the court is free to consult both dictionaries and experts. For example, in Toyota Motor Sales v. United States, the issue was whether an imported cab chassis came within the common meaning of the eo nomine provision for chassis for automobile trucks and motor buses. The court stated tariff terms are properly construed "in accordance with their common and commercial meaning, and it is presumed that Congress frames the tariff acts according to the general usage and denomination of the trade." While answering the "question of a term's common meaning courts may consult dictionaries, lexicons, scientific authorities and other reliable sources as an aid," these sources are to be used to ascertain the "meaning . . . given [to] a descriptive term used in a tariff act is that which it had at the time of the law's enactment."

The court then used the definition of chassis contained in the Handbook of the Society of Automotive Engineers (1963) (SAE Handbook) which did not include cabs in the definition of chasses. Going beyond this authoritative source, the CIT considered a variety of sources including: Funk & Wagnalls Standard Dictionary of the English Language, Encyclopedia Americana, McGraw-Hill Encyclopedia of Science and Technology, Webster's New Collegiate Dictionary, McGraw-Hill Dictionary of Scientific & Technical Terms, Collier's Encyclopedia, and The New Encyclopedia Britannica. The litany of lexicons listed by the CIT responded to the wealth of industry testimony showing industry usage of the terms. The CIT found that testimony to common meanings would be insufficient to overcome the dictionary definition. Admittedly, there was a great deal of conflict in the industry as to industry usage, thus the court chose to rely on the lexicographic sources.

The CIT's resort to dictionaries and experts seems reflexive at times. Given the normative goals of customs laws, and tariff classification in particular, this is a natural reflex. Customs statutes promote the fair assessment and imposition of duties consistent with foreign trade and policy objectives. These goals are intertwined with market forces and structures. The CIT, therefore, is challenged to make its determinations across a variety of commerce sectors consistently taking into account industry standards and definitions. Resort to objective criteria such as industry experts or dictionaries is natural. Likewise, the CIT respects the commercial and industry practices outside of the classification realm, when interpreting tariff terms that implicate business practices or common commercial dealings.

E. The Canons of Construction

The CIT can consider and employ the canons of construction in ascribing the meaning of a tariff term. For example, in Totes, Inc. v. United States, the court considered whether trunk organizers used to organize and store automotive tools and supplies in motor vehicles were properly classifiable within subheading 4202.92.9020, HTSUS which includes "trunks, suitcases, jewelry boxes, cutlery cases, and tool bags, rather than as parts of motor vehicles." The court considered the canon of construction ejusdem generis requiring that where particular words of description are followed by general terms, the general terms will be regarded as applying to things of a like class as those listed in the particular words of description. The CIT found that the trunk organizers possessed the same characteristics and common purpose as the exemplars listed in the tariff heading. Thus, using the canon of construction ejusdem generis, the court found that the organizers were properly classified within the "trunks" heading, rather than as "other automotive parts" or "other textiles."

Conversely, in Supermarket Systems, U.S. Inc. v. United States, the CIT considered the classification of Openmatic automatic entry gates (steel devices equipped with a gate arm and alarm and are placed at the entrance way of public buildings). Customs classified the merchandise under TSUS 653.30 as "other structures and parts of structures . . . of iron or steel." Plaintiff challenged the classification and argued it should be classified under item TSUS 685.50 as "other sound or visual signaling apparatus." The court examined whether the term "structure" as used in TSUS item 653.30 was intended by Congress to include devices such as the Openmatic. Using some of the tools discussed in prior sections the CIT considered the alternate headings itself, but found they did not specifically enumerate the gates.

The CIT then resorted to the common and commercial meaning. Both plaintiff and Customs offered dictionary definitions of "structure." The plaintiff also used expert witness testimony to describe the proper definition of the term. The witness offered evidence that the device was not intended to be a structure because it "bore no load." The CIT held that the dictionary definitions and expert witness failed to supply the meaning of the term "structure."

Employing the canons of construction, the CIT considered whether the automatic gate at issue was of the same class of merchandise as the exemplars listed in the proposed tariff heading defining "structure," i.e. hangars, buildings, bridges, towers, roofs, columns, pillars, shutters, and balustrades. The CIT found that the exemplars had no unifying criteria such that the ejusdem generis could not aid in the interpretive process.

Finding no basis to assign any of the alternative eo nomine subheadings, the CIT eventually resorted to GRI 3(c) to find that the merchandise should be classified in the "basket" provision. Thus, even when the plain language of the statute, the legislative history, the common and commercial meaning doctrine, expert testimony, and the canons of construction failed to define the meaning of a tariff term, the CIT could still use the GRIs to resolve the classification issue at hand.

BETTER HOME PLASTICS CORP. v. UNITED STATES

United States Court of International Trade, 1996.
916 F.Supp. 1265.

DiCARLO, CHIEF JUDGE.

Plaintiff, Better Home Plastics Corp., challenges the classification of imported shower curtain sets by the United States Customs Service. Customs classified the merchandise under the provision for the set's outer textile curtain at a duty of 12.8% ad valorem. Better Home Plastics asserts classification of the set is properly determined by the set's inner plastic liner, under Section VII, Chapter 39, Subheading 3924.90.1010, HTSUS (1992), at a duty of 3.36% ad valorem.

* * *

The shower curtain sets in question consist of an outer textile curtain, inner plastic magnetic liner, and plastic hooks. The plastic liner prevents water from escaping the shower enclosure while the shower is in use. The liner—which is opaque—also protects the textile curtain from mildew, and further serves to conceal the shower enclosure, a function the textile curtain cannot perform alone. The liner is color coordinated to match the outer curtain, and adds to the set's decorative appearance.

The textile curtain is intended to be decorative, and does not retain water in the shower enclosure. The curtain is also semi-transparent, permitting the color of the plastic liner to show when the curtain and the liner are drawn.

* * *

The General Rules of Interpretation (GRI) govern the classification of the imported shower curtain sets under the HTSUS. * * *

General Rule of Interpretation 3 (GRI 3) governs where the merchandise at issue consists of more than one material or substance, such as a textile curtain and an inner plastic liner, as here. *See* GRI 2(b). GRI 3 mandates that, when "goods are, *prima facie*, classifiable under two or more headings," the court must classify the merchandise in question pursuant to the heading providing the most specific description. This is known as the rule of relative specificity. An exception to this rule exists.

When, however,

two or more headings each refer . . . to part only of the items in a set put up for retail sale, those headings are to be regarded as equally specific . . . even if one [heading provides] a more complete or precise description of the goods.

GRI 3(a), HTSUS (emphasis added). Accordingly, the rule of relative specificity does not apply when two of the headings each refer only to part of the items within the set.

Goods put up in sets for retail sale, which cannot be classified by reference to GRI 3(a), are classified by the "component which gives them their essential character." GRI 3(b), HTSUS [hereinafter the "essential character test"]. For goods which cannot be classified by reference to either GRI 3(a) or the exception pursuant to GRI 3(b), GRI 3(c) directs their classification "under the heading which occurs last in numerical order among those which equally merit consideration." GRI 3(c), HTSUS. The parties contest how the court should apply these rules to the imported shower curtain sets in question.

1. THE RULE OF RELATIVE SPECIFICITY

Customs classified the shower curtain sets on the basis of the outer textile curtain pursuant to subheading 6303.92.0000, HTSUS, which provides,

> 6303 Curtains (including drapes) and interior blinds; curtain or bed valances:

> * * *

> 6303.92 Of synthetic fibers.

Better Home Plastics contends the court must apply the essential character test, in classifying the applicable merchandise. Application of the test, Better Home Plastics asserts, would mandate classification of the set on the basis of its inner plastic liner pursuant to Subheading 3924.90.1010, HTSUS. This provision provides, in pertinent part,

> 3924 Tableware, kitchenware, other household articles and toilet articles, of plastics:

> * * *

> 3924.90   Other:

> 3924.90.10 Curtains and drapes, including panels and valances . . .

> 3924.90.1010 Curtains and drapes.

Defendant argues the rule of relative specificity governs the classification of the imported merchandise. According to defendant, as both of the named headings fail to "refer" to different named materials contained in the imported sets, the essential character test would not apply.

Defendant further contends the court is limited only to comparisons among competing headings, and may not refer to the subheadings thereunder. Defendant therefore argues the rule of relative specificity applies. Application of the rule would support Customs' classification.

Although the court agrees that subheadings may not be referred to when comparing two competing headings, *see* Customs Co-operation Council, *Introducing the International Convention on the Harmonized Commodity Description and Coding System* 31 (1987) (finding that "in every case a product must first be classified to its appropriate [heading with] no account being taken of the terms of any lower-level subdivisions",) the court finds that the rule of relative specificity does not govern the classification of the curtain sets. The rule will not apply if (1) the headings are equally specific; or (2) two or more competing headings refer only to part of *the items within the set,* not as defendant asserts, a named material. This second exception is relevant here, as the imports in question are items in a set, put up for retail sale, not a mixture or composite good.

The applicable portions of the two competing headings refer to "[c]urtains," Heading 6303, HTSUS, and to "toilet articles, of plastics," Heading 3924, HTSUS. Heading 6303 covers the set's outer textile curtain. Heading 3924 contains the inner plastic liner.

Neither heading, however, encompasses all the items in the set. As Chapter 63 requires articles classified pursuant to its provisions to be made of textile fabric, "[c]urtains" would not encompass the plastic liner, nor the supporting plastic rings. Similarly, Note 1 to Chapter 39, HTSUS, which encompasses the inner plastic liner, specifically precludes classification of imports regarded as textiles under its provisions, and thus would exclude the textile curtains. Accordingly, as the two competing headings each refer only to part of the items in the set, the rule of relative specificity does not apply, and the court looks to the rule's exception in the essential character test.

2. THE ESSENTIAL CHARACTER TEST

Defendant contends the essential character of the curtains are embodied in the textile curtain. Defendant raises numerous arguments to support its position, particularly that (1) the plastic liner is replaceable at 1/3 to 1/4 the price of the set; (2) the consumer purchases the set because of the decorative function of the outer curtain, and not for the protection afforded by the liner; and (3) the liner is only employed for the limited period that someone is utilizing the shower, whereas the decorative outer curtain is employed, at a minimum, when the bathroom is in use, and as much as 24 hours a day. Defendant also contends Better Home Plastics' invoice description supports Customs' classification. Pursuant to the invoice description, the set is sold as "Fabric Shower Curtain and Liner." Therefore, defendant argues, this description serves as an admission that the curtain provides the essential character of the set.

The Explanatory Notes to the General Rules of Interpretation interpret essential character vaguely. Further, there are no reported cases defining essential character under the HTSUS. The predecessor to the HTSUS, the Tariff Schedule of the United States (TSUS), however, did utilize this concept. Accordingly, the court looks to case law under the TSUS for guidance.

In *United States v. Canadian Vinyl Industries, Inc.,* the Court of Customs and Patent Appeals reviewed the classification of flexible sheets with a polyurethane skin on one side and nylon fabric on the other, used as imitation patent leather in the manufacture of shoes. The Court of International Trade's predecessor, the Customs Court, had upheld the importer's claim that the merchandise was properly classified according to the polyurethane skin, which imparted the imitation patent leather upon the sheets. In affirming the Customs Court, the Court of Customs and Patent Appeals found that the qualities imparted by the polyurethane skin were "indispensable," and therefore imparted the essential character of the merchandise.

Although the court agrees that the curtain in the imported set imparts a desirable decorative characteristic, nonetheless, like the polyurethane skin in *Canadian Vinyl,* it is the plastic liner that provides the *indispensable* property of preventing water from escaping the shower enclosure. The liner (1) prevents water from escaping when the shower is in use; (2) protects the fabric curtain from mildew and soap scum; and (3) conceals the shower and provides privacy when the shower is in use. Further, the plastic liner can serve its intended function without the outer curtain and contributes to the overall appearance of the set. The outer curtain, in contrast, merely furthers the sets decorative aspect. The court therefore concludes the essential character of the set is derived from the plastic liner.

* * * Finally, while the court takes into consideration the relative cost of the component parts, this point alone is not dispositive, nor very persuasive against the competing arguments.

3. CONFLICT WITH THE CHAPTER NOTES

Defendant also argues the chapter notes to Chapter 39 prohibit the proposed classification. As GRI 1 indicates, Customs may apply the General Rules of Interpretation only to the extent that the relevant section and chapter notes do not otherwise require. Note 1 to Chapter 39 provides "any reference to *'plastics'* ... does not apply to materials regarded as textile materials of section XI." In addition, Note 2(*l*) of the same chapter provides that Chapter 39 does not cover "[g]oods of section XI (textiles and textile articles)[.]"). Accordingly, under GRI 1, defendant argues, the prohibition contained in the chapter notes to Chapter 39 would take precedence over an application of GRI 3(b). Thus, classification on the basis of the plastic liner would be improper.

Defendant further argues that, because the exclusion of textile materials made of plastic is already accomplished by Note 1, Note 2(*l*). must refer to sets made up in part of textile materials, if it is to have any effect.

According to defendant, basic principles of statutory construction mandate that the court must interpret each provision of a statute in such a manner so as not to render any provision superfluous.

The court is unpersuaded. Although the Explanatory Notes recognize that "headings cannot be extended to include goods which otherwise might fall there by reason of" the application of the General Rules of Interpretation, this limitation on the General Rules of Interpretation only applies "where the addition of another material or substance [would deprive] goods of *the character of goods of the kind mentioned in the heading.*"

This is not the case here. The application of GRI 3(b) results in the classification of a *set* pursuant to the component that imparts the set's essential character, here the plastic liner. Under this fiction, the set is to be treated as if it consists wholly of the plastic curtain. Explanatory Note GR1(V) envisioned, and sought to prohibit, a different situation.

Explanatory Note GR1(V), as demonstrated by its example and reference of Chapter 31, was primarily concerned with certain materials or substances, such as the chemical compounds in Chapter 31, whose basic nature and qualities would be fundamentally altered by the addition of another substance. For instance, adding sodium (Na+) to chloride (Cl-) would create a salt, a substance with entirely different chemical and physical properties than the individual ions unmixed.

Classification of the textile curtain under the provision for plastic goods would not deprive the set of its "plastic" qualities. It is the essential character of the set—derived in part from the plastic's ability to repel water—that denotes the set's utility, purpose, and accordingly, character. Inclusion of the textile curtain within the classification for the plastic liner does little to change the qualities or the basic nature of the set in meeting this purpose.

* * *

The court finds that, when the indispensable function of keeping water inside the shower enclosure, along with the protective, privacy and decorative functions of the plastic liner are weighed against the decorative function and the relative cost of the outer curtain, it is the plastic liner that imparts the essential character upon the set. The court therefore does not reach defendant's argument that, in accordance with GRI 3(c), the set is classified under the subheading which appears last in numerical order.

CONCLUSION

The court finds Better Home Plastics has overcome the presumption of correctness accorded to Customs, and the shower curtain sets were improperly classified under subheading 6303.92.0000, HTSUS. In addition, the court agrees with Better Home Plastics' proposed classification of the sets under subheading 3924.90.1010, HTSUS.

QUESTIONS AND COMMENTS

1.   Consult Chapter 20 of the Harmonized Tariff Schedule of the United States (HTS). Note that if PB&J Swirl is classified under Heading 2007 as a "fruit jelly", there is a Column 1 duty rate of 3.2% on all such jellies that are not derived from currants or berries. On $0.50 per kg., that could amount to $0.016 duty per kg., making the imported product's total cost $0.516, or lower than the cost of domestically produced PB&J ($0.55). Fast Food would want to purchase from Double Happiness at such a price, but the difference is rather small. Alternatively, if grape jelly was used in the PB&J Swirl, perhaps the tariff would be only 1.4%, which would be more advantageous to Fast Food.

On the other hand, if PB&J is classified under Heading 2008 as "peanut butter," it might be able to enter the United States duty free, and would be even more price-competitive, but if PB&J is classified as "peanut butter . . . other," the tariff would be a prohibitive 131.8%.

Each of these classifications seems arguably possible, but none feels exactly right. Further, there is no classification in HTS for "peanut butter *and* jelly." Thus, one of these classifications must be chosen. How do you resolve such an issue? Is a dictionary determinative? Or even helpful?

2.   Note that the HTS provides interpretive devices within its own text, both in the notes to particular chapters and in the General Rules of Interpretation. (See the Documents Supplement.) Are these helpful? Do they specifically resolve the issue raised by your own client?

For example, GRI 2(b) states that "Any reference . . . to a . . . substance shall be taken to include mixtures or combinations of that . . . substance with other . . . substances." "Thus, your client could argue that PB&J is "peanut butter," in a mixture with another substance. However, U.S. Customs may argue that PB&J is "fruit jelly," in a mixture with another substance, and subject to a 3.2% duty. Note that the last sentence of GRI 2(b) helps to solve this argument.

3.   GRI 3 establishes rules for products which may be classified under more than one heading. Does that describe PB&J? Part of the product can be classified under Heading 2007, and a different part can be classified under Heading 2008. But do either of these Headings cover the totality of the product? Consult again the last sentence of GRI 2(b) for a different nuance concerning the coverage of GRI 3.

4.   Under GRI 3(a), the proper classification is the Heading which provides the "most specific description." Is that Heading 2007 or 2008? This is often referred to as "the rule of relative specificity." Is either of these two headings more specific that the other? If so, which one and why? Note the analysis of the CIT in *Better Home Plastics* on this issue.

5.   If PB&J is a "mixture" or a "composite good," then GRI 3(b) is applicable. It employs the "essential character" test. What is the "essence" of PB&J—the peanut butter or the jelly? What is the analysis used by the CIT in *Better Home Plastics?*

However, is PB&J either a "mixture" or a "composite good"? What is a "mixture" or a "composite good"? Neither the GRIs nor the HTS as a whole offer a definition. Is this where a dictionary would be helpful? One definition of a "mixture" is a "mass or assemblage with more or less thorough diffusion of the constituent elements among one another." "Swirled" PB&J may not meet the standard. It is also defined as "any combination of differing elements." PB&J may meet that standard.

Likewise, dictionary definitions of "composite goods" range from "a compound, or a pure substance composed of two or more elements, whose composition is constant", to "made up of various elements." While PB&J may meet the latter standard, it is less likely to meet the former.

6.   If neither GRI 3(a) nor GRI 3(b) seems dispositive, or even useful, the "default rule" is contained in GRI 3(c). It gives a straight numerical test—the Heading with the larger number is applicable. That might be Heading 2008, which provides that importation is free, as long as it is covered by Additional U.S. Note 5 to Chapter 20.

7.   On the other hand, it is possible to argue that PB&J is neither a mixture nor a composite good, but that the peanut butter and the jelly are merely commingled goods. Under General Note 3(f), commingled goods are "subject to the highest rate of duty applicable to any part thereof." That might be the 3.2% rate on jelly. What is a commingled good—as contrasted to a mixture or a composite good? Does General Note 3(f) give you a working definition?

8.   If the provisions of GRI 3 and the provisions of General Note 3(f) lead to different results, how does one resolve the conflict? In case of conflict between general rules of interpretation and U.S. notes, which concepts should be considered controlling? Or, would this determination depend upon additional information concerning the issue, the rules, and the context of their usage?

9.   According to Heading 2008.11, some peanuts enter duty free, under 2008.11.05, but others have a duty rate of 131.8%, under 2008.11.15. Which rate is applicable to PB&J from Double Happiness? If the latter rate applies, Fast Food does not want to purchase from Double Happiness.

Additional U.S. Note 5, which is found in the Chapter 20 Notes, is relevant. It creates two determinants: the county of origin and the quality of the imports. If PB&J is classified as "peanut butter," and its origin is Chinese, then the amount which can be imported is quite limited, and the discount for large purchases may not be available. Thus, the rules concerning classification of the country of origin of the import become crucially important.

10.   If you are attempting to enter PB&J as "peanut butter" from China duty free under Heading 2008.11.05, you will have to compete with all the other importers in the U.S., and Double Happiness may have to compete with all the other exporters in many nations, to get any part of the 250 metric tons allowed to those countries not named in Additional U.S. Note 6. That may be very difficult. You may prefer to classify the goods as a "fruit jelly" under

Heading 2007, and to pay the 3.2% duty. How would you make that classification argument?

11. If you argue that PB&J is commingled goods, which are "subject to the highest duty rate applicable to any part thereof," is that rate 3.2% or 131.8%? In other words, are commingled peanut butter and jelly subject to the quantity limitations in Additional U.S. Note 5?

PART B.　PLACE OF ORIGIN CLASSIFICATION (WHERE IS IT FROM?)

WHAT EVERY MEMBER OF THE TRADE COMMUNITY SHOULD KNOW ABOUT: U.S. RULES OF ORIGIN

U.S. Customs and Border Protection Informed Compliance Publication (2004).

INTRODUCTION

The country of origin of merchandise imported into the customs territory of the United States (the fifty states, the District of Columbia and Puerto Rico) is important for several reasons. The country of origin of merchandise can affect, among other things, the rate of duty, the eligibility for special programs, admissibility, quota, procurement by government agencies and marking requirements. This publication summarizes the various rules of origin for goods imported into the customs territory of the United States. The discussion is divided into "non-preferential" and "preferential" rules of origin. "Non-preferential" rules are those that generally apply to merchandise in the absence of bilateral or multilateral trade agreements. On the other hand, "preferential" rules are those that apply to merchandise to determine eligibility for special treatment under various trade agreements or special legislation. [See the Free Trade problem and the Trade Preferences problem that follow.]

NON–PREFERENTIAL RULES OF ORIGIN

U.S. Non-preferential rules of origin schemes are used for several purposes:

- Most–Favored–Nation or Normal–Trade–Relations Treatment
- Country of Origin Marking
- Government Procurement
- Textile and Textile Products

All U.S. non-preferential rules of origin schemes employ the "wholly obtained" criterion for goods that are wholly the growth, product, or manufacture of a particular country. On the other hand, all U.S. non-preferential rules of origin schemes employ the "substantial transformation" criterion for goods that consist in whole or in part of materials from more than one country. In the majority of the non-preferential schemes, the substantial transformation criterion is applied on a case-by-case basis, and it is based on a change in name/character/use method (i.e., an article that consists in whole or in part of materials from more than one country is a product of the country in which it has been substantially transformed into a new and different article of commerce with a name, character, and use distinct from that of the article or articles from which is was so transformed).

SUPERIOR WIRE, A DIV. OF SUPERIOR PRODUCTS CO. v. UNITED STATES

United States Court of International Trade, 1987.
669 F.Supp. 472.

RESTANI, JUDGE:

Plaintiff, an importer of steel wire from Canada, challenges the denial of its protest against the exclusion of a shipment of wire made from wire rod produced in Spain. The United States Customs Service (Customs) excluded the wire because it was not accompanied by certificates that would allow its entry under a voluntary restraint agreement (VRA) with Spain covering wire and wire rod.

In connection with this action plaintiff sought a temporary restraining order and a preliminary injunction to allow it to continue importing. * * * The court denied preliminary relief.

FACTS

Plaintiff has been importing wire made from Spanish hot-rolled wire rod since late 1984. It obtains the finished cold-drawn wire from its related company, Big Point Steel Company, in Ontario, Canada. It is the operations of Big Point which are the main focus here.

The evidence discloses that plaintiff orders the wire rod from Spain for delivery to Canada. The rod arrives in coils of about 2,700 pounds each. The rod is uncoiled, and cleaned during passage through a mechanical descaling machine, which removes a hard oxide crust by reverse bending. The scale is formed during the rod-making process and must be removed to prevent damage to the wire-drawing equipment. The rod is then coated with a spray-on lubricant/rust preventative. The coils are joined by butt-welding, to facilitate feeding the dies, and because the end product is a 2,000 pound coil. Generally, the butt-welding process may also involve annealing across the joint so that the composition of the wire will be the same throughout. There was no testimony as to whether annealing took place at Big Point.

The operation crucial to resolution of this matter is the process which turns the wire rod into wire. In order to feed the machine which contains the dies that cold draw the rod into wire, the rod must be pointed and inserted into the machine. The rod is drawn through one, two and possibly, in a few cases, three dies. The testimony was contradictory as to whether one or two die passes were most commonly needed for the sizes of wire drawn by plaintiff, but plaintiff's witnesses seemed to have more familiarity with the process and the court accepts their testimony that two die passes are normally involved. Testimony also indicated that this process increases the tensile strength by thirty to forty percent as the rod is reduced in cross-sectional area by about thirty percent and is elongated. Other evidence indicated this degree of strength increase may be slightly high, but it is not greatly overstated. The final result is a substantially stronger product, which is also cleaner, smoother, "less springy," less ductile, and cross-sectionally more uniform.

Seventy percent of the wire imported by plaintiff is intended for use in making wire mesh for concrete sewer pipe reinforcement, which requires the strength of the finished wire. Twenty percent of the wire imported by plaintiff is sold as wire. The wire has about one dozen applications, such as shelving or decking and baskets used in the automotive industry. Wire rod has few uses except for making wire. Only a very small percentage of rod is used directly in concrete reinforcement.

The wire rod is of low carbon content. It is referred to as industrial quality or mesh quality rod. The rod is purchased by plaintiff for its affiliate from the Spanish producer in six sizes which range from $\frac{7}{32}$ of an inch to $\frac{7}{16}$ of an inch. The sizes of rod imported produce a range of sizes of wire, but the physical properties of the rod limit the range of sizes of wire which may be effectively or economically produced from a particular size of rod. It is also the chemical content of the rod and the cooling processes used in its manufacture which determine the properties that the wire will have after drawing.

Production of finished cold drawn wire from raw materials, such as scrap metal, involves several processes. The first step is to produce a steel billet. The particular process described at trial was that utilized by a domestic wire rod producer. There was no testimony indicating that the process used to produce the wire rod at issue was significantly different. The billet is a piece of steel about fifty feet long and five and one-eighth inches on each side, if measured cross-sectionally. Depending on the desired composition of the rod to be produced, a selection of different types of scrap are chosen. The scrap is melted in an electric furnace at 2700° Fahrenheit. The molten metal is refined by adding lime, oxygen, and possibly other additives to remove impurities. After the impurities are removed the steel is poured into a ladle and then into a tundish (a brick lined, steel container with holes). The steel then flows into a caster and the billets are formed. The testimony indicated that the scrap costs about one hundred dollars per ton, and at an efficient plant the making of a billet costs about the same.

The next step is the production of wire rod from billets. The billet is reheated to 2100° F. The rod mill described involves twenty-five separate rolling stages (stands) and two lines of billets can be processed at once. The first seven stands are called the roughing stage. The hot billets are passed through horizontal stands which gradually remove the corners of the billets to achieve a more cylindrical shape. The next four stands are also horizontal and are called the intermediate stage. The third stage also involves four stands but they are alternately horizontal and vertical. Finally, ten carbide rolls size down the rod into its final form. The process is computerized and moves at high speed so that water cooling is required to keep friction from raising the temperature above 2100°. The rod coils produced are then laid out with certain spacing depending on the rate of cooling needed. Air blowers can increase the cooling, and the use of hoods can decrease it.

The testimony indicated that the rolling mill cost between sixty and one hundred million dollars and a new mill would cost perhaps four times that amount. The testimony also indicated that much smaller operations are not economically feasible. The domestic producer's rolling operation involves one hundred and twenty-five employees and another sixty employees for quality control. The cost of producing one ton of rod from billet was placed at between forty and eighty dollars, depending on efficiency.

Testimony at trial indicates that a cold-drawing facility can be established for less than two hundred fifty thousand dollars. Plaintiff's operation seems within that range. A used drawing machine may be purchased for as little as thirty-five thousand dollars. Testimony indicated that three employees are needed to run a cold-drawing machine. Plaintiff operates its Canadian plant around the clock five days per week. Plaintiff's accountant stated that recent figures indicated that the cost of cold-drawing the wire from wire rod was about thirty-six dollars per ton. This figure has not been challenged seriously by defendant, and there was some evidence indicating that the figure is slightly understated if viewed in relation to a more general assessment of cost. In early 1987, the price of wire from Big Point to its affiliate was about two hundred eighty dollars per ton. Plaintiff paid two hundred thirty-five dollars per ton for the Spanish rod during the same period.

There seems to be agreement between the parties that the value added in terms of cost of the drawing process is about fifteen percent. During the relevant period domestic wire rod could be purchased for about three hundred dollars per ton. Also during this period, plaintiff sold wire at a substantially higher price to independent customers than it did internally.

Wire rod cannot be hot-rolled to a sufficiently round state to meet specifications of wire. To those in the steel and wire industries, wire rod and wire are different products. They are also classified differently for tariff purposes.

ARGUMENTS

Plaintiff raises two arguments. It asserts that the wire rod was substantially transformed in Canada into wire so that the product it seeks to import is a product of Canada, not Spain, and therefore is not covered by a VRA. Plaintiff also asserts that Customs' action regarding the shipment at issue represented a change in position resulting in a restriction, which change may not take place without notice and opportunity for comment, pursuant to 19 C.F.R. § 177.10(c)(2) (1986).

Defendant argues that the operations performed in Canada were minor and that the court should consider the purpose of the VRA and find that the wire is a product of Spain not Canada. Defendant also argues that Customs did not take a "position" within the meaning of § 177.10(c)(2), and thus no opportunity for comment is required.

EXISTENCE OF A "POSITION"

Two opinions of this court have treated directly the issue of the existence of a position for purposes of § 177.10(c)(2). In *National Juice* the court found a "position" to exist, based on the existence of several rulings published in the Customs Bulletin that provided a factually explicit description of a Customs position of at least eight years standing. *Arbor Foods* reached the opposite result, finding that "a series of ruling letters, oral assurances from various Customs officials, and remissions of liquidated damages claims" did not constitute a position, where the exact merchandise was not covered by a ruling letter.

The court finds the situation at hand more akin to that described in *Arbor Foods* than to that described in *National Juice*. Here there was one ruling letter, vaguely describing a wire-making process in Mexico and finding substantial transformation for purposes of the law relating to the Generalized System of Preferences (GSP). No. 553052 CW (Aug. 20, 1984). This letter ruling was only available to the public via microfiche, an indication that Customs did not consider the ruling letter to be of widespread applicability. Rulings of broad precedential value are generally published in the Customs Bulletin, as were those in *National Juice*. The letter ruling at issue is a "precedential" decision, which must be made otherwise "available for public inspection." 19 C.F.R. § 177.10(a). It need not be published in the Customs Bulletin.

* * *

Plaintiff had the option of obtaining its own letter ruling, which would have given it the right to notice before a change. Plaintiff did not avail itself of this mechanism but chose to rely on a cryptic letter directed to another. In sum, the letter ruling at issue was neither sufficiently descriptive to be broadly applied, nor was it clearly adopted as the position of Customs regarding merchandise of the type sought to be imported by plaintiff under the circumstances in which plaintiff sought to import it.

Plaintiff also cites the fact that the local Customs officials acquiesced in similar importations for more than two years, relying in part on the letter ruling. Such actions did not establish a "position" in *Arbor Foods,* and they do not suffice here. As no "position" had been established for purposes of § 177.10(c)(2), defendant is free to exclude plaintiff's merchandise immediately, if the substantive law permits.

SUBSTANTIAL TRANSFORMATION

* * *

The court now turns to the fundamental question of whether under generally applicable precedent a substantial transformation of the wire rod from Spain occurs when it becomes wire, so as to make the wire a product of Canada, and thus not subject to VRA restrictions. The basic test cited by the parties was set forth in a drawback case, *Anheuser–Busch Brewing Ass'n v. United States,* 207 U.S. 556, 562, 28 S.Ct. 204, 206, 52 L.Ed. 336 (1908), which held that a product would be considered the manufacture or product of the United States if it was transformed into a new and different article "having a distinctive name, character or use." The test has been applied in various situations. Cases giving rise to the most generally cited precedent are those involving country of origin for marking purposes, application of the GSP, and drawback. In addition, the parties have cited two import restriction cases which apply the same basic test.

Although all recent cases cite the *Anheuser–Busch* test, they apply it differently, and modify it somewhat. A name change, for example, is not always considered determinative. Therefore, although it is clear that a name change from "wire rod" to "wire" occurred here, this fact is not necessarily determinative. It may support, however, a finding of substantial transformation, as it did in *Ferrostaal.* Likewise the change in tariff classification which occurred here is not dispositive, although it also may be supportive.

In recent years the courts have concentrated on change in use or character, finding various subsidiary tests appropriate depending on the situation at hand. An inquiry that is sometimes treated as a type of cross-check or additional factor to be considered in substantial transformation cases is whether significant value is added or costs are incurred by the process at issue. In *National Juice,* values of between one and eight percent were not found to be significant. In *Uniroyal v. United States,* (addition of outer sole did not substantially transform shoe upper under marking laws), no percentage was specified, but the cost of the alleged transformation was deemed insignificant. In *Ferrostaal,* on the other hand, a value, attributable to the transformation of at least thirty-six to nearly fifty percent of the value of the heat treated steel, reinforced the court's conclusion that galvanizing and annealing steel constituted a substantial transformation.

A value added test has appeal in many situations because it brings a common sense approach to a fundamental test that may not be easily applied to some products. The fifteen percent added value figure for the wire standing alone does not pull in either direction, but related concepts, including the amount of labor required to accomplish the change and the capital investment required relative to that required to produce the entire article, are also relevant to a determination of whether the change involves minor processing. Minimal processing is part of the factual background of cases such as *Murray, National Juice* and *Uniroyal,* all of which involve findings of no substantial transformation. The differences in capital investment and labor needed in the production of wire rod versus wire are enormous. Comparing only the production of wire from wire rod, versus the production of wire rod from billet, it becomes apparent that the processing performed in Canada is a minor finishing step which may be accomplished easily anywhere with a minimal amount of effort and investment. By itself such analysis may not provide the entire answer as to whether a substantial transformation has taken place, but it should comprise part of the analysis in a case involving the type of products and processes at issue here.

* * * To determine whether the goods at hand are substantially transformed for purposes of VRA enforcement, the court should examine cases involving processing of metal objects without combination or assembly operations. *Torrington Co. v. United States,* is one such case. As indicated, it involved the manufacture of needles in a beneficiary developing country. In the first stage of production of needles, a wire is straightened, cut, beveled, and drawn to form a needle blank. The blank is only useful in the needle-making process. In the next stage, an eye is struck into the needle, a groove is made for thread, and the needle is finished by various processes, including hardening, sharpening, and polishing. The *Torrington* court found that in order for plaintiff to prevail under the GSP statute, two substantial transformations were necessary; the court found both the first and second stages to be substantial transformations.

The second stage of processing discussed in the *Torrington* case involved a transformation from producers' to consumers' goods. The *Torrington* court cited with approval the case of *Midwood Indus. v. United States,* in which rough forgings of the approximate dimensions of the finished products were found to be substantially transformed after being cut, tapered or trimmed, beveled, bored, and subjected to other finishing processes in order to create pipe flanges and fittings. The producer to consumer goods distinction drawn in *Midwood,* a marking case, however, was found not determinative as to substantial transformation in shoe construction in another marking case, *Uniroyal.* Although some of the processes involved here are the same as those involved in the second phase of *Torrington,* there is no clear change from producers' to consumers' goods. Wire rod is primarily intended for wire production, which, in turn, is primarily intended to be used for making wire mesh for concrete pipe reinforcement.

The processes involved in the first stage of *Torrington* are closer to the ones involved here. In fact, the *Torrington* court cited in support of its holding a Treasury Decision involving use of dies to draw plate steel into a cup-shaped rear engine housing. Two factors distinguish this aspect of *Torrington* from the case at hand. First, once the needle blanks were drawn they were fit for only one purpose; the raw material was then destined for one end use. This type of transformation does not occur when wire rod is drawn into wire. The composition of the wire rod determines what uses the wire may have. Although the steel and wire industries may have different names for the products, wire rod and wire may be viewed as different stages of the same product. The difference in stages may be important for tariff purposes but it is not determinative here. In contrast, the *Torrington* court stated, "the initial wire is a raw material and possesses nothing in its character which indicates either the swages [blanks] or the final product." Here, the wire rod dictates the final form of the finished wire. * * *

The engine housing decision cited by *Torrington* also differs from the case at hand. Like the wire to needle blank change, the product was transformed from basic steel into a part with a unique destiny. In addition, the decision noted the involvement of a series of dies. Essentially only two die passes are involved here. The wire emerges stronger and rounder after the passes, but the wire loses a few other advantages, such as greater ductility, in the process. It looks much the same. Its strength characteristic, which is important to its end use, is altered, but the parameters of the strength increase was metallurgically predetermined in the creation of the steel billet and very specifically through the fabrication of the wire rod. Under these circumstances the court does not find a significant change in use or character to have occurred.

The court should also mention here the *Ferrostaal* case. The hot-dipped galvanizing processes involved there, which involved substantial chemical changes, were different from the cold drawing processes involved here. Although, applying broader analytical concepts, the changes in use and character were not greatly different from those involved here, the value added was significant. It appears that a larger capital investment, as well as possibly significant labor, was required to accomplish the transformation in *Ferrostaal*. Taken together these differences are sufficient to distinguish *Ferrostaal* from the case at hand.

Here only the change in name test is clearly met, and such a change has rarely been dispositive. No transformation from producers' to consumers' goods took place; no change from a product suitable for many uses to one with more limited uses took place; no complicated or expensive processing occurred, and only relatively small value was added. Overall, the court views the transformation from wire rod to wire to be minor rather than substantial. Accordingly, the country of origin of the wire must be considered Spain rather than Canada.

Judgment is entered for defendant.

[**Author's Note:** After *Superior Wire*, Customs decided that the change from producers' goods to consumers' goods was not a factor in the "substantial transformation" determination—and said so in a published Interpretation, 65 Fed. Reg. 13830. That Interpretation came before the C.I.T. in 2000 in *Boltex Mfg. Co. v. U.S.* (below).]

BOLTEX MFG. CO. v. UNITED STATES

United States Court of International Trade, 2000.
24 C.I.T. 972, 140 F.Supp.2d 1339.

In the *Final Interpretation*, Customs changed the marking requirements for imported forgings based on its own determination that *Midwood* is no longer good law. Customs thereby abused its discretion in two ways. First, Customs encroached upon judicial authority by attempting to overrule a viable judicial decision. Second, Customs abused its discretion by relying on a legal conclusion that the producers' goods-consumers' goods distinction is no longer good law, rather than engaging in and providing a reasoned factual analysis, or in the words of the *Modification*, "a more complete presentation of the evidence," in determining that the forgings would no longer be considered substantially transformed. *43 Fed. Reg. at 57209.*

1) Customs has overstepped its authority by overruling Midwood.

a. *Midwood* is a continuing judicial decision that has not been overruled by this court or a superior court.

Customs attempts to defend its actions by arguing that *Midwood* is no longer good law. The court has carefully analyzed our predecessor court's opinion in *Midwood* and cannot agree with Customs. * * *

The producers' goods-consumers' goods distinction serves as a supplement to the court's analysis and conclusion based on the *Gibson-Thomsen* test of a new name, character and use. This reading of the *Midwood* decision is supported by several subsequent decisions of the Customs Court, the Court of International Trade, and the Court of Appeals for the Federal Circuit.[12]

In support of its statement that *Midwood* would be decided differently today, and that Customs has therefore not acted irrationally, Defendant cites and discusses several judicial opinions wherein "numerous Judges in this Court and the Federal Circuit have also elected not to be bound by that particular criterion in making a decision regarding whether imported merchandise was 'substantially transformed' for marking purposes." * * * Customs' argument proves too much. While true that in *Nat'l Hand Tool*, the court did not even mention *Midwood*; neither did the court rule that the *Midwood* distinction would hereafter cease to exist. No party to this lawsuit claims that every single factor utilized by every court in determining whether a substantial transformation has occurred must be evaluated in making that determination.

* * *

Finally, Customs cites *Superior Wire v. United States*, stating that "although listed as one of many factors, the producer good/ consumer good

---

12. *See, e.g.,* * * * *Superior Wire v. United States*, 11 C.I.T. 608, 616, 669 F. Supp. 472, 479 (1987) (indicating that *Midwood* has been cited with approval in *Torrington* and held not determinative in *Uniroyal*).

distinction was neither explicitly endorsed, nor relied upon by the court in making its determination." In that opinion, the court mentioned *Midwood*, but did not state that the distinction should no longer be relied upon in a substantial transformation determination. The court even mentioned in its conclusion that no substantial transformation had occurred, that "no transformation from producers' to consumers' goods took place...." Such a statement indicates that far from being abrogated, the court did consider the *Midwood* distinction in determining whether a substantial transformation had occurred. The court agrees with Boltex that "if this Court intended to question *Midwood*, it could have done so expressly."

QUESTIONS AND COMMENTS

1. The court in *Superior Wire and Boltex* suggests that there is no precise answer to the question: "How much manufacturing is enough to make the product of Chinese origin?" However, is it possible to determine instances in which the threshold has been passed? Compare the transformation of wire rod into wire with the transformation of peanuts into peanut butter, or peanut butter into swirled PB&J. Can you articulate any differences in the transformations?

2. The court also suggests that neither a "name change" nor a "change in tariff classification" is necessarily sufficient to make the resulting product originate in Canada. Then what is sufficient, and what more than that has occurred to PB&J in China? The court allows, as additional factors, the value added or the costs incurred by the processing. But we do not, at this time, know much about either. Even if we did, these factors are also not necessarily dispositive.

3. The criteria emphasized in this decision seem to be the "change in use or character" of the transformation of the goods. Did the processing of the peanut butter and the jelly into swirled PB&J change it from producers' goods to consumers' goods? Was there a change from a product suitable for many uses to one with more limited uses?

4. Alternatively, suppose the peanut butter for PB&J really comes from the Philippines, and the court rules no sufficient transformation takes place in China. What result? The Philippines has "normal trade relations" status, so the duty rates are established by Column 1. However, the Philippines is also a country listed in Additional U.S. Note 6 to Chapter 20. Under Additional U.S. Note 5, that would allow a much larger amount of peanut butter to enter the U.S. duty free. Thus, Fast Food might want to argue that no substantial transformation took place, so it could take advantage of the $0.40 per kg. price for larger orders.

5. Suppose the peanut butter comes from North Korea, and the court rules no sufficient transformation takes place in China. What result? See HTS Column 2. Please note that General Note 3(b) lists North Korea as a Column 2 country.

PART C.   VALUATION (WHAT IS ITS CUSTOMS VALUE?)

An understanding of Section 402 of the Tariff Act of 1930 (19 U.S.C. 1401a) is essential to any analysis of this Problem. It is set forth in the Documents Supplement.

HOUSE COMMITTEE ON WAYS AND MEANS, 108TH CONG., 1ST SESS., OVERVIEW AND COMPILATION OF U.S. TRADE STATUTES, 60–69

(Comm. Print, June 2003).

The Customs Valuation Agreement was signed by most major U.S. trading partners at the conclusion of the Tokyo Round. The WTO Agreement on Customs Valuation, which is essentially the same document, is included in the Uruguay Round Agreements applicable to all WTO members. Internationally-agreed rules governing customs valuation will apply to the overwhelming majority of trading countries. Newly joining developing countries may delay implementation for up to 5 years.

* * *

Section 402 of the Tariff Act of 1930, as amended by the Trade Agreements Act of 1979, establishes "Transaction Value" as the primary basis for determining the value of imported merchandise. Generally, transaction value is the price actually paid or payable for the goods, with additions for certain items not included in that price.

If the first valuation basis cannot be used, the secondary bases are considered. These secondary bases, in the order of precedence for use, are: transaction value of identical or similar merchandise; deductive value; and computed value. The order of precedence of the last two bases can be reversed if the importer so requests. Each of these bases is discussed in detail below:

Transaction value of imported merchandise. * * *

The transaction value of imported merchandise (i.e., the merchandise undergoing appraisement) is defined as the price actually paid or payable for the merchandise when sold for exportation to the United States, plus amounts equal to:

(1) the packing costs incurred by the buyer;

(2) any selling commission incurred by the buyers;

(3) the value of any assist;

(4) any royalty or license fee that the buyer is required to pay as a condition of the sale; and

(5) the proceeds, accruing to the seller, of any subsequent resale, disposal, or use of the imported merchandise.

These amounts (1 through 5) are added only to the extent that each is not included in the price and is based on information establishing the accuracy of the amount. If sufficient information is not available and thus the transaction value cannot be determined, then the next basis of value, in order of precedence, must be considered for appraisement.

The price actually paid (or payable) for the imported merchandise is the total payment, excluding international freight, insurance, and other C.I.F. charges, that the buyer makes to the seller.

Amounts to be disregarded in determining transaction value are:

(1) The cost, charges, or expenses incurred for transportation, insurance, and related services incident to the international shipment of the goods from the country of exportation to the place of importation in the United States.

(2) Any decrease in the price actually paid or payable that is made or effected between the buyer and seller after the *date of importation* of the goods into the United States.

As well as, *if identified separately*:

(3) Any reasonable cost or charge incurred for constructing, erecting, assembling, maintaining, or providing technical assistance with respect to the goods importation into the United States; or transporting the goods after importation.

(4) The customs duties and other Federal taxes, including any Federal excise tax for which sellers in the United States are ordinarily liable.

LIMITATIONS ON THE APPLICABILITY OF TRANSACTION VALUE

The transaction value of imported merchandise is the appraised value of that merchandise, provided certain limitations do not exist. If any of these limitations are present, then transaction value cannot be used as the appraised value, and the next basis of value will be considered. The limitations can be divided into four groups:

(1) *Restrictions on the disposition or use of merchandise.*—The first category of limitations which preclude the use of transaction value is the imposition of restrictions by a seller on a buyer's disposition or use of the imported merchandise. Exceptions are made to this rule. Thus, certain restrictions are acceptable, and their presence will still allow the use of transaction value. The acceptable restrictions are: (a) those imposed or required by law, (b) those limiting the geographical area in which the goods may be resold, and (c) those not substantially affecting the value of the goods. An example of the last restriction occurs when a seller stipulates that a buyer of new-model cars cannot sell or exhibit the cars until the start of the new sales year.

(2) *Conditions for which a value cannot be determined.*—If the sale of, or the price actually paid or payable for, the imported merchandise is subject to any condition or consideration for which a value cannot be determined, then transaction value cannot be used. Some examples of this group include when the price of the imported

merchandise depends on (a) the buyer's also buying from the seller other merchandise in specified quantities, (b) the price at which the buyer sells other goods to the seller, or (c) a form of payment extraneous to the imported merchandise, such as, the seller's receiving a specified quantity of the finished product that results after the buyer further processes the imported goods.

(3) *Proceeds accruing to the seller.*—If part of the proceeds of any subsequent resale, disposal, or use of the imported merchandise by the buyer accrues directly or indirectly to the seller, then transaction value cannot be used. There is an exception. If an appropriate adjustment can be made for the partial proceeds the seller receives, then transaction value can still be considered. Whether an adjustment is made depends on whether the price actually paid or payable includes such proceeds and, if it does not, the availability of sufficient information to determine the amount of such proceeds.

(4) *Related-party transactions where the transaction value is unacceptable.*—Finally, the relationship between the buyer and seller may preclude the application of transaction value. The fact that the buyer and seller are related does not automatically negate using their transaction value; however, the transaction value must be acceptable under prescribed procedures. To be acceptable for transaction value, relationship between the buyer and seller must not have influenced the price actually paid or payable. * * *

Transaction value of identical merchandise or similar merchandise.— If the transaction value of imported merchandise cannot be determined, then the customs value of the imported goods being appraised is the transaction value of identical merchandise. If merchandise identical to the imported goods cannot be found or an acceptable transaction value for such merchandise does not exist, then the customs value is the transaction value of similar merchandise.

The same additions, exclusions, and limitations, previously discussed in determining the transaction value of imported merchandise, also apply in determining the transaction value of identical or similar merchandise.

Besides the data common to all three transaction values, certain factors specifically apply to the transaction value of identical merchandise or similar merchandise. These factors concern the exportation date, the level and quantity of sales, the meaning, and the order of precedence of identical merchandise and of similar merchandise.

(a) *Exportation date.*—The identical merchandise, or similar merchandise, for which a transaction value is being determined must have been sold for export to the United States and exported at or about the same time as the merchandise being appraised.

(b) *Sales level/quantity.*—The transaction value of identical merchandise (or similar merchandise) must be based on sales of identical merchandise (or similar merchandise) at the same commercial level and, in substantially the same quantity, as the sales of the merchandise being appraised. If no such sale exists, then sales at either a different commercial level or in different quantities, or both, can be used, but must be adjusted to take account of any such difference. Any adjustment must be based on sufficient information, that is, information establishing the reasonableness and accuracy of the adjustment.

* * *

Deductive value.—* * *

Basically deductive value is the resale price in the United States after importation of the goods, with deductions for certain items in order to arrive at an import price. Generally, the deductive value is calculated by starting with a unit price and making certain additions to and deductions from that price.

* * *

After determining the appropriate price, packing costs for the merchandise concerned must be added to the price used for deductive value, provided such costs have not otherwise been included. These costs are added, regardless of whether the importer or the buyer incurs the cost. Packing costs include the cost of all containers and coverings of whatever nature; and of packing, whether for labor or materials, used in placing the merchandise in condition, packed ready for shipment to the United States.

Certain other items are not a part of deductive value and must be deducted from the unit price. The items are:

(1) *Commissions or profit and general expenses.*—Any commission usually paid or agreed to be paid, or the addition usually made for profit and general expenses, applicable to sales in the United States of imported merchandise that is of the same class or kind as the merchandise concerned; and regardless of the country of exportation.

(2) *Transportation/insurance costs.*—The usual and associated costs of transporting and insuring the merchandise concerned from the country of exportation to the place of importation in the United States; and from the place of importation to the place of delivery in the United States, provided these costs are not included as a general expense under the preceding paragraph.

* * *

Computed value.—The last basis of appraisement is computed value. If customs valuation cannot be based on any of the values previously discussed, then computed value is considered. This value is also the one the importer can select at entry summary to precede deductive value as a basis of appraisement.

Computed value consists of the sum of the following items:

(1) materials, fabrication, and other processing used in producing the imported merchandise;

(2) profit and general expenses;

(3) any assist, if not included in (a) and (b); and

(4) packing costs.

The cost or value of the materials, fabrication, and other processing of any kind used in producing the imported merchandise is based on information provided by or on behalf of the producer and on the commercial accounts of the producer, if the accounts are consistent with generally accepted accounting principles applied in the country of production of the goods.

The producer's profit and general expenses are used, provided they are consistent with the usual profit and general expenses reflected by producers in the country of exportation in sales of merchandise of the same class or kind as the imported merchandise.

HAYWARD AND LONG, COMPARATIVE VIEWS OF U.S. CUSTOMS VALUATION ISSUES IN LIGHT OF THE U.S. CUSTOMS MODERNIZATION ACT

5 Minn. J. Global Trade 311, 312–17, 324–27 (1996).*

The Customs Modernization Act [of 1994] was the first major overhaul of U.S. customs procedure since the Tariff Act of 1930. Designed to bring U.S. law into compliance with NAFTA and to streamline and update U.S. customs practice in general, the Mod Act amended many sections of the Tariff Act of 1930 and changed other related laws. Although the Mod Act changes little in terms of the actual substance of customs valuation law, it creates a new environment in which traders and Customs officials must work.

Premised on the idea that Customs can maximize voluntary compliance if the trade community is fully informed of its legal obligations, the Mod Act imposes a greater obligation on Customs to publish and otherwise make available information regarding the trade community's rights and responsibilities under Customs practices and related laws. Concurrently, traders have the responsibility to engage in informed compliance. This mutual or "shared responsibility," is the essence of the new U.S. customs procedure. Customs must make its rulings and practices available and the trading community must exercise "reasonable care" in making itself aware of and in following the rules.

* * *

The issue of when and under what authority a payment described as a "royalty" or "license fee" is added to the transaction value is one that has

---

* Copyright © 1996 and reprinted with permission from the Minnesota Journal of Global Trade.

occupied the Customs Service for a number of years. Prior to 1993, Customs focused solely on s 402(b)(1)(D) of the 1979 Trade Agreements Act, the "royalties provision," when dealing with royalty or fee payments, and specifically declined to analyze such payments under s 402(b)(1)(E). Referred to as the "proceeds provision," this latter section requires that proceeds of subsequent resales remitted by the buyer to the seller be added to the transaction value.

Under its prior interpretation of the Trade Agreements Act, as a condition of the sale for export to the United States, Customs added a fee or royalty payment to the transaction value if the buyer paid the fee directly or indirectly to the seller for patents covering processes necessary to manufacture the imported merchandise. This interpretation essentially included any royalty or fee paid by the buyer to the seller, unless the buyer could establish that the payment was distinct from the price actually paid, or that the payment was not a condition of the sale for export to the United States. Customs, however, did not add charges paid for the right to reproduce imported goods in the United States to the transaction value. In addition, if the buyer paid a third party for the right to use a copyright or trademark in the United States, Customs did not consider that payment to be a condition of the sale for export to the United States and the payment was therefore not dutiable.

Under Customs' prior interpretation, it was fairly simple to set up a transaction so that a fee was distinct from the price actually paid, or was not a condition of the sale for export to the United States. As a result, parties were often able to exclude payments which arguably constituted part of the transaction value. Perceiving this situation to be a loophole that Congress did not intend to create when it adopted the Trade Agreements Act. Customs re-evaluated its position on the proceeds provision in 1993. Asserting that the pre-1979 law required inclusion of the payments that were slipping through the cracks, and that Congress did not intend to change the dutiability of these payments when it adopted the 1979 Act, Customs announced that royalty payments would be subject to analysis under both the royalty and the proceeds provisions of the Trade Agreements Act. This means that these royalty payments are potentially dutiable.

Currently, Customs' policy indicates that the dutiability of a payment under the royalty provision is based on a three-prong test. A payment will generally be dutiable under the royalty provision if: (1) the merchandise was manufactured under a patent; (2) if the royalty was for an item or process involved in the production or sale of the imported goods; and (3) if the importer could not have bought the goods without paying the fee.

If the payment escapes duty under the royalty provision, however, Customs may now include it in the transaction value if it is the functional equivalent of proceeds to the seller. A payment is the functional equivalent of proceeds, and thus is likely to be included in the transaction value, if any portion of the fee or royalty accrues directly or indirectly to the seller. * * * In addition, Customs will evaluate payments made by the buyer to a party related to the seller. If these payments function as indirect payments to the seller itself, Customs will also include them in the transaction value.

* * *

LA PERLA FASHIONS, INC. v. UNITED STATES

United States Court of International Trade, 1998.
22 C.I.T. 393, 9 F.Supp.2d 698.

Musgrave, Senior Judge.

Importers and foreign manufacturers have an interest in lowering the overall duties placed on merchandise upon importation. One method of lowering import duties is to reduce the invoice price on the subject merchandise. When merchandise is sold between unrelated parties, an arm's length price is agreed upon, reflecting pressures of market forces, and it is this price that is declared to Customs upon importation. When merchandise is imported from a related party, however, market forces are absent from pricing. Related parties have the ability and opportunity to lower the prices charged to the related importer which proportionally reduces the associated import duties that are imposed as a percentage of the value of the imported merchandise. When the related importer resells to U.S. customers, a three-tiered transaction is created. The net profits made by the exporter on the subject merchandise are unaffected in a three-tiered transaction since the related importer resells to the open market, returning to the exporter any loss of revenue from the reduced-price sale to the importer. This ability and opportunity of import duty evasion motivated Congress to enact protective legislation and to direct Customs to closely scrutinize related party transfer pricing.

On the other hand, Congress, cognizant of the public policy of fostering trade, provided for means by which related parties could prove that their transfer pricing adequately reflected the equivalent of or at least a reasonable approximation of arm's length transactions resulting from the pressures of market forces. Congress enacted the valuation statute to control the methodology Customs employs in determining the basis of valuing imported merchandise. Congress was aware of the competing interests when it drafted the valuation statute. Congress wanted to protect Customs' legitimate income from imports but not at the expense of proper trading relationships. The Court recognizes the tension inherent in the valuation statute as well as the underlying interests involved in its etymology and finds that Customs correctly valued the subject merchandise on the transaction value between La Perla and its U.S. customers for the reasons that follow.

* * *

La Perla first claims that the correct basis for transaction value is the sales between GLP and La Perla under § 1401a(b)(1) since the "transactions between GLP and [La Perla] were *bona fide* sales." As evidence of *bona fide* sales reflecting arm's length purchasing. La Perla asserts that it is responsible for its own bank accounts, accounting and financial records, resale pricing negotiating authority, inventory, risk of non-payment by customers, risk of loss and the authority to accept orders without approval.

Customs valued the subject merchandise based on the sale between La Perla and its U.S. customers. Customs rejected the price between GLP to La Perla since it was affected by their close relationship and, therefore, "irreparably negate [d] a TV." Customs asserts that under the stipulation of facts, where La Perla and Customs agreed that the "relationship between [La Perla] and GLP, and the circumstances of sale between them, affected the prices between them," La Perla is precluded from utilizing the transaction value under § 1401a(b)(1) between the parties as a basis for valuation.

Customs and La Perla argue exhaustively on the agency relationship between GLP and La Perla but the Court finds that the stipulation takes the related party transfer price out of the realm of § 1401a(b)(1) and into the related party provision under § 1401a(b)(2)(B). The key to the resolution of valuation issues involving related parties is establishing an objective market-based price of the subject merchandise. The determination that an agency relationship exists only answers the first requirement of the statute, as transaction value can properly be utilized between related parties if the relationship does not affect the transfer price. The Court recognizes that the statute emphasizes the focus on the transfer price, not the presence of an agency relationship. Once La Perla stipulated that the transfer price was affected by their relationship with GLP, its burden is to prove approximate value under § 1401a (b)(2)(B).

* * *

Since GLP and La Perla are related parties and the transfer price was affected by their relationship, the Court finds that transaction value under § 1401a(b)(1) is inapplicable. At trial, La Perla did not provide evidence, such as volume discounts or reduced expenses, that would account for the price discrepancy between the related parties. La Perla cites many factual similarities with the importer in another valuation case involving a three-tiered transaction, *Wood v. United States*, where the court found that the goods were correctly valued at the price between the related parties. As the Court found in *VWP of America, Inc. v. United States*, "[t]he glaring difference between the two cases is that the parent company in *Wood* sold the subject merchandise to an unrelated third party in the U.S. at the same price" as that charged to the related party, while GLP sold merchandise to La Perla and unrelated third parties at markedly different prices.

* * *

The Court finds that the sales from GLP to its direct U.S. customers provides the necessary comparison transaction with an unrelated party in the U.S. Since the price between La Perla and its U.S. customers is approximately the same as the price GLP sells to unrelated parties in the U.S., the Court finds that this price fairly reflects the market price of the subject merchandise.

* * *

In the instant case the Court finds that there is only one *bona fide* transaction: the sale between La Perla and its U.S. customers. Transaction value cannot be based on a transaction that is found not to be a *bona fide* sale. Therefore, the Court finds that transaction value can only be based on La Perla's price charged to its U.S. customers.

QUESTIONS AND COMMENTS

1. The WTO Agreement on Customs Valuation basically adopted the U.S. approach to valuation. Thus, Section 1401a was not amended when the United States joined the WTO.

2. Of the various valuation methods discussed by the Congressional Report, which one is appropriate to use when Fast Food imports PB&J from China: transaction value, transaction value of similar or identical merchandise, computed value, deductive value? What criteria are used to determine which valuation method will be used? Do you have enough information to determine whether such criteria exist or not?

3. Once a particular valuation method is selected, a second question becomes whether there is sufficient information to make the valuation. For example, what information is needed to determine the transaction value of the PB&J from China? Do we have the necessary facts, or do more need to be added to the problem?

4. Assume that the freight charges of $0.10 per kg. include both transportation from Hong Kong to a U.S. West Coast port and transportation within the U.S. from that port to Fast Food's plant. Are the freight charges on the imported goods includable in their valuation? 19 U.S.C.A. § 1401a seems to distinguish between freight charges within the United States and freight charges outside the United States. To determine how to treat these expenses, consider both 19 U.S.C.A. §§ 1401a(b)(3)(A)(ii) and 1401a(b)(4)(A). Note that one expense item is treated in the definition of "price", while the other is an independent exclusion. Does that make any sense? However, note that transportation expenses within the U.S. are excludable only if "identified separately" from the price *or* any other expense item. This requirement has been enforced at least once. How should the contract with Double Happiness be designed to avoid any problems?

5. Double Happiness has proposed that it will establish a sales office in the United States, import the PB&J into the U.S. by selling to its sales office for only $0.30 per kg., and then have its U.S. sales office sell the PB&J to the Fast Food at the $0.50 (or $0.40) per kg., plus any import duties charged by U.S. customs. Would that lower the valuation of the PB&J, and thus lower the customs duties? How would Customs determine the value of the imported

goods in such a transaction? How would the holding in *La Perla* affect this scheme?

Alternatively, the owners of Double Happiness have some "friends" who would establish a U.S. sales office of a different company. Double Happiness would be willing to sell to that office for $0.30 per kg., and have Fast Food purchase from that office for $0.50 (or $0.40) per kg., plus any import duties charged by U.S. Customs. Would that lower the customs duties? How would Customs determine the value of the imported goods in such a transaction? Consider the analysis in the Hayward and Long excerpt.

6. Finally, what is your advice to Fast Food? Can you state with certainty a precise classification of PB&J under HTS, and therefore a precise amount of tariff duty on them? With enough certainty that a business client can rely on it to the tune of several million dollars? If so, fine.

If not, how do you phrase your advice to Fast Food? Incidentally, Fast Food will be somewhat unhappy to receive an answer of: "Maybe free, maybe 3.2%, maybe even 131.8%. It can be argued to be any of those. And maybe the rate will be levied on just the cost of the product, or maybe it will include the royalty. It is all arguable." The danger of incorrectly assuming a low duty is obvious. The danger of incorrectly assuming a high duty ("playing it safe") is less obvious, but it can cost Fast Food a good opportunity to make large profits. What action do you advise Fast Food to take?

How can you obtain more precise information? Note that an action for declaratory judgment is not likely to help—it will take too long; it will reveal Fast Food's marketing plans to the competition too early; and without the actual importation of goods, it might not yet be "a case or controversy."

7. 19 C.F.R. § 177 provides for prospective rulings. An importer may request a ruling from the Commissioner of Customs on the proper classification of goods whose importation is merely contemplated, and which have not arrived in the United States. Such a request, if properly presented, will be answered by a "ruling letter," which is binding on all Customs Service personnel; but only if the actual import transaction corresponds with the transaction described in the letter requesting the ruling.

8. Judicial review of the decisions of Customs regarding classification, origin or valuation go to the United States Court of International Trade (CIT), which has exclusive jurisdiction. Appeals from the CIT may be made to the Court of Appeals for the Federal Circuit (CAFC). From these specialized courts, appeals are ultimately made to the United States Supreme Court. The U.S. Supreme Court rather remarkably held in *United States v. Mead Corp.*, 533 U.S. 218, 121 S.Ct. 2164, 150 L.Ed.2d 292 (2001), that Customs Service classification rulings are <u>not</u> entitled to full administrative deference. Rather, such rulings are entitled to limited deference depending on their "thoroughness, logic and expertness, fit with prior interpretations, and any other sources of weight." This strikes the authors as strong invitation to litigate classification rulings.

PROBLEM 6.3 NONTARIFF TRADE BARRIERS: SHRIMP FROM INDIA AND BEEF FROM EUROPE

SECTION I. THE SETTING

Two clients bring you seemingly unrelated problems.

A. LOUISIANA SHRIMPERS is a trade association of shrimp industry companies, including shrimpers, processors, canners and distributors. United States regulations, adopted under the Endangered Species Act, require U.S. shrimpers to use "trawler or turtle elimination devices" (TEDs). LOUISIANA SHRIMPERS contested these regulations, but lost before the Fifth Circuit Court of Appeals in a litigation battle that had environmental/conservation groups allied with the Department of Commerce. See 853 F.2d 322 (5th Cir.1988).

LOUISIANA SHRIMPERS, having lost in the courts, then turned to its political allies in Congress. They were persuasive. In 1989, Congress adopted Public Law 101–162 (103 Stat. 988) which instructed the President to negotiate international agreements to protect sea turtles and to ban shrimp imports "which have been harvested with commercial fishing technology which may affect adversely such species of sea turtles."

Specifically, the President must determine and certify to Congress annually whether:

(A) the government of the harvesting nation has provided documentary evidence of the adoption of a regulatory program governing the incidental taking of such sea turtles in the course of such harvesting that is comparable to that of the United States; *and*

(B) the average rate of that incidental taking by the vessels of the harvesting nation is comparable to the average rate of incidental taking of sea turtles by United States vessels in the course of such harvesting; *or*

(C) the particular fishing environment of the harvesting nation does not pose a threat of the incidental taking of such sea turtles in the course of such harvesting.

Shrimp from uncertified harvesting nations cannot be imported into the United States.

The State Department administers the shrimp-turtle certification process. At first, they did so without much enthusiasm. But several lawsuits by environmental groups and LOUISIANA SHRIMPERS pushed the State Department into a broad ban against shrimp imports. See Earth Island Institute et al. v. Secretary of State, 913 F.Supp. 559 (CIT 1995). Shortly thereafter, India, Thailand, Malaysia, and Pakistan filed a complaint with the World Trade Organization asserting that the United States was in breach of its GATT obligations.

The complaint has been heard before a WTO panel under the 1994 Dispute Settlement Understanding. So far, the United States is losing, but an appeal is pending. You are counsel to LOUISIANA SHRIMPERS. They are distressed and would like to be heard somehow in the appeal process. Assuming the United States loses on appeal (as it did), they want to know what are the consequences for Public Law 101–162. They would naturally prefer just about any alternative you can think of other than nullification of this law.

What do you advise?

B. UNITED RANCHERS OF AMERICA is another of your trade associations clients. UNITED RANCHERS used to export lots of beef to Europe. But that was before the Europeans adopted a law (which took effect in 1988) banning the importation of beef from animals treated with fast growth hormones. UNITED RANCHERS cashed in all its political credits in supporting a vigorous campaign by the United States to overcome this law. To make a long battle short, the U.S. finally prevailed before a WTO panel and the Appellate Body early in 1998 and again in 2008. The Appellate Body's 1998 report is excerpted in the Readings for this problem.

UNITED RANCHERS is a bit weary but feels like it "won." As a result of arbitration about what constitutes a "reasonable period of time," the Europeans had until May 13, 1999 to implement the recommendations and rulings concerned, which still has not happened. UNITED RANCHERS would like to know if there is anything they can do to make Europe adhere in a way that at long last opens up their market to hormone-treated U.S. beef.

Meanwhile, in the wake of the "mad cow" disease (BSE, bovine spongiform encephalopathy), the European Union stopped internal trade in British beef but allowed its export to other parts of the world. The United States quickly and without extensive study banned the importation of all British beef and (for good measure) the beef any other European Union nation. In announcing this ban, the United States expressed the fear that the disease had or at least could spread throughout a Europe without internal frontiers. This fear is not groundless. In 1998, the European Union banned internal trade in Portuguese beef for lack of adequate BSE avoidance, while at the same time lifting the ban on internal trade in British beef.

It is widely believed in the scientific community that "mad cow" disease originated when beef carcasses, notably brains, were used in cattle feed. Although scientists are not in agreement, it is believed possible that use of any animal carcasses (sheep, etc.) as feed may also infect live animals. Use of carcasses as animal feed is now prohibited throughout Europe. In the United States, only use of beef carcasses is illegal.

There is no doubt that some humans who ate contaminated "mad cow" beef in Britain came down with Creutzfeld-Jacob disease. What is much less clear is the gestation period of this disease. Studies in Britain suggest that Creutzfeld–Jacob is very slow growing or can lie dormant for years before causing human injury. It is not known how many people may be carrying the disease (estimates range into hundreds of thousands) and whether such carriers can transmit the disease via their blood. The British government has acknowledged hundreds of deaths from Creutzfeld–Jacob disease. The British have also acknowledged many confirmed cases of infected cattle, and have slaughtered millions of cattle in their country. Infected cattle and C–J disease have also been significantly identified in France, Germany, Italy, Spain and Portugal. More recently, Japan, Canada, and the United States are experiencing similar problems. Japan now tests every cow slaughtered in that country. The United States tests way below one percent of all slaughtered cows, with Europe testing about 75 percent.

UNITED RANCHERS used to advertise that no U.S. cattle have ever had "mad cow" disease. Naturally they support the ban against British and other European beef imports. This ban has, economically speaking, helped make up for the loss in revenues from Europe's denial of entry to U.S. hormone-treated beef.

The British, however, have recently filed a complaint with the WTO against the U.S. import ban. The British maintain that this ban violates the Sanitary and Phyto-Sanitary (SPS) Agreement of 1994. The British, being clever, have studied the arguments used by the United States in *Beef Hormones*. In addition, the British assert that the U.S. "mad cow" disease ban is excessive. They say that only a very small percentage of their cattle ever had the disease, that its source has been scientifically identified and remedied, and that there is no longer any public health risk. And the British have some allies in this complaint. The other European nations covered by the U.S. import ban agree and argue, further, that they should never have been included in the first place.

UNITED RANCHERS is beginning to feel like they may have shot themselves in the foot. They come to you seeking advice and counsel for what will undoubtedly be another monumental battle.

SECTION II. FOCUS OF CONSIDERATION

Multilateral GATT negotiations have led to a significant decline in world tariff levies. As steadily as tariff barriers have disappeared, nontariff trade barriers (NTBs) have emerged to retard freer world trade. Health and safety regulations, environmental laws, rules regulating product standards, and customs procedures are frequently said to present NTB problems. It was not surprising therefore that NTBs dominated the Tokyo Round of GATT negotiations during the late 1970s and the Uruguay Round in the late 1980s and early 1990s.

Part A explores United States attempts at exporting its conservation goals for dolphins and sea turtles. These laws are classically "extraterritorial." That is to say, they apply to people and actions located outside the territorial limits of the United States. Extraterritorial jurisdiction is extremely controversial, as we shall also see in other problems. For now, the politically charged question is whether WTO dispute settlement and the GATT agreement provide the means to challenge U.S. assertions of such jurisdiction in the environmental protection and conservation arena. To some, the evolving law of the GATT/WTO demonstrates a loss of sovereignty ... others say the *Shrimp–Turtles* decision proves that trade law will always trump environmental interests.

Part B considers United States-European nontariff trade barriers for beef. Everyone agrees that health protection provisions can be misused for protectionist purposes. Most such measures are enacted without protectionist intent, but with some protectionist effect. There are few such provisions on which all sides will agree. To resolve such disputes, the SPS Agreement calls upon science to furnish unequivocal data. But most scientific data (like most legal rules) is subject to interpretation, and can be argued in several ways. The standards that must be met by the scientific data and the assignment of evidentiary burdens are critical legal issues. Part B presents two scenarios where scientific data is thin.

Articles XI and XX of the GATT, the WTO Dispute Settlement Understanding, and the WTO Sanitary and Phyto-Sanitary Measures Agreement are essential to an analysis of this problem. These materials are found in the Documents Supplement. Web Resources for further study include coverage of the SPS Agreement at *www.wto.org*

PART A.   ENVIRONMENTAL/CONSERVATION LAWS AS NTBs

WIRTH, THE ROLE OF SCIENCE IN THE URUGUAY ROUND AND NAFTA TRADE DISCIPLINES
27 Cornell Int'l L.J. 817 (1994).*

As a general matter, national measures directed at preservation of the environment and protection of public health are subject to the generic requirements of GATT 1947. Fundamental GATT obligations that apply in these areas, as others, include the most-favored-nation principle (nondiscrimination among imported products on the basis of their national origin), national treatment (non-discrimination between foreign and domestic products), and a prohibition on quantitative restrictions for imports or exports.

Article XX of GATT 1947 contains a number of exemptions from the General Agreement for specific categories of national measures. Of particular importance in the field of environment and public health are two express exceptions in article XX of GATT 1947: one in paragraph (b) for measures "necessary to protect human, animal or plant life or health;" and another in paragraph (g) for measures "relating to the conservation of exhaustible natural resources if such measures are made effective in conjunction with restrictions on domestic production or consumption." The two exceptions in the GATT are to be narrowly construed.[10] Moreover, in contrast to the usual situation for resolving disputes over rights in GATT 1947, the burden is on the respondent whose measure is challenged, and not on the complainant, to demonstrate the applicability of one of the enumerated exemptions. * * *

Entirely apart from any consideration of scientific integrity, the "necessary" requirement with respect to measures to protect human, animal, or plant life or health has been interpreted by panels as implying a test that turns on the trade effect of the measure.[12] Similarly, the exception for trade measures to protect exhaustible natural resources has been interpreted to require that the standards in question are "primarily aimed at conservation."[13] Only one of the environmental, conservation, or public health measures examined by dispute settlement panels whose consistency with GATT turned on the availability of these exceptions have met these tests.

DUNOFF, INSTITUTIONAL MISFITS: THE GATT, THE ICJ AND TRADE–ENVIRONMENT DISPUTES

15 Mich.J.Int'l L. 1043 (1994).*

In addition to forbidding outright many types of environmental trade measures, the GATT severely restricts the use of even those measures

---

10. E.g., United States—Restrictions on Imports of Tuna, [hereinafter United States—Tuna Dolphin I Panel Report]. In response to a complaint lodged by Mexico, this panel report addressed an embargo on importation of yellowfin tuna into the United States designed to encourage foreign states to ensure that vessels under their jurisdiction conduct tuna fishing operations so as not to kill or injure dolphin. A second challenge, initiated by the European Union and the Netherlands, addressed a secondary import ban designed to discourage "tuna laundering" by intermediary nations that purchase yellowfin tuna abroad and export it to the United States. United States—Restrictions on Imports of Tuna, [hereinafter United States—Tuna Dolphin II Panel Report]. Both panels concluded that the import prohibitions in question were inconsistent with the United States' obligations pursuant to the GATT. The GATT Council rejected a request by the European Union to adopt the first panel report, in which Mexico was the complainant. In a discussion of the second report, the GATT Council is reported to have rejected a proposal from the United States that would have opened further Council meetings on that case to the public, and Mexico was said to consider requesting adoption of the first report. As of this writing, neither report has been adopted by the GATT Council and hence neither has yet acquired legal force.

12. E.g., United States—Tuna Dolphin I Panel Report, (failure to "exhaust[ ] all options reasonably available ... through measures consistent with the General Agreement" implies lack of necessity pursuant to article XX(b)); Thailand—Restrictions on Importation of and Internal Taxes on Cigarettes, (import restrictions not justified by article XX(b) in light of availability of GATT-consistent or less GATT-inconsistent measures). Cf. United States—Measures Affecting Alcoholic and Malt Beverages, (measures relating to import of beer not least trade restrictive and therefore not "necessary" within meaning of article XX(d), which exempts "measures necessary to secure compliance with laws or regulations which are not inconsistent with" GATT).

13. E.g., United States—Taxes on Automobiles, (regulatory scheme requiring manufacturers and importers to meet minimum average fuel efficiency for all automobiles is intended to promote energy conservation and therefore is primarily aimed at conservation); United States—Tuna Dolphin II Panel Report, (measures taken so as to force other countries to change their policies, and that are effective only if such changes occur, not primarily aimed at conservation); United States—Tuna Dolphin I Panel Report, (limitations on taking marine mammals by foreign fleets established with reference to dolphin kills by U.S. vessels not primarily aimed at conservation) * * *.

that are permitted. This result is achieved through a very narrow interpretation of the Article XX requirement that trade restrictions be "necessary" for the protection of human, animal, or plant life or health.

The meaning of this term was at issue in a GATT challenge by the United States to Thailand's restrictions on imported cigarettes. Although the law at issue had strong protectionist elements, the reasoning used by the Thai Cigarette Panel may threaten measures not designed to protect domestic industries. Transplanting a definition from a different GATT provision, the Panel declared that a measure is "necessary" only "if an alternative measure which it could reasonably be expected to employ and which is not inconsistent with other GATT provisions is available to it." Applying this test, the Panel concluded that Thailand's restrictions on imported cigarettes did not fall within the scope of the Article XX exception. The Panel reasoned that, although cigarette smoking produced adverse health effects, Thailand's restrictions on imported cigarettes were not necessary because the government could protect its citizens by other, less trade restrictive measures. Thus, the Panel suggested, Thailand could safeguard the health of its citizens through the use of labeling requirements and reducing the demand for cigarettes by banning cigarette advertisements.

As the Thai Cigarette and Tuna–Dolphin cases demonstrate, in practice it is almost impossible to meet the requirement that a trade measure be the least GATT inconsistent remedy reasonably available. Astonishingly, no GATT Panel has required that the proposed alternative measure be as effective as the measure actually employed. Creative counsel challenging trade measures should always be able to posit an *ex post facto* measure that is less restrictive on trade.

Labeling requirements appear to be one of the few types of environmental trade measures that GATT panels will deem "necessary." There is a certain logic to this result from the trade perspective: "green" trade bans, taxes, quotas, and the like are government actions that "distort" trade, while labeling schemes permit the market and individual consumers rather than government bureaucrats to decide whether trade in environmentally harmful products will occur. Of course, this rationale ignores the fact that one or more nations may legitimately reach a *political* decision that certain markets should not exist. The narrow reading of Article XX's "necessary" requirement limits significantly the ability of the community of nations to make such political decisions.

WORLD TRADE ORGANIZATION APPELLATE BODY

United States—Import Prohibition of Certain Shrimp and Shrimp Products)	
)	
) AB–1998–4	
)	
United States, *Appellant*) Present:	
India, Malaysia, Pakistan, Thailand,)	
Appellees)	
) Feliciano, Presiding Member	
) Bacchus, Member	
Australia, Ecuador, the European) Lacarte-Muró, Member	
Communities, Hong Kong, China,)	
Mexico and Nigeria, *Third*)	
Participants)	

I. Introduction: Statement of the Appeal

This is an appeal by the United States from certain issues of law and legal interpretations in the Panel Report, *United States—Import Prohibition of Certain Shrimp and Shrimp Products*. Following a joint request for consultations by India, Malaysia, Pakistan and Thailand on 8 October 1996, Malaysia and Thailand requested in a communication dated 9 January 1997, and Pakistan asked in a communication dated 30 January 1997, that the Dispute Settlement Body (the "DSB") establish a panel to examine their complaint regarding a prohibition imposed by the United States on the importation of certain shrimp and shrimp products by Section 609 of Public Law 101–162[5] ("Section 609") and associated regulations and judicial rulings. * * *

The relevant factual and regulatory aspects of this dispute are set out in the Panel Report, in particular at paragraphs 2.1–2.16. Here, we outline the United States measure at stake before the Panel and in these appellate proceedings. The United States issued regulations in 1987 pursuant to the Endangered Species Act of 1973 requiring all United States shrimp trawl vessels to use approved Turtle Excluder Devices ("TEDs") or tow-time restrictions in specified areas where there was a significant mortality of sea turtles in shrimp harvesting.[10] These regulations, which became fully effective in 1990, were modified so as to require the use of approved TEDs at all times and in all areas where there is a likelihood that shrimp trawling will interact with sea turtles, with certain limited exceptions.

Section 609 was enacted on 21 November 1989. Section 609(a) calls upon the United States Secretary of State, in consultation with the Secretary of Commerce, *inter alia*, to "initiate negotiations as soon as possible for the development of bilateral or multilateral agreements with other nations for the protection and conservation of . . . sea turtles" and

---

5. 16 United States Code (U.S.C.) § 1537.

10. 52 Fed. Reg. 24244, 29 June 1987 (the "1987 Regulations"). Five species of sea turtles fell under the regulations: loggerhead (*Caretta caretta*), Kemp's ridley (*Lepidochelys kempi*), green (*Chelonia mydas*), leatherback (*Dermochelys coriacea*) and hawksbill (*Eretmochelys imbricata*).

to "initiate negotiations as soon as possible with all foreign governments which are engaged in, or which have persons or companies engaged in, commercial fishing operations which, as determined by the Secretary of Commerce, may affect adversely such species of sea turtles, for the purpose of entering into bilateral and multilateral treaties with such countries to protect such species of sea turtles; . . . ." Section 609(b)(1) imposed, not later than 1 May 1991, an import ban on shrimp harvested with commercial fishing technology which may adversely affect sea turtles. Section 609(b)(2) provides that the import ban on shrimp will not apply to harvesting nations that are certified. Two kinds of annual certifications are required for harvesting nations, details of which were further elaborated in regulatory guidelines in 1991, 1993 and 1996: First, certification shall be granted to countries with a fishing environment which does not pose a threat of the incidental taking of sea turtles in the course of shrimp harvesting. According to the 1996 Guidelines, the Department of State "shall certify any harvesting nation meeting the following criteria without the need for action on the part of the government of the harvesting nation: (a) Any harvesting nation without any of the relevant species of sea turtles occurring in waters subject to its jurisdiction; (b) Any harvesting nation that harvests shrimp exclusively by means that do not pose a threat to sea turtles, *e.g.*, any nation that harvests shrimp exclusively by artisanal means; or (c) Any nation whose commercial shrimp trawling operations take place exclusively in waters subject to its jurisdiction in which sea turtles do not occur."

Second, certification shall be granted to harvesting nations that provide documentary evidence of the adoption of a regulatory program governing the incidental taking of sea turtles in the course of shrimp trawling that is comparable to the United States program *and* where the average rate of incidental taking of sea turtles by their vessels is comparable to that of United States vessels. According to the 1996 Guidelines, the Department of State assesses the regulatory program of the harvesting nation and certification shall be made if the program includes: (i) the required use of TEDs that are "comparable in effectiveness to those used in the United States. Any exceptions to this requirement must be comparable to those of the United States program . . ."; and (ii) "a credible enforcement effort that includes monitoring for compliance and appropriate sanctions." The regulatory program may be in the form of regulations, or may, in certain circumstances, take the form of a voluntary arrangement between industry and government. Other measures that the harvesting nation undertakes for the protection of sea turtles will also be taken into account in making the comparability determination. The average incidental take rate "will be deemed comparable if the harvesting nation requires the use of TEDs in a manner comparable to that of the U.S. program . . . ."

* * *

V. Panel Proceedings and Non-requested Information

In the course of the proceedings before the Panel, on 28 July 1997, the Panel received a brief from the Center for Marine Conservation ("CMC") and the Center for International Environmental Law ("CIEL"). Both are non-governmental organizations. On 16 September 1997, the Panel received another brief, this time from the World Wide Fund for Nature. The Panel acknowledged receipt of the two briefs, which the non-governmental organizations also sent directly to the parties to this dispute. The complaining parties—India, Malaysia, Pakistan and Thailand—requested the Panel not to consider the contents of the briefs in dealing with the dispute. In contrast, the United States urged the Panel to avail itself of any relevant information in the two briefs, as well as in any other similar communications. * * *

The comprehensive nature of the authority of a panel to "seek" information and technical advice from "any individual or body" it may consider appropriate, or from "any relevant source", should be underscored. This authority embraces more than merely the choice and evaluation of the *source* of the information or advice which it may seek. A panel's authority includes the authority to decide *not to seek* such information or advice at all. We consider that a panel also has the authority to *accept or reject* any information or advice which it may have sought and received, or to *make some other appropriate disposition* thereof. It is particularly within the province and the authority of a panel to determine *the need for information and advice* in a specific case, to ascertain the *acceptability* and *relevancy* of information or advice received, and to decide *what weight to ascribe to that information or advice* or to conclude that no weight at all should be given to what has been received.

* * *

Article XX(g): Provisional Justification of Section 609

In claiming justification for its measure, the United States primarily invokes Article XX(g). Justification under Article XX(b) is claimed only in the alternative; that is, the United States suggests that we should look at Article XX(b) only if we find that Section 609 does not fall within the ambit of Article XX(g). We proceed, therefore, to the first tier of the analysis of Section 609 and to our consideration of whether it may be characterized as provisionally justified under the terms of Article XX(g).

Paragraph (g) of Article XX covers measures:

> relating to the conservation of exhaustible natural resources if such measures are made effective in conjunction with restrictions on domestic production or consumption;

"Exhaustible Natural Resources"

We begin with the threshold question of whether Section 609 is a measure concerned with the conservation of "exhaustible natural resources" within the meaning of Article XX(g). The Panel, of course, with its "chapeau-down" approach, did not make a finding on whether the sea turtles that Section 609 is designed to conserve constitute "exhaustible natural resources" for purposes of Article XX(g). In the proceedings before the Panel, however, the parties to the dispute argued this issue vigorously and extensively. India, Pakistan and Thailand contended that a "reasonable interpretation" of the term "exhaustible" is that the term refers to "finite resources such as minerals, rather than biological or renewable resources." * * *

We are not convinced by these arguments. Textually, Article XX(g) is *not* limited to the conservation of "mineral" or "non-living" natural resources. The complainants' principal argument is rooted in the notion that "living" natural resources are "renewable" and therefore cannot be "exhaustible" natural resources. We do not believe that "exhaustible" natural resources and "renewable" natural resources are mutually exclusive. One lesson that modern biological sciences teach us is that living species, though in principle, capable of reproduction and, in that sense, "renewable", are in certain circumstances indeed susceptible of depletion, exhaustion and extinction, frequently because of human activities. Living resources are just as "finite" as petroleum, iron ore and other non-living resources.

The words of Article XX(g), "exhaustible natural resources", were actually crafted more than 50 years ago. They must be read by a treaty interpreter in the light of contemporary concerns of the community of nations about the protection and conservation of the environment. While Article XX was not modified in the Uruguay Round, the preamble attached to the *WTO Agreement* shows that the signatories to that Agreement were, in 1994, fully aware of the importance and legitimacy of environmental protection as a goal of national and international policy. The preamble of the *WTO Agreement*—which informs not only the GATT 1994, but also the other covered agreements—explicitly acknowledges "the objective of *sustainable development*":

* * *

From the perspective embodied in the preamble of the *WTO Agreement*, we note that the generic term "natural resources" in Article XX(g) is not "static" in its content or reference but is rather "by definition, evolutionary". * * *

We turn next to the issue of whether the living natural resources sought to be conserved by the measure are "exhaustible" under Article XX(g). That this element is present in respect of the five species of sea turtles here involved appears to be conceded by all the participants and third participants in this case. The exhaustibility of sea turtles would in fact have been very difficult to controvert since all of the seven recognized species of sea turtles are today listed in Appendix 1 of the Convention on International Trade in Endangered Species of Wild Fauna and Flora

("CITES"). The list in Appendix 1 includes "all species *threatened with extinction* which are or may be affected by trade." (emphasis added)

* * *

"Relating to the Conservation of [Exhaustible Natural Resources]"

Article XX(g) requires that the measure sought to be justified be one which "relat[es] to" the conservation of exhaustible natural resources. In making this determination, the treaty interpreter essentially looks into the relationship between the measure at stake and the legitimate policy of conserving exhaustible natural resources. * * *

In the present case, we must examine the relationship between the general structure and design of the measure here at stake, Section 609, and the policy goal it purports to serve, that is, the conservation of sea turtles.

* * *

In its general design and structure, therefore, Section 609 is not a simple, blanket prohibition of the importation of shrimp imposed without regard to the consequences (or lack thereof) of the mode of harvesting employed upon the incidental capture and mortality of sea turtles. Focusing on the design of the measure here at stake, it appears to us that Section 609, *cum* implementing guidelines, is not disproportionately wide in its scope and reach in relation to the policy objective of protection and conservation of sea turtle species. The means are, in principle, reasonably related to the ends. The means and ends relationship between Section 609 and the legitimate policy of conserving an exhaustible, and, in fact, endangered species, is observably a close and real one, a relationship that is every bit as substantial as that which we found in *United States— Gasoline* between the EPA baseline establishment rules and the conservation of clean air in the United States.

In our view, therefore, Section 609 is a measure "relating to" the conservation of an exhaustible natural resource within the meaning of Article XX(g) of the GATT 1994.

"If Such Measures are Made Effective in conjunction with Restrictions on Domestic Production or Consumption"

* * *

In this case, we need to examine whether the restrictions imposed by Section 609 with respect to imported shrimp are also imposed in respect of shrimp caught by United States shrimp trawl vessels.

We earlier noted that Section 609, enacted in 1989, addresses the mode of harvesting of imported shrimp only. However, two years earlier, in 1987, the United States issued regulations pursuant to the Endangered Species Act requiring all United States shrimp trawl vessels to use approved TEDs, or to restrict the duration of tow-times, in specified areas where there was significant incidental mortality of sea turtles in shrimp trawls. These regulations became fully effective in 1990 and were later modified. They now require United States shrimp trawlers to use approved TEDs "in areas and at times when there is a likelihood of intercepting sea turtles", with certain limited exceptions. Penalties for violation of the Endangered Species Act, or the regulations issued thereunder, include civil and criminal sanctions. The United States government currently relies on monetary sanctions and civil penalties for enforcement. The government has the ability to seize shrimp catch from trawl vessels fishing in United States waters and has done so in cases of egregious violations. We believe that, in principle, Section 609 is an even-handed measure.

Accordingly, we hold that Section 609 is a measure made effective in conjunction with the restrictions on domestic harvesting of shrimp, as required by Article XX(g).

The Introductory Clauses of Article XX: Characterizing Section 609 under the Chapeau's Standards

* * *

Although provisionally justified under Article XX(g), Section 609, if it is ultimately to be justified as an exception under Article XX, must also satisfy the requirements of the introductory clauses—the "chapeau"—of Article XX, * * *

We commence the second tier of our analysis with an examination of the ordinary meaning of the words of the chapeau. The precise language of the chapeau requires that a measure not be applied in a manner which would constitute a means of "arbitrary or unjustifiable discrimination between countries where the same conditions prevail" or a "disguised restriction on international trade." There are three standards contained in the chapeau: first, arbitrary discrimination between countries where the same conditions prevail; second, unjustifiable discrimination between countries where the same conditions prevail; and third, a disguised restriction on international trade. In order for a measure to be applied in a manner which would constitute "arbitrary or unjustifiable discrimination between countries where the same conditions prevail", three elements must exist. First, the application of the measure must result in *discrimination*. As we stated in *United States—Gasoline*, the nature and quality of this discrimination is different from the discrimination in the treatment of products which was already found to be inconsistent with one of the substantive obligations of the GATT 1994, such as Articles I, III or XI. Second, the discrimination must be *arbitrary* or *unjustifiable* in character. We will examine this element of *arbitrariness* or *unjustifiability* in detail below. Third, this discrimination must occur *between countries where the same conditions prevail*. In *United States—Gasoline*, we accepted the assumption of the participants in that appeal that such discrimination could occur not only between different exporting Members, but also between exporting Members and the importing Member concerned. Thus, the standards embodied in the language of the chapeau are not only different from the requirements of Article XX(g); they are also different from the standard used in determining that Section 609 is violative of the substantive rules of Article XI:1 of the GATT 1994.

* * *

In our view, the language of the chapeau makes clear that each of the exceptions in paragraphs (a) to (j) of Article XX is a *limited and conditional* exception from the substantive obligations contained in the other provisions of the GATT 1994, that is to say, the ultimate availability of the exception is subject to the compliance by the invoking Member with the requirements of the chapeau. This interpretation of the chapeau is confirmed by its negotiating history. The language initially proposed by the United States in 1946 for the chapeau of what would later become Article XX was unqualified and unconditional. Several proposals were made during the First Session of the Preparatory Committee of the United Nations Conference on Trade and Employment in 1946 suggesting modifications. In November 1946, the United Kingdom proposed that "in order to prevent abuse of the exceptions of Article 32 [which would subsequently become Article XX]", the chapeau of this provision should be qualified. This proposal was generally accepted, subject to later review of its precise wording. Thus, the negotiating history of Article XX confirms that the paragraphs of Article XX set forth *limited and conditional* exceptions from the obligations of the substantive provisions of the GATT. Any measure, to qualify finally for exception, must also satisfy the requirements of the chapeau. This is a fundamental part of the balance of rights and obligations struck by the original framers of the GATT 1947.

The chapeau of Article XX is, in fact, but one expression of the principle of good faith. This principle, at once a general principle of law and a general principle of international law, controls the exercise of rights by states. One application of this general principle, the application widely known as the doctrine of *abus de droit*, prohibits the abusive exercise of a state's rights and enjoins that whenever the assertion of a right "impinges on the field covered by [a] treaty obligation, it must be exercised bona fide, that is to say, reasonably." An abusive exercise by a Member of its own treaty right thus results in a breach of the treaty rights of the other Members and, as well, a violation of the treaty obligation of the Member so acting. Having said this, our task here is to interpret the language of the chapeau, seeking additional interpretative guidance, as appropriate, from the general principles of international law.

The task of interpreting and applying the chapeau is, hence, essentially the delicate one of locating and marking out a line of equilibrium between the right of a Member to invoke an exception under Article XX and the rights of the other Members under varying substantive provisions (e.g., Article XI) of the GATT 1994, so that neither of the competing rights will cancel out the other and thereby distort and nullify or impair the balance of rights and obligations constructed by the Members themselves in that Agreement. The location of the line of equilibrium, as expressed in the chapeau, is not fixed and unchanging; the line moves as the kind and the shape of the measures at stake vary and as the facts making up specific cases differ.

With these general considerations in mind, we address now the issue of whether the *application* of the United States measure, although the measure itself falls within the terms of Article XX(g), nevertheless constitutes "a means of arbitrary or unjustifiable discrimination between countries where the same conditions prevail" or "a disguised restriction on international trade". We address, in other words, whether the application of this measure constitutes an abuse or misuse of the provisional justification made available by Article XX(g). We note, preliminarily, that the application of a measure may be characterized as amounting to an abuse or misuse of an exception of Article XX not only when the detailed operating provisions of the measure prescribe the arbitrary or unjustifiable activity, but also where a measure, otherwise fair and just on its face, is actually applied in an arbitrary or unjustifiable manner. The standards of the chapeau, in our view, project both substantive and procedural requirements.

"Unjustifiable Discrimination"

We scrutinize first whether Section 609 has been applied in a manner constituting "unjustifiable discrimination between countries where the same conditions prevail". Perhaps the most conspicuous flaw in this measure's application relates to its intended and actual coercive effect on the specific policy decisions made by foreign governments, Members of the WTO. Section 609, in its application, is, in effect, an economic embargo which requires *all other exporting Members*, if they wish to exercise their GATT rights, to adopt *essentially the same* policy (together with an approved enforcement program) as that applied to, and enforced on, United States domestic shrimp trawlers. As enacted by the Congress of the United States, the *statutory* provisions of Section 609(b)(2)(A) and (B) do not, in themselves, *require* that other WTO Members adopt *essentially the same* policies and enforcement practices as the United States. Viewed alone, the statute appears to permit a degree of discretion or flexibility in how the standards for determining comparability might be applied, in practice, to other countries. However, any flexibility that may have been intended by Congress when it enacted the statutory provision has been effectively eliminated in the implementation of that policy through the 1996 Guidelines promulgated by the Department of State and through the practice of the administrators in making certification determinations.

* * *

The actual *application* of the measure, through the implementation of the 1996 Guidelines and the regulatory practice of administrators, *requires* other WTO Members to adopt a regulatory program that is not merely *comparable*, but rather *essentially the same*, as that applied to the United States shrimp trawl vessels. Thus, the effect of the application of Section 609 is to establish a rigid and unbending standard by which United States officials determine whether or not countries will be certified, thus granting or refusing other countries the right to export shrimp to the United States. Other specific policies and measures that an exporting country may have adopted for the protection and conservation of sea turtles are not taken into account, in practice, by the administrators making the comparability determination.

* * *

A propos this failure to have prior consistent recourse to diplomacy as an instrument of environmental protection policy, which produces discriminatory impacts on countries exporting shrimp to the United States with which no international agreements are reached or even seriously attempted, a number of points must be made. First, the Congress of the United States expressly recognized the importance of securing international agreements for the protection and conservation of the sea turtle species in enacting this law. * * *

Second, the protection and conservation of highly migratory species of sea turtles, that is, the very policy objective of the measure, demands concerted and cooperative efforts on the part of the many countries whose waters are traversed in the course of recurrent sea turtle migrations. The need for, and the appropriateness of, such efforts have been recognized in the WTO itself as well as in a significant number of other international instruments and declarations. * * *

Third, the United States did negotiate and conclude one regional international agreement for the protection and conservation of sea turtles: The Inter–American Convention. This Convention was opened for signature on 1 December 1996 and has been signed by five countries, in addition to the United States, and four of these countries are currently certified under Section 609. * * *

The Inter–American Convention thus provides convincing demonstration that an alternative course of action was reasonably open to the United States for securing the legitimate policy goal of its measure, a course of action other than the unilateral and non-consensual procedures of the import prohibition under Section 609. It is relevant to observe that an import prohibition is, ordinarily, the heaviest "weapon" in a Member's armoury of trade measures. The record does not, however, show that serious efforts were made by the United States to negotiate similar agreements with any other country or group of countries before (and, as far as the record shows, after) Section 609 was enforced on a world-wide basis on 1 May 1996. Finally, the record also does not show that the appellant, the United States, attempted to have recourse to such international mechanisms as exist to achieve cooperative efforts to protect and conserve sea turtles before imposing the import ban.

Clearly, the United States negotiated seriously with some, but not with other Members (including the appellees), that export shrimp to the United States. The effect is plainly discriminatory and, in our view, unjustifiable. The unjustifiable nature of this discrimination emerges clearly when we consider the cumulative effects of the failure of the United States to pursue negotiations for establishing consensual means of protection and conservation of the living marine resources here involved, notwithstanding the explicit statutory direction in Section 609 itself to initiate negotiations as soon as possible for the development of bilateral and multilateral agreements. The principal consequence of this failure may be seen in the resulting unilateralism evident in the application of Section 609. As we have emphasized earlier, the policies relating to the necessity for use of particular kinds of TEDs in various maritime areas, and the operating details of these policies, are all shaped by the Department of State, without the participation of the exporting Members. The system and processes of certification are established and administered by the United States agencies alone. The decision-making involved in the grant, denial or withdrawal of certification to the exporting Members, is, accordingly, also unilateral. The unilateral character of the application of Section 609 heightens the disruptive and discriminatory influence of the import prohibition and underscores its unjustifiability.

The application of Section 609, through the implementing guidelines together with administrative practice, also resulted in other differential treatment among various countries desiring certification. Under the 1991 and 1993 Guidelines, to be certifiable, fourteen countries in the wider Caribbean/western Atlantic region had to commit themselves to require the use of TEDs on all commercial shrimp trawling vessels by 1 May 1994. These fourteen countries had a "phase-in" period of three years during which their respective shrimp trawling sectors could adjust to the requirement of the use of TEDs. With respect to all other countries exporting shrimp to the United States (including the appellees, India, Malaysia, Pakistan and Thailand), on 29 December 1995, the United States Court of International Trade directed the Department of State to apply the import ban on a world-wide basis not later than 1 May 1996. On 19 April 1996, the 1996 Guidelines were issued by the Department of State bringing shrimp harvested in *all* foreign countries within the scope of Section 609, effective 1 May 1996. Thus, all countries that were not among the fourteen in the wider Caribbean/western Atlantic region had only four months to implement the requirement of compulsory use of TEDs. We acknowledge that the greatly differing periods for putting into operation the requirement for use of TEDs resulted from decisions of the Court of International Trade. Even so, this does not relieve the United States of the legal consequences of the discriminatory impact of the decisions of that Court. The United States, like all other Members of the WTO and of the general community of states, bears responsibility for acts of all its departments of government, including its judiciary.

* * *

Differing treatment of different countries desiring certification is also observable in the differences in the levels of effort made by the United States in transferring the required TED technology to specific countries. Far greater efforts to transfer that technology successfully were made to certain exporting countries—basically the fourteen wider Caribbean/western Atlantic countries cited earlier—than to other exporting countries, including the appellees. The level of these efforts is probably related to the length of the "phase-in" periods granted—the longer the "phase-in" period, the higher the possible level of efforts at technology transfer. Because compliance with the requirements of certification realistically assumes successful TED technology transfer, low or merely nominal efforts at achieving that transfer will, in all probability, result in fewer countries being able to satisfy the certification requirements under Section 609, within the very limited "phase-in" periods allowed them.

When the foregoing differences in the means of application of Section 609 to various shrimp exporting countries are considered in their cumulative effect, we find, and so hold, that those differences in treatment constitute "unjustifiable discrimination" between exporting countries desiring certification in order to gain access to the United States shrimp market within the meaning of the chapeau of Article XX.

"Arbitrary Discrimination"

We next consider whether Section 609 has been applied in a manner constituting "arbitrary discrimination between countries where the same conditions prevail". We have already observed that Section 609, in its application, imposes a single, rigid and unbending requirement that countries applying for certification under Section 609(b)(2)(A) and (B) adopt a comprehensive regulatory program that is essentially the same as the United States' program, without inquiring into the appropriateness of that program for the conditions prevailing in the exporting countries. Furthermore, there is little or no flexibility in how officials make the determination for certification pursuant to these provisions. In our view, this rigidity and inflexibility also constitute "arbitrary discrimination" within the meaning of the chapeau.

* * *

In reaching these conclusions, we wish to underscore what we have *not* decided in this appeal. We have *not* decided that the protection and preservation of the environment is of no significance to the Members of the WTO. Clearly, it is. We have *not* decided that the sovereign nations that are Members of the WTO cannot adopt effective measures to protect endangered species, such as sea turtles. Clearly, they can and should. And we have *not* decided that sovereign states should not act together bilaterally, plurilaterally or multilaterally, either within the WTO or in other international fora, to protect endangered species or to otherwise protect the environment. Clearly, they should and do.

What we *have* decided in this appeal is simply this: although the measure of the United States in dispute in this appeal serves an environmental objective that is recognized as legitimate under paragraph (g) of Article XX of the GATT 1994, this measure has been applied by the United States in a manner which constitutes arbitrary and unjustifiable discrimination between Members of the WTO, contrary to the requirements of the chapeau of Article XX. For all of the specific reasons outlined in this Report, this measure does not qualify for the exemption that Article XX of the GATT 1994 affords to measures which serve certain recognized, legitimate environmental purposes but which, at the same time, are not applied in a manner that constitutes a means of arbitrary or unjustifiable discrimination between countries where the same conditions prevail or a disguised restriction on international trade. As we emphasized in *United States—Gasoline*, WTO Members are free to adopt their own policies aimed at protecting the environment as long as, in so doing, they fulfill their obligations and respect the rights of other Members under the *WTO Agreement*.

QUESTIONS AND COMMENTS

1. The heart of the complaint against the U.S. import ban on shrimp caught without turtle excluder devices (TEDs) is that it violates Article XI of the GATT. What exactly does Article XI prohibit? Do you agree that the U.S. ban is caught by Article XI?

2. The heart of the U.S. defense is that Article XX of the GATT provides general exceptions to Article XI that embrace the U.S. ban. Do you agree as regards Article XX(b) ... measures "necessary to protect human, animal or plant life or health"? And Article XX(g) ... measures "relating to the conservation of exhaustible natural resources"? And what about the "chapeau" (opening language) to Article XX which requires that the U.S. ban not be applied "in a manner which would constitute a means of arbitrary or unjustifiable discrimination between countries where the same conditions prevail, or a disguised restriction on international trade"?

3. The *Tuna–Dolphin* decisions I and II, footnoted in the Wirth excerpt, were never "adopted" under the old GATT (pre-WTO) dispute settlement process. Should that diminish their value as "precedent" in the *Shrimp–Turtles* dispute before the World Trade Organization? How much reliance would you place on their reasoning? What is the significance of the differences between *Tuna–Dolphin I* and *Tuna–Dolphin II*?

4. Arguably, the *Tuna-Dolphin* dispute was more about "animal rights" than endangered species. The sea turtles at issue are endangered, as the Convention on International Trade in Endangered Species of Wild Fauna and Flora recognizes. Should that make a difference?

5. The *Shrimp–Turtles* panel consulted with an outside panel of advisory experts (as allowed under Article 13.2 of the WTO Dispute Settlement Understanding). Three experts were chosen from the lists put forward by the complainants, and two from the United States list. All three of the former were members of the International Union for the Conservation of Nature, two

from Australia and one from Malaysia. The two U.S. experts were a conservationist who publishes "Marine Turtle Newsletter" and a sea turtle biologist. These five panelists were unable to agree on all the issues put to them, including: (1) the status of sea turtles in the complainants waters; (2) their migratory patterns; (3) the relative effectiveness of TEDs; (4) the relationship between shrimp trawling to sea turtle conservation in the complainants waters; and (5) the socio-economic conditions of the shrimping industry in the complainants' territory.

Do you see any influence of these experts in the *Shrimp–Turtles* decision? Should WTO panels rely on experts for fact-finding?

6. The Preamble to the Agreement Establishing the WTO recognizes that trade relations should be conducted, inter alia, to allow for "the optimal use of world resources in accordance with the objective of sustainable development" seeking "both to protect and preserve the environment and to enhance the means for doing so consistent with respective needs and concerns at different levels of economic development." Does this language support the U.S. position? That of the complainants? Should it influence the *Shrimp–Turtles* dispute?

7. Several non-governmental organizations (NGOs) submitted amicus briefs supporting the import ban to the *Shrimp–Turtles* panel. Is there any authority under the DSU for such submissions? The panel refused to accept these briefs. A factual portion of one of the NGO briefs was then appended to the second written submission of the United States. The panel accepted this appendage. What is the objection to NGO participation in WTO dispute settlement? More broadly, are there any private remedies or is WTO dispute settlement purely an intergovernmental process?

8. *Tuna–Dolphin* and *Shrimp–Turtles* show the international reaction to United States attempts to exclude foreign-made products on the basis of the process by which they were made. There was no difference between the final composition of the excluded products and the composition of other products which were allowed entry. Is the distinction between production processes and product attributes relevant to GATT law?

9. Another issue concerns WTO dispute settlement secrecy. Panel and Appellate Body hearings have traditionally been held *in camera*. This secrecy is a product of the diplomatic heritage of the GATT and WTO. It contrasts with fair and open legal processes found in courts and tribunals around the world. After much criticism, DSU hearings have become much more public, even sometimes televised!

10. Tuna exporting nations that join the Panama Declaration, a multilateral set of principles to protect dolphins from tuna fishermen, may avoid the U.S. Marine Mammal Protection Act. The Panama Declaration was agreed in October 1995 by the United States and eleven Nations (Belize, Colombia, Costa Rica, Ecuador, France, Honduras, Mexico, Panama, Spain, Vanuatu and Venezuela). The U.S. Congress authorized the lifting of the tuna import ban for Panama Declaration adherents in 1997. This is exactly the kind of multilateral accord that opponents of U.S. unilateralism and extraterritorial jurisdiction support. Nevertheless, in 2008, Mexico initiated WTO dispute proceedings against U.S. "dolphin-safe" label rules and the Ninth Circuit

decision, *Earth Island Institute v. Hogarth*, 494 F.3d 757 (2007) requiring zero use of purse seine nets for "dolphin-safe" tuna labels. In 2010, the U.S. instituted NAFTA dispute proceedings seeking to force Mexico to withdraw its WTO complaint and refile it under NAFTA. As the Folsom excerpt in the next problem indicates, the U.S., Mexico and Canada agreed to resolve "standards" disputes exclusively under NAFTA Chapter 20, applying nontariff trade barrier rules that favor individual national laws. In 2011, a WTO panel held in favor of Mexico complaint, which Mexico declined to refile under NAFTA.

11. The United States lost the *Shrimp* dispute. What must it do to comply?

12. Exports from Asian (especially Vietnamese) shrimp farmers (exempt from turtle exclusion issues) have been subjected to U.S. antidumping tariffs. Some of these customs revenues were remitted under the Byrd Amendment by the U.S. government to American shrimpers. See Problem 7.2.

PART B. PUBLIC HEALTH REGULATIONS AS NTBs

HUDEC, 'CIRCUMVENTING' DEMOCRACY: THE POLITICAL MORALITY OF TRADE NEGOTIATIONS

25 Int'l Law and Politics 311 (1993).*

Modern international trade policy in the United States began in 1930 with the enactment of one of the most perfectly "democratic" statutes ever enacted, the Tariff Act of 1930, better known as the Smoot–Hawley tariff. The legislation originated as an effort to raise tariffs on certain agricultural imports as a way of protecting U.S. farmers from very low prices prevailing on the world commodity markets. To secure the necessary votes, the Act's sponsors engaged in a process known as "log-rolling" by offering to support tariff increases for a particular legislator's local industries in return for that legislator's support for their own proposed increases. By the time it was enacted, Smoot–Hawley contained a tariff increase for just about every U.S. economic interest with enough wit to have its supporters place a telephone call to their representatives in Congress. The overall increase in tariffs was massive, sharply reducing imports into the United States. The rest of the world responded promptly by imposing equivalent or more restrictive trade barriers, causing U.S. exports to fall as much or more than U.S. imports.

* * * The scramble for higher and higher tariffs in 1930 was an expression of will by a democratic electorate that was systematically unable or unwilling to appreciate the all-but-certain reciprocal trade actions foreign governments would take. The knowledge was available, but there was something about the legislative setting—the Gold Rush atmosphere, the desire not to be left out—that obliterated whatever appreciation there might have been of an international dimension. If an international trade negotiation does nothing else, it at least presents a demonstration of the international consequences of a government's proposed action, reduced to concrete form in the reciprocal obligations being offered by other governments. The electorate can see the cost of higher tariffs in terms that are easily understood.

* * *

It might be argued that tariff-making is not a good example for our purposes, because it is not the sort of "domestic health or welfare regulation" referred to in our question. Health and welfare issues are different, it is often said, because they involve questions of risk tolerance or wealth redistribution that are, at the same time, both extremely important to the electorate and, there being no scientific answers, most in need of being answered by direct expression of electoral preference. Only the people can legitimately decide how much more the rich must pay in taxes, or how big a margin of safety there should be against the risk of tainted chicken meat.

* * *

Nevertheless, to maintain the sympathy of my audience, I will shift the rest of this brief analysis to a discussion of international negotiations about health and sanitary measures.

Since Arkansas chickens have been much in the news lately and are likely to remain so, let's take as our text a statute called the Poultry Products Inspection Act (PPIA). As enacted in 1957, Section 17 of the PPIA barred the importation of poultry that was not, *inter alia,* "healthful, wholesome, [and] fit for human food * * *." The Secretary of Agriculture promulgated regulations requiring that the imported poultry have been subject to processing and inspection standards "at least equal to" those employed in the United States. In the massive Food Security Act of 1985, known popularly as the 1985 Farm Bill, Senator David Pryor of Arkansas submitted an amendment adding a final subsection to Section 17 which, in effect, substituted "same as" for "at least equal to." The amendment meant that any difference between the foreign sanitary regime and the U.S. regime, regardless of whether or not it had any effect on the sanitary condition of the chicken, would result in the imported chicken being excluded from the United States. * * *

The new "same as" standard is typical of much sanitary legislation around the world. Whatever its justification, the statute does impose a competitive disadvantage upon foreign suppliers. It requires the foreign producer to set up a separate production line—perhaps even a separate facility—in order to continue exporting. Local U.S. producers, by comparison, can do all their production on just one production line tailored to U.S. regulations. The protective effect of such legislation makes it very popular with local producers.

Given that the statute has a protective effect, it remains to be determined whether the protective effect is justified. The answer could be yes, or no. It could be that the USDA has proved unable to evaluate other sanitary regimes effectively, and as a result of its own ineptitude has allowed a significant amount of tainted chicken to enter the country. If so, then the "same as" test would or could be justified as the only effective means of assuring the importation of wholesome chicken. If that were the case, the trade restraint would be deemed justified and would be legal under either GATT or any other international trade agreement.

On the other hand, the legislation could be pure and unqualified protectionism. * * *

* * * As noted above, the 1985 "same as" amendment was part of the 1985 Farm Bill, that wonderful once-every-five-years circus in which Congress brings together every rent-seeking interest in agriculture for a log-rolling contest. Everyone helps everyone else find a place at the trough. And also like Smoot–Hawley, very few foreign interests or international consequences are visible, or heard from, in this setting. Protectionism tends to be traded between legislators as though it were a free good.

It is difficult to believe that the legislative expression of electoral preferences we find in these protectionist sanitary laws is any more legitimate or "democratic" than the expression of electoral will achieved by the process of international negotiations plus implementing legislation. If anything, I would argue that the contrary is true. But the real point, surely, is that discussing the issue in terms of democracy is a red herring. Even worse, it is a broad and sweeping red herring that the protectionists can use as effectively as the well-intentioned environmental or consumer advocates.

* * *

WORLD TRADE ORGANIZATION APPELLATE BODY

EC Measures Concerning Meat and Meat Products (Hormones)	))) AB–1997–4
European Communities, *Appellant/Appellee*	)) Present:)
United States, *Appellant/Appellee*	) Feliciano, Presiding Member
Canada, *Appellant/Appellee*	) Ehlermann, Member) Matsushita, Member
Australia, New Zealand and Norway, *Third Participants*	))

I. Introduction: Statement of the Appeal

The European Communities, the United States and Canada appeal from certain issues of law and legal interpretations in the Panel Reports, *EC Measures Concerning Meat and Meat Products (Hormones)*. These two Panel Reports, circulated to Members of the World Trade Organization ("WTO") on 18 August 1997, were rendered by two Panels composed of the same three persons. These Panel Reports are similar, but they are not identical in every respect. The Panel in the complaint brought by the United States was established by the Dispute Settlement Body (the "DSB") on 20 May 1996. On 16 October 1996, the DSB established the Panel in the complaint brought by Canada. The European Communities and Canada agreed, on 4 November 1996, that the composition of the latter Panel would be identical to the composition of the Panel established at the request of the United States.

The Panel dealt with a complaint against the European Communities relating to an EC prohibition of imports of meat and meat products derived from cattle to which either the natural hormones: oestradiol-173, progesterone or testosterone, or the synthetic hormones: trenbolone acetate, zeranol or melengestrol acetate ("MGA"), had been administered for growth promotion purposes. This import prohibition was set forth in a series of Directives of the Council of Ministers that were enacted before 1 January 1995. * * *

Effective as of 1 July 1997, Directives 81/602, 88/146 and 88/299 were repealed and replaced with Council Directive 96/22/EC of 29 April 1996 ("Directive 96/22"). This Directive maintains the prohibition of the administration to farm animals of substances having a hormonal or thyrostatic action. As under the previously applicable Directives, it is prohibited to place on the market, or to import from third countries, meat and meat products from animals to which such substances, including the six hormones at issue in this dispute, were administered. * * *

IV. Allocating the Burden of Proof in Proceedings Under the SPS Agreement

The first general issue that we must address relates to the allocation of the burden of proof in proceedings under the *SPS Agreement*. The Panel appropriately describes this issue as one "of particular importance", in view of the nature of disputes under that Agreement. Such disputes may raise multiple and complex issues of fact.

The Panel begins its analysis by setting out the general allocation of the burden of proof between the contending parties in any proceedings under the *SPS Agreement*. The initial burden lies on the complaining party, which must establish a *prima facie* case of inconsistency with a particular provision of the *SPS Agreement* on the part of the defending party, or more precisely, of its SPS measure or measures complained about. When that *prima facie* case is made, the burden of proof moves to the defending party, which must in turn counter or refute the claimed inconsistency. This seems straightforward enough and is in conformity with our ruling in *United States—Shirts and Blouses*, which the Panel invokes and which embodies a rule applicable in any adversarial proceedings.

The Panel, however, proceeds to make a general, unqualified, interpretative ruling that the *SPS Agreement* allocates the "evidentiary burden" to the Member imposing an SPS measure. * * *

We find the general interpretative ruling of the Panel to be bereft of basis in the *SPS Agreement* and must, accordingly, reverse that ruling. It does not appear to us that there is any necessary (i.e. logical) or other connection between the undertaking of Members to ensure, for example, that SPS measures are "applied only to the extent necessary to protect human, animal or plant life or health . . ., and the allocation of burden of proof in a dispute settlement proceeding. Article 5.8 of the *SPS Agreement* does not purport to address burden of proof problems; it does not deal with a dispute settlement situation. * * *''

V. The Standard of Review Applicable in Proceedings Under the SPS Agreement

The European Communities appeals from certain findings of the Panel upon the ground that the Panel failed to apply an appropriate standard of review in assessing certain acts of, and scientific evidentiary material submitted by, the European Communities. * * *

We do not mean, however, to suggest that there is at present no standard of review applicable to the determination and assessment of the facts in proceedings under the *SPS Agreement* or under other covered agreements. In our view, Article 11 of the DSU bears directly on this matter and, in effect, articulates with great succinctness but with sufficient clarity the appropriate standard of review for panels in respect of both the ascertainment of facts and the legal characterization of such facts under the relevant agreements. Article 11 reads thus:

> "The function of panels is to assist the DSB in discharging its responsibilities under this Understanding and the covered agreements. Accordingly, a panel should make an <u>objective assessment of the matter before it</u>, including <u>an objective assessment of the facts</u> of the case and the <u>applicability of and conformity with the relevant covered agreements</u>, and make such other findings as will assist the DSB in making the recommendations or in giving the rulings provided in the covered agreements. Panels should consult regularly with the parties to the dispute and give them adequate opportunity to develop a mutually satisfactory solution". (underlining added)

So far as fact-finding by panels is concerned, their activities are always constrained by the mandate of Article 11 of the DSU: the applicable standard is neither *de novo* review as such, nor "total deference", but rather the "objective assessment of the facts". Many panels have in the past refused to undertake *de novo* review, wisely, since under current practice and systems, they are in any case poorly suited to engage in such a review. On the other hand, "total deference to the findings of the national authorities", it has been well said, "could not ensure an 'objective assessment' as foreseen by Article 11 of the DSU".

In so far as legal questions are concerned—that is, consistency or inconsistency of a Member's measure with the provisions of the applicable agreement—a standard not found in the text of the *SPS Agreement* itself cannot absolve a panel (or the Appellate Body) from the duty to apply the customary rules of interpretation of public international law. * * *

VI.   The Relevance of the Precautionary Principle in the Interpretation of the SPS Agreement

We are asked by the European Communities to reverse the finding of the Panel relating to the precautionary principle. * * *

It appears to us important, nevertheless, to note some aspects of the relationship of the precautionary principle to the *SPS Agreement*. First, the principle has not been written into the *SPS Agreement* as a ground for justifying SPS measures that are otherwise inconsistent with the obligations of Members set out in particular provisions of that Agreement. Secondly, the precautionary principle indeed finds reflection in Article 5.7 of the *SPS Agreement*. We agree, at the same time, with the European Communities, that there is no need to assume that Article 5.7 exhausts the relevance of a precautionary principle. It is reflected also in the sixth paragraph of the preamble and in Article 3.3. These explicitly recognize the right of Members to establish their own appropriate level of sanitary protection, which level may be higher (i.e., more cautious) than that implied in existing international standards, guidelines and recommendations. Thirdly, a panel charged with determining, for instance, whether "sufficient scientific evidence" exists to warrant the maintenance by a Member of a particular SPS measure may, of course, and should, bear in mind that responsible, representative governments commonly act from perspectives of prudence and precaution where risks of irreversible, e.g. life-terminating, damage to human health are concerned. Lastly, however, the precautionary principle does not, by itself, and without a clear textual directive to that effect, relieve a panel from the duty of applying the normal (i.e. customary international law) principles of treaty interpretation in reading the provisions of the *SPS Agreement*.

We accordingly agree with the finding of the Panel that the precautionary principle does not override the provisions of Articles 5.1 and 5.2 of the *SPS Agreement*.

VII.   Application of the SPS Agreement to Measures Enacted Before 1 January 1995

* * *

We agree with the Panel that the *SPS Agreement* would apply to situations or measures that did not cease to exist, such as the 1981 and 1988 Directives, unless the *SPS Agreement* reveals a contrary intention. We also agree with the Panel that the *SPS Agreement* does not reveal such an intention. The *SPS Agreement* does not contain any provision limiting the temporal application of the *SPS Agreement*, or of any provision thereof, to SPS measures adopted after 1 January 1995. * * * Finally, we observe, more generally, that Article XVI.4 of the *WTO Agreement* stipulates that:

Each Member shall ensure the conformity of its laws, regulations and administrative procedures with its obligations as provided in the annexed Agreements.

Unlike the GATT 1947, the *WTO Agreement* was accepted definitively by Members, and therefore, there are no longer "existing legislation" exceptions (so-called "grandfather rights").

We are aware that the applicability, as from 1 January 1995, of the requirement that an SPS measure be based on a risk assessment to the many SPS measures already in existence on that date, may impose burdens on Members. It is pertinent here to note that Article 5.1 stipulates that SPS measures must be based on a risk assessment, *as appropriate to the circumstances*, and this makes clear that the Members have a certain degree of flexibility in meeting the requirements of Article 5.1.

* * *

IX. Certain Procedures Adopted by the Panel

The Selection and Use of Experts

The European Communities considers that in its selection and use of experts, the Panel has violated Article 11.2 of the *SPS Agreement* and Articles 11, 13.2 and Appendix 4 of the DSU. We note that the Panel decided to request the opinion of experts on certain scientific and other technical matters raised by the parties to the dispute, and rather than establishing an experts review group, the Panel considered it more useful to leave open the possibility of receiving a range of opinions from the experts in their individual capacity. [Upheld] * * *

X. The Interpretation of Articles 3.1 and 3.3 of the SPS Agreement

* * *

The above conclusion of the Panel has three components: first, international standards, guidelines and recommendations exist in respect of meat and meat products derived from cattle to which five of the hormones involved have been administered for growth promotion purposes; secondly, the EC measures involved here are not based on the relevant international standards, guidelines and recommendations developed by Codex, because such measures are not in conformity with those standards, guidelines and recommendations; and thirdly, the EC measures are "not justified under", that is, do not comply with the requirements of Article 3.3. *En route* to its above-mentioned conclusion, the Panel developed three legal interpretations, which have all been appealed by the European Communities and which need to be addressed: the first relates to the meaning of "based on" as used in Article 3.1; the second is concerned with the relationship between Articles 3.1, 3.2 and 3.3 of the *SPS Agreement*; and the third relates to the requirements of Article 3.3 of the *SPS Agreement*. As may be expected, the Panel's three interpretations are intertwined.

* * *

After having erroneously "equated" measures "based on" an international standard with measures that "conform to" that standard, the Panel proceeds to Article 3.3. According to the Panel, Article 3.3 "explicitly relates" the "definition of sanitary measures *based on* international standards to the level of sanitary protection achieved by those measures". The Panel then interprets Article 3.3 as saying that "all measures which are based on a given international standard should *in principle* achieve the *same* level of sanitary protection", and argues *a contrario* that "if a sanitary measure implies a *different* level (from that reflected in an international standard), that measure cannot be considered to be *based on* the international standard". The Panel concludes that, under Article 3.1, "for a sanitary measure to be *based on* an international standard . . ., that *measure* needs to reflect the same level of sanitary protection as the *standard*".

It appears to us that the Panel reads much more into Article 3.3 than can be reasonably supported by the actual text of Article 3.3. Moreover, the Panel's entire analysis rests on its flawed premise that "based on", as used in Articles 3.1 and 3.3, means the same thing as "conform to" as used in Article 3.2 As already noted, we are compelled to reject this premise as an error in law. * * *

We turn to the relationship between Articles 3.1, 3.2 and 3.3 of the *SPS Agreement*. As observed earlier, the Panel assimilated Articles 3.1 and 3.2 to one another, designating the product as the "general rule", and contraposed that product to Article 3.3 which denoted the "exception". This view appear to us an erroneous representation of the differing situations that may arise under Article 3, that is, where a relevant international standard, guideline or recommendation exists.

Under Article 3.2 of the *SPS Agreement*, a Member may decide to promulgate an SPS measure that conforms to an international standard. Such a measure would embody the international standard completely and, for practical purposes, converts it into a municipal standard. Such a measure enjoys the benefit of a presumption (albeit a rebuttable one) that it is consistent with the relevant provisions of the *SPS Agreement* and of the GATT 1994.

Under Article 3.1 of the *SPS Agreement*, a Member may choose to establish an SPS measure that is based on the existing relevant international standard, guideline or recommendation Such a measure may adopt some, not necessarily all, of the elements of the international standard. The Member imposing this measure does not benefit from the presumption of consistency set up in Article 3.2; but, as earlier observed, the Member is not penalized by exemption of a complaining Member from the normal burden of showing a *prima facie* case of inconsistency with Article

3.1 or any other relevant article of the *SPS Agreement* or of the GATT 1994.

Under Article 3.3 of the *SPS Agreement*, a Member may decide to set for itself a level of protection different from that implicit in the international standard, and to implement or embody that level of protection in a measure not "based on" the international standard. The Member's appropriate level of protection may be higher than that implied in the international standard. The right of a Member to determine its own appropriate level of sanitary protection is an important right. * * *

As noted earlier, this right of a Member to establish its own level of sanitary protection under Article 3.3 of the *SPS Agreement* is an autonomous right and *not* an "exception" from a "general obligation" under Article 3.1.

The right of a Member to define its appropriate level of protection is not, however, an absolute or unqualified right. Article 3.3 also makes this clear:

> Members may introduce or maintain sanitary or phytosanitary measures which result in a higher level of sanitary or phytosanitary protection than would be achieved by measures based on the relevant international standards, guidelines or recommendations, if there is a scientific justification, or as a consequence of the level of sanitary or phytosanitary protection a Member determines to be appropriate in accordance with the relevant provisions of paragraphs 1 through 8 of Article 5.[2] Notwithstanding the above, all measures which result in a level of sanitary or phytosanitary protection different from that which would be achieved by measures based on international standards, guidelines or recommendations shall not be inconsistent with any other provision of this Agreement.

---

2. For the purposes of paragraph 3 of Article 3, there is a scientific justification if, on the basis of an examination and evaluation of available scientific information in conformity with the relevant provisions of this Agreement, a Member determines that the relevant international standards, guidelines or recommendations are not sufficient to achieve its appropriate level of sanitary or phytosanitary protection.

* * *

Article 3.3 is evidently not a model of clarity in drafting and communication. The use of the disjunctive "or" does indicate that two situations are intended to be covered. These are the introduction or maintenance of SPS measures which result in a higher level of protection:

(a) "if there is a scientific justification"; or

(b) "as a consequence of the level of ... protection a Member determines to be appropriate in accordance with the relevant provisions of paragraphs 1 through 8 of Article 5".

It is true that situation (a) does not speak of Articles 5.1 through 5.8. Nevertheless, two points need to be noted. First, the last sentence of Article 3.3 requires that "all measures which result in a [higher] level of ... protection", that is to say, measures falling within situation (a) as well as those falling within situation (b), be "not inconsistent with any other provision of [the SPS] Agreement". "Any other provision of this Agreement" textually includes Article 5. Secondly, the footnote to Article 3.3, while attached to the end of the first sentence, defines "scientific justification" as an "examination and evaluation of available scientific information in conformity with relevant provisions of this Agreement ...". This examination and evaluation would appear to partake of the nature of the risk assessment required in Article 5.1 and defined in paragraph 4 of Annex A of the *SPS Agreement*.

On balance, we agree with the Panel's finding that although the European Communities has established for itself a level of protection higher, or more exacting, than the level of protection implied in the relevant Codex standards, guidelines or recommendations, the European Communities was bound to comply with the requirements established in Article 5.1. We are not unaware that this finding tends to suggest that the distinction made in Article 3.3 between two situations may have very limited effects and may, to that extent, be more apparent than real. Its involved and layered language actually leaves us with no choice.

* * *

XI. The Reading of Articles 5.1 and 5.2 of the SPS Agreement: Basing SPS Measures on a Risk Assessment

We turn to the appeal of European Communities from the Panel's conclusion that, by maintaining SPS measures which are not based on a risk assessment, the European Communities acted inconsistently with the requirements contained in Article 5.1 of the *SPS Agreement*.

Article 5.1 of the SPS Agreement provides:

Members shall ensure that their sanitary or phytosanitary measures are <u>based on an assessment, as appropriate to the circumstances, of the risks to human</u>, animal or plant <u>life or health</u>, taking into account risk assessment techniques developed by the relevant international organizations. (underlining added)

The Interpretation of "Risk Assessment"

At the outset, two preliminary considerations need to be brought out. The first is that the Panel considered that Article 5.1 may be viewed as a specific application of the basic obligations contained in Article 2.2 of the *SPS Agreement*, which reads as follows:

Members shall ensure that any sanitary or phytosanitary measure is applied only <u>to the extent necessary to protect</u> human, animal or plant life or health, is <u>based on scientific principles</u> and is not maintained without <u>sufficient scientific evidence</u>, except as provided for in paragraph 7 of Article 5. (underlining added)

We agree with this general consideration and would also stress that Articles 2.2 and 5.1 should constantly be read together. Article 2.2 informs Article 5.1: the elements that define the basic obligation set out in Article 2.2 impart meaning to Article 5.1.

* * *

We consider that, in principle, the Panel's approach of examining the scientific conclusions implicit in the SPS measure under consideration and the scientific conclusion yielded by a risk assessment is a useful approach. The relationship between those two sets of conclusions is certainly relevant; they cannot, however, be assigned relevance to the exclusion of everything else. We believe that Article 5.1, when contextually read as it should be, in conjunction with and as informed by Article 2.2 of the *SPS Agreement*, requires that the results of the risk assessment must sufficiently warrant—that is to say, reasonably support—the SPS measure at stake. The requirement that an SPS measure be "based on" a risk assessment is a substantive requirement that there be a rational relationship between the measure and the risk assessment.

We do not believe that a risk assessment has to come to a monolithic conclusion that coincides with the scientific conclusion or view implicit in the SPS measure. The risk assessment could set out both the prevailing view representing the "mainstream" of scientific opinion, as well as the opinions of scientists taking a divergent view. Article 5.1 does not require that the risk assessment must necessarily embody only the view of a majority of the relevant scientific community. In some cases, the very existence of divergent views presented by qualified scientists who have investigated the particular issue at hand may indicate a state of scientific uncertainty. Sometimes the divergence may indicate a roughly equal balance of scientific opinion, which may itself be a form of scientific uncertainty. In most cases, responsible and representative governments tend to base their legislative and administrative measures on "mainstream" scientific opinion. In other cases, equally responsible and representative governments may act in good faith on the basis of what, at a given time, may be a divergent opinion coming from qualified and respected sources. By itself, this does not necessarily signal the absence of a reasonable relationship between the SPS measure and the risk assessment, especially where the risk involved is life-threatening in character and is perceived to constitute a clear and imminent threat to public health and safety. Determination of the presence or absence of that relationship can only be done on a case-to-case basis, after account is taken of all considerations rationally bearing upon the issue of potential adverse health effects.

We turn now to the application by the Panel of the substantive requirements of Article 5.1 to the EC measures at stake in the present case. * * *

Several of the above scientific reports appeared to the Panel to meet the minimum requirements of a risk assessment, in particular, the Lamming Report and the 1988 and 1989 JECFA Reports. The Panel assumes accordingly that the European Communities had demonstrated the existence of a risk assessment carried out in accordance with Article 5 of the *SPS Agreement*. At the same time, the Panel finds that the conclusion of these scientific reports is that the use of the hormones at issue (except MGA) for growth promotion purposes is "safe". * * *

Most, if not all, of the scientific studies referred to by the European Communities, in respect of the five hormones involved here, concluded that their use for growth promotion purposes is "safe, if the hormones are administered in accordance with the requirements of good veterinary practice." Where the condition of observance of good veterinary practice (which is much the same condition attached to the standards, guide lines and recommendations of Codex with respect to the use of the five hormones for growth promotion) is *not* followed, the logical inference is that the use of such hormones for growth promotion purposes may or may not be "safe". The *SPS Agreement* requires assessment of the potential for adverse effects on human health arising from the presence of contaminants and toxins in food. We consider that the object and purpose of the *SPS Agreement* justify the examination and evaluation of all such risks for human health whatever their precise and immediate origin may be. We do not mean to suggest that risks arising from potential abuse in the administration of controlled substances and from control problems need to be, or should be, evaluated by risk assessors in each and every case. When and if risks of these types do in fact arise, risk assessors may examine and evaluate them. Clearly, the necessity or propriety of examination and evaluation of such risks would have to be addressed on a case-by-case basis. What, in our view, is a fundamental legal error is to exclude, on an *a priori* basis, any such risks from the scope of application of Articles 5.1 and 5.2. We disagree with the Panel's suggestion that exclusion of risks resulting from the combination of potential abuse and difficulties of control is justified by distinguishing between "risk assessment" and "risk management". As earlier noted, the concept of "risk management" is not mentioned in any provision of the *SPS Agreement* and, as such, cannot be used to sustain a more restrictive interpretation of "risk assessment" than is justified by the actual terms of Article 5.2, Article 8 and Annex C of the *SPS Agreement*.

The question that arises, therefore, is whether the European Communities did, in fact, submit a risk assessment demonstrating and evaluating the existence and level of risk arising in the present case from abusive use of hormones and the difficulties of control of the administration of hormones for growth promotion purposes, within the United States and Canada as exporting countries, and at the frontiers of the European

Communities as an importing country. Here, we must agree with the finding of the Panel that the European Communities in fact restricted itself to pointing out the condition of administration of hormones "in accordance with good practice" "without further providing an assessment of the potential adverse effects related to non compliance with such practice". The record of the panel proceedings shows that the risk arising from abusive use of hormones for growth promotion combined with control problems for the hormones at issue, may have been examined on two occasions in a scientific manner. The first occasion may have occurred at the proceedings before the Committee of Inquiry into the Problem of Quality in the Meat Sector established by the European Parliament, the results of which constituted the basis of the Pimenta Report of 1989. However, none of the original studies and evidence put before the Committee of Inquiry was submitted to the Panel. The second occasion could have been the 1995 EC Scientific Conference on Growth Promotion in Meat Production. One of the three workshops of this Conference examined specifically the problems of "detection and control". However, only one of the studies presented to the workshop discussed systematically some of the problems arising from the combination of potential abuse and problems of control of hormones and other substances. The study presented a theoretical framework for the systematic analysis of such problems, but did not itself investigate and evaluate the actual problems that have arisen at the borders of the European Communities or within the United States, Canada and other countries exporting meat and meat products to the European Communities. At best, this study may represent the beginning of an assessment of such risks.

In the absence of any other relevant documentation, we find that the European Communities did not actually proceed to an assessment, within the meaning of Articles 5.1 and 5.2, of the risks arising from the failure of observance of good veterinary practice combined with problems of control of the use of hormones for growth promotion purposes. * * *

The Appellate Body *recommends* that the Dispute Settlement Body request the European Communities to bring the SPS measures found in this Report and in the Panel Reports, as modified by this Report, to be inconsistent with the *SPS Agreement* into conformity with the obligations of the European Communities under that Agreement.

QUESTIONS AND COMMENTS

1. The SPS Code governs measures undertaken to protect human health inside national territories from risks arising from disease-causing or disease-carrying organisms in food, pests and diseases. In cases involving conflicting scientific data, who should have the burden of proving what? What standard of scientific proof should be required? What level of protection should each country be permitted to adopt, and how strictly can it enforce such standards (for example, "zero risk")? Will the standards differ for countries adopting "international standards" (e.g., Codex), and those adopting alternative standards?

These are legal issues and their answers will depend upon the policies adopted by the group that promulgates the relevant rules. In part, it depends upon whether such standards are primarily considered "barriers to trade," which are suspected of being protectionist, and therefore presumptively to be disallowed; or whether they are primarily considered "consumer protections," which are presumedly not intended to be trade restrictive, and therefore benign and permissible.

Hudec points out the ability of a domestic industry to disguise protectionism as sanitary measure, a fact which must be recognized. Has that happened in Part B of this problem? In Part A? Does the SPS Code and/or Article XX provide legal bases for challenging disguised restraints on international trade?

2.   There are proponents of the beef hormone ban who are not interested in European protectionism, but believe that the U.S.-produced goods cause physical harm. Thus they are opposed to any WTO provisions which impede the ability of any country to exclude goods which are harmful to consumers or the environment. Further, they want the public (broadly defined) of any country to set its own consumer and environmental protection standards as high as they want, without interference from what they consider to be industry-dominated international trade organizations. Would such proponents be satisfied with the WTO Appellate Body's ruling in *Beef Hormones*? Does that ruling oblige SPS signatories to use Codex Alimentarius standards?

3.   If science could provide answers to consumer and environmental questions which were clear and convincing, there would be fewer disagreements. But science, like law, is a subject of interpretation, and typically provides arguments to both sides. Each side in the beef hormone controversy had its own scientific data to back up its contentions. Thus there is a gap between the two sides which cannot be bridged by scientific certainty. How does the Appellate Body handle this uncertainty in *Beef Hormones*? The Europeans allow hormones for pigs. Should that matter?

4.   The Dispute Settlement Body of the WTO adopted the Appellate Body and (as modified) Panel Reports in February of 1998. Could either side have blocked this adoption? Which side, if any, "won" in the *Beef Hormones* dispute?

5.   The Europeans invoked their right to arbitrate the amount of "reasonable time" they have to implement the recommendation and rulings of the WTO Dispute Settlement Body. See Articles 21.3(c) of the DSU. The Arbitrator gave them 15 months from February 1998 to comply. What must the Europeans do to bring their *Beef Hormones* directive into conformity with the SPS? Suppose there is a dispute about the adequacy of EU compliance with the WTO ruling. What happens then? See Articles 21.5 and 22 of the DSU.

Do the Europeans have options other than compliance? If so, what are they? Which option would you recommend? Suppose recent studies show risk to humans from hormone-treated beef. Can the EU petition for withdrawal of the authorization of trade sanctions? After conducting more studies and asserting compliance with the SPS Code, the EU commenced entirely new WTO proceedings in 2004. Why new proceedings? For the second time, absent adequate risk assessments and scientific proof, the EU lost this dispute. See

United States—Continued Suspension of Obligations in the EC–Hormones Dispute, WT/DS320/R (March 31, 2008), WT/DS321/AB/R (October 16, 2008).

U.S. retaliatory tariff sanctions remained in place. In 2009, an arguably pro-European settlement was reached. The U.S. effectively gets a higher quota to export hormone-free beef to the EU, in return for phasing out over four years its retaliatory tariffs on EU goods. The U.S. threat of carousel sanctions, i.e. rotating goods subject to tariff retaliation, was instrumental to this settlement. Meanwhile, because the U.S. beef industry failed to timely ask for a continuation of the retaliatory tariffs, the Federal Circuit ruled late in 2010 that they expired in 2007. Refunds are expected by importers of EU products subject to those tariffs.

6. Are you satisfied with the Appellate Body's rulings regarding the SPS and:

- Burden of Proof
- Standard of Review
- Retroactive Application
- Use of Experts
- The Precautionary Principle

Which of these rulings were most influential to the outcome? Why?

7. What is the Appellate Body's interpretation of SPS Articles 3.1 and 3.3? And Articles 5.1 and 2.2? Do you agree with these interpretations? Why?

8. What do you think of the quality of the Appellate Body's report and legal reasoning? Is it comparable to Courts of Appeal in your home jurisdiction?

9. The bottom line for this problem ... is the United States import ban on British and other European beef legal under the SPS Agreement? Why?

10. In 2003, the United States, Canada and Argentina commenced WTO dispute resolution proceedings against the EU moratorium since 1998 on regulatory approvals of genetically modified organisms (GMOs). In addition, the European Union has recently required labeling and production/distribution tracing for all foods containing more than .09 percent GMO content. The label must read: "This product contains genetically modified organisms" or "This product produced from genetically modified [name of organism]." U.S. companies are leaders in the bio-engineered foods, which have met widespread opposition among European consumers. As in *Beef Hormones*, the U.S. asserts that there was no scientific basis for the EU moratorium. In 2006, a WTO panel rejected this assertion, while agreeing that the moratorium violated the SPS Agreement.

11. Japan, Canada and other nations have experienced outbreaks of Mad Cow disease and fallen under the U.S. import ban. Late in 2003, the first United States case was found in a "downer cow" (unable to walk) that had been imported from Canada. Dozens of U.S. beef export markets were quickly shut, including South Korea, Russia, Mexico, Japan and China. The European Union, with its beef hormone rules still in place, continues to deny entry to U.S. beef. By 2005, "home-grown" Mad Cow disease had emerged in the

United States. Some import bans against U.S. beef remain, most controversially in South Korea where it became an issue under the U.S.–South Korea free trade agreement (KORUS). Thus your analysis on behalf of United Ranchers regarding the U.S. import ban may also have export application.

PROBLEM 6.4   FREE TRADE AGREEMENTS AND CUSTOMS UNIONS: JAPAN'S PERSPECTIVE

SECTION I.   THE SETTING

Sunrise Manufacturing (SUNRISE) is a Japanese multinational corporation driven by the motto: "Quality Is Everything." It produces bicycles, especially mountain bikes, in its Osaka plant. For many years, SUNRISE has exported high quality bikes to Europe and North America. But the rising value of the Yen hurt its price competitiveness in these markets. United States and French manufacturers in particular have been increasing their market shares at the expense of SUNRISE. This has occurred despite the decline under the GATT/WTO in European and North American MFN tariffs which has made it less expensive to import SUNRISE bicycles.

Management at SUNRISE has decided that production in the United States and France should be seriously considered as an alternative strategy to exports. Initial (tentative) plans are to continue the engineering and design of its bikes in Japan. All major components will be made in Osaka. These components will be shipped abroad to the new plants where they will be assembled with just a screwdriver (which of course will be forwarded with the components). In this way, management feels that its reputation for quality will be ensured.

SUNRISE has read about "Fortress Europe" and "Fortress North America" in several Japanese trade journals. It is aware that NAFTA is a "free trade area" while the European Union is a "customs union." It also has a general sense that each is a good deal for insiders, which it would like to become. Beyond that, SUNRISE has lots of questions. For starters, it would like to know what critical distinctions exist between free trade areas and customs unions. Is one more preferable than the other from its perspective as a potential foreign investor?

What tariffs will SUNRISE pay on the components it plans to ship to its French and United States subsidiaries? Once assembled in each location, can SUNRISE freely trade its bicycles to Mexico and Canada, and to the other EU states? In other words, can SUNRISE take advantage of NAFTA and the EU as regional markets?

Naturally, SUNRISE would prefer to stick with its initial screwdriver assembly plant intentions. If, however, management is persuaded that high quality components can be obtained in France and the United States (or for that matter anywhere inside NAFTA or the EU), it is willing to reconsider. Whether it should do so because of the way NAFTA and/or the EU work is another of its concerns.

One more immediate problem facing SUNRISE is the safety of its bicycles. Accident rates on its mountain bikes have been rising, along with increased litigation and insurance costs. Consumer product safety regulators in the United States and France have begun reviewing the construction and design of SUNRISE bikes. The last thing that management wants is a product recall or (worse yet) a product ban on its bikes. The President of SUNRISE hopes somehow that production overseas will alleviate product safety regulatory burdens associated with its full line of bicycles. He would appreciate advice on this point.

You are a young attorney with a large multinational law firm with offices in Tokyo, Los Angeles, Chicago, New York, Toronto, Mexico City, Paris, London, Frankfurt, Madrid, Rome and other locations. The senior partner who handles SUNRISE as a client has asked you to draft a response to the questions and concerns outlined above. What is your response?

SECTION II. FOCUS OF CONSIDERATION

The GATT/WTO notwithstanding, regionalization and bilateralization of the world economy has been growing rapidly. The Europeans got things rolling in the post-war reconstruction era with the Benelux Union, the European Economic Community (now the European Union) and the European Free Trade Area in the 1950s. Regional integration (at least on paper) spread throughout the developing world during the 1960s and 1970s. This period, for example, saw the emergence of the Central African Customs and Economic Union, the East and West African Communities, the Caribbean Free Trade Association (later the Caribbean Community), the Central American Common Market, the Latin American Free Trade Association (now the Latin American Integration Association), the Andean Common Market and the Association of Southeast Asian Nations. The formation of these groups was motivated principally by the desire to develop economically and to increase bargaining power. Many of these agreements were handicapped by serious political discord.

More recently, the Gulf Cooperation Council was formed in the Middle East, the Southern African Development Community emerged after apartheid, a South Asian Free Trade Area was agreed, and a Southern Cone (MERCOSUR) common market was established in South America. Many of these regional groups intersect or overlap an even more pronounced trend: Bilateral free trade agreements. Hundreds of such agreements lattice the world, including for example the European Union and South Africa, Canada and Costa Rica, China and Chile, Japan and Singapore. Mexico has dozens of bilateral free trade agreements. At this point the only nation without a bilateral free trade deal is Mongolia.

A variety of factors help explain why bilaterals have become the leading edge of international trade law and policy. Difficulties encountered in the Uruguay, "Seattle" and Doha Rounds of multilateral trade negotiations are certainly crucial. GATT/WTO regulatory failures regarding bilaterals have also fueled this reality. Yet these "negatives" do not fully explain the feeding frenzy of bilaterals. A range of attractions are also at work. For example, bilaterals often extend to subject matters beyond WTO competence. Foreign investment law is a prime example, and many bilaterals serve as investment magnets. Government procurement, optional at the WTO level, is often included in bilaterals. Competition policy and labor and environmental matters absent from the WTO are sometimes covered in bilaterals. In addition, bilaterals can reach beyond the scope of existing WTO agreements. Services is one "WTO-plus" area where this is clearly true. Intellectual property rights are also being "WTO-plussed" in bilateral free trade agreements. Whether this amounts to competitive trade liberalization or competitive trade imperialism is a provocative question.

In North America, competitive and political forces combined to generate the Canada–U.S. Free Trade Agreement of 1989 (CUSFTA) which was followed with Mexico by the North American Free Trade Agreement of 1994 (NAFTA). Delays in the Uruguay Round of GATT negotiations also contributed to the emergence of NAFTA. Chile was supposed to become the fourth member, followed by other Latin American countries, but repeated Congressional refusals to authorize President Clinton to engage in "fast track" negotiations sidetracked expansion. Fast track requires Congress to vote within 90 legislative days up or down, without amendments, on U.S. trade agreements negotiated and submitted by the president. In return, Congress receives substantial notice and opportunity to influence U.S. trade negotiations conducted by the USTR. For U.S. free trade partners, fast track suggests that once they reach a deal Congress cannot alter it, though in recent years Congress has effectively tacked on additional requirements, notably regarding labor and environment. Finally, President George W. Bush received bipartisan fast track authority in the Trade Act of 2002, 19 U.S.C. §§ 3801 et seq. (see the Documents Supplement). This authority expired in June 2007 and has not been renewed.

By 2008, the United States had *bilateral* free trade agreements in force with Chile, Singapore, Australia, Morocco, Peru, Oman, Bahrain, Jordan, and five Central American states (CAFTA) plus the Dominican Republic. Free trade agreements with Colombia, Panama and South Korea were concluded prior to the expiration of fast track, but implementation by Congress was delayed until 2011. Negotiations on a Free Trade Area of the Americas (FTAA) with 34 nations continue, but prospects are slim.

All regional and bilateral trade agreements are monitored by the WTO and are supposed to be governed by Article XXIV of the GATT. The purpose of Article XXIV is to minimize the conflict between such agreements and WTO law. Many wonder if bilateralization and regionalization do not have the upper hand. Certainly the practical impact of most of these agreements is to facilitate escape from MFN principles. The apparent failure of the Doha Round of WTO negotiations virtually assures that bilaterals will dominate future trade law and policy.

This problem focuses on the only major industrial nation that is not a member of a regional economic alliance, Japan.* From the perspective of SUNRISE, what do all these agreements suggest for its trade and investment interests. Specifically, what are the implications of NAFTA and the 27–nation European Union.

The laws of NAFTA and the European Union are considered in many parts of this coursebook. Materials designed to introduce the complex EU law-making and litigation-oriented dispute resolution system are provided in the Appendix to this book. In this problem, we are primarily concerned with sorting out tariff and nontariff trade barrier (NTB) consequences for SUNRISE. This will lead to an understanding of the basics of free trade area agreements, customs unions, rules of origin, and the significance of regional product safety regulation.

Article XXIV of the GATT and Chapters 4 and 9 of NAFTA are essential to analysis of this problem. They appear in the Documents Supplement. Web Resources for further study include European Union coverage at *www.europa.eu.* and NAFTA coverage at *www.nafta-sec-alena. org.*

SECTION III.   READINGS, QUESTIONS AND COMMENTS

PART A.   THE EUROPEAN UNION

R. FOLSOM, PRINCIPLES OF EUROPEAN UNION LAW

Section 1.4 (2011).**

THE TREATY OF ROME, THE GATT AND THE CUSTOMS UNION DILEMMA

The General Agreement on Tariffs and Trade (GATT), adopted in 1947 and much amended and interpreted since then, governs many features of the free world trading system. Over 100 nations, including those of the European Union, now adhere to the GATT and a host of "Uruguay Round" agreements administered by the World Trade Organization. In 1957, when the Treaty of Rome was signed, the United states, Britain and other GATT members protested that the Treaty was not in accord with the terms of Article 24 of the GATT.

---

* Japan is a member of the Asia–Pacific Economic Cooperation group which declared its support for "free and open trade and investment" late in 1994. This declaration is not legally binding. Although negotiations have been ongoing, relatively little of substance has emerged as yet from the APEC group. In 2003, Japan initiated its first free trade agreement, with Singapore. Japan also has "economic partnership" (free trade) agreements with Mexico, Chile, Thailand, the Philippines, Malaysia, Vietnam, Switzerland, India, Indonesia, Brunei and ASEAN. Compare this list to that of China in Part C, Comment 10.

** © West Publishing Co.

GATT Article 24

Article 24 permits contracting parties to enter into free trade area and customs union agreements of a fixed or evolutionary character. The premise here is that regional economic groups can be viewed as gradual steps (second-best alternatives) along the road to freer, less discriminatory *world* trade. All regional forms of economic integration are inherently discriminatory in their trade impact. As nonuniversalized trade preferences, they tend to simultaneously *create* trade among member states and *divert* trade between member states and the rest of the world. Thus, while trade creation may represent an improvement in the allocation of scarce world resources, trade diversion may generate an opposite result.

With free trade areas, diversionary trade effects are usually not distinct because of the absence of a common trade wall against outsiders. Trade diversion nonetheless occurs. "Rules of origin" in free trade area treaties keep third-party imports from seeking the lowest tariff or highest quota state and then exploiting the trade advantages within a free trade area. Under rules of origin, free trade areas are "free" only for goods substantially originating therein. This causes member state goods to be preferred over goods from other states. Rules of origin within a free trade area can be as trade diversionary as a common trade policy in other forms of regional economic integration. This appears to be true in the case of NAFTA, for example.

With customs unions, common markets, economic communities and economic unions, trade diversion is more obvious given a common trade policy for third-party states. In these circumstances the resulting "trade creation" and "trade diversion" effects are known generally in economic literature as the "customs union dilemma." In light of the discussion of rules of origin in free trade areas, it might be better to call this the "dilemma of regional economic integration."

Article 24 attempts to manage the internal trade-creating and external trade-diverting effects of regional economic groups. Free trade area and custom union proposals must run the gauntlet of a formal GATT (now WTO) approval procedure during which "binding" recommendations are possible to bring the proposals into conformity with Article 24. Such recommendations might deal with Article 24 requirements for the elimination of internal tariffs and other restrictive regulations of commerce on "substantially all" products originating in a customs union or free trade area. Or they might deal with Article 24 requirements that common external tariffs not be "on the whole higher or more restrictive" in effect than the general incidence of prior existing national tariffs. The broad purpose of Aticle 24, acknowledged therein, is to facilitate trade among the GATT contracting parties and not to raise trade barriers.

Article 24 and European Integration

It is through this GATT approval mechanism that most regional economic treaties, including those of Western Europe, have passed *without* substantial modification. Only the EFTA Treaty seems to have come genuinely close to meeting the terms of Article 24. The GATT, not the regional economic treaties, most often has given way. With the European Coal and Steel Community only two products were involved. Clearly no case can be made for its compliance with the requirement of elimination of internal trade barriers on "substantially all" products. Hence, the GATT members, passing over Article 24's own waiver proviso for proposal leading to a customs union or free trade area "in the sense of Article 24," reverted to Article 25. That article allows a two-thirds vote by the contracting parties to waive any GATT obligation.

During passage through the GATT of the Treaty of Rome, many "violations" of the letter and spirit of Article 24 were cited by nonmembers. The derivation of the common external tariff by arithmetically averaging existing national tariffs was challenged as more restrictive of trade than previous arrangements. Such averaging on a given product fails to take account of differing national import volumes. If a product was faced originally with a lower than average national tariff and a larger than average national demand, the new average tariff is clearly more "restrictive" of imports than before. Averaging in high tariffs of countries of low demand quite plausibly created more restrictions on third-party trade. If so, the letter and spirit of Article 24 were breached.

The economic association of Overseas Territories (mainly former French, Dutch, and Belgian colonies) with the EEC also raised considerable difficulty under Article 24. The Community argued that these "association" agreements were free trade areas in the long run, while the GATT officials viewed them as rather open efforts at purely preferential tariff status. Similar problems arose later in the GATT review of the multitude of "evolving" free trade area treaties with Mediterranean nations. In 1975, the openly preferential and discriminatory Lomé Convention negotiated between the European Community and forty-six African, Pacific and Caribbean nations (including many former colonies) challenged the evolutionary character of Community "free trade areas" with developing states. Once again it was the GATT and not the European Community that gave way. In fairness, since 2000 the Cotonou Agreement at least pledges the EU and its Lomé partners to reciprocal free trade principles.

Despite these and other arguments, the Treaty of Rome passed through the GATT study and review communities without final resolution of its legal status under Article 24. Postponement of these issues became permanent. GATT attempts—through the lawyer-like conditions of Article 24 to maximize trade creation and minimize trade diversion—must be seen in the European context as generally inadequate. Treaty terms became negotiable demands that were not accepted.

FOLSOM, BILATERAL FREE TRADE AGREEMENTS: A CRITICAL ASSESSMENT AND WTO REGULATORY REFORM PROPOSAL

San Diego Legal Studies Paper No. 08–070
http://SSRN.com/abstract=1262872.

Developing Nation Bilaterals

Developing nations in Africa, the Caribbean, Central America, South America and Southeast Asia (among others) had free trade and customs union agreements in place as early as the 1960s. In 1979, under what is commonly called the Enabling Clause, the GATT parties decided to permit developing nations to enter into differential and more favorable bilateral, regional or global arrangements *among themselves* to reduce or eliminate tariffs and nontariff barriers applicable to trade in goods. Like Article 24, the Enabling Clause constitutes an exception to MFN trade principles. It has generally been construed to authorize third world free trade area and customs union agreements. Whether the Enabling Clause was intended to take such agreements out of Article 24 and its requirements, or be construed in conjunction therewith, is unclear. However, the creation of alternative notification and review procedures for Enabling Clause arrangements suggests Article 24 is inapplicable.

Notification to GATT of Enabling Clause arrangements is mandatory. Since 1995, the WTO Committee on Trade and Development (CTD) is the forum where such notifications are reviewed, but in practice not examined in depth. Enabling Clause arrangements should be designed to promote the trade of developing countries and not raise external trade barriers or undue trade difficulties. Consultations with individual GATT members experiencing such difficulties must be undertaken, and these consultations may be expanded to all GATT members if requested. Unlike GATT Article 24, neither compensation to nonparticipants nor formal reporting on the consistency with the Enabling Clause of developing nation arrangements is anticipated. Despite these relaxed procedures, the Enabling Clause of 1979 did not trigger a rush of third world bilaterals. More recently, the ASEAN-China (2004), India-Sri Lanka (2002), and "revived" Economic Community of West African States (ECOWAS 2005) agreements illustrate notified but unexamined preferential arrangements sheltered by the Enabling Clause.

Regulatory Reform: Interpreting Article 24

The early regulatory failure of Article 24 and the limited requirements of the Enabling Clause arguably created an incentive to reach free trade area and customs union agreements as a means to avoid MFN trade principles. In the 1960s, 1970s and into the 1980s, a goodly number of bilaterals were established, especially in the developing world. Yet there was no avalanche of agreements, in part because of a steady stream of MFN successes in GATT negotiating rounds. The turning point came when major delays and perceptions of possible failure in the Uruguay Round (1986–1994) accelerated the creation of bilaterals, most visibly the Canada-U.S. FTA of 1989 and NAFTA (1994). The emergence, also, of export-driven (not import substituting) developing economies, such as Mexico and Chile, also contributed to this acceleration.

The Uruguay Round, which created the World Trade Organization, presented an opportunity to come to grips with the regulatory failure of Article 24 and the implications of the Enabling Clause. Agreement was reached in 1994 on an "Understanding on the Interpretation of Article 24," which presently binds the roughly 150 member nations of the WTO. This Interpretation reaffirms that free trade area and customs union agreements *must* satisfy the provisions of Article 24, clarifies the manner in which before and after evaluations of common external tariffs are to be undertaken, limits in most cases interim agreements to 10 years, and details Article 24 notification, report and recommendation duties and processes. Most importantly, the 1994 Understanding on Interpretation expressly permits invocation of standard WTO dispute settlement procedures (DSU) regarding any Article 24 matters. That said, the 1994 Understanding did not come to grips with the systemic ambiguities that led to Article 24's early and ongoing regulatory failure.

Integrated Services' Agreements

DSU procedures may also be invoked since 1995 regarding "economic integration agreements" (EIAs) covering services under Article 5 of the General Agreement on Trade in Services (GATS). Such agreements, which can be staged, must have "substantial sectoral coverage," eliminate "substantially" all discrimination in sectors subject to multilateral commitments, and not raise the "overall" level of barriers to trade in GATS services compared to before the EIA. EIAs involving developing nations are to be accorded "flexibility." Like GATT Article 24 customs unions, there is an Article 5 duty to compensate EIA nonparticipants.

Review of GATS Article 5 notifications is undertaken, when requested by the WTO Council for Trade in Services, by the Committee on Regional Trade Agreements. Thus, whereas CRTA examinations of GATT Article 24 agreements are required, such examinations are optional under GATS. Nevertheless, numerous Article 5 examinations have been conducted, including notably the services components of NAFTA, the EEC Treaty (1957) and EU Enlargement (2004), Japan's FTAs with Singapore, Mexico and Malaysia, China's FTAs with Hong Kong and Macau, and various U.S. bilaterals. None of these examinations have resulted in a final report on consistency with GATS Article 5.

The Impact of the Seattle and Doha Rounds

The failure to launch a new round of WTO negotiations in Seattle (1999), followed by delays and perceptions of possible failure in the Doha Round that commenced in 2001, has contributed to a veritable feeding frenzy of bilaterals. Well over 100 new agreements have been notified to the WTO, and a large additional number are believed *not* to have been notified. In general, most of the notified agreements are bilateral, not regional in character. Meanwhile, the WTO Regional Trade Agreements Committee, working by consensus, has been unable since 1995 to complete even one assessment of a bilateral agreement's conformity to GATT Article 24 or GATS Article 5. The same is true for WTO Committee on Trade and Development "review" of Enabling Clause arrangements.

It has been suggested that this record can be explained by the ambiguous relationship between Committee reports and WTO dispute settlement proceedings. For example, can such reports be used in evidence in WTO dispute proceedings? Can fact-finding by WTO Secretariat and information gathered for WTO regulatory purposes be similarly used? This "dispute settlement awareness" makes WTO members reluctant to provide information or agree on conclusions that could later be used or interpreted in DSU proceedings.

The Transparency Mechanism of 2006

The second post-Uruguay Round of regulatory failure put bilaterals on the Doha negotiating agenda. Special emphasis has been placed on "transparency" issues, i.e., notification and reporting duties. Surprisingly, in June 2006, agreement was reached on a "Transparency Mechanism for Regional Trade Agreements." This agreement has been provisionally implemented, although it is less than clear that it will bring about all required notifications and still retains the ex post facto nature of WTO regulatory review. Whether this Mechanism will solve the present regulatory gridlock is seriously problematic.

The Transparency Mechanism envisions multiple electronic filings and detailed data submissions by parties to bilaterals, and substantial posting of such information on the WTO website. Announcement of negotiations should be "early," notification of agreements "as early as possible" but no later than after ratification and before application of preferential treatment between the parties. In addition, the separate 1994 WTO Agreement on Rules of Origin specifies transparency requirements for bilaterals, including a duty to notify the WTO Secretariat of preferential rules of origin.

Review by the WTO of bilaterals should "normally" be concluded within a year of notification. The WTO Secretariat will prepare a "factual presentation" *primarily* based on information submitted by the parties, but if necessary from other sources. The Secretariat is admonished to "refrain from any value judgment." Most importantly, its factual presentation may not be used "as a basis for dispute settlement procedures" or "to create new rights and obligations for members." A general notice and comment period is prescribed. Subsequently, the CRTA and CTD will, as a rule, devote a single formal meeting to consider each notified agreement.

A Reform Proposal

Bilaterals presently fall under two WTO jurisdictions: (1) The disparate regulatory regimes of GATT Article 24, GATS Article 5 and the

Enabling Clause, and (2) the WTO Dispute Settlement Understanding (DSU). The regulatory regimes have a 60-year history of failure. At most they have contributed to information sharing and peer pressure regarding bilaterals, and even that accomplishment has a spotty record.

The DSU, this author believes, has broadly achieved a reasonable degree of success in obtaining member state compliance with WTO agreements, and has already developed some expertise in proceedings where bilaterals have been at issue. Specifically, the Appellate Body has suggested that parties raising Article 24 defenses in DSU proceedings must be prepared to have their bilateral agreements examined for compliance with WTO rules.[51] Moreover, the professionalism of WTO panels and its Appellate Body has been commendable, the DSU does not suffer from gridlock, and it relies on member state interests (not WTO consensus) for its driving force. Indeed, because GATT Article 24 and GATS Article 5 often trigger compensation rights for nonparticipants, member states are already quite interested in bilaterals and have reason to challenge their WTO conformity.

* * *

I therefore propose abandoning the WTO regulatory regimes applicable to bilaterals, save only notification and data reporting duties established in the 2006 Transparency Mechanism. Any failure to fulfill these duties should be sanctioned by creating a rebuttable presumption of WTO nonconformity. The opportunity for interested member states to pursue DSU proceedings regarding bilaterals should be as clearly delineated for GATS Article 5 and the Enabling Clause as it is in the 1994 Understanding on Interpretation of GATT Article 24. In all cases, the right to pursue such remedies should *not* depend upon proper notification of the bilateral agreement in question.

TREATY ON THE FUNCTIONING OF THE EUROPEAN UNION (TFEU) (2009)

Article 36

Quantitative restrictions on imports and all measures having equivalent effect shall be prohibited between Member States.

Article 37

Quantitative restrictions on exports, and all measures having equivalent effect, shall be prohibited between Member States.

---

51. *Id.*, Article 12. See Turkey—Textiles, WT/DS34/AB/R (Nov. 19, 1999) (Turkey's invocation of Article 24 customs union "defense" to Article 11 and 13 GATT quota violations rejected by Appellate Body; Turkey bears burden of proof of compliance with Article 24); Canada - Certain Measures Affecting the Automotive Industry, WT/DS 139/R, WT/DS 1442/R (June 19, 2000) (Article 24 defense rejected by WTO Panel). See generally, Hafez, "Weak Discipline: GATT Article XXIV and the Emerging WTO Jurisprudence on RTAs," 78 North Dak.L.Rev. 879 (2003).

Article 38

The provisions of Articles 36 and 37 shall not preclude prohibitions or restrictions on imports, exports or goods in transit justified on grounds of public morality, public policy or public security; the protection of health and life of humans, animals or plants; the protection of national treasures possessing artistic, historic or archaeological value; or the protection of industrial and commercial property. Such prohibitions or restrictions shall not, however, constitute a means of arbitrary discrimination or a disguised restriction on trade between Member States.

R. FOLSOM, EUROPEAN UNION LAW IN A NUTSHELL

Chapter 5 (2011).*

FREE MOVEMENT OF GOODS

The free movement of goods within Europe is based upon the creation of a customs union. Under this union, the member states have eliminated customs duties among themselves. They have established a common customs tariff for their trade with the rest of the world. Quantitative restrictions (quotas) on trade between member states are also prohibited, except in emergency and other limited situations. The right of free movement applies to goods that originate in the Common Market *and* to those that have lawfully entered it and are said to be in "free circulation."

Measures of Equivalent Effect

The establishment of the customs union has been a major accomplishment, though not without difficulties. The member states not only committed themselves to the elimination of tariffs and quotas on internal trade, but also to the elimination of "measures of equivalent effect." The elastic legal concept of measures of equivalent effect has been interpreted broadly by the European Court of Justice and the Commission to prohibit a wide range of trade restraints, such as administrative fees charged at borders which are the equivalent of tariffs. Charges of equivalent effect to a tariff must be distinguished from internal taxes that are applicable to imported and domestic goods. The latter must be levied in a nondiscriminatory manner (Article 110 TFEU), while the former are prohibited entirely (Articles 28, 30, 34). There has been a considerable amount of litigation over this distinction.

The elasticity of the concept of measures of an equivalent effect is even more pronounced in the Court's judgments relating to quotas. This jurisprudence draws upon an early Commission directive (no longer applicable) of extraordinary scope. In this directive (No. 70/50), the Commission undertook a lengthy listing of practices that it considered illegal measures of equivalent effect to quotas. It is still occasionally referenced in Commission and Court of Justice decisions. The directive's focus was on national rules that discriminate against imports or simply restrain internal trade.

---

* © West Publishing Co.

Cassis Formula

This "effects test" soon found support from the ECJ. In the famous *Dassonville* case, the Court of Justice ruled that Belgium could not block the importation via France of Scotch whiskey lacking a British certificate of origin as required by Belgian customs law. The Court of Justice held that any national rule directly or indirectly, actually or potentially capable of hindering internal trade is generally forbidden as a measure of equivalent effect to a quota. However, *if* European law has not developed appropriate rules in the area concerned (here designations of origin), the member states may enact "reasonable" and "proportional" (no broader than necessary) regulations to ensure that the public is not harmed.

This is commonly called the "*Cassis* formula," after the "Cassis de Dijon" case, in which a German *minimum* alcoholic beverage rule was held unreasonable. Products meeting reasonable national criteria, the *Cassis* formula continues, may be freely traded. The *Cassis* formula is also the origin of the "mutual reciprocity" principle used in significant parts of the legislative campaign for a Europe without internal frontiers.

The *Cassis* decision suggests use of a Rule of Reason analysis for national fiscal regulations, public health measures, laws governing the fairness of commercial transactions and consumer protection. Environmental protection and occupational safety laws of the member states have been similarly treated. Under this approach, for example, a Danish "bottle bill" requiring use of only *approved* containers was unreasonable. However, the Danes' argument that a deposit and return system was environmentally necessary prevailed. This was a reasonable restraint on internal trade recognized by the Court under the *Cassis* formula for analyzing compelling state interests.

Under *Cassis,* national rules requiring country of origin or "foreign origin" labels have fallen as measures of effect equivalent to quotas. So have various restrictive national procurement laws, including a "voluntary" campaign to "Buy Irish." Minimum and maximum retail pricing controls can also run afoul of the Court's expansive interpretation of measures of equivalent effect. Compulsory patent licensing can amount to a measure of equivalent effect. Where demand for the patented product was satisfied by imports from another member state, the U.K. could not compulsorily require manufacturing within its jurisdiction. Member states may not impose linguistic labelling requirements so as to block trade and competition in foodstuffs. In one instance, a Belgian law requiring Dutch labels in Flemish areas was nullified as in conflict with the Treaty. These cases vividly illustrate the extent to which litigants are invoking the TFEU and the *Cassis* formula in attempts at overcoming commercially restrictive national laws.

There are cases which suggest that "cultural interests" may justify national restrictions on European trade. For example, British, French and Belgian bans on Sunday retail trading survived scrutiny under the *Cassis* formula. And British prohibitions of sales of sex articles, except by licensed sex shops, are compatible. However, national marketing laws (e.g., prohibiting sales below cost), when applied without discrimination (especially market access discrimination) as between imports and domestic products, are not considered to affect trade between the member states. In the remarkable *Keck* decision signaling a jurisprudential retreat, the ECJ held that marketing rules may not be challenged under the traditional *Cassis* formula. As to what constitutes "marketing rules," deceptive trade practices laws ordinarily fall outside the scope of *Keck*, while national laws regulating sale outlets and advertising of goods may be embraced.

In recent years, member state regulations capable of being characterized as governing "marketing modalities" or "selling arrangements" have sought shelter under *Keck*. For example, the French prohibition of televised advertising (intended to favor printed media) of the distribution of goods escaped the rule of reason analysis of *Cassis* in this manner, but the Swedish ban on magazine ads for alcoholic beverages did not since it discriminated against market access by imports. Some commentators see in *Keck* and its progeny an unarticulated attempt by the Court to take subsidiarity seriously. Others are just baffled by its newly found tolerance for trade distorting national marketing laws. But the Court of Justice has poignantly refused to extend *Keck* to the marketing of services, and case law suggests *Keck* may be fading into obscurity.

The Court has made it clear that all of the Rule of Reason justifications for national regulatory laws are temporary. Adoption of Common Market legislation in any area would eliminate national authority to regulate trading conditions under *Dassonville, Cassis* and (presumably) *Keck*. All of these judicial mandates, none of which are specified in the TFEU, acutely demonstrate the powers the Court of Justice to expansively interpret the Treaty and rule on the validity under European law of national legislation affecting internal trade in goods.

ARTICLE 36 AND THE PROBLEM OF NONTARIFF TRADE BARRIERS

The provisions of the TFEU dealing with the establishment of the customs union do not adequately address the problem of nontariff trade barriers (NTBs). As in the world community, the major trade barrier within Europe has become NTBs. To some extent, in the absence of a harmonizing directive completely occupying the field, this is authorized. Article 36 of the Treaty permits national restraints on imports and exports justified on the grounds of:

- public morality, public policy ("order public") or public security;
- the protection of health and life of humans, animals or plants;
- the protection of national treasures possessing artistic, historical or archeological value; and
- the protection of industrial or commercial property.

Article 36 amounts, within certain limits, to an authorization of nontariff trade barriers among the EU nations. This "public interest" authorization exists in addition to but somewhat overlaps with the Rule of Reason exception formulated under Article 34 in *Dassonville* and *Cassis* (above). However, in a sentence much construed by the European Court of Justice, Article 36 continues with the following language: "Such prohibitions or restrictions shall not, however, constitute a means of arbitrary discrimination or a disguised restriction on trade between member states."

* * *

NTBs AND THE SINGLE MARKET

Nontariff trade barrier problems have been the principal focus of the campaign for a fully integrated Common Market. Many legislative acts have been adopted or are in progress which target NTB trade problems. There are basically two different methodologies being employed. When possible, a common European standard is adopted. For example, legislation on auto pollution requirements adopts this methodology. Products meeting these standards may be freely traded in the Common Market. Traditionally, this approach (called "harmonization") has required the formation of a consensus as to the appropriate level of protection.

Once adopted, harmonized standards must be followed. This approach can be deceptive, however. Some harmonization directives contain a list of options from which member states may choose when implementing those directives. In practice, this leads to differentiated national laws on the same so-called harmonized subject. Furthermore, in certain areas (notably the environment and occupational health and safety), the TFEU and certain directives expressly indicate that member states may adopt laws that are more demanding. The result is, again, less than complete harmonization.

* * *

Harmonization Principles

Many efforts at the harmonization of European environmental, health and safety, standards and certification, and related law have been undertaken. Nearly all of these are supposed to be based upon "high levels of protection." Some have criticized what they see as the "least common denominator" results of harmonization of national laws under the campaign for a Europe without internal frontiers. One example involves the safety of toys. Directive 88/378 permits toys to be sold throughout the Common Market if they satisfy "essential requirements." These requirements are broadly worded in terms of flammability, toxicity, etc. There are two ways to meet these requirements: (1) produce a toy in accordance with private CEN standards (drawn up by experts); or (2) produce a toy that otherwise meets the essential safety requirements. Local language labeling requirements necessary for purchaser comprehension have generally, though not always, been upheld.

The least common denominator criticism is also raised regarding the second legislative methodology utilized in the internal market campaign. The second approach is based on the *Cassis* principle of mutual reciprocity. Under this "new" minimalist approach, European legislation generally requires member states to recognize the standards laws of other member states and deem them acceptable for purposes of the operation of the Common Market. However, major legislation has been adopted in the area of professional services. By mutual recognition of vocational diplomas based upon at least three years of courses, virtually all professionals have now obtained legal rights to move freely in pursuit of their careers. This is a remarkable achievement.

COMMISSION v. FEDERAL REPUBLIC OF GERMANY
Court of Justice of the European Community, 1987.
1987 Eur.Comm.Rep. 1227.

All the Member States, with the exception of Greece and the Federal Republic of Germany, permit ingredients other than malted barley and, in addition, certain additives to be used in the manufacture of beer. Consequently, the Commission expressed the view in a formal letter of notice sent to the German Government on February 12, 1982, that Paragraphs 9 and 10 of the Biersteuergesetz create barriers to imports into Germany of beer lawfully manufactured in other countries insofar as it was not brewed in accordance with the relevant German legislation, and hence constitute an infringement of Article 30 of the EEC Treaty.

In its replies to that formal letter of notice, the German Government defended its rules, explaining that they were intended to reduce the total consumption of additives in Germany. If only the ingredients permitted by the Biersteuergesetz were used, beer could be made without using additives. In its view, the rules were also intended to protect consumers from being misled as to the composition of beer.

Notwithstanding the explanations furnished by the German Government, on August 25, 1983, the Commission delivered a reasoned opinion in which it expressed the view that, by prohibiting the marketing of beer lawfully produced and marketed in other Member States unless such beer complied with the requirements of Paragraphs 9 and 10 of the Biersteuergesetz, the Federal Republic of Germany had failed to fulfill its obligations under Article 30 of the EEC Treaty. In the statement of the grounds on which that reasoned opinion was based, the Commission explained that any beer manufactured from ingredients other than those listed in Paragraph 9 of the Biersteuergesetz could not be marketed in Germany and that such a barrier to trade was contrary to Article 30 of the EEC Treaty, as it has been interpreted by the Court of Justice. The Commission rejected the arguments advanced by the Federal Republic of Germany because it considered, on the one hand, that it had not been established that there was no technological need to use additives in beer and, on the other, that it was possible to protect consumers by much less drastic measures than an absolute prohibition on marketing.

On March 23, 1984, the Commission delivered a supplementary reasoned opinion with which it enclosed an expert's report.

Since the Federal Republic failed to amend its legislation within the period prescribed in the supplementary reasoned opinion, the Commission brought this action by an application of July 4, 1984, registered at the Court of Justice on July 6, 1984.

* * *

OPINION

The German Government's argument that Paragraph 10 of the Biersteuergesetz is essential in order to protect German consumers because, in their minds, the designation "Bier" is inseparably linked to the beverage manufactured solely from the ingredients laid down in Paragraph 9 of the Biersteuergesetz must be rejected.

Firstly, consumers' conceptions which vary from one Member State to the other are also likely to evolve in the course of time within a Member State. The establishment of the Common Market is, it should be added, one of the factors that may play a major contributory role in that development. Whereas rules protecting consumers against misleading practices enable such a development to be taken into account, legislation of the kind contained in Paragraph 10 of the Biersteuergesetz prevents it from taking place. As the Court of Justice has already held in another context (judgment of February 27, 1980, in Case No. 170/78, *Commission v. United Kingdom* [1980] E.C.R. 417 [¶ 8651]), the legislation of a Member State must not "crystallize given consumer habits so as to consolidate an advantage acquired by the national industries concerned to comply with them."

Secondly, in the other Member States of the Community the designations corresponding to the German designation "Bier" are generic designations for a fermented beverage manufactured from malted barley, whether malted barley on its own or with the addition of rice or maize. The same approach is taken in Community law, as can be seen from heading No. 22.03 of the Common Customs Tariff. The German legislature itself utilizes the designation "Bier" in that way in Paragraph 9(7) and (8) of the Biersteuergesetz in order to refer to beverages not complying with the manufacturing rules laid down in Paragraph 9(1) and (2).

The German designation "Bier" and its equivalents in the languages of the other Member States of the Community may therefore not be restricted to beers manufactured in accordance with the rules in force in the Federal Republic of Germany.

It is admittedly legitimate to seek to enable consumers who attribute specific qualities to beers manufactured from particular raw materials to make their choice in the light of that consideration. However, as the Court of Justice has already emphasized (judgment of December 9, 1981, in Case No. 193/80, *Commission v. Italy* [1981] E.C.R. 3019 [¶ 8788]), that possibility may be ensured by means which do not prevent the importation of products which have been lawfully manufactured and marketed in other Member States and, in particular, "by the compulsory affixing of suitable labels giving the nature of the product sold." By indicating the raw materials utilized in the manufacture of beer "such a course would enable the consumer to make his choice in full knowledge of the facts, and would guarantee transparency in trading and in offers to the public." It must be added that such a system of mandatory consumer information must not entail negative assessments for beers not complying with the requirements of Paragraph 9 of the Biersteuergesetz.

* * *

It follows from the foregoing that by applying the rules on designation in Paragraph 10 of the Biersteuergesetz to beers imported from other Member States which were manufactured and marketed lawfully in those States the Federal Republic of Germany has failed to fulfill its obligations under Article 30 of the EEC Treaty.

* * *

The Court of Justice has consistently held (in particular in the judgment of July 14, 1983, in Case No. 174/82, *Criminal proceedings against Sandoz BV* [1983] E.C.R. 2445 [¶ 14,006]) that "insofar as there are uncertainties at the present state of scientific research it is for the Member States, in the absence of harmonization, to decide what degree of protection of the health and life of humans they intend to assure, having regard, however, to the requirements of the free movement of goods within the Community."

* * *

However, the application to imported products of prohibitions on marketing products containing additives which are authorized in the Member State of production but prohibited in the Member State of importation is permissible only insofar as it complies with the requirements of Article 36 of the Treaty as it has been interpreted by the Court of Justice.

It must be borne in mind, in the first place, that in its judgments in the *Sandoz, Motte* and *Muller* cases, cited above, the Court of Justice inferred from the principle of proportionality underlying the last sentence of Article 36 of the Treaty that prohibitions on the marketing of products containing additives authorized in the Member State of production but prohibited in the Member State of importation must be restricted to what is actually necessary to secure the protection of public health. The Court also concluded that the use of a specific additive which is authorized in another Member State must be authorized in the case of a product imported from that Member State where, in view, on the one hand, of the findings of international scientific research, and in particular of the work of the Community's Scientific Committee for Food, the Codex Alimentarius Committee of the Food and Agriculture Organization of the United Nations (FAO) and the World Health Organization, and, on the other hand, of the eating habits prevailing in the importing Member State, the additive in question does not present a risk to public health and meets a real need, especially a technological one.

* * *

It must be observed that the German rules on additives applicable to beer result in the exclusion of all the additives authorized in the other Member States and not the exclusion of just some of them for which there is concrete justification by reason of the risks which they involve in view of the eating habits of the German population; moreover, those rules do not lay down any procedure whereby traders can obtain authorization for the use of a specific additive in the manufacture of beer by means of a measure of general application.

As regards more specifically the harmfulness of additives, the German Government, citing experts' reports, has referred to the risks inherent in the ingestion of additives in general. It maintains that it is important, for reasons of general preventive health protection, to minimize the quantity of additives ingested, and that it is particularly advisable to prohibit altogether their use in the manufacture of beer, a foodstuff consumed in considerable quantities by the German population.

However, it appears from the tables of additives authorized for use in the various foodstuffs submitted by the German Government itself that some of the additives authorized in other Member States for use in the manufacture of beer are also authorized under the German rules, in particular the Regulation on Additives, for use in the manufacture of all, or virtually all, beverages. Mere reference to the potential risks of the ingestion of additives in general and to the fact that beer is a foodstuff consumed in large quantities does not suffice to justify the imposition of stricter rules in the case of beer.

* * *

Consequently, insofar as the German rules on additives in beer entail a general ban on additives, their application to beers imported from other Member States is contrary to the requirements of Community law as laid down in the case law of the Court of Justice, since that prohibition is contrary to the principle of proportionality and is therefore not covered by the exception provided for in Article 36 [now Article 30] of the EEC Treaty.

[**Authors' Note:** German "pure beer" laws continue to apply to imports from outside the EU. It appears that the only U.S. beer allowed into Germany is Samuel Adams.]

PART B.   NAFTA

CANTIN AND LOWENFELD, RULES OF ORIGIN, THE CANADA–U.S. FTA, AND THE HONDA CASE *

87 Am.J.Int'l L. 375 (1993).

When the FTA came into effect in January 1989, Honda of Canada treated the engines used in the Civic and manufactured in the United States as qualified under the FTA for purposes of importation into Canada, and American Honda treated the Civics manufactured in Canada as qualified under the FTA for purposes of importation into the United States. Both of these positions were reviewed by the respective customs authorities. The claim concerning the engines came before the Customs and Excise branch of Revenue Canada, and the claim concerning the finished automobile came before the United States Customs Service, a branch of the U.S. Treasury Department. Both services conducted careful investigations, and their decisions were issued within five days of each other, in February 1992.

Honda explained its engine production and assembly processes as follows: First, the head and block subassemblies, classifiable as parts of engine under subheading 8409.91 HS, were produced in the United States. Second, these subassemblies were assembled and processed with other components imported from Japan to produce an engine classifiable under subheading 8407.34 HS. Third, the engines were shipped to Canada to be incorporated into the Honda Civics produced in Ontario. Honda maintained that the sum of U.S.-origin components of the engine and the direct costs of assembling and processing in the United States brought the engine up to the 50 percent North American requirement, and thus that the engine was entitled to duty-free treatment in Canada.

Revenue Canada held that all except fifteen hundred of the seventy-one thousand 1.5 liter automobile engines manufactured in Ohio qualified for duty-free treatment under the FTA. The exact percentage of the local content of the engines has not been released, but it is generally believed that Revenue Canada found the figure to be around 66 percent, including the "direct cost of processing." Revenue Canada included under this heading "certain additional production costs from the final engine assembly process to the head (valve) sub-assembly and the block sub-assembly."

In its submissions to the U.S. Customs Service, Honda of Canada contended that the non-North American components of the Civics imported into Canada had incurred a change in tariff classification in the process of assembly of the cars, and that many non-Canadian components, notably the engine manufactured in Ohio, met the 50 percent North American content requirement and thus could be counted as 100 percent North American by virtue of the roll-up rule. Accordingly, Honda argued, the

---

* Reproduced with permission from 87 AJIL 375 (1993), © The American Society of International Law.

completed cars met the 50 percent content requirement and could enter the United States duty-free. To substantiate this contention, however, Honda of Canada needed to count the engines imported from the United States as "material originating in the United States."

Revenue Canada, as we saw, agreed on this point with Honda. On the basis of the same facts, the U.S. Customs Service reached the opposite conclusion. U.S. Customs determined that the Honda Civics did not qualify for the duty-free treatment given to cars under the FTA, because they contained too many Japanese parts by value, and thus did not meet the 50 percent local content requirement of the FTA. In particular, Customs regarded the engines sent from Ohio to Ontario as not meeting the 50 percent requirement and, under the roll-down rule, Customs therefore treated the engines as having zero North American content. Honda was handed a retroactive bill of $17 million for the 2.5 percent ad valorem back tariffs on Civics shipped to the United States through March 1, 1990.

* * *

The U.S. Customs action in what became known as "the *Honda* case" propelled the rules of origin of the FTA to the front line of the trade conflicts between Canada and the United States. All over Canada, the decision was big news. Prime Minister Mulroney said, "We are getting sideswiped by American Japan-bashing." Others thought it was more like Canada-bashing, or at least confirmation of their negative views on the FTA in general. The U.S. officials tried to play the controversy down, explaining that it was merely a technical dispute having no bearing on their overall attitude to the FTA.

* * *

Some Reflections

The Honda story, whatever the correct interpretation of the obscure annexes by obscure bureaucrats, shows that we have arrived in the era not only of multinational enterprises, but of multinational goods. To speak of a Honda as a Japanese car made in Canada with an American engine may be simpler than struggling through roll-ups and roll-downs, tracing and "reasonable allocation," direct and indirect costs—all designed to aim for a mythical citizenship of a car that clearly has no citizenship. This is true not only of a Honda Civic, but of a good many other automobiles, computers, copying machines and so on, including many with United States parents or grandparents.

We might want to look at the parentage of a car, and conclude that the North American Honda's parents are Japanese. But what about joint ventures, like GM–Toyota in Fremont, California, or the GM–Suzuki in Ingersoll, Ontario, one of whose parents seems to have been able to extract a special deal from the drafters of NAFTA?

Of course, no one wants to permit evasions—taking a foreign product and wrapping it in a domestic package. In fact, both the FTA and NAFTA have clauses to prevent goods from being considered to have originated in the country of a party merely by virtue of simple packaging or dilution with water, or any process justifying the presumption that its sole object was to circumvent the Rules of Origin chapter. But granted that none of the techniques here illustrated account for the "true" value of a product—including concept, research and development, long-term planning, corporate culture, and on and on—it is fair to ask what the objection is to a car (or a camera, machine tool or whatever) assembled in one member state of a free trade area entering duty-free into the territory of another country. Did the United States want to collect the 2.5 percent duty on Hondas coming from Canada that it would have collected if the completed car had been imported from Japan? Or did it want to encourage assembly operations in the United States rather than in Canada? If the latter is true, where is the spirit of the Free Trade Agreement?

We do not know what the administrative cost of tracing and tracking is for the 50 percent value-added method, though we are not surprised at the report that many companies have decided that it is cheaper to pay the duty than to go through the audits and hassles required by U.S. Customs. The Rules of Origin, in other words, may themselves have become nontariff barriers. Complicated rules not only reflect side deals and hidden motives; they also obscure and undermine the objectives of a free trade agreement.

Looking at the pages of regulations aimed at bringing assembly plants in Mexico into the discipline of Rules of Origin, is the United States—worker, consumer, member of Congress—more worried about a Nissan or Toyota assembly plant in Mexico than about a GM or Ford plant? One might have thought that the fear in the United States was about plants moving from Michigan to Mexico, which will not be hampered at all by tight rules of origin.

There may be some answers to these questions—narrow calculations of special interests of various kinds. But it *is* the numbers that seem to count, not the principle. True as that is for much of modern trade law in operation, it seems especially true—and unsettling—about rules of origin.

McCALL, WHAT IS ASIA AFRAID OF? THE DIVERSIONARY EFFECT OF NAFTA's RULES OF ORIGIN ON TRADE BETWEEN THE UNITED STATES AND ASIA

25 Cal.W. Int'l L.J. 389 (1995).*

THE NAFTA's RULES OF ORIGIN

The NAFTA rules of origin raised some of the more controversial and difficult issues in the NAFTA negotiations. The governments involved, as

---

* © 1995 California Western International Law Journal. Reprinted with permission.

well as those representing economic and political interests in the three countries, wanted the reduced duties available under NAFTA to benefit only products that involve significant manufacturing and other economic activity in the three countries. Most particularly, the NAFTA members did not want Mexico, with its lower wage rates and other costs, to be used as an "export platform" for entry into the United States of goods that consisted largely of third-country materials.

Consequently, the NAFTA rules of origin are detailed, complex, and comprehensive. NAFTA includes a twenty-six page Rules of Origin section, including express definitions of thirty terms, a seventeen page Customs Procedure section, two pages of a Notes section, and a 169 page annex with specific rules of origin for individual Harmonized System chapters.

* * *

TARIFF–SHIFT RULES

A good may qualify as an originating good only when each nonoriginating material used to produce the good undergoes an applicable "change in tariff classification" as a result of production in one or more of the NAFTA countries. The particular change required depends on the tariff classification of the good involved. A change in origin based on a shift in tariff classification is a relatively recent development resulting from the adoption by most countries of the International Convention on the Harmonized Commodity Description and Coding System ("Harmonized System").

* * *

The following illustration is an example of the tariff-shift rules of origin under NAFTA: Canada produces bread, pastries, cakes, and biscuits, which come under Harmonized System Number 1905.90, with flour imported from Europe. The flour is categorized as Harmonized System Chapter 11. These items are then shipped to the United States. The applicable rule of origin states: "A change to heading 19.02 through 19.05 from any other chapter." Thus, for all products classified in Harmonized System Headings 1902 through 1905, all non-North American inputs must be classified in an Harmonized System chapter other than Harmonized System Chapter 19 in order to be considered "originating goods." These baked goods would qualify for NAFTA benefits because the non-originating material, the flour, is classified outside of Chapter 19.

VALUE–CONTENT RULES

Where the non-originating part or parts do not qualify as originating goods under the change in tariff classification test, the product can still be treated as originating in NAFTA if it meets the required regional value-content test.

Regional value-content rules require a percentage of the value of the good to be North American. A good will qualify as an originating good if the assembly of such parts and components within NAFTA accounts for sixty percent of the value of the finished product or fifty percent of the net cost of the product. Under Article 402 of NAFTA, the regional value content can be calculated by either the transaction value or the net-cost method.

THE TRANSACTION-VALUE METHOD

The transaction-value method generally means the price actually paid or payable for the good. The transaction-value method is generally easier to calculate than the net-cost method. A manufacturer may choose whichever method is most advantageous to his goods with certain exceptions.

The transaction-value method calculates regional content by: (1) subtracting the price paid for non-NAFTA-origin materials used in the production of the good from the price charged the consumer for the finished good and (2) dividing that figure by the price charged the consumer. If the product contains more than sixty percent regional value content, it qualifies as an originating good. Put simply, the assembly of parts and components within the NAFTA zone must account for at least sixty percent of the value of the finished product. For example, a Mexican manufacturer produces electric hair curling irons from Japanese hair curler parts. Each curling iron is sold for U.S. $4.40. The value of the non-originating hair curler parts is U.S. $1.80.

The hair curling iron is not an originating good because its regional value content is below 60% using the transaction value method.

THE NET-COST METHOD

The net-cost method is based on the total cost of the good minus sales promotion, marketing, after-sales service, royalties, shipping, packing, and non-allowable interest costs. The net-cost method calculates regional content by subtracting the price paid for non-NAFTA-origin materials from the net cost to the producer of the good and dividing that figure by the net cost to the producer. If the product contains more than fifty percent regional content, it will qualify as an originating product.

For example, assume the Mexican manufacturer above uses the net cost method for the hair curling irons imported into the United States. The total cost for the hair curler is U.S. $3.90. This figure includes U.S. $0.25 for shipping and packing costs. There are no other costs. The net cost therefore is U.S. $3.65.

The hair curling iron would be considered an originating good using the net cost method because the regional value content is a little over 50%.

* * *

TEXTILES AND MOTOR VEHICLES: THE TWO ASIAN
INDUSTRIES HARDEST HIT BY NAFTA

While NAFTA may not cause the kinds of problems Asia envisions, the rigorous rules of origin requirements for textiles and autos will cause some difficulties.

Textiles and motor vehicles are the two areas under NAFTA that have the most restrictive rules of origin requirements. Coincidentally, these two trade sectors are the two Asian industries that will be most affected by NAFTA's rules of origin.

Textiles

Asia accounts for a huge share of the U.S. textile and apparel market. In 1989, textiles accounted for over 30% of all exports from Hong Kong, South Korea, and the People's Republic of China. The developing economies of Southeast Asia exported $47.9 billion in clothes alone in 1989; $19.5 billion worth was exported to Canada and the U.S. In 1991, China's $13 billion trade surplus with the United States was mostly from textiles.

Textile imports into the United States are subject to both quotas and tariffs under the Multifiber Arrangement (MFA). The MFA quotas restrict the quantity of imported textiles that can compete with textiles produced in the United States, providing strong protection for United States textile and apparel manufacturers. NAFTA will eliminate both tariffs and quotas for "qualifying" goods—goods manufactured in North America that meet the strict NAFTA textile rule of origin.

Textiles are considered "originating goods" under the NAFTA rules of origin according to the "yarn-forward" or "fiber forward" rule. The yarn-forward rule means that textiles and apparel goods must be constructed from yarn produced in a NAFTA country to be an originating good and receive the full benefits of NAFTA. Cotton products are subject to a "fiber forward" rule which is similar to the "yarn forward" requirement.

NAFTA will immediately remove import quotas on textiles from Mexico that qualify as an originating good under the yarn forward or fiber forward rule. The net effect of these eliminations will be the increased importation into the United States of textiles and apparel manufactured in Mexico using North American yarn and fabric. These increased imports from Mexico will occur at the expense of existing imports from Asia. In addition, they will result in an increase in U.S. exports of yarn and fabric to Mexico, while reducing North American imports of yarn and fabric from Asian countries.

NAFTA will put Asia at a severe disadvantage in the textile market. The origin rules for textiles are among the most restrictive in NAFTA. Many textile and apparel goods produced in Asia compete directly with those of Mexico in North American markets. As the U.S. tariffs for non-originating textiles are currently 17%, the removal of these tariffs for

Mexican textiles which qualify as originating goods will place Asian producers at a distinct price disadvantage.

Motor Vehicles

In 1990, Japan and South Korea exported nearly $24 billion worth of passenger motor vehicles, wholly produced in Asia, into Canada and the United States. These Asian automobile imports do not contain any North American components. Consequently, they did not satisfy the rules of origin requirements for duty-free entry into the United States under the pre–NAFTA rules, nor will they satisfy the NAFTA rules of origin. Therefore, NAFTA will have relatively little practical impact on these exports to North America.

In addition, the United States tariff on automobiles from Asia is only 2.5%. Since this tariff is so low, the United States elimination of its barriers to passenger automobiles manufactured in Mexico will have little effect on the relative competitiveness of Asian automobiles. The low tariff on Asian automobiles does not increase the cost of an Asian automobile by a significant amount compared to a Mexico-produced automobile.

Although NAFTA will not decrease North American sales of Asian automobiles by much, it will affect the Asian automobile parts industry significantly. The general NAFTA rule of origin for automobiles will require 62.5% regional content to qualify for NAFTA benefits. The former regional content requirement was 50%. Thus, the 62.5% NAFTA rule of origin will provide a strong incentive for North American automobile manufacturers to use North American auto parts.

The 62.5% local content requirement will also impact Japanese automobile manufacturing facilities located in North America. While these automobiles are assembled in North America with a North American workforce, most of the components for the automobiles are currently imported from Japan. These plants were designed to take advantage of the 50% local content rule in place before NAFTA's 62.5% requirement. The higher local content rule will force Japanese automakers to upgrade their North American manufacturing process to include more North American parts, costing them billions of dollars, to take advantage of NAFTA's preferential treatment.

In addition, NAFTA will have serious adverse effects on Asian imports of light trucks to the United States. The current U.S. truck tariffs of twenty-five percent for most light trucks will be eliminated for Mexican-produced light trucks. Thus, light trucks, and possibly minivans which satisfy NAFTA rules of origin will gain a strong advantage over comparable Asian-produced products, as they will not be subject to the 25% tariff. NAFTA will divert some production from Asia to Mexico, as producers seek to avoid the 25% U.S. tariff on the Asian-produced vehicles.

AUTHORS' NOTE ON MOVEMENT OF PLANTS FROM MEXICO TO CHINA

The NAFTA-driven investment and trade diversion to Mexico from Asia that McCall analyzes has been partly reversed. A rising number of firms have shut their plants in Mexico and moved to China, Vietnam or other parts of Asia. Many factors are at work, including much lower Asian labor costs, the rising peso, undervalued PRC yuan, and access to China's vast growing market. Perhaps most importantly China's WTO membership ensures MFN tariff treatment for its exports. Remember that the average U.S. tariff on manufactured goods is now only about three percent. Mexico's geographic advantage still favors "just-in-time" production, but air freight and computers have reduced that competitive edge. WTO membership also allows China to benefit from the elimination in 2005 of MFA quotas on trade in textiles. Since then there has been explosive growth in Chinese exports of apparel to the United States, Canada and even Mexico.

Moreover, as United States free trade agreements proliferate (e.g., Chile, Singapore, Central America), it is not certain that NAFTA's preferences will suffice for Mexico. Whether its businesses can significantly move from labor intensive assembly plants with limited technology to production centers that also perform research, product design and development is in doubt. As China and more broadly Asia become the world's manufacturing platform, Mexico may look back at an all-too-short "NAFTA honeymoon." How does this trend affect your analysis of the questions raised by SUNRISE in this problem?

R. FOLSOM, NAFTA AND FREE TRADE IN THE AMERICAS

Chapters 4 and 8 (2011).

Products and Service Standards-Related Measures (SRM)

Chapter 9 of the NAFTA agreement is titled "Standards-Related Measures." SRM embrace standards, technical regulations and conformity assessment procedures. All of these terms are defined. Standards are voluntary, technical regulations are mandatory, and conformity assessment procedures determine if standards or technical regulations have been fulfilled.

Chapter 9 of NAFTA concerns service and product standards and technical regulations and certifications of compliance. Adherence to the GATT Agreement on Technical Barriers to Trade of 1979 (the GATT Standards Code) was affirmed (but not incorporated by reference) in Chapter 9. However, this Code has been superseded by the WTO Agreement on Technical Barriers to Trade (1995) upon which Chapter 9 was largely modeled. All other international agreements of Canada, Mexico and the United States affecting the regulation of goods were also affirmed. By specific provision in Chapter 9, these include the Washington Convention on International Trade in Endangered Species of Wild Fauna and Flora (1973, 1979), the Montreal Protocol on Substances that Deplete the Ozone Layer (1987, 1990), the Canada-U.S. Agreement on Movement of Transboundary Hazardous Waste (1986) and the Mexico-U.S. Agreement on Cooperation for the Protection and Improvement of the Environment in the Border Area (1983).

With relatively few qualifications (notably a duty not to discriminate), NAFTA permits use of product and service standards and regulations as a <u>nontariff trade barrier</u>. Article 904 recognizes the right of each country to adopt, maintain or apply SRMs based on "legitimate objectives." Protection of domestic industries is specifically excluded as a legitimate objective. "Legitimate objectives" is defined in Article 915 as including "sustainable development" as well as safety, health, environmental and consumer protection. "Sustainable development" is not defined in the NAFTA agreement. At a minimum, it refers to Mexico's economic development goals. More generally, the term is often used to connote development that is *environmentally* sustainable. Thus, all the NAFTA partners may enact SRM that promote sustainable development. The level of protection of all of these interests is left to each NAFTA member-state and is preserved for all levels of government. The power to prohibit the importation of nonconforming goods or services from a NAFTA partner is expressly reserved.

All <u>legitimate objectives</u> for product or service SRM should (where appropriate) be reviewed in light of: (1) Fundamental climatic or geographical factors; (2) technological or infrastructural factors; or (3) scientific justification. "Assessments of risk" may be employed (but are not required) when evaluating legitimate trade regulatory objectives. Thus NAFTA's SRM rules, unlike its SPS rules, are not firmly linked to science. When utilized, assessments of risk "may" take into account available scientific evidence or technical information, intended end uses, methodology, or environmental conditions. Such assessments are strongly encouraged in establishing appropriate levels of national standards protection. In determining these levels, arbitrary or unjustifiable distinctions between similar goods or services must not be made if disguised restrictions on NAFTA trade, or discriminations between goods or services posing the same level of risk and providing similar benefits, result.

NAFTA requires SRM to be administered without discrimination under national and most-favored-nation treatment rules. But each member need only "seek" to ensure observance of these rules by <u>state or provincial</u> (not local) <u>governments</u>. Likewise, they need only seek compliance by nongovernmental standards organizations. Adoption of international SRM (such as the numerous International Standards Organization rules) is required except when inappropriate or ineffective to meet a nation's legitimate regulatory objectives. In a provision dear to environmentalists, NAFTA specifically provides that levels of protection that are higher than internationally mandated may be chosen.

No SRM creating unnecessary obstacles to NAFTA trade are permissible. No unnecessary obstacle to trade exists for these purposes if the demonstrable purpose of the SRM is to achieve a legitimate objective and goods meeting that objective are not excluded. The NAFTA partners promised to work jointly towards enhanced and compatible SRM. They agreed to treat each other's technical regulations and certification tests as equivalent when they adequately fulfill the importing partner's legitimate objectives, a commitment not found in the WTO Technical Barriers Agreement. The 1993 CUSFTA dispute settlement arbitration on Puerto Rican regulations governing the importation of long-life milk from Quebec stands for the principle that each partner must give the others the chance to prove equivalency. *See* Chapter 2.

Testing and approval procedures (conformity assessments) are subject to minimum procedural requirements. The licensing of product testing in the other countries must be on terms that are no less favorable than applied domestically. Lastly, there are extensive notification, publication, information-sharing, information center and technical cooperation duties intended to keep standards issues transparent. Further review, discussion and consultation is anticipated in a special NAFTA "Committee on Standards-Related Measures."

This professor believes that the Achilles Heel of NAFTA rests in its SPS and SRM provisions. We know from decades of experience in the European Union that as tariffs decline, nontariff trade barriers take on major importance. In NAFTA, unlike Europe or even portions of CUSFTA, there is no commitment to uniform harmonization or mutual recognition of standards and certifications. Indeed, NAFTA's express reservation of the right to block trade in goods or services that do not meet diverse national SPS or SRM moves in exactly the opposite direction. The primary hope is that NAFTA's numerous cooperative Committees can reach agreement.

That said, in the early years of NAFTA, there have been comparatively few SPS or SRM disputes of major consequence. For example, Mexico was supposed to have issued its standard for terminal attachment telephone equipment by January 1, 1995. Negotiations within the NAFTA Telecommunications Standards Subcommittee (TSSC) were prolonged by divisions of interest in market opening versus market protection. More than 2 years later, under U.S. pressure, the telecom standard was finally promulgated. Known in Mexico as a "norma," the standard contains 13 mandatory parameters and applies to telephones, fax machines, modems and other end-user devices.

CUSFTA, where some standards disputes went to arbitration, seems to have facilitated considerable cross-border recognition of SPS and SRM. In addition, NAFTA and the WTO Technical Barriers Agreement (1995) and WTO SPS Agreement (1995) have moved all three NAFTA partners towards greater recognition of international standards. If NAFTA manages to avoid the European experience, that would be miraculous.

* * *

Chapter 20 Intergovernmental Dispute Settlement

The intergovernmental dispute resolution procedures found in Chapter 20 of the NAFTA agreement apply absent more specific NAFTA provisions. As was the case with CUSFTA, these procedures were intended to be an alternative to GATT 1947 dispute settlement (since replaced by much more effective World Trade Organization (WTO) procedures). Private parties do not participate in Chapter 20 dispute settlement. Moreover, Article 2021 expressly prohibits rights of action asserting inconsistency with NAFTA against a member state. The United States Trade Representative (USTR), however, does afford interested persons the opportunity to comment on Chapter 20 proceedings. Private parties can and have lodged complaints with the USTR about member state measures that adversely affect them. Whether to proceed to Chapter 20 dispute settlement is strictly a matter of USTR discretion.

The right of each member state to elect between NAFTA or WTO dispute settlement is generally preserved. However, once made, the election is final. Use of Chapter 20 under NAFTA will be denied if the complainant takes the issue to the WTO. That said, as part of a broad evaluation of NAFTA/WTO choice of forum opportunities and risks, Professor David Gantz has noted that nations may sometimes judiciously frame their disputes so as to gain access to both NAFTA and WTO fora. *See* 14 American U. Int'l Law Rev. 1025 (1999) (citing Mexico-U.S. sugar/corn syrup trade complaints and the Canada-U.S. farm products blockade dispute). In Chapter 2 we noted that preserving the option of WTO dispute settlement allows the U.S. to challenge Canadian cultural industry trade restraints that have been excluded from CUSFTA and NAFTA. For any complaint that the remaining NAFTA nation wishes to join, the two complainants must resolve the choice of forum. Absent resolution, the dispute "normally" will be heard under NAFTA.

The right to elect as between NAFTA or WTO dispute settlement is qualified. If the dispute falls in certain categories, the responding nation may force the issue to be heard under Chapter 20. This is the case when the dispute concerns:

- Specified environmental or conservation agreements;
- Sanitary and phytosanitary (SPS) health regulations; or
- Environmental, health, safety or conservation product or service standards (SRM).

Why are these the only disputes where the responding nation may insist on the NAFTA forum? One reason may be the perception that these areas involve unusually sensitive trade matters. Another may be the desire to ensure that national standards are absolutely respected (as NAFTA requires) and insulated from potentially global challenges at the WTO. A third may be the "lessons" learned in the pre-NAFTA challenge by Mexico under GATT 1947 of the U.S. Marine Mammal Protection Act (dolphin-safe tuna). *See* BISD 39 Supp. 155 (1993). The United States certainly wanted no repetition of that adverse GATT Panel ruling, which it "blocked" by pressuring Mexico into a negotiated settlement. Nevertheless, in 2008, Mexico initiated WTO dispute proceedings against "dolphin safe" U.S. label rules and the Ninth Circuit decision, *Earth Island*

Institute v. Hogarth (494 F.3d 757, 2007) which required zero use of purse seine nets for "dolphin-safe" tuna labels. In 2010, the U.S. commenced NAFTA dispute proceedings seeking to force Mexico to withdraw its WTO complaint and refile it under NAFTA. The NAFTA agreement provides that "standards" disputes are to be exclusively pursued under NAFTA Chapter 20, applying nontariff trade barrier rules that favor individual national laws. In 2011, a WTO panel held in favor of Mexico's complaint, which Mexico declined to refile under NAFTA.

Recourse to Chapter 20 dispute settlement may ordinarily be had if an actual or proposed act is or would be inconsistent with NAFTA obligations. Canada and Mexico have, for example, threatened to carry to arbitration their challenge of the 1996 U.S. "Helms-Burton" law (110 Stat. 785) against trafficking in U.S. property confiscated by Cuba. For some provisions of the agreement, Chapter 20 can also be used to challenge measures that are consistent with the NAFTA but cause "nullification or impairment" of expected benefits. But the government procurement, investment, telecommunications, financial services, competition law and monopolies, temporary entry of business persons, and automotive trading (Annex 300-A) provisions in NAFTA typically *cannot* be challenged in this way.

Any member state with a substantial interest in a Chapter 20 dispute can join as a complaining party and thereby participate in solutions to the dispute. However, in all cases, NAFTA's general dispute settlement procedures are *not* binding. Consultations are followed by mediation by the NAFTA Free Trade Commission followed by arbitration before a 5-member panel. A "reverse selection" process is used to select the arbitration panel from a roster of acceptable panelists. It is possible to propose a panelist from off the roster, but such nominees can be vetoed without cause by the other side.

First, the chair is selected by consensus or by lot. The chair cannot be from the selecting country, but can come from outside NAFTA. For example, in the first Chapter 20 panel the chair came from Britain and in the second from Australia. Two panelists are chosen by both parties. Each side must select persons who are citizens of the *other* country.

Chapter 20 Arbitrations

A Chapter 20 report should be completed 120 days after the request for arbitration. There is no appeal to a higher body such as the Extraordinary Challenge Committee under Chapter 19. If the dispute is not resolved, the prevailing party can pursue equivalent compensatory action within 30 days. Normally this should be in the same economic sector and can be challenged by panel review only if "manifestly excessive." Compensatory action cannot be undertaken by a member state that failed to join the dispute as a complaining party. The third NAFTA partner may not "normally" commence WTO or NAFTA proceedings on substantially equivalent grounds absent a significant change in economic or commercial circumstances.

Professor David Lopez has provided a revealing portrait of early Chapter 20 dispute settlement, one which emphasizes just how few disputes are pushed to arbitration. *See* 32 Texas Int'l Law J. 163 (1997). Of the eight complaints he cites as lodged by the end of 1996, only three have gone to arbitration ... Canadian agricultural tariffication, U.S. escape clause restraints on Mexican brooms, and U.S. refusal to admit Mexican trucks. To this date, these three disputes remain the only Chapter 20 arbitration decisions. Professor Lopez suggests that complaints linger at the consultation/mediation stages of Chapter 20 dispute settlement because there is no compulsion to move the dispute forward and because political realities temper that decision. Some disputes are settled (e.g., tomatoes above) while others just keep on lingering (Helms-Burton).

* * *

PART C.   EAST ASIA

ABBOTT AND BOWMAN, ECONOMIC INTEGRATION FOR THE ASIAN CENTURY: AN EARLY LOOK AT NEW APPROACHES

4 Transnat'l Law & Contemp.Probs. 159 (1994).*

GREATER CHINA: TAIWAN, HONG KONG, AND SOUTHERN PROVINCES OF THE PEOPLE'S REPUBLIC OF CHINA

The Greater China SREZ developed with little, if any, formal governmental cooperation. Prior to 1978, political barriers between the PRC, Taiwan, and Hong Kong limited economic interaction among the three. In that year, however, China began its slow move toward capitalism by establishing special economic zones in the coastal provinces of Guangdong and Fujian. The Beijing government softened its stance toward foreign investment and delegated considerable authority to these areas to encourage rapid market-based development. As Beijing lifted its restrictive controls in Guangdong and Fujian, these provinces began receiving significant levels of investment from nearby Hong Kong and Taiwan. Firms from these newly industrialized economies were attracted by the inexpensive land, labor, and raw materials found in China, while the Chinese provinces benefited from the large injection of capital and technology. In the process, Guangdong was transformed from one of mainland China's poorest provinces to one of its fastest growing regions.

Integration in this region has likely been advanced by the unique political situation prevailing there. Hong Kong will revert to governance by the PRC in 1997, and Beijing already exercises significant political influence in that British protectorate. China and the ROC also agree that their two governments represent a single nation, although they differ violently as to the nature of any reunification. Indeed, because Beijing

* © 1994 Transnational Law & Contemporary Problems. Reprinted with permission.

views Taiwan as part of China, Taiwanese businesses enjoy special concessions not offered to other investors. The PRC–ROC political rift obstructs official cooperation, however, making formal integration virtually impossible any time in the near future.

Linguistic and cultural ties also may have helped promote integration. According to Paul Hsu, *quan xi*—personal contacts with relatives and friends—among the ethnic Chinese population promotes close economic relations, giving local economic actors a competitive advantage over Westerners and Japanese. Although these bonds exist among the ethnic Chinese throughout the Asia–Pacific region—the PRC has even attempted to attract investment from overseas Chinese in many countries—cultural links are especially strong among the closely related peoples of Taiwan, Hong Kong, and the southern provinces of China.

For example, approximately eighty percent of Hong Kong's residents trace their heritage to the neighboring Guangdong province, and most still have relatives there. Many of these ties were created after World War II, as Guangdong residents fled to Hong Kong to escape poverty and Communism. Likewise, Taiwan lies within 100 miles of Fujian, and most Taiwanese are of Fujian descent. Furthermore, these regions share strong linguistic bonds: Cantonese, the language of Guangdong, is also the primary tongue in Taiwan and Hong Kong, and the Fujian dialect is also widely spoken in Taiwan. As Chia & Lee note, such strong cultural ties may have helped overcome the area's strong political differences.

These factors, which make it easier for business people within the triangle to engage in transactions with one another than with outside firms, are creating an increasingly integrated region. The governments involved have taken no formal steps toward integration, however, and recent agreements remain tentative. Nonetheless, after less than two decades of integration this triangle of approximately 120 million people now boasts the fastest rate of economic growth of any region in the world and a combined GDP of nearly $400 billion.

Guangdong province has become so attractive to business that half of the foreign investment funds entering China come to that province. With this spectacular development, however, Chinese leaders have discovered that they are unable to control economic change in Guangdong. The Beijing government does not want to discourage much-needed growth and investment, but it does want to tame it, control it, and reduce Guangdong's inflation rate, which exceeds even the soaring national average. The government is simply unsure how to achieve these aims, and it is loath to scare away the large amounts of investment pouring into Guangdong. As a result, the government merely de-emphasizes its ten year old decentralization plan in a quiet fashion.

Economic change also spills over into the political sphere. People in Guangdong listen more to nearby Hong Kong than to their own distant government. Thanks to these investments, Guangdong residents watch Hong Kong television, see investors from Hong Kong, and enjoy a higher standard of living. China's leaders now must worry about the political distance between Beijing and the provinces in the triangle, as well as the economic differences that separate them.

LAWRENCE, JAPAN TRADE RELATIONS AND IDEAL FREE TRADE PARTNERS: WHY THE UNITED STATES SHOULD PURSUE ITS NEXT FREE TRADE AGREEMENT WITH JAPAN, NOT LATIN AMERICA

20 Md.J.Int'l L. & Trade 61 (1996).*

The notion of an FTA with all of Latin America accompanied the idea of a U.S.–Mexico FTA. Shortly after the announcement of FTA negotiations between the United States and Mexico, President Bush unveiled the Enterprise for the Americas Initiative (EAI). This raised the prospect of a Western Hemispheric FTA (WHFTA), and it implicitly committed the United States to the negotiation of FTAs with Latin American countries.

* * *

This study posits that pursuing a WHFTA and aggressive unilateralism with Japan are not the best trade policies for the United States (or the world trading system). The United States is wise to encourage Latin American regional cooperation and improvement, but Latin America as a whole does not fit the criteria of an ideal free trade partner and few Latin American countries have liberalized sufficiently to expect that a WHFTA will be long-lasting. The potential benefit to the United States of a WHFTA, therefore, is questionable. Since forming a WHFTA encourages the digression of the world trade order into one of competing blocs, it is unwise for the United States to focus its policy in this direction.

The United States should focus its efforts to build an institutionalized and cooperative relationship with Japan, its most important trade partner and a state vital to U.S. efforts to maintain a stable security environment in East Asia. Japan fits the criteria of an ideal free trade partner very well. Rather than engaging in quarrelsome debates over market access targets and threatening to impose Section 301 sanctions, a threat which, by its mere assertion, further deteriorates U.S.–Japan relations and revives images of the ugly American, the United States ought to pursue building a cooperative framework with Japan through an FTA. Such an agreement would fundamentally alter U.S.–Japan relations by institutionalizing the means for the two countries to cooperate and lead the world in economic policy matters. It would fill the trust gap and, by doing so, make easier the task of establishing a more vibrant security alliance. Also, whereas U.S. influence over Japan is currently declining, a Japan–United States FTA (JUSFTA) would enshrine its influence, providing the United States a far greater amount of leverage with Japan in the future than it would otherwise possess.

* © 1996 Maryland Journal of International Law. Reprinted with permission.

The sections below add to the rationale and substance of the arguments above. Section one begins by introducing the reader to the economics of FTAs and the reasons behind their implementation; it also discusses the prospects for the current regionalism to be open and the issue of trade diversion. From there section two develops a two-tier free trade partner model, with the first tier focused on trade indicators and the second tier on readiness factors—including states' level of democracy.

Section three quantitatively and qualitatively demonstrates that Japan, but not Latin America, fits the ideal free trade partner model. This finding indicates that hemispheric free trade would not be the panacean windfall U.S. trade policy makers may desire it to be. It also strongly suggests that the dynamic trade creation benefits of pursuing true liberalization in the U.S.–Japan trade relationship would be quite large given the two economies' existing levels of interdependence, competitiveness, and wealth. For this reason the study argues that, rather than expend its limited resources on a small-gain game such as a WHFTA, the United States should focus its cooperative efforts foremost toward Japan. In support of this position the study holds that nontraditional access barriers are both the explanation as to why the United States and Japan do not already have an FTA and the reason their relationship needs one.

Section 4 then critiques some of the problems with the current U.S. trade policy toward Japan and explains why, rather than pursuing managed trade deals and threatening Section 301 sanctions, the negotiation of a Japan–United States Free Trade Agreement (JUSFTA) would be a better approach to mitigating U.S.–Japan trade tensions. An in-depth discussion of the 1995 U.S.–Japan auto and auto parts dispute helps illustrate the correctness of this argument.

Finally, section five proposes the JUSFTA framework. It discusses possible Japanese and U.S. motivation in JUSFTA negotiations, pinpoints likely JUSFTA objectives, and recommends the key JUSFTA components needed to achieve those objections: One, a consultative mechanism with two necessary sub-components—Structural Impediment Talks aimed at encouraging the amelioration of external imbalances and Working Groups aimed at harmonization of regulatory and industry standards; two, a dispute resolution mechanism that is self-executing (thus allowing private parties, not just the two governments, to bring suit), speedy (capable of rendering decisions within one year), and pro-active (authorized to appoint new working groups to iron out problems which the originally-negotiated JUSFTA rules do not address); and three, a G2 for increased macroeconomic policy coordination.

The article concludes that, even though its pursuit would be immense in terms of time, effort, and difficulty, the JUSFTA would necessitate cooperation, better resolve trade disputes, and encourage true long-term liberalization and trust in the U.S.–Japan relationship. In addition to de-politicizing trade disputes which are bound to occur between such competitive trade partners, it would bring much welcomed relief to the security side of the alliance. It would begin realizing the once much talked about "global partnership" between the two countries, and, having established the means of cooperation in its most vital trade relationship, it would provide the platform from which the United States could launch a new round of multilateral GATT trade negotiations aimed at harmonization of standards and competition policies, as well as furthering progress on trade in services and intellectual property rights. Overall, a JUSFTA would be a giant leap toward establishing free trade throughout the world, and it would burnish the tarnished image of U.S. leadership in international economic affairs.

QUESTIONS AND COMMENTS

1. Just exactly what is the "customs union dilemma?" Do you agree with Folsom that this is really the "dilemma of regional economic integration?" Does the dilemma affect SUNRISE?

2. How does Article 24 of the GATT (and Article 5 of the GATS) attempt to manage the "dilemma?" Has Article 24 been successful in the European context? In a global context? Are the types of arguments under Article 24 that were raised in the European context likely to re-emerge regarding North America? Why?

The explosion of regional and bilateral trade agreements has caused the WTO Director-General to be concerned with "systemic risk". Why? Is nondiscriminatory MFN treatment in reality becoming "least-favored-nation" (LFN) treatment? What are the implications of such systemic risk for SUNRISE? Will the Transparency Mechanism of 2006 solve the problems of systemic risk? Do you agree with Folsom that channeling Article 24-type disputes to the DSU is a better approach? Review the DSU procedures outlines in the nontariff trade barrier problem.

3. Can you explain to SUNRISE just exactly what are the critical differences between free trade areas like NAFTA and customs unions like the EU? And from its perspective as a potential foreign investor, which is preferable? Does the emergence in 1999 of the EURO, a common currency, affect your advice? What is U.S. "fast track" authority? Does its expiration in 2007 affect your advice?

4. Assuming SUNRISE invests in both France and the United States, what tariffs will have to be paid on its screwdriver plant component imports? Would a switch to the United Kingdom or Mexico alter your reply? How would you answer SUNRISE's question about whether its bikes can be freely traded inside NAFTA and the EU?

5. Would you advise SUNRISE to source components in Europe or North America? Why? Remember the company motto and NAFTA's rules of origin.

6. What are the implications of the *Honda* case for SUNRISE? If the special NAFTA rules of origin on motor vehicles were to apply to bicycles, would SUNRISE be pleased? And if the "ordinary" NAFTA rules of origin apply? See McCall.

7. Does the *Honda* case suggest that SUNRISE might be better off investing in Canada or Mexico? Does it matter where SUNRISE locates its plant in North America? In Europe?

8. What about product safety regulation in the European Union? Will that hinder or help SUNRISE? Does the German beer case enlighten your response? The *Dassonville*, *Cassis* and *Keck* opinions discussed in Folsom's *EU Law*? And Article 36 TFEU?

9. Should SUNRISE support harmonization or mutual recognition of bicycle safety regulation inside the EU? Does the same choice exist under NAFTA? What precisely is the approach towards technical product standards (TBT) under NAFTA? Is a risk assessment required, as with the SPS standards? May national TBT under NAFTA be "arbitrary" or "unjustifiable?" See Folsom's *NAFTA and Free Trade in the Americas*. We have explored similar issues at the GATT/WTO level in the nontariff trade barrier problem.

If the German beer case was re-run under NAFTA, what result? Is NAFTA behind the European learning curve on TBT issues? How would a dispute about the safety of SUNRISE bikes (or Canadian beer purity) be treated under NAFTA? In what forum would the dispute be heard?

10. Should Japan actively promote an East Asian regional trade organization? Should it be a free trade area or a customs union? How might the Koreas, the People's Republic of China, Taiwan, and the Southeast Asian states react to such an effort? Is "Greater China" a group that would take in Japan? See Abbott and Bowman.

In 2004, China negotiated free trade with ASEAN, a trade group comprised of virtually all Southeast Asian states, many of which have affluent Chinese minorities. China also has free trade agreements with its own Hong Kong and Macau Special Administrative Regions, Chile, Pakistan, Costa Rica, Peru, Singapore, New Zealand and others. Greater China appears to be getting greater. How do such agreements affect Japan? and SUNRISE?

11. Mexico has a free trade agreement with Japan. Do you agree with Lawrence, a social scientist, that Japan would be an ideal free trade partner for the United States? Would that help SUNRISE? Would it help the United States compete with Europe? With Greater China?

Since 2010, the EU has had a free trade agreement with South Korea. The U.S. signed a deal with South Korea in 2007, but implementation was delayed to 2011. If South Korea, why not U.S. free trade with Japan?

12. Recognizing that China is a rapidly developing economic superstar, the United States under the Obama administration is pursuing what resembles a "containment" strategy by promoting a "Trans–Pacific Partnership." This strategy seeks to bring the U.S., Australia, New Zealand, Chile, Peru, Brunei, Singapore and notably Vietnam into a broad trade, technology and investment alliance.

PROBLEM 6.5 TARIFF PREFERENCES FOR DEVELOPING NATIONS: IMPORT WORLD AND LEATHER GOODS

SECTION I. THE SETTING

IMPORT WORLD, Inc., is an Illinois corporation which specializes in importing different consumer goods. For most of them, it pays most favored nation (MFN) tariffs under U.S. law. But some goods come from developing nations. The company understands that Generalized Systems of Tariff Preferences (GSPs) for products from the developing world have been established. IMPORT WORLD has heard that it may be possible to import a variety of goods *duty free* under the GSP as applied by the United States. Company officials would like to know how the United States GSP system works and, in particular, whether and how it applies to imports of leather goods. Leather products account for nearly a third of IMPORT WORLD's United States sales.

Naturally, private exporters based in the developing world and their National Export Promotion Boards also are very interested in the answers to these questions. Their economic development plans call for increases in the export of leather goods over the next five years. If such increases materialize, it is projected that hundreds of jobs will be created and that revenues from the leather goods industry will assist in stabilizing balance of payments and debt servicing problems. But they worry about trade discrimination.

Some developing nations are concerned that the Caribbean Basin Economic Recovery Act of 1983 (CBI), the Andean Trade Preferences Act of 1991, and the African Growth and Opportunity Act of 2000 (AGOA) may divert United States imports to Caribbean, Andean and African sources. Other nations are convinced that Mexico's participation in NAFTA is the real problem. They seek "NAFTA–parity," which five Central American states plus the Dominican Republic obtained under the Central American Free Trade Agreement of 2005. Likewise, Jordan (2001), Chile (2003), Morocco (2004) and Peru (2005) also have free trade agreements with the United States, and more U.S. free trade agreements with developing nations are in the wings. Still others believe that the real threat to their common interests lie in third world assembly plants which benefit from special U.S. tariff treatment when U.S. components are used. Some wish to compete to attract these labor intensive investments.

Quite naturally, IMPORT WORLD wants to know how the CBI, Andean, AGOA and assembly plant programs compare and inter-relate with the GSP. It is especially interested in their impact on trade in leather goods.

SECTION II. FOCUS OF CONSIDERATION

Many third world nations have persistently argued that their development needs require special trade arrangements. Ideally, they would like all their products to enter developed nations duty free, while maintaining tariffs to protect their infant industries from foreign competition. But that level of preference has proven too much to expect. They have more realistically argued for preferential tariff treatment lower than most favored nation tariff levels. Their goods enter developed nations at the lowest tariff rates allowed by a nation, and even in some cases without any tariff. But they do not reciprocate and grant goods from developed nations similar special treatment. Their pleas ultimately reached listening ears. Special tariff preferences have been adopted by many developed nations.

This problem explores special tariff preferences for goods from developing nations. Particular attention is paid to the Generalized System of Preferences, the Caribbean Basin Economic Recovery Act of 1983, and assembly plant (maquiladora) tariff preferences. In addition to the intended benefits to developing nations, these programs have created new trade opportunities for importers and complex legal questions for international business lawyers.

Title V of the Trade Act of 1974 (GSP) (19 U.S.C.A. §§ 501–506) as amended and the Caribbean Basin Economic Recovery Act of 1983 are essential to analysis of this problem. They are found in the Documents Supplement.

General reference can be made to R. Folsom, M. Gordon, and J.A. Spanogle, *International Business Transactions 2d* (West Concise Hornbook Series, 2010), Chapter 10. Web resources for further study include coverage of the GSP, CBI and other trade preferences at *www.ustr.gov.*

SECTION III. READINGS, QUESTIONS AND COMMENTS

PART A. THE GATT AND GENERALIZED TARIFF PREFERENCES

NOTE, UNITED STATES PREFERENCES: THE PROPOSED SYSTEM

8 J. World Trade L. 216 (1974).*

Preferential trading arrangements between developed countries and their colonies and dependencies were an integral part of the economic policies of earlier centuries, and these arrangements—in somewhat altered form—have continued to influence trade relations between the former colonial powers and many LDCs [Less Developed Countries]. The United States, however, has historically shunned (at least in principle) such

---

* © Journal of World Trade Law. Reprinted with permission.

preferential ties. American prestige and economic power at the close of World War II may have helped to establish the most-favored-nation (mfn) approach to trade relations as one of the guiding principles of the General Agreement on Tariffs and Trade (GATT). Yet by the early 1960s, the United States was under pressure from the countries of Latin America, seeking preferential access to the U.S. market for their exports. This request for special treatment was justified by the various types of preferential treatment that most other LDCs already enjoyed, with Latin America alone lacking access to any important development country market. Hence the Latin American countries claimed that they were at a disadvantage in world trade.

By the time of the United Nations Conference on Trade and Development (UNCTAD) in 1964, the Latin American countries had dropped their request for special treatment to join other LDCs in support of a proposal for a generalized system of preferences (GSP), which would not discriminate among the LDCs. Under GSP, all DCs [Developed Countries] were to grant preferences to all the exports of semi-manufactured and manufactured goods from all the LDCs. This plan was intended to supersede any existing preferential systems. In his report as Secretary-General of UNCTAD Dr. Raul Prebisch included GSP among his comprehensive recommendations on development policy. The United States, clinging to the mfn concept, was the only major industrialized country to oppose the principle of GSP. And, two years later, when GATT members approved the waiver allowing Australia to depart from mfn practice by implementing a system of preferences, the U.S. cast the lone dissenting vote.

Meanwhile, the EEC concluded new preferential agreements with some African nations. As the prospects for GSP dimmed, the Latin American countries renewed their pressure on the United States for special status. Within the executive branch, the economic and political wisdom of the U.S. position on GSP began to be questioned. "Politically, we found ourselves virtually isolated from all the developing countries, and most of the industrialized countries as well. Economically, our reservation in principle and skepticism precluded our having much influence over the proliferation of discriminatory arrangements and also reduced our influence with regard to the specific workings of a preference scheme which other industrialized countries indicated they might put into effect whether or not the United States took part." In an address to the Latin-American summit meeting at Punta del Este, Uruguay, in April 1967, President Johnson reversed the U.S. stand on GSP, indicating United States willingness to pursue the possibility of temporary tariff preferences extended to all developing countries by all industrialized countries.

THE "ENABLING CLAUSE"

DECISION ON DIFFERENTIAL AND MORE FAVOURABLE TREATMENT, RECIPROCITY AND FULLER PARTICIPATION OF DEVELOPING COUNTRIES (28 November 1979)

Following negotiations within the framework of the [Tokyo Round] Multilateral Trade Negotiations, the CONTRACTING PARTIES *decide* as follows:

1. Notwithstanding the provisions of Article I of the General Agreement, contracting parties may accord differential and more favorable treatment to developing countries,[1] without according such treatment to other contracting parties.

2. The provisions of paragraph 1 apply to the following:[2]

(a) Preferential tariff treatment accorded by developed contracting parties to products originating in developing countries in accordance with the Generalized System of Preferences,[3]

(b) Differential and more favourable treatment with respect to the provisions of the General Agreement concerning non-tariff measures governed by the provisions of instruments multilaterally negotiated under the auspices of the GATT;

(c) Regional or global arrangements entered into amongst less-developed contracting parties for the mutual reduction or elimination of tariffs and, in accordance with criteria or conditions which may be prescribed by the CONTRACTING PARTIES, for the mutual reduction or elimination of non-tariff measures, on products imported from one another;

(d) Special treatment of the least developed among the developing countries in the context of any general or specific measures in favour of developing countries.

3. Any differential and more favourable treatment provided under this clause:

(a) shall be designed to facilitate and promote the trade of developing countries and not to raise barriers to or create undue difficulties for the trade of any other contracting parties;

(b) shall not constitute an impediment to the reduction or elimination of tariffs and other restrictions to trade on a most-favoured-nation basis;

---

1. The words "developing countries" as used in this text are to be understood to refer also to developing territories.

2. It would remain open for the CONTRACTING PARTIES to consider on an *ad hoc* basis under the GATT provisions for joint action any proposals for differential and more favourable treatment not falling within the scope of this paragraph.

3. As described in the Decision of the CONTRACTING PARTIES of 25 June 1971, relating to the establishment of "generalized, non-reciprocal and non-discriminatory preferences beneficial to the developing countries" (BISD 18S/24).

(c) shall in the case of such treatment accorded by developed contracting parties to developing countries be designed and, if necessary, modified, to respond positively to the development, financial and trade needs of developing countries.

4. Any contracting party taking action to introduce an arrangement pursuant to paragraphs 1, 2 and 3 above or subsequently taking action to introduce modification or withdrawal of the differential and more favourable treatment so provided shall:[4]

(a) notify the CONTRACTING PARTIES and furnish them with all the information they may deem appropriate relating to such action;

(b) afford adequate opportunity for prompt consultations at the request of any interested contracting party with respect to any difficulty or matter that may arise. The CONTRACTING PARTIES shall, if requested to do so by such contracting party, consult with all contracting parties concerned with respect to the matter with a view to reaching solutions satisfactory to all such contracting parties.

5. The developed countries do not expect reciprocity for commitments made by them in trade negotiations to reduce or remove tariffs and other barriers to the trade of developing countries, *i.e.*, the developed countries do not expect the developing countries, in the course of trade negotiations, to make contributions which are inconsistent with their individual development, financial and trade needs. Developed contracting parties shall therefore not seek, neither shall less-developed contracting parties be required to make, concessions that are inconsistent with the latters development, financial and trade needs.

6. Having regard to the special economic difficulties and the particular development financial and trade needs of the least-developed countries, the developed countries shall exercise the utmost restraint in seeking any concessions or contributions for commitments made by them to reduce or remove tariffs and other barriers to the trade of such countries, and the least-developed countries shall not be expected to make concessions or contributions that are inconsistent with the recognition of their particular situation and problems.

7. The concessions and contributions made and the obligations assumed by developed and less-developed contracting parties under the provisions of the General Agreement should promote the basic objectives of the Agreement, including those embodied in the Preamble and in Article XXXVI. Less-developed contracting parties expect that their capacity to make contributions or negotiated concessions or take other mutually agreed action under the provisions and procedures of the General Agreement would improve with the progressive development of their economies and improvement in their trade situation and they would accordingly

---

4. Nothing in these provisions shall affect the rights of contracting parties under the General Agreement.

expect to participate more fully in the framework of rights and obligations under the General Agreement.

8. Particular account shall be taken of the serious difficulty of the least-developed countries in making concessions and contributions in view of their special economic situation and their development, financial and trade needs.

9. The contracting parties will collaborate in arrangements for review of the operation of these provisions, bearing in mind the need for individual and joint efforts by contracting parties to meet the development needs of developing countries and the objectives of the General Agreement.

* * *

U.S. GENERALIZED SYSTEM OF PREFERENCES GUIDEBOOK

Office of the United States Trade Representative

May, 2011

1. GSP–Eligible Articles

Which imports into the United States qualify for duty-free treatment under the GSP?

To be eligible for duty-free treatment pursuant to GSP, an import must meet the following requirements (described in more detail below):

    (1) It must be included in the list of GSP-eligible articles;

    (2) It must be imported directly from a BDC;

    (3) The BDC must be eligible for GSP treatment for that article;

    (4) The article must be the growth, product, or manufacture of a BDC and must meet the value-added requirements;

    (5) The exporter/importer must request duty-free treatment under GSP by placing the appropriate GSP Special Program Indicator (SPI) before the HTSUS number that identified the imported article on the appropriate shipping documents (CBP Form 7501).

Which articles are eligible for duty-free treatment?

Articles classified by CBP under approximately 3400 eight-digit tariff rate lines are generally eligible for duty-free treatment from all GSP beneficiaries. In 1996, an additional 1,400 articles were made eligible for duty-free treatment when imported from LDBDCs. The combined lists include most dutiable manufactured and semi-manufactured products and also certain agricultural, fishery, and primary industrial products that are not otherwise duty-free. LDBDCs are designated as such pursuant to section 502(a)(2) of the Trade Act of 1974, as amended, and, in practice, are typically GSP beneficiaries that are on the United Nations' list of least developed countries.

* * *

Can any article be designated as eligible for GSP?

No. Certain articles are prohibited by law (19 U.S.C. 2463) from receiving GSP treatment. These include most textiles and apparel articles, watches, footwear, handbags, luggage, flat goods, work gloves, and leather apparel. In addition, the GSP statute precludes eligibility for import-sensitive steel, glass, and electronic articles. A list of non-GSP-eligible products can be found at http://www.ustr.gov/sites/default/files/Non–GSP-products-in–2009.pdf.

How is an article identified as GSP-eligible in the HTSUS?

The letter **A** in the "Special" tariff column of the HTSUS identifies GSP-eligible articles at an eight-digit level. The following table presents three HTSUS tariff lines to illustrate variations in the treatment given to different GSP articles. Under each entry for a GSP-eligible article in the HTSUS, the letter **A**, **A+**, or **A*** in the "Special" column identifies the article as GSP-eligible under certain conditions. The letter **A** designates articles that are GSP-eligible from any BDC. The letter **A+** indicates articles that are GSP-eligible only from LDBDCs. The letter **A*** indicates that one or more specific BDCs, listed in General Note 4(d) to the HTSUS, have lost GSP eligibility for that article.

HTSUS Subheading	Article description	Rate of Duty (%)		
		Column 1		Column 2
		General	Special	
8406.10.10	Steam turbines for marine propulsion	6.7%	Free (A,...)	20%
8413.30.10	Fuel-injection pumps for compression-ignition engines	2.5%	Free (A*, ..)	35%
8708.92.50	Mufflers and exhaust pipes	2.5%	Free (A+,...)	25%

Can the President limit products' GSP eligibility?

Yes. The President may:

(1) remove products from GSP eligibility in response to petitions submitted by interested parties in an annual review;

(2) preclude certain BDCs from GSP eligibility for certain newly designated products when those products are designated; and

(3) limit the redesignation of GSP eligibility to certain BDCs when specific articles are redesignated as GSP-eligible.

* * *

3. GSP Beneficiary Developing Countries

Where are the official lists of GSP-eligible beneficiaries (countries, territories, associations and LDBDCs) and country-specific restrictions on eligibility found?

General Note 4, found at the beginning of the HTSUS, contains information about GSP. General Note 4(a) contains the official list of GSP-eligible beneficiaries. General Note 4(b) contains the list of LDBDCs. General Note 4(d) contains the list of the imported articles that are not eligible for GSP treatment from certain GSP countries. When a BDC is first designated, or undergoes a change in GSP eligibility, a notice is published in the *Federal Register* indicating the change and the effective date of the change. The lists contained in General Note 4 are periodically modified to reflect these changes. Although the HTSUS General Note 4 is the official source for the list of GSP-eligible beneficiaries, this list can also be found on the USTR web site at http://www.ustr.gov/webfm_send/2469.

Are the lists of eligible articles and countries ever modified?

Yes. The GSP Subcommittee of the Trade Policy Staff Committee (TPSC), chaired by USTR and comprised of representatives of other executive branch agencies, conducts an annual review during which changes are considered to the lists of articles and countries eligible for duty-free treatment under GSP. Modifications made pursuant to the annual review are implemented by executive order, or Presidential Proclamation, and are published in the *Federal Register*. Modifications to the list typically take effect on July 1 of the calendar year after the next annual review is launched. The modifications are reflected in the electronic and hard copy versions of the HTSUS published by the USITC.

How does someone request modification of the list of GSP-eligible articles or countries?

Any person may petition the GSP Subcommittee to request modifications to the list of countries eligible for GSP treatment. However, only an "interested party" may petition for modifications to the list of articles eligible for GSP treatment. For purposes of this provision, an interested party is any party who has significant economic interest in the subject matter of the request, or any other party representing a significant economic interest that would be materially affected by the action requested, such as a domestic producer of a like or directly competitive article, a commercial importer or retailer of an article which is eligible for GSP or for which GSP eligibility is requested, or a foreign government. In order to be considered in a particular annual review, petitions must be submitted to the GSP Subcommittee by the deadline for submissions for that review, which is typically announced in the Federal Register in July or August.
* * *

What factors are taken into account in modifying the list of eligible articles or countries?

In modifying the GSP list of articles and countries, the following factors must be considered under the statute:

(1) the effect such action will have on furthering the economic development of developing countries through the expansion of their exports;

(2) the extent to which other major developed countries are undertaking a comparable effort to assist developing countries by granting generalized preferences with respect to imports of products of such countries;

(3) the anticipated impact of such action on U.S. producers of like or directly competitive products; and

(4) the extent of the country's competitiveness with respect to eligible products.

In addition, the statute provides mandatory and discretionary factors the President must take into account in designating a country as eligible for GSP. These factors include whether a country has taken or is taking steps to afford to workers in that country internationally recognized worker rights and the extent to which a country is providing adequate and effective protection of intellectual property rights. The full list of factors may be found at 19 USC 2462(b) and (c). Finally, the statute also provides a list of articles that may not be designated as eligible for GSP (19 USC 2463(b)).

Who makes the determinations regarding GSP product and country eligibility?

The President determines which countries and which products are eligible for GSP benefits, based on the recommendations of the U.S. Trade Representative (USTR). The GSP Subcommittee conducts the annual reviews of GSP product and country eligibility. These reviews typically involve both public hearings and a public comment period. The GSP Subcommittee reports the findings of these reviews to the TPSC and the U.S. Trade Representative. The Deputy Assistant USTR for GSP oversees the day-to-day operation of the GSP program and chairs the GSP Subcommittee.

Do all beneficiary countries receive duty-free treatment on the entire list of articles?

No. Some otherwise GSP-eligible products from particular BDCs may be ineligible because: (1) they exceed the competitive need limitations (see below); (2) the products' GSP eligibility has been removed from one or more particular countries in response to petitions submitted as part of an annual review; (3) a particular BDC has been found to be sufficiently competitive with respect to that product or products ; (4) the imported articles fail to meet the statutory requirements of GSP; or (5) the imported articles fail to meet other CBP or other agency requirements.

4.   Competitive Need Limitations and Requests for Waivers

What are competitive need limitations?

Competitive need limitations (CNLs) are quantitative ceilings on GSP benefits for each product and BDC. The GSP statute provides that a BDC is to lose its GSP eligibility with respect to a product if the CNLs are exceeded and if no waiver is granted (see below). There are two different measures for CNLs: when U.S. imports of a particular product from a BDC during any calendar year (1) account for 50 percent or more of the value of total U.S. imports of that product; or (2) exceed a certain dollar value. In accordance with the GSP statute, the dollar-value limit is increased by $5 million annually; the limit was $145 million in 2010 and will be $150 million in 2011. Products from a specified beneficiary are considered "sufficiently competitive" when imports exceed one of these limits. By statute, GSP treatment for an article exceeding either CNL terminates on July 1 of the next calendar year.

Are the competitive need limitations ever waived?

Yes. CNLs can be waived under four circumstances:

Petitioned waivers: The President may grant a CNL waiver for a product imported from a BDC. Interested parties may petition for a waiver during the annual review process. In deciding whether to grant a waiver, the President is required to place "great weight" on the extent to which the country is providing equitable and reasonable access to its market and basic commodity resources and the extent to which the country is providing reasonable and effective protection to U.S. intellectual property rights. If a waiver is granted, both the percentage limit and the dollar limit are waived. A waiver remains in effect until the President determines that it is no longer warranted due to changed circumstances. The statute also provides that the President should revoke any waiver that has been in effect for at least five years, if a GSP-eligible product from a specific country has an annual trade level in the previous calendar year that exceeds 150 percent of the annual dollar-value limit or exceeds 75 percent of all U.S. imports.

"504(d)" waiver: The percentage provision is waived for certain GSP eligible articles which were not produced in the United States on January 1, 1995, as provided for in what used to be Section 504(d) of the GSP statute, now 19 USC 2463(c)(2)(E). Interested parties may petition for a waiver during the annual review process. For those products on this list, a "504(d)" waiver will automatically be granted when required each year.

De minimis waiver: A waiver may also be provided when total U.S. imports from all countries of a product are "*de minimis*". Like the dollar-value CNLs, the *de minimis* level is adjusted each year, in increments of $500,000. The *de minimis* level in 2011 is $20.5 million, and will be $21 million in 2012. Each year, the GSP Subcommittee automatically considers *de minimis* waivers for all products from BDCs that exceeded the percentage-based CNL. Such waivers cannot be requested by petition, but public comments are accepted following publication of a *Federal Register* notice, usually in March, announcing the products that fall in this category. Granting such waivers is a discretionary decision of the President.

Least developed country waiver: All CNLs are automatically waived for GSP beneficiaries designated as LDBDCs.

What happens if GSP imports from a beneficiary country reach or exceed competitive need limitations in a given year?

GSP eligibility for articles from such countries will terminate no later than July 1 of the next calendar year unless those products and beneficiaries are granted a CNL waiver before that date.

* * *

5. Graduation of a Beneficiary Country from GSP

What is graduation and how is it implemented?

Graduation is the removal of a country's GSP eligibility on the basis of factors related to national income or competitiveness. The President may remove a BDC from the GSP program because the country is sufficiently developed or competitive, or may suspend or limit the BDC's access to duty-free treatment with respect to one or more products.

Country graduation occurs:

> 1. when the President determines that a beneficiary country is a "high-income country," as defined by the GSP statute (based on World Bank statistics) ("mandatory graduation"); or

> 2. as the result of a review of a BDC's advances in economic development and trade competitiveness.

The per capita GNP limit for mandatory graduation is set at the lower bound of the World Bank's definition of a "high income" country (which was $12,196 in 2010). Mandatory graduation takes effect January 1 of the second year after the year in which the President makes the graduation determination, which is announced in the *Federal Register*.

What factors are considered in graduation actions?

For circumstances other than mandatory graduation, the GSP Subcommittee normally reviews: (1) the country's general level of development; (2) its competitiveness in regard to the particular product; (3) the country's practices relating to trade, investment, and worker rights; (4) the overall economic interests of the United States, including the effect continued GSP treatment would have on the relevant U.S. producers, workers and consumers; and (5) any other relevant information.

6. Rules-of-Origin Requirements

What are the rules-of-origin requirements?

For an imported article to be GSP-eligible, it must be the growth, product, or manufacture of a BDC, and the sum of the cost or value of materials produced in the BDC plus the direct costs of processing must equal at least 35 percent of the appraised value of the article at the time of entry into the United States. CBP is charged with determining whether an article meets the GSP rules of origin.

* * *

Can imported materials be counted toward the 35 percent value-added requirement?

Yes, if the imported material undergoes a double substantial transformation. This means that the imported material must undergo a substantial transformation in the BDC, which means that the imported material is transformed into a new and different constituent material with a new name, character and use. Then the constituent material must be transformed in the BDC into a new and different finished article with a new name, character and use. Inputs from member countries of GSP-eligible regional associations will be treated as single-country inputs for purposes of determining origin.

* * *

7. "Imported Directly" Requirement

What is meant by the requirement that the article be "imported directly"?

Generally, the imported article must either be shipped directly from the BDC to the United States without passing through the territory of any other country or, if a shipment from a BDC passes through the territory of any other country en route to the United States, the imported articles must not enter the commerce of the other country. See 19 CFR 10.175 for more information. Questions about the "imported directly" requirement may be researched in CROSS or directed to CBP for a binding ruling.

Does the GSP program make any special provisions for BDCs that are members of a regional association?

Yes. If members of regional associations request and are granted recognition as regional associations under the GSP program, the association's member countries will be considered as one country for purposes of the GSP rules of origin. Articles produced in two or more eligible member countries of an association will be accorded duty-free treatment if the countries collectively meet the rules of origin. BDCs and LDBDCs in a regional association may jointly produce an article otherwise eligible for duty-free treatment only from LDBDCs, as long as the article is imported directly to the United States from the LDBDC. CNL criteria are applied only to the country of origin and not the entire association.

General Note 4 of the HTSUS has the most recent list of GSP-eligible countries, territories, and associations. There are currently six associations whose GSP-eligible beneficiary members can benefit from this provision: the South Asian Association for Regional Cooperation (SAARC) the Andean Group (or Cartagena Agreement); the Association of Southeast Asian Nations (ASEAN); the Caribbean Common Market (CARICOM); the Southern African Development Community (SADC); and the West African Economic and Monetary Union (WAEMU).

* * *

Criteria for Country Eligibility under GSP

Mandatory criteria

19 USC 2462(b)(2) of the GSP statute sets forth the criteria that each country must satisfy before being designated a GSP beneficiary. These criteria are summarized below for informational purposes only. Please see the GSP statute for the complete text.

1) A GSP beneficiary may not be a Communist country, unless such country receives Normal Trade Relations (NTR) treatment, is a WTO member and a member of the International Monetary Fund (IMF), and is not dominated or controlled by international communism;

2) A GSP beneficiary may not be a party to an arrangement of countries nor participate in actions the effect of which are (a) to withhold supplies of vital commodity resources from international trade or to raise the price of such commodities to an unreasonable level and (b) to cause serious disruption of the world economy;

3) A GSP beneficiary may not afford preferential treatment to products of a developed country that has, or is likely to have, a significant adverse effect on U. S. commerce;

4) A beneficiary may not have nationalized, expropriated or otherwise seized property of U.S. citizens or corporations without providing, or taking steps to provide, prompt, adequate, and effective compensation, or submitting such issues to a mutually agreed forum for arbitration;

5) A GSP beneficiary may not have failed to recognize or enforce arbitral awards in favor of U.S. citizens or corporations;

6) A GSP beneficiary may not aid or abet, by granting sanctuary from prosecution, any individual or group that has committed an act of international terrorism;

7) A GSP beneficiary must have taken or is taking steps to afford internationally recognized worker rights, including 1) the right of association, 2) the right to organize and bargain collectively, 3) freedom from compulsory labor, 4) a minimum age for the employment of

children, and 5) acceptable conditions of work with respect to minimum wages, hours of work and occupational safety and health; and

8) A GSP beneficiary must implement any commitments it makes to eliminate the worst forms of child labor.

Discretionary criteria

19 USC 2462(c) of the GSP statute sets forth the following criteria that the President must take into account in determining whether to designate a country as a beneficiary country for purposes of the GSP program. These criteria are summarized below for informational purposes only; please see the GSP statute for the complete text.

1) An expression by a country of its desire to be designated as a GSP beneficiary country;

2) The level of economic development, including per capita GNP, the living standards of the inhabitants and any other economic factors that the President deems appropriate;

3) Whether other major developed countries are extending generalized preferential tariff treatment to such country;

4) The extent to which such country has assured the United States that it will provide equitable and reasonable access to its markets and basic commodity resources and the extent to which it has assured the United States it will refrain from engaging in unreasonable export practices;

5) The extent to which such country provides adequate and effective protection of intellectual property rights, including patents, trademarks, and copyrights;

6) The extent to which such country has taken action to reduce trade distorting investment practices and policies, including export performance requirements, and to reduce or eliminate barriers to trade in services; and

7) Whether such country has taken or is taking steps to afford internationally recognized worker rights, including 1) the right of association, 2) the right to organize and bargain collectively, 3) freedom from compulsory labor, 4) a minimum age for the employment of children, and 5) acceptable conditions of work with respect to minimum wages, hours of work and occupational safety and health.

FLORSHEIM SHOE COMPANY v. UNITED STATES

United States Court of Appeals, Federal Circuit, 1984.
744 F.2d 787.

DAVIS, CIRCUIT JUDGE.

This is an appeal from a decision of the Court of International Trade (CIT) dismissing, on the defendant's motion, plaintiff Florsheim Shoe Company's (Florsheim's) complaint against the United States (the Government). In that complaint, Florsheim challenged the United States

Customs Service's denial of Florsheim's protests against the agency's classification of imported Indian buffalo leather and goat and kid leather, not fancy, as dutiable merchandise. The CIT properly decided that Florsheim was attacking the basis for Customs' denial of the protests—certain Executive Orders in which the President withdrew duty-free treatment (under the Generalized System of Preferences) from those Indian leather products—and held that Florsheim had stated no claim upon which relief could be granted * * *

Section 504(a) declares (as it appears in Title 19, U.S.C.):

> The President may withdraw, suspend, or limit the application of the duty-free treatment accorded under section 2461 of this title with respect to any article or with respect to any country; except that no rate of duty may be established in respect of any article pursuant to this section other than the rate which would apply but for this subchapter. In taking any action under this subsection, the President shall consider the factors set forth in sections 2461 and 2462(c) of this title.

* * *

Florsheim then argues that * * * Section 504(a) does not authorize the withdrawal of duty-free treatment from a *specific* article from a *particular* country. It maintains that, under that section, the President may delete a country from the list of beneficiary developing nations, *or* he may withdraw an article from the list of eligible articles. In other words, the President may only limit duty-free treatment for a particular article from all countries or for all articles from a particular country.

Florsheim's over-emphasis on the word "or" in Section 504(a) ("with respect to any article *or* with respect to any country" (emphasis added)) as restricting the President's power, leads to an interpretation of the President's authority that is at odds with the clause's overall provision that "the President may withdraw, suspend, or *limit* the application of the duty-free treatment * * * with respect to any article or with respect to any country * * *." (Emphasis added.) The only (or at least the best) way by which the President can "limit" the application of duty-free treatment respecting a particular country is to exclude certain articles from that country from duty-free treatment. The same is true for limiting the application of duty-free treatment with respect to an article; that can be done by limiting the countries to which duty-free treatment is given for that article.

Florsheim's response that the word "limit"

> simply means that the President can restrict the quantity of a particular article which will be permitted duty-free treatment under the GSP when imported from all countries, or restrict the quantity of all duty-free articles imported from a particular beneficiary developing country

is unacceptable. That restricted view of "limit," as simply giving the President the authority to impose quantitative limits on GSP treatment, would make the term "limit" superfluous. Section 504(a) already gives the President authority to "suspend" GSP treatment. If the President "limits" preferential treatment by setting a quota for the number of articles which will be permitted to enter the United States duty-free, he is effectively suspending duty-free treatment at a pre-determined point in time. On Florsheim's reading, "limit" would play no separate role at all.

Above all, we must remember that this is a statute giving broad discretionary authority to the President in a field trenching very closely upon foreign affairs and on our relations with other countries. Though an "or" in a statute may often call for a disjunctive interpretation, "this canon is not inexorable, for sometimes a strict grammatical construction will frustrate legislative intent."

QUESTIONS AND COMMENTS

1. Recall that GATT tariff arrangements are premised on the general and automatic operation of the most favored nation clause of Article I. How do preferential tariffs for developing nations affect the operation of Article I? See the Enabling Clause. Most developing nations have very limited or nonexistent tariff schedules which are "bound" under GATT. They often maintain very high tariffs. Are developing nations capable of reciprocity in GATT tariff negotiations?

2. In 1971, the GATT contracting parties decided to permit the development of generalized systems of tariff preferences for products from developing nations. The EU adopted its GSP in July of 1971. Each GSP is the creation of its "donor." The United States GSP was adopted as Title V of the Trade Act of 1974. What strings does Title V attach to the grant of duty free GSP benefits?

3. Can leather goods qualify under the United States GSP? Does the customs classification assigned to those goods affect the answer? Could IMPORT WORLD initiate a proceeding to have such goods included in the GSP program? Such inclusion would be objected to by United States manufacturers of those same goods. Could the domestic producers institute proceedings to have leather goods excluded from the United States GSP? What "import sensitive" goods can never qualify for duty free GSP treatment and why?

4. In 1979, the Tokyo Round of GATT multilateral negotiations reduced most favored nation tariff levels. The Uruguay Round of tariff cuts commenced in 1995 made further reductions. About 50 Least Developed Developing Countries (LDDCs) received accelerated application of these tariff reductions. What are the implications for the GSP of continued multilateral tariff reductions through the GATT/WTO? Are duty free tariffs under GSP the essence of the program, or is it the tariff differential between the GSP and the MFN? Do LDDCs get special GSP treatment? How so?

5. What "rules of origin" govern the GSP program? Some regional economic groups of nations, the Andean Group, ASEAN and CARICOM for example, have each been designated "one country" for purposes of the rules of origin under the United States GSP. What is the significance of such designations?

6. What is the purpose of the "competitive need formula" under the United States GSP? How does it work?

7. The United States GSP has in the past primarily benefited exports from Newly Industrializing Countries (NICs) (also referred to as ADCs or Advanced Developing Countries), i.e., Brazil, Hong Kong, Thailand, Philippines, Malaysia, Israel, Korea, Mexico, Singapore and Taiwan. Should the GSP be administered so as to effectively distinguish between advanced and less advanced developing countries? When may the President "graduate" GSP covered products to the regular tariff rate? See the *Florsheim Shoe Co.* case.

Late in 1988, President Reagan "graduated" Hong Kong, Korea, Taiwan and Singapore entirely from the GSP program. Previously, goods from these countries had amounted to about 60% of all duty free GSP imports. Thereafter, goods from Mexico accounted for 25% of all such imports until 1994 when NAFTA removed Mexico from the list of GSP beneficiaries. In 1997, President Clinton graduated Malaysia from the GSP program. Free trade with Jordan (2001), Chile (2003), Morocco (2004), five Central American Nations plus the Dominican Republic (2005) and Peru (2005) likewise removed those countries from GSP eligibility.

8. The Generalized System of Preferences Act of 1984 (Title V of the 1984 Trade and Tariff Act) renewed the United States GSP for 8½ years. Since 1993, the GSP program has been intermittently continued pending more extensive study by Congress.

How is Import World affected by the graduation criteria and competitive need limitations contained in the GSP program? What graduation rules are established and why? Should the graduation rules be of greater concern to IMPORT WORLD?

9. What country eligibility criteria apply to the GSP program and why? Are these changes likely to harm IMPORT WORLD?

PART B.   DISCRIMINATORY TRADE PREFERENCES OF THE UNITED STATES

Despite GATT efforts and the adoption of Generalized Systems of Preferences, discriminatory tariff agreements linking major industrial markets to selected developing nations have emerged. The proximity of Mediterranean Basin countries to the European Union (EU) has, from the outset, created close trading links. Special "association" agreements were negotiated with Greece (now an EU member) and Turkey early on. In later years, preferential trade agreements with Maghreb (Algeria, Tunisia, Morocco) and Mashrek (Egypt, Jordan, Syria, Lebanon) countries, Malta, Cyprus, Israel and the former Yugoslavia were implemented. Plans are afoot for a closely knit Mediterranean Economic Area.

After years of objecting to these arrangements, the United States began to imitate them. The Mediterranean pattern of European trade relations should be compared to that established under the United States Caribbean Basin Economic Recovery Act of 1983. The Act permits substantial duty free access for Caribbean goods to the United States market. The Andean Trade Preference Act of 1991 does likewise for Andean goods. In addition, the Africa Growth and Opportunity Act of 2000 (Public Law No. 106–200, 114 Stat. 252) selectively granted duty-free and quota-free access to the U.S. market.

R. FOLSOM, PRACTITIONER TREATISE ON INTERNATIONAL BUSINESS TRANSACTIONS
§§ 10.17–10.21 (2011–12).

CARIBBEAN BASIN INITIATIVE, ANDEAN AND AFRICAN TRADE PREFERENCES

The European Union has had for many years a policy which grants substantial duty free entry into its market for goods originating in Mediterranean Basin countries. The United States has duplicated this approach for the Caribbean Basin. This is accomplished through the Caribbean Basin Economic Recovery Act of 1983.[1] For these purposes, the Caribbean Basin is broadly defined to include nearly all of the islands in that Sea, and a significant number of Central and South American nations bordering the Caribbean. So defined, there are 28 nations which could qualify for purposes of the United States Caribbean Basin Initiative. As with the GSP program, the Caribbean Basin Initiative (CBI) involves presidential determinations to confer beneficiary status upon any of these eligible countries. However, unlike the GSP, there are no presidential determinations as to which specific products of these countries shall be allowed into the United States on a duty free basis. All Caribbean products except those excluded by statute are eligible. Moreover, there are no "competitive need" or annual per capita income limits under the CBI. Lastly, unlike the GSP program which must be renewed periodically, the Caribbean Basin Initiative is a permanent part of the U.S. tariff system.

The United States has maintained a steady trade surplus with Caribbean Basin countries. Leading export items under the CBI are typically beef, raw cane sugar, medical instruments, cigars, fruits and rum. The leading source countries have often been the Dominican Republic, Costa Rica and Guatemala. The value of all CBI duty free imports now exceeds $1 billion annually, but the CBI countries fear a diversion of trade and investment to Mexico as the North American Free Trade Agreement (NAFTA) matures.

CBI country eligibility

The President is forbidden from designating Caribbean Basin Initiative beneficiaries if they are communist, have engaged in expropriation

---

1. Public Law 98–67, 97 Stat. 384 codified at 19 U.S.C.A. §§ 2701 et seq.

activities, nullified contracts or intellectual property rights of the U.S. citizens, failed to recognize and enforce arbitral awards, given preferential treatment to products of another developed nation, broadcast through a government-owned entity United States copyrighted material without consent, failed to sign a treaty or other agreement regarding extradition of United States citizens, failed to cooperate on narcotics enforcement, or failed to afford internationally recognized workers rights. For these purposes, the definition of workers rights enacted in connection with the GSP program applies. Since 2000, CBI countries must also show a commitment to implementing WTO pledges.

These prohibitions notwithstanding, the President can still designate a Caribbean Basin country as a beneficiary if he or she determines that this will be in the national economic or security interest of the United States. However, this can be done only in connection with countries that are disqualified as being communist, expropriators, contract or intellectual property nullifiers, nonenforcers of arbitral awards, unauthorized broadcasters, or those who fail to provide for internationally recognized workers rights. Thus, if a Caribbean nation is disqualified because it grants preferential trade treatment to products of another developed nation or refuses to sign an extradition treaty with the United States, there is no possibility of its designation as a beneficiary nation under the Caribbean Basin Initiative. As with the GSP statutory requirements, if the basis for the disqualification is expropriation or nullification of benefits, the President may override this disqualification if that nation is engaged in payment of prompt, adequate and effective compensation or good faith negotiations intended to lead to such compensation.

In addition, the President is required to take various factors into account in designating beneficiary countries under the Caribbean Basin Initiative. These include:

(1) the desire of that country to participate;

(2) the economic conditions and living standards of that nation;

(3) the extent to which the country has promised to provide equitable and reasonable access to its markets and basic commodity resources;

(4) the degree to which it follows accepted GATT rules on international trade;

(5) the degree to which it uses export subsidies or imposes export performance requirements or local content requirements which distort international trade;

(6) the degree to which its trade policies help revitalize the region;

(7) the degree to which it is undertaking self-help measures to promote its own economic development;

(8) whether it has taken steps to provide internationally recognized workers rights;

(9) the extent to which it provides adequate and effective means for foreigners to secure and enforce exclusive intellectual property rights;

(10) the extent to which the country prohibits unauthorized broadcasts of copyrighted material belonging to U.S. owners; and

(11) the extent to which it is prepared to cooperate with the United States in connection with the Caribbean Basin Initiative, particularly by signing a tax information exchange agreement.

Under these criteria, the President has designated a large number of the 28 eligible nations as beneficiary countries under the Caribbean Basin Initiative. These include Antigua and Barbuda, Aruba, the Bahamas, Barbados, Belize, the British Virgin Islands, Costa Rica, Dominica, the Dominican Republic, El Salvador, Grenada, Guatemala, Guinea, Haiti, Honduras, Jamaica, Monserrat, the Netherlands Antilles, Nicaragua, Panama, St. Christopher-Nevis, St. Lucia, St. Vincent and the Grenadines, and Trinidad and Tobago. The nations not designated as beneficiary countries under the Caribbean Basin Initiative to date include Anguilla, Suriname, the Cayman Islands and the Turks and Caicos Islands. Cuba is not even listed among the nations eligible for consideration in connection with the Caribbean Basin Initiative.

U.S. Presidents have typically required of each potential beneficiary a concise written presentation of its policies and practices directly related to the issues raised by the country designation criteria listed in the Caribbean Basin Economic Recovery Act. Wherever measures were in effect which were inconsistent with the objectives of these criteria, U.S. presidents have sought assurances that such measures would be progressively eliminated or modified. For example, the Dominican Republic promised to take steps to reduce the degree of book piracy and the Jamaican and Bahamian governments promised to stop the unauthorized broadcast of U.S. films and television programs.

The U.S.—CAFTA/DR free trade agreement of 2005 removed Costa Rica, Guatemala, Nicaragua, Honduras, El Salvador and the Dominican Republic as GSP and CBI beneficiary countries.

CBI product eligibility

Unless specifically excluded, all products of Caribbean Basin nations are eligible for duty free entry into the United States market. Certain goods are absolutely excluded from such treatment. These include footwear, canned tuna, petroleum and petroleum derivatives, watches, and certain leather products. It should be noted that this listing of "import sensitive" products is different from but overlaps with that used in connection with the United States GSP program. Since 2000, products ineligible for CBI benefits enter at reduced tariff levels corresponding to Mexican goods under NAFTA ... so-called "NAFTA parity".

One of the most critical of the products that may enter the United States on a duty free basis is sugar. But the President is given the authority to suspend duty free treatment for both sugar and beef products originating in the Caribbean Basin or to impose quotas in order to protect United States domestic price support programs for these products. Sugar exports have traditionally been critical to many Caribbean Basin economies. Nevertheless, sugar import quotas into the United States from the Caribbean have been steadily reduced in recent years. For example, by 1988 the sugar quota allocations for some CBI countries reached a low of 25 percent of their 1983 pre-Caribbean Basin Initiative allocations. Many consider the few duty free import benefits obtained under the Initiative to be more than counterbalanced by the loss in sugar exports to the United States market.

The rules of origin for determining product eligibility in connection with the Caribbean Basin Initiative are virtually the same as discussed previously under the GSP. As a general rule, a substantial transformation must occur and a 35 percent value added requirement is imposed (but 15 percent may come from the United States). This percentage is calculated by adding the sum of the cost or value of the materials produced in the beneficiary country or two or more beneficiary countries plus the direct cost of processing operations performed in those countries. It should be noted that this approach effectively treats all of the CBI-eligible nations as a regional beneficiary since the 35 percent required value can be cumulated among them.

As under the GSP program, the President is given broad powers to suspend duty free treatment with reference to any eligible product or any designated beneficiary country. Import injury relief under Section 201 of the Trade Act of 1974 can be invoked in connection with Caribbean Basin imports. And the equivalent of that relief is authorized specifically for agricultural imports upon similar determinations by the Secretary of Agriculture. The effects of these protective proceedings may be diminished in the context of Caribbean Basin imports. Whenever the International Trade Commission is studying whether increased imports are a substantial cause of serious injury to a domestic industry under Section 201 or its agricultural equivalent, the ITC is required to break out the Caribbean Basin beneficiary countries. The President is given the discretion if he or she decides to impose escape clause relief to suspend that relief relative to Caribbean Basin imports. A similar discretion is granted to the President in connection with national security import restraints under Section 232 of the Trade Expansion Act of 1962. However, these discretionary provisions relate only to those goods that are eligible for duty free entry under the Caribbean Basin Initiative.

In 1986, President Reagan initiated a special program for textiles produced in the Caribbean. Essentially, this program increases the opportunity to sell Caribbean textile products when the fabric involved has been previously formed and cut in the United States. If this is the case, there are minimum guaranteed access levels that are different from those quotas which traditionally apply under the Multi-Fiber Arrangement. This program is run in conjunction with Section 9802.00.80 of the Harmonized Tariff Schedule of the United States.

The U.S.-Caribbean Basin Trade Partnership Act of 2000 grants duty-free and quota-free access to the U.S. market for apparel made from U.S. fabric and yarn. Apparel made from CBI fabric is capped for duty free into the United States. CBI textiles and apparel are subject to market surge safeguards comparable to those under NAFTA. Late in 2006, duty free treatment of Haitian apparel products was expanded under the HOPE Act. In certain cases, Haiti may utilize third country fabrics and still ship apparel duty free into the United States.

Andean trade preferences

The Andean Trade Preference Act (ATPA) of 1991[1] authorizes the President to grant duty free treatment to imports of eligible articles from Colombia, Peru, Bolivia and Ecuador. Venezuela is not included as a beneficiary country under this Act. The Andean Trade Preference Act is patterned after the Caribbean Basin Economic Recovery Act of 1983. Goods that ordinarily enter duty free into the United States from Caribbean Basin nations will also enter duty free from these four Andean countries. The same exceptions and exclusions discussed above in connection with the Caribbean Basin Initiative generally apply. However, while the CBI is a permanent part of United States Customs law, the ATPA is only authorized initially for a period of ten years. Furthermore, the guaranteed access levels for Caribbean Basin textile products, separate cumulation for antidumping and countervailing duty investigations, and the waiver of the Buy American Act for procurement purposes are not authorized by the ATPA. Broadly speaking, the passage of the ATPA represents fulfillment of the elder President Bush's commitment to assist these nations economically in return for their help in containing narcotics.

The Andean Trade Preference Act was renewed by the TPA-TAA through February 2006 retroactive to its expiry Dec. 4, 2001. Further extensions were made until December 31, 2010. Textile and apparel products, and most other products previously excluded, are now included under the ATPA. Country eligibility for enhanced benefits includes consideration of steps taken to comply with WTO obligations, the protection of worker rights and combating corruption. In 2005, the United States and Peru signed a free trade agreement, and in 2006 a similar agreement was reached with Colombia. These free trade agreements are intended to replace Andean trade preferences. Negotiations with Ecuador and Bolivia have failed to produce agreements, leaving their Andean benefits uncertain.

African trade preferences

The Africa Growth and Opportunity Act of 2000 (Public Law No. 106–200, 114 Stat. 252) granted duty-free and quota-free access to the U.S.

---

1. Public Law 102–82, 19 U.S.C.A. §§ 3201 et seq.

market for apparel made from U.S. fabric and yarn. Apparel made from African fabric is capped for duty free entry. The least developed sub-Saharan countries enjoy duty-free and quota-free apparel access regardless of the origin of the fabric.

The Act also altered U.S. GSP rules to admit certain previously excluded African products on a duty-free basis, including petroleum, watches and flat goods. Sub-Saharan countries can export almost all products duty-free to the United States. These countries are encouraged to create a free trade area with U.S. support.

African exports are subject to import surge (escape clause) protection and stringent rules against transshipments between countries for purposes of taking advantage of U.S. trade benefits. Late in 2006, the "third country fabric provisions" under AGOA were extended to 2012. In 2008, the "abundant supply" provision of AGOA was repealed, thus facilitating least-developed African nation exports of textiles to the USA.

THE YEAR IN TRADE

U.S. International Trade Commission.
USITC Publication 4247 (July 2011).

Trade Preference Programs

Generalized System of Preferences: Duty-free U.S. imports under the Generalized System of Preferences (GSP) program totaled $22.6 billion in 2010; almost one-fourth of these imports were petroleum products. Thailand was the leading GSP beneficiary in 2010, followed by Angola, India, Brazil, Indonesia, and Equatorial Guinea. As of January 1, 2010, the Republic of the Maldives was added to the list of GSP beneficiaries; Cape Verde was removed from the least-developed beneficiary developing countries(LDBDCs) list, though it remains a GSP beneficiary; and Trinidad and Tobago was removed from GSP eligibility based on its classification as a high-income economy. On January 1, 2011, Croatia and Equatorial Guinea were removed from the list of GSP beneficiaries based on high income. The President's authority to provide duty-free treatment under the GSP program expired on December 31, 2010.

African Growth and Opportunity Act: At the end of 2010, 38 sub-Saharan African (SSA) countries were designated for benefits under the African Growth and Opportunity Act (AGOA), and 26 SSA countries were eligible for AGOA textile and apparel benefits. Duty-free U.S. imports under AGOA, including those covered by GSP, were valued at $44.3 billion in 2010. U.S. imports under AGOA, exclusive of GSP, were valued at $38.7 billion in 2010, up 37.8 percent from 2009. This increase was driven mainly by a rise in the value and quantity of U.S. imports of petroleum-related products, which made up 93.1 percent of imports under AGOA in 2010.

Andean Trade Preference Act: At the end of 2010, certain products of two Andean countries—Colombia and Ecuador—were eligible for duty-free treatment under theAndean Trade Preference Act (ATPA), as amended by the Andean Trade Promotion and Drug Eradication Act (ATPDEA). Peru's eligibility continued after the U.S.-Peru Trade Promotion Agreement (TPA) entered into force on February 1, 2009, but was not renewed on December 24, 2010, when ATPA was extended through February 12, 2011. U.S. imports under ATPA were valued at $14.4 billion in 2010, an increase of 48.3 percent from 2009. Imports from Colombia and Ecuador under ATPA increased substantially, while imports from Peru under ATPA decreased as Peru entered more of its exports to the United States under the U.S.-Peru TPA. Petroleum-related products accounted for 86.2 percent of U.S. imports under ATPA in 2010. Other leading imports under ATPA included fresh cut flowers, apparel, and pouched tuna.

Caribbean Basin Economic Recovery Act: The Caribbean Basin Economic Recovery Act (CBERA), as amended by the Caribbean Basin Trade Partnership Act (CBTPA), provides duty-free and reduced-duty treatment for certain products from designated Caribbean Basin countries. In 2010, 18 countries were eligible for permanent CBERA preferences, and 8 were eligible for CBTPA preferences. U.S. imports under CBERA were valued at $2.9 billion in 2010, a 22.6 percent increase from $2.4 billion in 2009. This increase reflects substantial increases in 2010 in the prices of petroleum-related products and methanol, which are major imports from CBERA countries. Apparel was also a leading import under CBERA in 2010. Trinidad and Tobago was the leading supplier of U.S. imports under CBERA in 2010. In response to the devastating earthquake of January 2010, trade benefits for apparel from Haiti were expanded by the Haiti Economic Lift Program, which was signed into law on May 24, 2010.

QUESTIONS AND COMMENTS

1. Is the Caribbean Basin Economic Recovery Act of 1983 consistent with United States obligations under Article I of GATT?

2. What criteria must be met under the Caribbean Basin Economic Recovery Act of 1983 (19 U.S.C.A. § 2701 *et seq.*) before the President may designate a country as a qualified source of goods subject to duty free status? Does the Act distinguish between mandatory and discretionary criteria? How do these criteria compare with those established by Title V of the Trade Act of 1974 regarding GSP treatment? *See* Part A. How do they compare with the criteria of Title IV regarding MFN status for nonmarket economies?

3. What goods probably will never qualify for duty free treatment under the Caribbean Basin Act? Why? IMPORT WORLD may seek to increase imports under the Caribbean Basin Act. But United States producers will be concerned. What protective measures may those producers take in response to duty free Caribbean import competition?

4. How does the Caribbean Basin Act differ from and affect the United States GSP? Has it been a "success"? What about the Andean Act? And the AGOA?

5. Quite a few Caribbean nations presently qualify under the Caribbean Basin Act *and* participate in the duty free programs of the European Union. What is the significance to an investor producing in one of those nations of such dual status? In 2000, the EU and Mexico reached agreement on free trade. What is the impact of that accord on Caribbean nations?

6. After several years in Congress, CBI II was finally adopted in the Customs and Trade Act of 1990. Heavy lobbying defeated efforts to include textiles in the CBI initiative and to mitigate the effects of cuts in sugar import quotas. The CBI program was made permanent, and special rules now promote investment in the region from tax-sheltered Puerto Rican revenues. The most important changes for IMPORT WORLD are found in 19 U.S.C.A. § 2703(h). Every student should read it in connection with this problem. What are those changes and what is their impact on IMPORT WORLD?

PART C.　U.S. TARIFF PREFERENCES FOR GOODS INCOR-PORATING AMERICAN–MADE COMPONENTS

The United States Tariff Code, various Mexican Decrees, and the economics of assembly plant operations established a growth industry: Maquiladoras. Sometimes called "in-bond" or "border" plants, Mexican maquiladoras enjoyed phenomenal popularity in the 1980s and early 1990s. Maquiladoras provide Mexico with hundreds of thousands of jobs, many of which are filled by women. They are also a major source of foreign currency earnings, second only to oil exports and ahead of tourism. For the investor, the devaluation and depreciation of the peso in 1982 and again in 1994–5 rendered Mexican labor costs lower than those of Taiwan, Hong Kong, Singapore and South Korea (the "Four Dragons"), traditional low-cost assembly plant centers. As a result, thousands of maquiladoras have been established in Tijuana, Ciudad Juarez, Nuevo Laredo and other border cities. Electronics, apparel, toys, medical supplies, transport equipment, furniture, and sporting goods are examples of the types of industries that have been attracted south of the border. Maquiladoras are being imitated throughout the Caribbean Basin and Central America. Much to the frustration of organized labor, such offshore assembly operations exemplify the internationalization of the United States manufacturing sector.

Complex legal frameworks facilitate maquiladoras. On the United States side, Section 9802.00.80 of the Harmonized Tariff Schedule ("HTS") [formerly Section 807 of the TSUS] allows fabricated United States components to be shipped abroad and returned to the U.S. subject to a customs duty limited to the amount of the value added by foreign assembly operations. This section was first utilized with great success by the Four Dragons, and is the same law which facilitates Caribbean and Central American assembly plants. Mexico initiated its Border Industrialization Program in 1965, partly to compete with East Asian countries taking advantage of Section 9802.00.80 through labor-intensive assembly operations.[a]

The net result of Section 9802.00.80 and the law of an increasing number of developing nations is an interdependent legal framework mutually supportive of assembly plant operations. This can be viewed as a "co-production" or "production-sharing" arrangement between the two countries, an arrangement in which others can participate. Japanese corporations and their U.S. subsidiaries have, for example, become significant investors in such industries. Korean firms are also setting up assembly plant operations targeted at the U.S. market, and other Asian investors are expected. These companies appear to find assembly plants attractive even when they use components that are not from the United States, *e.g.*, Taiwanese electronic parts.

If at least 35 percent of the value of an assembly plant product is of local origin, it may qualify for *duty free* tariff status under the U.S. Generalized System of Tariff Preferences (GSP). See Part A. Most Carib-

a.

Section 9802.00.80
HARMONIZED TARIFF SCHEDULE of the United States
(formerly section 807.00 of the Tariff Schedule of the U.S.)

Heading/ Subheading	Stat. Suf. & cd	Article Description	Units of Quantity	Rates of Duty		
				1		2
				General	Special	
9802.00.80		Articles assembled abroad in whole or in part of fabricated components, the product of the United States, which (a) were exported in condition ready for assembly without further fabrication, (b) have not lost their physical identity in such articles by change in form, shape or otherwise, and (c) have not been advanced in value or improved in condition abroad except by being assembled and except by operations incidental to the assembly process such as cleaning, lubricating and painting	......	A duty upon the full value of the imported article, less the cost or value of such products of the United States (see U.S. note 4 of this subchapter)	A duty upon the full value of the imported article, less the cost or value of such products of the United States (see U.S. note 4 of this subchapter) (B, C, CA)	A duty upon the full value of the imported article, less the cost or value of such products of the United States (see U.S. note 4 of this subchapter)

bean and Central American nations are beneficiary countries under the GSP program, whereas the Four Dragons and Malaysia are not. As a matter of business planning, then, development and use of local components in an assembly plant is a strategy that is now being aggressively pursued. Local suppliers, like their East Asian competitors some years ago, are being pressed to improve the quality and utility of their components. The Four Dragons, by comparative example, suggest that if these suppliers meet this challenge, then fabrication of products of completely local origin may follow.

There is an evolutionary cycle in assembly plants—from cheap raw labor to more skill-oriented operations to capital-intensive manufacturing. One of the most interesting comparative questions is whether there is also an evolutionary process in the applicable laws of these countries. In other words, what legal regimes do developing nations have to adopt in order to first attract assembly operations and do they evolve from extremely accommodating to more demanding as the cycle reaches completion? Or, does the manufacturer's ability to go elsewhere to even cheaper labor markets (*e.g.,* from Mexico to Guatemala to Haiti or from Hong Kong to the People's Republic of China to Vietnam) constantly temper the legal regimes regulating assembly plants? By 2011, assembly plants withdrawn from Mexico were based in China and Vietnam, with a few actually returning to North America due to high fuel/transport costs.

OXFORD INDUSTRIES v. UNITED STATES

United States Court of International Trade, 1981.
517 F.Supp. 694.

RICHARDSON, JUDGE.

The merchandise in this case consists of one dozen long sleeve men's shirts (style 818) and one dozen short sleeve men's shirts (style 129) which were exported from Mexico, entered at Douglas, Arizona, and classified in liquidation under TSUS item 380.84 as other men's or boy's wearing apparel, not ornamented; not knit, at the duty rate determined in accordance with TSUS item 807.00. It is claimed by plaintiff that allowances in duty in accordance with item 807.00 should have been made for the collar band body and lining components and cuff body and lining components of the style 318 shirts, and for the collar band body and lining components of the style 129 shirts. The customs service had disallowed item 807.00 treatment for these components because they were subjected to a buttonholing operation in Mexico.

* * *

The record shows that the fabric and lining components in issue were cut to shape at the Woods Company in Douglas where, along with other components of the shirts not in issue, they were exported to Camisas Bahia Kino ("Kino") in Mexico across the border from Douglas for purposes of being assembled into shirts. Woods and Kino were at that time wholly owned subsidiaries of the plaintiff corporation.

* * *

Plaintiff contends that the facts of record demonstrate that the components in issue met the requirements of item 807.00. Plaintiff argues (brief, p. 71), "The record herein clearly presents evidence that buttonholing does not substantially transform the buttonholed components, but is a minor or incidental operation." Defendant contends that the subject components are not entitled to item 807.00 treatment because they were subjected to further fabrication prior to assembly, and were advanced in value or improved in condition by operations other than assembly operations or operations incidental to assembly.

Defendant argues that "not only did the buttonholing operations complete the components in issue while abroad, they had a commercial and utilitarian function well after assembly of the components into the shirts." (brief, p. 55) Defendant further argues that "the only assembly which occurred abroad was the joining or sewing of the seams or sewing the buttons onto the cuffs and collar bands." (brief, p. 77) And, in this connection, defendant goes on to argue, "Operations as essential as the buttonholing operations involved in this case could not possibly be considered to be of such a minor nature as to term it incidental, when, without those operations the assembly can be completed, but the article would not be accepted by the customer or ultimate consumer." (brief, p. 79)

In *Rudolph Miles v. United States,* 65 CCPA 32, C.A.D. 1202, 567 F.2d 979 (1978), to which both parties call attention in the briefs, steel Z-beams were exported to Mexico where they were processed into floating center sills which were assembled into railroad box cars that were imported into the United States. Item 807.00 treatment for the Z-beams was disallowed by the customs service by reason of the fact that holes and slots of varying dimensions had been burned into each beam during the processing in Mexico. The Customs Court upheld the customs service determination, and held that the burning of holes and slots in the beams and other operations in Mexico constituted further fabrication within the meaning of clause (a) of item 807.00, and also advanced the value and improved the condition of the Z-beams within the meaning of clause (c) of item 807.00.

The court of appeals reversed the lower court's holding in *Miles.* The appellate court held that the processing of the Z-beams in Mexico, especially the burning of holes and slots, was concomitant with the assembly of center sills, and was not substantial enough to preclude qualification under clause (a) of item 807.00. The appeals court also concluded that the processing in Mexico was merely part of the assembly of the Z-beams into center sills, and "incidental to the assembly process" as provided in item 807.00(c). The court stated that all the operations in Mexico constituted assembly of the beams into center sills, and that if increase in value resulted from these Mexican activities, it was within the exception expressly provided in the statute for advance in value "by being assembled."

In *Mast Industries, Inc. v. United States,* 515 F.Supp. 43 (1981), precut fabric components of women's pants were exported from the United States to El Salvador where they were assembled into finished garments that were imported into the United States. In El Salvador various fabric components of the pants were subjected to buttonholing (with a Reece S–2 machine) and pocket slitting operations. Upon entry into the United States the customs service disallowed item 807.00 treatment for these components by reason of these operations, and the importer instituted action in this court challenging the customs service disallowance.

In *Mast* the court found that slitting the fabric for buttonholing and pocket insertion purposes, and the preliminary remedial sewing in the buttonhole area, were relatively minor procedures, and concluded that such operations were "incidental to assembly" of the pants, following *Rudolph Miles v. United States, supra.* Accordingly, the court held that *Mast* was entitled to item 807.00 treatment for the disputed components.

The facts in *Mast* and the arguments advanced in that case by the defendant parallel closely the facts and defendant's arguments in the instant case. In fact, so similar are the facts and arguments in the two cases, that the court is constrained to notice the inadvertent references by defendant's counsel on at least five occasions in the brief at bar when counsel referred to "pocket slitting" which was involved in the women's pants of *Mast,* while clearly intending to refer only to the men's shirts at bar (brief, pp. 62, 65, 67, 80 where there are two references), a point which did not go unnoticed by plaintiff's counsel (reply brief, p. 15). Consequently, the court agrees with plaintiff that the holdings in *Miles* and in *Mast* are dispositive of the issues at bar, and the court so holds. What the court said in *Mast* applies equally to the facts at bar, namely, "Said operations were not such substantial changes as to constitute further fabrication. No new portion of the [shirts] was made, and the cost of performing these operations, in terms of both labor and expense was a small portion of the total cost of assembly."

L. VARGAS, NAFTA, THE U.S. ECONOMY AND MAQUILADORAS

Business Frontier, Issue 1, 2001.*

Phase 2: 2001

Starting this year, NAFTA affects the maquiladora industry in one very important way: It abandons the provision of duty-free importation of inputs into Mexico, regardless of origin. Instead, North American rules of origin now determine duty-free status for a given import. Thus, as long as the source of the inputs is either the United States or Canada, no duties are assessed. However, whenever maquiladoras use non-North American inputs, NAFTA's Article 303 stipulates that duty drawback provisions

---

* Federal Reserve Bank of Dallas, El Paso Branch.

apply. Specifically, these provisions allow maquiladoras to receive a duty refund for the lesser of (1) the amount of duties paid in Mexico for imported inputs or (2) the amount of duties paid on the final product in the United States or Canada at the time of importation from Mexico.

To assess the possible impact of the 2001 NAFTA rules, we need to look at the volume of inputs maquiladoras import from third countries. If maquiladoras rely heavily on imported inputs from sources outside the NAFTA region, it would appear that starting this year, because the new rules impose duties on these third-country imports where no duties were assessed before, maquiladoras will face dramatically increased costs. Actually, the opposite is true. The overwhelming majority of materials, parts and machinery imported by maquiladoras—90 percent, according to Banco de México—is sourced in the NAFTA region, specifically in the United States. Thus, this measure of overall maquiladora inputs would continue to enjoy the duty-free privileges that have applied ever since the maquiladora program started in 1965.

The fact remains, though, that now not all inputs imported by maquiladoras can enter Mexico duty-free. Even if only 10 percent of these inputs would now face duties because they are sourced in third countries, this translates into higher costs for some industry participants, especially if the duties in question are excessively high. In fact, one of the sectors most vulnerable to the new rules is the industry's largest—electric and electronics—since this sector has important supplier links with countries outside the NAFTA region, predominantly in East Asia.

During NAFTA's first phase, companies in the electric and electronics sector alerted Mexican authorities that the new duties they would face in 2001 on their third-country inputs would boost their costs and threaten the competitiveness of their investments in Mexico. To ensure compliance with the new North American rules-of-origin provisions that would be triggered in 2001, some third-country suppliers relocated to the NAFTA region. This strategy was pursued especially by Asian maquiladoras, which, along with maquiladoras in the electric and electronics sector, had the most extensive supplier links with countries outside the NAFTA region. However, members of the electric and electronics sector argued that it was not feasible for some components to be found or developed in the region or for third-country suppliers to relocate to the region. They contended that the use of inputs from outside the NAFTA region would still be required by 2001.

Mexican authorities responded in November 1998 by designating special rules that granted zero or nominal duties for third-country inputs for companies in the electric and electronics sector (maquiladoras and nonmaquiladoras alike). Soon other sectors brought their own case to Mexican authorities and asked for the same special treatment for their third-country inputs. These developments ultimately resulted in the establishment of the so-called Sectoral Promotion Programs.

Sectoral Promotion Programs

On December 31, 2000, Mexico passed a decree creating 20 Sectoral Promotion Programs (Programas de Promoción Sectorial, or PROSECs) aimed at ensuring the continued competitiveness of the maquiladora industry. The PROSECs cover 19 specific areas and one miscellaneous area. They extend preferential duties—of no more than 5 percent—to those third-country inputs that maquiladoras have designated as critical for their operation. Some third-country inputs have even been granted duty-free status. Both maquiladora and nonmaquiladora companies can use the PROSECs. They also can petition Mexican authorities to establish additional PROSECs for areas not covered under the existing programs.

Some maquiladoras have complained that applying the PROSECs is cumbersome. However, the industry agrees that the PROSECs have resolved the potential risk of lost competitiveness that could have resulted from strict adherence to North American rules of origin in the determination of duty-free treatment of inputs. Moreover, since the preferential duties under the PROSECs apply to inputs that are imported on a temporary (to be processed for export) or permanent (to be processed for national distribution) basis, maquiladoras can now more easily entertain direct sales into the Mexican market—as NAFTA now allows—because any inputs imported from third countries are now in a more acceptable and predictable tariff range than they were before 2001.

Questions and Comments

1. When do components lose their "physical identity" so as to be disqualified for special entry under Section 9802.00.80(b) of the HTS? Suppose IMPORT WORLD arranges for U.S. cured leather with stencilled shapes to be cut and assembled into handbags in an assembly plant. Can such handbags qualify? Suppose the leather is already cut in the U.S. into pieces for handbags which are merely sewn abroad. What result?

2. When are U.S. components "ready for assembly without further fabrication" as required by Section 9802.00.80(a)? If IMPORT WORLD arranges for hides to be shipped abroad for curing into leather, are they "ready for assembly"? If cured leather (without stencilling of handbag patterns) is sent abroad, is it "ready"? And with stencilling?

3. What is an "operation incidental to the assembly process" under Section 9802.00.80(c)? Cleaning? Painting? Packaging? See the *Oxford Industries* case. If leather handbags are polished before their return, is that an "incidental operation"? If not, what result?

4. Japanese corporations and their U.S. subsidiaries have become significant investors in assembly plant industries. For them, the savings in labor costs and avoidance of U.S. import quotas are the primary motivations. If they use Japanese or local components, will the goods qualify under Section 9802.00.80?

Section 9802.00.80 is not likely to overcome the economic incentive to use lower-cost foreign components whenever possible. Nevertheless, products presently assembled in many maquiladoras contain a high percentage of U.S. components. See the Vargas excerpt. Is it more likely, because of differences in their stages of economic development, that Latin American maquiladoras will use U.S. components than South Korean assembly operations? Does the GSP program create an incentive to add local value to assembly plant goods.?

5.   United States labor unions have complained that Section 9802.00.80 promotes the export of jobs. Do you agree? If so, which jobs? Do some jobs remain? Are new jobs created because of Section 9802.00.80?

6.   Many U.S. firms maintain that staying competitive is their primary motivation in moving labor-intensive assembly operations abroad, and that Section 9802.00.80 is a relatively minor factor in making that decision. They say that the only question is where to go. Are there political, social and economic reasons for the U.S. to favor Latin American maquiladoras over East Asian assembly plants?

7.   What are PROSECS and why has Mexico adopted them? See Vargas and review the NAFTA rules of origin in Problem 6.4.

PETERSEN, THE MAQUILADORA REVOLUTION IN GUATEMALA *

1 (1992).

In 1984, few Guatemalans were familiar with the term *maquila*. The Guatemalan Congress had recently passed legislation to lure foreign and domestic investment to this export-assembly industry, also known as outsourcing and drawback assembly production. But only the handful of young, ambitious exporters who fervently lobbied for the bill foresaw that within a decade the maquila industry would be the fastest-growing sector of the Guatemalan economy. When the law was passed, about six factories, all assembling apparel for export, employed fewer than two thousand employees. In a mere eight years, this fledgling industry expanded more than twenty-five times. By 1992, more than two hundred and seventy-five garment maquila factories were employing over fifty thousand workers who assembled nearly $350 million in garments for export to the United States.

The boom in garment-assembly production is thrusting the term *maquila* into the everyday vocabulary of millions of Guatemalans and simultaneously transforming the economic and social history of the country. To most Guatemalans, the maquila industry represents the dozens of converted warehouses where children and young women labor for long, monotonous hours sewing precut pieces of cloth into complete garments, which are then immediately shipped to U.S. department stores. Large signs posted on the sides of these buildings, offering employment and excellent compensation to young women, mark their location. For maquila workers, the labels are the tip-off: non-Spanish-sounding names such as "McKids," "Ralph Lauren," and "Van Heusen" indicate that the clothing

---

* Reprinted with permission of Orville H. Schell, Jr. Center for International Human Rights at Yale Law School.

is for U.S. consumers. In Zone 12, the major industrial sector of Guatemala City, there are so many of these factories that owners have nicknamed the area The Bermuda Triangle. "When a young woman gets off the bus in Zone 12," a maquila investor explained, "she vanishes into the morass of factories and is often never seen again."

* * *

MAQUILAZATION AND THE NEW INTERNATIONAL DIVISION OF LABOR AND PRODUCTION

For Guatemalan * * * policymakers, the maquila industry represents both a mode of production and a strategy of industrial development. As a mode of production, the maquila industry is a labor-intensive, export-assembly operation. With a burgeoning maquila industry, the host country receives an immediate fix of jobs and foreign exchange with the long-term goal of industrialization. The maquila strategy for industrial development, or "maquilazation," is export-led industrialization constructed through the introduction of increasingly advanced assembly industries and the concurrent development of indigenous inputs for these operations. Over the last three decades, the so-called Asian Tigers—the Republic of Korea, Taiwan, Singapore, and Hong Kong—have pursued variants of this strategy, emerging with remarkable speed as self-sufficient, industrialized nations.

Advocates of maquilazation espouse a "ladder theory" of industrial development. The simplest form of the theory goes as follows. A developing country begins with a low-skill apparel-assembly industry. As the work force matures and increases in skill, more advanced assembly operations—for example, footwear, electronics, and toys—are introduced. In addition to transferring technology to the work force, these assembly operations integrate, or form backward linkages, with the domestic economy. Local industries grow and displace foreign firms as the major source of assembled inputs. For instance, domestic textile and plastics industries expand to supply the cloth and parts for apparel and toy assembly, respectively. The next rung is computers, and so on until the country "climbs" into an industrialized state. The primary examples of this development model can be found in the newly industrialized Southeast Asian countries, which, according to this interpretation, began their development in apparel assembly and then progressed until, in what many term a "miracle," they became industrial powers.

Success, however, has its costs. It is largely contingent on the attractiveness of a country's labor to potential investors. Emphasizing the primacy of labor in the industry, an AID official described the maquila as "the exportation of labor without ever having to send the workers abroad." In essence, a host country, at least in the short term, deliberately chooses to permit exploitation of its cheap, abundant labor force in exchange for foreign currency, employment, and hoped-for industrialization.

Similar efforts of maquilazation have sprouted up throughout the Caribbean and Central America, the most renowned being Mexico's Border Industrial Program and the Dominican Republic's Free Trade Zone programs. The Dominican Republic opened its first free-trade zone in 1969. Costa Rica, Haiti, and Jamaica embarked on maquilazation programs in the early 1980s, contemporaneous with the promulgation of the Caribbean Basin Economic Recovery Act. Thus, Guatemala is a relative latecomer, not launching an earnest attempt to attract this type of industry until the late 1980s. For the most part, persistent internal strife has placed the Guatemalan maquila industry well behind its neighbors in size and maturity.

The maquila industry is a major result of the new international division of labor and production. Since colonial days, the traditional division has dictated that the more developed nations produce and export manufactured goods while the less developed nations produce and export raw materials for manufacture abroad. This division was justified by the theory of comparative advantage, in which nations contribute to the world economy what they do best and most efficiently. In Central America and the Caribbean, climate-sensitive agro-exports like sugar, fruit, and coffee were (and still are, to a great extent) the contribution most desired by the more developed nations, particularly the United States.

Over the last forty years, this traditional division has undergone radical transformation. Exceptional advances in transportation, production technology, and communications, combined with the birth of transnational corporations (TNCs), have made a global division of labor and production economically efficient. This modern international division of production and labor is organized on the separation of a single manufacturing process, which once could only be performed in a single factory or geographic area, into stages of production allocated to different sets of workers around the world.

The paradigmatic model of this new international division of labor and production occurs when workers in a developed country design and manufacture components, these components are exported to a less developed country where workers assemble them into a finished unit, and then the completed good is reexported to the developed nation for marketing and sale. The division of labor and production is simple: the more capital-intensive stages of the design and manufacture of components, requiring sophisticated technology and highly trained and skilled labor, are performed in developed countries; the more labor-intensive stages, primarily assembly, are performed in the less developed countries.

Although the division of labor and production has drastically changed in the last three decades, the theory of comparative advantage continues to provide a rationale for the distinct tasks each country performs. Countries with the comparative advantage of legions of inexpensive labor are entitled to the labor-intensive stages of production; those with the greater technical sophistication and more skilled labor perform the more capital-intensive segments of the production. Most important, TNCs based in the developed countries, powerful enough to control production and develop markets, decide precisely how the production will be separated. The governments willingly facilitate the exchange by suspension or reduction of import and export duties.

* * *

QUESTIONS AND COMMENTS

1. Why does Guatemala support maquiladoras? What are their costs and benefits?

2. Environmental issues concerning the wastes of and conditions in assembly plants have emerged. In 1986, the United States and Mexico reached an Agreement on Transboundary Shipments of Hazardous Wastes and Hazardous Substances. This agreement has been implemented by various U.S. Environmental Protection Agency regulations and Mexican Presidential decrees. These laws require maquiladora hazardous materials (*e.g.*, solvents) to be returned to their country of origin. Some commentators suggest that this provision has not been vigorously enforced. Is the United States exporting environmental problems through Section 9802.00.80?

3. Many maquiladora workers are female. What are the social, economic and immigration implications of the fact that maquiladora jobs have been mostly "women's work"? Does this fact help explain the significant absence of unions in assembly plants or the high rate of turnover among maquiladora workers?

4. Do you agree with Petersen's analysis that "maquilazation" represents a new international division of labor and production? What are the implications of this analysis for IMPORT WORLD? For Guatemala? Do you believe in the "ladder theory" of industrial development?

5. Should the United States condition Section 9802.00.80 tariff reduction benefits upon respect for internationally recognized workers rights? This string is attached to duty free GSP and CBI benefits, and recent U.S. free trade agreements. Why omit Section 9802.00.80?

PROBLEM 6.6   CONTRACT PREFERENCES FOR LOCAL PRODUCERS: CROSS–BORDER PROCUREMENT OF PHOTOCOPIERS

SECTION I.   THE SETTING

PHOTOCOP, Inc. is a New York corporation which produces and aggressively markets high quality photocopying machines. All of the materials and technology necessary to make PHOTOCOP's machines are derived from United States sources. About 60 percent come from New York sources. PHOTOCOP has sold primarily to wholesale concerns and to corporations, and recently hired a representative with considerable experience selling to governments, a market PHOTOCOP wishes to enter. Bids on public contracts for the supply of photocopying machines have recently been submitted to:

    (a) The City of Los Angeles, California;

    (b) The State of New Jersey;

    (c) Several United States federal agencies;

    (d) The Danish government;

    (e) The Japanese government; and

    (f) PEMEX, the state oil and gas monopoly of Mexico.

There are numerous other producers of photocopying machines. Some are based in the European Union (EU) and Japan. PHOTOCOP's new sales representative has told the directors and officers that its prospects of winning these bids will be affected by a variety of laws establishing preferences in government procurement for local producers. Before committing large resources to this endeavor, PHOTOCOP would like you to evaluate whether and how these laws may apply to its bids.

SECTION II. FOCUS OF CONSIDERATION

A number of NTB "Codes" (sometimes called "side agreements") emerged from the Tokyo Round of GATT negotiations. The United States accepted nearly all of these agreements, including the Procurement Code. Most of the necessary implementation of these agreements was accomplished in the Trade Agreements Act of 1979. However, despite notable amendments to the Procurement Code in 1987, the Omnibus Trade and Competitiveness Act of 1988 amended the Buy American Act and the Trade Agreements Act in ways intended to reduce the degree to which the United States waived its procurement preferences. Congress clearly was not happy with the way the Code was working.

About 15% of GDP in developed nations, and 20% in developing nations, is believed to be governmentally procured. A new procurement Code was negotiated under the auspices of the Uruguay Round. This WTO Code is one of a few "plurilateral" agreements, which means that it applies only to nations that opt for its coverage. Relatively few WTO members have acceded to the Procurement Code. These include the European Union nations, Armenia, Aruba, Canada, Hong Kong, Iceland, Israel, Japan, Lichtenstein, Norway, Singapore, South Korea, Switzerland, Taiwan and the United States. The Code was ratified in the United States through the Uruguay Round Agreements Act of 1994.

The WTO Procurement Code expands coverage to include procurement of services, construction, government-owned utilities, and some state and local (subcentral) contracts. Various improvements to the procedural rules surrounding procurement practices and dispute settlement attempt to reduce tensions in this difficult area. For example, an elaborate system for bid protests is established. Bidders who believe the Code's procedural rules have been abused will be able to lodge, litigate and appeal their protests. The United States has agreed, with few exceptions, to bring all procurement by executive agencies subject to the Federal Acquisition Regulations under the Code's coverage (i.e., to suspend application of the normal Buy American preferences to such procurement).

In addition, Canada, Mexico and the United States have agreed upon special procurement rules. Chapter 13 of the 1989 Canada–United States Free Trade Area Agreement opens government procurement to U.S. and Canadian suppliers on contracts as small as $25,000. However, the goods supplied must have at least 50 percent U.S. and Canadian content. These special procurement rules effectively create an exception to the WTO Procurement Code which otherwise applies. The NAFTA also establishes distinct procurement regulations. The thresholds are $50,000 for goods and services provided to federal agencies and $250,000 for government-owned enterprises (notably PEMEX and CFE). These regulations are particularly important because Mexico, unlike Canada, has not traditionally joined in GATT/WTO procurement codes.

Thirteen U.S. states have not ratified the WTO Procurement Agreement. The United States, amid considerable controversy, adopted "Buy American" steel rules in the Obama economic stimulus plan, exempting WTO Procurement Code participants and U.S. free trade partners. See section 1605 of the 2009 American Recovery and Reinvestment Act. In 2010, the United States agreed to provide temporary relief for Canadian exporters from Buy American restraints, long-term access to state and local U.S. procurement and a fast-track process for procurement disputes. Canada, in turn, opened up its procurement significantly to U.S. exporters. In December 2011 these Canada–U.S. procurement provisions were incorporated in a long awaited agreement to expand the WTO Procurement Code. This expansion selectively brings more types of procurement contracts, notably service contracts, and more sub-central government entities within the Code's coverage. Contract value thresholds are also selectively lowered.

The materials in this problem explore one form of NTB, government procurement laws, and various attempts to remove their restrictive impact on international trade. There is a tendency for all levels of government to enact discriminatory legislation favoring local producers. This is, after all, the taxpayers' money. When such laws are passed at the state and local level, they are typically challenged under federal, regional or international law. When they are enacted at a federal or regional level, they are likely to be challenged under international law. All of these challenges represent attempts at reducing the trade restrictive impact of discriminatory government procurement law and procedures. Special attention is paid in this problem to "Buy American," "Buy EU", "Buy Japan" and "Buy Local" laws, and to the GATT/WTO Codes on Government Procurement. Similar problems relating to local procurement mandates (*e.g.*, "domestic content" requirements) applicable to private firms investing and licensing abroad are developed in Part Five.

Article III(4) and (8) of the GATT, the WTO Procurement Code (1994), and the federal Buy American Act are essential to an analysis of this problem. They are found in the Documents Supplement. Web resources for further study include procurement coverage at *www.wto.org.*

SECTION III. READINGS, QUESTIONS AND COMMENTS

PART A. BUY AMERICAN PROCUREMENT

Individuals in California may say, "I will only buy a California made photocopier." They violate no law. But if the government of the City of Los Angeles says, by way of a local ordinance, the City will buy only California made photocopiers, we are reluctant to say that is permissible. Why is that any different? What is behind the objection to Buy California or Buy American rules?

NOTE, THE TRADE ACT OF 1979: THE AGREEMENT ON GOVERNMENT PROCUREMENT

14 J. Int'l Law & Econ. 321 (1980).*

The United States receives most of the international publicity on discriminatory government procurement, primarily due to the Buy-American Act. But it is not the only country that "pursues autarky" through procurement practices. Other countries, while not implementing their discriminatory procurement practices through specific legislation, effectively restrict foreign competition by other methods. Among these methods are selective tender procedures, by which only a selective group of suppliers are sent invitations to bid; single tender procedures, by which only one supplier is contacted for procurement; limited publicity on public offers; requirements that bidders must have an established branch within the country; and the vesting of broad discretion in procurement officers to ignore foreign bids.

Government procurement policies have traditionally reflected protectionist attitudes. There are several reasons for this. It is one area in which a government believes it can ensure, through legislation, policy, or practice, that its citizens will get the best treatment possible. A 1976 study pointed out that political, economic, and personal attitudes and biases against foreign suppliers each contribute to discrimination in federal procurement. The study recognized that there is a natural tendency to favor familiar suppliers. Furthermore, there has traditionally been a close relationship between government and business, especially in Western European countries and Japan. Pressure from special interest groups of the business and labor sectors, often in positions of strong political power, also leads to protectionist tendencies in procurement because government

---

contracts mean jobs and money. In addition, balance of payment deficits are an incentive to pro-national policies. On a different level are those practical factors that lead to discrimination against foreign bidders, such as lack of uniformity in specifications, language barriers, familiarity and ease of dealing with local suppliers, the easy availability of service, maintenance, and repair parts when dealing with a domestic company, and the greater facility to legal recourse against a domestic company in case of default. Finally, national security interests inescapably lead to pro-national procurement policies. For example, domestic capabilities in high technology areas as well as those industries that produce goods to be used in national security will quite naturally be encouraged by excluding potential foreign competitors from defense business.

By creating barriers to international trade, pro-national policies interfere with what one economist calls "the unshakable basis for international trade": the theory of comparative advantage. Under this theory, though a country is not most efficient in the production of a particular product or even any product, it is still to its advantage to open itself to free trade. The country should specialize in the production of those products in which it has the greatest relative efficiency because real income is maximized only if each country's labor force specializes in sectors in which it can compete most effectively with foreign countries. When barriers are placed on foreign firms who want to bid on government procurement, the economy is injured for two reasons. First, a domestic producer who could not compete with the foreign producer in a free economy is in effect subsidized. As a result, the government and taxpayer pay a higher price for the goods. Second, the barrier prevents the reallocation of that domestic producer's work force and resources—a reallocation that would result in the production of goods able to compete more effectively in a foreign market.

NOTE, FEDERAL LIMITATIONS ON STATE "BUY AMERICAN" LAWS

21 Colum.J.Transnat'l L. 177 (1982).*

"Buy American" laws were first passed in the early 1930's. As a result of the unprecedented unemployment that plagued the nation, the federal government undertook a massive program of public works in order to stimulate the economy. Although the federal government had never before made distinctions between domestic and foreign products in its procurement policies, the congressional sentiment favored protection of American labor and manufacturing to the greatest extent possible. Specifically, congressmen worried that, as a result of lower labor costs in Europe, European firms would underbid American firms and be awarded three and one half to four million dollars in contracts for the turbines and electrical equipment for the Hoover and Boulder Dams which were then being built.

---

* © Columbia Journal of Transnational Law. Reprinted with permission.

The congressmen felt that such a sizable expenditure by the United States should go towards the employment of American workers.

These concerns led to the introduction of a bill limiting purchases of foreign products by the federal government. The bill, however, was not without its opponents. Congressman Celler of New York attacked the proposed legislation as extremely detrimental to United States' relations with European powers, especially with respect to the payment of debts accumulated during the First World War. He also opposed the bill because it exacerbated an already dire situation by further decreasing trade and forcing American capital abroad. The bill was also challenged on the ground that it unduly restricted necessary flexibility in the government's procurement policies. * * *

The impetus for state "Buy American" statutes arose from the same causes and at the same time as the federal Act. Indeed, some state statutes pre-date the federal Act. * * *

The manner in which states express their "Buy American" policies varies considerably and may include one or a combination of devices designed to implement the policies. Twenty states have no explicit "Buy American" policies in their statutes or regulations. Of the remaining states, most have adopted a flexible approach, giving preference to American-made products when all else is substantially equal.

No state presently enforces a blanket prohibition on the purchase of foreign products with public funds, however, several states do prohibit governmental purchases of specific products when such products are of foreign origin. Of those states taking a flexible approach, three require by statute that the cost of the domestic product not exceed the cost of the foreign product by more than a specific differential. Three states shift the burden of deciding when the domestic product is too expensive to the appropriate administrative agency by mandating the purchase of the American product unless the price is "unreasonable." The rest merely express a statutory preference for American products, giving no further guidance to public agencies. Two states also have "public interest" exceptions to their general mandate to "Buy American." Those states whose "Buy American" policy is confined to specific products may adopt either the flexible or the absolute approach. Six states express a statutory preference for domestic steel, one favors American automobiles, one favors American beef, and one favors domestic meat and dairy products. In addition, two states give a greater preference if the American product is from a "labor surplus" area.

CROSBY v. NATIONAL FOREIGN TRADE COUNCIL

Supreme Court of the United States, 2000.
530 U.S. 363, 120 S.Ct. 2288, 147 L.Ed.2d 352.

JUSTICE SOUTER delivered the opinion of the Court.

The issue is whether the Burma law of the Commonwealth of Massachusetts, restricting the authority of its agencies to purchase goods or services from companies doing business with Burma, is invalid under the Supremacy Clause of the National Constitution owing to its threat of frustrating federal statutory objectives. We hold that it is.

In June 1996, Massachusetts adopted "An Act Regulating State Contracts with Companies Doing Business with or in Burma (Myanmar)," 1996 Mass. Acts 239, ch. 130 (codified at Mass. Gen. Laws §§ 7:22G-7:22M, 40 F. ½ (1997)). The statute generally bars state entities from buying goods or services from any person (defined to include a business organization) identified on a "restricted purchase list" of those doing business with Burma. §§ 7:22H(a), 7:22J. Although the statute has no general provision for waiver or termination of its ban, it does exempt from boycott any entities present in Burma solely to report the news, § 7:22H(e), or to provide international telecommunication goods or services, *ibid.,* or medical supplies, § 7:22I.

* * *

In September 1996, three months after the Massachusetts law was enacted, Congress passed a statute imposing a set of mandatory and conditional sanctions on Burma. See Foreign Operations, Export Financing, and Related Programs Appropriations Act, 1997, § 570, 110 Stat. 3009–166 to 3009–167 (enacted by the Omnibus Consolidated Appropriations Act, 1997, § 101(c), 110 Stat. 3009–121 to 3009–172). * * *

On May 20, 1997, the President issued the Burma Executive Order, Exec. Order No. 13047, 3 CFR 202 (1997 Comp.). He certified for purposes of § 570(b) that the Government of Burma had "committed large-scale repression of the democratic opposition in Burma" and found that the Burmese Government's actions and policies constituted "an unusual and extraordinary threat to the national security and foreign policy of the United States," a threat characterized as a national emergency. The President then prohibited new investment in Burma "by United States persons," Exec. Order No. 13047, § 1, any approval or facilitation by a United States person of such new investment by foreign persons, § 2(a), and any transaction meant to evade or avoid the ban, § 2(b). The order generally incorporated the exceptions and exemptions addressed in the statute. §§ 3, 4. Finally, the President delegated to the Secretary of State the tasks of working with ASEAN and other countries to develop a strategy for democracy, human rights, and the quality of life in Burma, and of making the required congressional reports. § 5.

Respondent National Foreign Trade Council (Council) is a nonprofit corporation representing companies engaged in foreign commerce; 34 of its members were on the Massachusetts restricted purchase list in 1998. *National Foreign Trade Council v. Natsios,* 181 F.3d 38, 48 (C.A.I 1999). Three withdrew from Burma after the passage of the state Act, and one member had its bid for a procurement contract increased by 10 percent under the provision of the state law allowing acceptance of a low bid from a listed bidder only if the next-to-lowest bid is more than 10 percent higher. *Ibid.*

* * *

The State's petition for certiorari challenged the decision on all three grounds and asserted interests said to be shared by other state and local governments with similar measures.[5] * * *

III

A fundamental principle of the Constitution is that Congress has the power to preempt state law. * * * [E]ven if Congress has not occupied the field, state law is naturally preempted to the extent of any conflict with a federal statute. *Hines v. Davidowitz*, 312 U.S. 52, 66–67, 61 S.Ct. 399, 85 L.Ed. 581 (1941); * * * We will find preemption where it is impossible for a private party to comply with both state and federal law, see, *e.g., Florida Lime & Avocado Growers, Inc. v. Paul*, 373 U.S. 132, 142–143, 83 S.Ct. 1210, 10 L.Ed.2d 248 (1963), and where "under the circumstances of [a] particular case, [the challenged state law] stands as an obstacle to the accomplishment and execution of the full purposes and objectives of Congress." *Hines, supra*, at 67, 61 S.Ct. 399. What is a sufficient obstacle is a matter of judgment, to be informed by examining the federal statute as a whole and identifying its purpose and intended effects * * *

Applying this standard, we see the state Burma law as an obstacle to the accomplishment of Congress's full objectives under the federal Act. We find that the state law undermines the intended purpose and "natural effect" of at least three provisions of the federal Act, that is, its delegation of effective discretion to the President to control economic sanctions against Burma, its limitation of sanctions solely to United States persons and new investment, and its directive to the President to proceed diplomatically in developing a comprehensive, multilateral strategy toward Burma.

* * *

Because the state Act's provisions conflict with Congress's specific delegation to the President of flexible discretion, with limitation of sanctions to a limited scope of actions and actors, and with direction to develop a comprehensive, multilateral strategy under the federal Act, it is preempted, and its application is unconstitutional, under the Supremacy Clause.

It is so ordered.

---

5. "At least nineteen municipal governments have enacted analogous laws restricting purchases from companies that do business in Burma." *Id.*, at 47; Pet. for Cert. 13 (citing N.Y.C. Admin. Code § 6–115 (1999); Los Angeles Admin. Code, Art. 12, § 10.38 *et seq.* (1999); Philadelphia Code § 17-104(b) (1999); Vermont H.J. Res. 157 (1998); 1999 Vt. Laws No. 13).

K.S.B. TECHNICAL SALES CORP. v. NORTH JERSEY DISTRICT WATER SUPPLY COMMISSION OF THE STATE OF NEW JERSEY

Supreme Court of New Jersey, 1977.
75 N.J. 272, 381 A.2d 774.

SCHREIBER, J.

This case projects for our review the validity of New Jersey "Buy American" statutes, which generally require use in government purchase contracts of materials produced in this country. The bidding specifications of the North Jersey District Water Supply Commission (Commission) for a water treatment plant contained such a provision. K.S.B. Technical Sales Corp. (K.S.B.), a New York corporation which is a wholly owned subsidiary of a West German manufacturer of pumps and pumping equipment, and Linda Fazio, a taxpayer and resident of the City of Clifton, seek an adjudication that the Buy American condition in the specifications be declared invalid and its statutory foundation unconstitutional. * * *

Notwithstanding any inconsistent provision of any law, and unless the head of the department, or other public officer charged with the duty by law, shall determine it to be inconsistent with the public interest, or the cost to be unreasonable, only domestic materials shall be acquired or used for any public work.

This section shall not apply with respect to domestic materials to be used for any public work, if domestic materials of the class or kind to be used are not mined, produced or manufactured, as the case may be, in the United States in commercial quantities and of a satisfactory quality. [N.J.S.A. 52:33–2]

Every contract for the construction, alteration or repair of any public work in this state shall contain a provision that in the performance of the work the contractor and all subcontractors shall use only domestic materials in the performance of the work; but if the head of the department or other public officer authorized by law to make the contract shall find that in respect to some particular domestic materials it is impracticable to make such requirement or that it would unreasonably increase the cost, an exception shall be noted in the specifications as to that particular material, and a public record made of the findings which justified the exception. [N.J.S.A. 52:33–3]

A contractor's failure to comply with these provisions may disqualify him from being awarded any public work construction contracts for three years. N.J.S.A. 52:33–4. * * *

Plaintiffs argue that the New Jersey Buy American provisions, N.J.S.A. 52:33–2 and 3, * * * represent an impermissible intrusion by the State into the field of foreign affairs, an area constitutionally reserved to Congress and the President. * * * the plaintiffs rely heavily on *Bethlehem Steel Corp. v. Board of Comm'rs of Dept. of W. & P., * * *.

The California Buy American Act [a] did not have the restricted sphere and more limited impact of the New Jersey statute. * * * Unlike the California Code N.J.S.A. 52:33–2 and 3 provide that domestic materials need not be used if the cost is "unreasonable" or it is "inconsistent with the public interest" or it is "impracticable." * * * [W]e do not agree that every and any state statute which in any way touches upon foreign affairs is proscribed. States may properly exercise their police powers and in doing so have some permissible effect on foreign trade.

* * *

Congress has expressed a policy judgment that foreign commerce will not be unduly burdened when the federal government and its agencies prefer domestic products in their purchases. By enacting the Buy American Act, Congress has approved the policy of preferring domestic goods for federal governmental projects. State statutes patterned after the federal act are consonant with that policy. At least when governmental purchases are not to be used in the production of goods for commercial sale, that policy judgment has been impliedly extended to the states * * * Although Buy American statutes have been the subject of extensive criticism, * * * it is our function to review the constitutionality, not the wisdom, of statutes. We conclude that N.J.S.A. 52:33–2 and 3 do not violate the Commerce Clause.

COMMENT ON THE APPLICATION OF THE FEDERAL BUY AMERICAN ACT

As currently applied, the United States Buy American Act requires federal agencies to treat a domestic bid as unreasonable or inconsistent with the public interest when it exceeds a foreign bid by more than six percent (customs duties included) or ten percent (customs duties and specified costs excluded). See Executive Order 10582, reproduced in the Documents Supplement. Exceptions to this general approach exist for reasons of national interest, certain designated small business purchases, domestic suppliers operating in areas of substantial unemployment, and demonstrated national security needs. Bids by small businesses and companies located in labor surplus areas are generally protected by a 12 percent margin. *See* the *Allis Chalmers* case, *infra.* Bids by United States companies are considered foreign rather than domestic when the materials used are below 50 percent American in origin.

The Department of Defense has its own Buy American rules. These rules generally provide for a 50 percent price preference (customs duties excluded) or a six or twelve percent preference (customs duties included), whichever is more protective to domestic suppliers. *See* the *Self-Powered Lighting* case,

---

a. Government Code section 4303 provides: "The governing body of any political subdivision, municipal corporation, or district, and any public officer or person charged with the letting of contracts for (1) the construction, alteration, or repair of public works or (2) for the purchasing of materials for public use, shall let such contracts only to persons who agree to use or supply only such unmanufactured materials as have been produced in the United States, and only such manufactured materials as have been manufactured in the United States, substantially all from materials produced in the United States."

infra. Intergovernmental "Memoranda of Understanding" (MOU) on defense procurement provide important exceptions to standard Department of Defense procurement rules. This 50 percent margin of preference notwithstanding, some critics of Department of Defense procurement perceive that the U.S. is increasingly dependent on foreign suppliers for the materials of war. This is especially true of electronic and other high-tech components that are found throughout modern military weapons systems. In the face of budget cuts, military procurement officers are often opposed to broad Buy American policies and favor internationally competitive bidding. In the extreme cases, however, they have been willing to create special procurement rules to insure at least one or two U.S. suppliers of key materials.

SELF–POWERED LIGHTING, LTD. v. UNITED STATES

United States District Court, Southern District of New York, 1980.
492 F.Supp. 1267.

EDWARD WEINFELD, DISTRICT JUDGE.

This is an action by Self-Powered Lighting, Ltd. ("Self-Powered"), a New York corporation engaged in the manufacture of armaments and military equipment against the United States and various officers of the U.S. Army Armament Materiel Readiness Command (the "Army") for a declaratory judgment that a contract entered into on July 31, 1979 between the Army and Saunders-Roe Developments, Ltd. ("Saunders Ltd.") is void, and enjoining payments thereunder. * * *

Plaintiff alleges two violations of the Buy American Act in connection with this procurement: (1) that Saunders Ltd.'s offer was improperly exempted from the application of the Act, and (2) that the original solicitation was defective in that it failed to contain the mandatory notice to domestic offerors of potential foreign competition. Neither of these arguments is of substance.

The Act requires government agencies to purchase for public use only American manufactured and produced end-products, "unless the head of the department or independent establishment concerned shall determine it to be inconsistent with the public interest, or the cost to be unreasonable * * *." The government contends that the "public interest" exception to the Act is applicable in this case. In a Memorandum of Understanding ("MOU") [a] dated September 24, 1975, the governments of the United States and the United Kingdom agreed to a policy of fostering "greater standardization and interoperability of their weapons systems * * * [and] assur[ing] the maintenance of a long term and equitable balance in reciprocal purchasing of defense equipment." In furtherance of that policy, they agreed to exempt both government-to-government and government-to-industry contracts for the procurement of military equipment from the application of "price differentials under Buy-National Laws." The Memorandum was specifically implemented by a Determina-

---

a. *See* Dempsey, *Foreign Procurement Under Memoranda of Understanding and the Trade Agreements Act,* 12 Public Contract L.J. 231 (1982).

tion and Finding, dated November 24, 1976, in which the Secretary of Defense concluded that, with respect to "all items of UK produced or manufactured Defense Equipment other than those items which have been excluded from consideration under the MOU, * * * it is inconsistent with the public interest to apply the restrictions of the Buy American Act." In the face of the broad, inclusive language of both the MOU and the Secretary's Determination, the plaintiff argues that the exemption applies only to military equipment purchased outside the country for use by NATO forces stationed in Europe; or at least for equipment intended to be interoperable with that in use in NATO countries.

Although the Secretary's Determination does mention these two goals, they are not the exclusive purposes of the exception. Plaintiff's crabbed reading of the introductory language in the Secretary's Determination is at odds with the sweeping language of its conclusion, quoted above * * *.

ALLIS–CHALMERS CORPORATION, HYDRO–TURBINE DIVISION v. FRIEDKIN

United States Court of Appeals, Third Circuit, 1980.
635 F.2d 248.

JAMES HUNTER, III, CIRCUIT JUDGE.

This action concerns whether a contract for the construction of the hydroelectric power plant at the Amistad damsite on the Rio Grande River was awarded to defendant-intervenor Hitachi America, Ltd. in violation of the Buy American Act (hereinafter the "Act"). Allis-Chalmers, an unsuccessful participant in the contract bidding, contends that the Buy American Act was not correctly applied to Hitachi's bid. Specifically it has two claims; one, that the cost of installation and other post-delivery services were subject to the Act's surcharge, and two that a greater surcharge rate should have been applied to the foreign bid. If both of these adjustments were made to Hitachi's bid, Allis Chalmers asserts they submitted the lowest bid and therefore the contract was awarded to Hitachi America unjustly. * * *

As a foreign manufacturer bidding on a government contract Hitachi America's bid was subject to the Buy American Act and its implementary regulations. The statute provides that American made articles and supplies be preferred in government construction contracts "unless the head of the department or independent establishment concerned shall determine it to be inconsistent with the public interest, or the cost to be unreasonable. * * *" 41 U.S.C. § 10a (1976). As interpreted by the federal procurement regulations, the price of domestic goods is considered "unreasonable" and hence the Act's preference for domestic goods does not apply when their cost is six percent greater than that of foreign goods. 41 C.F.R. 1–6.104–4(b) (1979). Further, a twelve rather than six percent surcharge is taxed to the cost of foreign goods if the domestic bidder operates in an area of substantial unemployment ("labor surplus concern''). *Id.* After consulting with the United States Department of Labor, the Corps found that Allis-Chalmers' manufacturing plant in York, Pennsylvania, was in an area of substantial unemployment making Allis-Chalmers a labor surplus concern and therefore applied the twelve percent Buy American surcharge to Hitachi's bid. The Corps subtracted the cost of installing the turbines ($983,800) and the services of an erecting engineer ($15,750) from Hitachi's bid and then applied the twelve percent surcharge to the balance. The cost of installation and engineering services were then added back into the total price as well as an additional $60,000 for foreign inspections. This made Hitachi's final adjusted bid $3,748,054, or approximately $20,000 less than Allis-Chalmers'. * * *

Allis–Chalmers contends that limiting the Act's surcharge to cost of foreign goods will encourage unbalanced bidding. Unbalanced bidding occurs when companies use foreign manufactured goods and materials that are subject to the surcharge, but then perform the bulk of manufacturing on these materials in the United States to minimize the impact of the Act's surcharge. This type of unbalanced bidding, it is contended, undercuts the protection afforded American labor by the Buy American Act.

This analysis presents several problems. First, while unbalanced bidding may exist, there is no indication that Hitachi's bid was unbalanced. Second, we believe that materially unbalanced bids can be detected and adjusted by the procuring agency. Finally, we fail to appreciate the problem of "unbalanced" bidding. The central purpose of the Buy American Act was to protect the American worker. If the foreign firms make their bids unbalanced by performing a disproportionate amount of manufacturing at the American jobsite, then the purpose of the Buy American Act protection of the American worker has been largely achieved. Foreign firms will employ American workers to perform the assembly/installation on the domestic jobsite and minimize their foreign manufacturing subject to the Act's surcharge. The Buy American Act protects American labor, not specific employers who seek contracts. To the extent firms submit "unbalanced" bids by having the majority of the work performed on the domestic jobsite with a minimum of the bid subject to the Act's surcharge the Buy American Act has served its purpose American workers perform the jobsite manufacturing and the cost of foreign goods and materials is subject to the Act's surcharge.

We find therefore that the Section's award of the contract to Hitachi America was not clearly illegal and we affirm the judgment of the district court.

NOTE ON "BUYING AMERICAN"

What does it mean to "Buy American"? Take automobiles, for example. What about Honda Accords made in Ohio? BMWs in South Carolina? Toyotas in Kentucky? Hyundai cars made in Mississippi? Or is buying an "American" car limited to GM, Ford or Chrysler .... oops, Chrysler that's FIAT, right? Or does buying American only mean buying from a

UAW, organized plant? Or from General Motors, majority owned at present by the U.S. government?

What about Volkswagen Beattles made in Pueblo, Mexico? Or Chrysler Minivans manufactured in Canada? As we saw in an earlier problem, in order to free trade autos under NAFTA, a minimum of 62.5% of the value of a car must originate in North America. All manufacturers of cars in Mexico, Canada and the United States adhere to this rule of origin. Does that make their cars "American"? But production of car parts has moved heavily to Mexico. So, is a Ford assembled in Michigan using lots of Mexican parts "American"?

R. FOLSOM, NAFTA AND FREE TRADE IN THE AMERICAS

Chapter 4 (2011).

Procurement

Chapter 10 of NAFTA governs procurement of services and goods by state enterprises and governments. Since Mexico, unlike Canada and the United States, has not signed the GATT/WTO Procurement Code, the provisions of Chapter 10 give Canadian and United States suppliers of goods and services priority status in Mexican procurement. NAFTA's procurement rules apply if three criteria are met: (1) The purchasing entity is covered; (2) the goods or services also are covered; and (3) the value of the contract meets designated thresholds. If these criteria are met, then Canadian, Mexican and United States suppliers are free to compete on procurement.

NAFTA's special access rules on procurement do not apply universally. Generally speaking, for example, military and national security procurement is excluded. And not all civil government procurement is covered; only those purchasing entities listed in the Annexes to Chapter 10 are included. These Annexes hoped to list state and provincial entities, another expansion upon the CUSFTA rules, but their participation was "voluntary" and left to further negotiations. United States and Canadian minority and small business set-aside programs are also excluded.

NAFTA's procurement rules apply to some government enterprises (e.g., parastatal Mexican enterprises, Canadian Crown Corporations, the Tennessee Valley Authority). These states enterprises are phased into NAFTA's procurement rules through 2002. For example, PEMEX and the Mexican Federal Electricity Commission (CFE) procure billions of dollars of goods and services annually. In 1994, 50 percent of their purchases were opened to competitive NAFTA bidding and thereafter U.S. firms won PEMEX and CFE contracts. The balance was brought under NAFTA by 2003.

Goods and construction services listed in the Annexes to Chapter 10 are subject to competitive NAFTA bidding. For example, pre-erection site work, civil engineering and construction equipment rentals are listed in

Annex 1001.16–3 and therefore included. Notably, transport, data processing, basic telecommunications, research and development, ship repair, management and other services are expressly excluded. But, apart from construction services, unless specifically excluded, services are subject to competitive NAFTA procurement. The United States, however, has complained that Canada has interpreted its exception for services procurement too broadly.

Canada and the United States had agreed in CUSFTA to a threshold of $25,000 U.S. for federal goods procurement. NAFTA extended this agreement. The threshold for civil procurement between Mexico and the United States is $50,000 U.S. for goods and services. The threshold for construction services is $6.5 million U.S. The $50,000 and $6.5 million thresholds for covered services and construction services also apply between Canada and the United States. The contract thresholds for government enterprises are higher: $250,000 U.S. for goods and services, and $8 million U.S. for construction services. These contract thresholds apply, for example, to PEMEX and CFE.

Bid procedures are detailed at great length in the NAFTA agreement. NAFTA rules mandate notice of bid information, product specifications, qualifications for bidders, etc. Government and state enterprise agencies must accord national and most-favored treatment to NAFTA bidders. Discrimination on grounds of national origin, or foreign affiliation or ownership of the supplier, is prohibited. Notably, procurement of local content or purchase "offsets," used frequently in Canada and Mexico, are also prohibited. So are technical specifications that create unnecessary obstacles to trade. And the normal rules of product origin must be employed.

NAFTA bidders must be given an opportunity to challenge the results or any feature of the procurement process in an impartial forum. However, bids by service suppliers owned or controlled by non-NAFTA nationals that lack substantial business activity in a NAFTA nation can be rejected.

QUESTIONS AND COMMENTS

1. What are the objectives of the federal Buy American statute? Why are government preferences established for United States products under the law? When may such preferences be waived? What are the sanctions for violating the Buy American statute? Will it assist PHOTOCOP?

2. Most waivers of Buy American law are made in advance of the award of procurement contracts. *See* the *Self-Powered Lighting* case. It has been held, however, that a determination that the public interest requires a waiver of the Buy American law may be made *after* a procurement contract has been awarded. *See John T. Brady & Co. v. United States,* 693 F.2d 1380 (Fed.Cir. 1982).

3. The trade distorting impact of Buy American laws is dramatically expanded when state and local procurement rules are considered. Federal and

regional governments are often as disturbed about local procurement rules as foreign suppliers. What is the constitutional basis for such rules? See the *Crosby* excerpt. In *K.S.B.*, why was the California Buy American law unconstitutional but the New Jersey law upheld?

Can the United States negotiate international agreements with other nations which regulate state and local procurement? See the WTO Procurement Code and Section 102(b) of the 1994 Uruguay Round Agreements Act. See also the President's Submission concerning the Code in Part B of this problem.

The National Foreign Trade Council, winner in the *Crosby* case invalidating state procurement rules hostile to Burma, has challenged similar state laws targeting Sudan for its atrocities in Darfur. See NFTC v. Giannoulias, 523 F.Supp.2d 731 (N.D. Ill. 2007).

4. Do you agree with the court in *Allis–Chalmers* that "unbalanced bidding" promotes Buy American objectives? Why?

5. If a law were to require purchase by government of an "American" photocopier, would that be possible? In an increasingly global marketplace, are buy local procurement preferences operable? What "rules of origin" should be used to establish when local procurement preferences are being met?

6. The Automobile Labeling Act of 1992, effective in 1994, requires producers to identify the "U.S./Canadian content" (not NAFTA content) by value of their automobiles. The origin of the engine and transmission must be specifically named, as must any country supplying over 15 percent of the value of vehicle's parts. Where an automobile is assembled must also be disclosed. Would you be influenced by these disclosures when purchasing an auto?

Is this the way to determine where products are from? Compare the automotive tracing requirements in NAFTA's regional value content calculations covered in the Free Trade problem. Does the Act function as a nontariff trade barrier? Why omit Mexico? Should the Act be extended to photocopiers?

7. What are PHOTOCOP's prospects for selling copiers to PEMEX?

PART B. GATT/WTO AND GOVERNMENT PROCUREMENT

Liberalizing government procurement law was one focus of the Tokyo and Uruguay Rounds of GATT negotiations. The results, to date, illustrate the difficulties of reaching global consensus on procurement rules and some of the practical problems of implementation of such rules.

K.S.B. TECHNICAL SALES CORP. v. NORTH JERSEY DISTRICT WATER SUPPLY COMMISSION OF THE STATE OF NEW JERSEY

Supreme Court of New Jersey, 1977.
75 N.J. 272, 381 A.2d 774.

SCHREIBER, J.

The General Agreement on Tariffs and Trade (GATT) is a multi-lateral international agreement to which the United States is a party by virtue of executive action. Presidential authority to bind the United States to GATT has been predicated in part on the Reciprocal Trade Agreements Act of 1934 and its successors, * * * and in part upon the executive power to conduct foreign affairs. The legal significance of GATT has been considered by all parties as equivalent to that of a treaty. * * * A state law must yield when it is inconsistent with or impairs the policy or provisions of a treaty. * * * Thus, whether federal preemption exists in this case depends upon an analysis of GATT, the New Jersey Buy American statute in question, N.J.S.A. 52:33–2 and 3, and the status and functions of the Commission.

Facially the Buy American statute, N.J.S.A. 52:33–2 and 3, appears to be in direct conflict with GATT, Pt. II, Article III, paragraph 4,[a] * * * Article III, paragraph 4 of GATT is not, however, all-inclusive. An exception reads as follows:

> The provisions of this article shall not apply to laws, regulations or requirements governing the procurement by governmental agencies of products purchased for governmental purposes and not with a view to commercial resale or with a view to use in the production of goods for commercial sale.

The Commission has urged that materials to be acquired in connection with the construction of its proposed water treatment plant fall within the exception clause. The exclusionary requisites are: (1) procurement by a governmental agency, (2) of a product, (3) purchased for governmental purposes, (4) not for commercial sale, and (5) not with a view to use in the production of goods for commercial sale. That the Commission is a governmental agency and that it proposes to acquire products, materials with which to construct and equip the plant, are clear.

The plaintiffs contend, however, that the Commission's construction of a water treatment plant is not for a governmental purpose and that the proposed plant will produce "goods", namely water, for commercial sale. Consideration of these contentions necessitates examination of the Commission, its operations and functions. * * *

We are satisfied that the Commission's activities in harnessing, treating and channeling the water to eight municipalities constitute appropriate governmental functions and purposes. It is transmitting "common"

---

a. See Documents Supplement. Article III(4) establishes a "national treatment standard."

property, potable water, to municipalities for the use of their inhabitants—a necessity upon which their very existence depends. In performing
these functions, the Commission, unlike a commercial enterprise, operates
at cost. We find, then, that the Commission's purchases of materials and
equipment for its water treatment plant are for governmental purposes
and not with a view to use in the "production of goods for commercial
sale."

* * * We hold that purchases for the construction of this water
treatment plant are exempted from the operation of Article III of GATT
and accordingly GATT has not preempted State jurisdiction.

PRESIDENT CLINTON'S SUBMISSION TO CONGRESS OF DOCUMENTS CONCERNING URUGUAY ROUND AGREEMENTS (DEC. 15, 1993)

58 Fed.Reg. 67299 (Dec. 20, 1993).

GOVERNMENT PROCUREMENT

U.S. Objectives

In the negotiations on Government Procurement, the U.S. government objectives were to expand coverage of the agreement to open
significant export opportunities in new areas of procurement, including
telecommunications and heavy electrical equipment, subcentral (state and
municipal) procurement, services and construction. In addition, the United States sought better enforcement of the Code by requiring signatories
to establish an effective bid protest system and tighten other disciplines.

Results

The United States has concluded a new Agreement on Government
Procurement to replace the existing agreement. This new Agreement
expands coverage to significant new areas of procurement and improves
the disciplines applicable to government procurement. In addition to the
current members of the Agreement (European Community, Japan, Canada, the Nordic countries, Hong Kong, Switzerland, Austria and Israel),
Korea has agreed to join.

In contrast to the existing agreement, which covers only central
government procurement of goods, the new Agreement includes procurement of services and construction and some coverage of subcentral governments and government-owned utilities. The United States and EC, in
particular, have agreed to seek expansion of their bilateral coverage
packages to subcentral and government-owned utilities by April 15, 1994.
At the same time, the new Agreement contains provisions that will
improve enforcement of the Agreement's disciplines, as well as provisions
anticipating future changes in procurement practices, such as streamlin-
ing procurement and electronic contracting.

Key Provisions

Effective Date: The new Agreement will go into force on January 1, 1996 with respect to all signatories, except for Hong Kong and Korea, for which the Agreement will be effective by no later than January 1, 1997.

Publication: Central government entities must publish a notice of each procurement in a readily available centralized publication. State and local government entities and government-owned utilities may publish once a year a notice regarding a qualification system or a forecast of anticipated procurements, which serves as an invitation to participate in all related procurements over the forthcoming year. These entities must follow up by transmitting specific information on such procurements to all those firms that have responded to the notice but can limit invitations to tender (i.e., an RFP) to selected firms from a list of qualified firms.

Bid Deadlines: Although the general rule on bid deadlines remains 40 days, under certain circumstances, deadlines can be reduced to not less than ten days.

Development of Technical Specifications: Entities at all levels of government are encouraged to establish technical specifications in terms of performance rather than design and on the basis of accepted international or national standards, where appropriate. They must not be formulated or communicated on a discriminatory basis.

Quality of Life Restrictions: Government entities can claim exemptions for recycled products and other "quality of life" restrictions under the Agreement, as long as they are not "a means of arbitrary or unjustifiable discrimination."

Notification of Losing Bidders: Entities at all levels must "promptly" inform bidders of decisions on contract award, either orally or in writing, if requested.

Bid Protest: In a significant improvement over the existing agreement, Government entities at all levels must provide non-discriminatory, timely, transparent and effective procedures enabling suppliers and service providers to challenge alleged breaches of the procedural provisions of the Agreement. A challenge must be heard by an impartial and independent review body with no interest in the outcome of the procurement and whose members are secure from external influence during the term of appointment. In addition, in the event the review body is not a court, the Agreement requires the body to apply court-like procedures. Finally, the procedures must provide for the possibility of procurement suspension while a challenge is being heard and compensation for the loss or damages, including costs for tender preparation or protest, or reversal after an award decision has been made.

Offsets: The Agreement prohibits the use of offsets as a condition for award unless a derogation is specified in a country's schedule. This is a substantial improvement over the existing Code, which authorizes offsets.

Dispute Settlement: The Agreement provides that the provisions of the Dispute Settlement Understanding will apply with a few exceptions. In recognition of the special nature of procurement, the Agreement urges that the dispute resolution panel make every effort to reduce the time frames set forth in the Understanding for reaching decisions. The Agreement limits the Dispute Settlement Body, which is charged with establishing panels, making recommendations and authorizing suspension of concessions, to signatories to the Agreement. Finally, the Agreement expands potential remedies in the event that the normal remedy of withdrawing the inconsistent measures is not possible.

Coverage: The Agreement will govern procurement by central government entities of goods and services above a threshold of 130,000 SDRs (approximately $182,000) and of construction services above a threshold of 5 million SDRs (approximately $6.5 million). The United States has agreed to cover procurement by all executive agencies subject to the Federal Acquisition Regulations. The United States has specifically excluded from coverage procurement subject to small and minority preference programs. In addition, the United States has not offered procurement of a number of sensitive services sectors, such as transportation, research and development and management and operation of Federal research centers and laboratories.

The new Agreement also envisions coverage of procurement by subcentral government entities and government-owned utilities and corporations. In negotiating coverage in these areas, the United States gave priority to access to procurement by government-owned telecommunications and heavy electrical generating utilities. For Korea, Israel and Hong Kong, which offered access to those sectors and others like ports, airports, and rails, the United States agreed to cover procurement by 24 states, including the five largest states, and the federally-owned utilities. The United States offer of states' procurement was based on voluntary commitments by the states and excluded federally-funded mass transit and highway projects.

With the EC, the United States agreed to pursue an expansion of coverage to subcentral governments and government-owned utilities by April 15, 1994. We expect that this expanded package can be extended to the Nordic countries, Switzerland and Austria as well. With regard to Japan, the United States did not offer access to these categories of procurement in light of Japan's refusal to lower its threshold for construction services, which is three times higher than that agreed by most other parties. We also declined to apply these categories to Canada because it was not prepared to cover its provincial hydro-electric crown corporations.

GRIER, JAPAN'S IMPLEMENTATION OF THE WTO AGREEMENT ON GOVERNMENT PROCUREMENT

17 U.Pa.J.Int'l Econ.L. 605 (Summer 1996).*

Over the past fifteen years, Japan has undertaken a number of measures designed to increase opportunities for foreign suppliers to participate in its government procurements. In 1980, Japan joined the United States and other countries in instituting international disciplines on government procurement in the GATT Agreement on Government Procurement ("GATT Code"). From 1980 to 1994, Japan entered thirteen bilateral procurement agreements with the United States, covering six sectors of Japanese government procurement. These agreements were aimed at making the Japanese government procurement system more fair, open, transparent, competitive, and accessible to foreign suppliers. During that same period, the Japanese government issued several action plans which contained similar objectives. Most recently, Japan signed the World Trade Organization's ("WTO") Agreement on Government Procurement ("GPA"), which was negotiated in the Uruguay Round of Multilateral Trade Negotiations.

* * *

JAPAN'S IMPLEMENTATION OF THE GPA

Background

When Japan implemented the GPA on January 1, 1996, it undertook its third set of international obligations to improve its government procurement system. To understand the implications of the new commitments for Japan, it is necessary to consider the extent to which Japan had already reformed its procurement system as a result of outside influences.

Before Japan became a signatory to the GATT Code, it made relatively little use of an open competitive bidding system in government procurements. As a consequence, when Japan implemented the Code in 1981, it instituted unprecedented changes in its procurement system as it opened government purchases to foreign suppliers. The reform of Japan's procurement system, however, did not end with its assumption of GATT Code obligations. Japan subsequently entered into a series of bilateral arrangements with the United States and issued several unilateral action plans in order to further reform its procurement system.

Between 1980 and 1994, the United States and Japan negotiated thirteen bilateral government procurement agreements. With the negotiation of these agreements, the United States sought to remove impediments faced by foreign suppliers in specific procurement areas. The resulting agreements required the Japanese government and certain government-related entities to adopt more transparent, competitive, and non-discriminatory procurement procedures.

While each bilateral agreement was tailored to remove the obstacles encountered by foreign suppliers in a particular sector, the separate agreements have several common characteristics. Each sets out procedures that generally are more detailed than those required by the GATT Code. The agreements, for the most part, supplement or fill "gaps" in the GATT Code by covering procurements not subject to multilateral disciplines, providing more detailed procedures, and addressing specific market access barriers posed by Japan's procurement system. Each agreement applies only to procurements that meet certain thresholds and are conducted by specified central government and quasi-governmental entities. These Japanese entities closely correspond to the entities subject to the GATT Code and the GPA. Japan accords the benefits of the bilateral agreements to all foreign suppliers, not just those from the United States.

An example of an agreement negotiated to compensate for limitations in GATT Code coverage is the first bilaterally negotiated agreement, which applies to procurements by Japan's domestic telecommunications carrier, Nippon Telegraph and Telephone Corporation ("NTT"). The United States had sought a bilateral agreement to open NTT's purchases of public telecommunications equipment to foreign suppliers because the United States believed that Japan's GATT Code coverage was inadequate. Other bilateral agreements cover services that were not subject to the GATT Code, in particular construction services.

In addition to the bilateral accords, Japan, on its own initiative, but at least partially in response to foreign criticism of its procurement system, adopted several action plans that augmented its international commitments. For example, Japan improved on its GATT Code obligations by voluntarily adding entities that would follow GATT Code requirements, increasing the period between the publication of notices of procurement and the deadline for the submission of tenders, and lowering the threshold for procurements announced in the *Kanpō,* Japan's official gazette.

Japan's GPA Obligations

Japanese Entities Subject to the GPA

Like all GPA signatories, Japan subjected three categories of entities to GPA disciplines: central government entities, sub-central entities, and government-related entities. This Article describes the specifics of the coverages below.

Central Government Entities

Consistent with its coverage under the GATT Code, Japan applies the GPA to the procurement of all central government entities. These entities include both houses of the Diet (Japan's legislative body), the Supreme Court, the Cabinet, twelve ministries, and fifteen other central government entities that are subject to the Accounts Law. Japan, however, withheld its National Space Development Agency from GPA coverage, and has taken a few other exceptions, including contracts awarded to cooperatives or associations. Japan applies the same thresholds for central government procurements as the other signatories: 130,000 SDRs for goods; 4,500,000 SDRs for construction services; 450,000 SDRs for architectural, engineering, and technical services; and 130,000 SDRs for other services.

Sub–Central Entities

Second, in a major departure from its prior practice, Japan has subjected its most important sub-central governmental entities to GPA disciplines. Japan has required its forty-seven prefectures and twelve designated cities (*shitei toshi*) to comply with the GPA, subject to several exceptions. The excepted procurements include: contracts awarded to cooperatives and associations; contracts awarded as part of entities' "daily profit-making activities which are exposed to competitive forces in markets;" and "[p]rocurement related to the production, transport or distribution of electricity." Japan negotiated GPA thresholds for its sub-central government procurements of 200,000 SDRs for goods and all services, except for construction services and architectural, engineering, and technical services, which have thresholds of 15,000,000 SDRs and 1,500,000 SDRs, respectively.

Government–Related Entities

Japan has included eighty-four government-related entities in the third category of entities subject to the GPA. These include the partially privatized NTT, several railway companies created after the breakup of Japan National Railways Corporation, the Japan External Trade Organization, and various financial corporations, such as the Housing Loan Corporation. Japan has also taken several general exceptions for its government-related entities, similar to those taken for central and sub-central entities. These exceptions from the GPA include contracts awarded to cooperatives and associations and contracts for "daily profit-making activities." In contrast to the other categories, Japan has also exempted certain procurements of specific government-related entities. For example, NTT's procurement of public electrical telecommunications equipment remains outside the GPA.

The thresholds that apply to procurements of Japanese government-related entities are equivalent to the thresholds for central government entities. An exception exists for construction services, which have the same threshold as sub-central entities, 15,000,000 SDRs.

Coverage Relative to the United States

When the GPA signatories concluded their negotiations, the United States and Japan had reached only partial agreement on bilateral coverage. The United States and Japan had agreed on the coverage of central government procurements and services, including construction services, but they had not reached agreement on sub-central government entities and government-related entities. On January 23, 1996, however, the two nations finalized their coverage negotiations, and agreed to extend bilateral access to their sub-central and government-related entities at the thresholds set out in their respective annexes, effective February 25, 1996.

Japanese Service Procurements Subject to the GPA

The services that Japan has brought under GPA disciplines include vehicle repair and maintenance, air transport services, courier services, telecommunications services, computer and related services, public works, and publishing and printing services. These services, including several construction services, are subject to several exclusions.

* * *

Local Government Procurement

Background

Japan's adherence to the GPA may have the greatest impact at the sub-central level because for the first time Japan's prefectures and twelve largest cities must comply with international disciplines for certain procurements. The GATT Code did not impose obligations on local governments. The sub-central governments also escaped binding coverage by the bilateral accords. The only bilateral commitment that the Japanese government undertook with regard to local governments was in several agreements to "encourage" them to adopt open, transparent, fair, and non-discriminatory procurement procedures Specified Services by Local Public Entities (*Chihō Kōkyō Dantai no Buppin to matawa Tokutei Ekimu no Chōtatsu Tetsuzuki no Tokurei o Sadameru Seirei*) ("Special Local Order").

Central government entities, primarily the Ministry of Home Affairs ("MHA"), have issued various administrative rules, including notifications (*tsūchi*) and circulars (*tsūtatsu*) that pertain to local government compliance with the GPA's provisions. The MHA has issued the ministerial counterpart to the Special Local Order, the Ministerial Ordinance Concerning the Announcement of Special Procedures for the Procurement of Goods and Specified Services by Local Public Entities (*Chihō Kōkyō Dantai no Buppin to matawa Tokutei Ekimu no Chōtatsu Tetsuzuki no Tokurei o Sadameru Seirei no Kōfu no tsuite*). The MHA has also issued other notifications detailing local government obligations. The MHA and the Ministry of Construction ("MOC") jointly issued a circular promoting the reform of bidding and contract procedures used for public works.

The central government directives and guidance are intended to ensure that the local governments are fully aware of their obligations under the GPA. Based on the authority granted by the central government, and subject to its constraints, each local government establishes its own regulations, rules, and internal circular notices to govern its procurement practices and comply with the GPA.

* * *

Implications of Application of GPA to Local Governments

Local governments are important players in public sector procurement. For example, they account for approximately eighty percent of public works undertaken in Japan. The extension of the GPA to the most important local governments is likely to have two major effects on local procurement. First, the GPA requires local entities to use fair, transparent, and predictable procurement procedures that will reduce the exercise of local discretion and increase competition. Second, the GPA requires the removal of certain local procurement practices, in particular the use of qualification requirements favoring local firms and the minimum price system. These practices are discussed below. The result should be new opportunities for foreign firms to participate in an important segment of government procurement in Japan.

Preferential Qualifications

Although local procurement requirements have largely paralleled those of the central government, they were not subject to the disciplines imposed by the GATT Code. Because local entities were not under any obligation to accord non-discriminatory treatment to foreign suppliers, they could favor local firms in their procurements without fear of penalty.

It is an "unwritten law" in Japan that local governments give priority to local firms when conducting procurements. Local governments routinely give preferential treatment to local firms by establishing qualifications for participation in a procurement that non-local firms cannot meet. Most local governments accomplish this aim by requiring suppliers to maintain a branch or headquarters office within their jurisdiction if the suppliers want to be eligible to participate in local procurements. One example is Akaho City, which awarded eighty percent of its 200 contracts to approximately seventy local firms.

Preference for local firms is attributable in part to Japan's "highly decentralized system [which] allows local procurement decisions to reflect parochial concerns and to favor local suppliers." Local governments often defend local preferences as a necessary means of ensuring funds from their legislative assemblies. As noted above, in its implementation of the GPA, the Japanese government has expressly prohibited local government entities subject to the GPA from employing office location as a qualification criterion in GPA-covered procurements. For entities and procurements not under the GPA, however, the Local Autonomy Law allows such qualifications.

Qualification requirements based on locality impede foreign and non-local domestic firms from gaining access to public sector procurements at the local level, even if they have the necessary technical capability and offer competitive prices. Maintaining offices in every local jurisdiction in which a firm wants to bid on local government contracts is not a practical alternative. Such practices that discriminate against foreign firms are prohibited by the GPA, which requires signatories to accord national treatment to the products, services, and suppliers of the other signatories.

Minimum Price System

Another common local practice that has been abolished as part of Japan's implementation of the GPA is the minimum price system. Under this practice, local governments set a minimum bidding price or "lowest permissible value" at a level that is about twenty percent lower than the estimated price or provisional value. Procuring entities then exclude from participation in the procurement all suppliers that submit tenders with prices below the minimum price, solely for that reason.

* * *

Japan's Adoption of a Complaint Mechanism

* * *

To meet the GPA requirement for a complaint mechanism, the Japanese Cabinet established two entities on December 1, 1995, an Office of Government Procurement Review ("OGPR") and a Government Procurement Review Board ("GPRB" or "Board"). Subsequently, on December 14, 1995, the OGPR adopted procedures to govern the complaint review process. This Article will next examine the OGPR, the GPRB, and the complaint review process.

* * *

Potential Consequences of the Complaint Mechanism

Fulfillment of the GPA directive to provide a bid challenge system will enable suppliers to challenge tendering procedures and contract awards, and thus enhance the enforcement of the GPA. This is particularly true for signatories, such as Japan, that lack a tradition of bid protest systems. The potential of the GPA-mechanism, however, will be realized only if suppliers use the system and the system is fair. The reviews requested by suppliers must be conducted in a manner that gives participants confidence that their disputes receive full and fair hearings and are properly resolved on the merits.

Since the pre-GPA complaint mechanisms have been used only once in Japan, it is difficult to draw firm conclusions. Nonetheless, the import of that one case cannot be ignored. Because lingering concerns with the case appear to contribute to the disincentive of foreign firms to use complaint mechanisms in Japan, it must be considered as part of this Article's assessment of the potential for success of Japan's new complaint mechanism.

In 1992, a U.S. firm, Cray Research, Inc. ("Cray"), participated in a procurement for a supercomputer conducted by the National Institute of Fusion Sciences ("NIFS"), which is an entity under the Ministry of Education. NIFS awarded the contract to a Japanese supercomputer manufacturer, NEC Corporation ("NEC"). When NIFS announced the award, Cray resorted to the complaint mechanism in the 1990 Supercomputer Agreement and filed a complaint with the Supercomputer Procurement Review Board ("Supercomputer Board").

Cray sought review of several aspects of the procurement. First, Cray challenged the NIFS evaluation as unfair, favoring the winning Japanese system, in particular with regard to its point allocation and scoring of performance evaluation standards. Second, Cray claimed that the abnormal matching of the NEC proposed system with the comprehensive evaluation standards set by NIFS raised the question whether NEC had prior information on the point allocation. Finally, Cray questioned whether the winning Japanese system could meet all of NIFS's specifications, particularly the requirements of an external mass storage system and an automated parallelization function.

In reviewing the complaint, the Supercomputer Review Board followed the process set out in the Supercomputer Agreement, which is very similar to Japan's GPA mechanism. The review process included the submission of written explanations and data by NIFS and Cray, a hearing by the Board in which the interested parties participated, and the preparation of a written report by the Board.

Based on its review of the complaint, the Supercomputer Review Board concluded that there were no significant problems in the conduct of the procurement, and that it was "unable to recognize the validity of Cray's claims." The Board limited its scope of review to a determination of whether the procurement had been conducted as prescribed by the procedures in the Supercomputer Agreement. The Board did not attempt to address the merits of the competing supercomputers.

When the Board issued its report, the U.S. government immediately expressed "serious concerns," noting that the review process represented "an important test of the Japanese government's resolve to fully implement the provisions of the 1990 Supercomputer Agreement." The United States also expressed concerns with the Board's "extraordinarily narrow interpretation" of its mandate, and registered its dissatisfaction with the manner in which NIFS subsequently "conducted verification procedures in determining that two features promised by the successful bidder actually were present in the machine delivered."

While the duties of the Supercomputer Review Board do not include conducting a *de novo* review of a procurement subject to a bid challenge, it must review "any aspect of a procurement" subject to a complaint. The Board must "specify whether the procurement process or award was inconsistent with *the intent or specific provisions*" of the Agreement. Accordingly, the Board was obligated to determine whether the procuring entity followed the required procedures in a manner that ensured selection of the bid "that best enables [the entity] to perform its mission" and whether the entity considered in its evaluation of bids "technical excellence, with overall system performance being of fundamental importance."

The Board was also required to consider "all the circumstances surrounding the procurement process or award," including whether the entity evaluated the bids based on achieving the overall greatest value.

Such determinations raise difficult issues. Boards must confront such issues if they are to generate confidence that suppliers' claims will be fully and fairly considered, and will not be dismissed on narrow procedural grounds.

QUESTIONS AND COMMENTS

1. What is the purpose of the "national treatment standard" established by Article III of the GATT? Are Buy American laws governed by Article III? Could PHOTOCOP (like KSB) challenge a New Jersey or Los Angeles Buy American law on the basis of conflict with Article III? See especially Section 102(c) of the Uruguay Round Agreements Act. Would it want to raise such a challenge?

2. In 1979, an Agreement on Government Procurement was negotiated within GATT as one of six nontariff trade barrier "Codes." It was significantly amended in 1987 and renegotiated entirely under the Uruguay Round. To what degree is the 1994 Procurement Code based on reciprocity in government procurement opportunities? Why might developing nations not adopt the Procurement Code? Might corrupt practices be part of the issue?

China does not participate in the WTO Procurement Code. It favors "indigenous innovators" in its procurement contracts, all perfectly legal says China. Do you agree?

3. Could PHOTOCOP challenge Buy Danish or Buy Japanese laws not administered according to the Code? What remedies are established for Procurement Code violations?

4. Title III of the United States Trade Agreements Act of 1979 followed from United States participation in the 1979 GATT Agreement on Government Procurement. Review the provisions of Title III as amended through 1994 and the Uruguay Round. Do they carry out United States obligations under the Code? How are other nations "encouraged" to join the Procurement Code?

5. What effect does Title III have on federal Buy American legislation?

6. How effective was the 1979 Procurement Code in dismantling NTBs? Why have the levels of open procurement in Japan been less than anticipated?

7. To what extent does Article III of GATT or the Procurement Code deal with problems of unwritten and unlegislated discriminatory patterns of customary government procurement? Can cultural barriers to trade be dismantled? See Weil and Glick, *Japan—Is the Market Open? A View of the Japanese Market Drawn from U.S. Corporate Experience*, 11 Law & Pol'y Int'l Bus. 845 (1979).

8. Various bilateral United States Treaties of Friendship, Commerce and Navigation provide that nationals shall receive fair and equitable treatment (when compared with nationals of any third party) regarding:

(a) government purchases of supplies;

(b) the award of concessions and government contracts; and

(c) the sale of government services.

See, *e.g.,* Treaty of Friendship, Commerce and Navigation, Feb. 2, 1948, United States—Italy, 63 Stat. 2255, T.I.A.S. No. 1965, 79 U.N.T.S. 143.

Is a bilateral or regional approach more likely to succeed in dealing with unwritten preferences (pressures?) for "buying local?" What about Chapter 10 of the NAFTA?

9. Some state and local jurisdictions have used procurement rules as a means to promote human rights. For many years, South Africa under apartheid was their focus. More recently, Massachusetts adopted a law that effectively denied state contracts to any United States or foreign company doing business in Myanmar (formerly Burma). About 20 other state and local jurisdictions adopted similar laws.

Such laws made an impact. Apple Computer, Eastman Kodak and Hewlett–Packard, among dozens of others, pulled out of Myanmar. About 30 Japanese companies, citing the Massachusetts law, did likewise. Several European countries and Japan threatened to challenge these laws under the 1994 Procurement Code before the World Trade Organization. What result? Revisit the *Crosby* case excerpted in Part A and see the Burmese Freedom and Democracy Act of 2003, Public Law 108–61.

10. Article XIII of the GATS basically exempts government procurement of services from its coverage.

CHAPTER 7

RESPONSES OF DOMESTIC PRODUCERS TO IMPORT COMPETITION

■ ■ ■

INTRODUCTION 7.0 THE FRAMEWORK FOR PROVIDING PROTECTION FROM IMPORT COMPETITION

Chapter 6 focused primarily upon the mechanisms and efforts used to reduce tariffs and non-tariff barriers, and to generally promote open and free trade. This chapter considers circumstances in which raising tariffs and trade barriers is expressly authorized in order to protect domestic industries from competition from abroad.

The Chapter begins by considering two major problems which arise as a result of valuing goods for import purposes through the use of the invoice price. Firstly, the government in the exporting country might subsidize the production of the goods, thus artificially lowering the sales price. The subsidy may have been designed especially for assisting exports of goods, or it may be a more general subsidy applicable to both domestic sales and exports. Secondly, the foreign manufacturer or seller of the goods may be selling them at distressed prices which are less than would be charged under normal market conditions. The potential motivations for such sales are many. They range from use of "loss leaders" or "introductory offers" to develop a new, foreign, market for the seller; to true "distress" sales where the seller must reduce inventory for financial reasons; or simply to a need to keep the manufacturing plant in operation, for example. These special low prices may be available only in export transactions, or in both domestic and export transactions. Problem 6.2 examined the Valuation Code processes, and Problems 7.1 and 7.2 should be considered as a further elaboration of those processes. Problem 7.3 then addresses the separate but related question of what can be done when properly valued imports nevertheless harm domestic producers or industries, under the "safeguards" or "escape clause" mechanism.

When goods are exported at unusually low prices they may well be regarded by domestic industries in the importing country as a source of unfair competition. Accordingly, the importing country's government may impose special tariffs in order to offset this unfair pricing. Countries respond to unfair import competition in this manner with two different mechanisms. Where the imported goods are priced unfairly due to the direct or indirect provision of governmental subsidies, "countervailing duties" (CVDs) are used to raise the imports prices to market levels. Similarly, where the unfair pricing occurs because a private exporter is selling the goods below their normal value, "anti-dumping duties" (ADs) are used to raise the effective price of those items in the importing country's market. The basic criteria and processes for imposing CVDs and ADs are largely derived from the WTO/GATT agreements.

In addition to CVDs and ADs, the WTO/GATT agreements provide a safeguards or escape clause mechanism which may be available even when there are no subsidies or sales at less than fair value. This is an extraordinary provision which permits WTO members to temporarily deviate from their obligations under the agreements when their domestic industries would suffer sufficient harm from *fairly* priced import competition that some sort of relief for the domestic industry becomes appropriate. The primary difference between the escape clause and the CVD/AD mechanism is the level of pain which must be suffered before each can be invoked. CVDs and ADs each require that material injury to a domestic industry actually occur or be threatened, or that establishment of such an industry be "materially retarded," before a duty may be imposed. The standard for use of the escape mechanism requires that the imports be a "substantial cause of serious injury, or the threat thereof" to an existing domestic industry.*

WORLD TRADE ORGANIZATION

Understanding the WTO
Fifth Edition © 2011*

Chapter 2 The Agreements

* * *

8. Anti-dumping, subsidies, safeguards: contingencies, etc.

Binding tariffs, and applying them equally to all trading partners (most-favoured-nation treatment, or MFN) are key to the smooth flow of trade in goods. The WTO agreements uphold the principles, but they also allow exceptions—in some circumstances. Three of these issues are:

- actions taken against dumping (selling at an unfairly low price)

- subsidies and special "countervailing" duties to offset the subsidies

- emergency measures to limit imports temporarily, designed to "safeguard" domestic industries.

Anti-dumping actions

If a company exports a product at a price lower than the price it normally charges on its own home market, it is said to be "dumping" the product. Is this unfair competition? Opinions differ, but many governments take action against dumping in order to defend their domestic industries. The WTO agreement does not pass judgement. Its focus is on how governments can or cannot react to dumping—it disciplines anti-dumping actions, and it is often called the "**Anti-Dumping Agreement**". (This focus only on the reaction to dumping contrasts with the approach of the Subsidies and Countervailing Measures Agreement.)

> **What is the agreement called?**
> Agreement on the Implementation of Article VI of the General Agreement on Tariffs and Trade 1994

The legal definitions are more precise, but broadly speaking the WTO agreement allows governments to act against dumping where there is genuine ("material") injury to the competing domestic industry. In order to do that the government has to be able to show that dumping is taking place, calculate the extent of dumping (how much lower the export price is compared to the exporter's home market price), and show that the dumping is causing injury or threatening to do so.

GATT (Article 6) allows countries to take action against dumping. The Anti–Dumping Agreement clarifies and expands Article 6, and the two operate together. They allow countries to act in a way that would normally break the GATT principles of binding a tariff and not discriminating between trading partners—typically anti-dumping action means charging extra import duty on the particular product from the particular exporting country in order to bring its price closer to the "normal value" or to remove the injury to domestic industry in the importing country.

There are many different ways of calculating whether a particular product is being dumped heavily or only lightly. The agreement narrows down the range of possible options. It provides three methods to calculate a product's "normal value". The main one is based on the price in the exporter's domestic market. When this cannot be used, two alternatives are available—the price charged by the exporter in another country, or a calculation based on the combination of the exporter's production costs, other expenses and normal profit margins. And the agreement also specifies how a fair compari-

> **'AD-CVD'?**
> People sometimes refer to the two together—"AD-CVD"—but there are fundamental differences.
> Dumping and subsidies—together with anti-dumping (AD) measures and countervailing duties (CVD)—share a number of similarities.
> Many countries handle the two under a single law, apply a similar process to deal with them and give a single authority responsibility for investigations. Occasionally, the two WTO committees responsible for these issues meet jointly.
> The reaction to dumping and subsidies is often a special offsetting import tax (countervailing duty in the case of a subsidy). This is changed on products from specific countries and therefore it breaks the GATT principles of binding a tariff and treating trading partners equally (MFN). The agreements provide an escape clause, but they both also say that before imposing a duty, the importing country must conduct a detailed investigation that shows

son can be made between the export price and what would be a normal price.

Calculating the extent of dumping on a product is not enough. Anti-dumping measures can only be applied if the dumping is hurting the industry in the importing country. Therefore, a detailed investigation has to be conducted according to specified rules first. The investigation must evaluate all relevant economic factors that have a bearing on the state of the industry in question. If the investigation shows dumping is taking place and domestic industry is being hurt, the exporting company can undertake to raise its price to an agreed level in order to avoid anti-dumping import duty.

Detailed procedures are set out on how anti-dumping cases are to be initiated, how the investigations are to be conducted, and the conditions for ensuring that all interested parties are given an opportunity to present evidence. Anti-dumping measures must expire five years after the date of imposition, unless an investigation shows that ending the measure would lead to injury.

properly that domestic industry is hurt.
But there are also fundamental differences, and these are reflected in the agreements.
Dumping is an action by a company. With subsidies, it is the government or a government agency that acts, either by paying out subsidies directly or by requiring companies to subsidize certain customers.
But the WTO is an organization of countries and their governments. The WTO does not deal with companies and cannot regulate companies' actions such as dumping. Therefore the Anti-Dumping Agreement only concerns the actions governments may take against dumping. With subsidies, governments act on both sides: they subsidize and they act against each others' subsidies. Therefore, the subsidies agreement disciplines both the subsidies and the reactions.

Anti-dumping investigations are to end immediately in cases where the authorities determine that the margin of dumping is insignificantly small (defined as less than 2% of the export price of the product). Other conditions are also set. For example, the investigations also have to end if the volume of dumped imports is negligible (i.e. if the volume from one country is less than 3% of total imports of that product—although investigations can proceed if several countries, each supplying less than 3% of the imports, together account for 7% or more of total imports).

The agreement says member countries must inform the Committee on Anti–Dumping Practices about all preliminary and final anti-dumping actions, promptly and in detail. They must also report on all investigations twice a year. When differences arise, members are encouraged to consult each other. They can also use the WTO's dispute settlement procedure.

ON THE WEBSITE:
www.wto.org > trade topics > goods > antidumping
> See also Doha Agenda negotiations

Subsidies and countervailing measures

This agreement does two things: it disciplines the use of subsidies, and it regulates the actions countries can take to counter the effects of subsidies.

What is this agreement called?

It says a country can use the WTO's dispute settlement procedure to seek the withdrawal of the subsidy or the removal of its adverse effects. Or the country can launch its own investigation and ultimately charge extra duty (known as "countervailing duty") on subsidized imports that are found to be hurting domestic producers.

> Agreement on
> Subsidies and
> Countervailing
> Measures

The agreement contains a definition of subsidy. It also introduces the concept of a "specific" subsidy—i.e. a subsidy available only to an enterprise, industry, group of enterprises, or group of industries in the country (or state, etc.) that gives the subsidy. The disciplines set out in the agreement only apply to specific subsidies. They can be domestic or export subsidies.

The agreement defines two categories of subsidies: prohibited and actionable. It originally contained a third category: non-actionable subsidies. This category existed for five years, ending on 31 December 1999, and was not extended. The agreement applies to agricultural goods as well as industrial products * * *.

- **Prohibited subsidies:** subsidies that require recipients to meet certain export targets, or to use domestic goods instead of imported goods. They are prohibited because they are specifically designed to distort international trade, and are therefore likely to hurt other countries' trade. They can be challenged in the WTO dispute settlement procedure where they are handled under an accelerated timetable. If the dispute settlement procedure confirms that the subsidy is prohibited, it must be withdrawn immediately. Otherwise, the complaining country can take counter measures. If domestic producers are hurt by imports of subsidized products, countervailing duty can be imposed.

- **Actionable subsidies:** in this category the complaining country has to show that the subsidy has an adverse effect on its interests. Otherwise the subsidy is permitted. The agreement defines three types of damage they can cause. One country's subsidies can hurt a domestic industry in an importing country. They can hurt rival exporters from another country when the two compete in third markets. And domestic subsidies in one country can hurt exporters trying to compete in the subsidizing country's domestic market. If the Dispute Settlement Body rules that the subsidy does have an adverse effect, the subsidy must be withdrawn or its adverse effect must be removed. Again, if domestic producers are hurt by imports of subsidized products, countervailing duty can be imposed.

Some of the disciplines are similar to those of the Anti–Dumping Agreement. Countervailing duty (the parallel of anti-dumping duty) can only be charged after the importing country has conducted a detailed investigation similar to that required for anti-dumping action. There are detailed rules for deciding whether a product is being subsidized (not always an easy calculation), criteria for determining whether imports of subsidized products are hurting ("causing injury to") domestic industry, procedures for initiating and conducting investigations, and rules on the implementation and duration (normally five years) of countervailing measures. The subsidized exporter can also agree to raise its export prices as an alternative to its exports being charged countervailing duty.

Subsidies may play an important role in developing countries and in the transformation of centrally-planned economies to market economies. Least-developed countries and developing countries with less than $1,000 per capita GNP are exempted from disciplines on prohibited export subsidies. Other developing countries are given until 2003 to get rid of their export subsidies. * * *

[**Authors' Note**: Under the SCM Agreement, developing countries were to have eliminated export subsidies by 2003. As of 2012, however, eighteen countries—principally in the Caribbean and Central America—continue to operate under an extension of this deadline granted by the WTO's Committee on Subsidies and Countervailing Measures.]

ON THE WEBSITE:

www.wto.org > trade topics > goods > subsidies and countervailing measures

> **See also** Doha Agenda negotiations

Safeguards: emergency protection from imports

A WTO member may restrict imports of a product temporarily (take "safeguard" actions) if its domestic industry is injured or threatened with injury caused by a surge in imports. Here, the injury has to be serious. Safeguard measures were always available under GATT (Article 19). However, they were infrequently used, some governments preferring to protect their domestic industries through "grey area" measures—using bilateral negotiations outside GATT's auspices, they persuaded exporting countries to restrain exports "voluntarily" or to agree to other means of sharing markets. Agreements of this kind were reached for a wide range of products: automobiles, steel, and semiconductors, for example.

| What is this agreement called? Agreement on Safeguards |

The WTO agreement broke new ground. It prohibits "grey-area" measures, and it sets time limits (a "sunset clause") on all safeguard actions. The agreement says members must not seek, take or maintain any voluntary export restraints, orderly marketing arrangements or any other similar measures on the export or the import side. The bilateral measures that were not modified to conform with the agreement were phased out at the end of 1998. Countries were allowed to keep one of these measures an extra year (until the end of 1999), but only the European

Union—for restrictions on imports of cars from Japan—made use of this provision.

An import "surge" justifying safeguard action can be a real increase in imports (an *absolute increase*); or it can be an increase in the imports' share of a shrinking market, even if the import quantity has not increased (*relative increase*).

Industries or companies may request safeguard action by their government. The WTO agreement sets out requirements for safeguard investigations by national authorities. The emphasis is on transparency and on following established rules and practices—avoiding arbitrary methods. The authorities conducting investigations have to announce publicly when hearings are to take place and provide other appropriate means for interested parties to present evidence. The evidence must include arguments on whether a measure is in the public interest.

The agreement sets out criteria for assessing whether "serious injury" is being caused or threatened, and the factors which must be considered in determining the impact of imports on the domestic industry. When imposed, a safeguard measure should be applied only to the extent necessary to prevent or remedy serious injury and to help the industry concerned to adjust. Where quantitative restrictions (quotas) are imposed, they normally should not reduce the quantities of imports below the annual average for the last three representative years for which statistics are available, unless clear justification is given that a different level is necessary to prevent or remedy serious injury.

In principle, safeguard measures cannot be targeted at imports from a particular country. However, the agreement does describe how quotas can be allocated among supplying countries, including in the exceptional circumstance where imports from certain countries have increased disproportionately quickly. A safeguard measure should not last more than four years, although this can be extended up to eight years, subject to a determination by competent national authorities that the measure is needed and that there is evidence the industry is adjusting. Measures imposed for more than a year must be progressively liberalized.

When a country restricts imports in order to safeguard its domestic producers, in principle it must give something in return. The agreement says the exporting country (or exporting countries) can seek compensation through consultations. If no agreement is reached the exporting country can retaliate by taking equivalent action—for instance, it can raise tariffs on exports from the country that is enforcing the safeguard measure. In some circumstances, the exporting country has to wait for three years after the safeguard measure was introduced before it can retaliate in this way—i.e. if the measure conforms with the provisions of the agreement and if it is taken as a result of an increase in the quantity of imports from the exporting country.

To some extent developing countries' exports are shielded from safeguard actions. An importing country can only apply a safeguard measure to a product from a developing country if the developing country is supplying more than 3% of the imports of that product, or if developing country members with less than 3% import share collectively account for more than 9% of total imports of the product concerned.

The WTO's Safeguards Committee oversees the operation of the agreement and is responsible for the surveillance of members' commitments. Governments have to report each phase of a safeguard investigation and related decision-making, and the committee reviews these reports.

ON THE WEBSITE:

www.wto.org > trade topics > goods > safeguards

AUTHORS' COMMENT ON ADMINISTRATIVE AND JUDICIAL PROCEDURE IN TRADE REMEDY CASES

A.   Procedures under United States Law

The actual imposition of ADs, CVDs, or safeguards measures under U.S. domestic law occurs as a result of complex administrative processes and determinations involving multiple governmental agencies. The principal agencies involved in AD/CVD cases are the International Trade Administration (ITA), which is part of the Commerce Department, and the United States International Trade Commission (ITC), which is an independent bipartisan agency created by an act of Congress in 1916 as the United States Tariff Commission. The ITC, but not the ITA, is also involved in safeguards or escape clause proceedings. The administrative decisions made by the ITA and the ITC are subject to review by the U.S. Court of International Trade (CIT), whose decisions may in turn be appealed to the U.S. Court of Appeals for the Federal Circuit and ultimately to the U.S. Supreme Court.

In broad terms, reflecting its role as part of the Commerce Department, the ITA's mission is to foster, promote, and develop U.S. participation in world trade. It assists American businesses by providing information concerning the "what, where, how, and when" of imports and exports, or the steps necessary to start a business in a foreign country. In addition to these "trade promotion" duties, the ITA helps protect American businesses from unfair competition from foreign imports by deciding whether there are impermissible foreign subsidies in CVD cases or sales at less than fair value in AD cases. The ITA is not, however, involved in decision-making in escape clause proceedings.

The ITC is an independent, quasi-judicial, bipartisan agency created to provide trade expertise to both Congress and the Executive. The Commission's duties include preparing reports pertaining to international economics and foreign trade for the Executive Branch, the Congress, other government agencies, and the public. To carry out this responsibility, the ITC conducts investigations which entail extensive research, specialized studies, and a high degree of expertise in all matters relating to the commercial and international trade policies of the United States. Statutory investigations conducted by the ITC include unfair import trade practice cases, domestic industry injury determinations in AD/CVD cases, and "escape clause" import relief for domestic industry cases. The ITC also advises the President as to probable economic effect on domestic industry and consumers of modifications on import duties and other trade barriers in connection with proposed trade agreements with foreign countries.

Trade remedy cases may be initiated by either the Department of Commerce or a group or association of aggrieved businesses—an aggrieved "industry". The ITA's function in the process is to decide whether there is a countervailable subsidy or sale at less than fair value and how large any extra duty should be to offset the unfair pricing practices. As a practical matter it is the ITA's preliminary determination, either that dumping has occurred in an AD case or that a countervailable subsidy exists in a CVD case, that starts to place pressure on the importers of the foreign goods—because at that point any covered goods will be subject to the duties that might ultimately be assessed under any final order once both the ITA and the ITC have completed their respective administrative processes. Often such a preliminary determination will effectively cut off further imports of the disputed goods until the administrative process has been completed. The ITC's separate role in this scheme is to determine whether a domestic industry suffers from a real or threatened material injury. The ITC also assesses whether any harm or injury to domestic industry that may result from fairly priced foreign imports is sufficient to invoke the escape clause mechanism, which is the key administrative determination in safeguards cases. All of these administrative decisions may be appealed to the CIT.

The CIT is an Article III court under the United States Constitution, with jurisdiction over civil actions arising out of import transactions and certain federal statutes affecting international trade. The President, with the advice and consent of the Senate, appoints the nine judges who constitute the Court. Not more than five of the nine judges may belong to any one political party. The geographical jurisdiction of the Court of International Trade extends throughout the United States; it is also authorized to hold hearings in foreign countries. The court has exclusive subject-matter jurisdiction to decide any civil action commenced against the United States, its agencies or its officers arising from any law pertaining to revenue from imports, tariffs, duties or embargoes or enforcement of these and other regulations. The court's exclusive jurisdiction also includes any civil action commenced by the United States that arises out of an import transaction, and authority to review final agency decisions concerning antidumping and countervailing duty matters, the eligibility of workers, firms, and communities who are economically harmed by foreign imports for trade adjustment assistance, disputes concerning the release of confidential business formation, and decisions to deny, revoke or suspend the licenses of customs house brokers. However, the CIT does not have jurisdiction over disputes involving restrictions on imported merchandise where public safety or health issues are raised. This limitation on CIT jurisdiction arises because such issues involving domestic goods would be determined by other regulatory bodies, and only referral to United States District Courts can ensure uniform treatment of both imports and domestically produced goods.

The CIT possesses all the remedial powers, legal and equitable, of a United States District Court, including authority to enter money judgments for or against the United States, but with three limitations. Firstly, in an action challenging a trade adjustment ruling, the court may not issue an injunction or writ of mandamus. Secondly, the CIT may order disclosure of confidential information only as specified in Section 777(c)(2) of the Tariff Act of 1930. Thirdly, for suits brought under a special provision allowing accelerated review of pre-importation administrative actions the court may only grant declaratory relief. Again, a disappointed party may seek review of a CIT decision before the Federal Circuit and, ultimately, the Supreme Court.

B. International Tribunals

International tribunals also play an increasingly significant role in the resolution of trade disputes. This is especially true in CVD and AD matters. If a dispute involves imports from Canada or Mexico, a claimant may file an action before a special "binational" panel under Chapter 19 of the North American Free Trade Agreement ("NAFTA"). Separately, aggrieved domestic interests may convince their government to challenge an adverse CVD or AD decision or law before the WTO's Dispute Settlement Body ("DSB").

The Jacobs and the Walders and Pratt excerpts in Problem 7.1 below explore in detail the procedures and powers of NAFTA binational panels in CVD and AD disputes. Several significant aspects are nonetheless worthy of review in this Introduction. First, the initiation of a review under NAFTA both divests the CIT of jurisdiction over the same dispute and requires it to dismiss any pending litigation involving the same administrative action. Second, NAFTA panel decisions are not appealable, except in very limited circumstances (so-called "Extraordinary Challenges") such as gross misconduct by a panel member, a serious departure from a fundamental rule of procedure, or that the panel manifestly exceeded its authority or jurisdiction. Third, although NAFTA panels cannot formally set aside decisions of U.S. administrative agencies, they may remand cases to those agencies for subsequent action consistent with panel decisions, including through revocations or reductions of CVD or AD duties. Finally, NAFTA panel decisions are binding only in the specific disputes under review, which means that they do not have precedential effect for U.S. administrative proceedings in later unrelated matters.

The WTO's Dispute Settlement Body presents still another, indeed alternative, forum for CVD and AD disputes. That is, the initiation of an action before the CIT or a NAFTA panel does not preclude a parallel proceeding with the WTO. Walders and Pratt also examine the procedures for and legal force of WTO decisions in the excerpt in Problem 7.1 below. The important points to emphasize here are, first, that this option is not open to private litigants: Only Member State governments may file an action before the WTO (although of course they may do so at the behest of domestic interests).

In addition, the WTO has no formal power to compel compliance with its decisions. Beyond recommending ways in which the offending state may comply, the WTO may only order compensation for the aggrieved state(s) or authorize retaliatory trade sanctions. As a matter of domestic law, moreover, the Uruguay Round Agreements Act ("URAA")—the statute that amended

U.S. law to conform to the substantial reform of the WTO system in 1994—does not make WTO decisions directly enforceable. Section 129 of the URAA instead contemplates a procedure by which the affected U.S. agency (either the Commerce Department or the ITC) may revisit the original administrative action in an attempt to reconcile its interpretation of U.S. law with the WTO's decision. On the other hand, as Nedzel excerpt in 7.1 below notes, the risk of sanctions authorized by the WTO may create intense pressure to comply, and in the past the U.S. has in fact complied with adverse WTO rulings through statutory revisions.

Web Resources for further study include the WTO Anti–Dumping, Subsidies and Safeguards web pages, http://www.wto.org/english/thewto_ e/whatis_e/tif_ e/agrm8_e.htm; the U.S. Commerce Department's "Introduction to Trade Remedies" web page, http://ia.ita.doc.gov/intro/index.html; the International Trade Administration's web pages, http://www.ita.doc. gov/; and the U.S. International Trade Commission web pages, http://www. usitc.gov/.

PROBLEM 7.1 SUBSIDIES AND COUNTERVAILING DUTIES: TIRES FROM CANADA

SECTION I. THE SETTING

Your client, the United States Rubber Manufacturers Association (the Association), is very concerned about a tire plant which has been constructed by Michelin in Canada. In particular, they are appalled at the amount of assistance various Canadian governmental bodies have given to Michelin to induce Michelin to locate its manufacturing facilities in Canada rather than in the United States. They believe that the Canadian plant does, and is intended to, manufacture tires more for the United States market than for the Canadian market. They give you the following facts.

Michelin Tire Manufacturing Company of Canada, Ltd., has constructed two industrial plants in the province of Nova Scotia for the manufacture of steel cord for use in manufacturing tires. A substantial majority of the tires produced are being and are expected to continue to be exported to the United States. In connection with the establishment of the two manufacturing plants, the Government of Canada has made certain grants and made available to Michelin a special accelerated depreciation provision under Canadian income tax law. Additionally, the Province of Nova Scotia has provided certain grants and provided a low interest-rate loan and the municipalities concerned have made certain concessions which lower the property taxes on each plant.

Michelin's parent company in France had begun considering the establishment of manufacturing facilities in North America to satisfy the growing demand for its belted radial tires. Plans for facilities in the United States were deferred when the United States Department of

Transportation began to consider proposals for safety rules whose method for measurement of tire pressure would have virtually barred the belted radial tire.

Industrial Estates Limited (IEL), a provincial Crown corporation of the province of Nova Scotia charged with promoting economic development, invited Michelin to establish manufacturing facilities in Nova Scotia. Discussions on this subject were conducted by representatives in France and Nova Scotia. Michelin then decided to establish a tire manufacturing operation in Nova Scotia, consisting of a tire factory and a cord factory.

Formal agreements were entered into between IEL and various Michelin enterprises. One provided for IEL to give Michelin $5 million in capital grants and a maximum of $2.6 million in training grants. This $7.6 million was used by Michelin's parent company to capitalize Michelin Canada, through purchases of its stock.

Another agreement provided for a loan directly from IEL to Michelin Canada. The loan was in the amount of $50 million at the rate of two percent (well below market rates), and took the form of purchases of $50 million of first mortgage bonds issued by Michelin Canada. The loan was utilized for construction of the tire factory and cord factory.

In addition, IEL obtained agreements from the town of Bridgewater and the county of Pictou that for ten years the real property taxes on the construction financed by IEL loans would be in the amount of one percent per year of the actual cost of construction, accrued to tax date, without provision for depreciation. This replaced the normal method of real property taxation based on fair market value.

For its first three years of operation, Michelin Canada also received grants under the Canadian Area Development Incentives Act (ADIA) and its successor, the Regional Development Incentives Act (RDIA), in a total of approximately $8.5 million.

The Association estimates that the effect of all of these efforts by various governmental bodies in Canada has been to reduce Michelin's per unit costs by about seven percent when compared to the costs of producing the tires with normal market financing and prevalent taxes.

The Association initiated a countervailing duty (CVD) proceeding under 19 U.S.C. § 1671a(b) (set forth in the Documents Supplement) by filing a petition with the ITA. Two weeks later the ITA announced that the petition was proper and alleged all the necessary elements for a CVD, and that it contained what information was available to the Association (petitioner) to support the allegations. The ITA then commenced its own investigation as to whether there was a subsidy and notified the ITC to begin an investigation as to whether the United States tire industry was materially injured or threatened with material injury by imported tires from the Michelin plant in Canada. Six weeks later, the ITC issued a preliminary determination under 19 U.S.C. § 1671b(a) that there is a reasonable indication of a threat of such injury.

The Association wants to know what the likelihood is that the ITA will make an affirmative final determination that the assistance to Michelin from the various Canadian governments can be considered "subsidies" under U.S. law. They also want to know whether there is any practical effect of this preliminary determination, or whether they must wait for final determinations from the two U.S. agencies to get any "real" relief.

SECTION II. FOCUS OF CONSIDERATION

The United States has long considered the use by a foreign nation of a subsidy granted to exporters from that nation to be an unfair trade practice. The application of "countervailing duties" to "bounties" or "grants" was established as early as 1897. In the Uruguay Round Agreement Act the United States government amended its countervailing duty law to conform with the Agreement on Subsidies and Countervailing Measures (SCM Agreement), one of the multilateral agreements under the World Trade Organization (WTO) Agreement. A countervailing duty is used to offset a subsidy of a foreign state. The statute, at 19 U.S.C. § 1671 et seq., imposes two administrative conditions on the creation of countervailing duties. First, the Secretary of Commerce, acting through the International Trade Administration, must determine that a country is providing a subsidy to its exporters. Second, the International Trade Commission must determine that imports benefiting from the subsidy injure, threaten to injure, or retard the establishment of a domestic industry. If both conditions are met, a duty equal to the net subsidy "shall be imposed" upon the imports. Although the subsidy may arise from either public or private sources, all the determinations of subsidy to date have involved public, governmental subsidies. Thus, these cases are usually determined on a country-wide basis (automobiles from Germany), and orders usually apply to all imported goods of a particular tariff classification from a particular country—including indirect imports shipped via other countries.

Although the authority for imposing duties is given in Section 1671, that section does not define the term "subsidy." The definitions applicable to both CVD and AD proceedings are found in Section 1677, and "countervailable subsidy" is defined in Section 1677(5) as a subsidy that is "specific," a term defined in Section 1677(5A). In these definitions, countervailable subsidies are defined to include both "export subsidies" and "domestic subsidies." All export subsidies are classified as specific, and therefore countervailable, which is compatible with GATT. To be countervailable, domestic subsidies must be found to be "specific" under one of the tests in Section 1677(5A)(D), which are derived from Article 2 of the SCM Agreement.

In any CVD proceeding, there are at least three separate issues for analysis: the extent of the concept "subsidy", the amount of injury suffered by the domestic tire manufacturers, and the procedure to be followed by one who wishes to induce the application of countervailing duties.

Because Canada is furnishing assistance without regard to whether the goods are exported, we will have to explore under what criteria the Canadian assistance might be labeled an "export subsidy". We may also wish to analyze it as a domestic subsidy, and compare Canada's assistance to determine whether it differs materially from the assistance provided by United States law, both federal and local, designed to induce producers to bring their manufacturing plants to one or another location in the United States.

Under 19 U.S.C. § 1671(b), the ITC is required to make an injury determination. Since the domestic tire industry is already established, such an injury determination will depend upon whether we can prove a material injury, or a threat thereof, to that industry.

Procedurally, one important practical issue is whether there is any effect on the sales of Michelin tires in the United States during the duty determination process. That will affect which party is more interested in a speedy resolution to the problem, and which one can accept lengthy proceedings.

Sections 1671, 1671a and 1677, as amended, of the Tariff Act of 1930, along with GATT Articles VI and XVI, and the WTO Agreement on Subsidies and Countervailing Measures, and Chapter 19 of the NAFTA Agreement, are essential to an understanding of this problem. They are set out in the Documents Supplement.

Web resources for further study are the ITA's Subsidies Enforcement Office webpage http://esel.trade.gov; the ITC's antidumping and countervailing duty webpage http://www.usitc.gov/trade_remedy/index.htm, its Time-table http://www.usitc.gov/trade_remedy/documents/timetables.pdf, and its Hand-book http://www.usitc.gov/trade_remedy/documents/handbook.pdf; the United States Trade Representative's Subsidies Enforcement webpage http://www.ustr.gov/trade-topics/enforcement/subsidies-enforcement; and the WTO's Subsidies and Countervailing Measures Gateway http://www.wto.org/english/tratop_e/scm_e/scm_e.htm.

SECTION III. READINGS, QUESTIONS AND COMMENTS

YOUNG, U.S. TRADE LAW AND POLICY

68–70 (2001).*

1. *Export Subsidies and Domestic Subsidies*

For trade purposes, subsidies are generally divided into two categories: *export subsidies* and *domestic subsidies*. The former, *export subsidies*, are benefits bestowed by a government on an industry or exporter for the products that are exported abroad. In its most straightforward incarnation, this would include a specific government payment to a domestic company, the amount of which is directly tied to the amount of goods that are exported. A *domestic subsidy* is also a benefit bestowed by the government, but, in this case, it is bestowed on the company (or industry) more generally and is not linked to the amount of the company's product that is exported.

2. Economic Rationale

Subsidies are generally considered bad for a variety of reasons. *Export subsidies* may, for example, be criticized from a purely economic perspective in that they may distort the optimal allocation of resources by encouraging more investment in export oriented activities than is warranted by the market demand for these export products or than is optimal for the exporting country in light of that country's comparative advantage. * * *

The case against *domestic subsidies* is more difficult to make. Like export subsidies, domestic subsidies may also distort optimal resource allocation. In addition, domestic subsidies may discourage imports because they permit domestic producers to sell at a price below what they would otherwise sell for.

All economists are not in agreement, however, that countervailing duty laws are the best, or perhaps even a good way, to deal with subsidies, especially domestic subsidies. Most economists seem to agree that in some broad, global sense subsidies may distort the optimal allocation of resources and thus are bad. However, some economists disagree with even that simple proposition, arguing instead that many subsidies merely correct for market failures and thus are not necessarily bad. Even when subsidies distort the proper allocation of resources, moreover, many argue that * * * such distortion visits no real economic harm on the importing country. Thus, they assert, the importing country should not take the lead in attacking subsidies, but rather either the entire world trade community should act in concert to eliminate trade distorting subsidies or, in the alternative, countries that grant subsidies should take steps to eliminate them.

3. Political Rationale

As in the case of dumping, however, the political imperatives do not always coincide with the prevailing economic wisdom. The world trading community has generally concluded that export subsidies are often problematic and has made some attempt to discourage the more blatant export subsidies through multilateral disciplines. Parties may even seek relief from export subsidies through the WTO * * *. as we will discuss later. Some countries, most notably the U.S., however, continue to maintain and apply domestic countervailing duty laws against subsidized goods that have made their way into their markets.

The rationale in the U.S. for the countervailing duty laws * * * stems in part from notions of fairness. Congress simply does not believe that U.S. producers should have to compete not only with the resources of private foreign companies, but also with the vastly more extensive resources of foreign governments. The competitive playing field is simply made too uneven when a country chooses to use public funds to supplement the resources of private companies.

EHRENHAFT, "REMEDIES" AGAINST UNFAIR INTERNATIONAL TRADE PRACTICES

ALI-ABA, Fundamentals of International Business Transactions, 2008.*

1. Introduction and General Concepts

1.(a) General Concepts

The concept of practices in international trade that are regarded as "unfair" is not necessarily the same as that in domestic commerce. In domestic commerce, the rules, particularly in the United States, are built upon a commitment to competition, and "unfair" practices are those that impermissibly restrict competition. On the other hand, in international trade, the rules are principally built upon a mercantilist model, and seek to protect domestic industries against foreign dependence and exploitation by restraining competition. "Unfair" practice in international trade, therefore, generally refers to the sale of imported goods at prices so low that the sales supplant domestic goods and, thus, injure domestic producers of like products. * * *

When the foreign producer or exporter has received a competitive advantage in the form of a payment from a foreign government to finance production or export of the goods, the U.S. import prices may * * * be considered impermissibly lowered, and regarded as "subsidized." The central thesis of these unfair trade laws is that it is unfair to require domestic producers to compete with the artificially low prices of a foreign competitor's imports as measured against that foreign party's prices in its home market or without the benefit of foreign government price-reducing assistance. The * * * countervailing duty laws are aimed at such imports. If findings of [the existence of foreign] subsidies are also supported by findings that such imports cause or threaten "material" injury to U.S. producers of like products, the government must collect an added customs duty on the imports to "restore" the price of imports to their * * * unsubsidized price. * * *

Most often, the unfair trade laws are enforced through a proceeding initiated by a petition from one or more domestic producers. This chapter only briefly discusses the remedies available to an American producer when faced with alleged artificially-low-priced imports, and the defenses available to a foreign exporter or U.S. importer of goods when faced with claims that goods they are offering in the U.S. market are * * * subsidized. Although the public discussion of "unfairly" priced imports is often couched in terms suggesting that * * * "subsidized" imports are "illegal," U.S. law does not treat the imports themselves as illegal. Rather, the law only provides for the imposition of equalizing customs duties, although these added duties may be so high as to effectively prevent further imports.

* * *

1.(b) Traditional Statutory Remedies

The Trade Act of 1974 ("TA '74") and the Trade Agreements Act of 1979 ("TAA '79") are the major American laws providing import relief through government intervention. The Trade and Tariff Act of 1984 ("TA '84"), the Omnibus Trade and Competitiveness Act of 1988 ("OTCA"), and most recently, the Uruguay Round Agreements Act ("URAA") added details. Most, but not all, of these laws are amendments to the Tariff Act of 1930, and are consolidated at 19 U.S.C. § 1671 et seq.

* * *

3. The CVD Law

* * *

3.(b) The Concept of "Subsidy"

A "subsidy," as is defined in the WTO Agreement on Subsidies and Countervailing Duties ("Subsidies Code") and incorporated into U.S. law[112], consists of

> (1) a "financial contribution" or a form of income/price support provided by a government or public body within the territory of a WTO Member;

> (2) "specific targeting" of a firm or industry, or to promote exports; and

> (3) a benefit actually received by the producer of the exported goods.

The financial contribution may be in the form of grants, loan guarantees, equity infusions, and tax credits. But mere financial contribution or income/price support is not enough to trigger a countervailable subsidy. These costs must also confer a "benefit" beyond that available to the recipient through private market vehicles, and must specifically aim to aid identifiable firms or industries and not at a region or the country as a whole.

* * *

---

112. See 19 U.S.C. §§ 1677(5), (5)(A), (5)(B), (6).

A domestic subsidy is also not countervailable unless it is provided to a *specific* enterprise/industry or group thereof. Subsidies that are *de jure* available to more than a specific industry or group are countervailable if *in practice* they are provided to a specific enterprise or industry. The law outlines the factors to be considered in determining whether *de facto* specificity exists when *de jure* specificity does not:

> (1) use of a subsidy program by a limited number of enterprises or industries;

> (2) predominant use by certain enterprises or industries;

> (3) grant of disproportionately large amounts to certain enterprises or industries; and

> (4) the manner in which discretion has been exercised by the granting authority in the decision to grant a subsidy.[118]

* * *

3.(c) The Injury Test

The GATT permits the imposition of a CVD by an importing country only if subsidized exports cause material injury to domestic producers of like products. Under U.S. law, standards of injury are generally identical to those under the antidumping title. Just as in dumping cases, the ITC is directed to consider the magnitude of the net countervailable subsidy in its determination of threat of material injury in a CVD case.[120] In the first CVD case brought with respect to subsidized imports from the PRC, the ITC found "no injury" and thus terminated the proceeding.

3.(d) Procedures

Procedures in CVD cases only differ slightly from those in antidumping proceedings. As in antidumping cases, the initial investigation culminating in the publication of a Countervailing Duty Order (CVDO), provides an estimate of the duties required to counteract the unfair trade practice, that is used to collect deposits until the actual amounts can be assessed retrospectively in an Administrative Review. * * *

The statute provides for judicial review, similar to that available for antidumping cases, of Affirmative and Negative Determinations by each administrative agency. It should also be noted that U.S. law creates a unique ability of a foreign government to challenge, in a U.S. court, a U.S. agency determination in an antidumping or countervailing duty case.[123] Few other countries afford standing to foreign governments in such administrative proceedings.

* * *

---

118. Subsidies Code, Art. 2.1(c); 19 U.S.C. § 1677(5A)(D)(iii)(I)–(V).

120. * * * 19 U.S.C. § 1677(7)(E).

123. 19 U.S.C. §§ 1516a(a)(1) & (2), 1677(9)(B) (defining "interested party" as including government of country where subject merchandise is produced, manufactured, or exported).

5.   The North American Free Trade Agreement

* * *

5.(b) Dispute Resolution Mechanisms

5.(b)(1) General

A unique and a separate dispute resolution mechanism was created in the NAFTA, applicable solely to AD and CVD duties imposed by the three NAFTA signatures. They are intended to provide international oversight of each country's obligations and enforcement procedures. They are not comparable to the pre-WTO GATT's emphasis on negotiation and consensus for the WTO's dispute resolution process in which a country's actions are judged against the standards of an international agreement. Rather, NAFTA antidumping/CVD dispute resolution panels, consisting of ad hoc representatives of the importing and exporting country, are to apply the *domestic* law of the country imposing the duty challenged.[124] * * *

NAFTA Chapter 19 provides the procedures for these antidumping and CVD reviews that may be sought by "interested parties," using definitions similar to those found at 19 U.S.C. § 1677(9).

5.(b)(2) Binational Panel Dispute Settlement

Binational panels under NAFTA Chapter 19 review whether the importing country's Final Determinations are in accordance with the importing country's laws. If a panel finds that the importing country's administrative agency erred, it remands the determination to the agency to correct the error and issue a new determination.[126]

The panel replaces domestic judicial review of Final Antidumping/CVD Determinations, and the panel's decision is binding, except in extraordinary situations.[127] NAFTA panel review is optional. Thus, if no party requests review under Chapter 19, review of a U.S. order may commence in the CIT as in any other antidumping/CVD case.

Trade lawyers generally have found the binational panels function effectively, although the panels' willingness to follow the domestic rules of the importing country has been questioned at times. Rejection of extraordinary challenges brought by the United States in two cases increased U.S. industry objections to the procedure and has narrowed the number of persons regarded as suitable for inclusion in the roster of panelists maintained by each government. * * * Similar dispute resolution provisions have not been included in other free trade agreements recently negotiated by the United States.

---

124.   See 19 U.S.C. §§ 1516a, 1677(f) (2005); 19 CFR Part 356 (2005).

126.   NAFTA Arts. 1904(3)–(8). * * *

127.   Id. at art. 1904(2). See, e.g., *Certain Iodinated Contrast Media ... from the United States,* CDA–USA 2000–1904–1, 2 (January 8, 2003) at 2–5 (CCRA review) and at 2–3 (CIT review) (panels must follow limited powers of Canadian courts to overrule agency decisions).

ZHENG, THE PITFALLS OF THE (PERFECT) MARKET BENCHMARK: THE CASE OF COUNTERVAILING DUTY LAW

19 Minn. J. Int'l L. 1, 15–21 (2010).*

[O]ne of the greatest accomplishments of the SCM Agreement is that it offers a definition of subsidy for the first time. * * *

Although the term "benefit" is a central element of the definition of subsidy, the SCM Agreement does not specify how to determine its existence. Instead, in Article 14, the SCM Agreement offers several "guidelines" on the "calculation of the amount of a subsidy in terms of the benefit to the recipient."

All four guidelines on identifying and measuring subsidies as specified in Article 14 of the SCM Agreement embody a market benchmark. The first three guidelines are straightforward. When determining whether government-provided equity confers a benefit, the criterion is whether the government provision of equity is "inconsistent with the usual investment practice . . . of private investors . . . " When determining whether a government-provided loan confers a benefit, the criterion is whether the borrowing firm pays the same amount on the government loan as it "would pay on a comparable commercial loan which the firm could actually obtain on the market." When determining whether a government-provided loan guarantee confers a benefit, the criterion is whether the firm receiving the government guarantee pays the same amount on the government guarantee as it "would pay on a comparable commercial loan absent the government guarantee." In each case, the treatment a firm receives or would receive in the private market is used as the benchmark for judging whether the treatment afforded by the government confers a benefit.

[Under] the fourth guideline * * * [w]hen determining whether the government provision (or purchase) of goods or services confers a benefit, the criterion is whether the government provision (or purchase) is made for less than (or more than) "adequate" remuneration. * * *

Following the adoption of the WTO agreements, Congress enacted the Uruguay Round Agreements Act (URAA) in 1994 to bring U.S. trade laws into compliance with the new world trade rules under the WTO. * * * [T]he URAA sets forth a set of guidelines for determining the existence of countervailable benefits. Those guidelines repeat, almost verbatim, the guidelines found in Article 14 of the SCM Agreement and espouse the market benchmark as the only subsidy benchmark.

* * *

[Nonetheless,] it was not until the Appellate Body's decision in

Canada—Measures Affecting the Export of Civilian Aircraft[84] that the [WTO's] Appellate Body made clear that the SCM Agreement adopts the market benchmark as the sole benchmark for identifying and measuring subsidies. In that case, the Appellate Body of the WTO held that when deciding whether a government action confers a benefit within the meaning of Article 1.1(b) of the SCM Agreement, the appropriate basis for comparison is the marketplace:

> We also believe that the word "benefit", as used in Article 1.1(b), implies some kind of comparison. This must be so, for there can be no "benefit" to the recipient unless the "financial contribution" makes the recipient "better off" than it would otherwise have been, absent that contribution. In our view, the marketplace provides an appropriate basis for comparison in determining whether a "benefit" has been "conferred", because the trade-distorting potential of a "financial contribution" can be identified by determining whether the recipient has received a "financial contribution" on terms more favourable than those available to the recipient in the market.[85]

* * *

More than one hundred years after the inception of countervailing duty law, the market benchmark has become the only officially recognized benchmark for identifying and measuring subsidies. Its triumph * * * shows countervailing duty law's reliance on the market's allocative efficiency as a justification for its use as a benchmark.

FOLSOM, GORDON, & SPANOGLE, PRINCIPLES OF INTERNATIONAL BUSINESS TRANSACTIONS, TRADE & ECONOMIC RELATIONS
Concise Hornbook Series (2005).*

* * *

§ 13.4   Two Statutory Regimes

The U.S. currently has two statutes on countervailing duties: Section 1671 of the Tariff Act of 1930 for products imported from countries that participate in the WTO Subsidies Code or its equivalent,[1] and Section 1303 for products imported from other nations.[2] Most importantly, duties may be imposed under the latter *without* any finding of injury to a domestic industry (unless the product enters duty free); but may not be imposed under the former without a determination that a U.S. industry is "materially" injured, or threatened with such injury, or its development is materially retarded. * * *

---

84. Appellate Body Report, Canada—Measures Affecting the Export of Civilian Aircraft, WT/DS70/AB/R (Aug. 2, 1999).

85. Id. ¶ 157.

* Copyright © 2005 and reprinted with permission of Thomson Reuters.

1. 19 U.S.C.A. § 1671 et seq.

2. 19 U.S.C.A. § 1303.

Like antidumping duties, countervailing duties are a statutory remedy, one which the President cannot veto or affect except in Section 1671 (but not Section 1303) proceedings by negotiation of an international trade agreement. If the complaining U.S. industry is not satisfied with such an agreement, it may generally pursue CVD proceedings to their conclusion in spite of the President by refusing to withdraw its complaint. This refusal power typically gives U.S. industries seeking CVD relief substantial leverage over Commerce Department subsidy complaint negotiations. * * *

CVD proceedings under Section 1671 can also be suspended if the foreign government or exporters accounting for substantially all of the exports agree to cease exporting to the U.S. or to eliminate the subsidy within six months.[5] The subsidy may be eliminated by imposition of an export tax or price increases amounting to the net subsidy. In complex "extraordinary circumstances" benefiting the domestic industry, a settlement agreement reducing the subsidy by at least 85 percent and preventing price cutting in the U.S. can be negotiated.[6] These approaches, which are increasingly common, may effectively give exporters a brief window of opportunity to enter the U.S. market at subsidized price levels prior to shifting production to the United States.

* * *

§ 13.5   U.S. Implementation of the WTO Subsidies Code—Countervailable Subsidies

* * *

Under the SCM Agreement there is an attempt to shift the focus of subsidy rules from a national forum, as it was exclusively under GATT, to the multinational forum provided by the Subsidies Committee under WTO and the SCM Agreement. Subsidies complaints can now be brought either in the national forum or the WTO. There are two remaining classes of subsidies: (1) prohibited ("red light"); and (2) permissible, but actionable if they cause adverse trade effects ("yellow light"). A third category of non-actionable and non-countervailable ("green light") subsidies lapsed in 2000. * * *

The U.S. statutory provisions on countervailing duties on products imported from WTO Members is set forth in 19 U.S.C.A. § 1671, et seq. Duties may be imposed if it is found that the product is subsidized and that a U.S. industry is materially injured or threatened with such injury or its development is materially retarded.

* * *

---

5.   19 U.S.C.A. § 1671(c)(b).

6.   19 U.S.C.A § 1671(c)4.

§ 13.16 Countervailing Duty Procedures

For a "Subsidies Agreement Country," the procedures governing the applicability of countervailing duties to its goods will be determined under 19 U.S.C.A. § 1671, not 19 U.S.C.A. § 1303.

Section 1671 proceedings can be settled by international agreement; Section 1303 proceedings cannot. Section 1303 CVD can be applied retroactively without limitation whereas Section 1671 CVD can be applied retroactively only in "critical circumstances." The major difference between the two sections is that only a determination that a subsidy exists is necessary under Section 1303, while Section 1671 requires both a determination of a subsidy and an injury determination. Thus the administrative procedure for deciding whether to impose countervailing duties under Section 1671 is the same as that for antidumping duties[2] and involves the ITA and ITC making both preliminary and final determinations. Under either Section 1671 or 1303, an ITA preliminary determination that a countervailable subsidy exists subjects all goods imported after that date to any countervailing duties imposed later. This usually has the effect of immediately reducing imports of such goods.

§ 13.17 Administrative Determinations

Two different governmental agencies are involved in regulating, through countervailing duties, imports into the United States. The International Trade Administration (ITA) is part of the Commerce Department, which in turn is part of the Executive Branch of the government. The international Trade Commission (ITC) is an independent agency.

The chain of decision-making in CVD proceedings depends upon which statutory section controls. If Section 1303 governs, which petitioners (the domestic industry) will ordinarily favor, the proceeding is totally before the ITA with the ITC excluded. This will be a two-stage proceeding:

ITA Preliminary Countervailable Subsidy Determination

ITA Final Countervailable Subsidy Determination

If, however, a "country under the Agreement" is the source of the goods, then Section 1671 controls. Respondents (the importers) will generally prefer this because a four-stage proceeding allowing argument over the alleged domestic industry injury will follow:

ITC Preliminary Injury Determination

ITA Preliminary Countervailable Subsidy Determination

ITA Final Countervailable Subsidy Determination

ITC Final Injury Determination

The CVD process may be initiated by either the Department of Commerce, a union or business, or by a group or association of aggrieved workers or businesses—an aggrieved "industry."[1] The required contents of the petition are stipulated at 19 C.F.R. § 355.12. * * * Pre-filing

---

1. 19 U.S.C A. § 1671a(a) and (b).

contact with the ITA and (if needed) the ITC can often resolve any problems regarding the contents of the petition. Petitioners may also access the ITA's library of information on foreign subsidy practices. The ITA determines whether the petition alleges the elements necessary for the imposition of a duty, based on the best information available at the time.[2] In other words, the ITA accepts or rejects the petition.

Once the petition is accepted, the ITC makes a preliminary determination as to a real or threatened material injury within 45 days of the date the petition was filed based on the best information available to it at that time.[3] If the ITC makes such a finding, the ITA must then make a preliminary determination whether there is "a reasonable basis to believe" based on the best information available that there is a countervailable subsidy with respect to the exported merchandise.[4] The time for making this decision may be extended if the petitioner so requests, or the ITA determines both that the parties are cooperating and that it is an extraordinarily complicated case.[5] The time period may also be extended for "upstream subsidy" investigations.[6]

If the ITA makes a preliminary determination that a countervailable subsidy exists, within 75 days it must make a "final determination" concerning the existence of a countervailable subsidy and calculate the amount of the proposed CVD.[7] If subsidization is found by the ITA, the ITC then must make a final determination concerning material injury within 120 days after the ITA has made an affirmative preliminary determination,[8] or within 75 days after an affirmative final determination by the ITA if its preliminary determination was negative.[9] * * *

In reaching their determinations, both the ITA and the ITC frequently circulate questionnaires to interested parties, including foreign governments and exporters. Since any failure to respond risks a determination on the "best information available," this results in the flow of significant and often strategically valuable business information to the government. Amendments adopted in 1988 now require release under protective order of all confidential business information to counsel for interested parties.[10] This protection is particularly important because not all domestic producers may support the CVD petition, but they are generally able to access the submissions of others who do. Confidentiality is defined in the regulations at 19 C.F.R. § 355.4 and 19 C.F.R. § 207.6.

---

2. 19 U.S.C.A. § 1671a(b).

3. 19 U.S.C.A. § 1671b(a).

4. 19 U.S.C.A. § 1671b(b).

5. 19 U.S.C.A. § 1671b(c).

6. 19 U.S.C.A. § 1671b(h).

7. 19 U.S.C.A. § 1671d(a).

8. 19 U.S.C.A. § 1671d(b)(2).

9. 19 U.S.C.A. § 1671d(b)(3).

10. See 19 U.S.C.A. § 1677f(c)(1).

§ 13.18   The Importance of the ITA Preliminary Subsidy Determination

An ITA preliminary determination that a countervailable subsidy exists places great pressure on the importers of the foreign goods. Liquidation (entry at a determined rate of tariff) of all such merchandise is suspended by order of customs. Goods imported after an ITA preliminary determination of a countervailable subsidy will be subject to any CVD imposed later, after final determinations are made.[1] Such a preliminary determination, although subject to final determinations by the ITA and the ITC and appealable to the CIT, will effectively cut off further importation of the disputed goods unless an expensive bond is posted until the process has been completed. In this process the respondent importer often wants a speedy resolution as its total costs for the imports are unknown. The statute is replete with time provisions established to protect the importer by requiring action to be completed and decisions to be made within specified time limits. Many CVD proceedings are concluded within a year.

At one level, then, a useful intermediate goal in representing a petitioner is to obtain an ITA preliminary determination concerning a "subsidy" or "bounty" which meets the statutory requirements. The respondent's "defense" to such efforts must be organized quickly, usually within 30 days of the filing of a CVD petition. The importer's ability to present a defense is handicapped by the nature of CVD proceedings * * * the complaint is really lodged against the subsidy practices of foreign governments. Unlike most foreign exporters whose pricing decisions are the focus in AD proceedings, many foreign governments are loath to provide information necessary to an adequate response to a CVD complaint. Since the ITA and ITC are authorized to make decisions on the basis of the best information available, any failure to adequately respond to a CVD complaint can contribute to adverse rulings. Moreover, responses by foreign governments and exporters to ITA questionnaires that cannot be verified by on the spot investigations are ignored and thus removed from the best information available for decision-making. This may leave only the petitioner's or other respondent's submissions for review, a one-sided proceeding almost sure to result in affirmative determinations.

The respondent importer's uncertainties over the amount of duty owed after a preliminary ITA determination that a countervailable subsidy exists can increase in Section 1671 (GATT-derived) proceedings if the ITA decides that "critical circumstances" are present. In such cases, the suspension of liquidation of the goods applies not only prospectively from the date of such determination, but also retrospectively for 90 days.[2] Moreover, in traditional Section 1303 proceedings against bounties or grants, there is *no* time limit to the ability to retroactively apply CVD

---

1.   19 U.S.C.A. § 1671b(d).

2.   19 U.S.C.A. § 1781(b)(e)(1)(B).

against any unliquidated entries and there need not be any determination that critical circumstances are present.

§ 13.19 CVD Duties and Anticircumvention

The ITA final determination of the existence of a subsidy establishes the amount of any CVD. Since duties are not imposed to support any specific domestic price, they are set only to equal the amount of the net subsidy.[1] The CVD remains in force as long as the subsidization occurs. The ITA may modify or revoke a CVD order if changed circumstances warrant, but the burden of proof is on the party seeking alteration of the CVD order.[2] Circumvention of an existing CVD order, on the other hand, can trigger anticircumvention orders....

* * *

§ 13.20 Appeals

Judicial review "on the record" of final (not preliminary) decisions by the ITA and the ITC in both CVD and AD proceedings may be sought before the Court of International Trade (CIT). However, for proceedings arising out of exports from Canada and Mexico, the United States—Canada FTA and the NAFTA provide for resolution of antidumping and countervailing duty disputes through binational panels. Such panels apply the domestic law of the importing country, and provide a substitute for judicial review of the decisions of administrative agencies of the importing country.

WILCOX, GATT–BASED PROTECTIONISM AND THE DEFINITION OF A SUBSIDY

16 B.U. Int'l L.J. 129, 153–160 (1998).*

* * *

B.   SPECIFICITY

After the Uruguay Round, specificity for the first time was made a requirement under the GATT. By essentially adopting this section of U.S. law, WTO members seemed to implicitly accept the need to limit the use of CVDs by the imposition of required objective standards for an actionable subsidy to be recognized under the GATT.

It is clear that it would be a mistake to apply the broadest definition of the term subsidy to domestic subsidies. There are many legitimate actions that a government could take that might be considered subsidies; the GATT explicitly acknowledges this fact.

If some domestic subsidies are going to be countervailable and others are not, a mechanism is required to distinguish between the "good" and

---

1.   19 U.S.C.A. § 1671e.

2.   19 U.S.C.A. § 1675.

the "bad" domestic subsidies. The GATT adopted the specificity require-ment mechanism during the Uruguay Round, previously only used in the United States.

Although U.S. courts have had trouble interpreting the specificity requirement, in subsidies law, it acts as a restriction on the ability of the U.S. government to use CVDs to protect domestic producers, rather than to counter the protection being bestowed on foreign producers. This is probably what WTO members are and should be concerned about. If a contracting party wishes to help a particular industry directly in a way that harms foreign industries, the GATT will allow that practice to be countervailed under the Uruguay Round, because of its specificity.

Specificity is a crude, but useful and manageable tool that can be used to separate acceptable subsidies from unacceptable ones, and to limit the potential abuse of CVD provisions. Although there are some economic reasons for adopting the specificity requirement, it is clear that it was also done for administrative ease. Generally Americans believe that subsidies that are aimed at a specific industry are more likely to be the kind of subsidies that the GATT was meant to discourage: those that distort markets for the sole purpose of helping domestic producers.

More sophisticated tests could be devised, but according to econo-mists, an enormous amount of information would be required to calculate the legitimacy of a subsidy, where legitimacy is based on economic efficiency. Many variables would have to be measured to precisely deter-mine the efficiency of a subsidy (assuming it is even possible) such as: economies of scale, the presence and importance of learning curves, externalities, the effects of spillover technology, barriers to entry, union strength, the available supply of key inputs, the amount of research and development required, the possible harm to downstream industries that buys an emerging industry's product, and the "stickiness" of real wages. Some of this information, such as the presence and scale of externalities, spillovers and research, is absolutely impossible to predict. Others would just be enormously expensive to gather and calculate. This information would have to be weighed against the loss to consumers and producers.

The possibility that the government could accurately measure these effects is low, even if there were not thousands of lobbyists trying to manipulate the system in their clients' favor. The pessimism among economists of a government ever achieving a system that could do this well is overwhelming. * * *

The effectiveness of specificity as a mechanism to separate acceptable from unacceptable subsidies is clearly limited. Legitimate internal policies will always help some industries more (or harm some industries less) than others, and in some cases this differential impact will be clear enough that other countries will be able to classify the actual benefit provided by subsidy as de facto specific. However, if an otherwise legitimate internal policy of one contracting party happens to benefit a certain industry or group of industries, the other contracting parties should not interfere with that country. The GATT has explicitly acknowledged this principle since the Tokyo Round. In cases such as these, another limit on the application of CVDs would be extremely helpful; the Uruguay Round uses a requirement of a financial contribution as this second limitation.

U.S. case law makes it clear that the specificity test may not be the appropriate mechanism to limit the use of CVDs, or at least that it is not sufficient by itself. For example, in Carlisle Tire & Rubber Co. v. United States, the court held that a greatly accelerated depreciation schedule is not a countervailable subsidy when it is available to all businesses in a country. This is a much more sophisticated and much less general subsidy than the building of a public road, and it is in cases like Carlisle that the weakness of the specificity test, and the need for a better (or additional) standard is revealed.

* * *

C. FINANCIAL CONTRIBUTION

Such protectionist policies should not be possible under the Uruguay Round definition, depending on how it is interpreted. Failure to regulate should not be considered to be a financial contribution, and therefore should not be considered to be an actionable subsidy.

Again, the use of a "financial contribution" requirement is not based on the application of economic theory, but, like specificity, is an imperfect and artificial mechanism that is used to separate legitimate internal policy from protectionist market distortions.

The requirement under the Uruguay Round of a financial contribution is even more clearly for the purpose of ease of administration, than that for specificity. Government aid distorts the market no matter what form it takes. The relevant question then is: will the financial contribution requirement, when combined with the specificity requirement act as a good solution to eradicate the behavior that contracting parties want to discourage?

When the specificity and financial contribution requirements are combined with the traffic light framework, it becomes apparent that the position of the contracting parties is that domestic subsidies should not be interfered with unless it is reasonably clear that their purpose is to benefit domestic producers and give them an unfair competitive advantage over foreign competition. By contrast, the American position has been that domestic subsidies are presumed to be market distorting and may be countervailed unless the benefits of the subsidy are generally available. The conflict between these two perspectives will undoubtedly surface as Commerce decides how to interpret the Uruguay Round Agreements Act, and as disputes arise over subsidies in the future.

NEDZEL, ANTIDUMPING AND COTTON SUBSIDIES: A MARKET–BASED DEFENSE OF UNFAIR TRADE REMEDIES

28 NW. J. Int'l L. & Bus. 215, 217–218, 224–234 (2008).*

* * *

II. CONTEXT: GATT'S FREER TRADE PRINCIPLES AND UNFAIR TRADE REMEDIES

A. The World Trade Organization and Freer Trade

Consistent with the goal of freer trade, the World Trade Organization, established in 1994, is based on a presumption that market economies help establish stronger nations, and it is focused on reducing trade barriers (such as tariffs) between nations. The primary function of the WTO is to set rules of trade between nations. It is the vehicle of enactment for several multinational agreements, of which the GATT treaty is one. In setting up a trade regime, the WTO's stated primary goal is to encourage international commerce: although trade does not ensure peace, it discourages war. Thus, the goal of the WTO is to encourage trade among Members by setting predictable rules, encouraging freer trade and competition, and providing benefits for less developed nations. The WTO does not mandate free trade, but instead establishes a framework of rules enabling WTO Members to progress towards freer trade by reducing tariffs and making voluntary trade concessions. This discourages Members from engaging in certain kinds of trade discrimination against fellow Members.

* * *

D. Exceptions to Freer Trade: the WTO's Three Trade Remedies

In theory, the three trade remedies—antidumping measures, counter-vailing duties, and safeguard measures—are WTO-sanctioned measures a member country can use to temporarily protect a vulnerable domestic industry from competition by imposing duties on a particular product above and beyond the amount listed in its schedule.

No measure is to be implemented without a WTO-prescribed investigation by the domestic government into whether the measure is justified under rules set by the WTO. The investigation is in fact a detailed litigation procedure conducted by a government agency, and requires that the agency give full hearing to both the plaintiff domestic industry and the defendant importers before reaching a decision. Analogizing to United States legal terminology, WTO rules require due process before any such extraordinary tariffs may be imposed. The decision must be justified on the basis of the evidence adduced in the investigation. In all three cases, when the measure is put into place, additional duties or tariffs are superimposed above and beyond those the importing country agreed to in its WTO schedule, so that the domestic industry is no longer threatened or injured by lower import prices. Thus, all three measures result in a higher domestic price for the particular product at issue and are anti-competitive in nature. A number of economists argue, therefore, that such measures are inherently unproductive and should not be used.

The purported justification for the imposition of such trade remedies is that they are needed to correct inefficiencies in the free market. The theory behind antidumping and countervailing duty laws is quite simple: it suggests that producers of merchandise in foreign lands are able to take advantage of protected home markets to produce and export goods at artificially low prices. * * * Subsidized products—such as imports whose low prices reflect financial support provided by the home government—cause similar harm to a target industry by distorting the local market: local manufacturers conclude that they cannot produce the product at a competitive price and they decrease or cease production. Thus, * * * countervailing duties protect a domestic industry from imported products that are being sold at what is concluded to be an unfairly low price by certain specific importers from certain specific countries. * * *

Both antidumping and countervailing duty measures are justified under WTO rules as an exception to the freer-trade policy because they theoretically protect a domestic industry from the unfair trade practices of one or more specific countries. Because they are an exception to the scheduled tariffs, however, the WTO includes a built-in "sunset" or termination rule: antidumping tariffs and countervailing duties are to be reviewed regularly and terminated when no longer needed because they otherwise artificially inflate the price of the product at issue to domestic consumers. * * *

III. TRADE REMEDIES AND THE WTO LEGAL GUIDELINES

Each WTO member nation adopts its own version of antidumping, countervailing duty, and safeguards laws; nevertheless, the WTO Antidumping, Subsidies and Countervailing Measures, and Safeguards Agreements set certain detailed parameters for such laws.

* * *

1. Definition of Subsidy

The CVD [Agreement] provides that a government may levy a countervailing duty on an imported product that was subsidized by its home government. A subsidy is defined as a financial contribution, and can be in the form of a direct transfer of funds (grant, loans, equity infusion), or government revenue foregone or not collected (i.e. tax credits), the provision of goods or services other than general infrastructure, or the purchase of goods, or the making of payments to a funding mechanism, or any other form of income or price support.[66] Thus, any subsidization of an industrial product in such a way as to specifically encourage its exportation or disfavor imported components in its production is prohibited.[67] If an importing country finds that an import has been impermissibly subsidized and has caused injury to or seriously prejudiced the interests of a domestic industry, it can levy a countervailing duty to compensate for the subsidization.[68]

2.   Countervailing Duty Procedure

As with antidumping proceedings, a CVD application must include sufficient evidence of the existence of a subsidy, its amount (if possible), injury, and a causal link between the subsidized imports and the alleged material injury.[69] As with an antidumping application, a CVD application must be supported by producers of at least 25% of domestic production,[70] must list all known domestic producers,[71] and must describe the volume and value of domestic production of the like product.[72] It must also contain a complete description of the allegedly subsidized product,[73] the names of the country or countries of origin, and the identity of each known exporter or foreign producer, as well as evidence with regard to the existence, amount, and nature of the subsidy.[76] Finally, it must provide evidence of the alleged injury, including information on any increase in volume of the allegedly subsidized imports, the effect of the imports on prices of domestic like product, and the consequent injury to (or threat of injury) to the imports on the domestic industry.[77]

Once the application is filed, the domestic governmental agency must investigate the information provided, giving all interested parties notice and ample opportunity to reply, following procedures similar to those detailed in the antidumping provisions. As with the antidumping rules, the CVD [Agreement] includes a five-year sunset review, requiring that any countervailing duty be removed after five years unless it is found that the expiry of the duty would be likely to lead to a continuation or recurrence of subsidization and injury.[79]

* * *

D.   WTO Remedies for the Remedies: Dispute Resolution

Once a WTO member has completed the internal litigation process and put a trade remedy in place, if the affected exporting country believes

---

66.   CVD Agreement, art. 1.1.

67.   Id. art. 3.1.

68.   Id. art. 5.

69.   Id. art. 11.2.

70.   See id. art. 11.4.

71.   Id. art. 11.2(i).

72.   CVD Agreement, art. 11.2(i).

73.   Id. art. 11.2(ii).

76.   Id. art. 11.2(iii).

77.   Id. art. 11.2(iv).

79.   Id. art. 21.3.

the remedy is unjustified, it can pursue an appeal either through the mechanisms provided under the importing country's law, or through the WTO Dispute Settlement Procedure. The WTO procedure is designed to be completed within fifteen months, even including an appeal. The process begins with a Member's complaint to the WTO's Dispute Resolution Body.

Once a complaint has been lodged with the WTO, the first sixty-day stage consists of confidential consultations, conciliation, and mediation between the two governments, because mutually acceptable solutions are preferred over the litigation process provided in the GATT Understanding on Rules and Procedures Governing the Settlement of Disputes. If consultation fails, the complaining government can then seek a panel review of the matter, a process which can take up to six months. A Panel consists of three to five experts from different countries who are selected, preferably by the parties to the dispute, from a list provided by the DSB. After a series of hearings and drafts, the Panel issues a report stating its opinion of which party is right, and which is wrong under the pertinent Agreement, and why. The Panel Report is then passed to the Dispute Settlement Body, which can only reject the Report by consensus.

After the Panel Report has become final, either party can appeal it to the Appellate Body, a permanent quasi-judicial body consisting of seven experts in law and international trade who are appointed for four-year terms. Once the Appellate Body issues its decision, if the defendant Member has lost, it is given a reasonable period of time to bring its law and tariffs into compliance with the decision. If it fails to do so, then it must enter into negotiations with the complaining country to determine mutually acceptable compensation, such as pertinent tariff reductions. If the defendant Member still fails to take action within twenty days, then the complaining Member can ask the Dispute Settlement Body for the authority to impose limited trade sanctions or retaliation in the form of suspending concessions, or other obligations it has towards the defendant Member in the same industrial sector.

E.　The Impact of the Dispute Resolution Process

A large proportion of WTO Panel and Appellate Body casework deals with antidumping and CVD measures. The decisions, in particular those of the Appellate Body, are long, highly detailed, and studied carefully by scholars, attorneys, and regulative bodies. Although different mechanisms are used to choose them, each decision is written by jurists from several different country-members of the WTO, and since the majority of members are from civil rather than common-law jurisdictions, the decisions are crafted not with an eye towards precedential value, but instead with a narrow understanding that their only job is to interpret the AD Agreement and whether it was properly applied. Consequently, while these decisions do not have the consistency that one would expect in a common law jurisdiction, they do have a jurisprudential effect, and are highly influential. For example, the 1916 Antidumping Act, the Byrd Amendment, certain cotton subsidy provisions, and the U.S. steel safeguard measure were all repealed or agreed to be scaled back after the Appellate Body found them to be inconsistent with the U.S. WTO obligations.... Thus, since the WTO panels and the Appellate Body view antidumping and countervailing duties skeptically as limitations on the free flow of trade and look for reasons to find an antidumping measure noncompliant, their decisions are consistent with the WTO's underlying goal of encouraging freer trade.

The prospect of imminent sanctions can exert immense political pressure on the defendant Member to repeal trade remedies ruled to be in violation of WTO rules by the Appellate Body. For example, on November 10, 2003, the Appellate Body found that the safeguard measures taken by the United States on behalf of its steel industry were inconsistent with Article XIX:1(a) of the GATT 1994 and the Agreement on Safeguards. Sanctions were [not] imposed, however, because the President of the United States issued a proclamation terminating the safeguard measures subject to the dispute within the applicable twenty-day period.

Pursuing an appeal, either through the WTO mechanism or through the importing country's own mechanism, is not the only remedy a country or affected importer can pursue when it objects to the imposition of an unfair trade remedy. Studies indicate that countries may be resorting to "vigilante justice" by imposing retaliatory remedies, possibly because they may be less costly and provide more immediate results than does the WTO Dispute Resolution process.

JACOBS, ONE OF THESE THINGS IS NOT LIKE THE OTHER: U.S. PARTICIPATION IN INTERNATIONAL TRIBUNALS AND WHY CHAPTER NINETEEN OF NAFTA DOES NOT FIT

45 Colum. J. Transnat'l L. 868, 871–882 (2007).*

This Note discusses NAFTA's dispute resolution mechanism in light of U.S. constitutional norms. * * *

The legality of the NAFTA provisions under U.S. law has been questioned since NAFTA's inception, and a recent lawsuit filed by the Coalition for Fair Lumber Imports Executive Committee has brought such considerations right back to the fore. Though the underlying lumber dispute ultimately settled at the end of 2006, and the legal wrangling over the implications of that settlement was dismissed by the D.C. Circuit for lack of jurisdiction,[16] the relevant constitutional challenges remain hotly debated. * * *

---

* Copyright © 2007, reprinted with permission.

16. See *Coalition for Fair Lumber Imps., Executive Comm. v. United States*, 471 F.3d 1329 (D.C. Cir. 2006).

I. Applying the Provisions of Chapter Nineteen

A. National Regulation of Trade Duties

The provisions of NAFTA attempt to further the principles of fair "free trade" by permitting signatory parties to monitor for and regulate against both subsidies and dumping. Accordingly, each signatory party "reserves the right to apply its antidumping law and countervailing duty law to goods imported from the territory of any other Party."[20]

In the United States, the D.O.C. investigates and identifies impermissible dumping in violation of free trade. Then, the United States International Trade Commission (U.S.I.T.C.) considers whether such a violation causes or threatens to cause material injury to an American industry. Finally, if the D.O.C. finds a violation of law and the U.S.I.T.C. finds injury, the D.O.C. determines the appropriate relief, which may include setting countervailing and antidumping duties to offset the price discrimination resulting from the violation.

B. Invoking Chapter Nineteen Panel Review

Ordinarily—indeed, under every other circumstance—determinations made by the D.O.C. and the U.S.I.T.C are reviewable by Article III federal courts. However, the NAFTA Implementation Act establishes an exception to this general principle of U.S. law for those determinations respecting trade with Canada and Mexico: although an "involved [p]arty"[26] may appeal D.O.C. and U.S.I.T.C determinations to U.S. federal courts, the party may, in the alternative, request review by a NAFTA panel.[27] Under NAFTA, these panels are required to apply the duty laws of the importing party, the administrative determination of which is being challenged, as well as the same standard of review that the importing party's courts would otherwise apply.[29] The apparent purpose and effect of these provisions, when applied to the United States, is to create a substitute forum that displaces and replaces otherwise available Article III courts.

An involved party must request panel review within thirty days[30] of publication of the final determination made by the D.O.C. and the U.S.I.T.C.[31] The reviewing panel has five members; each involved party appoints two panelists, with the other party enjoying some degree of input as well as a limited number of peremptory challenges. The fifth panelist is then selected pursuant to both parties' mutual agreement. After a hearing, the panel then decides by majority vote and issues a written opinion explaining its reasoning.

---

20. NAFTA, * * * art. 1902(1).

26. NAFTA defines "involved Party" as "(a) the importing Party; or (b) a Party whose goods are the subject of the final determination." NAFTA, * * * art. 1911.

27. See id. art. 1904(2) * * *.

29. Id. art. 1904(3).

30. Id. art. 1904(4).

31. See id. art. 1904(2) * * *.

C. The Effect of the Panel's Decision

After hearing from the parties and reviewing the relevant facts and domestic law, a panel "may uphold a final determination, or remand it for action not inconsistent with the panel's decision."[36] In the United States, this panel decision cannot be appealed to an Article III court.[37] Indeed, the very initiation of panel review at the request of an involved party necessarily forecloses any and all judicial review of the administrative determination by a domestic court.[38] In this way, the panel is not only able to step in front of an Article III court in the procedural evolution of the dispute, but its decision is also absolutely binding on U.S. administrative agencies and cannot be reviewed domestically, even if it is based on a no-longer current understanding of U.S. law. Indeed, anticipating constitutional objection to review of D.O.C. or U.S.I.T.C. determinations by a NAFTA binational panel or extraordinary challenge committee, the Tariff Act even includes a "fallback" mechanism to be triggered if and when a U.S. federal court were to find that, under the U.S. Constitution, the NAFTA panel could not have the authority to bind American administrative agencies.[40]

* * *

In certain limited circumstances, a party may request review of a panel decision by an "extraordinary challenge" committee.[43] However, even an incorrect application of domestic duty law is not necessarily a basis for overturning a panel decision if the circumstances do not meet specific enumerated criteria: the party must establish (i) that a panel member was guilty of material misconduct, (ii) that the panel seriously departed from a fundamental rule of procedure, or (iii) that the panel manifestly exceeded its powers, such as in failing to apply the appropriate standard of review. In addition, the party must show that the violation "has materially affected the panel's decision and threatens the integrity of the binational panel review process." To qualify for extraordinary challenge committee review, a challenge must therefore meet an extremely narrow standard—in fact, no litigant has ever managed to meet this standard.

---

36. Id. art. 1904(8).

37. See 19 U.S.C. § 1516a(g)(7)(A). The D.C. Circuit dismissed the case initiated by Coalition for Fair Lumber Imports for this very reason. Coalition for Fair Lumber Imps., Executive Comm. v. United States, 471 F.3d 1329 (D.C. Cir. 2006).

38. See NAFTA, * * * art. 1904 (1) * * * See also id. art. 1904(11).

40. See 19 U.S.C. § 1516a(g)(7)(B). 19 U.S.C. § 1516a(g)(7)(A) declares panel or committee decisions absolutely binding and not subject to any form of domestic judicial review. If and when its application is held unconstitutional, the President is given the power to 'disregard' this determination and accept the binational panel or extraordinary challenge committee remand on behalf of the United States. The D.O.C. or U.S.I.T.C. would, as a result, still be bound by the panel or committee decision.

43. NAFTA, * * * art. 1904(13). The "Extraordinary Challenge Procedure" is established in Annex 1904.13. Id. The three committee members are selected by a process similar to that of the binational panel and, like the panelists, do not undergo any confirmation proceedings before the U.S. Congress.

II.   Constitutional Stumbling Blocks

The Chapter Nineteen provisions can be most forcefully challenged on three separate federal constitutional grounds. This Section discusses each of these claims and identifies their various pitfalls.

A.   Article III

The United States Constitution vests judicial power in "one supreme Court, and in such inferior Courts as the Congress may from time to time ordain and establish." Additionally, federal jurisdiction extends to "all Cases, in Law and Equity, arising under this Constitution, the Laws of the United States, and Treaties made, or which shall be made, under their Authority." Congress took advantage of the option it was granted and established inferior federal courts. The judicial structure established by Article III made those courts accountable to—and their decisions ultimately reviewable by—the Supreme Court of the United States.

Although the Supreme Court has held that Congress can grant jurisdiction to non-Article III tribunals, its power to do so is limited to certain narrow circumstances. In *Northern Pipeline Construction Co. v. Marathon Pipe Line Co.*,[51] a plurality of the Court limited Congress's jurisdiction conferral power, first, to those historically recognized legislative court exceptions lying exclusively outside the states, such as the courts of the District of Columbia, second, to military courts and courts martial, and, third, to the adjudication of public rights. The power to grant jurisdiction over "public rights" to non-Article III tribunals includes the lesser power to create administrative agencies overseeing those public rights, as well as the power "to provide for review of those agency decisions in Article III courts."

With these principles in mind, an objection to Chapter Nineteen would begin by contending that the central issue in trade disputes is most properly understood as hinging on private rights. The duties, when levied, only involve the United States insofar as the government is intervening as a mediating regulatory authority in a clash between two private parties: the subsidizing and/or illegally dumping importing party, on the one hand, and the members of the domestic industry whom the importing party is harming on the other. The purpose of the duties, then, is to restore balance to the private relationship between the cross-border economic competitors, which demands Article III judicial review. Under the NAFTA panel scheme, however, there can be no federal judicial oversight of the review process or the panels' substantive holdings, as the very mobilization of the NAFTA machine by an involved party necessarily wrests all jurisdictional power from the domestic judiciary.

Though this argument sounds enticing, it faces some acute stumbling blocks. In *Thomas v. Union Carbide*, the Supreme Court envisioned a delegation doctrine that placed less emphasis on the public/private right distinction and, instead, hinged more on a pragmatic examination of how

---

51.   458 U.S. 50 (1982).

the immediate delegation meshes with "the independent role of the Judiciary in our constitutional scheme."[60] A year later, in *Commodity Futures Trading Commission v. Schor*, the Court re-invoked and elaborated on this balancing paradigm, declaring that the nature of the rights to be adjudicated must be measured along with the Constitutional powers granted to Article III courts.[61] Thus, under the murky schemes that Thomas and Schor have conjured, courts have the task of determining when a delegation crosses some as-yet-undefined line demarking those delegations that both distort the Constitution's structural framework and improperly impinge on a party's interest in impartial Article III adjudication.

Whether Chapter Nineteen goes too far is anybody's guess. * * * Nevertheless, the Supreme Court has stressed that rights most resemble those public rights properly adjudicated by non-Article III tribunals when * * * the rights were created by federal statute and do not arise under State or common law. Thus the current law on non-Article III adjudication of personal interests would likely put Chapter Nineteen in the clear.

B. Appointments Clause

The Appointments Clause objection to Chapter Nineteen is even weaker. The Appointment power is an Article II power vested in the President of the United States. An "Officer," under the Appointments Clause, is anyone in a position of employment within the federal government vested with significant authority "pursuant to the laws of the United States."

Some commentators have suggested that the appointment processes under Chapter Nineteen are unconstitutional. Under the NAFTA provisions and its implementing statute, federal law has created the public station of employment, and at least two members of every five-member panel are selected by the United States but are not presidential appointees. In addition, panelists surely possess significant authority pursuant to U.S. law, as their decisions concern the investigation of domestic countervailing and anti-dumping duty law as applied through the treaty obligations of the United States. However, whether the panelists can actually qualify as "Officers" under the Appointments Clause is less certain. The title of "Officer" applies to "all persons who can be said to hold an office under the government," which requires the position to be "continuing and permanent," rather than "occasional and intermittent." Given the nature and subject matter of their adjudicative investigation, NAFTA certainly may grant panelists authority "pursuant to the laws of the United States;" nevertheless, they hardly seem to qualify as "employed" in the federal government, as they are empowered to hear only a single dispute and do not permanently occupy a position of authority.

---

60. 473 U.S. 568, 590 (1985).

61. 478 U.S. 833 (1986).

* * * Because the panelists are asked to "perform only certain, limited duties" they can, at most, be considered "inferior officers," and, as such, Congress may rightly impart the power of their appointment to the head of a department—in this case, the United States Trade Representative.

C. Due Process Clause

The Fifth Amendment to the U.S. Constitution proscribes the deprivation of "life, liberty, or property, without due process of law." An objection to Chapter Nineteen would suggest that the provisions are problematic under the Fifth Amendment in three ways. First, Chapter Nineteen opens the door to the possibility of judicial bias[79] without providing an adequate level of built-in procedural protection. Second, Chapter Nineteen bars Article III review and thereby permits potentially damaging misapplications of domestic law, which, despite their error, may nevertheless go unchecked and be binding on the United States. Finally, this miscarriage of justice causes injury to members of the relevant domestic industry: because U.S. federal law grants domestic producers the right to petition the Trade Representative to investigate unfair trade practices, they have a protected interest in the lawful determination of any resulting duties. Chapter Nineteen thus enables the private rights that these duties protect to be deprived without due process of law.

Regrettably, this Fifth Amendment objection may also lack basis in the relevant caselaw in two ways. First, federal law may not create a protected entitlement simply by enacting a process by which a domestic producer may petition the government to initiate an investigation. * * *

Second, even if domestic producers have an entitlement to a fair and accurate final determination of import tariffs, it is not clear how Chapter Nineteen violates due process protections. Their interest is in an unbiased and diligently-executed countervailing duty and antidumping investigation, not in the subsequent binational panel review of that investigation. In addition, a third party does not have the ability simply to swoop in and supersede the D.O.C. willy-nilly. The binational panel review clearly represents a judicial model of dispute settlement, something the Due Process Clause does not even always demand. Finally, insofar as the binational panel system opens the door to potentially biased adjudication, due process is only violated when it is clear that a judge's mind is "irrevocably closed," a standard that has resulted in the overturning of only one administrative adjudication in the United States.

---

79. Under the provisions of Chapter Nineteen, since the parties directly participate in panel selection, there is a high likelihood they will select judges sympathetic to their position. * * *

WALDERS AND PRATT, TRADE REMEDY LITIGATION—CHOICE OF FORUM AND CHOICE OF LAW

18 St. John's J. Leg. Comm. 51, 52–61 (2003).*

Respondents in AD/CVD cases now have available a variety of fora in which they may attack or defend decisions of the Department of Commerce ("Commerce") and the International Trade Commission ("ITC"). They may select the traditional route under U.S. law by filing or intervening in lawsuits before the Court of International Trade ("CIT"). Alternatively, if the case involves imports from Canada or Mexico, the respondent may file a lawsuit before a panel under Chapter 19 of the North American Free Trade Agreement ("NAFTA"). Finally, a respondent may also persuade the government of the exporting country to challenge the decision before a World Trade Organization ("WTO") dispute settlement panel. Each procedure offers advantages and drawbacks, which will be discussed in this paper.

A related issue is the interaction of the laws of the three jurisdictions. While the choice of forum determines the choice of law, to what extent can or should the decisions of a WTO or NAFTA panel influence the decisions of the CIT? The issue has arisen in only a few cases so far, but it is likely to arise more frequently in the future as the United States faces increasing challenges to its AD/CVD decisions.

* * *

* * * While the WTO process can proceed independently of the CIT or NAFTA litigation, the same is not true with respect to litigation before the CIT or a NAFTA panel. Once a party requests a NAFTA panel review, the CIT is divested of its jurisdiction, and it must dismiss any litigation that has been initiated regarding the same administrative determination that is the subject of the NAFTA panel review.

* * *

The main detriment is time. While the parties to CIT litigation are subject to various deadlines imposed by the statute, the orders of the trial judge, and the CIT rules, the CIT itself, as an Article III court, is not subject to any deadlines. Once a case is submitted for judgment, after all of the briefs have been filed, oral argument has been held, and the record is closed, there is no deadline on the Court's decision. * * * Appeals to the CAFC entail additional years of delay.

2. NAFTA Panels

The NAFTA panel route appears to avoid the potential delay of CIT litigation, given the strict deadlines that NAFTA proceedings are subject to under Chapter 19. The entire process from filing a request for panel review to the issuance of the panel decision must be completed within 315 days. This deadline, however, is honored more in the breach than in the observance. In fact, many panel decisions are issued well beyond the 315-day deadline, and the delays have been increasing in recent years.

---

* Copyright © 2003 and reprinted with permission from the St. John's Journal of Legal Commentary.

The primary problem is selection of the panels. While NAFTA itself expresses a preference for using active and retired judges, most NAFTA panels consist of private lawyers who practice international trade law. Service on NAFTA panels by private lawyers can present conflicts problems. Even if the prospective panelists and other members of their law firms have no relationship with the parties to the case, participation on NAFTA panels can present "issue conflicts." While NAFTA panel decisions have no formal precedential value, a private lawyer may feel constrained from taking a position as a panelist that could be cited by an opponent in a later case. Apart from the possibility of issue conflicts, members of law firms are also aware that their participation as panelists could prevent their firm from representing parties to the panel proceeding in other matters. These concerns have made it difficult to recruit panelists and delayed the establishment of such panels.

Unlike the CIT (or for that matter WTO panels), the decisions of NAFTA panels ordinarily are not appealable. * * *

Another issue to consider in selecting a forum is that NAFTA panels, unlike the CIT, cannot vacate determinations of Commerce or the ITC, but they do have the power to remand decisions to the agencies for further action consistent with the panel decisions. Some cases have resulted in multiple remands. As a practical matter remands will eventually result in a decision that complies with the panel's decision. Thus, a NAFTA panel's determination has the same force of law in the United States as a decision by the CIT. Accordingly, a successful plaintiff before a NAFTA panel can obtain direct benefits in the form of revocation, refunds of cash deposits or reductions of estimated AD/CVD duties on later entries.

However, a major difference between the CIT and a NAFTA panel decision is that the effect of the panel decision is limited to the specific administrative determination that is before the panel. In short, decisions of NAFTA panels have no stare decisis effect. They are not binding on the DOC or ITC in later proceedings, and are not cited as precedent by the CIT. This lack of precedential effect can have adverse practical consequences for the parties in the case. While the agency must comply with a NAFTA panel remand order in one case, it is not bound to follow the panel decision in any other case, even one that involves the same AD or CVD order.

* * *

B.   CIT/NAFTA Panel or WTO

There is no either-or choice of forum between the CIT (or NAFTA), and the WTO in AD/CVD cases. The choice of one forum does not preclude the choice of the other. Both avenues can be pursued as long as the case involves issues under both U.S. law and the WTO AD/CVD agreements. A case at the CIT or before a NAFTA panel involving U.S. law can, and often does, implicate the WTO as well. The procedures and the consequences, however, are quite different.

1. WTO DISPUTE RESOLUTION

WTO dispute settlement proceeds according to a schedule set forth in the Dispute Settlement Agreement. The procedures begin with a request for consultations, which must be initiated within 30 days of the request. If the consultations fail to settle a dispute within 60 days of such request, the complaining party may request the establishment of a panel. The Dispute Settlement Body ("DSB") establishes a panel during the first meeting of the DSB following the first meeting when the panel request is on the agenda. If the parties cannot agree on the panelists, the WTO Director–General will establish the panel. The panel proceeding itself entails two meetings (hearings) with the parties and one meeting with third parties that have an interest in the dispute. The panel issues its report to the parties within six months of its establishment, and the panel report is circulated to the DSB within the next three months after it is translated into each of the WTO official languages—English, French, and Spanish. The DSB adopts the report within 60 days unless there is an appeal to the Appellate Body. The appellate review process takes 90 days, after which the report of the Appellate Body is adopted by the DSB.

While the deadlines are relatively precise, the actual time required varies depending on disagreements over the composition of the panels and the complexity of the cases. According to the most recent statistics reported by WorldTradeLaw.net, the average time between the establishment of the panels and circulation of the final panel report is 366.77 days.

* * *

Unlike decisions of U.S. courts, the WTO has no power to compel compliance with its decisions. WTO members, as sovereign nations, have the right to decide whether and how to comply with WTO decisions. If the losing party fails to comply, it may be required to pay compensation in the form of tariff concessions, or the winning party may be entitled to retaliate against imports from the losing party. However, the question of whether a losing party has failed to comply, and if so whether and to what extent the winning party may be entitled to compensation or retaliation must be decided in a separate proceeding under Article 21.5 of the DSU.
* * *

Ultimately, if the losing party is found to have failed to implement the original decision, the winning party may seek compensation or retaliation under Article 22 of the DSU. WTO agreements, including those on dispute settlement, are not self-implementing in the United States. U.S. law will prevail in the event of a conflict with the agreements as interpreted by a panel or AB report. Implementation of WTO decisions is governed by Section 129 of the Uruguay Round Agreements Act ("URAA"). Section 129(a) applies to implementation of panel or Appellate Body reports relating to decisions of the ITC. The U.S. Trade Representative ("USTR") is responsible for implementation, but the USTR cannot issue direct orders to the ITC because the Commission is an independent agency that is not part of the Executive Branch. Instead, Section 129(a) provides that the USTR may request the ITC to issue an advisory opinion as to whether the U.S. antidumping, countervailing duty, or safeguards laws permit the ITC to modify its decision in a particular proceeding in a manner that would render its action "not inconsistent with" the findings of the panel or Appellate Body. The USTR must notify the House Ways and Means and Senate Finance Committees of any such request. The ITC must make its report within 30 days of the USTR request in the case of a panel decision and 21 days after the request in the case of an Appellate Body decision. Since it is an advisory opinion, the ITC report is not subject to judicial review. If a majority of the Commission concludes that U.S. law would permit it to modify its decision in a manner that is "not inconsistent with" the panel or Appellate Body decision, the USTR will consult with the Finance and Ways and Means Committees to decide whether to ask the Commission to make a new determination. The ITC will then have 120 days to issue a new determination. If, as a result, the Commission issues a negative injury determination regarding imports from one or more of the subject countries, the USTR will instruct Commerce to revoke the order with respect to those imports.

Section 129(b) governs implementation of WTO decisions relating to Commerce Department proceedings. After consulting with the Finance and Ways and Means Committees, the USTR may direct Commerce to make a determination that is "not inconsistent with" the panel or Appellate Body report. Commerce has 120 days to make the determination.

QUESTIONS AND COMMENTS

1. 19 U.S.C. § 1671(a) states that "there shall be imposed * * * a countervailing duty" if it is determined that an exporting country "is providing, directly or indirectly, a subsidy," and the Commission makes an injury determination. The Young excerpt provides the economic and political rationales for "countervailing duties" in response to governmental subsidies. The Ehrenhaft, Folsom *et al.*, and Zheng excerpts then explore the fundamental requirements of U.S. law for the imposition of such duties. These excepts explain how the seeming complexity of the statutory provisions in § 1671 *et seq.* in fact distills into the essential elements of a "countervailable subsidy" (as defined in § 1677(5)) that is "specific" (as defined in § 1677(5A)) and that causes or threatens a material injury (as defined in § 1677(7)) to a domestic industry. Your responsibility as attorney for the Association is to determine whether the assistance provided to Michelin in this Problem satisfies those requirements.

2. Under Section 1677(5) the first step in any analysis is to determine that there is a "subsidy". In our Problem, this in turn requires a two-part inquiry of whether, first, the Canadian Government, or any other "public entity" within Canada, has made a "financial contribution" to Michelin in the form of a loan or loan guarantee, an equity infusion or a tax credit, etc.

Second, do the laws, guarantees or tax credits confer a "benefit" upon Michelin? Section 1677(5)(E) defines the concept by requiring a comparison to what would be available through normal market mechanisms. The Zheng excerpt elaborates on this point as well. Note that grants from purely private sources will not create a subsidy, but governmental contributions channelled through a private body are still countervailable. 19 U.S.C. § 1677(5)(B)(iii).

3. In addition to finding a beneficial Canadian governmental financial contribution, the contribution must be "specific" to Michelin. 19 U.S.C. § 1677(5A). It cannot be "general," such as the provision of a general education system, road network or national defense. Section 1677(5A) draws an important distinction in this regard between "export subsidies" and "domestic subsidies." Either type of subsidy may be subjected to countervailing duties, but different criteria apply to identify each. The significant difference, however, is that "export subsidies" are deemed to be "specific" without further proof.

4. What is an "export subsidy"? 19 U.S.C. § 1677(5A)(B). An export subsidy is typically one in which the contribution and benefit are contingent upon export performance. Since Canada is furnishing assistance without regard to whether the goods are exported, under what criteria could this assistance be labelled contingent upon export performance? A footnote to the SCM Agreement explains that a subsidy also is contingent on exports if it is "in fact tied to actual or anticipated exportation or export earnings." *See* SCM Agreement Article 3.1(a), footnote 4. (Annex I to the SCM Agreement also provides an "Illustrative List of Export Subsidies.") For a recent decision of the WTO Appellate Body on this point *see Report, European Communities and Certain Member States—Measures Affecting Trade in Large Civil Aircraft*, ¶ 1047, WT/DS316/AB/ (May 18, 2011)(observing that "[w]here the evidence shows, all other things being equal, that the granting of the subsidy provides an incentive to skew anticipated sales towards exports . . . this would be an indication that the granting of the subsidy is in fact tied to anticipated exportation within the meaning of Article 3.1(a) and footnote 4 of the SCM Agreement").

Unfortunately, the definition of an "export subsidy" in Section 1677(5A)(B) does not expressly incorporate the language from footnote 4 of the SCM Agreement. How might you nonetheless argue from reading § 1677(5A)(B) that the explanatory language in that footnote is also relevant under U.S. law?

Consider Michelin's projected output. The majority of the final products are in fact being exported from Canada to the United States, and the Association believes that the capacity of the Michelin plant is greater than the Canadian market can absorb. The Association states that Michelin needed additional production capacity to service the United States market, but abandoned plans to establish another U.S. factory when the Canadian plants were built, showing that Michelin intended to use the plant for production for the United States. Further, the Association asserts that the Canadian government offered some of the very types of assistance addressed in Annex I to the WTO SCM Agreement. Doesn't that make the Canadian assistance into an "export subsidy"? In what way is the Canadian assistance linked to Michelin exports? Is it in fact "tied to actual or anticipated exportation or export earnings"? As an advocate for the Association, can you propose an analysis that includes, as an export subsidy, the assistance to Michelin, but does not cover assistance to every manufacturer who happens to export some products to the United States?

5. As to "domestic subsidies," the definition in Section 1677(5A)(D) provides that they are subject to a countervailing duty if the subsidy is provided to a specific enterprise or industry, even if not linked to export. In what way is the Canadian governmental assistance given to a specific enterprise? The accelerated depreciation provision is available to everyone who meets its conditions, and the Province and municipalities will probably make similar grants and concessions to any other enterprise that brings a similar number of jobs to the locality.

Section 1677(5A)(D) lists four "guidelines" for making this decision. Under (5A)(D)(i), if the particular subsidy offered to Michelin is expressly limited to Michelin, there is a "specific" subsidy "as a matter of law." But where the grant of the subsidy is in fact automatically offered to all enterprises which meet written objective criteria or conditions, it is "not specific as a matter of law." 19 U.S.C. § 1677(5A)(D)(ii). Where the actual recipients of the subsidy are limited in number, or one enterprise is the predominant user or receives a "disproportionately large amount" of subsidy, or is otherwise favored, the subsidy may be specific "as a matter of fact." 19 U.S.C. § 1677(5A)(D)(iii). Finally, a subsidy is specific if it is limited to an enterprise or industry in a "designated geographic region" and is granted by the governmental authority of that region. 19 U.S.C. § 1677(5A)(D)(iv).

6. Do the benefits granted to Michelin create "domestic subsidies" under the definitions in Section 1677(5A)(D)? Are they offered exclusively to Michelin, or are they offered through a set of automatically-applied, written objective criteria or conditions? Would it be useful to know what other enterprises have obtained similar benefits from Canada or Nova Scotia, and the total amount granted? Would it make a difference if the grants from the Government of Canada were made under a statute providing such grants for any enterprise that created a significant number of new jobs in an "economically depressed area," such as Nova Scotia? Then the grants would be available to any enterprise which met the conditions of the statute. To answer these questions, you should focus on the criteria described in subsections 1677(5A)(D)(iii) and (iv).

7. There are no facts in this Problem from which you could begin to analyze the issues concerning an injury determination. Further, the Readings do not contain any material specifically devoted to those issues. The injury determination issues for countervailing duties are similar to those for antidumping duties, and will be postponed for more detailed consideration in the next Problem on antidumping duties.

8. Procedurally, what steps did the Association take in order to start the *process* of obtaining a countervailing duty determination? Does initiation of this process have any effect on Michelin's transactions with the United States—in other words, is this one of those situations where the importer has an incentive to keep the case ongoing for ten years through multiple agency hearings, each followed by an appeal to the courts and a remand for further hearings?

9. What are the benefits available to a domestic industry upon an agency preliminary determination that a countervailable subsidy exists? *See* 19 U.S.C. § 1671b(d). What are the procedural steps necessary to obtain that determination? *See* 19 U.S.C. § 1671b(a) and (b). Further, what facts and results must be found in order to obtain such a determination? Do you have sufficient facts to sustain that burden? If not, state how those additional specific facts can be determined.

What is the most likely outcome of this process? Is this process similar to other "cases" in which an independent judiciary has complete control over the outcome, and the executive enforces whatever order is issued? Note that this process affects our relations with other nations—after all, the culprit is likely to be a subsidy provided by a foreign *government*—and thus, it is in fact somewhat different from typical domestic cases, and even from many other foreign trade disputes. The executive part of the government zealously protects its control of foreign policy. At what point in the countervailing duty process does the executive lose that control?

10. Is this countervailing duty process a disguised form of "protectionism" (non-tariff trade barrier) for United States industries? Does Canada's assistance differ materially from the assistance provided by United States law, federal and local, to induce producers to bring their manufacturing plants to one or another location in this country?

11. One of the most difficult issues in this field is whether CVDs may be imposed against imports from non-market economies (NMEs). The long-standing view was that such duties were not appropriate because the government in effect subsidizes the entire economy. Recent developments suggest a substantial change. Bolstered by positive indications from the CIT, *see GPX Int'l Tire Corp. v. U.S.*, 645 F. Supp. 2d 1231 (Ct Int'l Trade 2009), the Commerce Department has now levied CVDs against imports from both China and Vietnam. *See* 73 Fed. Reg. 40,480 (July 15, 2008); 75 Fed. Reg. 23,670 (May 4, 2010).

12. Canada and the U.S. are both members of NAFTA, which establishes a procedure for resolving CVD disputes. The NAFTA dispute resolution procedure was developed from a similar one in the Canada–U.S. FTA, but with some deliberate modifications. If the ITA and the ITC decide that Michelin's tires are subsidized, what can Michelin do about it? The procedure for binational panels is set forth in NAFTA Article 1904.

13. What is the precedential value to a binational panel of a decision by the U.S. CIT? What is the precedential value to the CIT of a decision by a binational panel? What is the precedential value to a binational panel of a prior binational panel likely to be? The difficult problem for a binational panel is likely to arise when it discovers one precedent by a prior binational panel, and a later conflicting precedent by the CIT. Which one is binding upon the later binational panel? Which one is it more likely to follow?

14. Jacobs surveys the arguments concerning the constitutionality of the NAFTA panels. After all, that procedure does mean that some U.S. litigants will not be able to assert their cases before an Article III judge. The lack of clarity of the precedent induced the drafters of NAFTA to include a provision for judicial review for challenges to the constitutionality of the NAFTA

system. Thus far, however, no U.S. court has made a definitive ruling on the subject.

15. A second approach is available to Michelin—through the WTO. Nedzel describes the dispute resolution process before the WTO. What are the prerequisites for proceeding in this forum? Is this simply a "business decision" to be made by Michelin alone?

16. Can Michelin proceed to seek relief through both the NAFTA binational panels and the WTO Dispute Settlement Body? Walders and Pratt discuss these issues. Is there a likelihood of each body issuing conflicting pronouncements and orders? Or, is each body analyzing distinguishable issues?

In this regard, the Walders and Pratt excerpt reviews the formal legal effect of the remedy available through WTO proceedings. Is it the same as the remedy available through NAFTA panels? Would Michelin consider it preferable? Who would prefer the WTO remedy?

17. Finally, note that NAFTA also establishes a separate type of binational panel procedure to review situations in which one country formally amends its statutory or administrative laws on CVD and antidumping matters. *See* NAFTA Articles 1902 and 1903. Decisions by binational panels on such matters are declaratory only, although the failure of an offending country to comply authorizes the injured country to retaliate by similarly amending its local laws.

PROBLEM 7.2 ANTIDUMPING DUTIES: SUPERCOMPUTERS TO THE UNITED STATES

SECTION I. FACTS

The Grey Research Co. is a U.S. firm that has developed a new type of "super" super-computer uniquely capable of both vector and scalable calculations. It will process data in a new way that allows both instant random access and matching of enormous amounts of data. Very similar supercomputers are produced by CEN and Jujitsu, two Japanese firms.

Agony Airlines (AA) is a large, publicly-held Delaware corporation. It is in the market to buy one of the new supercomputers, so that it can do instant, deep-background checks on all of its potential passengers as they check in at the gate. AA has had extended discussions with Grey, CEN and Jujitsu. After considering all the options, it has decided to buy a supercomputer from CEN for $10 million. Grey offered to sell its supercomputer for $17 million, and Jujitsu offered to sell its supercomputer to AA for $9 million; but AA rejected both offers. The Grey price was higher by too great an amount, and the Jujitsu computer was considered less "user friendly."

Your client is Grey Research. It is very disappointed about losing this sale and feels that its market position is threatened. Grey believes that

CEN is pricing its computers below cost, and will continue to do so until Grey has been driven out of business. Grey's cost of building such a supercomputer would be $15 million, if research and development costs are properly allocated. Grey believes that the cost of building the Japanese supercomputers should be comparable. It has been told, however, that CEN does not allocate research and development costs to sales of individual supercomputers.

Grey Research sells about a dozen supercomputers in the U.S. each year, and another dozen to foreign buyers each year, and has a 60% share of the "supercomputer market" in both the U.S. and the global markets. Both Jujitsu and CEN have recently entered into the supercomputer business and each has only a small share of the market. CEN is selling supercomputers in Japan for $10 million each, although it did sell one supercomputer to the Indian government for $15 million. Both CEN and Jujitsu have lost money on their supercomputer operations since entering the business, but both are also parts of much larger Japanese conglomerates. They want to sell supercomputers in the U.S. to demonstrate how well their products work. In fact, nine other airlines will also buy supercomputers this year. And they will buy products that are compatible with the computer bought by AA, so that all the airlines' computers can exchange information on the potential passengers. Since only about twenty supercomputers are sold in the U.S. in an average year, these ten sales may represent about 50% of the U.S. market for supercomputers during the current year.

Everyone at Grey Research is concerned. Can Grey seek to have antidumping duties imposed on the computer sold to AA? Realistically, what are its chances of success?

SECTION II. FOCUS OF CONSIDERATION

In addition to countervailing duties against subsidies, considered in Problem 7.1, a second type of conduct often regarded as an unfair trade practice is "dumping", or selling goods at "less than fair value". The Young excerpt discusses why dumping is generally considered to be an unfair practice. In U.S. law authority for the imposition of "antidumping duties" (ADs) on goods sold at "less than fair value" is found in the Tariff Act of 1930 (19 U.S.C. § 1673), set forth in the Documents Supplement. As noted in Problem 7.0, antidumping duties are permitted by GATT–WTO, and are quite common in the legal systems of other nations which have their own antidumping duty processes.

How does one determine whether a sale is at "less than fair value"? Section 1673b(b) requires a comparison of the "normal value" of the goods with their "export price." The statute defines "normal value" in Section 1677b, and "export price" in Section 1677a. Under Section 1673(a)(2) the necessary injury element required for the imposition of ADs can arise from a "material injury" to an industry, a threat thereof, or the "material retardation" of the establishment of an industry in the United States. "Material injury" is defined in Section 1677(7), and the threat thereof in Section 1677(7)(F). Even the concept "industry" is defined in Section 1677(4). The procedure used to assess ADs is the same as that used for CVDs described in Problems 7.0 and 7.1: It involves a determination of whether imports are being sold at "less than fair value" (LTFV) by the International Trade Administration (ITA), and a determination of injury to a domestic industry made by the International Trade Commission (ITC). The amount of the additional duty is equal to the difference between the normal value and the export price. The calculation of the normal value and the export price, so that they are both stated in comparable terms, requires an almost endless series of adjustments and calculations. The excerpt from the ITA's Antidumping Manual describes the U.S. process in some detail, and how that process generally comports with the applicable international antidumping agreements.

The Comment and the Federal Circuit opinion then highlight an area where the U.S. antidumping process did not comply with the mandates of these international agreements, the provisions of the Continued Dumping and Subsidies Offset Act of 2000, colloquially known as the Byrd Amendment. The Byrd Amendment had established a mechanism under which the ADs the government collected were funneled back to members of the affected domestic industry, in effect subsidizing the injured industry in a way that the WTO has ruled violates international agreements. The ITC's injury determination in the Wooden Bedroom Furniture case then illustrates the application of the injury rules to an antidumping case. The readings conclude with the Josephs excerpt, which revisits the utility of the antidumping laws as a means of addressing import competition.

Grey would undoubtedly be pleased to have the U.S. government conclude that the Japanese manufacturers are dumping supercomputers in the United States market. How might Grey go about making a case that the imposition of antidumping duties is appropriate? Reaching such a conclusion may well require additional facts. One particular subject for analysis below, therefore, is precisely what further data would be required, why it would be required, and who is responsible for providing that information.

Sections 1673, 1673a, 1677, 1677a, 1677b, and 1677f–1 of the Tariff Act of 1930 are essential to an understanding of this Problem, along with GATT Article VI and the WTO Agreement on the Implementation of Article VI of the GATT. They are found in the Documents Supplement.

Web resources for further study include the ITA's Antidumping(AD)/Countervailing Duty(CVD) Petition Counseling and Analysis Unit web pages http://ia.ita.doc.gov/pcp/pcp-index.html; the ITC's Trade Remedy Investigations web pages http://www.usitc.gov/trade_remedy/index.htm; and the WTO's Antidumping Gateway http://www.wto.org/english/tratop_e/adp_e/adp_e.htm.

SECTION III. READINGS, QUESTIONS AND COMMENTS

YOUNG, U.S. TRADE LAW AND POLICY

52–53 (2001).*

Perhaps the most succinct explanation of the prevailing justification for prohibiting dumping in international trade is contained in a European Commission report on that subject. It describes the rationale as follows:

The reasons why the GATT considers injurious dumping as unfair are:

- dumping requires that the exporting market be segregated and that the importing market be open. These substantially different degrees of market access make international trade fundamentally different to trade within an integrated market;

- operating from a segregated market can confer on exporters an advantage which is not due to higher efficiency and cannot be matched by his competitors in the importing country;

- this provides the dumper with the opportunity to maximize profits or minimize losses and can be highly injurious for the importing country's industry.

As one can see from the above explanation, the main concern is that an industry can use its protected home market to earn high returns, which, in turn, support its attempts to import into another country. Thus, these practices are contrary to normal, free market principles, or, put slightly different, they are problematic because they seem to distort or undermine the operation of those free market economic principles, the principles upon which the U.S. economy and, for that matter, the entire international trading regime, as embodied in the GATT–WTO, are built.

As a matter of hard economic logic, however, from the perspective of the consumer in the importing country, selling at something below cost becomes a problem if (and probably only if) the foreign competitor uses this unnatural economic advantage to drive other competitors from the market and thus secures a monopoly or otherwise distorts the operation of the market in such a way as to raise prices or lower the quality of the product over the long run. It may do this by using profits from its protected market to drive down prices and either drive out competitors (and thus gain a monopoly position) or discourage the development of a competing domestic industry (in which case it retains a preexisting monopolistic position).

Of course, from the perspective of domestic competitors, dumping may be a problem, even if the foreign company does not secure a monopoly. At a minimum, it allows the foreign competitor to gain a

---

foothold in the domestic market, even though the foreign competitor cannot produce the goods more efficiently. Basically, the foreign company can compete, not because it produces more efficiently, but rather, because it has some alternate source of profits not available to the domestic competitor. Given the importance of market position in many cases, this can significantly disadvantage the domestic company. Dumping can also substantially reduce profit margins, thus causing the domestic industry to shrink, reduce its work force, reduce its rate of capital investment, and reduce its research and development.

INTERNATIONAL TRADE ADMINISTRATION IMPORT ADMINISTRATION ANTIDUMPING MANUAL

(2009).*

CHAPTER 1: INTRODUCTION

* * *

IV. IMPORT ADMINISTRATION

A. Antidumping and Countervailing Duty Enforcement

The primary responsibility of IA's Office of Operations [the relevant administrative unit of the ITA] is to administer the antidumping (AD) and countervailing duty (CVD) laws to ensure that domestic industries are not injured by unfair foreign competition in the U.S. market. * * *

The U.S. AD and CVD laws are comprised of the following: Title VII of the Tariff Act of 1930, as amended (19 U.S.C. 1671–1677n); the legislative history to amendments of the Act, including the Statement of Administrative Action to the Uruguay Round Agreements Act (URAA), which amended the law to conform with the Antidumping and Subsidies Agreements; and IA's regulations (Section 351 of the Department's Regulations). * * * IA's AD and CVD determinations are reviewable by two federal courts of special jurisdiction, the U.S. Court of International Trade and the Court of Appeals for the Federal Circuit. Determinations involving Canada and Mexico may be subject to review by NAFTA panels acting in the place of the Court of International Trade. The statute, legislative history, regulations, and court opinions provide detailed guidance on how to administer the AD and CVD laws.

1. The Antidumping Law

The U.S. AD law is designed to counter international price discrimination, commonly referred to as "dumping." Dumping occurs when a foreign firm sells merchandise in the U.S. market at a price lower than the "normal value" (NV) of the merchandise; generally, this is the price the foreign firm charges for a comparable product sold in its home market. * * * The amount by which NV exceeds the U.S. price is the "dumping margin." A weighted average dumping margin is calculated for each

---

* U.S. International Trade Administration document.

producer or exporter as a percentage of the value of the U.S. prices of that producer or exporter.

* * *

3.   AD and CVD Investigations

AD and CVD investigations are almost always initiated in response to petitions filed by an affected U.S. industry, although IA may also self-initiate a case. Under the statute, petitions must be filed by a domestic interested party, including a manufacturer or a union within the domestic industry producing the "domestic like product" which competes with the imports to be investigated. Petitions may be several hundred pages long, as the statute requires that the petitioner submit reasonably available data in support of the dumping or subsidization allegations. Based upon the information submitted in the petition and any supplements to the petition, IA normally has 20 days to evaluate the petition and to determine whether it will initiate an investigation.

While IA determines whether and to what extent dumping or unfair subsidization is occurring, the United States International Trade Commission (ITC) conducts a parallel investigation to determine whether the U.S. industry competing with the allegedly dumped or subsidized product has been materially injured by such imports. For instance, injury may result when unfairly low-priced foreign competition reduces the domestic industry's profits and market share. If the final determinations of both IA and the ITC are affirmative (that is, dumping and/or subsidization and injury are confirmed), an AD or CVD order is issued.

* * *

5.   The Information Collected in an Antidumping Case

In an investigation or an administrative review, IA issues questionnaires to foreign producers and their affiliated importers regarding sales made, generally, during a 12–month period of investigation (POI) for market-economy cases and a 6–month POI for NME cases, or a 12–month period of review (POR). The questionnaire requests information on, among other things, the investigated company's corporate structure and business practices, the quantity and value of sales of the merchandise being investigated in all markets and very specific information about the company's sales in the United States and in the market being used for comparison purposes. Under certain conditions, the Department will ask for the company's production costs. * * *

If the responding firms fail to provide requested data, IA uses other facts available in place of the missing information. Under the statute, if the respondent has not cooperated to the best of its ability in supplying information, IA can make an adverse inference in choosing which facts to use. The potential use of adverse facts available gives respondents incentive to cooperate fully in providing the information requested by IA.

In addition to the questionnaires issued by IA, the record in an investigation or administrative review contains numerous documents submitted by the domestic and foreign interested parties to the proceeding. * * * Prior to the final determination, interested parties may request that hearings be held on the arguments addressed in the briefs submitted by the parties. * * *

The substantial amount of information collected allows IA to make a comparison between the prices of imports and NV. To make certain that its comparisons are not distorted by factors extraneous to the central issue of price discrimination between markets, IA adjusts the "starting" prices to account for any differences in physical characteristics, quantities sold, levels of trade, circumstances of sale, applicable taxes and duties, and packing and delivery costs.

* * *

CHAPTER 2
ANALYSIS OF PETITIONS AND INITIATIONS OF INVESTIGATIONS

* * *

III. INDUSTRY SUPPORT

A. General Information

Petitions must be filed by an interested party who has the support of the industry producing the domestic like product in the United States. Although the ITC is the agency which determines domestic like product for injury purposes, the Department must make a determination with respect to like product during the initiation for purposes of calculating industry support. * * *

* * *

[19 U.S.C. § 1673(c)(4)(A)] requires the Department to determine, prior to the initiation of an investigation, that a minimum percentage of the domestic industry for the like product supports an antidumping duty petition. In making this determination, the Department and the ITC must both apply [19 U.S.C. § 1677(10)] which defines "domestic like product," but they do so for different purposes and pursuant to separate and distinct authority. Furthermore, the Department's determination is subject to limitations of time and information. This may result in different definitions of the like product, but such differences do not render the decision of either agency contrary to law * * *

* * *

A petition meets the minimum requirements if the domestic producers or workers who support the petition account for: 1) at least 25 percent of the total production of the domestic like product; and 2) more than 50 percent of the production of the domestic like product produced by that portion of the industry expressing support for, or opposition to, the petition * * *

* * *

IV. SCOPE OF THE INVESTIGATION AND LIKE PRODUCT DETERMINATIONS

A. Scope of the Investigation/Like Product

When filing a petition, the petitioner is required to include a detailed description of the merchandise that will be covered under the investigation. This detailed description generally defines the scope of the investigation * * *

B. Like Product Determinations

[T]he Department is required to determine whether a petition has been filed by or on behalf of a domestic industry. "Industry" is defined by the statute as "the producers as a whole of a domestic like product, or those producers whose collective output of a domestic like product constitutes a major proportion of the total domestic production of the product." Therefore, in order to determine whether there is adequate industry support for the petition, it is necessary to identify the domestic like product and then examine that industry's production. The statute defines the "domestic like product" as a product which is like or most similar in characteristics and uses with the subject merchandise.

Unless the Department finds the petitioner's definition of the domestic like product to be inaccurate, the agency will adopt the domestic like product definition set forth in the petition. * * *

* * *

While the Department makes a like product determination at the time of initiation for purposes of accurately calculating industry support, the ITC makes domestic like product determinations in determining whether or not there is material injury or threat of material injury to the domestic industry, i.e., it determines which product manufactured in the United States is most like the merchandise being imported. If, during the course of the investigation, the ITC determines that some domestic like products are not being injured by corresponding imports within the scope of the investigation, the investigation terminates on those imported products.

* * *

Chapter 6. Fair Value Comparisons

I. INTRODUCTION

The U.S. antidumping duty law is designed to counter injurious international price discrimination, commonly referred to as "dumping." Only when the Department determines that there are sales at less than fair value (LTFV), accompanied by a determination of material injury or threat of material injury to a domestic industry by the ITC, can antidumping duties be levied. Sales at LTFV most often occur when a foreign firm sells merchandise in the U.S. market at a price lower than the price it charges for a comparable product sold in its domestic market. Under certain circumstances, LTFV may also be identified by comparing the foreign firm's U.S. sales price to the price it charges in other export markets or to the firm's cost of producing the merchandise, taking into account the selling, general, and administrative expenses, and profit. Under the law, this latter basis for comparison is known as constructed value (CV). Finally, where the producer is located in a NME country, a comparison is made between U.S. prices and a "surrogate" NV. The difference between a company's U.S. sales price and the NV (or surrogate NV) is called the dumping "margin," which often is expressed as a percentage of the U.S. sales price.

In learning what dumping is, it is also important to understand what dumping is not. For example, dumping is not the sale of foreign merchandise in the United States at a price less than the price charged by U.S. producers of the same merchandise. In a dumping case, the fact that foreign producers sell their products at lower prices in the U.S. market than U.S. producers becomes relevant only in the context of the ITC's determination of whether dumped imports have materially injured a U.S. industry.

Also, many people tend to confuse dumping and subsidies, mistakenly seeing them as a single phenomenon. The two are, in fact, distinct—one involves the pricing behavior of individual firms, while the other stems from the decisions of governments to provide preferential assistance to exporters or specific industries. While a foreign government's decision to provide export subsidies or to protect its domestic market may create conditions conducive to dumping, a finding of dumping will ultimately turn solely on the pricing decisions of the firm in the two markets. Other U.S. trade laws, such as the countervailing duty law, are available to address more directly the trade-distortive actions of foreign governments.

FAIR VALUE COMPARISONS

The Antidumping Calculus: Comparing Normal Value to U.S. Price

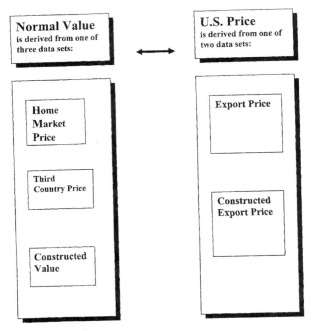

II. OVERVIEW OF EXPORT PRICE, CONSTRUCTED EXPORT PRICE AND NORMAL VALUE

To determine whether LTFV sales exist in an investigation or an administrative review, an EP or CEP as defined in [19 U.S.C. § 1677a] is compared to a NV as defined in [19 U.S.C. § 1677b]. [19 U.S.C. § 1677(35)] defines the dumping margin as being the amount by which the NV exceeds the EP or CEP of the subject merchandise.

A. Determining Which U.S. Sales Transaction to Examine: EP vs. CEP

Generally, a U.S. sale is calculated as an export price [EP] sale when the first sale to an unaffiliated person by a producer or exporter *outside* of the United States occurs *before* the goods are imported into the United States. A simple example would be when a U.S. company decides to distribute a foreign product in the United States and contacts the overseas producer or an exporter directly to set up the deal in terms of price, quantity, delivery, etc. A sale is calculated as a CEP sale if the first sale to the unaffiliated person is made *in* the United States by a person affiliated with the foreign exporter, irrespective of whether it occurs *before* or after importation. * * * In a CEP situation, the U.S. sale price is typically the price charged by a U.S. subsidiary of the foreign producer/exporter to the first unaffiliated U.S. buyer * * *

B. Determining the Basis for Normal Value: Home Market, Third Country or Constructed Value

NV is based either on the prices at which the foreign like product is first sold for consumption in the exporting country or to a third country if the home market is not "viable," i.e., not sufficiently large or it is otherwise unuseable as a comparison market. NV may also be based on CV using cost data (rather than price data) if: 1) there are no viable markets; 2) sales below the COP [cost of production], sales outside the ordinary course of trade, or sales the prices of which are otherwise unrepresentative are disregarded; 3) sales used to establish a fictitious market are disregarded; 4) no contemporaneous sales of comparable merchandise are available; or 5) where the Secretary determines that home market or third country prices are inappropriate.

In NME cases, NV is based upon a constructed value of sorts. Each NME respondent reports to the Department the quantities of direct materials and labor used to manufacture the subject merchandise, and the Department values these inputs using prices prevailing in a suitable market economy ("surrogate") country. To this derived cost of direct material and labor, the Department adds surrogate-country amounts for factory overhead, selling and general and administrative expenses, and packing and profit, resulting in a "constructed value" for the subject merchandise. * * *

III. OVERVIEW OF ADJUSTMENT

In order to achieve an "apples-to-apples" price comparison, various statutory adjustments are made to calculate NV * * * The need for adjustments arises because there are often physical differences between the merchandise exported to the United States and the merchandise sold in the exporting country or third-country markets and differences in the circumstances under which the merchandise is sold in each market. Therefore, to make certain that our comparisons are not distorted by factors extraneous to the central issue of price discrimination between markets, we adjust the NV "starting" prices to account for any differences in the prices resulting from differences in physical characteristics, quantities sold, levels of trade, circumstances of sale, applicable taxes and duties, and packing and delivery costs. * * *

III. OVERVIEW OF CALCULATIONS OF MARGINS

To calculate a dumping margin in an investigation, we must determine what sets of data will be compared, and how the comparison will be made. The following illustration presents three possible methods for comparing NV to U.S. price.

FAIR VALUE COMPARISONS

Possible Methods for AD calculations:

Weighted Average Price to Weighted Average Price

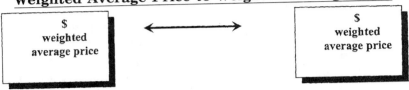

Comparing Individual Transaction to Individual Transaction

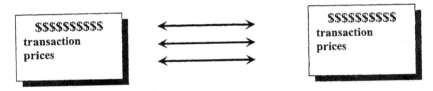

Weighted Average Price to Individual Transaction Prices

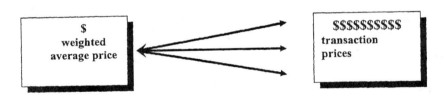

A. Calculation of Margins for U.S. Sales for Investigations and Administrative Reviews

* * *

Under [19 U.S.C. § 1677f–1], in an investigation, we normally compare the weighted-average EP or CEP to the weighted-average NV for a comparable product sold during the POI. We may also establish dumping margins by comparing NV and EP or CEP on a transaction-to-transaction basis. This is normally done only for large capital goods made to order. * * *

* * *

V. DETERMINATIONS ON THE BASIS OF FACTS AVAILABLE

A. Introduction

The Department normally bases its margin calculations on information provided by respondents about their sales, expenses, costs, etc. The questionnaire is designed to elicit all necessary information. In some cases, however, the Department finds that it does not have information it needs to perform its calculations. In such cases, the Department must use the "facts otherwise available," which is any acceptable information which the Department can find to substitute for a respondent's missing or otherwise deficient information. However, the Department will not decline to consider information that is submitted by an interested party and is necessary to the determination but does not meet all the applicable requirements if certain conditions are met, as described further below.

B. Use of Facts Available

[19 U.S.C. § 1677e(a)] states that the Department will use facts otherwise available in reaching a determination whenever:

(1) necessary information is not available on the record, or

(2) an interested party or any other person—

(A) withholds information requested, or

(B) fails to provide information requested in a timely manner or in the form and manner required * * *, or

(C) significantly impedes a proceeding under this title, or

(D) provides such information but the information cannot be verified * * *

When the Department resorts to facts available, it must determine the most appropriate information to form the basis of the dumping margin calculation. In doing so, the Department may also determine whether an adverse inference is warranted. According to [19 U.S.C. § 1677e(b)], if the Department finds that a respondent has failed to cooperate by not acting to the best of its ability to comply with a request for information, it may use an inference that is adverse to the interests of that party in selecting from among the facts otherwise available.* * *

* * *

CHAPTER 18
INTERNATIONAL TRADE COMMISSION INJURY DETERMINATIONS

* * *

III. STATUTORY FRAMEWORK

The ITC must make a preliminary determination as to whether there is a "reasonable indication" of injury either 1) within 45 days of the date of the filing of an AD duty petition or notice of self initiation of an investigation by the Department; or, 2) within 25 days after receiving notification of initiation by the Department should the Department extend the initiation period in order to poll the U.S. industry * * *. If the ITC's determination is affirmative, the case continues; if negative, the case is terminated.

The ITC must make a final determination of injury within 120 days of the Department's affirmative preliminary determination or 45 days of the Department's affirmative final determination, whichever is longer.

If the Department's preliminary determination is negative but its final determination is affirmative, the ITC has 75 days from the Department's final affirmative determination to make its final injury determination.

A. Standard for Injury

At both the preliminary and final stages of an AD investigation, the ITC is required to determine whether a U.S. industry is materially injured or threatened with injury, or whether the establishment of a U.S. industry is materially retarded "by reason of" the alleged less-than-fair-value imports.

The ITC's threshold for determining injury in a preliminary determination is lower than the threshold used by the ITC in its final determination. For the purpose of an affirmative preliminary determination, the ITC need only find a reasonable indication that a domestic industry is injured by imports allegedly sold at less than fair value. A stricter standard, however, applies in final determinations. To reach an affirmative determination in its final determination, the ITC must determine that a U.S. industry is either materially injured, threatened with injury, or that establishment of an industry is "materially retarded." Except for the different statutory standards involved in determining injury, the other statutory requirements in preliminary and final injury investigations are identical. The ITC must

- define the relevant domestic like product and domestic industry;

- determine whether that industry is experiencing or threatened with injury, or whether the establishment of the industry has been materially retarded; and

- determine whether there is a causal link between the injury and the imports allegedly sold at less-than-fair value.

1. The Reasonable Indication Standard

Congress did not intend to set a high standard for a preliminary determination as to whether there is a "reasonable indication" of injury. The legislative history of the provision states that a reasonable indication of injury exists in "each case in which the facts could reasonably indicate that an industry in the United States could possibly be suffering injury . . . ."

* * *

2. Material Injury

The term "material injury" is defined as "harm which is not inconsequential, immaterial, or unimportant." Although this definition can reasonably be interpreted in a number of different ways, it indicates that a domestic industry need not be catastrophically injured to qualify for AD relief. * * *

B. The Relevant Domestic Industry

The ITC defines "the domestic like product" as a product that is "like, or in the absence of like, most similar in characteristics and uses with, the article subject to . . . investigation . . ." * * *

After it defines the "domestic like product," the ITC defines the "domestic industry," which consists of the domestic producers, as a whole, of a domestic like product or those producers whose collective output of the domestic like product constitutes a major proportion of the total domestic production of that product. The ITC must then determine whether an "industry in the United States" is materially injured by reason of the imports of the merchandise subject to investigation.

The ITC usually examines the health of the domestic industry "as a whole" but, where the statutory criteria are present, the Commission can divide the United States into regional industries. * * *

To establish material injury for a regional industry, the Act requires the ITC to find that there is a concentration of dumped imports into the isolated regional market and that all, or almost all, of the producers within that market are being injured by reason of the dumped imports.

C. Threat of Material Injury

Specific guidelines, including a listing of the economic factors, for determining whether a domestic industry is threatened with injury are found in [19 U.S.C. § 1677(7)(F)]. * * *

The ITC considers these factors as a whole in making a determination of whether further dumped or subsidized imports are imminent and whether injury by reason of imports would occur unless an order is issued or a suspension agreement is accepted. * * *

D. Material Retardation

The ITC can also make an affirmative determination if it finds that dumped imports have materially retarded the establishment of an industry in the United States. To date, this provision has rarely been asserted by a petitioner in an antidumping duty investigation. Nearly all AD investigations have been initiated on the basis of petitions by established manufacturers of the domestic like product. * * *

* * *

F. Causation

In addition to ascertaining whether the domestic industry is materially injured, the ITC must determine whether this injury was "by reason of" the imports sold at less than fair value. The courts have held that this causation standard is satisfied if the dumped imports contribute, more than minimally or tangentially, to the injured condition of the domestic industry.

The statutory focus of an ITC AD investigation consists of the following: 1) the volume of the subject imports; 2) the effect of these imports on the prices of domestically produced products in the U.S. market; and, 3) the impact of this competition on the domestic producers of the like product. The ITC compares the average prices of domestically produced products, imports subject to the investigation, and, in some cases, imports not subject to the investigation (which, presumably, are fairly traded). In addition, the ITC may evaluate sales and revenues lost by the domestic producers to sales of the imports subject to investigation.

* * *

V. POST–ANTIDUMPING DUTY ORDER INJURY DETERMINATIONS AND CONSIDERATIONS BY THE ITC

A. Reviews Based on Changed Circumstances

[19 U.S.C. § 1675(b)(1) and (2)] direct the ITC to review its injury determinations based on changed circumstances if the ITC receives information, or a request from an interested party which shows changed circumstances sufficient to warrant a review of an antidumping duty order, countervailing duty order, suspension agreements, or continued investigations. In conducting the changed circumstances review of an antidumping duty order, the ITC shall determine whether revocation of the order is likely to lead to continuation or recurrence of injury. * * *

B. Sunset Reviews

[19 U.S.C. § 1675(c)] directs the ITC to conduct a review five years after the date of publication of an antidumping duty order to determine whether revocation of the antidumping duty order would be likely to lead to continuation or recurrence of material injury. * * *

* * *

CHAPTER 29
INTERNATIONAL AGREEMENTS

I. OVERVIEW OF THE WTO AGREEMENT AND THE GENERAL AGREEMENT ON TARIFFS AND TRADE

The Department's imposition of AD duties represents a measure against an internationally recognized unfair trade practice and is governed by internationally agreed upon principles, rules and procedures. Since the entry into force of the General Agreement on Tariffs and Trade (GATT) in

1948, these rules and procedures have been embodied in Article VI of the GATT (Article VI). The provisions of Article VI continue to form the basis of the international rules on the imposition of antidumping measures, but Article VI is now modified and interpreted by the WTO Agreement on Implementation of Article VI of GATT 1994, known as the AD Agreement. The AD Agreement, as well as the current version of the GATT (known as "GATT 1994"), are two of the multilateral agreements on trade in goods which are incorporated into the Agreement Establishing the World Trade Organization, commonly known as the WTO Agreement. * * *

As is the case throughout the WTO Agreement, Article VI and the AD Agreement each involve a balance of rights and obligations for every WTO Member. Neither the AD Agreement nor Article VI prohibits dumping. However, Article VI recognizes that injurious dumping is to be "condemned," and may be countered, if dumped imports cause, or threaten to cause, material injury to, or materially retard the establishment of, an industry within the importing country. Article VI, as interpreted by the AD Agreement, therefore, allows for the imposition of AD duties if dumping, injury, and causation have been found.

* * *

IV. THE NORTH AMERICAN FREE TRADE AGREEMENT (NAFTA)

* * *

Chapter 19 of NAFTA concerns review and dispute settlement related to AD and CVD determinations. Under Chapter 19 of the NAFTA, an interested party may request that a binational panel review a NAFTA country's final determination in an AD or CVD administrative proceeding that involves imports from another NAFTA country. In the United States this can replace review by the Court of International Trade.

* * *

The panels are supposed to determine whether a determination by an administering authority was in accordance with the AD or CVD law of the importing country. In other words, a panel reviewing a U.S. action against imports from Mexico or Canada will determine whether the actions taken by the Department or the ITC, as appropriate, were consistent with U.S. law. The panel review process is designed to take no more than 315 days.

AUTHORS' COMMENT ON THE RELATIONSHIP BETWEEN THE WTO AGREEMENTS AND U.S. LAW: THE EXAMPLE OF THE CDSOA OF 2000

As noted in Problems 7.0 and 7.1, the United States implemented its obligations under the various WTO Agreements concluded in the early 1990s through Uruguay Round Agreements Act ("URAA") of 1994. The URAA makes clear, however, that U.S. laws will prevail in the event of an unavoidable conflict with a provision in a WTO Agreement, including the AD Agreement. Specifically, section 102(a)(1) of the URAA provides: "No provision of any of the Uruguay Rounds Agreements, nor the application of any such provision to any person or circumstance, that is inconsistent with any law of the United States shall have effect."

In addition, the WTO has no formal power to compel compliance with the decisions made under its dispute settlement procedures. As also noted in Problems 7.0 and 7.1, section 129 of the URAA instead authorizes the affected U.S. agency (either the Commerce Department or the ITC) to revisit the original administrative action in an attempt to reconcile its interpretation of U.S. law with the WTO decision. If that is not possible, the risk of sanctions authorized by the WTO nonetheless may create intense pressure for the U.S. to comply through formal statutory amendments.

A prominent example of this is the repeal of the Continued Dumping and Subsidy Offset Act of 2000 (CDSOA, also known as the "Byrd Amendment"). The controversial aspect of that Act was a mechanism under which the U.S. government funneled the antidumping duties that it collected back to the members of the affected domestic industry. As a result, CDSOA in effect subsidized domestic industries through antidumping procedures, because it made those industries the financial beneficiaries of any duties ultimately assessed.

Nine other member states of the WTO promptly challenged CDSOA pursuant to the procedures set forth in the WTO's Dispute Settlement Understanding (DSU). Following unsuccessful negotiations, a WTO panel concluded that CDSOA was inconsistent with Articles 5.4, 18.1, and 18.4 of the AD Agreement (as well as various provisions of other WTO Agreements). The U.S. then appealed to the WTO's Appellate Body (AB). In its report, the AB first observed that CDSOA was subject to the obligations in the AD Agreement because it was a "specific action against" dumping. It also found that the only permitted responses to dumping under the AD Agreement are "definitive antidumping duties, provisional measures and price undertakings."

The AB ultimately concluded that, because CDSOA did not fall into any of these allowed responses to dumping, it was inconsistent with the U.S.'s obligations under the AD Agreement. *See Appellate Body Report, United States—Continued Dumping and Subsidy Offset Act of 2000*, WT/DS217/R, WT/DS234/R, Jan. 16, 2003. When the U.S. failed to comply with this decision, the WTO authorized the claimant countries to retaliate in their domestic trade laws as permitted under Article 22 of the DSU. *See, e.g., United States—Continued Dumping and Subsidy Offset Act of 2000, Original Complaint by Canada—Recourse to Arbitration by the United States under Article 22.6 of the DSU*, WT/DS234/ARB/CAN, 31 August 2004.

As discussed in the Federal Circuit opinion below, Congress ultimately bowed to the pressure created by the WTO decisions and repealed

CDSOA effective October 1, 2007 (although amounts collected on goods imported before then continue to be distributed to covered industries). Even before this repeal, however, Canadian producers of goods also brought a variety of challenges against CDSOA under NAFTA. The Federal Circuit decision below explores a special provision of domestic law designed to avoid unintended conflicts with the U.S.'s obligations under NAFTA.

CANADIAN LUMBER TRADE ALLIANCE v. UNITED STATES

517 F.3d 1319 (Fed. Cir. 2008).

MICHEL, CHIEF JUDGE.

This is a trade case concerning the interplay between the North American Free Trade Agreement Implementation Act * * * (codified at 19 U.S.C. §§ 3301–3473) ("NAFTA Implementation Act" or "NIA"), and the Continued Dumping and Subsidy Offset Act * * * ("CDSOA"), repealed by the Deficit Reduction Act of 2005, Pub.L. No. 109–171, § 7601(b), 120 Stat. 4, 154 (2006). * * *

The NIA was enacted in 1993. Section 408 of that act provides that any subsequent amendment to certain United States trade laws "shall apply to goods from a NAFTA country only to the extent specified in the amendment." 19 U.S.C. § 3438. The CDSOA, enacted in 2000, amended the trade laws by providing that antidumping and countervailing duties assessed on imported goods-which previously had been placed into the general fund of the United States Treasury-would instead be "distributed on an annual basis ... to the affected domestic producers for qualifying expenditures." 19 U.S.C. § 1675c (2000). Following enactment of the CDSOA, United States Customs and Border Protection ("Customs") began distributing duties assessed on imported goods, including on goods imported from NAFTA countries Canada and Mexico, to domestic producers.

In 2005, Plaintiffs–Appellees * * * (together, the "Canadian Producers") * * * sued the United States in the Court of International Trade, alleging that because the CDSOA does not specify that it applies to goods from NAFTA countries, it must be construed (in light of section 408 of the NIA) not to apply to goods from NAFTA countries. The Plaintiffs sought, inter alia, a declaratory judgment interpreting the CDSOA in their favor, and an injunction against Customs' continued distribution of duties assessed on softwood lumber, magnesium, and hard red spring wheat from Canada.

Defendants–Appellants * * * (together, the "Domestic Producers") intervened in the litigation, arguing (along with the United States) that the Plaintiffs lacked standing to challenge Customs' CDSOA distributions, had no cause of action, and were wrong on the merits in any event. After briefing and an evidentiary hearing, the Court of International Trade held that the Canadian Producers had standing and a cause of action * * * and that the merits favored the Canadian Producers. *Canadian Lumber Trade Alliance v. United States*, 425 F.Supp.2d 1321 (Ct. Int'l Trade 2006) ("CLTA I"). The Court of International Trade issued a declaratory judgment holding the CDSOA inapplicable to goods from Canada and Mexico, and granted an injunction against Customs' further distribution of duties assessed on softwood lumber, magnesium, and hard red spring wheat from Canada. *Canadian Lumber Trade Alliance v. United States*, 441 F.Supp.2d 1259 (Ct. Int'l Trade 2006) ("CLTA II").

The United States and the Domestic Producers now appeal the judgment in favor of the Canadian Producers * * *. We affirm the declaratory judgment issued by the Court of International Trade, because at least one Plaintiff–Appellee has standing to seek it, and because the Court of International Trade properly interpreted the CDSOA, in light of section 408 of the NIA, to be inapplicable to goods imported from Canada or Mexico. * * * Finally, we modify the injunction issued by the Court of International Trade so that it pertains only to hard red spring wheat, because subsequent events have rendered this case moot with respect to the softwood lumber and magnesium industries.

BACKGROUND

A. Relevant Provisions of the NAFTA Implementation Act

The United States entered into the North American Free Trade Agreement ("NAFTA") with Canada and Mexico in December of 1992. Congress passed the NIA in November 1993, President Clinton signed the bill on December 8, 1993, and the NIA was made effective on January 1, 1994. Pub.L. No. 103–182, 107 Stat. 2057 (1993). * * *

Section 408 of the NIA, entitled "[t]reatment of amendments to antidumping and countervailing duty law," lies at the center of this appeal. The entire section reads as follows:

Any amendment enacted after the Agreement [i.e., NAFTA] enters into force with respect to the United States that is made to-

(1) section 303 or title VII of the Tariff Act of 1930 [19 U.S.C. §§ 1671 et seq.], or any successor statute, or

(2) any other statute which-

(A) provides for judicial review of final determinations under such section, title, or successor statute, or

(B) indicates the standard of review to be applied,

shall apply to goods from a NAFTA country only to the extent specified in the amendment.

19 U.S.C. § 3438 (emphasis added).

As the Court of International Trade recognized, section 408 of the NIA is a "magic words" rule. "[A]ny amendment to title VII of the Tariff Act of 1930 must contain certain 'magic words' for Congress to indicate that it intends to alter antidumping and countervailing duty laws with respect to NAFTA parties." CLTA I, 425 F.Supp.2d at 1334.

B. *The Continued Dumping And Subsidy Offset Act*

In 2000, Congress enacted the CDSOA (often referred to as the "Byrd Amendment"). Before passage of the CDSOA, "the duties collected pursuant to the antidumping statute were deposited with the Treasury for general purposes." *Huaiyin Foreign Trade Corp. v. United States*, 322 F.3d 1369, 1379 (Fed.Cir.2003). The CDSOA changed this by providing that "[d]uties assessed pursuant to a countervailing duty order, an antidumping duty order, or a finding under the Antidumping Act of 1921 shall be distributed on an annual basis under this section to the affected domestic producers for qualifying expenditures." 19 U.S.C. § 1675c(a) (2000). In other words, the CDSOA "direct[ed] Customs to pay the collected antidumping duties to [domestic producers] harmed by the anticompetitive conduct" rather than to keep the duties within the government. *Huaiyin Foreign Trade Corp.*, 322 F.3d at 1380.

The CDSOA directed the Commissioner of Customs to establish a "special account" for each antidumping or countervailing duty order, and to deposit into each special account all duties collected after October 1, 2000 "under the antidumping order or finding or the countervailing duty order with respect to which the account was established." 19 U.S.C. § 1675c(e)(2) (2000). Every year, the special accounts were to be distributed to "affected domestic producers" who had incurred and claimed "qualifying expenditures."

As the Court of International Trade observed, the CDSOA "does not specify that it applies to goods from Canada or Mexico ... nor did the United States provide advance notice of the [CDSOA] to Canada or Mexico or engage in consultations with regard thereto." CLTA I, 425 F.Supp.2d at 1329. Soon after enactment of the CDSOA, nine countries, including Canada and Mexico, instituted dispute resolution proceedings against the United States in the World Trade Organization, arguing that the CDSOA violated a range of international agreements. A WTO dispute resolution panel, affirmed by the Appellate Body of the WTO, ruled that the United States acted inconsistently with the Uruguay Round Agreements in enacting the CDSOA, and as a remedy authorized the complaining nations to retaliate against the CDSOA by suspending tariff concessions on imports from the United States. * * *

Congress repealed the CDSOA as part of the Deficit Reduction Act of 2005, which was signed into law on February 8, 2006. *See* Pub.L. No. 109–171, 120 Stat. 4, 154 (2006). The repeal was made effective as of October 1, 2007, but provided that Customs may still distribute "duties on entries of goods made and filed before October 1, 2007." *Id.* § 7601(b).

At various times between enactment of the CDSOA and its repeal, antidumping and countervailing duty orders were in place on softwood lumber, magnesium, and hard red spring wheat from Canada. Pursuant to the CDSOA, Customs distributed duties collected under these antidumping and countervailing duty orders, including duties collected on goods produced or sold by the Canadian Producers, to domestic producers for fiscal years 2003, 2004, and 2005. * * *

C. Proceedings Below

On April 29, 2005, the Canadian Producers and the Government of Canada filed a total of five complaints against the United States and Customs in the Court of International Trade, alleging that Customs' distribution of duties assessed on imports from Canada was an unlawful agency action within the meaning of the Administrative Procedure Act * * * [and] asked the court to issue a declaratory judgment interpreting the CDSOA and to issue an injunction against further distribution of particular duties . . . [and] to instruct Customs to "collect back" particular duties from the domestic producers to whom they had been distributed. * * *

On April 7, 2006, the Court of International Trade issued an opinion holding that (1) the Canadian Producers had standing because they were likely to be economically injured by the challenged CDSOA distributions and were asserting interests within the "zone of interest" of section 408 of the NIA; * * * and (4) Customs' distribution of duties assessed on imports from Canada was unlawful, because the CDSOA must be read in light of section 408 of the NIA not to apply to goods from Canada or Mexico. CLTA I, 425 F.Supp.2d at 1321.

After further briefing concerning remedies, the Court of International Trade issued a second opinion on July 14, 2006, along with a judgment * * * (5) declaring that pursuant to section 408 of the NIA, the CDSOA does not apply to antidumping and countervailing duties assessed on imports of goods from Canada or Mexico; and (6) enjoining Customs from making any continued CDSOA distributions to the extent they derive from duties assessed pursuant to countervailing duty orders, antidumping duty orders, or findings under the Antidumping Act of 1921, upon softwood lumber, magnesium, or hard red spring wheat from Canada. CLTA II, 441 F.Supp.2d at 1259; Ct. Int'l Trade Consol. Ct. No. 05–00324, slip. op. 06–104 (Judgment, Jul. 14, 2006). The Court of International Trade declined to instruct Customs to "collect back" any duties already distributed, however. The United States and Domestic Producers then filed timely appeals. * * *

* * *

DISCUSSION

* * *

E. Merits–Interpretation of the CDSOA

[W]e turn finally to the merits of its claim that the CDSOA must be read, in light of section 408 of the NIA, *not* to apply to goods from Canada or Mexico. To review, section 408 provides in relevant part that "[a]ny amendment enacted after the Agreement [i.e., NAFTA] enters into force with respect to the United States that is made to . . . title VII of the Tariff Act of 1930 . . . shall apply to goods from a NAFTA country only to the extent specified in the amendment." 19 U.S.C. § 3438. It is quite clear that the CDSOA, enacted six years after the NIA, amended title VII of the Tariff Act of 1930. *See* Pub.L. No. 106–387, § 1003(a), 114 Stat. 1549, 1549A–73 (enacting the CDSOA) ("Title VII of the Tariff Act of 1930 is amended by inserting after section 753 the following new section. . . ."). It is also clear that the CDSOA does not specifically refer to NAFTA, the NIA, Canada, or Mexico. *See id.*; 19 U.S.C. § 1675c (2000). Therefore, the Court of International Trade concluded, "based on Congress' plain language in Section 408 [of the NIA], Customs is not authorized to apply the [CDSOA] to goods from Canada or Mexico." CLTA I, 425 F.Supp.2d at 1373.

The Domestic Producers now offer a barrage of arguments against this result. Most, if not all, were well-addressed and rejected by the Court of International Trade in its exhaustive opinion, *see id.* at 1366–73, and we adopt that court's reasoning and conclusions here without repeating all of them. Broadly, the Domestic Producers argue that the CDSOA is not subject to the "magic words" rule of section 408 because (1) the CDSOA does not "apply to goods" within the meaning of section 408; (2) the CDSOA supercedes section 408; or (3) the CDSOA is an exercise of Congress' spending power and cannot be challenged by foreign entities.

Starting with the words of section 408, the Domestic Producers contend that the statute affects subsequent trade amendments only insofar as they "apply to goods," and that the CDSOA falls outside this reach because it applies to money (i.e., duties assessed on imported goods) rather than to goods. But while it is true that the CDSOA does not regulate goods directly, such as by flatly prohibiting their sale or use, the CDSOA surely does "apply to goods" in the sense relevant to antidumping and countervailing duty laws, which are designed to regulate the market for goods in an attempt to compensate for anti-competitive behavior. *See, e.g., Dixon Ticonderoga Co. v. United States*, 468 F.3d 1353, 1356 (Fed.Cir. 2006)("it is true that the CDSOA is intended to protect domestic producers"). And it is exactly the antidumping and countervailing duty laws that are circumscribed by section 408. * * * Therefore the CDSOA does not escape section 408 merely by virtue of the language, "apply to goods."

Domestic Producers next argue that although the CDSOA does not specify that it applies to goods from NAFTA countries, neither does the statute specify that it does not so apply, and therefore we must infer from this silence that Congress intended the CDSOA to apply to goods from NAFTA countries regardless of section 408 of the NIA. In other words, the Domestic Producers claim that Congress' silence was the result of a deliberate judgment to supercede section 408 (or at least that section 408 was inapplicable). But we have explained that "[f]or a later statute to be held implicitly to supercede an apparently inconsistent earlier enactment, the intent of Congress must be apparent in the circumstances." *See Marine of San Francisco, Inc. v. United States*, 896 F.2d 532, 533 (Fed.Cir. 1990); cf. *United States v. United Cont'l Tuna*, 425 U.S. 164, 168, 96 S.Ct. 1319, 47 L.Ed.2d 653 ("It is, of course, a cardinal principle of statutory construction that repeals by implication are not favored."). Here, the much simpler inference to draw from Congress' silence-and the only reasonable inference, if we are to draw one at all-is that Congress, being aware of its earlier enactment of section 408 of the NIA, chose not to supercede section 408 nor to exempt the CDSOA from it.

Indeed, this simpler inference is bolstered by the fact that Congress was not silent when, years before the CDSOA, Congress enacted a different statute amending title VII of the Trade Act of 1930; namely, the URAA. See Pub.L. No. 103–465, 108 Stat. 4901 (URAA § 234) (1994) ("Pursuant to article 1902 of the North American Free Trade Agreement and section 408 of the North American Free Trade Agreement Implementation Act, the amendments made by this title shall apply with respect to goods from Canada and Mexico."). Given that Congress had demonstrated its ability to specify a statute's applicability to NAFTA parties-and indeed to make explicit reference to section 408-it is unreasonable to infer that Congress meant for the CDSOA to apply to Canadian and Mexican goods but also decided that a specific reference to this effect was unnecessary.

Finally, the Domestic Producers argue that the CDSOA was enacted as part of an appropriations bill, and was therefore an exercise of Congress' spending power that was only tangentially related to title VII of the Tariff Act of 1930 and is outside the reach of section 408. Once antidumping and countervailing duties are assessed, the Domestic Producers claim, those duties become the property of the United States, to dispose of as the United States chooses without interference by foreign entities. This argument has no traction, however, because the Canadian Wheat Board does not challenge Congress' spending authority or its choices thereunder. Rather, the Canadian Wheat Board challenges Customs' distribution of duties on the ground that they are inconsistent with Congress's intention as expressed in the CDSOA and section 408 of the NIA.

It is true that the CDSOA directs Customs to distribute money that has been received into the United States Treasury, and in this sense the statute bears the hallmark of a spending bill. But it is certainly not a general appropriation. The statute specifically directs the creation of "special accounts," separate from the Treasury's general fund, and provides that assessed duties are to be deposited into the special accounts and distributed therefrom to affected domestic producers. 19 U.S.C. § 1675c(e) (2000). Duties only reach the Treasury's general fund, if at all, after an antidumping or countervailing duty order has been revoked and money remains unclaimed in the corresponding special account for ninety days thereafter. *Id.* § 1675c(e)(4) (2000).

Further, as the Court of International Trade correctly observed, "the language of Section 408 does not speak to the type of Congressional authority invoked, but to the laws to which amendments are to be made.'' CLTA I, 425 F.Supp.2d at 1373. Though Congress might have exercised its spending power to assist domestic producers without also amending title VII of the Tariff Act of 1930, and though the Canadian Wheat Board might not have had any recourse to challenge Customs' actions in that event, Congress did in fact choose to enact the CDSOA as an amendment to the trade laws, subject to the constraints imposed by section 408 of the NIA. Therefore the Canadian Wheat Board does in fact have recourse to challenge Customs' actions in this case.

CONCLUSION

We AFFIRM the Court of International Trade's judgment granting the motion of the Canadian Wheat Board for judgment on the agency record, and denying the motions of the United States and Domestic Producers for judgment on the agency record as against the Canadian Wheat Board;

* * *

We AFFIRM the Court of International Trade's declaratory judgment that, pursuant to Section 408 of the NIA, the CDSOA does not apply to antidumping and countervailing duties assessed on imports of goods from Canada or Mexico; and

We AFFIRM the Court of International Trade's entry of a permanent injunction[.]

U.S. INTERNATIONAL TRADE COMMISSION

WOODEN BEDROOM FURNITURE FROM CHINA INVESTIGATION NO. 731–TA–1058 (FINAL)

Publication 3743 (December 2004).

Wooden Bedroom Furniture From China Determination

On the basis of the record developed in the subject investigation, the United States International Trade Commission (Commission) determines, pursuant to section 735(b) of the Tariff Act of 1930 (19 U.S.C. § 1673d(b)) (the Act), that an industry in the United States is materially injured by reason of imports from China of wooden bedroom furniture, provided for in subheadings 9403.50.90 and 7009.92.50 of the Harmonized Tariff Schedule of the United States, that have been found by the Department of Commerce (Commerce) to be sold in the United States at less than fair value (LTFV).

* * *

Views of the Commission

Based on the record in this investigation, we find that an industry in the United States is materially injured by reason of imports of wooden bedroom furniture that are sold in the United States at less than fair value ("LTFV").

I. Background

The petition in this investigation was filed on October 31, 2003. The petitioners include the American Furniture Manufacturers Committee for Legal Trade, an ad hoc association of U.S. manufacturers of wooden bedroom furniture, and six unions * * *

Respondents include the Furniture Retailers of America, an ad hoc association of 35 retailers and importers of wooden bedroom furniture; the Committee for Free Trade in Furniture, an ad hoc association of retailers and manufacturers; Furniture Brands International, the largest U.S. producer of wooden bedroom furniture; the Chinese producers and importers Maria Yee Inc., Guangzhou Maria Yee Furnishings Ltd., and Pyla HK Ltd. (the "Maria Yee Group" or "Maria Yee"); the Chinese producers Lacquer Craft Manufacturing Co. and Markor International Furniture (Tianjin) Manufacturing Co.; and the Coalition of Certain China Furniture Producers. Several Chinese exporters and U.S. importers of wooden bedroom furniture entered appearances in the proceeding but did not appear at the hearing or file briefs with the Commission.

Wooden bedroom furniture ("WBF") is wooden furniture that is designed and manufactured for use in the bedroom. WBF includes beds, night stands, chests, armoires, and dressers with mirrors, among other things. There are a large number of WBF producers in the United States, with more than 50 firms reporting production of WBF during the period of investigation. The ten largest U.S. producers accounted for approximately 56 percent of U.S. producer shipments in 2003. There are also a large number of producers of wooden bedroom furniture in China. The petition identified 133 Chinese producers and exporters of wooden bedroom furniture and the Commission received foreign producer responses from 154 Chinese producers of WBF. China was the largest source of imported WBF during the period of investigation, accounting for 50.2 percent of WBF imports in 2003. Chinese production capacity for WBF grew considerably during the POI [period of investigation], more than doubling (based on pieces) between 2001 and 2003. Capacity in China is projected to increase. * * *

Subject imports of WBF entered the U.S. market during the period of investigation in rapidly increasing volumes and were consistently priced below the domestic merchandise. Due to underselling by subject imports, the domestic industry lost 15.3 percentage points of market share to the subject imports by 2003. The industry also lost 7.0 percentage points of market share to lower-priced subject imports between interim 2003 and interim 2004. This lost market share and consistent underselling by subject imports occurred at the same time that the industry's production, shipment, sales and profitability levels all fell significantly.

Members of the domestic industry were themselves importers of a substantial volume of subject imports during the period, but their share of total imports remained essentially stable throughout the POI. Accordingly, importers who were not domestic producers accounted for the large majority of subject imports, as well as the bulk of the increases in subject volumes, during the period of investigation.

II. Domestic Like Product

To determine whether an industry in the United States is materially injured or threatened with material injury by reason of imports of the subject merchandise, the Commission first defines the "domestic like product" and the "industry." * * * [T]he Act defines "domestic like product" as "a product which is like, or in the absence of like, most similar in characteristics and uses with, the article subject to an investigation."

The decision regarding the appropriate domestic like product(s) in an investigation is a factual determination, and the Commission has applied the statutory standard of "like" or "most similar in characteristics and uses" on a case-by-case basis. No single factor is dispositive, and the Commission may consider other factors it deems relevant based on the facts of a particular investigation. The Commission looks for clear dividing lines among possible like products, and disregards minor variations. Although the Commission must accept the determination of the Department of Commerce ("Commerce") as to the scope of the imported merchandise sold at less than fair value, the Commission determines what domestic product is like the imported articles that Commerce has identified.

* * *

III. Domestic Industry and Related Parties

The domestic industry is defined as "producers as a [w]hole of a domestic like product, or those producers whose collective output of a domestic like product constitutes a major proportion of the total domestic production of the product." In defining the domestic industry, the Commission's general practice has been to include in the industry all domestic production of the domestic like product, whether toll-produced, captively consumed, or sold in the domestic merchant market. We find the domestic industry to include all U.S. producers of WBF.

* * *

IV. Material Injury by Reason of Less Than Fair Value Imports

A. Conditions of Competition

Several conditions of competition are pertinent to our analysis.

1. Demand Conditions

Demand for WBF is affected by changes in the housing market, consumer tastes, personal income levels, and demographics. Generally, demand for WBF is moderately responsive to price changes in the market, primarily because of the discretionary nature of the retail customer's decision on whether to purchase WBF. Nonetheless, a substantial number of purchasers reported that the presence of low priced subject imports from China did not significantly affect overall demand for WBF in the U.S. market. Moreover, the record indicates that demand for WBF, as measured by apparent consumption, has tracked housing starts and new home sales during the POI, indicating that growth in demand during the POI has been affected primarily by changes in the housing market rather than by the increased presence of low-priced subject imports from China.

Apparent U.S. consumption of WBF grew during the period of investigation, increasing by 13.2 percent between 2001 and 2003, and by an additional 12.0 percent between interim 2003 and 2004. Measured by value, apparent U.S. consumption increased from $4.1 billion in 2001 to $4.5 billion in 2002. It then increased to $4.7 billion in 2003. Apparent U.S. consumption was also higher in interim 2004 (at $2.5 billion) than in interim 2003 ($2.2 billion).

* * *

2. Substitutability and Purchase Factors

The record indicates that there is a moderate to high degree of substitutability between domestic wooden bedroom furniture and the subject imports. The subject imports are similar in style and design features to the domestic merchandise. A substantial majority of purchasers report that the domestic and subject merchandise are always or frequently used interchangeably. Further, most purchasers rated the domestic and subject merchandise as being comparable to one another on a variety of factors affecting the purchase decision, except for lowest price, delivery times and brand names.

The record also indicates that price is an important factor in the purchase decision for wooden bedroom furniture, with the large majority of responding purchasers reporting that "lowest price" is a very important factor in their purchase decision. Similarly, the large majority of responding purchasers reported that price was either the first or second most important factor in their purchase decision.

3. Supply

There are a large number of WBF producers in the United States, with more than 50 firms reporting production of this furniture during the period of investigation. The ten largest U.S. producers accounted for approximately 56 percent of U.S. producer shipments in 2003.

* * *

There are a large number of producers of wooden bedroom furniture in China. The petition identified 133 Chinese producers and exporters of wooden bedroom furniture, and the Commission received foreign producer responses from 154 Chinese producers of WBF. China was the largest source of imported wooden bedroom furniture during the period of investigation, accounting for 50.2 percent of total imports in 2003. Chinese production capacity for the subject product grew considerably during the POI. * * *

* * *

The domestic industry was responsible for a substantial but stable percentage of the subject imports during the period. During the POI, the domestic industry imported between 33.3 percent and 36.0 percent of the subject merchandise (measured by value) imported during the POI. However, subject imports accounted for an increasing portion of the domestic industry's total shipments during the POI, with the volume of the industry's subject imports growing from 7.8 percent of domestically produced shipments in 2001 to 16.7 percent in 2002, 25.6 percent in 2003, and 32.7 percent in interim 2004.

The domestic industry is divided with respect to its support for the petition. Thirty-eight members of the industry, accounting for 37.8 percent of domestic production (measured in pieces) but 47.6 percent of the industry's U.S. shipments (measured by value) in 2003, support the petition. Nine members of the industry, accounting for 59.1 percent of domestic production (measured in pieces) but 45.6 percent of the industry's U.S. shipments (measured by value) in 2003, oppose the petition. Seven members of the industry, accounting for 3.1 percent of domestic production (measured in pieces) and 6.8 percent of the industry's U.S. shipments (measured by value) in 2003, take no position with respect to the petition. Domestic producers opposing the petition accounted for a substantially larger percentage of subject imports during the OI than those supporting or taking no position on the petition.

B. Volume of the Subject Imports

[19 U.S.C. § 1677(7)(C)(i)] provides that the "Commission shall consider whether the volume of imports of the merchandise, or any increase in that volume, either in absolute terms or relative to production or consumption in the United States, is significant."

We find that the volume of subject imports increased rapidly and consistently during the POI, both in absolute terms and relative to production and consumption in the United States.

* * *

Given these rapid and consistent increases in subject imports during the POI, we find that the volume of the subject imports was significant during the period of investigation, both in absolute terms and relative to production and consumption in the United States. As we discuss below, the increases in subject import volumes and market share came directly out of the market share of the domestic industry and reduced the industry's production, shipment, and sales levels significantly.

We have considered respondents' argument that the domestic industry is itself primarily responsible for the large and consistent increases in subject volumes during the POI. According to respondents, the increases in subject import volumes are the result of a decision by the domestic industry to utilize a "blended" sourcing strategy to compete more efficiently in the market. We do not agree. Although it is true that the domestic producers imported approximately one third of all subject merchandise imported into the United States during the POI, importers who are not members of the domestic industry were responsible for roughly two-thirds of the subject imports and two-thirds of all increases in subject import volumes during the POI. Thus, the bulk of the subject import increases during the POI are attributable to the actions of importers that are not part of the domestic industry. Furthermore, even those domestic producers who have decided to "blend" their domestic production with imports freely admit that they are shifting production to China to obtain the benefit of low production costs, which indicates they are reducing their own production and sales of WBF in response to the LTFV pricing of subject merchandise.

We also considered respondents' argument that an increased supply of moderately priced subject WBF has increased overall demand in the market. We do not agree that the significant increases in subject import volumes occurred primarily because they expanded aggregate demand in the market. First, if these increases in subject volumes occurred because low-priced imports significantly expanded demand in the market, we would have expected to find that increased subject import volumes satisfied the newly-created demand without significantly affecting the industry's shipment and production levels during the POI. However, the opposite occurred in this case, with the industry experiencing significant declines in its production, shipments, and sales levels as it lost substantial market share to subject imports. Moreover, between 2001 and 2003, subject import volume rose much more sharply than the increase in apparent consumption. Finally, although we recognize that demand for WBF is somewhat elastic and might be expected to respond to the availability of low-priced imports, the record indicates a closer tie between the increases in apparent consumption and increased housing starts and new house sales during the POI than between consumption changes and subject import volumes.

Accordingly, we find both the volume and increase in volume of subject imports, both in absolute terms and relative to production and consumption in the United States, to be significant.

C. *Price Effects of the Subject Imports*

[19 U.S.C. § 1677(7)(C)(ii)] provides that, in evaluating the price effects of the subject imports, the Commission shall consider whether—

(I)   there has been significant price underselling by the imported merchandise as compared with the price of domestic like products of the United States, and

(II) the effect of imports of such merchandise otherwise depresses prices to a significant degree or prevents price increases, which otherwise would have occurred, to a significant degree.

As discussed above, we find that there is a moderate to high degree of substitutability between domestic wooden bedroom furniture and the subject imports. In this regard, the majority of purchasers report that the subject imports and domestically produced WBF are always or frequently used interchangeably. Moreover, a majority of purchasers reported that the subject imports and the domestic and subject merchandise are comparable to one another with respect to most factors figuring into their purchase decision. We also note that the record indicates that price is an important factor in the purchase decision for wooden bedroom furniture, with the large majority of responding purchasers reporting that "lowest price" is a very important factor in their purchase decision.

* * *

Moreover, the price comparison data show that the subject imports depressed and suppressed domestic prices to a significant degree during the POI. In particular, the pricing data show that, for each price comparison product, weighted-average domestic prices declined significantly during the period between the first quarter of 2001 and the final quarter of 2003, when petitioners filed the petition in this investigation. * * * Thus, the pricing data show a significant correlation between underselling by subject imports and domestic price declines in the market during the period before the filing of the petition, especially given the importance of price to the purchase decision and the substitutability between the domestic and subject merchandise. Further, given that declines in the industry's pricing during the POI outstripped declines in the industry's costs of goods sold during the POI, the record indicates that this underselling caused the industry to experience a cost-price squeeze during the period.

The price comparison data also show that the significant and consistent underselling by the subject imports caused a significant shift in purchases from the domestic merchandise to the subject imports during the POI.

* * *

Finally, we have considered respondents' argument that the Commission's weighted-average price comparison data masks the fact that the subject imports did not, in fact, have any clear impact on domestic prices during the POI. Although respondents concede that the Commission's price comparison charts show weighted-average domestic prices declining during the POI, they argue that a company-specific analysis of pricing trends shows no clear correlation between domestic producer pricing trends and underselling by the subject imports. We do not agree with this argument. Although it is true that the Commission has the discretion to utilize any reasonable price comparison methodology in its analysis, the quarterly weighted-average price comparison methodology used in this proceeding is the standard methodology the Commission uses to assess whether subject imports are underselling domestic merchandise and having adverse price effects in the market. We generally rely on weighted-average pricing because it allows us to assess, in a meaningful fashion, whether general pricing trends across a number of domestic producers indicate that the subject imports are having an adverse impact on domestic prices overall.

By weight-averaging reported domestic and imported prices, we are able to ensure that we do not place too much weight on pricing and price trends that are associated with smaller, less significant sales in the market. Breaking our price series apart by segregating out individual producer pricing and basing our price conclusions on those individual sets of data, as respondents suggest, would simply result in our giving greater weight to those producers who should have less weight, comparatively, in the analysis.

* * *

D. *Impact of the Subject Imports*

In examining the impact of the subject imports on the domestic industry, we consider all relevant economic factors that bear on the state of the industry in the United States. These factors include output, sales, inventories, capacity utilization, market share, employment, wages, productivity, profits, cash flow, return on investment, ability to raise capital, and research and development. No single factor is dispositive and all relevant factors are considered "within the context of the business cycle and conditions of competition that are distinctive to the affected industry."

As we discussed above, there were rapid and significant increases in the volume and market share of the subject imports during the POI and the subject imports consistently undersold domestic merchandise at significant margins throughout the POI. As these lower-priced subject imports entered the market in increasing volumes during the POI, the domestic industry experienced substantial declines in almost all of its trade and financial indicia, even during a period of growing apparent consumption.

* * *

In sum, subject imports had a significant adverse impact on the condition of the domestic industry during the POI. As discussed above, the significant increases in the volumes of the subject imports consistently and significantly undersold the domestic merchandise during the period of investigation. The domestic industry lost significant market share to LTFV imports, which in turn significantly affected the industry's production, shipments and sales volumes as well as nearly all of its other indicators. Although the industry's operating margin remained positive throughout the period of investigation, the industry's aggregate operating income fell by a significant amount during the POI. Thus, we find that subject imports adversely affected the performance of the domestic industry during the period of investigation.

* * *

Finally, we have considered the fact that a substantial proportion of the industry opposes the petition and the imposition of antidumping duties in this investigation. As we noted previously, nine members of the industry, accounting for 59.1 percent of domestic production (measured in pieces) but 45.6 percent of the industry's U.S. shipments (measured in value) in 2003, oppose the petition. Thirty-eight members of the industry, accounting for 37.8 percent of domestic production (measured in pieces) but 47.6 percent of the industry's U.S. shipments (measured in value) in 2003, support the petition. Respondents argue that the opposition of a substantial portion of the industry to the petition indicates that the industry as a whole is not being materially injured by subject imports and that the subject imports from China have been a net benefit to the industry's operations.

We do not find respondents' argument compelling. While it is true that we have the discretion to consider the level of an industry's support for the petition as part of our analysis, the level of support by the industry is not dispositive with respect to a finding of present material injury. Thus, even though a substantial percentage of the industry opposes the petition, this does not outweigh the other record evidence indicating that the subject imports have had significant volume and price-related effects on the industry.

Moreover, while it is true that nine members of the industry, representing a majority of domestic production in 2003, oppose the imposition of dumping duties, thirty-eight producers, representing a larger percentage of domestic shipments (measured by value) in 2003 than those in opposition, support the imposition of duties in this case. Also, we note that six unions support the petition. * * * Thus, there remains substantial industry-wide support for the petition. Finally, we would add that the nine domestic producers who oppose the petition have been responsible for the large majority of the subject merchandise imported by the industry during the POI, indicating that their views on this matter are affected by a desire to continue importing subject imports.

Accordingly, we conclude that the subject imports of WBF have had a significant adverse impact on the domestic industry.

CONCLUSION

For the foregoing reasons, we find that the domestic wooden bedroom furniture industry is materially injured by reason of LTFV imports from China.

JOSEPHS, THE MULTINATIONAL CORPORATION, INTEGRATED INTERNATIONAL PRODUCTION AND U.S. ANTIDUMPING LAWS

5 Tul. J. Int'l & Comp. L. 51, 69–73 (1997).*

VII. PERCEIVED INADEQUACIES OF THE ANTIDUMPING LAWS
AS A MEANS OF ADDRESSING UNFAIR TRADE PRACTICES

Antidumping laws, whether of the United States or other jurisdictions, have been criticized as encouraging anticompetitive and protectionist behavior, rather than furthering the international free flow of goods. Some critics have argued that the antidumping laws should be entirely eliminated, and unfair trade practices prosecuted solely under the antitrust laws.

Among the criticisms leveled at the antidumping laws is that they are frequently invoked where the petitioner is a U.S. producer which has failed to adapt to international competition. As a practical matter, standing to invoke the antidumping laws is limited to the "affected industry" and the public interest is not considered. On balance, the benefits of imports to society may far outweigh the harm to the "affected industry" through the creation of new businesses, the availability of superior inputs to downstream producers of other products, and the increased availability of superior products at lower prices to consumers. United States law differs from that of the European Union and Canada in that it does not expressly allow for consideration of the public interest as part of an antidumping proceeding.

Paradoxically, compliance with the antidumping laws may encourage, or even actually require, oligopolistic or oligopsonistic behavior: the freezing of market shares by domestic companies and collusion between producers to maintain or raise prices. For example, in one case, unfair trade actions brought against Brazilian exporters of frozen orange juice concentrate actually compelled the exporters to coordinate prices rather than compete.

* * *

Another criticism of the antidumping laws is that they fail to take account of normal and usual business practices. There is no recognition of the fact of business life that competitive prices are a necessary lever to gain market share. There is no recognition of short-term dumping as a justifiable response to unanticipated market developments, currency fluctuations, or sharp swings in demand.

Other critics claim that the antidumping laws are biased towards a finding of sales at less than fair market value. The dumping margin generally is calculated as the difference between prices in the home market (where the exporter operates) and prices in the U.S. market. Yet the calculation of home market prices excludes sales which are below average cost, and the calculation of U.S. prices ignores sales which are above home market prices, all of which tends to create or increase the dumping margin. Where home market prices are not available, the ITA may resort to constructed prices, which require inclusion of overhead and profit factors.

On the other hand, numerous arguments may be made in defense of the antidumping laws. For example, the laws are necessary when foreign producers subsidize low prices abroad through high prices at home. Another argument is that since the statute requires that the petition for relief be filed "on behalf of" a domestic industry, the antidumping laws cannot be used to further a purely private grievance. Even if the petitioner is the sole or one of the few remaining domestic producers, it still must be demonstrated that its injury is due to unfair trade practices and not its own mistaken business decisions. In fact, the key factor in antidumping cases is the finding of injury; when a petition for relief is rejected, it is nearly always because of a negative injury determination.

* * *

Though not a defense of the antidumping laws themselves, the laws are generally administered in a way which is fair, impartial, and transparent in comparison to the way other countries administer similar laws. If antidumping laws worldwide have protectionist outcomes despite differences in procedure, U.S. law can at least be defended as superior on due process grounds. This is so because U.S. law diffuses the decision-making process over two administrative agencies which are independent of each other: the ITA makes the dumping determination, and the ITC makes the injury determination. The ITC has demonstrated pragmatism and flexibility in dealing with nationality questions, emphasizing the production process rather than the nationality of the producer. United States law limits the discretion of these administrative agencies much more than either their European or Canadian counterparts. Moreover, U.S. law on price determinations and findings of injury is more detailed; the administrative process is more verifiable; and there are liberal opportunities for judicial review. In fact, ITA and ITC determinations are not infrequently reversed and remanded by the courts. There is every indication that the courts function as a protective mechanism against arbitrary agency decision-making.

QUESTIONS AND COMMENTS

1. Has the CEN supercomputer that AA purchased been "dumped", that is, sold at "less than fair value"? Young gives the underlying rationale for antidumping legislation. The ITA Antidumping Manual discusses the necessary calculations, which are detailed in Sections 772 and 773 of the Tariff Act of 1930 (19 U.S.C. §§ 1677a, 1677b in the Documents Supplement).

2. As the ITA Dumping Manual explains, the fundamental determination in a dumping investigation involves a comparison of the U.S. price of

imported goods with the "normal value" of those goods. The ITA has three different approaches to calculating "normal value" of the goods in the foreign market. One is to calculate the price for sales in the ordinary course of business. A second is based on prices in sales to third countries. A third is to calculate a "constructed value." The first step in the analysis, therefore, is to determine which method the ITA should use to calculate the "normal value" of CEN's supercomputer.

3. Is the $10 million Japanese price of the CEN supercomputer an appropriate baseline from which to calculate normal value? Are there sufficient sales of supercomputers in Japan to justify using the Japanese price as a baseline? Typically the quantity or value of sales in the exporting country's market must exceed 5% of the quantity or value of sales in the U.S. for the figures to be deemed reliable (*see* 19 U.S.C. § 1677b(a)(1)(C)). Even if there is a sufficient quantity of sales in the Japanese market, is the $10 million price figure a good indicator of normal value given that it costs Grey $15 million to produce its supercomputers? The Japanese manufacturers assert that their costs of production are less than $10 million, but research and development costs are apparently not included in those calculations. The Tariff Act of 1930 provides (*see* 19 U.S.C. §§ 1677b(b)) that sales in the exporting country may be disregarded in calculating normal value if they are made at less than the cost of production. In determining the costs of production, how should expenditures for research and development be treated?

4. If, for whatever reason, the ITA determines that domestic sales in Japan do not provide a viable baseline for calculating normal value, which of the alternative methodologies for calculating normal value might be available? Would it make any difference if CEN were a Chinese manufacturer rather than a Japanese manufacturer? *See also* ITA Antidumping Manual, ch. 18, § III.B. and 19 U.S.C. § 1677b(c).

5. The next step is to determine the appropriate U.S. sales price to compare with the "normal value." Generally, the ITA uses the "export price." How is that price determined? *See* 19 U.S.C. § 1677a(a). The ITA manual also refers, however, to the use of an alternative, the "constructed export price." When is it appropriate to use that price and what is the method for determining it? *See* the ITA Antidumping Manual, ch. 6, § II.A., and 19 U.S.C. § 1677a(b).

Finally, it is time to pull the pieces together. How is the "dumping margin" ultimately determined from the comparison of the normal value to the export price?

6. As you investigate the sales of Japanese supercomputers further, you also discover that the cost of warranty protection, especially of product liability insurance, is much greater for goods sold in the United States than in Japan. On the other hand, American buyers are much less "fussy" about the initial quality of the goods as to "finish," etc. Thus, goods which could not be sold to Japanese buyers, except as reduced-price "seconds," will "pass" in the United States market and be salable at full price. Should any of these facts affect any of the calculations? If so, in which direction—should they narrow or widen the gap between normal value in the Japanese market and the export

price for the U.S. market? Also, if any of the above information affects calculations, how would you quantify the effect?

7. These calculations obviously require a great deal of information. For example, if in our Problem the ITA decides to use the "constructed value" for CEN's supercomputer (instead of the standard home market price), it must obtain information on CEN's cost of production, including its selling, general, and administrative (SG & A) expenses, and profit. How does the ITA gather this information? *See* ITA Antidumping Manual, ch. 1, § IV.A.5.

Note in this regard that if CEN fails to cooperate, the ITA may rely on the best information available ("BIA") in making its determinations. *See* ITA Antidumping Manual, ch. 1, § IV.A.5. and 19 U.S.C. § 1677e(a). *See also* AD Agreement, art. 6.8. What other consequence may befall CEN if it fails to cooperate with the ITA? *See* 19 U.S.C. § 1677e(b).

8. In addition to finding sales at less than fair value, both the Tariff Act of 1930 and the WTO AD Agreement require that dumping must cause or threaten to cause material injury to the domestic industry (or retard the establishment of a domestic industry) before an antidumping duty may be imposed. The ITC makes this determination. This thus requires proof of both injury and causation.

9. In order analyze these two issues, however, one must first identify the relevant domestic product market and affected industry. *See* ITA Antidumping Manual, ch. 18, § III.B and the ITC's Wooden Bedroom Furniture decision, §§ II. and III. Has an "industry" in the United States suffered material injury through CEN's sale of its supercomputer to AA? If the relevant market is "all computers," these sales are an insignificant part of it. That may still be true even if the market is "all supercomputers". However, if the relevant market is "all supercomputers capable of both vector and scalable calculations," then Grey may constitute the majority of the entire U.S. industry. *See* the basic facts for this Problem. What factor(s) should be most significant in identifying the relevant "domestic like product" and the relevant "industry" from among this range of options?

10. Once the industry is identified, what factors go into establishing whether that industry has suffered a "material injury"? *See* the ITC's Wooden Bedroom Furniture decision, § IV.

11. If "material injury" is doubtful, is there a "threat of material injury"? Ten relevant economic factors are listed in § 1677(7)(F). Must the ITC find that all factors are satisfied, or merely one or some of them? *See* ITA Antidumping Manual, ch. 18, § III.C. If supercomputers are not considered fungible goods, and the market for them is growing and so also may be Grey's sales, does that affect your analysis? Does the Japanese computer manufacturers membership in larger conglomerates, and the comparison of the manufacturers' sales tactics to traditional analyses of "predatory pricing" under antitrust law have any bearing on the analysis?

12. This analysis is closely related to the question whether the injury or threat of injury to the domestic industry occurred "by reason of" (*i.e.*, was caused by) CEN's dumping. A potential complication on this issue is the fact that Jujitsu offered to sell a supercomputer to AA for $9 million. If that offer

is still available, CEN likely will argue that its conduct could not have caused any injury to the U.S. supercomputer industry. How could you nonetheless demonstrate that CEN's dumping caused material injury to domestic producers notwithstanding such competition from other foreign producers? *See* ITA Antidumping Manual, ch. 18, § III.F. (The facts provided at the beginning of this Problem also may spur some thoughts.)

13. What are the potential benefits to Grey Research if the government ultimately decides that actionable dumping has occurred?

14. Josephs summarizes many of the positions taken for and against the U.S. antidumping law. This is a continuing national debate. It is also a growing international debate as more foreign governments adopt their own antidumping laws, which they can use to protect themselves from U.S. exports. Should the U.S. join efforts to abolish antidumping duties altogether? Or efforts to find a substitute method of protecting domestic manufacturers from dumped imports?

15. Assume that CEN is instead exporting from Canada or Mexico and that Grey Research has inquired about resolving the dispute through NAFTA. (a) First, how does the NAFTA dispute resolution *process* differ from the WTO process? *See also* the Jacobs excerpt from Problem 7.1. (b) Second, what *substantive* law would a NAFTA panel apply to the dumping claim asserted by Grey? *See* ITA Antidumping Manual, ch. 29, § IV. (c) Finally, what does the *Canadian Lumber Trade Alliance* opinion tell us about how U.S. domestic law is more protective of NAFTA than of the various WTO Agreements, including the WTO AD Agreement?

16. As a final example of the controversies that can arise over U.S. compliance with international law in this area, consider ITA's former practice of "zeroing." To understand this practice, first note that a foreign producer likely will have numerous sales in its home country. As a result, in order to calculate the "home market price," the ITA may use the *average* price from all such sales. *See* 19 U.S.C. § 1677(35). This average price is then compared to the "export price" to yield the dumping margin. Under zeroing, however, the ITA in effect considered only those home market sales that were *above* the export price; for sales *below* the export price, it simply assigned a "zero" (*i.e.*, not a negative number). Because on average this meant a higher home country comparison price, it also resulted in a higher average dumping margin.

In a series of decisions, WTO panels declared that this practice violates the U.S.'s obligations under the article 2.4 of the AD Agreement. *See, e.g.*, Appellate Body Report, *United States—Laws, Regulations and Methodology for Calculating Dumping Margins ("Zeroing")*, ¶ 222, WT/DS294/AB/R, adopted May 9, 2006. Notwithstanding these decisions, the Federal Circuit repeatedly upheld the methodology as a reasonable interpretation of the actual language in the Tariff Act of 1930 (as amended). *See, e.g.*, *Corus Staal BV v. Department of Commerce*, 395 F.3d 1343 (Fed. Cir. 2005). In response to the repeated adverse rulings by the WTO, however, in 2006 the Commerce Department revised its views (as permitted in Section 129 of the URAA) and declared that it would discontinue the practice of zeroing. *See* 71 Fed. Reg. 77,722 (Dec. 17, 2006).

PROBLEM 7.3 ESCAPE CLAUSE (SAFEGUARD) PROCEEDINGS: SNEAKERS FROM INDONESIA

SECTION I. THE SETTING

Sneaker World, Inc., was created by several MBA students who had been track team members in college, their track team coach, and a local attorney. They incorporated in Washington and began to import athletic footwear from Asia, initially from Korea but now largely from Indonesia where production costs are lower. In the company's ten years of existence, sales have increased markedly each year. The company is currently negotiating a contract with Seers, Inc., a major retail chain, to supply nearly all the sneakers sold by Seers.

Kids, Inc., is an old family owned Wisconsin corporation that has manufactured a full line of sneakers for over 40 years. The company produces mainly at its large factory in Milwaukee, where it has employed as many as 460 persons when operating at full capacity. For a number of years it did operate at full capacity, indeed enjoying a rather dominant market position in the United States. But for the past ten years sales have decreased some 20 percent, and the workforce at Kids is presently 350 persons. Kids has occasionally supplied Seers with sneakers.

The management of Kids sees a dark future if the company relies on domestic production. A recent board meeting topic was dismantling the Milwaukee plant and relocating production to a subsidiary in China or Mexico. Mexico offers even cheaper labor, NAFTA membership and greater convenience. China offers many investment incentives and wage rates are only a fraction of those paid to the unionized labor force in Wisconsin. But there are some concerns about sustaining product quality. The city council of Milwaukee learned of the board discussion and at a meeting voted favorably on a temporary property tax holiday for Kids. The management and employees at Kids, and many other persons in Milwaukee, believe that the problems are the result of unfair import competition. Although consumers now pay less for sneakers than ten years ago (prices adjusted for inflation), they are not always well organized to argue that free trade provides them with greater choices, increases competition and assists economic development in many areas of the world. Nor are the importers, such as Sneaker World, well organized. But Kids and other United States producers are.

The United States Athletic Footwear Association (AFA) is a trade association to which Kids and most other domestic producers of such footwear belong. The AFA has stated that the problems of Kids are mirrored in other companies in the United States, including many smaller companies which have less ability to survive than Kids. Statistics prepared by the AFA show that over the last ten years the domestic athletic footwear industry has lost 40 percent of the market to foreign producers. Demand for athletic footwear has been increasing, however, and United States producers make roughly the same number of sneakers as they did ten years ago. Nevertheless, foreign made footwear now represents 65 percent of all sales in the United States. United States producers are increasingly confined to high-quality, high-priced footwear. Several smaller domestic firms producing in that sector of the market have prospered, although they are concerned that foreign producers may ultimately turn to that segment of the market as well.

SECTION II.   FOCUS OF CONSIDERATION

Import competition is an irritant to many domestic producers. The major concern is the impossibility of matching the low labor rates in many developing nations. Often these domestic producers turn to the federal government for help in blocking these imports. There may be no evidence of dumping present, nor any indication of subsidies by the foreign government. But the domestic company nevertheless is being harmed by the foreign competition. Your client, AFA, first wants a stop to what it believes is unfair competition. Its members are losing a great deal of business. Secondly, AFA members, the unions and Milwaukee all would like "compensation" for their injuries.

But the United States has limitations on what it may do. It is a member of the WTO, and through that organization has sought to open rather than close markets. The General Agreement on Tariffs and Trade (a WTO agreement) anticipates the domestic concerns discussed above, principally through Article XIX, the so-called "safeguard or escape clause." A supplemental WTO "Safeguards Agreement" was reached in 1994. United States law providing for relief from import injury was consolidated in Title II of the Trade Act of 1974. The principal authority for "safeguard" measures in U.S. law is set forth in Section 201 of that Act. A Senate Report at the time describes its underlying policy in this way:

> The rationale for the "escape clause" has been, and remains, that as barriers to international trade are lowered, some industries and workers inevitably face serious injury, dislocation and perhaps economic extinction. The "escape clause" is aimed at providing temporary relief for an industry suffering from serious injury, or the threat thereof, so that the industry will have sufficient time to adjust to the freer international competition.

Senate Rep. No. 93–1298, Trade Act of 1974, at 119 (1974).

This Problem explores Title II procedures for potential relief from import injury. Particular attention is paid to the competing policy considerations surrounding escape clause injury and relief decisions and to the provision of "trade adjustment assistance" to those affected by import competition.

Title II of the Trade Act of 1974 (as amended) (19 U.S.C. §§ 2251–2395), Article XIX of the GATT and the WTO Agreement on Safeguards are essential to an analysis of this problem. They are found in the Documents Supplement.

Web resources for further study include the Department of Labor's trade adjustment assistance webpage *http://www.doleta.gov/tradeact/* and the ITC's safeguards webpage, *http://www.usitc.gov/trade_remedy/about_global_safeguard_inv.htm.*

SECTION III. READINGS, QUESTIONS AND COMMENTS

PART A. IMPORT INJURY DETERMINATIONS

U.S. INTERNATIONAL TRADE COMMISSION

STEEL
Investigation No. TA–201–73.
Publication No. 3479, pp. 25–30, 32–34 (December, 2001).

* * *

VIEWS ON INJURY OF THE COMMISSION

I. INTRODUCTION

Pursuant to section 202(b) of the Trade Act of 1974 ("Trade Act") (19 U.S.C. § 2252(b)), the Commission determines that certain carbon flat-rolled products, including slab, hot-rolled sheet and strip (including plate in coils), plate (including cut-to-length plate and clad plate), cold-rolled sheet and strip (other than grain-oriented electrical steel), and corrosion-resistant and other coated sheet and strip, are being imported into the United States in such increased quantities as to be a substantial cause of serious injury to the domestic industry. The Commission also determines that grain-oriented electrical steel ("GOES") is not being imported into the United States in such increased quantities as to be a substantial cause of serious injury or threat thereof to the domestic industry.[1] * * *

[*The ITC then also describes in great detail its similar findings with respect to dozens of other specific categories of steel imports—The Authors.*]

* * *

In making determinations in safeguard actions, the Commission has traditionally divided the statutory standard into three criteria. Specifically, to make an affirmative determination, the Commission must find that:

---

1. Pursuant to section 311(a) of the North American Free Trade Agreement ("NAFTA") Implementation Act (19 U.S.C. § 3371(a)), the Commission unanimously makes negative findings with respect to Canada and makes affirmative finds (5–1 vote) with respect to Mexico regarding these imports (Commissioner Devaney dissenting with respect to Mexico).

(1) imports of the subject article are in *increased quantities* (either actual or relative to production);

(2) the domestic industry producing an article that is like or directly competitive with the imported article is *seriously injured or threatened with serious injury;* and

(3) the article is being imported in such increased quantities as to be a *substantial cause* of serious injury or threat of serious injury to the domestic industry.

The Commission must find that all three criteria are satisfied to make an affirmative determination. In a recent section 201 determination, and in this action, the Commission has considered the second and third criteria together with respect to its threat of serious injury analysis.

II. BACKGROUND

The Commission instituted this investigation effective June 22, 2001, following receipt of a request from the United States Trade Representative ("USTR"). On July 26, 2001, the Commission received a resolution from the Committee on Finance of the United States Senate requesting that the Commission conduct a safeguard investigation of the same steel products. The Commission exercised its authority under section 603 of the Trade Act and consolidated the investigation requested by the Senate Committee on Finance with the Commission's previously-instituted investigation requested by the USTR. The Commission was requested to determine whether certain steel products are being imported into the United States in such increased quantities as to be a substantial cause of serious injury, or the threat of serious injury, to the domestic industries producing like or directly competitive products. * * *

III. LEGAL STANDARDS

A. *Domestic industry Producing Like or Directly Competitive Article*

Statutory Framework and Commission Practice. To determine whether an article is being imported into the United States in such increased quantities as to be a substantial cause of serious injury or the threat thereof, the Commission first defines "the domestic industry producing an article that is like or directly competitive with the imported article." The statute defines the term "domestic industry" to mean "the producers as a whole of the like or directly competitive article or those producers whose collective production of the like or directly competitive article constitutes a major proportion of the total domestic production of such article." The Commission defines the domestic industry in terms of each like or directly competitive article and evaluates the impact of the pertinent imports on the facilities and workers producing each article.

* * *

In determining what constitutes the like product, the Commission traditionally has taken into account such factors as the physical properties of the product, its customs treatment, its manufacturing process (*i.e.*, where and how it is made), its uses, and the marketing channels through which the product is sold. These are not statutory criteria and do not limit what factors the Commission may consider in making its determination. No single factor is dispositive and the weight given to each individual factor will depend upon the facts in the particular case. The Commission traditionally has looked for clear dividing lines among possible products and has disregarded minor variations.

The Commission has broad discretion to determine what constitutes the domestic industry producing a like or directly competitive article in a section 201 investigation * * *.

* * *

B. *Increased Imports*

Statutory Framework and Commission Practice. The first of the three statutory criteria for an affirmative determination in a safeguard investigation is that imports must be in "increased quantities." Under 19 U.S.C. § 2252(c)(1)(C), imports are considered to have increased when the increase is "either actual or relative to domestic production." In determining whether imports have increased, the Commission considers imports from all sources. The Commission traditionally has considered import trends over the most recent five-year period as a framework for its analysis, but can consider longer or shorter periods and may focus on the most recent period, as it deems appropriate.

C. *Serious Injury or Threat Thereof*

Statutory Framework and Commission Practice. The second of the three statutory criteria concerns whether the domestic industry is seriously injured or threatened with serious injury. The statute defines "serious injury" as being "a significant overall impairment in the position of a domestic industry."[43] The term "threat of serious injury" is defined as "serious injury that is clearly imminent."[44]

In determining whether serious injury or threat exists, the Commission considers "all economic factors which it considers relevant, including (but not limited to)" the following—

(a) with respect to serious injury—

    (i) the significant idling of productive facilities in the domestic industry,

    (ii) the inability of a significant number of films to carry out domestic production operations at a reasonable level of profit, and

---

43.   19 U.S.C. § 2252(c)(6)(C).

44.   19 U.S.C. § 2252(c)(6)(D).

(iii) significant unemployment or underemployment within the domestic industry;

(b) with respect to threat of serious injury—

(i) a decline in sales or market share, a higher and growing inventory (whether maintained by domestic producers, importers, wholesalers, or retailers), and a downward trend in production, profits, wages, productivity, or employment (or increasing underemployment) in the domestic industry,

(ii) the extent to which firms in the domestic industry are unable to generate adequate capital to finance the modernization of their domestic plants and equipment, or are unable to maintain existing levels of expenditures for research and development, and

(iii) the extent to which the United States market is the focal point for diversion of exports of the article concerned by reason of restraints on exports of such article to, or on imports of such article into, third country markets.[46]

The presence or absence of any of these factors is not "necessarily dispositive" of whether increased imports are a substantial cause of serious injury, or the threat of serious injury, to the industry. In addition, the Commission must "consider the condition of the domestic industry over the course of the relevant business cycle."

* * *

D. *Substantial Cause*

Statutory Framework and Commission Practice. The third statutory criterion concerns whether the subject article is being imported in such increased quantities as to be a "substantial cause" of serious injury or threat. The statute defines "substantial cause" as meaning "a cause which is important and not less than any other cause."[50] Thus, increased imports must be both an important cause of the serious injury or threat *and* a cause that is equal to or greater than any other cause.

In determining whether increased imports are a substantial cause of serious injury or threat of serious injury, the statute directs that the Commission take into account all economic factors that it considers relevant, including but not limited to "... an increase in imports (either actual or relative to domestic production) and a decline in the proportion of the domestic market supplied by domestic producers."[51] The statute further directs that the Commission consider "the condition of the domestic industry over the course of the relevant business cycle," but provides that the Commission "may not aggregate the causes of declining demand

46. 19 U.S.C. § 2252(c)(1)(A) and (B).

50. 19 U.S.C. § 2252(b)(1)(B).

51. 19 U.S.C. § 2252(c)(1)(C).

associated with a recession or economic downturn in the United States economy into a single cause of serious injury or threat of injury."[52]

Moreover, the statute directs that the Commission "examine factors other than imports" that may be a cause of serious injury or threat of serious injury to the domestic industry and include the results of its examination in its report.[53] Neither the statute nor the legislative history rules out consideration of other possible causes of injury. * * *

PICKARD & KIMBLE, CAN U.S. SAFEGUARD ACTIONS SURVIVE WTO REVIEW?: SECTION 201 INVESTIGATIONS IN INTERNATIONAL TRADE LAW*

29 Loy. L.A. Int'l & Comp. L. Rev. 43, 44–46, 49–58 (2007).

I. Introduction

A "Section 201" investigation is one of the strongest fundamental trade remedy actions available under U.S. law. This provision of the Trade Act of 1974 authorizes the U.S. International Trade Commission ("ITC") to examine whether a particular import is causing or threatening to cause serious injury to a domestic industry. Once an import is deemed harmful, Section 201 provides the President with a range of remedies to restore balanced competition to the marketplace.

* * *

[O]ther nations have challenged the findings of several Section 201 investigations before the WTO. To date, the result is the same every time: the WTO strikes down every Section 201 safeguard measure. The WTO consistently finds that the ITC's positions under U.S. law regarding the definition of "unforeseen developments" and application of the causation standard, are contrary to the United States' international legal obligations. * * *

II. Overview of Section 201

* * *

The federal agency responsible for conducting Section 201 safeguard investigations is the ITC, an independent federal agency with quasi-judicial authority. The ITC is charged with determining whether "an article is being imported into the United States in such increased quantities as to be a substantial cause of serious injury, or the threat thereof, to the domestic industry producing an article like or directly competitive with the imported article." A substantial cause is defined as "a cause which is important and not less than any other cause." Consequently, both the injury and causal standards are higher in a Section 201 investiga-

---

52. 19 U.S.C. § 2252(c)(2)(A).

53. 19 U.S.C. § 2252(c)(2)(B).

* Copyright © 2007 and reprinted with permission.

tion as compared to an anti-dumping or countervailing duty case. If the ITC makes an affirmative injury determination under Section 201, the investigation proceeds to a remedy phase. During the remedy phase, ITC recommends specific actions to address the serious injury to the domestic industry.

* * *

As previously noted, the United States has lost every safeguard action challenged at the WTO. One recent loss, the United States–Steel case, involved arguably the largest safeguard investigation ever undertaken by the ITC, and serves as a good example of the difficulties that the United States is encountering in coordinating its Section 201 actions with its international obligations. * * *

In June 2001, President Bush initiated a Section 201 investigation to determine whether certain steel articles were being imported into the United States in such increased quantities as to cause or threaten substantial injury to the domestic industry. The Commission conducted numerous days of hearings, and the parties submitted tens of thousands of pages in pleadings. The ITC concluded that twelve steel import products (out of thirty-three categories) were a cause of serious injury, or threat thereof, to the domestic industry. Several nations challenged the ITC's determination at the WTO and won at both the panel and the Appellate Body. The final report of the Appellate Body found that the ITC's determination failed to satisfy the requirements of the Agreement on Safeguards, specifically with respect to, inter alia, the unforeseen developments requirement, the causation standard applied, and the parallelism doctrine. This section will analyze each of these three elements.

B.   Unforeseen Developments

Under Article XIX(1)(a) of the GATT, in order to serve as the basis for a safeguard action, a flood of damaging imports must be "a result of unforeseen developments." Both the GATT 1947 and the GATT 1994 include this "unforeseen developments" requirement, but the Agreement on Safeguards—which entered into force at the same time as the GATT 1994 and was intended to clarify it—conspicuously omits any mention of unforeseen developments. This omission is particularly glaring in Article 2.1 of the Agreement on Safeguards, which otherwise closely reflects the language of Article XIX(1)(a) of the GATT. * * *

* * *

In the United States–Steel safeguard proceeding, the WTO panel admitted that "there is no reference to unforeseen developments in the Agreement on Safeguards." However, following its decisions in [earlier cases], the panel explained that the Agreement on Safeguards and the GATT must be read conterminously and required the United States to show that the flood of imports at issue resulted from unforeseen developments. The ITC found that unforeseen developments, such as the economic crises in Russia and Asia, the continued strength of the U.S. economy, and the persistent appreciation of the U.S. dollar, caused the increase in steel imports. Even though the panel agreed that these represented "a plausible set of unforeseen developments that may have resulted in increased imports to the United States from various sources," it held that the ITC's Report "[fell] short of demonstrating that such developments actually resulted in increased imports into the United States causing serious injury to the relevant domestic producers." Because the ITC only demonstrated that unforeseen developments caused a general increase in steel imports but not how unforeseen developments led to increased imports of specific products, the panel determined that the Section 201 action was inconsistent with both the GATT and the Agreement on Safeguards. The Appellate Body upheld this ruling on appeal.

C. The Non–Attribution Requirement of Injury Causation

To serve as a basis for a safeguard action, U.S. law requires the ITC to find that the increase in imports is "a substantial cause of serious injury, or threat thereof, to the domestic industry producing an article like or directly competitive with the imported article." Article 4.2(b) of the Agreement on Safeguards also requires the aggrieved party to demonstrate "the existence of the causal link between increased imports of the product concerned and serious injury or threat thereof." However, the ITC and the WTO interpret this requirement quite differently. The ITC concept of causation requires that there be a causal link between increased imports and injury to the domestic industry; it must be determined that imports are no less important than any other potential source of injury. Alternatively, the WTO's interpretation effectively requires the ITC to identify and systematically rule out all of the possible alternative causes of injury other than the increase of imports at issue. * * *

The Appellate Body stated that Article 4.2(b) does not require that increased imports be the sole cause of the serious injury. The Appellate Body found that the language in Article 4.2(b) forbidding the attribution of injury caused by "factors other than increased imports" to increased imports does not mean that the existence of such factors will prevent a party from meeting the causation standard. Rather, the Appellate Body agreed only with the panel's interpretation of this language to mean that "the effects caused by increased imports must be distinguished from the effects caused by other factors." Thus, the Appellate Body found that there may be several factors contributing simultaneously to the injury suffered by the domestic industry, and that subject imports need not be the only source of injury, but rather a sufficient one.

* * *

D. NAFTA Provisions/Doctrine of Parallelism

The Doctrine of Parallelism provides, in essence, that all imports included in an injury analysis in a safeguard case must also be covered by the safeguard remedy. This requirement has proven to be yet another stumbling block for the ITC at the WTO with respect to its determinations affecting nations that have signed free trade agreements with the United States, such as the North America Free Trade Agreement ("NAFTA") co-signatories. Specifically, the WTO disagrees with the provision under U.S. law which allows the President to exclude from a safeguard remedy those imports from NAFTA countries which do not account for a substantial share of total imports or do not "contribute importantly to the serious injury, or threat thereof, found by the [ITC]."

* * *

The WTO's decision in United States–Steel essentially affirmed [an earlier] holding that imports included in the injury determination must correspond with those products covered in the remedy. If there is a "gap" between the imports that were determined to have caused injury and those covered in the remedy, then the relevant authority must explicitly demonstrate that the imports included in the safeguard remedy are, in and of themselves, sufficient to satisfy all of the conditions for a safeguard action.

AUTHORS' COMMENT ON SPECIAL SAFEGUARD RULES FOR CHINESE IMPORTS

In addition to the general rule in Section 201, U.S. law has a special provision for safeguard measures relating to imports from China. *See* 19 U.S.C. § 2451. Enacted in the U.S.-China Relations Act of 2000 and as a condition to China's accession to the WTO, the authorization for these "Section 421" safeguard measures arose out of concerns over a potential flood of inexpensive Chinese imports. The most significant difference for safeguard determinations under Section 421 is that a challenged Chinese import need merely be a "significant cause"—that is, it "need not be equal to or greater than any other cause"—for only a "material" injury to domestic industry. *See* 19 U.S.C. § 2451(c).

The number of recent safeguard investigations demonstrates the rising importance of imports from China. Since 2003, the ITC has initiated six investigations under Section 421, but none under Section 201. The ITC announced its first affirmative recommendation of safeguard measures under Section 421 (as to vehicle tires from China) in June 2009. President Obama then adopted a three-year schedule of tariffs that began at thirty-five percent. *See* Proclamation No. 8414, 74 Fed. Reg. 47,861 (Sept. 17, 2009). More such proceedings are expected before the authorization under Section 421 expires in 2013.

QUESTIONS AND COMMENTS

1. Does GATT Article XIX authorize unilateral action in response to import injury? Is relief for import injury tied to GATT-derived trade concessions?

2. Note the operative language of Article XIX: imports "in such increased quantities * * * to cause or threaten serious injury to domestic producers * * * of like or directly competitive products." Under U.S. law, the basic authority to impose safeguard measures is set forth in 19 U.S.C. § 2251 (Section 201 of the Trade Act of 1974); the procedures and standards to be applied by the "competent authority"—the International Trade Commission (ITC)—are set forth in § 2252; and the ultimate role of the President is defined in § 2253. Do the domestic standards that the ITC must apply in making safeguard "determinations" comply with the basic criteria defined by GATT Article XIX?

3. Which of the enterprises or groups in this Problem may petition the ITC for a determination of eligibility for import relief? How else may ITC determinations of import injury be initiated? *See* 19 U.S.C. § 2252(b).

4. The ITC observes in its *Steel* determination that the first step in the analysis is to identify "the domestic industry producing an article that is like or directly competitive with the imported article." Why is that a necessary first step?

5. Suppose certain highly efficient and modernized U.S. athletic footwear companies side with Sneaker World in an import injury determination. Will that hurt the chances of an affirmative import injury finding for Kids? Should escape clause proceedings be used to protect inefficient firms from import competition? *See also* 19 U.S.C. § 2252(c)(6)(A).

6. The *Steel* determination also sets forth the remainder of the statutory test for safeguard measures. On the "increased imports" element, the AFA in our Problem should have little difficulty convincing the ITC of an "actual" increase of imported athletic footwear. But note that this element can also be satisfied if an increase has occurred "relative to domestic production." *See* 19 U.S.C. § 2252(c)(1)(C). What might that mean?

7. Has the domestic athletic footwear producing industry been "seriously injured"? The *Steel* determination describes the basic definition of this term as well as the (non-exhaustive) list of relevant factors set forth in 19 U.S.C. § 2252(c)(1)(A). What facts could the AFA and Kids cite in our Problem to support an affirmative finding by the ITC on this issue?

8. If this test is not met, has the domestic athletic footwear producing industry been "threatened with serious injury"? The *Steel* determination again describes the basic definition of the term as well as the (non-exhaustive) list of relevant factors set forth in 19 U.S.C. § 2252(c)(1)(B). What facts could the AFA and Kids cite in our Problem to support an affirmative finding by the ITC on this issue?

9. Are the imports of athletic footwear in this Problem a "substantial cause" of serious injury to the domestic industry? *See* 19 U.S.C. § 2252(c)(1)(C). What might other causes be? What further information would you like to have? Should the significance of the industry for our national economy—*e.g.*, athletic footwear vs. steel—affect the outcome? Finally, it is enough for the AFA to show that the U.S. is experiencing a recession and thus that consumers are more cost-conscious than normal? *See* the ITC's *Steel* determination.

10. Article 4 of the WTO Safeguards Agreement concerns the determination of serious injury or threat hereof. Article 4.2(b) requires "objective evidence" to prove the existence of "the causal link" between increased imports and the injury determination. Further, "when factors other than increased imports are causing injury to the domestic industry at the same time, such injury shall not be attributed to increased imports."

As the Pickard and Kimble excerpt explains, the WTO in the Steel safeguards case criticized the ITC's analysis of the causation issue as compared to this standard. In another decision (on South Korean line pipe in 2002), the WTO criticized the ITC for a "mere assertion" that challenged imports were "an important cause of serious injury and * * * not less than any other cause." *See* 19 U.S.C. § 2252(b)(1)(B). This approach, the WTO declared, did not "establish explicitly, through a reasoned and adequate explanation, that injury caused by factors other than increased imports is not attributed to increased imports." *See* Appellate Body Report, WT/DS202/AB/R (Feb. 15, 2002). Does this mean that basic "substantial cause" rule of U.S. law does not comport with the "causal link" test in Article 4.2(b) of the Safeguards Agreement?

11. The United States has lost a number of Safeguards Agreement disputes before the WTO. Australia and New Zealand successfully challenged U.S. escape clause restraints on lamb. The European Union did likewise regarding wheat gluten, and India prevailed concerning wool shirts and blouses. The Pickard and Kimble excerpt also describes the U.S. loss on steel safeguards. What are the consequences of losing a dispute before the WTO? Problems 7.0 through 7.2 above examined this issue in detail.

12. Why would it ever be appropriate for a developed country such as the U.S.—with a mature economy and highly competitive domestic markets— to resort to "safeguard" measures? What circumstances could justify such an action?

13. Finally, the Steel safeguards case again demonstrates the variety of "moving parts" in trade remedy cases. Opponents promptly challenged the imposition of the safeguard measures in both U.S. courts and the WTO. The Federal Circuit upheld the action as a matter of domestic law. *See Corus Group PLC v. ITC*, 352 F.3d 1351 (Fed. Cir. 2003). As noted in the Pickard & Kimble excerpt, however, the WTO Appellate Body declared that the duties violated the U.S.'s obligations under Article XIX of GATT and the Safeguards Agreement. *See* Appellate Body Report, *U.S.-Definitive Safeguard Measures on Imports of Certain Steel Products*, WT/DS248/AB/R, *et al.* (adopted Dec. 10, 2003).

But before the WTO could authorize sanctions, President Bush rescinded the duties in December, 2003, pursuant to corresponding authority in 19 U.S.C. § 2254(b)(1). Nonetheless, in the meantime domestic interests separately petitioned the ITA and ITC to impose *CVDs* or *ADs* on many of the same products. Precisely because it found that the temporary safeguard measures effectively mitigated the damaging effects of imports, the ITC concluded that there was no material injury or threat thereof to justify responsive duties on either basis. *See Nucor Corp. v. U.S.*, 414 F.3d 1331 (Fed. Cir. 2005)(upholding the ITC's determinations).

PART B.   IMPORT INJURY RELIEF

Establishing injury is a precondition to receiving some relief. Import injury relief available under Title II of the Trade Act of 1974 is basically of two kinds: (1) Presidential relief designed to protect the domestic producers of like or directly competitive products; and (2) trade adjustment assistance to workers and firms displaced economically by the import competition. Adjustment assistance is seen as a means to accommodate the injury caused by import competition. Protective relief tends to be awarded when the President considers the import competition to be fundamentally disruptive. The President must be ready to expect "compensatory action" (retaliation) by the exporting nation. Such action may be authorized because escape clause relief is not (in contrast to CVD and AD) taken against unfair trade practices. Rather, the increased import competition is fair but injurious.

Since the statutory purposes and criteria for each kind of relief differ, the opening materials in Part B concern Presidential protective measures and the succeeding materials in Part C consider adjustment assistance.

U.S. INTERNATIONAL TRADE COMMISSION

STEEL
INVESTIGATION NO. TA–201–73.
Publication No. 3479, pp. 353–356 (December, 2001).

* * *

VIEWS ON REMEDY OF THE COMMISSION

I.   INTRODUCTION

Having found that increased imports are a substantial cause of serious injury or the threat of serious injury to certain domestic industries, we must now recommend to the President the action that will address the serious injury or threat of serious injury and be most effective in facilitating the efforts of each domestic industry to make a positive adjustment to import competition. In deciding what relief to recommend, we have taken into account the considerations set forth in section 202(e)(5)(B) of the Trade Act of 1974,[2] including the form and amount of action that will, in our view, remedy the serious injury we have found to exist; commitments submitted by firms in the domestic industries during the course of the investigation; information available to the Commission concerning the conditions of competition in domestic and world markets and likely developments affecting such conditions during the period for which action is being requested; whether international negotiations may be constructive to address the serious injury or to facilitate adjustment; and the arguments of the parties.

---

2.   19 U.S.C. § 2252(e)(5)(B).

The action we recommend must conform to certain statutory limitations with respect to the amount and duration of the relief. * * * We must also describe the likely short-and long-term effects of taking and not taking the recommended action on each pertinent domestic industry and its workers, other domestic industries, and consumers.

A. **Form of Recommended Remedies**

The statute authorizes the Commission to recommend several forms of import relief, including additional duties, quantitative restrictions, tariff rate quotas, and adjustment measures, as well as a combination of these remedies. In determining which of these forms would be most effective in remedying the serious injury being suffered by the industries in question, we have examined closely the costs and benefits of each remedy. As we discuss below, we believe that tariff-based remedies will provide each industry with the most appropriate and easily-administered form of relief for the products for which we made affirmative injury or threat of injury findings, while minimizing market disruption to that necessary to remedy injury and facilitating positive adjustment. These remedies are generally additional duties. For two products we have recommended tariff-rate quotas that include additional duties.

In general, the tariff-based remedies we are recommending are intended to increase domestic prices, shipment volumes, and industry profitability and therefore allow the domestic industries to make additional investments in the modernization and rationalization of their productive facilities. The recommended additional duty levels are also intended to help restore the market share of seriously injured domestic industries to the levels that existed prior to the import surges and maintain the market shares of industries threatened with serious injury. We note that the additional duties do not prohibit the importation of any products.

* * *

Duration and Degressivity. For all products, we recommend that the tariffs, or tariff-rate quotas, be imposed for a four-year period. We believe that a four-year period of relief is necessary to give domestic industries time both to generate the profits needed to complete the investments called for in their adjustment plans and the time to implement the plans themselves. We recognize that a relief action of more than three years will require the Commission to conduct a mid-course review under section 204(a)(2) of the Trade Act. Such an investigation would provide the Commission with an opportunity to review the progress of the various industries in implementing their adjustment plans. It would also provide the President, after receiving the Commission's report, with the opportunity to reduce or terminate relief if relief is no longer necessary to prevent or remedy serious injury or if the industry has not made adequate efforts to make a positive adjustment to import relief.

For most products, we also recommend that the additional tariffs (including that recommended in our tariff rate quotas) be phased down by three percentage points per year during the period of relief. We believe that this phase down, together with the level of tariffs we have recommended, will strike a balance between yielding positive and immediate revenue effects for the industries in the short-term while minimizing the impact on consumers and the market in the long run.

* * *

Trade Adjustment Assistance. We have also considered whether to recommend adjustment measures, such as the trade adjustment assistance programs administered by the U.S. Department of Commerce and the U.S. Department of Labor. The assistance and funding that these programs offer is limited in amount and scope. In the context of the record of this investigation, trade adjustment assistance alone would not provide the amount or type of assistance that would remedy the serious injury or threat of serious injury and facilitate adjustment. In particular, trade adjustment assistance would not limit the influx of imports that we have found is a substantial cause of serious injury or threat of serious injury to the pertinent domestic industries. However, such adjustment assistance may prove useful in conjunction with import relief, particularly insofar as it may offer retraining to workers displaced by any consolidation or rationalization the domestic industry may undertake to increase its competitiveness. Thus, pursuant to section 202(a) of the Trade Act, we have notified the Secretary of Commerce and the Secretary of Labor of our affirmative determinations. Under section 202(a) of the Trade Act, applications for adjustment assistance by firms or workers in the pertinent domestic industries are to be given expedited treatment once the Commission makes an affirmative determination.

[**Authors' Note**: On March 5, 2002, President George W. Bush issued a Proclamation on the basis of these recommendations by the ITC. The Proclamation imposed annually decreasing tariffs on the covered steel products, although only for a three year period. *See* Proclamation No. 7529, 67 Fed. Reg. 10553 (Mar. 5, 2002). As noted in Comment 13 above, the President then terminated the tariffs in December, 2003, reasoning that the effectiveness of the tariffs "ha[d] been impaired by changed economic circumstances." *See* Proclamation No. 7741, 68 Fed. Reg. 68,-483, ¶ 6 (Dec. 4, 2003).]

ROSENTHAL AND GILBERT, THE 1988 AMENDMENTS TO SECTION 201: IT ISN'T JUST FOR IMPORT RELIEF ANYMORE

20 Law & Pol'y Int'l Bus. 403, 425–429 (1989).*

Without doubt, the overriding congressional concern with the 1988 amendments to section 201 is that the law be used to promote adjustment. Although the 1974 Act had specifically encouraged adjustment both by statute and legislative history, the Trade Act makes adjustment the fundamental purpose of the escape clause. * * *

---

* Copyright Law and Policy in International Business. Reprinted with Permission.

ADJUSTMENT PLANS, COMMITMENTS, AND CONSULTATIONS

* * *

As enacted, the law retains the requirement for USTR to consult with the petitioner prior to submitting a statement of proposed adjustment measures to "consider the adequacy of proposed adjustment measures in the context of any relief which might be provided and thereby enable the petitioner to develop a more effective statement of adjustment measures." The consultation must be with the USTR and any other governmental agency deemed appropriate by the USTR. Because the statute requires notice of the request for consultation to be published in the *Federal Register,* it is unlikely that any petitioner would seek consultations prior to filing a petition for fear of alerting adverse interests.

While consultations on the adjustment plan are mandatory if requested by the petitioner, the 1988 Trade Act does not retain the Finance Committee's proposed requirement that petitioners actually submit a plan. Instead, the Act makes submission of a plan optional. Nevertheless, Congress strongly encouraged the submission of adjustment plans.

Even though submission of an adjustment plan is not a requirement under the Trade Act, sophisticated industries and counsel would—if they could—submit a plan under the law prior to 1988. Indeed, submissions of plans and commitments undoubtedly were essential to the success of the motorcycle and specialty steel petitions. Despite the lack of a requirement to submit adjustment plans and commitments, the Act's emphasis on adjustment, as a practical matter, makes the failure of industries and firms to submit plans *of some sort* a serious miscalculation if they are to achieve relief under the new act.

* * *

PRESIDENTIAL STANDARDS

The 1988 Trade Act's emphasis on adjustment quite naturally is reflected in the new standard for action by the President. If the criteria for action by the President are met, the President "shall take all appropriate and feasible action within his power which the President determines *will facilitate efforts by the domestic industry to make a positive adjustment to import competition* and provide greater economic and social benefits than costs."[159] Thus, the focus of the President's remedy determination must be on adjustment. In making this determination, the President specifically must consider the probable effectiveness of the actions that might be taken to facilitate positive adjustment to import competition. Further, the range of possible actions that the President may take has been expanded to include initiation of international negotiations, submission to Congress of legislative proposals to facilitate efforts of the domestic industry to adjust to import competition, and the taking of any

---

159. Trade Act of 1988, § 201(a), 102 Stat. 1225 (emphasis added) [19 U.S.C. § 2253(a)(1)(A)]
* * *

action that the President considers appropriate under the statutory standard for relief. Thus, just as the Commission has been given broader options in the area of remedy recommendations, the President now has a wider spectrum of import and non-import related actions to employ.

RECENT DECISION, "THE HARLEY-DAVIDSON CASE: ESCAPING THE ESCAPE CLAUSE"

16 Law & Pol'y Int'l Bus. 325 (1984).*

In *Heavyweight Motorcycles, and Engines and Power Train Subassemblies Therefor,* more widely known as the *Harley-Davidson* case[1] the U.S. International Trade Commission (ITC) found, pursuant to the so-called "escape clause" in section 201 of the Trade Act of 1974, that heavyweight motorcycles were being imported into the United States in such increased quantities as to constitute a substantial cause of the threat of serious injury to the U.S. industry producing like or directly competitive articles. As required by the 1974 Act, the Commission also recommended to the President the relief that it thought necessary to prevent the threatened injury—in this case, a 45 percent ad valorem tariff increase, decreasing over a five year period to pre-relief levels. On April 1, 1983, the President announced that he would implement the Commission's recommended remedy, modified only by tariff rate quotas which would assure continued access to the U.S. market for countries which export relatively few motorcycles to the United States.

The actions of both the Commission and the President represent significant departures from past practice. The Commission majority's refusal to give weight to recessionary elements in the U.S. economy in determining causation of injury constitutes an explicit rejection of prior Commission reasoning.[8] Such thinking, together with the Commission's reliance on the threat provision of the escape clause, would tend to promote more findings of remediable injury for U.S. companies, and thus offer an avenue of escape to U.S. industries in future cases from the restrictive "substantial cause" provision of section 201.

As for the President, acceptance of the Commission's recommendation sharply contrasts with the tendency of former Executives either to reject protective remedies recommended by the ITC, or at least to substitute less restrictive measures such as orderly marketing agreements or trade adjustment assistance to the domestic industry. * * *

The philosophy expressed by the dissenting commissioners in the motor vehicles case was adopted by Chairman Eckes and Commissioner Haggart in *Harley-Davidson.* Many of the same economic conditions could

---

* Copyright © 1984 Law and Policy In International Business. Reprinted with permission.

1. Heavyweight Motorcycles, and Engines and Power Train Subassemblies Therefor, 48 Fed.Reg. 6043 (1983), Investigation No. TA-201-44, USITC Pub. 1342 (1983).

8. *See, e.g.,* Certain Motor Vehicles and Certain Chassis and Bodies Therefor, 45 Fed. Reg. 85, 194 (1980), Investigation No. TA-201-44, USITC Pub. 1110 (1980) (finding of no substantial cause or threat of serious injury) [Part A, *supra*].

be found in both cases, most notably, the drop in overall demand. Commissioner Stern found, as she had in the case of the motor vehicles investigation, that a decrease in demand for motorcycles was a more important cause of the threat of injury than increased imports; thus, she voted against granting Harley-Davidson any relief. The majority, however, were emphatically opposed to this view. Chairman Alfred Eckes states in the first paragraph of his opinion that "[t]o deny relief to the motorcycle industry in its present precarious position on the rationale that recessionary factors are more of a cause or threat of serious injury is to frustrate the intent of Congress."

As Commissioner Stern points out in her opinion, however, Harley-Davidson's major loss of market share over the period investigated was to another U.S. producer; market share between importers and the U.S. industry remained constant in the first nine months of 1982 as compared with the corresponding period in 1981. Indeed, Commissioner Haggart, who voted with Chairman Eckes in the affirmative, noted that both U.S. consumption and imports decreased by approximately 12 percent during that same period and, for that reason, concluded that imports could not be considered a substantial cause of serious injury.

Chairman Eckes, while acknowledging that the unusual length and severity of the present recession had created "unique problems" for the industry, maintained that if the Commission were to analyze the causation question in this way, "it would be impossible in many cases for a cyclical industry experiencing serious injury to obtain relief under section 201 during a recession. In my opinion Congress could not have intended for the Commission to interpret the law this way." Nevertheless, with both the statute and the legislative history deliberately enigmatic on how the Commission was to interpret this particular point of law, the Chairman chose to base his opinion on what he termed "an unambiguous case for relief"—not serious injury, but threat thereof.

For both commissioners in the majority, the presence of the large inventories of unsold imports was the factor distinguishing *Harley-Davidson* from the motor vehicles case. The most significant differences between the two cases remain analytical, however, not factual. Analytical inconsistency is, by itself, not a surprising outcome from the Commission. In fact, it has been said that an analysis of Commission precedent is enlightening only to the extent that it confirms the case-by-case latitude of the ITC. Indeed, the statutory framework seems to have had such freedom precisely in mind. *Harley-Davidson*, however, represents a departure from past Commission practice in two important respects: first, in the deliberate reduction, apparently on policy grounds, in weight given to economic factors of causation, and second, in the use of the perceived imminence of threat as an escape from the inflexibilities of the statutory criteria. If the factors utilized by the *Harley-Davidson* Commission can be taken in any way as an omen of future Commission interpretation of the 1974 Act, then it appears that the Commission may have adopted an arguably major expansion of the criteria for affirmative findings.

Consistent refusal to accord due weight to recessionary factors in determining threat of injury in the ITC's substantial cause analysis would go far toward transforming section 201 from an import relief to an industrial relief provision. Such a policy would effectively reduce the burden on U.S. petitioners to a showing that an increase in imports has been a contributing, rather than substantial, cause of difficulty experienced by the domestic industry.

The use of threat analysis compounds this effect by moving the serious injury into the future. Such analysis shifts the burden from the U.S. industry, which must no longer prove present serious injury already caused by increased imports, to the foreign exporter, who must prove, in effect, that its intentions are honorable. When such an exporter is brought to the bar by an obviously ailing U.S. industry, it will not find it easy to demonstrate that its buildup of inventory is the result of miscalculation rather than malevolence, or that such a buildup is due more to the inability of a foreign manufacturer to react quickly enough to an unresponsive U.S. economy than it is to a plot to take over a vulnerable U.S. market.

However plausible the reassurance of the exporting company, the Commission technically can ignore such arguments altogether, as the Senate Report to the 1974 Act states that the Commission may base its finding of threat simply on projections of what will occur "if import trends continued unabated." Such forecasts of future injury must always be speculative to some extent; they also will be influenced by the Commission's definition of what constitutes a U.S. industry and competitive or "like" products in a particular case. In *Harley-Davidson,* for instance, the Commission's acceptance of the petitioner's definition of the industry cut off further exploration of the fact that 80 percent of the threatening motorcycle inventory was of a type only minimally competitive with the kind of heavyweight motorcycles made by Harley-Davidson.

The absence of present serious injury and the lack of competitiveness between the over 1000cc bikes manufactured by Harley-Davidson and the under 800cc bikes which constitute 80 percent of the threatening inventory suggest that a primary motivation behind the Commission's broad provision of relief and the petitioner's broad definition of the affected industry was simply to allow Harley-Davidson more time to begin competing in the popular small motorcycle market; such an adjustment clearly was envisioned by the relief statement of the majority. Certainly one of the goals of article XIX and the U.S. escape clause was to provide time for an afflicted domestic industry to adjust to competition, provided that the industry meets the "fair and reasonable test" embodied in the U.S. statutory criteria for temporary relief. Provision of such relief outside of the statutory criteria, however, is a function of industrial policy, not of the temporary emergency regulation of fair trade through the escape clause.

The escape clause embodied in section 201 represents U.S. implementation of article XIX of the GATT. Because of economic pressures that have beset the United States in the past two decades, this implementing provision has distanced itself from some of the more basic tenets of the GATT escape clause in a way that clearly reflects the Senate Committee's wish that "no domestic industry which has suffered serious injury should be cut off from relief for foreign policy reasons."

The escape clause is not a suitable tool for setting U.S. policy. The GATT clause embodies that agreement's goals of non-discrimination and reciprocity among trading partners. To that end, the U.S. escape clause must be construed as a balance which should favor neither U.S. trading partners nor U.S. industry, but rather should provide an element of protection for both—protection to U.S. industries faced with emergency conditions of competition, and protection to foreign exporters which depend on U.S. acceptance of GATT achievements. The very nature of section 201 as an emergency measure, triggered more or less mechanically by extraordinary circumstances of fair competition, suggests that the more that it is used, the less effective it will become for its prophylactic purpose.

PRESS SUMMARY OF URUGUAY ROUND AGREEMENTS

(GATT, Dec. 14, 1993).

AGREEMENT ON SAFEGUARDS

Article XIX of the General Agreement allows a GATT member to take a "safeguard" action to protect a specific domestic industry from an unforeseen increase of imports of any product which is causing, or which is likely to cause, serious injury to the industry.

The agreement breaks major ground in establishing a prohibition against so-called "grey area" measures, and in setting a "sunset clause" on all safeguard actions. The agreement stipulates that a member shall not seek, take or maintain any voluntary export restraints, orderly marketing arrangements or any other similar measures on the export or the import side. Any such measure in effect at the time of entry into force of the agreement would be brought into conformity with this agreement, or would have to be phased out within four years after the entry into force of the agreement establishing the [W]TO. An exception could be made for one specific measure for each importing member, subject to mutual agreement with the directly concerned member, where the phase-out date would be 31 December 1999.

All existing safeguard measures taken under Article XIX of the General Agreement 1947 shall be terminated not later than eight years after the date on which they were first applied or five years after the date of entry into force of the agreement establishing the [W]TO, whichever comes later.

The agreement sets out requirements for safeguard investigations which include public notice for hearings and other appropriate means for interested parties to present evidence, including on whether a measure would be in the public interest. In the event of critical circumstances, a provisional safeguard measure may be imposed based upon a preliminary determination of serious injury. The duration of such a provisional measure would not exceed 200 days.

The agreement sets out the criteria for "serious injury" and the factors which must be considered in determining the impact of imports. The safeguard measure should be applied only to the extent necessary to prevent or remedy serious injury and to facilitate adjustment. Where quantitative restrictions are imposed, they normally should not reduce the quantities of imports below the annual average for the last three representative years for which statistics are available, unless clear justification is given that a different level is necessary to prevent or remedy serious injury.

In principle, safeguard measures have to be applied irrespective of source. In cases in which a quota is allocated among supplying countries, the member applying restrictions may seek agreement with other members having a substantial interest in supplying the product concerned. Normally, allocation of shares would be on the basis of proportion of total quantity or value of the imported product over a previous representative period. However, it would be possible for the importing country to depart from this approach if it could demonstrate, in consultations under the auspices of the Safeguards Committee, that imports from certain contracting parties had increased disproportionately in relation to the total increase and that such a departure would be justified and equitable to all suppliers. The duration of the safeguard measure in this case cannot exceed four years.

The agreement lays down time limits for all safeguard measures. Generally, the duration of a measure should not exceed four years though this could be extended up to a maximum of eight years, subject to confirmation of continued necessity by the competent national authorities and if there is evidence that the industry is adjusting. Any measure imposed for a period greater than one year should be progressively liberalized during its lifetime. No safeguard measure could be applied again to a product that had been subject to such action for a period equal to the duration of the previous measure, subject to a non-application period of at least two years. A safeguard measure with a duration of 180 days or less may be applied again to the import of a product if at least one year had elapsed since the date of introduction of the measure on that product, and if such a measure had not been applied on the same product more than twice in the five-year period immediately preceding the date of introduction of the measure.

The agreement envisages consultations on compensation for safeguard measures. Where consultations are not successful, the affected members may withdraw equivalent concessions or other obligations under GATT 1994. However, such action is not allowed for the first three years of the safeguard measure if it conforms to the provisions of the agreement, and is taken as a result of an absolute increase in imports.

Safeguard measures would not be applicable to a product from a developing country member, if the share of the developing country member in the imports of the product concerned does not exceed 3 per cent, and that developing country members with less than 3 per cent import share collectively account for no more than 9 per cent of total imports of the product concerned. A developing country member has the right to extend the period of application of a safeguard measure for a period of up to two years beyond the normal maximum. It can also apply a safeguard measure again to a product that had been subject to such an action after a period equal to half of the duration of the previous measure, subject to a non-application period of at least two years.

The agreement would establish a Safeguards Committee which would oversee the operation of its provisions and, in particular, be responsible for surveillance of its commitments.

R. FOLSOM, M. GORDON, J.A. SPANOGLE, INTERNATIONAL TRADE AND ECONOMIC RELATIONS IN A NUTSHELL

Chapter 3 (2008).*

THE WTO SAFEGUARDS AGREEMENT

A Safeguards Code on escape clause and related "gray area" protective measures was agreed upon during the Uruguay Round. This WTO code was approved and implemented by Congress in December of 1994 under the Uruguay Round Agreements Act. One of its more important prohibitions is against seeking, undertaking or maintaining voluntary export or import restraint agreements (VERs and OMAs). Substantive and procedural escape clause rules are also established, notably on proof of "serious domestic injury," opportunities to present evidence and a maximum four-year period of protection (extendable to eight years). The right to retaliate when another country invokes escape clause relief is suspended for the first three years of such invocation. Special rules limit the use of escape clause measures to exports from developing nations and extend the potential for their use on imports by such nations.

Interpretation

The WTO Appellate Body rulings concerning the Safeguards Agreement stringently limit use of escape clause remedies. In 2001, three rulings went against U.S. safeguard measures. In *U.S.—Wheat Gluten from the EC*, the Appellate Body emphasized the critical issue of causation. The U.S. International Trade Commission's analysis of factors other than imports that may have caused domestic industry injury lacked clarity and was inadequate. In addition, U.S. notice of intent to impose safe-

---

guards had to be "immediate," sufficient to allow a "meaningful exchange" of consultations. In *U.S.—Lamb Meat from New Zealand,* the Appellate Body reiterated that all causation factors must be isolated and examined. Further, it rejected the "domestic industry" definition adopted by the ITC because growers were included. Exclusion of free trade partners (Canada, Mexico) from escape clause remedies is not permissible if their imports were included in the injury determination. Both of these decisions emphasize the need for the ITC to find "unforseen developments" in its injury determinations. No guidance is given by the Appellate Body on this term.

The third 2001 Appellate Body ruling against U.S. safeguards concerned cotton yarn from Pakistan. This decision came under the Agreement on Textiles and Clothing. The Appellate Body rejected exclusion of vertically integrated yarn producers from the definition of "domestic industry." Similarly, exclusion of Mexican yarn from the relief was not permissible. In 2002, the Appellate Body ruled against U.S. safeguards on line pipe from Korea, finding under strict scrutiny a number of substantive and procedural errors.

U.S. Steel Tariffs

In March of 2002, President Bush imposed tariffs of up to 30 percent on imported steel over three years. This escape clause relief was tempered by exclusions for selected steel from selected countries. Most Australian and Japanese steel products, for example, were not subject to these U.S. tariffs. About half of all EU steel imports were exempt. Canada and Mexico were fully exempt. Numerous WTO members commenced dispute proceedings under the WTO Safeguards Agreement. In 2003, the Appellate Body ruled the U.S. tariffs on steel illegal under the WTO Safeguards Agreement. The Appellate Body held that the U.S. erred in utilizing the protective tariffs some four years after the surge of steel imports during the Asian economic meltdown, and that exclusion of NAFTA partners Canada and Mexico was improper. The European Union threatened over $2 billion annually in retaliatory tariffs on U.S. exports of clothing, citrus and boats, products thought to be politically damaging to the Bush Administration. In November 2003, the United States lifted its escape clause steel tariffs.

Questions and Comments

1. Suppose that the ITC determines that all of the import injury requirements of Section 201 are met in our Sneaker problem. What relief may the ITC recommend to the President? *See* 19 U.S.C. § 2252(e)(2). What relief did the ITC recommend in the *Steel* case and what were the goals of that relief? (The excerpt on the *Harley–Davidson* case provides an historical perspective on this perennially controversial subject.)

2. Consider now the powers of the President as set forth in Section 203 (19 U.S.C. § 2253(a)). Consult that provision in order to answer the following questions:

(a) What relief may the President grant? Is he or she bound by the recommendations of the ITC? Is the President obligated to order at least *some* relief if the ITC finds an import injury and recommends relief?

(b) On the other hand, may the President order safeguards relief if the ITC finds that the import injury requirements were *not* met?

(c) Are there any limits on the amount or duration of the relief the President may order under U.S. law? In any event, are open-ended safeguard measures consistent with guiding principles of the Safeguards Agreement? Note that the President prematurely terminated the safeguard relief in both the *Harley–Davidson* case (after four years) and the *Steel* case (after not even two).

3.   What could the AFA and Kids do for their part both to justify and to structure an appropriate safeguards remedy? *See* 19 U.S.C. §§ 2252(a) and 2253(a) and the Rosenthal & Gilbert excerpt.

4.   Suppose that the AFA and Kids have a powerful lobby in Washington and are able to convince the White House of the importance of a special agreement with Indonesia limiting imports. *See* 19 U.S.C. § 2253(a)(3)(E). Would that be consistent with the policy of the Safeguards Agreement? *See* Article 11.

5.   Suppose that the ITC determines that the import injury requirements are not met in the first place. Do the AFA and Kids have any right of *judicial* review? *See* the Comment on Administrative and Judicial Procedure from Problem 7.0.

6.   Chapter 11 of the United States—Canada Free Trade Agreement and Chapter 8 of the NAFTA limit the use of escape clause proceedings with respect to goods coming from North American countries. Bilateral escape clause actions were essentially eliminated after 10 years. Restraints can be imposed on global escape clause relief as applied to North American goods. *See* R. Folsom, NAFTA and Free Trade in the Americas in a Nutshell (2008), Chapter 4.

But may the U.S. properly order relief on a "selective" basis (such as to exclude imports from NAFTA countries) when imposing safeguard remedies? Is "selective" relief consistent with the basic principles of GATT Article XIX? *See also* the Pickard & Kimble excerpt from Part A above (discussing the doctrine of "parallelism").

7.   A separate and different approach for relief from injury due to imports is provided by Section 406 of the Trade Act of 1974, 19 U.S.C. § 2436. Section 406 is modeled after the escape clause provisions of Section 201, but is directed at market disruption caused by imports from "Communist countries." (Is that the same as NMEs?) The two primary differences between Section 201 and Section 406 are, first, that Section 406 is directed only at imports of merchandise from countries with economies that are assumed not to operate on market principles, rather than all exporting countries; and, second, that the injury and causation standards under Section 406 are less severe than the standard under Section 201. Although still on the books, the geo-political developments of the last two decades have left little relevance for this provision.

8. Review the discussion of protective U.S. escape clause actions (notably regarding steel) in the excerpt from *International Trade and Economic Relations in a Nutshell*. Note that the U.S. has almost never won a WTO dispute over escape clause relief. Nevertheless, does Article 8 of the WTO Safeguards Agreement create a three-year "free ride" for protective escape clause remedies? *See* Article 8(3). When may WTO members respond to escape clause actions by suspending substantially equivalent trade benefits? *See* Articles 8(1) and 8(2).

PART C.　ADJUSTING TO IMPORT COMPETITION

Section 201 provides, at most, temporary (and often costly) protection from import competition. Adjustment to import competition is the longer term goal, resulting in competitive U.S. industries and markets. Temporary adjustment assistance payments and loans to workers and firms displaced by import competition have long been a feature of Title II of the Trade Act of 1974. Promoting more structural and permanent readjustments within domestic industries was the main thrust of 1988 amendments to Title II and its Section 201 proceedings. A further expansion of trade adjustment assistance was adopted in the Trade Promotion Authority-Trade Adjustment Assistance Act of 2002. Moreover, Congress occasionally makes temporary, although sometimes significant, changes to the rules governing trade adjustment assistance. A prominent recent example is The American Recovery and Reinvestment Act of 2009 (the "stimulus bill"), whose TAA provisions Congress, in late 2011, extended until 2014.

HEKIMOVA, CAN THE U.S. COURT OF INTERNATIONAL TRADE REVERSE AN AGENCY'S DETERMINATION OF ELIGIBILITY FOR TRADE ADJUSTMENT ASSISTANCE?

17 Fed. Circuit B.J. 685, 687–689 (2008).*

Introduction

Economists unanimously agree that the benefits of free trade to society outweigh the costs, but this is little consolation to workers whose employers have closed down because of import competition. In 1962, Congress sought to alleviate the burden on such workers by establishing a federal program providing income support, health care supplements, retraining allowances, and other benefits, known as trade adjustment assistance (TAA). Workers wishing to receive TAA benefits must petition the United States Department of Labor (DOL) to certify their eligibility under the criteria set out in § [222] of the Trade Act of 1974 ("Trade Act"). The United States Court of International Trade (CIT) has exclusive jurisdiction to review DOL's decisions on TAA petitions.

DOL has recently contested the CIT's authority to overrule DOL's determinations before the Federal Circuit. DOL argued that the statute governing TAA administration allows the CIT only to affirm DOL's

---

* Copyright © 2008 and reprinted with permission.

determination or to remand the case to DOL for further investigation.* * * The Federal Circuit reversed on different grounds and refrained from ruling on the CIT's authority to overrule DOL.

The question of whether CIT has authority to overrule DOL's determinations remains open. Furthermore, Congress extended the TAA program to farmers in 2002 and designated the United States Department of Agriculture (USDA) to determine their eligibility under § [222] of the Trade Act. The question of whether the CIT has authority to overrule the USDA is also open * * *.

* * *

II. The Statutory Scheme for Implementation of the TAA Program

Congress established the TAA program in 1962 to assist individuals who lost their jobs because of increased imports from foreign countries with which the United States signed free trade agreements. At that time, instances where foreign imports could crowd out a major share of domestic production were relatively rare. As the volume of imports and the number of free trade agreements increased, the TAA program became more prominent and underwent legislative overhauls in 1974 and 1988. The program was further amended in 1993 (separate sub-program related to NAFTA) and in 2002 (extending to secondarily affected workers and farmers). In fiscal year 2007, the program's budget was $855 million and DOL issued certification to 1,427 petitioners covering an estimated 146,-606 workers.*

Section [222] of the Trade Act, codified as 19 U.S.C. § 2272, establishes the eligibility criteria for TAA benefits. To certify workers as eligible for TAA benefits, DOL must determine that the workers fall in one of three broad categories: (1) they lost their jobs because of increased imports of the goods produced by their former employer; (2) they lost their jobs because their former employer shifted production to a foreign country * * *; or (3) they lost their jobs because their former employer was a "secondary firm" that supplied products to or finished the products of a primary certified firm. The statute specifies further requirements within each of these categories and instructs how certain terms should be interpreted and applied to specific industries.[19]

Judicial review of DOL's determination by the CIT is governed by 19 U.S.C. § 2395. Specifically, in subsection (b), the statute establishes that "[t]he findings of fact by the Secretary ... , if supported by substantial evidence, shall be conclusive; but the court, for good cause shown, may remand the case to such Secretary to take further evidence...." Subsection (c) confers jurisdiction to the CIT to "affirm the action of the Secretary ... or set such action aside in whole or in part." * * *

---

* [*Authors' Note*: In 2010, the corresponding numbers were $975 million on the basis of 2,718 certified petitions covering 227,882 workers. *See http://www.doleta.gov/tradeact/factsheet.cfm*]

19. [19 U.S.C.] § 2272(c).

MATEIKIS, THE FAIR TRACK TO EXPANDED FREE TRADE: MAKING TAA BENEFITS MORE ACCESSIBLE TO AMERICAN WORKERS

30 Hous. J. Int'l L. 1, 11–14 (2007).*

* * *

B. The Quid Pro Quo of Trade Adjustment Assistance for Fast Track Authority

Fast track authority has been "the central domestic political prerequisite" for the leadership role the United States has assumed on global trade liberalization since [the] Smoot–Hawley [Act of 1930]. "By delegating responsibility to the executive and by helping fashion a system that protected legislators from one-sided restrictive pressures, Congress made it possible for successive presidents to maintain and expand the liberal trade order."

And * * * Congress has often appeased workers' interests, at least in part, by improving the TAA program in exchange for support of major trade legislation, which has included fast track authority.

Until NAFTA and the Uruguay Round, U.S. trade liberalization generally rested on a broad consensus, based on the unambiguous economic theory that the gains from trade outweighed the costs and, therefore, the net welfare effect of expanded free trade was generally positive for consumers and exporters, even though it produced "losers" in import-competing sectors:

The central notion that governed the conception of the relationship of trade policy to domestic policy generally was that wherever trade barriers such as tariffs had direct price-distorting effects in the market of the importing country, removal of those barriers enhanced aggregate domestic welfare in that the total gains to consumers could be shown always to exceed the total losses to producers/workers. Put in this crude way, the case for trade liberalization appeared to be totally indifferent to any notion of a just distribution of benefits and burdens from the removal of trade restrictions.

The implied domestic political bargain embedded in the liberalism of the GATT trading regime was that the losers of expanded free trade would be compensated by the winners and, hence, the losers would not block trade liberalization due to questions of distributive justice[.] * * * So long as the economic benefits of expanded free trade were clear and the losers appeared to be roughly compensated for their losses, the politics of U.S. trade liberalization was fairly straightforward: Congress would grant the Executive branch fast track authority and workers displaced by expanded free trade would be entitled to receive TAA.

But, the political economy of trade in the United States has shifted since the mid–1990s. Following the extension of fast track authority in mid–1993, passage of the NAFTA implementing statute in late 1993, and the re-extension of fast track authority in early 1994, Congress refused to grant President Clinton fast track authority after it expired in late 1994. Since the mid–1990s the economic benefits of further U.S. trade liberalization have gotten murkier, and the opposition to it has become more pronounced. Then, after an eight-year hiatus, fast track negotiating authority was renewed on August 6, 2002, but not without a bruising political battle in the U.S. House of Representatives.

1.   The Necessary Grant of Fast Track Authority

It would be difficult, if not impossible, for the United States to expand free trade without the Congressional delegation of fast track authority to the Executive branch, because trading partners would be reluctant to enter into trade agreements with the United States unless they were confident that the agreement reached through negotiations would not be materially changed in Congress; and, unless Congress insulated itself from protectionist self-interests, and restrained itself from encumbering trade-agreement implementing legislation with excessive amendments and debate, trade agreements reached by the Executive branch would rarely, if ever, be voted on by Congress as negotiated. Indeed, they might never be voted on at all. Accordingly, all major U.S. trade legislation since the Trade Act of 1974 has been enacted using the fast track approach.

AUTHORS' COMMENT ON TRADE ADJUSTMENT ASSISTANCE BENEFITS

Workers properly certified by the Department of Labor are eligible for a variety of benefits and services (sometimes at the discretion of a person's home state) under the trade adjustment assistance program. Importance enhancements to this program were added by the 2009 stimulus bill, which the Trade Adjustment Assistance Extension Act of 2011 extended and further enhanced. These include reemployment services such as employment counseling, job search programs, and job referrals. A certified worker also may receive job search allowances to reimburse travel and subsistence costs. If the worker finds employment in a new geographic area, the TAA program provides "relocation allowances" to cover moving expenses, as well as a lump sum payment of three times the worker's prior weekly wage (subject to limits). In addition, the program provides extensive retraining assistance (again, subject to certain requirements and limits). The goal of this assistance is that a certified worker will find employment at a similar or higher skill level. Remedial education for occupational training may be available for an additional 26 weeks.

The most significant form of assistance is simple income support for workers, but generally only for those participating in a retraining program. Certified workers are eligible for up to 78 weeks of income support after the end of state unemployment insurance compensation. Workers in this category also may receive two years of support to cover health insurance costs in the form of tax credits amounting to 72.5% of monthly health insurance premiums. The "Reemployment Trade Adjustment Assistance" program created by the 2002 Act provides special benefits for workers over 50. If retraining is not appropriate and such older workers accept reemployment at a lower wage, they are eligible, as an alternative, for a "wage subsidy" of 50% of the difference between the old and new wages for up to two years (but not more than $10,000).

QUESTIONS AND COMMENTS

1. The rules governing trade adjustment assistance are set forth in Chapter 2 of Title II of the Trade Act. *See* 19 U.S.C § 2271 *et seq.* What entities may initiate a petition for such adjustment assistance? What are the general eligibility requirements for a "group of workers" to obtain such assistance?

2. Is adjustment assistance contingent upon an import injury determination by the ITC? Are the criteria for adjustment assistance the same as for ITC determinations of import injury?

3. Consider now 19 U.S.C. § 2272(b), which relates to "Adversely Affected Secondary Workers." What groups of workers are entitled to adjustment assistance under this provision? In our Problem, what kinds of workers would be "secondary workers" as compared to employees of Kids?

4. Now compare "import injury relief" discussed in Part B above with the "trade adjustment assistance" we are analyzing in this Part C:

(a) How does the nature of the relief granted under the authority in Section 201 differ from the nature of trade adjustment assistance?

(b) If the President denies relief under Section 201, are Kids, Inc.'s workers automatically entitled to adjustment assistance?

(c) On the other hand, if the President *grants* import injury relief under Section 201, does that preclude trade adjustment assistance for workers who are nonetheless negatively affected by imports? The ITC's remedy recommendation in its *Steel* determination from Part B above gives you a big clue.

5. As the Mateikis excerpt explains, the "fast track authority" the President needs to negotiate free trade agreements is often closely linked to an expansion of trade adjustment assistance. The conclusion of a specific trade agreement likewise often sets off intense debates in Congress on the same subject. The controversies over the—recently approved—free trade agreements with South Korea, Colombia, and Panama present the most recent examples.

6. Congress has also authorized a separate, but much more limited, program—Trade Adjustment Assistance for Firms (TAAF)—to assist business entities in adjusting to foreign competition. *See* 19 U.S.C. § 2341 *et seq.* This Program is administered by the Department of Commerce based on standards that somewhat parallel those for the general TAA program. The scope of the TAAF Program has experienced substantial swings, however, based on the prevailing political winds in Congress.

CHAPTER 8

EXPORTS

■ ■ ■

INTRODUCTION 8.0 CONTROLLING
AND PROMOTING EXPORTS

The issues discussed in Chapters 4 and 5 involve commercial contracts between buyers and sellers. Most often they are between private parties, but in many cases the buyer or seller, or both, are government agencies. In those cases the government agency is acting as a buyer or seller and not as a regulatory agency. This chapter continues discussing the role of the government as a third party to a contract for the sale of goods across borders. We have discussed the role of governments, and indeed multi-government organization such as the WTO, in addressing *imports*. Imports are often regulated by a country for balance of payments reasons. If a country imports far more goods and services than it exports, how can such practice be sustained when the money runs out? Many countries have tried to continue relying on borrowing. It is easy to understand that the regulation of imports can become contentious; in general every country wants to decrease imports and increase exports. Or at least export more than it imports. Every country cannot be a net exporter.

One can understand the difference in regulating imports and exports by looking at the Documents Supplement. Far more laws enacted by the federal legislature are directed to imports than exports. While most of the succession of trade acts, such as the Trade Act of 1930, the Trade Act of 1974, the Trade Agreements Act of 1979, the Omnibus Trade and Competitiveness Act of 1988, and the Trade Act of 2002 (all of which are partly included in the Documents Supplement), are directed to import issues, the only federal legislative act directed to exports that we study is the Export Administration Act of 1979 (and to some extent the Arms Export Control Act). Of greater length are the included Export Administration Regulations. That is because Congress tends to promote exports and place in the hands of the executive the administrative details of export trade. Of course this is speaking with quite a broad brush, there are many legislative enactments that specifically regulate exports and imports without distinction, such as U.S. laws that limit or prohibit trade with whomever Congress disfavors at a given time. Or the anticorruption laws that not

656

only apply to export and import trade, but to any business undertaken abroad, including foreign investment.

Because exports are basically deemed positive since they generate jobs in the United States, as well as hard currency, the regulatory framework is generally limited to encouraging export trade. But with significant reservations. The forces of globalization that have facilitated the growth of international commerce—increasingly integrated transportation, communication, financial, and information systems—can also be used by criminals, terrorists, and national enemies to threaten a country's security and economic well being. Accordingly, the United States, along with most other countries and international organizations, regard global trade and global security as related topics.

There was a time, following the collapse of the Soviet Union in the late 1980s, when many thought that the governmental controls on exports established after World War II would fall away along with the Berlin Wall and the end of the Cold War. Unfortunately, events such as the terrorist attacks on the United States and other nations such as the United Kingdom and Spain, prove that the world remains a dangerous place. Governments thus continue to regard addressing the intersection between business and security issues as an important part of national security strategy in the post-Cold War era. There are, accordingly, laws and regulations that either limit what private parties may do in their various international dealings, or shape the manner and nature of those undertakings. However, in contrast to the issues associated with regulating imports that were explored in Chapters 6 and 7, the international consensus as to the appropriate scope of national governmental regulation of export related transactions is much less well developed. The lack of any direct equivalent to the WTO/GATT mechanisms in this area, for example, reflects the fundamental importance of security issues to any national government.

Counsel need be familiar with the effect of these national laws and regulations *before* contracts are drafted, in order to structure the transaction and adjust the contract terms in line with the impact of these regulations; and perhaps more importantly to advise or assist the client in developing a compliance program to meet any applicable requirements affecting the ongoing operation of the business. Proper planning to avoid potential issues will certainly be the business client's preference, rather than litigating the problems associated with a failure to comply with the controls or defending an enforcement action brought by the government, even if the business might ultimately succeed in the litigation.

This chapter will explore governmental regulation of export transactions in three different but related contexts, including controls on individual export related transactions, broader boycotts and economic sanctions, and behavioral controls that apply irrespective of the substance of a particular transaction where the behavior involves that illusive term "corrupt practices."

The first area examined involves export controls, which are the subject of Problem 8.1. The United States Constitution grants to the federal Congress "Power ... [t]o regulate Commerce with Foreign Nations." Art. I, § 8, cl. 3. Congress has exercised this power with regard to exports, and in certain circumstances "re-exports" abroad, of U.S. products or technology, principally through the Export Administration Act of 1979 (EAA), 50 U.S.C.A. App. § 2401 *et seq.*, and the Arms Export Control Act (AECA) 22 U.S.C.A. § 2778 *et seq.* The International Emergency Economic Powers Act (IEEPA), 50 U.S.C.A. § 1701 *et seq.*, and the Trading with the Enemy Act (TWEA)[1] 50 U.S.C.A. App. § 1 *et seq.*, are important additional statutory grants of authority for the government's regulation of export related activities. In fact, the EAA expired in 1994, but by using the IEEPA the EAA has been extended annually. Numerous other statutes are passed from time to time that are tailored to specific political concerns regarding security and trade. Each of these statutory grants augments the President's "inherent authority" in the area of foreign relations derived from his powers to "make treaties" with the consent of the Senate, and as the Commander in Chief of the armed forces under Art. II §§ 1 and 2 of the Constitution.

Neither the AECA nor the EAA provides the detailed substantive provisions which an attorney needs to use to comply with governmental requirements for a client who is exporting goods or services. Instead, the statutes are a broad grant of powers to the President, stating the types of actions he may take in furthering stated Congressional purposes. The President has, in turn, delegated most of these powers either to the Secretary of State who, though the International Traffic in Arms Regulations (ITAR), 22 C.F.R. Parts 120–130, administered by the Directorate of Defense Trade Controls, regulates the export of "munitions items"; or to the Secretary of Commerce who, through the Export Administration Regulations (EAR), 15 C.F.R. Parts 730–774, administered by the Bureau of Industry and Security, controls the export of virtually all other items. Because the vast majority of export transactions concern the controls imposed by the EAR, Problem 8.1 emphasizes the Commerce Department's controls on export related activity. Although the details of the regulations are very different, the same general approach would be useful in dealing with "munitions" controlled by the State Department under the ITAR, for example, and many other agencies' controls as well.

Although legal restrictions intended to prevent the sale of weapons to an enemy during wartime are not uncommon, export controls became particularly important following World War II as a means of limiting the spread of technology to the Soviet Union and its allies. The Cold War era export controls expanded to restrict not only the sale of actual weapons, under the AECA, but also non-military or "dual-use" items and technolo-

---

1. The TWEA was enacted in 1917. Its powers have mostly been shifted to the IEEPA. The remaining power of the TWEA restricts trade with Cuba. The use of the word "enemy" in the TWEA has been criticized since it often meant little more than a country Congress didn't like, not one that was either at war with the United States or even created a threat to U.S. national security.

gy that could be used to enhance their military capabilities, under various versions of the EAA. These "national security" controls were also augmented with "short supply" controls that restricted private transactions in strategic products and materials. Over time, the export control system was further supplemented with a broad range of "foreign policy" based controls targeted at a variety of different countries and expressly aimed at economic or political objectives beyond those concerning potential military threats. By the late 20th century virtually all exports were subject to some sort of governmental control, under a complex set of regulations that dictated when the government was going to exercise that control by requiring an individual export license for the transaction to proceed.

Under the current system, even if the EAR indicates that a specific item going to a specific destination ordinarily requires government approval in the form of an export license, there are a number of "license exceptions" which may excuse the need for a license. These license exceptions reflect the government's attempt to balance it's security requirements against the burdens imposed on trade by the license application process. Each exception has its own particular requirements, which must be met in order to avoid the need to submit a formal license application, and the exception relied upon must be stated on the Shipper's Export Declaration or SED (included in Problem 4.0) that is routinely required at the time of export from the United States. This Declaration, which is a joint Bureau of Census—United States Department of Commerce form, is used for compiling official export statistics and for enforcing the export control laws of the United States. It contains general information concerning the parties to the transaction, descriptions of the merchandise, and documents any specific license or license exception authorization for the shipment.

This process basically reflects the residue of the Cold War era "product and destination" controls, now reflected in a matrix which is included in the regulations themselves. These controls may also be considered as "product eligibility" controls, because licensing depends upon whether a particular product is "eligible" to be sent to a particular destination. Exporters are strictly liable for compliance with "product eligibility" controls. If the product/destination matrix calls for a license to export the item to a particular destination, the essential question becomes whether the exporter did in fact have the proper license prior to the export or correctly used an available license exception. Otherwise the exporter will be liable for failure to comply with the product/destination export controls.

In the post Cold War era, the aims and techniques employed in the export regulations changed dramatically. Rather than being a system designed primarily to limit access by Communist nations to a broad range of Western products or technology through numerous governmental licensing requirements, today's export controls attempt to address diverse regional issues by emphasizing an approach which depends upon broad legal prohibitions in lieu of licenses. The controls shifted to focus upon much more diffuse concerns over the proliferation of weapons of mass destruction, regional warfare, and the prospect of international terrorism. Lacking a well defined adversary, the old approach of having licensing officials look at a large number of export transactions in order for the government to decide which individual transactions might contribute to the Communist "threat" was no longer workable. Accordingly, while a number of "product and destination" controls remain, much of the thrust of the new controls is directed at informing exporters what type of activities concern the government, and having the individual exporters identify the relatively few transactions which fall into those categories from among the larger bulk of transactions which pose no issues. Thus, these newer controls impose a governmental license requirement only if the importer or customer is involved in one of the types of activities which causes the government concern. Therefore these newer regulations can be considered as controls which depend upon the particular "end-use" or "end-user".

Under this system very few transactions actually require government approval in the form of a license. However, the trade-off is a shift in the burden of determining which transactions *should* be considered for licensing. That responsibility is moved away from government officials formulating detailed regulations and "control lists," and onto individual exporters who must assess the particular facts of their individual transaction. The rationale is that the individual exporter, as a party to the transaction, is in a much better position than a government official to "know their customer", and to determine if its customer is engaged in a "bad" end-use. Therefore, many of the new regulatory provisions are structured so as to simply prohibit unapproved exports to certain types of end-users or certain types of end-uses, thereby placing the burden of determining precisely which transaction might need a license onto the exporter. But, as a practical matter, the exporter's decision as to whether or not a particular transaction is "licensable" due to the presence of a proscribed end-use or end-user is unlikely to be challenged until after something has gone awry. Since the consequences for a failure to comply with the export controls are potentially severe, formulating an ongoing compliance process is a critical task, and a major opportunity for counsel to engage in the preventative practice of law.

These more recent export controls may be considered as "customer eligibility" controls. That is, even when no license is called for based upon the particular item's export classification and destination, a license requirement may still be triggered if the customer is "ineligible". Customer eligibility issues arise in one of two ways. Firstly, the customer may be involved in proscribed activities relating to the non-proliferation of weapons of mass destruction (*i.e.*, those activities dealing with the proliferation of chemical, biological, or nuclear weapons, or their associated weapons delivery systems). If so, even the export of the most benign civilian item, such as pencils, may sometimes require government approval in the form of a license. This type of control may also be considered a "knowledge based" control, in that licensing depends upon the exporter's awareness of the customer's activities. However, the regulations also impose liability in this area on exporters who are willfully ignorant or "self-blind", which leads to the maxim that under the new regulations exporters must "know their customer". Secondly, as the government may have information regarding particular end-users which is not generally available, lists are also promulgated of particular individuals or firms which are involved in proscribed activities. In a sense, by publishing "blacklists" the government affirmatively conveys the "knowledge" required to trigger licensing requirements for specific customers or end-users. Both the "product eligibility" and "customer eligibility" based licensing requirements must be met for the exporter's transaction to be in compliance with the regulations.

While complex, all of this sounds rather straightforward, at least where only the United States and the buyer's nation are involved. However, as we will see in other contexts as well, the United States often attempts to apply its laws to transactions which involve parties located in *third* countries. This may occur where the United States attempts to control (1) goods exported from the United States to a foreign nation which are to be re-exported to a second foreign nation, or (2) goods manufactured by a U.S. controlled subsidiary which is located in one foreign nation which are destined to be exported to a second foreign nation. It may also occur when any foreign products contain more than a certain percent (which varies depending on destination, often 10–25%) of U.S. origin parts or U.S. controlled content.

To further add to the complexity of the government's controls on export related transactions, there are also "behavioral controls" which govern the actions of the U.S. parties to a transaction but which may be unrelated to the tasks associated with the actual export. Sometimes these are reflected in additional licensing requirements, such as in the case where a U.S. party might become involved in projects related to the proliferation of weapons of mass destruction. At other times these may simply dictate what types of business practices may or may not be permitted. For example, the EAA also governs dealings which may further a boycott promoted by one nation and against the interests of a nation friendly to the United States. 50 App. U.S.C.A. § 2407. These antiboycott provisions, and their extensive implementing regulations, were adopted to respond to the Arab boycott of Israel. They are a very clear illustration of the use of trade controls to achieve political goals, in this case to help a friendly nation subjected to extensive primary, secondary, and even tertiary boycotts by other nations. These behavioral controls are the principal focus of Problem 8.2 which addresses both the antiboycott regulations administered by the Commerce Department and also the various embargo or sanctions programs administered by the Department of the Treasury's Office of Foreign Assets Control. These boycott, embargo, and sanctions regulations are of considerable importance to any international trade practitioner.

Another form of behavioral control is found in the Foreign Corrupt Practices Act, 15 U.S.C.A. §§ 78q(b), 77*dd*, 78*ff*(a), and the OECD Anti–Bribery Convention, addressed in Problem 8.3. It is increasingly recognized that corrupt payments to foreign officials, made directly or through third parties, should be prohibited even where common under local practice. These payments are often made to encourage a foreign government to purchase certain products, and are thus linked to exports. They may also be present, however, when a foreign direct investment is being negotiated, or when an established foreign investment is attempting to avoid the impact of some law, or have favorable laws enacted. Problem 8.3 helps illustrate how far reaching government controls can become, and how national law is influencing the development of international law regarding export transactions.

The U.S. is not only concerned with restrictions on exports, it is interested in promoting exports. The export of products, intellectual property, and services from the United States has confronted considerable resistance in many foreign nations. The United States has considered opening foreign markets a high priority. Section 301 of the Trade Act of 1974 allows United States exporters to commence proceedings which may result in sanctions against foreign governments that unreasonably, unjustifiably restrain their exports. The Omnibus Trade and Competitiveness Act of 1988 added an important and highly controversial concept to section 301 law, largely the result of restrictions on services, but also addressed to restrictive practices in foreign investment rules and trade of manufactured goods. "Super 301" proceedings were established. These involve mandated determinations by the U.S. Trade Representative regarding specific nations which engage in unfair trade practices. The Super 301 concept was very much criticized, particularly by India, Brazil and Japan, which were the first nations designated under Super 301 as unfair traders. They were all ultimately removed from the priority designation. The Uruguay Round Agreements Act continued Section 301.

One historical anomaly in import and export trade that further illustrates the different national attitude toward imports and exports is the judicial route disputes follow in each area. For the most part the kind of import disputes discussed in Chapters 6 and 7 are dealt with by the United States Court of International Trade (CIT). Some refer to it as the Court of Import Trade, recognizing its limitations. Export trade disputes, on the other hand, such as those this Chapter 8 will deal with, are taken to the general federal courts. Both are constitutionally equivalent in that they are Article III courts. Not only is this true of the trial court level, the CIT and the federal district courts, it remains so for the first level of appeal, to the Court of Appeal for the Federal Circuit (CAFC) for appeals from the CIT, and to the federal circuit courts for appeals from the federal district courts. But a second appeal, from either the CAFC or one of the federal circuits, goes to the U.S. Supreme Court. Judges on the CIT and CAFC are apt to have a trade background, judges on the general federal courts do not. Finally, there is but one CIT and CAFC, sitting in New York City and Washington, D.C., respectively. The federal courts sit throughout the country in their respective districts and circuits.

There are of course qualifications to the above. Where trade with certain countries is prohibited, disputes go to the general federal courts. Thus, a dispute about whether certain products may be imported from Cuba is a matter for the federal district courts rather than the CIT.

PROBLEM 8.1 EXPORT CONTROLS: ROLL–ON BALL BEARINGS TO EUROPE AND THE MIDDLE EAST

SECTION I. THE SETTING

Roll–On Inc. is a small company, located in the mid-western United States, manufacturing industrial equipment. It recently began producing a new "active magnetic" ball bearing that is extremely strong and milled to very high tolerances, and therefore generates much less friction than most other ball bearings. The design for the new ball bearings, and their manufacturing process, was developed by Professor Jones at the engineering department of MidWest College, assisted by a Chinese graduate student assistant, under a research contract with Roll–On.

Although Roll–On is an established business with sales to customers across the country, demand for this revolutionary new ball-bearing has exploded and brought numerous new orders from all over the world, along with very lucrative proposals to enter into distributorships or licensing arrangements with companies elsewhere. Roll–On is considering affiliating with a potential foreign distributor/licensee in the European Union, and as part of its negotiations recently e-mailed detailed blueprints and specifications for its ball bearing manufacturing process to a company in Germany, and gave the German company's Director of Manufacturing Operations a tour of the Roll–On manufacturing plant in the United States.

In the midst of its new found success, Roll–On was visited by a special agent from the U.S. Commerce Department's Bureau of Industry and Security (BIS). Roll–On's ball bearings were apparently discovered in equipment captured from a terrorist group operating in Syria and Iraq. Even though Roll–On now has several European customers, it has never done business with anyone in Iraq or Syria. The founder and CEO of Roll–On is appalled, and fearful of what might happen to the company's reputation and business "if this gets out in the press." Roll–On is in turmoil, and turns to you for help. The CEO insists that their freight forwarder handled all the details for their foreign shipments and that Roll–On "didn't do anything wrong," but also wants to know what they can do to be sure this never happens again.

SECTION II. THE FOCUS OF CONSIDERATION

This problem introduces governmental regulation of exports. Unlike the legal controls affecting imports, the government's export controls are largely found in administrative regulations, issued pursuant to broad statutory grants of administrative authority, rather than in the text of the laws themselves. Our first task is to understand the regulatory framework governing exports, the responsibilities imposed upon exporters under those regulations, and the strengths and weaknesses of a control system that was largely constructed to deal with the challenges of the Cold War—but which is now forced to deal with the more amorphous threats posed by non-state actors in an era of global terrorism.

One of the central problems facing governments in crafting effective export controls is balancing the restrictions necessary to protect national security against the benefits of increasing the nation's exports. Achieving the right balance between these conflicting aims is perhaps most difficult when dealing with "dual use" items—exports of non-military goods, technology, or software that nevertheless could enhance an adversary's weapons or other capabilities to do harm. Additionally, unless one country has an effective monopoly on a particular item, restricting the sale of that item simply results in harming the domestic economy by shifting the sale to some other nation's exporters without affecting a potential adversary's actual capabilities. Thus, in order to have an effective system, governments either have to extend the reach of their own controls extraterritorially or enlist other nations in imposing similar restrictions as part of a multilateral, coordinated approach.

With the fall of the Soviet Union there is no widespread international agreement as to who or what constitutes a threat. The result is that export control remains essentially a subject for national law, albeit influenced by a number of different multilateral regimes with overlapping membership. In the absence of an international consensus, those engaged in export related transactions face a complex and sometimes conflicting range of polices and controls in various countries. Therefore, export control is an area where understanding the requirements in advance and structuring business operations and transactions with export compliance obligations in mind can greatly help avoid difficult and potentially irresolvable issues.

The Export Administration Regulations are essential to an analysis of this problem. The text of the applicable provisions are included in the Documents Supplement. Web resources for further study include the BIS web site at http://www.bis.doc.gov/, and the Stockholm International Peace Research Institute's Non-proliferation and Export Control Project at http://www.sipri.org/contents/expcon/.

SECTION III. READINGS, QUESTIONS AND COMMENTS

U.S. COMMERCE DEPARTMENT BUREAU OF INDUSTRY AND SECURITY, INTRODUCTION TO COMMERCE DEPARTMENT EXPORT CONTROLS

http://www.bis.doc.gov/licensing (Revised August 2010).*

OVERVIEW

The Bureau of Industry and Security (BIS) is responsible for implementing and enforcing the Export Administration Regulations (EAR), which regulate the export and reexport of most commercial items. We often refer to the items that BIS regulates as "dual-use"—items that have both commercial and military or proliferation applications—but purely commercial items without an obvious military use are also subject to the EAR.

The EAR do not control all goods, services, and technologies. Other U.S. government agencies regulate more specialized exports. For example, the U.S. Department of State has authority over defense articles and defense services. A list of other agencies involved in export controls can be found on this [the BIS] Web site or in Supplement No. 3 to Part 730 of the EAR which is available on the Government Printing Office Web site.

* * *

> The EAR contain provisions relating to matters not discussed in this short overview. Two examples of important concepts not discussed here are controls on the activities of U.S. persons in support of proliferation programs (see EAR §744.6) and the antiboycott provisions contained in EAR §760.

WHAT IS AN EXPORT?

Any item that is sent from the United States to a foreign destination is an export. "Items" include commodities, software or technology, such as clothing, building materials, circuit boards, automotive parts, blue prints, design plans, retail software packages and technical information.

How an item is transported outside of the United States does not matter in determining export license requirements. For example, an item can be sent by regular mail or hand-carried on an airplane. A set of schematics can be sent via facsimile to a foreign destination, software can be uploaded to or downloaded from an Internet site, or technology can be transmitted via e-mail or during a telephone conversation. Regardless of the method used for the transfer, the transaction is considered an export.

---

* Reprinted with permission.

An item is also considered an export even if it is ... going to a wholly-owned U.S. subsidiary in a foreign country. Even a foreign-origin item exported from the United States, transmitted or transhipped through the United States, or being returned from the United States to its foreign country of origin is considered an export. Finally, release of technology or source code subject to the EAR to a foreign national in the United States is "deemed" to be an export to the home country of the foreign national under the EAR.

HOW TO DETERMINE IF YOU NEED A COMMERCE EXPORT LICENSE

A relatively small percentage of total U.S. exports and reexports require a license from BIS. License requirements are dependent upon an item's technical characteristics, the destination, the end-user, and the end-use. You must determine whether your export requires a license. When making that determination consider:

● What are you exporting? ● Where are you exporting? ● Who will receive your item? ● What will your item be used for?

WHAT ARE YOU EXPORTING?

THE EXPORT CONTROL CLASSIFICATION NUMBER AND THE COMMERCE CONTROL LIST

A key in determining whether an export license is needed from the Department of Commerce is knowing whether the item you intend to export has a specific Export Control Classification Number (ECCN). The ECCN is an alpha-numeric code, e.g., 3A001, that describes the item and indicates licensing requirements. All ECCNs are listed in the Commerce Control List (CCL) (Supplement No. 1 to Part 774 of the EAR) which is available on the Government Printing Office website. The CCL is divided into ten broad categories, and each category is further subdivided into five product groups.

Commerce Control List Categories

0 = Nuclear materials, facilities and equipment (and miscellaneous items)
1 = Materials, Chemicals, Microorganisms and Toxins
2 = Materials Processing
3 = Electronics
4 = Computers
5 = Telecommunications and Information Security
6 = Sensors and Lasers
7 = Navigation and Avionics
8 = Marine
9 = Propulsion Systems, Space Vehicles, and Related Equipment

Five Product Groups

A. Systems, Equipment and Components
B. Test, Inspection and Production Equipment
C. Material
D. Software
E. Technology

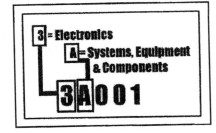

CLASSIFYING YOUR ITEM

Classifying Your Item

The proper classification of your item is essential to determining any licensing requirements under the Export Administration Regulations (EAR). You may classify the item on your own, check with the manufacturer, or submit a classification request to have BIS determine the ECCN for you.

When reviewing the CCL to determine if your item is specified by an ECCN, you will first need to determine in which of the ten broad categories of the Commerce Control List your item is included and then consider the applicable product group.

EXAMPLE

Assume that you have polygraph equipment that is used to help law enforcement agencies. What would be your ECCN? Start by looking in the Commerce Control List under the category of electronics (Category 3) and product group which covers equipment (Product Group A). Then read through the list to find whether your item is included in the list. In this example the item is 3A981 as shown below.

3A981 Polygraphs (except biomedical recorders designed for use in medical facilities for monitoring biological and neurophysical responses); fingerprint analyzers, cameras and equipment, n.e.s.; automated fingerprint and identification retrieval systems, n.e.s.; psychological stress analysis equipment; electronic monitoring restraint devices; and specially designed parts and accessories, n.e.s.

License Requirements

Reason for Control: CC

Control(s)	**Country Chart**
CC applies to entire entry	CC Column 1

License Exceptions

    LVS: N/A
    GBS: N/A
    CIV: N/A

List of Items Controlled

    Unit: Equipment in number
    Related Controls: N/A
    Related Definitions: N/A

The list of items controlled is contained in the ECCN heading.

IF YOUR ITEM IS NOT ON THE COMMERCE CONTROL LIST—EAR99

If your item falls under U.S. Department of Commerce jurisdiction and is not listed on the CCL, it is designated as EAR99. EAR99 items generally consist of low-technology consumer goods and do not require a license in many situations. However, if you plan to export an EAR99 item to an embargoed country, to an end-user of concern or in support of a prohibited end-use, you may be required to obtain a license.

> **EAR99**
>
> Items subject to the EAR that are not elsewhere controlled by this CCL Category or in any other category in the CCL are designated by the number EAR99.

WHERE ARE YOU EXPORTING?

Exports to the embargoed countries and those countries designated as supporting terrorist activities such as Cuba, Iran, North Korea, Northern Sudan, and Syria are more restricted. However, restrictions vary from country to country. There are restrictions on some products, however, that are worldwide.

HOW TO CROSS-REFERENCE THE ECCN WITH THE COMMERCE COUNTRY CHART

Once you have classified the item, the next step is to determine whether you need an export license based on the "reasons for control" and the country of ultimate destination. You begin this process by comparing the ECCN with the Commerce Country Chart (Supplement No. 1 to Part 738).

Below the main heading for each ECCN entry, you will find "Reason for Control" (e.g., NS for National Security, AT for Anti–Terrorism, CC for Crime Control, etc.). Below this, you will find the "Country Chart" designator which shows the specific export control code(s) applied to your item (e.g., NS Column 2, AT Column 1, CC Column 1, etc.). These control codes for your ECCN must be cross-referenced against the Commerce Country Chart.

Commerce Country Chart

Reason for Control

Countries	Chemical & Biological Weapons			Nuclear Nonproliferation		National Security		Missile Tech	Regional Stability		Firearms Convention	Crime Control			Anti-Terrorism
	CB 1	CB 2	CB 3	NP 1	NP 2	NS 1	NS 2	MT 1	RS 1	RS 2	FC 1	CC 1	CC 2	CC 3	AT 1
Guyana	X	X		X		X	X	X	X	X	X	X		X	
Haiti	X	X		X		X	X	X	X	X	X	X		X	
Honduras	X	X		X		X	X	X	X	X	X	X		X	
Hong Kong	X	X		X		X		X	X	X		X		X	
Hungary	X					X	X	X	X						
Iceland	X				X	X	X	X	X						
India	X	X	X	X	X	X	X	X	X	X		X		X	
Indonesia	X	X		X		X	X	X	X	X		X		X	

If there is an "X" in the box based on the reason(s) for control of your item and the country of destination, a license is required, unless a License Exception is available. Part 742 of the EAR sets forth the license requirements and licensing policy for most reasons for control.

Example:

Question: You have polygraph equipment classified as 3A981 for export to Honduras. Would you be required to obtain an export license from the Department of Commerce before selling and shipping it to your purchaser?

Answer: Yes. 3A981 is controlled for Crime Control (CC) reasons under CC Column 1 and the Country Chart shows that such items require a license for Honduras.

If there is no "X" in the control code column(s) specified under your ECCN and country of destination, you will not need an export license unless you are exporting to an end-user or end-use of concern.

Example:

Question: You have polygraph equipment classified as 3A981 for export to Iceland. Would you be required to obtain an export license from the Department of Commerce before selling and shipping it to your purchaser?

Answer: No. As you can see from the Commerce Country Chart (above) 3A981 is controlled for Crime Control (CC) reasons under CC Column 1 and the Country Chart shows that such items do not require a license for Iceland unless you are exporting to an end-user or end-use of concern.

Although a relatively small percentage of all U.S. exports and reexports require a BIS license, virtually all exports and many reexports to embargoed destinations and countries designated as supporting terrorist activities require a license. Part 746 of the EAR describes embargoed destinations and refers to certain additional controls imposed by the Office of Foreign Assets Control of the Treasury Department.

WHO WILL RECEIVE YOUR ITEM?

Certain individuals and organizations are prohibited from receiving U.S. exports and others may only receive goods if they have been licensed, even items that do not normally require a license based on the ECCN and Commerce Country Chart or based on an EAR99 designation. You must be aware of the following lists:

Entity List—EAR Part 744, Supplement 4—A list of parties whose presence in a transaction can trigger a license requirement under the Export Administration Regulations. The list specifies the license requirements that apply to each listed party. These license requirements are in addition to any license requirements imposed on the transaction by other provisions of the Export Administration Regulations.

Treasury Department Specially Designated Nationals and Blocked Persons List—A list maintained by the Department of Treasury's Office of Foreign Assets Control which administers and enforces economic and trade sanctions against targeted foreign countries, terrorism sponsoring organizations, and international narcotics traffickers.

The Unverified List is composed of firms for which BIS was unable to complete an end-use check. Firms on the unverified list present a "red flag" that exporters have a duty to inquire about before making an export to them.

Denied Persons—A list of those firms and individuals whose export privileges have been denied is available on this website. You may not participate in an export or reexport transaction subject to the EAR with a person whose export privileges have been denied by the BIS. Note that some denied persons are located within the United States. If you believe a person whose export privileges have been denied wants to buy your product, you must not make the sale and report the situation to BIS's Office of Export Enforcement. If you have questions about Denied Persons, you may contact BIS's Office of Enforcement Analysis at (202) 482–4255.

WHAT WILL YOUR ITEM BE USED FOR?

Some end-uses are prohibited while others may require a license. For example, you may not export to certain entities involved in the proliferation of weapons of mass destruction (e.g., nuclear, biological, chemical) and the missiles to deliver them, without specific authorization, no matter what your item is. For more information on prohibited end-uses, please refer to Part 744 of the EAR.

WAYS TO EXPORT

Authorization to export is determined by the transaction: what the item is, where it is going, who will receive it, and what it will be used for. The majority of U.S. commercial exports do not require a license.

NLR—("No License Required")

Most exports from the United States do not require a license, and may be exported under the designation "NLR." Except in those relatively few transactions when a license is required because the destination is under embargo or because of a proliferation end-use or end-user, no license is required when:

1. The item to be shipped is not on the CCL (i.e. it's EAR99); or

2. The item is on the CCL but there is no "X" in the box on the Country Chart under the appropriate reason for control column on the row for the country of destination. (See the country chart example above.)

In each of these situations, you would enter "NLR" on your export documents.

License Exception

If a license is required for your transaction, a license exception may be available. License Exceptions, and the conditions on their use, are set forth in Part 740 of the EAR. If your export is eligible for a license exception, you would use the designation of that license exception (e.g. LVS, GBS, TMP) on your export documents.

License

If your item requires a license to be exported, you must apply to the BIS for an export license. If your application is approved, you will have a license number and expiration date to use on your export documents. A BIS-issued license is usually valid for 24 months. See "Applying for an Export License" for additional information.

* * *

BOWMAN, E–MAILS, SERVERS, AND SOFTWARE: U.S. EXPORT CONTROLS FOR THE MODERN ERA

35 Geo. J. Int'l L. 319 (2004).*

* * *

In terms of political change, in the past twenty years the world's political order was dramatically restructured with the collapse of the

Union of Soviet Socialist Republics ("USSR") and the resulting end of the Cold War, as well as the People's Republic of China's ("PRC") slow but inexorable shift toward market economy principles. With the world's geopolitical structure no longer bipolar in nature, export controls based primarily on the country of destination arguably have become less important (with embargoed countries such as Cuba and Iran being notable exceptions) and certainly more difficult to apply than in the past. That is, during the Cold War it was far easier to determine what export destinations (such as Soviet Bloc countries or the PRC) were considered problematic for U.S. national security or foreign policy purposes. . . .

An important result of these recent technological, economic, and political changes is that activities defined under U.S. law as "exports" have increased exponentially, far in excess of economic growth. By far the largest increase has been in non-physical exports of technology and software. [S]uch non-physical "exports" can occur in a variety of ways. [Also]—and of key importance to maintaining an effective national system of export controls for commercial items—"exports" are not limited to business transactions. Rather, they can include such activities as intercompany communications or meetings at which technology or software is conveyed abroad or even conveyed domestically to a national of a foreign country. In some cases, Internet postings of software can be considered exports. Because of the broad range of activities that qualify as exports, it is difficult to estimate the current level of non-physical exports, but it is certain to be significant.

Despite these revolutionary technological, economic, and political changes, the basic structure of U.S. export controls on commercial items remains unchanged, and the United States continues to rely on a Cold War era statute as the basis for export controls on commercial goods, software, and technology. It is clear that this statute—the Export Administration Act of 1979 (hereinafter referred to as the "EAA of 1979")—is outdated and in need of reform. In fact, the EAA of 1979 is currently expired (the regulations promulgated under it remain in force pursuant to a separate emergency powers statute), and there has been much discussion in recent years as to what a new Export Administration Act should look like. One of the primary issues driving this debate has been the question of how to balance the largely incompatible goals of promoting commercial exports and ensuring U.S. national security. On one hand, this debate has been heavily shaped by the events of and following September 11, 2001, which led some observers to conclude that U.S. commercial export controls need to be strengthened, not eased, in light of the threat of terrorism and weapons proliferation. On the other hand, the increasing importance of exports to U.S. economic growth and the interconnectedness of the world's economies indicate that imposing further controls on commercial U.S. exports could further harm what recently has been an unsteady U.S. economy.

To date, however, the debate over modernizing commercial export controls largely has ignored what is arguably the controls' most fundamental structural aspect: that the controls invariably look to individual export transactions as the events to be regulated. The regulation of individual export transactions is so imbedded in the current U.S. system of export controls that many observers see control of individual transactions as an indelible feature of the export control landscape. To be sure, regulating individual export transactions is a straightforward concept; however, the approach is not always straightforward in application. The application of this approach to the large volume of non-physical exports results in an export control system that focuses too much on the mechanism for control (identifying the individual transaction) and not enough on the reasons for which these controls were imposed (furtherance of U.S. national security and foreign policy objectives). In short, form threatens to supersede substance, and the system meets neither the goals of those who want to reduce the legal compliance burden on U.S. exporters nor the goals of those who want to promote U.S. national security and foreign policy objectives.

* * *

JOYNER, THE ENHANCED PROLIFERATION CONTROL INITIATIVE: NATIONAL SECURITY NECESSITY OR UNCONSTITUTIONALLY VAGUE?

32 Ga. J. Int'l & Comp. L. 107 (2004).*

EXPORT ADMINISTRATION ACT AND EXPORT ADMINISTRATION REGULATIONS

* * *

In 1979, Congress passed the Export Administration Act (EAA) to replace the provisions of the earlier 1949 Export Control Act. The purpose of the EAA was to restrict the export of goods and technology, including nuclear non-proliferation items, which would make a significant contribution to the military capacities of nations posing a threat to the United States. . . .

The EAA's provisions delegated a degree of discretionary authority to the executive branch to craft regulations for the implementation of its goals and policies, and specifically for the implementation of a licensing system for goods of dual-use character. The resulting Export Administration Regulations (EAR) of the Department of Commerce established a comprehensive regime for the licensing of dual use goods to be administered by the department's Bureau of Export Administration (now the Bureau of Industry and Security (BIS)). The basic structure of the EAR provisions governing dual-use items consists of a Commerce Control List (CCL), which provides detailed specifications for approximately 2400 dual-use items, including equipment, materials, software, and technology (including data and know-how), the export of which is likely to require a license from BIS. Often, items on the CCL will require a license only if being exported to a particular country of concern, although some items, even if directed to a non-sensitive location, will yet require a license due to the significant risk of diversion to a destination of concern or because of the inherently sensitive nature of the item itself.

* * *

However, due to concerns about the dynamic nature of the development and demand for dual-use goods and technologies, the EAR also established in Sections 744.1–744.6 a set of regulations known as the Enhanced Proliferation Control Initiative (EPCI). The EPCI, rather than being based on a set control list specifying sensitive items to be monitored by exporters, places its emphasis on exporters' knowledge of the activities and characteristics of end users, or final recipients, of their commodity and the uses to which their commodity will be put once in the hands of its destined recipient, including the potential for diversion of the export from its stated end uses to uses of WMD proliferation concern. Section 744.6(a)(1) places obligations on U.S. exporters with regard to their knowledge of such facts and their efforts at acquiring such knowledge.

In pertinent part, the regulations state:

(i) No U.S. person ... may, without a license from BIS, export, reexport, or transfer to or in any country any item where that person knows that such items:

(A) Will be used in the design, development, production, or use of nuclear explosive devices in or by a country listed in Country Group D:2 ... ;

(B) Will be used in the design, development, production, or use of missiles in or by a country listed in Country Group D:4 ... ; or

(C) Will be used in the design, development, production, stockpiling, or use of chemical or biological weapons in or by a country listed in Country Group D:3....

(ii) No U.S. person shall, without a license from BIS, knowingly support an export, reexport, or transfer that does not have a license as required by this section. Support means any action, including financing, transportation, and freight forwarding, by which a person facilitates an export, reexport, or transfer without being the actual exporter or reexporter.

The regulations continue in the same section to forbid any U.S. person from "perform[ing] any contract, service, or employment that the U.S. person knows will directly assist" in the development, production or use of the aforementioned items in the specified nations of concern. They further define the term "know" and its derivations in the context of the regulation as not only positive knowledge that [a] circumstance exists or is substantially certain to occur, but also an awareness of a high probability of its existence or future occurrence. Such awareness is inferred from evidence of the conscious disregard of facts known to a person and is also inferred from a person's willful avoidance of facts.

The obvious purpose of the EPCI provisions is to supplement the inherently limited quality of an enumerated list-based system of regulation with a more inclusive or "catch-all" normative framework that places positive obligations upon U.S. exporters to make themselves aware not only of the characteristics of their particular items and their potential for use in WMD programs, but also of the particulars of the specific uses to which the items are to be put in their place of destination and of the likelihood of their diversion by either primary or secondary parties and potential use in the manufacture of WMD.

The utility of such a regulatory policy is easy to understand. Placing such obligations upon exporters creates, in effect, an entirely new first line of defense in elements of the private sector in the war on dual-use goods proliferation. This argument, of course, is supported by the government's ever-present scarcity of enforcement resources and the efficiency of having those in closest connection with sources of information on goods and technologies, as well as end users, accountable for their negligent use of the same.

* * *

[T]he current national security climate in the United States following the terrorist attacks of September 11, 2001, and the continuing war on terrorism both at home and abroad, as well as heightened international concern over the spread of WMD to countries posing significant perceived threats to international peace and security, suggest that expanded use of the provisions of the EPCI to supplement the EAR's control list procedures for regulation of U.S. persons' trade in dual-use goods in coming years is a distinct possibility. As written, the EPCI has the potential to serve as a useful instrument in the hands of government regulators frustrated by perceived loopholes in the CCL system, as well as a means by which to shift a significant proportion of the burden of regulation of trade in dual-use goods to the resources of the private sector who, according to innumerable documents issued by the BIS, are thereby placed under obligation to "know your end user."

* * *

ANALOGOUS INTERNATIONAL REGULATIONS

It should be noted with interest that a number of other states have instituted regulations establishing end-user export controls of a character comparable to those in the EPCI. * * *

Perhaps the most analogous example of end-user controls to the U.S. model is to be found in Germany, where investigations into the violation of German export control laws in the 1980s led to the institution of a number of reforms to the legal and administrative structure of end-use controls. A "catch-all" clause was introduced in 1990 pertinent to exports under the Foreign Trade Act. Although the catch-all language regulating chemical, biological, and nuclear weapons, as well as that regulating missile technologies, subsequently became subject to and subsumed under Article 4 of the European Community's Regulation on Dual–Use Goods, the catch-all legislative language in relation to conventional weapons remains in German national law and is a unique feature of the German export control model. Under this provision, exports of goods not on a specified Export List (comparable to the CCL) require a license when destined for use in the production of conventional weapons or armaments in thirteen listed countries of concern and the exporter has prior knowledge of this intended use. In effect, this requires companies to exercise comparable due diligence in confirming that all proposed exports to these destinations are for legitimate civilian use only.

NATIONAL SECURITY AND THE APPLICATION OF THE EPCI

* * *

Control of dual-use goods particularly has taken on increased urgency and importance in the minds of policymakers, following revelations in the late 1990s that much of Iraq's stockpile, particularly of chemical weapons, was supplied to it prior to the Gulf War by foreign companies in the form of civilian-use-intended chemical commodities, the sale of which was unimpeded by loose governmental controls on such dual-use character goods. Thus, a tightening of export controls for dual-use goods has been an issue of increasing priority for U.S. policymakers, who may soon find in the provisions of the EPCI a source of regulation already on the books which offers increased breadth and flexibility to their efforts in this regard.

However, despite their theoretical and practical utilities, the EPCI provisions, by the same token, exemplify some typical problems always present when more standardized methods of regulation are supplemented by, or abandoned and replaced by, broadly drawn positive obligations of due diligence imposed upon private individuals. Questions which would be raised in the EPCI context would undoubtedly include these queries: What does it really mean on the ground for an exporter to, in essence, "know or should have known" in the context of circumstances indicating an end use in WMD related programs? How much knowledge and what kinds of facts should be enough to send up a red flag? How far does an exporter have to go to obtain sufficient information to exculpate themselves? What about the resource differentiation between exporters? Are smaller entities under the same due diligence obligations as large multinational entities? Who gets to decide what the parameters of inquiry and fact finding must be, and what are the standards for deciding?

This last query is in fact the most problematic. As written, the EPCI regulations arguably provide little in the way of standards to guide a Department of Commerce lawyer or an administrative law judge in determining whether a requisite level of due diligence has been exerted in finding out information on end users and potential uses of an export, as well as what knowledge will suffice to trigger the EPCI's application in a particular case. * * *

The material problem is that, without clear standards to guide both regulators and, more importantly, the private subjects of the law, the regulations are in danger of becoming an arbitrary exercise of enforcement by government officials given excessive discretion in applying overly-broad norms, something the Due Process Clause of the Fifth Amendment to the U.S. Constitution cannot countenance. As previously mentioned, a significant body of case law has not yet formed by which to discern standards not present in the regulations themselves, so at present the observer is left with only the contours of the regulations as drawn and to speculate about the scope of their potential application. However, as noted, the time may come and may not be far distant when the harmony of the EPCI provisions with bedrock principles of due process jurisprudence will be central to their continued usefulness as tools in the United States' efforts to combat illicit trade in dual-use goods and the resulting threat of proliferation of WMD.

* * *

FITZGERALD, PIERRE GOES ONLINE: BLACKLISTING AND SECONDARY BOYCOTTS IN U.S. TRADE POLICY

31 Vand. J. Trans. L. 1 (1998).*

* * *

Tʀᴀᴅᴇ Cᴏɴᴛʀᴏʟs ᴀɴᴅ Rᴇ-ᴇxᴘᴏʀᴛs

Portions of the Export Administration Act (EAA) and EAR do expressly apply to foreign subsidiaries.... Most of the issues surrounding the extraterritorial application of the trade controls, however, are generated by an aspect of the regulations that is unique to the United States. The EAR, and to a slightly lesser extent the ITAR, purport to control the re-export of U.S. origin products and technology abroad by non-U.S. parties. In essence, the re-export provisions create controls based not upon the nationality of the parties involved, but upon the "nationality" of the goods or technology that are the subjects of the transaction. This applies both to transactions abroad in products containing more than a de minimis amount of U.S. parts, and also to the foreign-produced "direct products" of certain U.S. technology or software, even when they consist entirely of foreign parts.

These re-export provisions also indirectly tie into the trade control blacklists. If the parties to an unapproved re-export are unaffiliated with the United States and therefore beyond U.S. jurisdiction for enforcement purposes, the re-export provision nevertheless provides a basis for the

---

United States to assert that a violation of its controls has occurred. It can then proceed to administratively sanction those involved with the violation by naming them to the State Department's Debarred List or the Commerce Department's DPL, even though they are otherwise beyond the reach of other U.S. enforcement processes. Moreover, the United States may order those who are subject to U.S. jurisdiction to cease dealing with the "wrongdoers." For example, a company in Singapore that re-exports items that the United States deems to be subject to its regulations without the necessary authorizations or approvals may find itself blacklisted and effectively cut off from access to U.S. products, technology, and markets.

The mere threat of this sanction effectively extends the reach of the U.S. trade controls. The force of the U.S. controls and the threat of blacklisting becomes even more credible when there is some affiliation between the foreign persons or organizations and parties in the United States, as when it is a foreign subsidiary, branch, or contractually related party such as a distributor. The U.S. blacklists can reach not only the actual persons or organizations who committed the violation of the controls, but also "related" persons or parties, those who are connected by "ownership, control, position of responsibility, affiliation, or other connection in the conduct of business." Thus, when one part of a group of companies commits a violation, the entire corporate enterprise may find itself "denied." As a practical matter, this places tremendous pressure on the U.S. parent or affiliate to take whatever steps it can to ensure that foreign "related parties" comply with the extraterritorial controls, as those more closely involved or dependent upon U.S. products, technology, and markets will be the most adversely affected by a denial or debarment. The Delft case dramatically illustrates how these provisions interrelate to bolster the effectiveness of the U.S. controls well beyond the direct reach of U.S. legal processes.

Instrubel N.V. and OIP N.V., two Belgian subsidiaries of the Delft group of companies based in the Netherlands, manufactured night vision devices. These devices contain imaging equipment and parts, which are controlled under the ITAR, and manufactured by Hughes Aircraft Corp in the United States. Hughes shipped the imaging equipment and parts to OIP and Instrubel, via another Delft subsidiary, Franke & Co. Optik GMBH, in Germany, under a U.S. State Department license indicating that the exporters were to be incorporated into night vision devices intended for NATO military forces. However, in 1991 during the Gulf War, the Delft night vision devices were found in the possession of captured Iraqi forces.

The State Department suspended all licenses and other approvals, as of January 25, 1991, for Delft Instruments, OIP, and Franke & Co., based upon a "reasonable belief" that a violation of the ITAR occurred. The Commerce Department similarly issued a Temporary Denial Order naming the three companies on February 28, 1991, based upon the assumed ITAR, not EAR, violation. As was explained when the Commerce Department's ex parte Temporary Denial Order was subsequently renewed:

Establishing prior violations of the Export Administration Regulations is one way to establish that an imminent violation is likely to occur. It is not the only way. Here the Department has established that Delft ignored U.S. export controls in the past and, given the gravity of that action may likely do it again. That the past violations were of munitions controls is no guarantee that Delft would not supply goods controlled under the EAR in a future violation.

At the same time, Commerce significantly expanded the scope of the Denial Order to include the entire Delft enterprise, forty-seven companies located in thirteen countries or territories, as known "related parties" of OIP and Instrubel. Arguments that alleged violations by two subsidiaries should not support denial of export privileges for the entire group of Delft companies were initially rejected, but when the Denial Order was next renewed its coverage was reduced to just the seven Delft companies with substantial involvement in defense-related businesses. At the next renewal of the Denial Order, in February 1992, its coverage was again reduced to deny export privileges only for OIP and Instrubel as negotiations with the U.S. government on a resolution continued. In July 1992, Delft paid $3.3 million in fines and pled guilty to a criminal indictment charging Delft, and OIP and Instrubel, with violating the re-export prohibitions of the ITAR. As part of a consent settlement, the State Department lifted its suspension of Delft's export privileges and the Commerce Department's Temporary Denial Order was revoked. However, because of the conviction resulting from the entry of the guilty plea, OIP and Instrubel simultaneously received a seven year formal denial of their export privileges under the EAR, and Delft's seven defense-related companies were statutorily debarred under the ITAR. Although defense-related business accounted for less than ten percent of Delft's overall revenue, the loss of access to U.S. products, technology, and markets for the larger enterprise due to its blacklisting resulted in a net operating loss of $26.6 million for 1991. The collateral effects of the case still linger on in 1997, as Delft recently paid a civil fine to settle allegations that it knowingly made false statements to the government while opposing renewal of the Temporary Denial Orders.

This illustrates the interrelated operation of the trade blacklists, the incentive they provide to innocent foreign parties to comply with the controls abroad, and the rapid and dramatic consequences of being accused of violating the extraterritorial requirements of U.S. trade controls. Here, only one part of the Delft enterprise acted contrary to the U.S. rules, but several of the larger group of related companies, and for a period of time the entire enterprise, was cut off from access to U.S. products, technology, and markets for over a year-and-a-half without administrative charges or civil or criminal proceedings ever being instituted. This also serves to emphasize why it is the administrative sanction of blacklisting rather than more formal criminal or civil enforcement proceedings that has the greatest impact upon, and prompts the most concern from, foreign businesses who must comply with U.S. laws and regulations. As noted previously, this traditional use of blacklisting to enforce U.S.

trade controls is now further augmented by new blacklist tools expressly aimed at encouraging those beyond the reach of U.S. jurisdiction to comply with the EPCI nonproliferation controls.

* * *

[D]espite the substantial penalties attached to violating these statutes and regulations ... decisions as to what to do are rendered even more difficult because the outcome in cases dealing with extraterritorial controls appears to differ depending upon where the action is brought....

The classic illustration of this problem from the perspective of the United States are the cases that arose out of the Russian Trans–Siberian Pipeline dispute in 1982. Dresser Industries in the United States had a French subsidiary, which in turn had a French-based customer who was going to buy locally produced products that were going to be used in the Russian pipeline. When the Reagan Administration unilaterally expanded the trade controls on dealing with the Soviet Union as a result of its role in the imposition of martial law in Poland, the U.S. parent told Dresser (France) S.A. that they would be unable to fulfill the pre-existing contracts with the French customer. The expanded U.S. trade controls specifically imposed limitations on transactions related to the pipeline by foreign entities "owned or controlled" by U.S. residents, nationals, or companies, as well as on transactions by licensees or distributors who were involved in the re-export of U.S. origin goods or technology or their direct products. Therefore, the transactions were clearly proscribed from the U.S. perspective.

The French government disagreed with the U.S. policy and sanctions, and especially with the application of the U.S. trade controls to transactions between a French company and a French customer involving goods manufactured in France. In order to ensure that the goods were delivered, the French government "requisitioned" the goods and compelled delivery as originally contracted. The U.S. government considered this a breach of the controls and the direction the French subsidiary had received, and the Commerce Department issued an ex parte Temporary Denial Order against the subsidiary, blacklisting Dresser (France). Four other foreign companies in different countries were similarly blacklisted, based upon their refusal to comply with the extraterritorial U.S. Pipeline controls.

As with the *Delft* case some years later, the U.S. government resorted to an ex parte Temporary Denial Order to accomplish the blacklisting of Dresser (France). The U.S. government justified its choice on the grounds that the Temporary Denial Order was a quick and timely measure aimed at preventing future violations with further deliveries. Despite having virtually the same practical effect upon Dresser's ability to conduct business, the Temporary Denial Order was not intended as a substitute for more extensive administrative proceedings leading to a formal Denial Order retroactively punishing Dresser for the deliveries demanded by the French government requisition. Dresser had anticipated the Commerce Department action and filed suit in the United States in an attempt to enjoin the entry of the Temporary Denial Order, but was unsuccessful. It also sought relief after the Order was entered, but was again unsuccessful. Attempts to appeal the Temporary Denial Order through the administrative process were also unavailing, as was yet another resort to the courts. The U.S. administrative and judicial processes upheld the U.S. controls, and rejected Dresser's arguments regarding "foreign sovereign compulsion" or violations of international law due to the reach of the controls.

The U.S. legal position has been much criticized. As one commentator wrote:

> In the Dresser case, it seems apparent that neither of the traditional principles of jurisdiction—territoriality and nationality—justified the extension of U.S. export regulations to Dresser (France). Dresser (France) had no operation within the United States; and although it was owned by a U.S. parent company, it was incorporated in France and therefore, under recognized legal principles, was a national of that country. [While o]ne could argue that jurisdiction was based on a considerably expanded notion of the "effects doctrine" inasmuch as continued exports to the Soviet Union by Dresser (France) would affect U.S. foreign policy objectives ... the Restatement of Foreign Relations Law ... explicitly states that such effects must be direct and substantial. It is doubtful if the Dresser "effects" met either criterion under the standards heretofore applied.

Ultimately, the case was mooted when the Temporary Denial Order was vacated as a result of the sanctions themselves being lifted in late 1982, in response to the overwhelming opposition to their unilateral extraterritorial application from industry and from concerned governments abroad.

Nevertheless, the U.S. government's ability to invoke unilateral and extraterritorial sanctions, and to punish those who ignored such measures either at home or abroad with its blacklisting tools, was upheld....

However, the foreign cases produced a different result and show that choosing to comply with the extraterritorial application of the U.S. laws is also fraught with difficulty. In another case arising out of the pipeline dispute, Compagnie Européenne des Pétroles, S.A. v. Sensor Nederland, B.V., a Dutch company was sued in the Netherlands for specific performance of a contract to deliver goods covered by the U.S. trade controls. Compagnie Européenne des Pétroles (CEP) contracted with Sensor prior to the U.S. imposition of the pipeline sanctions for the delivery of "geophones," geological sensing equipment, which would be used in connection with the construction of the Soviet pipeline. When the U.S. sanctions were expanded in June 1982, Sensor, as a wholly owned subsidiary of Geosource Inc. in Texas, informed CEP that it was precluded from completing the contract.

CEP insisted the contract be completed, and the court issued an order to compel delivery with a penalty of 10,000 Nfls per day fine for nonperformance. The court rejected the argument that the extraterritorial reach of the U.S. trade controls compelled the Dutch defendant to breach its contract, and that it could therefore rely upon the doctrine of force majeure to excuse its obligations. The court stated that under general principles of international law, a state may not exercise jurisdiction with respect to acts performed outside its borders unless permitted by certain exceptions, which the court found to be inapplicable. In particular, the "owned or controlled" standard used in the U.S. controls was a "dubious" application of the "nationality principle" under international law and additionally was contrary to the Friendship, Commerce, and Navigation Treaty between the Netherlands and the United States, which provided for mutual recognition of companies established under each other's laws. Moreover, with regard to the "effects principle" the court stated that it could not "be seen how the export to Russia of goods not originating in the United States by a non-U.S. exporter could have any direct and illicit effects within the United States." Via this route too, therefore, the jurisdiction rule cannot be brought into compatibility with international law. Lacking any valid basis for the U.S. assertion of extraterritorial jurisdiction, the Dutch defendant's refusal was not really a compulsory act and therefore Sensor had no defense to its nonperformance. As with *Dresser*, it took the lifting of the sanctions to resolve the case as a practical matter. . . .

The extent of the opposition abroad, and the risks to businesses caught in the middle of competing governmental policies and requirements, is illustrated by an earlier, and more renowned, case involving the Detroit-based Freuhauf Corporation. In the mid 1960s, Freuhauf held two-thirds of the shares in Freuhauf–France, S.A., with the remainder of the shares being held by French interests. One of its major customers, Automobiles Berliet, S.A., contracted with Freuhauf–France for a large number of Freuhauf semi-trailers. Subsequent to entering into the contract, Freuhauf–France learned that the semi-trailers, together with truck tractors manufactured by Berliet, would eventually be delivered to China. The proposed delivery to China ran afoul of a now largely defunct OFAC embargo program embodied in the Transactions Control Regulations, and the U.S. government directed Freuhauf to rescind the contract or face penalties. . . . Automobiles Berliet, not unlike CEP in the Dutch case, refused to release the subsidiary from its contract and threatened suit. Raoul Massardy, the President of Freuhauf–France resigned, and with the other minority French directors, petitioned the local French courts for relief. A judicial administrator was appointed to temporarily take over management of Freuhauf–France for three months and perform the contract, and the Court of Appeals of Paris subsequently affirmed this extraordinary intervention in the management of the French Freuhauf subsidiary. This appears to have been an application of the French doctrine of abus de droit (abuse of a legal right), where the controlling (foreign) management's desire to avoid liability under the [U.S. law] lost out to concerns over potentially drastic consequences for Freuhauf–France itself if the contract were canceled. The Court of Appeals specifically noted that contract cancellation would:

definitely ruin the financial equilibrium and credit of Freuhauf–France and bring about its disappearance and laying off of more than 600 workers, that these circumstances establish sufficiently the emergency and the justification of the conservatory measure taken ... [which was] governed by social interests in preference to the personal interests of certain members [of the Board of Directors].

Underlying this approach was a rejection of the U.S. expansion of the "nationality" principle to reach Freuhauf–France as a "controlled" foreign subsidiary, and a concern for maintaining French "sovereignty" in the face of an extraterritorial U.S. policy. Interestingly, with the appointment of the judicial administrator the United States no longer deemed Freuhauf–France to be under U.S. "control" and declined to pursue the matter further or impose any sanctions for completing the deliveries. Thus, as in the Dresser case, the sanctions were effectively circumvented, but contrary to what occurred in the pipeline dispute, no retaliatory action was taken.

* * *

JOYNER, RESTRUCTURING THE MULTILATERAL EXPORT CONTROL REGIME SYSTEM

9 J. Conflict & Security L. 181 (2004).*

* * *

The Regime System

.... The multilateral export control regime system is currently comprised of four separate and almost wholly independent functional supplier state regimes, the Nuclear Supplier's Group (NSG) in the nuclear weapons and materials context, the Wassenaar Arrangement in the conventional weapons context, the Australia Group concerned with chemical and biological weapons proliferation, and the Missile Technology Control Regime (MTCR) in the missile and related delivery system technologies area. Several of these export control and nonproliferation regimes supplement the provisions of binding, multilateral treaties primarily focused on the development and possession of weapons technologies, including the 1968 Nuclear Non–Proliferation Treaty (NPT), the 1972 Biological Weapons Convention (BWC) and the 1993 Chemical Weapons Convention (CWC).

While differences exist among the particulars of the respective regimes, their essential attributes share a great deal of similarity. All are informal political arrangements, with no elements of legal formality in the commitments of member states either in the originating regime documents or with regard to subsequent guidelines and decisions made by or within the regimes.... [I]n general they may be ... typified by their character as thoroughly informal, voluntary and vague associations of states who maintain discretion in implementing regime policies, but which

---

* Copyright © 2004, reprinted with permission of the Journal of Conflict and Security Law.

at the same time have become influential in the promulgation of norms and in possessing some elements of institutionalization, including in some cases the appointment of permanent secretariats with staff and a standing physical presence.

Their primary purpose being to co-ordinate and harmonize national policies regarding non-proliferation export controls, the core membership of the regimes has traditionally been those states already in possession of significant amounts of such technologies, and therefore a proliferation threat (that is supplier states). In addition to facilitating co-ordination and co-operation, the regimes have also become important promulgators of multilateral norms used in efforts by the regimes and by international civil society of compliance pressuring, directed both at regime members and non-members.

The central features of each regime include a control list, composed of items both of a single use (that is of only military practical usefulness) and of a dual use character (that is with both legitimate civilian as well as WMD or high end conventional weapons-related potential application) which are to be monitored with utmost diligence by member states within their national regulatory systems, and which should be a part of each member state's export licensing programme. . . .

In most of the regimes, there are procedures for information sharing among member states particularly relating to license denials. When a denial of an export license for an item on a control list is made at the national level, member states under this rule are to notify the regime. This is a crucial element in ensuring member states that the restrictive policies of the regime will not be abrogated to the financial gain of one or a few members, to the corresponding loss of the remainder of member states whose positions have thereby been undercut and to the mooting of regime principles.

Three out of the four regimes can trace their origins to the Cold War period, and were initially formed by relatively small groups of 'like minded' states the chief goal of many of which was to counter the influence of the Soviet Union and protect the security interests of the West through harmonized control of WMD-related materials and technology transfer. However, particularly since the fall of the Soviet Union the regimes have been faced with an identity crisis, and their character as supply side regimes comprised of like minded states has been challenged through the addition of new members, many of whom were former targets of regime controls including Russia itself, and many of which are either questionable in their categorization as supplier states, have widely divergent perceptions of threat identification and security interests, or which are substantively lacking in resources to devote to export control efforts. . . .

Also with the end of the Cold War, proliferation of WMD-related materials and technology has until recently taken a back seat in the minds of many policymakers, as the newly arrived unipolar movement and resultant 'new world order' has seemed to justify turning attentions elsewhere. As a result, there has been a lack of high-level political attention given to the multilateral export control regimes in the past thirteen years. Part of this problem no doubt stems from the complexity of the issue-area generally and the disparate nature of the regimes, with four separate (and not always functionally named) groups with independent mandates and lists of covered materials. . . .

Finally, Iraqi post–1991 WMD revelations along with fears concerning WMD development programmes notably in North Korea and Iran, combined with the terror attacks of 11 September 2001, have thrust into the public spotlight the nexus of WMD proliferation and global terrorism as the most serious challenge facing the international community in the 21st century, and have highlighted the degree to which sophisticated states and non-state actors have acquired or are threatening to acquire WMD. In the wake of this modified calculus of geopolitical threat, the multilateral export control regimes have in recent years ... been the target of criticism by some both within national governments and without who claim that the regimes have been insufficiently adapted to the challenges posed by these and other forces. . . .

QUESTIONS AND COMMENTS

1. The first task facing Roll–On is to determine what laws or regulations might apply to its export related transactions. Export controls are an area where the government's detailed controls are typically found in an extensive body of administrative regulations, rather than in the statutory language which tends to be very broadly written in order to enable a wide range of executive action. Thus, Roll–On must first determine which agency's regulations might govern its actions.

The vast majority of U.S. exports fall under the Commerce Department's jurisdiction, whose controls are detailed in the Export Administration Regulations (EAR). Since the EAR are the most broadly applicable controls it is often easiest to begin with those regulations. With that in mind the Commerce Department's Bureau of Industry and Security (BIS) structured their regulations to begin with an analysis of who or what might be "subject to the EAR," along with some additional guidance as to what might be under other agencies' controls, in 15 C.F.R. Part 734. The EAR also include a series of 29 "steps" to follow in order to properly determine one's obligations under the Commerce Department's regulations, which are detailed in 15 C.F.R. Part 732 and supplemented by flowcharts of the process.

Referring to 15 C.F.R. Part 734 in the Documents Supplement, are Roll–On's ball bearings "subject to the EAR"? Are the designs for the ball bearings and their associated manufacturing processes also "subject to the EAR"?

2. Assuming that the EAR apply, the next task is to determine whether a license is required in order to export these items. Determining that an item is "subject to the EAR" is not the same as determining that a license is required. In fact, the overwhelming majority of transactions subject to BIS

jurisdiction do not require license approval. Such shipments are identified in export documents as "NLR" for "no license required". Whether a license will be required depends upon what is being shipped, where it is going, and how (and by whom) it will be used.

The basic licensing requirements are found in the Export Control Classification Number (ECCN) entry for each controlled item on the Commerce Control List (CCL) (15 C.F.R. Part 774, Supp. No. 1). The structure and content of the CCL list of ECCNs used to detail the government's export control requirements bears no relation whatsoever to the Harmonized Tariff System or the Brussels tariff nomenclature used to determine the customs duties applied to imports. After reviewing the CCL itself, or after submitting a classification request to BIS, Roll–On concludes that its ball bearings fall under ECCN 2A001. That ECCN therefore lists the basic export controls applicable to Roll–On's ball bearings based upon the general characteristics of these "dual use" products. Referring to the excerpt found in the Documents Supplement, why are items described in ECCN 2A001 subject to regulation, what "reasons for control" are listed in that ECCN?

Traditional "product based" licensing requirements also depend upon where the product is going. Using the Reasons for Control specified in ECCN 2A001 and the excerpt from the Commerce Country Chart (15 C.F.R. Part 738, Supp. No.1) found in the Documents Supplement, does Roll–On need an export license to send its ball bearings to Germany? What about for exports to Iraq or Syria?

3.   Even if the EAR imposes an export licensing requirement, there may be circumstances under which that requirement does not apply, where a "license exception" permits the exporter to ship the item without obtaining specific BIS license approval in advance. More than a dozen license exceptions are detailed in 15 C.F.R. Part 740. They typically provide that shipments meeting all the specified terms and conditions for that particular exception may proceed without the necessity of submitting a license and obtaining approval from BIS in advance of the transaction. Use of a license exception is indicated by specifying a three letter code in one's export documents (such as the Shipper's Export Declaration). For example the code "LVS" would be used for the "low value shipment" license exception described at 15 C.F.R. Part 740.3. Use of a license exception constitutes a specific certification that all the requirements for proper use of that license exception are met—and therefore subject to the penalties applicable to making a "false statement" to the government.

Could Roll–On use license exception LVS for shipments to Germany that might otherwise require an export license? What about for shipments to Iraq or Syria? Would any other license exceptions be available in addition to LVS?

4.   What about the design information for the ball bearings and their manufacturing processes? Would that information be subject to the same or different controls from those applicable to the finished products themselves? Would a license be required to email the blueprints and design information to the potential distributor/licensee in Germany? What about if the same information were sent to Iraq, or to Syria? Would any license exceptions be

available? Would there be any special requirements for using such a license exception?

5. As noted in the readings, it is possible to "export" technology, such as the ball bearing designs, even without sending the information out of the country. When technology subject to the EAR is released to a foreign national in the United States, under 15 C.F.R. 734.2(b) a "deemed export" occurs to that individual's home country. Does that mean an export license is required before the German Director of Manufacturing Operations tours Roll–On's U.S. manufacturing plant? Does that similarly mean that Professor Jones at MidWest College needed an export license in order to have the Chinese graduate student work on the contract to develop the ball bearing designs?

6. Even prior to the demise of the Cold War, these traditional "product based" export controls were increasingly considered inadequate to address new types of security threats that are less clearly tied to a potential national adversary such as the former Soviet Union. With increasing concerns over weapons proliferation and global terrorism by non-state actors, the product/destination based controls were augmented with additional controls, such as the EPCI initiative, which focus less on what is being sold and more on how it will be used and by whom. These "customer based" controls trigger licensing requirements depending upon one's knowledge of the other parties involved in the transaction.

One form of customer control is provided by the lists of persons, entities, or groups with whom one may not do business without first obtaining government license approval. Perhaps one of the oldest forms of a customer level control is found in the Commerce Department's "Denied Persons List". These are individuals and companies who have themselves violated the export controls and consequently had their export "privileges" denied. U.S. persons are prohibited from directly or indirectly dealing with denied parties in export related transactions. The State Department maintains an analogous list of "debarred parties" who have violated the ITAR and the Treasury Department Office of Foreign Assets Controls maintains an extensive list of specific parties who are subject to its various economic sanctions programs. Irrespective of what products are involved, transactions with these parties are generally prohibited without exception.

The EPCI initiative represents another, newer, form of customer eligibility control. With the EPCI controls the government specifies the type of activities that are of concern, such as those related to the proliferation of weapons of mass destruction described in 15 C.F.R. Part 744, and license requirements are triggered by the exporter's "knowledge" of the end use and end user involved in the transaction. This is supplemented by the more general "Know Your Customer" and "Red Flag" Guidance found in 15 C.F.R. 732, Supp. No. 3 which support a general obligation not to participate in any transaction where an export control violation is or is likely to occur.

Conceptually, the Entity List and the Unverified List lie halfway between the list based and the knowledge based customer eligibility controls. The Entity List (15 C.F.R. Part 744 Supp. No. 4) provides the names of various facilities and companies engaged in weapons proliferation activities in foreign countries. Unlike the Denied Party List, the named entities may not have violated any U.S. export control regulation, but by placing their names on the list the U.S. Government is affirmatively providing exporters with "knowledge" that the named entities are engaged in the type of activities which trigger the EPCI controls. Similarly the Unverified List affirmatively provides exporters with a "Red Flag" that the named parties may require additional scrutiny because the U.S. Government was unable to complete either a pre-license check or a post-shipment verification that were conditions of license approval for some prior transaction.

Each of these lists effectively moves the burden of deciding whether a license application is necessary away from government officials administering generalized regulations and onto the private parties actually involved in particular transactions who are directed to "know" their customers. This facilitates trade by minimizing the number of explicit product based licensing requirements, but at some cost in certainty. With the knowledge based customer eligibility controls, any challenge to the parties' decision as to whether a license application should have been submitted will always come after the fact—in the context of a government enforcement action when the items are already in the "wrong" hands.

How should an exporter structure their transactions and business operations in order to be in the best possible position to avoid such a problem? Roll–On asserts that it always relied upon its freight forwarder to handle its foreign shipments. Does the use of such a company enhance Roll–On's ability to avoid responsibility if a violation occurs? What is Roll–On's potential exposure if it is responsible for an export control violation?

7. The BIS Export Enforcement Special Agent says Roll–On's ball bearings were found in Iraq and Syria, but Roll–On has no customers in those countries. If one of Roll–On's customers elsewhere, for example in Europe, wanted to resell or send the ball bearings to the Middle East would a U.S. export license be required? What is the impact upon Roll–On's own obligations under the EAR if it knows or should have known that a European customer is purchasing the ball bearings for use or resale in Iraq or Syria?

8. The BIS "Red Flag Guidance" (15 C.F.R. Part 732 Supp. No. 3) directs that exporters should "[t]ake into account any abnormal circumstances in a transaction that indicate that the export may be destined for an inappropriate end-use, end-user, or destination." While the guidance also states that "there is no affirmative duty upon exporters to inquire, verify, or otherwise 'go behind' the customer's representations", the regulatory scheme does impose "a duty to check out the suspicious circumstances and inquire about the end-use, end-user, or ultimate country of destination" if a red flag occurs. Moreover, exporters may not avoid or evade their responsibilities by "self-blinding". The Red Flag guidance states that exporters should "not cut off the flow of information that comes to [the] firm in the normal course of business. For example, do not instruct the sales force to tell potential customers to refrain from discussing the actual end-use, end-user, and ultimate country of destination for the product [the] firm is seeking to sell. Do not put on blinders that prevent the learning of relevant information. An affirmative policy of steps to avoid "bad" information would not insulate a

company from liability, and it would usually be considered an aggravating factor in an enforcement proceeding.''

What does this suggest about the difference in the basis for potential liability between the product based licensing requirements and acting with "knowledge" that a violation has occurred or is likely to occur?

9. The *Freuhauf*, *Dresser*, *CEP* and *Delft* cases discussed in the Fitzgerald excerpt suggest that when export controls are applied extraterritorially, and without being part of a common multilaterally agreed regime, they may be regarded abroad as an affront to the foreign state's sovereignty. International law, as reflected in §§ 402—403 of the Restatement (Third) of Foreign Relations Law, generally recognizes three bases for a country's ability to legitimately exercise regulatory or adjudicatory authority—the territorial principle, the nationality principle, or the effects principle. However, more than one state may be able to simultaneously claim a basis for acting, and then notions of reasonableness and comity (*i.e.* international good will) apply to limit the legitimate exercise of national authority.

Which principle or principles might support the U.S. exercise of authority, and the foreign state's exercise of authority, in each of these cases? Is the requirement that European customers obtain a U.S. export license to send the ball bearings to the Middle East supportable under these principles? Does it make a difference whether the re-exporter is affiliated with Roll–On or simply another arms length customer? If a European re-exporter, unconnected with the Roll–On and effectively beyond U.S. jurisdictional reach, failed to obtain an export license to send the ball bearings to the Middle East, would any of these principles support BIS in denying the European's "export privileges"? Do these general international jurisdictional principles limit the exercise of national authority and lessen the potential for inter-state disputes over these sorts of controls? If there is a direct conflict between the legal requirements being imposed abroad and those imposed by the U.S., does that affect Roll–On's obligations under the EAR?

The *Delft* case illustrates the power the United States may exert when it does not have actual jurisdiction over a foreign party. But how would the United States react when it discovered that the foreign company also made items much desired by American people, or needed by the U.S. military? How do the *Dresser* and *Sensor* cases differ from *Delft*?

10. The Wassenaar Arrangement, Nuclear Supplier's Group, Australia Group, and the Missile Technology Control Regime supplement a variety of treaties and international agreements, and are aimed at co-ordinating various national non-proliferation and export controls efforts. How do they compare as vehicles for defining and harmonizing national legal rules affecting "outbound" transactions with, for example, the GATT/WTO in defining and harmonizing what nations may do with regard to "inbound" transactions?

Perhaps the most significant international effort to address the risks posed by the proliferation of WMD was the recent adoption of United Nations Security Council Resolution 1540. Although Pakistan and several other states argued that the Resolution was an unprecedented exercise of the Council's legislative authority under Chapter VII of the UN Charter, as it mandates actions by the member states that are more typically the subject of debate and negotiation in the context of the specific non-proliferation treaties, the Resolution was unanimously adopted on April 28, 2004. Focused specifically on the risks posed by non-state actors largely missed by the major non-proliferation treaties, the Resolution directs that:

> "all States ... shall adopt and enforce appropriate effective laws which prohibit any non-State actor to manufacture, acquire, possess, develop, transport, transfer or use nuclear, chemical or biological weapons and their means of delivery, in particular for terrorist purposes, as well as attempts to engage in any of the foregoing activities ..."

With specific regard to trade controls the Resolution mandates that:

> "all States shall take and enforce effective measures to establish domestic controls ... and to this end shall ... [e]stablish, develop, review and maintain appropriate effective national export and transhipment controls over such items, including appropriate laws and regulations to control export, transit, trans-shipment and re-export and controls on providing funds and services related to such export and trans-shipment ... as well as establishing end-user controls; and establishing and enforcing appropriate criminal or civil penalties for violations of such export control laws and regulations."

The Security Council has also established a committee to receive reports and monitor the implementation of the Resolution. The United States has also called upon the U.N. Security Council to use Resolution 1540 to impose sanctions upon North Korea and Iran for weapons proliferation.

How might Security Council Resolution 1540 affect the international network of export controls in the future? What are the advantages or disadvantages of resorting to a Security Council Resolution in lieu of bilateral or multilateral treaties?

11. Bowman notes the need to make changes and adopt a replacement for the EAA of 1979. The Obama administration in its first year initiated an Export Control Reform Initiative (ECR) to "fundamentally" reform the export control system. By mid-term, with democrats losing control of the House, little had been accomplished. The EAA of 1979 plods on. Exporters want to export—government officials want to control exports. But the Obama proposal intends to adopt a *single* control list, licensing agency, information technology system, and enforcement coordination agency. Will it be a new agency, or one of those currently having a finger in the pie—including the Departments of Commerce, State, Agriculture and Energy, the Nuclear Regulatory Agency, the Drug Enforcement Agency, and the Food and Drug Administration? Which of the nonchosen will relinquish power quietly?

12. Joyner notes how Germany approaches the export control problems. He then notes the experience in Iraq. In view of Iraq, Iran and North Korea, can exports really be controlled when nations are determined to have the product in question? Considering the Joyner extract, if you were an administrative law judge, would you conclude that Roll–On had performed an adequate due diligence?

13. Does the use of economic controls in these cases conflict with the idea of globalization? Where is the WTO/GATT in the dispute?

PROBLEM 8.2 INTERNATIONAL ECONOMIC BOYCOTTS: MACHINE LATHES TO CUBA AND QATAR

SECTION I. THE SETTING

Prentice Mfg., Inc. (incorporated in Delaware), manufactures machine lathes in Detroit, Michigan, as well as at both a wholly owned subsidiary in Vancouver, Canada, Prentice of Canada, Ltd., and a joint venture plant in London, England, Prentice UK, PLC. The Canadian subsidiary's board of directors consists of six Canadians and three U.S. nationals. The London affiliate is a 50–50 equity joint venture, with two of nine directors U.S. nationals and the remaining seven British. The machine lathes are used to make different metal items. The industry is very competitive and Prentice has only a small share of the market. The Canadian plant production is usually sold in Canada and some western portions of the United States. The UK plant production is usually sold in the European Union, with some sales to Africa. None of the Prentice entities has ever sold lathes to Cuba, to Israel, or to any of the Arab nations.

Prentice exhibited several machine lathes at international trade fairs in Frankfurt and Detroit. The exhibit in Frankfurt was organized by the UK affiliate. Representatives from a Cuban ministry attended the fair. They were impressed with the Prentice lathes, some of which were manufactured in the U.S., some in Canada, and some in the U.K. The Cuban's placed a tentative order for three machine lathes. One which they ordered was normally made in the United States. The British CEO of Prentice, UK, told the Cubans that this lathe could not be shipped directly from the United States to Cuba, but could be sent to the UK plant for some final assembly and then shipped to Cuba. The second lathe would be manufactured in Canada and shipped directly to Cuba. This lathe contains some technology from the United States, but all the parts and labor are Canadian. The third lathe would be manufactured in the UK, with about 25 percent of the parts from the United States.

The exhibit at the trade fair in Detroit, and the possible sales to Qatar, are discussed in Part B of this problem.

SECTION II. FOCUS OF CONSIDERATION

Prentice confronts two different issues involving boycotts in this problem. The sales to Cuba, Part A of the problem, involve U.S. laws which **mandate** participation in a boycott initiated by the United States. The sales to Qatar, Part B of the problem, involve U.S. laws which **prohibit** participation in a boycott **not** initiated by the United States. These laws illustrate that while the United States wishes to be able to engage in boycotts of other nations, such as Cuba, it also wishes to control U.S. persons who through trade might assist a boycott initiated by another nation (Arab bloc) against a third nation which is friendly to the

United States (Israel). However, an apparent incongruity arises when the United States tries to extend its own boycott of another nation (Cuba) to third nations, which constitutes a secondary boycott, while at the same time prohibiting U.S. persons from participating in a secondary boycott. Can the United States have it both ways?

Nations use primary boycotts to achieve political goals. The United States has boycotted or embargoed trade with Angola, Burma, Cambodia, China, Cuba, Haiti, Iran, Iraq, Libya, Namibia, Nicaragua, North Korea, Panama, South Africa, Sudan, Vietnam and parts of former Yugoslavia. The effectiveness of many of U.S. unilateral boycotts has been widely debated. The United States has also engaged in collective boycotts, such as the U.N. boycott against Iraq after the invasion of Kuwait, against Serbia and Montenegro after the Serbian promoted invasion of Bosnia, and against South Africa and Namibia because of apartheid.

Some boycotts have been quite brief, such as U.S. limits on exports to Europe for use in constructing a gas pipeline from the USSR, imposed soon after the Soviet invasion of Poland. Some have been quite long—the U.S. boycott of Cuba is four times longer than the siege of Troy. Successful or not, there is little doubt that unilateral and collective boycotts will continue to be part of U.S. foreign policy.

The United States has one significant experience with antiboycott laws. That evolved from the Arab nations' boycott of Israel, although the U.S. law nowhere specifically mentions either Israel or Arab. The antiboycott law is directed to prohibiting U.S. persons from participating in or supporting boycotts by foreign nations against other foreign nations friendly to the United States.

International law scholars have long debated whether boycotts violate international law.[1] But boycotts frequently are used as an instrument of foreign policy individually by nations, and collectively by such organizations as the United Nations.[2] A primary boycott involves a curtailment of direct trade with another nation and is generally regarded as not in violation of international law.[3] But that view may change when the boycotted nation is economically dependent upon the boycotting nation, and the boycott causes economic collapse and significant human suffering. Even when a boycott assumes secondary or tertiary characteristics, international law may not be violated, although complex issues of extraterritoriality are raised.

---

1. They may be referred to as "self-help" or unilateral measures. The Restatement (Third) of Foreign Relations Law addresses unilateral measures in § 905, as does the International Law Commission's Draft Articles on State Responsibility (Part Two), in Articles 12–14. Both assume similar approaches. Neither constitute law, they reflect the perceptions (and often goals) of their drafters. Boycotts are discussed in R. Folsom, M. Gordon and J. Spanogle, Principles of International Business Transactions (West Concise Hornbook Series, 2d ed. 2010), Chapter 18.

2. The U.N. Security Council has embargoed certain arms materials exports to Congo, Côte d'Ivore, Eritrea, Iraq, Lebanon, Liberia, North Korea, Sierra Leone, Somalia and Sudan. The United States complies through a regulation under the EAR.

3. A critical point is whether the boycotted state must have committed an illegal act. The majority view seems to be that the act need not be illegal, it may simply be "unfriendly.".

The imposition of an embargo or economic sanctions is usually made by the President, although Congress has intervened at times to *mandate* boycotts. Trade embargoes often are imposed after some act by a foreign nation that the President or Congress consider unacceptable, such as the USSR invasion of Poland, or the Cuban downing of two small civilian planes. The former led to the President imposing the pipeline sanctions, and the latter led to enactment by Congress of the Libertad (Helms–Burton) Act.

Trade boycott laws are found both in statutes and administrative regulations. Most boycotts are implemented under separate regulatory controls for each particular embargo target, such as the restrictions in the North Korean Assets Control Regulations or the Libyan Assets Control Regulations. These regulations are administered by the Office of Foreign Assets Control of the Department of the Treasury.[4] The regulations OFAC enforces are mostly progeny of the Trading With the Enemy Act of 1917, and the International Emergency Economic Powers Act of 1976. Although there is a pattern to the controls imposed on trade with different countries, each nation creates special issues treated in specific ways. For example, the U.S. controls applicable to Cuba allow rather unique telephone service. These Treasury regulations may overlap with foreign policy based controls enforced by the Department of Commerce .. Also, the Department of State, which plays an important role in relations with these embargoed nations, may view the trade restrictions very differently than other departments. The Department of Defense is yet another department with some role in the imposition of boycotts.

Boycotts are sometimes extended further by special laws. In the case of Iran and Libya there is the Iran and Libya Sanctions Act of 1996, commonly known as the D'Amato Act (after its principal sponsor). But the Cuban boycott has been extended the furthest. In addition to the Cuban Assets Control Regulations, Congress enacted the Cuban Democracy Act of 1992, and the Cuban Liberty and Democratic Solidarity (Libertad) Act of 1996, commonly known as the Helms–Burton Act. Furthermore, in the past few years many states have enacted laws that prohibit government procurement from specific nations for alleged violations of human rights. These laws have not been welcome in Washington, nor in some foreign nations.

Congress tends to allow the President discretion regarding many trade relations decisions, such as granting most favored nation status to other nations not otherwise entitled to such status under our trade laws. The President also has discretion in the implementation of boycotts. But often the Congress also acts when the issue assumes broader dimensions, especially when there is organized opposition to U.S. policy. But even when Congress does act, it usually allows the President to enact further regulations not inconsistent with, and intended to carry out, the purpose of the legislation. The Cuban Liberty and Democratic Solidarity (Libertad)

---

4. 31 C.F.R. Parts 500 et seq. See Documents Supplement.

Act differs in that it is an unusual example of a significant restraining of such Presidential enactment of regulations.

SECTION III.   READINGS, QUESTIONS AND COMMENTS

PART A.   THE BOYCOTT OF CUBA BY THE UNITED STATES

The boycott of Cuba raises the issue of the extraterritorial application of laws, discussed in the previous problem regarding the sale of ATMs to China from a U.S. corporation's French subsidiary. That case dealt with an executive order directed to the corporation to cease specific sales. This problem involves regulations and specific laws directed to almost all trade with Cuba. The issue of extraterritoriality will be present again in other problems, particularly Problem 11.3 that addresses Extraterritorial Jurisdiction and Discovery.

The boycott of Cuba began as a response to the nationalizations of all U.S. owned property in 1959 and 1960. The U.S. Congress gave the President authority to alter the Cuban sugar quota. President Eisenhower responded by nearly totally removing the generous quotas. He also imposed an extensive embargo on shipments of goods to Cuba. The boycott was amended in 1975 to clarify that foreign subsidiaries of U.S. companies could trade with Cuba under a licensing procedure controlled by Treasury. This trade angered anti-Castro groups in the United States and led to the enactment of the Cuban Democracy Act in 1992, which amended the Cuban Assets Control Regulations to curtail the trade by subsidiaries.[5] The Cuban Regulations fill nearly 50 pages and are the basic provisions for trade with Cuba, but their application is limited by the Cuban Democracy Act. The more recent Libertad (Helms–Burton) Act further restricted trade, and further angered friendly foreign governments.

The Cuban Regulations prohibitions are followed by quite extensive definitions. While nearly all of the definitions create few problems, one is of considerable importance to U.S. businesses with foreign subsidiaries and affiliates, and thus to Prentice and its Canadian and UK entities. A "person subject to the jurisdiction of the United States," upon whom the Regulations impose trade restrictions, includes "any corporation, partnership, or association, wherever organized or doing business, that is owned or controlled by persons" citizen or resident of the United States. The meaning of "owned" or "controlled" is not included in the Regulations. The Regulations and the Cuban Democracy Act have induced reactions from friendly nations in the form of "blocking" laws, that mandate that subsidiaries disregard the U.S. restrictions.

The third stage of the Cuban boycott was the 1996 enactment of the Cuban Liberty and Democratic Solidarity (Libertad) Act, the infamous Helms–Burton Act. This act includes two especially troublesome parts. Title III establishes a right of action in U.S. courts by U.S. nationals who

---

5. 31 C.F.R. Parts 500–585. See Documentary Supplement.

have a claim that their property was taken by Cuba and that the foreign party charged is now "trafficking" in such property. Title IV requires the United States to deny visas to foreign persons who have trafficked in confiscated property.[6] The reaction to the Libertad Act from abroad has been negative. Further blocking laws have been enacted. The OAS Juridical Committee denounced the law. Each successive president has used waiver authority to defer the implementation of Title III, and Title IV has been implemented sparingly.

ANDREAS F. LOWENFELD, AGORA: THE CUBAN LIBERTY AND DEMOCRATIC SOLIDARITY (LIBERTAD) ACT

90 Am.J.Int'l L. 419 (1996).*

* * * The issue of compensation for property of United States nationals, partly submerged in the first two parts of the Helms–Burton Act, is the focus of title III. The scheme of the Act is to create a right of action in United States courts on behalf of any U.S. national who has a claim for property confiscated by Cuba since January 1, 1959, against any person who "traffics" in such property. * * * [T]he idea is clear: Whoever "traffics" in property that once belonged to U.S. nationals is to be confronted with the prospect of litigation in the United States, and of exposure to damages equal in the first instance to the value of the property in question, and if the trafficking continues, to treble damages (section 302(a)). "Trafficking," a word heretofore applied in legislation almost exclusively to dealing in narcotics, is defined to include not only selling, transferring, buying, or leasing the property in question, but also "engag[ing] in a commercial activity using or otherwise benefiting from confiscated property" (section 4(13)). Thus the Act contemplates that if an English company purchases sugar from a Cuban state enterprise and the English company also does business in the United States and accordingly is amenable to the judicial jurisdiction of a U.S. court, it would be liable to a U.S. national who could show that some of the English company's purchases consisted of sugar grown on the plantation that the plaintiff once owned. There is no necessary connection between the value of the property on which the claim is based and the value of the transaction on which the assertion of "trafficking" rests.

Helms–Burton as a Secondary Boycott. * * * It is true that the sanctions imposed by the Helms–Burton Act are distinguishable from the Arab boycott of Israel, in that the sanction for violation under Helms–Burton is not a prohibition, only exposure to litigation and exclusion. But the litigation, as we have seen, may result in damages equal not to defendants' gain but to plaintiffs' loss, plus interest for some thirty-five years, all subject to trebling if the potential defendants do not exercise their Hobson's choice quickly. The objective, in any case, is the same. X, a

---

6. Titles III and IV sections are included in the Documents Supplement.

* Reprinted with permission of the American Society of International Law.

national of state C (say Canada), is being coerced by state A (the United States) to stop trading with B (Cuba) or handling merchandise containing products of state B, although the law of state C makes such trade perfectly legal and may even encourage it. I believe that (in time of peace) the exercise of jurisdiction by the United States for these purposes, to impose a secondary boycott on Cuba, like the exercise of jurisdiction by members of the Arab League to impose a secondary boycott on Israel, is contrary to international law, because it seeks unreasonably to coerce conduct that takes place wholly outside of the state purporting to exercise its jurisdiction to prescribe.

Helms–Burton and the Effects Doctrine. The authors of the Helms–Burton Act were prepared for criticism that they were engaged in extraterritorial legislation. They included in the Findings on which the operative portions of the Act are based, the statement:

> International law recognizes that a nation has the ability to provide for rules of law with respect to conduct outside its territory that has or is intended to have substantial effect within its territory. (Section 301(9))

This is, of course, a statement derived—indeed almost quoted—from the *Restatement of Foreign Relations Law.* But the "almost" is significant. * * *

I submit that the effort by the authors of Helms–Burton to build on the *Restatement* is flawed—fundamentally flawed—in two respects. *First,* the effect against which the legislation is directed—even if one can locate it in the United States—was caused by the Government of Cuba, not by the persons over whom jurisdiction is sought to be exercised. Thus, even leaving aside the thirty-six year interval between conduct and effect on the one hand, and exercise of prescriptive jurisdiction on the other, the effort to place Helms–Burton within the effects doctrine is no more than a play on words. It does not withstand analysis, and it would carry the effects doctrine farther than it has ever been carried before.

Second, the effort to impose United States policy on third countries or their nationals in the circumstances here contemplated is unreasonable by any standard. * * *

Suppose, for instance, Iran were to adopt a law stating that anyone who invests in the Great Satan U.S.A. will be subject to suit in Iran for up to the value of the assets that the former Shah robbed from the Iranian people, as determined by the Majlis. BMW, calculating its litigation exposure in Iran and the value of its investments in the United States, cancels operations about to begin at its new plant in Spartansburg, South Carolina, at the same time. Mercedes Benz cancels its plan to build a sports vehicle plant in Vance, Alabama. I believe all Americans would be outraged, both at Iran for adopting the law I have suggested, and at the German manufacturers for having capitulated. I do not believe we would be hearing Iran's exercise of jurisdiction characterized as reasonable.* * *

BRICE M. CLAGETT, TITLE III OF THE HELMS–BURTON ACT IS CONSISTENT WITH INTERNATIONAL LAW

90 Am.J.Int'l L. 434 (1996).*

* * *

A state has jurisdiction to prescribe rules of law with respect to "conduct outside its territory that has or is intended to have substantial effect within its territory," at least when the exercise of that jurisdiction is reasonable in all the circumstances.* * *

Under the *Restatement* scheme, international law is said to require that a state, even if it has jurisdiction to prescribe based on "substantial effects," must balance its interests against those of other states, and refrain from applying its laws when the legitimate and reasonable interests of another state are greater. * * *

If the "other state" is Cuba, Cuba has no legitimate interest, which other states need or should respect, in confiscating property without compensation, and profiting from foreign investment in that property.* * *

If the "other state" is the state of which the trafficker is a national, that state's interest in protecting its national's ability to traffic in confiscated property in a third country is, at the most, no greater (let alone more legitimate) than the United States' interest in protecting the ability of its national—the rightful owner—to prevent further interference with his property and perhaps ultimately to recover it. The interests of both states are equally "extraterritorial," since the activity with which both are concerned is taking place in a third country, Cuba. Thus, title III does not fail a balancing test, even if such a test is deemed part of international law. Title III is well within the right of the United States to prescribe rules for application by its own courts, against defendants subject to its jurisdiction, in a matter with a demonstrable impact on the United States and its residents.

A further reason for title III is the notorious weakness and ineffectiveness of international enforcement mechanisms. Because the jurisdiction of international tribunals is consensual, it is only rarely that a confiscation case can be brought in such a forum. Espousal of claims by the victims' government can take generations to bear any fruit at all and, even when it does, typically results in recovery by the victims of only a pathetically inadequate fraction of the just compensation to which international law entitles them. In these conditions, there is every reason for an aggrieved state to supply effective remedies on its own if it can. Cuba has given the United States that opportunity by peddling confiscated property to traffickers who may be subject to U.S. jurisdiction. Creation of

---

* Reprinted with permission of the American Society of International Law.

such a remedy, far from violating international law, works toward rescuing that law from relative impotence.

Enactment of title III does no injustice to the "traffickers" who may become defendants. That Castro's confiscations were made without compensation, and also typically involved discrimination against U.S. nationals or political persecution of Cubans, is not one of the world's best-kept secrets. Traffickers are fully aware that they are dealing in tainted property. It can be presumed that the culpability of dealing in stolen goods is a familiar concept to them from their own legal systems. Traffickers are knowingly taking the risk that the dispossessed owners or aggrieved states might take action against them.

* * * British, French, Swiss, Austrian, Dutch and German courts * * * have denied effect to foreign confiscations. Certainly * * * no consensus exists that an internationally unlawful confiscation does pass good title that a "purchaser" can rely on and that the United States is required to recognize or respect.

Thus, it seems difficult to make a serious argument that title III infringes international law to the extent that it permits suits by confiscation victims who were U.S. nationals at the time. To the contrary, title III applies and vindicates international law. As to these lawsuits, except for some of the details of the legislation, the United States is not even exercising its jurisdiction to prescribe, but only its jurisdiction to adjudicate. It is applying international law, not just its own law.* * *

Finally, title III does not rest on a premise that international law in all cases forbids a state to confiscate the property of its nationals without just compensation. A court acting under title III will not adjudicate title to property; it will award damages for an actionable wrong under U.S. law. In title III the United States takes sharp issue with Castro's confiscations—whether the victims were aliens or Cubans—as a matter of U.S. public policy and instructs the courts to grant a monetary remedy in cases, and vis-à-vis parties, subject to their jurisdiction. Put in *Restatement* terms, the substantial effects on the United States, which warrant the exercise of its jurisdiction to prescribe its own rule, occur with respect to trafficking in any property that is owned by a U.S. national today, whether he or his ancestor was a national in the 1960s or not.* * *

Title III of Helms–Burton does not violate international law. To the contrary, it furthers both the development and the implementation of international law in an area where the rudimentary state of enforcement mechanisms allows rogue states to ignore that law and to violate the most elementary human rights of their own citizens and of foreigners with impunity. Title III is a powerful dissuasive to the immoral trafficking in stolen property that today plays a major role in keeping Castro in funds and therefore in power, and that directly affects the rights and interests of the United States and its nationals. It is a legitimate exercise of U.S.

jurisdiction, and the international rule of law should be a principal beneficiary of its enactment.

The General Assembly of the Organization of American States, by Resolution of June, 1996, **directed** the Inter–American Juridical Committee of the OAS "to examine and decide upon the validity under international law" of the Libertad Act, and to do so "as a matter of priority." The Juridical Committee rendered a unanimous (11–0, including the U.S. member) opinion. It is a non-binding opinion, and addressed two areas, property rights and the issue of extraterritoriality. The opinion included the following:

OPINION OF THE INTER–AMERICAN JURIDICAL COMMITTEE IN RESPONSE TO RESOLUTION AG/DOC 3375/96 OF THE GENERAL ASSEMBLY OF THE ORGANIZATION, ENTITLED "FREEDOM OF TRADE AND INVESTMENT IN THE HEMISPHERE"

6. In the light of the principles and norms set out in paragraph 5.[a] above the Committee considers that the legislation under analysis does not conform to international law in each of the following respects:

a) The domestic courts of a claimant State are not the appropriate forum for the resolution of State-to-State claims.

b) The claimant State does not have the right to espouse claims by persons who were not its nationals at the time of injury.

c) The claimant State does not have the right to attribute liability to nationals of third States for a claim against a foreign State.

d) The claimant State does not have the right to attribute liability to nationals of third States for the use of expropriated property located in the territory or the expropriating State where such use conforms to the laws of this latter State, nor for the use in the territory of third States of intangible property or products that do not constitute the actual asset expropriated.

e) The claimant State does not have the right to impose liability on third parties not involved in a nationalization through the creation of liability not linked to the nationalization or unrecognized by the international law on this subject, thus modifying the juridical bases for liability.

f) The claimant State does not have the right to impose compensation in any amount greater than the effective damage, including interest, that results from the alleged wrongful act of the expropriating State.

----

a. Paragraph 5 considered the "rules of international law applicable to diplomatic protection, State responsibility, and the minimum rights of aliens regarding the protection of property rights of nationals."

g) The claimant State may not deprive a foreign national of the right in accordance with due process of law to effectively contest the bases and the quantum of claims that may affect his property.

h) Successful enforcement of such a claim against the property of nationals of a third State in a manner contrary to the norms of international law could itself constitute a measure tantamount to expropriation and result in responsibility of the claimant State.

* * *

9. The Committee examined the provisions of the legislation that establish the exercise of jurisdiction on bases other than those of territoriality, and concluded that the exercise of such jurisdiction over acts of "trafficking in confiscated property" does not conform with the norms established by international law for the exercise of jurisdiction in each of the following respects:

a) A prescribing State does not have the right to exercise jurisdiction over acts of "trafficking" abroad by aliens unless specific conditions are fulfilled which do not appear to be satisfied in this situation.

b) A prescribing State does not have the right to exercise jurisdiction over acts of "trafficking" abroad by aliens under circumstances where neither the alien nor the conduct in question has any connection with its territory and where no apparent connection exists between such acts and the protection of its essential sovereign interests.

Therefore, the exercise of jurisdiction by a State over acts of "trafficking" by aliens abroad, under circumstances whereby neither the alien nor the conduct in question has any connection with its territory and there is no apparent connection between such acts and the protection of its essential sovereign interests, does not conform with international law.

Conclusion

10. For the above reasons the Committee concludes that in the significant areas described above the bases and potential application of the legislation which is the subject of this Opinion are not in conformity with international law.* * *

MANFRED WOLF, HITTING THE WRONG GUYS: EXTERNAL CONSEQUENCES OF THE CUBAN DEMOCRACY ACT

8 Fla.J.Int'l L. 415 (1993).*

* * * The protest might have confined itself to resolutions and formal protests because the trade volume at stake between Cuba and the EC

---

* Reprinted with permission of the Journal.

amounted "only" to about 500 million U.S. dollars per year. In a previous similar conflict concerning the construction of a gas-pipeline from the former Soviet Union to Western Europe there was much more protest, including a blocking statute by Great Britain as well as a confiscation by the French government of the goods concerned in order to ship them to Russia.[6]

The pipeline embargo case raised much discussion among legal scholars coming to the result that the principles of international law did not justify the use of extraterritorial jurisdiction because neither the requirements of the principle of universality nor of the nationality principle, the passive personality principle or the protective principle were met. Therefore a Netherlands' court held that the U.S. order prohibiting exports to Russia may not be considered as binding under the laws of the Netherlands.

* * *

[E]xtraterritorial jurisdiction might also be justified under a general balancing of the interests involved.[8] Thereby the ties to the state claiming extraterritorial jurisdiction must be the stronger the more the interests of other states are affected. On the other hand the ties to the regulating state may be looser, if this state is pursuing objectives of the international community. As the U.S. State Department relies on a general justification of its extraterritorial jurisdiction in the Cuban Democracy Act, it is important to come to a general balancing of interests.

In this context it has to be considered that with the Cuban Democracy Act, unlike with the pipeline embargo, the U.S. government is striving to establish democracy in Cuba which in general is an internationally approved objective. But such an internationally approved objective does not justify any measures of extraterritorial jurisdiction. Even if it is conceded that the present situation in Cuba does not comply with democratic standards, it is doubtful what would come after a change. Could a democratic government and a democratic system really be expected to emerge?

Furthermore, the embargo must be a proper means to achieve the objective intended. This could be contested too. Lacking international support, Cuba might get all goods needed from other countries. In addition, it could be argued that a country might be influenced more by a friend than by an enemy. Therefore the establishment of friendly and profitable relations with a country could be more effective in achieving democratic standards than by using boycott measures.

Under a general balancing of interests it has also to be kept in mind that only such means can be justified which are less harmful to other nations which are not a direct goal of the boycott measures. Considering

---

6. See *Ziegenhain* RIW 1993, 897, 901; specifically dealing with the French situation Dresser Industries, Inc. v. Baldridge.

8. *Basedow* Rabels Z 47 (1983), 142, 165; *Ziegenhain* RIW 1993, 897, 899.

the Cuban Democracy Act in this context, it can be stated that by preventing U.S. owned or controlled subsidiaries in third countries from trading with Cuba, these third countries could be seriously affected and hurt in their economy. The prohibition of trade will probably reduce the turnover and the earnings of the subsidiary, which could lead to dismissals, thereby enlarging the unemployment rate in the third state and causing higher social security expenses. At the same time, because of lower profits, the third state will receive lower tax revenues so that this state might have serious problems with its budget. Also the trade balance of the third state could be affected and a serious currency decline might follow.

RAJ BHALA, NATIONAL SECURITY AND INTERNATIONAL TRADE LAW: WHAT THE GATT SAYS, AND WHAT THE UNITED STATES DOES[1]

19 Univ. Penn. J. Int'l Econ. L. 263 (1998).

* * *

One recent study, conducted by the Institute for International Economics, examined the impact of unilateral American sanctions imposed against twenty-six countries, including Cuba, Iran, Libya, and Burma.[209] The results of the study indicated that in 1995, the sanctions cost the United States between fifteen and twenty billion dollars as a result of lost exports and higher priced substitute import sources, and between 200,000 and 250,000 lost export-related jobs. * * *

A second recent study, conducted by the National Association of Manufacturers, reviewed sixty-one laws and executive actions ordering unilateral American sanctions against thirty foreign countries, including Cuba, Iran, Libya, and Burma that represent forty-two percent of the world's population, or 2.3 billion potential consumers of American goods and services in export markets worth $790 billion annually.[218] The upshot is that while these sanctions may make some Americans feel safe, they are not effective. "[I]n only a handful of cases can it be argued that the sanctions changed the behavior of the targeted governments." Thus, "[u]nilateral sanctions are little more than postage stamps we send to other countries at the cost of thousands of American jobs," and they "give U.S. companies the 'stigma' of being unreliable trading partners." Unilateral trade actions rarely have positive diplomatic results to offset the costs they impose on the American economy. As of this writing, for instance, there have been no significant, long-term changes in the fundamental policies of the target countries. Libya's Qaddafi remains recalcitrant and

---

1. Reprinted with permission of the author and the U.Pa.J. Int'l Econ. L.

209. *See* Gary Clyde Hufbauer et al., *U.S. Economic Sanctions: Their Impact on Trade, Jobs, and Wages* (Apr. 16, 1997)

218. *See* National Ass'n of Manufacturers, a Catalog of New U.S. Unilateral Sanctions for Foreign Policy Purposes 1993–96 (1997).

unapologetic. Like many sanction targets, he seems to be claiming victim status, using the sanctions to attract both admiration and sympathy from other Third World governments. The ILSA may well prove to push Libya from "mere" recalcitrance to outright defiance. As for Iran, the long-term effects of their 1997 elections on the relationship between Iran and the United States remains to be seen. . . . Even if Iran changes its behavior and American–Iranian relations improve, it will be difficult if not impossible to argue the ILSA was a primary force behind the improvement. Indeed, there are at least three other pragmatic reasons why Iran could be seeking better dealings with the Great Satan: (1) the need to deal with declining oil revenues; (2) the need to deal with the widening gap between the official exchange rate for its currency (the riyal) and the black market rate and; (3) the hope for support in a possible second war with Iraq.

In sum, unilateral trade action persists despite considerable evidence showing that it is not efficacious, and is often counterproductive. Nevertheless, this evidence has not prodded U.S. trade policy officials or jurists to rethink their fidelity to unilateral trade actions, and is unlikely to do so in the foreseeable future.* * *

QUESTIONS AND COMMENTS

1. Authors Lowenfeld and Clagett present different views of parts of the Libertad (Helms–Burton) Act. Does either argument help Prentice plan its sales? What if the Cuban's, frustrated in their attempt to purchase from Prentice or one of it's affiliates, ask a Spanish company that has a plant in Havana in an old factory expropriated by the Castro government from a Cuban who is now a U.S. national living in Miami, to assemble the lathes from parts it will obtain from Prentice's UK subsidiary. They will be bought by a French machine tools parts distributor who has dealt with Prentice before, and then be resold to the Spanish company in Madrid, and shipped to its plant in Cuba. The Spanish company with the plant in Cuba has a wholly owned subsidiary in New York. That subsidiary has a Spanish CEO, who resides in Manhattan, and whose children are in U.S. schools. Are there any implications for the Spanish company because of the Cuban boycott laws?

2. Does the Libertad Act raise the boycott to a secondary level? Does Title III pass or fail a balancing test? Could a U.S. federal judge effectively carry out a balancing test?

3. Does Clagett argue convincingly that the law is more a criminal law than a trade law? Was "trafficking" a good choice of words for the drafters? What would have been better? What about his statement that title to property confiscated in a manner that violates international law cannot be passed to another party by the confiscator? Clagett suggests that the Libertad Act does not violate international law but actually "furthers both the development and the implementation of international law." Is this consistent with your understanding of how international law develops? Is it consistent with the OAS Juridical Committee opinion?

4. What is the value of the nonbinding OAS opinion? What additional step might the OAS consider?

5. Is the following opinion, expressed by Ricardo Alarcón, former Cuban Foreign Minister, consistent with the OAS opinion? He stated:

> First of all, it is illegal because it violates the most fundamental principles of the UN charter: the sovereign equality of states, non-intervention in the internal affairs of other states and the non-use of force in resolving bilateral or multilateral disputes. The blockade has political motivations. It is an attempt to force another country to act in accordance with the views and desires of a big power. That is something that clearly violates the basic premises of international law. It is also a violation of international law because it defies the UN resolutions on friendly relations among states and international peaceful cooperation. It is a clear violation of the GATT accord, the General Agreement on Trade and Tariffs, which is based on one fundamental principle: that no restrictions should be imposed on international trade. No country is to establish artificial barriers to economic and trade transactions. All of these violations exist even if we were only speaking about an "embargo." But over and above this, the United States is trying to extend its embargo throughout the entire world and that is why I assert that the policy is one of "blockade." This blockade is clearly not only a denial on the part of the United States to respect or behave in accordance with those principles, but is also an attempt by the U.S. government to force others to ignore them. I think it's a violation of international law from every aspect of this term.

R. Alarcón, Interview May, 1992, Cuban Information Project.

6. The UN voted in November, 1992, 59 to 3 (79 abstentions, only Israel and Romania supporting the United States), to urge all states to repeal all laws "whose extraterritorial effects affect the sovereignty of other states and the legitimate interests of entities or persons under their jurisdiction." That Resolution did not refer specifically to the United States, but the preamble noted that the General Assembly had learned "of the recent promulgation of measures of that nature aimed at strengthening and extending the economic, commercial and financial embargo against Cuba." Each year since there has been a new resolution, and each year more votes have been cast against the boycott. While the 1992 Resolution only condemned the extraterritorial effects of the embargo, the 1993 and 1994 resolutions added a provision calling for the end of the primary embargo by the United States. This change caused Canada to abstain in 1993, after having voted in favor of the 1992 Resolution. But Canada voted in favor of the 1994 Resolution. The United Nations General Assembly, in October, 1998, voted 157 to 2 (only Israel joining the United States) to urge the United States to repeal the Cuban blockade. Do the U.N. General Assembly Resolutions support Alarcón's position?

7. Does Professor Wolf of Frankfurt provide a fair reading of international law?

8. Considering the Cuban Assets Control Regulations, as amended by the Cuban Democracy Act (See the Documents Supplement) when the Prentice parent in the United States receives an order for a lathe to be shipped to the UK for some partial assembly and later shipment to Cuba, how should Prentice respond?

9. The Canadian wholly owned subsidiary intends to ship one machine directly to Cuba. Does that violate the regulations and the CDA?

10. Does the shipment of the third machine from the UK affiliate directly from England violate the regulations or the CDA? Does shipping the machine from England violate any EU or UK law? Does the *Freuhauf* decision briefly discussed in the previous problem affect the shipments from England? Is Wolf's view consistent with *Freuhauf*?

11. Since the enactment of the CDA, there have been no significant instances where U.S. parents of foreign subsidiaries trading with Cuba have been challenged. In February, 1994, sanctions were enforced against a French company, Sofep Petrole et Derives, for the transshipment to Cuba of United States aviation oil without a license. 11 ITR 9, Mar. 2, 1994. But this was an action by the Commerce Department regarding export regulations, not by the Treasury for violations of the Cuban Assets Control Regulations and the CDA.

12. In an attempt to address this problem of indirect trade with a boycotted or embargoed target country, the OFAC programs also cover dealings with agents of the target destination operating in third countries. Dealing with a known agent is treated the same, under the regulations, as dealing directly with the embargoed country itself. All dealings with such an agent are covered, the regulations do not confine themselves only to transactions known to be intended for the target destination. The Office of Foreign Asset Controls periodically publishes lists of such agents, in essence "blacklists" of individuals, organizations, companies, and even vessels, which are deemed to be acting for embargoed destinations. These lists appear under different names depending upon the particular embargo program, for example, parties may appear as "Blocked Yugoslav Entities" or "Specially Designated Nationals" of Cuba or of some other embargoed destination. There are currently in excess of 2,500 such individuals or firms named in the Treasury blacklists. See, 31 C.F.R. Chapter V, Appendices A, B, & C. Interestingly, to the extent that these agents are located abroad and outside the scope of U.S. jurisdiction, their activities may be entirely legal and permissible under local law. Nevertheless, the extraterritorial application of the U.S. policies embodied in the Treasury programs means that parties who are subject to U.S. jurisdiction must control their dealings with such agents. Other parts of the U.S. government such as the Commerce and State Departments maintain similar lists, but which are geared to U.S. and foreign parties who may have violated the agencies' respective export control regimes.

Prentice's Canadian and UK affiliates, and their officials, may end up on the Treasury Department's list of "Specially Designated Nationals (SDNs)" of Cuba. The list, maintained by the Office of Foreign Assets Controls (OFAC) is a form of blacklist, and prohibits all persons subject to U.S. laws from participation in financial arrangements with the listed persons or entities, without government approval. The OFAC uses the SDN list mainly to sanction foreign nationals who trade with Cuba, but are beyond the reach of the United States. U.S. persons, and foreign nationals within the United States, are thought to be adequately controlled by the boycott laws, although they could be listed. If Prentice of Canada were listed, no U.S. person, nor person within the reach of the United States, could lawfully do business with the Canadian entity, without U.S. government permission. OFAC operates in a nonlegal environment. Blacklisted persons may believe that they are not receiving due process. Peter Lichtenbaum, of Steptoe & Johnson in Washington, suggests three troublesome features that attorneys often face when dealing with OFAC. First is the use of vague terms, second the lack of established precedent of OFAC decisions, and third the procedures for identifying entities as SDNs. These would place Prentice in the difficult position of either not going forward with its plans because it cannot predict the reaction from OFAC, or asking OFAC for an opinion. What OFAC might base its decision on is uncertain since it does not publish advisory opinions as does Justice regarding the Foreign Corrupt Practices Act. The lack of available precedent extends to judicial decisions as well as OFAC opinions. Few cases help define the language of the restrictions. One decision that discusses evasion and avoidance is *Looper v. Morgan*, 1995 WL 499816 (S.D. Tex.).

Would these U.S. government lists be considered a primary or a secondary boycott tool? What would you advise Prentice to do to avoid violating any regulations applicable to dealing with any of the blacklisted parties, and would that advice differ for the Prentice subsidiaries in Canada or the United Kingdom? Was Prentice's mere acceptance of the order for the lathes at the Frankfurt trade fair problematic under these rules? Is there a parallel to be drawn between the Canadian and U.K. blocking measures discussed in this section and the U.S. antiboycott laws discussed below in Part B?

13. Professor Bhala asks whether the boycott laws are working. If they are not, why does the United States persist in using unilateral boycotts?

14. The European Union challenged the Libertad Act by calling for a dispute panel. The EU agreed to stay the matter because the United States agreed to seek some modification in the application of Title IV, the visa denial provisions. Whether U.S. boycott laws are consistent with obligations under the WTO and the NAFTA may never be determined. The national security defense seems to offer an absolute immunity, or does it? Professor Gordon's comments on sanctions and NAFTA, and Professor Spanogle's comments on sanctions and the WTO, in 27 Stetson L. Rev. 1259 and 1313, respectively (1998), illustrate some significant differences in the way challenges under the WTO and NAFTA might proceed. For example, the NAFTA includes a provision specifically allowing any Party to maintain a trade boycott against a non-Party which includes limitations or prohibitions on importing to the Party goods of the non-Party through the territory of another Party. Art. 309(3). The WTO has no such provision. Does the Title IV denial of visas part of the Libertad Act conflict with the movement of persons allowed in the NAFTA if visas are denied to Canadian or Mexican business persons?

15. Relatively recently, states and even smaller subdivisions such as cities have enacted sanctions laws. They have usually directed the government not to purchase from certain countries until certain policies changed. Massachusetts enacted sanctions on trade with Burma because of alleged human rights violations, by imposing upon any company doing business with the Commonwealth of Massachusetts a penalty if they also engaged in business with Burma. A group of U.S. businesses reacted by suing Massachusetts in federal court over the sanctions laws. The U.S. Supreme Court ruled the law

invalid under the Supremacy Clause because it threatened to frustrate federal statutory objectives. *See National Foreign Trade Council v. Baker*, 26 F.Supp.2d 287 (D.Mass.1998), *aff'd, National Foreign Trade Council v. Natsios*, 181 F.3d 38 (1st Cir.1999), *aff'd sub nom., Crosby v. National Foreign Trade Council*, 530 U.S. 363, 120 S.Ct. 2288, 147 L.Ed.2d 352 (2000). The Florida legislature has occasionally enacted laws directed to relations with Cuba, including a mini-Helms–Burton law. One law that prohibited the use of private and public funds by any university employee to travel to Cuba was annulled by the federal court. See *Faculty Senate of Florida International University v. Roberts*, 574 F.Supp.2d 1331 (S.D.Fla. 2008). But right behind it was a new law to impose a $250,000 state bond upon any vendor in Florida selling trips to Cuba, effectively trying to shut down the Miami travel agencies that book legal travel to Cuba. A good history of the travel restrictions is in CRS Report for Congress, Cuba: U.S. Restrictions on Travel and Remittances, July 30, 2008, at fpc.state.gov/documents/organization/108310.pdf.

16. The Libertad Act appears to have been the apogee of restrictions on trade with Cuba. In 2000 the Trade Sanctions Reform and Export Enhancement Act prevented the use of unilateral agricultural and medical sector trade sanctions, except in extraordinary circumstances. The sales must be for cash rather than letters of credit. BIS has revised and liberalized its Cuban licensing policy and created a new EAR license exception that allows exports of donated consumer communication devices, including mobile phones, personal computers, and related software. The Obama administration in the 2009 Omnibus Appropriations Act loosened travel and remittance restrictions. They were extended further in early 2011. But general travel by U.S. citizens has not yet been restored. Curiously, the United States has become a major trading partner of Cuba. The U.S. embassy (called officially the Special Interests Section) is the largest of any nation, and there is considerably more travel than the United States would prefer to admit.

PART B. THE ANTIBOYCOTT LAWS OF THE UNITED STATES

Prentice also exhibited its machine lathes at an international trade fair in Detroit. That fair was attended by representatives from several Arab nations. They were impressed by the products of Prentice. An official of a large government-owned enterprise in Qatar told the Prentice representatives that he wished to negotiate the purchase of several machine lathes that would be made for special purposes. The official asked the Prentice representative about the company's background and where it did business. He said he wanted to be certain that the company had sufficient experience in international trade to provide reasonable assurance that it would carry out its contractual obligations. Without having any idea that there might be additional motives for the questions, the Prentice representative gave the Qatar official a copy of the last two annual reports of Prentice. The reports included the company's history, its entry into international business, and a list of all the countries with which Prentice had done business. The list did not contain any reference to Israel.

Two weeks later a letter was received from Qatar inviting a Prentice official to visit Qatar to discuss the needs of the Qatar plant. The letter also stated that, assuming those discussions were satisfactory, a firm order would be made for several machine lathes. A Prentice official, Herman Schmidt, soon thereafter visited Qatar. The negotiations proceeded extremely well. There was no question but that a mutually agreeable contract would be signed. Relaxing over dinner, the Qatar official asked Schmidt, who was of German ancestry, about his family background, and whether any members of the family had "suffered" in World War II. Schmidt said, "my parents escaped from Germany at the beginning of the War. They did not flee because they feared for their lives, they were not Jewish, but because they did not agree with the territorial expansion designs of the German government." The conversation turned to several contemporary conflicts, including that in the Middle East. The Qatar official asked what Schmidt's personal views were about the conflict, and whether his views appeared consistent with other people in his community and, particularly, other officials at Prentice. Schmidt said he had little substantive knowledge of the conflict, partially because his business obligations took a great deal of his time, and partially because he lived in a suburb of Detroit with a very small Jewish population. He said that he rarely had any opportunity to come in contact with Jewish members of the community and discuss the issue. And he stated that since the company had not yet received any orders from Israel, he had no opportunity to discuss the issue with Israeli officials or manufacturers. Later, in a different context, while discussing the company's busy schedule, Schmidt noted that the receipt of the orders from Qatar would, along with the company's current business, impose such demand upon the company that they would not be able to accept any orders from any other nations for the foreseeable future. The next day the contract was signed for the purchase of ten machine lathes.

To fulfill the contract, Prentice had to obtain parts from several companies to manufacture the machine lathes. The usual practice of Prentice was to solicit bids from at least two, and often as many as four or five, other companies. Before asking for bids for this contract, Prentice received a letter from the Qatar enterprise that requested certain information. The Qatar enterprise wished to have Prentice certify that none of the companies that were included on an enclosed list would participate in supplying parts for the lathes. Prentice's counsel sent a letter to Qatar stating that they could not under U.S. law complete the information statement, but that Prentice "understood" the concern of Qatar. Prentice listed all the companies which it purchased supplies from and suggested that Qatar stipulate suppliers it preferred. By return letter Qatar stipulated certain suppliers which Prentice used for the manufacture of the lathes. When Prentice shipped the goods, they were transported on a carrier that only carries cargo between Western and Arab nations, never stopping at an Israeli port.

The Arab nations have imposed upon Israel an international economic boycott. The United States responded with legislation and regulations to attempt to prohibit U.S. persons, primarily business enterprises, from supporting the boycott. The role of the United States in the Arab boycott has been to regulate how U.S. persons must act in their dealings with Arab nations. That regulation is based on the policy that U.S. persons should not assist the Arab nations in their boycott of Israel, although the law and regulations are drafted more generally in terms of not assisting restrictive trade practices imposed by foreign nations against nations friendly to the United States.

The antiboycott response of the United States included both provisions of the Internal Revenue Code and the Export Administration Act. Section 999 of the IRC (the Ribicoff amendment) essentially penalizes taxpayers who agree to not engage in business with Israel. The Export Administration Act provisions are broadly worded. For specific advice one must turn to the more detailed regulations issued by the Department of Commerce. Commerce has produced, along with the regulations, a number of examples that are designed to illustrate the intent of the regulations. They disclose the difficulty in drawing the line where illegal conduct begins.

Prentice involves a situation where a company has never sold products to Israel and confronts the antiboycott issue when it becomes interested in trading with an Arab nation. There are other contexts that may arise and create a different tension and possible resolution under the regulations. A company may be doing business with Israel, but also wish to do business with Arab nations. More difficult is where it is doing business with Israel but would like to terminate that business and commence doing business with Arab nations. The reason could be perfectly justifiable—the company may have difficulty obtaining hard currency from Israel because of trade imbalances, and believe the Arab nations would be able to pay their bills. But the reason for dropping Israel could also be that the Arab nations have told the company to make a choice. A reverse situation occurs when the company is doing business in Arab nations but would like to expand and include Israel. Or it might prefer to be in Israel and drop its business in the Arab nations. A final possibility is that the company is functioning in both areas (either the Arab nations do not know of the presence in Israel or they overlook it to obtain needed products), and the company decides to leave Israel. It might be for legitimate business reasons, or it might be because the Arabs place pressure on the company to choose.

The antiboycott rules are an excellent example of the effect political decisions have upon trade. No one would deny that the rules—although they do not contain the words Israel or Arab, but speak of boycott activity in general—were passed as part of U.S. foreign policy regarding the Israel–Arab tension.

Prentice may have considerable sympathy towards Israel, yet have no interest in doing business there. The officials at Prentice may thus object strenuously to any obstacle which causes them to lose business with Qatar when they had no intention of dealing with Israel. Or the officials may be strongly committed to the Arab boycott motives. It is not a very easy area in which to resolve issues for one's client. And it may be an area where less is best, where one wants to talk as little as possible and ask as few questions as possible for fear that an innocent remark may jeopardize a legitimate business interest. The choice the U.S. Congress made is that United States–Israel relations must come before private trade interests, and that some legitimate trade arrangements may be prohibited (or never come to pass because of the additional costs of compliance) to assure that trade is not used by the Arab nations as one weapon to keep the conflict with Israel continuing.

This part of the problem affords an opportunity to consider some planning recommendations by counsel to the Prentice company regarding how officials of Prentice should respond when they receive inquiries or forms from Arab nations or the boycott office. Some Arab nations have partly relaxed the boycott. But the Damascus boycott office remains functioning.

Within the Department of Commerce is the Bureau of Industry and Security (BIS), which has export enforcement responsibility, exercised through three offices, including the Office of Antiboycott Compliance (OAC). That is the Office which most directly addresses antiboycott issues.

The Export Administration Act, particularly 50 U.S.C.A.App. § 2407 and § 2410, is necessary for an analysis of this part of the problem. It is included in the Documents Supplement. The Export Administration Regulations, also necessary for the analysis, are included in the Documents Supplement.

GUZZARDI, THAT CURIOUS BARRIER ON THE ARAB FRONTIERS

Fortune, July 1975, at 82.*

* * * The primary boycott * * * is not everywhere leakproof: farm produce, for example, crosses the frontier between Israel and Jordan. The Israelis like to exaggerate the amount of forbidden traffic, and the Arabs like to say there is none at all.

The secondary boycott is the one that has kicked up an international storm. * * * The films of Elizabeth Taylor have been banned, and Arabs have expressed special displeasure over a scene in *Funny Girl* in which Barbra Streisand kisses Omar Sharif.

---

* Reprinted with permission of Fortune Magazine.

Companies that violate the rules * * * are put on a blacklist. * * * They can be delisted—or libérées, as the phrase goes—any time they choose to mend their ways. * * *

* * *

* * * RCA could take double umbrage, first at being listed, and then at discovering that five models of its Spectra computer series, sold off long ago, are also itemized. The Moslem faith forbids drinking, and the Arabs have obviously decided that the best scotch not to drink is Chivas Regal, which merits mention separate from Seagram. Along with Revlon—although they are unlikely candidates for big sales among the Bedouin—go Natural Wonder Medicated Total Skin Lotion and Moon Drops Moisturizing Bath Oil.

Almost all of the big companies insist that they never received any formal notification that they were being blacklisted. Ford has no record of being notified. RCA learned the news from an executive who heard about it on a trip. Hartz Mountain, the pet-food maker, found out when its president, Leonard Stern, picked up a copy of the New York *Post* recently on his way home from the office. Necchi still insists that it isn't listed, although its name appears on a Saudi Arabian list. All that, of course, leaves doubt in some corporate minds about the exact reason for inclusion.

Trivial and fortuitous connections with Israel seem reason enough—although hundreds of associations of equal triviality must have been overlooked. Topps Chewing Gum is banned because it licenses the production in Israel of Bazooka Bubble Gum, complete with baseball cards. The products of the Nassau Brassiere Co. for years were denied to Arab womanhood because the Arabs said that its parent, Bestform Foundations, never answered a questionnaire. A spokesman for Laurance Rockefeller guesses that Laurance Rockefeller Associates (which doesn't exist) is mentioned because Rockefeller and a few associates once owned a minor interest in Elron Electronic Industries, an Israeli company, which they sold in 1967. * * *

As for being libérée, that has its bizarre aspects, too. Bulova's experience sounds as though it came out of a Peter Lorre movie. Although the company had no interests in the Middle East except for a few watches on sale in the duty-free shops of airports, it awoke one day to find itself blacklisted. Later, it was approached indirectly by a Syrian lawyer who said that, by working through an influential agent related to one of the then governing families of Damascus, he could have the company removed. Bulova paid him a retainer to try. Negotiations were said to be going swimmingly when word reached Bulova that the agent had been hanged in a public execution in the main square of Damascus. Doubtless out of humane considerations, Bulova has made no effort to be delisted since.

The image of ineptitude projected by the blacklist may be embarrassing to the Arabs. But at the same time there may be a kind of wisdom in the policies as well. Cloaked by the general chaos, the Arab countries make some startling ad hoc exceptions to the boycott's rules, in order to serve their higher interests.

Many American companies in the defense industry—McDonnell Douglas, United Aircraft, General Electric, Hughes Aircraft, Textron—are selling or have sold war equipment to Israel. Of course, each of them should be on the list in boldface type for rendering such "material" help to the enemy. But they are all omitted for the overriding reason that the Arabs want the choice of the best weaponry without inhibitions about boycotts. The Arabs use as a convenient rationale the fact that the contract to purchase is made with the Department of Defense.

There is another case where being faithful to the embargo would serve the Arabs, as Joseph Conrad once wrote, about as well as "tying up a dog with a string of sausages." The Arabs are eager for economic development, and many companies already established in Arab lands are contributing to that goal. To expel them in the name of the boycott would be to defeat the Arabs' own larger purposes. So exceptions galore: Hilton International operates hotels in Kuwait, Egypt, and Abu Dhabi—and in Tel Aviv and Jerusalem. I.B.M. has plants in three Arab countries and in Israel; Olivetti has agents in twelve Arab nations as well as Israel. Hertz is blacklisted, its parent (RCA) is blacklisted, and it has outlets in both Israel and Egypt. Boeing sells planes to El Al and to Arab countries; some well-known brands of Swiss watches are on sale throughout the Middle East.* * *

TRANE v. BALDRIGE

United States District Court, Western District of Wisconsin, 1983.
552 F.Supp. 1378, cert. denied 469 U.S. 826, 105 S.Ct. 105, 83 L.Ed.2d 50.

[This case is included to illustrate the history of the Arab boycott. The plaintiff challenged the EAA and regulations directed to boycotts on constitutional grounds. The court ruled against such challenge on each ground.]

WARREN, DISTRICT JUDGE.

The League of Arab States is composed of 21 Arab states. On December 11, 1954, its council passed a resolution calling for an economic boycott of the State of Israel. Sometime thereafter, the League formed an organization called the Central Boycott Office, whose purpose is to facilitate communications among the local boycott offices of the boycotting states, gather boycott-related information, investigate and administer certain aspects of the boycott, and make recommendations concerning firms or individuals that should be blacklisted by participating Arab states. All Arab states that participate in the boycott of Israel represent that their boycott activities are governed by a document entitled "General Principles for Boycott of Israel." Each state, however, retains sovereign rights over boycott activities. In a significant number of cases, these states have not followed the provisions of the document.

The Arab boycott of Israel occurs on three levels. The "primary boycott" involves a refusal by the governments of the participating countries to deal, and a prohibition on their residents from dealing, directly with, or in the goods of, Israel or Israeli firms. The primary boycott is enforced by 16 Arab states. The "secondary boycott" involves a refusal by the governments of participating Arab states to deal, and a prohibition on their residents from dealing, with persons or firms, or in the goods or services of persons or firms, which, although not Israeli, have been "blacklisted" by boycott officials of these Arab states. The "tertiary boycott" involves a requirement by participating governments that persons or firms not deal with blacklisted firms in certain circumstances. The secondary and tertiary aspects of the boycott are enforced in varying degrees in 13 Arab states. * * *

As a means of gathering boycott-related information, the local boycott office in an Arab state may send a questionnaire to a target seeking formal written responses as to the target's business affiliations, relationships with Israel, relationships with blacklisted persons or firms, and other matters. Failure by a target to respond to such a questionnaire within the prescribed time period makes it more likely than not that the target will be blacklisted by the country sending the questionnaire and that the target will be recommended for blacklisting to the Central Boycott Office. * * *

In the mid–1970's, Congress became concerned about Arab efforts to pressure American companies into participating in the boycott of Israel. * * * In 1977, Congress enacted anti-boycott legislation as an amendment to the Export Administration Act. * * * The 1977 Amendments authorized the President to issue regulations making it a criminal offense for any "United States person" to take or agree to take certain boycott-related actions with respect to his activities in United States commerce. The Department of Commerce promulgated such regulations, which took effect on January 18, 1978. * * * In 1979, the Export Administration Act extended the foreign-boycott provisions of the 1977 Amendments, with no changes effecting the present litigation. * * *

One of the provisions of the anti-boycott legislation, along with the implementing regulations promulgated by the Commerce Department, prohibits United States persons from intentionally complying with demands from foreign boycott officials for information in response to a boycott questionnaire. See 50 U.S.C.App. § 2407(a); 15 C.F.R. § 369.2.[a] The legislation does not prevent a United States person from providing information on its business operations to a boycotting country in a normal commercial context. See 15 C.F.R. § 369.2(d)(3). The restriction touches upon such information only if it would be furnished for boycott-related purposes through a questionnaire or otherwise. See 15 C.F.R. § 369.2(d)(4).

---

a. C.F.R. sections were renumbered so that all 369 sections now appear as 769.

UNITED STATES v. MEYER

United States Court of Appeals, First Circuit, 1988.
864 F.2d 214.

COFFIN, CIRCUIT JUDGE.

Appellant Robert Meyer is a Massachusetts lawyer charged with violating anti-boycott regulations * * * by completing, and failing to inform the Commerce Department about, a Saudi Arabia trademark registration form that asked whether his client had a business relationship with Israel. Appellant refused to pay a $5,000 civil fine, and the government then brought this suit to collect the penalty. The district court upheld the assessment, and we affirm.

* * * In December 1977, in the course of assisting a client who sought to register a trademark in Saudi Arabia, Meyer received an Authorization of Agent form from a Saudi Arabian firm that processed applications for trademark registration in that country. The form included a section characterized in the cover letter as a "Creed Declaration." In relevant part, it stated: "I/We also hereby solemnly declare that this company has no relations with Israel, which would contradict the following boycott principles:

    1.   Establishment of a branch of the factory in Israel.

    2.   Establishment of an assembling factory in Israel or presence of an agent who assembles the products of the company in Israel.

    3.   The availability of general agents or central offices for the Middle East in Israel.

    4.   Granting the right to use the company's name by Israeli companies.

    5.   Participation in Israeli factories or companies.

    6.   Rendering technical assistance to Israeli companies.

    7.   In case one of the promoters is an Israeli national."

In January 1978, Meyer mailed the completed form to the Saudi Arabian Embassy in Washington, D.C. The next month, in response to a request from the Embassy, Meyer attempted to obtain State Department notarization of the form through a Virginia associate. The State Department responded to the associate's request by explaining that it could not authenticate documents "relating to the Arab boycott of Israel," and it further stated that the law "prohibit[s] U.S. persons from providing certain boycott information." The Virginia lawyer later wrote to Meyer that he authenticated the form through the U.S. Arab Chamber of Commerce, "[a]fter failing to obtain authentication by the State Department because of the Arab boycott."

In April, Meyer wrote a letter to his client in which he described his efforts to obtain authentication of the form, explaining that one problem he encountered was "that the Department of State would not apply its Certificate because of the boycott provisions [and] that Saudi Arabia would not waive the boycott provisions." In September 1978, Meyer sent a copy of the completed form to the Saudi Arabian firm that had sent it to him.

Meyer received a letter from the firm in November, explaining that the form he submitted was unacceptable because it was not authenticated by the State Department. The letter added, however, that the Creed Declaration was no longer required, and it suggested that the change was made because Saudi Arabia recognized "that the United States State Department will not legalize any document which contains the Boycott provisions." A new form, without the declaration, was enclosed. Meyer sent the new form to his client, but he never received a reply from her. He therefore closed his file on this matter.* * *

Meyer's primary argument is that he lacked the requisite intent to violate the statute and regulations. He claims that his sole purpose in transmitting the form containing the Creed Declaration was to secure a trademark registration for his client, and that nothing he did "either furnished any information or in any way had anything to do with any boycott." The purpose of the Declaration, he asserts, was "not to derive information or knowledge, but merely to exclude [those] unworthy" to obtain a trademark registration.

We disagree that Meyer's actions fell outside of the regulatory prohibition. Although an individual does not violate section 369.2(d) if he takes a prohibited action *inadvertently, see* 15 C.F.R. § 369.1(e)(3),[a] the regulations expressly state that an individual who does an act "[knowing] that such action was required or requested for boycott reasons" will be deemed to have acted "with intent to comply with an unsanctioned foreign boycott." *Id.* at § 369.1(e)(6). The regulations spell out the significance of the intent requirement:

(4) Intent in this context means the reason or purpose for one's behavior. It does not mean that one has to agree with the boycott in question or desire that it succeed or that it be furthered or supported. But it does mean that the reason why a particular prohibited action was taken must be established.

(5) Reason or purpose can be proved by circumstantial evidence. For example, if a person receives a request to supply certain boycott information, the furnishing of which is prohibited by this Part, and he knowingly supplies that information in response, he clearly intends to comply with that boycott request. It is irrelevant that he may disagree with or object to the boycott itself. Information will be deemed to be furnished with the requisite intent if the person furnishing the information knows that it was sought for boycott purposes.

---

a. C.F.R. sections were renumbered so that all 369 sections now appear as 769.

15 C.F.R. § 369.1(e)(4), (5). Included in the regulations are "Examples of 'Intent,'" one of which resembles the circumstances of this case:

> (viii) A, a U.S. chemical manufacturer, receives a "boycott questionnaire" from boycotting country Y asking, among other things, whether A has any plants located in boycotted country X. A, which has never supported Y's boycott of X, responds to Y's questionnaire, indicating affirmatively that it does have plants in X and that it intends to continue to have plants in X.

> A's responding to Y's questionnaire is deemed to be action with intent to comply with Y's boycott, because A knows that the questionnaire is boycott-related. It is irrelevant that A does not also wish to support Y's boycott.

In addition, an example in the section of the regulations discussing what it means to furnish information about business relationships is strikingly similar to this case, and illustrates that appellant's completion of the Creed Declaration was prohibited.

> (xvii) U.S. company A, a manufacturer of certain patented products, desires to register its patents in boycotting country Y. A receives a power of attorney form required to register its patents. The form contains a question regarding A's business relationships with or in boycotted country X. A has no business relationships with X and knows or has reason to know that the information is sought for boycott reasons.

> A may not answer the question, because A would be furnishing information about its business relationships with or in a boycotted country. 15 C.F.R. § 369.2(d).

There is no doubt that Meyer knew that the Creed Declaration was boycott-related. The document expressly asked for a declaration that the company had no relationship with Israel that would "contradict ... boycott principles." If he somehow failed to notice the language on the form when he received it, his Virginia associate's letter explaining the State Department's refusal to authenticate the form certainly brought the boycott issue directly to his attention. Indeed, when appellant wrote to his client in April 1978, he referred to the "boycott provisions" in the document.

In light of Meyer's obvious awareness of the Creed Declaration, appellant can not contend that he inadvertently violated the regulations when he arranged for completion of the form and transmitted it, thus fulfilling Saudi Arabia's boycott requirements. Instead, appellant emphasizes the district court's finding "that at no time did he consciously intend to violate the laws of the United States or any applicable regulations established by the commerce department." We find no fault with this conclusion, but—as the district court recognized—it does not help appellant. The maxim that ignorance of the law is no excuse is fully applicable here. Appellant sent the application form to Saudi Arabian officials with full awareness that it contained a signed declaration that his client did no business with Israel. In so doing, he intentionally complied with Saudi Arabia's boycott of Israel. That he had no intent to break the law does not erase the fact that he did so.[2] * * *

AFFIRMED.

JOHN R. BROWN, CIRCUIT JUDGE, dissenting.

* * *

Indulgent as we must be to the trier's finding of guilt, the question remains: were any of these acts done by Attorney Meyer with a *consciousness* that they were illegal? The test for determining whether the finding of guilt can stand is whether there was sufficient evidence to establish beyond a reasonable doubt that the acts done by Attorney Meyer were done with a *consciousness* that they violated the anti-boycott statute. In words which could not have been plainer or clearer or more selective, the trial judge, as the trier, answered emphatically:

> ... at no time did he [Meyer] *consciously* intend to violate the laws of the United States or any applicable regulations established by the Commerce Department.

The anti-boycott statute construed as it must be in the light of *Liparota* requires the Government to prove that one charged with violations of the anti-boycott statute *consciously* did the acts knowing that they were a violation of the statute.

QUESTIONS AND COMMENTS

1. Primary boycotts are not unlawful under international law because there is no customary, multilateral or treaty law outlawing such boycotts. What if the Arab League instructs all Arabs living in Israel, or Israeli occupied territories, not to trade with Israeli or Jewish persons, except to obtain life-sustaining requirements not otherwise available from other Arabs? Do the secondary or tertiary boycotts violate international law? *See generally,* Marcuss, U.S. Antiboycott Law—Problems & Pitfalls, 1982, Private Investment Abroad 99 (1982); Symposium, *International Trade Embargos and Boycotts,* 20 Colum.J.Transnat'l L. 407 (1981); Sherman, *Outline and Checklist of Arab Boycotts and U.S. Antiboycott Laws,* 17 Int'l Lawyer 711 (1983).

2. Considering the current regulations blacklisted companies would find it difficult to become libérée. Prior to the EAA and the regulations, companies that discovered they were on the blacklist would discuss their becoming libérée with the Arab nations. But under regulation Section 769.2(d), furnishing information about business relationships with boycotted countries is

---

2. We note, in response to the dissent, our view that subsection (3) simply states the limitation that the statute and regulations do not apply to *inadvertent* actions in compliance with a boycott. We believe that subsection (5) and the "Examples of 'Intent'" demonstrate that the intent requirement is met so long as the actor complies with a request for information with knowledge that the request is boycott-related. We therefore disagree that the principle of *Liparota v. United States,* 471 U.S. 419, 105 S.Ct. 2084, 85 L.Ed.2d 434 (1985) is applicable here.

severely limited. For example, were a company asked whether it had facilities in Israel, it could not answer. But in soliciting business in an Arab nation, it could supply the country with a brochure listing those countries in which it has facilities, if the brochures were used throughout the world and were not intended to convey to the Arab nation the company's relationships with Israel. The regulations are replete with such enticements to deceptive drafting. Given a desire to trade with Arab nations and a set of the regulations, a company may tell the Arab nation much of what it wants to hear without violating the regulations. The regulations may be a trap for the innocent or a solvable puzzle for the intended guilty. They try to accomplish a perhaps impossible, however generally perceived laudable, task—but they are there and they must be dealt with. Prentice would like to undertake the sale without violating the law. It is a maze which may become more difficult to penetrate with every succeeding question—asked either by Prentice or the officials of Qatar.

There are many questions that Prentice may have. Each may require a careful reading of the lengthy regulations and helpful examples. It is impossible to reproduce all the regulations and examples in the Document Supplement. But what should illustrate the role of counsel in helping Prentice is to focus on one section and consider how Prentice will be affected. The Section chosen is 760.2 Prohibitions, (a) Refusals to do business, (c) Furnishing information about race, religion, sex or national origin, and (d) Furnishing information about business relationships with boycotted countries or blacklisted persons, which provides regulations to the EAA Section 8(a).

3. The principal function of the boycott regulations is to prohibit applicable persons from furthering or supporting a boycott against a friendly nation. The two main areas which the regulations address are refusals to do business and furnishing certain information. Boycott support before the enactment of the antiboycott rules was common practice by many companies. That has been replaced by considerable corporate conduct that illustrates an extensive range of subtle contacts designed to convey information to the boycotting nations that a company with which they might do business does not deal with Israel.

A highly publicized blacklist case involved Baxter International Inc. (a large medical supply company), and the company's general counsel. See Bus.Wk., Oct. 7, 1991, at 106. As a result of an informant Baxter was investigated and charged with violating the EAA because of the way in which it attempted to have its name removed from the blacklist. The company and general counsel pleaded guilty to 337 criminal and civil charges of furnishing information contrary to the antiboycott laws in an effort to be delisted. Baxter paid $6.5 million and the general counsel paid $100,000. The company was the subject of a denial order prohibiting any business in Saudi Arabia or Syria for two years. Subsequently the company was debarred from government contracts and customer cancellations amounted to millions of dollars.

Consent decrees continue to be the norm. Most are settled with relatively nominal fines. For example, settlements in mid–1998 of three companies, a Dell Computer German subsidiary, a Nashville paper broker, and a Chicago manufacturer, were $3,000, $10,000, and $13,000. All involved furnishing information issues. But larger settlements come along every few years. One of the more recent was $1.4 million paid by Paris based L'Oreal, which acquired Helena Rubinstein of the United States and wanted to assure the Syrians that L'Oreal was not doing business through the American company. Among the most recent is an $88,500 settlement of charges against GM Daewoo Auto & Technology Company, a Korean company majority owned by General Motors.

4. Has Prentice by its conduct refused to deal with Israel under the EAA and the Regulations? See 50 U.S.C.A. § 2407(a)(1)(A) and (B), and the Regulations. Is the necessary intent discussed in *United States v. Meyer* present? Consider the following actions of Prentice:

    a. Providing annual reports which disclose that Prentice does not do business with Israel. See 50 U.S.C.A. § 2407(a)(1)(D), and Regulations.

    b. Discussion after dinner when Prentice official Schmidt discloses that he is not Jewish, that he lives in an area with few Jewish residents, and that the company had received no orders from Israel and if they did they could not be filled. See 50 U.S.C.A. § 2407(a)(1)(D), and Regulations.

    c. Prentice listing suppliers and suggesting Qatar choose suppliers it preferred. See 50 U.S.C.A. § 2407(a)(1)(D), (2)(C), and Regulations.

    d. Shipping goods on a carrier that never stops at an Israel port. See 50 U.S.C.A. § 2407(a)(1)(D), (2)(B), and Regulations.

5. If Prentice had subsidiaries in several Arab boycotting countries and, not knowing that country X, a friend of Israel, had been added to the boycotted country list of those Arab nations, what affect should there be on plans of Prentice to open a subsidiary in X if the company receives a notice from the Arab nations stating that X is on the boycott list? Prentice might have decided separately not to go forward with the plans to build in X for legitimate business reasons. How would they establish that their reason was the latter and not the notice from the Arab nation? What if the president of Prentice at a conference said that Prentice would like to do business in Israel but since it was long established in several Arab nations, it would not consider commencing business in Israel for fear that it would lose the Arab business? See 50 U.S.C.A. § 2407(a)(1)(A), and Regulations.

6. In manufacturing the machine lathes, Prentice buys parts from several companies. One company which it refuses to buy parts from is on the boycotted nation list, but Prentice simply does not respond to numerous inquiries from the company. The parts it buys from other suppliers are the same quality, but a bit more expensive. Has Prentice violated the regulations? It would quite clearly be a violation if Prentice wrote and said they were sorry but they could not buy because it would cause a loss of the contract with Qatar, but what happens when the refusal is one of silence? What if Prentice writes to the company and says, "Your parts are identical and the price is the same, but all this nonsense about boycotts and antiboycotts causes additional expense and makes dealing with you more costly, so we regret we can't buy from you"?

7. What if Qatar officials write to Prentice and say "We will undertake the acquisition of parts for your manufacture of the lathes for us. Tell us what you need and we will obtain them"? What if instead Qatar sends a list of

acceptable suppliers for parts? Next Qatar asks Prentice to send to Qatar a list of prospective parts suppliers. Qatar selects the company it wants to be the supplier. Prentice does not know what criteria Qatar used. Has Prentice violated the regulations? If not, what if Prentice has reason to believe that the boycott was at least an element of the decision making process in Qatar?

8. When Prentice receives the order, it includes a statement that one of the reasons Prentice was chosen was because after a careful investigation, Qatar had concluded that Prentice does not do business with Israel and thus is entitled to the contract? What if part of the investigation had been to ask Prentice for the past ten years annual reports so that the government could "learn more" about the company?

9. Prentice has asked to be paid by a letter of credit. Qatar obtains a letter confirmed by Michigan Merchant's Bank in favor of Prentice. One of the requirements of the letter of credit that Prentice must supply, in addition to the usual invoice, bill of lading, consular invoice, etc., is a statement that all parts of the lathe were made by companies on the list of acceptable sources previously sent to Prentice. Prentice is concerned that giving such a statement might be a refusal to deal. Do you agree? What if a statement is required for payment under the letter of credit that certifies that the ship on which the goods are in transit is qualified under Qatar law to enter Qatar ports?

10. What if the contract has a "Buy Arab" provision, that requires all parts available in any Arab nation to be used in the manufacture of the lathes?

11. Has Prentice by its conduct furnished information to Qatar in violation of the EAA and regulations? Consider the annual reports and the letter to Qatar listing suppliers. Was Prentice's counsel correct in that the requested certification would violate United States law?

12. These examples should illustrate that the regulations attempt to draw lines between lawful and unlawful conduct, but that they are extremely difficult to draw with any certainty. It would be desirable to be able to conclude that all conduct which should be prohibited is prohibited, and all conduct that should be permitted is permitted. Is that possible to conclude?

The section of the regulations discussed above constitutes only part of what Prentice must know. There are many other sections which involve definitions of persons subject to the law, what controlled in fact means, activities in interstate or foreign commerce subject to the law, intent, discriminatory actions, furnishing information, letters of credit, exceptions, evasions, and, of considerable importance—the reporting requirements.

Reporting requirements are quite extensive. The Department of Commerce is entitled to know about any requests that might assist carrying out a boycott. Since Qatar has need for information from its contracting partner, there can be no rule disallowing any requests of any nature. Thus the regulations attempt to outline requests and other information which must be forwarded to Commerce. What if Prentice receives a letter from Qatar stating that under Qatar law, the goods which will be shipped to Qatar must not include any six pointed stars or other symbols or words of an Israeli origin? The regulations suggest that such letter must be reported, because it contains a request to comply with the boycott requirements of Qatar. Section 760.6(c), example xxiv. The examples in the regulations are a fertile source for questions, and an equally fertile source of frustration for a company attempting to comply with the spirit of the antiboycott laws, while doing legitimate business with any nations it chooses.

13. Our concern with Prentice has been whether the U.S. government might challenge the activities of Prentice. Does the EAA allow a private right of action? See *Israel Aircraft Ind. v. Sanwa Business Credit Corp.*, 16 F.3d 198 (7th Cir.1994) (no private right); *Bulk Oil (ZUG) A.G. v. Sun Co., Inc.*, 583 F.Supp. 1134 (S.D.N.Y.1983), affirmed without opinion 742 F.2d 1431 (2d Cir.1984) (no private right); *Abrams v. Baylor College of Medicine*, 581 F.Supp. 1570 (S.D.Tex.1984) (implied private cause does exist).

14. "The anti-boycott law received little response from foreign nations. Germany and the Netherlands seemed satisfied that their governments could by negotiation defuse any Arab actions such as blacklisting companies. The United Kingdom briefly considered anti-boycott legislation, but none was enacted. The U.K. Foreign Office is more inclined to favour Arab interests than the U.S. State Department, and British firms are allowed to make commercial decisions involving the boycott exclusively on commercial grounds. France did enact laws which might have been used to challenge any assistance given to the Arab boycott, but the government interpreted the legislation so as to render it useless. The motivation for such emasculation was the paramount interests of French trade and employment. The anti-boycott laws generated a minimum of response based on moral foundations. The Arab boycott was not viewed as sufficiently threatening to Israel to raise a question of human rights. Israel was successful economically, more so than many Arab nations."

15. BIS reports annually on the antiboycott laws. During fiscal 2007 ten companies agreed to pay $194,500 in civil penalties to settle allegations that they violated the antiboycott provisions. In the same year 17 voluntary disclosure cases were reported, a number that remains a norm (12 in 2008, 17 in 2009). No BIS report was issued for 2008 or 2009. The complaints mostly involved furnishing information about business relations with Israel and failure to report receipt of requests that might result in participation in prohibited activities.

Is the boycott collapsing? Commerce officials have occasionally suggested that the boycott was collapsing. The list of sanctions in the form of consent decrees is not suggestive of an active prosecution of alleged violations. The boycott is ignored by Arab countries when convenient. But it is not likely that anyone in the government will declare it to be over. As Yogi Berra said it best—"It ain't over till it's over." See "Arab boycott largely reduced to 'lip service'," The Jerusalem Post, Feb. 28, 2006. See www.jpost.com.

PROBLEM 8.3 QUESTIONABLE PAYMENTS TO FOREIGN OFFICIALS: PROCESSED FOODS IN NIGERIA

SECTION I. THE SETTING

Processed Foods, Inc. (Processed) is a large Delaware corporation, included among the "Fortune 500." The company both purchases agricultural products and sells processed foods throughout the world. In many cases food grown in one country is brought to the United States for processing and subsequent distribution to third nations. The company also processes some food in the country in which it is grown, selling part in the domestic market and exporting the balance. It has extensive experience in doing business in nations of varying stages of development and of political and economic philosophies.

Processed has obtained cocoa from Nigeria for decades. For years after independence in 1960, Processed purchased Nigerian cocoa for processing in Europe and the United States. Some of the final product was sent back to Nigeria for retail sale. In 2006, at the urging of the Nigerian government, Processed agreed to establish a small cocoa processing plant in Nigeria. The government wanted the company to offer a minority equity position to Nigerians. But Processed was able to convince government officials that the enterprise should be a wholly foreign owned subsidiary, even though the then applicable Nigerian foreign investment law prohibited more than 49 percent foreign equity. Processed's officials, at company expense, wined and dined members of the Nigerian government over a three month period during the process of persuading officials to exempt the company from being a joint venture with Nigerian equity and to grant the necessary licenses. Processed also made several campaign contributions to some key Nigerian legislators who faced re-election, and who at first opposed the wholly foreign owned subsidiary.

In return for receiving a permit to construct the processing plant, and after considerable negotiations, Processed agreed to establish employee housing, construct recreational facilities adjacent to its plant and subsidize employee transportation from the center of Lagos, Nigeria, to the plant on the outskirts of the city. The government had tried to convince Processed to locate the plant in a rural area, far from Lagos, where unemployment was particularly high. Processed was able to convince the government officials that the plant should be near Lagos.

The final contract with the government was signed in early 2007 at Processed's executive offices in New York City. The company had flown the four most involved Nigerian officials, and their spouses, to New York for the ceremony. They were given a tour of the company's facilities and for several days attended sports and cultural events in various parts of the United States. They enjoyed unquestionably gracious living.

The company's plant in Nigeria functioned efficiently and profitably for only a year. There were occasional difficulties with the importation of glass jars and metal cans. The normal process for clearing customs often took several months. On more than one occasion, when the company feared the possibility of halting production and laying off Nigerian workers, cash payments of about $1,000 were given to several different Nigerian customs officials, who in return gave priority status to the clearance of the containers.

In late 2008 several other African nations that were the principal markets for Processed's prepared cocoa drinks shifted their purchases to other sources. There also was some decline in the consumption of cocoa on the continent. Nigerian cocoa was becoming less competitive than that grown in several nations close to the major markets of Processed. Furthermore, Nigerian law and policy affecting foreign investment was of concern to the company because of its restrictive attitude towards wholly foreign owned companies. Processed has been reluctant to participate in joint ventures in developing nations. It has always preferred to have wholly owned subsidiaries. But it has agreed to joint ventures in several developing nations.

The above factors led the board of directors to approve the sale of the processing plant. It informed the government that it was seeking potential buyers and inquired whether the government might like to purchase the plant. But an offer by the government was only 60 percent of what the company believed was a fair price and the offer was courteously rejected. After further months of searching, a French food processing company with extensive operations in Africa agreed to Processed's price. For reasons not given to Processed, the Nigerian government continued to delay granting required approval of the transfer. After months of frustration, Processed was approached by a consulting firm in Lagos. Owned and staffed exclusively by Nigerians, the firm was known to Processed as having excellent contacts within the Nigerian government. The senior staff members were former high level government officials. It had a reputation for "getting things done" and suggested to Processed that government delays often were occasioned by inefficient procedures, a maze of bureaucratic regulations and other minor obstacles with which they had experience surmounting. The fee of $500,000 for obtaining approval of the sale at first appeared to Processed to be unusually large. But it was not unreasonable in view of the company's desire to withdraw, and the serious reduction of production efficiency in the plant since the news of its impending withdrawal had become known to the employees. The company paid the fee, expressly telling the consultants that the company did not need to have any accounting as to how the money was used. In 2010, within two weeks of Processed's retaining the consulting firm, the proposed sale of the plant was approved by the government. Three months later it was disclosed in newspapers in Lagos and abroad that some of the money that had been paid to the consulting firm, in turn had been paid to several Nigerian government officials. The public announcement created an outcry.

In late 2010, the company, the president, the vice-president of the international division, all the members of the board of directors and the former managing director of the Nigerian plant were indicted in federal court in the United States with having violated the United States Foreign Corrupt Practices Act by making improper payments in Nigeria. The only record of any of the payments are listings under "ordinary promotional expenses."

SECTION II.   FOCUS OF CONSIDERATION

SEC investigations in the mid–1970s disclosed a large number of payments by U.S. corporations to foreign officials. Congress responded with the enactment of the Foreign Corrupt Practices Act in 1977, amended in 1988 and again in 1998, the latter to bring the FCPA into compliance with the OECD Convention on Combating Bribery of Foreign Public Officials in International Business Transactions. The United States had worked for years to encourage the adoption of FCPA type legislation by other nations and the OECD Convention reflects those efforts.

This problem explores payments that raise important issues and reflect the tensions between ethics and business. Language plays an important role in this area. The title of the chapter refers to "questionable payments". They are often called bribes or corrupt payments. But the negative or immoral meaning we associate with the word "bribe", or the unlawful meaning the FCPA gives to "corrupt payments", is not always agreed to in other nations. Until the adoption of the OECD Convention, and implementing legislation in signatory nations, there was little legislation comparable to the U.S. FCPA in other nations.

The FCPA does not prohibit bribes qua bribes. It prohibits payments prohibited by the Act. One's notion of what may constitute a bribe is usually based on moral and ethical considerations, and may not at all be consistent with the definitions in the FCPA. Two questions are important with regard to payments made to foreign officials. The first is for what purpose was the payment made? The second is what is the magnitude of the affect on the foreign nation caused by the payments to one of the nation's officials? If the purpose was to speed up an otherwise lawful legal process, such as to move goods through customs inspection in two days rather than two weeks, perhaps the consequences should be less than where the payment was made to violate a law, such as not collecting proper customs duties. Furthermore, what if the direct result of the payment is the downfall of the foreign government, especially a foreign government friendly to the United States? It may be useful to explore the ethics and moral standards that are present before turning to the actual provisions of the FCPA and their application to the payments made by Processed Foods' officials.

Making payments to foreign officials did not begin in the 1970s only to be prohibited by the passage of the FCPA. Payments that raise questions of legitimacy are as old as payments that do not. It was the disclosures after Watergate that brought the issue to the front pages of newspapers and covers of weekly news magazines. The lead cover story from Newsweek in the readings illustrated the magnitude of the problem.

The FCPA in 1977 amended the Securities Exchange Act of 1934 to make it unlawful for an issuer of securities that are registered under § 12 of the SEA, or an issuer that is required to file reports under § 15(d), to make certain payments to foreign officials or other foreign persons. The Act further requires those issuers to maintain accurate financial records that would tend to disclose the existence of such payments. Furthermore, the Act extends prohibited payments to any domestic concern making use of the mails or any means or instrumentality of interstate commerce, thus bringing within the Act's scope essentially all enterprises, not unlike the extensive scope of the insider trading provisions of § 10 of the Act.

The 1977 Act was brief, containing only three substantive sections. The 1988 amendments retained much of the structure of the original Act, but made some very important changes and additions, as discussed in the Bliss & Spak reading. The most controversial change was removing the "reason to know" language from the provision governing payments to third persons which might be passed on to government officials, replacing it with a complicated definition of "knowing" violations. See 15 U.S.C.A. § 78dd–1(f)2. This change caused one Senator to suggest that it created a loophole "big enough to fly a Lockheed through." The 1998 amendments, generated by the U.S. adoption of the OECD Convention, add as prohibited payments those made to secure "any improper advantage." The amendments also expand the scope of the Act beyond issuers or domestic concerns to cover prohibited acts by "any person".

Foreign persons are now included if their acts occur in the United States. Finally, jurisdiction is extended to assure coverage of acts that take place wholly outside the United States, and the officials of international organizations are brought within the definition of foreign officials.

The 1977 FCPA generated considerable discourse. Some critics dislike the Act because is allegedly places U.S. business at a competitive disadvantage. That criticism tends to ignore the ethical issues. The 1988 amendments reduced some of the criticism, and the adoption by other nations of laws to fulfill obligations of committing to the OECD Convention further reduced criticism. The meaning of a bribe remains in conflict, as does the effectiveness of the FCPA in significantly reducing unlawful payments, or simply sending them underground.

The U.S. FCPA came out of the Watergate era, diminished in use after a few years, was expanded because of international action by the OECD and recently has settled in as the basis for some large civil cases brought by the SEC. Some 19 prosecutions were initiated in 2009, about a dozen in 2010. Few cases ever go to trial but those that have been tried have generally favored the Justice Department. The greater activity, however, has been settlement with often very large fines.

Part A addresses the U.S. experience and approach to a solution by enactment of the FCPA. Part B briefly looks at the experience in developing an international solution, focusing on the OECD Convention but with references to other nations and organizations efforts to combat foreign bribery, including efforts of Transparency International.

The FCPA is essential to an analysis of this problem. It is included in the Documents Supplement.

SECTION III.   READINGS, QUESTIONS AND COMMENTS

PART A.   THE UNITED STATES APPROACH

SELLA, MORE BIG BUCKS IN JURY VERDICTS
A.B.A. Journal 69 (1989).*

* * * In 1976, the 33–year–old McKay was hired as a vice president at Ashland Oil Inc., arguably one of the most powerful companies in the United States. Within a few years, he was in the inner circle of Ashland execs, a protégé of CEO Orin Atkins. He was put in charge of a division of the corporation that supervised Middle East investments. But in late 1980, the tide turned against McKay. Atkins instructed him to pay $1.3 million to a shadowy figure named Yehia Omar. It wasn't clear what Omar's precise role was (Atkins insisted he was just an independent business-man), but McKay knew that Omar was actually in the employ of the oil-rich sultanate of Oman. McKay refused to make a payment that he perceived to be, plain and simple, a bribe to a foreign official. That, he said, would constitute a direct violation of the 1977 Foreign Corrupt Practices Act (FCPA). McKay's contract with Ashland had three key components. The first two weren't extraordinary: To fire McKay, the company must have just cause and follow well-defined disciplinary proce-dures.

More important is the third: John R. Hall, Atkins successor as Ashland CEO, promised McKay that he would not be compelled to make questionable payments.

Not only had McKay declined to take part in any bribery schemes, but he refused in subsequent investigations to hide Ashland's conduct from officials at the Internal Revenue Service and the Securities and Exchange Commission. If McKay's ambitions weren't already dead in the water, his disclosures to the IRS in late 1982 sealed his fate at Ashland. By May 1983, the SEC was taking a long, hard look at the Ashland–Oman connection. Three months later, McKay was fired.

At about the same time, another Ashland executive named Harry D. Williams found that his job had suddenly been eliminated. Williams had

---

* Reprinted with permission from the July, 1989, issue of the ABA Journal, the Lawyer's Magazine, published by the American Bar Association.

not been asked to take part in any foreign payments, but he'd become sympathetic to McKay's efforts to change Ashland's policy. He, too, wanted to cooperate with the SEC and IRS inquiries, and he lent a good deal of moral support to McKay. In April 1983, Williams—unbeknownst to McKay—made an anonymous phone call to the SEC and spoke freely about Ashland's recent actions abroad.

The upshot of the SEC inquiry was a 1986 consent decree in which Ashland agreed not to bribe officials, and the SEC promised not to pursue the case.

But McKay and Williams did pursue it—they sued for breach of contract and wrongful discharge,* * * McKay insisted that he was sacked for his refusal to play the foreign corruption game and take part in Ashland's deliberate cover-up. For its part, Ashland's board of directors claimed that McKay had become unproductive and that his work had suffered during his preoccupation with the IRS and SEC probes. On June 10, a jury returned a verdict of $69,575,367; McKay was awarded over $44.5 million, and the rest was apportioned to Williams. (Because the plaintiff attorneys succeeded in demonstrating RICO violations, large portions of the verdict were trebled—hence the gargantuan awards.) It was the largest jury verdict ever in Kentucky.

Many incidents recounted in testimony seemed like something out of a cheap novel—secret midnight flights, meetings with a former CIA director, covert deals with Arab sultans—and the caliber of the attorneys involved matched the opulence and mystery of the main actors. * * *

Upshot: After threatening to appeal, Ashland brought in new lawyers, who settled with McKay and Williams for $25 million. * * *

FORMER OFFICER AND DIRECTOR OF GLOBAL ENGINEERING AND CONSTRUCTION COMPANY PLEADS GUILTY TO FOREIGN BRIBERY AND KICKBACK CHARGES

Department of Justice Release, September 3, 2008.

WASHINGTON–Albert "Jack" Stanley, a former officer and director of a global engineering, construction and services company based in Houston, pleaded guilty today to conspiring to violate the Foreign Corrupt Practices Act (FCPA) by participating in a decade-long scheme to bribe Nigerian government officials to obtain engineering, procurement and construction (EPC) contracts and to conspiring to commit mail and wire fraud as part of a separate kickback scheme, Acting Assistant Attorney General Matthew Friedrich of the Criminal Division announced. The EPC contracts to build liquefied natural gas (LNG) facilities on Bonny Island, Nigeria, were valued at more than $6 billion.

Stanley, 65, a U.S. citizen and resident of Houston, entered the plea in U.S. District Court in Houston. ... Stanley pleaded guilty to a two-count criminal information charging him with conspiracy to violate the

FCPA and conspiracy to commit mail and wire fraud. As part of his plea agreement, Stanley agreed to cooperate with law enforcement authorities in the ongoing investigations.

Stanley's former employer was part of a four-company joint venture that was awarded four EPC contracts by Nigeria LNG Ltd. (NLNG) between 1995 and 2004 to build LNG facilities on Bonny Island. The government-owned Nigerian National Petroleum Corporation was the largest shareholder of NLNG, owning 49 percent of the company.

Stanley was the senior representative for his former employer on the joint venture's steering committee, which made major decisions on behalf of the joint venture, including decisions relating to the hiring of agents to assist the joint venture in obtaining business. Stanley admitted that he authorized the joint venture to hire two agents, Consulting Company A and Consulting Company B, to pay bribes to a range of Nigerian government officials to assist the joint venture in obtaining the EPC contracts. Stanley also admitted that, at crucial junctures before the award of the EPC contracts, he and others met with three successive former holders of a top-level office in the executive branch of the Nigerian government to ask the office holder to designate a representative with whom the joint venture should negotiate bribes to Nigerian government officials. According to the criminal information to which Stanley pleaded guilty, the joint venture paid approximately $132 million to Consulting Company A and more than $50 million to Consulting Company B during the course of the bribery scheme. Stanley admitted that he had intended for the agents' fees to be used, in part, for bribes to Nigerian government officials. * * *

On the two conspiracy counts, Stanley faces a maximum penalty of 10 years in prison and a $500,000 fine. Under his plea agreement, which the court accepted at today's guilty plea hearing, Stanley faces a sentence of seven years in prison and the payment of $10.8 million in restitution.

What's Missing from the Department of Justice Press Release?

"PBS" Frontline is preparing a more telling story about Stanley and the bribes in Nigeria. Stanley ran KBR, a subsidiary of Halliburton. The $182 million in bribes were paid by Halliburton and its partners. Stanley agreed to testify, which creates links to Vice President Cheney who ran Halliburton between 1995 and 2000. The case may continue for some time, and apparently is one of the more unusual FCPA cases because the FBI has been involved and is using techniques, such as wiretapping and undercover agents, more commonly associated with organized crime.

UNITED STATES v. LIEBO

United States Court of Appeals, Eight Circuit, 1991.
923 F.2d 1308.

. . . Between January 1983 and June 1987, Liebo was vice-president in charge of the Aerospace division of NAPCO International, Inc., located in Hopkins, Minnesota.* * * In early 1983, the Niger government contracted with a West German company, Dornier Reparaturwerft, to service two Lockheed C–130 cargo planes.

In June 1983, representatives from Dornier met with officials of NAPCO and agreed that NAPCO would become the prime contractor on the C–130 maintenance contracts. Under this arrangement, NAPCO would supply parts to Niger and Dornier, and Dornier would perform the required maintenance at its facilities in Munich.

* * * Liebo and Axel Kurth, a Dornier sales representative, flew to Niger to get the President of Niger's approval of the contract. They flew to Niger and met with Captain Ali Tiemogo * * * the chief of maintenance for the Niger Air Force.

Tiemogo testified that during the trip, Liebo and Kurth told him that they would make "some gestures" to him if he helped get the contract approved. When asked whether this promise played a role in deciding to recommend approval of the contract, Tiemogo stated, "I can't say 'no', I cannot say 'yes', at that time," but "it encouraged me." Following Tiemogo's recommendation that the contract be approved, the President signed the contract.

Tahirou Barke, Tiemogo's cousin and close friend, was the first consular for the Niger Embassy in Washington, D.C. Barke testified that he met Liebo in Washington sometime in 1983 or 1984. Barke stated that Liebo told him that he wanted to make a "gesture" to Captain Tiemogo and asked Barke to set up a bank account in the United States. With Barke's assistance, Liebo opened a bank account in Minnesota in the name of "E. Dave," a variation of the name of Barke's then girl friend, Shirley Elaine Dave. Barke testified that NAPCO deposited about $30,000 in the account and that he used the money to pay bills and purchase personal items and that he gave a portion of the money to Captain Tiemogo.

Barke also testified that in August 1985 he returned to Niger to be married. After the wedding, he and his wife honeymooned in Paris, Stockholm and London. He testified that before leaving for Niger, he informed Liebo of his honeymoon plans, and Liebo offered to pay for his airline tickets as a gift. Liebo made the flight arrangements for Barke's return to Niger and for his honeymoon trip. Liebo paid for the tickets, which cost $2,028, by charging them to NAPCO's Diner's Club account. Barke testified that he considered the tickets a "gift" from Liebo personally.

We need not develop the record further other than to provide details of NAPCO's dealings with Niger and the Foreign Military Sales program. NAPCO received two other contracts from Niger. The second contract in the amount of $1,000,000 for the supply of spare parts and maintenance was signed on August 20, 1984. The third contract in the amount of $1,550,000 was signed on August 2, 1985.

Over a two and a half year period beginning in May 1984, NAPCO made payments totalling $130,000 to three "commission agents." The practice of using agents and paying them commissions on international contracts was acknowledged as proper, legal, and an accepted business practice in third world countries. NAPCO issued commission checks to three "agents," identified as Amadou Mailele, Tiemogo's brother-in-law, Fatouma Boube, Tiemogo's sister-in-law, and E. Dave, Barke's girl friend. At Tiemogo's request, both Mailele and Boube set up bank accounts in Paris. Neither Mailele, Boube, nor E. Dave, however, received the commission checks or acted as NAPCO's agent. Instead, evidence established that these individuals were merely intermediaries through whom NAPCO made payments to Tiemogo and Barke. Evidence at trial established that NAPCO's corporate president, Henri Jacob, or another superior of Liebo's approved these "commission payments." There was no evidence introduced at trial, however, that anyone approved the payment for the honeymoon trip.

To obtain Foreign Military Sales financing, NAPCO was required to submit a "Contractor's Certification and Agreement with Defense Security Assistance Agency." In the Contractor's certification submitted in connection with the third Niger contract, Liebo certified that "no rebates, gifts or gratuities have been given contrary to United States law to officers, officials, or employees" of the Niger government. Liebo certified that NAPCO's commission agent under the contract was Amadou Mailele and that he would be paid $47,662. Liebo also certified that no commissions or contingent fees would be paid to any agent to solicit or obtain the contract other than as identified in the certificate.

Following a three week trial, the jury acquitted Liebo on all charges except the count concerning NAPCO's purchase of Barke's honeymoon airline tickets and the related false statement count. This appeal followed.

Liebo first argues that his conviction on Count VII for violating the bribery provisions of the Foreign Corrupt Practices Act by giving Barke airline tickets for his honeymoon should be reversed because insufficient evidence existed to establish two elements of the offense. First, Liebo contends that there was insufficient evidence to show that the airline tickets were "given to obtain or retain business." Second, he argues that there was no evidence to show that his gift of honeymoon tickets was done corruptly.* * * There is sufficient evidence that the airplane tickets were given to obtain or retain business. Tiemogo testified that the President of Niger would not approve the contracts without his recommendation. He also testified that Liebo promised to "make gestures" to him before the first contract was approved, and that Liebo promised to continue to "make gestures" to him before the first contract was approved, and that Liebo promised to continue to "make gestures" if the second and third contracts were approved. There was testimony that Barke helped Liebo establish a bank account with a fictitious name, that Barke used money from that account, and that Barke sent some of the money from that account to Tiemogo. Barke testified that he understood Liebo deposited money in the account as "gestures" to Tiemogo for some "of the business that they do have together."

Moreover, sufficient independent evidence exists that the tickets were given to obtain or retain business. Evidence established that Tiemogo and Barke were cousins and best friends. The relationship between Barke and Tiemogo could have allowed a reasonable jury to infer that Liebo made the gift to Barke intending to buy Tiemogo's help in getting the contracts approved. Indeed, Tiemogo recommended approval of the third contract and the President of Niger approved that contract just a few weeks after Liebo gave the tickets to Barke. Accordingly, a reasonable jury could conclude that the gift was given "to obtain or retain business."

Liebo also contends that the evidence at trial failed to show that Liebo acted "corruptly" by buying Barke the airline tickets. In support of this argument, Liebo points to Barke's testimony that he considered the tickets a "gift" from Liebo personally. Liebo asserts that "corruptly" means that the offer, payment or gift "must be intended to induce the recipient to misuse his official position.... " Because Barke considered the tickets to be a personal gift from Liebo, Liebo reasons that no evidence showed that the tickets wrongfully influenced Barke's actions.

We are satisfied that sufficient evidence existed from which a reasonable jury could find that the airline tickets were given "corruptly." For example, Liebo gave the airline tickets to Barke shortly before the third contract was approved. In addition, there was undisputed evidence concerning the close relationship between Tiemogo and Barke and Tiemogo's important role in the contract approval process. There was also testimony that Liebo classified the airline ticket for accounting purposes as a "commission payment." This evidence could allow a reasonable jury to infer that Liebo gave the tickets to Barke intending to influence the Niger government's contract approval process. We conclude, therefore, that a reasonable jury could find that Liebo's gift to Barke was given "corruptly." Accordingly, sufficient evidence existed to support Liebo's conviction.

Next, Liebo contends that his conviction should be reversed because the court erred by refusing to give his requested jury instructions distinguishing a "gift or gratuity" from a bribe.* * * Here, the court instructed the jury that the term "corruptly" meant that "the offer, promise to pay, payment or authorization of payment, must be intended to induce the recipient to misuse his official position or to influence someone else to do so," and that "an act is 'corruptly' done if done voluntarily [a]nd intentionally, and with a bad purpose of accomplishing either an unlawful end or result, or a lawful end or result by some unlawful method or means." * * * Contrary to Liebo's argument, the instructions as a whole adequately instructed the jury that a gift or gratuity does not violate the Act unless it is given "corruptly." * * * Accordingly, the court did not abuse its discretion by refusing to give the requested instruction.

Finally, Liebo argues that the district court erred in denying his motion for a new trial based on newly discovered evidence. Approximately two months after his conviction, a NAPCO employee provided Liebo with a memorandum showing Henri Jacob's approval to the charge of the airline tickets to NAPCO's Diner's Club Card. Liebo argues that the discovery of this evidence warrants a new trial.

The government argues that the district court correctly concluded that the evidence would probably not produce an acquittal. Although the government concedes that Liebo's counsel established that Jacob or another superior approved the seven commission payments underlying the acquitted bribery counts, the government contends that this evidence was "not significant" to Liebo's defense. The government states that Liebo's primary defense, exemplified in defendant's closing argument, was that he acted in good faith because he did not know that Amadou Mailele, Fatouma Boube, and E. Dave were not NAPCO agents or that the money was going to Tiemogo and Barke.

We do not place such significance on defendant's closing argument. This was a complicated thirteen-day trial involving nineteen charges. We cannot say that the evidence would not have led to an acquittal merely because it was not strenuously argued in defendant's closing argument. In addition, we note that defendant's closing argument did touch on the fact that Jacob signed numerous documents, that his "Mark of Zorro" could be seen all over the documents, and that Liebo relied on Jacob to obtain the agents.

As discussed in Part I, the evidence against Liebo, while sufficient to sustain the conviction, was not overwhelming. Indeed, we believe that the company president's approval of the purchase of the tickets is strong evidence from which the jury could have found that Liebo acted at his supervisor's direction and therefore, did not act "corruptly" by giving the tickets to Barke. Furthermore, we are highly persuaded that the jury considered such approval pivotal, especially in light of the question it submitted to the court during its deliberations and its acquittal of Liebo on the other bribery counts in which evidence of approval existed. Accordingly, we hold that the district court clearly abused its discretion in denying Liebo's motion for a new trial. We remand for a new trial on counts VII and XVII.

UNITED STATES v. KOZENY

United States District Court
S.D. New York, 2009.
643 F.Supp.2d 415.

SCHEINDLIN, DISTRICT JUDGE.

This prosecution relates to alleged violations of the Foreign Corrupt Practices Act ... by defendant Frederic Bourke, Jr. and others in connection with the privatization of ... SOCAR. Bourke has submitted a motion in limine to preclude the Government from offering background evidence relating to corruption in Azerbaijan.

* * * SOCAR is the state-owned oil company of the Republic of Azerbaijan .... In the mid–1990s, Azerbaijan began a program of privati-

zation. The program gave the President . . . discretionary authority as to whether and when to privatize SOCAR. Bourke and others allegedly violated the FCPA by making payments to Azeri officials to encourage the privatization of SOCAR and to permit them to participate in that privatization.

The Federal Rules of Evidence favor the admission of all relevant evidence. Evidence is relevant if it has "any tendency to make the existence of any fact that is of consequence to the determination of the action more probable or less probable than it would be without the evidence." * * *

[T]he Second Circuit has "stressed that it is 'essential to the concept of conscious avoidance that the defendant must be shown to have decided not to learn the key fact, *not merely to have failed to learn it through negligence.'* "The Second Circuit has repeatedly quoted a scholarly treatise on this point to say:

> A court can properly find wilful blindness [i.e., conscious avoidance] only where it can almost be said that the defendant actually knew. He suspected the fact; he realised its probability; but he refrained from obtaining the final confirmation because he wanted in the event to be able to deny knowledge. This, and this alone, is wilful blindness.[15]

Bourke moves to preclude the Government from presenting background evidence of corruption in Azerbaijan, which he believes will be central to the Government's proof that Bourke acted with the requisite knowledge required by the FCPA. The FCPA states that "[w]hen knowledge of the existence of a particular circumstance is required for an offense, such knowledge is established if a person is *aware of a high probability of the existence of such circumstance,* unless the person actually believes that such circumstance does not exist." Bourke therefore notes that the Government will likely proceed on a "conscious avoidance" theory in an attempt to impute to Bourke knowledge of the alleged bribes.

Bourke notes correctly that the Government cannot present background evidence of corruption in Azerbaijan for the purpose of demonstrating that Bourke "should have known" that Azeri officials would require bribes in order to facilitate the privatization of SOCAR. In response, the Government argues that such evidence will be used not to show that Bourke "should have known," but to show that Bourke was aware of the high probability that Azeri officials were being bribed. * * *

That Azerbaijan was known to be a corrupt nation, that the post-Communist privatization processes in other countries have been tainted by corrupt practices, that SOCAR was a strategic asset of Azerbaijan, and that Kozeny was notorious as the "Pirate of Prague" makes it probable that Bourke was aware that Azeri officials were being bribed in order to ensure the privatization of SOCAR. I therefore find this evidence to be relevant and admissible.

---

15.   Glanville Williams, *Criminal Law: The General Part* § 57, at 159 (2d ed.1961).

Nevertheless, Bourke points to certain language that the Government uses that might confuse a jury into believing that the correct standard is a negligence standard-in other words, that if Bourke had made an investigation, he would have discovered the alleged bribery.

* * * The Government is not contending that Bourke was negligent in failing to investigate whether Kozeny and others were resorting to the use of bribery to encourage the privatization process. The Government is arguing instead that it will prove beyond a reasonable doubt that a person of Bourke's means, who was considering making a large investment in a venture in Azerbaijan, would have at least been aware of the high probability that bribes were being paid.

* * * The Government notes that it has accumulated substantial evidence regarding Bourke's awareness of corruption in Azerbaijan generally. For instance, the Government seeks to present evidence of conversations in which Bourke was warned by his counsel that Azerbaijan was the "Wild West" and that doing business in Azerbaijan was like the movie "Chinatown," where there are "no rules."

In addition, the Government will introduce a tape recording that it obtained from one of Bourke's counsel, which records a conversation among Bourke, another investor, and their respective attorneys. In this recording, Bourke expresses his concern that Kozeny and his employees are paying bribes and violating the FCPA: "I mean, they're talking about doing a deal in Iran.... Maybe they ... bribed them, ... with ten million bucks. I, I mean, I'm not saying that's what they're going to do, but suppose they do that." Later in the conversation, Bourke says:

> I don't know how you conduct business in Kazakhstan or Georgia or Iran, or Azerbaijan, and if they're bribing officials and that comes out ... Let's say ... one of the guys at Minaret says to you, Dick, you know, we know we're going to get this deal. We've taken care of this minister of finance, or this minister of this or that. What are you going to do with that information?

> Still later ... Bourke again ponders:

> What happens if they break a law in, uh, in uh, you know, Kazakhstan, or they bribe somebody in Kazakhstan and we're at dinner and ... one of the guys [says] 'Well, you know, we paid some guy ten million bucks to get this now.' I don't know, you know, if somebody says that to you, I'm not part of it, I didn't endorse it. But let's say, they tell you that. You got knowledge of it. What do you do with that? ... I'm just saying to you in general ... *do you think business is done at arm's length in this part of the world.*

While these comments do not demonstrate conclusively that Bourke knew that bribes were being paid in Azerbaijan to further the privatization of SOCAR, they certainly suggest that he suspected that might be the case. Furthermore, statements such as "What are you going to do with that information?" and "You got knowledge of it. What do you do with that?'' intimate that he was concerned about what he might discover. Thus, if Bourke did not actually know, this evidence is at least sufficient for a jury to conclude beyond a reasonable doubt that he knew of the high probability that bribes were being paid. In addition, his lack of actual knowledge would suggest that he decided not to learn more. Because this evidence is both relevant and probative to whether Bourke acted with conscious avoidance, Bourke's motion to preclude such evidence is denied.

The defense next contends that the Government should not be permitted to introduce evidence of third parties' knowledge of the bribes unless the Government also presents evidence " 'from which to conclude that [Bourke] would have the same knowledge.' "

In this case, the Government has responded that there is "ample" evidence that the knowledge of others was likely communicated to Bourke and that Bourke was exposed to the same sources from which others had derived their knowledge of the fraud. For instance, Bourke traveled by private jet through the former Soviet Union with Viktor Kozeny, the alleged mastermind behind the SOCAR investment. The Government intends to show that Kozeny knew about the corruption in Azerbaijan and thereafter undertook to establish a relationship with a high-ranking Azeri official.

Moreover, the Government will present evidence that Bourke became friendly with others in Kozeny's "inner circle," including Clayton Lewis, a former employee of Omega Advisors, which was a co-investor in the venture, and Thomas Farrell, who was employed by Kozeny to facilitate the scheme. The Government has informed the Court that Farrell will testify about the significant amount of time he spent in Azerbaijan and elsewhere in the Soviet Union and his awareness of the corruption in that part of the world. This evidence, the Government argues, will make clear that Bourke likely possessed the same knowledge.

I am satisfied that there will be sufficient testimony from Government witnesses regarding the close business relationships between Bourke, Kozeny, and Lewis, and the participation of others like Farrell. Based on these relationships the jury has a fair basis to infer that the knowledge of these individuals can be imputed to Bourke.

* * * I further conclude that the prejudice caused by such proof does not outweigh its probative value. [E]vidence of Kozeny's knowledge or the knowledge of others is only one part of the proof the Government will introduce. The Government has also stated its intention to present direct evidence that will support its conscious avoidance theory. This evidence includes the conversations that Bourke had with his counsel which have been discussed and addressed above.

For the reasons set forth above, Bourke's motion ... seeking to bar the Government from offering evidence of corruption in Azerbaijan is denied.

BLISS & SPAK, THE FOREIGN CORRUPT PRACTICES ACT OF 1988: CLARIFICATION OR EVISCERATION?

20 L. & Pol'y Int'l Bus. 441 (1989).*

The Foreign Corrupt Practices Act of 1977 established a two-track approach to solving the problem of corporate bribery, requiring * * * that certain statutory accounting standards be observed and prohibiting * * * the bribery of foreign officials.* * * The accounting provisions apply only to "issuers" registered under the Securities and Exchange Act of 1934, and for this reason, the accounting standards were codified as an amendment to the Securities Exchange Act of 1934. As with the rest of the securities laws, the SEC has primary responsibility for civil enforcement of the FCPA accounting standards, and the penalties for violating the standards are those generally applicable to securities law violations. Criminal prosecutions for violation of the accounting standards are the responsibility of the Justice Department. * * *

The antibribery provisions, on the other hand, apply to both issuers and domestic concerns, and are codified separately. The SEC has civil enforcement authority over the violation of the antibribery provisions by issuers, and the Department of Justice has both civil and criminal enforcement responsibility for violations of the antibribery provisions by domestic concerns, as well as for criminal actions involving issuers. * * * Congress never intended to prohibit the payment of all bribes; it intended from the beginning to permit "facilitating" or "grease" payments. * * * The major ambiguity in the antibribery provisions involves the question of the standard used to govern liability for illegal payments by third parties. The basic prohibition on payment to foreign officials extends to any foreign political party or official thereof or any candidate for foreign political office, *and to third parties who make such payments while "knowing or having reason to know" that some or all of the money will be paid as a bribe.* This last provision embodies both a subjective and objective standard for imposing liability on corporations; subjective because the "while knowing" language asks what the corporation or corporate official actually knew with regard to the ultimate disposition of the funds, and objective because the "having reason to know" language asks whether a hypothetical, reasonable corporation or official under the existing circumstances would have known that the money would be used to pay foreign bribes. This, more than any other aspect of the law, has been cited as having a chilling effect on legitimate business transactions. Representatives of the business community long argued that it was simply impractical to expect them to deal with an objective "reason to know" legal standard in the context of complex international transactions in which most of the activity takes place outside the U.S.* * *

---

* Reprinted with permission of the Law & Policy in International Business Journal of the Georgetown University Law Center.

With regard to enforcement actions under the FCPA, the SEC announced from the beginning that it would take a reasonable approach to enforcement, and would not initiate enforcement proceedings to pursue inadvertent record-keeping mistakes or to question reasonable business decisions. * * * For the most part, violations of the FCPA have been mentioned as one count in cases which most likely would have been brought without the FCPA.

The Department of Justice has been more active in enforcing than in regulating under the FCPA. Private business interests lobbied the Department of Justice immediately after enactment of the FCPA to issue detailed guidelines—like those issued under the Arab boycott provisions of the Export Administration Act—to clarify some of the alleged ambiguities in the FCPA. The Department of Justice never issued any such guidelines, and in general assumed an inactive regulatory role.

The Foreign Corrupt Practices Act of 1988

The Trade Act makes three substantive amendments to the accounting provisions of the FCPA. First, the Act clarifies the terms "reasonable assurances" and "reasonable detail" as used in section 13(b)(2) of the Securities Exchange Act of 1934.[63] As noted above, the FCPA requires issuers to make and keep books, records, and accounts, which, *in reasonable detail,* accurately and fairly reflect transactions and dispositions of the issuer's assets, and to devise and maintain a system of internal accounting controls sufficient to provide *reasonable assurances* that corporate assets are properly accounted for as specified in the statute. * * * The Trade Act clarifies these provisions by stating that the terms "reasonable assurances" and "reasonable detail" mean "such level of detail and degree of assurance as would satisfy prudent officials in the conduct of their affairs."[66] * * * Second, the Trade Act added a new paragraph (b)(6) to the accounting provisions defining the responsibility of an issuer over the accounting practices of a subsidiary in which it owns a minority share.[a] * * * The third amendment made by the Trade Act to the accounting provisions stipulates that no criminal liability shall be imposed for violating the accounting provisions, unless the violation is done knowingly.[71] * * *

The Trade Act makes numerous changes to the antibribery provisions. For purposes of discussion, the various amendments can be arranged into three groups: (1) those attempting to clarify the types of payments which are illegal under the Act; (2) those which go to the question of who should be liable for violations, and under what circumstances; and (3) those which attempt to provide better guidance and uniform treatment to the business community.* * * The Trade Act contains [several] amendments which affect the definition of prohibited

---

63. 15 U.S.C. § 78m(b)(2)(A)–(B).

66. * * * 15 U.S.C. § 78m(b).

a. 15 U.S.C. § 78m(b).

71. 15 U.S.C. § 78m(b).

payments. First, the new law modifies the description of the activities of foreign persons for which payments are prohibited. Prior law prohibited payments made for the purpose of "influencing any act or decision of such [a person] in his official capacity, including a decision to fail to perform his official functions.... " The Trade Act amendment prohibits giving anything of value to certain persons for the purpose of "influencing any act or decision of such [person] in his official capacity, *or inducing such a [person] to do or omit to do any act in violation of a lawful duty of such [person]*.... " * * *

Second, * * * the 1977 FCPA prohibited payments made "to assist ... in obtaining or retaining business for or with, or directing business to, any person.... " Some had interpreted this clause, which became known as the "business purpose test," to mean that payments could be made to foreign officials as long as the payment was not directly related to a current or future business deal. As an example of the ambiguity, legislators and prosecutors discussed throughout the legislative process of the 1988 FCPA the payments made by United Brands Company in 1974. In that case, Eli M. Black, Chief Executive Officer of United Brands, agreed to pay $2.5 million to Honduran Minister of Economy, Abraham Bennaton Ramos, in return for a reduction in the Honduran banana export tax and a 20 year extension of certain trade concessions. After the banana export tax was reduced from $.50 to $.25 per box and $1.25 million was deposited into Bennaton Ramos' Swiss bank account, Black committed suicide, and the SEC discovered the payments during an investigation. There was some question as to whether this payment, which was certainly the type of payment Congress intended to prevent in passing the 1977 law, would be covered under the FCPA as drafted. It might be argued in United Brand's defense that the payments were not made to retain or obtain business, but rather to create a more favorable environment for the continuation of business.

* * * [I]n retaining the business purpose test contained in prior law, the conferees made it clear that this test was not to be narrowly construed, stating:

> The conferees wish to make clear that the reference to corrupt payments for "retaining business" in present law is not limited to the renewal of contracts or other business, but also includes a prohibition against corrupt payments related to the execution or performance of contracts or the carrying out of existing business, such as a payment to a foreign official for the purpose of obtaining more favorable tax treatment.

The third clarification of the types of payments prohibited by the FCPA involves the exemption for so-called facilitating or grease payments. * * * The Trade Act clarifies this issue by explicitly stating in the text of the law that the prohibitions "shall not apply to any facilitating or expediting payment to a foreign official, political party, or party official the purpose of which is to expedite or to secure the performance of a *routine governmental action by a foreign official, political party, or party official.*" * * *

The fourth clarification addresses the issue often raised by the business community that U.S. law should not prohibit activities permitted under a foreign country's laws. * * * The conferees * * * created an affirmative defense that "the lawfulness of the payment [to a foreign official] must be shown to exist in the ... statutory law or specific regulations of the foreign official's country ... ," where a payment to a foreign official is "lawful under the *written* laws and regulations of the foreign official's country."

The fifth amendment clarifying the types of payments prohibited by the FCPA concerns payments that are "reasonable and bona fide expenditures." * * *

Two of the amendments to the FCPA contained in the Trade Act concern the standards and scope of corporate and individual liability for violations of the accounting and/or antibribery provisions. The first of these—perhaps the most controversial of the amendments contained in the Trade Act—involves the question of third-party payments. * * * As explained above, the original version of the FCPA not only prohibited corporate entities and officers from giving bribes to certain foreign persons, it also prohibited corporate entities or officers from giving anything of any value to "any person, while knowing or having reason to know that all or a portion of such money or thing of value will be offered, given, or promised, directly or indirectly" to certain foreign persons. The U.S. business community complained that the "reason to know" language subjected corporations and corporate officers to potentially open-ended liability, permitting a jury or judge to determine at some point in the future whether the circumstances were such that the corporation or official had "reason to know" what the agent would do with corporate funds. Prosecutors and supporters of tough antibribery laws, on the other hand, stressed that the "reason to know" language was necessary to prevent corporations from escaping liability under the statute by having bribes paid by agents and deliberately avoiding knowledge of such illegal payments. This situation came to be known as the "head in the sand" problem and was probably the most contentious issue throughout the reform effort.* * *

The House and Senate differences on the third party liability standard were resolved in the conference committee through the adoption of a modified version of the House proposal, maintaining criminal liability for "knowing" violation of the antibribery provisions, but deleting the provision of the House bill which would have imposed civil liability on corporations or officers for "recklessly disregarding" that the agent would pay a bribe. As a result, the provision of the original FCPA regarding third-party payments was amended by simply deleting the controversial "reason to know" standard. As for the deliberate ignorance or "head in the sand" problem, the conferees adopted the reasoning of the federal courts in a number of cases involving possession of narcotics or the receipt of stolen property which concluded that the term "knowingly" already encompasses the problem of deliberate ignorance. In other words, a corporation or corporate official could not, under the reasoning of these cases, evade the criminal sanctions of the provision by purposely avoiding knowledge that his agent paid a bribe. Attempts to deliberately avoid such knowledge would satisfy the knowledge standard.* * *

The final amendment relating to the question of who could be held responsible for violations of the FCPA contains what has become known as the "Eckhardt Amendment." The Eckhardt Amendment contained in the original FCPA effectively prevented the prosecution of employees or agents for violating the FCPA unless the domestic concerns or issuers were found to have violated the Act. * * * The Trade Act adopted the proposal of the House trade bill by deleting the clause. This has the effect of permitting the prosecution of corporate officers or agents, regardless of whether the domestic concern or issuer has been shown to have violated the FCPA.

QUESTIONS AND COMMENTS

1. An initial question is the scope of the FCPA. Does the law include foreign companies, such as a subsidiary of Processed Foods? What about actions against employees of Processed Foods, such as those officials who wined and dined the Nigerians, or who approved or actually made the campaign donations, or those who participated in any of the other questionable activities? Is any distinction made, or should it be made, between persons actively making payments, persons in a direct supervisory role of those participants and officers who might not reasonably be aware of such payments? What about outside directors or corporate employees who are not officers? May actions be brought against any of the foreign officials, those Nigerian citizens who accepted benefits or payments? Another question is who brings actions under the FCPA? We assume the government may be the principal enforcer of the Act, but does it also allow a private right of action? If a direct private right of action is not possible, could one use other laws as the basis for an action supported by violations of the FCPA? See *Environmental Tectonics v. W.S. Kirkpatrick, Inc.*, 847 F.2d 1052 (3d Cir.1988), aff'd, 493 U.S. 400, 110 S.Ct. 701, 107 L.Ed.2d 816 (1990)(antitrust laws); *Town of Kearny v. Hudson Meadows Urban Renewal*, 829 F.2d 1263 (3d Cir.1987)(Civil RICO). There are also related criminal offenses that may involve foreign payments, such as conspiracy, aiding and abetting, violations of the Travel Act, Mail Fraud, Wire Fraud, and the criminal side of RICO. See *United States v. Young & Rubicam*, Inc., 741 F.Supp. 334 (D.Conn.1990)(FCPA and state commercial bribery offenses constituted multiple violations of the federal Travel Act; motion to dismiss denied which argued that such multiple violations could not come under the Racketeer Influenced and Corrupt Organizations ((RICO)) Act).

2. The *United States v. McLean* decision interpreted a 1977 FCPA provision that the court ruled prohibited bringing a suit directly against an

employee without first having found the employer in violation of the Act. 738 F.2d 655 (5th Cir.1984). This was the Eckhardt provision, which the *McLean* decision suggests had several benefits to the employee. But the 1988 amendments deleted the Eckhardt provision, allowing suits against employees without first going against the employer. Are employees now at a serious disadvantage? What if the Vice–President of the International Division of Processed had expressed concern over the Nigerian delay and suggested to the President of Processed that "that's business", but the President responded saying "we must have approval within the next two months. Consider whether you have explored all avenues. I cannot believe you can't find some way to obtain the approval and I think the board might have serious doubts as to your future with Processed if the sale is much further delayed?" Should the President or board members be liable? The *Ashland* case in the readings suggests that an officer dismissed for failing to violate the FCPA may have some recourse. *See D'Agostino v. Johnson & Johnson, Inc.*, 133 N.J. 516, 628 A.2d 305 (1993); *Hutson v. Analytic Sciences Corp.*, 860 F.Supp. 6 (D.Mass.1994); *DePuydt v. FMC Corp.*, 35 F.3d 570 (9th Cir.1994). A hypothetical scene in a company office, where there are concerns of improper payments to domestic city and town officials, is the subject of Ewing, *Case of the Rogue Division*, 62 Harv.Bus.Rev. 166 (1983), and raises some concern relative to payments made abroad. H. Lowell Brown, *Extraterritorial Jurisdiction Under the 1998 Amendments to the Foreign Corrupt Practices Act: Does the Government's Reach Now Exceed Its Grasp?*, 26 N.C.J. Int'l L. & Com. Reg. 239 (2001).

3. The FCPA was enacted with the intention that it would be enforced by the SEC and the Department of Justice. *Lamb v. Phillip Morris, Inc.*, 915 F.2d 1024 (6th Cir.1990), cert. denied 498 U.S. 1086, 111 S.Ct. 961, 112 L.Ed.2d 1048 (1991), held that there is no private right of action under the FCPA. See also *J.S. Service Center Corp. v. General Electric Technical Services Co., Inc.*, 937 F.Supp. 216 (S.D.N.Y. 1996); *Citicorp Int'l Trading Co., Inc. v. Western Oil & Refining Co., Inc.*, 771 F.Supp. 600 (S.D.N.Y. 1991). If a competitor of Processed believes that the payments made by Processed caused it damage, although the competitor would not have a private right of action against Processed under the FCPA, might it use violations of the FCPA in another form of action? See the *W.S. Kirkpatrick & Co., Inc. v. Environmental Tectonics Corp., Int'l* decision discussed in Problem 10.6. An interesting book by two Canadian investigative reporters that relates a tale of bribery and intrigue involving 34 Airbus aircraft purchased by then state-owned Air Canada is Stevie Cameron & Harvey Cashore, The Last Amigo: Karlheinz Schreiber and the Anatomy of a Scandal (2001). More on aircraft companies' (Boeing as well as Airbus) "incentives" to purchase involving Sabena, Air Mauritius, Saudi Arabian Airlines, Bahamas Air, Kuwait Airways Corp., EgyptAir, Indian Airlines, in addition to Air Canada, is included in "Airbus's secret past," The Economist, June 14th 2003 at 59.

4. Commencing actions against foreign officials might be difficult because of problems obtaining personal jurisdiction. It also might create some problems of diplomacy, especially where the payments are not inconsistent with norms in the foreign nation regarding receiving favors. *United States v. Castle*, 925 F.2d 831 (5th Cir.1991)(prosecution limited to U.S. persons and companies). What if the foreign official has been acting as the agent for the

company, such as the members of the consulting firm in Lagos retained by Processed Foods? *Dooley v. United Technologies Corp.*, 803 F.Supp. 428 (D.D.C.1992)(foreign national "otherwise subject to the jurisdiction of the United States" is within the scope of the Act).

5. Do the facts suggest that Processed has violated any of the record keeping requirements? The American Bar Association and the SEC have disagreed on the scope of the accounting provisions of the FCPA. The ABA believes that if the conduct in question does not cause an impact upon the financial statements, then that conduct does not come within the accounting provisions. The SEC has repeatedly argued that Congress intended a broader application of the accounting provisions to make corporations accountable in general for questionable payments. ABA Comm. on Corp. Law and Accounting, *A Guide to the New Section 13(b)(2) Accounting Requirements of the Securities Exchange Act of 1934*, 34 Bus.Lawyer 307 (1978).

6. Working through the hypothetical problem, there are a number of payments which raise questions under the FCPA. Which do you identify as possible violations? Assume that they have all been included in a federal indictment and consider each under the provisions of the FCPA.

7. Entertaining may be considered more a matter of courtesy than a bribe. Does the language of the FCPA clearly allow entertainment expenses under the "affirmative defenses"? What if the business entertainment in the United States took place entirely after the contract was signed, and there had been no suggestion of such a trip prior to the signing of the contract? Is the "retaining business" language of the FCPA sufficient to make this a criminal violation? Were the entertainment expenses more than "gestures" as discussed in the *Liebo* case? In *Liebo* the payments were not made to the Niger official whose favorable decision was needed (the Niger Air Force Chief of Staff), but to a cousin and friend (Barke). How can this be unlawful under the FCPA?

8. What if "everyone" knows that a particular nation is one of those nations where you just do not do business without making payments to officials? This suggests that there is an unwritten law approving such payments. Does that mean the payments were lawful? *See* Okechukwu Oko, *Subverting the Scourge of Corruption in Nigeria: A Reform Prospectus*, 34 N.Y.U.J. Int'l L. & Pol. 397 (2002).

9. Would it be a violation of the FCPA to make a political contribution solely on the basis that that candidate has been a long-term advocate opposing any nationalization of private property?

10. Payments to customs officials might seem to be exempt as "routine government action." But are customs officials included in the FCPA definition of "routine government action?" What if the payments in the hypothetical were $10,000? The *United States v. Kay*, 359 F.3d 738 (5th Cir. 2004), decision in the district court applied a very narrow interpretation of "obtain or retain" business. How would that affect Processed?

11. What if one of the Nigerian officials requested that the payment to speed the process be made to a bank in Switzerland? Assume Nigeria has local exchange controls which the employee consequently violates. Does Processed

assume any new risks? How do you suppose the Nigerian officials would react if told it was company policy to make all such payments in the currency of the official's nation and to make the payments in that nation? Speeding a customs process by making small payments to customs officials is a widespread practice. Does the definition of "routine government action" in the FCPA cover such payments?

Processed did not make any direct payments to Nigerian officials for the sale of the business. Nevertheless, undoubtedly it was a company source of money which was paid to the government officials by the Nigerian consultants retained by Processed. The Processed's representatives may have no reason to believe that the consultants made these kinds of payments. On the other hand, they may have directly known that this was the consultants' practice, or assumed that the reason for the consulting fee being so large was that some of it had to be used to make such payments. What problems are involved when independent agents participate in the conduit of questionable payments? Did the payment violate the FPCA considering the Act's definition of "knowing"? What about the earlier "reason to know" standard? Does the "knowing" definition in the FCPA include "reason to know?" Did Processed's officials have their "heads in the sand"?

12.   Could Processed Foods successfully argue "extortion" as a defense? Or, using the *Kozeny* case, argue that "everyone" knows Nigeria is a corrupt nation?

13.   What if the officials of Processed had been referred to the consulting firm by the U.S. Ambassador in Nigeria, who knew that the consulting firm had been highly successful in persuading government officials on other occasions to approve acquisitions or new foreign investments, and the ambassador knew that part of the funds were paid directly to government officials as bribes? Would the U.S. Ambassador be liable under the FCPA?

14.   Would it make any difference if Processed's board had adopted a corporate policy of adherence to the FCPA soon after the enactment of the FCPA and made every corporate official sign that policy, including all of those involved? Suppose that the document clearly stated that it was the policy of the corporation not to make any payments to foreign officials for any purpose? Should Processed adopt a written company policy regarding payments to foreign officials and agents? What would be the key elements? Is it realistic to expect a company to follow such a policy when it has the leadership illustrated by the comments about Ashland Oil in the ABA Journal extracts?

15.   Assume Processed's directors were insured by the American Life Insurance Company against expenses incurred in the performance of their official duties. American Life refused to pay for the legal expenses associated with the SEC investigations and charges. Processed sued American Life and the latter has sought access to Processed's records gathered by the SEC, but never made public in accordance with a consent decree with the SEC. Processed says the disclosure "could have a devastating impact upon the reputation and career of a number of foreign officials, some of whom hold positions of importance to the foreign relations of the United States." What problems are raised?

16. The Department of Justice has a review procedure allowing a company to request a determination whether the Department of Justice would prosecute on a stipulated set of facts. Does such a review procedure solve most of the problems with the Act, and would you recommend the company use that procedure?

The Bechtel Group was given an advisory opinion by the Department of Justice which offered some guidelines regarding the viewpoint of that Department towards enforcement of the FCPA. Bechtel agreed with respect to its contract with SGV Group, a Philippines based consortium of companies from 11 nations that was to provide auditing, tax and other services to the Bechtel Group, that: (1) all payments from Bechtel to SGV would be by check or bank transaction and none would be by cash; (2) no SGV management positions would be held by government or political party officials; (3) Bechtel would obtain from local lawyers opinions that payments for travel and entertainment expenses would not violate local laws; (4) SGV could not assign its rights without written consent of Bechtel; (5) SGV would tell Bechtel's general counsel of any Bechtel employee suggestion that the Act was being violated; (6) the agreement would be immediately terminated for any SGV or Bechtel violation of the law; (7) any gifts made by SGV under $500 and which were proper according to local custom would be reimbursed by Bechtel, and (8) Bechtel could audit any SGV requests for expense reimbursement if such an audit seemed prudent. Are these guidelines helpful in drafting a company policy?

17. Similar to the antiboycott provisions discussed in the previous problem, the FCPA has generated mostly consent decrees. Corporations usually prefer to accept a negotiated fine rather than litigate and have their "corrupt" practices made public. Suggestions that the FCPA would cause a serious loss of business for U.S. concerns have never been proven to have merit, nor to be incorrect.

Although there have not been many decisions in the case reports, that should not be interpreted as a lack of administrative enforcement of the FCPA. Many actions have been commenced charging violations of the reporting requirements of the Act. This is similar to the practice of the Department of Commerce in enforcing the antiboycott rules. One of the problems in commencing actions under the FCPA is that the cooperation of the foreign nation may be required. Such an action may also raise questions of the act of state doctrine, although the *W.S. Kirkpatrick & Co. v. Environmental Tectonics Corp.,* 493 U.S. 400, 110 S.Ct. 701, 107 L.Ed.2d 816 (1990), decision has limited the use of that doctrine when the motive as opposed to the legality of a foreign action is questioned. See Problem 10.6.

Only about a dozen cases have been disclosed since the enactment of the law, very few in the standard case reports. (Others have been reported in the useful private report, FCPA Rep., discussed in Longobardi, *Reviewing the Situation: What is to be Done with the Foreign Corrupt Practices Act?* 20 Vand.J. of Transnat'l L. 431 (1987)). Some companies have agreed to considerable fines, including International Harvester ($510,000) and Crawford Enterprises ($3.45 million) (both involving bribes allegedly paid to Pemex, the Mexican national oil company), and IBM ($300,000, involving alleged payments of $4.5 million to the directors of an Argentine bank). In 1995 Lockheed paid a $24.8 million fine and a $3 million civil settlement. See *Bribery Case Puts Lockheed Under Scrutiny*, Atlanta J., Jan. 28, 1995, at B1. In 2011, Tyson Foods paid a fine of $5.2 million for bribes paid in Mexico. Although the government has brought few cases, it has selected them carefully. Most have resulted in guilty pleas. More recent actions have been against Baker Hughes by the SEC and DOJ for alleged payments in Indonesia, and against KPMG–SSH also for alleged payments in Indonesia. A good review of recent enforcement actions is in International legal developments in review, 44 Int'l Lawyer 451 (2010)(discussing company settlements and individual prosecutions both in the United States and abroad).

18. Why doesn't the FCPA take into consideration the various cultural attitudes regarding payments to government officials? Could U.S. courts be expected to analyze cultural elements that might moderate or mitigate the questionability of the payments? See J. Kim and J. B. Kim, *Cultural Differences in the Crusade Against International Bribery: Rice–Cake Expenses in Korea and the Foreign Corrupt Practices Act*, 6 Pac. Rim Law & Pol'y J. 549 (1997)(discussing "ttokkap" or literally rice-cake expenses, as "culturally ingrained into the fabric of Korean society", and considered permissible under the "social courtesy" exception to otherwise illicit payments); H. Kolenda, *One Party, Two Systems: Corruption in the People's Republic of China and Attempts to Control It*, 4 J. Chinese Law 187 (1990) (discussing "guanxi" and its relation to a communist party dominated regime); and C. Dugan and V. Lechtman, *The FCPA in Russia and Other Former Communist Countries*, 91 Am. J. Int'l Law 378 (1997).

19. Perhaps Processed Foods should just consider any sanctions as a cost of doing business. Why not?

20. See U.S. Department of State website—www.state.gov/www/issues/economic/bribery/html.

PART B.   ENTER FOREIGN AND INTERNATIONAL LAW— THE OECD CONVENTION AND OTHER RULES

The U.S. enactment of the FCPA in 1977 did not immediately lead to the adoption of similar laws in other nations. Nearly all nations have laws prohibiting corrupt payments to their own officials, but other nations seemed totally disinclined to follow the U.S. lead in prohibiting payments to **foreign** officials. More than a dozen nations, including France, even allowed such payments to constitute a tax deduction as a business expense.

The United States began a long campaign to convince other industrialized nations to adopt laws similar to the FCPA. The UN discussed the matter in the 1970s but focused more on a broader corporate code of conduct that established rules for multinationals, but no rules for host nations receiving investment. The Organization for Economic Cooperation and Development (OECD) in 1976 issued voluntary guidelines for multinational corporations that addressed bribery, and the International Chamber of Commerce discussed the matter in 1977. Nearly two decades later in

1996 the ICC issued voluntary rules, and the Organization of American States concluded its Inter–American Convention Against Corruption (signed by Canada, the United States and most Latin American nations). The Organization of African Unity (OAU) has been working on a convention for its members. In late 1997, the OECD concluded its Convention on Combating Bribery of Foreign Public Officials in International Business Transactions. Adopted by some three dozen plus nations, including the European Union Member States, the United States amended the FCPA in 1998, soon after its acceptance of the Convention. The UN finally returned to the subject, concluding its United Nations Convention Against Corruption in October, 2003. Whether that leads to U.S. ratification and a new amendment of the FCPA remains to be seen. The United States wanted the focus to be on *government* corruption and insisted that provisions which prohibit business and political party payments be optional. The U.N. Convention does take the corruption issue a step further. It provides for the recovery of assets wrongfully transferred abroad by government officials.

The European Union Member States, in addition to adopting the OECD Convention, have ratified an EU Convention Against Corruption of Both EU and Member States' Officials (1997), and an EU Convention for the Protection of EU Financial Interests (1995).

Some of the success for the increased awareness in the world of the seriousness of doing business by using payments to influence foreign officials must be given to Transparency International (TI), an NGO in Germany that has supported antibribery efforts throughout the world, especially by making corruption and its consequences better understood by the public. TI annually publishes a "Corruption Perception Index." Nigeria, the subject of our problem, is often ranked worst. The United States is among the least corrupt, but Finland is given the best rating.

Peter Eigen, Chairman of the Board of Directors, describes the role of Transparency International as:

> TI, through its International Secretariat and more than 85 independent national chapters around the world, works at both the national and international level to curb both the supply and demand of corruption. In the international arena, TI raises awareness about the damaging effects of corruption, advocates policy reform, works towards the implementation of multilateral conventions and subsequently monitors compliance by governments, corporations and banks. At the national level, chapters work to increase levels of accountability and transparency, monitoring the performance of key institutions and pressing for necessary reforms in a non-party political manner.

> TI does not expose individual cases (that is the work of journalists, many of whom are members of TI chapters). Rather, in an effort to make long-term gains against corruption, TI focuses on prevention and reforming systems.

A principal tool in the fight against corruption is access to information. It is in this spirit that we offer this web site to everybody with an interest in the fight against corruption. We hope that it will make a valuable contribution to assessing the gains made in recent years, and to contemplating the challenges that still lie ahead. See www. transparency.org.

STUART EIZENSTAT, TESTIMONY BEFORE THE SENATE FOREIGN RELATIONS COMMITTEE*

The OECD Convention

Let me briefly highlight for you what this Convention does:

—The Convention obligates the Parties to criminalize bribery of foreign public officials, including officials in all branches of government, whether appointed or elected. This prohibition includes payments to officials of public agencies, public enterprises, and public international organizations. This, therefore, would cover government controlled parastatals, such as airlines, utilities, state telecommunications companies, which are increasing important in public procurement. Only those operating on a purely commercial basis would be exempt.

—The Parties must apply "effective, proportionate and dissuasive criminal penalties" to those who bribe foreign public officials. If a country's legal system lacks the concept of criminal corporate liability, it must provide for equivalent non-criminal sanctions, including monetary penalties.

—The Convention requires that parties be able to seize or confiscate both the bribe and the bribe proceeds—the net profits that result from the illegal transaction—or to impose equivalent fines so as to provide a powerful disincentive to bribery. Under our law, substantial fines have had significant impact on corporate compliance.

—The Convention has strong provisions to prohibit accounting omissions and falsification, and to provide for mutual legal assistance and extradition. These mutual legal assistance provisions, in particular, will greatly enhance cooperation with foreign governments in cases of alleged bribery, improving both our own enforcement of the FCPA and foreign governments' enforcement of anti-bribery laws.

The Convention will cover business-related bribes to foreign public officials made through political parties, party officials, and candidates, as well as those bribes that corrupt foreign public officials direct to them.

While the Convention does not cover directly bribery of foreign political parties, party officials, and candidates for political office, OECD

---

* Mr. Eizenstat was at the time Under Secretary of State for Economic, Business and Agricultural Affairs.

members have agreed to discuss these issues on a priority basis in the OECD's anti-bribery working group, which negotiated the Convention, and to consider proposals to address these issues by the May 1999 OECD annual Ministerial meeting.

The greatest impact of the FCPA has been achieved through enforcement measures and through the business community's response to the law: the institution of meaningful internal corporate controls, effective internal and external auditing, and codes of conduct requiring compliance not only with the FCPA, but also with other federal criminal laws. We would expect to see a similar dynamic in other OECD countries. The OECD Convention requirements, which closely follow the FCPA, represent a very high standard. As our OECD partners enact effective criminal and civil laws to fully implement those requirements, their business communities will need to take appropriate steps to comply. The Convention also provides us with a mechanism to monitor, through regular peer review, both the quality of the legislation enacted by the other nations and the effectiveness of their enforcement of their legislation. * * *

QUESTIONS AND COMMENTS

1. What caused the apparent shift in opinion from some foreign nations viewing payments to foreign officials as ordinary tax deductible business expenses to unlawful payments? The initial 33 OECD Convention signatories in December, 1997, were largely the industrialized nations, but included some important non-OECD nations. Is the Convention simply an agreement among mostly industrialized nations that the playing field ought to be leveled, meaning that bribes demanded by foreign officials from principally developing nations should be uniformly rejected, or is it an agreement which will cause the major recipient nations (i.e., Bangladesh, Nigeria, Uganda, Indonesia and Kenya as Transparency International's "worst-five") to take action to stop the acceptance of bribes? China and Russia, two of TI's major corrupt nations, have both moved away from total state control to more market economies— has this required greater attention to the issue of bribes? Have greater transparency within government, development of multiparty systems, freer coverage of news events, and increased judicial independence contributed to the greater awareness of the problems of bribery of government officials? But should we really classify nations as either "bribe-paying" or "bribe-receiving", Transparency International does list Italy along with Namibia? See No Longer Business as Usual: Fighting Bribery and Corruption (OECD 2000).

2. What steps ought to be taken to make certain the objectives of the OECD Convention are carried out? Stuart Eizenstat noted the differences between the FCPA, as amended in 1988, and the OECD Convention. Has the U.S. law implementing the Convention and amending the FCPA properly resolved these differences? Have these changes diluted the U.S. law, or strengthened it? Did the manner in which the U.S. incorporated the OECD Convention language "improper advantage" into the FCPA, discussed in the *United States v. Kay* decision, subvert the purpose of the OECD Convention?

3. If the payment of bribes takes place within the operational code—the unwritten law or the "way things really work", can we expect the international standards to be very effective?

4. The Uruguay Round which led to the formation of the WTO did not produce any rules addressing foreign payments. But is the WTO the best forum to further the current discussion?

5. Should foreign payments be governed by civil or criminal law rules? The answer will depend on how a nation views such conduct. The United States seems to consider it partly criminal (and not allowed), while France seems to consider it a civil issue (and allowed). Culture causes nations to perceive actions differently. While the United States considers defamation civil, Mexico considers it criminal. England views it civil but of such a serious level to merit use of a jury, rare in English civil law matters. Would foreign payments receive more consistent treatment?

6. Does the FCPA interfere with U.S. foreign relations? Extraterritoriality continues to create conflicts between trading nations. Sensitivity regarding sovereignty is ever lurking at trade agreement conferences and in the legislative halls of every nation. Does the FCPA create sensitive extraterritorial problems?

7. Does the UN Convention, portions of which are contained in the Documents Supplement, add anything that should cause the United States to amend the FCPA?

8. The World Bank has permanently debarred more than a dozen companies and nearly a half dozen individuals for violations of its Procurement Guidelines and/or Consultant Guidelines.

9. While the OECD Convention has generally been welcomed, some nations have adopted separate laws, influenced by both the OECD Convention and the U.S. FCPA. Britain adopted an anti-bribery statute in 2010, but the effective date was delayed for a year waiting for interpretive guidance by the government. See, e.g., 44 Int'l Lawyer 1173 (2010).

10. See OECD website—www.oecd.org.; Transparency International website—www.transparency.de/organisation/chapter; OAS website—www.oas. org.

PART 4

TRANSFERS OF TECHNOLOGY

■ ■ ■

CHAPTER 9

LICENSING, THEFT
AND PROTECTION OF
INTELLECTUAL PROPERTY

■ ■ ■

INTRODUCTION 9.0 INTELLECTUAL
PROPERTY AND INTERNATIONAL
TRANSACTIONS

Issues surrounding the transfer of knowledge across national borders have provoked intense discussions during the last three decades. The discussions promise to continue unabated. At the core is the desire of third world countries (often advanced developing countries like Brazil, South Korea, Taiwan and Singapore) to obtain protected information quickly and affordably irrespective of the proprietary rights and profit motives of current holders (usually persons from the most developed countries). Developing countries want production processes which maximize uses of abundant, inexpensive labor but which result in products that are competitive in the international marketplace; capital intensive production processes (e.g., robot production of automobiles) may be of less interest. MNEs may be willing to share (by way of license or sale) a good deal of proprietary information, but are reluctant to part with their "core technology."

Among the industrialized countries, efforts often occur to acquire (even by way of stealing) "leading edge" technology. One example involved attempted theft of IBM computer technology by Japanese companies ultimately caught by the F.B.I. In the United States, the Office of Export Administration uses the export license procedure to control strategic technological "diversions." But falsification of licensing documents by prominent Norwegian and Japanese companies allowed the Soviets to obtain the technology for making vastly quieter submarine propellers. In the ensuing scandal, "anti-Toshiba" trade sanctions were adopted in the U.S. Leading Japanese executives resigned their positions, which is considered the highest form of apology in Japanese business circles.

The predominant vehicle for controlling technology transfers across national borders is the "license" or "franchise" contract. Some $180

752

billion in licensing royalties flow annually across borders. The holder of a patent, copyright or trademark in one country first acquires the legally protected right to the same in another country. With few exceptions, IP rights are national in origin, products of territorial domestic regimes. This makes the acquisition of IP rights around the globe remarkably expensive. Once acquired, the holder then licenses that right, usually for a fee known as royalty, to a person in the other country. Thus, the licensor typically conveys to the licensee rights to make, use or sell the technology. The very sharing of intellectual property rights across borders raises a risk that proprietary control of the technology may be lost or, at a minimum, that a competitor will be created. For these reasons, international licensing agreements are complex legal documents that need to be carefully negotiated and drafted. Absent licensed transfers, piracy of intellectual property is increasingly commonplace. Indeed, in some countries such theft has risen to the height of development strategy.

The developing nations (as a "Group of 77"), the industrialized nations, and the nonmarket economy nations have tried to agree in UNCTAD upon an international "Code of Conduct" for the transfer of technology. Wide disparities in attitudes toward such a Code have been reflected by the developing nations' insistence that it be "internationally legally binding," and the industrialized nations' position that it consist of "guidelines" for the international transfer of technology. Some economics of the debate are illustrated by the fact that persons in the United States pay millions in royalties for use of imported technology, but receive billions in royalty payments from technology sent abroad. Many considered development of an international technology transfer Code the most important feature of the North–South dialogue between developed and developing nations. But it was not to be. Instead, to some degree, the TRIPs agreement (discussed below) reached during the Uruguay Round of GATT negotiations functions as a technology transfer code.

PATENT PROTECTION

For the most part, patents are granted to inventors according to national law. Thus, patents represent *territorial* grants of exclusive rights: The inventor receives Canadian patents, United States patents, Mexican patents, and so on. Since over one hundred countries have laws regulating patents, there are relatively few jurisdictions without some form of patent protection. Approximately 2 million patents are issued each year around the world. However, legally protected intellectual property in one country may not be protected similarly in another country. For example, many third world nations *refuse* to grant patents on pharmaceuticals. These countries often assert that their public health needs require such a policy. Thailand has traditionally been one such country and unlicensed "generics" have been a growth industry there.

Nominal patent protection in some developing nations may lack effective forms of relief—giving the appearance but not the reality of legal rights. Since international patent protection is expensive to obtain, some holders take a chance and limit their applications to those markets where they foresee demand or competition for their product. Nevertheless, U.S. nationals continue to receive tens of thousands of patents in other countries. But the reverse is increasingly true. Residents of foreign countries now receive over 50 percent of the patents issued under U.S. law. In many countries, persons who deal with the issuance and protection of patents are called patent agents. In the United States, patent practice is a specialized branch of the legal profession. Obtaining international patent protection often involves retaining the services of specialists in each country.

What constitutes a "patent" and how it is protected in any country depends upon domestic law. In the United States, a patent issued by the U.S. Patent Office will grant the right for 20 years from the date of application (17 years from the date of issuance prior to TRIPS) to exclude everyone from making, using or selling the patented invention without the permission of the patentee. Until 2011, the United States granted patents to the "first to invent" not (as in many other countries) the "first to file". The U.S. is now a "first to file" jurisdiction. Patent infringement, including the supply of "components" for patented inventions, can result in injunctive and damages relief in the U.S. courts. See Microsoft v. AT & T, 550 U.S. 437, 127 S.Ct. 1746, 167 L.Ed.2d 737 (2007) (shipment by Microsoft of infringing software to overseas facilities that installed it on computers sold outside the USA did not violate Patent Act; software was not a "component"). "Exclusion orders" against foreign-made patent infringing goods are also available. Such orders are frequently issued by the International Trade Commission under Section 337 of the Tariff Act of 1930, and are enforced by the U.S. Customs Service. A U.S. patent thus provides a short-term legal, but not necessarily economic, monopoly. For example, the exclusive legal rights conveyed by the patents held by Xerox on its photocopying machines have not given it a monopoly in the marketplace. There are many other producers of non-infringing photocopy machines with whom Xerox competes.

There are basically two types of patent systems in the world community, registration and examination. Some countries (e.g., France) grant a patent upon "registration" (accompanied by appropriate documents and fees), without making an inquiry about the patentability of the invention. The validity of such a patent grant is most difficult to gauge until a time comes to defend the patent against alleged infringement in an appropriate tribunal. In other countries, the patent grant is made following a careful "examination" of the prior art and statutory criteria on patentability or a "deferred examination" is made following public notice given to permit an "opposition." The odds are increased that the validity of such a patent will be sustained in the face of an alleged infringement. The United States and Germany have examination systems. To obtain U.S. patents, applicants must demonstrate to the satisfaction of the U.S. Patent Office that their inventions are novel, useful and nonobvious. Nevertheless, a significant number of U.S. patents have been subsequently held invalid in the courts and the Patent Office has frequently been criticized for a lax approach to issuance of patents. Much of the growth in patents issued is centered in high-tech industries, including computer software and business methods patents. See Bilski v. Kappos, ___ U.S. ___, 130 S.Ct. 3218, 177 L.Ed.2d 792 (2010) (some business methods unpatentable) and KSR International Co. v. Teleflex Inc., 550 U.S. 398, 127 S.Ct. 1727, 167 L.Ed.2d 705 (2007) (raising patentability standards for nonobviousness). The U.S. has also been criticized for sometimes allowing patents on "traditional knowledge" (e.g., Mexican Enola Beans) found primarily in the developing world.

The terms of a patent grant vary from country to country. For example, local law may provide for "confirmation," "importation," "introduction" or "revalidation" patents (which serve to extend limited protection to patents already existing in another country). "Inventor's certificates" and rewards are granted in some socialist countries where private ownership of the means of production is discouraged. The state owns the invention. This was the case in China, for example, but inventors now may obtain patents and exclusive private rights under the 1984 Patent Law. Some countries, such as Britain, require that a patent be "worked" (commercially applied) within a designated period of time. This requirement is so important that the British mandate a "compulsory license" to local persons if a patent is deemed unworked. Many developing nations have similar provisions in their patent laws ... the owner must use it or lose it.

INTERNATIONAL RECOGNITION OF PATENTS

The principal treaties regarding patents are the 1970 Patent Cooperation Treaty and the 1883 Convention of the Union of Paris, frequently revised and amended. To some extent, the Paris Convention also deals with trademarks, servicemarks, trade names, industrial designs, and unfair competition. Other recent treaties dealing with patents are the European Patent Convention (designed to permit a single office at Munich and The Hague to issue patents of 35 countries party to the treaty), and the European Union Patent Convention (intended to create a single patent valid throughout the EU).

The Paris Convention, to which over 170 countries including the U.S. are parties, remains the basic international agreement dealing with treatment of foreigners under national patent laws. It is administered by the International Bureau of the World Intellectual Property Organization (WIPO) at Geneva. The "right of national treatment" (Article 2) prohibits discrimination against foreign holders of local patents and trademarks. Thus, for example, a foreigner granted a Canadian patent must receive the same legal rights and remedies accorded Canadian nationals. Furthermore, important "rights of priority" are granted to patent holders provided they file in foreign jurisdictions within twelve months of their home country patent applications. But such rights may not overcome prior filings by others in "first to file" jurisdictions. Patent applications in foreign jurisdictions are not dependent upon success in the home country:

patentability criteria vary from country to country. Nevertheless, the Paris Convention obviates the need to file simultaneously in every country where intellectual property protection is sought. If an inventor elects not to obtain patent protection in other countries, anyone may make, use or sell the invention in that territory. The Paris Convention does not attempt to reduce the need for individual patent applications in all jurisdictions where patent protection is sought. Nor does it alter the various domestic criteria on patentability.

The Patent Cooperation Treaty (PCT), to which about 140 countries including the U.S. are parties, is designed to achieve greater uniformity and less cost in the international patent filing process, and in the examination of prior art. Instead of filing patent applications individually in each nation, filings under the PCT are done in selected countries. The national patent offices of Japan, Sweden, Russia and the United States have been designated International Searching Authorities (ISA), as has the European Patent Office at Munich and The Hague. The international application, together with the international search report, is communicated by an ISA to each national patent office where protection is sought. Nothing in this Treaty limits the freedom of each nation to require expensive translations, establish substantive conditions of patentability and determine infringement remedies. However, the Patent Cooperation Treaty also provides that the applicant may arrange for an international preliminary examination in order to formulate a non-binding opinion on the questions whether the claimed invention is novel, involves an inventive step (non-obvious) and is industrially applicable. In a country without sophisticated search facilities, the report of the international preliminary examination may largely determine whether a patent will be granted. For this reason alone, the Patent Cooperation Treaty may generate considerable uniformity in world patent law. Indeed, in 1986 the United States ratified the PCT provisions on preliminary examination reports, thereby supporting such uniformity.

KNOWHOW

Knowhow is commercially valuable knowledge. It may or may not be a trade secret, and may or may not be patentable. Though often technical or scientific, e.g., engineering services, knowhow can also be more general in character. Marketing and management skills as well as simply business advice can constitute knowhow. If someone is willing to pay for the information, it can be sold or licensed internationally.

Legal protection for knowhow varies from country to country and is, at best, limited. Unlike patents, copyrights and trademarks, you cannot by registration obtain exclusive legal rights to knowhow. Knowledge, like the air we breathe, is a public good. Once released in the community, knowhow can generally be used by anyone and is almost impossible to retrieve. In the absence of exclusive legal rights, preserving the confidentiality of knowhow becomes an important business strategy. If everyone knows it, who will pay for it? If your competitors have access to the knowledge, your market position is at risk. It is for these reasons that only a few people on earth ever know the Coca–Cola formula, which is perhaps the world's best kept knowhow.

Protecting knowhow is mostly a function of contract, tort and trade secrets law. Employers will surround their critical knowhow with employees bound by contract to confidentiality. But some valuable knowledge leaks from or moves with these employees, e.g. when a disgruntled retired or ex-employee sells or goes public with the knowhow. The remedies at law or in equity for breach of contract are unlikely to render the employer whole. Neither is torts relief likely to be sufficient since most employees are essentially judgment-proof, though they may be of more use if a competitor induced the breach of contract. Likewise, even though genuine trade secrets are protected by criminal statutes in a few jurisdictions, persuading the prosecutor to take up your business problem is not easy and criminal penalties will not recoup the trade secrets (though they may make the revelation of others less likely in the future).

The Economic Espionage Act of 1996 creates *criminal* penalties for misappropriation of trade secrets for the benefit of foreign governments or anyone. For these purposes, a "trade secret" is defined as "financial, business, scientific, technical, economic or engineering information" that the owner has taken reasonable measures to keep secret and whose "independent economic value derives from being closely held." In addition to criminal fines, forfeitures and jail terms, the Act authorizes seizure of all proceeds from the theft of trade secrets as well as property used or intended for use in the misappropriation (e.g., buildings and capital equipment).

Despite all of these legal hazards, even when certain knowhow is patentable, a desire to prolong the commercial exploitation of that knowledge may result in no patent registrations. The international chemicals industry, for example, is said to prefer trade secrets to public disclosure and patent rights with time limitations. Licensing or selling such knowhow around the globe is risky, but lucrative.

TRADEMARK PROTECTION

Virtually all countries offer some legal protection to trademarks, even when they do not have trademark registration systems. Trademark rights derived from the use of marks on goods in commerce have long been recognized at common law and remain so today in countries as diverse as the United States and the United Arab Emirates. The latter nation, for example, had no trademark registration law in 1986, but this did not prevent McDonald's from obtaining an injunction against a local business using its famous name and golden arches without authorization. However, obtaining international trademark protection requires separate registration under the law of each nation. Over three million trademarks are registered around the globe each year. In the United States, trademarks are protected at common law and by state and federal registrations. Federal registration is permitted by the U.S. Trademark Office for all marks capable of distinguishing the goods on which they appear from other goods. U.S. law notably allows trademarks on distinct smells, color, sounds and tastes. Unless the mark falls within a category of forbidden registrations (e.g., those that offend socialist morality in the People's Republic of China), a mark becomes valid for a term of years following registration.

In some countries (like the U.S. prior to 1989), marks must be used on goods before registration. In others, like France, use is not required and speculative registration of marks can occur. It is said that ESSO was obliged to purchase French trademark rights from such a speculator when it switched to EXXON in its search for the perfect global trademark. Since 1989, U.S. law has allowed applications when there is a bona fide intent to use a trademark within 12 months and, if there is good cause for the delay in actual usage, up to 24 additional months. Such filings in effect, reserve the mark for the applicant. The emphasis on bona fide intent and good cause represent an attempt to control any speculative use of U.S. trademark law.

The scope of trademark protection may differ substantially from country to country. Under U.S. federal trademark law, injunctions, damages and seizures of goods by customs officials may follow infringement. Other jurisdictions may provide similar remedies on their law books, but offer little practical enforcement. Thus, trademark registration is no guarantee against trademark piracy. A pair of blue jeans labeled "Levi Strauss made in San Francisco" may have been counterfeited in Israel or Paraguay without the knowledge or consent of Levi Strauss and in spite of its trademark registrations in those countries. Trademark counterfeiting is not just a third world problem, as any visitor to a United States "flea market" can tell. Congress created criminal offenses and private treble damages remedies for the first time in the Trademark Counterfeiting Act of 1984.

In many countries trademarks (appearing on goods) may be distinguished from "service marks" used by providers of services (e.g., the Law Store), "trade names" (business names), "collective marks" (marks used by a group or organization), and "certificate marks" (marks which certify a certain quality, origin, or other fact). Although national trademark schemes differ, it can be said generally that a valid trademark (e.g., a mark not "cancelled," "renounced," "abandoned," "waived" or "generic") will be protected against infringing use. A trademark can be valid in one country (ASPIRIN brand tablets in Canada), but invalid because generic in another (BAYER brand aspirin in the United States).

Unlike patents and copyrights, trademarks may be renewed continuously. A valid mark may be licensed, perhaps to a "registered user" or it may be assigned, in some cases only with the sale of the goodwill of a business. A growing example of international licensing of trademarks can be found in franchise agreements taken abroad. And national trademark law sometimes accompanies international licensing. The principal U.S.

trademark law, the Lanham Act of 1946, has been construed to apply extraterritorially (much like the Sherman Antitrust Act) to foreign licensees engaging in deceptive practices. See especially *Scotch Whiskey Association v. Barton Distilling Co.,* 489 F.2d 809 (7th Cir.1973).

Foreigners who seek a registration may be required to prove a prior and valid "home registration," and a new registration in another country may not have an existence "independent" of the home country registration's continuing validity. Foreigners are often assisted in their registration efforts by international and regional trademark treaties.

INTERNATIONAL RECOGNITION OF TRADEMARKS

The premium placed on priority of use of a trademark is reflected in several treaties, principal of which are the Paris Convention, the 1957 Arrangement of Nice Concerning the International Classification of Goods and Services, and the 1973 Trademark Registration Treaty done at Vienna. The treaties of widest international application are the Paris Convention and the Arrangement of Nice, as revised to 1967, to which the United States is signatory. The International Bureau of WIPO plays a central role in the administration of arrangements contemplated by these agreements.

The Paris Convention reflects an effort to internationalize some trademark rules. In addition to extending the principle of national treatment in Article 2 and providing for a right of priority of six months for trademarks (see patent discussion *ante*), the Convention mitigates the frequent national requirement that foreigners seeking trademark registration prove a pre-existing, valid and continuing home registration. This makes it easier to obtain foreign trademark registration, avoids the possibility that a lapse in registration at home will cause all foreign registrations to become invalid, and allows registration abroad of entirely different (and perhaps culturally adapted) marks. Article 6*bis* of the Paris Convention gives owners of "well known" trademarks the right to block or cancel the unauthorized registration of their marks. One issue that frequently arises under this provision is whether the mark needs to be well known locally or just internationally to obtain protection.

The Nice Agreement addresses the question of registration by "class" or "classification" of goods. In order to simplify internal administrative procedures relating to marks, many countries classify and thereby identify goods (and sometimes services) which have the same or similar attributes. An applicant seeking registration of a mark often is required to specify the class or classes to which the product mark belongs. However, not all countries have the same classification system and some lack any such system. Article 1 of the Nice Agreement adopts, for the purposes of the registration of marks, a single classification system for goods and services. This has brought order out of chaos in the field.

The 1973 Vienna Trademark Registration Treaty (to which the United States is a signatory) contemplates an international filing and examination scheme like that in force for patents under the Patent Cooperation Treaty. This treaty has not been fully implemented. Over 60 countries are parties to the Madrid Agreement for International Registration of Marks (1891, as amended). This Agreement and its related 1989 Protocol permit international filings to obtain national trademark rights and are administered by WIPO. The United States joined the Madrid Protocol in 2002, thus facilitating international filings to obtain approximately 60 national trademark registrations. A common market trademark can now be obtained in the European Union, an alternative to national trademark registrations and the "principle of territoriality" underlying national IP laws.

COPYRIGHT PROTECTION

Nearly one hundred nations recognize some form of copyright protection for "authors' works." The scope of this coverage and available remedies varies from country to country, with some uniformity established in the roughly 100 nations participating in the Berne and Universal Copyright Conventions. In the United States, for example, the Copyright Act of 1976 protects all original expressions fixed in a tangible medium (now known or later developed), including literary works, musical works, dramatic works, choreographic works, graphic works, audiovisual works, sound recordings, computer programs and selected databases. It is not necessary to publish a work to obtain a U.S. copyright; it is sufficient that the work is original and fixed in a tangible medium of expression. To retain a U.S. copyright, the author must give formal notice of a reservation of rights when publishing the work. Publication of the work without such notice dedicates it to free public usage.

U.S. copyright protection now extends for 70 years after the death of the author. The author also controls "derivative works," such as movies made from books. Only the author (or her assignees or employer regarding "works for hire") may make copies, display, perform, and first sell the work. Registration with the U.S. Copyright Office is not required to obtain copyright rights, but is essential to federal copyright infringement remedies. Infringers are subject to criminal penalties, injunctive relief and civil damages. Infringing works are impounded pending trial and ultimately destroyed. But educators, critics and news reporters are allowed "fair use" of the work, a traditional common law doctrine now codified in the 1976 Copyright Act.

The marketing of copyrights is sometimes accomplished through agency "clearinghouses." This is especially true of musical compositions because the many authors and potential users are dispersed. In the United States, the American Society of Composers, Authors and Publishers (AS-CAP) and Broadcast Music, Inc. (BMI) are the principal clearinghouses for such rights. Thousands of these rights are sold under "blanket licenses" for fees established by the clearinghouses and later distributed to their members. Similar organizations exist in most European states. Their activities have repeatedly been scrutinized under United States and European Union antitrust law. See *Broadcast Music, Inc. v. Columbia Broadcasting System, Inc.*, 441 U.S. 1, 99 S.Ct. 1551, 60 L.Ed.2d 1 (1979); *Re GEMA*, 10 Common Mkt.L.Rep. D35 (1971), 11 Common Mkt.L.Rep. 694 (1972). A Joint International Copyright Information Service run since 1981 by WIPO and UNESCO is designed to promote licensing of copyrights in the third world. This Service does not act as an agency clearinghouse for authors' rights, a deficiency sometimes said to promote copyright piracy.

Copyright protection in other countries may be more or less comprehensive or capable of adaptation to modern technologies. The copyrightability of computer programs, for example, is less certain in many jurisdictions. In some developing countries, "fair use" is a theme which is expansively construed to undermine copyright protection. But these differences seem less significant when contrasted with the worldwide problem of copyright piracy ranging from satellite signal poaching to unlicensed music and books.

In the United States, the Copyright Felony Act of 1992 criminalized all copyright infringements. The No Electronic Theft Act of 1997 (NET) removed the need to prove financial gain as element of copyright infringement law, thus ensuring coverage of copying done with intent to harm copyright owners or copying simply for personal use. The Digital Millenium Copyright Act of 1998 (DMCA) brought the United States into compliance with WIPO treaties and created two new copyright offenses; one for circumventing technological measures used by copyright owners to protect their works ("hacking") and a second for tampering with copyright management information (encryption). The DMCA also made it clear that "webmasters" digitally broadcasting music on the Internet must pay performance royalties.

INTERNATIONAL RECOGNITION OF COPYRIGHTS

Absent an appropriate convention, copyright registrations must be tediously acquired in each country recognizing such rights. However, copyright holders receive national treatment, translation rights and other benefits under the Universal Copyright Convention (UCC) of 1952 (U.S. adheres). Most importantly, the UCC *excuses* foreigners from registration requirements provided notice of a claim of copyright is adequately given (e.g., © Folsom, Gordon, Spanogle, Fitzgerald and Van Alstine, 2012). Some countries like the U.S. took advantage of an option *not* to excuse registration requirements. The exercise of this option had the effect at that time of reinforcing the U.S. "manufacturing clause" requiring local printing of U.S. copyrighted books and prohibiting importation of foreign copies. This protectionist clause finally expired under U.S. copyright law in 1986. The UCC establishes a minimum term for copyright protection: 25 years after publication, prior registration or death of the author. It also authorizes compulsory license schemes for translation rights in all states and compulsory reprint rights and instructional usage in developing countries. About 25 nations are UCC but not Berne Convention signatories.

National treatment and a release from registration formalities (subject to copyright notice requirements) can be obtained in Pan–American countries under the Mexico City Convention of 1902 and the Buenos Aires Convention of 1911, the U.S. adhering to both. Various benefits can be had in about 160 countries through the Berne Convention of 1886 (as revised). Like the UCC, the Berne Convention suspends registration requirements for copyright holders from participating states. Unlike the UCC, it allows for local copyright protection independent of protection granted in the country of origin and does not require copyright notice. The Berne Convention establishes a minimum copyright term of the life of the author plus 50 years, a more generous minimum copyright than that of the UCC. It also recognizes the exclusive translation rights of authors. Unlike the UCC, the Berne Convention does not contemplate compulsory licensing of translation rights. Most United States copyright holders previously acquired Berne Convention benefits by simultaneously publishing their works in Canada, a member country. In 1989, the United States ratified the Berne Convention. U.S. ratification of the Berne Convention creates copyright relations with an additional 25 nations. Ratification has eliminated U.S. registration requirements (reserved under the UCC) for foreign copyright holders and required protection of the "moral rights" of authors, i.e., the rights of integrity and paternity. The right of paternity insures acknowledgement of authorship. The right of integrity conveys the ability to object to distortion, alteration or other derogation of the work. It is generally thought that unfair competition law at the federal and state levels will provide the legal basis in U.S. law for these moral rights. *But see* The Visual Artists Rights Act of 1990, Title VI, P.L. 101–650, 104 Stat. 5089.

THE GATT/WTO AND INTELLECTUAL PROPERTY (TRIPs)

The Uruguay Round accords of 1994 included an agreement on trade-related intellectual property rights (TRIPs). This agreement took effect in July 1995. In the United States, the TRIPs agreement has been ratified and implemented by Congress. There is a general requirement of national and most-favored-nation treatment among the parties.

The TRIPs Code covers the gamut of intellectual property. On copyrights, there is protection for computer programs and databases, rental authorization controls for owners of computer software and sound recordings, a 50–year motion picture and sound recording copyright term, and a general obligation to comply with the Berne Convention (except for its provisions on moral rights).

On patents, the Paris Convention prevails, product and process patents are to be available for pharmaceuticals and agricultural chemicals, limits are placed on compulsory licensing, and a general 20–year patent term is created. Patents on certain medical procedures, as well as plants and animals, may be denied protection. For trademarks, service marks become registrable, internationally prominent marks receive enhanced protection, the linking of local marks with foreign trademarks is prohibited, and compulsory licensing is banned. Geographical indicators of origin (Feta cheese, Bordeaux wines, Tennessee Whiskey) are protected. In addition, trade secret protection is assisted by TRIPs rules enabling owners to prevent unauthorized use or disclosure. Integrated circuits are covered by rules intended to improve upon the Washington Treaty. Lastly, industrial designs are also part of the TRIPs regime.

Infringement and anticounterfeiting remedies are included in the TRIPs, for both domestic and international trade protection. There are specific provisions governing injunctions, damages, customs seizures, and discovery of evidence.

Late in 2001, the Doha Round of WTO negotiations were launched. These negotiations will reconsider the TRIPs agreement, particularly as it applies to developing nations. In addition, a Declaration on the TRIPs Agreement and Public Health was issued at the Qatar Ministerial Conference. This Declaration includes the following statement:

> We agree that the TRIPs Agreement does not prevent Members from taking measures to protect public health. Accordingly, while reiterating our commitment to the TRIPs Agreement, we affirm that the Agreement can and should be interpreted and implemented in a manner supportive of WTO Members' right to protect public health and, in particular, to promote access to medicines for all.

By mid–2003, a "Medicines Agreement" was finally reached on how to implement this Declaration. Compulsory licensing and/or importation of generic copies of patented medicines needed to address developing nation public health problems are authorized. Such activities may not pursue industrial or commercial policy objectives, and different packaging and labeling must be used in an effort at minimizing the risk of diversion of the generics to developed country markets. Under pressure from the United States, a number of more advanced developing nations (such as Mexico, Singapore and Qatar) agreed not to employ compulsory licensing except in situations of national emergency or extreme urgency. Canada, on the other hand, has licensed production of drugs for Rwanda and other nations incapable of pharmaceutical production.

Dozens of TRIPs complaints have been initiated under WTO dispute settlement procedures. Most have been settled, but a few have resulted in WTO Panel and Appellate Body Reports:

1. India—Patent Protection for Pharmaceutical and Agricultural Chemical Products, WT/DS 50/AB/R (1998) ("mailbox rule" patent applications for subjects not patentable in India until 2005 inadequate; denial of exclusive marketing rights in breach of TRIPs Article 70.9).

2. Canada—Term of Patent Protection, WT/DS 170/AB/R (2000) (pre-TRIPs Canadian patents must receive 20 year term).

3. U.S.—Section 110 (5) Copyright Act, WT/DS 160/ R (2000) (copyright exemption for "homestyle" dramatic musical works consistent with Berne Convention; small "business use" exemption inconsistent with Berne and therefore in breach of TRIPs) (settled by payment).

4. Canada—Pharmaceutical Patents, WT/DS 114/ R (2000) (Canadian generic pharmaceutical regulatory review and stockpiling patent rights' exceptions not sufficiently "limited").

5. U.S.—Section 211 Appropriations Act, WT/DS 176/AB/R (2002) (prohibition against registering marks confiscated by Cuban government, e.g. HAVANA CLUB rum, without original owner's consent violates Paris Convention and TRIPs; trade names covered by TRIPs).

6. EC—Trademarks and Geographical Indications WT/DS 174, 290/R (2005) (EC regulation violates national treatment and most-favored treatment obligations to non-EC nationals; procedural violations also found).

7. China—Measures Affecting The Protection and Enforcement of Intellectual Property Rights, WT/DS 362 R (Jan. 26, 2009) (China's implementation of TRIPs upheld as to criminal law thresholds and disposal of confiscated, infringing goods by customs authorities, rejected as to denial of copyright protection for works not authorized for release in China).

8. China—Measures Affecting Trading Rights and Distribution Services for Certain Publications and Audiovisuals Entertainment Products, WT/DS 363/AB/R (Dec. 31, 2009) (China's ADV restrictions limited to state-owned or approved channels violate WTO Accession Protocol, GATT 1994 and GATS; Restrictions not necessary to protect public morals).

9. European Communities—Information Technology Tariffs, WT/DS DS 375–377 (Aug. 16, 2010) (EU tariffs on cable converter boxes with Net capacity, flat-panel computer screens and printers that also scan, fax or copy violated 1996 Information Technology Agreement zero tariff requirements).

WTO REDUCES TARIFFS ON INFORMATION TECHNOLOGY

Tariff cuts on a wide range of information technology products were agreed to late in 1996 by a "coalition of the willing." The United States, the European Union and most of East Asia agreed to abolish tariffs on computers, electrical capacitors, calculators, ATM's, fax and answering machines, digital copiers and video cameras, computer diskettes, CD–ROM drives, computer software, fiber optical cables and hundreds of other items by 2000. This agreement covers more than 90 percent of all information technology trade.

In early 1997, agreement on liberalizing trade and reducing tariffs on basic telecommunications equipment was reached by 69 nations. This agreement took effect Feb. 5, 1998. World trade in office machines and telecom equipment is significant—$626 billion in 1996, or about 12.2 per cent of world merchandise trade. The agreement covers six main categories: computers, telecom equipment, semiconductors, semiconductor manufacturing equipment, software and scientific instruments. It does not currently cover consumer electronic goods.

Later that year, a WTO declaration imposed standstill obligations on all members to continue to refrain from applying customs duties to electronic commerce while negotiations are underway for more permanent rules in this area. In 2010, a WTO Panel ruled against EU information technology tariffs on cable converter boxes with Net capacity, flat-panel computer screens and printers that also scan, fax or copy. The EU elected not to appeal this ruling. Zero tariffs should apply.

PROBLEM 9.1   FRANCHISING AND TRADEMARK LICENSING: COLONEL CHICKEN GOES ABROAD

SECTION I.   THE SETTING

Colonel Chicken Inc. is a Texas fast food franchising corporation. Colonel Chicken has successfully established over 100 franchises in the United States. Its "formula for success" has involved:

(a) careful selection and ownership of the site by the company and required use of the site by the franchisee;

(b) mandatory franchisee use of secret recipes, special patented cooking equipment and purchases of chicken from a list of designated sources;

(c) extensive cooperative English language advertising programs;

(d) aggressive protection of its trademarks, COLONEL CHICKEN (TM) and CHICKEN–LICKEN–GOOD (TM), which appear in red, white and blue against an outline of the boundaries of the State of Texas;

(e) active supervision of quality controls maintained by its franchisees in accordance with Colonel Chicken's copyrighted instruction manual;

(f) exclusive use of a "Western" building design which draws upon the company's Texas heritage; and

(g) strongly "recommended" prices.

Colonel Chicken has never opened a franchise abroad. The company's marketing division believes that the possibility of international franchising of Colonel Chicken should be explored.

SECTION II. FOCUS OF CONSIDERATION

Franchising constitutes a rapidly expanding form of doing business abroad. Most franchisors have established fairly standard contracts which are utilized in their home markets, and receive counsel on the myriad of laws relevant to their domestic business operations. International franchising confronts the attorney with the need to research and evaluate an equally broad range of foreign laws which may apply in any particular jurisdiction. Such laws tend to focus on placing equity and control in the hands of local individuals and on regulating the franchise agreement to benefit the franchisees. Such laws tend not to respond to the cultural impact of foreign franchises. For example, appearance of the franchise building or trademark symbol may conflict in a foreign setting with traditional architectural forms (such as in European cities) or nationalist feelings hostile to the appearance of foreign trademarks on franchised products (such as in India or Mexico). Cultural conflicts can diminish the value of international franchises. To anticipate and solve legal and cultural problems, foreign counsel may be chosen to assist in the task of franchising abroad.

This problem explores some of the concerns counsel to a franchisor or prospective franchisee may encounter in opting for, negotiating, drafting or enforcing an international franchise agreement. Although patents, copyrights and trademarks may all be involved in international franchising, trademark licensing is the core of most international franchise agreements and is accordingly the principal focus of these materials. Students should be aware that the laws affecting international licensing of patents, copyrights and trademarks can be quite different. See generally, R. Folsom, M. Gordon and J.A. Spanogle, *Principles of International Business Transactions* 2d (West Concise Hornbook Series, 2010), Chapter 22. Web resources for further study include EU vertical restraints franchising coverage at *www.europa.eu*.

SECTION III. READINGS, QUESTIONS AND COMMENTS

PART A. PREPARING TO FRANCHISE ABROAD

P. ZEIDMAN, MEMORANDUM TO FOREIGN COUNSEL: AN INTRODUCTION TO INTERNATIONAL FRANCHISING

(1970).*

The decision to "go international" is one of the most important that any franchisor will ever make. Obviously, it should not be arrived at

---

* © P. Zeidman. Philip Zeidman is a partner in the law firm of Brownstein, Zeidman and Schomer, Washington, D.C. Reprinted with permission. Originally published in *International Franchising* (Continental Franchise Reports).

hastily or without thorough evaluation of the opportunity. The aura of international franchising may appeal to the romantic notions of even the most jaded franchise executive, but it should not be allowed to override his basic business judgment. Frequently, the initial question to be resolved will be the delicate one of timing: Is the company ready now for international franchising? If the urge to get into international franchising is great, so too may be the temptation to rush into it prematurely. There can be little doubt that a franchise which has matured in its domestic operations will stand a greater chance of success in international operations than one which has not. * * *

Though the U.S. company may have ultimate ambitions for a worldwide franchise system, it can help assure the success of its important first steps by organizing potential markets into a schedule of realistic priorities. Canada and the United Kingdom may be the most apparent targets for immediate extension of an American franchisor's activities because of their English-speaking populations, high standards of living, American-style tastes, geographic accessibility, and legal systems very similar to our own. The selection of other countries will typically require more extensive analysis. To illustrate, consider the U.S. franchise company which wishes to extend its operations in the Pacific area. It has narrowed its choice for a first country to either Japan or Australia. Australia has almost all of the advantages of England or Canada, and certain others of its own, but with its population of less than 13 million, Australia is a comparatively small market * * * and it is a very long way from the United States. Japan has the disadvantages of a markedly different culture, a non-English-speaking population, and a legal system significantly different from that of the U.S. On the other hand, Japan has a large population of approximately 100 million people, a high standard of living, consumer orientation, excellent transportation facilities, and a demonstrated receptivity to American tastes and methods of doing business.

In the example just given, and assuming there are no overriding legal considerations, the franchisor enjoys the luxury of a wide margin of error. Whichever market is chosen initially, the company will, if successful, probably expand to the alternative market in a matter of time. Of more critical importance, and far more difficult, is the decision to adopt a particular approach or structure for internationalizing the franchise system. Here lie the legal and operational considerations which will do much to determine the success or failure of the international program.

PENGILLEY, LEGAL AND COMMERCIAL ASPECTS OF INTERNATIONAL FRANCHISING— PROBLEMS IN THEIR NEGOTIATION*

8th Commonwealth Law Conference Ocho Rios, Jamaica.
Sept. 7–13, 1986.

Broad Nature of the Type of Desired Arrangement

The most fundamental question to be considered involves a consideration of the broad nature of the arrangement to be engaged in. Is it to be:

(a) Direct Franchising whereby the franchisor franchises individual outlets direct from the home country to the target country. Generally this system only operates between proximate countries with similar societies and legal systems. There is, for example, a lot of direct franchising from the United States into Canada and from Australia into New Zealand, and vice versa in each case.

* * *

(d) Master or Area Franchise, whereby the franchisor gives the franchisee a specific area (usually a particular country or a significant part of it) to exploit with the right usually to subfranchise. The advantage of such a system is less franchisor involvement. Master franchising particularly suits franchisors who are without substantial financial or managerial expertise. Moreover, it is a particularly useful form of franchising where long distances or different cultural and legal systems are applicable. There is a lot of "Master" franchising, for example, into and out of Australia for distance reasons.

* * *

Master Franchise agreements can work very well. The chief downside is if the Master Franchisee goes bad financially or in his performance. In such a case a Master Franchise arrangement is a total commercial disaster whereas, in other types of arrangements, something can often be salvaged. Obviously, therefore, Master Franchise arrangements should be looked at with a cautious, conservative and doubting eye.

The above questions should never be considered without thinking of alternative methods of conducting business. Frequently it is assumed that franchising is the best business method but the point is not fully debated. Often the best business decision is not to do business at all. Some "cross examination" questions by the lawyer for a franchisee can often be valuable in focusing the franchisee's thoughts on to the difficulties and advantages involved in doing business in various ways.

Commercial reasons should, I believe, be the prime consideration in choosing the method of conducting business. If it won't work commercially

---

* © Warren Pengilley, B.A., LL.B. [Sydney], J.D. [Vanderbilt], M.Com. [Newcastle], AASA CPA; Solicitor, Sly & Russell, Sydney; Formerly Commissioner, Australian Trade Practices Commission. Reprinted with permission.

then all the lawyers and accountants with all their tax planning and other advice are completely unable to make a profit for either franchisor or franchisee. Lawyers, however, can be of great assistance in advising on the method of doing business and, at least as regards the basic methods of doing business, legal advice should be sought very early.

* * *

Lawyer Involvement in Negotiations

When should lawyers become involved in negotiations?

Lawyer involvement in negotiation is desirable in my view at an early stage. As lawyers, we should, however, recognize what the commercial community wants us to do—where we can assist and where we hinder. One franchising consultant with whom I discussed a draft of this paper said that the best thing a lawyer can do is to put it to his client at the beginning of negotiations: "Are you sure you couldn't develop a similar system yourself? What is it that you see gives you the advantage in franchising? Is it worth the premium?" This is a different role to that in which many lawyers see themselves, i.e., as a passive recipient of instructions. Almost as important was the comment of another franchising consultant who said with some frustration:

> "My advice to any franchisor is to have a lawyer on the team who truly understands franchising, otherwise the learning curve can be expensive!"

The art of lawyer involvement in franchising negotiations, it seems to me, is for the lawyer to give immediate steering advice so that the negotiations can head down the right track. Lawyers, because they are brought into negotiations early, should not think that they can or should run the negotiations or control the commercial direction of the proposed deal. Regrettably this all too often occurs and there is thus a very real client reluctance to involve lawyers until a late, often all too late, stage.

Lawyers, I believe, do appreciate being part of a negotiating team. Membership of such a team can make one more interested, more informed and more enthusiastic as to the whole activity. When a final agreement has to be drawn up, a lawyer involved in the negotiations from the beginning will be far more successful in expressing the intent of the parties than one who comes late to the scene.

He who controls the Draft controls the Negotiation

One basic rule of thumb which has been demonstrated to my satisfaction on numerous occasions is that "He who controls the draft controls the negotiation". It is tempting to a client to agree to the other party's lawyer drafting the agreement. It saves him money. Nonetheless, I believe that this is often a short sighted view. When you are drafting, it is so easy to draft favourably to your own cause and introduce favourable clauses which never get written out of the final. Often such clauses are not even discussed as they are "subsidiary items".

Often, however, one's ability to control drafting is limited by the question of the comparative power of the parties involved. A well established franchisor will frequently have a Master Franchise arrangement which he will offer on a "take it or leave it" basis. Similarly traditional etiquette will often be important. Commonly he who conveys rights will present the first draft.

* * *

G. GLICKMAN, TYPICAL FRANCHISE AGREEMENTS (FAST FOOD FRANCHISE)

Volume 15A, § 11.08 (1983).*

This agreement, made and entered into at (city, state) this _____ day of _____, 20__, by and between [Franchisor], a _____ corporation, hereinafter referred to as Company, party of the first part, and _____ hereinafter referred to as Franchisee, party of the second part. * * *

Now, therefore, in consideration of the mutual covenants herein contained, the parties agree as follows:

I. Fʀᴀɴᴄʜɪsᴇ Pᴀʏᴍᴇɴᴛ; Sᴇʀᴠɪᴄᴇs ʙʏ Cᴏᴍᴘᴀɴʏ

A. *Franchise Payment.* The Company acknowledges payment to it by Franchisee of the total sum of _____ ($_____) Dollars; consisting of _____ ($_____) Dollars as and for a franchise fee; _____ ($_____) Dollars for initial assistance essential to Franchisee consisting of the training and the services detailed at Paragraph B, subparagraphs 2, 3 and 4 below; and _____ ($_____) Dollars for a grand opening advertising fund. Franchisee acknowledges that the grant of the franchise constitutes the sole consideration for the payment of the franchise fee and that said sum shall be fully earned by Company upon execution and delivery hereof. * * *

B. *Services by Company.* Company agrees during the term of this Franchise Agreement to use its best efforts to maintain the high reputation of Franchised Restaurants and in connection therewith to make available to Franchisee:

1. Initial standard specifications and plans for the building, equipment, furnishings, decor, layout, and signs identified with Franchised Restaurants, together with advice and consultation concerning them.

2. A pre-opening training program conducted at Company's training school and at a Franchised Restaurant.

3. Opening supervision and assistance from employees of Company at Franchisee's premises.

4. Opening promotion programs conducted under the direction of Company's Marketing Department.

---

5. The Company's confidential standard business policies and operations data instruction manuals (hereinafter collectively called "Manual"), a copy of which is (or will be) delivered and loaned to Franchisee for the term hereof.

6. Such merchandising, marketing and advertising research data and advice as may be from time to time developed by the Company and deemed by it to be helpful in the operation of Franchised Restaurants.

* * *

8. Such special recipe techniques, food preparation instructions, new restaurant services and other operational developments as may be from time to time developed by the Company and deemed by it to be helpful in the operation of Franchised Restaurants.

9. A standardized accounting, cost control and portion control system.

II.   FRANCHISE GRANT: AREA: TERM

A. *Franchise Grant.* Subject to the terms and conditions of this Franchise Agreement and the continuing good faith performance thereof by Franchisee, Company grants to Franchisee the franchise to operate a Franchised self-service restaurant at the location of the premises; and in consideration of the payment by Franchisee of the royalties and advertising and sales promotion contribution hereinafter specified, Company licenses to Franchisee for the term hereof the Company's right to use at the premises and in the operation of such restaurant, the names (enumerate trade names) together with such other insignia, symbols and trademarks which may be approved and authorized by Company from time to time in connection with franchised Restaurants, and the good will derived from such previous use by Company.

B. *Area.* This franchise shall be exclusive within a radius of one (1) mile from the boundary of the premises.

C. *Term.* The term of this Franchise Agreement shall commence on the date Franchisee's restaurant opens for business and shall expire at midnight on the day preceding the fifteenth (15th) anniversary of said opening, unless sooner terminated in accordance with the terms and conditions hereof.

III.   PREMISES

The premises at which Franchisee shall operate a Franchised Restaurant are fully described in Exhibit "A" appended hereto. * * * Franchisee shall conduct business from said location only if and when the premises have been improved with a restaurant building and decorated, furnished, and equipped with restaurant equipment, furnishings and supplies which meet Company's specification. The restaurant building erected at the premises will be in strict conformity with plans and specifications prepared by Company's architect. During the term of this agreement, the premises shall be used only by the Franchisee and solely for the purpose of operating a Franchised Restaurant pursuant to the terms of this agreement.

IV. TRAINING

Franchisee will designate itself or another person approved by Company as a trainee to attend Company's training school. * * *

V. ROYALTIES AND ADVERTISING CONTRIBUTION

A. *Royalties.* Franchisee agrees in consideration of Company's licensing its use of the names [Franchisor's Trade Names], together with such other trademarks and service marks as may be authorized for use by Company, to pay a monthly royalty in the amount of three and five-tenths percent (3.5%) of Franchisee's gross sales. Royalties shall be paid on or before the tenth (10th) day of each month and shall be based upon sales for the preceding calendar month.

B. *Advertising and Sales Promotion.* The Franchisee agrees, as partial consideration for the grant of this franchise, to pay to Company a monthly advertising and sales promotion contribution. This sum shall be equal to four (4%) percent of Franchisee's gross sales. The advertising and sales promotion contribution shall be paid on or before the tenth (10th) day of each month and shall be based upon Franchisee's gross sales for the preceding calendar month. The advertising and sales promotion contribution shall be expended by Company at its discretion for advertising and sales promotion both in Franchisee's market area and on a national basis, except for that portion used for creative and production costs of advertising and sales promotion elements, and for those market research expenditures which are directly related to the development and evaluation of the effectiveness of advertising and sales promotion.

C. *Gross Sales Defined.* * * *

D. *Accounting Procedures: Right of Audit.*

1. *Accounting.* Franchisee agrees to keep complete records of its business. Franchisee shall furnish monthly profit and loss statements for the preceding month and a profit and loss statement from the beginning of Franchisee's fiscal year to the end of the preceding month. * * *

2. *Certified Statements.*

(a) A Franchisee shall submit an annual financial statement as to gross sales, which statement shall be certified to by a certified public accountant within ninety (90) days after the close of its fiscal year.

* * *

3. *Audits.* Franchisee agrees that Company or its agents shall, at all reasonable times, have the right to examine or audit the books and accounts of Franchisee to verify the gross sales as reported by Franchisee.

VI. STANDARDS AND UNIFORMITY OF OPERATION

Franchisee agrees that Company's special standardized design and decor of buildings and uniformity of equipment and layout, and adherence to the Manual are essential to the image of a Franchised Restaurant. In recognition of the mutual benefits accruing from maintaining uniformity of appearance, service, products and marketing procedures, it is mutually covenanted and agreed:

A. *Building and Premises.* Except as specifically authorized by Company, Franchisee shall not alter the appearance of the improvements or the premises. * * *

B. *Signs.* Franchisee agrees to display Company's names and trademarks at the premises, in the manner authorized by Company. Franchisee agrees to maintain and display signs reflecting the current image of Company. The color, size, design and location of said signs shall be as specified by Company. Franchisee shall not place additional signs or posters on the premises without the written consent of Company.

C. *Equipment.* Franchisee is acquiring through Company and other approved sources by purchase or lease, machinery, equipment, furnishings, signs and other personal property (hereinafter collectively called equipment). Appended hereto as Exhibit "B" * * * is a list of equipment which must be used by Franchisee in the operation of its business. Franchisee agrees to maintain such equipment in excellent working condition. As items of equipment become obsolete or mechanically impaired to the extent that they require replacement, Franchisee will replace such items with either the same or substantially the same types and kinds of equipment as are being installed in [Franchised] Restaurants at the time replacement becomes necessary. All equipment used in Franchisee's Restaurant, whether purchased from Company or other approved suppliers pursuant to Paragraph F herein, shall meet Company specifications.

D. *Vending Machines, Etc.* * * *

E. *Menu and Service.* Franchisee agrees to serve the menu items specified by Company, to follow all specifications and formulas of Company as to contents and weight of unit products served, and to sell no other food or drink item or any other merchandise of any kind without the prior written approval of Company. Franchisee agrees that all food and drink items will be served in containers bearing accurate reproductions of the Company's service marks and trademarks. Such imprinted items shall be purchased by Franchisee through Company or through a supplier or manufacturer approved in writing by Company. * * *

Franchisee shall remain open for business from 11:00 A.M. to 11:00 P.M. daily unless Company consents to other hours or days at the request of Franchisee. * * *

F. *Alternate Suppliers.* Irrespective of any other provision hereof, if Franchisee gives Company notice sufficiently in advance to permit supplier and specification verification and testing, that it wishes to purchase equipment, food, supplies or containers from reputable, dependable sources other than Company or its designated or previously approved sources of supply, Company will not unreasonably withhold the prompt approval of such purchases provided said purchases conform to the appearance, quality, size or portion (and, where applicable, taste), and uniformity standards and other specifications of Company. Company may require that samples from alternate suppliers be delivered to Company or to a designated independent testing laboratory for testing before approval and use. A charge not to exceed the actual cost of the test may be made by Company or by an independent testing laboratory designated by Company, and shall be paid for by Franchisee.

G. *Right of Entry and Inspection.* Company or its authorized agent and representative shall have the right to enter and inspect the premises and examine and test food products and supplies for the purpose of ascertaining that Franchisee is operating the restaurant in accordance with the terms of this agreement and the Manual. * * *

VII. INSURANCE: INDEMNIFICATION

A. Franchisee agrees to secure and pay premiums thereon for the term of this Franchise Agreement, a Comprehensive General Liability Policy, including Products Liability, in the amount of $500,000/$500,000 bodily injury liability, and $100,000 property damage liability, or in such other amounts as Company may reasonably request, for the operation on the premises. Franchisee agrees to name Company in said policy as additional named insured * * *.

B. Franchisee is responsible for all loss or damage and contractual liabilities to third persons originating in or in connection with the operation of the Franchised self-service restaurant and for all claims or demands for damages to property or for injury, illness or death of persons directly or indirectly resulting therefrom; and Franchisee agrees to defend, indemnify and save Company harmless of, from and with respect to any such claims, loss or damage.

VIII. TAXES

Franchisee shall promptly pay when due all taxes levied or assessed by reason of its operation and performance under this agreement. * * *

IX. OPTION AT END OF TERM

Provided that Franchisee shall have substantially complied with all of the terms and conditions of this agreement * * * Company will offer Franchisee the opportunity to remain a Franchisee for one additional period of fifteen (15) years, provided that: * * *.

X. ASSIGNMENT: CONDITIONS AND LIMITATIONS

A. Franchisee shall neither sell, assign, transfer nor encumber this agreement or any right or interest therein or thereunder, nor suffer or permit any such assignment, transfer or encumbrance to occur by operation of law unless the written consent of Company be first had and obtained. * * *

B.　In the event of the death or disability of a franchisee, Company shall consent to the transfer of the interest to Franchisee's spouse, heirs or relatives, by blood or by marriage, whether such a transfer is made by Will or by operation of law if, at the sole discretion and judgment of Company, such person or persons obtaining said interest shall be capable of conducting said business in a manner satisfactory to Company. * * *

XI.　LIMITATIONS OF FRANCHISE

A.　Trademarks, Trade Names and Trade Secrets. 1. Franchisee acknowledges the Company's sole and exclusive right (except for certain rights granted under existing and future license agreements) to use the trademarks, trade names and trade secrets set forth herein and represents, warrants and agrees that neither during the term of this Agreement nor after the expiration or other termination hereof, shall Franchisee directly or indirectly contest or aid in contesting the validity or ownership of the Trademarks or take any action whatsoever in derogation of the Company's claimed rights therein.

2.　Nothing contained in this Agreement shall be construed to vest in Franchisee any right, title or interest in or to the [Company's] trademarks, the goodwill now or hereafter associated therewith, or any right in the design of any restaurant building, other than the rights and license expressly granted herein. Any and all goodwill associated with the [Company] trademarks shall inure directly and exclusively to the benefit and is the property of the Company.

3.　No advertising by Franchisee or other use of the Company trademarks shall contain any statement or material which may, in the judgment of the Company, be in bad taste or inconsistent with the Company's public image. * * *

4.　Franchisee shall adopt and use the Company trademarks only in the manner expressly approved by the Company. Franchisee shall advertise and promote the Restaurant only under the Company trademark and the name _____ without any accompanying words or symbols except as otherwise required by law and approved in writing by the Company.

5.　The Franchisee acknowledges and agrees that the Company is the owner of all proprietary rights in and to the product formulae and restaurant systems and methods described in the Company's training guides and materials, and that the product formulae and restaurant systems and methods in their entirety constitute trade secrets of the Company which are revealed to the Franchisee in confidence and that no right is given to or acquired by the Franchisee to disclose, duplicate, license, sell or reveal any portion thereof to any person other than an employee of the Franchisee required by his work to be familiar with relevant portions thereof. * * *

B. No Agency. 1. Franchisee shall not represent or hold himself out as an agent, legal representative, partner, subsidiary, joint venturer or employee of Company. Franchisee shall have no right or power to, and shall not bind or obligate Company in any way, manner or thing whatsoever, nor represent that it has any right to do so.

2. In all public records and in its relationship with other persons, on letterheads and business forms, Franchisee shall indicate its independent ownership of said business, and that it is only a franchisee of Company. Franchisee agrees to exhibit on the premises in a place designated by Company, a notification that it is a franchisee of Company.

XII. DEFAULT: TERMINATION

A. *Default.* The occurrence of any of the following events shall constitute good cause for Company, at its option and without prejudice to any other rights or remedies provided for hereunder or by law or equity, to terminate this agreement.

1. If Franchisee shall be adjudicated a bankrupt, becomes insolvent, or if a receiver (permanent or temporary) of its property or any part thereof is appointed by a court of competent authority; * * *

2. If Franchisee defaults in the payment of royalties or advertising due hereunder or fails to submit profit and loss statements or other financial statements or data or reports on gross sales as provided herein, * * *

3. If Franchisee fails to maintain the standards as set forth in this agreement, and as may be supplemented by the Manual, * * *

4. If Franchisee suffers a violation of any law, ordinance, rule or regulation of a governmental agency in connection with the operation of the Franchised Restaurant, * * *

5. If Franchisee ceases to do business at the premises or defaults under any lease or sublease or loses its right to the possession of the premises. * * *

6. If Franchisee violates any other term or condition of this agreement and Franchisee fails to cure such violation within thirty (30) days after written notice from Company to cure same.

B. *Effect of Termination.*

* * *

XIII. ARBITRATION

A. If this agreement shall be terminated by Company and Franchisee shall dispute Company's right of termination or the reasonableness thereof, the parties shall submit said dispute for binding arbitration as hereinafter set forth:

1. Each party shall select one arbitrator and the two shall select a third, and failing selection of an arbitrator by either or by the two selected

by the parties, the third arbitrator shall be selected by the American Arbitration Association or any successor thereof. The arbitration proceeding shall be conducted in accordance with the rules of the American Arbitration Association or any successor thereof. Judgment upon an award of the majority of arbitrators filed in a court of competent jurisdiction shall be binding.

2.   If Company or Franchisee shall operate the restaurant pending the adjudication of the matter in dispute, said party shall be considered the trustee of the prevailing party and shall be required to make a full and complete accounting of such trusteeship.

B.   In the event that any other dispute arises between the parties hereto in connection with the terms or provisions of this agreement, either party, by written notice to the other party, may elect to submit the dispute to binding arbitration in accordance with the foregoing procedure. Such right shall not be exclusive of any other rights which a party may have to pursue a course of legal action in an appropriate forum.

XIV.   MISCELLANEOUS: GENERAL CONDITIONS

A.   *Interpretation.* * * *

B.   *Entire Agreement.* This agreement constitutes the entire agreement of the parties and supersedes all prior negotiations, commitments, representations and undertakings of the parties with respect to the subject matter hereof. Franchisee agrees that Company has made no representations inducing execution of this agreement which are not included herein.

C.   *Non-Waiver.* The failure of Company to exercise any right, power or option given to it hereunder, or to insist upon strict compliance with the terms hereof by Franchisee shall not constitute a waiver of the terms and conditions of this agreement with respect to any other or subsequent breach thereof, nor a waiver by Company of its rights at any time thereafter to require exact and strict compliance with all the terms hereof. The rights or remedies hereunder are cumulative to any other rights or remedies which may be granted by law.

D.   *Governing Law.*

1.   This agreement shall become valid when executed and accepted by Company at [city, state], and it shall be governed and construed under and in accordance with the laws of the State of _____.

2.   Anything herein to the contrary notwithstanding, Franchisee shall conduct its business in a lawful manner; and it will faithfully comply with all applicable laws or regulations of the state, city or other political subdivisions in which it conducts its said business.

E.   *Severability.* * * *

F.   *Notices.* * * *

G.   *Employees.* Company shall have no control over employees of Franchisee, including the terms and conditions of their employment.

H. *Competition With Company.* Franchisee agrees that during the term of this agreement it shall not engage in any restaurant or prepared food business which is the same or similar to Company's business. Franchisee further agrees that, for a period of eighteen (18) months after termination of this agreement, it will not engage in any business the same or similar to Company's business within an area of five (5) miles from the premises without the prior written consent of Company. In applying for Company's consent, Franchisee has the burden of establishing that any such activity by it will not involve the use of benefits provided hereby or constitute unfair competition with Company or other franchisees.

I. *Interference With Employment Relations of Others.* Franchisee shall not attempt to attain an unfair advantage over other Company franchisees or Company by soliciting for employment any person who is, at the time of such solicitation, employed by other Company franchisees or Company, nor shall Franchisee directly or indirectly induce any such person to leave his or her employment as aforesaid.

J. *Liability of Multiple Franchisees.* * * *

K. *Modification.* This agreement may only be modified or amended by a document of equal dignity.

L. *Execution.* * * *

In Witness Whereof, Company has caused these presents to be executed in its name and on its behalf by its proper corporate officers, and Franchisee has hereunto affixed its hand and seal all on the day and year first above written.

* * *

QUESTIONS AND COMMENTS

1. Article 4 of the Paris Convention (discussed in the Introduction 9.0) applies to the international acquisition of patents and trademarks and provides for a "right of priority." What is the purpose of such a right? Why might Colonel Chicken prefer country-by-country trademark, patent and copyright applications to any "international filing"? Will Colonel Chicken want to register its marks abroad "just as" registered at home?

2. Long before any international franchise contract is negotiated or drafted, counsel may be asked to evaluate the general legal environment of franchising in specific countries. Such a request often is made to enable executives to decide whether and where to franchise abroad. What areas of law, e.g. taxation, should you investigate in order to respond to such a request? In light of Colonel Chicken's "formula for success," what particular legal questions should be researched?

3. Pengilley discusses the use internationally of "master franchise" agreements. Should COLONEL CHICKEN consider such an agreement? Why? What about an "area development" agreement where franchisees agree to open a certain number of locations within a given geographic region?

4. What do you think of Pengilley's maxim that the lawyer who controls the draft controls the negotiation of international franchise agreements? Suppose the lawyers on each side want to control the draft. What then?

5. Zeidman is a well-known United States franchising attorney. Pengilley is a well-known Australian franchising attorney. Are their different backgrounds reflected in their analyses of the role of lawyers in international franchising?

6. Consider the sample *domestic* fast food franchise agreement contained in the Readings. This agreement is old, and full of problems, deliberately so. How might it be adapted to Colonel Chicken's franchise formula? What clauses probably will have to be modified for purposes of franchising abroad? Why? How? See especially Parts I, V, VI, VII, IX, XIII and XIV.

7. If you were representing a foreign franchisee under the sample agreement, what clauses would you most likely seek to alter and why? *See* especially Parts I, V, VI, XI, XIII and XIV of the sample agreement. How would you redraft them?

8. Apart from commercial motivations, trademark franchisors must maintain some quality control over the actions of franchisees in order to preserve registered trademark rights. Failure to do so could result in a finding that the mark has been "abandoned" because it no longer represents to the public a source of consistent quality. International franchisors operating at a distance from their franchisees will be especially concerned with quality controls.

9. Franchisors will naturally also want to control those activities constituting their "formula for success." On the other hand, excessive control or the public appearance of such control may give rise to an agency or employment relationship between the franchisor and franchisee. Such a relationship could be used to establish vicarious franchisor liability for franchisee conduct, including international product and other tort liabilities. How has the sample franchise agreement tried to deal with these considerations? *See* Parts VII and XI of the sample agreement.

10. Section V(A) of the sample agreement specifies royalties which are calculated on the basis of *gross* sales. In countries where sales or other consumption taxes exist, or tax rebates are used, some *net* sales figure should be used. Section V(B) gives the franchisor control of an advertising and promotion fund also based upon a percentage of the franchisee's gross sales. Should the franchisee, who very likely knows the foreign market better than the franchisor, be given more influence over the use of this fund?

11. Section XI(A) is a judicial ouster clause. Would most United States courts be willing to enforce this clause? How could it be restructured?

12. The sample fast food franchise agreement is arguably lopsided in favor of the franchisor. Might it boomerang at a later date? Is it really in the franchisor's interest to exercise all of the bargaining leverage it may have in international negotiations? Many franchisors believe that carefully selecting foreign franchisees is their most critical decision.

PART B. REGULATION OF THE INTERNATIONAL FRANCHISE AGREEMENT

THE FRANCHISES ACT, ALBERTA, CANADA

Alta.Rev.Stat. Ch. F–17 (1980).

Sec. 6. Registration.—(1) No person shall trade in a franchise in Alberta either on his own account or on behalf of any other person until there have been filed with the Commission both an application for registration in the prescribed form and a prospectus in respect to the offer of that franchise and until a receipt for the prospectus has been obtained from the Registrar.

* * *

(3) A trade in a franchise is deemed to have occurred in Alberta if

(*a*) an offer to sell or a sale is made in Alberta,

(*b*) an offer to buy is accepted in Alberta,

(*c*) the franchisee is domiciled or ordinarily resident in Alberta,

(*d*) the franchise will be operated in Alberta,

(*e*) an offer to sell is made from Alberta, or

(*f*) an offer to sell or an offer to buy is accepted by communicating the acceptance to a person in Alberta either directly or through an agent in Alberta.

* * *

Sec. 8. Prospectus.—(1) A prospectus shall provide full, plain and true disclosure of all material facts relating to the franchise proposed to be offered. * * *

* * *

(3) The Director may require any additional information which he considers necessary to be included in the prospectus. * * *

Sec. 34. Offences and penalties.—(1) A person who

(*a*) in any material, evidence or information submitted or given under this Act or the regulations to the Commission, its representative, the Director or the Registrar or to a person appointed to make an investigation or audit under this Act makes a statement,

(i) that, at the time and in the light of the circumstances under which it is made, is false or misleading with respect to a material fact, or

(ii) that omits to state a material fact, the omission of which makes the statement false or misleading,

(*b*) in an application, report, prospectus, return, financial statement or other document required to be filed or furnished under this Act or the regulations

   (i) that, at the time and in the light of the circumstances under which it is made, is false or misleading with respect to a material fact, or

   (ii) that omits to state a material fact, the omission of which makes the statement false or misleading,

(c) contravenes this Act or the regulations, or

(d) fails to observe or comply with an order, ruling, direction or other requirements made under this Act or the regulations

is guilty of an offence and liable to

(e) a fine of not more than $2,000 or to imprisonment for a term of not more than one year, or to both, or

(f) in the case of a company, a fine of not more than $25,000.

(2) No person is guilty of an offence under subsection (1)(a) or (b) if he establishes that he did not know that the statement was false or misleading and in the exercise of reasonable diligence could not have known that the statement was false or misleading.

(3) If a company is found guilty of an offence under subsection (1) every director or officer of the company who authorized, permitted or acquiesced in the offence is also guilty of an offence and is liable to a fine of not more than $2,000 or to imprisonment for a term of not more than one year, or to both.

* * *

Civil Remedies and Liabilities

Sec. 36. Withdrawal from trade agreement.—(1) A person not acting as agent of the purchaser who receives an order for a franchise to which section 4, 6 or 19 is applicable shall, unless he has previously done so, send by prepaid mail or deliver to the purchaser the statement of material facts, prospectus or amended prospectus, whichever is the last required to be filed with the Commission,

(a) before entering into an agreement of purchase and sale resulting from the order, or

(b) not later than midnight on the 4th day, exclusive of Saturdays, Sundays and holidays, after entering into the agreement.

(2) An agreement of purchase and sale or a sale referred to in subsection (1) is not binding on the purchaser if the person from whom the purchaser purchased the franchise receives written or telegraphic notice evidencing the intention of the purchaser not to be bound by the agreement of purchase and sale or the sale not later than midnight on the 4th day, exclusive of Saturdays, Sundays and holidays, after receipt by the purchaser of the statement of material facts, prospectus or amended prospectus, whichever is the last required to be filed with the Commission.
* * *

Sec. 37.   Rescission of trade agreement.—(1) A person who is a party to a contract as purchaser resulting from the offer of a franchise to which section 5, 6, or 17 is applicable has a right to rescind the contract while still the owner of the franchise if the statement of material facts or the prospectus and any amended prospectus then filed with the Commission in compliance with section 17 and received by the purchaser, as of the date of receipt contains an untrue statement of a material fact or omits to state a material fact necessary in order to make any statement contained therein not misleading in the light of the circumstances in which it was made.

(2) No action shall be commenced under this section after the expiration of 2 years from

> (a) the receipt of the statement of material facts, prospectus or amended prospectus by the purchaser, or

> (b) the date of the contract referred to in subsection (1), whichever is the later.

(3) Subsection (1) does not apply to an untrue statement or a material fact or an omission to state a material fact

> (a) if the untruth of the statement or the fact of the omission was unknown to the person whose franchises are being offered by the statement of material facts or prospectus and, in the exercise of reasonable diligence, could not have been known to that person,

> (b) if the statement or omission is disclosed in an amended prospectus filed in compliance with section 17 and the amended prospectus was received by the purchaser, or

> (c) if the purchaser knew of the untruth of the statement or knew of the omission at the time he purchased the franchise.

* * *

Sec. 39.   Reliance on prospectus.—(1) When a receipt for a prospectus has been issued by the Registrar, notwithstanding that the receipt is thereafter revoked, every purchaser of the franchise to which the prospectus relates shall be deemed to have relied on the statements made in the prospectus whether the purchaser has received the prospectus or not, and, if a material false statement is contained in the prospectus, every person who, at the time of the issue of a receipt for the prospectus, is a director of a company issuing the franchises or a person who signed the certificate required by section 9 is liable to pay compensation to all persons who have purchased the franchise for any loss or damage those persons have sustained as a result of such purchase unless it is proved

> (a) that the prospectus was filed with the Commission without his knowledge or consent, and that, on becoming aware of its filing with the Commission, he forthwith gave reasonable public notice that it was so filed,

(*b*) that, after the issue of a receipt for the prospectus and before the purchase of the franchise by the purchaser, on becoming aware of any false statement therein, he withdrew his consent thereto and gave reasonable public notice of such withdrawal and of the reason for it,

(*c*) that, with respect to every false statement, he had reasonable grounds to believe and did believe that the statement was true,

(*d*) that he had no reasonable grounds to believe that an expert who made a statement in a prospectus or whose report or valuation was produced or fairly summarized in it was not competent to make the statement, valuation or report, or

(*e*) that, with respect to every false statement purporting to be a statement made by an official person or contained in what purports to be a copy of or extract from a public official document, it was a correct and fair representation of the statement or copy of or extract from the document.

HEFTER AND ZEIDMAN, PREPARING A TRADEMARK LICENSE AGREEMENT: CONTRACTUAL AND ANTITRUST CONSIDERATIONS

(1983).*

The Lanham Act provides for use of a mark by a "related company." Section 1055 states: "Where a registered mark or a mark sought to be registered is or may be used legitimately by related companies, such use shall inure to the benefit of the registrant or applicant * * *." A "related company" is defined in the Lanham Act as being "any person including a juristic person who legitimately controls or is controlled by a registrant or applicant for registration in respect to the nature and quality of the goods or service in connection with which the mark is used." 15 U.S.C. § 1127 (1974). Thus the Act, while authorizing approved use of a mark by others, maintains the concept of source of origin. It permits an owner of a mark to license his mark, but requires him to control the nature and quality of the goods or services with which the mark is used.

* * *

Licensee purchasing practices are probably one of the two areas of trademark licensing which have the most antitrust implications. These practices, which constitute the great bulk of antitrust considerations in the area of trademark licensing, involve efforts, by the seller or the licensor to restrict what and from whom the buyer or licensee purchases, and what he sells.

---

* © L. Hefter and P. Zeidman: Reprint permission granted by Laurence Hefter, a partner with the law firm of Finnegan, Henderson, Farabow, Garrett & Dunner, Washington, D.C., and a Professorial Lecturer of Law (Trademarks) at the National Law Center, George Washington University. Reprint permission also granted by Philip Zeidman, a partner with the law firm of Brownstein, Zeidman and Schomer, Washington, D.C. Originally published in *Law of Business and Licensing* (1983).

Most of the problems in this area arise under the rubric of a section of the antitrust law which is referred to as "tying." This is an arrangement under which a seller agrees to sell one product only on the condition that the buyer also purchases a second product. The first product is generally referred to as the "tying product," the second as the "tied product."

In trademark licensing this arises out of the allegation that the license or trademark is a tying product to which the goods can be tied as the tied product. However, there is no general agreement as to whether a franchise or a trademark license can be a product for certain purposes. It cannot be a "commodity" for purposes of the Clayton Act because it is an intangible but it can be subject to the Sherman Act. The question is: "Can a trademark license be a tying product?"

The principal case in this field is *Siegel v. Chicken Delight, Inc.,* 448 F.2d 43 (9th Cir.1971), *cert. denied,* 405 U.S. 955 (1972), in which the Ninth Circuit held that a trademark license could be a tying product.

If a licensor imposes upon its licensee a condition that it purchase from the licensor certain goods, then antitrust problems arise. That is exactly what Chicken Delight said to Mr. Siegel, namely, if Siegel wanted to be a Chicken Delight franchisee, he would be required to buy from the company its special spice mix, special cooking equipment and packaging supplies. Unhappy with this arrangement, Mr. Siegel successfully sued Chicken Delight, whose contractual requirements were held to constitute a tying arrangement in violation of the Sherman Act.

Since 1971, much of the case law has endeavored to determine the boundaries of such impermissible ties.

* * *

The major area of dispute in this segment of the law is the "two product test," because, as mentioned above, two products must be involved. * * *

The Ninth Circuit, in *Krehl v. Baskin–Robbins,* [664 F.2d 1348 (9th Cir.1982)] *supra,* held that one product was being marketed; when a customer entered a Baskin–Robbins store, he was entitled to know it was Baskin–Robbins ice cream he was buying. Therefore, Baskin–Robbins was entitled to require the licensee to purchase Baskin–Robbins ice cream. There were not two products involved because the licensee was purchasing one product, which was the right to do business under the Baskin–Robbins name and an integral part of that was the Baskin–Robbins system.

Perhaps the most important decision in this area is that of the Fourth Circuit in *Principe v. McDonald's Corp.,* 1980–2 Trade Cas. ¶ 63,556 (4th Cir.1980). The court held that McDonald's was entitled to say to its aspiring franchisees that, if they wanted a McDonald's franchise, they would first be required to lease the land and building from McDonald's.

Assuming that two products are involved, and that the licensor meets the economic power standards and imposes that kind of restriction, the question remains, "Is it illegal?" The answer may well depend upon whether there was available to the licensor some less restrictive alternative which still provided the quality control of the goods or services which the Lanham Act not only permits, but requires.

This is where the systems of specifications, approved suppliers, and designated suppliers are involved, all of which, assuming they are not abused, have been essentially upheld. The 1977 decision of the Fifth Circuit in *Kentucky Fried Chicken v. Diversified Packaging,* 549 F.2d 368 (5th Cir.1977), is perhaps one of the most helpful cases on this point. The question is whether the licensor will be required to use one of those techniques, as opposed to requiring the licensee to purchase from the licensor. The answer may well depend upon whether the item which is being sold is one which is, in fact, subject to specification.

In *Susser v. Carvel Corp.,* 332 F.2d 505 (2d Cir.), *cert. granted,* 379 U.S. 885 (1964), *cert. dismissed,* 381 U.S. 125 (1965), the Second Circuit held that the particular product, namely the desired texture and taste of an ice cream cone or sundae, was not subject to precise specification. *Id.* at 520. On the other hand, if the product is fairly fungible, it is going to be difficult for a licensor to argue he couldn't provide adequate specifications to enable purchasing from another supplier.

The existence and importance of a trade secret may be significant in determining the outcome of a case. In the *Chock Full O' Nuts* case, 85 F.T.C. 575 (1973), the Federal Trade Commission said the mere fact that a trade secret is involved will not immunize what otherwise might be a "tying" situation from the antitrust laws, unless the owner can also show that there was no way in which he could have protected his trade secret and at the same time publish his specifications.

TREATY ON THE FUNCTIONING OF THE EUROPEAN UNION (TFEU)

RULES ON COMPETITION—RULES APPLYING TO UNDERTAKINGS

ARTICLE 101

1. The following shall be prohibited as incompatible with the common market: all agreements between undertakings, decisions by associations of undertakings and concerted practices which may affect trade between Member States and which have as their object or effect the prevention, restriction or distortion of competition within the common market, and in particular those which:

(a) directly or indirectly fix purchase or selling prices or any other trading conditions;

(b) limit or control production, markets, technical development, or investment;

(c) share markets or sources of supply;

(d) apply dissimilar conditions to equivalent transactions with other trading parties, thereby placing them at a competitive disadvantage;

(e) make the conclusion of contracts subject to acceptance by the other parties of supplementary obligations which, by their nature or according to commercial usage, have no connection with the subject of such contracts.

2. Any agreements or decisions prohibited pursuant to this article shall be automatically void.

3. The provisions of paragraph 1 may, however, be declared inapplicable in the case of:

— any agreement or category of agreements between undertakings,

— any decision or category of decisions by associations of undertakings,

— any concerted practice or category of concerted practices,

which contributes to improving the production or distribution of goods or to promoting technical or economic progress, while allowing consumers a fair share of the resulting benefit, and which does not:

(a) impose on the undertakings concerned restrictions which are not indispensable to the attainment of these objectives;

(b) afford such undertakings the possibility of eliminating competition in respect of a substantial part of the products in question.

R. FOLSOM, PRINCIPLES OF EUROPEAN UNION LAW
Section 7.13 (2011).

The Pronuptia Case

Prior to its landmark decision in *Pronuptia,* the Commission had never sought to apply Article 81 [formerly Article 85] to franchise agreements. *Pronuptia* arose from the refusal of a franchisee to pay license fees to the franchisor. The distribution of the Pronuptia brand wedding attire in the Federal Republic of Germany was handled by shops operated by the German franchisor and by independent retailers through franchise agreements with that franchisor. The franchisee had obtained franchises for three areas (Hamburg, Oldenburg and Hannover). The franchisor granted the franchisee exclusive rights to market and advertise under the name of "Pronuptia de Paris" in these specific territories. The franchisor promised not to open any shops or provide any goods or services to another person in those territories. The franchisor also agreed to assist the franchisee with business strategies and profitability.

The franchisee agreed to assume all the risk of opening a franchise as an independent retailer. The franchisee also agreed to the following: (1) To sell Pronuptia goods only in the store specified in the contract and to decorate and design the shop according to the franchisor's instructions; (2) to purchase 80 percent of wedding related attire and a proportion of evening dresses from the franchisor, and to purchase the rest of such merchandise only from sellers approved by the franchisor; (3) to pay a one time entrance fee for exclusive rights to the specified territory and a yearly royalty fee of 10 percent of the total sales of Pronuptia and all other products; (4) to advertise only with the franchisor's approval in a method which would enhance the international reputation of the franchise; (5) to make the sale of bridal fashions the franchisee's main business purpose; (6) to consider the retail price recommendations of the franchisor; (7) to refrain from competing directly or indirectly during the contract period or for one year afterward with any Pronuptia store; and (8) to obtain the franchisor's prior approval before assigning the rights and obligations arising under the contract to a third party.

In due course, the case was referred to the European Court of Justice. The Court's judgment concentrates on the crucial issue of whether franchise agreements come within Article 81. The Court draws a preliminary distinction between "distribution" franchises such as Pronuptia as opposed to "service" and "production" franchises. The Court concludes that a franchising system as such does not interfere with competition. Consequently, clauses essential to enable franchising to function are not prohibited. Thus, the franchisor can communicate know-how or assistance and help franchisees apply its methods. The franchisor can take reasonable steps to keep its know-how or assistance from becoming available to competitors. Location clauses forbidding the franchisee during the contract, or for a reasonable time thereafter, from opening a store with a similar or identical object in an area where it might compete with another member of the franchise network were necessary for distribution franchises and therefore permissible. The obligation of the franchisee not to sell a licensed store without prior consent of the franchisor was similarly allowable.

Clauses necessary to preserve the identity and reputation of the franchise network, such as decorations and trademark usage, were upheld. The reputation and identity of the network may also justify a clause requiring the franchisee to sell only products supplied by the franchisor or by approved sources, at least if it would be too expensive to monitor the quality of the stock otherwise. Nevertheless, each franchisee must be allowed to buy from other franchisees. The requirement of uniformity may also justify advertisement approvals by the franchisor, but the franchisee must be allowed to set and advertise resale prices. The Court rejected the view that clauses tending to divide the Common Market between franchisor and franchisee or between franchisees are always necessary to protect the know-how or the identity and the reputation of the network. The location clause in *Pronuptia* was seen as potentially supporting exclusive territories. In combination, location clauses and exclusive territories may divide markets and so restrict competition within the network. Even if a potential franchisee would not take the risk of joining the network by making its own investment because it could not expect a profitable business due to the absence of protection from competition from other franchisees, that consideration (in the Court's view) could be taken into account only under an Article 81(3) individual exemption. The Commission, in fact, ultimately granted such an exemption to Pronuptia.

* * *

The Commission received an onslaught of [Article 81(3) exemption requests] in 1962 when Regulation 17 took effect. The vast majority of the business activities involved in this deluge were in the distribution and licensing areas. As a result, the Commission sought and obtained authorization in 1965 from the Council to formulate, for limited time periods, group "declarations of inapplicability" under Article 81(3). These are commonly known as "group or block exemptions." The Council granted this authorization, noting that Article 81(3) allows "classes" of exempt agreements.

Group exemptions, guidelines and policy announcements issued by the Commission in areas where group exemptions have not yet been promulgated, invite businesses to conform their agreements and behavior to their terms and conditions. In other words, group exemptions rely upon confidential business self-regulation.

* * *

FRANCHISING REGULATION

The Commission, following the European Court of Justice decision in *Pronuptia*, adopted a group exemption regulation for franchise agreements under Article 81(3). Regulation 4087/88 required each franchisee to identify itself as an independent enterprise apart from the trademark/service mark/trade name owner. This disclosure could avoid joint and several franchisor liability for the provision by franchisees of defective goods or services. Regulation 4087/88 defined a "franchise" as a package of industrial or intellectual property rights relating to trademarks, trade names, signs, utility models, designs, copyrights, know-how or patents exploited for the resale of goods or the provision of services to customers. "Franchise agreements" were defined as those in which the franchisor grants the franchisee, in exchange for direct or indirect financial consideration, the right to exploit a franchise so as to market specified types of goods and/or services. A "master franchisee agreement" involved the right to exploit a franchise by concluding franchising agreements with third parties.

VERTICAL RESTRAINTS REGULATION

Starting with these basics, Regulation 4087/88 proceeded to detail permitted and prohibited clauses in EU franchise agreements.... This approach remained in force until 2000, when Regulation 2790/99 (the "vertical restraints" group exemption) took over franchise agreements, along with exclusive dealing and other distribution agreements. Regulation 2790/99 is accompanied by lengthy vertical restraints guidelines. This regulation and its guidelines are more economic and less formalistic than the predecessors. Supply and distribution agreements of firms with less than 30 percent market shares are generally exempt; this is known as a "safe harbor." Companies whose market shares exceed 30 percent may or may not be exempt, depending upon the results of individual competition law reviews. In either case, no vertical agreements containing so-called "hard core restraints" are exempt. These restraints concern primarily resale price maintenance, territorial and customer protection leading to market allocation, and in most instances exclusive dealing covenants that last more than five years. In 2010, a new vertical restraints Regulation 330/10 was issued. Its content is similar to that of 1999, except that restrictions on the use of the Internet by distributors are treated as a hardcore restraints.

COMMISSION REGULATION 330/2010 ON THE APPLICATION OF ARTICLE 101(3)

O.J. L 102/1 (April 23, 2010).

"VERTICAL RESTRAINTS REGULATION"

Article 1

Definitions

1. For the purposes of this Regulation, the following definitions shall apply:

(a) 'vertical agreement' means an agreement or concerted practice entered into between two or more undertakings each of which operates, for the purposes of the agreement or the concerted practice, at a different level of the production or distribution chain, and relating to the conditions under which the parties may purchase, sell or resell certain goods or services;

(b) 'vertical restraint' means a restriction of competition in a vertical agreement falling within the scope of Article 101(1) of the Treaty;

(c) 'competing undertaking' means an actual or potential competitor; 'actual competitor' means an undertaking that is active on the same relevant market; 'potential competitor' means an undertaking that, in the absence of the vertical agreement, would, on realistic grounds and not just as a mere theoretical possibility, in case of a small but permanent increase in relative prices be likely to undertake, within a short period of time, the necessary additional investments or other necessary switching costs to enter the relevant market;

(d) 'non-compete obligation' means any direct or indirect obligation causing the buyer not to manufacture, purchase, sell or resell goods or services which compete with the contract goods or services, or any direct or indirect obligation on the buyer to purchase from the supplier or from another undertaking designated by the supplier more than 80% of the buyer's total purchases of the contract goods or services and their substitutes on the relevant market, calculated on the basis of the value or, where such is standard industry practice, the volume of its purchases in the preceding calendar year;

(e) 'selective distribution system' means a distribution system where the supplier undertakes to sell the contract goods or services, either directly or indirectly, only to distributors selected on the basis of specified criteria and where these distributors undertake not to sell such goods or services to unauthorised distributors within the territory reserved by the supplier to operate that system;

(f) 'intellectual property rights' includes industrial property rights, know, how, copyright and neighbouring rights;

(g) 'know-how' means a package of non-patented practical information, resulting from experience and testing by the supplier, which is secret, substantial and identified: in this context, 'secret' means that the know-how is not generally known or easily accessible; 'substantial' means that the know-how is significant and useful to the buyer for the use, sale or resale of the contract goods or services; 'identified' means that the know-how is described in a sufficiently comprehensive manner so as to make it possible to verify that it fulfils the criteria of secrecy and substantiality;

(h) 'buyer' includes an undertaking which, under an agreement felling within Article 101(1) of the Treaty, sells goods or services on behalf of another undertaking;

(i) 'customer of the buyer' means an undertaking not party to the agreement which purchases the contract goods or services from a buyer which is party to the agreement.

* * *

Article 2

Exemption

1. Pursuant to Article 101(3) of the Treaty and subject to the provisions of this Regulation, it is hereby declared that Article 101(1) of the Treaty shall not apply to vertical agreements.

This exemption shall apply to the extent that such agreements contain vertical restraints.

2. The exemption provided for in paragraph 1 shall apply to vertical agreements entered into between an association of undertakings and its members, or between such an association and its suppliers, only if all its members are retailers of goods and if no individual member of the association, together with its connected undertakings, has a total annual turnover exceeding EUR 50 million. Vertical agreements entered into by such associations shall be covered by this Regulation without prejudice to the application of Article 101 of the Treaty to horizontal agreements concluded between the members of the association or decisions adopted by the association.

3. The exemption provided for in paragraph I shall apply to vertical agreements containing provisions which relate to the assignment to the buyer or use by the buyer of intellectual property rights, provided that those provisions do not constitute the primary object of such agreements and are directly related to the use, sale or resale of goods or services by the buyer or its customers. The exemption applies on condition that, in relation to the contract goods or services, those provisions do not contain restrictions of competition having the same object as vertical restraints which are not exempted under this Regulation.

4. The exemption provided for in paragraph 1 shall not apply to vertical agreements entered into between competing undertakings. However, it shall apply where competing undertakings enter into a non-reciprocal vertical agreement and:

(a) the supplier is a manufacturer and a distributor of goods, while the buyer is a distributor and not a competing undertaking at the manufacturing level; or

(b) the supplier is a provider of services at several levels of trade, while the buyer provides its goods or services at the retail level and is not a competing undertaking at the level of trade where it purchases the contract services.

5. This Regulation shall not apply to vertical agreements the subject matter of which falls within the scope of any other block exemption regulation, unless otherwise provided for in such a regulation.

Article 3

Market share threshold

1. The exemption provided for in Article 2 shall apply on condition that the market share held by the supplier does not exceed 30% of the relevant market on which it sells the contract goods or services and the market share held by the buyer does not exceed 30% of the relevant market on which it purchases the contract goods or services.

2. For the purposes of paragraph I, where in a multi party agreement contract goods or services from one undertaking party to the agreement and sells the contract goods or services to another undertaking party to the agreement, the market share of the first undertaking must respect the market share threshold provided for in that paragraph both as a buyer and a supplier in order for the exemption provided for in Article 2 to apply.

Article 4

Restrictions that remove the benefit of the block exemption—hardcore restrictions

The exemption provided for in Article 2 shall not apply to vertical agreements which, directly or indirectly, in isolation or in combination with other factors under the control of the parties, have as their object:

(a) the restriction of the buyer's ability to determine its sale price, without prejudice to the possibility of the supplier to impose a maximum sale price or recommend a sale price, provided that they do not amount to a fixed or minimum sale price as a result of pressure from, or incentives offered by, any, of the parties;

(b) the restriction of the territory into which, or of the customers to whom, a buyer party to the agreement, without prejudice to a restriction on its place of establishment, may sell the contract goods or services, except:

    (i) the restriction of active sales into the exclusive territory or to an exclusive customer group reserved to the supplier or allocated by the supplier to another buyer, where such a restriction does not limit sales by the customers of the buyer,

    (ii) the restriction of sales to end users by a buyer operating at the wholesale level of trade,

    (iii) the restriction of sales by the members of a selective distribution system to unauthorised distributors within the territory reserved by the supplier to operate that system, and

    (iv) the restriction of the buyer's ability to sell components, supplied for the purposes of incorporation, to customers who would use them to manufacture the same type of goods as those produced by the supplier;

(c) the restriction of active or passive sales to end users by members of a selective distribution system operating at the retail level of trade, without prejudice to the possibility of prohibiting a member of the system from operating out of an unauthorised place of establishment;

(d) the restriction of cross-supplies between distributors within a selective distribution system, including between distributors operating at different level of trade;

(e) the restriction, agreed between a supplier of components and a buyer who incorporates those components, of the supplier's ability to sell the components as spare parts to end-users or to repairers or other service providers not entrusted by the buyer with the repair or servicing of its goods.

Article 5

Excluded restrictions

1. The exemption provided for in Article 2 shall not apply to the following obligations contained in vertical agreements:

(a) any direct or indirect non-compete obligation, the duration of which is indefinite or exceeds five years;

(b) any direct or indirect obligation causing the buyer, after termination of the agreement, not to manufacture, purchase, sell or resell goods or services;

(c) any direct or indirect obligation causing the members of a selective distribution system not to sell the brands of particular competing suppliers.

For the purposes of point (a) of the first subparagraph, a non-compete obligation which is tacitly renewable beyond a period of five years shall be deemed to have been concluded for an indefinite duration.

* * *

Article 6

Non-application of this Regulation

Pursuant to Article 1a of Regulation No 19/65/EEC, the Commission may by regulation declare that, where parallel networks of similar vertical restraints cover more than 50% of a relevant market, this Regulation shall not apply to vertical agreements containing specific restraints relating to that market.

Article 7

Application of the market share threshold

For the purposes of applying the market share thresholds provided for in Article 3 the following rules shall apply:

(a) the market share of the supplier shall be calculated on the basis of market sales value data and the market share of the buyer shall be calculated on the basis of market purchase value data. If market sales value or market purchase value data are not available, estimates based on other reliable market information, including market sales and purchase volumes, may be used to establish the market share of the undertaking concerned;

(b) the market shares shall be calculated on the basis of data relating to the preceding calendar year;

(c) the market share of the supplier shall include any goods or services supplied to vertically integrated distributors for the purposes of sale;

(d) if a market share is initially not more than 30% but subsequently rises above that level without exceeding 35%, the exemption provided for in Article 2 shall continue to apply for a period of two consecutive calendar years following the year In which the 30% market share threshold was first exceeded;

(e) if a market share is initially not more than 30% but subsequently rises above 35%, the exemption provided for in Article 2 shall continue to apply for one calendar year following the year in which the level of 35% was first exceeded;

(f) the benefit of points (d) and (e) may not be combined so as to exceed a period of two calendar years;

(g) the market share held by the undertakings referred to in point (e) of the second subparagraph of Article 1(2) shall be apportioned equally to each undertaking having the rights or the powers listed in point (a) of the second subparagraph of Article 1(2).

* * *

GORDON, HAMBURGERS ABROAD: CULTURAL VARIATIONS AFFECTING FRANCHISING ABROAD*

9 Conn.J.Int'l L. 165 (1994).

[T]he franchise is especially useful to illustrate that its cultural impact tends not to be very specifically governed by written law, but is likely to draw into the governance scheme the unwritten law. I use the franchise predominantly because it is such an openly expressed symbol of culture, from golden arches to "finger lickin' good." It is essential to maintain consistency in selling the franchise's product abroad, and maintaining that consistency may create conflicts with local culture.

The consistency has several facets. It is a consistency in architectural *style,* expressed in golden arches above Route 44 in Hartford, Connecticut, or on a street in Kensington in London, or around the corner from the Piazza di Spagna (Spanish Steps) in Rome. That consistency in style is maintained no matter how those arches may conflict with local architectural tastes. It is also a consistency in *name* recognition, as seen by a Big Mac being on essentially every menu in every McDonald's throughout the world. That consistency in name recognition is maintained regardless of what that name means in the local language. It is a consistency in *menu,* expressed by the availability of essentially the same products in every nation. That consistency in menu is maintained no matter what the local preferences or mores might suggest is more suitable. It is a consistency in *advertising* as expressed by the same slogans used around the globe. Consistency in advertising is maintained whether or not it makes any sense if in English in the foreign country, or in translated form in the local language. It is a consistency in *taste* as expressed by a uniformity of taste (or absence of identifiable taste). That consistency in taste is maintained no matter what the taste buds of local persons are attuned to recognize and deem pleasurable. And finally, it is a consistency in *price* as expressed by a kind of equivalency in value under different currencies. That consistency in price is maintained even if the goods are priced out of the mass market most franchises seek to serve.

Consistency may be critical to protecting the trademark, but it may be carried to such extremes that it creates an inertia of its own as new franchise outlets are opened in country after country. One important element of success in operating a franchise abroad is to be able to make

---

* Reprinted with permission of the Connecticut Journal of International Law.

deviations from this demand for consistency to satisfy local standards. Many of those deviations will be undertaken to adjust to local culture.

The conflicts with culture from attempting to maintain consistency in each of these areas—style, name recognition, menu, advertising, taste, and price, may be shown by some examples. The examples will also consider what is important to us as lawyers—how the host nations respond to a cultural impact which is negatively perceived. The cultural conflicts may be attributable to:

(1) a lack of understanding of the local culture;

(2) an assumption that an understood culture is unimportant; or,

(3) an inability to effectively deal with a culture which is understood, and which the company does not wish to disturb.

Your role as a lawyer may be to address all three issues: to explain cultural variations, to emphasize the value which the host nation places on the preservation of its culture, and to advise how to do business without conflict. The answers usually will not be greatly assisted by an understanding limited to the local written laws. The answers will come from experience in understanding other cultures, an attribute often lacking in United States lawyers working in international business law. You must be prepared to learn as much about the culture as about the law of foreign nations in which you work, because law is an expression of culture.

* * *

NAME RECOGNITION

In addition to how the foreign franchise entity appears to the eye, what it is called may also be misunderstood or objected to abroad. The name of the franchise, as well as the product, may make little sense, or too much sense, abroad. Advertisements referring to "Colonel" Sanders of Kentucky Fried Chicken met with objection in Germany where "Colonel" suggests reference to the less than loved United States military. Chevrolet certainly gave little thought to selling the Nova in Latin America, where "no va" means "it does not go." Kentucky Fried Chicken opened outlets in several Central American countries in the late 1960s and early 1970s. It referred to the one in Costa Rica as "Pollo Frito de Kentucky," but to the outlets in Guatemala and El Salvador in English. The tendency is to use the full English name, partly to protect the overall franchise image and partly to create the image of consistency across the globe.

The latter desire, whether it is a service enterprise such as American Express, a product such as the Nova, or a fast food franchise such as McDonald's or Kentucky Fried Chicken, was challenged in Mexico in the 1976 Tradenames and Inventions Law's infamous articles 127 and 128.[18] These provisions mandated foreign businesses to link Mexican origin names with foreign names, and constituted one of the first attempts by

---

18. Diario Official, 10 Feb. 1976.

developing nations during the nationalistic and restrictive 1970s to reduce the dominance of foreign brand names, and to attempt to create local names for familiar foreign origin products. The Mexican legislative history discloses that there was considerable urging to require the foreign name be dropped after the linked name gained local recognition. Thus, Cristal–Gleem toothpaste would ultimately become Cristal toothpaste. The response from foreign producers was so negative that the implementation of these articles was delayed a year, and the following year annually delayed year after year until the provisions were repealed. The problems associated with linking names were considerable. For example, Coca–Cola was, at the time, mainly sold in the familiar green molded glass bottle, which would have to be totally replaced with new bottles with the linked name.

In lectures in a number of developing and nonmarket economy countries I discussed these Mexican provisions. It was clear that there was considerable empathy for the idea. But there was also an awareness that such provisions in the written law were unrealistic, and would likely be difficult or impossible to enforce without losing needed foreign investment. These Mexican provisions were an attempt to bring aspirational declarations into the written law. But they were too aspirational. They were more than what foreign multinationals would accept. They were similar to the Indian government's demanding, however indirectly, disclosure of the formula for Coca Cola. The company left India rather than comply. Mexican officials quickly realized that they had assumed incorrectly that what was aspirational was achievable. There seemed to be two obvious choices: repeal the provisions or ignore them. The Mexican government wisely chose neither. These two provisions were very popular with the press and academics, both quite liberal and anti-multinational. It would have been unwise to repeal the provisions. The government could also have ignored them, but left them on the books. But questions would be asked. They were popular and the public was waiting for their implementation. Instead of the above courses of action, the government decided to defer their implementation. The decision to delay the implementation for only one year allegedly to work out details in regulations, and to annually extend the deferred implementation until attitudes changed in the 1980s, allowed the government to save face.

While I am not aware of many other attempts in other nations to mandate by written law the adoption of local names for the names of foreign businesses or their products, there have been local language laws which have affected various aspects of business, such as the language of the menu and the language used in advertising. Both will be discussed below. It seems essential that a business going abroad, franchise or otherwise, consider *every* English word used in the name of the business, as a product of the business, and in signs, slogans or advertising, to determine what such English words mean in the local language. The word in English may prove objectionable to good manners, or offensive to morals, or simply be totally misunderstood. It might be unlawful, and thus the company is forewarned, but it is far more likely not to violate any written law, but to violate norms of expected behavior.

What written laws do exist may be limited to mandating bilingual labeling or instructions for use, much less often do they mandate bilingual brand names as in the aborted attempt in Mexico. Moreover, it is not only the *language* which must be considered, but *pictorial* elements intended to convey a meaning. For example, baby food in the familiar small jars with photos of babies on the label did not sell well on the shelves of some African nations. Illiterate mothers wondered why anyone would buy jars containing ground up babies.

* * *

ADVERTISING

The most frequently made errors involve how language is used in advertising products abroad. English is often used, usually to maintain the image of a product, and its trademark, such as the Big Mac. Use of English names in the franchise may create less objection than outside advertising, such as billboards. Nearly twenty years ago, on my first visit to Panama, I was surprised to see a billboard on the road to Panama City from the airport which advertised the local Kentucky Fried Chicken, with the well known phrase "Finger lickin' good" in English. Even Panamanians with a working knowledge of English might not understand the slogan. Revisiting Panama in the early 1980s to give a series of lectures for the Department of State, on subjects including the one I am discussing, I was told by several lawyers that advertising signs in English such as that of Kentucky Fried Chicken were unlawful. I asked to see the law, but no one could identify it. I made reference to this mysterious law at subsequent luncheon and dinner lectures. Finally, one lawyer indicated that he believed it was a decree announced but never officially published, an example of the confusion and difficulty in identifying the control of the impact of foreign culture.

Where there is no pressure to use the host nation language, good sense may suggest translating English advertising into the foreign language. Attempted translations, however, can create the most embarrassing situations. Obscenities are obviously not intended by foreign multinationals, and they are often accepted abroad as unintended blunders. Some translations are not offensive, but simply convey unintended meanings. For example: (1) A toy Taiwanese made bear which sang such Christmas carols as "Oh Little Town of Birmingham"; (2) KFC's "finger lickin good" in Chinese as "eat your fingers off"; and (3) Coor's Light beer sold with the slogan "Turn it loose" translated into Spanish to mean "Drink Coors and get diarrhea."

Additionally, not all nations read from left to right. Obvious confusion was created in a nation which reads from right to left in a three picture advertising display of dirty clothes on the left, the suggested washing soap in the middle and the clean clothes on the right. Even the order of word translations may cause trouble, Bud Lite's "delicious, less filling" slogan was translated into Spanish to read "filling, less delicious."

* * *

The experience of foreign firms, using principally fast food franchises as an example, suggests no clear method of governance of the cultural impact. Governance, where it does exist, suggests that the nation sometimes views the presence of the foreign franchise as conflicting with local culture. But that may be more the view of officials than consumers. McDonalds and other fast food franchises have very successful records abroad. Long lines at newly opened branches from Mexico City to Moscow have been the subject of newspaper articles. Left to consumer choice, there might be little opposition to the invasion of United States culture abroad. Just who are the custodians of culture who object to foreign culture, and have been able to influence government decision makers, and in some cases legislators, to reject or limit the opening of foreign franchises, and the playing of foreign music, the showing of foreign movies or the selling of foreign magazines? They are often local competitors who have the same interests in protecting local industry as do other "producers," whether farmers or manufacturers of products.

QUESTIONS AND COMMENTS

1. Suppose Colonel Chicken's first franchise is in the Canadian province of Alberta. One form of direct regulation of franchising is analogous to securities registration and disclosure laws. What is the purpose of the Alberta Franchises Act? Does the Act require Colonel Chicken to alter its "formula for success?" Will the Act influence the negotiating position of either party to a Colonel Chicken franchise agreement? Will it alter the drafting of the agreement? What remedies under the Act might a franchisee seek to invoke?

2. Hefter and Zeidman indicate that United States antitrust law is especially relevant to the drafting of a franchise agreement. Such law represents an indirect form of regulation of the franchise relationship. Do you see any "tying" antitrust risks in the Colonel Chicken "formula for success?" What about under EU business competition law? See Article 101(1)(e) of the TFEU. How might Colonel Chicken's antitrust exposure be minimized in drafting an international franchise agreement?

3. European customs union and competition law is applicable to Common Market licensing agreements. Any franchisor in the Common Market will want to consider the impact of such law on its agreements and operations. An appendix to this coursebook explores the nature of the EU legal system. For now, what legal problems for Colonel Chicken's "strongly recommended" prices are suggested by the *Pronuptia* decision of the European Court of Justice? What about problems under the Vertical Restraints Regulation?

4. *Pronuptia* implies a departure from leading United States antitrust law on market division arrangements in distribution schemes. Compare Continental T.V., Inc. v. GTE Sylvania Inc., 433 U.S. 36, 97 S.Ct. 2549, 53 L.Ed.2d 568 (1977) (location clauses and vertical territorial restraints not per

se illegal under Sherman Act). Why might such differences exist? Is Colonel Chicken "sharing markets" among its franchisees in a manner contrary to *Pronuptia?* To the Vertical Restraints Regulation? Is *intrabrand* Colonel Chicken or Pronuptia competition as important as *interbrand* fast food or wedding attire competition?

5.　Review Commission Regulation 330/2010, the "Vertical Restraints Regulation." This Regulation, issued under Article 101(3), creates a "group" or "block" exemption to Article 101(1) of the TFEU. Why does Article 3 of the Regulation use a market share test for exemption?

Does the Colonel Chicken formula for success conform to its requirements? See Articles 4 and 5 of Regulation 330/2010. Does conformity to the Regulation matter? See Treaty Articles 101(1) and (2).

6.　Another form of direct regulation of franchising is found in laws regulating transfers of technology, particularly in third world nations. These laws usually specify the kinds of contract terms that cannot be included in a licensing agreement which is registered with a local transfer of technology commission. A further type of regulatory law sometimes encountered in franchising abroad is that which requires use of "adequate local substitutes" by the franchisee, *e.g.,* olive oil instead of cooking batter for fast food chicken, or that which absolutely bans the sale of certain products, *e.g.,* beer and wine in Islamic countries. "Local content" regulation of international franchise agreements appears to be increasing. Should Colonel Chicken be advised that some parts of its "formula for success" may be regulated? Which parts seem most vulnerable?

7.　Professor Gordon discusses cultural variations that affect franchising abroad. Is there any response in the 1976 Mexican Law of Inventions and Tradenames to the likely cultural impact of Colonel Chicken's trademarks and building design? You might give thought to whether a Colonel Chicken franchise would be culturally acceptable in a European nation or in Asia? U.S. franchising in China is expanding rapidly.

PROBLEM 9.2　PROTECTION OF INTELLECTUAL PROPERTY: PIRATED AND GRAY MARKET ROCKERS™ MUSIC

SECTION I.　THE SETTING

The ROCKERS™ are one of the world's most popular rock-and-roll recording groups. They have produced three of the all-time "top 100" selling releases. The ROCKERS record on the DACCA™ label of Dacca, Inc., a New York corporation. Dacca, Inc. owns several European subsidiaries which are licensed to produce DACCA videos, DVDs and CDs. It has always been assumed by Dacca, Inc. that sales by these subsidiaries would be in Europe. The ROCKERS hold copyrights for their sound recordings wherever national laws permit such protection.

Sales of the ROCKERS' most popular recordings have recently declined in the United States. The ROCKERS believe that one cause of the decline is competition from pirate products produced without license in the Far East, but which bear the notation "Reproduced in the United States." A second cause is the unauthorized "sharing" of the ROCKERS music on the Internet, a sharing that circumvents their computer technicians' best digital management encryption efforts. The ROCKERS and Dacca, Inc. would like to rapidly halt this competition. They consider it a form of intellectual property theft.

A third cause of concern is import competition from genuine ROCKERS recordings produced under license abroad by the Dacca, Inc. subsidiaries in Europe. Because of fluctuations in currency exchange rates, substantial price differences exist between the United States and European markets. K–Market, Inc. is the primary importer of these "gray market" goods, which it obtains from European wholesalers of videos, DVDs, and CDs. The ROCKERS and Dacca, Inc. would like to also halt this competition which they consider unfair and infringing of their intellectual property rights.

SECTION II. FOCUS OF CONSIDERATION

Patent, copyright and trademark piracy is increasing in many parts of the developing, and to a lesser extent, developed world. Some developing countries believe that technology should be transferred freely as a matter of principle and to foster their economic growth. They either encourage piracy or choose not to oppose it. Unlicensed manufacturers of goods pay no royalties. Additionally, they often have lower production costs than the owners of such property.

This problem initially explores some of the customs service and judicial remedies against counterfeit goods that United States patent, copyright and trademark holders may pursue in defense of their rights. Since national remedies are often insufficient, the possibility of greater access to remedies internationally is considered in connection with the TRIPs agreement and the WIPO Copyright Treaty.

The problem also takes up the related controversy surrounding trade in genuine or "gray market" goods (goods lawfully bearing patents, trademarks or copyrights which originate abroad and which compete without permission in domestic markets). Trade in gray market goods has mushroomed in recent years in response to floating currency exchange rates and other market forces. Today it represents one of the "cutting edges" of international trade law.

Section 526 of the Tariff Act of 1930 (19 U.S.C.A. § 1526) and Part III of the TRIPs agreement are essential to an analysis of this problem. They are found in the Documents Supplement. Web resources for further study include TRIPs coverage at *www.wto.org.* and U.S. customs coverage of intellectual property rights *www.customs.gov.*

SECTION III. READINGS, QUESTIONS AND COMMENTS

PART A. COUNTERFEIT GOODS

COUNTERFEITING AND THEFT OF TANGIBLE INTELLECTUAL PROPERTY: CHALLENGES AND SOLUTIONS

Written Testimony of Timothy P. Trainer, President
International AntiCounterfeiting Coalition, Inc. (IACC).
United States Senate Committee on the Judiciary (March 23, 2004).

GLOBAL COUNTERFEITING

An IACC member auto company's raid of a Chinese auto parts factory uncovered 7,000 sets of counterfeit brake pads intended for export to Egypt. This single raid represents potential losses of nearly $330,000. Another auto industry member reported raids resulting in the seizure of thousands of counterfeit windshields and several thousand suspension control arms, valued at nearly $4 million dollars. A third auto industry member estimates that 50%–60% of counterfeit parts bearing its trademarks found in the world are made in China.

The auto industry is also confronted by a massive parts counterfeiting problem in India. IACC member auto companies report counterfeit parts make up 20% to 30% of the Indian market. The auto industry as a whole is suffering parts counterfeiting that is reported to be over 35% of the market and valued at roughly $434 million dollars in that country.

While not as mechanically sophisticated as automobiles, the Uganda Manufacturer's Association complains of counterfeit bicycle parts posing risks for citizens of that country.

Another IACC member, whose certification mark is relied upon as a mark of safety, reported that our federal border enforcement authorities seized 91 shipments of counterfeits bearing its mark in fiscal year 2003. These seizures included a seizure of US$1.5 million in air compressors that had counterfeit ground fault circuit interrupters, $700,000 of counterfeit extension cords, power strips and hair trimmers that, in turn, led to an additional $7 million seizure of counterfeit extension cords and power strips. In addition to the Customs seizures, another $1 million seizure of Chinese made counterfeit portable and hand tools was made by police in southern California.

In Australia, an investigation of two Australian nationals led to the discovery of a massive counterfeit operation of Chinese-made counterfeit batteries and razors. Three containers heading to different ports—Dubai, Oman and Los Angeles—were seized having counterfeit goods valued at $1.5 million. Australian authorities also seized two shipments (50,000 bottles) of counterfeit shampoo from China bearing the trademark of a famous brand.

Counterfeit vodka in the United Kingdom caused hospitalization when the vodka was tested and found to have dangerous levels of methanol. As a result of the detection, authorities issued a description of the bottle and labels that were applied to the bottle to assist potential consumers in identifying the counterfeits. In December 2003, another counterfeit vodka problem arose when a woman went into a coma after consuming counterfeit Kirov brand vodka. It was the second time in 2003 that supplies of counterfeit vodka with high levels of methanol had been found.

Counterfeit batteries have also posed a threat to consumers. A boy playing with a toy that had a counterfeit battery suffered facial injuries from an exploding battery and a man suffered injuries to a hand when his remote control exploded from the use of a counterfeit battery, both incidents in Malaysia? Canadian authorities seized 60,000 counterfeit "Duracell" batteries before the holiday season and warned consumers because of potential hazards if used in toys. Nokia found that counterfeit batteries used in connection with their cell phones were exploding, as reports of such incidents were widespread—from Vietnam to the Netherlands.

Russia's chief trade inspector and department head at the Economic Department and Trade Ministry noted that for certain categories of consumer items, 30–50% of the Russian market consists of imitations. These product lines include alcohol, juices, butter, vegetable oil, canned foods, tea, coffee, cosmetics, clothing and footwear. Other sources similarly indicate that up to 50% of the perfume and cosmetics markets are fakes.

* * *

RECOMMENDATIONS

At the outset, the IACC respectfully requests that this Committee and Congress consider implementing the following package of recommendations to combat the scourge of counterfeiting and piracy that exists:

- Raise the stakes for the individuals involved—the federal criminal statute against trafficking in counterfeit goods should be strengthened;

- Encourage federal law enforcement agencies to cooperatively pursue investigations of counterfeiting to root out and prosecute manufacturers, distributors and others involved in the trafficking of counterfeit goods;

- Increase the level of vigilance at the border regardless of the products involved—counterfeiting and piracy impact national economic security;

- Impose higher intellectual property enforcement standards on trading partners who seek trade preferences to access the world's greatest market;

- Support Interpol's effort to improve cross-border coordination to combat the international trafficking in counterfeit goods; and

- Examine the extent to which organized crime is involved in the international trade of counterfeit and pirated products.

"ANTI–PIRACY"
MOTION PICTURE ASSOCIATION OF AMERICA

www.mpaa.org/anti-piracy.

TYPES OF PIRACY

OPTICAL DISC PIRACY

Optical Disc Piracy is a major threat to the audiovisual sector. Pirate optical discs, which include Laser Discs (LD), Video Compact Discs (VCD) and Digital Versatile Discs (DVD), are inexpensive to manufacture and easy to distribute. In 2000, over 20 million pirate optical discs were seized, and by comparison, 4.5 million videos were seized worldwide in the same period.

Unlike traditional analog piracy, a digital pirated disc is as pure and pristine as the original. In addition, a production facility can churn out a huge volume of illegal discs in relatively short time. To illustrate this, an average illegal videocassette duplication facility with 100 VCRs can, in a 10 hour period, produce about 400 pirated cassettes, while pirates with the right CD pressing equipment can produce thousands of perfect VCDs or DVDs daily.

The MPA supports the introduction of effective measures to control the spread of optical disc piracy, such as licensing requirements for optical disc manufacturing facilities and the tracking of the import and export of manufacturing equipment. Strengthened cooperation among customs and enforcement authorities worldwide to share information relating to trans-national operation of organized criminal enterprises engaged in production, export, or import of illicit optical discs is also critical.

INTERNET PIRACY

Online motion picture piracy is the unauthorized use of copyrighted motion pictures on the Internet. It is illegal to sell, trade, lease, distribute, upload for transmission, transmit or publicly perform motion pictures online without the consent of the motion pictures' copyright owner.

Online piracy is a relatively new phenomenon, and, unfortunately, a growing trend. The MPA Worldwide Internet Anti–Piracy program investigates all forms of online piracy including: Downloadable Media, Hard Goods Piracy, Streaming Media and online offerings of illegal Circumvention Devices. The MPA is working closely with the online community to prevent the unauthorized use and distribution of film industry product on the Internet.

Downloadable Media

Downloadable Media refers to digital files that allow for motion pictures to be compressed and uploaded for direct download onto a computer. Pirates use Downloadable Media formats to illegally offer and distribute motion pictures to other Internet users. Typically, the pirate host will use illegal VCD copies of motion pictures to create digital copies that are recorded into a computer file. Using online communication avenues, including chat rooms, Internet Relay Chats (IRC), FTP sites, newsgroups, File Swapping Utilities (FSUs) and Web sites, the pirate offers these files to other Internet users who then download the motion picture file onto their own computers.

Hard Goods

Hard goods piracy refers to the illegal sale, distribution and/or trading of copies of motion pictures in any format, including videocassettes and all optical media product. Illegal hard goods are sold on web sites, online auction sites such as eBay and Yahoo!, and via e-mail solicitations.

Streaming Media

Streaming media refers to the transmission or transfer of data that is delivered to the online user or viewer in a steady stream in near real time. Similar to hard goods and downloadable media, it is illegal to stream copyrighted content without the express authorization of the copyright holder.

Circumvention Devices

A circumvention device is any physical medium or digital file that allows for the circumvention of content protection devices put on films, videos, discs, etc. to secure the copyrighted content. One such circumvention device is the unauthorized, so-called software utility DeCss. Any person that has the DeCss utility can use it to break the copy protection on DVDs making it possible for motion pictures in DVD format to be decrypted and illegally copied onto a computer's hard-drive for further distribution over the Internet or otherwise, in perfect, digital format. Other common circumvention devices include "black boxes" and other illegal signal theft devices and macrovision defeators.

* * *

NOTE ON U.S. COUNTERFEITING REMEDIES

Many states have enacted criminal statutes to combat increased counterfeiting of goods and services in the United States. After much debate, Congress enacted the Trademark Counterfeiting Act of 1984 (18 U.S.C.A. § 2320 *et seq.*). Criminal penalties are established for anyone who "intentionally traffics or attempts to traffic in goods or services and knowingly uses a counterfeit mark on or in connection with such goods or services." Treble damages or profits (whichever is greater) and attorney fees may be recovered in civil actions unless there are "extenuating circumstances." Temporary restraining orders, injunctions and ex parte seizure orders for counterfeit goods may be issued by the federal courts. Such remedies can work domestically, but may not succeed against elusive foreign defendants outside U.S. jurisdiction. Parallel imports of genuine or "gray market goods" (goods legitimately produced overseas but imported into the United States via unauthorized distribution channels—See Part B infra) and "overruns" (goods produced without authorization by a licensee) are expressly *excluded* from the Act's coverage.

The owner of a U.S. trademark or copyright can file a certificate of registration with the Secretary of Treasury. Such filings subject counterfeit merchandise to seizure by the U.S. Customs Service. See 19 U.S.C. § 1526(a) (trademarks) and 17 U.S.C. § 602(b) (copyrights). In the event that the merchandise has already entered the United States, Customs will demand its return of the importer, who otherwise faces a liquidated damages claim. The importer can appeal any such claim or seizure of goods alleged to be counterfeit. All that said, how is the Customs Service handling voluminous U.S. imports through many different points of entry going to know that a particular shipment is counterfeit? As a practical matter, much of the burden of alerting the Custom Service to counterfeit imports, and ultimately proving their counterfeit character, rests with the trademark or copyright owner. Many owners hire private detectives in the source countries with the hope of ascertaining counterfeit operations, and shutting them down under local law or at least minimizing their exports. Those same detectives may be able to signal when a shipment of counterfeit goods is headed for the United States.

The Anticounterfeiting Consumer Protection Act of 1996, Public Law 104–153 (110 Stat. 1386) made a number of statutory changes intended to combat counterfeiting. Trafficking in counterfeit goods is now an offense under the RICO Act (Racketeer Influenced and Corrupt Organizations Act). In addition, importers must disclose the identity of any trademark on imported merchandise, ex parte seizures by law enforcement officers of counterfeit goods and vehicles used to transport them are widely authorized, the amount of damages and civil penalties that can be recovered from counterfeiters and importers was increased, and the Customs Service's authority to return counterfeit merchandise to its source (and potential re-entry into commerce) has been repealed. Customs must now destroy all counterfeit merchandise that it seizes unless the trademark owner otherwise consents and the goods are not a health or safety threat.

In 2009, U.S. officials seized about $260 million in counterfeit goods. Chinese gangs accounted for the bulk of these goods, which were most often footwear, consumer electronics, luxury goods and pharmaceuticals. U.S. military and civilian procurement agencies have begun actively targeting counterfeit suppliers. An Anti–Counterfeiting Trade Agreement (ACTA) is in the works, though China is not expected to participate.

IMPORTATION OF "ROMLESS" COMPUTERS NOT BARRED UNDER § 602(b) OF COPYRIGHT ACT

9 BNA U.S. Import Wkly 1062 (May 30, 1984).*

"ROMless" computers may not be denied entry into the United States under Section 602(b) of the Copyright Act on the theory that their manufacture constitutes contributory infringement of the copyrighted operating system software, the U.S. Customs Service ruled recently.

Customs explained—in the ruling issued by the Entry Procedures and Penalties Division—that Section 602(b)'s importation prohibition pertains only to articles constituting "piratical" copies of copyrighted works.

Pursuant to 19 CFR Part 133, Apple Computer recorded with the Customs Service the copyrights on its "Autostart ROM" and "Applesoft" operating system computer programs. Under 19 CFR 133.42(b), the importation of piratical copies of recorded copyrighted works is prohibited.

In their efforts to prevent piratical copies of Apple's computer programs from entering the United States, Customs officers have noted incoming shipments of computers and computer kits complete in all respects except that they do not contain any firmware incorporating an operating system into the machines. In that condition, the imported machines are incapable of functioning as computers. However, when ROM (Read Only Memory) or EPROM (Erasable Programmable Read Only Memory) chips containing copies of "Autostart ROM" and "Applesoft" are inserted into these computers, they function identically to Apple II computers.

Apple Computer contended that Customs is authorized to prevent the importation of these "ROMless" computers. In the meantime, Customs officers have been detaining all "ROMless" computers pending a resolution of this matter.

As used in 19 CFR 133.42(b), Customs said, "piratical copies" is defined to mean "actual copies or substantial copies of a recorded copyrighted work, produced or imported in contravention of the rights of the copyright owner." Under this definition, "ROMless" computers cannot be excluded from entry because they do not contain any devices capable of fixed storage of software; therefore, they cannot contain a piratical copy of the copyrighted programs.

Customs noted, however, that the Customs regulations dealing with copyrights were promulgated prior to passage of the 1976 Copyright Act. The regulations, Customs noted, must be read in the context of the new copyright law, Section 602(b) of which provides, in part, that:

> In a case where the making of the copies or phonorecords [of a work that has been acquired outside the United States] would have

---

* Reprinted by permission from *U.S. Import Weekly,* copyright 1984 by the Bureau of National Affairs, Inc., Washington, D.C.

constituted an infringement of copyright if this title had been applicable, their importation is prohibited.

Apple argued that Section 602(b) places all types of infringement within the scope of the importation prohibition, except infringement by the unlawful distribution of lawful copies of a copyrighted work, which the statute specifically excludes from its coverage. Apple maintained that the foreign manufacturers and sellers of "ROMless" computers are contributory copyright infringers because they knew or should know that their machines can be used with unlawfully made copies of the copyrighted programs and because there is no substantial noninfringing use for a "ROMless" computer.

According to Customs, the importation of "ROMless" computers is not prohibited by § 602(b) of the Copyright Act.

[Text] Assuming without deciding that the making of the "ROMless" computers constitutes a contributory infringement against the copyright holder's copyrights, the importation of such merchandise is not prohibited by 17 U.S.C. 602(b). While the phrase "an infringement of copyright" arguably includes contributory copyright infringement, preventing the importation of "ROMless" computers would be inconsistent with other language in the statute. The objects against which the provisions of 17 U.S.C. 602(b) are directed are copies or phonorecords of a work that have been acquired outside the United States.

* * *

With regard to the very computer programs in issue, the statutory copyright requirement of fixation has been held to be satisfied through the embodiment of these programs in ROM devices. * * * Furthermore, computer programs contained in ROMs can be perceived, reproduced, or otherwise communicated therefrom with the aid of other computer equipment. Accordingly, the provisions of 17 U.S.C. 602(b) are operative against ROMs (or diskettes, tapes, or other devices for fixed storage of software) that contain unlawful reproductions of copyrighted computer software, for these items are copies within the meaning of that section. * * * Therefore, inasmuch as "ROMless" computers do not include such copies upon arrival in the United States, they may enter the country without violating 17 U.S.C. 602(b). [End of Text]

A.T. CROSS COMPANY v. SUNIL TRADING CORPORATION

United States District Court, Southern District of New York, 1979.
467 F.Supp. 47.

KEVIN THOMAS DUFFY, DISTRICT JUDGE.

The plaintiff, A.T. Cross Co. [hereinafter referred to as "ATC"], brings this action against defendants, the Sunil Trading Corporation [hereinafter referred to as "Sunil"], and Narsing N. Narson [hereinafter referred to as "Narson"], alleging trademark infringement, unfair competition and false designation of origin under the Lanham Act, 15 U.S.C. §§ 1051 et seq.

The plaintiff, ATC, is a Rhode Island corporation who has for over one hundred years manufactured Cross writing instruments. Defendant Sunil is a New York corporation in the business of exporting "general merchandise." The individual defendant, Narson, is an officer and moving force behind the Sunil Corporation. Although not a United States citizen, Narson has resided in the United States for the past six years.

This case involves a highly sophisticated scheme in which bogus Cross pens, manufactured in a foreign country, were being passed through the United States by use of New York's foreign trade zone for shipment to still another foreign country for ultimate sale as genuine Cross pens "made in the U.S.A."

The scheme had its impetus in Taiwan at the Wang Pao Long Manufacturing Company [hereinafter referred to as "Wang Pao"] where ball point pens which purported to be genuine Cross pens were being manufactured.[1] Indeed, upon visual examination it is virtually impossible to distinguish a genuine Cross from the counterfeit. Each and every detail of the Cross pen—from the distinctive "Cross" mark and configuration to the inscriptions "made in U.S.A." and "A.T. Cross, Lincoln, R.I."—has been duplicated.

While on a business trip in Taiwan, the defendant, Narson, went to the Wang Pao plant and placed an order for 3,500 dozen of the bogus pens for shipment to his New York corporation, Sunil. The pens were subsequently shipped to Sunil but were received by Sunil in New York purportedly for the sole purpose of exportation and sale to Sunil's agent, Metro International Agencies, [hereinafter referred to as "Metro"], in the Canary Islands. Since none of the pens were to be distributed within the United States, they remained in what Congress has designated New York's foreign trade zone. 19 U.S.C. §§ 81a et seq.[2] The zone is simply a bonded warehouse where foreign goods destined exclusively for foreign

---

1. Apparently as a result of plaintiff's efforts in Taiwan, the principals connected with the Wang Pao operation have all been arrested and their machinery seized with whatever stock of counterfeit Cross pens were on hand. Indeed, it was through ATC's efforts in Taiwan that it was able to ascertain Wang Pao's customers, which included Sunil, and begin tracking down the counterfeit pens before their goodwill was irreversibly damaged.

2. Title 19 provides, in pertinent part, that each port of entry in the United States shall be entitled to at least one foreign trade zone wherein foreign goods may be stored, sold, exhibited, broken up, repacked, assembled, distributed, sorted and even mixed with foreign or domestic merchandise without being subject to the customs laws of the United States.

The practical effect of foreign goods entering the foreign trade zone is that although physically imported into the United States, while they remain in the foreign trade zone and provided they are finally exported to a foreign port without distribution within the United States, they are not subject to import duties. The more subtle, and for purposes of the instant action the most important effect of using the New York Foreign Trade Zone in transporting these pens was to aid and abet defendants in their fraudulent scheme to pass the counterfeit Cross pens off as genuine Cross pens—manufactured in the United States and exported from New York, New York.

ports are stored and are not deemed to be "imports" for purposes of the United States Customs Tariff Laws.

While in the foreign trade zone, Narson would inspect the counterfeit pens which were then broken down into smaller units, repacked, relabeled and shipped to Metro in the Canary Islands. Apparently, Sunil's sale to Metro was effected by the use of letters of credit. Issuance of the letters, however, was conditioned upon Sunil's providing to Metro certain certificates calculated to represent that the counterfeit pens were actually products of the United States. * * *

Sunil's use of the New York foreign trade zone served two very important functions. First, it enabled Sunil to obtain the counterfeit pens from Taiwan without having to pay any import duties thereon. More importantly, however, it enabled Sunil to disguise the true origin of the pens which, in turn, aided it in passing off the bogus Cross pens as having truly been manufactured in the United States.

* * *

It must * * * be determined whether in creating the foreign trade zone, it was intended to exclude the jurisdictional reach of the Lanham Act from the zone.

* * *

The entire operation of the foreign trade zone is under the close supervision of the United States Customs officials. To this end, custom officials alone control access to the goods once they are within the zone and supervise all repacking, relabeling and combinations which take place in the zone. More importantly, however, the customs' officers have the power, albeit rarely exercised, to inspect the goods as they enter the foreign trade zone.

* * *

There is absolutely no indication in the Foreign Trade Zone Act that Congress ever intended to exclude goods therein from regulation under United States laws by the Federal Courts. Indeed, the totality of evidence indicates the contrary. The Customs officials are given a substantial amount of authority not only in admitting and exporting goods from the zone, but also in dealing with the goods while therein.

Consequently, since the Commerce Clause extends into the foreign trade zone, and the jurisdictional reach of the Lanham Act is coextensive therewith, the only possible conclusion is that absent an express repudiation of federal jurisdiction (which is not contained in the Foreign Trade Zone Act), the jurisdictional parameters of the Lanham Act reach within the foreign trade zone.

COHEN, ANTI–CIRCUMVENTION: HAS TECHNOLOGY'S CHILD TURNED AGAINST ITS MOTHER?
36 Vanderbilt J. Transnational L. 961 (2003).*

Perhaps the technological innovation that most concerned the owners of intellectual property was widespread access to the Internet. Described as "a global copying machine, with millions of irresponsible and anonymous pirates pushing the buttons," the Internet makes digital information available worldwide to anyone with Internet access. Such access allows the copying of digital works by people who would not otherwise have access to an original.

The concerns about such widespread access are further heightened by characteristics of the Internet that make it almost impossible to control. First, the Internet is an ever-changing medium; its boundaries are undefined, and it is composed entirely of intangible encrypted bits of information. Second, all age groups and people of every race, color, and creed participate in the Internet. Third, the Internet has a presence in every corner of the globe, and every nation has a different perception of the copyright protections that it would extend to material made available on the Internet. These three problems, in particular, illustrate the difficulties inherent in providing intellectual property protection to digital works. The practical effect of such difficulties is manifest in any attempt to provide international copyright protection to material made available on the Internet. For example, because of the breadth of the Internet, it is difficult to determine who should have jurisdiction to police the Internet and who should determine the scope of copyright protection afforded to digital works.

The World Intellectual Property Organization

At the forefront of the attempt to move beyond some of these problems and to offer more protection to digital works is the World Intellectual Property Organization (WIPO). In 1974, WIPO became one of the 16 specialized agencies under the organizational structure of the United Nations. The Convention Establishing the World Intellectual Property Organization, signed in 1967 and amended in 1979, officially established the WIPO as a fully authorized entity with the official support of the United Nations. The WIPO's mission is "[t]o promote through international cooperation the creation, dissemination, use, and protection of works of the human spirit for the economic, cultural, and social progress of all mankind." As of January 2003, the WIPO had 179 member states, over 90 percent of the world's countries, including China, France, Germany, Japan, the United Kingdom, and the United States. As of the same date, the WIPO administered 23 international treaties, including 6 relating to copyright.

* * *

---

* Reproduced with permission.

DIGITAL RIGHTS MANAGEMENT

The information industry has sought to capitalize on the rapid development of technology by distributing works in digital form. Although the Internet and advancing digital media have opened up a new market for creative works, they also have expanded the piracy of creative works. Because of the difficulties associated with legally protecting digital works with copyright law, some copyright owners have attempted to "fight fire with fire" by using technology to provide additional protection for their works.

Often called digital rights management tools, there are a variety of mechanisms that have been somewhat effective at preventing, or at least monitoring, illegal access, use, reproduction, and manipulation of digital works. Each digital rights management tool is technologically unique, but all share a single purpose—to raise the costs of unauthorized use of protected works, in terms of time and trouble, above the benefits of such use, thereby discouraging the piracy of digital material.

Three of the most common digital rights management tools are encryption, virtual containers, and watermarks. Encryption is the conversion of digital information into a code, making the information useless to anyone who does not have the decryption key. Virtual containers are like digital envelopes that contain the protected material; the container can only be opened when the user agrees to the terms and conditions of use set by the owner of the content. Digital watermarks contain data, such as copyright information, that identifies a work and is incorporated into the work itself; watermarking allows the content owner to track the use of his work and ensure payment. Other digital rights management tools exist, and new tools are continually being developed to provide copyright owners with stronger protections for their digital material.

The use of digital rights management tools provides some added protection for digital works, but the protection mechanisms are hardly impenetrable. A key can be created for every digital lock. Talented "hackers" often use their programming abilities to get around such devices and actively work to create technology that circumvents these attempts at digital protection.

* * *

ANTI-CIRCUMVENTION IN THE WIPO COPYRIGHT TREATY

The desire for an extra level of protection for copyright owners inspired the anti-circumvention provisions included in Article 11 of the WIPO Copyright Treaty. [1996]. Article 11 requires each contracting nation to address the circumvention of encryption and other digital rights management tools used by the authors or owners of the material to protect their rights. It requires member states to

Provide adequate legal protection and effective legal remedies against the circumvention of effective technological measures that are used by authors in connection with the exercise of their rights under this Treaty or the Berne Convention and that restrict acts ... which are not authorized by the authors concerned or permitted by law.

Each nation must also ensure that enforcement procedures are available under its law, including not only "expeditious remedies to prevent infringements," but also "remedies which constitute a deterrent to further infringements."

While a provision restricting the circumvention of digital protection mechanisms seems very sensible and standard amidst the other language of the treaty, it is in fact a large step—forward or backward, depending upon whom you consult—for international copyright protections. These anti-circumvention provisions and other similar provisions have been aptly deemed the "third legal regime" because they offer "legal protection of technological protection of copyright protection."

* * *

DIGITAL MILLENNIUM COPYRIGHT ACT

The Digital Millennium Copyright Act (DMCA) was signed into U.S. law on October 28, 1998. It implemented the WIPO Copyright Treaty and established a legal framework for copyright issues related to the Internet. The DMCA was passed amidst great controversy, especially over the anti-circumvention provisions it included. The battle in Congress over its implementation has been aptly described as a battle between Hollywood and Silicon Valley. Hollywood sought strong protections for the owners of original works and the technology used to protect such works, while Silicon Valley opposed broad protections that would impede on the ability to engage in reverse engineering, computer security testing, and encryption research.

* * *

Title I of the DMCA amends U.S. law to extend protection to those works that require protection under the WIPO Copyright Treaty. This Title also includes the aforementioned broadly construed anti-circumvention provisions. The basic prohibition of the anti-circumvention provisions is against the unauthorized "circumvention of any measure that effectively controls access to a copyrighted work ... irrespective of whether the access gained, apart from the circumvention needed to effect it, infringes a property right in the work."

The DMCA defines three types of anti-circumvention violations: a basic provision, a ban on trafficking, and "additional violations." The basic provision bans the act of circumvention itself. The ban on trafficking prohibits the manufacture, import, and distribution of any "technology, product, service, device, component, or part thereof" that is primarily designed to circumvent copyright protections, has little commercially significant use other than such circumvention, or is marketed for the use of such circumvention. The additional provisions are worded very similarly to the ban on trafficking but apply to persons who have authorized access to a copy of the work, but then manufacture, import, or distribute any of the above prohibited items. Clearly, the DMCA enacts a broad interpretation of the WIPO Copyright Treaty's anti-circumvention provisions because it applies to acts beyond actual technical circumvention and to those who have a legal right to use the works. [Authors' Note: The DMCA contains felony criminal sanctions. It also provides civil injunctive and damages relief.]

UNIVERSAL CITY STUDIOS, INC. v. SHAWN C. REIMERDES

United States District Court, S.D. New York, 2000.
111 F.Supp.2d 294.

KAPLAN, DISTRICT JUDGE.

Plaintiffs, eight major United States motion picture studios, distribute many of their copyrighted motion pictures for home use on digital versatile disks ("DVDs"), which contain copies of the motion pictures in digital form. They protect those motion pictures from copying by using an encryption system called CSS. CSS-protected motion pictures on DVDs may be viewed only on players and computer drives equipped with licensed technology that permits the devices to decrypt and play—but not to copy—the films.

Late last year, computer hackers devised a computer program called DeCss that circumvents the CSS protection system and allows CSS-protected motion pictures to be copied and played on devices that lack the licensed decryption technology. Defendants quickly posted DeCSS on their Internet web site, thus making it readily available to much of the world. Plaintiffs promptly brought this action under the Digital Millennium Copyright Act (the "DMCA") to enjoin defendants from posting DeCSS and to prevent them from electronically "linking" their site to others that post DeCSS. Defendants responded with what they termed "electronic civil disobedience"—increasing their efforts to link their web site to a large number of others that continue to make DeCSS available.

CSS involves encrypting, according to an encryption algorithm, the digital sound and graphics files on a DVD that together constitute a motion picture. A CSS-protected DVD can be decrypted by an appropriate decryption algorithm that employs a series of keys stored on the DVD and the DVD player. In consequence, only players and drives containing the appropriate keys are able to decrypt DVD files and thereby play movies stored on DVDs.

The DMCA contains two principal anti-circumvention provisions. The first, Section 1201(a)(1), governs "[t]he act of circumventing a technological protection measure put in place by a copyright owner to control access to a copyrighted work," an act described by Congress as "the electronic equivalent of breaking into a locked room in order to obtain a copy of a book." The second, Section 1201(a)(2), which is the focus of this case, "supplements the prohibition against the act of circumvention in paragraph (a)(1) with prohibitions on creating and making available certain technologies ... developed or advertised to defeat technological protections against unauthorized access to a work." As defendants are accused here only of posting and linking to other sites posting DeCSS, and not of using it themselves to bypass plaintiffs' access controls, it is principally the second of the anti-circumvention provisions that is at issue in this case.

VIOLATION OF ANTI-TRAFFICKING PROVISION

Section 1201(a)(2) of the Copyright Act, part of the DMCA, provides that:

"No person shall ... offer to the public, provide or otherwise traffic in any technology ... that—

(A) is primarily designed or produced for the purpose of circumventing a technological measure that effectively controls access to a work protected under [the Copyright Act];

"(B) has only limited commercially significant purpose or use other than to circumvent a technological measure that effectively controls access to a work protected under [the Copyright Act]; or

"(C) is marketed by that person or another acting in concert with that person with that person's knowledge for use in circumventing a technological measure that effectively controls access to a work protected under [the Copyright Act]." (17 U.S.C. § 1201(a)(2))

* * *

The centerpiece of defendants' statutory position is the contention that DeCss was not created for the purpose of pirating copyrighted motion pictures. Rather, they argue, it was written to further the development of a DVD player that would run under the Linux operating system, as there allegedly were no Linux compatible players on the market at the time.

* * *

The question whether the development of a Linux DVD player motivated those who wrote DeCss is immaterial to the question whether the defendants now before the Court violated the anti-trafficking provision of the DMCA. The offering or provision of the program is the prohibited conduct—and it is prohibited irrespective of why the program was written, except to whatever extent motive may be germane to determining whether their conduct falls within one of the statutory exceptions.

* * *

There was a time when copyright infringement could be dealt with quite adequately by focusing on the infringing act. If someone wished to make and sell high quality but unauthorized copies of a copyrighted book, for example, the infringer needed a printing press. The copyright holder, once aware of the appearance of infringing copies, usually was able to trace the copies up the chain of distribution, find and prosecute the infringer, and shut off the infringement at the source.

In principle, the digital world is very different. Once a decryption program like DeCSS is written, it quickly can be sent all over the world. Every recipient is capable not only of decrypting and perfectly copying plaintiffs' copyrighted DVDs, but also of retransmitting perfect copies of DeCSS and thus enabling every recipient to do the same. They likewise are capable of transmitting perfect copies of the decrypted DVD. The process potentially is exponential rather than linear. Indeed, the difference is illustrated by comparison of two epidemiological models describing the spread of different kinds of disease. In a common source epidemic, as where members of a population contract a non-contagious disease from a poisoned well, the disease spreads only by exposure to the common source. If one eliminates the source, or closes the contaminated well, the epidemic is stopped. In a propagated outbreak epidemic, on the other hand, the disease spreads from person to person. Hence, finding the initial source of infection accomplishes little, as the disease continues to spread even if the initial source is eliminated. For obvious reasons, then, a propagated outbreak epidemic, all other things being equal, can be far more difficult to control.

This disease metaphor is helpful here. The book infringement hypothetical is analogous to a common source outbreak epidemic. Shut down the printing press (the poisoned well) and one ends the infringement (the disease outbreak). The spread of means of circumventing access to copyrighted works in digital form, however, is analogous to a propagated outbreak epidemic. Finding the original source of infection (e.g., the author of DeCSS or the first person to misuse it) accomplishes nothing, as the disease (infringement made possible by DeCss and the resulting availability of decrypted DVDs) may continue to spread from one person who gains access to the circumvention program or decrypted DVD to another. And each is "infected," i.e., each is as capable of making perfect copies of the digital file containing the copyrighted work as the author of the program or the first person to use it for improper purposes. The disease metaphor breaks down principally at the final point. Individuals infected with a real disease become sick, usually are driven by obvious self-interest to seek medical attention, and are cured of the disease if medical science is capable of doing so. Individuals infected with the "disease" of capability of circumventing measures controlling access to copyrighted works in digital form, however, do not suffer from having that ability. They cannot be relied upon to identify themselves to those seeking to control the "disease." And their self-interest will motivate some to misuse the capability, a misuse that; in practical terms, often will be untraceable.

Accordingly, this Court holds that the anti-trafficking provision of the DMCA as applied to the posting of computer code that circumvents measures that control access to copyrighted works in digital form is a valid exercise of Congress' authority.

QUESTIONS AND COMMENTS

1. Counterfeiting, especially in the digital age, has never been easier. The testimony by Trainer and the MMP excerpt represent decidedly U.S./industrial world perspectives. Might a third world nation think counterfeiting a quick, inexpensive means of development? As borrowing from a "public good?"

2. What must Dacca, Inc. and the ROCKERS do to have the United States Customs Service assist in the protection of their trademark rights? See the Note on U.S. Counterfeiting Remedies. Is the question of copyright piracy more difficult to determine than trademark piracy? *See* 17 U.S.C.A. §§ 602 and 603 (Copyright Act of 1976). How will alleged copyright piracy of the ROCKERS recordings be determined in customs proceedings?

3. Why did the Customs Service hold that ROMless computers could *not* be barred entry under § 602? What remedies may the Customs Service ultimately employ if it determines that infringing or counterfeit goods are involved? Suppose some of the goods are already in the hands of the importer. May they be recalled? Suppose some of the goods have been sold to the public and are not returned. What results?

4. What ultimately happens to forfeited goods? Is this a fair disposition to the harmed party? See the Note on U.S. Counterfeiting Remedies.

5. Suppose the United States Customs Service does not prohibit the importation of allegedly pirated DACCA label ROCKERS DVDs and CDs. May Dacca, Inc. or the ROCKERS bring direct or contributory infringement suits against the importer or exporter? Why are such suits unlikely to succeed in terminating trade in counterfeit ROCKERS albums?

6. Suppose that some decidedly counterfeit ROCKERS CDs have been purchased abroad by a United States company and shipped to a free trade zone located in Los Angeles, California. No CDs have ever left the free trade zone for resale in the United States. Rather, they are repackaged by the company for sale in other countries. May the ROCKERS or Dacca, Inc. sue under the Lanham Trademark Act or the Copyright Act of 1976 to halt these practices? *See* the *A.T. Cross* case.

7. What are free trade zones intended to be used for, and why was the Sunil Trading Corporation using the New York free trade zone in the *A.T. Cross* case?

8. Why are national remedies for international counterfeiting generally inadequate? Note that China and Vietnam are WTO members, and that Chinese products comprise the large majority of counterfeit goods seized in the U.S.A. Will Part III of the TRIPs agreement assist in combatting international piracy originating in those countries? Does your answer depend on where the goods are going? Specifically, what should the ROCKERS and Dacca, Inc. do to benefit from TRIPs in their campaign against piracy from the Far East?

9. What about the WIPO Copyright Treaty ... will it benefit the ROCKERS in the digital age? And the Digital Millenium Copyright Act? See the Cohen and *Universal City Studios* excerpts. See also A & M Records, Inc. v. Napster, Inc., 239 F.3d 1004 (9th Cir.2001) (Copyright Act relief against music file-sharing software).

10. France and Italy have made it illegal to knowingly purchase counterfeit goods. For example, if a student buys a "Louis Vuitton" bag for $15 in a Paris or Florence flea market, he or she may be arrested, fined and imprisoned. France has gone one step further. A new agency monitors Internet piracy. French offenders are subject to a "three strikes" rule: Two warnings are issued before Net access can be terminated and fines imposed by court order. South Korea and Taiwan also employ warnings and penalties against illegal downloading.

PART B. GRAY MARKET GOODS

WEICHER, K MART CORP. v. CARTIER, INC.: A BLACK DECISION FOR THE GRAY MARKET

38 Amer.U.L.Rev. 463 (1989).*

In the crowded discount camera stores of New York City, consumers face not only a confusing selection of cameras and equipment, but also a choice between two different prices for what appears to be the same item. These prices may differ by as much as forty percent. The higher price buys a camera from an authorized distributor with a manufacturer's warranty. The lower price, however, buys a good that only comes with the store's warranty, and that was imported through the "gray market."

Gray market goods are products manufactured with a genuine trademark that an independent importer purchases in an authorized foreign market and resells in the United States, without the express consent of the trademark owner. Unlike the black market, which deals in counterfeit and stolen goods, the gray market is legal. Gray market importers charge less than authorized distributors because they are able to take advantage of fluctuating exchange rates. Authorized importers must maintain stable inventories to satisfy customer demand, and cannot wait for favorable exchange rates. Gray market importers, however, only make purchases when the dollar is relatively strong. American consumers purchase everything from cameras to cars through gray market channels. Retail gray market sales are estimated at six to ten billion dollars per year.

A gray market situation can arise in two ways. First, an American manufacturer can authorize its subsidiaries or licensees to manufacture its trademarked goods. A third party could then purchase these goods in a foreign country and resell them in the United States. Under a second scenario, an independent importer could purchase a foreign manufacturer's products and divert them to the United States. Diverted goods sold in competition with authorized imports are referred to as "parallel imports."

The United States Customs Service permits gray market goods to enter this country when the foreign trademark owner and the United States trademark owner are the same or are affiliated. The Coalition to Preserve the Integrity of American Trademarks, an association of trademark owners, brought suit against the Customs Service, claiming that the Customs regulations allowing parallel importation violated tariff and trademark laws. In an unprecedented opinion, the United States Court of Appeals for the District of Columbia Circuit held that section 526 of the Tariff Act of 1930 prohibited all gray market importation. On appeal, the Supreme Court held that section 526 prohibits only gray market goods that an independent foreign manufacturer produced under license from an American trademark owner.[21]

* * *

An overview of the development of the law governing parallel importation is critical to an analysis of the Supreme Court's decision in K Mart. The legislative history of section 526 of the Tariff Act does not conclusively delineate which types of gray market importation Congress intended to prohibit. This uncertainty created confusion in the lower courts concerning the legality of the gray market.

PRE–1922 LAW

Prior to 1922, the United States permitted gray market importation despite the protests of American trademark owners. The federal courts concluded that the law of the period only protected American trademark owners from trademark infringement, and not from parallel importation. Congress was initially alerted that gray market importation could produce inequities because of ongoing litigation against a parallel importer in the case of *A. Bourjois & Co. v. Katzel.*

The facts in *Katzel* depicted the typical "gray market victim" who purchased the domestic rights to a foreign trademark but later faced competition, direct or indirect, from the foreign trademark owner (the "*Katzel* situation"). In *Katzel,* the plaintiff, an American citizen, purchased the United States trademark rights of a French face powder manufacturer. Shortly thereafter, the French manufacturer began to sell its face powder to the defendant, an American druggist, who imported the powder to the United States. The plaintiff sought injunctive relief to protect the value of its trademark. The United States Court of Appeals for the Second Circuit concluded that trademarks merely show the origin of the goods and, therefore, parallel importation of genuine goods was not trademark infringement. Finding no trademark infringement, the court held that the United States trademark owner could not prevent the parallel importation.

THE TARIFF AND LANHAM ACTS

Before the Supreme Court could rule on *Katzel,* Congress enacted section 526 as an unrelated amendment to the Tariff Act of 1922 to

---

21. K Mart Corp. v. Cartier, Inc., 108 S.Ct. 1811, 1830 (1988).

remedy the perceived inequity of the circuit court's decision. Congress adopted section 526 in response to the demands of American trademark owners who had purchased their trademarks from foreigners. The provision requires that American trademark owners expressly consent to the importation of identically trademarked goods before those goods may enter the United States.[38] It is unclear, however, whether Congress intended section 526 to apply to all gray market situations or only to the *Katzel* situation.

Section 526 prohibits importation of foreign manufactured merchandise bearing a United States trademark without the express consent of the United States trademark owner. The language of the statute is ambiguous, however, in a modern context. First, it is unclear whether Congress intended to include parent-subsidiary relationships in the context of trademark ownership. Second, it is uncertain if Congress would have classified goods that a United States company manufactured in a foreign country as "goods of foreign manufacture." Third, because trademark licensing was not widely accepted until approximately twenty-five years after Congress enacted section 526, it is unclear how section 526 applies to goods manufactured under a trademark license. Moreover, although the statute does not provide any express exceptions, the Customs Service has consistently recognized "common control" and "authorized use" exceptions to the statute's prohibition.

The language of the statute must be viewed in the context in which it was drafted. The legislative history reveals that Congress adopted the section as a "midnight amendment," after only a ten-minute debate. Some commentators argue that the short Senate debate reveals that Congress intended section 526 to apply to all gray market situations. Other commentators have characterized section 526 as a "hastily drafted provision designed to prevent an inequity sanctioned by *Katzel*."

Several of the Senators debating the legislation erroneously believed that the importer in *Katzel* was the manufacturer and not a third party. It is, therefore, difficult to ascertain whether or not Congress intended to limit the coverage of section 526 to the *Katzel* situation. Moreover, it is unclear how Congress perceived the facts in *Katzel*.

* * *

CUSTOMS SERVICE REGULATION AND THE STANDARD FOR JUDICIAL REVIEW

The Customs Service is responsible for enforcing the Tariff and Lanham Acts and may establish regulations which reasonably interpret

---

38. Fordney–McCumber Tariff Act of 1922, ch. 356, § 526, 42 Stat. 858, 975 (1922) (current version at 19 U.S.C. § 1526 (1982)). Congress reenacted section 526 in the Hawley–Smoot Tariff Act of 1930, 46 Stat. 741 (1930) (codified as amended at 19 U.S.C. § 1526 (1982)). Section 526 provides in pertinent part:

(a) **Importation prohibited.** Except as [otherwise] provided . . . , it shall be unlawful to import into the United States any merchandise of foreign manufacture if such merchandise, or the label, sign, print, package, wrapper, or receptacle, bears a trademark owned by a citizen of, or by a corporation or association created or organized within, the United States, and registered in the Patent and Trademark Office by a person domiciled in the United States . . . unless written consent of the owner of such trademark is produced at the time of making entry.

the Acts. Since 1936 Customs has consistently interpreted the statutes to allow parallel importation of trademarked goods when the foreign and domestic trademark owners are the same or affiliated—the "common control" exception. Similarly, since the time trademark licensing became an acceptable practice, Customs has excluded from the statutes' prohibition foreign goods made under license from a United States trademark owner—the "authorized use" exception. The current regulation, section 133.21, prohibits importation of articles bearing a trademark identical to a domestic trademark, unless the foreign and domestic trademark owners are the same or subject to common control or ownership, or the domestic trademark owner authorized a foreign manufacturer to use its trademark. During the fifty year period since Customs promulgated the regulation, Congress has never expressed any disagreement with the Customs Service policy.

* * *

THE ECONOMIC IMPACT OF THE GRAY MARKET

The gray market provides American consumers with a larger selection of goods at lower prices than authorized distributors provide. In addition, the gray market benefits trademark owners in two ways. First, trademark owners profit when parallel importers purchase goods for resale because these importers must purchase the goods from the trademark owner or its affiliates. Second, the increased competition in distribution benefits the manufacturer because more goods are sold at the lower price. Moreover, parallel imports benefit the United States economy because competition increases market efficiency. The increased competition also promotes the United States Government's interest in free trade.

The gray market, however, is potentially harmful to consumers and trademark owners. First, gray market goods are not necessarily identical to authorized imports and may not meet United States technical specifications or safety standards. Second, gray market goods are not eligible for manufacturers' warranty services and rebates. Consumer dissatisfaction with gray market goods damages the manufacturer's reputation, and not the unauthorized importer's reputation, because consumers are generally uninformed about the gray market.

K MART CORP. v. CARTIER, INC.

Supreme Court of the United States, 1988.
486 U.S. 281, 108 S.Ct. 1811, 100 L.Ed.2d 313.

OPINION OF THE COURT

Justice Kennedy announced the judgment of the Court, and delivered the opinion of the Court with respect to Parts I and II–A which Rehnquist, C.J., and White, Blackmun, O'Connor, and Scalia, JJ., joined, an opinion with respect to Part II–B which White, J., joined, and an opinion of the Court with respect to Part II–C which Rehnquist, C.J., and Blackmun, O'Connor, and Scalia, JJ., joined.

A gray-market good is a foreign-manufactured good, bearing a valid United States trademark, that is imported without the consent of the U.S. trademark holder. These cases present the issue whether the Secretary of the Treasury's regulation permitting the importation of certain gray-market goods, 19 CFR § 133.21 (1987), is a reasonable agency interpretation of § 526 of the Tariff Act of 1930.

The gray market arises in any of three general contexts. The prototypical gray-market victim (case 1) is a domestic firm that purchases from an independent foreign firm the rights to register and use the latter's trademark as a U.S. trademark and to sell its foreign-manufactured products here. Especially where the foreign firm has already registered the trademark in the United States or where the product has already earned a reputation for quality, the right to use that trademark can be very valuable. If the foreign manufacturer could import the trademarked goods and distribute them here, despite having sold the trademark to a domestic firm, the domestic firm would be forced into sharp intrabrand competition involving the very trademark it purchased. Similar intrabrand competition could arise if the foreign manufacturer markets its wares outside the United States, as is often the case, and a third party who purchases them abroad could legally import them. In either event, the parallel importation, if permitted to proceed, would create a gray market that could jeopardize the trademark holder's investment.

The second context (case 2) is a situation in which a domestic firm registers the U.S. trademark for goods that are manufactured abroad by an affiliated manufacturer. In its most common variation (case 2a), a foreign firm wishes to control distribution of its wares in this country by incorporating a subsidiary here. The subsidiary then registers under its own name (or the manufacturer assigns to the subsidiary's name) a U.S. trademark that is identical to its parent's foreign trademark. The parallel importation by a third party who buys the goods abroad (or conceivably even by the affiliated foreign manufacturer itself) creates a gray market. Two other variations on this theme occur when an American-based firm establishes abroad a manufacturing subsidiary corporation (case 2b) or its own unincorporated manufacturing division (case 2c) to produce its U.S. trademarked goods, and then imports them for domestic distribution. If the trademark holder or its foreign subsidiary sells the trademarked goods abroad, the parallel importation of the goods competes on the gray market with the holder's domestic sales.

In the third context (case 3), the domestic holder of a U.S. trademark *authorizes* an independent foreign manufacturer to use it. Usually the holder sells to the foreign manufacturer an exclusive right to use the trademark in a particular foreign location, but conditions the right on the foreign manufacturer's promise not to import its trademarked goods into the United States. Once again, if the foreign manufacturer or a third party imports into the United States, the foreign-manufactured goods will compete on the gray market with the holder's domestic goods.

Until 1922, the Federal Government did not regulate the importation of gray-market goods, not even to protect the investment of an independent purchaser of a foreign trademark, and not even in the extreme case where the independent foreign manufacturer breached its agreement to refrain from direct competition with the purchaser. That year, however, Congress was spurred to action by a Court of Appeals decision declining to enjoin the parallel importation of goods bearing a trademark that (as in case 1) a domestic company had purchased from an independent foreign manufacturer at a premium.

* * *

The regulations implementing § 526 for the past 50 years have not applied the prohibition to all gray-market goods. The Customs Service regulation now in force provides generally that "[f]oreign-made articles bearing a trademark identical with one owned and recorded by a citizen of the United States or a corporation or association created or organized within the United States are subject to seizure and forfeiture as prohibited importations." But the regulation furnishes a "common-control" exception from the ban, permitting the entry of gray-market goods manufactured abroad by the trademark owner or its affiliate:

"(c) *Restrictions not applicable*. The restrictions ... do not apply to imported articles when:

"(1) Both the foreign and the U.S. trademark or trade name are owned by the same person or business entity; [or]

"(2) The foreign and domestic trademark or trade name owners are parent and subsidiary companies or are otherwise subject to common ownership or control. ...."

The Customs Service regulation further provides an "authorized-use" exception, which permits importation of gray-market goods where

"(3) [t]he articles of foreign manufacture bear a recorded trademark or trade name applied under authorization of the U.S. owner...."

* * *

A majority of this Court now holds that the common-control exception of the Customs Service Regulation, is consistent with § 526. A different majority, however, holds that the authorized-use exception, is inconsistent with § 526.

* * *

In determining whether a challenged regulation is valid, a reviewing court must first determine if the regulation is consistent with the language of the statute. "If the statute is clear and unambiguous 'that is the end of the matter, for the court, as well as the agency, must give effect to the unambiguously expressed intent of Congress.' ... The traditional deference courts pay to agency interpretation is not to be applied to alter the clearly expressed intent of Congress."

* * *

Following this analysis, I conclude that subsections (c)(1) and (c)(2) of the Customs Service regulation, are permissible constructions designed to resolve statutory ambiguities. All Members of the Court are in agreement that the agency may interpret the statute to bar importation of gray-market goods in what we have denoted case 1 and to permit the imports under case 2a. As these writings state, "owned by" is sufficiently ambiguous, in the context of the statute, that it applies to situations involving a foreign parent, which is case 2a. This ambiguity arises from the inability to discern, from the statutory language, which of the two entities involved in case 2a can be said to "own" the U.S. trademark if, as in some instances, the domestic subsidiary is wholly owned by its foreign parent.

A further statutory ambiguity contained in the phrase "merchandise of foreign manufacture," suffices to sustain the regulations as they apply to cases 2b and 2c. This ambiguity parallels that of "owned by," which sustained case 2a, because it is possible to interpret "merchandise of foreign manufacture" to mean (1) goods manufactured in a foreign country, (2) goods manufactured by a foreign company, or (3) goods manufactured in a foreign country by a foreign company. Given the imprecision in the statute, the agency is entitled to choose any reasonable definition and to interpret the statute to say that goods manufactured by a foreign subsidiary or division of a domestic company are not goods "of foreign manufacture."[4]

Subsection (c)(3), 19 CFR § 133.21(c)(3) (1987), of the regulation, however, cannot stand. The ambiguous statutory phrases that we have already discussed, "owned by" and "merchandise of foreign manufacture," are irrelevant to the proscription contained in subsection (3) of the regulation. This subsection of the regulation denies a domestic trademark holder the power to prohibit the importation of goods made by an independent foreign manufacturer where the domestic trademark holder has authorized the foreign manufacturer to use the trademark. Under no reasonable construction of the statutory language can goods made in a foreign country by an independent foreign manufacturer be removed from the purview of the statute.

* * *

We hold that the Customs Service regulation is consistent with § 526 insofar as it exempts from the importation ban goods that are manufac-

---

4. I disagree with Justice Scalia's reasons for declining to recognize this ambiguity. First, the threshold question in ascertaining the correct interpretation of a statute is whether the language of the statute is clear or arguably ambiguous. The purported gloss any party gives to the statute, or any reference to legislative history, is in the first instance irrelevant. Further, I decline to assign any binding or authoritative effect to the particular verbiage Justice Scalia highlights. The quoted phrases are simply the Government's explanation of the practical effect the current regulation has in applying the statute, and come from the statement of the case portion of its petition for a writ of certiorari.

tured abroad by the "same person" who holds the U.S. trademark, 19 CFR § 133.21(c)(1) (1987), or by a person who is "subject to common ... control" with the U.S. trademark holder, § 133.21(c)(2). Because the authorized-use exception of the regulation, § 133.21(c)(3), is in conflict with the plain language of the statute, that provision cannot stand. The judgment of the Court of Appeals is therefore reversed insofar as it invalidated §§ 133.21(c)(1) and (c)(2), but affirmed with respect to § 133.21(c)(3).

It is so ordered.

QUALITY KING DISTRIBUTORS, INC. v. L'ANZA RESEARCH INTERNATIONAL, INC.

Supreme Court of the United States, 1998.
523 U.S. 135, 118 S.Ct. 1125, 140 L.Ed.2d 254.

JUSTICE STEVENS delivered the opinion of the Court.

Section 106(3) of the Copyright Act of 1976(Act), 17 U.S.C. § 106(3), gives the owner of a copyright the exclusive right to distribute copies of a copyrighted work. That exclusive right is expressly limited, however, by the provisions of §§ 107 through 120. Section 602(a) gives the copyright owner the right to prohibit the unauthorized importation of copies. The question presented by this case is whether the right granted by § 602(a) is also limited by §§ 107 through 120. More narrowly, the question is whether the "first sale" doctrine endorsed in § 109(a) is applicable to imported copies.

Respondent, L'anza Research International, Inc. (L'anza), is a California corporation engaged in the business of manufacturing and selling shampoos, conditioners, and other hair care products. L'anza has copyrighted the labels that are affixed to those products. In the United States, L'anza sells exclusively to domestic distributors who have agreed to resell within limited geographic areas and then only to authorized retailers such as barber shops, beauty salons, and professional hair care colleges. L'anza has found that the American "public is generally unwilling to pay the price charged for high quality products, such as L'anza's products, when they are sold along with the less expensive lower quality products that are generally carried by supermarkets and drug stores." App. 54 (declaration of Robert Hall). L'anza promotes the domestic sales of its products with extensive advertising in various trade magazines and at point of sale, and by providing special training to authorized retailers.

L'anza also sells its products in foreign markets. In those markets, however, it does not engage in comparable advertising or promotion; its prices to foreign distributors are 35% to 40% lower than the prices charged to domestic distributors. In 1992 and 1993, L'anza's distributor in the United Kingdom arranged the sale of three shipments to a distributor in Malta; each shipment contained several tons of L'anza products with copyrighted labels affixed. The record does not establish whether the initial purchaser was the distributor in the United Kingdom or the distributor in Malta, or whether title passed when the goods were delivered to the carrier or when they arrived at their destination, but it is undisputed that the goods were manufactured by L'anza and first sold by L'anza to a foreign purchaser.

It is also undisputed that the goods found their way back to the United States without the permission of L'anza and were sold in California by unauthorized retailers who had purchased them at discounted prices from Quality King Distributors, Inc. (petitioner). There is some uncertainty about the identity of the actual importer, but for the purpose of our decision we assume that petitioner bought all three shipments from the Malta distributor, imported them, and then resold them to retailers who were not in L'anza's authorized chain of distribution.

After determining the source of the unauthorized sales, L'anza brought suit against petitioner and several other defendants.[3] * * *

This is an unusual copyright case because L'anza does not claim that anyone has made unauthorized copies of its copyrighted labels. Instead, L'anza is primarily interested in protecting the integrity of its method of marketing the products to which the labels are affixed. Although the labels themselves have only a limited creative component, our interpretation of the relevant statutory provisions would apply equally to a case involving more familiar copyrighted materials such as sound recordings or books. * * *

Section 109(a) provides:

"Notwithstanding the provisions of section 106(3), the owner of a particular copy or phonorecord lawfully made under this title, or any person authorized by such owner, is entitled, without the authority of the copyright owner, to sell or otherwise dispose of the possession of that copy or phonorecord...."

* * *

The most relevant portion of § 602(a) provides:

"Importation into the United States, without the authority of the owner of copyright under this title, of copies or phonorecords of a work that have been acquired outside the United States is an infringement of the exclusive right to distribute copies or phonorecords under section 106, actionable under section 501...."

It is significant that this provision does not categorically prohibit the unauthorized importation of copyrighted materials. Instead, it provides that such importation is an infringement of the exclusive right to distribute copies "under section 106." Like the exclusive right to "vend" that was construed in *Bobbs–Merrill*, the exclusive right to distribute is a limited right. The introductory language in § 106 expressly states that all of the exclusive rights granted by that section—including, of course, the

---

3. L'anza's claims against the retailer defendants were settled. The Malta distributor apparently never appeared in this action and a default judgment was entered against it.

distribution right granted by subsection (3)—are limited by the provisions of §§ 107 through 120. One of those limitations, as we have noted, is provided by the terms of § 109(a), which expressly permit the owner of a lawfully made copy to sell that copy "[n]otwithstanding the provisions of section 106(3)."

* * *

After the first sale of a copyrighted item "lawfully made under this title," any subsequent purchaser, whether from a domestic or from a foreign reseller, is obviously an "owner" of that item. Read literally, § 109(a) unambiguously states that such an owner "is entitled, without the authority of the copyright owner, to sell" that item. Moreover, since § 602(a) merely provides that unauthorized importation is an infringement of an exclusive right "under section 106," and since that limited right does not encompass resales by lawful owners, the literal text of § 602(a) is simply inapplicable to both domestic and foreign owners of L'anza's products who decide to import them and resell them in the United States.

* * *

The parties and their *amici* have debated at length the wisdom or unwisdom of governmental restraints on what is sometimes described as either the "gray market" or the practice of "parallel importation." In *K Mart Corp. v. Cartier, Inc.*, 486 U.S. 281, 108 S.Ct. 1811, 100 L.Ed.2d 313 (1988), we used those terms to refer to the importation of foreign-manufactured goods bearing a valid United States trademark without the consent of the trademark holder. *Id.*, at 285–286, 108 S.Ct., at 1814–1815. We are not at all sure that those terms appropriately describe the consequences of an American manufacturer's decision to limit its promotional efforts to the domestic market and to sell its products abroad at discounted prices that are so low that its foreign distributors can compete in the domestic market.[29] But even if they do, whether or not we think it would be wise policy to provide statutory protection for such price discrimination is not a matter that is relevant to our duty to interpret the text of the Copyright Act.

LEVER BROS. CO. v. UNITED STATES

United States Court of Appeals, D.C. Circuit, 1993.
299 U.S.App.D.C. 128, 981 F.2d 1330.

Lever Brothers Company ("Lever US" or "Lever"), an American company, and its British affiliate, Lever Brothers Limited ("Lever UK"), both manufacture deodorant soap under the "Shield" trademark and hand dishwashing liquid under the "Sunlight" trademark. The trade-

---

29. Presumably L'anza, for example, could have avoided the consequences of that competition either (1) by providing advertising support abroad and charging higher prices, or (2) if it was satisfied to leave the promotion of the product in foreign markets to its foreign distributors, to sell its products abroad under a different name.

marks are registered in each country. The products have evidently been formulated differently to suit local tastes and circumstances. The U.S. version lathers more, the soaps smell different, the colorants used in American "Shield" have been certified by the FDA whereas the colorants in British "Shield" have not, and the U.S. version contains a bacteriostat that enhances the deodorant properties of the soap. The British version of "Sunlight" dishwashing soap produces less suds, and the American version is formulated to work best in the "soft water" available in most American cities, whereas the British version is designed for "hard water" common in Britain.

The packaging of the U.S. and U.K. products is also somewhat different. The British "Shield" logo is written in script form and is packaged in foil wrapping and contains a wave motif, whereas the American "Shield" logo is written in block form, does not come in foil wrapping and contains a grid pattern. There is small print on the packages indicating where they were manufactured. The British "Sunlight" comes in a cylindrical bottle labeled "Sunlight Washing Up Liquid." The American "Sunlight" comes in a yellow, hour-glass-shaped bottle labeled "Sunlight Dishwashing Liquid."

Lever asserts that the unauthorized influx of these foreign products has created substantial consumer confusion and deception in the United States about the nature and origin of this merchandise, and that it has received numerous consumer complaints from American consumers who unknowingly bought the British products and were disappointed.

Lever argues that the importation of the British products was in violation of section 42 of the Lanham Act, 15 U.S.C. § 1124 which provides that with the exception of goods imported for personal use:

> [N]o article of imported merchandise which shall copy or simulate the name of the [sic] any domestic manufacture, or manufacturer . . . or which shall copy or simulate a trademark registered in accordance with the provisions of this chapter . . . shall be admitted to entry at any customhouse of the United States.

Id. The United States Customs Service ("Customs"), however, was allowing importation of the British goods under the "affiliate exception" created by 19 C.F.R. § 133.21(c)(2), which provides that foreign goods bearing United States trademarks are not forbidden when "[t]he foreign and domestic trademark or tradename owners are parent and subsidiary companies or are otherwise subject to common ownership or control."[3]

In *Lever I*, we concluded that "the natural, virtually inevitable reading of section 42 is that it bars foreign goods bearing a trademark identical to the valid U.S. trademark but physically different," without regard to affiliation between the producing firms or the genuine character of the trademark abroad. 877 F.2d 101, 111 (D.C.Cir.1989). * * *

---

3. This case does not involve a dispute between corporate affiliates. Neither Lever US nor Lever UK has authorized the importation which is being conducted by third parties. *See Lever I,* 877 F.2d at 103.

Customs' main argument from the legislative history is that section 42 of the Lanham Act applies only to imports of goods bearing trademarks that "copy or simulate" a registered mark. Customs thus draws a distinction between "genuine" marks and marks that "copy or simulate." A mark applied by a foreign firm subject to ownership and control common to that of the domestic trademark owner is by definition "genuine," Customs urges, regardless of whether or not the goods are identical. Thus, any importation of goods manufactured by an affiliate of a U.S. trademark owner cannot "copy or simulate" a registered mark because those goods are *ipso facto* "genuine."

This argument is fatally flawed. It rests on the false premise that foreign trademarks applied to foreign goods are "genuine" in the United States. Trademarks applied to physically different foreign goods are not genuine from the viewpoint of the American consumer. As we stated in *Lever I*:

> On its face ... section [42] appears to aim at deceit and consumer confusion; when identical trademarks have acquired different meanings in different countries, one who imports the foreign version to sell it under that trademark will (in the absence of some specially differentiating feature) cause the confusion Congress sought to avoid. The fact of affiliation between the producers in no way reduces the probability of that confusion; it is certainly not a constructive consent to importation.

877 F.2d at 111.

There is a larger, more fundamental and ultimately fatal weakness in Customs' position in this case. Section 42 on its face appears to forbid importation of goods that "copy or simulate" a United States trademark. Customs has the burden of adducing evidence from the legislative history of section 42 and its administrative practice of an exception for materially different goods whose similar foreign and domestic trademarks are owned by affiliated companies. At a minimum, this requires that the specific question be addressed in the legislative history and administrative practice. The bottom line, however, is that the issue of materially different goods was not addressed either in the legislative history or the administrative record. It is not enough to posit that silence implies authorization, when the authorization sought runs counter to the evident meaning of the governing statute. Therefore, we conclude that section 42 of the Lanham Act precludes the application of Customs' affiliate exception with respect to physically, materially different goods.

* * *

For the foregoing reasons, we affirm the District Court's ruling that section 42 of the Lanham Act, 15 U.S.C. § 1124, bars the importation of physically different foreign goods bearing a trademark identical to a valid U.S. trademark, regardless of the trademark's genuine character abroad or affiliation between the producing firms. Injunctive relief, however, is limited to the two products which were the subject of this action. We therefore vacate the District Court's prior order to the extent that it renders global relief and remand for the entry of an injunction consistent with this opinion.

TAKAMATSU, PARALLEL IMPORTATION OF TRADEMARKED GOODS: A COMPARATIVE ANALYSIS

57 Wash.L.Rev. 433 (1982).*

The rapid development of international trade has raised a serious problem in trademark law. The importation of genuine goods by someone other than the designated exclusive importer is usually referred to as "parallel importation." For example, when a manufacturer wants to sell his branded products in a foreign country, he often appoints an exclusive distributor in that foreign country and sells the products through that distributor. The manufacturer, who owns identical trademark rights in his home country and in the foreign nation, either grants a license or assigns his trademark to the distributor. The problem of parallel importation arises when a third party purchases the trademarked products in the manufacturer's home country and imports them into that foreign country without the distributor's consent. Whether this importation constitutes infringement of the trademark right in the importing country has long been disputed. Fact patterns vary depending on the relation between domestic and foreign trademark owners. The problem becomes more complex if the products sold by a distributor are different in quality from those imported by a third party. * * *

Initially, the Japanese courts took a strong stance against parallel importation. In *Nestle Nihon K.K. v. Sankai Shoten,*[44] a Swiss manufacturer owned the trademark "Nescafe," and its Japanese subsidiary was registered as an exclusive use right owner of the trademark. The Japanese subsidiary imported Nescafe coffee from its parent company. A third party also imported genuine Nescafe coffee. The court held that the third party's possession of the coffee infringed the exclusive use right of the Japanese subsidiary and affirmed the temporary injunction preventing the third party from selling Nescafe coffee in Japan. The Tokyo District Court in *Nestle* seems to have assumed that any unauthorized importation of genuine goods infringes domestic trademark rights.

The series of *Parker Pen* cases are the most significant statement of Japanese parallel importation law. Schulyro Trading Company was an exclusive distributor of Parker pens in Japan, and it registered an exclusive use right on the "Parker" trademark in Japan. When a third party

---

* Reprinted by permission of the author and the Washington Law Review Association. Takamatsu, Kaoru, *"Parallel Importation of Trademarked Goods: A Comparative Analysis,"* in 57 Wash.L.Rev. 433–459 (1982).

44. *Nestle Nihon K.K. v. Sankai Shoten* (unreported case, Tokyo Dist.Ct., May 29, 1965), summarized in T. Doi, Digest of Japanese Court Decisions In Trademarks And Unfair Competition Cases 66 (1971).

imported Parker pens from Hong Kong, Schulyro obtained the equivalent of a temporary injunction from the Tokyo District Court. Schulyro then filed with the Customs Office an application to prevent importation of goods that infringed the trademark "Parker." When another party tried to import pens from Hong Kong, the Customs Office refused to issue an import permit without Schulyro's consent. The third party responded by bringing an action against Schulyro in Osaka District Court, seeking a declaration that Schulyro had no right to bar importation of genuine Parker pens.

The decision of the Osaka District Court [47] was comprehensive and has been influential. The court first acknowledged that Schulyro did not manufacture the Parker goods, but only imported them, and found that the goods imported by others were exactly the same in quality as those Schulyro imported. The court rejected the principle of territoriality of trademark rights as being irrelevant to the problem of parallel importation. Instead, it examined the function of trademark protection. The court recognized that the purpose of trademark law is to protect marks as indications of source and as a guarantee of quality. While refusing to adopt the exhaustion theory of trademark rights, the court applied the criminal law theory of "illegal in substance" (*jisshitsuteki-ihosei no riron*) to the problem of parallel importation.

The court considered several factors in deciding whether the parallel importation was illegal in substance: (i) the internationally well-known trademark "Parker" indicated the manufacturer, and not the domestic distributor, as the origin of the goods; (ii) the other Parker pens were equal in quality to those sold by Schulyro; (iii) Schulyro's goodwill as the exclusive distributor was based on the reputation of Parker goods in the world market; (iv) parallel importation of genuine goods by third parties may well promote fair and free competition in price and servicing of the products; and (v) the parallel importer did not take advantage of Schulyro's advertisements of Parker goods. In addition, the parallel importer did not employ unfair practices.

The court held that there was nothing illegal in substance in the case, and rendered the judgment that Schulyro had no right to exclude importation and sale of pens bearing the genuine Parker trademark. Though this case was dismissed on appeal for other reasons, the High Court, in dicta, affirmed the holding of the District Court.

The *Parker* case brought substantial legislative change. In 1972 the Customs Division of the Ministry of Finance of Japan issued a new notice under the Customs Duties Act. This notice provided that parallel importation by third parties may not be excluded at the Customs Office where the domestic trademark owner also holds the foreign trademark and is supplying the goods to the parallel importer, or where the domestic and foreign

---

47. *N. MC. Co. v. Schulyro Trading Co.*, Feb. 27, 1970, Osaka Dist.Ct., 234 Hanrei Taimuzu (Law Times Reports) 57, *reprinted in English in* 16 Japanese Annual of International Law 113 (1972).

trademark owners should be considered the same entity by virtue of their special relationship. *Parker* dealt with parallel importation where both the domestic and the foreign trademarks were owned by the same person. Under the new notice, parallel importation is allowed not only in a case like *Parker,* but also where the foreign and domestic trademarks are owned by parent-subsidiary companies. The notice also makes clear that parallel importation of genuine goods for an importer's personal use will not be treated as infringement of trademark rights.

In 1972, the Fair Trade Commission of Japan, which administers the Japanese Antimonopoly Act, published guidelines for sole import distributorship agreements. The guidelines stipulate that it is an unfair business practice to unduly hinder parallel importation of goods covered by a distributorship agreement. Thus, parallel importation of genuine goods cannot be enjoined by a Japanese sole distributor as a matter of the antitrust law.

* * *

Thus, the problem of parallel importation is best solved by examining the functions of trademarks and considering the anticompetitive effects of barring parallel importation. Applying these principles to the fact patterns in which the problem of parallel importation arises reveals how those patterns should be resolved.

In the first general fact pattern, the same entity owns both the domestic and foreign trademarks. Three patterns of parallel importation are possible here. First, the owner itself attempts to enjoin importation by a third party of goods produced and distributed by the owner in another country. Second, a domestic licensee who only imports trademarked goods attempts to enjoin the importation of goods the owner or a foreign licensee has produced in a foreign country. Third, a domestic licensee who manufactures the trademarked goods locally attempts to enjoin importation of goods the owner or a foreign licensee has produced elsewhere. In each case, the imported goods may be of the same or of different quality than those sold by the domestic producer.

When the imported and domestically produced goods are the same in quality, the origin and guarantee functions of trademark suggest that parallel importation should be allowed. Because quality is the same, the guarantee function is satisfied. Because the imported and domestically produced goods derive from the same source, by licensing or otherwise, the public is not deceived as to the origin of the goods.

The problem is more difficult when the imported goods differ in quality from the domestically produced or marketed goods. Courts and commentators favoring a single function theory are not concerned with the guarantee function, and conclude that the trademark owner cannot prevent parallel importation. A Japanese court, however, enjoined parallel importation of coffee under the trademark "Nescafe" where the imported coffee differed in taste from the domestically distributed coffee. Where there is a substantial difference between the imported and domestic goods, this result is appropriate because the difference in quality may deceive consumers. If the difference is indicated on the label of the imported product, on the other hand, deception will not occur and parallel importation is appropriate. Parallel importation should also be allowed when the quality variance is intended to divide markets or allow price discrimination, rather than to meet variances in local demand.

In the second general fact pattern, the domestic and foreign trademarks are owned by different persons. Here too, examination of the function of trademarks points out the correct results. If the public will be deceived about the origin or quality of the trademarked goods, enjoining parallel importation is appropriate. Where the domestic and foreign trademarks are owned by entirely different entities, the public may be deceived about the origin of any imported goods, so enjoining parallel importation is appropriate. Where the domestic trademark owner is associated with the foreign owner, as in a distributorship agreement, or through a legal relation such as parent-subsidiary, parallel importation should be allowed, as the public is not deceived about the origin of the goods. However, even where the domestic and foreign trademark owners are closely related, parallel importation may be enjoined if the difference in quality is not clearly indicated on the imported goods or if the purpose of the quality variance is market division or price discrimination.

SILHOUETTE INTERNATIONAL v. HARTLAUER

European Court of Justice.
Case No. C-355/96 (July 16, 1998).

JUDGMENT: By order of 15 October 1996, received at the Court on 30 October 1996, the Oberster Gerichtshof referred to the Court for a preliminary ruling under Article 177 of the EC Treaty two questions on the interpretation of Article 7 of the First Council Directive 89/104/EEC of 21 December 1988 to approximate the laws of the Member States relating to trade marks (OJ 1989 L 40, p. 1, the Directive), as amended by the Agreement on the European Economic Area of 2 May 1992 (OJ 1994 L 1, p. 3, the EEA Agreement).

Those questions were raised in proceedings between two Austrian companies, Silhouette International Schmied GmbH & Co. KG (Silhouette) and Hartlauer Handelsgesellschaft mbH (Hartlauer).

Article 7 of the Directive, concerning exhaustion of the rights conferred by a trade mark, provides:

> (1) The trade mark shall not entitle the proprietor to prohibit its use in relation to goods which have been put on the market in the Community under that trade mark by the proprietor or with his consent.
>
> (2) Paragraph 1 shall not apply where there exist legitimate reasons for the proprietor to oppose further commercialisation of the

goods, especially where the condition of the goods is changed or impaired after they have been put on the market.

* * *

Silhouette produces spectacles in the higher price ranges. It markets them worldwide under the trade mark Silhouette', registered in Austria and most countries of the world. In Austria, Silhouette itself supplies spectacles to opticians; in other States it has subsidiary companies or distributors.

Hartlauer sells inter alia spectacles through its numerous subsidiaries in Austria, and its low prices are its chief selling point. It is not supplied by Silhouette because that company considers that distribution of its products by Hartlauer would be harmful to its image as a manufacturer of top-quality fashion spectacles.

In October 1995 Silhouette sold 21 000 out-of-fashion spectacle frames to a Bulgarian company, Union Trading, for the sum of USD 261 450. It had directed its representative to instruct the purchasers to sell the spectacle frames in Bulgaria or the states of the former USSR only, and not to export them to other countries. The representative assured Silhouette that it had so instructed the purchaser. However, the Oberster Gerichtshof noted that it had not proved possible to ascertain whether that had actually been done.

In November 1995 Silhouette delivered the frames in question to Union Trading in Sofia. Hartlauer bought those goods—it has not, according to the Oberster Gerichtshof, been possible to find out from whom— and offered them for sale in Austria from December 1995. In a press campaign Hartlauer announced that, despite not being supplied by Silhouette, it had managed to acquire 21 000 Silhouette frames abroad.

Silhouette brought an action for interim relief before the Landesgericht Steyr, seeking an injunction restraining Hartlauer from offering spectacles or spectacle frames for sale in Austria under its trade mark, where they had not been put on the market in the European Economic Area (EEA) by Silhouette itself or by third parties with its consent. It claims that it has not exhausted its trade mark rights, since, in terms of the Directive, trade-mark rights are exhausted only when the products have been put on the market in the EEA by the proprietor or with his consent. * * *

Like the rules laid down in Article 6 of the Directive, which set certain limits to the effects of a trade mark, Article 7 states that, in the circumstances which it specifies, the exclusive rights conferred by the trade mark are exhausted, with the result that the proprietor is no longer entitled to prohibit use of the mark. Exhaustion is subject first of all to the condition that the goods have been put on the market by the proprietor or with his consent. According to the text of the Directive itself, exhaustion occurs only where the products have been put on the market in the Community (in the EEA since the EEA Agreement entered into force).

No argument has been presented to the Court that the Directive could be interpreted as providing for the exhaustion of the rights conferred by a trade mark in respect of goods put on the market by the proprietor or with his consent irrespective of where they were put on the market.

On the contrary, Hartlauer and the Swedish Government have maintained that the Directive left the Member States free to provide in their national law for exhaustion, not only in respect of products put on the market in the EEA but also of those put on the market in non-member countries.

The interpretation of the Directive proposed by Hartlauer and the Swedish Government assumes, having regard to the wording of Article 7, that the Directive, like the Court's case-law concerning Articles 30 and 36 of the EC Treaty, is limited to requiring the Member States to provide for exhaustion within the Community, but that Article 7 does not comprehensively resolve the question of exhaustion of rights conferred by the trade mark, thus leaving it open to the Member States to adopt rules on exhaustion going further than those explicitly laid down in Article 7 of the Directive.

As Silhouette, the Austrian, French, German, Italian and United Kingdom Governments and the Commission have all argued, such an interpretation is contrary to the wording of Article 7 and to the scheme and purpose of the rules of the Directive concerning the rights which a trade mark confers on its proprietor.

* * *

Articles 5 to 7 of the Directive must be construed as embodying a complete harmonisation of the rules relating to the rights conferred by a trade mark. That interpretation, it may be added, is borne out by the fact that Article 5 expressly leaves it open to the Member States to maintain or introduce certain rules specifically defined by the Community legislature. Thus, in accordance with Article 5(2), to which the ninth recital refers, the Member States have the option to grant more extensive protection to trade marks with a reputation.

Accordingly, the Directive cannot be interpreted as leaving it open to the Member States to provide in their domestic law for exhaustion of the rights conferred by a trade mark in respect of products put on the market in non-member countries.

This, moreover, is the only interpretation which is fully capable of ensuring that the purpose of the Directive is achieved, namely to safeguard the functioning of the internal market. A situation in which some Member States could provide for international exhaustion while others provided for Community exhaustion only would inevitably give rise to barriers to the free movement of goods and the freedom to provide services.

QUESTIONS AND COMMENTS

1. Suppose that one of Dacca, Inc.'s licensed, wholly owned European subsidiaries has sold a large quantity of ROCKERS DVDs and CDs at a discount to an Irish wholesaler who in turn has sold them to K–Market, Inc. The products lawfully bear the ROCKERS™ and DACCA™ labels and are thus "genuine goods," commonly referred to as "gray market goods." Will the Customs Service after the *K Mart* decision prohibit the entry of these goods under Section 526 of the Tariff Act of 1930, originally known as the "Genuine Goods Exclusion Act?"

Suppose the goods were produced by a European licensee in which Dacca, Inc. had no ownership interest. What result? Suppose they were produced by a European joint venture in which Dacca, Inc. held majority/minority ownership?

2. Are you persuaded by the results and reasoning of Justice Kennedy in *K Mart*? If the statute's "plain meaning" is so clear, how could the Court be so split? Some have argued that the Supreme Court opinion in *K Mart* represents both bad law and bad policy. Do you agree?

3. For purposes of construing Section 526, should it matter whether the genuine goods were put on the market by a subsidiary or affiliate of a U.S. company operating abroad or by a foreign firm operating in the United States through a subsidiary or affiliate?

4. The Trademark Counterfeiting Act of 1984 specifically *excludes* imports of gray market and "overrun" goods from its coverage. *See* Part A. Should this exclusion influence the customs law debate surrounding importation of gray market goods?

5. The *Alkaline Batteries* decision of the International Trade Commission (discussed in Problem 9.3) holds that importation of gray market goods may violate Section 337 of the Tariff Act of 1930. Accord *Bourdeau Bros. Inc. v. International Trade Comm.*, 444 F.3d 1317 (2006). President Reagan, however, denied relief in the batteries' case. The President specifically referred to the longstanding position of the Customs Service allowing parallel importation of gray market goods in his denial of relief.

6. There is conflicting case law on the right to injunctive relief against gray market imports under the 1976 Copyright Act and the Lanham Trademark Act. *See* R. Folsom, M. Gordon and J.A. Spanogle, *Principles of International Business Transactions* 2d, (West Concise Hornbook Series, 2010), Chapter 24. If *Quality King* and *Lever Bros.* had been argued under Section 526, what results?

Is the Supreme Court's decision in *Quality King* another example of the "plain meaning" rule in action? In *Quality King,* the goods were made in the USA and imported back into the United States. Suppose the gray market goods were foreign-made. What result? See, e.g., Parfums Givenchy, Inc. v. Drug Emporium, Inc., 38 F.3d 477 (9th Cir.1994); Costco Wholesale Corp. v. Omega S.A., ___ U.S. ___, 131 S.Ct. 565, 178 L.Ed.2d 470 (2010) *affirming* 541 F.3d 982 (9th Cir. 2008).

What about the "plain meaning" of the Court of Appeal in *Lever Bros.*? Is labeling enough to deal with material differences between gray market goods? See the U.S. Customs Service Regulation at 19 C.F.R. § 133.23.

Would you advise the ROCKERS to pursue injunctive relief? What kind of injunctive relief is available? How does such a remedy compare to that available under Section 526 if it applies?

7. How are gray market goods treated under Japanese law? What result *should* occur when gray market goods differ in quality from those sold in the home market? Is labeling a solution?

Do you agree with Takamatsu that the "problem of parallel importation is best solved by examining the functions of trademarks and considering the anticompetitive effects of barring parallel importation?" How does this approach differ from that adopted in the *K Mart, Quality King* and *Lever Bros.* opinions?

8. The doctrine of exhaustion of intellectual property rights has been very influential in European law. It has consistently been invoked by the European Court of Justice to deny use of intellectual property rights to inhibit trade *within* the Common Market. See R. Folsom, *Principles of European Union Law* 2d (West Concise Hornbook Series), Chapters 4 and 7. The doctrine posits that once title to genuine goods has lawfully passed from the original trademark holder, infringement actions cannot be used to block trade in those goods. To allow such relief, the Court of Justice has ruled, would extend trademark rights beyond their intended scope. Until *Silhouette*, it was generally thought that the doctrine of exhaustion would apply internationally as well as internally.

Why has the European Court ruled otherwise? What will be the likely effect of this decision in the Common Market? How might it impact the European subsidiaries of Dacca, Inc.? See also, Zino Davidoff SA v. A&G Imports Ltd., 2001 E.C.R.I–8691 (no implied consent to gray market imports from sales of LEVI jeans outside Europe).

PROBLEM 9.3 PROTECTION OF INTELLECTUAL PROPERTY: SECTION 337 PROCEEDINGS, SPECIAL 301 PROCEDURES, TRIPS AND PHARMACEUTICALS FROM THAILAND

SECTION I. THE SETTING

Fizzer, Inc. (FIZZER) is a large United States multinational pharmaceutical company. It has an extensive research and development budget and staff. Over the years FIZZER has invented many pharmaceuticals of great use to human health, including most recently TETRACINE ™ and ANTIAIDS ™. TETRACINE is a powerful antibiotic, with limited side effects, which FIZZER sees as a replacement or at least an alternative to existing antibiotics. ANTIAIDS is truly a miracle drug: It immunizes most humans from the AIDS virus.

FIZZER has obtained patents on TETRACINE and ANTIAIDS in the U.S. and in every other country of the world where that is possible. In Thailand and other developing nations, however, there had been an express exclusion of pharmaceuticals from coverage under local patent laws. More recently, acting under pressure from the industrial world and anticipating the intellectual property requirements of the WTO TRIPS Agreement, Thailand has allowed pharmaceutical patents. FIZZER acted quickly to register its TETRACINE and ANTIAIDS patents in Thailand.

However, Thai patent law has a provision on "compulsory licensing" of patents that have not been "used" in the country. At least as to ANTIAIDS, FIZZER has been informed by Thai authorities that since it has not established a local production facility (but instead chose to export ANTIAIDS to Thailand), it has not "used" its patent in conformity with Thai law. Thai officials have also noted that there is a rapidly rising rate of AIDS infections which constitutes a public emergency in their opinion. The authorities therefore intend to compel licensing by FIZZER of its ANTIAIDS patent to several local pharmaceutical firms. Compulsory licensing of TETRACINE is also being discussed. FIZZER would like to know whether Thailand can do that under the TRIPS agreement and (if so) under what conditions and (if not) what remedies it may pursue.

FIZZER also has some very immediate problems. A flourishing Thai pharmaceutical industry is busy producing and exporting unlicensed "generic" drugs, including the two owned by FIZZER. The export earnings and local employment generated by this industry are significant, and local authorities seem unable to halt these activities. The people in Thailand can obtain both of FIZZER's drugs without prescription and at nominal cost. They are no doubt healthier for it, and there have been no reported quality control problems with these generics.

Some of the Thai versions of TETRACINE and ANTIAIDS have been imported into the U.S. market. FIZZER is outraged by this result, which it sees as theft of its intellectual property. It has filed a complaint with the U.S. International Trade Commission (ITC) under Section 337 of the Tariff Act of 1930 requesting preliminary and permanent relief from these imports. Its second question to counsel is whether it is likely to be successful in excluding these goods from the U.S. market.

FIZZER has also urged the United States Trade Representative (USTR) to take action under the "Special 301" procedures adopted in the 1988 Omnibus Trade and Competitiveness Act. Through this request, FIZZER seeks to have Thailand's inadequate enforcement of patents on pharmaceuticals and compulsory licensing identified as priorities for special treatment under Section 301 of the Trade Act of 1974. Its third question to counsel is whether it is likely to be successful in stopping the unauthorized production or compulsory licensing of its drugs in Thailand through Section 301.

SECTION II. FOCUS OF CONSIDERATION

Pharmaceuticals have long been a point of contention in world patent law between the developed and developing worlds. Whereas there are very few countries which do not recognize patents in some way under their laws, there have been quite a large number of third world nations which limit patent rights for pharmaceuticals. India is a prime example. Almost all developing and some developed (e.g., Canada and Britain but not the United States) nations have compulsory licensing provisions in their patent laws. Many nations argue that the health of their people should not be held hostage to patent rights. Furthermore, pharmaceuticals are one of relatively few high-tech industries that developing nations are capable of reproducing without significant licensing of technology. This is something they can do and have done prior to the TRIPS agreement.

This problem explores the potential impact of the TRIPS accord. It specifically focuses on Section 337 of the Tariff Act of 1930, the traditional forum for import relief from patent infringements under U.S. law. Section 337 is also invoked when imports involve copyright or trademark infringements, including imports of gray market goods. Furthermore, it allows challenges to unfair import practices which have little or nothing to do with intellectual property. See R. Folsom, M. Gordon, and J.A. Spanogle, *Principles of International Business Transactions* 2d (West Concise Hornbook Series, 2010), Chapter 24.

The problem also examines the "Special 301" procedures established by the 1988 Omnibus Trade and Competitiveness Act. These procedures are located in Section 182 of the Trade Act of 1974. They can lead to initiation of Section 301 proceedings under the Trade Act of 1974. Section 301 proceedings are generally used to obtain market access for United States exporters of goods and services, but are also capable of being used to pressure and perhaps sanction other nations whose intellectual property policies diverge from U.S. standards.

Sections 337 and 338 of the Tariff Act of 1930 (19 U.S.C. § 1337 & 1338), Sections 182 and 301 of the Trade Act of 1974 (19 U.S.C. §§ 2242 and 2411) and Articles 27–31 of the TRIPS agreement are essential to an analysis of this problem. They are found in the Documents Supplement. Web resources for further study include TRIPS coverage at *www.wto.org*, Section 337 coverage at *www.usitc.gov*, and Section 301 coverage at *www. ustr.gov*.

SECTION III. READINGS, QUESTIONS AND COMMENTS

PART A. EXCLUSION OF INFRINGING IMPORTS FROM THE U.S. MARKET

GLICK, SECTION 337 OF THE TARIFF ACT OF 1930

Fed.Bar Ass'n. Manual for the Practice of Int'l Trade Law Ch. 1.
(Ince and Glick, eds. 1984).*

PROCEDURE FOR CONDUCT OF AN INVESTIGATION UNDER § 337

An important provision of Section 337 is that the investigations must be carried out by the Commission under the terms of the Administrative Procedure Act. This provides that in conducting an investigation, parties are entitled to certain rights relating to equal access to information and are only permitted to communicate with decision-makers at the Commission in certain prescribed ways. These methods include conferences which are attended by all of the parties or written submissions which are circulated to all parties to the investigation. Each party also has a right to fully investigate the facts of the case. This is done by various discovery tools such as interrogatories, the taking of oral depositions and requests for documents. The facts gathered by the parties are presented at hearings before an Administrative Law Judge. Hearings provide an opportunity for parties to cross-examine witnesses as in a normal district court proceeding. However, unlike in federal courts, the rules of evidence are more relaxed and, for example, hearsay evidence can be admitted. Evidence admitted must merely be shown to be relevant, material and reliable.

One feature of the ITC investigations that makes them particularly attractive to domestic companies (and burdensome to accused importers) is that an investigation must be completed within one year. The amount of time which can be spent in discovery and trial is limited to approximately 7 months of this period. This one year statutory limit can be expanded by vote of the Commission only to a maximum of 18 months in more complicated cases. The ITC is therefore a preferable forum to a district court for those who want a quick disposition of a case. As the former Chief Administrative Law Judge at the ITC was fond of pointing out, § 337 hearings are "due process with dispatch". In cases involving temporary exclusion orders, all discovery and the hearing must be completed within three months from the date the notice of institution of the investigation is published.

A Section 337 investigation may be instituted based either upon a complaint filed with the Commission or by the Commission on its own

---

* © by Leslie Alan Glick, Partner in the law firm of Adduci, Dinan and Mastriani, Washington, D.C. Reprinted with permission.

motion. Most past complaints have been instituted by persons filing complaints with the Commission. The majority of the complaints which have been filed concerned allegations by U.S. industries that foreign companies were selling articles in the United States which infringed patents owned by the U.S. company involved. The Commission has found that patent infringement is an unfair method of competition or unfair act under the statute. There have also been some significant cases involving other types of unfair trade practices. The Commission has entertained cases based on misappropriation of trade secrets, the unauthorized use of trademarks, including common law trademarks, the passing off of goods, improper designations of origin and violation of copyrights. In addition, there have been various antitrust-type investigations which were based on allegations of pricing at levels which were lower than the foreign manufacturer's cost of production and attempted monopolization or monopolization of United States industries.

When a complaint is brought to the International Trade Commission, it is directed to a staff legal division, known as the Unfair Imports Investigation Division, or U.I.I.D., which preliminarily investigates the allegations of the complaint and determines whether it meets certain procedural rules set up by the Commission. U.I.I.D. employs approximately a dozen attorneys. The staff may attempt to contact the respondents named in order to determine whether information would be available from them during the investigation and to determine the factual basis of certain allegations in the complaint. During a 30–day period complaints are reviewed by the staff and recommendations are made to the Commission as to whether the complaint sufficiently meets the rules and presents a cause of action which should be considered by the Commission as a basis for an investigation.

* * *

In the past, the Commission has generally taken the position that Section 337 requires that if a complaint meets the requirements of its rules, it should be instituted. However, there has been some indication recently, perhaps due to the Commission's increased caseload, that the Commission may adopt a different interpretation of the statute. Under this interpretation, even complaints which meet the rules may not be instituted if there is a reason for the Commission to exercise some discretion. Such reasons may include a lack of staff resources to devote to the investigation, or a belief that the unfair act is not significant enough in terms of United States trade to spend public resources on an investigation. * * *

If the Commission determines that a Section 337 investigation should be instituted, a notice is published in the Federal Register and copies of the complaint are sent to those named as respondents in the investigation. At this point, the Commission assigns the investigation to an Administrative Law Judge, who will control the conduct of the investigation up through the time an initial determination as to violation is made by the Judge to the Commission.

* * *

The date of the publication of a Notice of Investigation in the Federal Register begins the one-year time limit for the Commission to complete its investigation. Respondents named in the investigation have 20 days in which to answer the complaint.

Discovery generally follows the Federal Rules of Civil Procedure. However, because of the short time limits involved in these investigations, the time for answering interrogatories, producing documents, and conducting depositions is very short. During this time, there may be one or more conferences with the Administrative Law Judge who attempts to control discovery by the parties, and handles various requests of the parties to gain additional information or to withhold information requested by an opposing party. * * *

The domestic company may have discovery problems because a great deal of the information needed to prove its case may be in foreign countries. This information may be difficult to obtain not only because of volume and distance, but also because some foreign governments do not make it easy for discovery, as known in the U.S., to take place. Although the Commission cannot force foreign companies to divulge information or documents in the same way it can compel the conduct of companies or persons located in the U.S., the Commission can impose sanctions for failure to provide information. Sanctions may include an inference or presumption that the information which the complainant could have obtained would be unfavorable to the respondent's position or even finding the case in favor of the complainant.

For a foreign company this discovery period can be extremely burdensome because of the short time limits and the difficulties of transporting large numbers of documents or persons around the world, and coordinating with its U.S. counsel to make certain that accurate information is compiled and presented to the Commission.

* * *

Once the period of discovery is closed, preparation begins for the trial-type hearing before the Administrative Law Judge (ALJ). Normally there is approximately one month between the close of discovery and the beginning of the hearing. A hearing may last from a day or two to several weeks. One of the longest hearings conducted at the ITC was approximately 13 weeks during which the daily in-hearing sessions lasted up to 12 hours and were often also held on weekends.

Following the termination of a hearing, the parties are allowed a short period of time, up to one month, to prepare final briefs, detailed findings of fact and conclusions of law for consideration by the Administrative Law Judge. The Judge has approximately 60 days in which to consider these documents and the evidence presented at the hearing to prepare an initial determination to the Commission.

* * *

Parties may take exception to the ALJ's determination by filing a petition for review with the Commission. The Commission, which acts as an appellate body, has set out specific criteria for review. These are: 1) whether a finding or conclusion of the Administrative Law Judge as to a material fact is clearly erroneous; 2) whether a legal conclusion is erroneous, without governing precedent rule or law, or constitutes an abuse of discretion; or 3) whether the determination is one affecting Commission policy. It may grant or deny such petitions and may also review the ALJ's initial determination on its own motion. If the Commission decides to review the determination it will specify the scope of review and the issues that will be considered, and will make provisions for the filing of briefs and for oral arguments if deemed appropriate. This is a relatively new procedure adopted to limit Commission review of the Judge's determination. Under previous rules, the Judge made a recommended determination that was automatically reviewed by the Commission. Now he or she makes an "initial determination" which becomes final if not ordered for review by the Commission. This tends to increase the authority of the ALJ and probably will benefit domestic complaints that want a final decision in the shortest amount of time.

* * *

Many of the investigations instituted never go to a hearing and are settled or terminated before a final decision by the Commission. Parties can initiate a variety of means during the course of the investigation to terminate it. For example, the parties to patent infringement actions often reach terms for the settlement of a case based on license of the patent. It is also possible that the respondents named in an investigation find that their sales in the U.S. market are not significant enough to justify the expense of fully defending an action. In such an event it is possible for them to agree to not import the product into the United States for the life of the patent and accept a consent order agreement. Actions can be disposed of in the pre-trial stage by motions to terminate based on settlements or by motions for summary determination when there are no material issues of fact in dispute.

* * *

Section 337 has proven to be an effective remedy for U.S. industries seeking protection of property rights. As of March 1984, 188 cases had been instituted. Of these, 43 resulted in findings of violation and orders were issued, 41 resulted in findings of no violation, 64 were settled or withdrawn, and the rest are still in progress. Thus, the Commission's record has been fairly even in deciding for and against domestic industries. In at least 5 cases the Commission found U.S. patents invalid. Commission decisions themselves do not have any *res judicata* effect on actions in a district court. However, although the situation has not yet arisen, if the CAFC [Court of Appeals, Federal Circuit] affirms a finding of invalidity in an ITC case, it could well prevent enforcement of the patent in the district courts.

IN RE CERTAIN PERSONAL COMPUTERS AND COMPONENTS THEREOF

United States International Trade Commission, 1984.
Inv. No. 337–TA–140.

On January 31, 1983, Apple Computer Inc. (Apple) filed a complaint with the Commission under section 337 of the Tariff Act of 1930 (19 U.S.C. § 1337). On the basis of that complaint, the Commission instituted this investigation on March 2, 1983. The notice of investigation defined its scope as the determination of whether there is a violation of section 337 in the importation of certain personal computers and components thereof into the United States, or in their sale, by reason of alleged:

(1) Infringement of the claims of U.S. Letters Patent 4,136,359;

(2) Infringement of the claims of U.S. Letters Patent 4,278,972;

(3) Direct or contributory infringement of U.S. Copyright Reg. No. TX 873–203 and U.S. Copyright Reg. No. TX 886–569;

(4) Misappropriation of trade dress;

the effect or tendency of which is to destroy or substantially injure an industry, efficiently and economically operated, in the United States.[a]

* * *

On January 20, 1984, the Commission determined to review the initial determination (ID) of the administrative law judge (ALJ) in *Certain Personal Computers and Components Thereof,* Inv. No. 337–TA–140. The

---

a. The following firms were named respondents in the notice of investigation: (1) Golden Formosa Microcomputer Co., Ltd. a/k/a Guan Haur Industrial Co. ("Guan Haur"), Taipei, Taiwan. (2) Sunrise Computer Service Co., Ltd. ("Sunrise"), Taipei, Taiwan. (3) Jardine Strauss International, Ltd. ("Jardine"), Taipei, Taiwan. (4) Fantastic Merchandise Inc. ("Fantastic"), Taipei, Taiwan. (5) A–Tek Enterprises Co., Ltd. ("A–Tek"), Taipei, Taiwan. (6) Leader Trading Co. ("Leader"), Kowloon, Hong Kong. (7) Fuji Trading Co. ("Fuji"), Kowloon, Hong Kong. (8) Reliant Engineering Co. ("Reliant"), Hong Kong. (9) STC Limited ("STC"), Taipei, Taiwan. (10) Yen Enterprises ("Yen"), Taipei, Taiwan. (11) Business Computer Alliance Systems Co., Ltd. ("Business Computer"), Taipei, Taiwan. (12) Microtronics, Singapore. (13) Taiwan Machine Trading Co. ("TMT"), Philadelphia, Pennsylvania. (14) North American Research Corp. ("NAR"), Arlington, Virginia. (15) J.E. Computer Co., Ltd. ("JEC"), Taipei, Taiwan. (16) Apollo Computer Co., Ltd. ("Apollo"), Taipei, Taiwan. (17) Oriental Investments Ltd. ("Oriental"), Zurich, Switzerland. (18) Collins International Trading Corp. ("Collins"), Encino, California. (19) Formula International, Inc. ("Formula"), Hawthorne, California. (20) Powtek Electronics Co., Ltd. ("Powtek"), Taipei, Taiwan. Of the respondents, only Collins and Guan Haur participated in the evidentiary hearing before the presiding officer (ALJ). The ALJ issued her initial determination (ID) on December 9, 1983, finding that there is a violation of section 337. Complainant Apple, respondents Collins and Guan Haur, and the Commission investigative attorney petitioned for review of the ID. That only two of the respondents participated in this proceeding illustrates the jurisdictional problems of Section 337 proceedings.

ALJ issued the ID on December 9, 1983, and determined that there was a violation of section 337 of the Tariff Act of 1930 * * *.

* * *

We concur with the ALJ that there is an "industry * * * in the United States," within the meaning of section 337, and that the industry is composed of those portions of Apple Computer Inc. devoted to Apple II and Apple III series personal computers.

The Commission has a longstanding practice of defining the domestic industry in terms of the involved intellectual property right. In this investigation, the patented and copyrighted elements are essential components of the personal computer. The Autostart ROM program, in particular, is an operating system program which is used every time the computer is used. In fact, the computer cannot be used without it. The article of commerce involved here is the complete personal computer. Thus, for the purposes of assessing injury under section 337, the industry should be defined in terms of such complete computers.

* * *

We concur with the ALJ that the infringing imports have a tendency to substantially injure the domestic industry. It is clear from the record that numerous respondents are attempting to sell, and are selling, infringing computers in the United States under circumstances that indicate they are likely to be successful. The record indicates that respondents also have a large capacity and can sell personal computers in the United States at a much lower price ($300–$700) than Apple's dealer price. Importantly, Apple's experience in the Far East market amply demonstrates its susceptibility to competition from low-priced infringing imports. Customs Service officials have testified that approximately 3,000 infringing computers, including a large number of respondents' computers, have been seized nationwide and that this number represents approximately 5–15 percent of the total number of infringing computers which had been imported into the United States. * * *

Given the price sensitivity of the market for computers and the substantially lower prices of imported computers compared with Apple's price, the predictable impact is large numbers of future lost sales. In this investigation, the record establishes that these lost sales will have a significant negative impact on the economic performance of the domestic industry.

We have determined that a general exclusion order is the appropriate remedy in this case. The large number of sources of infringing imports actually established, and the apparent existence of even more, fully justify a general exclusion order. The only question is the form of the order. Our order, by its express terms, excludes from entry personal computers and components which directly infringe the involved patents and copyrights. Further, since the record shows that imports having motherboards substantially similar to the Apple motherboards contributorily infringe or induce infringement of the involved patents and copyrights, such imports are included in our exclusion order subject to the presentation of a license.

It is the intent of this order to remedy the violation we have found to exist without disrupting lawful trade in personal computers and components thereof. To avoid evasion of our order, it excludes from entry ROMless computers and components which can be shown to be associated with imports of infringing ROMs or which are intended to receive infringing ROMs in the United States. Any beneficiary or any person adversely affected by this order may petition this Commission for a modification or clarification to ensure that its intent is achieved. The Commission may also modify or clarify the order on its own motion.[158]

We find that there are no public interest factors which would preclude the issuance of a general exclusion order in this case.

* * *

Collins argues that an exclusion order applicable to its Orange + Two computer would have an adverse effect on the public health and welfare because the public "would be deprived of access to a unique model personal computer which, at a retail price significantly lower than that of the Apple IIe, provides the double capabilities of a 6502 microprocessor capable of playing most Apple-compatible software and a Z–80 microprocessor that is compatible with CP/M–based software." There is nothing in the record of any public need for respondent's particular computer. It is clear that computers will be available at various price levels which can run these applications programs or other, equivalent programs.

Collins also argues that an exclusion order applicable to its Orange + Two computer would have an adverse effect on competitive conditions in the United States economy because it "would deprive the public of the well-established advantages of competition by leaving Apple more secure in its ability to command high premium prices within its 'niche' in the market place." However, the record shows that Apple has numerous foreign and domestic competitors besides the Collins Orange + Two. Whether these can run Apple-compatible software is not relevant since they can run other, equivalent software.

Collins argues that an exclusion order applicable to the Orange + Two computer would have an adverse effect on the production of like or

---

158. On February 2, 1984, and March 7, 1984, the Commission received letters from the U.S. Customs Service (Customs) regarding the inherent difficulties in enforcing an exclusion order in this investigation in view of Customs' limited resources. The letters stated that, at the time of importation, Customs "must attempt to identify * * * whether the printed circuitry of a computer or component is in violation of an Apple patent * * *" Customs further stated that this might entail an examination of every computer and component importation regardless of make, model, and type. Further "difficulties" were noted, but Customs stated that they would endeavor to enforce the order to the best of their ability. (February 2, 1984, letter from the Director, Office of Trade Operations to the Chairman and letter dated March 7, 1984, from the Assistant Commissioner, Office of Commercial Operations to the Chairman). As discussed above, we have concluded that an exclusion order is the only way to remedy the violation found to exist. Commissioner Haggart notes that Apple states that it will provide Customs with technical support necessary to enforce such an order. Complainant's Brief on Remedy, Bonding, and the Public Interest 5–9.

directly competitive articles in the United States. None of these arguments show that Apple's competitors which produce their computers in the United States will be affected by an exclusion order.

Collins argues that an exclusion order applicable to the Orange + Two computer would have an adverse effect on United States consumers because "consumers would be left without commercial recourse against Apple's unfair pricing practices." Again, it is clear that consumers have a variety of choices at varying prices which will not be affected by an exclusion order in this case.

Finally, we reject Collins' arguments with regard to monopolistic practices for the same reasons discussed above.

BONDING

We find that the bond should be set at 200 percent of the entered value of the products involved.

The bond provided for by 19 U.S.C. § 1337(g)(3) is a re-exportation bond requiring the re-exportation of the articles covered by this exclusion order which are entered during the Presidential review period provided for by 19 U.S.C. § 1337(g)(2). Entry of such articles during this period is only conditionally lawful, the condition being that the President disapprove the Commission's determination, thus rendering the determination and order of no force or effect. If this condition is not satisfied, the bond requires that the articles be re-exported, and if they are not, the penalty amount of the bond may be assessed * * *.

REAGAN DISAPPROVES ITC RULING IN "DURACELL BATTERY CASE" FOLLOWING TREASURY OBJECTION

2 BNA Int'l Trade Rptr. 69 (Jan. 9, 1985).*

In an unusual rejection of the agency's position, President Reagan on Jan. 4 disapproved the International Trade Commission's recent determination in the Duracell batteries case that the importation of gray market goods [a] violates Section 337 of the Tariff Act of 1930 (*In re Certain Alkaline Batteries,* Inv. No. 337–TA–165).

In October, the ITC, following a finding of a violation of Section 337, ordered excluded from entry into the United States imports of the batteries that were found to infringe a U.S. registered trademark and to misappropriate the trade dress of the batteries on which the trademark is used (1 ITR 482, Oct. 17, 1984).

In taking the action, the President resolved an apparent split within the Administration over whether the commission's determination in this important gray market case should be allowed to stand. Some agencies,

---

* Reprinted by permission from International Trade Reporter, copyright 1985 by The Bureau of National Affairs, Inc., Washington, D.C.

a. See Problem 9.2 covering gray market trade law.

including the U.S. Trade Representative's Office, reportedly wanted the order against the imports to go into effect. However, objections are understood to have been raised by the Treasury Department, which has taken the position—embodied in a longstanding Customs Service regulation—that U.S. trademark owners may not bar the importation of genuinely-marked goods made by foreign subsidiaries.

The President made reference to the department's position in a short statement on his action that was released by the White House. In that statement, Reagan asserted that the commission's interpretation of Section 42 of the Lanham Act, one of several grounds for the ITC's determination, "is at odds with the longstanding regulatory interpretation by the Department of the Treasury, which is responsible for administering the provisions of that section."

* * *

Reagan also noted that the Treasury and Commerce Departments, on behalf of the Cabinet Council on Commerce and Trade, have solicited data from the public concerning the issue of parallel market importation and are reviewing responses with a view toward formulating a cohesive policy in this area. "Failure to disapprove the Commission's determination could be viewed as a change in the current policy prior to the completion of this process," the President argued.

A spokesman for the ITC said the agency had no comment on the White House action. The commission has in prior instances reexamined those issues raised by the President in his statement of disapproval.

The ITC on Oct. 10 unanimously found violation of Section 337 in the case, and also voted 3–2 in favor of a general exclusion order, with Chairwoman Paula Stern and Commissioner David Rohr favoring a more limited order.

The agency rendered its decision after Administrative Law Judge Donald Duvall on July 10 issued an initial determination that there is a violation of the statute. In his decision, the ALJ found unauthorized importation into the United States and sale of certain alkaline batteries by reason of infringement of a registered trademark; misappropriation of trade dress; false designation of geographic origin; and failure to identify the quantity of the contents of the imported packages.

The case has attracted considerable attention within the trade bar because of the presence of the gray market issue, even though the batteries investigation differs in certain fundamental ways from the typical gray market case. In Duracell, for example, there was no dispute between authorized and unauthorized importers; and the company did not grant permission to any importer to sell Duracell batteries in the United States because Duracell sells only U.S.–made products in this country.

NEWMAN, THE AMENDMENTS TO SECTION 337: INCREASED PROTECTION FOR INTELLECTUAL PROPERTY RIGHTS

20 Law & Pol'y Int'l Bus. 571 (1989).*

Among the many changes to U.S. trade law wrought by the Omnibus Trade and Competitiveness Act of 1988 (1988 Trade Act, or Trade Act) were the long anticipated but relatively unpublicized amendments to section 337 of the Tariff Act of 1930 (1930 Tariff Act).

Prior to the amendments, section 337 of the 1930 Tariff Act prohibited unfair practices having the effect or tendency of destroying or substantially injuring an efficiently and economically operated U.S. industry, or monopolizing or restraining trade and commerce in the United States. The statute gave the U.S. International Trade Commission (the Commission) the authority to exclude articles from entry into the United States whose importation would injure a U.S. industry, or to order persons over whom it had jurisdiction to cease and desist from importing such articles. In the last 15 years, section 337 has been used primarily by U.S. patent holders to shield themselves against infringements by imported products.

The Trade Act's amendments to section 337 were the result of more than three years of consideration by Congress and the Reagan administration. The amendments reflect a concern that section 337 was becoming increasingly ineffective "in addressing the growing problems being faced by U.S. companies from the importation of articles which infringe U.S. intellectual property rights." In the statement of findings and purposes preceding the Trade Act's substantive amendment to section 337, Congress declared it was amending the statute "to make it a more effective remedy for the protection of United States intellectual property rights." Congress believed "the existing protection under section 337 of the Tariff Omnibus Trade Act of 1930 against unfair trade practices is cumbersome and costly and has not provided United States owners of intellectual property rights with adequate protection against foreign companies violating such rights."

At the time section 337 was originally enacted in 1922, the statute was aimed at a broad range of unfair acts not then covered by other unfair import laws. At that time it was not aimed specifically at imports infringing intellectual property rights. Yet, the drafters of the 1988 Trade Act, citing a Government Accounting Office study, noted that between 1974 and 1986 no less than 95 percent of the section 337 investigations initiated by the Commission involved statutory intellectual property rights. Accordingly, the Trade Act's amendments to section 337 were aimed at harmonizing the statute with the needs of its present principal users.

* * *

The Trade Act's amendments to section 337 respond to the Congressional concerns in three principal ways. First, section 1342(a)(1) of the Act eliminates the need to prove suffering or the threat of injury of any kind, for all complainants alleging that the imports at issue either infringe a valid and enforceable U.S. patent, registered copyright, registered trademark, registered mask work, or were made, produced, processed, or mined using a process covered by the claims of a valid and enforceable U.S. patent. Second, section 1342(a)(1)(A)(i) eliminates for all complainants the need to prove that they are "efficiently and economically operated," and requires, of those complainants alleging any of the intellectual property violations listed above, only a fairly minimal showing that they constitute a "domestic" industry in the United States. Third, section 1342(a)(3)(B) alters section 337's temporary relief proceedings, shortening the time for required completion, on the theory that an accelerated procedure would be more useful to complainants. Apart from these changes, the Trade Act contains a number of other amendments, essentially technical in nature, which are not controversial.

* * *

INJURY

Perhaps the Trade Act's biggest change to section 337, and the one pressed most vigorously by the proponents of reform, was the elimination of the injury requirement in investigations based upon certain intellectual property rights. Under amended section 337, complainants alleging the importation into the United States, the sale for importation, or the sale within the United States after importation, of certain articles are not required to prove any injury. Specifically, this includes articles that: (1) infringe a valid and enforceable U.S. patent; (2) infringe a valid and enforceable registered U.S. copyright; (3) are made, produced, processed, or mined under, or by means of, a process covered by the claims of a valid and enforceable U.S. patent; (4) infringe a valid and enforceable U.S. trademark registered under the Trademark * * * Act of 1946; or (5) are semiconductor chip products that infringe a mask work registered under chapter 9 of title 17, United States Code.

By not requiring proof of injury, complainants are spared the exercise, required under prior section 337 practice, of establishing substantial injury, the threat of substantial injury, or that they had been prevented from establishing an industry. Moreover, respondents were required to prove that it was the importation of the articles in question that caused or threatened to cause the complainant's injury or prevented its establishment as an industry. Although complainants were denied relief in only a few cases because of a failure to meet these requirements, it is estimated that over half of the total expenses in litigating section 337 cases were incurred in establishing the injury and other economic requirements. These expenses tended to make section 337 proceedings inaccessible to prospective complainants with small pocketbooks.

Although removed for intellectual property purposes, the injury requirement remains for complainants alleging any other type of unfair act or method of competition, including infringement of a common law trademark, theft of trade secrets, restraint of trade, or monopolization. This poses an interesting issue, since complainants have alleged in many past section 337 cases both intellectual property violations and other assorted unfair acts and methods of competition. The practice of alleging multiple causes of action under the new statute would require complainants to prove injury as to some but not all of its unfair acts, potentially adding to the expense and extending the scope of discovery. Therefore, complainants, having on the one hand an uncertain infringement or validity case, and on the other strong evidence regarding, for example, theft of trade secrets and interference with contract, must consider whether the need for the additional causes of action warrants the extra burden.

Without question, the deletion of the injury requirement in investigations based on intellectual property violations represents a great new advantage to complainants. But the potential remains for injury issues to resurface in the guise of development of the record on issues of remedy and the public interest. Under prior law, administrative law judges in the discovery and hearing phases of the investigation were permitted (but not required) to develop a record relating to remedy and public interest factors; under the Commission's interim rules, however, the practice appears to be encouraged. The invitation is explicit for temporary relief proceedings, where the pertinent interim rule provides that "[w]hile the motion for temporary relief is before the administrative law judge, he may compel discovery on matters relating to remedy, the public interest and bonding." The Commission implicitly encourages temporary relief for section 337 proceedings generally in its interim rule, which states that the administrative law judge shall set limitations on discovery as he sees fit, so long as consistent with the time limitations in temporary relief proceedings. If such extended discovery can be managed in more accelerated temporary relief proceedings, it certainly can fit into the relatively relaxed permanent relief cases. Respondents can be expected to push aggressively for such discovery, arguing that it is the only means of developing a full record on vital remedy and public interest issues.

INDUSTRY

Efficiency and Economy

Under the prior section 337, all complainants were required to prove they constituted or were part of an "efficiently and economically operated" domestic industry. Traditionally, complainants proved the element with evidence relating to the up-to-date nature of their facilities and the excellence of the working conditions of their employees, and respondents were singularly unsuccessful in stopping them. Therefore, in writing the efficiency and economy requirement out of the statute, Congress was in effect codifying actual practice. Accordingly, this particular amendment should create few ripples.

The "Domestic" Industry Requirement

The "domestic" industry requirement, on the other hand, has been significantly altered. Under the old practice, a complainant was required to show it had engaged in sufficient activity of a specific kind—generally, actual production—in the United States to be eligible for section 337 relief. The Commission, concerned that it would become the forum for battles between importers rather than the protector of U.S. interests, created elaborate tests for determining whether complainants qualified as a genuine "domestic" industry. In particular, the Commission was influenced by tangible production, manufacturing, quality control, and research and development activity, and was skeptical of mere marketing and sales efforts, licensing, and ownership of intellectual property.

The amendments to section 337 still require that the complainant have more than a tenuous connection with the United States, while at the same time steering away from rigid rules and allowing flexibility of proof. In so doing, section 337 now has two different standards, depending upon whether complainant is alleging (1) the type of intellectual property violation that excuses the need to prove injury, or (2) any other kind of unfair act or method of competition.

Amended section 337 provides that the Commission will grant relief for copyright, patent, trademark, or semiconductor violations "only if an industry in the United States, relating to the articles protected by the patent, copyright, trademark, or mask work concerned, exists or is in the process of being established." The statute also provides some guidance on how to determine whether an industry exists, explaining that:

> For purposes of paragraph (2), an industry in the United States shall be considered to exist if there is in the United States, with respect to the articles protected by the patent, copyright, trademark, or mask work concerned: A) significant investment in plant and equipment; B) significant employment of labor or capital; or C) substantial investment in its exploitation, including engineering, research and development, or licensing.

In its discussion of these factors, the House Report stresses, for section 337 cases grounded on intellectual property rights, that the domestic industry requirement is not to be interpreted in an "unduly narrow manner," and that actual production of the article in the U.S. is not required. Nevertheless, simple marketing and sales in the United States alone will not satisfy the domestic industry requirement. "Substantial investment" in the exploitation of the intellectual property right "could, however, encompass universities and other intellectual property owners who engage in extensive licensing of their rights to manufacturers."

However, both the statutory enumeration and the legislative history do not clearly explain when investment in plant or equipment is "significant," or when engineering, research, and development is "substantial" or "extensive." Further, the manner in which any of the above should be related to the intellectual property at issue, or at what point in time relative to the importation the activities should have occurred, is also unclear. Moreover, the "labor and capital" statutory language sounds very much like a test used by the Commission in one particular investigation, and was implicitly rejected in subsequent decisions. Because of these ambiguities, respondents can be expected, under the newly enacted law, to develop the same domestic industry issues developed under the prior law. For example, one can imagine a respondent attacking the standing of a complainant who at some time prior to bringing its section 337 case was engaged in fairly extensive licensing activities, but who, for at least a year prior to bringing his case, has performed little such work. Respondent would argue strongly that such complainant does not qualify for relief under the statutory test.

Regarding the statute's "in the process of being established" language, the House Report states the provision is intended to protect parties actively engaged in activities leading to the exploitation of the intellectual property—*e.g.*, application engineering, or design work—within a reasonable period of time, but not those who are no more than simple owners of the intellectual property and have limited contact with the United States. Again, there is elasticity here, providing an opening for respondents to defend themselves on grounds other than those strictly related to the intellectual property. Indeed, since the "in the process of being established" formulation is open-ended, the Commission presumably will need to have recourse to cases decided under prior law, addressing whether complainant had engaged in sufficient activities to qualify as an emerging industry whose establishment was prevented by the unfair imports.

Where the unfair act or method of competition is something other than the enumerated intellectual property violations, the amended section 337 simply states that unfair acts and methods of competition shall be unlawful where they threaten to destroy, substantially injure, or prevent the establishment of "an industry in the United States." Although the statute and legislative history are silent on this point, it is assumed that in such instances the domestic industry requirement is to be interpreted as under prior law.

In short, where a complainant seeks to enforce a right other than an enumerated intellectual property right, he will shoulder more of a burden in showing his presence in the United States than if he were alleging an intellectual property violation. The Trade Act thus creates a double standard: what is sufficient domestic activity for a U.S. patent-holder, for example, is inadequate for a company seeking to protect a trade secret. This is consistent with the general purpose of the section 337 amendments: to make the statute more accessible and readily useful to U.S. intellectual property owners.

Temporary Relief Proceedings

The 1988 Trade Act also made substantial changes to the temporary relief procedures found in section 337. However, it is here that the changes may not actually prove helpful to complainants. Under the prior law, the Commission was allowed to impose either a temporary exclusion order or a temporary cease and desist order where it determined that during the course of its section 337 investigation there was reason to believe that the statute was being violated. Yet, the statute's silence regarding deadlines for temporary relief proceedings and the Commission's rules effectively allowing it seven months from the initiation of the investigation to complete temporary relief proceedings made it possible in practice for temporary relief awards not to issue until the investigation was almost completed. By this time, the temporary relief was of relatively little use to complainant.

To address this problem, Congress amended section 337(e) so as to require the Commission to issue a determination regarding preliminary relief within 90 days (or within 150 days in more complicated investigations) of the institution of the investigation. The amendment also provides that in deciding whether to issue preliminary relief under section 337(e), the Commission is expected to use the standards and procedures employed by federal district courts in deciding whether to issue a preliminary injunction or temporary restraining order, and that the Commission may require the complainant to post a bond as a prerequisite to the issuance of preliminary relief.

* * *

In amending section 337, Congress sought to make investigation procedures less expensive and more accessible to U.S. intellectual property owners. Given that the great majority of recent section 337 cases has been based on alleged infringements of intellectual property rights, and that future complainants alleging such violations are now excused from proving injury or anything other than a fairly minimal showing of a presence in the United States, it is likely that the number of section 337 cases will increase and that generally those cases will be less complicated than their predecessors under prior law.

Under the amended section 337, the issues in an investigation of an intellectual property based complaint have been streamlined, to validity (and/or enforceability), infringement, a minimal U.S. presence, public interest, and remedy. Thus, the virtual disappearance of the injury and industry requirements may have the unintended effect of converting the Commission from a body with jurisdiction over international trade matters into an international patent court whose decisions may or may not have the same weight as those of the federal courts. Indeed, as a result of the section 337 amendments, the Commission and the federal courts now have overlapping jurisdiction over intellectual property issues, thus encouraging complainants to engage in duplicative litigation, turning to the federal courts if dissatisfied with the Commission, and vice-versa.

Despite these observations, section 337 has not been wholly eviscerated by the Trade Act's amendments. For although deletion of the injury and efficiency requirements and limitation of the domestic industry element will simplify proceedings, it can be expected that litigation of the "economic" issues in section 337 cases will survive to some extent in the ambiguities of the new "domestic" industry test and in issues relevant to remedy and public interest factors. Admittedly, Congress has expressed its concern that the injury and industry requirements not be reintroduced through the back door in the guise of public interest determinations. Nevertheless, one can still expect respondents to argue vigorously that where a complainant has yet to suffer demonstrable injury as a result of unfair imports, public interest factors (for example, consumer need for competing suppliers of the article in question) militate against relief such as, for example, an exclusion order. Additionally, it will still be necessary in cases where the imported article is a component of a larger product to address how to devise a remedy under such circumstances. Under prior law, the relevant facts could be explored in developing the record on injury.

* * *

QUESTIONS AND COMMENTS

1. Is there a violation of Section 337 in the FIZZER problem? How would you define the industry involved? Has it been injured and does that matter?

2. What defenses may be raised to a Section 337 complaint? Should it matter that ANTIAIDS is a miracle drug, but TETRACINE is not?

3. What relief may be had should a violation of Section 337 be found by the ITC in the FIZZER problem? How effective would a cease and desist order be? Who decides what relief, if any, will be granted?

4. How are exclusionary orders under Section 337 enforced? Why did the President deny such relief in the *Alkaline Batteries* case?

5. Why did the Customs Service express reservations in connection with enforcement of exclusionary relief in the *Personal Computers* decision? How can the beneficiary of such relief assist in making it truly effective?

6. When should general exclusionary orders be granted and why? What criteria should the ITC apply in determining the effect of exclusionary orders on "public health and welfare, competitive conditions in the United States economy, the production of like or directly competitive articles in the United States, and United States consumers?" *See* Section 1337(d) of the Tariff Act of 1930. Is it in the public interest to exclude Thai pharmaceuticals?

Are Section 337 orders likely to be more effective than Section 526 orders? See the problem on counterfeiting and gray market trading. Will information provided by foreign private investigators be needed to realize the benefits of a general exclusionary order?

7. Can importers of other foreign products constitute domestic industries for purposes of filing a Section 337 complaint? Compare Schaper Manu-

facturing Co. v. United States International Trade Commission, 717 F.2d 1368 (Fed.Cir.1983) (small amounts of research and development in connection with imported products insufficient to constitute domestic industry) with *In re Certain Cube Puzzles,* 337–TA–112, 4 BNA Int'l Trade Rep.Dec. 2102 (domestic Rubik's Cube industry existed in view of repair, packaging and significant value added in the United States).

8. Do Section 337 procedures create pressures to settle complaints? May temporary relief be granted pending FIZZER's Section 337 determinations? If so, what kind of temporary relief? *See* Sections 1337(e) and (f).

9. A 1989 decision by a GATT panel ruled that Section 337 violates the national treatment provisions of Article III:4 of the GATT. The panel was persuaded that imported goods are treated less favorably (i.e., more severely) under Section 337 in terms of patent infringement remedies than domestic goods which are remedied in the federal courts. The panel's decision was ultimately adopted by the GATT Council and the U.S. indicated that it would consider ways to reach compliance after the TRIPS accord was finalized. The Uruguay Round Agreements Act of 1994 did not alter the substance of Section 337 law. It did make procedural changes (such as allowance of counterclaims in Section 337 proceedings) intended to address the issue of an imbalance in patent infringement remedies. The federal district courts must stay infringement proceedings at the request of the respondent to the Section 337 action.

10. Patent-based Section 337 proceedings are multiplying. ITC decisions take about 12 to 15 months, versus three to five years for federal court lawsuits. General exclusion orders are typically sought. Hearings are held before one of four administrative law judges specializing in patent law, with final decisions taken by the ITC. Infringing products are excluded from importation during the appeals process. About one-fourth of all 337 proceedings find infringements. An increasing number of foreign owners of U.S. patents are invoking 337 procedures. About half of all such complaints are settled, often using cross-licensing among the parties.

In 2007, in a major decision, the ITC excluded the importation of cell phones containing Qualcomm microchips found to infringe Broadcom patents. Invocation of Section 337 in patent disputes will be influenced by the U.S. Supreme Court's ruling in *KSR International Co. v. Teleflex, Inc.* (April 30, 2007) where it unanimously held that a patent combining pre-existing elements is invalid if the combination is no "more than the predictable use of prior art elements according to their established functions" (obvious). Likewise, the Supreme Court's cautious consideration of business method process patents in *Bilski v. Kappos* (June 28, 2010) will influence Section 337 disputes.

11. Section 337 can also be used to obtain exclusionary orders based upon misappropriation abroad of trade secrets of U.S. companies. Such complaints are governed by federal common law (not state law). See *TianRui Group Co. v. International Trade Commission,* 661 F.3d 1322 (2011) (misappropriation in China from licensees of wheel production trade secrets of U.S. manufacturer).

PART B.   GLOBAL PROTECTION OF INTELLECTUAL PROPERTY

BELLO AND HOLMER, "SPECIAL 301": ITS REQUIREMENTS, IMPLEMENTATION AND SIGNIFICANCE

13 Fordham Int'l L.J. 259 (1989–90).*

On August 23, 1988, President Reagan signed into law the Omnibus Trade and Competitiveness Act of 1988 (the "1988 Trade Act"), including provisions facilitating the Uruguay Round multilateral trade negotiations and the so-called "Special 301." A key aim of the Uruguay Round, and the sole aim of Special 301, is to promote the adequate and effective protection of intellectual property rights in foreign countries. The Uruguay Round offers the opportunity to realize this goal through a multilateral agreement with the trading partners of the United States. Special 301, by contrast, is designed to use the credible threat of unilateral retaliation by the United States to "persuade" trading partners to reform currently deficient intellectual property practices.

* * *

While Special 301 compels the USTR to initiate Special 301 investigations of certain "priority foreign countries," it nevertheless affords the USTR substantial discretion in determining which foreign countries engage in actionable activities, which of such countries are priorities, whether a Special 301 investigation would be detrimental to U.S. economic interests, and what response to actionable activities, if any, is appropriate.

Special 301, like its counterpart, "Super 301," the controversial and more commonly known provision of the 1988 Trade Act, is designed to increase leverage for U.S. trade negotiators seeking to promote international trade liberalization. Super 301, however, requires the USTR to probe into a wider variety of unfair trade practices over a twelve- to eighteen-month period, in 1989 and in 1990 only. In contrast, Special 301 is a permanent feature of the 1988 Trade Act, lacking the two-year sunset provision embedded in Super 301. Moreover, Special 301 was devised solely to enhance the protection of intellectual property rights by foreign governments, and it demands that investigations be conducted on an expedited basis, faster than a normal section 301 investigation.

* * *

Rather than identifying countries as "priority foreign countries" under Special 301, the USTR created a "priority watch list" and a "watch list," naming countries that are particularly lax in their protection of intellectual property rights or that have imposed barriers to market access. The USTR placed Brazil, India, the Republic of Korea, Mexico, the People's Republic of China, Saudi Arabia, Taiwan, and Thailand on the priority watch list. Seventeen other countries were named to the watch list. The USTR stated that the decision was reached after consulting closely with key sectors of the business community that are affected by Special 301. The USTR added that the business community supported its decision.

Accelerated action plans were announced for each country on the priority watch list, and U.S. negotiators conducted intensified discussions with those countries until November 1, 1989. The USTR sought expeditious improvement in the protection of intellectual property rights and the prevention of piracy. The USTR announced that it would take remedial steps to alleviate any remaining problems if further progress was not made by November 1, 1989, taking into account the objectives identified by the Administration in its accelerated action plans and the U.S. proposals for intellectual property law protection in the Uruguay Round.

PRESIDENT CLINTON'S SUBMISSION TO CONGRESS OF DOCUMENTS CONCERNING URUGUAY ROUND AGREEMENTS (DEC. 15, 1993)

58 Fed.Reg. 67289 (Dec. 20, 1993).

TRADE–RELATED INTELLECTUAL PROPERTY RIGHTS

U.S. Objectives

The principle negotiating objectives of the United States with respect to trade-related intellectual property rights (TRIPs) were to:

- implement adequate standards for the protection of copyrights, patents, trademarks, semiconductor chip layout designs, trade secrets and to prohibit unfair competition,

- establish effective enforcement procedures internally and at the border, and

- implement effective dispute settlement procedures that improve on existing GATT procedures.

Results

The TRIPs agreement establishes improved standards for the protection of a full range of intellectual property rights and the enforcement of those standards both internally and at the border. The intellectual property rights covered by the agreement are: copyrights, patents, trademarks, industrial designs, trade secrets, integrated circuits (semiconductor chips) and geographical indications.

The TRIPs text is covered by the Dispute Settlement Understanding, thus ensuring application of the improved dispute settlement procedures, including the possibility of imposing trade sanctions, such as increasing tariffs, if another Member violates TRIPs obligations.

The TRIPs agreement achieves improved standards of protection in the areas of key interest to the United States. In the area of protection of geographic indications, the U.S. wine industry and trademark owners are safeguarded and we will simply make permanent existing regulations.

The agreement also includes strong enforcement provisions that are critical to obtaining effective enforcement of the agreed standards. Members must also enforce copyrights and trademarks at their borders against counterfeiting and piracy.

Key Provisions

Copyrights: The text resolves some key trade problems for U.S. software, motion picture and recording interests by:

- protecting *computer programs* as literary works and *databases* as compilations under copyright;

- imposing an *obligation* on Members to grant owners of computer programs and sound recordings the right to authorize or prohibit the *rental* of their products;

- establishing a term of *50 years for the protection of sound recordings* as well as requiring Members to provide protection for existing sound recordings; and

- setting a minimum term of 50 years for the protection of motion pictures and other works where companies may be the author.

The Agreement also obligates Members to comply with the provisions of the Berne Convention, the preeminent international copyright treaty, with the exception of that Convention's requirements on moral rights.

Patents: The Agreement resolves long-standing trade irritants for U.S. patent interests, especially pharmaceutical and agricultural chemical companies. Key benefits provided under the Agreement are:

- *product and process* patents for virtually all types of inventions, including pharmaceuticals and agricultural chemicals;

- meaningful limitations on the ability to impose *compulsory licensing;*

- a *patent term of 20 years* from the date the application is filed; and

- prompt implementation of procedures to permit the filing of patent applications covering pharmaceuticals and agricultural chemicals upon the entry into force of the agreement.

Trademarks: The Agreement:

- requires Parties to register *service marks* in addition to trademarks;

- enhances protection for *internationally well-known marks;*

- prohibits the mandatory linking of trademarks;

- prohibits the compulsory licensing of marks.

Other Protections: The Agreement also provides rules for protecting:

- *trade secrets* which enable owners to prevent unauthorized use or disclosure of confidential information;

- *integrated circuits* that eliminate the deficiencies of the Washington Treaty;

- *industrial designs* consistent with existing U.S. laws; and

- non-generic *geographical indications* used to identify wines and spirits.

Finally, the Agreement contains obligations to provide effective *enforcement* for these intellectual property rights, both internally and at the border (including safeguards to prevent abuses), and specific provisions on *injunctions, damages and obtaining evidence.*

PECHMAN, SEEKING MULTILATERAL PROTECTION FOR INTELLECTUAL PROPERTY: THE UNITED STATES "TRIPs" OVER SPECIAL 301

7 Minn. J. Global Trade 179 (1998).*

Although TRIPs represents a major step forward in international intellectual property agreements, two major problems threaten its effectiveness for the United States. First, from the perspective of a developed country like the United States, TRIPs is overly conciliatory to developing countries. The Agreement over-emphasizes the special needs of developing countries that must now generate or improve protection for intellectual property. The second concern is best phrased as a question: how will a "young and still untested international organization like the WTO ... hope to manage the complexities of the TRIPs Agreement ... when so many of its constituent members lack the legal infrastructure, technical skills, and philosophic commitment to make it work[?]" Such concerns are heightened by the recognition that the WTO has little or no expertise in governing the complex trade issues involved with intellectual property.

TRIPs CONCESSIONS TO DEVELOPING COUNTRIES

As noted above, one major downfall of TRIPs from the point of view of the United States is the number of concessions granted to developing countries. The conflict over the difference in scope of intellectual property protection afforded by developed and developing countries, and the extent to which TRIPs preserves this difference, poses significant obstacles.

As one major concession, TRIPs allows extended transition periods for developing countries to comply with the minimum standards. Articles 65 to 67 of TRIPs define these grace periods. The earliest a Member country could be held to the obligations under TRIPs was January 1, 1996, or one year after the WTO Agreement came into force. For developing countries,

---

* © 1998 Minnesota Journal of Global Trade, Inc. and Robert Pechman. Reprinted with permission.

the transition period extends to January 1, 2000. In addition, any Member country in the process of transforming to a market economy enjoys the same grace period allowed for developing countries. In terms of patent protection, developing countries are allowed five years beyond the standard grace period to recognize the patentability of inventions in technology areas previously not afforded protection. Finally, less-developed countries may also take advantage of a ten year transition period, with the possibility of further extensions, from the date the WTO Agreement came into force in which to comply with the substantive standards of TRIPs.

Many consider these transition periods to be excessive. It is speculated that, rather than using these periods to develop meaningful intellectual property protection in compliance with TRIPs, some developing countries will exploit the grace periods by stepping-up already thriving pirating industries. Indeed, transitional periods for developing countries are more likely to delay the growth of third-world economies by inhibiting their integration into the world market instead of encouraging their assimilation through the recognition of the rights of intellectual property owners. Developing countries tend to resist strengthening intellectual property protection because of the fear that in so doing they will compromise any competitive advantage they have over developed countries. Thus, developing countries may consider the grace periods an opportunity to exploit their competitive advantages by encouraging pirating efforts, while more powerful countries remain obligated to honor TRIPs.

TRIPs does, however, contain a provision to encourage and facilitate the implementation of its substantive standards in developing countries by obligating developed countries to provide, upon request, technical and financial assistance regarding the drafting of regulations and the establishment of agencies for enforcement. Although this provision is undoubtedly aimed at accelerating developing countries' compliance, it does not address the potential exploitation of grace periods through increased pirating efforts.

The second major concession to developing countries emanates from the public policy exceptions to patentability allowed under Article 27:

> Members may exclude from patentability inventions, the prevention within their territory of the commercial exploitation of which is necessary to protect *ordre public* or morality, including to protect human, animal or plant life or health or to avoid serious prejudice to the environment, provided that such exclusion is not made merely because the exploitation is prohibited by domestic law.

The "escape clause" of Article 27 "arms the developing countries with grounds for excluding from patentability important technology areas such as pharmaceuticals, chemicals, agro-chemicals, computers, and electronics simply on the pretense of public policy." It is likely that this escape clause will be easily invoked by developing countries, because patenting such subject matter is per se against public policy in many developing countries. Although developed as well as developing countries may invoke this broad escape clause, it stands to reason that countries that have historically had less patent protection are more likely to voice objections to patenting inventions in certain areas of technology than developed countries that complied with the substantive standards of TRIPs before they acceded to the Agreement. Developed countries like the United States already comply with the patentable subject matter provisions of TRIPs and have long outgrown many of their policy-development growing pains. On the other hand, developing countries such as India have deeply-rooted objections to patenting products like pharmaceuticals.

In addition, as discussed above, TRIPs ultimately relies on each individual Member for implementation. Although this preserves national sovereignty for all Members, it primarily benefits those countries with minimal existing intellectual property protection. Generally, the laws of developed areas such as the United States, Japan, Canada, and the European Union already embody the intellectual property protections sought under TRIPs. Consequently, the majority of the problems likely to arise will concern whether the ultimate implementation of intellectual property protection in developing countries fulfills TRIPs obligations. Without adequate implementation, the United States will not attain its goal of externalizing its strong intellectual property protection through TRIPs.

While concessions to developing countries may have been necessary both to gain their accession to the TRIPs Agreement and to ensure their ultimate compliance, it is doubtful that the concessions given will provide the necessary incentives for developing countries to meet the TRIPs standards as soon as possible. It is more likely that developing countries will attempt to use these concessions to expand pirating efforts and retain every competitive advantage possible.

* * *

USE OF SPECIAL 301 TO SUPPLEMENT TRIPS

The Special 301 process may be used as a means to monitor trading partners with respect to their compliance with TRIPs. In this manner, the Special 301 process could be used to accelerate the conformity of developing countries with TRIPs during their transition periods. It may also be used to identify nonconforming developed countries and to initiate WTO dispute settlement proceedings. The United States may, in any case, continue to use Special 301 against GATT non-Members.

The first scenario in which the United States may justify its continued use of Special 301 is to encourage developing countries, and those countries moving towards a free market economy, to comply as quickly as possible with TRIPs standards. Because the grace periods granted to these Members may be exploited by increased piracy or grace period extensions, the United States will attempt to force developing countries to comply with TRIPs as soon as possible by threatening Special 301-type sanctions. The Brazil pharmaceuticals case is an early indication of the efficacy of such a plan. Due to continued threats of retaliation under Special 301, Brazil ultimately agreed to immediate implementation of TRIPs standards without regard to the transition period it was allowed as a developing country.

Despite this apparent success, some scholars warn that the potency of Special 301 will be diminished during the phase-in period for developing countries, and thus Special 301 will have little utility in coercing Members to accelerate their compliance. This view is premised on the opinion that the emergence of TRIPs will heighten the effectiveness of Special 301 only when used in conjunction with the WTO dispute settlement process. This would render Special 301 all but useless against developing countries, which have no obligation to comply with TRIPs during their transition periods.

Another use of Special 301 review is to monitor other Members' degree of compliance with TRIPs. "Participating in the Special 301 review allows [U.S. intellectual property rights holders to file complaints with] the USTR in a unique forum that addresses current international trade issues and gives [them] a chance to influence economic policy in line with [their] business interests." The review system relies on information provided by domestic businesses, producers and organizations that possess an intimate familiarity with any inadequacies in the intellectual property protection provided by foreign countries. Using this information, the United States can more efficiently monitor questionable trade practices and engage offending countries in consultations on a regular basis. Special 301, as it stands today, requires that the USTR monitor the protection of intellectual property provided by other countries and bring disputes that arise to the WTO dispute settlement process when a country violates U.S. rights under TRIPs.

It is also argued that Special 301 will be more efficient when used in conjunction with TRIPs because the minimum substantive standards provided by TRIPs serve as a uniform target for compliance. The utility of TRIPs in a Special 301 action is that it provides a baseline of intellectual property protection that Special 301 by itself lacks. For instance, in the Brazil pharmaceuticals case, the United States withdrew sanctions and threats of sanctions as soon as Brazil promised to change its laws because the United States had no benchmark standards which it could reasonably expect Brazil to meet. If a similar case arose today, the trigger for lifting sanctions would not be promises, but rather compliance with TRIPs. Thus, it is posited that the United States will no longer need to use Special 301 as a way to unilaterally force other countries to provide intellectual property protection, but only as a method of encouraging compliance with TRIPs, and perhaps as a method of providing additional protection above and beyond the scope of TRIPs. It should be noted that the United States announced its intention to use Special 301 not only as a method to ensure full participation in the DSU and compliance with TRIPs, but also to secure the continued development of intellectual property protection in nations that are not Members of the WTO Agreements. . . .

USTR SPECIAL 301 REPORT

April, 2011.

2011 Special 301 List

The 2011 Special 301 review process examined IPR protection and enforcement in 77 trading partners. Following extensive research and analysis, USTR has listed the 42 trading partners below as follows:

> Priority Watch List: Algeria, Argentina, Canada, Chile, China, India, Israel, Indonesia, Pakistan, Russia, Thailand, Venezuela.

> Watch List: Belarus, Bolivia, Brazil, Brunei, Colombia, Costa Rica, Dominican Republic, Ecuador, Egypt, Finland, Greece, Guatemala, Italy, Jamaica, Kuwait, Lebanon, Malaysia, Mexico, Norway, Peru, Philippines, Romania, Spain, Tajikistan, Turkey, Turkmenistan, Ukraine, Uzbekistan, Vietnam.

> Section 306 Monitoring: Paraguay.

* * *

Initiative for Special 301 Action Plans

The United States develops action plans and similar programs to address IPR issues in various contexts, including the Special 301 process. These plans and programs establish benchmarks, such as legislative, policy, or regulatory action by which to measure progress. Additionally, these plans can serve as tools to encourage U.S. trading partners to make improvements to their IPR regimes, thereby increasing the likelihood that they may be removed from the Special 301 list.

As called for in the Administration's 2010 Joint Strategic Plan on IPR Enforcement, USTR, in coordination with the Intellectual Property Enforcement Coordinator (IPEC), initiated an interagency process to increase the effectiveness of, and strengthen implementation of Special 301 action plans. As a result of that process, **USTR is announcing that it invites any trading partner appearing on the Special 301 Priority Watch List or Watch List to work with the United States to develop a mutually agreed action plan designed to lead to that trading partner's removal from the relevant list**. Agreement on such a plan will not by itself change a trading partner's status in the Special 301 Report. However, in the past, successful completion of action plans has led to the removal of trading partners such as Saudi Arabia, Taiwan, and many others from Special 301 lists. An action plan may take more than one year to complete. Action plans differ from OCRs, which are conducted between Special 301 annual reports.

Positive Developments

The United States welcomes the following important steps by our trading partners in 2010 and early 2011:

- **Australia, Canada, the European Union (EU) and its Member States, Japan, Korea, Mexico, Morocco, New Zealand, Singapore, Switzerland**—These trading partners, along with the United States, worked cooperatively to finalize the text of the Anti-Counterfeiting Trade Agreement—an important new tool to fight trademark counterfeiting and copyright piracy.

- **Mexico**—Mexico enacted legislation granting *ex officio* authority to its law enforcement officials to initiate criminal investigations against trademark counterfeiting and copyright piracy without requiring the rights holder to first file a complaint.

- **Philippines**—The Philippines enacted legislation to address unauthorized camcording of motion pictures in theaters.

- **Russia**—Russia enacted four pieces of 1PR legislation, which complete the legislative commitments it made in the 2006 Bilateral Agreement on Protection and Enforcement of Intellectual Property Rights. These measures are: (1) amendments to Part IV of the Civil Code (governing intellectual property generally); (2) enactment of the Federal Law on Customs Regulation granting *ex officio* authority to customs officials; (3) amendments to the Law on Activity Licensing, which ensures that infringers cannot renew optical media production licenses; and (4) amendments to the Law on Circulation of Medicines to protect undisclosed test or other undisclosed data generated to obtain marketing approval.

- **Spain**—Spain took action to address the problem of copyright piracy over the Internet by passing legislation that will provide a mechanism for rights holders to remove or block access to infringing content online.

The United States will continue to work with its trading partners to further enhance IPR protection and enforcement during the coming year.

Initiatives to Strengthen IPR Protection and Enforcement Internationally

The United States has worked to promote adequate and effective protection and enforcement of IPR through a variety of mechanisms, including the following initiatives:

- **Anti–Counterfeiting Trade Agreement (ACTA):** The ACTA negotiations, which concluded in November 2010, reflect a commitment by the negotiating parties not only to have strong laws on the books, but also to pursue the international cooperation and meaningful enforcement practices necessary to make intellectual property protection effective. ACTA will be the first agreement of its kind to both require strong enforcement provisions and promote the cooperation and key practices that make these provisions effective, raising international standards for the enforcement of IPR.

* * *

OFFICE OF THE UNITED STATES TRADE REPRESENTATIVE

Out-of-Cycle Review of Notorious Markets.
February 28, 2011.

Global piracy and counterfeiting continue to thrive due in part to marketplaces that deal in infringing goods. The Notorious Markets List identifies selected markets, including those on the Internet, which exemplify the problem of marketplaces dealing in infringing goods and helping to sustain global piracy and counterfeiting. These are marketplaces that have been the subject of enforcement action or that may merit further investigation for possible intellectual property rights infringements.

The Notorious Markets List, previously included in the annual Special 301 Report, will now be published separately. This reflects an effort to further expose these markets, and is in response to the Intellectual Property Enforcement Coordinator's 2010 Joint Strategic Plan on Intellectual Property Enforcement. This document is the result of an Out-of-Cycle Review of Notorious Markets and follows a separate, dedicated request for comments from interested stakeholders which was initiated on October 1, 2010.

The Notorious Markets List does not purport to reflect findings of legal violations, nor does it reflect the United States Government's analysis of the general climate of protection and enforcement of intellectual property rights in the countries concerned. That broader analysis of IPR protection and enforcement is contained in the annual Special 301 report, published at the end of April every year.

* * *

Pay-per-download

These sites exemplify the problem of online sales of pirated music on a pay-per-download basis.

Allofmp3 clones: While the Russia-based allofmp3 (formerly the world's largest server-based pirate music website) was shut down in 2007, nearly identical sites have taken its place.

Linking

These are online services engaged in "deep linking" to allegedly infringing materials, often stored on third-party hosting sites.

Baidu: Baidu recently ranked as the number one most visited site in China, and among the top ten in the world. [Removed from list in 2012]

B2B and B2C

Business-to-business (B2B) and business-to-consumer (B2C) websites have been cited by industry as offering a wide range of infringing products (such as cigarettes, clothing, manufactured goods, pharmaceutical products and sporting goods) to consumers and businesses while maintaining intellectual property policies that are inconsistent with industry norms.

> **Taobao**: While recognizing that Taobao is making significant efforts to address the availability of infringing goods through its website, it still has a long way to go in order to resolve those problems. Taobao recently ranked in the 15 most visited sites in the world, and in the five most visited sites in China.

BitTorrent indexing

BitTorrent indexing sites can be used for the high speed location and downloading of allegedly infringing materials from other users. The sites identified below illustrate the extent to which some BitTorrent indexing sites have become notorious hubs for infringing activities, even though such sites may also be used for lawful purposes.

> **ThePirateBay**: ThePirateBay recently ranked among the top 100 websites in both global and U.S. traffic, and has been the target of a notable criminal prosecution in Sweden.
>
> **IsoHunt**: Canada-based IsoHunt, which has been subject of civil litigation in both Canada and the U.S., recently ranked among the top 300 websites in global traffic and among the top 600 in U.S. traffic.
>
> **Btjunkie**: This site is among the largest and most popular aggregators of public and non-public "torrents," which find and initiate the downloading process for a particular file.
>
> **Kickasstorrents**: Another popular indexing site, notable for its commercial look and feel.
>
> **torrentz.com**: This site is a major aggregator of torrents from other BitTorrent sites.

BitTorrent trackers

BitTorrent tracker sites can also be used for the transfer of allegedly infringing material by directing users to those peers sharing the infringing content. The sites listed below exemplify how some BitTorrent tracking sites have become notorious for infringing activities, even though such sites may also be used for lawful purposes.

> **Rutracker**: Russia-based Rutracker recently ranked among that country's 15 most visited sites, and among the 300 most visited sites in the world.
>
> **Demonoid**: Ukraine-hosted Demonoid recently ranked among the top 600 websites in global traffic and the top 300 in U.S. traffic.
>
> **Publicbt**: This site is one of the most popular BitTorrent trackers with over 30 million users worldwide.

openbittorrent: This site ranks among the most widely used BitTorrent trackers in the world.

zamunda: Bulgarian-based zamunda is currently the target of a noteworthy criminal prosecution.

Other web services

Other internet-based services, such as social media sites or cyberlockers, are widely used for lawful purposes. However, some may facilitate unauthorized access to allegedly infringing materials.

vKontakte: The site, which permits users to provide access to allegedly infringing materials, recently ranked among the five most visited sites in Russia and among the 40 most visited sites in the world.

Live sports telecast piracy

Live sports telecast piracy affects amateur and professional sports leagues by making these protected telecasts and broadcasts freely available on the Internet.

TV Ants: This peer-to-peer service, which reportedly operates from China, exemplifies this problem.

Smartphone software

A number of websites are making Smartphone software applications available to the public without compensating rights holders.

91.com: This site is reportedly responsible for more than half of all downloaded applications in China.

QUESTIONS AND COMMENTS

1. What chance does FIZZER have of persuading the USTR to prioritize Thai pharmaceutical policy under the Special 301 procedures? Would designation as a "notorious market" help? Suppose Thailand has met all its TRIPs obligations. Would that keep it from being prioritized under Section 301? See Section 182(d)(4) of the Trade Act of 1974. What will happen if FIZZER succeeds in getting Thai pharmaceutical policy prioritized?

Are "watch lists" or "priority watch lists" contemplated by the Special 301 legislation? What is the significance of their use by the USTR? To FIZZER?

2. What are its prospects for Section 301 relief? Does TRIPs diminish the potential for Section 301 relief? Take a good look at Sections 301(d)(3)(B)(i)(II) and 301(d)(3)(F)(i) of the Trade Act of 1974 and Pechman's analysis.

3. President Clinton submitted that the TRIPs establishes "improved standards" for intellectual property protection and "meaningful limitations" on compulsory licensing. Would FIZZER agree? Would Thailand?

4. On what grounds might Thailand argue that its compulsory licensing of ANTIAIDS is justifiable under TRIPs? See Articles 30 and 31. Could Thailand revert to its former policy of no pharmaceutical patents? See Article

27 and Pechman's analysis. Is the Thai law providing for compulsory licensing for want of local "use" permissible under TRIPs? See Article 27(1). The United States withdrew in 2001 amidst the AIDS controversy a TRIPS complaint against a comparable Brazilian law. Recently, Thailand has issued compulsory licenses on a range of cancer, heart disease and AIDS drugs, all in the name of public health emergencies. Are those licenses legal under TRIPs? What about a compulsory license on TETRACINE?

5. A number of legislative provisions indicate that the United States is pursuing an aggressive international role in protecting intellectual property rights. Benefits under the Caribbean Basin Economic Recovery Act of 1983 are conditioned upon Caribbean countries not taking steps to repudiate or nullify any patent, trademark or other intellectual property of a United States citizen and not broadcasting copyrighted works of United States owners without express consent. The grant of U.S. generalized tariff preferences (GSP) is also conditioned, by Title IV of the 1974 Trade Act, upon adequate arrangements for the protection of the intellectual property rights of United States nationals. Section 301 proceedings under the Trade Act seeking retaliatory action against unfair trade practices of foreign nations may be based on intellectual property issues.

Are any of these provisions likely to help FIZZER? Which of these provisions might be particularly useful in dealing with "piracy havens" around the world and why? How should the United States seek to get other countries to improve their protection of intellectual property rights?

6. The AIDS epidemic has sharpened the debate about pharmaceutical patents. The Doha Round of WTO negotiations were launched in 2001 amid renewed declarations that TRIPs does not prevent members from protecting public health, "in particular, to promote access to medicines for all." In this problem, Thailand invokes compulsory licensing in the context of a flourishing "generics" pharmaceutical industry. What about the many developing nations, say in Africa, that do not have the capacity to make ANTIAIDS? Is compulsory licensing of any relevance to them?

7. In August of 2003, a Medicines Agreement was reached within the WTO. This Agreement operates presently as an "Interim Waiver" from the TRIPs rules. Under it, compulsory licenses may be used by developing nations to override pharmaceutical patent rights for purposes of local manufacture *or* importation of generic copies. To prevent such pharmaceuticals from being diverted to developed country markets, the Medicines Agreement commits WTO members not to use compulsory licenses to pursue industrial and commercial policy objectives, to take reasonable labeling, marking and other steps to prevent such diversions, and to notify and allow review of complaints expeditiously within the TRIPs Council. Canada and the European Union have established procedures for generic exports.

Suppose developing nations import cheap, good quality generic drugs from Thailand, or the major producer in the AIDS field, India. Does TRIPs affect this trade? For your information, India was obliged by TRIPs to start granting pharmaceutical patents in 2005. But new versions of older drugs must be "more efficacious" to qualify for Indian patents. Is this requirement permissible under TRIPs? See Article 27(1) in the Documents Supplement.

PROBLEM 9.4   PATENT AND KNOWHOW LICENSING: OIL DRILLING BITS IN GERMANY AND MEXICO

SECTION I.   THE SETTING

Drill-Bit Manufacturing Company, Inc., is a Delaware corporation. It was formed in 1949 to manufacture drilling cutting bits for oil rigs for the United States market. The company has grown steadily. The success of the company is attributable largely to one of the founders, who designed and patented several styles of drilling bits. Drill-Bit now has a modest share of the market in the United States. But since its product is of such exceptional quality, it has a larger share of the high quality end of the market.

In the 1950's, the company began to receive orders for its products from abroad, principally from European companies operating oil projects in the Middle East, and occasionally from oil companies with enterprises in Latin America. After several nations nationalized petroleum exploration and production, the company continued its sales to the new government owned petroleum companies.

The company has only limited experience in dealing with third world nations. It occasionally has sold its products to petroleum enterprises in several Latin American nations. Because the drilling bits are high on the priority list of imports of these nations, the purchasers have had little difficulty receiving necessary import permits. These sales generally have been satisfactory, although in several instances temporary shortages of hard currency and exchange controls have led to delayed payments. Local officials frequently have urged the company to establish local manufacturing facilities.

MEXICO

In the mid-1970's orders from the Mexican national petroleum enterprise, PEMEX, increased very substantially. This coincided with the discovery of large petroleum reserves in several locations in Mexico, and a consequent rapid expansion by the Mexican government of oil production. Mexican sales in 1980 constituted some 60 percent of Drill-Bit's exports, and the board of directors decided in 1982 that it should thoroughly explore the licensing of its knowhow and patents to a manufacturing facility in Mexico for the production of drilling bits. Drill–Bit undertook an extensive review of the Mexican laws affecting the transfer of technology which would affect a licensing agreement. But after reviewing the strict 1972 Transfer of Technology Law, amended during Drill–Bit's review process in early 1982, the company decided that the law was too restrictive to conclude a satisfactory agreement. Drill–Bit was concerned with the need to have the agreement approved by the Mexican government. Drill–Bit did go to the extent of finding a quite satisfactory Mexican partner which would be the licensee, but when the parties initially discussed the proposed agreement (much like the agreement below), Drill–Bit thought the Mexican agency was too strict in its interpretation of the law. The result was Drill–Bit backed off from the agreement, and continued as previously to sell its products directly to Mexican users by documentary sales with letters of credit.

In late 1991 Drill–Bit began to rethink its business in Mexico, particularly in view of the repeal of the 1972 Transfer of Technology Law and the adoption of a new Industrial Property Law in 1991. In fact Drill–Bit was so impressed with the changes in Mexico that it decided to establish a subsidiary in Mexico.

The president of Drill–Bit has asked you to keep track of the technology rules in Mexico. Even though the company is planning a direct foreign investment to establish a wholly owned subsidiary in Mexico under NAFTA, Drill–Bit will have to transfer the technology to the subsidiary, and thus a transfer of technology agreement will be needed. The president at this time would like to know how the Mexican 1991 Industrial Property Law is affected by Mexico's obligations under NAFTA and TRIPs. Is registration required? Does a government agency have to approve the agreement? Are there restrictions on grant-back provisions, territorial restrictions, amount of royalty paid for the technology, choice of law and forum provisions, etc.

GERMANY

Drill–Bit has now turned to licensing production in Germany, to sell principally to the Middle East. Drill–Bit assumed it would confront none of the restrictive measures it found present in the 1970s and 1980s in Mexico. Drill–Bit is concerned with protecting its patent rights and knowhow; its advanced technology has always been a basis for its success. Maintaining quality control is essential. The company is well aware that its success is partially the result of the infrequency of complaints regarding the quality of its products.

Drill–Bit knew of a highly regarded company, NordMetall, G.m.b.H., in Hamburg. Company officers visited the plant and discussed a licensing agreement with the company officials. Hans von Ebke, the director of NordMetall, said he was aware of the quality of Drill–Bit products over the years from talking to Drill–Bit's German competitors, and that Nord-Metall would be delighted to negotiate a licensing agreement.

You are in charge of Drill–Bit's law department and have the task of negotiating and concluding the agreement with NordMetall. One concern you have is the fact that Germany is part of the European Union and you want to be certain that the agreement does not conflict with any European law. You were quite surprised when you called NordMetall's chief legal officer, and were told that the European Union has adopted Regulations on transfer of technology agreements. Just when Mexico had nearly eliminated restrictions, the Europeans were advancing them. All of a sudden the president's questions regarding Mexican law are echoing in Germany.

Although Drill-Bit has been pleased with its sales to Europe and the Middle East, the market has such growth potential that a more extensive commitment is called for. There are also recurring problems with exports to the Middle East from the United States, and Drill–Bit feels that market will favor products from Germany. Drill-Bit has found an enterprise in Germany which can produce its products under a licensing agreement. That agreement will allow the German enterprise NordMetall to have access to the technology of Drill-Bit, and Drill–Bit will obviously be very insistent that the agreement protects the company's property, and that it does not result in the creation of a competitor. That concern *might* be avoided by forming a subsidiary in Germany (as it plans to do in Mexico) wholly owned by Drill-Bit. Then it would transfer the technology to manufacture the drilling bits to its own entity, thus granting it more assurance of protection. For the time being, however, Drill-Bit will move into Germany cautiously, and seek a transfer of its technology by way of a licensing agreement.

SECTION II. FOCUS OF CONSIDERATION

Patent and knowhow licensing are the primary vehicles for lawful technology transfers across borders. An overview of knowhow, patent protection and international recognition of patents was presented at the opening of this chapter. This material should be revisited before commencing this problem.

Part A concentrates on the appropriateness of the draft agreement between Drill Bit and NordMetall. This focus leads us into European case and regulatory law governing technology transfers. Our questions are very specific. Clause by clause, will this agreement pass muster? Part A may be approached from the perspective of counsel for Drill-Bit, counsel for NordMetall, or a staff member of the European Commission (after the agreement was brought to the attention of the Commission by complaint that it is inconsistent with the Regulation 772/2004).

Part B looks at Mexican, NAFTA and TRIPs law on patents, knowhow and licensing. Past and present Mexican law are quite different. NAFTA and TRIPs add to and cement the changes in Mexican law. They also give us a broader view of global trends and issues in the technology transfer field.

Chapter 17 of NAFTA and the TRIPs agreement are essential to an analysis of this problem. These materials are found in the Documents Supplement. Be sure, also, to re-read Article 81 of the Treaty establishing the European Community, reproduced in the franchising problem. Web resources for further study include patent and know-how coverage at *www.europa.eu* and *www.nafta-sec-alena.org*, and TRIPs coverage at *www. wto.org.*

SECTION III. READINGS, QUESTIONS AND COMMENTS

PART A. THE LICENSING AGREEMENT AND TRANSFER OF TECHNOLOGY TO GERMANY

DRAFT LICENSE AGREEMENT

This is an agreement by and between, on the one hand, DRILL–BIT MANUFACTURING CO., INC. (hereinafter call "DRILL–BIT"), a Delaware corporation with its home office in Philadelphia, Pennsylvania, U.S.A., and on the other hand, NORDMETALL, G.m.b.H. (hereinafter called "LICENSEE"), a corporation organized under the laws of Germany, with main offices in Hamburg, Germany.

WHEREAS, DRILL–BIT owns and possesses trademarks, patents and certain considerable knowhow in the field of design, manufacturing, installation and sale of oil well drilling bits (hereinafter called "PRODUCT") and whereas LICENSEE desires to obtain rights in the "AREA" defined below to develop, manufacture, assemble, sell, deliver, install and service said PRODUCT, the parties hereto agree as follows:

1. *Grant*: DRILL–BIT grants to LICENSEE the exclusive license rights in Germany ("AREA"), to manufacture, develop, assemble, sell, deliver, install and service the PRODUCT and associated parts. Sales outside of the AREA may be authorized by DRILL–BIT in writing and such sales are hereby authorized on a trial basis for ultimate use in other member states of the European Union, except France and the UK, until DRILL–BIT shall request termination of such sales. LICENSEE has the exclusive rights to organize all sales through its distribution network, at prices to be established by agreement with DRILL–BIT. LICENSEE agrees to produce only DRILL–BIT oil well drilling bits. In the event DRILL–BIT establishes a licensee in an East European nation, LICENSEE agrees to share the German market with the East European licensee on a percentage to be determined by DRILL–BIT. DRILL–BIT agrees that no distributors of DRILL–BIT products in the European Union, including two independent distributors in France and the UK, will be permitted to solicit sales in Germany.

LICENSEE may sub-license such rights to third parties and vendors only if such agreements with third parties are previously approved in writing by DRILL–BIT upon suitable arrangements.

2. *No Competition Arrangements*: Until the Agreement shall terminate, DRILL–BIT shall not enter into any arrangements in the AREA similar to those contemplated in this Agreement, except that DRILL–BIT may itself operate directly, freely and fully, in the AREA regarding the PRODUCT, and further, may utilize other parties if LICENSEE is unwilling to handle a job. LICENSEE shall not undertake the manufacture, development, assembly, sale, delivery, installation or service anywhere in

the world, including the AREA, of PRODUCT or products competitive with the licensed PRODUCT contemplated in this Agreement. Sales for ultimate use outside the AREA or any countries on a trial-basis shall be referred to DRILL–BIT for handling.

3. *Supply of Know-How, Technical Assistance, Engineering Development*:

A. *Know-How.* DRILL–BIT shall from time-to-time, and to such extent as it shall consider to be reasonably necessary for the performance of this Agreement, furnish to LICENSEE, by mail and other mutually convenient means, technical information and specifications DRILL–BIT now possesses as to design engineering, manufacturing and other operations, and processes or experience incidental to the design, manufacture, assembly, sale, delivery, installation and service of the licensed PRODUCT. LICENSEE shall pay out-of-pocket costs incurred by DRILL–BIT in the transportation and mailing of such technical information and specifications, upon submission from time-to-time by DRILL–BIT of itemized invoices for same.

B. *Separate Technical Assistance.* DRILL–BIT personnel may assist, consult, and cooperate with LICENSEE in the design, manufacture, assembly, sale, delivery and service of licensed PRODUCT or other products under such arrangements as are agreed upon by the parties from time to time in regard to compensating DRILL–BIT for DRILL–BIT personnel going to AREA or for DRILL–BIT personnel training LICENSEE'S employees in the Pennsylvania area.

C. *Separate Engineering Development:* DRILL–BIT may, under arrangements and payment terms mutually agreeable to the parties from time to time, undertake special engineering development for LICENSEE with respect to licensed PRODUCT or other products and provide LICENSEE with information and technical assistance resulting therefrom.

4. *Inter-Party Sale of Products or Components:* Should either party hereto desire to sell products, parts or components to the other, including those relating to the PRODUCT or other products, such sales shall be upon terms agreed in writing. Normal payment terms shall be net 30 days after shipment.

5. *Manufacturing and Sales Responsibility:* LICENSEE agrees to use its best efforts to design, manufacture, assemble, sell, deliver, install and service licensed PRODUCT, including advertising, vigorous promotion by technical sales personnel, prompt handling or inquiries, complaints and service follow-up, including reasonable stocking of spare parts. The warranty terms shall be as approved by DRILL–BIT in writing. LICENSEE shall keep DRILL–BIT informed of its prices for PRODUCT so that DRILL–BIT may analyze the consistency of its world-wide pricing structure.

6. *Quality Control:* LICENSEE shall maintain manufacturing standards equal to those of DRILL–BIT in the United States, which standards

LICENSEE acknowledges and is familiar with, and any material proposed change involving any alteration in the structure, quality or design of the licensed PRODUCTS and the supplied know-how relating thereto, shall be subject to the written approval of DRILL–BIT. LICENSEE agrees that DRILL–BIT may, at LICENSEE's expense, visit the laboratories, offices and factories of LICENSEE at reasonable times to observe the operations contemplated by this Agreement.

7. *Grant-Back:* LICENSEE agrees to disclose to DRILL–BIT any developments or improvements which LICENSEE may make in the licensed PRODUCT and to permit DRILL–BIT a permanent, exclusive, royalty-free license to use such improvements or developments in all countries of the world and to permit DRILL–BIT to secure in such countries, except the AREA, where possible, patents and other industrial property rights at DRILL–BIT's expense.

8. *Marking Requirements:* On each item of licensed PRODUCT manufactured hereunder, LICENSEE shall attach in a prominent position, suitable to DRILL–BIT, a stamping, which shall indicate that the item has been manufactured under license from DRILL–BIT.

9. *Confidential Relations:* LICENSEE shall keep secret the methods, processes and techniques and all information, knowledge, trade practices and secrets communicated to LICENSEE under this Agreement. LICENSEE shall have the right to communicate such to its employees who need to know such, but each employee to whom such information is communicated shall correspondingly be bound in writing to confidentiality and secrecy. Any such written information or other physical information communicated to suppliers or, sub-licensees with the permission of DRILL–BIT, or others, shall be properly stamped with the following legend: "This information is accepted in confidence to be used only as agreed and will not be revealed to any other party without the express written permission of DRILL–BIT, of Philadelphia, Pennsylvania, U.S.A."

10. *Royalty:*

A. *Initial payment:* In consideration of this agreement and the initial delivery of know-how and data on PRODUCT as described herein, LICENSEE agrees to pay Fifty Thousand Dollars ($50,000) U.S. A payment of $35,000 shall be made on the signing hereof and the remaining $15,000 on the date of the first transfer by registered mail of technical data.

B. *Sales Royalty:* In addition, LICENSEE agrees to pay DRILL–BIT in Philadelphia, Pennsylvania, U.S.A., a continuing royalty of ten percent (10%) of LICENSEE's f.o.b. factory selling price, including installation fees, of all licensed PRODUCT and parts sold by LICENSEE, payable in U.S. funds.

All royalty fees payable hereunder shall be paid to DRILL–BIT within ten (10) days of the end of each month in which the times upon which royalty fees are earned have been paid for by the customer. With all payments due to DRILL–BIT, LICENSEE shall furnish DRILL–BIT a statement certified by LICENSEE's chief financial officer showing the computation of the amount of such payment. The correctness of such statements shall be audited and confirmed for DRILL–BIT by LICENSEE's public accounting firm in the course of LICENSEE's annual financial report, and shall be submitted immediately to DRILL–BIT in writing. Seventeen percent (17%) interest shall be paid on late payments. DRILL–BIT may audit such transactions itself at any time and shall have free access to LICENSEE's books, either itself or its certified public accounting firm.

11. *Records:* LICENSEE agrees to keep accurate records in sufficient detail to enable DRILL–BIT to accurately determine the number of PRODUCT and parts manufactured and sold and LICENSEE will permit examination of its records by DRILL–BIT at any time and will submit such written reports as DRILL–BIT shall request, and certified by independent accountants or others where requested. Whenever LICENSEE is in doubt or there is an interpretation to be made of inclusion or exclusion from the royalty, LICENSEE shall inform DRILL–BIT in writing and obtain a written authorization or direction.

12. *Trademarks, Patents:* LICENSEE must use the names used by DRILL–BIT in the U.S. when designating PRODUCT manufactured, but shall not use such names in any manner not approved by DRILL–BIT in writing and shall discontinue such use upon written notice from DRILL–BIT and in no case will LICENSEE interfere, directly or indirectly, with the application for, procurement or enforcement of DRILL–BIT's trademarks or patents in the AREA or elsewhere. LICENSEE will notify DRILL–BIT immediately of any known use in AREA of DRILL–BIT's established names, patents or trademarks by others. LICENSEE will assist DRILL–BIT in procuring DRILL–BIT's trademarks and patents in AREA, without expense of LICENSEE, and will assist DRILL–BIT in enforcing DRILL–BIT's rights. LICENSEE acknowledges DRILL–BIT's invention of the PRODUCT, and will respect any patent application and grants filed or received by DRILL–BIT in the AREA.

13. *Government Approval, Taxes.* LICENSEE agrees to obtain the approval of any government authorities in AREA, if necessary, to authorize this Agreement or payments hereunder, and including any necessary registrations or filings of this Agreement.

14. *Termination:*

A. *Term:* This Agreement shall be in force and effect for ten (10) years from date of execution and continue from year to year on an annual basis thereafter unless either party gives notice to the other not less than three (3) months prior to the expiration of the then current year's tenure of the Agreement that it will not be renewed when such current year expires.

If relations under this Agreement prove mutually satisfactory, there will be serious discussion given at the earliest moment to the establishment of a separate joint venture company.

Either party may terminate this Agreement, effective thirty (30) days from written notice of termination being mailed or delivered to the other party, except in case of (2) below where DRILL–BIT may terminate immediately, upon (1) the breach of any material portion of this Agreement, or (2) if either party is adjudged bankrupt or insolvent or shall make any assignment for the benefit of creditors or have a receiver appointed.

B. *Continuing Rights, Obligations:* Upon termination of this Agreement, all rights and obligations hereunder shall terminate except (1) the fulfillment of accrued rights, (2) the grant-back of licenses in Paragraph 7, and (3) the keeping of confidential relations as provided in Paragraph 9 and any other rights, the continuing protection of which is reasonably contemplated by this Agreement to protect either of the parties hereto and their industrial property rights, including service follow-up on existing customers, if requested by DRILL–BIT.

C. *Surrender of Rights, Know-How:* On the termination of this Agreement, LICENSEE shall deliver to DRILL–BIT in Philadelphia, Pennsylvania, all books, notes, drawings, writings, other documents, samples or models which were supplied to LICENSEE by DRILL–BIT, or which relate to know-how or technical assistance supplied by DRILL–BIT (and all copies thereof), and LICENSEE agrees to cease to exploit any industrial know-how licensed or given under this Agreement and to cease the manufacture, assembly and sale of any licensed items without the written permission of DRILL–BIT.

15. *U.S. Laws and Regulations:* LICENSEE will cooperate in complying with all U.S. laws and regulations of which it has notice, and especially with the laws and regulations relating to trade with Communist countries, including Cuba, and the U.S. anti-boycott laws.

16. *General.*

A. *Assignment.* LICENSEE shall not assign this Agreement nor any rights or benefits hereunder, without the written permission of DRILL–BIT.

B. *Force Majeure.* The parties hereto shall not be liable for failure of performance hereunder if such is caused by force majeure or circumstances beyond their respective control, but such suspension or performance shall be limited to the period during which such cause of failure exists.

C. *Arbitration.* All unresolvable disputes arising in connection with this Agreement shall be finally settled by the American Arbitration Association, in accordance with its Rules. If such arbitration remedy is frustrated by non-cooperation or otherwise, then the parties may pursue all available legal remedies. In all questions of interpretation of this contract, the law of Delaware shall apply.

R. FOLSOM, PRINCIPLES OF EUROPEAN UNION LAW

Section 7.11 (2011).

In its 1982 *Maize Seed* judgment, the European Court of Justice addressed patent license restrictions under the Community's competition rules.[1] The Commission waited for this judgment before publishing the 1984 group exemption under Article 81(3) [Article 101(3), TFEU] for patent licensing agreements. In this case, a research institute financed by the French government (INRA) bred varieties of basic seeds. In 1960, INRA assigned to Kurt Eisele plant breeder's rights for maize seed in the Federal Republic of Germany. Eisele agreed to apply for registration of these rights in accordance with German law. In 1965, a formal agreement was executed by the parties. This agreement consisted of five relevant clauses.

Clause 1 gave Eisele the exclusive rights to "organize" sales of six identified varieties of maize seed propagated from basic seeds provided by INRA. This enabled Eisele to exercise control over distribution outlets. Eisele undertook not to deal in maize varieties other than those provided by INRA. Clause 2 required Eisele to place no restriction on the supply of seed to technically suitable distributors except for rationing in conditions of shortage. The prices charged to the distributors by Eisele were fixed in consultation with INRA, according to a specified formula. Clause 3 obligated Eisele to import from France for sale in Germany at least two-thirds of that territory's requirements for the registered varieties. This restricted Eisele's own production and sale to only one-third of the German market. Clause 4 concerned the protection by Eisele of INRA's proprietary rights, including its trademark, from infringement and granted Eisele the power to take any action to that end. Clause 5 contained a promise by INRA that no exports to Germany of the relevant varieties would take place otherwise than through the agency of Eisele. This meant that INRA would ensure that its French marketing organization would prevent the relevant varieties from being exported to Germany to parallel importers.

In September 1972, it became apparent that dealers in France were selling the licensed varieties of maize seed directly to German traders who were marketing the products in breach of the breeder's rights claimed by Eisele. This resulted in an action by Eisele in the German courts against one of the traders. The parties reached a court approved settlement under which the French trader promised to refrain from offering for sale without permission any variety of maize seed within the rights held by Eisele, and to pay a fine. In February 1974, another breach took place, this time advertising in the German press by a French dealer. In response to threats of legal proceedings, this dealer lodged a complaint with the Commission alleging breach of the Treaty of Rome competition rules.

The Commission considered both the agreement and the settlement to violate Article 81(1) because they granted an exclusive license and provid-

---

1. Nungesser v. Commission (1982) Eur.Comm.Rep. 2015.

ed absolute territorial protection. The Court of Justice reversed the Commission with respect to exclusivity, but upheld the Commission with respect to absolute territorial protection. The Court drew a distinction between "open" licenses which do not necessarily fall under Article 81(1), and "closed" licenses which do so.

Open license agreements are those which do not involve third parties. In *Maize Seed,* the obligation upon INRA or those deriving rights through INRA to refrain from producing or selling the relevant seeds in Germany was treated as an open license term. The Court held such clauses necessary to the dissemination of new technology inasmuch as potential licensees might otherwise be deterred from accepting the risk of cultivating and marketing new products. The Court defined closed licenses as those involving third parties. Thus, the obligation upon INRA or those deriving rights through INRA to prevent third parties from exporting the seeds into Germany without authorization, Eisele's concurrent use of his exclusive contractual rights, and his breeder's rights, to prevent all imports into Germany or exports to other member states were invalid under Article 81(1).

* * *

TRANSFER OF TECHNOLOGY REGULATION 240/96

In 1996 the Commission enacted Regulation 240/96 on the application of Article 81(3) of the Rome Treaty to transfer technology agreements. The intention of this Regulation was to combine the existing patent and knowhow block exemptions into a single regulation covering technology transfer agreements, and to simplify and harmonize the rules for patent and knowhow licensing. It contained detailed lists of permitted, permissible and prohibited clauses.

* * *

TRANSFER OF TECHNOLOGY REGULATION 772/2004

The detailed regulation of technology transfer agreement clauses contained in Regulation 240/96 was replaced by Regulation 772/2004, which applies to patent, know-how and software copyright licensing. The new Regulation distinguishes agreements between those of "competing" and "noncompeting" parties, the latter being treated less strictly than the former. Parties are deemed "competing" if they compete (without infringing each other's IP rights) in either the relevant technology or product market, determined in each instance by what buyers regard as substitutes. If the competing parties have a *combined* market share of 20 percent or less, their licensing agreements are covered by group exemption under Regulation 772/2004. Noncompeting parties, on the other hand, benefit from the group exemption so long as their *individual* market shares do not exceed 30 percent. Agreements initially covered by Regulation 772/2004 that subsequently exceed the "safe harbor" thresholds noted above lose their exemption subject to a two-year grace period. Outside these exemptions, a "rule of reason" approach applies.

Inclusion of certain "hardcore restraints" causes license agreement to lose their group exemption. For competing parties, such restraints include price fixing, output limitations on both parties, limits on the licensee's ability to exploit its own technology, and allocation of markets or competitors (subject to exceptions). Specifically, restraints on active and passive selling by the licensee in a territory reserved for the licensor are allowed, as are active (but not passive) selling restraints by licensees in territories of other licensees. Licensing agreements between noncompeting parties may not contain the "hardcore" restraint of price fixing. Active selling restrictions on licensees can be utilized, along with passive selling restraints in territories reserved to the licensor or (for two years) another licensee. For these purposes, the competitive status of the parties is decided at the outset of the agreement.

Other license terms deemed "excluded restrictions" also cause a loss of exemption. Such clauses include: (1) mandatory grant-backs or assignments of severable improvements by licensees, excepting nonexclusive license-backs; (2) no-challenges by the licensee of the licensor's intellectual property rights, subject to the licensor's right to terminate upon challenge; and (3) for noncompeting parties, restraints on the licensee's ability to exploit its own technology or either party's ability to carry out research and development (unless indispensable to prevent disclosure of the licensed Know-how).

In all cases, exemption under Regulation 772/2004 may be withdrawn where in any particular case an agreement has effects that are incompatible with Article 81(3) [Article 101(3), TFEU].

COMMISSION REGULATION (EC) NO. 772/2004 OF 27 APRIL 2004 ON THE APPLICATION OF ARTICLE [101(3)] OF THE TREATY TO CATEGORIES OF TECHNOLOGY TRANSFER AGREEMENTS

2004 O.J. (L 123) 11.

* * *

ARTICLE 1

Definitions

1. For the purposes of this Regulation, the following definitions shall apply:

    (a) 'agreement' means an agreement, a decision of an association of undertakings or a concerted practice;

    (b) 'technology transfer agreement' means a patent licensing agreement, a know-how licensing agreement, a software copyright licensing agreement or a mixed patent, knowhow or software copyright licensing agreement, including any such agreement containing provisions which relate to the sale and purchase of products or which relate to the licensing of other intellectual property rights or the assignment of intellectual property rights, provided that those provisions do not constitute the primary object of the agreement and are directly related to the production of the contract products; assignments of patents, know-how, software copyright or a combination thereof where part of the risk associated with the exploitation of the technology remains with the assignor, in particular where the sum payable in consideration of the assignment is dependent on the turnover obtained by the assignee in respect of products produced with the assigned technology, the quantity of such products produced or the number of operations carried out employing the technology, shall also be deemed to be technology transfer agreements;

(c) 'reciprocal agreement' means a technology transfer agreement where two undertakings grant each other, in the same or separate contracts, a patent licence, a know-how licence, a software copyright licence or a mixed patent, know-how or software copyright licence and where these licences concern competing technologies or can be used for the production of competing products;

(d) 'non-reciprocal agreement' means a technology transfer agreement where one undertaking grants another undertaking a patent licence, a know-how licence, a software copyright licence or a mixed patent, know-how or software copyright licence, or where two undertakings grant each other such a licence but where these licences do not concern competing technologies and cannot be used for the production of competing products;

(e) 'product' means a good or a service, including both intermediary goods and services and final goods and services;

(f) 'contract products' means products produced with the licensed technology;

(g) 'intellectual property rights' includes industrial property rights, know-how, copyright and neighbouring rights;

(h) 'patents' means patents, patent applications, utility models, applications for registration of utility models, designs, topographies of semiconductor products, supplementary protection certificates for medicinal products or other products for which such supplementary protection certificates may be obtained and plant breeder's certificates;

(i) 'know-how' means a package of non-patented practical information, resulting from experience and testing, which is:

   (i) secret, that is to say, not generally known or easily accessible,

   (ii) substantial, that is to say, significant and useful for the production of the contract products, and

   (iii) identified, that is to say, described in a sufficiently comprehensive manner so as to make it possible to verify that it fulfills the criteria of secrecy and substantiality;

  (j) 'competing undertakings' means undertakings which compete on the relevant technology market and/or the relevant product market, that is to say:

   (i) competing undertakings on the relevant technology market, being undertakings which license out competing technologies without infringing each others' intellectual property rights (actual competitors on the technology market); the relevant technology market includes technologies which are regarded by the licensees as interchangeable with or substitutable for the licensed technology, by reason of the technologies' characteristics, their royalties and their intended use,

   (ii) competing undertakings on the relevant product market, being undertakings which, in the absence of the technology transfer agreement, are both active on the relevant product and geographic market(s) on which the contract products are sold without infringing each others' intellectual property rights (actual competitors on the product market) or would, on realistic grounds, undertake the necessary additional investments or other necessary switching costs so that they could timely enter, without infringing each others' intellectual property rights, the(se) relevant product and geographic market(s) in response to a small and permanent increase in relative prices (potential competitors on the product market); the relevant product market comprises products which are regarded by the buyers as interchangeable with or substitutable for the contract products, by reason of the products' characteristics, their prices and their intended use;

  (k) 'selective distribution system' means a distribution system where the licensor undertakes to license the production of the contract products only to licensees selected on the basis of specified criteria and where these licensees undertake not to sell the contract products to unauthorised distributors;

  (l) 'exclusive territory' means a territory in which only one undertaking is allowed to produce the contract products with the licensed technology, without prejudice to the possibility of allowing within that territory another licensee to produce the contract products only for a particular customer where this second licence was granted in order to create an alternative source of supply for that customer;

  (m) 'exclusive customer group' means a group of customers to which only one undertaking is allowed actively to sell the contract products produced with the licensed technology;

(n) 'severable improvement' means an improvement that can be exploited without infringing the licensed technology.

2. The terms 'undertaking', 'licensor' and 'licensee' shall include their respective connected undertakings.

* * *

ARTICLE 2

Exemption

Pursuant to Article 101(3) of the Treaty and subject to the provisions of this Regulation, it is hereby declared that Article 101(1) of the Treaty shall not apply to technology transfer agreements entered into between two undertakings permitting the production of contract products.

This exemption shall apply to the extent that such agreements contain restrictions of competition falling within the scope of Article 101(1). The exemption shall apply for as long as the intellectual property right in the licensed technology has not expired, lapsed or been declared invalid or, in the case of know-how, for as long as the know-how remains secret, except in the event where the know-how becomes publicly known as a result of action by the licensee, in which case the exemption shall apply for the duration of the agreement.

ARTICLE 3

Market-share thresholds

1. Where the undertakings party to the agreement are competing undertakings, the exemption provided for in Article 2 shall apply on condition that the combined market share of the parties does not exceed 20% on the affected relevant technology and product market.

2. Where the undertakings party to the agreement are not competing undertakings, the exemption provided for in Article 2 shall apply on condition that the market share of each of the parties does not exceed 30% on the affected relevant technology and product market.

3. For the purposes of paragraphs 1 and 2, the market share of a party on the relevant technology market(s) is defined in terms of the presence of the licensed technology on the relevant product market(s). A licensor's market share on the relevant technology market shall be the combined market share on the relevant product market of the contract products produced by the licensor and its licensees.

ARTICLE 4

Hardcore restrictions

1. Where the undertakings party to the agreement are competing undertakings, the exemption provided for in Article 2 shall not apply to agreements which, directly or indirectly, in isolation or in combination with other factors under the control of the parties, have as their object:

(a) the restriction of a party's ability to determine its prices when selling products to third parties;

(b) the limitation of output, except limitations on the output of contract products imposed on the licensee in a non-reciprocal agreement or imposed on only one of the licensees in a reciprocal agreement;

(c) the allocation of markets or customers except:

    (i) the obligation on the licensee(s) to produce with the licensed technology only within one or more technical fields of use or one or more product markets,

    (ii) the obligation on the licensor and/or the licensee, in a non-reciprocal agreement, not to produce with the licensed technology within one or more technical fields of use or one or more product markets or one or more exclusive territories reserved for the other party,

    (iii) the obligation on the licensor not to license the technology to another licensee in a particular territory,

    (iv) the restriction, in a non-reciprocal agreement, of active and/or passive sales by the licensee and/or the licensor into the exclusive territory or to the exclusive customer group reserved for the other party,

    (v) the restriction, in a non-reciprocal agreement, of active sales by the licensee into the exclusive territory or to the exclusive customer group allocated by the licensor to another licensee provided the latter was not a competing undertaking of the licensor at the time of the conclusion of its own licence,

    (vi) the obligation on the licensee to produce the contract products only for its own use provided that the licensee is not restricted in selling the contract products actively and passively as spare parts for its own products,

    (vii) the obligation on the licensee, in a non-reciprocal agreement, to produce the contract products only for a particular customer, where the licence was granted in order to create an alternative source of supply for that customer;

(d) the restriction of the licensee's ability to exploit its own technology or the restriction of the ability of any of the parties to the agreement to carry out research and development, unless such latter restriction is indispensable to prevent the disclosure of the licensed know-how to third parties.

    2. Where the undertakings party to the agreement are not competing undertakings, the exemption provided for in Article 2 shall not apply to agreements which, directly or indirectly, in isolation or in combination with other factors under the control of the parties, have as their object:

(a) the restriction of a party's ability to determine its prices when selling products to third parties, without prejudice to the possibility of imposing a maximum sale price or recommending a sale price, provided that it does not amount to a fixed or minimum sale price as a result of pressure from, or incentives offered by, any of the parties;

(b) the restriction of the territory into which, or of the customers to whom, the licensee may passively sell the contract products, except:

   (i) the restriction of passive sales into an exclusive territory or to an exclusive customer group reserved for the licensor,

   (ii) the restriction of passive sales into an exclusive territory or to an exclusive customer group allocated by the licensor to another licensee during the first two years that this other licensee is selling the contract products in that territory or to that customer group,

   (iii) the obligation to produce the contract products only for its own use provided that the licensee is not restricted in selling the contract products actively and passively as spare parts for its own products,

   (iv) the obligation to produce the contract products only for a particular customer, where the licence was granted in order to create an alternative source of supply for that customer,

   (v) the restriction of sales to end-users by a licensee operating at the wholesale level of trade,

   (vi) the restriction of sales to unauthorised distributors by the members of a selective distribution system;

(c) the restriction of active or passive sales to end-users by a licensee which is a member of a selective distribution system and which operates at the retail level, without prejudice to the possibility of prohibiting a member of the system from operating out of an unauthorised place of establishment.

3. Where the undertakings party to the agreement are not competing undertakings at the time of the conclusion of the agreement but become competing undertakings afterwards, paragraph 2 and not paragraph 1 shall apply for the full life of the agreement unless the agreement is subsequently amended in any material respect.

ARTICLE 5

Excluded restrictions

1. The exemption provided for in Article 2 shall not apply to any of the following obligations contained in technology transfer agreements:

(a) any direct or indirect obligation on the licensee to grant an exclusive licence to the licensor or to a third party designated by the licensor in respect of its own severable improvements to or its own new applications of the licensed technology;

(b) any direct or indirect obligation on the licensee to assign, in whole or in part, to the licensor or to a third party designated by the licensor, rights to its own severable improvements to or its own new applications of the licensed technology;

(c) any direct or indirect obligation on the licensee not to challenge the validity of intellectual property rights which the licensor holds in the common market, without prejudice to the possibility of providing for termination of the technology transfer agreement in the event that the licensee challenges the validity of one or more of the licensed intellectual property rights.

2.   Where the undertakings party to the agreement are not competing undertakings, the exemption provided for in Article 2 shall not apply to any direct or indirect obligation limiting the licensee's ability to exploit its own technology or limiting the ability of any of the parties to the agreement to carry out research and development, unless such latter restriction is indispensable to prevent the disclosure of the licensed know-how to third parties.

Article 6

Withdrawal in individual cases

1.   The Commission may withdraw the benefit of this Regulation, pursuant to Article 29(1) of Regulation (EC) No 1/2003, where it finds in any particular case that a technology transfer agreement to which the exemption provided for in Article 2 applies nevertheless has effects which are incompatible with Article 101(3) of the Treaty....

* * *

2.   Where, in any particular case, a technology transfer agreement to which the exemption provided for in Article 2 applies has effects which are incompatible with Article 101(3) of the Treaty in the territory of a Member State, or in a part thereof, which has all the characteristics of a distinct geographic market, the competition authority of that Member State may withdraw the benefit of this Regulation, pursuant to Article 29(2) of Regulation (EC) No 1/2003, in respect of that territory, under the same circumstances as those set out in paragraph 1 of this Article.

Article 8

Application of the market-share thresholds

* * *

2.   If the market share referred to in Article 3(1) or (2) is initially not more than 20% respectively 30% but subsequently rises above those levels, the exemption provided for in Article 2 shall continue to apply for a period

of two consecutive calendar years following the year in which the 20% threshold or 30% threshold was first exceeded.

QUESTIONS AND COMMENTS

1. The comments in the Folsom extract discuss the landmark *Maize Seed* case. How might the 1982 *Maize Seed* judgment would affect the proposed draft licensing agreement? Would the European Court find the license to be an "open" or "closed" license?

The *Maize Seed* case involved five clauses, all subjects addressed in the proposed draft agreement. Assume Drill-Bit and NordMetall would like to challenge sales in Germany by the French distributor of Drill-Bit's products. In view of the draft agreement, would you recommend such suit? Remember that the Commission may become aware of the licensing agreement between Drill-Bit and NordMetall (probably because the French distributor will lodge a complaint with the Commission). Obviously the French distributor may find its distributorship agreement with the parent Drill-Bit in jeopardy, but it may be willing to take that risk and hope that French law will not allow a termination of the distributorship agreement.

2. For Regulation 772/2004 purposes, is the proposed Drill-Bit agreement between competing or noncompeting parties? Does your answer matter? See Articles 3, 4 and 1(j).

3. The facts of this problem state: "Drill-Bit now has a modest share of the market in the United States. But ... it has a larger share of the high quality end of the market." NordMetall's market share is not discussed. Do the licensor's and licensee's market shares matter under Regulation 772/2004? If so, which market shares ... product market shares? technology market shares? or both? How are these markets defined? See Article 3.

4. Are there any "hardcore restrictions" in the draft Drill-Bit agreement? See particularly Agreement Article 1. If so, what is their significance to exemption under Regulation 772/2004? See Article 4. Does Article 4 suggest how to revise Agreement Article 1?

5. Are there any "excluded restrictions" in the draft agreement? See particularly Agreement Article 7. If so, what is their significance to exemption under Regulation 772/2004? See Article 5.

6. We have assumed that Regulation 772/2004 is consistent with EU obligations under TRIPs. As you work through Part B, you might want to evaluate that assumption.

PART B. THE TRANSFER OF TECHNOLOGY TO MEXICO

Additional protection for technology transferred abroad was created under NAFTA. Drill-Bit is interested in following these developments because it plans an investment in Mexico. It will transfer technology from the U.S. parent to its Mexican subsidiary. It remains wary of the possibility of changes, and a reversal to more restrictive practices.

RADWAY, ANTITRUST, TECHNOLOGY TRANSFERS AND JOINT VENTURES IN LATIN AMERICAN DEVELOPMENT

15 Lawyer Am. 47 (1983).*

The technology transfer laws [of Latin America] were conceived as part of an overall mechanism to regulate foreign exchange amid a severe balance of payments crisis. The balance of payment problem was brought on by recurrent sharp fluctuations in the prices of the commodities which dominate the economies of developing countries. In Brazil and Columbia, coffee prices were most affected; in Chile and Peru, copper prices were involved; and in Venezuela, the price of oil was the concern. In other Latin American countries coffee, cotton, cocoa, bananas, copper, iron ore and oil were of paramount importance.

* * *

Certain "abuses" were gleaned from studies performed on technology transfer arrangements throughout the 1960's and into the 1970's. These studies were made by organizations in Brazil, Mexico and Argentina, as well as regional or international organizations (i.e., LAFTA and UNC-TAD.) The alleged abuses purportedly subjected developing countries to virtually complete dependence on external centers of decision-making and control as a price for the technology being received.

"Dependency theorists" dominated the discussions and debates in the 1960's. These talks led to the enactment of the Colombian law in 1967, which was the forerunner of the well-known Decision 24 of the Andean Pact. Argentina enacted the first of its four transfer of technology laws in 1971, patterned after Decision 24. Mexico followed with a decree * * *. The intent of the laws was clear: regulation and control through State intervention to steer the course of economic development.

In practice, however, economic development was still the ultimate objective in many cases. Foreign suppliers of technology strongly resisted the rigid requirements of the newly enacted technology transfer laws. With inexperienced and inadequately trained technocrats in the newly created government agencies charged to review and approve the licensing and related agreements, the bargaining power was clearly unequal. Most of the suppliers of technology, or their representatives before the agencies, knew far more than the government technocrats about the relevant development needs of the host country in their industry, and the ability of the foreign supplier to fill those needs. Thus, exceptions were made in those countries where the critical nature of the technology outweighed the concern over the loss of foreign reserves in payment of royalties, fees and other remittances.

* * *

---

* Reprinted with permission of the Inter–American Law Review.

Among the stated objectives of the laws enacted in these countries during the period described above, was the registration of all agreements embodying a flow of technology in order to begin to prepare profiles on that process. A similar process had been undertaken during that period with respect to the flow of capital by the enactment of foreign investment laws in the same countries. * * *

Greater local control of industrialization remained another principal objective, one which was enormously broad and elusive. According to theorists, the alleged abuses * * * led to an attempt to shift some control to local industrialists in order to facilitate the economic development process. * * *

The most controversial of these clauses in Mexico, Brazil and the Andean Pact countries were those which involved export restrictions, royalties, the treatment of confidential information (secrecy clauses), tie-ins and grant-backs. Several of these laws have now been modified. The present policy trend in Latin America appears to be that many of these items are still negotiable and may be accepted where the technology supplier can establish the use of arm's length dealing, reciprocity and generally accepted international market prices (for parts, raw materials, etc.) Limited export restrictions are permitted when exportation to the supplier's home country market is involved. Frequently, limited restrictions also apply to countries where the supplier can show registered patents or a pre-existing network of license agreements. Grant-backs are accepted but the royalty-bearing conditions, terms and other aspects must be reciprocal.

J. McKNIGHT AND C. MUGGENBURG, MEXICO'S INDUSTRIAL PROPERTY AND COPYRIGHT LAWS: ANOTHER STEP TOWARD LINKAGE WITH A GLOBAL ECONOMY

M. Gordon (ed.), Doing Business in Mexico (1993).*

Mexico's recent enactment in June 1991 of the Law for the Promotion and Protection of Industrial Property ("Industrial Property Law") completely revamps the Mexican industrial property regime and signals a significant step forward in Mexico's efforts to join the global economy. While the Industrial Property Law can be improved upon, it notably increases the protection afforded most industrial property rights in Mexico to a level generally commensurate with that found in the industrialized nations. As a consequence, Mexico has dramatically improved its business climate and removed another barrier to attracting foreign investment and advanced technology.

* * *

While the Industrial Property Law significantly broadens the patent protections afforded inventions, it continues to suffer from provisions

---

* Reprinted with permission of Transnational Juris Publications, Inc.

subjecting patentable inventions to compulsory licenses if the patent has not been worked in Mexico by the later of four years from the filing date of the patent application or three years from the date of granting the patent (unless failure to work the patent is justified for technical or economic reasons). A patentable invention is also subject to a compulsory license for reasons of the public interest where the production, supply or distribution of basic commodities would otherwise be impeded.

* * *

Prior to the enactment of the Industrial Property Law, there was virtually no legal protection in Mexico of general industrial or trade secrets. * * *

* * *

The extension of legal protection to industrial or trade secrets is clearly one of the most important aspects of the Industrial Property Law, as a very significant portion of the industrial property assets of most businesses may be classified as trade secrets. Nonetheless, this section of the Industrial Property Law has a number of shortcomings, chief among which is concern with respect to what constitutes an industrial or trade secret qualifying for protection (e.g. what is the significance of the requirement that the secret have "an industrial application" and are all secrets relating to rendering services protected or are only those relating to the marketing or distribution of services?). In addition, in light of the subjective nature of several of the elements of proof required to support a statutory claim (e.g. proving that the secret provided a competitive or economic advantage over third parties) and the continuing absence of any injunctive relief for unauthorized disclosures or uses of secrets, concern remains with respect to the effectiveness of the statutory remedies provided for under the Industrial Property Law.

* * *

The Industrial Property Law completely revamps the legal treatment of transfers of technology to Mexico and, while it does not eliminate all legal barriers to technology transfers, it would appear to reduce these barriers to minimum levels. First, the regulatory scope of the Industrial Property Law is limited to requiring the recordation of patent and trademark licenses and transfers (including licenses and transfers relating to the registration thereof) only, and does not extend to other types of technology transfer agreements that were previously regulated. Also, while failure to register a technology transfer agreement under the [former] Transfer of Technology Law resulted in the imposition of fines and the agreement being deemed null and void, the primary purpose of recording a patent or trademark license or transfer agreement with the Ministry is to render the transfer of rights thereunder enforceable against third parties.

The application to record a license must be submitted to the Ministry in accordance with the regulations to the Industrial Property Law. As previously noted, the transitional provisions of the Industrial Property Law provide that until new regulations are prepared, the existing regulations relating to the Law of Inventions and Trademarks will apply. Since the Law of Inventions and Trademarks did not generally address the licensing of industrial property rights, there is no definitive regulatory criteria indicating what form of application must be submitted to the Ministry, and whether it is necessary to submit a copy of the license agreement or whether a simple writ setting forth certain basic information regarding the license agreement will suffice. In keeping with the economic policies underlying the Industrial Property Law, it is hoped that the regulations will permit the filing of a writ so as to avoid public disclosure of the terms of the license agreement.

In contrast to the numerous grounds for denial of registration of a technology transfer agreement under the Transfer of Technology Law, the Industrial Property Law provides that a license agreement will be recorded unless by its terms the applicability of the Industrial Property Law is excluded. * * *

The remainder of the provisions relating to licenses in the Industrial Property Law is fairly abbreviated, reflecting the expressed policy of deregulation. The working of a patent by a licensee, and the use of a trademark by a licensee, will be deemed to constitute use by the owner of the patent or trademark owner, as the case may be, so long as the related license is recorded. In addition, if a patent or trademark license is recorded with the Ministry, the licensee is empowered under the Industrial Property Law, absent an agreement to the contrary, to take legal action to protect such industrial property rights as if it were the owner thereof. * * * Finally, the recordation of a license may in general be canceled only by a court order or at the joint request of the licensor and licensee (as a terminated licensee may be less than wholly cooperative, the licensor is well advised to obtain agreement in advance with the licensee upon mechanisms to ensure the prompt cancellation of the license). Of course, a patent license will terminate upon the nullity or lapsing of the related patent, and a trademark license will terminate in the event the trademark registration is cancelled by virtue of the trademark becoming a generic designation for the related product or service.

R. FOLSOM, NAFTA AND FREE TRADE IN THE AMERICAS

Chapters 7 and 11 (2011).

Why are intellectual property rights so controversial? From the perspective of the industrial world (including Canada and the United States), patents, copyrights, trademarks and trade secrets are essential to their modern technology-driven economies. Such rights are used as incentives and rewards for innovative research, development and progress. Needless to say, this perspective corresponds with a very high degree of ownership of intellectual property rights around the world.

From the perspective of the developing world (including Mexico), patents, copyrights, etc. are often expensive barriers to economic improvement. Third world nations are basically technology importers, and done legally this means paying royalties to owners of intellectual property rights. The stream of royalty payments from the developing to the industrial world is in fact huge, with much smaller sums headed the other way. Such payments add to the costs of development, and in some cases are quite simply unaffordable.

These competing perspectives on intellectual property rights have resulted in certain patterns of law and behavior. The industrial nations have pushed hard at every opportunity for recognition in the laws of developing nations of the right to obtain intellectual property protection. This push illustrates a fundamental point: No nation need grant patent, trademark, copyright or trade secret protection unless that is their wish. If a developing world nation decides to allow patents on pharmaceuticals, in reality it is opening its market to the multinational drug companies. They will end up owning the lion's share of the Mexican, Thai or Nigerian (for example) pharmaceutical patents. Without effective patent protection, these companies will face local competitors who need not pay them royalties. Such "pirates" are found in some developing nations, but it is important to remember that under the laws of their nation they are not necessarily pirates. Indeed, they may even be encouraged in their efforts by their governments as part of a low-cost development strategy.

It is easy to understand why the United States and Canada (to a lesser extent) as technology exporters share the common goal of obtaining effective protection for intellectual property rights around the world. In NAFTA, Mexico promises to meet (if not exceed) their greatest expectations. For Mexico, building upon its 1991 Law for the Fostering and Protection of Industrial Property, joining NAFTA represents a coming of age on intellectual property rights.

* * *

Chapter 17 of the NAFTA agreement contains a comprehensive set of rules for North American intellectual property rights. NAFTA's provisions are closely related, but somewhat more extensive than those of the WTO Agreement on Trade-Related Intellectual Property Rights (TRIPS) (1995). Both NAFTA and TRIPS stipulate that whichever agreement affords the broadest protection of intellectual property will prevail. While its primary impact has been on Mexico, Canada and the United States also amended their intellectual property laws after NAFTA. U.S. free trade agreements in the Americas since NAFTA have notably expanded "TRIPS Plus" coverage of intellectual property rights.

Prior to 1991, Mexico had a <u>Technology Transfer Commission</u> with a veto power over most intellectual property licensing and franchising agreements. The Commission also controlled in detail the terms and conditions of technology transfer agreements. It even decided the level of acceptable royalties. Commissions of this kind are best understood by remembering that developing nations like Mexico are basically technology importers. While Mexico needed technology, it did not wish to pay excessively for what was not always at the cutting edge. So it, like most of Latin America, empowered the Commission to get better terms. What happened instead was that technology transfers to Mexico slowed to a trickle.

In 1991, well prior to NAFTA, Mexico abolished the Commission and most technology transfer controls. Licensors and licensees were free to bargain over the terms and conditions of their agreements. However, Mexico's patent, copyright, trademark and trade secret laws remained (by United States standards) less than fully protective of intellectual property rights. This was of concern because many Mexican patents and copyrights, for example, are owned by U.S. corporations and investors. NAFTA brought fundamental alterations to Mexican law in these areas. In 1994, Mexico joined the Patent Cooperation Treaty. Obtaining Mexican patents is now as simple as checking a box designating Mexico as a country in which protection is desired.

General Obligations

Specific commitments on patents, copyrights, trademarks, trade secrets and other intellectual property rights are made in the NAFTA agreement. These are discussed individually below. NAFTA also contains some general intellectual property rights obligations. Many of these obligations have counterparts under the TRIPS agreement. For example, except for secondary use of sound recordings, there is a general rule of national treatment.

There is also a general duty to protect intellectual property adequately and effectively, as long as barriers to legitimate trade are not created. At a minimum, this duty necessitates adherence to NAFTA Chapter 17. This general duty also embraces adherence to the substantive provisions of: The Geneva Convention of Phonograms (1971); the Berne Convention for the Protection of Literary and Artistic Works (1971); the Paris Convention for the Protection of Industrial Property (1967); and the 1978 or 1991 versions of the International Convention for the Protection of New Varieties of Plants. Protecting intellectual property rights more extensively than these Conventions is expressly authorized.

The process of intellectual property rights enforcement is covered in detail under NAFTA. Speaking generally, these provisions require fair, equitable, and not unnecessarily complicated, costly or time-consuming enforcement procedures. Written notice, independent legal counsel, the opportunity to substantiate claims and present evidence, and protection of confidential information are stipulated for civil enforcement proceedings. Overly burdensome mandatory personal appearances cannot be imposed. Remedies to enjoin infringement (new to Mexico), prevent importation of infringing goods, and order payment for damages and litigation costs must exist. However, proof of knowing infringement or reasonable grounds for such knowledge is an acceptable criterion. Recovery of profits or liquidated damages must be available when copyright or sound recording infringement is involved. Disposition of infringing or counterfeit goods outside the ordinary channels of commerce or even by destruction is anticipated by NAFTA. All administrative intellectual property rights decisions must be reviewable by a court of law.

* * *

Patents

Article 1709 of NAFTA assures the availability of patents "in all fields of technology." New products and processes resulting from an inventive step that are capable of industrial application are patentable. Patents for pharmaceuticals, computer software, microorganisms and microbiological processes, plant varieties and agricultural chemicals were specifically included under NAFTA and caused changes in Mexican law. In addition, protection for layout designs of semiconductor integrated circuits was provided by Article 1710. All patent rights must be granted without discrimination as to field of technology, country of origin, and importation or local production of the relevant products. Since the United States still awards patents on a first-to-invent (not first-to-file) basis, activities in Canada and Mexico now count for purposes establishing the date of an invention.

NAFTA specifically reserves the right to deny patents for diagnostic, therapeutic and surgical methods, transgenic plants and animals, and for essentially biological processes that produce plants or animals. If commercial exploitation might endanger public morality or "ordre public" (state security) no patents need be granted. Patent denials to protect human, animal or plant life or health, or to avoid serious injury to nature or the environment, are also justifiable under NAFTA.

It was agreed that patents in NAFTA nations would run either for 20 years from the date of the filing of the patent application, or 17 years from the grant of patent rights (the traditional U.S. approach). However, the subsequent TRIPS agreement stipulates a 20-year patent term from the date of filing. Canadian, Mexican and United States patent laws now follow this rule. For pharmaceutical patents, effectively speaking, an additional five years of protection from generic competition is often achieved because NAFTA requires five years exclusivity for product approval test data. Under NAFTA, patent owners generally possess the right to prevent others from making, using or selling the invention without their consent. No mention is made of the right to block infringing or unauthorized imports. If the patent covers a process, this includes the right to prevent others from using, selling or *importing* products obtained directly from that process. Assignment or transfer of patents, and licensing contracts for their use and exploitation, are also expressly protected.

On the touchy subject of <u>compulsory licensing</u>, which is not authorized under U.S. law, governments may allow limited nonexclusive usage without the owner's authorization if the invention has not been used or exploited locally through production or importation. This is generally permissible only after reasonable attempts at securing a license. However, under emergency, competition law or public noncommercial circumstances, no prior attempt at securing a license is required. In all cases of compulsory licensing, there is a duty to adequately remunerate the patent owner. Significant changes in Canadian compulsory licensing of pharmaceuticals were made in 1993. These changes caused some pharmaceutical prices to rise in Canada.

Apart from compulsory licensing, NAFTA authorizes "limited exceptions" to exclusive patents rights. Such exceptions may not "unreasonably conflict" with the normal exploitation of the patent. Nor may they "unreasonably prejudice" the owner's "legitimate interests." It is not clear how this broad authorization will be construed or applied.

* * *

Trade Secrets

NAFTA was the first international agreement on trade secret protection. Its primary impact has been on Mexican law. At a minimum, each nation must ensure legal means to prevent trade secrets from being disclosed, acquired or used without consent "in a manner contrary to honest commercial practices." (Article 1711). Breach of contract, breach of confidence, and inducement to breach of contract are specifically listed as examples of dishonest commercial practices. Moreover, persons who acquire trade secrets knowing them to be the product of such practices, or who were grossly negligent in failing to know this, also engage in dishonest commercial practices. This is true even if they do not use the secrets in question. NAFTA does not mention, however, the practice of "reverse engineering". This practice is thought to be common and has been authoritatively endorsed by the U.S. Supreme Court. *See Kewanee Oil Co. v. Bicron Corp.*, 416 U.S. 470 (1974).

For NAFTA purposes, information is "secret" if it is not generally known or readily accessible to persons who normally deal with it, has commercial value because of its secrecy, and reasonable steps have been taken to keep it secret. This <u>definition</u> ought to cover, for example, the secret formula for making Coca-Cola. Nevertheless, trade secret holders may be required to produce evidence documenting the existence of the secret in order to secure protection. Release of such information to government authorities obviously involves risks that will need to be considered.

No NAFTA government may discourage or impede the voluntary licensing of trade secrets (often referred to as "<u>knowhow licensing</u>"). Imposing excessive or discriminatory conditions on knowhow licenses is prohibited. More specifically, in testing and licensing the sale of pharmaceutical and agricultural chemical products, there is a general duty to protect against disclosure of proprietary data.

In 1996, independently of NAFTA, the United States enacted the Economic Espionage Act. 18 U.S.C. § 1831 et seq. This Act creates criminal penalties for misappropriation of trade secrets. For these purposes, a "trade secret" is defined as "financial, business, scientific, technical, economic or engineering information" that the owner has taken reasonable measures to keep secret and whose "independent economic value derives from being closely held". All proceeds from the theft of trade secrets and all property used or intended for use in the misappropriation can be seized and forfeited.

* * *

U.S. Free Trade Agreements—NAFTA Plus

United States free trade agreements since NAFTA have evolved substantively under a policy known as "competitive liberalization." For example, coverage of labor law has been narrowed to core ILO principles: The rights of association, organization and collective bargaining; acceptable work conditions regarding minimum wages, hours and occupational health and safety; minimum ages for employment of children and elimination of the worst forms of child labor; and a ban on forced or compulsory labor. Coverage of labor and environmental law enforcement is folded into the trade agreement (compare NAFTA's side agreements) and all remedies are intergovernmental (compare private and NGO "remedies" in the side agreements).

Other NAFTA–plus provisions have emerged. These are most evident regarding foreign investment and intellectual property. Regarding investor-state claims, for example, post–NAFTA U.S. free trade agreements insert the word "customary" before international law in defining the minimum standard of treatment to which foreign investors are entitled. This insertion tracks the official Interpretation issued in that regard under NAFTA. In addition, the contested terms "fair and equitable treatment" and "full protection and security" are defined for the first time:

> "fair and equitable treatment" includes the obligation not to deny justice in criminal, civil, or administrative adjudicatory proceedings in accordance with the principle of due process embodied in the principal legal systems of the world; and

> "full protection and security" requires each Party to provide the level of police protection required under customary international law.

More significantly perhaps, starting with the U.S.–Chile FTA, these agreements contain an Annex restricting the scope of "indirect expropriation" claims:

> Except in rare circumstances, nondiscriminatory regulatory actions by a Party that are designed and applied to protect legitimate public

welfare objectives, such as public health, safety, and the environment, do not constitute indirect expropriations.

Hence the potential for succeeding with "regulatory takings" investor-state claims has been reduced. Morever, the CAFTA–DR agreement anticipates creating an appellate body of some sort for investor-state arbitration decisions.

Regarding intellectual property, NAFTA–plus has moved into the Internet age. Protection of domain names, and adherence to the WIPO Internet treaties, are stipulated. E-commerce and free trade in digital products are embraced, copyrights extended to rights-management (encryption) and anti-circumvention (hacking) technology, protection against web music file sharing enhanced, and potential liability of Internet Service Providers detailed.

Less visibly, pharmaceutical patent owners obtain extensions of their patents to compensate for delays in the approval process, and greater control over their test data, making it harder for generic competition to emerge. They also gain "linkage," meaning local drug regulators must make sure generics are not patent-infringing before their release. *See* Rajkumar, 14 Albany L.J. Sci & Tech. 433 (2005). In addition, adherence to the Patent Law Treaty (2000) and the Trademark Law Treaty (1994) is agreed. Anti-counterfeiting laws are tightened, particularly regarding destruction of counterfeit goods.

Other NAFTA–plus changes push further along the path of free trade in services and comprehensive customs law administration rules. Anti-dumping and countervailing duty laws remain applicable, but appeals from administrative determinations are taken in national courts, not binational panels. Except for limited provisions in the Chile–U.S. agreement, business visas drop completely out of U.S. free trade agreements, a NAFTA–minus development.

In sum, the United States has generally used its leverage with smaller trade partners in the Americas to obtain more preferential treatment and expanded protection for its goods, services, technology and investors. It has given up relatively little in return, for example a modest increase in agricultural market openings.

* * *

QUESTIONS AND COMMENTS

1. The 1982 Mexican law, the "Law on the Control and Registration of the Transfer of Technology and the Use and Exploitation of Patents and Trademarks," illustrated its focus on registration and its general restrictiveness, both by its title and some of the section headings, such as "Causes Which Cancel the Registration," which listed 17 reasons for denying registration. In contrast, the 1991 law shows its emphasis on the protection of technology by its title, "Law on the Promotion and Protection of Industrial Property." Well before NAFTA and TRIPs, the 1991 law protects know-how, previously absent from protected property.

Why did Mexico undertake such fundamental changes to its law? Won't it pay a lot more for technology under one-sided licensing agreements? Did it go too far? Compare EU Regulation 772/2004.

2. Radway provides a useful summary of the history of restrictive controls. But a new era has begun as developing nations reduce restrictive provisions and substitute provisions granting protection to technology. Do you agree with Drill-Bit's decision a decade ago that transferring technology to Mexico was probably too risky? Why? It is ironic that the draft agreement in Part A would likely be registered "as is" in Mexico today, but must be rewritten significantly for Europe.

3. NAFTA and TRIPs also focus on intellectual property protection, not regulation of technology transfers. See Folsom and the Documents Supplement. Is the Mexican 1991 law consistent with these provisions? What is their impact on Mexican law?

Do you see any reason why Drill-Bit should not go forth with licensing technology to Mexico?

4. In 2005, the United States and five Central American nations (Costa Rica, Guatemala, Honduras, El Salvador and Nicaragua) plus the Dominican Republic agreed to free trade (CAFTA–DR). Suppose Drill-Bit is thinking to license in a CAFTA–DR country. Would the NAFTA–Plus provisions of that agreement make a difference? See the Folsom excerpt.

PART 5

FOREIGN INVESTMENT

■ ■ ■

CHAPTER 10

ESTABLISHING AND OPERATING
A FOREIGN INVESTMENT

■ ■ ■

INTRODUCTION 10.0 THE DECISION AND WAYS TO INVEST ABROAD— DOMESTIC GOODS IN FRANCE

In 4.0 a basic international sales transaction was presented, consisting of a walk through an ordinary documentary sale of toys to Greece where nothing appears to have gone wrong. These investment problems begin the same way. This introduction to foreign investment is intended to walk through the initiation, operation and termination of an investment made abroad. Problems 10.1–10.7 turn to some of the legal conflicts that arise with planning, operating, or concluding a foreign investment. But before focusing on these specific legal issues, this introduction will introduce some of the considerations that should be addressed when a client decides that it is time to change the company's practice of manufacturing the goods in the United States and selling them abroad, to manufacturing the goods abroad in an entity wholly or partly owned by the U.S. entity.

PART A. HOW DOES A FOREIGN DIRECT INVESTMENT (FDI) DIFFER FROM A DOMESTIC INVESTMENT?

Our company, which will appear in several of the specific problems in this Chapter, is Domestic Goods, Inc.(DGI). DGI is a corporation registered in Delaware with home offices in New York City. DGI has plants in several states. One of those states is Texas. It manufactures various items used in cleaning and maintaining homes, such as detergents and cleaning supplies, room deodorants, roach and other pest eliminators, etc. DGI sells throughout the United States mainly to large distributors who serve grocery and drug stores, and retail enterprises such as K–Mart, Target, and Wal–Mart. The U.S. market is highly competitive and the company has spent the last few years trying to increase market shares of individual products. It has had some success. A new Vice President for International Production, Mitchell Graves, was recently hired away from Proctor & Gamble with the express directive to begin manufacturing abroad and within five years achieve a goal of 15 percent of production to be foreign.

Vice President Graves has retained you because of your reputation as a lawyer who has helped numerous companies commence an investment abroad either by way of acquisition or the creation of a new company. DGI would like to establish its first overseas investments in Europe, specifically within the European Union. Perhaps at some later time DGI will consider the developing nations in Asia, Africa or South America, or an investment within NAFTA, meaning almost certainly Mexico. Basically, what Graves wants you to do is to walk him through a typical successful foreign investment, discussing the various choices that DGI will face and the factors that influence decisions in a foreign investment.

When DGI established its plant in Texas it considered whether to operate the plant as a branch of the Delaware parent DGI, or as a separate corporation. That separate corporation could have been chartered in Delaware, like DGI, but the officers decided that the Texas corporation law was not significantly different from the Delaware law and that there might be benefits to having a Texas corporation. Had it decided upon a Delaware corporation, or a branch of DGI operating in Texas, it almost certainly would have registered the Delaware corporation to do business in Texas.

The laws that affect DGI investing anywhere in the United States are a combination of state and federal laws. The basic corporation laws are state laws, many of which are adoptions or adaptations of the Revised Model Business Corporation Act. Federal law provides an overlay for some corporations in the governance of officers and directors by means of the federal securities laws. DGI seems large enough, and probably sufficiently broadly owned, to be subject to the federal securities laws.

The laws encountered in foreign nations that govern foreign investment are often very different than what DGI encounters in the United States. That may be true even when the investment is in a common law tradition nation, such as the United Kingdom, Canada or Australia. It is especially true when the investment is in a civil law tradition nation, such as Spain or Brazil.

U.S. corporate law may not include within the scope of "corporation law" some areas that other nations so include. The principal area is labor law. Whether it is considered part of corporation law or not, labor laws of the foreign host nation will be applicable to DGI's foreign investment no matter what business form (branch, subsidiary, etc.) it assumes. For example, DGI may find it much harder to lay off employees in other nations. There may be no area more startlingly different than foreign labor law, such as the participation of workers in the management of the corporation under such labels as codetermination in Germany and co-optation in The Netherlands. But are laws governing worker participation in management more correctly classified as labor laws or corporation laws? The answer may be very important when there is an issue of what law applies, the law of the state of incorporation or the law of the nation in which the corporation is doing business.

DGI is a *foreign* investor in any nation outside the United States, an outsider bringing in capital and technology and often some high-level employees. Many nations, including the United States, have laws that apply specifically to foreign investors, such as limitations on the ownership of shares of U.S. incorporated airlines. Developing nations have sometimes enacted severely restrictive foreign investment laws. The addition of the Trade Related Investment Measures (TRIMs) to the World Trade Organization (WTO) agreements (GATT, TRIPs, etc.), however, has eliminated or reduced many restrictive characteristics of foreign investment laws, such as mandatory joint ventures, required levels of domestic content and export requirements. Sometimes restrictive written laws of developing nations seem to conflict from the actual rules that are in reality applied to foreign investment, creating a kind of "Operational Code" or unwritten law that must be understood by every successful foreign investor.

There are risks, and usually restrictions, involved with every investment. We are concerned with the variations of risks and restrictions that apply to an investment by a U.S. company that decides to commence an equity investment in a foreign nation. We define risks as threats to the investment that may cause a loss of part or all of the invested capital and technology. Restrictions are rules of the host nation applicable to foreign investment. For example, there is a risk of expropriation, and there may be restrictions that limit foreign investment to a minority equity position, the familiar joint venture. There is also a risk of failure due to a lack of understanding of different cultures, although perhaps that is more a challenge than a risk. For example, Hungary as an investment location may be a risk if democratization is not successful and the nation again nationalizes foreign businesses. India may impose too many restrictions in the form of mandatory joint ventures or local content requirements. Nigeria may have a corrupt government whose officials constantly demand bribes. Brazil may be unable to control inflation and periodically establish severe exchange controls which prohibit repatriation of profits. Thus, Poland, Thailand, Kenya and Argentina may be better from the viewpoint of fewer risks and fewer restrictions on the formation and operation of the investment, even though they may be less favorable when only business issues are evaluated, such as the demographics of the market. For the immediate future, however, DGI will avoid many of those risks by investing in a developed nation within the European Union. While risks and restrictions also exist with respect to developed nations, they tend to be more similar to the risks and restrictions in the United States, and they tend to be less severe than in the developing and nonmarket economy nations in transition.

Some risks at a foreign plant are easily covered by insurance, such as fire or theft, just as they would be in the United States. Risks of injuries to employees may be covered by a state or national plan similar to workman's compensation, but liability insurance for injuries to visitors and other individuals may be less expensive because of lower court awards. Some risks of investing abroad are for the most part unique to foreign investment, such as convertibility of currency, or expropriation of the company's property, or damage due to war, revolution or insurrection. Special insurance, such as that written by the U.S. Overseas Private Investment Corporation (OPIC), the World Bank's Multilateral Investment Guarantee Agency (MIGA), or private insurers may cover those risks.

PART B. WHAT NATION WILL GOVERN THE FOREIGN INVESTMENT?

DGI at first may assume that the only rules of governance will be the rules of the host (foreign) nation in which the investment is located. But actually governance of DGI's foreign investment may be divided into three spheres. They are governance (1) by the home nation (United States), (2) by the host nation (DGI is to choose France as the location), and/or (3) by multi-nation organizations (UN, WTO, etc.). One might also wish to add a fourth, governance by international law. Although the latter form of governance might constitute an ideal form of governance in an ideal world, international legal norms that govern multinational enterprises are few in number and often contested in status.

The U.S. regulation of DGI's investment abroad, or governance by the home nation, is almost exclusively a matter of U.S. *federal* law. These laws tend to fall into one of two classes. First are those laws originally enacted to deal with domestic issues, and without serious consideration given to their impact on foreign activities of U.S. enterprises. Examples are the federal securities and antitrust laws that DGI is familiar with because they have been subject to them with regard to DGI's activities in the United States. But both these laws have an *extraterritorial* effect, although the impact abroad was not an issue when they were enacted. Second are laws that address specific foreign policy issues and are intended to achieve what are largely political goals. Examples are the antiboycott laws and the Foreign Corrupt Practices Act. DGI may be familiar with these laws if it has been trading goods in international markets, but they also affect DGI's foreign investment.

There are many other U.S. laws that affect DGI's actions abroad, such as tax laws that encourage foreign investment in "friendly" foreign nations (or prohibit investment in "unfriendly" foreign nations), customs provisions allowing assembly abroad of U.S. made parts with duties on the returned finished product applied only to the value added abroad, and programs such as the U.S. Generalized System of Preferences (GSP), which are intended to assist economic development in less developed nations. What is missing are laws of home nation enacted to carry out the demands or aspirations of the developing nations. Foreign nations must understand that home nations in which multinationals are registered and their governing offices usually located (or "seated") nearly always enact laws that are in the best interests of the home nation, usually without very much regard for the interests of the host nations. Thus, it is almost exclusively a *host* nation's laws that will regulate DGI's foreign investment.

One form of governance by home nations, in a kind of collective sense, is the product of the Organisation for Economic Cooperation and Development (OECD). The OECD, for most of the 1970s, 1980s and into the 1990s, was composed of developed Western European nations, plus such other nations as the United States, Japan, Australia, New Zealand, Canada, Finland and Turkey. In the past few years the Paris based OECD has expanded, adding such nations as the Czech Republic, Slovak Republic, Hungary, Korea, Mexico and Poland, to bring the total to 34. Possible additions in the next few years include Brazil, China, India and Russia. The OECD offers a modest form of "governance"; its recommendations have not always subsequently been incorporated into national laws. The OECD traditionally focused on the creation of *guidelines* for the conduct of multinational enterprises. Some of the guidelines consisted of recommendations regarding how multinationals should act in foreign nations. In 1998, it enacted an antibribery convention, that was discussed in Problem 8.3. One important but yet to be accomplished goal has been the completion of a Multilateral Agreement on Investment. The MAI was intended to further investment liberalization, but stalled over disputes between the United States and several other members, partly about the extraterritorial application of a nation's laws.

Laws enacted in the 1970s by host nations to govern foreign investment tended to be very restrictive. Mandatory joint ventures, minimum local content requirements, and mandatory export levels often were key elements. But foreign investors in developing nations with restrictive laws frequently were able to avoid the application of such restrictive provisions. An "Operational Code" or unwritten law existed that allowed specific, needed foreign investment to avoid some of the harsh written laws generally imposed upon foreign investment. Host nation laws of the 1970s that governed foreign investment tended to arise from two quite different perspectives. Some nations that enacted restrictive laws mandating joint ventures already had considerable foreign investment in place, such as India, Nigeria and Mexico. These nations viewed the new laws as a way to gain greater control over existing foreign multinationals and to allow their own nationals opportunities to participate directly in the equity ownership and management of the means of production in the nation. At the same time nonmarket economy nations were beginning to adopt joint venture laws that were used to admit for the first time in decades some limited foreign equity. The justification for deviating from socialist economic principles was usually that the nation needed foreign technology that would not be transferred without some accompanying equity participation. Nations adopting such laws included several Eastern European countries, as well as Vietnam, China and Cuba. Nearly all of the world's nations that have experimented with a nonmarket economy have subsequently adopted investment laws that lack most of the most restrictive features of investment laws of the 1970s. Foreign investors often preferred to establish an investment in non-market economy nations rather than in the developing nations, which was perplexing to the developing nations. The developing nations failed to realize that they were becoming more restrictive than they had been before, while the nonmarket economy nations were becoming less restrictive than before. Overall, whether nonmarket or developing (or both), new investment entered these nations in transition far more cautiously than it has in the most recent two decades, when the restrictive laws began to be dismantled, in application if not in existence.

Governance by host nations has been a dynamic process. Foreign investment laws of any given nation cannot be viewed as static, but as laws acknowledging the stage of transition of the nation towards a free market economy. By the early 1990s the restrictiveness of the earlier laws was largely replaced by laws encouraging foreign investment. The changes were both internally induced after the financial crises of the early 1980s when foreign debts could not be paid, and externally induced in order to participate in regional pacts and the WTO. The earlier GATT had not addressed foreign investment issues, but the WTO includes some coverage of investment in its Trade Related Investment Measures, or TRIMS. Nations wishing to participate in the WTO have to commit to the Agreement on TRIMS.

In addition to legislation governing foreign investment, there may be host nations' constitutional provisions that affect investment. These may reserve areas for national ownership, allocate regulation to or among specific government agencies, and generally outline the form of economy the nation has adopted. When China initially opened to limited foreign investment with the adoption of a law on joint ventures in 1979, it first amended the Constitution of 1978 to admit foreign investment. A nation's foreign investment law, or its legislative commitment to the WTO or a regional trade agreement such as the NAFTA, may not always be consistent with the nation's constitution. That may create problems with a successor government that is not inclined to view the investment laws as liberally as the previous government. But in many civil law nations the weight given to the constitution is less than in the United States, often because there may be no process of judicial review to test legislation against the constitution. Investment laws often follow amendments to the constitution, as in China as noted above.

The principal multi-nation organization that has attempted to regulate multinationals is the United Nations. The United Nations and its subsidiary organizations, however, have had little success in developing an effective, widely accepted regulatory scheme for multinationals. This should not be surprising because the UN is a large organization with an extensive diversity of cultural, economic and political norms. However laudable have been the efforts to develop a code of conduct for multinationals, the record to date has not been impressive. The role of the UN, especially the Centre on Transnational Corporations (UNCTC), became increasingly obscure as developing nations and the former nonmarket economies began to adopt less restrictive investment laws. The aspirations of some developing nations of the 1970s, to achieve development by means of reparations for alleged abuses of colonialism, and transfers of technology based on intellectual property being the patrimony of mankind rather than subject to private ownership, have been largely subordinated to a desire to achieve development through self-help. Most developing nations are presently more interested in joining the developed world than in leading the developing world. The UN General Assembly's 1974 Declaration on the Establishment of a New International Economic Order, and the Charter of Economic Rights and Duties of States, are little more than historical anachronisms. The UN's program on transnational corporations was ultimately transferred to the United Nations Conference on Trade and Development (UNCTAD), and its little known Division on Investment, Technology and Enterprise Development. The United Nations has been far more effective with the work of its Commission on International Trade Law (UNCITRAL).

Not only did these UNCTC efforts to regulate multinationals collapse, but the development of international law in general has been disappointing in its failure to establish rules establishing responsibilities of *both* multinationals and host governments. For example, the most contentious issue, compensation rights subsequent to expropriation, was before the International Court of Justice in the *Barcelona Traction* case, but the court focused on a narrow issue of ownership (standing) and did not rule on compensation.

The only significant control of foreign investment, at least until the creation of the WTO and its TRIMS, has been by the laws of the host nation. It is therefore the form of those host nation laws that is of most concern to counsel representing an enterprise planning a foreign investment, and is the subject of the some of the comments below. For DGI, the laws of France will constitute those host nation laws. Ever important is how multi-nation organizations such as the WTO have placed limitations on what nations may adopt in the form of investment controls. That will not be a problem with DGI in France; French law is receptive to foreign investment.

Because DGI is to decide to place its foreign investment in a developed nation in Europe, France, it will not be affected by the restrictiveness that lingers in some developing and transitional nations. But when it does enter some of those nations in later problems in this chapter, it will have to face some challenges not confronted in most of the European Union.

PART C. THE OPERATIONAL CODE OR THE UNWRITTEN LAW GOVERNING FOREIGN INVESTMENT[1]

Multinational officials are often perplexed over the structure of laws that govern foreign investments in developing nations. Their lawyers are

---

1. Adapted from Michael W. Gordon, Of Aspirations and Operations: The Governance of Multinational Enterprises by Third World Nations, 16 Inter–American L.Rev. 301 (1984).

diligent in discovering all of the written laws of the host nation that govern such investment, but nevertheless new restrictions and roadblocks frequently are placed before them. Many mandate expensive detours that threaten to change a potentially profitable investment into a losing venture. The Operational Code is a pivotal concept for foreign investor's lawyers to understand. It is important largely because it is not written, or where written is not publicly disclosed. Indeed, by definition it may not be publicly disclosed. The government will continue to deny its existence even in the face of increasing public awareness of its existence.

The definition of the Operational Code suggests that it is limited to formal unwritten regulations and decisions, but it may also include formal written regulations and decisions that remain not publicly available or discoverable, until when the nation's written investment laws are next revised, and some of the Operational Code concepts are integrated into the new written investment laws. The Operational Code is always at variance with the written laws, but it must not deviate from the written laws so extensively that it generates so much uncertainty that it reduces foreign investor confidence in the regulatory structure.

An indirect variance exists when positive statements of the written foreign investment law are conditioned by exception provisions, but the government so routinely grants exceptions that the positive law effectively becomes a nullity. It is a potential source of conflict because unknowing foreign investors may believe the written law to be routinely and exclusively applied. If the variance between the Operational Code and the written investment laws becomes extreme, it is in the best interests of the nation that it pass a new investment law. The new law should incorporate those elements of the Operational Code the government wishes to acknowledge as now being appropriately part of the written law, and those which it believes create unacceptable conflicts by remaining within the Operational Code. The government will continue to disavow Operational Code provisions it does not want admitted to the public.

The Operational Code has numerous facets. It has different rules applicable to foreign investors that possess different levels of power to demand a lenient Operational Code. It reflects the host nation's need to be flexible so as to obtain foreign investment, particularly in crucial areas. The Operational Code under which a company with advanced and needed technology functions is in stark contrast to the Operational Code applicable to a foreign investor entering an industry saturated by domestic-owned competing enterprises.

The Operational Code occupies an important position in a host nation's governance of foreign direct investment because it allows the government to treat foreign investors unequally. For example, an investor with leverage may be able to enter without accepting a joint venture with majority host nation equity, but other enterprises, even those manufacturing similar products, may be required to comply with a written law mandating the joint ventures. More important than permitting unequal treatment, however, is that a potentially unpopular but flexible Operational Code is hidden from public criticism. Nationalistic pressures may have caused the enactment of a restrictive written foreign investment law, but the Operational Code allows the public to think nationalistically while the government is able to function pragmatically.

The most successful multinational enterprises are those that are aware of all the various sources of law affecting foreign investment. This awareness, however, should not be misinterpreted as constituting control by the multinational enterprise. A multinational that appears to have a foreign investment with attributes that differ from provisions of the written law, may simply have "read" the Operational Code more effectively than other multinationals. The Operational Code cloaks much activity of foreign investment. It can lead to increased criticism from the public sector, particularly the press and academia, which may identify practices of multinationals that appear to the public to be at variance with the written law. The multinationals, however, have not necessarily violated the law, they have followed the Operational Code completely in accordance with the practices of the host nation government.

PART D. WHERE TO ESTABLISH THE FOREIGN INVESTMENT?

The choices for location of DGI's foreign investment are extensive. Although during the 1970s and 1980s foreign investments tended to be divided into investments in developed nations, developing nations and non-market economy nations, some characteristics of any one such classification often were present in another. Furthermore, less developed nations, in their pursuit of development, were usually in a state of transition. Within the term "developing nation" existed nations of a wide range of development, from dependent nations to advanced developing countries. Such nations as Brazil and India moved to the status called newly industrialized countries (NICs), or advanced developing countries (ADCs). Most of the once labeled nonmarket economies, essentially those in Eastern Europe and the former USSR, moved into quite diverse stages of political and economic transition. Placing a foreign investment in a market economy developed nation usually means facing fewer problems, or at least different problems, compared to an investment in a nation in transition, whether the latter is a developing or more advanced nonmarket economy nation.

When DGI decided to establish a foreign investment, the decision was at first based principally on a number of *business* rather than *legal* decisions. While some of the decisions to invest abroad are exclusively business, such as to use cheaper labor or to establish a base in the foreign market, most decisions have a legal dimension. Furthermore, an international lawyer is often expected by the client to have a fairly good knowledge about the business side of the decision to invest, and also to be able to discuss political risk analysis. The lawyers for DGI have probably not been asked in what region of the world DGI should invest, but they may have been asked where within a region is the best legal climate for a foreign investment. For example, DGI might want to manufacture cheap labor and the company may have identified six nations that satisfy that requirement. DGI's lawyers (both in-house and outside counsel) may be asked about the legal climate in each of those nations. Or DGI may have decided, as they have in this hypothetical, to establish a plant somewhere in the European Union, and have asked which nations have the most favorable legal climate. The DGI officers may not even be able to define "legal climate", but they will know that it exists in very different forms in different nations.

A frequent reason for investing abroad is to make products within the nation or free trade area where they will be sold. While tariffs have decreased markedly in the last half century, due largely to the creation of the General Agreement on Tariffs and Trade (GATT) in 1947, and more recently the World Trade Organization (WTO), there are many forms of trade barriers designed to protect local industries. In DGI's case it wanted to establish a company in the European Union to produce for sale throughout the EU. They have tentatively chosen France. They may believe that France will be the best market within the EU for DGI's products, and that it will be easy to transport them to other EU nations. They also may believe that French labor is both reasonable in its costs and demands, and stable, in contrast to other potential EU locations. DGI's tentative decision to invest in France was not difficult, and confronted no obstacles. France is investor friendly, a developed nation with a large market, has an educated labor supply, attractive culture with good schools, poses no political risk, is in the European Union with access to a very large market, and has a very highly developed and fair legal system. Most nations in the world would hope to present such a favorable investment climate. But most do not.

A major consideration of any company considering foreign investment is taxation. If a desirable location has exceptionally high corporate income and other taxes (social security, real property, etc.), the location's desirability may diminish to the point where the nation is rejected as a possible site. Many international business lawyers are uncomfortable with rendering tax advice, and are likely to add the services of a tax specialist. That may include both a specialist on the taxation rules in the foreign nation, as well as a U.S. lawyer familiar with the U.S. tax rules covering such areas as the taxation of income of the foreign investment repatriated (or deemed repatriated) from abroad, income taxation of U.S. employees working abroad in the foreign investment, etc. As in so many domestic instances, such as mergers, business reasons suggest certain actions but tax rules determine how each action will be carried out. That should be true of DGI's investment in France, tax rules will be important but will not be the determining factor of whether or where the foreign investment is made or located.

In the last two decades foreign investment has increasingly been recruited and offered incentives. This amounts to a vastly different picture of foreign investment than existed in the 1970s and 1980s, when foreign investment was subject to discouraging restrictions in most developing nations, and even in a few developed nations, such as Canada. But the world of trade and investment has changed markedly. Incentives are now the norm, and not only in developing nations. Incentives vary country-by-country, and within a country over time. Federal tax rates are sometimes reduced for specified periods of time. States or provinces, and counties and cities, offer attractive incentives. The BMW is not being made in South Carolina, nor the Mercedes–Benz in Alabama, without incentives. Many developing nations offer substantial benefits, such as property tax holidays, special exchange preferences, and such labor incentives as the absence of labor unions. Incentives are given for new investments, called "greenfields" investment, but usually not for acquiring a local company. Thus, in Part F, DGI may be more likely to receive incentives from the municipality of Montpellier in France if it establishes a new plant in the new industrial park, as opposed to buying one of the two companies that are for sale. But even if it chooses the acquisition route, the government might offer incentives to buy the state owned company, perhaps in the form of a most favorable price. DGI will probably not receive any state or local incentives to purchase the privately owned French company. If DGI plans to export most of its production, the likelihood of receiving incentives rises, especially from the federal government.

PART E.   RESTRICTIONS UPON THE ESTABLISHMENT OF THE FOREIGN INVESTMENT

At what point in the investment process restrictive government regulation or law takes effect presents another key distinction. Some nations make *entry* very difficult, by mandatory review of proposed investments, requirements of joint ventures or exemptions gained only after long negotiations and concessions, restrictions on acquisitions, numerous levels of permission from various ministries and agencies, long delays in obtaining various required approvals, finding appropriate local partners, and in far too many instances dealing with government officials demanding "payments" to process and/or approve the investment. Mexico, until the late 1980s, had in place restrictive laws governing many of these areas. But by 1994 it had removed nearly all such restrictions. France is expected to pose little problem in these areas for DGI. That does not mean that the investment in France will be unregulated; it means that the various stages will not be subject to unduly restrictive regulation.

Restrictions upon *entry* tend to assume one of two forms. Nations which recognize the corporate form sometimes restrict the maximum equity allowed to foreign ownership. Additional rules may also limit the foreign management or control to a minority interest. The enterprises resulting from the restrictions are referred to as equity joint ventures.

The manner of control over permitted foreign investment in non-market economy nations which do not have corporate forms, is by means of contract. The foreign investor's rights are detailed in what is referred to as a contractual joint venture on investment. The foreign party receives a percentage of the profits and is granted certain management rights. As nonmarket nations have converted to market economies, they have tended to adopt corporation laws and shifted from the use of contractual to equity joint ventures. They have also shifted from mandatory to voluntary joint ventures. In some cases the shift has involved a change from contractual joint ventures directly to wholly foreign owned corporate entities, without an intermediate stage of mandating equity joint ventures. DGI has avoided joint venture mandates by its focus on Europe and choice of France. But it may face them later in other investments in other countries.

One of the more contentious issues arising during the 1990s and continuing into the new century, regarding restrictions on investment, was the adoption of provisions or policies allegedly protecting the host nation's culture. Canada and France have led this effort, with support from India, Brazil and Indonesia, and many smaller developing nations. These nations believe that the WTO agreements can be read to include a cultural exception. There are thus two areas where culture affects foreign investment. One is the need of foreign traders or investors to understand the culture of the foreign nation, such as how to greet business associates and negotiate a contract, or how to present or adapt the company's product to the culture of the local market. Another area is that of restrictions faced in trading or investing when the host nation is concerned that the foreign trade or investment may harm the local culture. Although France is one of the leaders of the "cultural protectionism" movement, it is unlikely to create any serious problems for DGI. It may affect such areas as foreign franchises, where American cultural symbols, from golden arches to southern friend cooking, may be challenged.

Cultural protection is often less the protection of the nation's culture than the protection of its "cultural industries". It is hard to view a Canadian prohibition on showing a U.S. made movie positively depicting the life of the founder of the Canadian Royal Mounted Police as the protection of Canadian culture. It indeed enhances the local culture. But if the movie was made by a U.S. movie production company, with a U.S. director and all U.S. actors, it may be banned in Canada. The protection in reality is the protection of the "cultural industry", the nation's actors and directors and production companies. It would seem to gain the label of protecting Canadian culture by having a Canadian production company, Canadian director and all Canadian actors retained, even if the focus of the movie has changed to the life of Hemingway, who was far more at home in Key West than Calgary.

Now that DGI has tentatively decided to establish a foreign investment in France, more specifically in Montpellier in southern France, it must decide on whether to acquire a company already established in Montpellier, probably French owned, or begin from "scratch", often called a "greenfields" investment.

PART F. FOREIGN INVESTMENT BY ACQUISITION OR GREENFIELDS?

DGI has explored the possibility of either acquiring one of two French owned companies that make some of the same products, or alternatively starting a totally new company in a new industrial park on the edge of Montpellier. One of the French companies is owned by the French government, the other is owned by private individuals. The industrial park is land owned by the municipality of Montpellier, which offers long term leases and very attractive tax incentives. The price may be the major factor, but there may be such other considerations as obtaining known brand names by an acquisition, or faster entry to the market by an acquisition. An acquisition may involve a purchase of assets, or of shares, and if it is for shares it may be for cash or in exchange for shares of the acquiring company. If there is an acquisition there may be antitrust issues that may raise questions of the applicability of French and/or EU antitrust laws, as well as the possible extraterritorial application of U.S. antitrust laws. France may prefer DGI to adopt the greenfields route, since it will create a new competitor. But the private French owners of competitors of DGI may dislike the entry of a new foreign-owned competitor. Indeed, private owners of companies producing goods throughout France, not just in Montpellier, may not welcome a new competitor. An acquisition is less time consuming; starting from scratch requires acquiring the land, building the factory, hiring employees, purchasing machines and developing markets.[2]

If DGI is considering buying the state owned company they are involved in the state privatization process. Many nonmarket economy nations, especially in the former USSR and Eastern Europe, have sold state owned industries. But there may be a difference in buying the French state owned industry. It is more likely to be operating at a profit than one in, for example, the Ukraine. Nevertheless, the French government is probably not selling it because it makes too much profit, but perhaps because the government believes private ownership will lead to a more efficient production, or perhaps the French government is seeking revenues to cover a large public debt. Privatization raises many issues, such as how do you value the company and will the employees be entitled to any equity. Privatization is a complex method of acquiring a company, but it may be a very good deal.

DGI is thinking that it will purchase a small privately owned French company that has a good reputation but has not had the capital to expand. It will actually combine a greenfields investment, by also acquiring some land in the new industrial park and building a new factory, moving the old acquired company to the new larger location. It has avoided the problems of privatization, and the merger raised no concerns on the part of the French government or other competitors.

---

2. See, John Hadley and Sabine Durand, *Acquiring in France, Doing Business with France* (PriceWaterhouseCoopers 1998).

Fear of acquisition of major companies has led to novel ideas. In 2007 Austria discussed the establishment of an Austro-fund to buy controlling interests of major Austrian firms, such as Böhler-Uddeholm (steel), Wienerberger (clay bricks), OMV (oil and gas), Voest (steel), and Lenzing (cellulose fiber). Austria has generally been hostile to major takeovers by foreign forms, while Austrian banks and companies have invested heavily abroad. Spain has long protested major takeovers, sometimes encouraging as an alternative joint ventures. Spanish politicians, fearing a German takeover of Endesa, Spain's largest electricity company, pushed for an acquisition by Spanish-shareholder owned Gas Natural. Then it pushed for Italy's state-owned energy company Enel, to join with the Spanish firm Acciona, which had already acquired some 20% of Endesa, to make an offer. DGI is less likely to draw such attention; it is not a major player in sensitive industries such as electricity and power. But were it to make an offer for a consumer icon in its targeted nation, political opposition might arise.

PART G.   BRANCH OR SUBSIDIARY?

DGI must decide whether the French factory will be a subsidiary or a branch of the U.S. company.[3] A branch operation is the simplest form of foreign direct investment. The branch has no independent juridical status. It is recognized for legal purposes as a mere extension of the foreign parent company. A foreign subsidiary, contrastingly, is incorporated under the laws of a foreign nation, and for most purposes is subject to the laws of that foreign nation. The word "subsidiary" implies that the parent holds a controlling interest in the foreign corporation. Either wholly or majority owned by the parent, subsidiaries are generally treated as distinct legal personalities separate from their parent.

As little more than an extension of the parent entity, the branch offers its parent fairly absolute assurance of control and administrative convenience. However, the choice of operating by use of a branch subjects the parent entity to all of the branch's obligations. The subsidiary, contrastingly, traditionally is regarded as a distinct legal entity with separate juridical status. It generally does not subject the parent to liability for the subsidiary's obligations, unless there are grounds for piercing the corporate veil. Veil piercing theory is not a very well developed concept in many foreign nations. Various devices have been created, however, to impose liability on the parent for obligations of the subsidiary.

Occasionally, a single characteristic (i.e., taxation, liability avoidance) of the contemplated direct foreign investment is so important that it dominates the choice of form decision. More often, however, careful consideration of all the benefits and detriments of each form is necessary to make an informed and intelligent decision. Once familiar with all of the generic relevant factors, the investor and counsel must further review the applicable laws and policies in the specific foreign, host nation. Foreign

---

3. A. Bernut–Pouillet, French Branches: Respective Liabilities of the Manager and the Parent Company, RDAI 2000, n.3, p. 281.

nations may not attribute the same characteristics to or make the same distinctions between the branch and the subsidiary.

The easiest choice seems to be a branch, which does not require the establishment of a new corporation. The French factory would still be DGI, with probably some indication of its "Frenchness" on the building such as DGI—French Division. But because there are no separate corporations, DGI is concerned that France might wish to tax the whole DGI company, which means its worldwide operations including its U.S. operations and income. The branch will have to submit annual accounts. A major reason for avoiding the branch is that if DGI is present in France, it creates liabilities it may not wish to assume, and it risks the worldwide assets of the company. It has not taken very long for DGI to decide that it should have a separate corporation for its business in France. A separate corporation may provide limited liability to the owner, DGI, for obligations of the French subsidiary. DGI may even create an additional level of insulation from liability. It may create another Delaware corporation called DGI International, Inc. That corporation will be located along with the offices of DGI in New York and will have few assets. It will be the conduit through which all foreign business, investment as well as the trading of goods, is undertaken. For example, if there is a Bhopal-like explosion in the French plant, DGI's liability may be limited to its investment in the French subsidiary, unless it is directly liable or France has a veil piercing theory. Furthermore, France will not tax the operations of DGI outside France.[4] Since DGI is thinking of locating in France partly because it gives access to the whole EU, why not forum shop in the EU for the form of business that is most favorable to management and least restrictive, especially in reporting and labor rules? For example, DGI thinks that incorporating in England and having the French factory a branch of the English company would allow it to be governed by the laws of a fellow common law nation. But maybe that choice would be disallowed or at least disliked by French officials. DGI tentatively decides that at least initially the company will be French. Perhaps it will later reincorporate in a more favorable EU nation.

While there may be an ease of operation with a branch, DGI's concerns about liability and taxes has made the decision rather easy. The company will establish a subsidiary, probably in France but perhaps in England if further study so suggests. There are still some questions about the subsidiary. One is what forms of business organizations are available under the French law? The second is whether there is any reason to have a joint venture with some French (or non-DGI) owned equity?

PART H.   JOINT VENTURE OR WHOLLY OWNED?

Sharing equity may not be in DGI's interests. But it may be asked by the owners of the French company that it is to acquire to allow the French

---

4.   Gilles Semadeni, Xavier Rohmer and Nicolas Granier, Coopers & Lybrand CLC Juridique et Fiscal, Paris, Company Formation: Taxation and Legal Implications for Foreign Investors, Doing Business with France (PriceWaterhouseCoopers 1998).

sellers to receive both shares of the new DGI French subsidiary as well as cash. DGI will obviously want to retain absolute control, but might find reason to give the French sellers a nominal minority interest, perhaps 10–15%. That should gain their loyalty and help in making the new enterprise successful. But that can be done without giving up shares, by hiring the former officers/owners as officers of or consultants to the new company.

The suggestion of a joint venture should not be met with a reaction from DGI that they are never successful. Royal Dutch Shell and Unilever are examples of successful joint ventures. They are *voluntary* joint ventures, both parties entered into the joint venture arrangement without coercion. It may have been for tax reasons, or to have local equity owners who offer something that cannot be purchased, such as close links to the government, critically needed land, considerable capital to invest in the business, etc. It is the *involuntary* joint venture that DGI has good reason to be reluctant to enter. Involuntary joint ventures were often the heart of restrictive foreign investment laws of developing nations in the 1970s and 1980s. They were both involuntary and mandatory for a new foreign investment, and often forced upon old established wholly owned subsidiaries of foreign corporations, a process called "creeping" expropriation. They created enormous hostility and were the reason for a much diminished level of foreign investment in those nations. They often came with mandates that at least 51% be owned by the host nation or their nationals, and that the number of host nation persons appointed directors mirrored that percentage. Most of those laws have been dismantled, and mandatory joint ventures are inconsistent with the provisions of such trade organizations and agreements as the WTO and NAFTA.

DGI will probably purchase the French firm for cash and will not use the joint venture form. The French sellers proved not to be interested in acquiring any equity of DGI's French subsidiary, believing that being a minority equity holder of a French corporation that was totally controlled by the U.S. DGI was not in their best interests.

PART I. WHAT FORM OF BUSINESS ORGANIZATION FOR THE SUBSIDIARY?

When DGI formed other corporations in other states in the United States, it confronted one principal form, the basic corporation. Some consideration was given to using the relatively new limited liability company (LLC) form, but it did not seem to provide benefits that offset the benefits of the experience of using the traditional corporation form. DGI has used the traditional corporation form largely to limit its liability and not expose the assets of the parent to obligations of the subsidiary.

In considering France, DGI discovered a very different choice of business enterprises, and a different approach to the governance of corporations. The first distinction is between a civil and commercial company. DGI is clearly to be a commercial entity, as civil is restricted to professional or property activities. There are several forms of commercial entities, sometimes divided between companies where the liability of shareholders is limited, and those where it is unlimited. DGI clearly wants to form one in the former group, that means primarily one of three forms. They are:

1. Société Anonyme (SA);

2. Société á Responsabilité Limitée (SARL); and

3. Société par Actions Simplifiée (SAS).

Of these, the SA and SAS allow shares to be freely traded, while the transfer of shares of a SARL involves some formalities. DGI will choose the form only after discussions with its French lawyers. They have recommended the use of the SARL and DGI has concurred.

PART J. FINANCING THE FOREIGN INVESTMENT

DGI intends to finance the French investment both using internal resources and by borrowing. It has traditionally borrowed from its New York banks and has found that they remain the most favorable source of loans. French interest rates were found to be higher and DGI has no experience dealing with French banks. But it will establish accounts in Montpellier for the French subsidiary's working capital, and that may lead in the future to borrowing from that bank.

One concern discussed is the need to convert a large part of the U.S. loan from dollars to French currency, the Euro. At the time of the loan the two currencies were about equal, but the dollar has been falling against the Euro. DGI is not very pleased with that at least with regard to the loan, since when it converts funds borrowed in dollars into Euros at various times during the establishment of the investment, it will receive increasingly fewer Euros for each dollar. It may decide to convert most of the loan immediately into Euros to be held in DGI's new bank account in Montpellier. The Euros hopefully will not only not lose value, they will earn interest.

DGI has not given much thought to the possibility of obtaining low cost loans from a development bank, such as the World Bank's International Finance Corporation (IFC), because it assumes that such lending is directed largely towards loans for investment in developing and transitional nations, and for projects that relate directly to development, such as infrastructure. Were it investing in Ecuador rather than France it would be likely to consider such funding.

Some foreign investment financing is so large that it involves many lenders. It is usually referred to as international project financing and may involve many lawyers working on numerous issues. Lenders will probably wish to have a security interest in the company's receivables, and they may demand that foreign exchange revenues be paid into an offshore collateral account that must maintain an agreed upon debt service reserve. Perfecting such security interests can be very complex.

PART K.   RESTRICTIONS DURING THE OPERATION OF THE FOREIGN INVESTMENT

Some nations allow entry with comparative ease. Once established, however, the *operation* of the enterprise may be subject to various restrictions that divert time and resources from the main purpose of the investment. Government oversight may be extensive, with such frequent visits from different officials that it becomes more harassment than regulation. Those visits may be for no reason other than to extract some payment that may place the foreign investor at risk of violating payments to foreign officials laws, such as the U.S. Foreign Corrupt Practices Act. Restrictions are often imposed on repatriating capital or sending profits or royalties abroad, or receiving hard currency to pay for needed imports. Currency restrictions have long been troublesome to foreign investments in Argentina and Brazil, and in other developing nations. DGI is not concerned with European currency restrictions, because separate EU Member States have little individual control over the exchange of Euros for dollars.

Nor is DGI very concerned about another form of restrictions on operations that tend to be more prevalent in developing nations, but have been diminishing in use. They are performance requirements that mandate minimum local content, specify use of local labor or mandate levels of technology used in production. The elimination of performance requirements has been a focus of multinational negotiations, especially in the WTO.

Of course DGI will be subject to regulations, including local, national and EU rules. They will affect many areas of operations, including product and plant safety, plant working conditions, the environment, employee health, worker training, and a myriad of other areas. But these are rules largely mirrored by rules it is accustomed to dealing with in the United States.

PART L.   THE AFFECT OF A DIFFERENT CURRENCY ON THE INVESTMENT

When DGI invests in any part of the United States, it thinks only of U.S. dollars. But when it decided to invest abroad, it had to consider that it would in almost all instances be dealing with one or more foreign currencies. The exceptions include a very few nations, such as Panama and Ecuador, that have adopted the U.S. dollar. In Panama's case it has used the dollar since the nation's creation. Ecuador is different, it replaced its national currency with the dollar in 2000. DGI's tentative investment in France would be in a nation with a freely exchangeable, or "hard", currency. The Euro is indeed one of the world's most important and stable currencies. An investment in one of many developing nations, such as Argentina or Nigeria, would have created many more problems, perhaps most importantly sinking values in the world markets and occasional periods when currency controls restricted access to hard currency in exchange for the local soft currency. Investment in the European Union will avoid that problem.

But even though the Euro and the dollar are easily exchangeable, they may vary in exchange rates to a degree that may mean a profit or a loss to the parent DGI. An example will illustrate how important shifting exchange rates are to a foreign investment. Assume that DGI established a French subsidiary in 2001 and believed it needed € 10,000,000 (euros) to build the plant, pay start-up costs and have adequate working capital until expected profits were earned. In 2001 the dollar was stronger than the Euro—assume one Euro was worth .80 U.S. That means DGI needed $8,000,000 to obtain the € 10,000,000. Assume that the plant is now producing and earning profits. They are from sales in the EU and are in Euros. But by early 2005 the Euro had increased significantly against the dollar. Assume one Euro is now worth $1.50. If DGI repatriates € 2,000,000 in profits it may convert that to $3,000,000, while if the Euro-dollar remained as it was in 2001, the repatriated € 2,000,000 would be converted to $1,600,000. The $1,400,000 difference is very significant. DGI officials and shareholders are quite happy. But the result could have been very different. Had the Euro dropped in value by the same amount, to .40 U.S., the € 2,000,000 would have been converted to only $800,000.

The change in currency above as the Euro strengthened might have encouraged DGI to diminish production in France and sell more products directly to the EU from DGI's U.S. plants. As a nation's currency drops, as the dollar did in relation to the Euro, the nation's goods become cheaper for foreigners to buy. If an American art collector had been considering buying a Monet from a Paris gallery, and delayed during the two years the Euro increased in value, the collector might think of buying an Andrew Wyeth in the United States instead. The same may be true of a French collector. While the Monet did not increase in cost to the French collector because the dealer and collector both worked in Euros, the increasing value of the Euro against the dollar made art in the United States less costly, and thus made the Wyeth painting more attractive.

For DGI there is little concern that either the U.S. dollar or the Euro will decline against the other in the fashion that such currencies as those of Argentina and Brazil did in the last part of the last century. The dollar and principal European currencies have long moved up and down against each other, and presumably will do so in the future. DGI will watch the currency fluctuations carefully, and do some planning around their changing values. But currency issues should not assume the dimensions they would were the investment to have been in many of the developing nations.

PART M. TRANSFER PRICING

When DGI transfers goods and services from the New York parent to the French subsidiary it actually sells those services. To be able to determine the success of the French subsidiary, and to comply with tax rules, those transactions would be conducted as "arm's length" transactions, meaning at prices that the subsidiary would pay a different, unconnected supplier for the same goods or services. But DGI may be tempted to alter the intra-company transfer prices to serve other purposes. Were France to have a high corporate income tax, there would be a temptation to DGI to charge more for goods and services transferred, to the French subsidiary, because such purchases would have no tax implication and would lower the French subsidiary's taxable income. This would obviously be considered tax evasion by the French government and it is not a wise practice for DGI.

Had DGI agreed to make the acquired French company's owners 10% shareholders, DGI could by the same means of transfer pricing reduce the profit that could be distributed as dividends to the shareholders. Granted, all shareholders would receive less in the distribution, but the benefit of the transfer pricing would accrue only to the benefit of DGI by the higher prices it charged for the intra-company transfers. Because DGI's French subsidiary is wholly owned, there is no such temptation.

PART N.   TERMINATION OF THE OPERATION

The *withdrawal* or *termination* of a foreign investment also may be subject to restrictions. These restrictions may affect the ability to repatriate capital, the liability of the foreign parent or other subsidiaries in the foreign country for debts of the withdrawing entity, and the removal of physical assets from the country. Potential investors evaluate the restrictiveness at each level in determining whether or not to invest. Assuming DGI has not been satisfied with it's EU operation, it may decide to withdraw. That may involve a process by which the company simply pays all its obligations and dissolves the EU entity. But it may result from insolvency. That can raise some difficult issues. But DGI is doing well. Everything has gone right. But there may be some conflicts. There might even be a taking of DGI's property by the French government because the government believes it is in the public interest to expropriate DGI. But developed governments are rarely in the business of expropriating private businesses, and even the developing nations have for the past few decades avoided engaging in such contentious actions.

The following problems address both some of the difficulties a company such as DGI might face with its foreign investment, and some cases where things have not gone wrong, but the company is involved in more detailed planning.

While we have been thinking about the above issues, there have been some changes in the European Union and in the discussions in DGI's corporate headquarters. For several reasons, DGI has decided that France is less attractive a location for its initial investments in Europe. A plant in Germany would be closer to the markets of the new EU nations added in 2004. But DGI tends to prefer the common law corporation law of the United Kingdom, or of Erie.

PART O. WHEN THINGS GO WRONG—THE PROBLEMS CONSIDERED IN 10.1–10.7

The DGI investment *as discussed above* moved smoothly through creation and operation. But few foreign investments progress through their corporate life without some obstacles and conflicts consuming corporate resources.

We consider in Problem 10.1 some issues of form when establishing a foreign investment. We again use DGI, which is considering an investment in the EU and decides upon not France but, tentatively, Germany. Some rulings of the European Court of Justice and German courts have opened the EU to forum shopping for DGI in the establishment of its EU subsidiary. It may be able to incorporate in one EU Member State but have its management offices and plant in another. DGI always thought Germany would be closest to its markets, especially as the EU increased in size by adding nations to the East. But DGI was not pleased with some attributes of German law, especially requiring workers to serve on boards and high taxes and capital requirements. Perhaps DGI might establish a subsidiary incorporated in the United Kingdom, locate its principal place of business and manufacturing plant in Germany but have the applicable corporate law that of the United Kingdom. The problem also considers some of the issues noted above, such as commencing the investment by "greenfields" or acquisition, and operation as a branch or a subsidiary? If we choose to create a subsidiary, are there alternative forms of enterprises provided by the host nation law? If we merge with an existing company is the process governed by special EU merger laws that might be familiar to a U.S. corporate merger and acquisitions attorney? Because our foreign investment may be in a nation that has a civil law tradition legal system (it could also be in the UK or Ireland with their common law traditions), we will be introduced to new concepts of control of the corporation. DGI is also briefly introduced to a possible choice in the future, the European Union Societas Europeae. This new concept of a European corporate entity was discussed for many years, but not enacted until 2001, becoming effective in 2004.

Next we turn to some issues that affect operations. In Problem 10.2 DGI has an operation in a Latin American nation (Latina) where various currency controls have been established. Another operation is in Asia where DGI has used transfer pricing to avoid taxes and payments to local shareholders. Finally, the entire DGI group of companies has failed, and bankruptcy in several nations is assured. DGI wants all assets worldwide gathered under bankruptcy administration in the United States.

The remaining four problems in the chapter focus on special issues. However, two of the issues addressed in Problem 10.2 relate to Problems 10.3 through 10.5. Problem 10.3 focuses on the international debt problems addressed by AMABANK, an Oregon bank increasingly loaning to projects in Asia. DGI's problems in Latina explored in Problem 10.2 in the section on currency controls involve Latina's default on its international debts. Problems associated with the burdensome international debt of foreign nations hosting foreign investment are important to understanding why currency controls are imposed. The IMF enters the scene in Problem 10.3 with its changing role of policing reforms in beneficiary nations that need further IMF and private lending support. The high outstanding debt may offer some opportunity to foreign investors to gain access to this resource under debt-equity swap plans to obtain funds for investment or expansion at favorable rates. Such swaps have been used in the process of privatization as well. While the IMF's principal role is to assist in funding to correct monetary instability, essentially balance of payments problems, another entity also established after World War II, the World Bank, offers lending for public and some private projects. Some of the huge developments taking place in many nations involve improvements to the infrastructure as part of an extensive plan to accept a large private foreign investment.

Problem 10.4 considers project financing. This has become a very large part of private law practice in the past few years, although somewhat slowed (and new issues created) with the financial problems beginning in Asia in the late 1990s. Project financing often involves very considerable sums, in the hundreds of millions of dollars, if not exceeding $1 billion. There are many issues, including identifying sources of financing, obtaining the financing and preparing the loan documentation, acquiring security interests, completion guarantees, restructuring, and others. These are projects where many lawyers combine their efforts.

In Problem 10.5 DGI is back and has been sued in U.S. courts by an Indonesian union and an indigenous peoples group under the U.S. Alien Tort Claims Act and Torture Victims Protection Act for alleged violations of international environmental, human rights and cultural genocide laws; and of Indonesian tort laws. Large and small multinational corporations are increasingly facing such suits, brought in the United States by foreign plaintiffs seeking punitive damages.

Problem 10.6 focuses on another problem associated with withdrawal, but more serious than bankruptcy. It is when the host nation expropriates the foreign company, in this case the U.S. chartered RODCO operating in Marnesia. This problem explores such areas as the right to expropriate, compensation, insurance, exhaustion of local remedies, and two defenses often raised when the taking nation's assets in the United States are sought, sovereign immunity and the act of state doctrine.

A final Problem 10.7 covers an investment within NAFTA. The first part deals with investing in Mexico by our old friend Drill–Bit, from Chapter 9. This allows a consideration of a single nation's investment laws (Mexico), the investment provisions of Chapter 11 of the NAFTA, and the investment provisions of the WTO, the Trade Related Investment Measures or TRIMS. The second part of the problem involves investing in the United States, and a discussion of the U.S. 2007 FINSA (formerly Exon–Florio) provisions that provide for review of certain acquisitions of U.S.

companies for national security reasons, and presidential discretion in disallowing an acquisition.

If any lesson is to be learned from the problems in this Chapter it is that investment concepts and rules are in a constant state of change. Nations which adopt investment laws with the idea that such laws will set the pattern for effective governance of foreign investment for an indefinite period will soon lose out to other nations which correctly see the investment regulatory process as dynamic rather than static.

PROBLEM 10.1   CHOICES UPON THE FORMATION OF THE FOREIGN INVESTMENT: MEMBER STATE COMPANY OR A *SOCIETAS EUROPAEA,* "GREENFIELDS" OR ACQUISITION, MERGER OR PRIVATIZATION: DOMESTIC GOODS INVEST IN EUROPE

SECTION I.   THE SETTING

DGI from the previous chapter has decided to invest in Europe. The single market in Europe is increasing in size. Starting in 1958 with six Member States, the European Union grew slowly to become 15. Then, with a single admission of 10 nations in May 2004, the EU increased to 25 Member States. That latter admission added 75 million people to form a union of some 450 million.[1] Further additions brought the EU to 27. DGI wants to benefit from this huge market. Business reasons, such as access to markets, are paramount in deciding where to locate a foreign investment in Europe. That led DGI to conclude that it establish at least one manufacturing plant on the continent. DGI management believe that the most favorable location from a business perspective would be Germany. It now wishes to explore legal issues that might affect its decision to locate in Germany. Although DGI believes that it can adapt to the legal norms of any country it chooses, it would prefer to incorporate under the laws most favorable to management. That would be consistent with DGI's U.S. incorporation in Delaware, even though its principal offices are in New York. A variety of reasons led the DGI board to consider establishing a second facility in one of the Eastern European nations that joined the EU in 2004, or in another Eastern European nation that has commenced the process to join. Further thought led to a decision to establish the second manufacturing facility in Eastvia, a former member of the USSR sphere in Eastern Europe not yet a member of the EU. Eastvia has been selling many of its state-owned businesses through the process of privatization.

---

1. The European Union is the subject of an appendix at the end of this book. It may be appropriate to spend a day on that Introduction to the European Union before proceeding with this Problem.

DGI is yet undecided as to the size of its facilities in Germany and Eastvia, but tends to think that it will employ no more than 150 workers in either plant. A tentative decision has been made to locate the German plant in Frankfurt, and the Eastvian plant in the capital, Usala. There are excellent rail and air connections to both cities from throughout Europe.

For several years, as outside counsel for DGI in New York, you have assumed from discussions with DGI officials that they would ultimately establish a plant in Europe. You have always thought that the manufacturing plant would be on the continent, but for reasons you have not yet fully explored, you would prefer to incorporate the EU facility under the UK company law. Perhaps your reasoning is based on little more than the fact that the UK is also a common law tradition nation. But after having reviewed both UK and Germany company law you have discovered that neither has rules that strongly dictate one or the other's use in regard to the governance of many corporate internal affairs, such as the number of required directors, required meetings of shareholders and the board, meeting notices, location of meetings, capital requirements, classification and subscription of shares, accounting requirements, and disclosure. The European Union Council has adopted several Directives that have helped to achieve uniform rules and avoid the kind of race to the bottom associated with the choice of the state of incorporation in the United States. Some issues have been debated extensively within the EU, but not resolved by EU Directive, such as worker access to company information and worker participation in management. DGI would prefer to be governed by rules that limit such worker rights. That is why incorporation in the UK, or perhaps Eire (also common law tradition and the only such nation in the Euro zone), initially appears attractive. However, the long held but now challenged continental view that the applicable company law is the nation where the management seat is located suggested that it would not be possible to have DGI's plant and management in Germany without having German law the applicable company law. Three decisions of the European Court of Justice, *Centros Ltd. v. Erhvervs-og Selbskabsstyrelsen,* Case C–212/97, 1999 E.C.R. I–1459; *Überseering BV v. Nordic Constr. Co. Baumanagement GmbH* (NCC), Case C–208/00; and *Kamer van Koophandel en Fabrieken voor Amsterdam v. Inspire Art Ltd.,* Case C–167/01, 2003 E.C.R. 10155, as well as a decision of the German Bundesgerichtshof (Supreme Court), Judgment of Jan. 29, 2003, 57 WM 699 (2003), appear to have opened the door to incorporation in the most favorable Member State, while locating the management seat in another Member State. Before making a final decision, DGI has sent you to talk with lawyers in London and Frankfurt, to learn a little more about the structure of UK and German corporations. While in Europe you plan to go on to Usala, Eastvia, and discuss with local lawyers that nation's privatization laws.

DGI will probably decide to establish a separate U.S. corporation as a subsidiary of DGI, through which it will form the foreign subsidiary. That may be called Domestic Goods International, Inc. (DGInt). Thus, DGI will wholly own DGInt, and DGInt will wholly own any European subsidiaries. It might also be the entity used to acquire a European company, if that is the route chosen.

SECTION II. FOCUS OF CONSIDERATION

If DGI had asked you to assist in forming a new branch or subsidiary in California or Texas you would not expect to confront a very different set of business enterprise laws than the Delaware laws under which DGI was incorporated. There are some differences between the corporation laws of Delaware and Texas, or Delaware and California, or Delaware and any other state, but they do not reach the magnitude of the differences between some of the EU nations, such as the Germany company laws with codetermination (workers' rights to participate in management) and the UK company laws that have no such provisions. The U.S. Model Business Corporation Act (MBCA), and the Revised version (RMBCA), have been adopted in most of the states in the United States. That has harmonized much corporation law. Delaware corporation law remains separate from the RMBCA, but the RMBCA incorporates much of the substance of the Delaware law. No state wants to have its corporations "flee" and reincorporate in another more favorable jurisdiction, and thus all states tend to keep their corporation laws close enough to the RMBCA and the Delaware law so that the old axiom "If in doubt don't incorporate out-of-state" remains good advice. That advice seems less applicable in Europe.

When a "race for the bottom" is discussed in the United States, that bottom is not very far below the main floor. If there are sub-sub-basements, with laws much more favorable to corporate management than the RMBCA, they are in other nations, perhaps in Bermuda or the Cayman Islands, rather than other states, such as Delaware. Some U.S. corporations have reincorporated in one of those foreign jurisdictions, and it is not likely that such practice will end.

The differences among the company laws in the European Union are attributable to several characteristics not present in the United States. One is that while most of the EU nations are parts of the civil law tradition, there are nations such as Eire and the United Kingdom that are parts of the common law tradition. But the difference in legal tradition has not been the major reason that the company laws have some significant differences. Where there are law tradition driven differences, such as the role of a notary in the formation of a corporation, or the use of more detailed incorporation papers, both present in the civil law nations, they have not constituted the differences that cause foreign investment to prefer incorporation elsewhere. What has been of far greater concern of foreign investors is where company law requires a relatively high paid-in capital, or incorporates social norms of worker participation in company management. It is partly these reasons why DGI might, upon further analysis, prefer to have its EU entity be governed by UK company law, even though it wishes to locate a manufacturing plant, and perhaps the management seat, in Germany.

Part of your inquiry about the best location for incorporating in Europe assumes you will come to understand the differences in approaches to governance of corporations in the possible incorporation locations. You will of course rely upon local counsel in the nations under consideration, the United Kingdom and Germany, and also Eastvia, but you wish to be able to understand what the local lawyers are recommending. You also must prepare to meet with DGI's Vice President and General Counsel before you go to Europe. Some of the initial questions to discuss include:

1.   Assuming Germany is the most favorable manufacturing location, from a business viewpoint, to locate both the production and management of the first DGInt subsidiary, if DGInt incorporates a subsidiary in the United Kingdom, but locates it's management and manufacturing facilities in a branch in Germany, will UK or German law apply to the internal affairs of the corporation?

2.   Would this be true in either of the following cases:

a.   DGInt acquires a UK incorporated company, closes the UK facilities and then establishes its plant and management seat in Germany?

b.   DGInt acquires a German incorporated company and moves the state of incorporation to the United Kingdom, while leaving the plant and management seat in Germany?

3.   If UK company law is the applicable law to the internal affairs of DGInt operating in Germany, does that mean that the German rules of codetermination and works councils do not apply?

4.   Assuming DGInt will form a subsidiary in either the United Kingdom or Germany, are there choices for the form of business entity, such as the choice in the United States of a general corporation (Inc.) or a limited liability company (LLC)?

5.   There is one more possibility, incorporating as a *Societas Europaea,* an EU-wide corporate form that became effective in 2004. Can (and should) DGInt form a *Societas Europaea* subsidiary? Sometime after mid-2011 there may be another choice, a second form of European entity called a European Private Company or *Societas Privata Europaea,* SPE, which appears intended to offer benefits similar to the currently popular use of a UK LLC with branches in other EU nations.

6.   Might DGI decide not to incorporate in Europe at all but operate as a branch of the U.S. DGInt corporation?

Most of these questions are the focus of Part A. Once we have considered them, we will give thought in Part B whether to acquire an existing company in Germany or elsewhere. What merger rules would apply to an acquisition—those of the nation in which the corporation to be acquired is located, or separate EU merger rules, or both? Would U.S. anti-trust law apply? In Part C we are introduced to a concept we have not encountered in the United States, the idea of workers participating in management under the German rules of codetermination and works councils. These issues seem quite exciting to you, even more so since the president of DGI has asked you to consider becoming the first Senior Counsel of DGInt, if "all goes well" with your trip to Europe.

SECTION III. READINGS, QUESTIONS AND COMMENTS

PART A. CHOOSING THE LOCATION OF THE EUROPEAN INVESTMENT: STATE OF INCORPORATION OR LOCATION OF THE MANAGEMENT SEAT; AND INTRODUCING THE *SOCIETAS EUROPAEA*.

ÜBERSEERING BV v. NORDIC CONSTRUCTION COMPANY BAUMANAGEMENT GMBH

European Court of Justice, 2002.
200 Eur. Comm. Rep. I–9919.

By order of 30 March 2000 ... the Bundesgerichtshof (Federal Court of Justice) referred to the Court for a preliminary ruling [on] two questions on the interpretation of Articles 43 EC and 48 EC.

1. The Zivilprozessordnung (German Code of Civil Procedure) provides that an action brought by a party which does not have the capacity to bring legal proceedings must be dismissed as inadmissible.* * *

2. According to the settled case-law of the Bundesgerichtshof, which is approved by most German legal commentators, a company's legal capacity is determined by reference to the law applicable in the place where its actual centre of administration is established (Sitztheorie or company seat principle), as opposed to the Grundungstheorie or incorporation principle, by virtue of which legal capacity is determined in accordance with the law of the State in which the company was incorporated. That rule also applies where a company has been validly incorporated in another State and has subsequently transferred its actual centre of administration to Germany.

Findings of Court

As to whether the Treaty provisions on freedom of establishment apply

56. ... [I]t must be borne in mind that, as the Court has already had occasion to point out, the freedom of establishment, conferred by Article 43 EC on Community nationals, includes the right for them to take up and pursue activities as self-employed persons and to set up and manage undertakings under the same conditions as are laid down by the law of the Member State of establishment for its own nationals. Furthermore, ac-

cording to the actual wording of Article 48 EC, companies or firms formed in accordance with the law of a Member State and having their registered office, central administration or principal place of business within the Community shall, for the purposes of [the provisions of the Treaty concerning the right of establishment], be treated in the same way as natural persons who are nationals of Member States.

57.   The immediate consequence of this is that those companies or firms are entitled to carry on their business in another Member State. The location of their registered office, central administration or principal place of business constitutes the connecting factor with the legal system of a particular Member State in the same way as does nationality in the case of a natural person.

59.   A necessary precondition for the exercise of the freedom of establishment is the recognition of those companies by any Member State in which they wish to establish themselves.

76.   Uberseering is entitled to rely on the principle of freedom of establishment in order to contest the refusal of German law to regard it as a legal person with the capacity to be a party to legal proceedings.

As to whether there is a restriction on freedom of establishment

78.   The Court must next consider whether the refusal by the German courts to recognise the legal capacity and capacity to be a party to legal proceedings of a company validly incorporated under the law of another Member State constitutes a restriction on freedom of establishment.

79.   In that regard, in a situation such as that in point in the main proceedings, a company validly incorporated under the law of, and having its registered office in, a Member State other than the Federal Republic of Germany has under German law no alternative to reincorporation in Germany if it wishes to enforce before a German court its rights under a contract entered into with a company incorporated under German law.

80.   Uberseering, which is validly incorporated in the Netherlands and has its registered office there, is entitled under Articles 43 EC and 48 EC to exercise its freedom of establishment in Germany as a company incorporated under Netherlands law. It is of little significance in that regard that, after the company was formed, all its shares were acquired by German nationals residing in Germany....

81.   Indeed, its very existence is inseparable from its status as a company incorporated under Netherlands law since, as the Court has observed, a company exists only by virtue of the national legislation which determines its incorporation and functioning. The requirement of reincorporation of the same company in Germany is therefore tantamount to outright negation of freedom of establishment.

82.   In those circumstances, the refusal by a host Member State ('B') to recognise the legal capacity of a company formed in accordance with the law of another Member State ('A') in which it has its registered office on the ground, in particular, that the company moved its actual centre of

administration to Member State B following the acquisition of all its shares by nationals of that State residing there, with the result that the company cannot, in Member State B, bring legal proceedings to defend rights under a contract unless it is reincorporated under the law of Member State B, constitutes a restriction on freedom of establishment which is, in principle, incompatible with Articles 43 EC and 48 EC.

As to whether the restriction on freedom of establishment is justified

83.   Finally, it is appropriate to determine whether such a restriction on freedom of establishment can be justified on the grounds advanced by the national court and by the German Government.

87.   In the German Government's submission, the German rules of private international company law enhance legal certainty and creditor protection. There is no harmonisation at Community level of the rules for protecting the share capital of limited liability companies and such companies are subject in Member States other than the Federal Republic of Germany to requirements which are in some respects much less strict. The company seat principle as applied by German law ensures that a company whose principal place of business is in Germany has a fixed minimum share capital, something which is instrumental in protecting parties with whom it enters into contracts and its creditors. That also prevents distortions of competition since all companies whose principal place of business is in Germany are subject to the same legal requirements.

88.   The German Government submits that further justification is provided by the protection of minority shareholders. In the absence of a Community standard for the protection of minority-shareholders, a Member State must be able to apply to any company whose principal place of business is within its territory the same legal requirements for the protection of minority shareholders.

89.   ... The German Government argues that the transfer to Germany of the actual centre of administration of a company incorporated under the law of another Member State could, if the company continued to be a company incorporated under that law, involve a risk of circumvention of the German provisions on joint management, which allow the employees, in certain circumstances, to be represented on the company's supervisory board. Companies in other Member States do not always have such a body.

92.   It is not inconceivable that overriding requirements relating to the general interest, such as the protection of the interests of creditors, minority shareholders, employees and even the taxation authorities, may, in certain circumstances and subject to certain conditions, justify restrictions on freedom of establishment.

93.   Such objectives cannot, however, justify denying the legal capacity and, consequently, the capacity to be a party to legal proceedings of a company properly incorporated in another Member State in which it has its registered office. Such a measure is tantamount to an outright negation

of the freedom of establishment conferred on companies by Articles 43 EC and 48 EC.

On those grounds,

THE COURT, in answer to the questions referred to it by the Bundesgerichtshof hereby rules:

1. Where a company formed in accordance with the law of a Member State ('A') in which it has its registered office is deemed, under the law of another Member State ('B'), to have moved its actual centre of administration to Member State B, Articles 43 EC and 48 EC preclude Member State B from denying the company legal capacity and, consequently, the capacity to bring legal proceedings before its national courts for the purpose of enforcing rights under a contract with a company established in Member State B.

2. Where a company formed in accordance with the law of a Member State ('A') in which it has its registered office exercises its freedom of establishment in another Member State ('B'), Articles 43 EC and 48 EC require Member State B to recognise the legal capacity and, consequently, the capacity to be a party to legal proceedings which the company enjoys under the law of its State of incorporation ('A').

COMMENT ON *ÜBERSEERING*, *INSPIRE ART* AND *CORPORATE FORUM SHOPPING*

Only a year after the *Überseering* decision, the European Court decided *Kamer van Koophandel en Fabrieken voor Amsterdam v. Inspire Art, Ltd.,* 2003 E.C.R. I–10155. While *Überseering* allows a corporation incorporated in one Member State to have its legal personality recognized in another Member State, which would allow the corporation to establish its management seat in a location in the European Union other then where it is incorporated, and retain the place of incorporation's corporation rules as the applicable rules to govern the entity's internal affairs, *Inspire Art* goes one step further and prohibits the EU Member State to which the company management seat has moved from imposing numerous legal requirements on the company, such as certain companies having to commence with a legal capital equal to the minimum required in nation where the management seat is located (in *Inspire Art,* the Netherlands). Inspire Art was incorporated under the laws of England and Wales, had its registered office in England, and had a branch in Amsterdam that conducted all its business. The Netherlands demanded its registration as a "formally-foreign corporation", an act that would have imposed upon Inspire Art numerous Dutch company rules, affecting minimum capital and limited director liability. The Court held that subjection to these rules would constitute a restriction on the freedom of establishment and also held that there was insufficient justification for imposing such restriction.

Überseering and *Inspire Art* leave unanswered the extent to which a corporation incorporated outside a Member State may be subject to corporation laws of the Member State without violating the EU freedom of establishment rules. Stated another way, how much law of a Member State may be avoided by incorporating in another Member State, or even in a foreign state outside the European Union? That question has been discussed within the context of the real seat versus state of incorporation choice of law debate that has lasted for decades. One of the areas of debate is the ability of a Member State to mandate the participation of workers on the board of directors. This is a question of most importance to Germany and the application of its codetermination laws, and to several Member States in addition to Germany in the application of mandatory works councils. See Part C. Under current German conflicts rules, these rules are not applicable to foreign corporations, but there is renewed pressure to amend that view and include corporations incorporated in another Member State. But that seems to be an attempt by one Member State to impose its national concepts of the public interest on the whole European Union. Even if that were accomplished, it would not answer whether such application might be extended to corporations incorporated outside of the European Union, such as in the United States.

QUESTIONS AND COMMENTS

1. Why did the German Bundesgerichtshof refer the *Überseering* matter to the European Court rather than deciding the matter itself?

2. The German courts in *Überseering* appear to have ruled very strictly. German law denied legal capacity to an entity not incorporated in Germany. Underlying Germany's strictness is a strong fear foreign corporations doing business in Germany without compliance with what are undoubtedly the most restrictive corporate rules that reach deeply into what other nations consider labor law issues. Perhaps the German courts are less to blame than the German legislators, who have persistently rejected adopting measures that permit foreign entities to function in Germany without accepting German rules that may have significant extraterritorial implications.

3. Which state has the greater interest in regulating DGInt's subsidiary incorporated in the United Kingdom but having its management seat and manufacturing plant in Germany? What if its German-made products are sold exclusively in Germany? Throughout the European Union? Worldwide? Exclusively in the United Kingdom?

4. What is the real seat—where the physical offices of management are located or where the actual day-to-day business decisions are being made, or perhaps where the affects of those decisions have their greatest impact? With modern communications technology, couldn't DGInt have the real seat in London, from which orders could go out daily to any and all European manufacturing and distribution facilities? But with an affects test, doesn't that point to Germany?

5. If a nation believes it should be protecting shareholders, creditors, employees, and others having some interest in the corporation, such as principal customers, does the real seat theory best provide that protection? DGI entity shareholders may all be in the United States, its largest customers evenly distributed throughout the European Union, and its creditors in Japan. That leaves the employees in the plant in Germany, whose interests seem clearly a legitimate concern of Germany. Notice that the United Kingdom seems to have only a nominal interest—the interests of some customers. If the

real seat doctrine means governance by whichever nation has the most interest in each group (shareholders, employees, etc.) then there might be several real seats. Do we really want a doctrine that determines which state has the most significant interest in the total interests of the different groups? Would the nation that comes in second willingly defer?

6.   The German view towards governance of corporations is not shared throughout the European Union. The United Kingdom favors the place of incorporation. Nor can the real seat doctrine be stated to be a general norm of civil law tradition nations. The Netherlands believes along with the United Kingdom that the laws of the place of incorporation should govern.

7.   DGI might wish to incorporate an entity called DGInt Europe in Delaware, where DGI and DGInt will thus both be incorporated, and then locate the management seat and manufacturing plant in Germany. Would Germany have to grant legal status to DGInt Europe? The United States has a Friendship, Commerce and Navigation Treaty with Germany. That seems to give any U.S. corporation legal status in Germany. The German Bundesgerichtshof (Supreme Court), in 2003, decided that under that Treaty a Florida corporation is entitled to have its judicial status recognized in Germany. Judgment of Jan. 29, 2003, 57 WM 699 (2003). The decision was confirmed by another chamber of the German Court dealing with a Delaware corporation. Judgment of July 5, 2004, 59 BB 1868 (2004). The decision leaves unanswered whether there must be some greater link with the state of incorporation than mere incorporation, but it seems clear that any required greater link does not extend to having its principal place of business in that state. Some European scholars have expressed concern that without some substantial link there will be pseudo-foreign corporations in Europe.

8.   In view of these decisions, is the reaction of German commentators that are disturbed with the loss of the real seat doctrine more because of the prospect of Germany having to recognize a Netherlands corporation or a Delaware corporation? Would recognition of a UK corporation be closer to the view regarding Delaware or Netherlands corporations?

9.   If *Überseering* allows DGInt to establish a subsidiary in the United Kingdom and then locate its management seat and plant in Germany, it does not address whether DGInt might acquire a German company both incorporated and having its management seat in Germany, and then reincorporate in the United Kingdom, while leaving the management seat in Germany. Should it make any difference?

10.   Whatever the reaction has been by Germany, the proof of the pudding may lie in the number of German firms, estimated in an Economist article as high as 18,000 to 20,000, that have changed their German entity status to a UK limited liability company. See www.economist.com/node/4408089. They tend to be small to medium size, but have included a German pharmacy chain with some 16,500 employees. The Financial Times has concurred, in 2006 suggesting that more than 30,000 entities had incorporated in the UK with their exclusive operations conducted in Germany using branches. One reason seems to be avoiding the high 25,000 Euro minimum capital in Germany. Another is surely annual fees and taxation. Germany again is less attractive than the UK. Furthermore, German and continental

tax notions can't be forced on the rest of the EU; tax legislation to harmonize EU taxes would require a unanimous vote.

11. A significant difference in forming a corporation in a civil law tradition nation, such as Germany, in contrast to the United States, is that in the United States the articles of incorporation are usually very brief, often including only 4–5 required items, while in a civil law tradition nation the articles of association may include much more detail regarding the operation of the corporation. For example, in the corporation in the United States, the authority of the officers and directors is not specified, but left to bylaws and statutory and case law. In a civil law nation the articles may include considerable detail regarding the role of officers and directors. Civil law statutes governing officers' and directors' conduct tend to be less detailed, and civil law precedent is sparse and of less authority, than in the United States. What effect on changes does having a longer set of articles have?

12. The *Centros, Überseering, Inspire Art* decisions have instigated considerable inquiry into national corporate law rules that limited freedoms guaranteed by the Rome Treaty. Valuable and stimulating analysis has followed, including Erik P.M. Vermeulen, The Evolution of Legal Business Forms in Europe and the United States (2003); John Armour, *Who Should Make Corporate Law? EC Legislation versus Regulatory Competition,* in 58 Current Legal Problems 2005, at 369 (Jane Holder & Colm O'Cinneide eds. 2006); William W. Bratton, Joseph A. McCahery and Erik P.M. Vermeulen, *How Does Corporate Mobility Affect Lawmaking? A Comparative Analysis,* forthcoming; Hanne Sondergaard Birkmose, *A Market for Company Incorporations in the European Union?—Is Überseering the Beginning of the End?* 13 Tul. J. Int'l & Comp. L. 55 (2005); Christian Kirchner, Richard W. Painter & Wulf A. Kaal, *Regulatory Competition in EU Corporate Law after* Inspire Art: *Unbundling Delaware's Product for Europe,* 2 Eur. Co. & Fin.L. Rev. 159 (2005); Wulf–Henning Roth, From Centros to Überseering: Free Movement of Companies, Private International Law, and Community law, 52 Int'l & Comp. L.Q. 177 (2003).

COMMENT ON THE EUROPEAN UNION SOCIETAS EUROPEAE AND SOCIETAS PRIVATA EUROPEAE

Societas Europeae. A long held goal of most of the EU members has been to harmonize company law. Many British, however, have viewed the way the process has developed as a means of forcing continental concepts of workers' participation in management on all UK companies. There was considerable discussion about the creation of a European Company Statute (ECS) in the 1960s and 1970s. For more than a decade little progress on the company law was made. The emphasis shifted to considering specific issues and enacting a series of directives. Some harmonization was achieved in this manner. But a truly European company was on the very back burner. It did not reappear until the discussions of the Single European Act amendments in 1985 provided encouragement to reconsider a European company law. The UK renewed its objection to any European company law that mandated workers' participation beyond collective bargaining. Several member states began to consider a legal basis for adopting the law without a UK veto. That legal basis was included in the provisions in the proposed Single European Act, which became the basis of a new draft European Company Statute in 1989. Although the EU had earlier proposed a convoluted definition of workers' rights to include collective bargaining, which satisfied the UK, several EU states remained determined to mandate workers' participation throughout the EU, and the 1989 draft statute thus omitted collective bargaining as an alternative. But it also separated employee participation in management from the principal proposal for a new form of entity. The 1989 draft regulation included two main proposals. First was the creation of a European company, to be called an SE (societas europeae, using neutral Latin). Second was a proposed "complementing" directive which covered workers' participation. Although the drafts separated workers' participation, the Commission stated that the directive was "an indissociable complement" to the regulation and the two had to be applied "concomitantly". That meant that a European company could not be created using a Member State's company as a base unless that Member State adopted the draft directive.

In 1996 a new report was issued that perhaps for the first time acknowledged the diverse forms existing in the EU of providing for worker information, consultation and participation. A different approach seemed to be developing that recognized national "corporate cultures". Imposing worker's participation on corporations throughout the EU was no longer thought to be feasible. The emphasis shifted to adopting a structure that did not take away workers' participation in nations that allowed such rights. A dual system was proposed. Where employee involvement in management was not present when an SE was formed, such participation would not be required. But where such participation did exist before an SE was established, there would have to be participation consistent with national practices. In late 2001 the European Company Statute and related Directive on worker involvement were issued, but deferred entry into force until 2004.

The next step was the adoption of the European Private Company or *Societas Privata Europaea (SPE)*. To become effective in 2011, it allows the formation of a form of limited liability company similar to the very popular UK limited company and those of most civil law tradition EU members, such as the German GmbH, Dutch BV and French SARL. It would obtain legal existence in all EU member states. The SPE rules do not regulate labor law, tax law, accounting or insolvency. The minimum capital is a nominal one Euro, closer to the UK LLC than most other EU member states. A most important issue is workers' participation. The SPE is intended to work without workers losing any existing rights, accomplished by stipulating that an SPE will be subject to the employee participation rules of the member state where the SPE has its registered office. That means the UK will be one of the most preferred member states for registration. If there is a cross border merger, the SPE is designed to protect pre-existing rights if the registered office is changed. The SPE is intended to minimize the kind of movement of German entities to the UK as reported by the Economist and Financial Times in Part A above.

QUESTIONS AND COMMENTS

1. DGI wants to structure its enterprise in the EU so as to assure that products produced at that enterprise are entitled to move freely throughout the EU, but without having to adopt worker participation in management. Does it appear that either the SE or SPE will be of interest to DGI?

2. Does the possible use of a *Societas Europaea* increase or diminish as a result of the *Überseering* and *Inspire Art* decisions?

PART B. ACQUISITION OF A EUROPEAN UNION BUSINESS BY MERGER

An alternative to a "greenfields" investment, where the business is started "from scratch", is an acquisition. The acquisition will probably be by merger. Any acquisition DGI pursues will probably fall below the EU threshold and not be reviewed. The same may be true if the merger is subject to national law, such as merger law in Germany or the United Kingdom. But to be assured of exemption requires answers to some questions. Are mergers permitted? Are there any EU rules regarding mergers? Which rules will apply, EU rules or those in the specific country where the target company is located? Does "located" mean the management seat, production facilities or state of incorporation?

RALPH FOLSOM, EUROPEAN UNION LAW IN A NUTSHELL

Chapter 7 (2011).

Commission Regulation of Concentrations (Mergers)

In December of 1989, the Council of Ministers unanimously adopted Regulation 4064/89 on the Control of Concentrations Between Undertakings ("Mergers Regulation"). This regulation became effective Sept. 21, 1990 and was expanded in scope by amendment in 1997, and significantly revised in 2004. It vests in the Commission the *exclusive* power to oppose large-scale "Community dimension" mergers and acquisitions of competitive consequence to the Common Market and the EEA. For these purposes, a "concentration" includes almost any means by which control over another firm is acquired.* * *

The duty to notify applies within one week of the signing of a Community dimension merger agreement, the acquisition of a controlling interest or the announcement of a takeover bid. The duty to notify is triggered only when the concentration involves enterprises with a combined worldwide turnover of at least 5 billion ECUs *and* two of them have an aggregate regional turnover of 250 million ECUs *unless* each enterprise achieves more than two-thirds of its aggregate Community-wide turnover within one and the same member state. Community-dimension concentrations subject to notification also occur if the enterprises have a combined aggregate world-wide turnover of at least 2.5 billion ECUs *and* they have a combined aggregate turnover of at least 100 million ECUs in at least three member states *and* at least two of the enterprises have at least 25 million ECUs turnover in the same three member states *and* at least two of them have at least 100 million ECUs turnover in the European Community *unless* each of the enterprises achieves more than two-thirds of its aggregate Community-wide turnover in the same member state.

As a general rule, concentrations meeting these criteria cannot be put into effect and fall exclusively within the Commission's domain. The effort here is to create a "one-stop" regulatory system. However, certain exceptions apply so as to allow national authorities to challenge some mergers. For example, this may occur under national law when two-thirds of the activities of each of the companies involved take place in the *same* member state. The member states can also oppose mergers when their public security is at stake, to preserve plurality in media ownership, when financial institutions are involved or other legitimate interests are at risk. If the threshold criteria of the Mergers Regulation are not met, member states can ask the Commission to investigate mergers that create or strengthen a dominant position in that state. This is known as the "Dutch clause." States that lack national mergers' controls seem likely to do this. Similarly, if the merger only affects a particular market sector or region in one member state, that state may request referral of the merger to it. This is known as the "German clause" reflecting Germany's insistence upon it. It has been sparingly used by the Commission.

Once a concentration is notified to the Commission, it has one month to decide to investigate the merger. If a formal investigation is commenced, the Commission ordinarily then has four months to challenge or approve the merger. During these months, in most cases, the concentration cannot be put into effect. It is on hold.

Evaluation

The Commission evaluates mergers in terms of their "compatibility" with the Common Market. Prior to May 1, 2004, if the concentration creates or strengthens a dominant position such that competition is "significantly impeded," it was incompatible. * * * Effective May 1, 2004, this test was replaced by a prohibition against mergers that "significantly impede effective competition" by creating or strengthening dominant positions. Thus the new test focuses on effects not dominance.* * *. It is thought that this change will bring EU and U.S. mergers law closer together (the U.S. test is "substantial lessening of competition").

Comment on Mergers and Acquisitions in the European Union

Original Articles 81 and 82 (currently 101 and 102) of the EC Treaty, now renumbered as Articles 101 and 102 of the Treaty on the Functioning of the European Union [the Lisbon Treaty of 2009], provide the foundation for the regulation of mergers and acquisitions. Article 101 prohibits agreements and practices "which have as their object or effect the prevention, restriction or distortion of competition within the common market."

Article 101 includes the important language that prohibits "abuse ... of a dominant position." These two provisions may be viewed as the parallel to Sections 1 and 2 of the U.S. Sherman Act. The Sherman Act has been extended by U.S. courts to extend extraterritorially using an "effects" test. The EU treaty has been interpreted in much the same way by the European Court of Justice, but the latter has attempted to make the foreign effects appear as internal market activity. See *Åhlström Osakeyhtiö v. Commission*, [1988] ECR 5193.

The Merger Control Regulation, noted above in the Folsom extract, removed any doubt that Articles 81 and 82 of the Treaty governed acquisitions. The Regulation specifically authorized the Commission to challenge acquisitions that harmed competition. It also attempted to move closer to a one-stop shopping scheme by centralizing merger enforcement in the Community. Finally, it established a structure to govern the control, allowing the Commission to gather needed information and halt anticompetitive mergers before they were completed.

Several types of acquisitions are governed. One is a proposed acquisition of a Member State company by another Member State company. That could be a proposed merger of a German company into a French company, or a merger of two German companies. Second, it could be a merger proposed between a Member State company and a non-Member State company, such as our hypothetical where a U.S. company, DGI, proposes to acquire a German company. Finally, under the "effects" theory, the EU may attempt to regulate a proposed merger between two non-Member State companies, such as the proposed Boeing/McDonnell Douglas merger.

The 2004 revision of the Merger Regulation increased the scope of coverage from the original authority that was limited to mergers that created or strengthened a dominant position that significant impeded internal market competition. Article 2 of the revision provides:

1. Concentrations within the scope of this Regulation shall be appraised in accordance with the following provisions with a view to establishing whether or not they are compatible with the common market.

   In making this appraisal, the Commission shall take into account:

   (a) the need to maintain and develop effective competition within the common market in view of, among other things, the structure of all the markets concerned and the actual or potential competition from undertakings located either within or without the Community;

   (b) the market positions of the undertakings concerned and their economic and financial power, the alternatives available to suppliers and users, their access to supplies or markets, any legal or other barriers to entry, supply and demand trends for relevant goods and services, the interests of the intermediate and ultimate consumers, and the development of technical and economic progress provided that it is to consumers' advantage and does not form an obstacle to competition.

2. A concentration which would not significantly impede effective competition in the common market or in a substantial part of it, in particular as a result of the creation or strengthening of a dominant position, shall be declared compatible with the common market.

3. A concentration which would significantly impede effective competition, in the common market or in a substantial part of it, in particular as a result of the creation or strengthening of a dominant position, shall be declared incompatible with the common market.

U.S. merger and acquisition law has largely evolved in the federal courts interpreting the Sherman Act, in the form of enforcement by the Justice Department, the FTC, the attorney general of any affected state, or by private parties. Consistent with civil law theory, the EU adopted the Merger Regulation, which attempts to address many of the issues that appear before the courts in the United States. In both the United States and the EU some mergers are enforced in the U.S. individual states and in the separate EU Member States.

The proposed merger in our hypothetical is the most common, called a "horizontal merger." It would be between two companies that are both producers of largely the same or similar products. Both are said to be in the same "relevant market." Other mergers considered less anti-competitive are first, "vertical mergers," mergers between buyers and suppliers, and second, "conglomerate mergers," essentially being all other mergers.

Any proposed horizontal merger by DGI may have various effects. It will reduce the number of competitors by one. That alone has little meaning, reducing the number of firms in the relevant market from two to one is vastly different than reducing the number from 15 to 14. But what if the latter merger resulted in a leading firm with 30 percent of the market adding a firm with 25 percent of the market, leaving the remaining 13 firms to evenly share (about three and a half percent each) the remainder? The focus would then be on how the resulting firm with 55 percent of the market would be able to dominate and control the industry using its market share power. But perhaps combining market shares made the leading firm more efficient and able to lower prices? Lowering prices focuses on benefits to consumers, which is arguably a more significant factor in the EU than in the United States. Lower prices, better quality, and better service may all be important considerations to regulators. The regulating nation may gave to choose between various benefits and detriments of a proposed merger. Where the merger crosses borders, whether the German–French border or that between the United States and the EU, or lesser scale regional interests within a state or nation, the various consequences of a merger may be viewed very differently by different people. Perhaps a useful way to understand this is to consider several actual merger cases. Not every case is resolved by a judicial decision. Many are debated by the various interested parties and a compromise is reached.

Aerospatiale-Alenia/de Havilland. Boeing of the United States owned a Canadian subsidiary de Havilland, which Boeing wished to sell. Two European companies, Aerospatiale of France and Alenia e Seleni of Italy, owned a joint venture, ATR, which was the leading producer of turboprop, commuter aircraft, agreed to buy de Havilland. Two competitors existed, Fokker and British Aerospace. The acquisition by ATR would increase its market share of 50–59 seat commuter aircraft from 46 to 63%. Fokker would have 22%. ATR would also increase its market share of 20 to 70 seat commuter aircraft from 30 to 50%. The nearest competitor was Saab which would have 19%. The EU Commission prohibited the merger because of its belief that the smaller competitors survival would be in question, resulting in a monopoly for ATR. While Britain, Sweden and Germany wanted to protect their smaller participants, France and Italy objected to the EU position. Curiously, the merger would be favorable to the EU as a whole, but not to specific parts of the Community. Should the interests of European industry offset the creation of a dominant entity? The EU Merger Regulation did not provide for an industrial policy consideration to offset the impact of creation of a dominant entity.

Canada, which had approved the merger, was upset with the EU decision because de Havilland was in financial trouble. Canadian jobs were at issue, de Havilland was already being subsidized. But it relented when de Havilland was acquired by a new prospect, Bombardier, another Canadian company that kept the jobs in Canada. But not without further subsidies.

The de Havilland case showed how political a cross border controversy could be. While the de Havilland case involved some clear potential impacts within the EU, it would not be long before a proposed merger that directly involved only two U.S. entities would be rejected by the EU, location of a major competitor.

Boeing/ McDonnell Douglas. Six years after the de Havilland EU decision, Boeing, with 64% of the world commercial jet market, followed by Airbus Industrie (a consortium of manufacturers in Britain, France, Germany and Spain) with 30%, sought to acquire another U.S. manufacturer McDonnell Douglas, which had about 5% but was losing ground and could be considered a failing industry. Under a Cooperation Agreement of 1991 between the United States and the EU, enacted soon after the de Havilland case, the Boeing and McDonnell Douglas filed premerger notifications with the EU (and with the United States). The U.S. FTC and the European Commission jointly discussed the proposal and assumed very contrasting, and local industry protective, positions. The conflict quickly became political, reaching the White House. The United States appeared to conclude that the overall impact would be good for the United States, keep facilities in the country, preserve and likely create new jobs, even though the result might raise prices to consumers. That struck a sore spot in the EU, which focused more on harm to competition and consumers. Or perhaps it was preservation of Airbus over a more efficient entity?

The FTC issued a public statement that concluded that the proposed "acquisition would not substantially lessen competition or tend to create a monopoly in either defense of commercial aircraft markets."[1] The EU position was quite at contrast. Only after Boeing agreed to numerous conditions did the EU approve the merger.

COMMISSION OF THE EUROPEAN COMMUNITIES DECISION

30 July 1997 (Case No IV/M.877—Boeing/McDonnell Douglas)(97/816/EC).

On 14 December 1996, Boeing and MDC entered into an agreement by which MDC would become a wholly owned subsidiary of Boeing. The operation constitutes a concentration within the meaning of Article 3 of the Merger Regulation since Boeing acquires ... control of the whole of MDC.

Not only does the operation have a Community dimension within the legal sense of the Merger Regulation, it also has an important economic impact on the large commercial jet aircraft market within the EEA. * * * It is therefore evident that the operation is of great significance in the EEA as it is in the world market of which the EEA is an important part.

The concentration affects the market for large commercial jet aircraft.* * * [T]he geographic market for large commercial jet aircraft to be taken into account is a world market.

There are currently three competitors on the worldwide market for large commercial jet aircraft: Boeing, Airbus and MDC.

Customers of large commercial jet aircraft are airlines and leasing companies. * * *Among the latest main factors that have contributed to the industry growth, developments such as the air transport liberalization process within the Community and the additional demand from China and the former eastern block are to be emphasized.

The overall world-wide assessment leads to the conclusion that, after a significant improvement in the late 1980s and early 1990s, Airbus maintained its position in large commercial aircraft on the same level. Boeing increased its market share during the 1990s to more than 60% whilst there was a continuous decrease in the market share of MDC, in particular in the wide-body market. The combined market share of Boeing and MDC from 1989 was more or less stable at around 70%.

The very high market shares of Boeing already indicate a strong position in the overall market for large commercial aircraft as well as in the two markets proposed in the notification. Furthermore, after making

---

1.   Matter of Boeing Company/ McDonnell Douglas Corporation, US Federal Trade Commission, Statement, CCH Trade Reg. Reporter. [1997–2001 Transfer binder] ¶ 24,295 (July 1, 1997).

an inroad into Boeing's position in the 1980s, Airbus was not able significantly to improve its position during the 1990s whilst Boeing, already starting from a high level, was able to increase its market share more or less continuously during this period. This indicates that it was difficult for Airbus to attack Boeing's position in the market even after having gained a market share of nearly 30% in the 1980s. * * * The market power of Boeing, allowing it to behave to an appreciable extent independently of its competitors, is an illustration of dominance, as defined by the Court of Justice of the European Communities in its judgment in Case 322/81 Michelin v. Commission.

Boeing, as the company itself states in its 1995 annual report, has led the world production of commercial aeroplanes for more than three decades and has built more jet aircraft than all the other manufacturers combined. Given the typical long operating life of these products, Boeing has by far the broadest customer base which gives it a significant competitive advantage vis-à-vis its competitors.

Boeing has recently entered into exclusive arrangements for the supply of large commercial jet aircraft to American Airlines (American), Delta Airlines (Delta), and Continental Airlines (Continental). In November 1996, American and Boeing agreed on a long-term partnership that will make Boeing the exclusive supplier of jet aircraft to American until the year 2018. American placed firm orders for 103 aircraft, including 75 orders for the next generation 737 family of jetliners, twelve orders for the 777–200, twelve 757s and four 767–300ERs. Based on Boeing's list prices, the order is valued at about US $6,6 billion. American also obtained price-protect 'purchase rights' for 527 additional jets during the more than 20–year exclusivity period. These purchase rights enable American to determine when it wants to exercise its options to buy aircraft, with as little as 15 months advance notice before delivery for narrow-body aircraft and 18 months before delivery for wide-body aircraft, compared to the traditional 18 to 36 month delivery period. It has been reported that American did not have to pay for these purchase rights but received them in exchange for the commitment to buy only Boeing jets. At the same time, it appears that Boeing offered retroactive price reductions on aircraft purchased by American in previous campaigns.

On 20 March 1997, Boeing concluded a second long-term exclusive arrangement with a major airline when Delta agreed to purchase exclusively Boeing aircraft for the next 20 years. Delta placed 106 firm aircraft orders until the year 2006, including ten 767–300ERs, five 757/200 twin jets, seventy next-generation 737s and twenty-one 767–400ERXs. The total order is valued at US $6,7 billion. The plan also includes 124 options with an estimated value of US $8,3 billion, as well as 414 rolling options for aircraft until 2018. Finally, on 10 June 1997, Continental agreed in principle on 35 firm orders and further purchase options from Boeing, with a condition that Continental will meet all its large aircraft supply requirements exclusively from Boeing for the next 20 years.

The fact that three of the biggest airlines in the world have locked themselves into a 20–year supply agreement with a single supplier is already an indication that Boeing enjoys a dominant position in the large commercial aircraft market. Furthermore it is likely that those three deals were facilitated by the proposed merger (as explained below). Although, as indicated, the customers are to receive economic benefits from the deals, these are likely to be more than offset by the rigidity incurred by being locked into a single supplier for so long a period, during which it might prove to be the case that competitors' prices become lower, their technology and related services superior.

The existing exclusive deals between Boeing and the three airlines in question will have important foreclosure effects on the worldwide market for large commercial jet aircraft over the next 20 years. It is estimated that 14,400 new aircraft will be delivered worldwide between 1997 and 2016, of which about 2,400 are on firm order with Boeing, MDC or Airbus. There thus remains an open market for about 12,000 aircraft. However, Boeing's exclusive deals including options and purchase rights, account for an estimated 13% of this open market (or over 30% of the US market).

In view of the various characteristics of the current structure of the markets for large commercial jet aircraft, as described above, in particular the existing market shares of Boeing, the size of its fleet in service, the recent conclusion of long-term exclusive supply deals with major customers, and the lack of potential new entrants, the Commission has reached the conclusion that Boeing already enjoys a dominant position on the overall market for large commercial aircraft as well as on the markets for narrow-body and wide-body aircraft.

* * *

It is unlikely that a third party would acquire MDC's commercial aircraft business. * * *Neither Airbus, the only competitor left in the market for large commercial aircraft, nor one of its parent companies showed an interest in the acquisition of DAC. Furthermore, no other potential buyers were interested in entering the market for large commercial aircraft through the acquisition of DAC. It appears, therefore, that, given the current competitive situation of DAC, only Boeing is prepared to take over MDC's commercial aircraft business. The competitive potential of MDC's commercial aircraft business can, however, be a significant factor in the market when it is integrated into the Boeing group

* * *

The proposed merger would significantly enhance Boeing's capacity to enter into agreements such as those concluded with American, Delta and Continental. It should be noted that such airlines are amongst the world's largest and are 'launch customers' for new aircraft models, that is to say, they are in effect the only airlines with sufficient resources to commit themselves to entirely new aircraft models or new families of aircraft. In particular, with respect to those airlines which currently operate both

Boeing and MDC aircraft, within the framework of an exclusivity deal, Boeing could also offer the provision of additional MDC aircraft, as well as spare-parts and support services for older MDC aircraft. On the other hand, where airlines which have ordered MDC aircraft want to streamline their fleet, Boeing, being in control of MDC, would simply cancel those MDC orders and the penalties which normally have to be paid by airlines in the event of cancellation of orders would be of no significance. It is reported that, within the framework of the exclusivity deal, Boeing has offered to take back the MD–90s that have already been delivered to Delta and to cancel existing orders for further MD–90s. However, Boeing, when asked by the Commission, was not in a position either to confirm or to deny those arrangements.

It is also noteworthy that prior to those agreements, exclusivity deals had never before been entered into in the large commercial aircraft sector and that their duration itself is unprecedented.

The potential effect of exclusive deals with the world's top ten airlines would be to block over 40% of the worldwide market (based on those airlines' existing fleet in service as a proportion of the worldwide fleet). Such a scenario is quite feasible, since there could be a knock-on effect wereby further large airlines would not want to miss out on the apparent advantages accruing to their competitors who have already entered into exclusive deals. The result could be a split worldwide market, with the biggest airlines with the largest fleets exclusively controlled by Boeing following the merger, leaving competition possible only for the supply of the aircraft requirements of smaller airlines.

Furthermore, those deals are likely to have an extended effect beyond their already very long-frame, given the very long operating life typical of the industry's products. Thus, Boeing estimates that aircraft designed after 1980 may have an operating life of between 28 and 31 years. This implies in fact that aircraft bought in the last years of the deal, even if it is not renewed, could cover the airlines' needs up to the years 2045 to 2047. Moreover, it is also reasonable to consider that after such an extremely long period of purchasing exclusively from Boeing, airlines would probably not be inclined to face the costs of switching to a different family of aircraft.

The proposed merger will lead to a large increase in Boeing's buying power. * * * Boeing's increase in buying power could significantly weaken the competitive position of Airbus. Following the concentration, Boeing would reinforce, in particular, its buying power with respect to the many suppliers that furnish parts for both civil and military applications. The addition of MDC's buying power, especially in the military sector, to Boeing's already strong position in commercial aircraft would increase suppliers' overall reliance on Boeing and might put them in a position where they could not resist giving Boeing priority over Airbus. Boeing would be able to exert pressure on numerous suppliers to discourage them from working with its only competitor, Airbus, or to induce them to favour Boeing over Airbus in terms of resource allocation.

* * *

For the reasons outlined above, the Commission has reached the conclusion that the proposed concentration would lead to the strengthening of a dominant position through which effective competition would be significantly impeded in the common market within the meaning of Article 2 (3) of the Merger Regulation.

With a view to removing the competition concerns, Boeing has given the Commission the following undertakings:

1. Boeing undertakes to provide the following structural remedy: for a period of 10 years Boeing will maintain DAC in a separate legal entity and will supply to the Commission a report certified by an independent auditor which describes the business performance and results on a commercial line of business basis for the continued DAC business activities. The report will also be made available to the public. On these conditions, Boeing will have the right to manage fully the separate legal entity and make all business decisions it deems appropriate. The above period may be reduced in agreement with the Commission should Boeing not maintain two or more of the DAC aeroplane programmes.

2. Boeing commits to providing customer support for DAC aircraft at the same high quality level provided for Boeing aircraft. This includes all of Boeing's traditional services available from time to time for Boeing aircraft (which currently include the global network of field representatives, 24–hour technical service hotline, all aspects of spares support, including next-day shipment, responsive AOG support and world-class maintenance and flight training). Boeing also will apply the same Boeing guidelines and procedures for spare parts availability and pricing, and ensure appropriate levels of engineering support.

3. Boeing agrees it will not withhold or threaten to withhold support for DAC aircraft (including spare parts) or penalize or threaten to penalize an operator with respect to support for its DAC aircraft (for example, by raising prices or increasing delivery times for spare parts) because the operator proposes to purchase another manufacturer's aircraft. Boeing undertakes to continue to make publicly available the information (including pricing) currently available in the DAC spare parts catalogue.

4. Boeing will not use its privileged access to the existing fleet in service of DAC aircraft in order to leverage its opportunities for persuading current DAC operators to purchase Boeing aircraft. In particular, Boeing will not provide spare parts and product support on more favourable terms to some DAC operators rather than others, in order to persuade them to purchase Boeing aircraft.

Boeing proposal on exclusive agreements

Boeing will not enter into any additional exclusive agreements until 1 August 2007 except for those campaigns in which another manufacturer has offered to enter into an exclusive agreement.

Boeing will not enforce its exclusivity rights under the agreements with American, Delta and Continental announced on 21 November 1996, 20 March 1997 and 10 June 1997, respectively.

Boeing proposal on suppliers

1.   Boeing will not exert or attempt to exert undue or improper influence on its suppliers, directly or indirectly, by promising an increase in supplies or subcontracted R & D activities, threatening to decrease supplies or subcontracted R & D activities, or leveraging in any other way its own supply relationships, . . .

2.   Boeing retains its right to select its suppliers, enforce its contracts with respect to price, quality scheduling and delivery and to protect its proprietary information.

Consequently, the Commission concludes that, subject to full compliance with the commitments made by Boeing, . . . the proposed concentration will not create or strengthen a dominant position as a result of which effective competition would be significantly impeded in the common market or in a substantial part of it.

––––––––––––

The Boeing/McDonnell Douglas case is discussed in Eric J. Stock, Explaining the Differing U.S. and EU Positions on the Boeing/McDonnell–Douglas Merger: Avoiding Another Near–Miss, 20 U.Pa.J.Int'l Econ.L. 835 (1999); Amy Ann Karpel, The European Commission's Decision on the Boeing–McDonnell Douglas Merger and the need for Greater U.S.-EU Cooperation in the Merger Field, 47 Am.Univ.L.R. 1029 (1998).

Kraft Foods/ Cadbury. More recently the acquisition of the venerable British chocolate maker, Cadbury, by U.S. Kraft Foods, caused the Takeover Panel of Britain to propose new rules that would remove the alleged "tactical advantage" of bidders in hostile takeovers. Typical of hostile takeovers, the board of the target sought a "white knight" substitute for Kraft in the form of Hershey, apparently more to cause Kraft to increase its offer than to be replaced as the acquirer. Hershey was an interesting alternative because it had been moving U.S. production to the cheaper labor in Mexico. When it seemed clear that Kraft might succeed by going directly to Cadbury's shareholders than through the board, Kraft upped its bid about 5% to $19 billion and the board relinquished. The merger went through. Britain was concerned both with the possible loss of a British icon and especially the possible closing of plants in Britain. The concern was prophetic, soon after the merger was completed Kraft closed a plant in western England. The Takeover Panel suggested changes that reduced the time between the announcement by the intended acquirer of its interest and tendering a firm offer, as well as more disclosure by both firms of fees and additional voice to employees. A Confederation of British Industry spokesman went further than the Takeover Panel with reform suggestions, questioning the proper role of short-term investors in determining the outcome in a takeover battle.

QUESTIONS AND COMMENTS

1.   The Aerospatiale–Alenia/de Havilland proposed merger created an internal EU dispute. France and Italy wanted the merger to go through because it increased the size and market shares of the French–Italian joint venture. But Sweden, Britain and Germany wanted to protect their own smaller companies. Did the end result help the latter three? What might have happened if Bombardier had not arrived as a substitute suitor? Where was the discussion of greater efficiencies and consumer benefits, or was it fair to for the EU to assume that any such benefits would be offset by the creation of a very singularly dominant player in the market. In an even more exclusively internal EU proposed merger, in 2007 the EU blocked the proposed merger of Ryan Air and Aer Lingus, two airlines operating out of Ireland to many of the other EU nations. The decision seemed focused on market dominance rather than accepting any perceived consumer benefits from efficiencies.

2.   The EU decision starts with a conclusion that the merger constituted a concentration in the industry. That is hard to disagree with, but shouldn't the focus be on the consequences of the concentration rather than the fact that the market reduces from two to one.?

3.   The Boeing/McDonnell Douglas merger might best be viewed as part of the long smoldering battle between Boeing and Airbus, or between the United States government and the European Union. Either airline is simply too big to be lost, like some banks were deemed a few years ago to be too big to fail. Does the EU decision essentially hold that EU law favors protecting competition at the expense of consumers, such as Boeings improvements in technology and consumer service resulting from the merger?

4.   Is Boeing/McDonnell Douglas so special that it can't be expected to set forth rules which favor competition, the Economist once reported that the aircraft industry has "never had free and fair competition."[2] Can one reasonably expect politics to be removed from the Boeing/Airbus debates?[3]

5.   One author has suggested that the United States and the EU differed in how they viewed the merger. First, the United States didn't see much difference in the addition of MDC to Boeing because MDC was going to fail and not be a part of the market in any event. Second, the United States saw positive consumer benefits to consumers resulting from the merger, while the EU doubted that cost savings would benefit consumers. Third, the EU was extremely disturbed about the exclusive dealing arrangements Boeing had contracted with several U.S. airlines, Boeing didn't place much weight on the arrangements as important to the merger analysis. Agree?

---

2.   The Economist, July 26, 1997, at 59.

3.   President Clinton threatened trade sanctions if the merger were blocked.

6. Why did Boeing agree to the conditions? Are they conditions that have much meaning? The U.S. airlines that agreed to purchase from Boeing have continued to do so. Isn't that their decision?

7. Couldn't the British Takeover Panel have insisted on conditions acceptable to Kraft, such as promises to maintain jobs in Britain at the level at the time of the takeover, perhaps for so many years? The Takeover Panel was mostly concerned with British employees. But it is the shareholders, not necessarily a majority British, who own the company and have a right to sell their shares when offers are presented. Is there a way to meet both employee and shareholder interests?

8. Hedge funds have argued against the Takeover Panel's suggestions for changes. Hedge funds gamble on the takeover proceeding by early buying of shares of the company to be acquired. Should the Takeover Panel be listening? Are hedge fund shareholders less entitled to a say than other shareholders? Don't they help run up the price to the advantage of the shareholders who don't sell to the hedge funds? Should "short-term" investors, meaning hedge funds, have different rights than longer term investors? If so, how would you define a "short-term" investor?

9. Notice that much of the debate about the Kraft/ Cadbury merger focused on British jobs, not whether the merger would result in greater efficiencies and competition in the EU and world market, or, contrastingly, create a monopoly or strengthen an oligopoly.

10. Cadbury had roots in England to its founding in 1824. The announced takeover of a national icon by a foreign company usually brings some public outcry. It did so when Kraft announced plans to takeover Cadbury, especially over the objection of Cadbury's board. When Pepsico of the United States went after the French yogurt icon, Danone (also a major player in bottled water and baby foods), France enacted a law to protect "strategic" businesses, now known as the "Danone Law."

11. Problem 10.7 includes consideration of the U.S. Exon–Florio law, now amended as FINSA. It allows the President of the United States to block proposed mergers that might result in foreign control of a U.S. entity if the President has "credible evidence" that the exercising of control "threatens to impair national security." It has not been welcomed in the EU. "National security" is not defined in FINSA or the ensuing regulations. Should U.S.-EU proposed mergers be exempt from national security concerns?

12. Assuming DGI has found possible target companies in both the United Kingdom and Germany, DGI will need to learn something about the merger law of these specific nations. For example, if the acquisition were to involve German law, we will discover that Germany has merger rules. The German Act Against Restraints of Competition has been amended several times, including a 1988 amendment to address the issue of achieving harmonization with EU competition law while strengthening German law. The amendments achieved greater transparency in German merger control, and provided new thresholds for notifications. It is currently DM 500 million in annual sales. The Act widens the definition of a concentration to bring German law closer to the EU law. It has been criticized for failing to add a definition of relevant market. The German Federal Supreme Court (BGH) has

ruled that the relevant geographic market only includes Germany, which is thought to be too narrow and not consistent with the globalization of markets or EU competition law practice. Any impact of an acquisition by DGI of a German company would thus only be measured, if the German law is applicable, by considering the German market. Were the acquisition reviewed by the EU Commission, however, consideration would be given to the EU market and the global market.

13.   A final base to touch is the 1977 EU Directive on the Transfer of Undertakings. If all or part of a German enterprise is transferred to DGI, and some employees are dismissed before or shortly after the transfer, the discharged employees may be entitled to some protection. Directive 77/187 may apply, and employees may be entitled to maintain their jobs and former contract rights. The bargaining agreement that bound the German company may now bind DGI. Part of the Directive's intent is to reduce the ability of companies to transfer business for the purpose of downsizing their work force. Even a "substantial change in working conditions to the detriment of the employee" may constitute a constructive dismissal. John W. Cioffi, *Restructuring "Germany Inc.": The Politics of Company and Takeover Law Reform in Germany and the European Union*, 24 L. & Pol'y 355 (2002).

PART C.   WORKER PARTICIPATION IN THE EU

DGI will start as a relatively small entity (a subsidiary of DGI or branch or subsidiary of a UK LLC) manufacturing in Germany. It will have no more than 150 employees. DGI is fully prepared to comply with mandatory German labor laws. It hopes that it will not be subject to Germany's codetermination and works council rules, but that has not been answered yet. Thus it wants to know something about these rules. DGI would not be unhappy were the company to grow to 600–700 workers in the next two decades.

C. SUMMERS, WORKER PARTICIPATION IN THE U.S. AND WEST GERMANY: A COMPARATIVE STUDY FROM AN AMERICAN PERSPECTIVE

28 Am. J. Comp. L. 367 (1980).*

For purposes of comparing worker participation ... it seems to me useful to focus on five questions. 1. At what level of decision making do workers participate in those decisions ... ? 2. Through what representative do workers participate? 3. How comprehensive is the participation system; that is, how many workers are in fact represented? 4. What is the scope of participation; that is, in which decisions does the workers' representative have a voice? 5. How much voice does the worker have in the decisions of the representative who speaks for him?

There are four levels at which workers may have a voice in the decisions which affect their working life—at the governmental level through the political process or membership on government bodies, at the

---

* Reprinted with permission of the American Journal of Comparative Law.

industry level through collective bargaining, at the enterprise level through membership on supervisory or governing boards, and at the plant or shop level through works councils or union representatives.

At the governmental level, in both countries, workers participate in the political process directly and through their unions; and in both countries workers' representatives, normally nominated by unions, sit on various governmental bodies. This formal similarity, however, obscures substantial differences. American unions have far less political effectiveness than German unions. Few union members are elected to the state legislatures or to Congress; the unions have only a limited influence on who is nominated by either political party; and at least during the last ten years the unions have been markedly unsuccessful in getting legislation through Congress.* * *

... [W]hy [is] there lacking in the United States this level of participation which is so common in Europe. One reason ... is that participation in such decisions requires some acceptance of responsibility for carrying out the decisions. American unions are not structured to accept such responsibility. The American Federation of Labor cannot speak with any binding authority for its national unions on most of these matters. * * * This disparity of policies, or absence of policy, is at least in part a product of the American labor movement's lack of any unified or coherent ideology or social philosophy. There are no socialist roots or other philosophical commitments to social responsibility which can provide the basis for a common policy. There is instead acceptance of the operating principle of free competition under which each union gets for its members the most it can.

Once we see why there is no participation in national economic policy making in the United States, we can begin to understand the importance in the Federal Republic of the fact that the labor movement is unified, is highly centralized at the federal level, and has a unifying ideology. It is these characteristics which make possible the socially integrative process of participation in decisions at the national level.

At the enterprise level, the contrast between the two countries is even more complete and its implications more significant. In the Federal Republic workers participate in the management of the enterprise through representatives on the supervisory board. Under the Co–Determination Acts, workers have a potential voice in naming the managing directors, declaring dividends, and making important investment decisions concerning the enterprise. * * * The important point here is that unions have insisted that there should be participation at this level and that workers' representatives have sought "parity" with shareholders' representatives. Moreover, worker participation has been generally accepted by employers; the disagreement is only over whether workers should have "parity," or what constitutes "parity."

In the United States ... the unions reject any such role, for they view their function as one of confrontation of management through collective bargaining, and any participation in management would be inconsistent with that function.... The unions, in taking this position, accurately reflect the premises of American labor law and labor relations, for the American system emphasizes confrontation rather than cooperation. In the United States, worker participation in the decisions of the enterprise is solely through collective bargaining. Both figuratively and literally unions and management sit on opposite sides of the bargaining table as adversaries bargaining at arms length for opposing interests.

In the United States, there is no comprehensive system of industry agreements between unions and employer associations; collective agreements are typically negotiated between a union and a single employer. Only in a limited number of industries such as construction, trucking, stevedoring, coal mining, steel producing and clothing manufacturing are there regional or national agreements....

WIEDEMANN, CODETERMINATION BY WORKERS IN GERMAN ENTERPRISES

28 Am.J.Comp.L. 79 (1980).*

At The Enterprise Level. The Codetermination Act of 1976 ... mandates the formation of a supervisory board composed of 50% shareholders' and 50% employees' representatives. It applies to all business organizations regularly employing more than 2,000 employees.* * * At least one enterprise worker, one salaried employee and one executive employee must be elected, and the number of representatives from each group must reflect the actual proportion of each group to the total work force. Depending on the size of the supervisory board, two or three seats are reserved for the unions represented in the enterprise. The chairman of the supervisory board is elected by a majority of qualified members, but if no majority is attained the shareholder representatives elect the chairman from their own ranks. This is particularly important, because in the event of a tie vote the chairman has two votes on the second ballot. Only the chairman is entitled to this second vote and it may not be delegated. It should be pointed out that the second vote was introduced to guarantee the enterprise's ability to function, not to assure shareholder superiority. ...Employees are supposed to participate equally in the direction of the enterprise, but in fact do not when the chairman belongs to the ranks of the shareholders, because he can use his extra vote. The supervisory board is deemed a homogeneous body and not a pluralistic group of competing interests. However, the beginnings of such a division are found in different provisions of the Act, where employee representatives and shareholder representatives are treated separately. Corporate law is supposed to remain untouched. But the shareholder meeting of the limited liability corporation is hampered through the loss of its ability to appoint the executives. The codetermination rules are not extended to management; but the unions do expect that the elected labor relations director will enjoy

---

* Reprinted with permission of the American Journal of Comparative Law.

the confidence of the employee representatives. It is indisputable that the unions have increased their influence in the managements of large enterprises.

Probably less known abroad but not less important to the domestic situation is the second scheme of codetermination on the enterprise level embodied in the old Works Constitution Act of 1952. Under this Act the supervisory board of every stock corporation[a] and of closed corporations with more than 500 employees is divided: one third must be appointed by the employees, none of them by the union, and two thirds are elected by the shareholders.

At the Plant Level. The Works Constitution Act of 1972 prescribes that works councils shall be elected in all establishments or plants of business organizations with five or more permanent employees qualified to vote. The works council is elected by all employees. Partners, shareholders, directors or executives are not regarded as employees by the Act. In reality there are many small business organizations without a works council because the employees are not interested in establishing one. On the other hand, nearly every enterprise with more than 50 employees now has a works council.

1. *Social Matters.* The works council has a mandatory codetermination right in a number of cases, * * * mainly the formal conditions of work, e.g. commencement and termination of the daily working hours, time, place and form of payment; measures for the prevention of unemployment, accidents and occupational diseases etc. One might expect that codetermination in social matters would be confined to arrangements which do not entail additional expense, since wages and other cost-relevant factors are part of the collective bargaining agreements. But this would be a mistaken conclusion. To the extent that the matter is not completely settled by the collective agreement, the works council has additional influence in questions related to remuneration, including in particular the establishment of principles of remuneration and the introduction of new remuneration methods. It is not quite clear yet whether the enterprise can be forced to provide unlimited wage increases, but it is undisputed that codetermination of the works council can, in the fields mentioned above, enlarge the burden of remuneration. * * *

2. *Personnel Matters.* The works council has to be notified before each layoff or dismissal, whether voluntary or exceptional, and is entitled to request a hearing. If the works council has not been notified in advance, the layoff or dismissal is void and consent cannot be secured afterwards. If the works council objects to a routine dismissal, it must notify the employer in writing within a given time. The employer is not bound by the objections * * *. However, it suffices here to confirm what is everywhere

---

a. Amendments in 1994 made codetermination applicable for the AG only if there are more than 500 employees, making the rule the same for the AG and GmbH. But the 1994 law did not apply to AGs already in existence.

conceded, namely that codetermination in this field is widely recognized as a vehicle to protect employees against unfair treatment.

3. *Business Modification.* In enterprises with more than twenty employees the employer must inform the works council of any proposed modifications which may entail substantial prejudice to the employees, or a large portion thereof. Among the modifications enumerated are reduction of operations or closure of whole departments of the plant, transfer of departments of the establishment, and important changes in the organization, purpose or plant of the enterprise.

Comment on the European Works Council Directive

While Germany remains relatively isolated in its use of codetermination, the idea is shared with Denmark, Luxembourg and the Netherlands, the concept of the less intrusive *works council* has spread. It remains unwelcome but partly accepted in the UK and Ireland. After years of attempts by continental Member States, led by Germany, to force works councils on the UK, Directive 94/45 on the establishment of a European Works Council was enacted in 1994. It was amended in 1998 after the UK elected a labour government, causing the UK to adopt the modified directive. Final implementation was delayed until mid–2011.

Some forms of workers' councils have existed since the Russian revolution, where workers' councils were called "soviets." Soon to develop in Germany, they spread throughout Europe in the years between the two world wars. By means of successive proposed directives beginning in the 1970s, the EU has urged some form of worker access to broader information on issues important to their welfare, especially plant closures and downsizing. But the UK, and later Ireland, along with the European Confederation of Industries and subsidiaries of U.S. companies, strongly objected. Most EU nations adopted, or continued, some form of a workers' council in the 1980s and 1990s. They usually were formed when there were at least 50 employees, but the UK continued to lead the opposition. In reality, Britain did have something similar, called a *joint consultative committee.* When the EU proposed adoption of a Social Charter, the movement shifted to adoption of a European Works Council.

The European Works Council (EWC) Directive ultimately adopted in 1994, attempts to require that employees of "Community-scale undertakings and . . . groups" are represented on an EWC that has the right of access to company information and to consult with the company management. Small enterprises are exempt. To be a "Community-scale undertaking or . . . group" essentially requires that a company have at least 1,000 part time or full time employees in the EU, averaged over two years, and as least 150 employee in each of at least two Member States. LLCs and partnerships are included along with general corporations. Any enterprise that employees at least 50 employees

When a EWC is required, a negotiating body is formed to represent all employees in consulting with central management on a range of issues. Of course the issues of most interest are those that directly affect the workers, especially plans to merge, eliminate workers or close plants. Additional amendments, effective mid–2011, may help to clarify the scope of consultation and how a EWC should be restructured after a merger alters the number of employees. As of early 2010, more than 800 EWCs, representing some 14 million workers, had been established, but it was estimated that less than half the EWCs that should (or could) have been established had actually been created. At mid–2011, when the EWC Directive became fully functioning, debate had not ended as to whether the UK, which held to the view that they had acceptable existing workers' agreements, was acceptably in compliance. The matter is not over.

Concluding Comment on Where to Incorporate or Acquire a Business in the EU

A half dozen years ago, if the choice of location in the EU based on business reasons was Germany, that would probably be where DGI would have formed or acquired a corporation. But with EU Court of Justice decisions like *Centros Ltd.* and *Überseering*, the ability to have DGI's principal European subsidiary in the UK and a manufacturing and distribution plant in Germany began to make sense. Add lower taxation of the UK, plus the less intrusive form of works council, and corporate forum shopping on the Continent has benefits that can't be ignored. The location choice is ever evolving, we have not even addressed the use of a former Eastern bloc nation, especially a country such as Slovakia (also low taxes). In another half dozen years the choice may be very different. But for now, the experience of many corporations, including both foreign corporation such as DGI investing in Europe for the first time, as well as established corporations in the EU looking to move from a restrictive nation to an accommodating one, tends to suggest that Germany is a great place to make and sell quality products, but you wouldn't want to incorporate there. DGI obviously did some corporate forum shopping in the United States, it chose Delaware for its state of incorporation. It will most certainly want the most favorable location in the EU.

QUESTIONS AND COMMENTS

1. Why have unions in the United States so strongly opposed any proposals for worker representation on company boards?

2. We have been introduced to two new forms of employee participation, the works council and codetermination. Is DGI required to have either? Which form gives the workers greater participation? Will DGI be required to have a works council?

3. Are Summers' comments regarding attitudes in Germany consistent with the Wall Street Journal piece about the measures companies use to avoid codetermination? Are there other ways of avoiding codetermination? Changing from an AG to a GmbH no longer seems to be an option. Does a branch rather than a subsidiary now become more attractive? Fragmentation of a

company has been used frequently. Some divisions could be located in other EU nations such as its plant in Eastvia, or DGI could have several enterprises in Germany rather than only one in Frankfurt. Perhaps the others could be in different regions. Another method has been to alter the structure of power allocation within the company.

4. The Codetermination Act in Germany was challenged by some employer associations on various constitutional grounds. The Constitutional Court decided against the employers, rejecting contentions that (1) future bargaining agreements would constitute unilateral dictates to companies because due to codetermination there would be union representatives on both sides of the table, (2) property rights were not infringed, and (3) semi-parity did not injure the economic system.[1] In reaching its decision the court noted that under the law the shareholders held the edge in voting power on the supervisory board. Consequently, parity—which the employers really feared— was not present.

5. Germany pushed hard for decades seeking adoption of codetermination rules for the entire European Union. From Germany's perspective, codetermination was part of the formula responsible for its post-war economic success story, infrequent strikes and relatively good industrial relations. France, and especially Britain, opposed Germany's effort, favoring instead "works councils" with substantial information sharing and consultation between management and employees. Wiedemann (above) discusses German works councils "at the plant level," but note that under German law codetermination is mandatory for works councils on certain social, personnel and business modification matters. In the end, German codetermination principles failed to carry the day at the European level. Instead, in 1994, an EU "Works Council Directive" (No. 94/45) was adopted. Its rules are mandatory in all member states. The Directive's content anticipated the conflict and resolution of "worker involvement" requirements in European Companies (above). Directive 94/45 requires councils in companies with more than 1000 employees operating with 150 employees in at least two member states. Workers must be given information on and an opportunity to respond to a broad range of topics including the firm's economic and financial situation, employment, work methods and mergers and layoffs. But the information can be withheld when disclosure might "seriously harm" the functioning of the company or be "prejudicial" to it. Thousands of works councils now operate with little controversy, even in Britain. The European Court of Justice has held that Directive 94/45 applies to parent companies located outside the EU.

6. As of early 2005, companies began shifting factories and jobs from Germany to less regulated and cheaper EU locations. DGI is following this carefully, and its proposed subsidiary in Eastvia, might assume more and more of the German plants manufacturing if German rules prove overly restrictive. DGI is counting on changes in Germany. Those changes are much debated currently in Germany. Even the venerable co-determination law may be eliminated. While unions may be able to prevent that elimination, perhaps of more concern are possible EU directives. They are likely to move worker participation in management from mandatory to permissible as part of union

---

1. Bundesverfassungegericht (BVerfG), 32 N.J.W. 699 (1979).

collective bargaining. There was some thought that the 2004 EU merger amendments would allow cross-border mergers to avoid co-determination, but the countries with strong worker participation laws thwarted these attempts. Now, these countries (Germany, Austria and the Netherlands) laws are preserved when the workers who enjoy such rights comprise one-third or greater of the employees in the merged unit. But that may not apply if the company reincorporates in a less worker-participation protective nation. Might using an SE thwart worker participation?

PROBLEM 10.2   ISSUES CONFRONTING THE ESTABLISHED INVESTMENT— CURRENCY CONTROLS, TRANSFER PRICING AND INSOLVENCY: DOMESTIC GOODS, INC. FIVE YEARS LATER

SECTION I.   THE SETTING

DOMESTIC GOODS, INC. (DGI) has subsidiaries in several nations. In addition to Europe, it has subsidiaries in developing nations in Asia and South America. It occasionally accepted some conditions that it preferred to avoid, but for the most part it maintained its U.S. based management practices. The company did avoid accepting an involuntary minority interest in a joint venture and mandated performance requirements in its investments. (Some of these issues will be noted in Problem 10.7). DGI has total ownership of its subsidiaries, with the exception of that in Asia, where it allowed a local investment group to purchase fifteen percent of the shares in return for (1) their contribution of an excellent manufacturing facility, and (2) their close contacts within the government.

After establishing the Asian and Latin American operations DGI thought that these foreign subsidiaries would function much the same as those in the United States or Europe. The company has generally been pleased with its investments, but now each has confronted a problem in operations.

1.   Latina and currency controls. The subsidiary in Latina in South America is Factores Latina, which DGI acquired during the Latina privatization process. DGI has been working to increase the quality of the products so that it is able to export and earn hard currency to pay off the price of the privatization. The company produces various home products. About half of the production is exported, mostly to the United States, but some to Brazil and other parts of Latin America. Latina has had currency problems in the past, but when DGI established Factores Latina the country had recently adopted the dollar as an official dual currency along with the Latina peso. Similar adoptions had occurred in Argentina, Ecuador and El Salvador, and the dollar is widely accepted and used in major transactions in many other Latin American nations. Before the adoption of the dollar as a dual currency, Latina had carefully controlled its currency. It possessed limited hard currency reserves, and had difficul-

ty paying its international debt. The country had very high inflation, usually three digits and sometimes four or even five. The government indexed salaries to inflation, and prices were quickly raised with inflation. In 1982, along with several other nations, Latina defaulted on its debt. Urged by the IMF and private lenders, Latina promised to tighten its belt. It did sell many state-owned businesses under its privatization law. But many were bought by persons with more connections to politicians than experience in business. Politics prevailed when it came to reducing significant government spending, such as retirement at full salary after 20 years for government workers. Hard currency earned from exports and tourism never supported the nation's lavish spending habits. Tax evasion has long been rampant, diminishing potential tax revenue. Dealing with shortages of currency, multiple exchange rates, inflation, and indexation, however, seemed mostly in the past when DGI commenced its wholly owned investment in Latina because the dollar or the local peso were equally acceptable as currency.

In the last year it has become more and more apparent to the population of Latina that the government is corrupt and has not changed policies to bring spending within the nation's capacity to pay. At most the government seems only to be rearranging the deck chairs on the Titanic. People have been quietly withdrawing hard currency from their bank accounts, sending it abroad or keeping it in safes in their houses. Although many of these accounts are in dollars, people fear that the government might freeze the accounts, and even convert all dollar accounts to pesos. Their worst fears were realized several weeks ago.

2.   Rinisia and transfer pricing. DGIA, S.A., the DGI investment in Rinisia, a former French colony in Asia, confronted problems with both the U.S. IRS and Rinisian tax authorities over the method it uses for pricing intracompany transfers. Both U.S. and Rinisian governments allege that the transfers were not done as though they were arms' length transactions between unrelated enterprises. DGI and DGIA are quite obviously related; DGI wholly owns DGIA. DGI's initial response to you as its lawyer is that it was seeking to minimize taxes and that each step it took was lawful.

SECTION II.   FOCUS OF CONSIDERATION

Three problems that illustrate issues confronting foreign investment established abroad are discussed in this problem. They each involve issues for the most part unique to foreign business transactions, or at least significantly more complex than parallel domestic issues. DGI has learned that foreign nations are not fungible. Very different problems occur in different nations. DGI wishes to earn the highest permissable profit in each foreign nation, and be able to repatriate that profit to the United States. In Part A, we consider problems DGI faces when operating in a nation that imposes currency controls, rather than allowing the currency to float freely. Domestic inflation may impact on the company's profits, reducing a profit to a loss when currency becomes available for repatriation. In Part B, we consider intracompany pricing practices, engaging in what is know as transfer pricing. Finally, in Part C, the DGI group of companies collapses and bankruptcy ensues. There are assets in each country. And there are creditors in each country. Where should the bankruptcy proceedings take place? DGI would like to have a single proceeding in the United States. It would also prefer to reorganize as opposed to terminate.

Reading Problem 10.3 along with this problem may help in answering the questions in this problem. This problem, in Part A, addresses the specific concerns of DGI when Latina has taken the severe currency measures contained in the readings. Problem 10.3 discusses third world debt issues in a broader perspective, covering some of the organizations such as the IMF that are central to not only the lending process but to imposing conditions on borrowing governments in order to receive the loans. DGI may borrow from banks that are similar to AMABANK in Problem 10.3.

SECTION III. READINGS, QUESTIONS AND COMMENTS

PART A. CURRENCY EXCHANGE CONTROLS

Nations with soft currencies restrict their inhabitants access to hard, foreign currency for principally one reason—they do not have enough to go around. Few hard currency nations restrict the flow of their currencies abroad, although many require the reporting of large transfers. It is the market rather than the government which determines the value of hard currencies. Soft currency nations by definition have currencies which are not exchangeable. They are not exchangeable because people believe that if they accept such currency it will not be usable, or when it is exchanged for hard currency its value will have decreased. If a U.S. seller of goods to India accepts rupees, what will they be used for? The company's employees in the United States will not accept them as wages because the local supermarket in Iowa or New York will not take rupees, nor will the telephone company, nor the dentist. The company might use them to buy products from India, but India might demand dollars. If the rupees are deposited in the U.S. company's local bank, it may take time to convert them, if they can do so at all, and at a rate probably unfavorable to the U.S. company if in the period since the transaction the rupee has declined in value against the dollar.

There are a number of forms of currency controls which may confront the person or entity engaged in international trade and investment. Controls may stipulate how transactions must be structured so that the nation is assured of access to foreign currency. Thus a nation may require its exporters to use letters of credit and receive payment within a certain time period or else obtain an export license. Or the controls may assume the form of more direct limitations on access to or ability to transfer currency. Controls may also be less direct but constitute government actions regarding the value of the nation's currency.

Restrictions on Foreigners' Access to Domestic Borrowings, Even in Local Currency. Both domestic and foreign currency which is held in local lending institutions may be reserved exclusively for the use of domestic borrowers. Allowing foreigners to compete for limited local holdings may increase the interest rates for such borrowings, to the detriment of local traders and investors. Foreign investors will not wish to place hard currencies in such accounts if their access to such accounts will be limited. They will bring into the country only what hard currency is absolutely necessary and remove currency as soon and often as possible.

Restrictions on Any Access to Local Borrowing of Foreign Hard Currency Holdings. The above may be extended to limit even *domestic* persons in borrowing locally held deposits of foreign hard currencies, saving those currencies for government use for such reasons as maintaining foreign embassies, sending government delegations to foreign conferences, purchases by state-owned companies, etc. These controls indicate a severe shortage of foreign hard currency.

Restrictions on Access to and Transfer of Local Foreign Hard Currency Holdings. In contrast to limits on borrowing locally, these controls limit access to local foreign currency holdings when the purpose is to transfer that currency abroad for any one of various reasons. The reasons may vary from nation-to-nation, but often address the repatriation of capital or profits, the payment of interest on debt, or the payment for goods or technology. One nation may prohibit all such transfers, another may allow servicing of debt. This access is usually controlled by the nation's central bank, which will have a monopoly on the regulation of exchange transactions, subject only to international agreements such as participation in the International Monetary Fund (IMF).

Mandated Transfers From Abroad Into the Country to Obtain Approval of Investment Projects. To gain approval of a proposed investment, the foreign investor may be required to invest so much foreign currency in the nation. It may be a minimum percentage of the total planned investment, or a specific amount. The amount required may be to meet the needs of the foreign investor, or an additional sum which is available for local government or private domestic investor demands.

Requirements That a Percentage of Borrowing of Foreign Currencies by a Resident Be Deposited Locally. To gain access to foreign currency the government may require its own residents to convert to local soft currency a percentage of its foreign borrowings. This is counterproductive if the resident intended to bring to the country the foreign currency for investment. It will probably cause the borrower to purchase abroad or bring in only what is needed for soft currency purchases locally. The person will be discouraged from maintaining a foreign currency account locally, which may be converted to soft currency at the whim of the government.

Requirements That the Proceeds of Sales or Services Abroad Be Returned to and Deposited in Local Institutions. Another control when the government is very short of foreign currency is to require local providers of services who work abroad to "bring some hard currency home." Exporters in some nonmarket countries are often required to sell a percent of their foreign currency proceeds to the government, often at artificially disadvantageous rates and often within a brief period whether or not payment has actually been received. This frequently leads to double-invoicing with part of the proceeds left in undisclosed accounts abroad, additionally hurting tax collection in the nation imposing the controls.

Requirements That Earnings of Residents in Foreign Currencies Be Deposited in Domestic Accounts. A local resident who is a foreign national may wish to have some salary paid into a foreign account to avoid such control, and be paid in local soft currency only what is necessary to meet local expenses. Many nations dislike this but really have little way of knowing whether a foreign company pays its home nation personnel some part of the salary at home. There may be legitimate expenses in the home nation, such as home mortgage payments, education costs of children remaining in the home country, health plan premiums, etc. Companies routinely pay employees going abroad some salary at home in hard currency, and additional salary abroad in local, soft currency sufficient only to meet local expenses.

Requirements That Above Deposits of Foreign Hard Currencies Be Converted to Domestic Currency Accounts. If the above amounts must be converted to a depreciating local currency, the interest in avoiding such transfers increases. The nation imposing these controls probably has a severe shortage of foreign currency. The foreign trader or investor will be even more careful not to transfer to the host nation any amount beyond what is needed for current expenses.

Requirements That a Foreign Investor's Demands for Hard Currency Be Met by Hard Currency Earnings From Exports. This parity requirement removes a burden from the host nation to draw upon its scarce foreign currencies in allowing foreign investment to enter the country. Usually, the demand is limited to several years, at which time it is assumed that exports would increase beyond the point of earning sufficient hard currency to meet local needs.

The above variations reflect the potential for extremely intrusive [currency] controls on international transactions. Furthermore, controls tend to change frequently and thus controls to which one adapts one day may change the next and create new problems. [T]he government may take other steps which essentially constitute control of its currency and will affect international business. These are actions which characterize or influence the *value* of the currency.

Every investment in a foreign nation creates some possibility of loss (or gain) due to the changing values of the currency of the investor's home nation and that of the nation in which the investment is made. The currency of the host nation may float or be pegged to the currency of another nation, possibly the U.S. dollar. Where the currency floats, it is possible to keep track of the changing relationship of the two currencies. Where the currency is pegged to another that is less easily done, because there is always the possibility that the government will change the rate, possibly quite substantially and almost always without warning. The investor is thus subject to depreciation losses caused by the fluctuation of the two currencies. But even if the foreign currency has been devalued, it is available. That is only true, however, if the host nation has not imposed any exchange controls which may delay or prohibit the exchange of its currency for that of the investor's home nation. The imposition of exchange controls is most likely where the nation has a shortage of foreign currency, often attributable to a balance of payments problem.

When [exchange] controls exist in a nation with high inflation, the problems become more serious. If an investor waits for its money while its exchange value plummets, a profit may soon vanish. If indexation is present (that process of various money values being adjusted to inflation, such as pensions and salaries), however, the profit may retain its value until repatriation. If indexing is not applied to all obligations, then severe distortions may be present. Latina, like its neighbors Argentina and Brazil in the 1980s, achieved a high state of indexing-nirvana in the 1990s.

DGI is interested both in how it might be affected by Latina currency controls, and how it might avoid the negative impact of such controls. One method Factores plans to use is to enter into agreements to sell goods abroad for dollar amounts but disclose the sales prices to the Latina government as being for lower amounts, and thus convert only part of the dollars actually received into pesos (Latina currency) under the mandatory sales and currency conversion rules in effect in Latina. The balance would be transferred directly to the parent DGI.

The President of Latina made the following announcement one month ago: Speech by the President of Latina to the Congress and the Nation.

I will send to the Congress today the first measures we are adopting to implement the national reconstruction plan, which was presented to the nation yesterday. My economic programmes rest on the principles that above all we need a moral reform in the economic field. Governments once coexisted calmly with tax evasion and corruption. Parasitic businessmen and lax bureaucrats, although they were a minority, set the tone for previous administrations. All this will end here and now! I am determined to adopt the following measures, which are designed to have a moralising effect:

(1) Economic abuse will be punishable by up to five years in jail. Managers, directors and owners of businesses can be jailed for hoarding goods, charging exorbitant prices or deceiving consumers.

(2) Public servants who participate in acts detrimental to the Treasury will be dismissed and jailed.

(3) All perquisites, falsified salary payments and so on will be abolished.

(4) The anonymity of hidden wealth obtained through tax evasion will be ended. Bearer securities and other devices contributing to secrecy that protects even criminals will be eliminated.

(5) The very wealthy will henceforth make payments to clean up the country.

(6) Capital gains from stock sales will henceforth be taxed. This ends an unfair discrimination; wage earners paid income tax on their meagre salaries, while employers made speculative gains without paying a cent to the Treasury.

These measures have already been adopted. I am thereby fulfilling on the first day of my term my commitment not to condone injustice from the start. On this platform of decency, I am determined that this year's public deficit will be zero. There is no way to bring down inflation if the government spends more than it collects in revenues. Therefore, we have adopted the following measures:

(1) The implementation of far-reaching administrative reforms involving the dismissal of bad public servants and the closing of ministries, decentralised agencies and public enterprises.

(2) The suspension of all subsidies, including those to exporters and the computer industry.

(3) The inclusion of agricultural income in the federal government's tax base in order to strengthen the system for financing the livestock and agricultural sector.

(4) A drastic reduction in the loss of tax revenues through the quasi-instant indexation of taxes owed to the federal government, and the updating of IPI [manufactured goods tax] percentages.

(5) Readjustment of public prices that lag behind cost.

The third group of measures that we are instituting is intended to modernise our economy, to bring it into line with what is happening in the rest of the world. We recognise that free enterprise is the only road to self-sustained and progressive growth. To stimulate competition is, in the medium-term, the most important task of a government that seeks an updated and dynamic economy. To this effect, we are determined to do the following

(1) Bring the fluctuation of the foreign exchange rate under government control.

(2) Reduce import barriers and stimulate the participation of foreign capital in the nation's development

(3) Initiate an ambitious programme to denationalise the economy.

(4) Privatise debts to the federal government by auctioning them to individuals who want to buy them.

(5) Create privatisation certificates as a means to speed the process of denationalisation; financial institutions, pension funds, insurance companies and so forth will be required to buy these certificates.

For lasting price stability, it is necessary to implement an austere monetary reform capable of returning currency controls to the state. Currency controls represent a guarantee for currency stability, a basic characteristic of the state's sovereignty, and a basic precondition for the development of civilised life. True monetary reform is not just a matter of changing the denomination in which prices and contracts are specified. It must involve deep processes to achieve liquidity and create purchasing power. In this regard, it is necessary to eliminate, with one stroke, the practices that undermine the monetary standard and the practices of those who grow rich on the devaluation of money. These were the practices that prevailed in Latina over the past few years. The measures are very comprehensive. And difficult as they are, however, they are designed to preserve the rights of the citizen.

Messrs Ministers, Secretaries, Leaders of the National Congress. Latina is weary of the rhetorical indignation that for too long has fueled the sea of complacency in which most of our elite leaders have been immersed. The people demand that moral indignation be promptly translated into decisions and actions. The nation demands that we decide and take action. Our decisions will again be legitimate as a result of the culmination of the process of democratic institutionalisation. I have received from the people the responsibility of exercising our powers, as well as the duties to make serious decisions in their name. We must now regain our ability to take action. If we fail to do so, our decisions will not have the desired effects. We must overcome the paradoxical immobility in which we are immersed. The crisis of the state is preventing us from taking effective measures and the crisis continues to persist because no measures are taken. This is a logic of self-seeking cowards, a logic that unfortunately is linked with the image of the public sector in Latina.

This is another reason why many of the measures I am submitting to the legislature and to the nation are designed to bring about the moral and functional recovery of the state apparatus. It will be to no avail to be tuned in with the people's desires if the instruments at our disposal are not in keeping with the feelings of our nation or with the urgent needs of this time. It would be to no avail for the patient to have confidence in the expertise of his doctor, if the doctor lacks the instruments required to treat him. Latina understands its circumstances very well. The government machinery requires dramatic reforms. This was strongly emphasised in our electoral campaign. The distortions that kept on accumulating in the public sector not only reduced its usefulness, but set an example of highly obnoxious consequences for the country's economic life. The most obvious of those distortions is inflation. The reform of the state is a fundamental aspect of the fight against the uncontrolled explosion of prices. As of now, the government will lead great efforts both to remove the state from places where it should never have been and from places it is no longer needed, and to take action in places where it has never been or where its presence has never met the most elementary needs of the population. This is not an ideological option; this is an imperative of reality and a decision of the majority of the Latina people.

With the culmination of the democratic transition, society has recovered its sovereign control over the state. This must be fully understood and assimilated, once and for all. Today the state is certainly no longer the engine of our history, even if it once was in the past. It is neither an engine nor a lifesaver. In a democracy, the nation is not saved by the government, but by society. The government, an instrument subject to the rule of the popular will and of the laws that stem from that will, should interpret the community's aspirations; should sum up those aspirations and raise signposts on the roads to be followed; should lead and orientate the march of the nation in the direction it has chosen; should maintain, and whenever necessary re-establish, the authority of the state, an authority rooted in respect for the nation itself; should safeguard public morality; should sustain the nation's ability to trust in itself and to inspire trust in other nations with which we share life of earth. This is not a small undertaking, but this is what we are going to do. We have no alternative. Latina can no longer accept defeats. The alternatives are now only to win, or to win. Thank you very much.

Two weeks after the above announcement Latina undertook the following by legislative and presidential actions:

1.　Suspended all debt payments (about $100 billion) and asked the IMF to accelerate the payment of $2 billion of previously promised hard currency. The savings in defaulting on the debt will be used for social programs and job creation. Unemployment is about 20 percent.

2.　The peso was delinked from its one-to-one linkage to the U.S. dollar and the announced rate two weeks ago was 1.4 pesos to $1. During the past 14 days the ratio has dropped slowly to 1.9 pesos to the dollar. Short term borrowing interest rates have reached 700 percent.

3.　All utility bills have been frozen. Utilities companies (gas, electric and telephone) have been ordered to freeze prices at the amount prior to devaluation and to allow payment in pesos. Most utilities are privately owned (domestic and foreign) as a result of privatization over the past decade.

4.　All mortgages of less than $100,000 were converted to pesos at the one-to-one rate in effect on the day of the president's speech. Many bank liabilities remain payable in dollars. Spanish banks are heavily invested in Latina and expect huge losses. Their shares have dropped 10–12 percent in the past month.

5.　The government plans to issue a new emergency third currency. It will be called the toucan (a bird which struggles to remain aloft just as past Latina currencies have struggled to remain afloat), and will be the currency paid to government workers, pensioners, and government contractors. The amount printed and issued will depend on national needs. It will be issued one-to-one with the peso but allowed to float freely. The peso will be subject to a controlled float. The toucan will be backed by the president's pledging his presidential mansion, many government buildings and foreign embassies in other nations as the currencies collateral.

6.　All dollar deposits were converted to peso deposits at one-to-one. Depositors may withdraw up to $1,000 pesos a month. They may write checks and may use debit and credit cards.

7.　The government announced a new export tax yesterday to raise needed revenue.

QUESTIONS AND COMMENTS

1.   Should DGI welcome the President's speech and the actions following that speech? Consider each of the speeches provisions and the actions of the government, and how they might affect DGI and Factores.

2.   Latina wants to reduce inflation, and appears to be doing so by keeping the peso high, adopting a new currency—the toucan, and maintaining restrictions on the local forex (foreign exchange) market. Some currency restrictions are established as unwritten policies not generally disclosed to the public. See F.A. Mann, The Legal Aspects of Money (4th ed. 1983); Keith Rosenn, Law and Inflation (1982).

3.   Latina has responded to the large gap in their government budget and expected revenues. Russia responded in 1998 to a similar problem by printing new currency. Might not Latina choose to correct its problems and close the gap between expenditures and revenue by printing more pesos and seek hard currency loans for the balance? How would such action affect Factores purchase of needed imports, selling its products in and outside Latina, and repatriating profits to DGI for sales in Latina? Might not Latina also follow a Mexican practice in the 1980s by ordering that all proceeds for sales of goods exported from Latina be accounted for and converted into pesos at the government established exchange rate. That rate is controlled and is perhaps inflated. Factores had a fairly large dollar account. What should Factores. be thinking about?

4.   Factores has found that many local suppliers, house owners renting to Factores officers, and even merchants, who were happy to deal either in dollars or pesos over the past few years are now demanding payments in U.S. dollars. The economy seems to be "dollarized". How does this affect Factores?

5.   DGI may have difficulty obtaining local financing if interest rates are high. In Argentina, interest rates were about 600 percent per month in early 1990. The 1991 stabilization plan included reducing the australes in circulation by converting seven day bank deposits into ten year bonds. For DGI, facing similar problems in Latina, it may mean a reduction of its Latina pesos, some of which it would try to convert into dollars to repatriate, and some of which it would use to pay local expenses, particularly salaries. But there was a bright side in Argentina. The new Argentine bonds were trading at about half face value on the market, but could be used by companies at full value to pay tax obligations. If circumstances are similar in Latina, DGI may be able to buy bonds at half value and use them to pay taxes at full value. But DGI would prefer less unpredictability in its operations. It would gladly trade this tax benefit for *nominal* inflation and the ability to repatriate its profits. Another part of the Argentina miracle was lowering interest rates. By 1994 short term rates were about 30 percent per annum, a significant drop from 600 percent per month. But the Argentine "miracle" was soon in trouble. In 2002 the government defaulted on the debt, the largest default in its history. As of early 2005, the government was asking debtors to write down some $100 billion of holdings. N.Y.Times at C4, Jan. 12, 2005. Even if the proposed arrangement of 25–30 cents on the dollar were acceptable to bondholders,

Argentina's history suggests that the new instruments would be most uncertain in a few years. The Argentine actions seem to push the nation closer to losing access to global capital markets. While the president argued that payment of the nation's debt would divert funds from important social programs, little thought was given to correcting government corruption and the nation's habit of living beyond its means. Argentina may be less a developing nation than a dependent nation. Another difficulty affecting Argentina and international payments has been its rejection of ICSID awards rendered against it. Argentina has sought annulment of arbitration awards rendered against it, but has not withdrawn from its ICSID obligations. Contrastingly, in 2007 Bolivia denounced the ICSID, allowing Bolivia to withdraw six months thereafter. It is the first ever withdrawal. By mid–2008 Argentina was again an economic disaster, borrowing $1 billion from Venezuela at 15% interest, bond prices had plunged, commodity prices down, a proposed export tax rejected by Congress, and a main topic of conversation the longevity of the Kirchners. The peg had collapsed not long after it was created and dollar accounts reached the neighborhood of $100 billion dollars when what investors should worry about happened. Dollar accounts were pesoized on a one to one basis. The dollar demand skyrocketed and the peso dropped to five to the dollar. In mid–2011 it was holding at four to five to the dollar. It may be a long time before foreign investors keep dollar accounts in Argentina.

    6.   What investors faced in Brazil in the past two decades started similar to Argentina, but Brazil in 2011 looked far better. Several reform plans were introduced in the late 1980s but none was effective. At the end of February, 1990, inflation on an annualized basis was near 5,000 percent. In March the new president announced a more severe plan. It is the plan which the president of Latina adopted and announced, as included above in the readings. Brazil, like Argentina, introduced new and drastic measures. None seemed to work. But in the summer of 1994 Brazil introduced the *plano real*, imposing tighter fiscal and monetary measures. By late 1994, the new currency unit, the real, had helped to reduce monthly inflation from 45 percent (compounded to 8,500 percent annually) early in the year to below ten percent. The new *real* had been issued at one to the dollar. But by 1999 attempts to keep the one-to-one rate were abandoned and after the exchange linkage was ended the *real* sank to four to the dollar. It soon returned to a little better than three to the dollar, due both to some internal factors such as political stability, and external factors such as the falling dollar on the world market. By 2005 the government was announcing that the currency was truly floating, while it intervened daily to try to weaken the *real* against the dollar to boost exports. Brazil has performed better than Argentina as the first decade of the new century comes to a close, a surprise to many who thought President Lula would take Brazil on the path of Venezuela and Bolivia. Inflation is markedly lower in Brazil (5% + -) than Argentina (22% + -). Argentina looks more like Venezuela (29% + -) than Brazil. How has Brazil done this? By controlling credit expansion (especially consumer credit), higher interest rates, a higher reserve requirement and an increase in financial operation taxes. Sound better than the United States? But austerity has contributed to routine power cuts, auto gridlock and overcrowded airports. Just in time for the 2014 World

Cup and 2016 Olympics. At least for the time being, DGI clearly would prefer to see Latina looking more like Brazil than Argentina.

7.   The brief experience of Mexico with exchange controls is undoubtedly one DGI would prefer to see occur, or better fully avoid, in Latina. Mexico adopted exchange controls in August, 1982, but rescinded them four months later. For a discussion of foreign investment issues in the era of exchange controls, see, e.g., Ignacio Gomez–Palacio, *Mexico's Foreign Exchange Controls: Two Administrations—Two Solutions: Thorough and Benign*, 16 Inter.Am.L.Rev. 267 (1984); Valencia Barrera and Sanchez–Mejorada V., *Fundamentals of Doing Business With Mexico: After the Exchange Control*, 14 St. Mary's L.J. 683 (1983); Stephen Zamora, *Peso–Dollar Economics and the Imposition of Foreign Exchange Controls in Mexico*, 32 Am.J.Comp.L. 99 (1984); and *Doing Business in Mexico: The Impact of its Financial Crisis on Foreign Creditors and Investors: A Symposium*, 18 Int'l Lawyer 287 (1984).

8.   If DGI felt threatened by unrest and the possibility of a government determined to more severely restrict exchange transactions, should it ship its machinery and equipment back to the United States? Would it be better to lease local machinery and equipment, if possible?

9.   How would the law affect the repatriation of profits by DGI? If repatriation is limited to a certain percentage, is there any other way for DGI to achieve a higher return? An alternative to repatriation is reinvestment. Is that a viable alternative? Does it merely exacerbate the problem?

10.   What effect does the high inflation have upon the profit repatriation of DGI? How does indexation affect DGI? Does the process of indexing against inflation establish expectations by the beneficiaries and reduce responsibilities of the government which might otherwise lead to a diminished inflation and termination of the need for indexation?

11.   Latina has asked the IMF for help. The IMF may extend a loan but is concerned with several issues. One is the nation's ability to fully fund the government budget. Another is resolution of what seems to be a fragile banking system (remembrances of things past—the Asian and Russian banking problems in 1998). A final concern is ensuring that the nation's financial obligations, both private and public, are met. Might the IMF also be concerned about the dual exchange rate discussed above?

12.   One Latina official, just home from being Ambassador to Panama, suggested that Latina follow the Panamanian practice and make the dollar the official and *exclusive* Latina currency. What would that require from Latina, and how might it affect DGI?

13.   Would you recommend that DGI be insured against non-receipt of convertible exchange? Inconvertible currency is one risk for which insurance is available from the Overseas Private Investment Corporation (OPIC) or from the World Bank's Multilateral Investment Guarantee Agency (MIGA), both discussed in Problem 10.6.

14.   The International Monetary Fund (IMF) Agreement governs some currency exchange control laws of its member nations. See J. Gold, *Exchange Controls and External Indebtedness: Are the Bretton Woods Concepts Still Workable?*, 7 Houston J. Int'l & Comp.L. 1 (1984). The Agreement, a product

of the Bretton Woods conference in 1944 near the end of World War II, which also created the World Bank and the GATT, was intended to address the use of exchange controls as a means of economic nationalism. Article VIII, 2(b) of the Agreement is one of the most difficult and dispute generating provisions. See W. Ebke, Article VIII, Section 2(b), *International Monetary Cooperation, and the Courts*, in W. Ebke & J. Norton (eds. & contribs.), Festschrift in Honor of Sir Joseph Gold 63 (1990). It provides that "Exchange contracts which involve the currency of any member and which are contrary to the exchange control regulations of that member maintained or imposed consistently with this Agreement shall be unenforceable in the territories of any member." Thus, private contract claims may have to defer to public interests. The Article VIII, 2(b) language has been used as a defense to avoid payment of obligations in many cases. The Article is noteworthy since it has extraterritorial effect, it attempts to supplant private international rules of the forum. It has generated considerable diversity of opinion because domestic courts have divided on whether to view the provision literally or interpret it in view of the purposes of the Agreement. Some view this broadly to mean *any* contract which in any way affects a nation's exchange reserves, while others view it more narrowly as limited only to any exchange contract. Under the former broad view a bond issue or loan agreement may be considered an exchange contract. This view is not well regarded by lenders since it allows debtor nations considerable leeway to alter their legal obligations.

PART B. TRANSFER PRICING

DGI transfers technology to its Rinisian wholly owned subsidiary DGIA that allows DGIA to make many of DGI's trade named and trademarked products for sale in Rinisia and other Asian nations. Assume that a month's production results in the sale of products made by DGIA for a total of $4 million. The cost of those products, including the amount ($1 million) paid to DGI for the technology, was $3 million. Rinisia taxes DGIA on its $1 million profit at the Rinisian corporate tax rate of 20%, or $200,000.

The products were very well made and DGI decided to double the production in Rinisia and offset that by curtailing production in the United States by 50%. DGI pays its subsidiary for the cost of the products, which remains $3 million. DGIA continues to make a $1 million profit on what it sells in Asia, but no profit on what it sells back to DGI for sale in the United States. Although DGIA had doubled its production, partly by adding many new Rinisian workers, it has not increased its profit. The production sent to the United States is sold in the United States for $4 million. The United States taxes DGI on its $1 million profit at the U.S. corporate tax rate of 50%, of $500,000.

DGI then decides to pay its subsidiary $4 million for the next years Rinisian production that is sold to the United States. Rinisia taxes DGIA on its profit from sales to the parent DGI ($200,000) and to the public in Asia ($200,000), a total of $400,000. But because it made no profit on the goods bought from DGIA for $4 million and sold in the United States for $4, no tax was paid to the United States.

In the first year of sales to DGI by DGIA, DGI paid the 50% tax on its $1 million profit in the United States, but nothing on the profits of DGIA, which were retained in Rinisia by DGIA for future expansion of production. In the following year, although the production remained the same in both DGI and DGIA, DGI paid no tax in the United States. It paid a higher tax in Rinisia, but at the 20% rate rather than 50%, and it did not repatriate the profits from Rinisia so it paid nothing.

DGI has shifted before tax profits from the United States to Rinisia, where the rate is lower. It might have chosen to shift less of the profit to Rinisia, or none of it, or all of it.

Suppose that the following year DGI does not charge DGIA anything for the technology. DGIA now sells the goods that cost $2 million to make for $4 million. That gives DGIA a $2 million before tax profit on which DGIA pays the 20% rate in Rinisia, or a tax of $400,000, leaving it with an after tax profit of $1.6 million. It has dropped its tax from the first example from $700,000 to $400,000, which caused the company to pay the CFO a handsome bonus. Of course most of the difference is located in Rinisia, which is fine with the company since it was discussing expansion in Rinisia in any event.

DGI never changed its manufacturing or marketing procedures. It only changed book entries. Did it avoid taxes? Yes. But the more important question is did it do anything illegal? Grantedly, in paying fewer or no taxes within the United States (DGI is registered in Delaware, has its home offices in NYC and several facilities in various states), one view is that the tax revenue that would have been paid to the United States and any states must be made up from other sources, such as higher income taxes—including on DGI workers.

What began was a parent company, DGI, reaction to the great disparity in corporate tax rates in the United States and Rinisia (50% versus 20%). Few would challenge its decision some years ago to locate production in Asia to serve the Asian market. It would never be able to sell in Asia in competition with such nations as China and India if it tried to sell products made in the United States in Asia, because of the high labor costs in the United States. But when it also moved production to Rinisia that was exported to the U.S. market, such move would surely generate conflict with the U.S. unions, and likely to cause the more liberal economic theologians in Congress to say something was wrong.

The above experience of DGI and DGIA involves transfer pricing. Increasingly nations are exerting control over such practices. Unfortunately, it is usually by intensely nationalistic policies intended to favor the one country. Thus the multinational faces a pull from two sides, the nation where it is located and the foreign nation where its goods are sold. And also from its shareholders and the investment advisory profession, demanding that DGI continually adopt policies to maximize after tax profits. Even if it does so not by gaining a greater share of the market by improving production and sales efforts, but by manipulating the prices of intracompany transfers.

A second reason for transfer pricing arises when a nation prohibits or restricts certain payments but allows others. Rinisia may severely limit the transfer of profits because it considers anything above a modest percentage to be an excessive return on capital invested, but be lenient on technology royalty payments because it considers technology necessary for development. This position may encourage DGI to attempt to increase the royalty rate charged its Rinisian subsidiary, DGIA, consequently reducing DGIA's profits to a level acceptable to the host nation.

Transfer pricing further may be challenged by minority shareholders of the subsidiary who are squeezed out of profit distributions by lowered profits in the subsidiary's nation as a result of an artificial accounting of revenues.

Transfer pricing and currency exchange controls are closely related. DGI and Factores may attempt to show low profits in Latina if exchange controls preclude, or make it more difficult to effect, the transfer of profits abroad. If exchange controls are more restrictive to profit repatriation than to the payment for needed imports and technology, there is little reason to doubt that DGI and Factores will "adjust" prices and profits to favor the parent company.

The focus to date has largely been on demanding that intracompany transfers be done at "arm's length," much like agreements between non-related companies. But that is easier than it sounds. A good place to start is U.S. Internal Revenue Code Section 482. That is followed by some comment on the OECD role in drafting guidelines (most recently revised in 2010) for transfer pricing.

26 USC Sec. *482*—Income Taxes

Sec. 482. Allocation of income and deductions among taxpayers.

In any case of two or more organizations, trades, or businesses (whether or not incorporated, whether or not organized in the United States, and whether or not affiliated) owned or controlled directly or indirectly by the same interests, the Secretary may distribute, apportion, or allocate gross income, deductions, credits, or allowances between or among such organizations, trades, or businesses, if he determines that such distribution, apportionment, or allocation is necessary in order to prevent evasion of taxes or clearly to reflect the income of any of such organizations, trades, or businesses. In the case of any transfer (or license) of intangible property (within the meaning of section 936(h)(3)(B)), the income with respect to such transfer or license shall be commensurate with the income attributable to the intangible.

OECD—TRANSFER PRICING GUIDELINES FOR MULTINATIONAL ENTERPRISES AND TAX ADMINISTRATIONS

The Transfer Pricing Guidelines for Multinational Enterprises and Tax Administrations provide guidance on the application of the "arm's length principle" for the valuation, for tax purposes, of cross-border transactions between associated enterprises. In a global economy where multinational enterprises (MNEs) play a prominent role, governments need to ensure that the taxable profits of MNEs are not artificially shifted out of their jurisdiction and that the tax base reported by MNEs in their country reflects the economic activity undertaken therein. For taxpayers, it is essential to limit the risks of economic double taxation that may result from a dispute between two countries on the determination of the arm's length remuneration for their cross-border transactions with associated enterprises.

WHEELER, AN ACADEMIC LOOK AT TRANSFER PRICING IN A GLOBAL ECONOMY

Tax Notes, July 4, 1988, pg. 87.*

The return on assets for all U.S. corporations of 1.8 percent is six times larger than the .3 percent for foreign-owned U.S. subsidiaries. * * * Improper transfer pricing appears to be the only potential explanation for a six-fold difference. * * * Preliminary data from an IRS study indicates that comparable foreign-owned U.S. corporations pay from 16 to 19 percent less tax than the U.S. firms with which they compete.

It is difficult to * * * not be concerned with the integrity of the income tax system as to transfer pricing. Certainly, something has to be done to stem the tide of over-aggressive pricing and income-shifting. It seems clear that the U.S. is losing large amounts of tax revenue through income shifting both for purposes of income measurement and in the determination of the foreign tax credit limitation. For the latter problem, we could adopt the approach that if it is not taxed by a foreign government, it cannot be foreign-source income. The U.S. could also eliminate deferral, as there is no theoretical reason to have both deferral and a foreign tax credit. However, the transfer pricing issue is currently the more difficult issue.

Two approaches seem possible. One, a worldwide income allocation scheme could be developed * * *. Second, the U.S. could tighten up the section 482 regulations. * * * Since income is related to assets, perhaps the taxpayers should be required to list, value, and give the physical location of every significant asset that is involved in producing their income. By forcing them to value intangibles, we may then be able to reach the point where we can meet the newly established "commensurate with income" standard. What value might Coca Cola put on their trademark and secret formula?

Another approach might be to simply make all corporate tax returns public information. This would foster better compliance and researchers would be delighted with hard data availability. * * *.

Comment on the Determination of Transfer Pricing

The standard generally accepted throughout the world is that of an "arm's length" transaction between unrelated entities. But how it is determined varies significantly. There are numerous tests that take into consideration numerous factors. Were services as opposed to products involved? What intangibles should be considered? The OECD suggests using "the most appropriate transfer pricing method to the circumstances of the case." But that leaves considerable leeway.

What tests are used? One is a multi-step *comparability analysis*, another one or more variations of the *transactional profit method*. These become complex and are beyond the scope of an introductory discussion.

Two additional areas should be mentioned. One is how to settle disputes among the parties—the company and one or both of the national tax authorities. Increasingly arbitration has been used. The other is obtaining an advance pricing arrangement. An additional focus of the latest OECD guidelines is on the transfer pricing aspects of business restructuring.

QUESTIONS AND COMMENTS

1. How can transfer pricing be controlled? Is tax legislation effective or is its role as a revenue raising device an obstacle to serving in a regulatory manner?

In 2008 studies suggested that U.S. corporations paid little in U.S. corporate taxes in comparison to foreign forms, even though U.S. corporate tax rates were higher. The reason was believed to be transfer pricing that shifted profits abroad and away from the United States parent. How might the United Nations assist in regulating transfer pricing? One of the members of the "Group of Eminent Persons" suggested in a U.N. study that in most cases transfer pricing is not a problem because there are identifiable arms-length prices against which alleged transfer pricing challenges may be tested. See United Nations, The Impact of Multinational Corporations in Development and on International Relations, U.N. publication E/5500/Rev. 1; ST/ESA/6., sales no. E.74.II.A.5 (1974). Do you agree?

2. Would the United States be willing to agree to use its information acquiring abilities to inform developing nations about transfer pricing practices of U.S. based multinational enterprises?

3. Cost or pricing information is obviously of importance to the United States. The administration must establish some method of determining whether the price of a foreign made product sold in the United States benefitted from government subsidies, or was dumped on the U.S. market. This is not the same as transfer pricing, but might be used as leverage in bilateral treaty negotiations.

4. What would you advise DGI to do with regard to its pricing practices? Is it possible that the company is doing anything illegal? What additional information do you need?

5. Were a minority Rinisian shareholder of DGIA to raise the issue of transfer pricing, how would it be framed? If a suit was thought to be necessary, where should it be brought? Should a minority shareholder in a developing nation expect help in U.S. courts. Do you agree? See, e.g., Alexandre Tadeu Seguim, *New Transfer Pricing Rules in Brazil*, 19 Nw. J. Int'l L. & Bus. 394 (1999).

6. France has enacted legislation intended to counter the negative tax consequences from transfer pricing. Mexico in 1994 amended the income tax law to require that intracompany transactions be at arm's length prices. China has more recently adopted transfer pricing rules. *See* C.D. Wallace, Legal Control of Multinational Enterprises 128 (1982); Richard M. Hammer, Cym H. Lowell, Marianne Burge & Marc M. Levy, U.S. International Transfer Pricing (RIA Treatise w/ annual supplementation).

PART C.   INTERNATIONAL INSOLVENCY

The collapse of the currency and subsequently the economy of Latina, high fines imposed by Rinisia for transfer pricing, and the failure of the Eastvian enterprise discussed in problem 10.1 left DGI in a difficult financial position. DGI had relied upon its international ventures to help its sagging domestic business. It has now defaulted on bank debt and has terminated payments to creditors by DGI and its foreign subsidiaries. It would like to reorganize DGI. It plans to terminate its business in Latina, Rinisia and Eastvia, but retain the German subsidiary, from which it will serve the Eastvian market. DGI has debtors and creditors who are mostly located in the United States. Its German subsidiary borrowed from Deutsche Bank, and there are many small creditors in various EU nations. It has some accounts receivable in the EU. The Eastvia subsidiary is indebted to the Eastvian government. Estvia has essentially no assets; many Eastvia employees hold shares in Eastvia. DGIA in Rinisia has indebtedness in Asia, and some assets in Rinisia. The Latina subsidiary had borrowed from Argentine banks that are majority owned by Spanish banks. There are substantial assets in Latina, possibly more than obligations.

You are a U.S. lawyer in a firm that does principally corporate work. Your work has been reorganizations and bankruptcy, but only of domestic companies with all the assets and liabilities in the United States. A firm colleague who does extensive international business but has never worked on a reorganization or bankruptcy has discussed some possible issues she sees from her international work. She has raised the following issues:

1.   Will reorganization or bankruptcy proceedings occur in each nation where DGI has a subsidiary?

2.   What is the nature of reorganization and bankruptcy laws in each nation? Is reorganization similar to U.S. Chapter 11 allowed? Does the EU have any rules on reorganization or bankruptcy that might affect the German and Eastvian subsidiaries, especially assuming Eastvia has become a member of the EU?

    3.   Are there any international conventions or laws applicable to cross-border bankruptcy?

    4.   Is there some way for a reorganization or bankruptcy proceeding to be consolidated in the United States with all assets owned by DGI's throughout the world collected there and all unsecured creditors throughout the world being paid equally? Would creditors in Latina agree to this since they might stand to collect the full amount owed if they have priority access to the assets located in Latina?

    5.   Is there any doubt that secured creditors in each nation will be able to seek payment from the value of the secured assets? Do the foreign nations have laws regulating secured transactions?

Your colleague reaffirms you that her comments were made without expertise in bankruptcy. But some of her concerns are a good starting point.

WESTBROOK, DEVELOPMENTS IN TRANSNATIONAL BANKRUPTCY

39 St. Louis U.L.J. 745 (1995).*

Transnational insolvency cases are proliferating. The largest of them involve billions of dollars in assets and debts and thousands of employees in hundreds of communities around the world. Many smaller cases do not appear in the newspapers or the law reports. But they may, in the aggregate, constitute even more cross-border financial travail than the more famous ones. At both land borders of the United States, for example, it appears that hundreds of United States–Mexican and United States–Canadian insolvencies—both liquidations and reorganizations—are pending in the U.S. courts at any given time.

    Two of the best-known recent cases illustrate both progress and difficulties. The collapse of Olympia & York, one of the world's greatest real estate empires, has been managed in a relatively coordinated manner among the various countries involved. On the other hand, each jurisdiction is tending toward resolution of that portion of the Olympia case located in that country, with less and less reference to a global solution. The problem is exemplified by the appointment of Cyrus Vance to mediate a solution to conflicts between the Canadian administrators and the U.S. creditors concerning operation and sale of Olympia's U.S. properties.

    The other matter, *In re Maxwell Communication*,[4] arising after the apparent suicide of the British press magnate, Robert Maxwell, ... represents a far greater achievement of international cooperation than most cross-border cases in that the U.S. courts deferred to the British courts almost entirely, with the caveat that a U.S. "examiner" must be closely consulted at each stage. The result has been confirmation of a joint reorganization scheme for the assets and creditors worldwide....

---

* Reprinted with permission of the St. Louis U.L.J.

  4.   *In re* Maxwell Communication Corp., 170 B.R. 800 (Bankr.S.D.N.Y.1994).

As impressive in size and number as these cases may be, their results are ultimately less important than the law they develop. Whether the law is created by decisions of cases in the common-law countries, or from legislation developed from the experience of the courts in the civil law countries, the legal rules that emerge from these proceedings will change the structure and the cost of transactions from Toledo to Singapore. Every major financing, every large "requirements" contract, must be sculpted by expert lawyers responding to the risks of general, global default as defined by this emerging experience. The entire function of international finance, investment, and trade is materially influenced by these developments.

Up to now, the burden has fallen mainly on the courts of various countries, which have been busily engaged in very creative and innovative responses to the challenges of cross-border insolvency. This outburst of judicial activity has stirred interest in this important area and has produced a number of efforts at general reform. The reform efforts are proceeding by treaty, by harmonization, and by coordination. This paper briefly summarizes developments: the concepts and rules emerging from the courts and the efforts to achieve more general reform. It also outlines the key issues emerging from the combination of litigation and reform.

As one studies the judicial decisions in the field and the progress of the various efforts for reform, certain issues recur as key to the problem of transnational insolvency. Although there are many important details and related problems, the most significant questions seem to be the following.

Moratorium. A moratorium on creditor action (a "stay", in U.S. terms) is found in most insolvency systems around the world and is essential to orderly liquidation and successful rehabilitation. Generally, the moratorium halts lawsuits and other legal actions against the debtor and its property, although secured creditors and other favored parties are allowed to proceed in some jurisdictions.

It can be argued that the adoption of automatic or nearly automatic moratorium procedures in each country in response to a bankruptcy filing elsewhere is the most important single reform that could be achieved in transnational insolvency cases. A moratorium, as fast, complete, and absolute as possible, ensures court control in each country and, by an interesting twist, its prevention of individual action promotes consultation and possible agreement among creditors. Because every creditor is blocked until some further court action is taken, everyone has an incentive to produce an agreed course of action. For the same reason, each knows it is safe from precipitate action by the others. This opportunity for creditor consultation and agreement is of critical importance in cross-border cases where there are so few legal rules and precedents. Often private agreements, subject to court approval, may produce the fairest as well as the most efficient results. A moratorium also allows time for vital communication between the courts involved, directly or through their officers (liquidators or administrators) or through the parties.

Standing/Title For Liquidator. The liquidator or administrator or trustee in bankruptcy acquires some important rights to the debtor's property in virtually all bankruptcy systems. In some jurisdictions it is merely control, title remaining in the debtor, while in others title actually passes to the officer, or the court, or a bankruptcy "estate." The important point is that the liquidator obtains the right to control the property, subject to applicable law and court order. Generally the same officer has the right to defend pre-existing lawsuits against the debtor and its property, ensuring that defaults and collusion are avoided. Even the most cautious and conservative approaches to insolvency cooperation contain provision for recognition of the foreign liquidator's rights in both regards.

Information Sharing. As noted above, communication between the courts involved is very important. While the parties can serve an important role in that regard, it would be highly desirable to have methods of judicial communication not entirely dependent on the parties. Closely related is the fact that most countries require extensive disclosures from the debtor, especially as to financial matters. That information should be available to the courts and parties in each interested jurisdiction. Again, a reliable mechanism for its dissemination is needed.

Creditor Involvement. Because nearly every country has devices for creditor involvement, if not control, in the insolvency process, the only difficulty is national treatment. Most countries today give national treatment to creditors as to claims matters, but there are very few provisions relating to fair representation of foreign interests and communication with them. This problem can be addressed in part through cross-filing and the foreign liquidator's role as creditor representative, as discussed below.

Executory Contracts. Every system has some mechanism for addressing the problem of contracts not fully performed at the time an insolvency proceeding is filed. If the only unperformed element is payment by the debtor or the other party, no great difficulty is presented. But if various important elements of performance remain, perplexing issues are often presented. It is challenging to proceed in a way that is reasonably fair, or no more unfair than necessary, to both the other party to the contract and the other creditors of the debtor. For example, if the contract represents a good bargain for the debtor, its performance will benefit the other creditors and therefore it is an asset of theirs. Yet insistence on performance where the debtor is insolvent may produce hardship and risk for the other party. Various bankruptcy systems have produced various responses to the quandaries created by executory contracts. They have not been much studied comparatively. Even fewer answers exist as to their application in a transnational case.

Coordinated Claims Procedures. Another single reform that would have a major impact on transnational insolvency cases would be adoption of cross-filing and marshalling provisions. Cross-filing permits the liquidator in each proceeding to file in every other proceeding on behalf of all creditors in the proceeding in which the liquidator was appointed. "Marshalling" or "hotchpot" rules limit recovery by a creditor in a given proceeding with reference to amounts the creditor has recovered in proceedings in other jurisdictions, so that the creditor cannot receive more than other creditors of the same class. The combination would go a long way toward more equal treatment of creditors and a *de facto* worldwide system of distribution.

Such a system would also permit local adjudication of claims, if each court was reasonably comfortable with the scrutiny that claims would receive in the foreign proceedings. If a court did believe that foreign courts would be rigorous in approving and valuing claims, and therefore accepted the results of foreign claims adjudication, creditors could resolve any disputes with the liquidator in their own countries, using local lawyers and in the local language, rather than having to assert their claims in a distant court through foreign lawyers.

Priorities/Preferences. Although most systems favor employees and governments in determining priorities in distributions, the details vary greatly and each insolvency system has various categories of creditors that are favored by local policy. The priority puzzle is one of the most difficult to solve in the entire field of transnational bankruptcy. The Istanbul treaty provides that creditors entitled to priority in distribution under local law should be paid from local assets, and what remains should be returned to the main proceeding, where the priorities of the main jurisdiction's law will prevail. It is important to note that this priority/preference problem includes as a major component the question of the rights of secured creditors.

Avoiding Powers. The problem of the avoidance of transactions which take place shortly before or even after bankruptcy is most obviously, and classically, a choice of law question: what law should be applied to determine if the transaction is avoidable? Yet it is unlike ordinary choice-of-law issues because it is intimately related to the legal governance (and ultimate law of distribution) of the entire proceeding. The central concern is development of a rule that is predictable for commercial purposes and yet not readily manipulable or evadable by unscrupulous debtors and creditors, all while serving the policy functions for which avoidance laws exist.

Discharge. Discussed earlier [see full article] was an important new case from Germany recognizing the effect of a Swiss bankruptcy discharge given to a Swiss citizen. This decision is one of the very few addressing the transnational effect of a discharge. While giving effect to a foreign discharge of a natural person is important, recognition of a foreign discharge may be equally important for legal persons in reorganization or rescue cases, where the entire scheme often rests upon agreement that each creditor will be paid a certain percentage of its debt (and no more) over a certain period of time (and no sooner). Obviously, a creditor free to enforce its pre-existing, pre-reorganization rights against a corporate debtor in jurisdiction "B," despite a discharge in the reorganization approved in jurisdiction "A," would effectively bar the debtor from operating in jurisdiction "B" and the prospect might make the reorganization impossible.

The difficulties of achieving international agreement about cross-border insolvencies have left a void that has necessarily been filled by the courts. Happily, the courts have been creative and audacious in moving away from traditional parochialism and toward a more universal approach. More recently, reform efforts have been started in a number of countries and by a number of institutions, suggesting that in the future we may enjoy more success in managing failure.

PAUL J. KEENAN, CHAPTER 15: A NEW CHAPTER TO MEET THE GROWING NEED TO REGULATE CROSS-BORDER INSOLVENCIES

15 J. Bankr. L. & Prac. 2 Art. 4, Norton Journal of
Bankruptcy Law and Practice April 2006.*

The 2005 Act ["Bankruptcy Abuse Prevention and Consumer Protection Act of 2005" (the "BAPCPA" or the "2005 Act")] supplants former section 304 of the "Bankruptcy Code" with an entirely new chapter to the Bankruptcy Code, Chapter 15, which now governs not only ancillary cases, but also plenary cases with cross-border issues. In large part, Chapter 15 codifies much of the current practice and procedure under former section 304. However, Chapter 15 does provide a much more detailed procedural framework for the governance of cross-border insolvencies. However, Chapter 15 is not just procedural, it also creates new statutory substantive rights for, as well as constraints upon, foreign and domestic debtors and creditors. [W]hile former section 304 consisted of only one section and approximately 270 words, Chapter 15 consists of thirty-two sections and over 4,500 words. [T]he meaning of several key provisions of Chapter 15 is less than clear, leaving many cross-border issues ripe for litigation.

In the early 1990s, the United Nations Commission on International Trade Law ("UNCITRAL") recognized the need for a regime to govern the conduct of cross-border insolvencies. UNCITRAL acknowledged the futility of creating a model law to govern the substantive rights of debtors and creditors in different countries.

Worldwide, two main approaches have emerged regarding jurisdiction over a debtor and its assets: the territorialist approach and universalist approach. Under the territorialist approach, the court of each country administers the assets within that country according to their own laws, often without regard to the proceedings in another country involving the same debtor. Under the universalist approach, the court in the "home" country of the debtor administers, or at least attempts to administer, all of the debtor's assets, wherever they may be found, and distributes them according to the substantive law of the debtor's home country. While

---

* Reprinted with permission.

many foreign countries are territorialist in their approach to bankruptcy jurisdiction, the United States notoriously subscribes to the universalist approach. The obvious result is a clash where the judiciaries of two different countries, or more, assert jurisdiction over the same assets.

UNCITRAL's answer to these jurisdictional conflicts and differing substantive rights is the Model Law on Cross–Border Insolvency, adopted at the thirtieth Session of UNCITRAL in 1997 (the "Model Law"). As of 2005, the Model Law has been adopted by at least nine countries, including the United States. Chapter 15 incorporates the Model Law into the Bankruptcy Code with relatively few modifications.

Chapter 15 ... contain[s] many novel principles that lack decisional authority for their interpretation. In this regard, Congress was unusually explicit in directing courts on the interpretation of Chapter 15. " ... the court *shall* consider its international origin, and the need to promote an application of this chapter that is consistent with the application of *similar statutes* adopted by foreign jurisdictions."

Remarkably, a footnote in the legislative history states that the UNCITRAL Guide to Enactment of the Model Law (the "UNCITRAL Guide") "should be consulted for guidance as to the meaning and purpose of its provisions."

By its terms, section 304 only addressed the commencement of an ancillary case in the United States by a foreign representative seeking relief with respect to property located in the United States. On the other hand, Chapter 15 applies not only where a foreign representative commences an ancillary case, but also where a foreign representative or creditor seeks to commence a plenary bankruptcy case in the United States, assistance is sought in a foreign country in connection with a United States bankruptcy case, and a foreign proceeding and a bankruptcy case in the United States are pending concurrently.

An order for recognition of a foreign proceeding is critical because much of the relief available to debtors and creditors under Chapter 15 does not become available until a foreign proceeding is recognized by a United States bankruptcy court. Although the concept of recognition of a foreign proceeding was borrowed from former section 304, the grounds for requesting or denying relief, and abstention from the case are different under. Pursuant to former section 304, a foreign representative could commence a case ancillary to a foreign proceeding by filing a section 304 petition. If a party in interest did not timely controvert the petition, then the court, at its discretion, could accord the debtor certain relief. A party in interest could contest the petition by arguing that the alleged foreign representative or foreign proceeding did not qualify as such under their respective definitions. Even if the court did grant the petition, a party in interest could still argue that the court should deny the requested relief or abstain from the ancillary case altogether due to the considerations enumerated in section 304(c). In accordance with section 304(c), in determining whether to grant relief or abstain from the ancillary case, a court was to consider "what will best assure an economical and expeditious administration of such estate." Under Chapter 15, a party in interest can still argue for denial of relief and abstention. However, the factors considered by the court are now different in some important respects.

Under Chapter 15, a foreign representative applies for recognition by filing a Chapter 15 petition, ... accompanied by a copy of the decision commencing the foreign proceeding and appointing the representative, or some other acceptable form of certification by the foreign court. Section 1517 directs that a bankruptcy court *shall* enter an order recognizing a foreign proceeding when the following conditions are met: (1) the foreign proceeding is main or nonmain under section 1502; (2) the foreign representative is a person or body; and (3) the petition includes the requisite documentation. As was the practice under section 304, a party in interest can object to a petition for recognition on the basis that the alleged foreign representative or proceeding does not qualify as such under the definition of those terms in section 101. However, this will be more difficult under Chapter 15 given the expanded definition of those terms and the courts' willingness to broadly interpret them.

In addition to the definitional arguments, an objecting party can still attempt to moot the effect of recognition by requesting that the court abstain from the ancillary case under section 305. This is where Chapter 15 diverges from section 304 practice. With the adoption of Chapter 15, section 305 has been amended so that a court may abstain from an ancillary case where "the purposes of chapter 15 of would best be served by such dismissal or suspension."

Under former section 304, a bankruptcy court actually examined some details of the substantive law governing the foreign proceeding in determining whether to abstain or grant requested relief. If the distribution of proceeds under applicable foreign law was not substantially in accordance with the order prescribed in the Bankruptcy Code, then abstention or denial of relief was warranted. None of the objectives of Chapter 15 focus specifically on priority of distribution under the applicable foreign law. In addition, comity is also conspicuously absent from the list of Chapter 15 purposes.

As an alternative to arguing for abstention, a party in interest could also object to the requested relief itself. An objecting party could argue that the requested relief is antithetical to the purposes of Chapter 15 or is contrary to an international obligation of the United States. In addition, with respect to the specific forms of provisional and permissive relief available under Chapter 15, there are additional arguments for the denial.... When arguing for abstention or denial of relief under Chapter 15, the practitioner must be judicious in the use of section 304 case law.

Chapter 15 also provides an entirely new statutory basis to deny recognition or relief—the public policy exception. Section 1504 provides that "[n]othing in this chapter prevents the court from refusing to take an action . . . that would be manifestly contrary to the public policy of the United States."

Refusal to recognize a foreign representative or a foreign proceeding can thwart a representative's plans to exercise control over assets in the United States. If a court denies the petition for recognition, the court may block the foreign representative's access to United States courts through an appropriate order. If the court does enter an order recognizing the foreign proceeding, then the foreign representative will have the capacity to sue and be sued in the United States and the ability to apply directly for relief from the court. Regardless of recognition, a foreign representative is subject to applicable nonbankruptcy law and may still sue in a United States court to collect or recover on the debtor's claim. The sole act of filing a petition for recognition does not subject a foreign representative to the jurisdiction of any court in the United States for any other purpose. Upon recognition of a foreign proceeding, the foreign representative is entitled to participate as a party in interest in any bankruptcy case regarding the debtor. Once a foreign proceeding is recognized, the foreign representative may intervene in any proceedings in the United States in which the debtor is a party.

Generally, there are three forms of relief available under Chapter 15: (1) provisional relief available during the gap period between the filing of the petition and the entering of an order for relief; (2) automatic relief upon recognition of a main foreign proceeding; and (3) permissive relief available after recognition of a main or nonmain foreign proceeding.

A court may grant provisional and permissive relief only if the interests of creditors and other interested entities, including the debtor, are sufficiently protected. The court may place conditions on a grant of provisional or permissive relief as it deems appropriate, including the posting of security or a bond. The court may modify or terminate provisional or permissive relief on its own motion, or the motion of the foreign representative or an entity affected by the relief granted.

In addition to the relief described above, Chapter 15 provides an amorphous fourth form of relief—"additional assistance." Congress intended the provision for additional assistance to "permit the further development of international cooperation begun under section 304, but is not to be the basis for denying or limiting relief otherwise available under [Chapter 15]."

[I]t is important to remember that a "foreign" debtor is not obliged to commence a foreign proceeding and file an ancillary case under Chapter 15 in lieu of a Chapter 7 or 11 plenary case. If no foreign proceeding exists, or even if one does exist, a foreign debtor can commence a plenary case under Chapter 7 or 11, as long as it meets the eligibility requirements of section 109, which are unchanged under the 2005 Act. However, once a foreign proceeding is recognized, the options for a foreign debtor to file a plenary case change. Although there is no discussion of it in Chapter 15 or the legislative history, the implication appears to be that the debtor itself loses the right to file a voluntary Chapter 7 or 11 petition after recognition of a foreign main proceeding.

Under these rules, a scenario that might develop is where a debtor becomes the subject of a foreign main proceeding that is recognized in the United States, and the representative then commences a voluntary proceeding on behalf of the debtor to ensure the debtor's assets located in the United States are administered in conjunction with the foreign proceeding. Under those circumstances, a receiver appointed in a foreign country would be empowered to file a voluntary bankruptcy case in the United States and the debtor could not seek dismissal of the case, as it could seek the dismissal of an involuntary case. In such circumstances, the only recourse for the other representatives of the debtor (e.g., management or the board of directors) may be to challenge the foreign proceeding's recognition. Once recognized, it is difficult to imagine procedurally how the debtor could controvert the filing of a voluntary petition.

There are a number of circumstances where a debtor or foreign representative may want to commence a plenary case concurrent with an ancillary case. If the debtor or foreign representative needs relief that is not one of the forms of relief prescribed in Chapter 15, then a plenary Chapter 7 or 11 case may be necessary.

Under Chapter 15, foreign creditors have access to the courts equal to that of domestic creditors. * * * This principle of nondiscrimination is not without limits. Chapter 15 does not change or codify current law with regard to priority of claims under section 507, except to specifically provide that the claim of a foreign creditor shall not be accorded priority less than that of a general unsecured claim solely because the holder is a foreign creditor.

In some instances, Chapter 15 does substantively affect a debtor's ability to commence a bankruptcy case in the United States. Section 109(a) of the Bankruptcy Code provides that a person or entity that has a domicile, place of business or property in the United States is eligible to be a debtor under the Bankruptcy Code. However, once a foreign main proceeding is recognized, a case under another chapter of the Bankruptcy Code may be commenced *only if* the debtor has *assets* in the United States. Furthermore, a bankruptcy case initiated subsequent to recognition of a foreign main proceeding shall be restricted to the debtor's assets that are "within the territorial jurisdiction of the United States." To the extent necessary to achieve Chapter 15's goals of cooperation and coordination, certain assets outside the territorial jurisdiction of the United States may be subject to a bankruptcy case. Assets that are "within the jurisdiction of the court," as opposed to only those assets within the territorial jurisdiction of the United States, may be subject to a bankruptcy case provided such assets are not subject to the jurisdiction and control of a recognized foreign proceeding. Here, Chapter 15 allows universalism to prevail where it does not create a jurisdictional conflict with a foreign proceeding.

The existence of plenary United States case concurrent with a foreign proceeding will affect the relief available to a debtor under Chapter 15. Where a plenary case and a foreign proceeding are pending concurrently, the court shall seek cooperation and coordination by applying the following rules: (1) if a bankruptcy case is already pending at the time a petition for recognition is filed, any provisional or permissive relief granted under Chapter 15 must be consistent with the bankruptcy case, and automatic relief shall not be triggered upon recognition of a foreign main proceeding; and (2) if a bankruptcy case is commenced post-recognition, any provisional or permissive relief granted under Chapter 15 must be modified or terminated to the extent inconsistent with the bankruptcy case. To achieve cooperation and coordination of where a bankruptcy case and foreign proceeding are pending concurrently, the court may abstain from the bankruptcy case or suspend all proceedings in a bankruptcy case.

COMMENT ON THE USE OF PROTOCOLS IN INTERNATIONAL INSOLVENCY CASES

In 1991–1992 the first significant protocol was used in the Maxwell communications empire insolvency. See Gitlin & Silverman, *International Insolvency and the Maxwell Communication Corporation Case: One Example of Progress in the 1990s*, in International Bankruptcies: Developing Practical Strategies 7, 10 (1992). The protocol was between courts in the United States and the United Kingdom. The function of a protocol is to agree upon how the insolvency will proceed, and avoid the problems discussed above. The Maxwell protocol is an exemplary case and other protocols have followed. Several have involved U.S.-Canadian cases. Some have used satellite television for hearings. Updates on protocols are mentioned in the annual column ''The International Scene'' of the American Bankruptcy Institute Journal. Protocols developed after the International Bar Association adopted in 1995–96 its Cross–Border Insolvency Concordat. The Concordat is a set of principles intended to encourage and assist insolvency administration involving more than one country. Several dozen protocols have been created. While they may become less important as national laws harmonize, they have filled an important large gap in the past decade and will probably still be used occasionally to fill smaller gaps.

QUESTIONS AND COMMENTS

1. How should the lawyers for DGI and the subsidiaries in various nations proceed to avoid the conflicts likely to occur if a strictly territorial approach is taken? Is this a good case for use of a protocol? Would a protocol have to have the participation of all the countries to be effective? Might there be a hub-spoke arrangement, with the U.S. court having separate protocols with each other nation's court? Are most of the nations involved, Germany, Rinisia and Latina, likely to have reorganization and bankruptcy laws? What about the EU? International law? Would the laws that do exist in any of these jurisdictions be similar to U.S. laws?

2. Chapter 11 of U.S. bankruptcy law provides a much used form of reorganizing a corporation. Few other nations have such proceedings. Where a

corporation has assets in the United States but is principally a foreign corporation, Chapter 11 may be attractive. In December, 2004, the Russian oil giant Yukos filed for Chapter 11 protection in Houston, where the company claimed it had assets and where its chief financial officer had a residence. The petition asked the U.S. court to stop an auction planned in Russia a few days later of Yukos most valuable asset, Yuganskneftegas. The Russian government scheduled the auction to collect on a tax claim that some officers of Yukos viewed as expropriation. An injunction was issued prohibiting Gazprom, the huge Russian natural gas company, from participating in the auction. But it was ignored in Russia and the auction was held as scheduled. However, Gazprom apparently was concerned that its gas exports could be threatened by legal actions in Europe. It did not bid. At the auction an unidentified buyer purchased Yuganskneftegas in a six minute auction. The buyer was believed to be a group of individuals who would quickly sell the company to another Russian oil giant, with Kremlin approval. The secrecy of the proceeding illustrates the lack of transparency in Russia in insolvency proceedings, and the need for international proceedings with transparency.

3. Westbrook identifies eleven key issues that recur in efforts to reform and in major judicial decisions. Have his concerns been met with the adoption of Chapter 15 as outlined in the Keenan extract? They should each be considered with respect to the DGI case.

4. The Keenan extract explains how new Chapter 15 replaces but essentially retains much of old 304. See also Jonathan L. Howell, International Insolvency Law, 42 Int'l Law. 113 (2008). Has the adoption of Chapter 15 moved the United States closer to the universality approach? If the "grab rule" seems to be used in the DGI case, what should DGI's lawyers do now?

5. The European Union Convention on International Insolvency failed because of itas rejection by the UK. But the EU presented the Convention in new clothes and little change, as a *regulation* of the European Parliament. The EU Regulation on Insolvency Proceedings became effective without legislative action by the member states in 2002. The UK, which had rejected the EU Convention, began a complex process to adopt the UNCITRAL Model Law.

The EU regulation will undoubtedly have some affect beyond the borders of the EU. An American creditor of a company in the EU will realize that all creditors within the EU will be able to prove their claims against the debtor. Will DGI's Germany subsidiary come within the scope of the regulation? The answer seems yes since the company's EU center of main interests is in Germany. Unanswered is the potential conflict between insolvency regulation by the EU or by the non-EU nation.

6. Mexico was the first major nation to adopt the UNCITRAL Model Law. It was part of bankruptcy legislation of 2000. Canada has also now adopted the essence of the UNCITRAL Model Law, thus making it effective throughout the NAFTA. But as a "model law" each nations' version is bound to have some differences, and it might require a NAFTA convention to eliminate any serious differences.

7. The Model Law has been adopted in some important countries. In addition to the developments in the UK and Mexico, Japan has adopted

legislation based on the Model Law, as has South Africa. UNCITRAL has also developed a Legislative Guide on Insolvency as an assist to the many countries in the process of adapting their insolvency laws to the Model Law. See www.uncitral.org.

8.   The American Law Institute's Transnational Insolvency Cases project produced Guidelines for Court-to-Court Communications in Cross–Border Cases. The guidelines address communications that must occur between jurisdictions and rely much on the experience of the above noted protocols. In turn the Guidelines were used in protocols in two Canadian–United States cases involving the Delaware bankruptcy and the U.S. Bankruptcy Court in the Southern District of New York. See *In re Matlack Systems Inc.* (Bank. D. Del., 01–01114, May 24, 2001); *In re PSINet Inc.* (Bank. S.D.N.Y. 01–13213, July 10, 2001).

9.   Perhaps an option for DGI is relocation. Might DGI's German subsidiary, threatened by bankruptcy in Germany, leave Germany and move the headquarters to London and file for bankruptcy under laws more favorable to restructure the company? Referred to as ''global court-shopping,'' it is a practice that is increasing. An auto parts maker in Germany, Schefenacker, was facing default on a bond debt and moved its headquarters to London, where it filed for bankruptcy and restructured the company in a manner not permitted under German law. A small group of bondholders in Germany might have been able to force a liquidation in German courts, but could not do so in London. Sometimes bonds held in the country from which the company moves are converted into shares, reducing the vote of bondholders in that departed nation. Management was retained as before. The end result of this global shopping has been revisions to the laws in France and Italy. The German experience of Schefenacker and another entity, Deutsche Nickel, may encourage the same in Germany, such as allowing the company to choose the insolvency administrators, and allowing the company rather than the administrator to decide how to restructure the company. Some German lawyers say the practice is not due to strict German laws, but to greedy London lawyers. Germany already revised its insolvency laws in 1999 to allow management to retain control of the company, but companies apparently believe the changes were not sufficient. Schefenacker already had a plant in the United Kingdom, thus providing a link with Britain. That can be important because an EU Directive limits the filing of insolvency petitions to the ''center of a debtor's main interests.'' In a case involving Parmalat of Italy the Bank of America was able to file to wind up the proceedings of a Parmalat Irish entity located in Dublin. What is behind allowing such proceedings—could it be preserving jobs?

10.   Should DGI file a bankruptcy petition in the United States to protect assets located in the United States?

PROBLEM 10.3   THIRD WORLD DEBT: THE IMF, AMABANK AND WORLDDEBT IN ASIANA

SECTION I.   THE SETTING

Asiana is a medium-sized nation rapidly engaged in the process of political, economic and social development. Until recently, it has been stable. Asiana has an export driven economy based on commodities, assembly goods and early stage industrial production. Its economy has been moderately dependent on access to the North American market, but exports to Europe and Japan are also important.

To finance development, Asiana has borrowed relatively large sums from foreign commercial banks, developed nations ("the Paris Club") and (less frequently) the International Monetary Fund (IMF). Asiana's foreign debt service payments consume between 35 and 45 percent of its export earnings, a percentage of the Ministry of Trade and Finance had always thought manageable. Many of its leading corporations have strong political connections. These connections have garnered them a steady stream of government and bank loans without much scrutiny. In addition, Asiana and its business sector have of late financed a lot of their capital needs through short-term notes that foreign institutional investors bought (and are now selling) with alacrity. The rapid withdrawal of these portfolio investments has, much like Mexico in 1994–95, triggered a financial crisis in Asiana and devaluation of its currency. Asiana does not impose capital or currency controls, a policy the Ministry is rethinking.

Amabank, Inc. (AMABANK) is a medium-sized federal banking corporation located in Portland, Oregon. Following the lead of its large California correspondent bank, AMABANK became increasingly involved in Asian international loan syndications. Approximately $200 million (16%) of its international loans are Asiana-related and none are backed by special loan-loss reserves. Many of these loans are to Asiana enterprises, but a few were direct loans to the government earmarked for oil exploration. Most of them are covered by "cross-default" clauses with its California correspondent bank which is a very large lender to Asiana. Under these clauses, a default as to AMABANK or its California bank is a default as to the other. None of AMABANK's loans are presently "non-performing loans" as a matter of federal banking law, but they have been consistently "rolled-over" in past restructurings of Asiana's debt. This has meant that repayment deadlines on principal have been extended and new loans created to keep interest payments on existing debt current.   Hence AMABANK's total loan exposure in Asiana has been steadily increasing.

WORLDDEBT is a closely held Delaware corporation that has been an active buyer and seller of developing world securities in the secondary market. It has accumulated substantial holdings of Asiana government debt, and debt of its leading companies, all purchased at large discounts off face value. Some critics label WORLDDEBT a speculator. Others see it as an important source of financial fluidity in a high risk environment. Either way, WORLDDEBT is definitely an investor that is driven by profit motives.

SECTION II.   FOCUS OF CONSIDERATION

During the 1970s a shift occurred from considerable public to a very large amount of private lending to developing nations. Terms were highly favorable and profitable, but the bankers did not give great consideration to the risk of defaults. Many small banks were brought into consortia lending on the tails of major money center banks. These banks certainly did not possess expertise allowing them to make sound judgments regarding lending to these nations. They relied on the judgments of the major banks which had considerable dealings with developing nations. But in the late 1970s and particularly in the 1980s, it became apparent that many banks had loaned excessively and many nations had borrowed beyond their means. In this context, the IMF assumed an increasingly important role. It stepped in to negotiate austerity agreements with third world governments before private banks would refinance outstanding loans. The IMF thus became the principal facilitator and regulator of credit to developing nations.

This problem addresses the IMF's traditional and intended role as a regulator of intergovernmental monetary relations, balance of payments problems, and credit. The primary focus, however, is on the IMF's unintended role as the source of economic adjustment "conditions." Such conditions were typically formulated by teams of IMF economists and other professionals operating quite secretively on the assumption that they know best how to deal with financial crises. This assumption has been openly criticized, not the least because IMF conditions were often remarkably intrusive in national affairs. By 2002, the IMF was micromanaging the affairs of some 80 member countries. By early 2008, it was virtually out of the loan business as members fled from its conditions. Then the world financial and economic meltdown arrived in the Fall of 2008. By year's end, the IMF was back in the loan business, most notably joining with the EU to conditionally bail out members of the EURO zone.

The problem explores some of the linkages between the IMF and public and private sources of international financing, including the question of "moral hazards" associated with IMF bailouts. It focuses upon international debt and some possible solutions: secondary markets, debt swaps, the Baker Plan and the Brady Plan (named after successive U.S. Secretaries of State). It also focuses on some worst case scenarios as creditors sue sovereigns and sovereign wealth funds enter financial markets.

Web resources for further study include *www.imf.org*.

SECTION III.   READINGS, QUESTIONS AND COMMENTS

WHAT IS THE INTERNATIONAL MONETARY FUND?

http://www.imf.org/external/pubs/ft/exrp/what.htm (August 2002).

The Origins of the IMF

The IMF was conceived in July 1944 at a United Nations conference held at Bretton Woods, New Hampshire, U.S.A. when representatives of 45 governments agreed on a framework for economic cooperation designed to avoid a repetition of the disastrous economic policies that had contributed to the Great Depression of the 1930s.

During that decade, as economic activity in the major industrial countries weakened, countries attempted to defend their economies by increasing restrictions on imports; but this just worsened the downward spiral in world trade, output, and employment. To conserve dwindling reserves of gold and foreign exchange, some countries curtailed their citizens' freedom to buy abroad, some devalued their currencies, and some introduced complicated restrictions on their citizens' freedom to hold foreign exchange. These fixes, however, also proved self-defeating, and no country was able to maintain its competitive edge for long. Such "beggar-thy-neighbor" policies devastated the international economy; world trade declined sharply, as did employment and living standards in many countries.

As World War II came to a close, the leading allied countries considered various plans to restore order to international monetary relations, and at the Bretton Woods conference the IMF emerged. The country representatives drew up the charter (or *Articles of Agreement*) of an international institution to oversee the international monetary system and to promote both the elimination of exchange restrictions relating to trade in goods and services, and the stability of exchange rates.

* * *

Countries that joined the IMF between 1945 and 1971 agreed to keep their exchange rates (in effect, the value of their currencies in terms of the U.S. dollar, and in the case of the United States, the value of the U.S. dollar in terms of gold) pegged at rates that could be adjusted, but only to correct a "fundamental disequilibrium" in the balance of payments and with the IMF's concurrence. This so-called Bretton Woods system of exchange rates prevailed until 1971 when the U.S. government suspended the convertibility of the U.S. dollar (and dollar reserves held by other governments) into gold. Since then, IMF members have been free to choose any form of exchange arrangement they wish (except pegging their currency to gold): some now allow their currency to float freely, some peg their currency to another currency or a group of currencies, some have adopted the currency of another country as their own, and some participate in currency blocs.

* * *

Who Makes Decisions at the IMF?

The IMF is accountable to its member countries, and this accountability is essential to its effectiveness. The day-to-day work of the IMF is carried out by an Executive Board, representing the IMF's 184 members, and an internationally recruited staff under the leadership of a Managing Director and three Deputy Managing Directors—each member of this management team being drawn from a different region of the world. The powers of the Executive Board to conduct the business of the IMF are delegated to it by the Board of Governors, which is where ultimate oversight rests.

The **Board of Governors**, on which all member countries are represented, is the highest authority governing the IMF. It usually meets once a year, at the Annual Meetings of the IMF and the World Bank. Each member country appoints a Governor—usually the country's minister of finance or the governor of its central bank—and an Alternate Governor. The Board of Governors decides on major policy issues but has delegated day-to-day decision-making to the Executive Board.

Key policy issues relating to the international monetary system are considered twice-yearly in a committee of Governors called the **International Monetary and Financial Committee**, or IMFC (until September 1999 known as the Interim Committee). A joint committee of the Boards of Governors of the IMF and World Bank called the **Development Committee** advises and reports to the Governors on development policy and other matters of concern to developing countries.

The Executive Board consists of 24 Executive Directors, with the Managing Director as chairman. The Executive Board usually meets three times a week, in full-day sessions, and more often if needed, at the organization's headquarters in Washington, D.C. The IMF's five largest shareholders—the United States, Japan, Germany, France, and the United Kingdom—along with China, Russia, and Saudi Arabia, have their own seats on the Board. The other 16 Executive Directors are elected for two-year terms by groups of countries, known as constituencies.

* * *

Unlike some international organizations that operate under a one-country-one vote principle (such as the United Nations General Assembly), the IMF has a weighted voting system: the larger a country's quota in the IMF—determined broadly by its economic size—the more votes it has. But the Board rarely makes decisions based on formal voting; rather, most decisions are based on consensus among its members and are supported unanimously.

* * *

Where Does the IMF Get Its Money?

The IMF's resources come mainly from the quota (or capital) subscriptions that countries pay when they join the IMF, or following periodic reviews in which quotas are increased. Countries pay 25 percent of their quota subscriptions in Special Drawing Rights (SDRs) or major currencies, such as U.S. dollars or Japanese yen; the IMF can call on the remainder, payable in the member's own currency, to be made available for lending as needed. Quotas determine not only a country's subscription payments, but also its voting power, the amount of financing that it can receive from the IMF, and its share in SDR allocations.

Quotas are intended broadly to reflect members' relative size in the world economy: the larger a country's economy in terms of output, and the larger and more variable its trade, the higher its quota tends to be. The United States of America, the world's largest economy, contributes most to the IMF, [17] percent of total quotas; Seychelles, the world's smallest, contributes 0.004 percent. [Japan and Germany contribute 6 percent, Britain and France 5 percent, China 4 percent, Russia 3 percent, India and Brazil 2 percent after 2008 adjustments.]

* * *

GERSTER, THE IMF AND BASIC NEEDS CONDITIONALITY

16 J. World Trade L. 497 (1982).*

The concept of "conditionality" is crucial for the access to credits of the IMF. "Conditionality" is not a legal term as it is not mentioned in the Articles of Agreement. However, the conditionality of IMF credits refers to the economic policies the IMF expects a member to follow in order to be able to use the Fund's general resources * * *. As Sir Joseph Gold, a senior consultant to the Fund, pointed out: "These policies should help a member to overcome its balance of payments problem, avoid the temptation to resort to measures detrimental to itself or to the general welfare, and help it to achieve and maintain a sustainable balance of payments position over a reasonable period ahead" * * *. Conditionality should not only be for the benefit of the member but also serve as a safeguard to protect the Fund's resources.

Since 1952, the IMF continuously developed the instrument of stand-by arrangements considered as decisions of the Fund on the basis of a letter of intent by the interested government * * *. Such stand-by arrangements today are frequently preceded by the fulfillment of preconditions by the government. The stand-by arrangements include a set of qualitative and quantitative performance criteria. These clauses have to be met if the country's entitlement to draw is to remain intact. The phasing of the credits and the performance criteria are the heart of conditionality and make it effective. Performance criteria mainly refer to credit and

---

* © Journal of World Trade Law. Reprinted with permission.

fiscal policies, to the exchange rate and to the liberalization of restrictions on payments and trade. The shaping of these criteria has to follow the purposes of the Fund as stated in Article I of the Articles of Agreement.

It is not the intention of the IMF to cover all the financial means of a member being in balance of payments troubles. On the contrary, the conditionality of drawings is to enhance the structural adjustment of the economy in order to overcome a worsening foreign position, thereby reducing the member's need for balance of payments finances. The Fund's credits should rather be considered as an incentive and a seal of approval of an economic policy in the interests of the creditors.

Conditionality plays an increasing role in IMF lending. Whereas during the first oil crisis of 1974–5 the Fund tried to respond to the balance of payments problems by increasing its facilities of low conditionality, after the second oil price increase in 1979 the IMF stressed the need for adjustment * * *. The main vehicle for this adjustment oriented IMF policy was and still is high conditionality of its resources. Jacques de Larosière, Managing Director of the Fund, stated at an OECD Meeting in June 1981: "Three quarters of our financing is now provided in conjunction with economic adjustment programs, while only a few years ago, by contrast, three quarters of our financing was made available with virtually no conditions".

To sum it up, the significance of the present IMF conditionality is sixfold:

1. *As a key to IMF resources:* From the members' point of view, conditionality is the key to access to the Fund's resources.

2. *As a seal of approval:* Beyond IMF resources, intact drawing entitlements of a stand-by with high conditionality is considered as a seal of approval for the economic policy of a country and facilitates the access to private and official loans.

3. *As a vehicle to dependency:* Through reintegration into the present world economy with unequal partners, conditionality tends to keep the developing countries in dependency instead of promoting their self reliant development.

4. *To exclude alternative balance of payments policies:* As conditionality of IMF credits is designed to promote the purposes of the Fund, the concept of IMF conditionality excludes—often undiscussed—alternative balance of payments policies.

5. *As a rationing device:* On its way to a more liberal system of international trade and payments, IMF conditionality facilitates rationing and allocating of scarce resources along the lines of market forces, thereby replacing other social and political priorities.

6. *To favour foreign interests:* The chosen IMF conform adjustment policies favour the interests of foreign creditors and are therefore the key to the repayment of the Fund's own credits.

SIR J. GOLD, ORDER IN INTERNATIONAL FINANCE, THE PROMOTION OF IMF STAND-BY ARRANGEMENTS, AND THE DRAFTING OF PRIVATE LOAN AGREEMENTS

International Monetary Fund Pamphlet No. 39 (1982).*

The reluctance of banks to "establish economic conditions for countries" has not prevented the attempt on some occasions. On the whole, however, banks have regarded efforts of this kind as unbecoming, in addition to which they have been loath to put themselves at a disadvantage in competition with other banks that would be willing to lend without engaging in these efforts. The reluctance of banks to establish conditions on economic policy for countries has been not less than, and has probably been surpassed by, the unwillingness of governments to engage in discussions with private interests on the initiation of sensitive policies relating to fiscal, monetary, and exchange rate matters. All these considerations may induce banks to place major reliance on the Fund's judgment.

* * *

The provisions of a bank's loan agreement may condition effectiveness of the agreement on the Fund's approval of a stand-by arrangement and may condition advances under the agreement on a country's status in the Fund or on its access to the Fund's resources under the arrangement. These and other provisions relating to the Fund fall into a number of categories.

Clauses calling for certain representations by the borrower on entry into a loan agreement constitute one category. A representation that is said to be normal in Eurodollar loan agreements for the benefit of developing states, but is probably in wider use, is one in which a government as borrower, or as guarantor if the central bank is the borrower, "represents," or "represents and warrants," that it is "a member in good standing of the International Monetary Fund * * * and is fully eligible to purchase dollars from the I.M.F." Representations of this kind can be narrower or broader than this formulation. A narrower formulation calls for a representation that:

Patria is a member in good standing of the IMF.

A broader formulation provides for a representation that:

On the effective date of this Agreement, Patria shall be a member in good standing of the IMF and IBRD and no event shall have occurred which suspends or limits Patria's ability to utilize the resources of the IMF or IBRD, including SDR facilities.

* * *

In a second category are provisions that establish conditions for each advance to the borrower under a loan agreement. It has been seen that a

---

* Reprinted with permission of the International Monetary Fund.

representation sometimes required when a member enters into a loan agreement is that it is eligible or fully eligible to make purchases from the Fund or that it is fully eligible to purchase U.S. dollars from the Fund. A representation of this kind may be required also on the occasion of each advance under a loan agreement.

* * *

A third category of provisions involving the Fund deals with the circumstances or events that are deemed defaults under a loan agreement. Some of these provisions have been drafted along the following lines:

> If any of the following events ("Events of Default") shall occur and be continuing: * * *

>> (v) Patria shall cease to be a member in good standing of the IMF; or

>> (vi) Patria shall not draw down the Second Credit Tranche from the IMF in two phases to be completed by (date) and (date), respectively * * *

> Patria shall cease to be a member of the International Monetary Fund, or shall cease to be entitled to draw under the IMF Facility for any reason other than that the availability thereunder has been fully drawn.

* * *

GOLD, THE GROWING ROLE OF THE IMF'S STAND-BY ARRANGEMENTS

1984 J.Bus.Law 315.*

Notable new developments involving stand-by arrangements have occurred in United States law [Public Law 98–181] as a result of the debt crisis. Congress took the opportunity to insist on these developments when called upon to authorise consent by the United States to an increase in its quota in the IMF and in its commitment under the standing agreement, called the General Arrangements to Borrow, entered into in the early Sixties by the IMF with ten of its leading industrial members under which they undertake to consider lending to the IMF in certain circumstances.

* * *

The second class of provisions is Title IX of the statute, which is to be cited as the "International Lending Supervision Act of 1983." The adequacy of the supervision of banking has been a national and international concern for some years, partly because of the failure of some banks. One reason for these failures has been the exchange risks undertaken by the banks in a world in which currencies are no longer subject to the

---

discipline of a par value system. In the United States, the attitude of Congress was affected by the conviction that the banks had been careless in their past international lending and by the suspicion that the banks were now hoping that sovereign borrowers would obtain resources from the IMF to repay their debts to the commercial banks. Objection to use of the IMF's resources to "bail out" the banks became a frequent incantation.

* * *

Each appropriate Federal banking agency (Comptroller of the Currency, or Federal Deposit Insurance Corporation, or Federal Reserve Board) must evaluate foreign country exposure and transfer risk for use in the strengthened supervision of banking institutions as defined by the Act. United States agencies or branches of foreign banks, but not foreign banks themselves, are within the definition. Each appropriate Federal agency must adopt procedures to ensure that exposure and risk are among the factors taken into account in evaluating the adequacy of the capital of banking institutions. These institutions must establish and maintain a special reserve, to be charged against current income and not considered part of capital and surplus or allowances for possible loan losses, whenever, in the judgment of the agency, one of specified events has happened or one of specified situations has developed. Among these events or developments is an impairment of a banking institution's assets "by a protracted inability of public or private borrowers in a foreign country to make payments on their external indebtedness." One of the evidences of such an impairment is "a failure by the foreign country to comply with any International Monetary Fund or other suitable adjustment program."

What is meant by a failure to comply with an adjustment programme of the IMF is not clear and can give rise to much debate. For example, will the test be the inability of a member to engage in transactions under a stand-by arrangement because of the nonobservance of performance criteria or some broader evaluation of progress?

Since 1977, banking institutions have had to report their foreign country exposure semiannually. The new statute and the first regulations adopted under it, which became effective on February 13, 1984, require that reports be made at least at quarterly intervals and that information be made available to the public on request. The regulations deal in detail with the special reserves for transfer risk, now called Allocated Transfer Risk Reserves (ATRRs). Transfer risk is defined as the possibility that an asset cannot be serviced in the contractual currency of payment because of a lack, or restraints on the availability, of foreign exchange in the country of the obligor.

SOMERVILLE, NEGOCIAR EN TIEMPOS DIFICILES (TO NEGOTIATE IN HARD TIMES)

Reviewed by Enrique R. Carrasco.
30 Columbia J.Transnat'l L. 719 (1992).*

About a decade ago (in August of 1982), Mexico declared that it could no longer service its external debt. Mexico's announcement, which marked the beginning of the so-called "Third World debt crisis," provided the foundation for a mountain of literature that addresses the many dimensions of Latin America's "lost decade." Hernán Somerville, Chile's chief debt negotiator from 1983 to 1988, has recently made a significant "post-crisis" contribution to this topic. Unlike the literature produced by other Latin Americans, Somerville's book, titled *Negociar en Tiempos Dificiles* or *To Negotiate in Hard Times,* provides outside observers of the crisis with a very interesting insider's account of negotiations that took place primarily between Chile and its commercial bank creditors.

In the prologue to his book, Somerville states, "[T]he only viable way to surmount the external debt crisis was negotiation." His conclusion is not self-evident, however. Cooperation through negotiations—rather than sustained confrontation—would not have flourished without an official (public) belief in a "value-creating" system within which a debtor country could confidently pursue a workout with its private and official creditors abroad. Somerville describes a relatively (sufficiently) well-defined and highly manipulable system that in his view worked well for his country and that, by inference, could have worked equally well for other Latin American debtor countries if they had followed Chile's example: Chile arguably was the first troubled Latin American debtor country that could proclaim officially in the late 1980s that it surmounted the debt crisis by regaining at least partial access to the voluntary international lending market and by resuming sustained economic growth. Virtually all major Latin American debtor countries have adopted Chile's highly cooperative approach. And virtually all of Latin America is in the midst of sweeping neo-liberal economic "reforms" that Chile implemented years ago, changes such as deregulation of the economy, privatization, and rejection of the import substitution model of development.

Somerville's book thus describes an approach to the debt crisis that has made Chile a model debtor country, at least from the creditors' point of view. Equally important and revealing, however, is the book's failure to address the plight of so-called vulnerable groups in debtor countries—i.e., children, women and elderly who lack (or are likely to lack) the resources to obtain housing, clothing and the minimum caloric intake. Somerville's omission illustrates the major flaw of the otherwise seemingly successful cooperative approach to the debt crisis.

* * *

---

* © 1992 Columbia Journal of Transnational Law. Reprinted with permission.

The crisis erupted in 1982 when the price of copper fell and Chile's foreign creditors, having realized that the country faced a very precarious financial position, abruptly stopped their lending. Chile's economy then fell into a deep recession. GDP fell fifteen percent in real terms during the 1982–1983 period. The effective unemployment rate rose to approximately thirty percent; real wages fell by eleven percent. Consumption and investment plummeted. Chile's terms of trade plunged twenty-seven percent between 1979 and 1983, one of the steepest declines in Latin America.

* * *

Implementing the Cooperative Approach

Winning the respect of commercial bank creditors was crucial, since Chile owed most of its external debt to such creditors. The first step for Chile, as for other Latin American countries, was to form a Bank Advisory Committee (BAC) (also called the Steering Committee for some debtor countries), a group of twelve commercial bank creditors chaired by the Manufacturers Hanover Trust. Through the BAC and its subcommittees, which in practice represented Chile's commercial bank creditors (approximately 500), Somerville sought to achieve the *quid pro quo* described above: The BAC worked with Somerville and others to gather information (principally economic), process it and through negotiations arrive at an agreement based on such information that would be acceptable to all of Chile's commercial bank creditors. Another round of negotiations would follow to write the contract or contracts that execute the agreement in principle.

This model of negotiations assumed that debtor countries could put their economic houses in order relatively quickly and thereby return to the voluntary lending markets and normal debt service. The assumption proved to be wrong, however. Commercial bank creditors suspected sometime in 1984 that debtor countries perhaps might be insolvent (unable to amortize their external debt) rather than merely illiquid (temporarily unable to gather enough foreign exchange to service their external debt). Consequently, the banks became increasingly reluctant to engage in debt restructuring exercises, especially the new money component. BACs became forums for acrimonious exchanges between and among bankers and debtor country officials.

In Chile's case, cooperative behavior was reinstated at times by actors outside the BAC, namely the International Monetary Fund, the World Bank, and the finance ministries in the developed countries, particularly the U.S. Treasury Department. Somerville also found the Federal Reserve Bank of New York, a representative of which regularly attended Chile's BAC meetings, to be a particularly useful ally. Sometimes Somerville could successfully persuade these other actors to place pressure on the BAC to agree to a proposal Chile had put on the negotiating table, such as Chile's proposal to re-time interest payments. The BAC, on the other hand, managed to convince the IMF and World Bank that Chile should provide a guarantee for restructured debt of the private financial sector originally due during the period 1985–1987. The BAC also persuaded the IMF and World Bank to back the banks' position that Chile restructure its official external debt through the Paris Club in order to meet its financing needs.

Through this fluid and manipulable system, Somerville secured deals with Chile's commercial bank creditors that, among other things, provided balance of payments financing, postponed payments of principal, and lowered interest payments—elements which other Latin American debtor countries pursued after 1982. He concludes, however, that the BAC, the focal point of the system, will no longer be as relevant to Chile's financial future, given the innovative 1988 agreement between Chile and its commercial bank creditors. Although other commentators have similarly questioned whether BACs can still play a useful role in light of the Brady Initiative's emphasis on debt reduction, the recent experiences of Venezuela and Brazil indicate that BACs have continued to play a useful role in the cooperative approach.

QUESTIONS AND COMMENTS

1. How is the IMF structured and run? Is it dominated by the developed world? By the United States? Why do developing nations like Asiana participate in the IMF?

2. Special drawing rights (SDRs) are not tangible like dollars or yen. Special drawing rights are essentially a monetary unit of account created within the IMF to increase its loan capacity. Each member of the fund receives a proportionate allocation of SDRs, thus entitling it to call upon other members to provide currencies in an effort to meet balance of payments problems.

Furthermore, the SDR has become a kind of fictional currency used occasionally as a transaction value in *private* trading because it represents a basket of leading world currencies, the U.S. dollar, the EURO, the Japanese yen and the pound sterling. Private promissory notes and bank drafts are sometimes even written in SDRs. Some countries actually peg their currencies to the value of SDRs. Asiana, like other IMF members, will have received an allocation of SDRs which it may utilize. It could present these special drawing rights to the United States, Japan, Germany, Switzerland or other IMF nations to obtain "hard currencies." Those nations then accumulate SDRs against the day when they run into similar problems. China has pushed for developing SDRs into a global currency. Why? Do you agree?

3. Prior to the second oil price increase in 1979 most IMF funds were available with few or no conditions attached. Why have the bulk of IMF financings been conditioned upon economic adjustment programs?

4. What is the meaning of IMF conditionality? Why hasn't AMABANK "conditioned" its loans to Asiana? Why do private and public lenders defer to the IMF to set loan conditions? Are they functioning as a creditors' cartel?

5. Suppose the IMF experts determine that the conditions for credit to Asiana are more taxes, high interest rates, the closure of politically connected

banks and corporations, reduced government spending, transparency (especially regarding financial data), and market access for foreigners. What do you think of that "formula for recovery?"

How will the imposition of such conditions affect AMABANK's interests? If AMABANK declines to lend on these conditions, might its California correspondent bank pick up the loan, thus allowing AMABANK to extract itself from a difficult situation?

How will these conditions affect stability and life in Asiana? What do they suggest regarding the economic sovereignty of Asiana? Imagine for a moment that an IMF team stipulated the same conditions for the United States, the world's leading debtor nation.

6. At this point, why do the banks lend at all? What is the significance to AMABANK of the potential reclassification of its Asiana loans as "non-performing"? What is the significance to Asiana of this potential reclassification? Federal bank regulators have in the past ordered U.S. banks to write off large percentages of their Latin American loans.

IMF loan performance criteria were effectively incorporated in 1983 into regulation of the United States banking system by Public Law 98–181. Why? Does Public Law 98–181 attempt to influence those criteria? See the Gold excerpt.

7. What are AMABANK's options for dealing with its Asiana-related loans? Which options do you advise it to pursue?

8. What are Asiana's options? Would you advise it to follow Chile's cooperative "hard times" approach as related by Somerville? Note that Chile negotiated directly with a Bank Advisory Committee (BAC) led by Manufacturers Hanover. What role did the IMF play?

ARONSON, FINANCIAL INSTITUTIONS IN THE INTERNATIONAL MONETARY SYSTEM

12 Case West.Res.J.Int'l L. 341 (1980).*

The United States government was probably more responsible for the changing role of banks in the markets and the monetary system than any other government. America's attempt to reverse its balance of payments position through the imposition of the Interest Equalization Tax (1963), the Voluntary Foreign Credit Restraint Program (1965), and the Foreign Direct Investment Program (1968) may or may not have delayed the first devaluation. It certainly accelerated the growth and attractiveness of the Eurodollar market and virtually forced many smaller banks to move abroad more rapidly, more vigorously, and in greater numbers than otherwise would have been prudent. Smaller non–American banks and some previously insular large foreign banks were prompted to become more international or risk declining market visibility and profits.

Each bank entering the international market needed to establish an immediate profit base. Since most of the best traditional borrowers were

---

* © Case Western Reserve Journal of International Law. Reprinted with permission.

already committed to large banks, newcomers had to hustle business or admit defeat and return home. Since the public relations costs of retreat were high, newcomers stole business from established institutions. In the foreign exchange markets they pushed the bid-offer differentials closer together and took open positions during the business day. In the Eurocurrency markets, newcomers accepted slightly lower fees, pushed margins down, tenors out, and gave borrowers the chance to take more funds. The most credit-worthy customers discovered that they could borrow money on such favorable terms that banks made acceptable profits only through undertaking huge volumes of business on minimal capital. The large banks' oligopoly was broken and competition increased. There was surplus liquidity in the markets, a need to lend these funds, and inevitably a decline in the quality of borrowers. The largest banks started lending to developing countries, socialist nations, smaller multinationals, and more recently to the People's Republic of China. Although the risks were higher, so were the profits, and the competition was less. Gradually, however, small banks ventured into these markets as well.

A borrower's market emerged. Banks which once sought borrowers able to repay the interest and a portion of the principal of their loans out of their expected cash flow, began accepting debtors unable even to pay the interest on their loans from projected cash flows. Intense competition among lenders during 1973 and 1974 further eroded bank lending standards. This deterioration was briefly constrained by the banking crisis of 1974, but banks were so liquid after the OPEC price rises that lending necessarily resumed. Problems intensified when traditional borrowers' loan demand stagnated. Prime borrowers switched to the bond markets and the commercial paper market from the Euromarkets. By 1979 over forty-three percent of Eurocurrency syndication funds went to non–OPEC developing nations.

Banks assured their stockholders and themselves that these new loans presented no major problems. They pointed out that there had been no major LDC (less developed country) defaults since World War II and that the growth of Eurocurrency loans to these nations, when adjusted for inflation, was not out of line. They neglected pre–World War II experiences which indicated that "productive loans to developing countries are not very productive and do not stay long out of default." In part this was because banks did not have to worry about the repayment of Eurosyndicates until the late 1970s. The eight and ten year loans made in the early 1970s took their profits up front, but the principal was not due until the end of the decade. So far, loans have been rolled over or rescheduled, but rarely repaid.

In theory, the banking system should funnel funds to projects and countries where long-term economic returns will be maximized. In practice, the banking system has not realized sufficient rent for the use of its funds as the risks justify. There are two reasons for this miscalculation. First, the "over-competition" of swelling numbers of banks competing for a slower growing amount of desirable business distorted risk-return analyses. Unfortunately, there is no easy way to correct the situation. Large banks are so committed to some developing countries that they cannot withdraw. If smaller banks decide to pull out of a shaky country, the large institutions must assume their positions as well or risk country defaults. In addition, banks are not terribly worried about even major losses since most institutions involved internationally are large enough that their national governments would probably bail them out rather than risk disrupting their domestic economies.

A second reason for bank miscalculations was their complacence towards political risks. Bankers averred that although manufacturing and extractive firms were vulnerable to nationalization, no rational national leader would destroy his nation's credit-worthiness by defaulting on international bank loans. While the banks accepted intermittent loan roll overs, as long as interest continued to be paid, this actually benefited them by making it unnecessary to find new borrowers. In the late 1970s banks even accepted the political risks of oil companies operating in Indonesia and Malaysia because they felt secure from national upheavals. In essence, the banks believed that their bargaining position was not an obsolescing one. They were in a stable mutual hostage position with their borrowers.

COMMENT ON APPROACHES TO THE DEBT PROBLEM

In the Fall of 1986, Secretary of Treasury Baker (Secretary of State in 1990) suggested at the IMF meeting in Seoul what has been called *"the Baker Plan"* for third world debt. It suggested (1) the need for more commercial bank lending, (2) the need for more lending by multinational organizations such as the World Bank, and (3) the need for economic reform in the debtor nations. The Baker Plan was not revolutionary, but it was the first acknowledgment by the U.S. government that the debt crisis demanded the participation of the major governments—it was not just a private bank-debtor nation issue. Latin American nations responded with the Cartegena Agreement, which approved the first two parts of the Baker Plan, but objected to more conditionality terms of economic reform. They wanted new funds tied to their needs and old money deferred with the rates lowered considerably. Little came out of the Baker Plan. The banks were pressured to loan more to Mexico in the Fall of 1986, but they responded with only a part of the requested money.

As a response to the Baker Plan, Senator Bradley suggested an alternative. Bradley said the Baker Plan was simply more of the same, and overlooked the need to consider the lessening of U.S. exports caused by the deteriorating conditions of third world economies which have so much to pay in interest and principal on debt. Bradley believed that the banks should adopt some form of debt relief. The banks did not respond very enthusiastically, but Bradley suggested the banks will eventually agree that the debt cannot be repaid and that relief is better than default. To this end, Section 3111 of the 1988 Omnibus Trade and Competitiveness Act directed the Secretary of the Treasury to study the feasibility and advisability of establishing an

International Debt Management Authority, and to initiate discussions with debtor and creditor countries about such an authority. Section 3121 of the 1988 Act expresses the general desire of Congress that federal banking agencies should "grant the widest possible latitude to the banks for negotiating principal and interest reductions with respect to obligations of heavily indebted sovereigns." Related Congressional intent in connection with loans to banks by federal authorities, recapitalization requirements, reserves for loan losses and reporting requirements are specified in Section 3121.

In the Spring of 1989, Secretary of Treasury Brady announced a revised U.S. policy on third world debt (*the "Brady Plan"*). The Brady Plan implicitly acknowledged the shortcomings of the Baker Plan. It emphasizes debt reduction rather than piling on new loans mostly to meet current interest payments. The World Bank, the IMF, Japan and private banks were asked to facilitate debt reduction through discounted buy-back arrangements, loan swapping ("exit bonds") and various guarantee programs. The Brady Plan was sparked by riots in Venezuela and a general recognition of the social costs of the debt problem in Latin America. Mexico, which had undertaken many liberalizing economic and trade reforms, was the leading candidate for Brady Plan.

The Mexican accord achieved in July of 1989 offered banks three choices: (1) exchange existing loans with floating interest rates for fixed rate 30–year credits at a well below market interest rate of 6.25% ("par bonds"); (2) exchange the loans for 30–year bonds at a 35% reduction in face value but with floating interest rates ("discount bonds"); or (3) provide new loans in a traditional 4–year roll-over refinancing in an amount at least equal to 25% of current exposure. Any bank reducing Mexican debt has its interest payments guaranteed for at least 18 months and its principal secured by U.S. Treasury zero-coupon bonds. These guarantees are financed by the IMF, World Bank, Mexico and Japan. Several leading U.S. banks bolstered their reserves late in 1989 in order to avoid new lending to Mexico. By 1990, it became apparent that the Brady Plan formula was not working as Mexico and the U.S. had hoped. Only about 10 percent of all banks opted for continued lending, leaving Mexico short of ready cash. The remaining banks split about evenly between par bonds and discounted bonds. On balance, Mexico's total debt remained about the same, but its debt service costs declined significantly. It essentially replaced commercial bank debt with new loans from international agencies and Japan. The banks were the real winners with relatively few losses after such poor investment decisions. They also signaled an ability to leave future financings to governments and multilateral agencies. Some agreements after Mexico showed a return to the Baker Plan's emphasis on continued lending. Debt renegotiations with Bolivia and Costa Rica, however, involved a large amount of overall loan forgiveness. The banks seem more flexible with creditors who are potentially capable of walking away from the international credit market. Major Brady Plans were later negotiated with Argentina, Brazil, Nigeria, Poland and Venezuela among others.

The impact of the *marketplace* on third world debt is an interesting factor. A market has emerged for such debt. Third world debt may be substantially discounted in the marketplace thereby giving a measure of fair value. Banks sometimes swap debt of different countries in order to balance their loan portfolios; and some third world governments have retired their debt at a discount by buying it back in the market. Securitization of third world debt has begun through a number of investment funds, a kind of ultimate "junk bond" approach to the debt problem. A huge market in "Brady bonds" has emerged. And U.S. mutual funds are increasingly active buyers of *short-term* international debt. This gives them, like the IMF, considerable clout with debtor governments. Mutual and hedge fund money managers move mega-money around the work with the click of a computer. Sometimes they do so only after "suggesting" policy changes to debtor nations, as was the case with Mexico in the mid–1990s. On other occasions, the flood of private funds into government bond markets dramatically raises currency values, an outcome some nations seek to minimize by imposing foreign bond-buyer transaction taxes. South Korea, Australia, Thailand, Indonesia, South Africa, Brazil and others moved in this direction in 2010 as investors poured huge sums into their financial markets. Low interest rates in the U.S., Europe and Japan fueled the movement of private capital across borders despite entry taxes.

Another alternative which has emerged are so called *debt-equity swaps*. Such swaps have been used in the Philippines, Mexico (suspended in 1987 because of its inflationary impact but resumed again in 1989 for infrastructure or state enterprise debt), Chile, Brazil and other countries. Banks and holders of national debt swap debt at a discount using market values for equity positions in local companies (sometimes government owned companies) or local currency which is used for new or expanded local investment. A publicly spirited variation on this theme are debt for nature swaps which create conservation areas in developing nations, e.g., Costa Rica. Brokers have emerged who arrange debt-equity swaps. They have the beneficial effect of reducing external debt while at the same time increasing investment in local firms. United States banking rules have been rewritten to allow banks to participate in such swaps without necessarily having to write off their remaining holdings of similar debt along terms which reflect fair market value.

Here is how a debt-equity swap might work. Bank of America holds millions of dollars in Mexican debt. The Mexican government would love to pay in pesos, but Bank of America has little use for more than what it needs for commercial operations or sells to tourists heading south. IMB, a huge U.S. corporation with a plant in Mexico, wants to add another production plant in Mexico. It will need some $5 million for that investment, which it will convert to 5 billion pesos, the going rate of exchange. It goes to the Bank of America and buys $5 million of Mexican debt, but only has to pay at the 60 percent discounted rate. It has given $3 million to Bank of America which has given IMB a note from the Mexican government promising to pay the Bank of America $5 million. The Bank of America is content with the 60 percent, they really thought they might get nothing at all if Mexico defaulted. Now IMB takes the $5 million debt note to Mexico and says to the Mexican government that it is willing to give Mexico that note not for scarce dollars but for the equivalent in pesos, which means 5 billion pesos. The Mexican government agrees and gives IMB the 5 billion pesos. The foreign debt of Mexico has been reduced by $5 million but by paying in pesos, not dollars. IMB has obtained 5 billion pesos for $3 million rather than what they would have to pay in a direct exchange, $5 million. But now the Mexican government has caught on and negotiates how much it will give IMB, perhaps 80 percent rather than 100 percent. So IMB does not get the full 5 billion pesos, but they will get considerably more than the 3 billion they would receive in a direct exchange.

There are some problems. Mexico does not have the dollars they would receive if they negotiated directly with IMB. If they received dollars they could use them for any purpose, perhaps even to buy back debt at the discounted rate through an intermediary. Additionally, IMB may have large peso accounts in Mexico from profits of the current plant. They could use them for new investment. But they would be better off converting them to dollars at the current exchange rate and then buy some debt and follow the above. They come out with more dollars. That is why developing nations control, for example, the *kinds* of debt that can be swapped. Furthermore, Mexico must release a lot of pesos to make this swap work. In large, repeated amounts that could have an inflationary impact on the local economy. Regulations will therefore control the *amount* and *frequency* of debt-equity auctions and swaps. Lastly, the developing nations will establish minimum periods (e.g., 10 years) during which none of these new investments (and perhaps dividends therefrom) may be removed from the country.

The participation of United States banks in debt-equity swaps is governed by the Federal Reserve Act (12 U.S.C.A. §§ 601–604) and the Bank Holding Company Act (12 U.S.C.A. §§ 1841–50) as particularly implemented in Regulation K of the Federal Reserve Board. The net effect of these laws is to allow U.S. banks to invest in foreign non-financial companies through holding companies. Prior to 1987, Regulation K permitted no more than 20 percent shareholdings in such companies. Since then, up to 100 percent ownership is allowed if the shares are bought from a foreign government (i.e., through a privatization scheme) in a debt-equity swap of existing sovereign obligations and the country involved has refinanced (restructured) its debt with foreign creditors since 1980 (e.g., Mexico, Brazil, Chile). Such shareholdings may be held (with the permission of the Federal Reserve Board) for up to 10 years, but must in general be divested as soon as practicable. Remember, the use of these swaps cannot reduce third world debt substantially. But it does help and is a positive approach to dealing with some of the debt.

During the first half of the 1990s, developing country debt problems grabbed fewer headlines as U.S. banks wrote or sold off large amounts of debt. In many parts of the developing world, however, the levels of debt remained high. Payments were softened by low interest rates. The Brady Plan, securitization, debt-equity swaps and debt buy-backs notwithstanding, the late 1990s saw a return in Latin America and East Asia to financial crises, instability and continued IMF-led loan conditions. Consider this analysis of the Mexican financial crisis of December, 1994.

R. FOLSOM, NAFTA AND FREE
TRADE IN THE AMERICAS

Chapter 3 (2011).

The Peso Crash, A Common Currency?

Less than a year after NAFTA's launch, in December 1994 the Zedillo government suddenly announced a decision to discontinue its crawling-peg devaluation of the peso and let the peso float against other currencies. The peso quickly lost 35 percent of its value against the U.S. dollar and plunged nearly 100% before the crisis was over. Currency devaluations are not new to Mexico, and are a not-forgotten lesson in international finance. The 1994 crisis was in many ways a repeat of financial problems faced in much of Latin American since the late 19th century.

Governments have frequently relied upon foreign capital to make up for insufficient domestic savings. Additionally in the case of Mexico, the inflation rate was greater than the rate of devaluation resulting in an overvalued peso. Over-valuation stimulated added private sector spending which in turn further decreased the domestic savings rate. At the same time, rising interest rates in the United States and improved investment conditions elsewhere in Latin America (particularly Brazil) reduced the flow of capital to Mexico. The country's problems were magnified by a new risk factor. Much of the foreign capital that Mexico had recently come to rely upon came from short-term investments by U.S. mutual fund managers. Quite a lot of this money took flight when the peso crisis arrived and was 'not likely to return.

In response to the peso crisis, the Zedillo government announced plans to increase the budget surplus (yes, Mexico actually had a budget surplus), expand privatization, tighten monetary policy and to continue to allow the peso to float. The goal was to cut the nation's current account deficit and thereby the amount of foreign (particularly short-term) capital needed. The program was painful for many, especially workers and the hitherto growing middle class in Mexico, whose incomes did not keep up with the increase in inflation. Increased interest rates from a tight money policy slowed the Mexican economy and pushed it into a recession. This made it harder for Mexico and Mexican corporations to repay their debts to foreigners.

A plan announced on January 31, 1995 by President Clinton helped Mexico work out its financial crisis. This $50 billion plan was a coordinated effort by the United States, the IMF, the Bank for International Settlements (BIS), Canada and several Latin American nations. The United States and the IMF provided about $28 billion in medium-term credits to Mexico. These were used primarily to replace Mexico's short-term debt as it matured. Loan and loan guarantee conditions were attached, including restraints on the growth of Mexico's money supply, domestic credit, public sector borrowing and current account deficit.

Mexico's central bank was made more independent and transparent. Privatization was accelerated and, in a notable commitment, Mexico pledged future revenues from its oil sales to the Federal Reserve Bank of New York as collateral. Mexico subsequently repaid the United States, thus freeing up its oil revenues.

Border areas saw a reversal in commerce as the devalued peso decreased Mexicans' purchasing power and correspondingly increased the purchasing power of U.S. consumers. Foreign businesses in Mexico wrote down the value of inventory, while manufacturers in Mexico who primarily exported their output realized cost-savings. However, much like the 1982 devaluation of the peso which sparked the maquiladora boom, the 1994 crisis in the longer term actually increased the attractiveness of Mexico as a place to invest in order to obtain inexpensive labor and supplies. Price, wage, financial and currency stability returned to Mexico.

In the process of dealing with this debacle, Mexico confirmed its commitment through NAFTA to an outward-looking economic policy. Many poor nations caught in Mexico's bind would have blocked imports and restricted access to foreign currency. But the crisis raised fundamental questions about whether a common currency for NAFTA might not be desirable. Despite Mexican ideas about inventing a new currency (the "Amero"), the most likely scenario is "U.S. dollarization." Some Canadians have gradually come to believe that adopting the U.S. dollar as their national currency is in their self-interest. Mexicans, despite their history of peso crashes, are less enthused. In either case, it is worth noting that permission from the United States to "dollarize" is not required, as Ecuador and El Salvador have already demonstrated.

POWER, SOVEREIGN DEBT: THE RISE OF THE SECONDARY MARKET AND ITS IMPLICATIONS FOR FUTURE RESTRUCTURINGS

64 Fordham L.Rev. 2701 (1996).*

SUING THE SOVEREIGN: THE WAY OF THE FUTURE?

The effective freeze on collection actions has thawed as banks have reduced their exposure to LDC debtors and unloaded their LDC loan assets in the secondary market. The growth of the secondary market has created a new class of sovereign creditors, having incentives and expectations entirely different from those of their commercial bank predecessors. Because their debt holdings are comparatively smaller, individual secondary market purchasers of sovereign debt are more likely than were their commercial bank assignors to obtain full satisfaction of their claims by attaching the sovereign's limited U.S. assets following a default. In addition, secondary market purchasers are not subject to the same peer and political pressures to participate in debt restructurings, and may have a strong profit incentive to use litigation to collect on their sovereign loan

---

* © 1996 Fordham Law Review. Reprinted with permission.

assets. Indeed, the substantial discount in secondary market prices may cause LDC debt to become more valuable in default than as a performing loan asset. While the debt is performing, the investor holds an asset valued at pennies on the dollar; the chance that the sovereign will be able to repay the face value at maturity is slim. After a default, however, the investor acquires the right to accelerate the debt and proceed against available sovereign assets in the United States. The effect of these different incentives on the ongoing sovereign debt restructuring process is illustrated by the two recent cases discussed in this part.

CIBC Bank and Trust Co. (Cayman) Ltd.
v. Banco Central do Brasil*

Like Mexico, Brazil became unable to pay its debts to foreign creditors in 1982. In September of 1988, after a series of reschedulings, Brazil and its creditors entered into a Multi–Year Deposit Facility Agreement ("MYDFA"), which restructured over $60 billion (the great majority) of Brazil's debt to commercial bank creditors. Banco Central do Brasil, the Brazilian central bank (the "Central Bank"), was the obligor under the MYDFA. Only a year after the MYDFA was executed, however, Brazil again found itself unable to meet its obligations, and initiated negotiations to restructure the MYDFA debt.

In July of 1992, Brazil and its creditors reached an initial agreement-in-principle on a Brady Plan securitization of the MYDFA debt (the "1992 Accord"). Under the 1992 Accord, Brazil's creditors were offered a menu of options for converting their MYDFA debt into Brady bonds. Most creditors opted for par bonds, which would give them the full face value of their MYDFA principal, but bear a lower, fixed interest rate. The par bonds would be collateralized by U.S. Treasury bonds to be purchased by Brazil with the proceeds of IMF loans. A second option offered under the 1992 Accord was uncollateralized bonds, to be converted from the MYDFA debt at full principal value, but bearing an initial interest rate of four percent, rising to eight percent over six years. After receiving commitments to the 1992 Accord, however, Brazil sought to alter its terms, and asked its creditors to convert at least thirty-five percent of their MYDFA debt to yet another option—collateralized bonds to be converted at a deep discount from the face value of the MYDFA principal, but bearing a floating interest rate. All of the MYDFA creditors ultimately agreed to this proposal except one, the Dart family of Sarasota, Florida.

Since 1991, the Darts had been quietly purchasing Brazilian debt at a sixty-five percent discount in the secondary market. By 1993, the Darts had acquired obligations having a face value $1.4 billion, making them Brazil's fourth largest creditor. The family did not reveal the extent of its holdings, however, until Brazil attempted to alter the terms of the 1992 Accord. The Darts' potential profit from the Brady deal, had they accepted the deep discount bond option, was estimated at $270 million. Instead, the

---

* 886 F.Supp. 1105 (S.D.N.Y.1995).

Darts insisted on converting all of their MYDFA debt to the uncollateralized bonds originally offered under the 1992 Accord. Under the uncollateralized bond option, the Darts stood to reap a profit of $360 million from the conversion. Holding out for the greater profit, the Darts refused to convert their MYDFA debt at the April 15, 1994 closing of Brazil's Brady deal.

Faced with the Darts' intransigence, Brazil took defensive measures. Under the terms of the MYDFA, an acceleration of the MYDFA debt could be declared only with the consent or at the request of holders of more than fifty percent of the principal outstanding under the MYDFA. Therefore, if, as contemplated by the 1992 Accord, all of Brazil's creditors (except the Darts) converted their MYDFA debt to bonds, the Darts would have an immediate right after the conversion to declare an acceleration of their $1.4 billion of MYDFA debt. To prevent that occurrence, the Brazilian government instructed Banco do Brasil, a state owned commercial bank, to retain an amount of MYDFA debt sufficient to ensure that the Darts would not hold more than forty-nine percent of the MYDFA debt outstanding after the conversion. At the April 15, 1994 closing, therefore, Banco do Brasil converted all of its MYDFA debt except approximately $1.6 billion, which it continued to hold under the MYDFA.

Foiled in their attempt to obtain better terms than Brazil's other creditors, the Darts filed suit in the Southern District of New York, naming as defendants the Central Bank, Banco do Brasil, and Citibank, as agent under the MYDFA. Alleging that Banco do Brasil had retained its $1.6 billion of MYDFA debt in a bad faith attempt to prevent them from becoming a majority creditor under the MYDFA, the Darts sought a declaration of their right to accelerate the MYDFA principal without the consent of Banco do Brasil. In addition, the Darts sought repayment of the full $1.4 billion face amount of their debt, together with some $60 million in accrued interest. The defendants all moved to dismiss the Darts' complaint. Perhaps appreciating their probable futility, the defendants did not raise any of the affirmative defenses discussed in part II. Instead, the defendants relied solely on the terms of the MYDFA. Banco do Brasil was the majority creditor under the MYDFA. Therefore, the defendants argued, the Darts could not accelerate the MYDFA principal without the consent of Banco do Brasil.

* * *

In any event, the court dismissed the Darts' claim for a declaration of their right unilaterally to accelerate the principal of their MYDFA debt, but did not dismiss their breach of contract claim for $60 million in overdue interest. The case was recently settled for a $25 million cash payment and $52.3 million in bonds, representing interest accrued to April of 1994. A number of important questions were left unanswered by the court's decision, however, including whether the Darts may recover the full $1.4 billion of outstanding principal of their MYDFA debt at maturity. That question was presumably answered affirmatively by the Second

Circuit's decision in *Allied* ten years earlier. A "Statement of Interest" submitted by the United States in *CIBC*, however, cast doubt on the continuing validity of *Allied* as applied to secondary market purchasers of sovereign debt.

In its Statement of Interest in *CIBC*, the United States urged the court to deny the Darts' request to accelerate their MYDFA debt. The United States noted that the rapid growth of the secondary market for sovereign debt since *Allied* was decided has dramatically altered the relationship between LDC debtors and their creditors. The Statement of Interest observes that

> [i]n 1984, the United States identified in its *Allied* brief a number of factors extant at that time that helped assure good faith efforts on the part of debtors and creditors to resolve sovereign debt problems. These included: creditors' realization that orderly resolution of such problems is the best assurance of full repayment; a dearth of debtor assets to satisfy judgments; and peer pressure from like-minded fellow creditors that helped constrain impulsive or short-sighted behavior. The United States also observed at that time that there were only a limited number of banks unwilling to participate in sovereign debt restructurings, preferring instead to litigate to enforce their contractual rights (so-called "rogue banks").

> As a result of these factors, until now there have been relatively few lawsuits stemming from the sovereign debt crisis. These factors, however, are not present in 1994 to the same extent they were ten years ago. Most significantly, there has been a dramatic increase in the number of secondary market purchasers of sovereign debt.

The growth of the secondary market is significant, the Statement of Interest observes, because

> purchasers of debt on the secondary market do not necessarily have the same long-term interests as the commercial bank creditors who were the original lenders. Entities that purchase sovereign debt on the secondary market often do not intend to undertake a direct credit relationship with the sovereign borrower. Rather, some are investors who intend either to use the debt in debt-for-equity transactions or for other debt exchanges, or to resell it at a later date at a profit.

As a result of these divergent interests of secondary market sovereign debt purchasers,

> the sovereign debtor can no longer count on creditors being like-minded, similarly situated commercial financial institutions susceptible to peer pressure.

> This is a significant development in light of the absence of a neutral decisionmaking body, such as a bankruptcy court, with authority to restructure sovereign debt.

In light of the changes wrought by the growth of the secondary market, the United States observed that its concern in *CIBC* was a "mirror image" of its concern in *Allied* ten years earlier. In *Allied,* the United States had been concerned that a judgment for Costa Rica would encourage sovereign debtors to use the courts to extract better terms from creditors than they could obtain through negotiation. In *CIBC,* conversely, the United States was concerned that a judgment in favor of the Darts would encourage *creditors* to use the courts to gain unfair concessions from sovereign debtors.

More surprisingly, the United States also suggested that the availability of discounted sovereign debt in the secondary market has lowered creditors' reasonable expectations of full repayment. The Statement of Interest notes that

> [w]hile in 1984 banks rescheduled debt with the expectation of eventual full repayment, the widespread acceptance of the Brady Plan, which calls for commercial debt service and debt reduction, has generally changed this expectation.

Without stating explicitly what amount of sovereign debt recovery by secondary market purchasers the United States would consider reasonable, the Statement of Interest notes that

> [sovereign] debt obligations effectively have two values. One is their original legal contract value, *i.e.,* the values stated in the obligations themselves, expressed in terms of outstanding principal and interest due over a particular period of time. The other is their generally recognized market value, *i.e.,* the amount outside investors are willing to pay for the debt instruments at a particular point in time.

* * *

Pravin Banker Assocs. Ltd. v. Banco Popular del Peru*

The proper measure of recovery was even more hotly contested in a recent collection action against Peru, decided shortly after *CIBC.* In 1990, Pravin Banker Associates, Ltd., the plaintiff in the case, purchased from Mellon Bank a $9 million debt owed by Banco Popular del Peru, a commercial bank owned by the Peruvian government. The debt had been guaranteed by Peru and was payable in the United States in U.S. dollars. As a result of Peruvian exchange control regulations, Banco Popular had not made a payment of the debt principal since 1984, instead limiting payment to interest amounts as they fell due. The debt was thus in technical default at the time Pravin purchased it. Pravin purchased the debt for twenty-seven cents on the dollar and within two days resold all but $1.4 million of the debt to other investors for an undisclosed price. Notified of the assignment, Banco Popular made interest payments on the $1.4 million directly to Pravin until February of 1992, when Pravin served Banco Popular with a notice of default and demanded payment of the full principal amount. In December of 1992, the Peruvian Superintendent of Banks instituted liquidation procedures against Banco Popular. Instead of

---

* 895 F.Supp. 660 (S.D.N.Y.1995, [aff'd 109 F.3d 850 (2d Cir. 1997).

filing a claim in the liquidation, however, Pravin filed suit against Banco Popular and Peru in the U.S. District Court for the Southern District of New York.

The timing of the suit was not coincidental. At the time the suit was filed, Peru's debt was trading on the secondary market at approximately thirty-four cents on the dollar. Had Pravin sold the debt at that price, therefore, it would have turned a profit, in addition to the interest payments it had received, of seven cents for each dollar of debt sold. By seeking a judgment for the full face amount of the debt, however, Pravin stood to reap a profit of seventy-three cents on each dollar of debt it held. Moreover, Pravin knew that Peru would have a strong incentive to settle the suit quietly. At the time the suit was filed, Peru was negotiating an $8 billion Brady Plan restructuring with its commercial bank creditors. As a prelude to the negotiations, Peru's creditors had entered into a tolling agreement whereby they agreed to stay their pending lawsuits as long as no other collection actions against Peru went forward. A judgment in Pravin's favor would entitle Peru's other creditors to reactivate the lawsuits they had stayed pursuant to the tolling agreement.

* * *

The court granted Pravin's motion for summary judgment. Although noting factual differences from the *Allied* case, the court accepted as a premise *Allied's* holding that a sovereign debtor's unilateral suspension of external debt repayment is not entitled to deference in the interest of comity unless the suspension is consistent with U.S. policy. The court then attempted to determine the extent to which U.S. policy on sovereign debt restructuring has changed in the ten years since *Allied* was decided. As evidence of such a policy change, the defendants observed that *Allied* was decided before the Brady Plan signalled a U.S. endorsement of debt forgiveness for distressed sovereign debtors. In addition, the defendants referred the court to the Statement of Interest in *CIBC*, in which the United States argued that the growth of the secondary market for sovereign debt has dangerously altered the balance of power in sovereign debt restructurings and lowered the legitimate repayment expectations of secondary market purchasers.

The court was not persuaded by either argument. Although acknowledging that the Brady Plan represented a shift from the U.S. policy on sovereign debt restructuring prevailing when *Allied* was decided, the court held that

> the Brady Plan is essentially a call for *voluntary* participation by creditor banks in negotiations with foreign debtor nations to restructure their debt. The Brady Plan does not abrogate the contractual rights of creditor banks, nor does it *compel* creditors to forbear from enforcing those rights while debt restructuring negotiations are ongoing, or prohibit them from "opting out" of settlements resulting from such negotiations.

The court thus affirmed for secondary market purchasers of sovereign debt the right that the *Allied* court had implicitly affirmed for commercial bank creditors ten years earlier—the right to reject a restructuring proposal that a majority of a country's other creditors are prepared to accept. The *Pravin* court found support for that right in the Statement of Interest in *CIBC* and suggested that the right to opt-out might be even more important to secondary market purchasers than to commercial bank creditors. The court observed that

> Pravin has never signed a general debt restructuring agreement, has not participated in any restructuring negotiations and is not represented on [Peru's] Bank Advisory Committee. In light of this fact, the CIBC Statement of Interest's observation that secondary market sovereign debt purchasers often have divergent interests from original lender creditors cuts in favor of Pravin. Because Pravin's interests may well diverge from those of the creditor banks [on] the Bank Advisory Committee, the Committee does not provide Pravin with a forum in which to exert influence on the negotiations affecting the restructuring of [its] debt.

The outcome in *CIBC,* the court reasoned, did not signal a retreat from *Allied's* affirmation that creditors have a unilateral right to hold the sovereign to its loan agreement because, in *CIBC,* the Darts had attempted to use litigation effectively to *amend* the terms of their loan agreement. Pravin, in contrast, sought merely to enforce the terms of its agreement as written.

In light of the fact that the court had twice stayed the action on comity grounds, it is striking that the court did not find the comity rationale sufficient to deny Pravin's summary judgment motion, or to stave it off indefinitely. A clue to the court's apparent reversal may perhaps be found in the opinion's mention of press reports of Peru's secondary market buy-back of $2 billion of its debt at a discount of forty-five cents on the dollar. Together with the court's statement that the effect of its two prior stays had been to delay resolution of the action for almost eighteen months, the observation suggests the court may have been concerned that Peru was using dilatory tactics to keep Pravin and the rest of its creditors at bay, while using funds otherwise available to pay creditors to repurchase its debt instead. Indeed, the court's decision may amount simply to a recognition that comity is a two-way street. By repurchasing its debt, Peru was willing to jeopardize its ongoing debt restructuring negotiations, the success of which, Peru had argued to the court, was vital to U.S. policy interests. A litigant invoking a court's equitable powers must generally come to the court with clean hands.

* * *

This observation, however, does not undercut Peru's argument that full face value recovery by Pravin, in light of Pravin's diminished expectations when it purchased the debt and Peru's continuing economic difficulties, would constitute unjust enrichment. Pravin certainly believed it had purchased the *right* to receive 100 cents on the dollar; whether it actually *expected* to receive that amount is another matter entirely. The court was probably incorrect, therefore, in its assertion that Pravin's incentive for acquiring Peru's debt, "at whatever cost, [was] the possibility of eventual *full* payment of principal." The seventy-three percent discount in the purchase price of the debt indicated that Pravin would earn a substantial profit if Peru repaid even a small percent of the principal. It is even possible, in light of the fact that the debt was in technical default at the time Pravin purchased it, that Pravin's "incentive for acquiring [that] type of debt" was the hope of recovering more than twenty-seven cents on the dollar in a collection action.

As the foregoing analysis suggests, both *CIBC* and *Pravin* were close cases; perhaps closer than the courts let on. Legal justification might convincingly have been found for each case to go the other way. Although the *Pravin* court took pains to distinguish *CIBC* on purely legal grounds, the different results obtained by the similarly situated plaintiffs in the two cases may perhaps be better explained by a single factual difference between them: Pravin held $1.4 million of Peruvian debt; the Darts held $1.4 *billion* of Brazilian debt. The three extra zeros on the end of the Darts' claim gave them the power, if they won their suit, effectively to ruin Brazil's Brady restructuring, thus wreaking economic havoc in a foreign land. Pravin's smaller claim against Peru, although irksome to both the country and its other creditors, was not about to bankrupt the Peruvian treasury or scuttle the country's contemplated Brady deal. In light of that reality, and the fact that Brazil had given equal treatment to all creditors in its Brady deal whereas Peru, by its debt buy-back, had preferred some of its creditors over others, a stronger case could be made for setting aside the Darts' contract rights than for setting aside those of Pravin.

Even so, contract law does not typically consider the adverse economic consequences to the obligor in determining whether to hold him to his contract. That such considerations may have swayed the courts in *CIBC* and *Pravin* suggests that those cases were about something more than plain contract interpretation, both courts' assurances to the contrary notwithstanding. With the success of two countries' debt restructurings hanging in the balance, the outcome in each case likely resulted from a pragmatic balancing of the creditors' rights to receive payment against the debtors' asserted inability to pay, a process more familiar in bankruptcy proceedings than in ordinary contract disputes.

* * *

QUESTIONS AND COMMENTS

1. How and when was the "debt problem" created? Who was involved in its creation and were the risks of debt failure ignored on all sides? What is "political risk" and how could AMABANK or WORLDDEBT assess it?

2.   What long-term strategy would you recommend for AMABANK? For Asiana? Does the size of AMABANK or Asiana affect your conclusions? Are AMABANK and Asiana in a "mutual hostage position"? Are the developed world and the developing world mutually dependent upon IMF-led bailouts? See Comment 15 below.

3.   Why not simply let Asiana default? What would be the consequences for Asiana? For AMABANK? For its New York correspondent bank? For WORLDDEBT? For the United States and other major debtor nations? For the IMF and the international monetary system it represents?

4.   Should there be the equivalent of bankruptcy protection for nations and how might it function?

5.   What are the differences between the Baker Plan and the Brady Plan? Does either hold out much hope for Asiana, WORLDDEBT or AMA-BANK?

6.   Would you recommend that Asiana adopt a debt swapping program? Why? What features might it have? Do you think that WORLDDEBT might be interested in such a program?

7.   There is growing case law suggesting that maverick lenders who do not agree to participate in a syndicated third world refinancing can sue to collect on their existing debt. The act of state doctrine (see Problem 10.6) may not shelter the debtor nation. See A.I. Credit Corp. v. Government of Jamaica, 666 F.Supp. 629 (S.D.N.Y.1987); Allied Bank International v. Banco Credito Agricola de Cartago, 757 F.2d 516 (2d Cir.1985) (Costa Rica) and the cases discussed by Power. What are the implications of these decisions for this problem? How do you explain the different outcomes in *CIBC* and *Pravin*? If WORLDDEBT sues, what likely result?

8.   Why has currency stability eluded Mexico and Asiana? Are U.S. mutual funds of the solution or part of the problem?

The amount of investor-driven money flowing into and out of developing nations is growing rapidly. Pension, mutual and hedge funds now provide the majority of all private lending to developing countries. Unlike banks, bank regulators and the IMF, investors and capital markets move rapidly and have demonstrated recently in Korea, Thailand, Mexico, Brazil and even Russia that for a high enough interest rate premium, they will lend to nations in financial crisis. What are the implications of these trends for this problem and the world's financial system?

9.   The Mexican, Asian and Russian financial crises significantly reduced the IMF's loan capacity. Mexico took $17.8 billion, Korea $20.9 billion, Indonesia $9.9 billion, Thailand $3.9 billion, and Russia $22.6 billion by mid-1998. Only Malaysia steadfastly refused IMF loans. For several years, the U.S. Congress refused to authorize more than minimal additional U.S. support for IMF funding. Many see in this reluctance an erosion of U.S. economic leadership via the IMF. Is it preferable for the United States to exercise its influence through international institutions like the IMF, or should it deal directly with nations in financial need?

10.   One major criticism of the IMF is that it failed to warn against the Asian financial crisis. Even if the IMF saw it coming, its country reports

buried the risks in bureaucratic language that clearly did not set off alarm bells. The IMF says it will develop a better "surveillance" system that first communicates privately with nations that are seriously off course. Public warnings could follow if its advice and recommendations are not followed.

At present, IMF country reports are released only with consent. For example, Argentina, Chile, Hong Kong, Germany, Japan, India and the United States permit such releases. Brazil, Malaysia, Mexico, Indonesia, Thailand, China and Russia generally do not. Is there a pattern here? Suppose the secrecy surrounding IMF country reports was lifted by posting all of them on the Internet. What would be the consequences?

11. Assume the IMF bails out of Asiana using a Brady Plan formula or one like that created for Mexico in 1995. Are there "moral hazards" in rescuing banks and investors that have inadequately assessed the risks associated with their lending/investment decisions? Should the IMF plan ensure that the creditors take at least some "hit"? How much? WORLDDEBT is more than a little interested in your responses.

What about "moral hazard" on the part of the borrowers in Asiana? If the IMF continually rescues them from their follies, what incentive is there to engage in better governance and better corporate financial practices? Are the IMF loan conditions incentive enough?

12. The IMF has also been setting conditions for financial support of nations that are in transition from nonmarket to market economies. Russia provides the prime and most critical example. IMF loan conditions for Russia have focused on tax collections, improvements in bankruptcy and commercial law, reduced government subsidies and spending, crony capitalism and banking sector reforms. Some commentators believe that Russia's instability combined with its nuclear arsenal have given it unusual leverage in negotiations with the IMF. Can the IMF say "No" to Russia? To Poland? To Bulgaria?

13. Late in 1998, as part of the Omnibus Appropriations Bill (H.R. 4328), Congress approved slightly more than $18 billion in additional U.S. support for IMF funding. This approval caused other major IMF members to increase their support, resulting in a total of approximately $80 billion in new IMF funds. Congressional support came in the middle of Russia's financial crisis (but before that of Brazil) with certain strings attached:

- IMF loan conditions must provide schedules for: (1) reducing restraints on trade in goods and services; (2) eliminating systemic government practices that direct lending on non-commercial bases; and (3) granting nondiscriminatory treatment to foreign and domestic creditors in bankruptcy proceedings.

- Greater transparency at the IMF, including a full written summary of most Executive Board meetings and related documents.

- Above market interest rates on short-term IMF loans (versus long-term "structural" loans).

- Improved IMF loan monitoring procedures.

Will any of these strings affect Asiana? AMABANK? WORLDDEBT?

14.   Late in 1998 the IMF, World Bank, Inter-American Development Bank and major industrial countries organized a $41.5 bailout for Brazil, largely at above market interest rates with short maturities. In turn, Brazil promised to cut its government deficit, reduce its inflation rate, raise taxes, reform its pension system, generate state and local government surpluses and maintain its exchange-rate regime.

The "tough love" approach to IMF lending took a new turn in 2001–2002 when loans to Argentina were steadily refused. Argentina, which had fixed its currency to the U.S. dollar at a one-to-one exchange, was forced to eliminate its dollar linkage and enact financial and fiscal reforms in a crisis environment. Still the IMF loans were not forthcoming, while an arguably less severe crisis in Brazil brought substantial new IMF commitments in 2002. Some analysts noted that U.S. banks did not have much exposure in Argentina, but had a high level of exposure in Brazil. Those same analysts wondered if the U.S. voting power in the IMF was not being put to use on behalf of those banks. Others commented on the timeliness of the IMF commitment to Brazil in terms of influencing its national elections.

15.   From 2006 onwards, nations paid off their IMF debt in record numbers. Argentina did so with an assist from Venezuela. Brazil, Russia, Bolivia, Uruguay, Indonesia, the Philippines and others joined in the flight from IMF loan conditions. The IMF's loan portfolio stood at $100 billion in 2003. By 2008, that portfolio was approaching zero, the IMF was running a budget deficit, cutting staff and proposing sales of gold reserves. Many commentators wonder aloud what is the role of the IMF without loans?

The global financial and economic crisis that commenced late in 2008 has muted this commentary. The IMF has "pre-approved" unconditional, short-term loans to nations it deems sound but facing liquidity problems, such as Mexico, Brazil and South Korea. Should the United States consider such a loan? Conditional IMF loans were made to Iceland, Pakistan, Ukraine and Hungary among others. Then the market-driven Greek financial crisis of 2010 arrived. For the first time, the IMF joined with the EU to finance a 110 billion rescue a EURO zone member with lots of conditions attached. Indeed, the EU seemed almost grateful that the IMF would enforce dramatic reductions in government spending and employment, improved accounting and anti-corruption measures, tax increases, monopoly break-ups and structural changes in the Greek economy. The IMF does this through constant monitoring and gradual, contingent release of funds. A 100 billion EURO bailout of Ireland followed late in 2010, with about the same amount to Portugal in 2011. Stay tuned to see if these bailouts work, and whether Spain or Italy may follow in the footsteps of Greece and Ireland. The EU hopes not, and has created a 1 trillion EURO safety net aimed at reassuring investors and financial markets.

16.   The IMF has drafted a Code of Best Practices for "Sovereign Wealth Funds" (SWFs). Such Funds are said to hold over $ 3 trillion, and are expanding rapidly. Abu Dhabi, Saudi Arabia, Kuwait, Singapore, Russia, China and Norway (for example) all have large SWFs, many of which played an important role in bailing out U.S. banks and securities firms with heavy sub-prime loan exposure.

By 2008, developing nations (particularly their central banks) bought over 50 percent of the net foreign purchases of U.S. government securities. In a role reversal, the United States has become heavily dependent on SWF and developing world capital inflows to finance its large national debt and enormous international trade deficit. The primary concern is that SWFs and developing nations might use their power for political purposes. Their emergence further diminishes the need for IMF loans. As yet the SWFs have not "conditioned" their lending or investment decisions. Might they do so?

PROBLEM 10.4 PROJECT FINANCING— MOGUL LIQUEFIES GAS

SECTION I. THE FACTS

Mogul Oil Co. has discovered an enormous natural gas field on the Kamchatka Peninsula, which is on the East Coast of the Russian Federation. There is a ready market for such gas in Japan, but it cannot be shipped to Japan efficiently in a gaseous state. Natural gas is shipped overseas as "liquified natural gas", so Mogul will need to liquefy the natural gas in Kamchatka; and thus it will need to build a gas liquification plant there. A plant of this kind, including four "trains" (each train being a separate refrigeration facility), and necessary infrastructure including port facilities, will cost approximately $10 billion.

Large companies like Mogul normally finance their projects on the basis of their own credit, but no company can assume debt of this magnitude, so other sources of funding must be found. The sources for any such funding will require quality collateral. The collateral which is available is the prospective payments by the Japanese buyers of the natural gas. The financing thus must be based on the economics of the project itself, *i.e.*, on its ability to generate sufficient revenue to service the debt and produce a profit for the participants. However, Mogul does not want to bear any risk, or to be liable to the institutions which do finance the building of the plant. Thus, Mogul wants to find "non-recourse financing" (financing in which the project owner is not legally liable for the debt) for the construction of the gas liquification plant. It asks you to structure the deal. How would you do it?

Mogul has lined up construction companies and potential buyers of the gas. Now it needs to line up potential financers. Does it need any other persons to create a complete cast of characters for a project finance venture? If so, you will need to advise it on what other roles are needed, and what type of person or institution might fill each role properly.

What is the relationship between Mogul, the buyers, the construction companies, the financers, and any other persons involved? What parts of each relationship will be formed by custom and understood by the parties, and what parts of each relationship will be the subject of intense bargaining? As a foundation for these negotiations, you will need to advise Mogul on the basic structure of a standard international project finance transaction.

There are a large number of identifiable risks in this venture. There is the risk that the quantity or quality of the gas may be insufficient for the buyers' use, or for efficiency of production. There is the risk of construction cost over-runs, or unsuitability of the plant as finally constructed. There is the risk that either the gas field or the plan may be nationalized or arbitrarily taxed by the Russian government. There is a risk that the Japanese buyers may not want or need the gas, or that they may not be able to pay for it. There is a risk that currency exchange rates may change sufficiently to make the project unfeasible, or that interest rates could soar during construction. There is a risk that the gas sales to Japan are not profitable.

Which of these risks will Mogul bear? Who will bear the other risks? Is the placement of these risks rational and efficient?

SECTION II.   FOCUS OF CONSIDERATION

Project financing is usually defined as "the financing of a particular economic unit in which a lender is satisfied to look initially to the cash flows and earnings of that economic unit as the source of funds from which a loan will be repaid and to the assets of the economic unit as collateral for the loan." The "sponsor" wants the benefits of the project, but with no effect on its credit or balance sheet. However, projects are rarely financed completely independently without some credit support from the sponsor or third party guarantors; but that is always the sponsor's goal. Thus, the attorney's skill is in minimizing the liability of the sponsor, while satisfying the lender concerning the credit risk, so that the "deal" can go forward.

The project will entail many risks, including construction delays and cost overruns, force majeure, governmental interference, insolvency of one of the parties, poor quality or lack of sufficient gas in the field and market downturns. Each of these risks must consciously be allocated and monitored.

The building blocks of project financing are debt instruments, which are supported by collateral. The collateral may include the fixed assets of the project (through mortgages), the payments due to the project from purchasers of its output (through assignments), and guarantes of interested financial institutions (e.g., the World Bank).

Certain steps in the transaction may be covered by "comfort" assurances. These are statements by participants which are requested by other parties as non-binding statements of intent. For example, Mogul may supply an assurance that it currently intends to remain in the oil & gas production & supply business. Or, to provide assurances concerning the quality of the gas in the ground. Why would anyone accept them or think them useful? Do they carry any legal risks? Would a reasonable lender rely upon such an assurance, or have its own independent studies made as to the quality of the gas in the ground?

The types of combinations of these building blocks, and of the corporate subsidiaries and their relationships, used by attorneys in this field is limited only by their ingenuity.

As one attorney has said:

> By virtually any measure, the documentation for a typical project financing is among the most complex and voluminous of any financings. In addition to the basic loan or credit agreement pursuant to which funds are loaned to the project, the documentation includes security and mortgage instruments, assignments and consents to assignment of project documents (such as construction contracts, power purchase agreements, fuel supply contracts and operation and maintenance agreements), real property conveyance instruments, subordination agreements, and a depositary, disbursement, fiscal agency or similar lock box type agreement pursuant to which project revenues are all deposited directly with an independent financial institution for distribution to project participants in accordance with an agreed upon "cashcade." In fact, in many respects, the negotiation of these documents can be more time consuming and important from both the lender's and the borrower's perspective than the loan agreement itself.

> Birenbaum, Credit and Related Documentation
> for Project Finance Transactions, PLI Commercial Law and
> Practice Course Handbook Series, 1993.

A further topic concerns the tax aspects of the transaction, but that is beyond the scope of this introductory problem.

SECTION III. READING, QUESTIONS, AND COMMENTS

HOFFMAN, A PRACTICAL GUIDE TO TRANSACTIONAL PROJECT FINANCE: BASIC CONCEPTS, RISK IDENTIFICATION, AND CONTRACTUAL CONSIDERATIONS

45 Bus. Law. 181 (1989).*

The ability of one lender, or a group of lenders acting as a syndicate, to make a single loan to finance the entire development, site acquisition, construction, and initial operation of a project offers a unique marketing advantage in the competitive financial services industry. In many cases, the large amount of capital needed to finance a project strains the ability of many corporations to borrow money and fund the equity contributions needed, just as it strains the lending levels for many banks. The need for

---

enormous debt and capital, coupled with the risks involved in large project development, often make a project financing[1] one of the few available financing alternatives in the energy, resource recovery, mining, transportation, resort, and retirement care industries.

Project financing involves more than financing a project; "project finance" has developed as a complex financial and legal specialty, providing business with an attractive alternative to other types of financing. The flexibility of project financing ranges from small hydroelectric power projects, to shipping loans, to the construction of the English Channel tunnel (the largest project financing of this century). It is a financing option not limited to new facility construction; project financing can also be used to refinance existing facilities.

In simplest terms, project finance is nonrecourse financing predicated on the merits of a project rather than the credit of the project sponsor. The credit appraisal of the project finance lender is therefore based on the underlying cash flow from the revenue-producing contracts of the project, independent of the project sponsor. Since the debt is nonrecourse, the project sponsor has no direct legal obligation to repay the project debt or make interest payments if the cash flows prove inadequate to service debt.

Because the ability of the project sponsor to produce revenue from project operation is the foundation of a project financing, the contracts constitute the framework for project viability and control the allocation of risks. Contracts that represent the obligation to make a payment to the

---

1. The term "project finance," or "segregated finance" as it is sometimes called, is generally used to refer to the arrangement of debt, equity, and credit enhancement for the construction or refinancing of a particular facility in a capital-intensive industry, in which lenders base credit appraisals on the projected revenues from the operation of the facility, rather than on the general assets or the corporate credit of the promoter of the facility, and in which they rely on the assets of the facility, including the revenue-producing contracts and cash flow, as collateral for the debt.

The term is sometimes applied to any financing of a particular project, whether recourse or nonrecourse, although the definition given is becoming the more accepted meaning of the term in the American legal and financial communities. It is in contrast to term lending, in which lenders analyze the loan based on historical earnings of the borrower and are satisfied with recourse to the collateral value of the borrower's assets securing the loan to ensure debt repayment. Other distinguishing factors of project finance from term lending include the high leverage of project finance debt, reliance on commitments by third parties for debt repayment in specified contingencies, and nonrecourse treatment of the project finance debt. An example of a project financing will assist the beginning project financier in understanding the basic concepts discussed in this article. Developer A owns the United States technology rights to a system that processes waste tires into chips that can be burned. The heat produced from the combustion of the tires can be used to produce steam and electricity. A locates a source to supply waste tires and also locates a stockpile of tires that A estimates will permit the facility to operate at 100% capacity for four years. A also locates a power company willing to execute a contract with A to purchase all of the power produced by A at attractive rates. Construction contracts, operation and maintenance contracts, a site, and all other agreements necessary for the construction and operation of the facility are also negotiated and executed.

Banker B examines the contracts, the projections for the facility, and the regulatory environment and decides that the facility will produce sufficiently dependable revenues to service debt needed to construct the facility, while providing sufficient funds for operation and maintenance and an attractive equity return that helps ensure that the project sponsor will remain committed to project success. B enters into a project finance loan agreement with A, taking a security interest in the facility and a collateral assignment of the contracts executed for the project. The loan is nonrecourse to Developer A since Banker B is content to look only to revenues that will be paid to A by the power company for the repayment of the debt.

project owner on the delivery of some product or service are of particular importance since these contracts govern cash flow. Each of the contracts necessary to construct and operate a project, such as the sales contract, site lease, and construction contract, must not interfere unduly with the expectation for debt repayment from project revenues. If risks are allocated in an unacceptable way from the lender's perspective, credit enhancement from a creditworthy third party is needed, such as letters of credit, capital contribution commitments, guarantees, and insurance. Also, the project finance contracts must be enforceable and have value to the lender as collateral security.

A project financing is also based on predictable regulatory and political environments and stable markets, which combine to produce dependable cash flow. To the extent this predictability is unavailable or the risks of dependability are allocated unacceptably, credit enhancement is necessary to protect the lender from external uncertainties, such as fuel supply, product market instability, and changes in law. In many instances, however, the project exists in an uncertain environment which subjects the project lender to some unallocated risks.

* * *

All project financings have nearly identical fundamental elements. Debt, in the form of traditional term notes, bonds, or subordinated notes from the project sponsor or other project participants is, of course, the most common element. Collateral security is similarly present in the form of assignments of the project revenues to support the underlying debt obligations. Also, various types of credit enhancement from the project sponsor or third parties are included to support the risk allocation. The precise structure selected is dependent upon a range of variables, influenced in large part by project viability and the goals of the project sponsor.

ADVANTAGES OF PROJECT FINANCE

* * *

Nonrecourse Debt Financing

Classic nonrecourse project financing provides a structure that does not impose upon the project sponsor any obligation to guarantee the repayment of the project debt if the project revenues are insufficient to cover principal and interest payments. The nonrecourse nature of a project financing provides financial independence to each project owned and protection of the sponsor's general assets from most difficulties in any particular project. A typical nonrecourse project finance loan provision provides that no recourse is available against the sponsor or any affiliate for liability to the lender in connection with any breach or default, except to reach project collateral. Thus, the lender relies solely on the project collateral in enforcing rights and obligations in connection with the project finance loan.

* * *

Off-Balance-Sheet Debt Treatment

A second objective of some project financings is the potential for using off-balance-sheet accounting techniques for project commitments. From the perspective of the project sponsor, accounting rules generally require the consolidation of financial statements of a company and certain of its subsidiaries and other entities over which it can exercise control. A subsidiary that is controlled more than fifty percent by the parent company is consolidated on a line by line basis with the parent. Otherwise, the equity method of accounting is used, whereby the investment in the subsidiary is shown as a one-line entry. Debt in such circumstances is not reported on the parent company's financial statements.

Highly Leveraged Debt

A third objective of project finance sponsors is the ability to finance a project using highly leveraged debt without a dilution of existing equity. The amount of leverage acceptable to a lender varies from project to project. Often the leverage percentage is between seventy-five and eighty percent, but transactions are sometimes structured with ratios between ninety and one hundred percent. The amount of the equity contribution required of the project sponsor is influenced by many factors, including the project economics and whether any other project participants, such as the contractor or equipment supplier, invest equity in the project.

Avoidance of Restrictive Covenants in Other Transactions

A fourth reason for selecting a project financing is that the structure permits a project sponsor to avoid restrictive covenants, such as debt coverage ratios, in existing loan agreements and indentures. Since the project financed is separate and distinct from other operations and projects of the sponsor, existing restrictive covenants do not typically reach to the project financing. Similarly, the distinct nature of the project financed permits the sponsor to leverage debt to an extent that may be prohibited under existing agreements.

Favorable Financing Terms

A project financing is selected in many circumstances because more attractive interest rates and credit enhancement are available to the project than are otherwise available to the project sponsor. A credit appraisal of an individual project is sometimes more favorable than a credit appraisal of the project sponsor. Thus, a more attractive risk profile can result in more favorable interest rates and lower credit enhancement costs.

Internal Capital Commitment Policies

The rate of return goals of the project sponsor for new capital investments can also make project financing attractive. Companies that typically establish goals for rates of return generated from a proposed capital investment often determine that the return on a project investment is improved with a project financing, which permits highly leveraged debt financing with a minimum of equity commitment.

DISADVANTAGES TO A PROJECT FINANCING

Project financings are complex transactions involving many participants with diverse interests. Risk allocation tensions exist between the lender and sponsor regarding the degree of recourse for the loan, between the contractor and sponsor concerning the nature of guarantees, and so on, resulting in protracted negotiations and increased costs to compensate third parties for accepting risks.

In addition to third party project participants, the degree of risk for the lender in a project financing is not insignificant. Although by definition and law a bank is not an equity risk-taker, many project financing risks cannot be effectively allocated, nor can the resultant credit risk be enhanced. This high risk scenario results in higher fees charged by lenders for the transaction than are charged in other types of transactions; it also results in an expensive process of due diligence that is conducted by the lender's counsel.

Similarly, interest rates charged in project financings are typically higher than on direct loans made to the project sponsor. Also, although some economies are achieved because only one lender, acting as the agent bank, and one lender's counsel are involved, the documentation is complex and lengthy. The complexity results in higher transaction costs than is typical of traditional asset-based lending.

Another disadvantage of a project financing is the degree of supervision that a lender will impose on the management and operation of the project. This obligation is incorporated into the project loan agreements, which require the sponsor to satisfy certain tests, such as debt service and operating budget, and comply with various covenants, such as restrictions on transfer of ownership and management continuity.

* * *

PROJECT FINANCE PARTICIPANTS AND PERSPECTIVES

Because a project financing is nonrecourse to the project sponsor, financial responsibility for the various risks in a project financing must be allocated to parties that will assume recourse liability and that possess adequate credit to accept the risk allocated. The allocation of risks varies from transaction to transaction, and is largely dependent on the bargaining position of the participants and the ability of the project to cover risk contingencies with the underlying cash flow and reserve accounts. There are three general categories of risk in the typical project financing: design engineering and construction risks, start-up risks, and operating risks.

Design engineering and construction risks are risks that are inherent during project design and construction phases. As construction proceeds, new risks arise and other subside. Each project participant is concerned with whether the project will be constructed on time for the price upon which project financial projections are based. The classic construction risk is the necessity of a change in the work contemplated in the construction price, such as a change necessitated by technical design refinements. Other project construction risks include price changes caused by currency fluctuation or inflation, construction delays, material shortages, design changes required by law, and strikes.

Start-up of a project is the most important risk-shifting phase of a project financing since achievement of the performance guarantees through performance tests signals the end of the contractor risk period and the beginning of the risk period for the operator and the project owner. At start-up, permanent lenders and equity investors, including the sponsor, require the contractor to provide evidence that the project is capable of operating at a level of performance necessary to service debt and pay operating costs.

Operating risks are those risks that arise after the project is accepted or is in preliminary operation. Operating risks are exemplified by a decrease in the availability of raw materials or fuel, or by a decrease in demand for the output of the project. Other operating risks include inflation, fluctuation in currency, strikes and other production risks, supply risks, regulatory changes, political changes, uninsured losses, and management inefficiencies. Each operating risk helps determine whether the project will perform at projected levels, thereby producing sufficient funds to cover debt service, operating costs, and to provide a return on equity invested.

An analysis of a project financing by each participant, and the negotiation approach for the project documents, begins typically with a compilation of risks and a determination of the party best capable of bearing each identified risk through various methods of credit support. The allocation of risks is generally determined on the basis of control over the risk, reward associated with that control, role, and creditworthiness. As a gross oversimplification, it is generally true that the participant that can best exercise control over a risk or that will realize the greatest reward if the risk does not materialize, considering the role of the participant in the project, typically is allocated the risk.

For example, a risk identified in a project may be that a key contract will terminate if a change in law occurs. While no party can control the occurrence of that risk, all parties in the project will benefit if the project is completed. The participant ultimately selected to bear the change of law risk, however, may be the project sponsor since the change of law risk is a risk sometimes allocated to equity. If the project sponsor lacks the financial resources to address this risk, other participants must examine the risk, determine the likelihood of the risk and the value of participation in the project, and establish the terms upon which allocation of the risk is acceptable. The allocation accepted often results in the transfer of some project reward to the participant accepting the risk through a higher contract price or an addition of a role, such as from contractor to contractor and equity participant.

* * *

CREDIT ENHANCEMENT IN PROJECT FINANCINGS

In theory, a project financing can be structured in which there are no risks and the lenders are content to rely solely upon the revenue-producing project contracts to service debt. In reality, of course, the foregoing illustrative list of potential project finance risks gives evidence that mere reliance on those contracts is insufficient to protect the lender from equity risk. Credit support (or enhancement of credit, as it is sometimes referred to) from a creditworthy source is necessary.

* * *

There are essentially two types of guarantors in a project financing: sponsor guarantors and third party guarantors. The most common guarantor in a project financing is the sponsor itself. Typically, the sponsor establishes a special purpose subsidiary to construct, own, and operate the project. The subsidiary, however, lacks sufficient capital or credit rating to support risks associated with the underlying loan obligation. To effect a loan, the sponsor must arrange some form of credit enhancement to cover the identified risks. Often the requisite credit enhancement is provided in the form of a guarantee by the project sponsor of the obligations of the project owner.

The sponsor guarantee can be structured in various forms to satisfy the objectives of the sponsor and the enhancement needs of the project. For example, a completion agreement is sometimes used in which the project sponsor is required to complete construction of the project. Once the project is completed at agreed upon performance levels, the agreement terminates. On termination, the liability is also terminated and the project sponsor is able to guarantee other projects in a similar fashion.

If the sponsor guarantee is insufficient to support the risks identified, however, credit enhancement by a third party is needed. Each project finance participant is a potential third party guarantor, since each participant has an economic stake in the success of the project's development. The various project participants that may provide project finance guarantees include suppliers that have an interest in the fulfillment of purchase orders contingent on financing, or that recognize that a sponsor cannot compete in the marketplace without financial assistance. Other potential providers are output purchasers where supply of the output is of particular importance, and contractors that are interested in constructing the project and realizing construction profit.

Third party guarantors are often reluctant to sign a direct, unconditional guarantee in a project financing. In some financings, a lender may be persuaded to accept a different type of guarantee in which the obligations of the guarantor are more limited. These include limited and indirect guarantees.

Limited Guarantees

Traditional guarantees represent direct, unconditional commitments by a guarantor to perform all the obligations of a third party. Guarantees limited in amount or time can be used to provide minimum enhancement necessary to finance the project. This approach provides the necessary credit support to a project without considerable impact on the guarantor's credit standing and financial statements. Examples of limited guarantees include guarantees that are effective only during the construction phase of a project or that are limited in amount, whether calculable in advance or not. An example of the latter type of guarantee is a cost overrun guarantee in which the guarantor agrees to finance construction of a project to the extent design changes or changes in law require additional funds for project completion.

Letters of Credit

Another type of credit enhancement device is a letter of credit, which is an agreement that substitutes the payment obligation and creditworthiness of a more solvent party, usually a bank, for the payment obligation and creditworthiness of a less solvent party, such as an insufficiently capitalized project owner. In a project financing, the standby or guarantee letter of credit is used to protect against the project owner's failure to perform some obligation, such as a payment or performance obligation. For example, in a project financing, a creditor, such as a turnkey contractor of a small power production project, may require the sponsor to procure a standby letter of credit from a bank to assure payment of the construction progress payments. The letter of credit, in effect, "stands by" awaiting a default by the owner under the construction contract or some other specific default with reference to which the letter of credit is directed.

Surety Obligations

The commercial risk of project completion to the point that permits operation at a level consistent with expected revenue is typically covered by a completion guarantee that the project will be completed and will operate at a specified level of production and efficiency. This guarantee is typically provided by the contractor, but the risk is often passed along by the contractor to a surety that issues performance and payment bonds.

BLUMENTHAL, SOURCES OF FUNDS AND RISK MANAGEMENT FOR INTERNATIONAL ENERGY PROJECTS

16 Berkeley J. Int'l L. 267 (1998).*

In recent years, changing market conditions and rising costs have changed the way funds are sourced for international energy projects. As a basic industry, energy projects, whether oil production, natural gas transmission, or electric power generation, have access to equity and debt funding from diverse sources. These sources including multilateral institutions, regional development banks, export-import banks, commercial banks, institutional investors, equity and bond markets, equipment suppliers' credit, and other ad hoc sources. Because commercial banks are now careful to limit their exposure to the risk inherent in lending to projects in developing countries, most projects ultimately obtain funding from a mix of public and private sources.

Institutionally, multilateral organizations and regional development banks have shifted their traditional focus and now provide numerous services and facilities designed to support private investment in the energy sector. Although the actual amounts that multilateral institutions commit to energy projects are usually relatively small, they serve to give private investors comfort and confidence and thus pave the way for commercially-sourced funding.

Bilateral agencies and the export-import banks of developed countries, including the U.S. and Japan, now provide funding to private entities in the form of suppliers' credit, buyers' credit, and guarantees. Because these agencies exist to promote their own nations' exports, this support is generally limited to use for the purchase of that country's equipment and products.

Commercial financing refers to funds from commercial banks and other institutional investors as well as capital raised through equity and bond offerings. Beyond risk aversion, commercial banks are also subject to certain structural and regulatory constraints which necessitate a financing package that includes other sources. Principally, energy projects require large investment and debt service over a relatively long term. Commercial banks, however, are limited in the amount of long-term loans they can fund due to country risk limits, sector limits, and reserve requirements.

Changing market conditions in the 1990s have caused oil companies to reduce their own investment in projects. Oil companies are no longer willing to fund new projects solely from their own balance sheets.

* * *

Nonrecourse or limited recourse project finance is now widely accepted as an alternative to traditional recourse corporate financing. Traditional financing approaches gave lenders recourse to all of the borrower's assets and cash flow. Project finance, on the other hand, is 'off balance sheet' financing that limits recourse to the assets and cash flow of the underlying project. The result is that companies do not have to carry project debt on their balance sheets and are able to pursue several projects simultaneously. Nonetheless, as a practical matter, project finance is very often structured on a hybrid, limited recourse basis.

During the riskiest phases of the project—construction and start-up—the project sponsor is committed to providing contingent financial support beyond its equity investment, typically in the form of a payment guaranty. At the completion date, once the facility has passed all completion tests, the sponsor's payment guaranty is released, and the lenders' rights convert to nonrecourse status. Most often, however, sponsors will continue to provide limited support in the form of performance guarantees regarding the fulfillment of obligations of their subsidiaries and affiliates.

Determining the proper ratio and the sources of equity and debt financing are key steps in designing the structure of project finance energy projects. Generally, total project investment is 20–40% equity and 60–80% debt financed. This mixture relates back to the question of how project risk is to be distributed among the parties. Between project sponsors and lenders there is a natural tension surrounding this issue. Lenders naturally prefer project sponsors to commit more equity to a project. The more equity a project sponsor invests, the greater the proportion of the project risk it undertakes. The project sponsor, however, wants to reduce its exposure and save as much of its capital as possible to invest in other projects. The tension between the interests of the lenders and those of the project sponsors plays out during the negotiation of the loan documents and project structure. Several factors influence the determination of the debt to equity ratio: the creditworthiness of the sponsors, the location and economics of the project, and the risks inherent in that project.

In this area, just as in the development of project finance itself, necessity drives innovation. The huge investments and long-term nature of energy project investment have forced project sponsors to broaden the search for financing. Equity financing now often includes funds raised not just from the sponsor, but also from investment funds, multilateral institutions like the International Finance Corporation ("IFC"), regional development banks, and international and local equity markets. Projects structured as joint ventures between project sponsors and local public utilities add a new dimension because the local partner's funding may come from the host government or from the public lending arms of the World Bank or regional development banks.

Similar creativity and innovation go into structuring the debt financing. Because commercial banks remain cautious about making large infrastructure investments in developing countries, and because of the structural problems commercial banks face in making such large, long-term loans, traditional commercial financing alone cannot provide sufficient debt financing for large energy projects. Syndicated bank loans increase the funds available, but they cannot resolve the timing constraints on commercial banks. Energy projects still generally require financing for longer periods than the standard five to ten year commercial loan maturity. Other common sources of debt financing include institutional investors (pension funds, insurance companies, and mutual funds), government-sponsored energy funds, the IFC, private investment departments of regional development banks, international and local bond markets, and suppliers' credit. However, these sources of financing also come with challenges in timing.

* * *

The [International Finance Corporation] is the World Bank's private enterprise development arm, and is perhaps the most important World Bank affiliate with which potential project sponsors should be familiar. The IFC was established in 1956, and its approach differs significantly from that of the World Bank, proper. The IFC will lend directly to private companies and cannot accept repayment guarantees from host country governments.

The IFC may fund equity investments in private businesses, and it also may provide debt financing for projects. Through mobilization, the IFC also plays a key role in attracting other investors and lenders to a project. IFC syndication gives commercial banks the comfort they require to extend commercial loans in developing countries. As the lender of record in the syndication, the IFC's special privileges as a multilateral institution will extend to the commercial banks in the syndication. They will be exempt from payment of local taxes, insulated against political risk and may have greater access to local political leadership. The IFC is responsible for exercising due diligence on a project and for coordinating legal documentation. The IFC also administers the loans and collection of payments from the borrower, distributing these payments pro rata among itself and the other banks. This means, in effect, that a default on any portion of the loan is a default to the IFC. All of this gives commercial lenders a greater degree of comfort. * * *

As with multilateral and bilateral agencies, international capital markets are much more receptive to recognized and experienced project sponsors. In the United States, Security and Exchange Commission ("SEC") Rule 144A permits certain qualified institutional investors to purchase securities not registered with the SEC. However, these securities may not be freely traded for three years after they are purchased. Generally, under Rule 144A, foreign companies issue equity in the United States by means of American Depositary Receipts ("ADR") issued by a U.S. bank. ADRs can be traded on national exchanges, but are privately placed. The underlying shares are held by a custodian bank in the home country.

International bond markets in the United States, the United Kingdom, Japan, and Europe are all available to raise capital for international energy development projects. Each has distinct advantages. Bonds for international projects may be considered domestic or foreign, depending on which entity issues them. Bonds may be publicly-issued or privately-placed, and many project sponsors opt for privately-placed bonds because they are subject to less government regulation.

In the United States, publicly-offered bonds must be registered with the SEC, and the borrower must be rated by a credit rating agency, such as Moody's or Standard and Poor's ("S&P"). However, SEC Rule 144A offers privately placed foreign bonds a way around otherwise restrictive SEC regulations. Project sponsors can offer bonds to qualified institutional investors, raising capital quickly without adverse regulatory or tax consequences.

Eurobonds can be issued in any convertible currency and sold to institutional investors. Eurobonds also offers project sponsors freedom from SEC disclosure requirements and other regulations. Also, Eurobonds may offer tax treatment more favorable than that of bonds issued publicly in the United States by a foreign corporation.

FITZGERALD, PROJECT FINANCING TECHNIQUES

1170 PLI/Corp 49, 55–56, 61–66 (2000).*

The construction phase of a project presents particular risks associated with completion of construction. For example, delays in construction may result in higher costs (including interest accruing on debt during the longer construction period) or may result in a failure to meet deadlines for commencement of power deliveries to the power purchaser. The risk of completion of construction of the project ideally should be allocated to an internationally recognized and experienced construction contractor under a "turnkey" contract. The scope of work of the contractor should be all-inclusive, so that the contractor is required to perform all services necessary to provide a power plant that operates in the manner anticipated by the Project Owner and the power and steam purchasers, at a fixed price. If it is not possible to contract with an internationally recognized construction contractor, in this manner, the project sponsors may have to assume construction risks or seek financing only after construction is completed. Project Owners should keep in mind that projects using new technology are difficult to project finance.

* * *

Typically, project agreements are negotiated long before the Project Owner begins discussions with potential lenders. There is often a need to renegotiate provisions of a project agreement to satisfy requirements or concerns of the lenders. Renegotiations can be time-consuming and expen-

---

* Copyright © 2000 and reprinted with permission from the Practicing Law Institute.

sive if the parties are unwilling to cooperate with the Project Owner to obtain financing for the project.

Each agreement relating to a project should be assignable to the lenders in the event of a loan default. Each agreement should require the cooperation of the contracting party with the Project Owner's efforts to arrange financing and with the negotiation and execution of a lender "consent" agreement. A consent agreement will provide, among other things, an additional "cure period" for the lenders before a default is declared under the agreement because of a breach by the Project Owner.

* * *

FINANCING

Sources of funds for a power project include equity, senior loans and, at times, subordinated loans, and the capital markets. Equity interests may be active or passive (passive investors might include investment funds or private institutions that seek investment opportunities offering high yields), and may take the form of shareholdings, partnership interests or other forms of equity investment in the Project Owner. Equity may be required to be contributed at financial closing or during the construction phase of the project (in the latter case, credit support may be required if the sponsor's balance sheet is weak).

Senior loans may be provided by commercial lenders (local and foreign) or institutions such as insurance companies or pension funds, export credit agencies and other government assistance programs and multinational corporations such as the World Bank.

Subordinated loans may be provided by equipment vendors or by investors. Subordinated debt is often used in lieu of equity, since some sponsors may prefer to contribute debt instead of equity.

Recently, project sponsors have begun looking to the capital markets to obtain funds for U. S. and overseas power generation projects through the public offering or private placement of securities, typically long-term bonds.

The use of debt sold publicly or pursuant to a private placement to finance power projects may raise issues not present in using commercial bank lending. For example, proceeds from the sale of debt securities are usually received up front prior to the construction stage of a project, and begin to accrue interest immediately, even though most of the proceeds may not be needed until later. Even if the undisbursed proceeds are invested in other instruments, the income will likely be less than the coupon on the public debt, resulting in a "negative carry."

While institutional lenders generally are equipped to respond quickly if issues develop, and wish to be consulted in such circumstances, the holders of public debt are difficult to mobilize if unforeseen events require changes (amendments, waivers or consents) to the terms of the transaction. Even though there is generally an indenture trustee in place to act in the interest of debtholders in both registered and privately placed debt securities, such trustees are usually reluctant to exercise discretion, and most security-holders place a lower value than do commercial lenders on the right to be consulted. As a result, the covenant package used in a public financing or private placement of securities are likely to be less restrictive than the covenants banks demand in their loan documentation.

To guide investors in analyzing these debt issuances, rating agencies have developed ratings to evaluate project-related offerings. These ratings evaluate the ability of project collateral to generate sufficient cash flows to provide for timely payment of debt-service obligations. Standard & Poor's utilizes seven rating criteria for project debt basing its overall rating on the interrelationships between these factors: output sales contracts, power costs, fuel risk, structure, technology risk, the purchaser's credit strength and the project's projected financial results.

Any potential lender or investor will review a project for technical and economic feasibility. Lenders can be expected to retain an engineering firm and other advisors to analyze the design of the project and other technical matters such as access to utilities and spare parts, overall project cost and contingency requirements.

* * *

Legal opinions. Lenders are likely to require an extensive review by its lawyers of the laws of the country where the project is located. Generally, a legal opinion will confirm for the foreign lender the legal assumptions on which the lender's decision to lend money are based. The legal opinion is often viewed by a lender as an extension of the lender's investigation and review of the risks of the transaction and of factors that may have an impact on repayment of the loan. Among the legal issues that may be reviewed:

- Regulatory structure governing the project.
- The need to obtain governmental approvals, licenses, concessions, etc.
- Ownership of the project assets.
- Enforceability of each of the project agreements (over its entire term) and loan documents (including enforceability of interest and default interest provisions). Where a contractor, such as a fuel supplier, is a governmental entity, this analysis will cover the enforceability of waivers of immunity as well.
- Enforceability of choice of law and dispute resolution (arbitration) provisions.
- Enforceability of foreign judgments or arbitral awards.
- The creation of liens or charges and restrictions on, and costs of, foreclosing the lien created by the security documents.
- Laws or rules giving priority to liens of certain creditors (e.g., tax authorities).

- Existence of exchange controls (and need to obtain exchange control approvals), withholding taxes or other charges.

- Registration requirements that may be imposed on foreign lenders by the government or local banking authorities.

- Restrictions or limits on use of offshore bank accounts.

- Procedures and creditors' rights following a bankruptcy of the Project Owner.

- Liabilities under local environmental laws.

- Liabilities under local labor laws.

- Restrictions on availability of insurance coverages.

- Costs of stamp duties required for documentation, notarial fees or other required payments to local counsel, recording or registration costs for security documents, and court costs payable in connection with enforcement of the lenders' rights as creditors.

* * *

Despite the "non-recourse" character of project financings, it is not unusual, particularly in cross-border financings and financings involving multilateral institutions, that the project sponsors are required to enter into a support agreement. This agreement might provide for contingent equity to be contributed if, for example, cost overruns are not recovered from insurers, and for other forms of support such as continued participation in the project or technical support. In some cases, where surplus cash generated by the project is distributed to the sponsors, lenders may require that these distributions be "clawed back" to fund unexpected expenses or to service debt.

FITZGERALD, INTERNATIONAL PROJECT FINANCING: AN OVERVIEW
866 PLI/Comm 7, 9–16, 22–28, 42–46 (2004).*

This paper focuses on issues that should be considered by lenders and their counsel in structuring, negotiating and documenting cross-border project financings * * *

1. CURRENCY RISKS

Currency-related risks can be categorized into three separate risks: inconvertibility, transfer and devaluation risk.

a. Inconvertibility of Currency. If the country hosting the project experiences foreign exchange shortages, the lender must examine the risk that the borrower will be unable to convert its local currency revenues

---

* Copyright © 2004 and reprinted with permission from the Practicing Law Institute and Peter F. Fitzgerald. This excerpt appeared as a chapter in the book *Project Financing Update, 2004: Reworking & Building New Projects in Developing Markets* (Peter F. Fitzgerald and Barry N. Machlin, eds., 2004).

into the foreign exchange required to make necessary debt service and other foreign currency payments. * * *

b. Transfer Risk. Transfer risk is the risk that the central bank of the host country will notionally convert the borrower's local currency into foreign exchange on its books, acknowledge the central bank's foreign exchange obligation to the lender, but will not transfer the foreign exchange out of the host country. This is often a prelude to a country's general rescheduling of its foreign exchange obligations. * * *

c. Devaluation Risk. Whenever a lender lends in foreign exchange and relies for repayment on a borrower that generates earnings only in local currency, there is a risk that the local currency may depreciate in value and that the borrower will be unable to generate sufficient local currency for conversion into foreign exchange to service the debt. In developing countries with soft currencies, the likelihood of devaluation is high and the ability to hedge against or insure the risk is very limited. * * *

2. EXPROPRIATION RISK

The risk of expropriation is greatest in high profile projects that are often associated with public ownership (*e.g.*, oil projects, mining projects, power projects, etc.). The risk is that the host country government will nationalize the assets or equity of the project company in an arbitrary or discriminatory manner or without the payment of "just compensation."

Expropriation can be by a single governmental act or a series of hostile acts designed to force the shareholders to abandon the project ("creeping expropriation"). * * *

3. CHANGES IN LAW/REGULATORY RISK

Perhaps an even greater risk than expropriation is that the host country government will take lawful actions that have the consequence of rendering the project unprofitable, such as import and export restrictions, price controls, or excessive taxation. Insurers providing expropriation coverage generally are not willing to insure this risk as they would be left without recourse to the host country government in the event of a claim (the insurer's claim against the host country government in the event of expropriation is based on the <u>illegality</u> of the government's action). If, by agreement with the project sponsor, the host country government agrees not to take certain regulatory actions against the project, however, political risk insurers may be willing to cover the risk of abrogation or repudiation of that agreement.

* * *

Cross-border financings also raise significant tax issues. Governments may excessively tax a project into unprofitability. * * *

4. POLITICAL VIOLENCE RISK

Political violence in the host country (war, revolution, insurrection, civil strife, terrorism or sabotage) can often interrupt (and in some cases terminate) the project's ability to generate the cash flow necessary to service the debt. * * *

5. RISKS RELATING TO AVAILABLE SECURITY FOR THE LOAN UNDER LOCAL LAW

In domestic projects, the laws governing debtor-creditor relations, the creation and perfection of security interests, the granting and registration of mortgages and the bankruptcies of borrowers, are highly developed and highly protective of creditor rights. Lenders to projects in developing countries face a much more uncertain legal environment. Civil law countries generally do not recognize the floating charge and do not provide for security over inventory, receivables or other moveable assets. Many countries do not permit mortgages to be registered in foreign currency and the value of the collateral can therefore be significantly eroded by devaluations. In addition many countries place significant restrictions on the ability of foreign entities to operate or purchase projects upon foreclosure, especially projects that are important to the country's economic development plans.

The legal infrastructure of many developing countries remains primitive and is changing rapidly. In connection with loans to the early projects in the emerging market economies of Eastern Europe and the former Soviet Union, for example, the lenders often found that laws enabling a lender to be granted liens had been enacted, but no system for the registration of the prioritization of liens had yet been implemented. In addition, given the recent enactment of the underlying laws, the court systems of these countries frequently had no track record of enforcement of creditor rights.

Given these problems, project financings in developing countries often require lenders to live with a degree of uncertainty as to effective remedies upon default that is much different from a domestic transaction. Lenders with experience in these types of financings have learned to accept that liens on the project assets are often more important for their strategic negotiation value when things go wrong, rather than for their realizable liquidation value upon default.

6. RISKS ASSOCIATED WITH FOREIGN LAWS AND LEGAL SYSTEMS

The lender faces additional risks associated with foreign laws (or the lack thereof) generally. The legal systems of most developing countries continue to be less developed than in industrialized countries and this leads to uncertainty as to the legal environment the borrower must operate in and the lender will encounter if it ever is compelled to enforce its rights. * * *

7.   PERFORMANCE RISK OF OTHER PARTIES

The various risks discussed in this memorandum may prevent a borrower from meeting its obligations to the lender. These risks can also prevent project sponsors, key suppliers and key offtake purchasers from meeting their obligations to the project and thereby cause the project to fail.* * *

8.   RISK ALLOCATION

If the lender, after assessing the risk in connection with the project proposed to be financed, is unable to structure the financing to mitigate the risk in a manner acceptable to it, it must consider allocating the risk to (or sharing the risk with) the project sponsors or the host country government. Limited recourse completion guarantees provided by the project sponsors are common in international project financings. Unacceptable political risks can be allocated to the project sponsors under these agreements.

Allocating some of the risks to the host country government is also a possibility, particularly for large high-profile projects that are important to a country's economic development plans. As host country governments continue to privatize state-owned enterprises, however, they are becoming more reluctant to accept these risks. In the past, Sponsors of large infrastructure projects often were able to negotiate lengthy implementation agreements with the host country government providing a variety of government assurances with respect to the risks encountered. Host country government guarantees were also often obtained in this context. These agreements are becoming more difficult to obtain, even as the risks seem to be increasing. If such an agreement is obtained, given the inherent difficulties of enforcing these types of state support agreements, it is important that they be governed by a body of law that is protective of creditor rights (*e.g.*, New York or English law is preferred), that offshore arbitration be agreed upon as the dispute resolution method, that the host country government waive its sovereign immunity and that the host country government, as well as the government of the country in which the arbitration taken place, is a party to the New York Convention on the Recognition and Enforcement of Foreign Arbitral Awards.

[*Fitzgerald then analyzes in detail the possible methods for addressing each of these specific risks. Principal among these methods is so-called "political risk insurance," which may cover currency risks (as discussed in the text immediately below), expropriation risk, and the risk of default by foreign governments. Fitzgerald also addresses in detail the "risks relating to available security," which are particularly important for our purposes here—The Authors.*]

1.   CURRENCY RISKS

* * *

This risk can be shifted to political risk insurers:

(i) Multilateral Sources:

—Multilateral Investment Guarantee Agency ("MIGA"): MIGA provides inconvertibility/ transfer risk coverage for lenders covering 95% of the risk. MIGA traditionally would insure project lenders only if a project sponsor also insured its equity investment. MIGA traditionally would insure up to $4 of bank debt for every $1 of equity. This is changing, however, and MIGA will now consider covering only the debt under certain circumstances. Maximum coverage available per project has recently been increased from $50 million to $200 million. Given MIGA's short track record in paying claims, some lenders prefer to insure with OPIC which can reinsure with MIGA. A lender is eligible for MIGA coverage if it is incorporated and has its principal place of business in a member country or if it is majority-owned by nationals of member countries. MIGA's coverage does not cover devaluation risk.

—Multilateral "B Loans": The "B Loan" programs of the International Finance Corporation ("IFC"), Inter–American Development Bank ("IDB"), European Bank for Reconstruction and Development ("EBRD") and the Asian Development Bank ("ADB") can also provide some protection against inconvertibility/transfer risk, as well as other political risks. A "B Loan" is a loan made by a multilateral agency (such as the IFC or IDB) which is 100% participated out to a commercial bank or a syndicate of banks. Because the loan is made under the multilateral's umbrella, it is perceived to have the same "preferred creditor status" asserted by multilateral agencies generally.

—World Bank Guarantees: The World Bank has been tasked with finding ways to provide needed credit enhancement to mobilize capital for infrastructure projects. Under the World Bank's Guarantee program, the World Bank can provide guarantees against political risks in favor of commercial bank lenders covering 100% of the exposure. The scope of the risks guaranteed can be negotiated with the World Bank. * * *

—Inter–American Development Bank Guarantees. The IDB also has a program of providing guarantees against political risk in favor of commercial bank lenders. Although similar to the World Bank's guarantee program, the IDB has been able to issue guarantees without obtaining a host country government counter-guaranty in its favor. IDB's flexibility in this regard could lead to this instrument's greater use by the market. IDB's political risk guaranty program permits IDB to provide inconvertibility coverage that is very similar in terms of scope to the coverages provided by MIGA and OPIC. IDB can also guarantee host country government obligations in this regard in the same manner as the World Bank.

(ii) Bilateral Sources:

—Overseas Private Investment Corporation ("OPIC") (U.S.): OPIC provides [currency] inconvertibility/transfer risk coverage for lenders covering 100% of the risk. If the lenders have structured the financing to include an offshore collateral account into which foreign exchange revenues are paid, OPIC will cover the risk that the host country government may abrogate, repudiate or rescind its agreement consenting to the maintenance of the offshore account. Generally, OPIC does not provide coverage in excess of $200 million (there is no longer a formal cap on coverage amounts, however). * * *

—Eximbank and Other OECD Export Credit Agencies: U.S. Eximbank [the Export–Import Bank of the United States] and its bilateral export credit agency counterparts (such as ECGD in Britain, COFACE in France, Hermes in Germany, JBIC in Japan, CESCE in Spain, etc.) provide similar coverage for lenders to the extent that the loan proceeds are used to purchase goods or services from the home country.

* * *

5. Risks Relating to Available Security for the Loan Under Local Law

Availability of Security

What type of security do the laws of the host country permit?

(i) Common Law Countries: Generally provide for security over all assets—fixed and floating charges are available. A "floating charge" is a lien on moveable assets, including inventory and receivables—the lien "crystallizes" or attaches to specific assets at the time the charge is enforced.

(ii) Civil Law Countries: Generally do not provide for security over inventory and receivables—no floating charges available.

Enforcement Issues

Need to retain expert local counsel to assist in determining what security the local law provides for and how the security is enforced:

(i) Look beyond the "enforceability" opinion of local counsel. Determine the costs of enforcement. For example, does the country have an excessive court tax which makes enforcement of liens economically unenforceable?

(ii) Make sure all local formalities are complied with. For example, many civil law countries require all security agreements to be "protocolized" in order to be enforceable. * * *

(iii) Determine how foreclosure works under local law. Are there any restrictions on the right of the lenders to participate as buyers? Can the lenders bid in the debt, in lieu of cash? If cash must be paid, are there any creditors with a higher statutory priority? Is there a right of private sale or must foreclosure proceed by public auction? If there is a right of private sale, can the lender sell the collateral for foreign exchange or for local currency only? If the latter, does the lender's foreign exchange approval cover proceeds from the sale of collateral?

(iv) Many jurisdictions require the lender to place a value upon the collateral subject to a mortgage (the "Mortgage Value"). Upon foreclosure, the lender is not entitled to receive proceeds in excess of the Mortgage

Value. Placing a sensible value on the collateral is important and should not be overlooked. * * *

(v) Many jurisdictions also require that the lender denominate the Mortgage Value in local currency. This is fraught with devaluation risk. In this situation, it is typical to set a very high local currency amount as the Mortgage Value. Nevertheless, devaluations can be unpredictably large and seriously erode the value of the lender's collateral. In these cases, the loan documentation should provide a covenant requiring the borrower to grant a new mortgage in the event the lender's mortgage is eroded due to devaluations. Given the possibility that any such new mortgage may be granted after intervening mortgages have attached to the collateral, however, the lender should consider retaining some recourse to the project sponsors to cover this risk (*e.g.*, a project funds agreement obligating the project sponsors to advance funds to either pay off the lender's junior mortgage or repay any creditors with prior-ranking liens in the event of any such occurrence).

(vi) Determine whether the security can be held by an agent or trustee for a syndicate of commercial banks whose members may change from time to time (as the banks transfer their participation to other banks) or whether each bank must separately register its lien.

(vii) Upon foreclosure, can the lender operate the project? Are the governmental permits and approvals for the operation of the project assignable to the lender? Are there restrictions on foreign ownership of the project which will make it impossible for the lender to sell the project to a foreign entity upon foreclosure or to designate a foreign operator for the project? Is a conditional assignment exercisable upon default obtainable? Is foreclosure a practical option? In some countries foreclosure proceedings may take ten years or longer of court proceedings. In others, the court costs and other costs are so high as to often make foreclosure an impractical remedy.

McLAUGHLIN AND GREENE, REPRESENTING THE OWNER AT THE PROJECT PLANNING STAGE

76 Mich. B.J. 572 (1997).*

ALLOCATION OF PROJECT RISKS

The construction risks associated with the project must be identified and an allocation of such risks among the members of the project team must be worked out.

Typical Risks

Certain risks are present on virtually every construction project, including, by way of example, the following:

Unanticipated subsurface conditions: Subsurface conditions may be encountered that vary from those indicated in the soil investigation

---

report. Typically the owner will bear the risk of conditions that vary from those indicated in the contract documents provided by the owner to the contractor. Even if the contractor is responsible for the soil investigation, the owner is often responsible for conditions that reasonably could not have been discovered by a thorough investigation.

The contractor may encounter subsurface conditions that vary from those usually encountered in the performance of its work. This risk differs from the risk that owner-provided information does not accurately describe the subsurface conditions, and usually the contractor is responsible to investigate the site and make reasonable assumptions regarding the subsurface conditions present.

Force majeure delays: The construction work may be delayed by causes not due to the fault of the contractor or the owner, including adverse weather, strikes not involving the contractor's employees, riots and other governmental action, and similar causes. Typically the contractor is responsible for the risk of delays that are reasonably anticipatable, such as normal adverse weather. Frequently, the owner's responsibility for force majeure delays will be limited to delays to critical path work, as substantiated by the project schedule.

Design errors: Under the common law of most states, the owner implicitly warrants that the drawings and specifications are adequate for purposes of construction, and the owner bears the risk of construction delays and costs due to drawing errors and omissions. Usually the contractor will be responsible under the contract documents for design errors that the contractor should have discovered before the start of the work.

In addition, if the owner has engaged the contractor to review the drawings and specifications during the design phase, the contract documents may allocate to the contractor the risk of drawing conflicts and coordination and constructibility problems that the contractor reasonably should have discovered in connection with such review. If the project is completed on a design-build basis, this risk is generally allocated to the contractor.

Material and labor shortages: Unless the contract documents provide otherwise, the contractor typically bears the risk of providing sufficient labor and materials to complete the work.

Price increases: There is a risk that prices for materials and equipment required for the project will escalate during the construction period. The allocation of this risk will depend on the pricing arrangement for the work. If the contractor performs the work on a stipulated lump sum basis, the contractor typically will bear the risk of price escalation, and the owner will bear the risk under certain cost-plus arrangements.

Site security: There is a risk that theft, vandalism, damage and other problems will occur at the site. The allocation of this risk will be interrelated with decisions about responsibility for site security, property insurance, and payment of deductible amounts of claims under property insurance policies.

Trade contractor defaults: There is a risk that the work of a trade contractor may be defective or otherwise not in accordance with the contract documents, that the trade contractor may not complete its work on schedule, and that the trade contractor may cause damage or delay to the work of others. This risk is allocated to the general contractor under general contract and design- build arrangements. The allocation of this risk under a construction management arrangement will depend on the specific terms of the contract.

Special Project Risks

Certain special risks arise due to the particular circumstances and requirements of the project, including, by way of example, the following:

Environmental conditions: There may be a risk that hazardous materials or substances are present at the site that could cause injury or result in delays or additional costs to complete the project. If the site of the project was previously used for industrial or commercial operations, underground storage tanks may be present and the soil may be contaminated. If the project involves the renovation or demolition of an existing facility, asbestos-containing materials or other hazardous materials may be encountered during the work. Unless the contractor has been engaged specifically to remediate hazardous materials at the site, the risk of environmental problems typically is borne by the owner, except to the extent that the contractor negligently exacerbates the problem.

Concealed conditions: If the project involves the renovation or demolition of an existing facility, the contractor may encounter concealed conditions that vary from the conditions indicated by as-built drawings for the facility, and from the conditions that the contractor could reasonably anticipate based on an investigation of the existing facility. Because the contractor is not in a position to assess the costs associated with such conditions, the owner typically bears the risk that unexpected concealed conditions will be encountered.

On-going operations: If the project involves the renovation of an existing facility or construction work adjacent to an existing facility, the owner may need to continue to conduct its normal operations at the project site during the performance of work. It may be necessary to take extra precautions to prevent injuries and to accommodate the on-going use of the facility. Potential risks include the need to perform work activities after normal business hours, especially system shutdowns; traffic and parking problems; and restrictions on activities that might interfere with the use of the facility. It is particularly important for the owner to identify risks associated with renovation of hospital facilities.

If the contractor is informed, submitting its price quotation of the owner's requirements to maintain normal operations at the site and any restrictions on working hours or use of the site, the contractor will bear the risk of additional costs to reasonably accommodate the on-going use of the facility.

Quantities of work items: It may not be possible to calculate the amount of work required in advance, and there is a risk that the actual quantity of work required may vary from estimated quantities. The allocation of this risk will depend upon the particular circumstances of the project. If estimated quantities of work are indicated in the bidding documents furnished by the owner or in the quotation submitted by the contractor, the owner will typically bear the risk that the actual quantity may differ from the estimated quantity of work.

Allocation of Risk

Once project risks have been identified, decisions must be made regarding which consequences of a problem will be borne by which project team member. For example, the owner and contractor may decide, with respect to delays to the work resulting from force majeure causes, that the contractor will be entitled to an extension of the contract time for completion of work as necessary to offset such delays, but that the owner and contractor will each bear their own additional costs resulting from such delays.

As a general rule, a particular project risk is assigned to the entity that is in the best position to control and manage that risk and to prevent, avoid, circumvent or mitigate the damage that could occur as a result. Risk and control should be linked and, typically, when a project team member assumes the risk of a potential project problem, that team member also assumes control over that aspect of the project. Some owners will choose to assume the risks relating to a sensitive aspect of the project simply because they want to maintain control over that portion of the design and construction process.

Allocation of risk also usually affects the project price to the owner and may affect the project schedule. For example, if the owner enters into a lump sum general contract and the contractor assumes the risk of additional costs due to delays caused by adverse weather, the contractor will presumably include an amount in its lump sum price to cover such risk. The contractor will receive that additional amount whether or not the adverse weather ever occurs.

Similarly, if the owner attempts to allocate the risk of delays to the contractor by including a liquidated damages provision in the contract documents, the contractor will typically include an additional amount in its bid to offset the potential liquidated damages and will include a "cushion" of extra time in its original schedule to protect against delays. The contractor will receive the increased price and the extra time in the schedule even if the project is not delayed.

The owner whose primary concern is the lowest possible project price may elect to assume the risk of delays caused by adverse weather so that it does not have to pay an extra amount for adverse conditions that may never occur. On the other hand, the owner who is more concerned about price certainty will be willing to pay the contractor to assume more project risks; the initial contract price will be increased to cover those risks, but the contract price will not be subject to escalation later if adverse conditions occur. The owner who is concerned about completing the project as early as possible should carefully consider whether the threat of liquidated damages will, in fact, help the owner to achieve this goal.

The various construction delivery mechanisms represent combinations of responsibility and risk allocations that are sufficiently distinct to have acquired labels. For example, the design-build construction delivery mechanism involves assigning all design and construction responsibility to a single entity which includes many risks normally allocated between the owner, designer and the contractor. Under the general contractor or design-build mechanisms, the general contractor is responsible for all risks of subcontractor defaults. Conversely, the construction management delivery mechanism has the owner responsible for the risk of trade contractor defaults, except to the extent that such defaults result from the negligence of the construction manager.

FINNERTY, PROJECT FINANCING, ASSET-BASED FINANCIAL ENGINEERING
88–94 (2nd ed., 2007).*

DESIGNING SECURITY ARRANGEMENTS

* * *

In a project financing, lenders require the sponsors or other creditworthy parties involved with the project to provide assurances, generally through contractual obligations, that (1) the project will be completed even if costs exceed those originally projected (or, if the project is not completed, its debt will be repaid in full); (2) the project, when completed, will generate cash sufficient to meet all of its debt service obligations; and (3) if for any reason, including force majeure, the project's operations are interrupted, suspended, or terminated, the project will continue to service (and fully repay on schedule) its debt obligations.

The credit supporting a project financing comes in the first instance from the project itself. Such credit strength often needs to be supplemented by a set of security arrangements between the project and its sponsors or other creditworthy parties. The benefit of these arrangements is assigned to project lenders. The security arrangements provide that creditworthy entities will undertake to advance funds to the project if needed to ensure completion. They also usually provide for some sort of undertaking on the part of creditworthy entities to supplement the project's cash flow after completion, to the extent required to enable the project entity to meet its debt service requirements. The precise form of these commit-

---

ments varies, depending on the nature and projected economics of the project and on the prevailing political and capital market environments.

Several identifiable parties will normally have an interest in a project. Interested parties may include the sponsors, the suppliers of raw materials, the purchasers of project output, and the host political jurisdictions government. The interests of these parties may diverge. Often, a particular party may have more than one area of interest. For example, a purchaser of the project's output may also be an equity investor in the project. Broadly speaking, a sponsor seeks to earn a rate of return on his or her equity investment that is commensurate with the project-related risks the sponsor assumes. A purchaser of the project's output is interested in obtaining a long-term source of supply at the lowest possible price. A government may regulate the price of the project's output or support the project for reasons of national interest, such as promoting employment. The willingness and ability of the various parties to assume risks associated with the project depend on the benefits each expects to derive from the project, the financial strength and business objectives of each party, and the perceived likelihood that those bearing project risks will be compensated fully for doing so.

Purpose of Security Arrangements

Arranging sufficient credit support for project debt securities is a necessary precondition to arranging debt financing for any project. Lenders to a project will require that security arrangements be put in place to protect them from various risks. The contractual security arrangements apportion the risks among the project sponsors, the purchasers of the project output, and the other parties involved in the project. They represent a means of conveying the credit strength of going-concern entities to support project debt.

These contractual arrangements, whether in the form of a "hell-or-high-water" contract, a tariff, a financial support agreement, or some other form of contract, serve as the means by which the requisite credit support is conveyed to the project. The nature and extent of these contractual arrangements will depend on the type and magnitude of project risks, the financial strength of the parties at interest relative to those risks, and the profitability of the project.

Contractual undertakings that provide legal recourse to the credit strength of third parties normally form the nucleus of the security arrangements of a project. In most circumstances, these obligations will be several; each obligor's liability will be limited to a defined proportion of the total liability.

* * *

Direct Security Interest in Project Facilities

Lenders will also require a direct security interest in project facilities, usually in the form of a first mortgage lien on all project facilities. This security interest is often of limited value prior to project completion. A half-completed petrochemical plant may be worth substantially less than what it has cost to build thus far, particularly if there are concerns about its ability to perform. In the extreme, a plant that has been constructed but fails to pass its completion test may be worth only its scrap value (which is why lenders normally insist that the project debt must be repaid immediately if a project fails to satisfy its completion test).

Following completion of the project, the first lien provides added security for project loans. The lien gives lenders the ability to seize the project assets and sell them (or hire someone to operate them on the lenders' behalf) if the project defaults on its debt obligations. It thus affords a second possible source of debt repayment (the first source is project cash flow). However, lenders would much prefer to have the project entity service its debt in a timely manner out of its cash flow. So, although the collateral value of a project's assets can affect the amount of funds prospective lenders would be willing to lend to a project, the adequacy of project cash flow is the primary criterion that lenders apply.

* * *

After the project commences operations, contracts for the purchase and sale of the project's output or utilization of the project's services normally constitute the principal security arrangements for project debt. Broadly speaking, such contracts are intended to ensure that the project will receive revenues that are sufficient to cover operating costs fully and meet debt service obligations in a timely manner. Lenders almost always insist that these contractual obligations be in place, valid, and binding (governmental or regulatory approval may be required) before any portion of their loans can be drawn down.

* * *

FIGURE 6.1 Types of Purchase and Sale Contracts	
Type of Contract	*Degree of Credit Support Provided*
Take-if-Offered Contract	The contract obligates the purchaser of the project's output or services to take delivery and pay for the output or services only if the project is able to deliver them. No payment is required unless the project is able to make deliveries.
Take-or-Pay Contract	The contract obligates the purchaser of the project's output or services to pay for the output or services, regardless of whether the purchaser takes delivery. Cash payments are usually credited against charges for future deliveries.
Hell-or-High-Water Contract	There are no "outs," even in adverse circumstances beyond the control of the purchaser; the purchaser must pay in all events, even if no output is delivered.

* * *

QUESTIONS AND COMMENTS

1. How can Mogul raise $10 billion for this project? It could use its own retained earnings, obtaining the funds internally. It could sell enough stock to generate $10 billion. Or, it could borrow that amount.

There are disadvantages to each of these approaches. Even if $10 billion were available internally (an unlikely event), the first approach would drain Mogul's savings and leave little for other investment opportunities. Sales of stock to generate funds would dilute the position of current stock-holders. Mogul also likely does not want to shoulder a new debt burden that large, and may even have a contractual obligation to its current lenders not to take on that much additional debt.

2. Thus, the purpose of project financing is to avoid using any of the three approaches in Comment 1. The bases of the transaction are outlined in the article by Hoffman. *The project* will have to borrow the funds, not Mogul. Therefore, from Mogul's perspective, the debt is "off-balance sheet." Why would a lender make such a loan? The lender's compensation for any higher risk will be higher rates and fees, and potentially greater profit if the project is successful.

Ordinarily, the lender (which, as the readings state, is risk-averse) would want guarantees of repayment from Mogul or third parties. But Mogul wishes to avoid legal liability for the debt, so the loan will be "non-recourse," with liability *only* to the project, and not to the parent, Mogul. If Mogul were willing to guarantee repayment, it would have borrowed under its own name, and probably received a better interest rate.

3. Thus, any loans to the project will be off-balance sheet and non-recourse to Mogul. But this also means that the lenders must be convinced that the project itself will be self-financing, that it is likely to succeed, and that the increased interest rate and fees cover the increase in risk. The Blumenthal excerpt and the first Fitzgerald excerpt survey the kinds of lenders and financing structures available to a project sponsor like Mogul.

To provide the necessary information, the sponsor of the project will undertake and present to the lenders a feasibility study of the project. The feasibility study will include a political risk analysis of building a plant in Russia and exporting gas from it. It will also contain a market analysis of the current and future markets for liquified natural gas, and the sources and effect of competition. In this case, Mogul would include information about the Japanese buyers of the gas, and the types of contractual obligations to buy which they had undertaken. Finally, it will include a breakdown of the costs and financing for the project. The lenders are interested in the amount of equity which the sponsor, Mogul, is willing to put into the project and the amount of equity that third parties, such as local governments or other investors, may be willing to put into the project.

4. The feasibility study must also assure the lender concerning the supply of gas in the field. It will present the findings of its own employees, but will seek not to make any guarantees as to the amount of gas available. The lenders will hire their own experts to conduct their own research and to report their own findings concerning the amount of gas available. But the expert's opinions, to the extent that they create any legal liabilities, will be very highly conditioned. This qualified assurance is another source of uncertainty and risk to the lender.

5. At least two types of lenders (or lender groups) will be involved: those who make the construction loan, which is of relatively short term, and those who make the long-term, or "take-out" loan. Both of these lenders will seek assurances concerning the cost and timing of the construction phase of the project. The contractor will present construction drawings, land surveys, and resumes of the experience record of itself and its subcontractors and suppliers. However, the lenders will also hire their own experts to examine each of these aspects and to report their findings.

As Blumenthal indicates, if commercial lenders are not willing to finance the project, a private placement or an "off shore transaction" to sell the securities can be attempted, without meeting all the requirement of a public offering of securities under the SEC Act. The buyers of such securities will, however, have restrictions on any resales of the securities.

6. Note the many different parties involved in the project. They include the project sponsor, the project company, commercial lenders, international agencies, output purchasers, one or more contractors, the host government, technical consultants, project finance lawyers, and local lawyers. Getting all of them moving in the same direction (much less agreeing on every clause in every contract) requires an enormous amount of time and effort—at normal hourly rates.

7. What risks can cause construction cost overruns and delays? McLaughlin and Greene discuss these risks for the owner of a project and how they believe the risks are, and should be, allocated. They advance as a conceptual foundation that a risk should be "assigned to the entity that is in the best position to control and manage that risk." Does this concept provide a clear and consistent answer in practice? In any event, what would you advise a client to do in the negotiation stage if it agrees to assume a particular project risk?

8. Mogul may control some of these construction risks through performance bonds. (a) What roles could performance bonds play to make Mogul's project more secure (and thus more attractive to lenders)? (b) Which party should pay the costs of establishing each such bond? (c) Finally, recall the treatment of international standby letters of credit in Problem 5.3. What role might such a credit device play in Mogul's project?

9. The second Fitzgerald excerpt highlights the array of special risks involved in international project finance. Which of those risks are likely to be most prominent in Mogul's proposed gas project in Russia? (We will focus on the risks relating to available security in Questions 11 and 12 below.) Principal among these special international risks are those associated with the host government, Russia, and its local governmental entities on the Kamchat-

ka Peninsula. What are those risks and how do they differ as compared to a purely domestic energy production project?

Fitzgerald also notes that some of these risks may be mitigated by involving an international finance organization such as the IFC, MIGA, or a regional development bank. What role do these organizations play in mitigating the risks and what considerations do you think they weigh in deciding to support a private project such as this?

10.   Fitzgerald, Hoffman and Finnerty each survey the lenders' sources of security for repayment, including the revenue generated by the project, the physical and intangible assets of the project, and guarantees (such as standby letters of credit) from the sponsor or third parties.

Of these sources of security, the most important is the project's revenue. Thus, the lenders will need to be assured that the Japanese buyers are ready, willing and able to pay for the gas. Credit checks can assist in determining the ability of the buyers to pay, although outside the U.S. it is even more difficult to obtain accurate information. Although in some cases the project will produce a product that is sold on the open market, lenders prefer that the sponsor have buyers identified and legally obligated to purchase the product if produced. There are different levels of obligation, including the "take or pay" contract and the "hell or high water" contract. Finnerty charts the range of such contracts available for Mogul as it negotiates a deal with the Japanese buyers. How is each different from the ordinary sale contract? Which one would Mogul prefer that the Japanese buyers sign? Would that contract leave the project and its finances with any risks?

11.   If the project fails and available guarantees are insufficient, the lenders will be forced to resort to any security or similar rights they have in other assets. As noted, the future payments due to the project from the Japanese buyers likely will be at the top of the list, for they represent an easily accessible source of cash. But how can Mogul assure the lenders that they will actually receive these payments—especially because other creditors, including governmental entities, may also lay claim to those payments?

This raises difficult legal issues for the lenders. The concept of a registered and enforceable "security interest", including in future payment obligations (so-called "floating" liens or charges), is well established under U.S. law. *See* UCC §§ 9–102(a)(2), 9–203, 9–308. The easy answer, therefore, is to have all involved parties agree up front that U.S. law will govern the enforcement of security rights. The trouble is that such an agreement may not be enforceable in foreign courts. (*See* Problems 11.1 and 11.2 below for a more general analysis of this issue.)

In light of this, your job is to create as much legal certainty for Mogul (and its lenders) as is possible, and this almost certainly requires that you engage local counsel. Nonetheless, you must be able to ask the right questions to ensure that you and the local counsel are speaking the same legal and conceptual language. These questions should include the following, but what else would you want to know?

(a) First, does local law even allow "floating charges," especially on future payment obligations? Fitzgerald notes that most civil law countries do not recognize this form of security. If not, will some other conceptual device—such as an "assignment" or a "pledge" of the project's contract rights against the Japanese buyers—suffice under Russian law? One recent study left substantial doubt on this score. *See* Ivanova, *Russia, Enforcement of Security Interests in Banking Transactions*, 17 Banking Law News, No. 1, at 2 (May, 2010)(concluding that, although Russian law "expressly recognises a pledge of rights, including rights under contracts, . . . there are many open issues concerning pledges of contractual claims, especially upon enforcement and bankruptcy").

(b) This raises an equally important concern about priority and the enforcement of creditor rights. Does local law provide for formal registries of creditor interests or otherwise enforce priority rights as between competing creditors? Even if so, would local law permit the lenders to enforce their rights against the Japanese buyers without formal (and potentially lengthy) litigation in local courts? The second Fitzgerald excerpt also examines such issues.

(c) Finally, if the Japanese buyers simply refuse to pay, will *Japanese* courts recognize and enforce the lenders' claims? Japanese law generally permits the parties to choose the governing law for their transactions. *See* Act on the General Rules of Application of Laws, Law No. 10 of 1898 (as amended in 2006), Art. 7 (Anderson and Okuda, trans.), available at *http://www.hawaii. edu/aplpj/articles/APLPJ_08.1_anderson.pdf.* But will Japanese law recognize the priority of the lenders' claims?

12. In addition to the payment obligations of the Japanese buyers, the lenders may wish to secure rights in the fixed assets of the project located at the project site. The second Fitzgerald excerpt likewise focuses on this issue. These "immoveable" assets might seem particularly valuable; but in what ways could a "secured" creditor be less "secure" in an international project as compared to one located entirely in the United States? What are the special risks involved with resorting to such security rights in a country like Russia, whose legal system is still in transition?

13. The logical solution to this problem of divergent local laws would be an international treaty (similar to the CISG covered in Problem 4.1 above). There is in fact such a treaty for the assignment of money owed to a debtor ("receivables") from the sale of goods or the supply of services (also known as "factoring"). *See* UNIDROIT Convention on International Factoring, 27 I.L.M. 922, 925 (1988). Only seven countries have ratified this treaty, however, and none of those involved in Mogul's project. An alternative treaty by UNCITRAL has not entered into force as of 2012. *See* the 2001 United Nations Convention on the Assignment of Receivables in International Trade, 41 I.L.M. 776 (2002). Another treaty from UNIDROIT has been more successful (with nearly 50 ratifications as of 2012), but it covers only narrow categories of mobile physical equipment. *See* Convention on International Interests in Mobile Equipment, 39 I.L.M. 966 (2000).

14. Finally, a separate risk for the lenders relates to the effect of unforeseen future events on the obligations of the Japanese buyers. (The recent tsunami in Japan puts a tragic, practical face on this question.) Most legal systems recognize some form of the related doctrines of impossibility/im-

practicability, frustration, hardship, and supervening impediment. Problem 4.3 above analyzed in detail the special challenges that arise from these related doctrines for international business transactions.

In project finance, Finnerty observes that lenders generally will want to carefully circumscribe resort to such doctrines through detailed *force majeure* clauses, especially in "hell-or-high water" contracts. Beyond this, courts (in this country at least) have not been receptive to the doctrines, even for "take-or-pay" contracts. *See, e.g., R.J.B. Gas Pipeline Co. v. Colorado Interstate Gas Co.*, 813 P.2d 14 (Okl. App. 1990)(observing, even in the face of the total collapse of natural gas market in the 1980s, that "[a]bsent a specific contract provision creating a cognizable excuse for performance ... the parties to [a] contract are assumed to have allocated the risk in a take-or-pay clause").

PROBLEM 10.5   FOREIGN INVESTOR IS SUED: DOMESTIC GOODS IS SUED BY INDONESIAN TRADE UNION AND INDIGENOUS PEOPLES UNDER ALIEN TORT CLAIMS ACT AND TORTURE VICTIMS PROTECTION ACT FOR HUMAN RIGHTS, CULTURAL GENOCIDE, AND ENVIRONMENTAL LAW VIOLATIONS

SECTION I.   THE SETTING

Domestic Goods, Inc., the subject of Problems 10.1, 10.2 and 10.3, is involved in another international issue. Their Indonesian subsidiary DGIN-DO, an assembly plant in rural Sumatra, makes many DGI products for the Asian market. DGI and DGINDO have been sued in two lawsuits in federal court in New York City. They are:

Indonesian Trade Union v. Domestic Goods, Inc., et al. The Indonesian union (ITU) has long tried unsuccessfully to establish a union at DGINDO. In this case, the ITU alleges that DGINDO, with the participation and approval of DGI, hired private security forces made up mostly of government military to intimidate union leadership so as to influence the outcome of a vote on whether or not to have a union at DGINDO. The plaintiffs allege that DGINDO met frequently with the security forces to be informed about and coordinate acts of violence including torture, kidnaping, beatings, and forced labor. The plaintiffs claim that both DGINDO and DGI are liable under both the Alien Tort Claims Act (ATCA) and the Torture Victim Protection Act (TVPA), as well as for violating various tort laws of Indonesia.

Indigenous Peoples v. Domestic Goods, Inc., et al. An indigenous peoples group (IPG) has also initiated a suit in the same court against both DGI and DGINDO, alleging that the defendants' are liable under the ATCA and TVPA for violations of environmental laws and "cultural genocide" by destruction of the region's habitat and religious monuments.

In both cases, motions have been made by the defendants requesting that the cases be dismissed on subject matter jurisdiction grounds—that the complaints failed to state causes of action.

SECTION II. FOCUS OF CONSIDERATION

Corporations investing abroad are occasionally sued. Most suits are against the local subsidiary and are brought in the foreign courts. Most deal with contract issues, such as the interpretation of transfer of technology agreements, privatization agreements, joint venture agreements, and commercial disputes with suppliers and customers. Some involve torts, such as an injury to a customer or employee on company property. But within the past decade a new form of litigation against multinationals has gained favor. They are actions (1) by groups of foreign persons, (2) against U.S. corporations (both foreign subsidiaries and U.S. parents), (3) filed in U.S. courts, (4) alleging a broad range of wrongs, (5) under (mainly) the U.S. ATCA and TVPA. Such actions, several funded by the International Labor Rights Fund, have been brought against numerous corporations, including Exxon Mobil Corp., Unocal Corp., ChevronTexaco, Bank of America, Citigroup, Price Waterhouse, Dupont, Del Monte, Drummond Co., Talisman Energy, Inc., DaimlerChrysler Corp., Union Carbide, United Technologies, Freeport–McMoran, Ford Motor Company, Coca–Cola Co., and others. They have involved acts in many nations, including Burma, Indonesia, the Sudan, Colombia, Ecuador, Guatemala and Indonesia. Every corporation investing abroad should be aware of how these statutes are being used.

Part A presents two case extracts that do not deal with claims against corporations, but are the foundation cases for claims under the ATCA. The first is *Filártiga v. Peña-Irala,* the first contemporary use of the ATCA that establishes the ATCA as a powerful force in changing traditional perspectives regarding where litigation may occur. It sends a warning to governments everywhere that if they are engaged in not always fully defined violations of international law, they are subject to suit in the United States, if personal jurisdiction exists. The second foundation case is the 2004 Supreme Court decision in *Sosa v. Alvarez-Machain,* which seemed to initially place considerable restraints on the use of the ATCA, but then left the door open for some undefined continued use. *Filártiga* and *Sosa* are discussed as preludes to Part B, where in contrast to *Filártiga's* and *Sosa's* involving foreign individuals (principally) as the defendant, the defendant becomes a *private* entity in the United States (and may include its directors and officers). Unlike *Filártiga* and *Sosa,* ATCA cases against U.S. corporations usually have little problem with personal jurisdiction.

SECTION III. READINGS, QUESTIONS AND COMMENTS

For two hundred years prior to the 1980 Filártiga decision jurisdiction under the ATCA had been upheld only twice in about two dozen attempts. Clearly, the ATCA was not enacted as a means to address human rights issues. And also clearly, the ATCA was unknown as a threat to the operations of U.S. multinational corporations operating abroad. Many suits are now based on the Alien Tort Statute (often called the Alien Tort Claims Act or ATCA), 28 U.S.C.A. § 1350.

As one of the main methods of challenging human rights issues allegedly committed by individuals or corporations, the reawakening of the ATCA has led to additional legislation to address some limitations in its use, principally the 1994 Torture Victims Protection Act (TVPA), 28 U.S.C. § 1350 (Supp. V 1993), and the 1996 amendments to the Foreign Sovereign Immunities Act (FSIA).

28 U.S.C. § 1350, constituting the ATCA and additions by the adoption of the TVPA, is essential to an analysis of this problem. It is included in the Documents Supplement.

PART A.   SUITS AGAINST INDIVIDUALS

The *Filártiga* decision is the starting point for any consideration of the current use of the ATCA. It was brought against a government official of Paraguay who was visiting in the United States. One consequence of the *Filártiga* decision is that well-advised foreign government officials who engage in violations of international law should forgo Disney World and shopping trips to the United States. There may be a service processor behind that Mickey Mouse mask. They should also avoid official trips to the United Nations headquarters in New York. The *Sosa* decision has placed yet undefined limits on the use of the ATCA. It does not give the human rights and environmental law organizations a green light to create norms of customary international law, nor does it present a red light to end the use of the ATCA for such cases. Of importance to corporations, such as DGI and DGINDO, the court necessarily left open who a defendant might be; DGI and DGINDO had undoubtedly hoped that the Supreme Court would have either abolished the use of the ATCA altogether, or at least limited it to claims against individuals.

FILARTIGA v. PENA–IRALA

United States Court of Appeals, Second Circuit, 1980.
630 F.2d 876.

Kaufman, Circuit Judge:

Implementing the constitutional mandate for national control over foreign relations, the First Congress established original district court jurisdiction over "all causes where an alien sues for a tort only (committed) in violation of the law of nations." Judiciary Act of 1789, codified at 28 U.S.C. § 1350. Construing this rarely-invoked provision, we hold that deliberate torture perpetrated under color of official authority violates universally accepted norms of the international law of human rights, regardless of the nationality of the parties. Thus, whenever an alleged torturer is found and served with process by an alien within our borders, § 1350 provides federal jurisdiction. Accordingly, we reverse the judgment of the district court dismissing the complaint for want of federal jurisdiction.

The appellants * * * are citizens of the Republic of Paraguay. Dr. Joel Filártiga, a physician, describes himself as a longstanding opponent of the government of President Alfredo Stroessner, which has held power in Paraguay since 1954. His daughter, Dolly Filártiga, arrived in the United States in 1978 under a visitor's visa, and has since applied for permanent political asylum. The Filártigas brought this action in the Eastern District of New York against Americo Norberto Pena–Irala (Pena), also a citizen of Paraguay, for wrongfully causing the death of Dr. Filártiga's seventeen-year old son, Joelito. * * *

The appellants contend that on March 29, 1976, Joelito Filártiga was kidnaped and tortured to death by Pena, who was then Inspector General of Police in Asunción, Paraguay. Later that day, the police brought Dolly Filártiga to Pena's home where she was confronted with the body of her brother, which evidenced marks of severe torture. As she fled, horrified, from the house, Pena followed after her shouting, "Here you have what you have been looking for for so long and what you deserve. Now shut up." The Filártigas claim that Joelito was tortured and killed in retaliation for his father's political activities and beliefs. Shortly thereafter, Dr. Filártiga commenced a criminal action in the Paraguayan courts against Pena and the police * * *. As a result, Dr. Filártiga's attorney was arrested and brought to police headquarters where, shackled to a wall, Pena threatened him with death. This attorney, it is alleged, has since been disbarred without just cause.

In July of 1978, Pena * * * entered the United States under a visitor's visa. He was accompanied by [a companion] * * *. The couple remained in the United States beyond the term of their visas, and * * * Dolly Filártiga * * * learned of their presence. * * * [T]he Immigration and Naturalization Service arrested Pena and his companion, both of whom were subsequently ordered deported on April 5, 1979 following a hearing. * * * Almost immediately, Dolly caused Pena to be served with a summons and civil complaint * * *. The complaint alleged that Pena had wrongfully caused Joelito's death by torture and sought compensatory and punitive damages of $10,000,000. The Filártigas also sought to enjoin Pena's deportation to ensure his availability for testimony at trial. The cause of action is stated as arising under "wrongful death statutes; the U. N. Charter; the Universal Declaration on Human Rights; the U. N. Declaration Against Torture; the American Declaration of the Rights and Duties of Man; and other pertinent declarations, documents and practices constituting the customary international law of human rights and the law of nations," as well as 28 U.S.C. § 1350, and the Supremacy Clause of the U. S. Constitution.

Judge Nickerson * * * dismissed the complaint on jurisdictional grounds. The district judge recognized the strength of appellants' argument that official torture violates an emerging norm of customary international law. Nonetheless, he felt constrained by dicta contained in two recent opinions of this Court, *Dreyfus v. von Finck*, 534 F.2d 24 (2d Cir.), cert. denied, 429 U.S. 835, 97 S.Ct. 102, 50 L.Ed.2d 101 (1976); *IIT v. Vencap, Ltd.*, 519 F.2d 1001 (2d Cir. 1975), to construe narrowly "the law of nations," as employed in § 1350, as excluding that law which governs a state's treatment of its own citizens.

Appellants rest their principal argument in support of federal jurisdiction upon the Alien Tort Statute, * * * which provides: "The district courts shall have original jurisdiction of any civil action by an alien for a tort only, committed in violation of the law of nations or a treaty of the United States." * * * In light of the universal condemnation of torture in numerous international agreements, and the renunciation of torture as an instrument of official policy by virtually all of the nations of the world (in principle if not in practice), we find that an act of torture committed by a state official against one held in detention violates established norms of the international law of human rights, and hence the law of nations.

The Supreme Court has enumerated the appropriate sources of international law. The law of nations "may be ascertained by consulting the works of jurists, writing professedly on public law; or by the general usage and practice of nations; or by judicial decisions recognizing and enforcing that law." *United States v. Smith*, 18 U.S. (5 Wheat.) 153, 160–61, 5 L.Ed. 57 (1820). * * * The requirement that a rule command the "general assent of civilized nations" to become binding upon them all is a stringent one. Were this not so, the courts of one nation might feel free to impose idiosyncratic legal rules upon others, in the name of applying international law. Thus, in *Banco Nacional de Cuba v. Sabbatino*, 376 U.S. 398, 84 S.Ct. 923, 11 L.Ed.2d 804 (1964), the Court declined to pass on the validity of the Cuban government's expropriation of a foreign-owned corporation's assets, noting the sharply conflicting views on the issue propounded by the capital-exporting, capital-importing, socialist and capitalist nations.

The case at bar presents us with a situation diametrically opposed to the conflicted state of law that confronted the *Sabbatino* Court. Indeed, to paraphrase that Court's statement there are few, if any, issues in international law today on which opinion seems to be so united as the limitations on a state's power to torture persons held in its custody.* * * [A]lthough there is no universal agreement as to the precise extent of the "human rights and fundamental freedoms" guaranteed to all by the [U.N.] Charter, there is at present no dissent from the view that the guaranties include, at a bare minimum, the right to be free from torture. * * * [W]e conclude that official torture is now prohibited by the law of nations.

Although the Alien Tort Statute has rarely been the basis for jurisdiction during its long history, ... there can be little doubt that this action is properly brought in federal court. This is undeniably an action by an alien, for a tort only, committed in violation of the law of nations. The paucity of suits successfully maintained under the section is readily attributable to the statute's requirement of alleging a "violation of the law of nations" (emphasis supplied) at the jurisdictional threshold. Courts have, accordingly, engaged in a more searching preliminary review of the merits than is required, for example, under the more flexible "arising under" formulation. Thus, the narrowing construction that the Alien Tort Statute has previously received reflects the fact that earlier cases did not involve such well-established, universally recognized norms of international law that are here at issue. Since federal jurisdiction may properly be exercised over the Filártigas' claim, the action must be remanded for further proceedings.

SOSA v. ALVAREZ–MACHAIN

United States Supreme Court, 2004.
542 U.S. 692, 124 S.Ct. 2739, 159 L.Ed.2d 718.

JUSTICE SOUTER delivered the opinion of the Court.

The two issues are whether respondent Alvarez–Machain's allegation that the Drug Enforcement Administration instigated his abduction from Mexico for criminal trial in the United States supports a claim against the Government under the Federal Tort Claims Act (FTCA or Act), and whether he may recover under the Alien Tort Statute (ATS). We hold that he is not entitled to a remedy under either statute.

In 1985, an agent of the Drug Enforcement Administration (DEA), Enrique Camarena–Salazar, was captured on assignment in Mexico and taken to a house in Guadalajara, where he was tortured over the course of a 2–day interrogation, then murdered. Based in part on eyewitness testimony, DEA officials in the United States came to believe that respondent Humberto Alvarez–Machain (Alvarez), a Mexican physician, was present at the house and acted to prolong the agent's life in order to extend the interrogation and torture. In 1990, a federal grand jury indicted Alvarez for the torture and murder of Camarena–Salazar, and the United States District Court for the Central District of California issued a warrant for his arrest. The DEA asked the Mexican Government for help in getting Alvarez into the United States, but when the requests and negotiations proved fruitless, the DEA approved a plan to hire Mexican nationals to seize Alvarez and bring him to the United States for trial. As so planned, a group of Mexicans, including petitioner Jose Francisco Sosa, abducted Alvarez from his house, held him overnight in a motel, and brought him by private plane to El Paso, Texas, where he was arrested by federal officers. Once in American custody, Alvarez moved to dismiss the indictment on the ground that his seizure was "outrageous governmental conduct," and violated the extradition treaty between the United States and Mexico. The District Court agreed, the Ninth Circuit affirmed, and we reversed, holding that the fact of Alvarez's forcible seizure did not affect the jurisdiction of a federal court. The case was tried in 1992, and ended at the close of the Government's case, when the District Court granted Alvarez's motion for a judgment of acquittal. In 1993, after returning to Mexico, Alvarez began the civil action before us here. He sued Sosa,

Mexican citizen and DEA operative Antonio Garate–Bustamante, five unnamed Mexican civilians, the United States, and four DEA agents. So far as it matters here, Alvarez sought damages from the United States under the FTCA alleging false arrest, and from Sosa under the ATS, for a violation of the law of nations. The former statute authorizes suit "for . . . personal injury . . . caused by the negligent or wrongful act or omission of any employee of the Government while acting within the scope of his office or employment." The latter provides in its entirety that "[t]he district courts shall have original jurisdiction of any civil action by an alien for a tort only, committed in violation of the law of nations or a treaty of the United States."

The District Court granted the Government's motion to dismiss the FTCA claim, but awarded summary judgment and $25,000 in damages to Alvarez on the ATS claim. A three-judge panel of the Ninth Circuit then affirmed the ATS judgment, but reversed the dismissal of the FTCA claim. A divided en banc court came to the same conclusion. As for the ATS claim, the court called on its own precedent, "that [the ATS] not only provides federal courts with subject matter jurisdiction, but also creates a cause of action for an alleged violation of the law of nations." The Circuit then relied upon what it called the "clear and universally recognized norm prohibiting arbitrary arrest and detention," to support the conclusion that Alvarez's arrest amounted to a tort in violation of international law. * * * We granted certiorari in these companion cases to clarify the scope of both the FTCA and the ATS. We now reverse in each.* * *

Sosa . . . argues (as does the United States supporting him) that there is no relief under the ATS because the statute does no more than vest federal courts with jurisdiction, neither creating nor authorizing the courts to recognize any particular right of action without further congressional action. Although we agree the statute is in terms only jurisdictional, we think that at the time of enactment the jurisdiction enabled federal courts to hear claims in a very limited category defined by the law of nations and recognized at common law. We do not believe, however, that the limited, implicit sanction to entertain the handful of international law *cum* common law claims understood in 1789 should be taken as authority to recognize the right of action asserted by Alvarez here.* * *

Alvarez says that the ATS was intended not simply as a jurisdictional grant, but as authority for the creation of a new cause of action for torts in violation of international law. We think that reading is implausible. As enacted in 1789, the ATS gave the district courts cognizance of certain causes of action, and the term bespoke a grant of jurisdiction, not power to mold substantive law. The fact that the ATS was placed in § 9 of the Judiciary Act, a statute otherwise exclusively concerned with federal-court jurisdiction, is itself support for its strictly jurisdictional nature. Nor would the distinction between jurisdiction and cause of action have been elided by the drafters of the Act or those who voted on it. In sum, we think the statute was intended as jurisdictional in the sense of addressing the power of the courts to entertain cases concerned with a certain subject.

But holding the ATS jurisdictional raises a new question, this one about the interaction between the ATS at the time of its enactment and the ambient law of the era. Sosa would have it that the ATS was stillborn because there could be no claim for relief without a further statute expressly authorizing adoption of causes of action. *Amici* professors of federal jurisdiction and legal history take a different tack, that federal courts could entertain claims once the jurisdictional grant was on the books, because torts in violation of the law of nations would have been recognized within the common law of the time. We think history and practice give the edge to this latter position.

Still, the history does tend to support two propositions. First, there is every reason to suppose that the First Congress did not pass the ATS as a jurisdictional convenience to be placed on the shelf for use by a future Congress or state legislature that might, some day, authorize the creation of causes of action or itself decide to make some element of the law of nations actionable for the benefit of foreigners. The anxieties of the preconstitutional period cannot be ignored easily enough to think that the statute was not meant to have a practical effect. * * * It would have been passing strange for * * * Congress to vest federal courts expressly with jurisdiction to entertain civil causes brought by aliens alleging violations of the law of nations, but to no effect whatever until the Congress should take further action. There is too much in the historical record to believe that Congress would have enacted the ATS only to leave it lying fallow indefinitely. The second inference to be drawn from the history is that Congress intended the ATS to furnish jurisdiction for a relatively modest set of actions alleging violations of the law of nations. Uppermost in the legislative mind appears to have been offenses against ambassadors, violations of safe conduct were probably understood to be actionable, and individual actions arising out of prize captures and piracy may well have also been contemplated. But the common law appears to have understood only those three of the hybrid variety as definite and actionable, or at any rate, to have assumed only a very limited set of claims. The sparse contemporaneous cases and legal materials referring to the ATS tend to confirm both inferences, that some, but few, torts in violation of the law of nations were understood to be within the common law.

In sum, although the ATS is a jurisdictional statute creating no new causes of action, the reasonable inference from the historical materials is that the statute was intended to have practical effect the moment it became law. The jurisdictional grant is best read as having been enacted on the understanding that the common law would provide a cause of action for the modest number of international law violations with a potential for personal liability at the time. We think it is correct, then, to assume that the First Congress understood that the district courts would recognize private causes of action for certain torts in violation of the law of nations, though we have found no basis to suspect Congress had any examples in mind beyond those torts corresponding to Blackstone's three primary offenses: violation of safe conducts, infringement of the rights of ambassadors, and piracy. We assume, too, that no development in the two centuries from the enactment of § 1350 to the birth of the modern line of cases beginning with Filartiga, has categorically precluded federal courts from recognizing a claim under the law of nations as an element of common law * * *. Still, there are good reasons for a restrained conception of the discretion a federal court should exercise in considering a new cause of action of this kind. Accordingly, we think courts should require any claim based on the present-day law of nations to rest on a norm of international character accepted by the civilized world and defined with a specificity comparable to the features of the 18th-century paradigms we have recognized. This requirement is fatal to Alvarez's claim.

A series of reasons argue for judicial caution when considering the kinds of individual claims that might implement the jurisdiction conferred by the early statute. First, the prevailing conception of the common law has changed since 1789 in a way that counsels restraint in judicially applying internationally generated norms. When § 1350 was enacted, the accepted conception was of the common law as "a transcendental body of law outside of any particular State but obligatory within it unless and until changed by statute." Now, however, in most cases where a court is asked to state or formulate a common law principle in a new context, there is a general understanding that the law is not so much found or discovered as it is either made or created.

Second, along with, and in part driven by, that conceptual development in understanding common law has come an equally significant rethinking of the role of the federal courts in making it. * * * And although we have even assumed competence to make judicial rules of decision of particular importance to foreign relations, such as the act of state doctrine, the general practice has been to look for legislative guidance before exercising innovative authority over substantive law. It would be remarkable to take a more aggressive role in exercising a jurisdiction that remained largely in shadow for much of the prior two centuries.

Third, this Court has recently and repeatedly said that a decision to create a private right of action is one better left to legislative judgment in the great majority of cases. The creation of a private right of action raises issues beyond the mere consideration whether underlying primary conduct should be allowed or not, entailing, for example, a decision to permit enforcement without the check imposed by prosecutorial discretion, Accordingly, even when Congress has made it clear by statute that a rule applies to purely domestic conduct, we are reluctant to infer intent to provide a private cause of action where the statute does not supply one expressly.

Fourth, the subject of . . . collateral consequences is itself a reason for a high bar to new private causes of action for violating international law, for the potential implications for the foreign relations of the United States of recognizing such causes should make courts particularly wary of impinging on the discretion of the Legislative and Executive Branches in managing foreign affairs. It is one thing for American courts to enforce constitutional limits on our own State and Federal Governments' power, but quite another to consider suits under rules that would go so far as to claim a limit on the power of foreign governments over their own citizens, and to hold that a foreign government or its agent has transgressed those limits. Yet modern international law is very much concerned with just such questions, and apt to stimulate calls for vindicating private interests in § 1350 cases. Since many attempts by federal courts to craft remedies for the violation of new norms of international law would raise risks of adverse foreign policy consequences, they should be undertaken, if at all, with great caution.

The fifth reason is particularly important in light of the first four. We have no congressional mandate to seek out and define new and debatable violations of the law of nations, and modern indications of congressional understanding of the judicial role in the field have not affirmatively encouraged greater judicial creativity. * * * Several times, indeed, the Senate has expressly declined to give the federal courts the task of interpreting and applying international human rights law, as when its ratification of the International Covenant on Civil and Political Rights declared that the substantive provisions of the document were not self-executing.

These reasons argue for great caution in adapting the law of nations to private rights. Justice SCALIA concludes that caution is too hospitable, and a word is in order to summarize where we have come so far and to focus our difference with him on whether some norms of today's law of nations may ever be recognized legitimately by federal courts in the absence of congressional action beyond § 1350. All Members of the Court agree that § 1350 is only jurisdictional. We also agree, or at least Justice SCALIA does not dispute, that the jurisdiction was originally understood to be available to enforce a small number of international norms that a federal court could properly recognize as within the common law enforceable without further statutory authority. Justice Scalia concludes, however, that two subsequent developments should be understood to preclude federal courts from recognizing any further international norms as judicially enforceable today, absent further congressional action. As described before, we now tend to understand common law not as a discoverable reflection of universal reason but, in a positivistic way, as a product of human choice. And we now adhere to a conception of limited judicial power first expressed in reorienting federal diversity jurisdiction, that federal courts have no authority to derive "general" common law. Whereas Justice SCALIA sees these developments as sufficient to close the door to further independent judicial recognition of actionable international norms, other considerations persuade us that the judicial power should be exercised on the understanding that the door is still ajar subject to vigilant doorkeeping, and thus open to a narrow class of international norms today.

We must still, however, derive a standard or set of standards for assessing the particular claim Alvarez raises, and for this case it suffices to look to the historical antecedents. Whatever the ultimate criteria for accepting a cause of action subject to jurisdiction under § 1350, we are persuaded that federal courts should not recognize private claims under federal common law for violations of any international law norm with less definite content and acceptance among civilized nations than the historical paradigms familiar when § 1350 was enacted. * * * And the determination whether a norm is sufficiently definite to support a cause of action should (and, indeed, inevitably must) involve an element of judgment about the practical consequences of making that cause available to litigants in the federal courts. * * *

Thus, Alvarez's detention claim must be gauged against the current state of international law, looking to those sources we have long, albeit cautiously, recognized. * * * To begin with, Alvarez cites two well-known international agreements that, despite their moral authority, have little utility under the standard set out in this opinion. He says that his abduction by Sosa was an "arbitrary arrest" within the meaning of the Universal Declaration of Human Rights (Declaration), G.A. Res. 217A (III), U.N. Doc. A1810 (1948). And he traces the rule against arbitrary arrest not only to the Declaration, but also to article nine of the International Covenant on Civil and Political Rights (Covenant), Dec. 19, 1996, 999 U.N.T.S. 171, to which the United States is a party, and to various other conventions to which it is not. But the Declaration does not of its own force impose obligations as a matter of international law. * * * And, although the Covenant does bind the United States as a matter of international law, the United States ratified the Covenant on the express understanding that it was not self-executing and so did not itself create obligations enforceable in the federal courts. Accordingly, Alvarez cannot say that the Declaration and Covenant themselves establish the relevant and applicable rule of international law. He instead attempts to show that prohibition of arbitrary arrest has attained the status of binding customary international law.* * *

Whatever may be said for the broad principle Alvarez advances, in the present, imperfect world, it expresses an aspiration that exceeds any binding customary rule having the specificity we require. Creating a private cause of action to further that aspiration would go beyond any residual common law discretion we think it appropriate to exercise. It is enough to hold that a single illegal detention of less than a day, followed by the transfer of custody to lawful authorities and a prompt arraignment, violates no norm of customary international law so well defined as to support the creation of a federal remedy.

The judgment of the Court of Appeals is *Reversed.*

QUESTIONS AND COMMENTS

1. The motion to dismiss on jurisdiction having been denied in *Filártiga*, the case was remanded and the Filártigas received a default judgment for $385,364 in compensatory damages, plus $10 million punitive damages. Nothing has been collected, Peña had been allowed to return to Paraguay. Could the suit have been successful against the government of Paraguay? A judgment against Paraguay might have been collected.

2. Why was the Alien Tort Statute limited to aliens and why was it applicable only to torts? If the answer is not clear, what is clear is that the recent use of the ATCA in human rights cases was not envisioned in 1789 when the Act was passed. When adopted in 1789 the nation was new. Many living in the country were not citizens. The country wanted diplomatic recognition. The ATCA offered some help to foreigners coming to the United States for any of many reasons. But not to forum shop in 1789.

3. Dozens of cases have followed *Filártiga* under the ATCA. Many sought a judicial expansion of the *Filártiga*. But *Sosa* dealt a blow to those expectations. But clearly more a glancing blow than a knockout punch. If we start with the acceptance of *Filártiga* that at least the form of torture applied in *Filártiga* is a violation of the law of nations, and furthermore acknowledge that the detention of Alvarez–Machain in *Sosa* is not, what is left in the middle? Might detention over a long period of time rise to a violation of the law of nations? Might some brief threats be *mental* abuse but not constitute torture and therefore not be a violation of the law of nations? An additional requirement in *Filártiga* is that the act must be done "under color of official authority." Is that the case in our hypothetical?

4. The ATCA is thoroughly considered in *Tel–Oren v. Libyan Arab Republic*, 726 F.2d 774 (D.C.Cir. 1984), *cert. denied*, 470 U.S. 1003, 105 S.Ct. 1354, 84 L.Ed.2d 377 (1985). For a discussion of the ATCA, *see, e.g.*, Anne–Marie Burley, *The Alien Tort Statute and the Judiciary Act of 1789: A Badge of Honor*, 83 Am.J. Int'l L. 461 (1989); Kenneth C. Randall, *Federal Jurisdiction over International Claims: Inquiries into the Alien Tort Statute*, 18 N.Y.U. J. L. & Pol. 1 (1985); Jean–Marie Simon, *The Alien Tort Claims Act: Justice or Show Trials?*, 11 B.U. Int'l L.J. 1 (1993); Joseph Modeste Sweeney, *A Tort Only in Violation of the Law of Nations*, 18 Hastings Int'l & Comp. L. Rev. 445 (1995); Lawrence W. Newman & David Zaslowsky, *The Alien Tort Claims Act: How Far Will It Go?*, N.Y.L.J., Jan. 2, 2003, at 3.

5. Did the *Filártiga* court effectively deal with the argument that written laws prohibiting torture in many areas of the world exist in nations where they are commonly ignored? If torture, like corruption, is routine in a many nations, how can it be a violation of international law? Which source of international law seemed to be the most convincing to the court? When the court stated that "although there is no universal agreement as to the precise extent of the 'human rights and fundamental freedoms' guaranteed to all by the [U.N.] Charter," was it ruling that universal agreement is required? Why? Are the claims made in the hypothetical actions where there is "universal agreement?"

6. Could the Filártigas have brought suit in state court? Had the suit been initiated in state court, could it have been removed by the defendant to federal court?

7. There is an intersection of the ATCA with the Foreign Sovereign Immunities Act (FSIA), the subject of Part C of Problem 10.6, and also with head-of-state immunity. Human rights cases often involve challenges to foreign governments and their officials. Invariably a defense of sovereign and/or head-of-state immunity is raised. The FSIA is the exclusive basis of subject matter jurisdiction over foreign states. In 1996, it was amended to add § 1605(a)(7) that denies immunity to foreign states for personal injury caused by torture, extra-judicial killing, aircraft sabotage, and hostage taking if the acts are engaged in by an official of the state acting within the scope of employment. But the claimant or victim must be a U.S. national, thus avoiding increasing the United States as a forum of choice for foreigners. The foreign state in question also has to have been designated by the United States as a state sponsor of terrorism.

8. At the time of the *Filártiga* decision, there was a draft of the subsequently adopted Torture Victim Protection Act. 28 U.S.C.A. § 1350. Might that have influenced the court? The *Sosa* court noted the enactment of the TVPA. Did that enactment help Sosa's arguments? The TVPA addressed a limitation of the ATCA. The ATCA allowed only claims by aliens. The TVPA allows claims to be brought by both aliens and citizens against some defined defendants and where there is personal jurisdiction.

9. Collecting a judgment rendered under the ATCA or TVPA may be difficult, if not impossible. But a money judgment in a U.S. court that cannot be satisfied may have nominal value in achieving the broader goal of reducing human rights violations. Not all such judgments remain unsatisfied. A judgment of $187 million was rendered in 1997 against the government of Cuba for shooting down two civilian airplanes. *Alejandre v. Cuba*, 996 F.Supp. 1239 (S.D.Fla.1997). It remained uncollected despite attempts by the plaintiffs to execute on debts owed Cuba by U.S. based communications companies (mainly for telephone services), *Alejandre v. Republic of Cuba*, 42 F.Supp.2d 1317 (S.D.Fla.1999); *Alejandre v. Telefonica Larga Distancia de Puerto Rico*, 183 F.3d 1277 (11th Cir.1999). Congress enacted legislation offering some compensation to the Cuban claimants and several others, including the recipients of $247.5 million in damages against Iran, *Flatow v. Islamic Republic of Iran*, 999 F.Supp. 1 (D.D.C.1998), from blocked assets. Was it appropriate to remove these blocked funds from the President's arsenal of negotiating factors for ultimate reestablishment of relations with Cuba? What about other claimants who filed claims against Cuba in the 1960s under the Foreign Claims Commission's procedures, and have long expected to share in the blocked assets? Why should the families of the downed pilots have priority? Does this all reflect badly upon the *Filártiga* decision and its aftermath? In *Sosa*, Alvarez–Machain wanted substantial damages, undoubtedly aware of the *Alejandre* case. The court was asked to apply Mexican law in forming the damages, which might have amounted to $20,000. The court rejected the request, noting that it had to fashion its own damages. But it awarded Sosa only $25,000. Why?

10. In *Sosa*, the Department of Justice provided the defense; Sosa was in the witness protection program. The DOJ wanted the court to rule that the ATCA does not provide a cause of action. That would favor DGI and DGINDO. Did the Supreme Court get it right?

11. Contrastingly, Alvarez–Machain wanted the federal district court to rule that the ATCA authorized the creation of international torts. While the court was asked by the DOJ to apply Mexican tort law, the court created an international tort of kidnapping. Does the Supreme Court address this?

12. The Supreme Court in *Sosa* offers two propositions or inferences supported by the history of the ATCA. Are these tenable?

13. The Supreme Court goes on to discuss five reasons for judicial caution. Are they reasonable? Do they help DGI and DGINDO?

14. Justice Scalia prefers a different route, one that more certainly closes the door that the decision left ajar to new causes of action. Why? Which do you prefer? Which view provides more predictability? Which view would DGI and DGINDO prefer?

15. Is there sufficient support to the Court's conclusion that the detention and transportation of Alvarez–Machain did not violate the law of nations?

16. A further criticism of the TVPA is its retroactive application. See *Alvarez–Machain v. United States,* 107 F.3d 696 (9th Cir.1996), *cert. denied,* 522 U.S. 814, 118 S.Ct. 60, 139 L.Ed.2d 23 (1997). There is a ten year statute of limitations in the TVPA that has been ruled subject to "equitable" tolling. See *Hilao v. Estate of Marcos,* 103 F.3d 767 (9th Cir.1996).

17. A criticism of the Department of Justice's argument that the ATCA is merely jurisdictional and does not provide for a cause of action is addressed in *Contemporary Practice of the United States Relating to International Law, Department of Justice Position in Unocal Case* (edited by Sean D. Murphy), 97 Am.J. Int'l L. 703 (2003).

PART B. ATCA BASED SUITS AGAINST CORPORATIONS

Most of the first modern era ATCA cases (post *Filartiga*) involved suits against foreign officials who had allegedly caused harm to their own nations in their countries. The foreign officials were served with process when they travelled to the United States. It was not long before suits were expanded in two ways—the allegations were for actions that did not fit into the traditional definition of abuses of human rights (e.g., torture, extrajudicial killing) and the defendants were often non-state actors, especially U.S. corporations. Cases were not very consistent on either the expansion of the role of the ATCA to new areas or new defendants. But a few observations may be made. The ATCA is more than a basis for jurisdiction, it creates limited causes of actions. Those causes of action clearly include violations of human rights that are by consensus serious, such as torture, slavery, genocide and extrajudicial killing, but they do not include the use of those terms in a wider context. Genocide does not mean cultural genocide. Violations of a nation's environmental laws do not rise to create an international law norm of environmental law. As to the role of a corporation as a defendant, the issue is the corporation as a defendant, not officials of the corporation as defendants. The latter seems well-settled; individuals who are officials of corporations abroad and commit acts which constitute violations of international are actionable under the ATCA. The more difficult question has been whether the corporation qua corporation is a proper defendant under the ATCA. This part explores both these issues.

DOE v. UNOCAL CORP.

Federal District Court, Central District for California, 2000.
110 F.Supp.2d 1294.

[*Doe* was a class action brought by Burmese nationals under the ATCA, RICO, and federal question jurisdiction. The plaintiffs claimed that Unocal paid the Burma military junta to provide security and labor for the construction of a gas pipeline in Burma, knowing that the workers may have been forced labor. Unocal's actions were alleged to constitute international human rights violations. The extract from the district court's decision is included because it addresses the issue of a private entity as a defendant. Omitted from the extract are very extensive factual details.]

LEW, DISTRICT COURT JUDGE

The Second Circuit's decision in *Filártiga* marked the beginning of a new era of reliance on section 1350 in international human rights cases and was the first Circuit decision interpreting the ATCA. * * * This holding left open whether the ATCA applies *only* to state actors or also to non-state actors. Four years later, in *Tel–Oren v. Libyan Arab Republic,* 726 F.2d 774 (D.C.Cir.1984), Judge Harry T. Edwards commented that individual liability was available under the ATCA for a handful of acts including piracy and slave trading. However, Judge Edwards limited the application of the ATCA to private defendants by "declin[ing] to read section 1350 to cover torture by non-state actors, absent guidance from the Supreme Court on the statute's use of the term 'law of nations.'"

In *In re Estate of Ferdinand E. Marcos Human Rights Litigation* ("Estate I"), 978 F.2d 493 (9th Cir.1992), the Ninth Circuit stated without significant analysis that "[o]nly individuals who have acted under official authority or under color of such authority may violate international law...." More recently, the Ninth Circuit noted, without comment on its decision in *Estate I,* that it did "not need to reach the issue of whether the law of nations applies to private as opposed to government conduct." *Hamid v. Price Waterhouse,* 51 F.3d 1411, 1417–18 (9th Cir.1995). However, the Second Circuit's decision in *Kadic* provides a reasoned analysis of the scope of the private individual's liability for violations of international law. *Kadic v. Karadzic,* 70 F.3d 232 (2d Cir. 1995). There, the court disagreed with the proposition "that the law of nations, as understood in the modern era, confines its reach to state action. Instead, [the court held] that certain forms of conduct violate the law of nations whether undertaken by those acting under the auspices of a state or only as private individuals." While crimes such as torture and summary execution are proscribed by international law only when committed by state officials or under color of law, the law of nations has historically been applied to private actors for the crimes of piracy and slave trading, and for certain war crimes.

"The 'color of law' jurisprudence of 42 U.S.C. § 1983 is a relevant guide to whether a defendant has engaged in official action for purposes of jurisdiction under the Alien Tort Claims Act." A private individual acts under "color of law" within the meaning of section 1983 when he acts together with state officials or with significant state aid.

Both the Ninth Circuit and the Supreme Court have recognized that "cases deciding when private action might be deemed that of the state have not been a model of consistency."

Here, Plaintiffs present evidence demonstrating that before joining the Project, Unocal knew that the military had a record of committing human rights abuses; that the Project hired the military to provide security for the Project, a military that forced villagers to work and entire villages to relocate for the benefit of the Project; that the military, while forcing villagers to work and relocate, committed numerous acts of violence; and that Unocal knew or should have known that the military did commit, was committing, and would continue to commit these tortious acts. * * * Unocal and SLORC (State Law and Order Restoration Council) shared the goal of a profitable project. However, this shared goal does not establish joint action. Plaintiffs present no evidence that Unocal "participated in or influenced" the military's unlawful conduct; nor do Plaintiffs present evidence that Unocal "conspired" with the military to commit the challenged conduct.

The joint action cases address situations in which a private individual, acting in concert with the government, commits the challenged acts. In this case, the government committed the challenged acts. In order for a private individual to be liable for a section 1983 violation when the state actor commits the challenged conduct, the plaintiff must establish that the private individual was the proximate cause of the violation. In order to establish proximate cause, a plaintiff must prove that the private individuals exercised *control* over the government official's decision to commit the section 1983 violation. In this case, Plaintiffs present no evidence Unocal "controlled" the Myanmar military's decision to the commit the alleged tortious acts. Accordingly, Plaintiffs' claims that Unocal acted under "color of law" for purposes of the ATCA fail as a matter of law.

As discussed above, individual liability under the ATCA may be established for acts rising to the level of slavery or slave trading. Plaintiffs contend that forced labor is "modern slavery" and is therefore one of the "handful of crimes" to which individual liability under section 1350 attaches. Unocal, on the other hand, argues that the Myanmar military's use of forced labor is more akin to a public service requirement of limited duration than to slavery.

In international law, the prohibition of recourse to forced labour has its origin in the efforts made by the international community to eradicate slavery, its institutions and similar practices, since forced labour is considered to be one of these slavery-like practices.... Although certain instruments, and particularly those adopted at the beginning of the nineteenth century, define slavery in a restrictive manner, the prohibition of slavery must now be understood as covering all contemporary manifestations of this practice.

In this case, there are no facts suggesting that Unocal sought to employ forced or slave labor. In fact, the Joint Venturers expressed concern that the Myanmar government was utilizing forced labor in connection with the Project. In turn, the military made efforts to conceal its use of forced labor. The evidence does suggest that Unocal knew that forced labor was being utilized and that the Joint Venturers benefitted from the practice. However, because such a showing is insufficient to establish liability under international law, Plaintiffs' claim against Unocal for forced labor under the Alien Tort Claims Act fails as a matter of law.* * *

For the reasons set forth above, Unocal's motion for summary judgment as to Plaintiffs' federal claims is GRANTED and Plaintiffs' state law claims are dismissed without prejudice.

DOE v. UNOCAL CORP.

United States Court of Appeals, Ninth Circuit, 2002.
395 F.3d 932.

[After the district court held that Unocal could not be held liable under Alien Tort Claims Act (ATCA) and RICO, the matter was appealed to the Ninth Circuit.]

PREGERSON, CIRCUIT JUDGE.

* * * Unocal urges us to apply not international law, but the law of the state where the underlying events occurred, i.e., Myanmar. Where, as in the present case, only *jus cogens* violations are alleged—i.e., violations of norms of international law that are binding on nations even if they do not agree to them—it may, however, be preferable to apply international law rather than the law of any particular state, such as the state where the underlying events occurred or the forum state. The reason is that, by definition, the law of any particular state is either identical to the *jus cogens* norms of international law, or it is invalid. Moreover, "reading § 1350 as essentially a jurisdictional grant only and then looking to [foreign or] domestic tort law to provide the cause of action mutes the grave *international law* aspect of the tort, reducing it to no more (or less) than a garden-variety municipal tort," i.e., reducing it to a tort "relating to the internal government of a state of nation (as contrasted with *international*)." * * * We conclude that given the record in the present case, application of international law is appropriate.

Plaintiffs further allege that the Myanmar military murdered, raped or tortured a number of the plaintiffs. * * * According to Plaintiffs' deposition testimony, all of the acts of murder, rape, and torture alleged by Plaintiffs occurred in furtherance of the forced labor program. * * * [F]orced labor is a modern variant of slavery and does therefore never require state action to give rise to liability under the ATCA.

* * * The same reasons that convinced us earlier that Unocal may be liable * * * for aiding and abetting the Myanmar Military in subjecting Plaintiffs to forced labor also convince us now that Unocal may likewise be liable under this standard for aiding and abetting the Myanmar Military in subjecting Plaintiffs to murder and rape. We conclude, however, that as a matter of law, Unocal is not similarly liable for torture in this case. * * * The record does not * * * contain sufficient evidence to establish a claim of torture (other than by means of rape) involving Plaintiffs.

Viewing the evidence in the light most favorable to Plaintiffs, we conclude that there are genuine issues of material fact whether Unocal's conduct met the *actus reus* and *mens rea* requirements for liability under the ATCA for aiding and abetting murder and rape. Accordingly, we reverse the District Court's grant of Unocal's motion for summary judgment on Plaintiffs' murder and rape claims under the ATCA. By contrast, the record does not contain sufficient evidence to support Plaintiffs' claims of torture. We therefore affirm the District Court's grant of Unocal's motion for summary judgment on Plaintiffs' torture claims.* * *

For the foregoing reasons, we REVERSE the District Court's grant of summary judgment in favor of Unocal on Plaintiffs' ATCA claims for forced labor, murder, and rape. We however AFFIRM the District Court's grant of summary judgment in favor of Unocal on Plaintiffs' ATCA claims for torture. We further AFFIRM the District Court's dismissal of all of the *Doe*-Plaintiffs' claims against the Myanmar Military and Myanmar Oil. We REMAND the case to the District Court for further proceedings consistent with this opinion.

REVERSED IN PART, AFFIRMED IN PART and REMANDED.

[A majority of the nonrecused active 9th Circuit judges voted by a majority to have the case reheard by the en banc court. See 2003 WL 359787 (9th Cir.). In December, 2004, several months after the Supreme Court *Sosa* decision and only one day before the scheduled rehearing, Unocal settled. The settlement terms remain confidential, but both sides concurred that Unocal agreed to provide funds for the improvement of living conditions, health care and education, as well as to "protect the rights of people from the pipeline region."]

BEANAL v. FREEPORT–McMORAN, INC.

United States Court of Appeals, Fifth Circuit, 1999.
197 F.3d 161.

STEWART, CIRCUIT JUDGE:

[Beanal] alleged that Freeport engaged in environmental abuses, human rights violations, and cultural genocide. Specifically, he alleged that Freeport mining operations had caused harm and injury to the Amungme's environment and habitat. He further alleged that Freeport engaged in cultural genocide by destroying the Amungme's habitat and religious symbols, thus forcing the Amungme to relocate. Finally, he asserted that Freeport's private security force acted in concert with the Republic to violate international human rights. Freeport moved to dismiss Beanal's claims. The district court in April 1997 issued [an] Order dismissing Beanal's claims. [T]he district court instructed Beanal to amend his complaint to state more specifically his claims of genocide and individual human rights violations. In March 1998, the district court granted Freeport's motion to strike Beanal's Third Amended Complaint and dismissed his claims with prejudice. Beanal now appeals the district court's rulings below.[1]

* * * Under § 1350. Beanal's allegations under the ATS can be divided into three categories: (1) individual human rights violations; (2) environmental torts; and (3) genocide and cultural genocide. We address each in turn.

1. *Individual Human Rights Violations.* * * * Essentially, Beanal complains that Freeport engaged in the following conduct; (1) surveillance; (2) mental torture; (3) death threats; and (4) house arrest. * * * Freeport claims that Beanal failed to plead the requisite state action to support his claims under the ATS. * * * After reviewing Beanal's pleadings de novo, we agree with the district court's ruling. Beanal's complaint merely makes conclusory allegations. Beanal's claims are devoid of names, dates, locations, times or any facts that would put Freeport on notice as to what conduct supports the nature of his claims. * * * [W]e agree with the district court's observation in that, "Beanal has made a superficial effort to personalize his complaint in order to comply with the court's April and August Order."[3]

2. *Environmental Torts and Abuses.* Next, Beanal argues that Freeport through its mining activities engaged in environmental abuses which violated international law. In his Third Amended Complaint, Beanal alleges the following:

---

1. *Amici Curiae* have submitted briefs to support Beanal's claims. They include the Sierra Club, Earthrights International, Center for Constitutional Rights, Center for Justice and Accountability, and the Four Directions Council.

3. A comparison of Beanal's complaints reveals that Beanal attempted to personalize his Third Amended Complaint by merely substituting the plural subject, "Plaintiffs," with his name. As such, we agree with the district court in that "it is apparent that Beanal has peppered his own name throughout these paragraphs without averring facts giving rise to the claim."

FREEPORT * * * deposits approximately 100,000 tons of tailings per day in the Aghwagaon, Otomona and Akjwa Rivers. Said tailings have diverted the natural flow of the rivers and have rendered the natural waterways of the plaintiff unusable for traditional uses including bathing and drinking. Furthermore, upon information and belief, the heavy metal content of the tailings have and/or will affect the body tissue of the aquatic life in said rivers. Additionally, tailings have blocked the main flow of the Ajkwa River causing overflow of the tailings into lowland rain forest vegetation destroying the same.

FREEPORT * * * has diverted the aforesaid rivers greatly increasing the likelihood of future flooding in Timika, the home of the plaintiff, TOM BEANAL.

FREEPORT * * * operations has caused or will cause through the course of its operations 3 billion tons of "overburden" to be dumped into the upper Wanagon and Carstensz creating the likely risk of massive landslides directly injurious to the plaintiff. Furthermore, said "overburden" creates acid rock damage which has created acid streams and rendering the Lake Wanagon an "acid lake" extremely high in copper concentrations,....

* * *

Beanal and the *amici* refer the court to several sources of international environmental law to show that the alleged environmental abuses caused by Freeport's mining activities are cognizable under international law. Chiefly among these are the *Principles of International Environmental Law I: Frameworks, Standards and Implementation* 183–18 (Phillip Sands ed,. 1995) and the *Rio Declaration on Environment and Development*, June 13, 1992, U.N. Nevertheless, "[i]t is only where the nations of the world have demonstrated that the wrong is of mutual and not merely several, concern, by means of express international accords, that a wrong generally recognized becomes an international law violation in the meaning of the [ATS]." *Filartiga*, 630 F.2d at 888. Thus, the ATS "applies only to shockingly egregious violations of universally recognized principles of international law." Beanal fails to show that these treaties and agreements enjoy universal acceptance in the international community. The sources of international law cited by Beanal and the *amici* merely refer to a general sense of environmental responsibility and state abstract rights and liberties devoid of articulable or discernable standards and regulations to identify practices that constitute international environmental abuses or torts. [F]ederal courts should exercise extreme caution when adjudicating environmental claims under international law to insure that environmental policies of the United States do not displace environmental policies of other governments. Furthermore, the argument to abstain from interfering in a sovereign's environmental practices carries persuasive force especially when the alleged environmental torts and abuses occur within the sovereign's borders and do not affect neighboring countries.[6] Therefore, the district court did not err when it concluded that Beanal failed to show in his pleadings that Freeport's mining activities constitute environmental torts or abuses under international law.

3. *Genocide and Cultural Genocide.*

A review of Beanal's Third Amended Complaint reveals that his claim of genocide suffers from the same pleading defects that plagued his other claims of individual human rights violations. Beanal's complaint is saturated with conclusory allegations devoid of any underlying facts to support his claim of genocide. Notwithstanding Beanal's failure to allege facts to support sufficiently his claim of genocide, Beanal and the *amici* in their respective briefs urge this court to recognize cultural genocide as a discrete violation of international law. Again, they refer the court to several international conventions, agreements, and declarations. Nevertheless, a review of these documents reveals that the documents make pronouncements and proclamations of an amorphous right to "enjoy culture," or a right to "freely pursue" culture, or a right to cultural development.[7] They nonetheless fail to proscribe or identify conduct that would constitute an act of cultural genocide. As such, it would be problematic to apply these vague and declaratory international documents to Beanal's claim because they are devoid of discernable means to define or identify conduct that constitutes a violation of international law. Furthermore, Beanal has not demonstrated that cultural genocide has achieved universal acceptance as a discrete violation of international law. Thus, it would be imprudent for a United States tribunal to declare an amorphous cause of action under international law that has failed to garner universal acceptance.[8] Accordingly, we find that Beanal's claims of genocide and cultural genocide are facially insufficient to withstand a motion to dismiss.

* * * In light of the gravity and far ranging implications of Beanal's allegations, not only did the court give Beanal several opportunities to amend his complaint to conform with the minimum requisites as set forth in the federal rules, the court also conscientiously provided Beanal with a road-map as to how to amend his complaint to survive a motion to dismiss assuming that Beanal could marshal facts sufficient to comply with the

---

6. Although Beanal cites the Rio Declaration to support his claims of environmental torts and abuses under international law, nonetheless, the express language of the declaration appears to cut against Beanal's claims. Principle 2 on the first page of the Rio Declaration asserts that states have the "sovereign right to exploit their own resources pursuant to their own environmental and developmental policies," but also have "the responsibility to ensure that activities within their jurisdiction or control do not cause damage to the environment or other States or areas beyond the limits of national jurisdiction." Beanal does not allege in his pleadings that Freeport's mining activities in Indonesia have affected environmental conditions in other countries.

7. Examples of the documents cited by Beanal and the *amici* are the International Covenant on Civil and Political Rights, (ethnic minorities "shall not be denied the right ... to enjoy their own culture."); International Covenant on Economic Social and Cultural Rights, (all peoples enjoy a right to "freely pursue their ... cultural development."); Universal Declaration on Human Rights, (all persons are entitled to cultural rights indispensable for dignity).

8. In earlier drafts of the Convention on Genocide, there were proposals to incorporate cultural genocide into the definition of genocide. However, after much debate, the concept of cultural genocide was explicitly excluded.

federal rules. Nevertheless, Beanal was unable to put before the court a complaint that met minimum pleading requirements under the federal rules. Accordingly, we AFFIRM the district court.

KIOBEL v. ROYAL DUTCH PETROLEUM CO.

United States Court of Appeals, Second Circuit, 2010.
621 F.3d 111.

Once again we consider a case brought under the Alien Tort Statute ("ATS"), a jurisdictional provision unlike any other in American law and of a kind apparently unknown to any other legal system in the world. Passed by the first Congress in 1789, the ATS lay largely dormant for over 170 years. In light of the universal recognition of *Filartiga* as the font of ATS litigation—including by Judge Leval, *see* Concurring Op., we do not understand Judge Leval's assertion that our decision conflicts with "two centuries" of precedent.

Since that time, the ATS has given rise to an abundance of litigation in U.S. district courts. For the first fifteen years after *Filartiga*—that is, from 1980 to the mid–1990s—aliens brought ATS suits in our courts only against notorious foreign *individuals;* the first ATS case alleging, in effect, that a corporation (or "juridical" person) was an "enemy of all mankind" apparently was brought as recently as 1997 [Doe v. Unocal].

Such civil lawsuits, alleging heinous crimes condemned by customary international law, often involve a variety of issues unique to ATS litigation, not least the fact that the events took place abroad and in troubled or chaotic circumstances. The resulting complexity and uncertainty-combined with the fact that juries hearing ATS claims are capable of awarding multibillion-dollar verdicts has led many defendants to settle ATS claims prior to trial. Thus, our Court has published only nine significant decisions on the ATS since 1980 (seven of the nine coming in the last decade) and the Supreme Court in its entire history has decided only one ATS case. [*Sosa*, 542 U.S. 692, 124 S.Ct. 2739].

Because appellate review of ATS suits has been so uncommon, there remain a number of unresolved issues lurking in our ATS jurisprudence* * *. This case involves one such unresolved issue: Does the jurisdiction granted by the ATS extend to civil actions brought against corporations under the law of nations?

Plaintiffs are residents of Nigeria who claim that Dutch, British, and Nigerian corporations engaged in oil exploration and production aided and abetted the Nigerian government in committing violations of the law of nations. They seek damages under the ATS, and thus their suit may proceed only if the ATS provides jurisdiction over tort actions brought against corporations under customary international law.

A legal culture long accustomed to imposing liability on corporations may, at first blush, assume that corporations must be subject to tort liability under the ATS, just as corporations are generally liable in tort under our domestic law (what international law calls "municipal law"). But the substantive law that determines our jurisdiction under the ATS is neither the domestic law of the United States nor the domestic law of any other country. By conferring subject matter jurisdiction over a limited number of offenses defined by *customary international law,* the ATS requires federal courts to look beyond rules of domestic law—however well-established they may be—to examine the specific and universally accepted rules that the nations of the world treat as binding *in their dealings with one another.*[11]

Our recognition of a norm of liability as a matter of *domestic law,* therefore, cannot create a norm of customary international law. In other words, the fact that corporations are liable as juridical persons under domestic law does not mean that they are liable under international law (and, therefore, under the ATS). Moreover, the fact that a legal norm is found in most or even all "civilized nations" does not make that norm a part of customary international law. As we explained in *Filartiga:*

> [T]he mere fact that every nation's municipal [*i.e.,* domestic] law may prohibit theft does not incorporate "the Eighth Commandment, 'Thou Shalt not steal' . . . into the law of nations." It is only where the nations of the world have demonstrated that the wrong is of mutual, and not merely several, concern, by means of express international accords, that a wrong generally recognized becomes an international law violation within the meaning of the [ATS].[630 F.2d at 888.]

Accordingly, absent a relevant treaty of the United States—and none is relied on here—we must ask whether a plaintiff bringing an ATS suit against a corporation has alleged a violation of customary international law.

From the beginning * * * the principle of individual liability for violations of international law has been limited to natural persons—not "juridical" persons such as corporations—because the moral responsibility for a crime so heinous and unbounded as to rise to the level of an "international crime" has rested solely with the individual men and women who have perpetrated it. As the Nuremberg tribunal unmistakably set forth in explaining the rationale for individual liability for violations of international law: "Crimes against international law are committed by men, not by abstract entities, and only by punishing individuals who commit such crimes can the provisions of international law be enforced." *The Nurnberg Trial (United States v. Goering),* 6 F.R.D. 69, 110.

After Nuremberg, as new international tribunals have been created, the customary international law of human rights has remained focused not on abstract entities but on the individual men and women who have committed international crimes universally recognized by the nations of

---

11. The idea that corporations are "persons" with duties, liabilities, and rights has a long history in American domestic law. The history of corporate rights and obligations under *domestic law* is, however, entirely irrelevant to the issue before us—namely, the treatment of corporations as a matter of *customary international law.*

the world. This principle has taken its most vivid form in the recent design of the International Criminal Court ("ICC"). Although there was a proposal at the Rome Conference to grant the ICC jurisdiction over corporations and other "juridical" persons, that proposal was soundly rejected, and the Rome Statute, the ICC's constitutive document, hews to the tenet set forth in Nuremberg that international norms should be enforced by the punishment of the individual men and women who violate them.

The United States has not ratified the Rome Statute. Under the Clinton Administration, the U.S. delegation voted against the text adopted in Rome in 1998, in part because of concerns that the treaty "could inhibit the ability of the United States to use its military to meet alliance obligations and participate in multinational operations, including humanitarian interventions." Despite those concerns, the United States signed the Rome Statute on December 31, 2000, the last day it was open for signature, under the outgoing Clinton Administration. On May 6, 2002, the Bush Administration notified the United Nations that the United States did not intend to become a party, an act popularly referred to as "un sign[ing]." However limited the value of the Rome Statute in determining what customary international law *is,* a demonstrated lack of consensus amongst its signatories about a particular norm is valuable evidence of what customary international law *is not.*

In short, because customary international law imposes individual liability for a limited number of international crimes—including war crimes, crimes against humanity (such as genocide), and torture—we have held that the ATS provides jurisdiction over claims in tort against individuals who are alleged to have committed such crimes. * * *[H]owever, customary international law has steadfastly rejected the notion of corporate liability for international crimes, and no international tribunal has ever held a corporation liable for a violation of the law of nations.

We must conclude, therefore, that insofar as plaintiffs bring claims under the ATS against corporations, plaintiffs fail to allege violations of the law of nations, and plaintiffs' claims fall outside the limited jurisdiction provided by the ATS.

* * *

We pause briefly to acknowledge and reply to the separate opinion of our colleague, Judge Leval. As an initial matter, we are perplexed by Judge Leval's repeated insistence that there is no "basis" for our holding because "[n]o precedent of international law endorses" it. In an ATS suit, we may apply only those international norms that are "specific, universal, and obligatory." As a result, the responsibility of establishing a norm of customary international law lies with those wishing to invoke it, and in the absence of sources of international law endorsing (or refuting) a norm, the norm simply cannot be applied in a suit grounded on customary international law under the ATS. Thus, even if there were, as Judge Leval claims, an absence of sources of international law addressing corporate liability, that supposed lack of authority would actually *support* our holding. By contrast, to support Judge Leval's proposed rule, there would need to be not only a few, but so many sources of international law calling for corporate liability that the norm could be regarded as "universal." As it happens, no corporation has ever been subject to *any* form of liability under the customary international law of human rights, and thus the ATS, the remedy Congress has chosen, simply does not confer jurisdiction over suits against corporations.[22]

We agree with Judge Leval that whether to enact a civil remedy for violations of customary international law is a matter to be determined by each State; the United States has done so in enacting the ATS. But the ATS does not specify who is liable; it imposes liability only for a "violation of the law of nations," and thus it leaves the question of the nature and scope of liability—who is liable for what—to customary international law. [T]herefore, whether a defendant is liable under the ATS depends entirely upon whether that defendant is subject to liability under customary international law. It is inconceivable that a defendant who is *not liable* under customary international law could be *liable* under the ATS.

* * *[N]othing in this opinion limits or forecloses suits under the ATS against the individual perpetrators of violations of customary international law-including the employees, managers, officers, and directors of a corporation-as well as anyone who purposefully aids and abets a violation of customary international law. Nor does anything in this opinion limit or foreclose criminal, administrative, or civil actions against *any* corporation under a body of law *other than customary international law*-for example, the domestic laws of any State. And, of course, nothing in this opinion limits or forecloses legislative action by Congress.

* * *

We must* * *leave it to the reader to decide whether any of Judge Leval's charges, individually or in combination, are a fair reading of our opinion. In so doing we are confident that if our effort is misguided, higher judicial authority is available to tell us so.

LEVAL, Circuit Judge, concurring only in the judgment:

The majority opinion deals a substantial blow to international law and its undertaking to protect fundamental human rights. According to the rule my colleagues have created, one who earns profits by commercial exploitation of abuse of fundamental human rights can successfully shield those profits from victims' claims for compensation simply by taking the precaution of conducting the heinous operation in the corporate form. Without any support in either the precedents or the scholarship of

---

22. * * * We do not rest our analysis of customary international law on the district court ATS decisions on which Judge Leval relies. Indeed, even if we were to accord those district court cases the merit Judge Leval seems to believe they deserve, the opinions of domestic courts citing domestic courts alone for propositions of customary international law do not constitute evidence of a "specific, universal, and obligatory" norm of the kind necessary to impose judgment under the ATS.

international law, the majority take the position that corporations, and other juridical entities, are not subject to international law, and for that reason such violators of fundamental human rights are free to retain any profits so earned without liability to their victims.

The rule in cases under the ATS is quite simple. The law of nations sets worldwide norms of conduct, prohibiting certain universally condemned heinous acts. That body of law, however, takes no position on whether its norms may be enforced by civil actions for compensatory damages. It leaves that decision to be separately decided by each nation. The ATS confers on the U.S. courts jurisdiction to entertain civil suits for violations of the law of nations. In the United States, if a plaintiff in a suit under the ATS shows that she is the victim of a tort committed in violation of the norms of the law of nations, the court has jurisdiction to hear the case and to award compensatory damages against the tortfeasor. That is what the Supreme Court explained in Sosa. No principle of domestic or international law supports the majority's conclusion that the norms enforceable through the ATS-such as the prohibition by international law of genocide, slavery, war crimes, piracy, etc.-apply only to natural persons and not to corporations, leaving corporations immune from suit and free to retain profits earned through such acts.

I am in full agreement that this Complaint must be dismissed. It fails to state a proper legal claim of entitlement to relief. The Complaint alleges that the Appellants—the parent holding companies at the apex of the huge Royal Dutch Shell international, integrated oil enterprise-are liable under the ATS on the theory that their actions aided the government of Nigeria in inflicting human rights abuses on the Ogoni peoples in the jungles of Nigeria. The allegations fall short of mandatory pleading standards. * * * [T]he complaint in this action would need to plead specific facts that support a plausible inference that the Appellants aided the government of Nigeria with a purpose to bring about the Nigerian government's alleged violations of the human rights of the plaintiffs. [T]he allegations of the Complaint do not succeed in meeting that test. I therefore agree with the majority that the claims against the Appellants must be dismissed.

QUESTIONS AND COMMENTS

1. *Doe v. Unocal* established the possibility for corporation liability for participation in human rights abuses abroad, at least in the Ninth Circuit. Does that seem to have been the intention of the FTCA's drafters in 1789? Assuming it was not, does the language of the ATCA fairly encompass actions against non-individuals? The issue of corporate liability under the ATCA is chronologued in *Presbyterian Church of Sudan v. Talisman Energy, Inc.*, 244 F.Supp.2d 289, 308 (S.D.N.Y. 2003). See, e.g. Courtney Shaw, *Uncertain Justice: Liability of Multinationals Under the Alien Tort Claims Act*, 54 Stan.L.Rev. 1359 (2002). But that was before the *Kiobel* decision.

2. Is it the use of forced labor that is a tort, or the way in which forced laborers were treated, such as intentional beatings, etc.? What tort law

applies—the law of Indonesia or the law of the U.S. forum or perhaps an international tort law?

3.   The first modern era cases using the ATCA were against either state officials or the state itself. Perhaps that justifies the suit against the government of Myanmar or the members of the military that abused the labor. But that does not mean private actors come under the Act. How did the federal district court in *Unocal* make the shift from states as defendants to foreign corporations as defendants? Did Unocal act in concert with the Myanmar government? Does the mere fact that there is a contractual joint venture to engage in production constitute the joint action for liability under the ATCA?

4.   What advice with respect to avoiding joint action should be given to Unocal if it enters into a similar venture elsewhere? Does a company always know of such abuses? Do the *Unocal* decisions comply with the *Sosa* ruling?

5.   Should corporate liability exist only when corporate employees actually participate jointly with government officials in the violations of international law? See Bauman v. Daimler–Chrysler Corp., 579 F.3d 1088 (9th Cir. 2009).

6.   A requirement of the ATCA is that there be a violation of international law. Does the use of forced labor violate international law? If slavery is defined broadly, does it include voluntary work at less than subsistence wages?

7.   *Unocal* cites the U.S. Supreme Court *Butler v. Perry* decision that allowed Florida to force citizens to work on maintaining its roads. The work was a public duty. Now that the United States has a volunteer military, would it be slavery to restore the draft? Note the courts preference to discuss the German forced labor during World War II rather than maintaining Florida's roads. The German experience (U.S. cases) suggests that necessity is a defense, such as when the corporations were ordered to increase production and compelled to use government provided workers, under threat of severe sanctions for refusing.

8.   On appeal to the Ninth Circuit the court first considered the existence of a tort that violated the law of nations. It easily recognized torture, murder and slavery as *jus cogens* violations, and thought U.S. case law to view forced labor as "a modern variant" of slavery. Then Unocal was liable?

9.   The district court had found that Unocal's conduct did not constitute "active participation." How can the Ninth Circuit conclude otherwise if it recognizes any discretion on the part of the lower court?

10.   Unocal argued that Myanmar law should apply to determine the existence of the tort, not international law. Effective?

11.   Is it appropriate for the court to use criminal law cases for support when these acts were civil?

12.   What is the test that the court finally uses?

13.   The plaintiffs also alleged that the Myanmar military murdered, raped or tortured some of the plaintiffs. Isn't that a stronger case? The *Unocal* settlement leaves many of these and other questions unanswered. The *Sosa* decision of the Supreme Court also leaves much for future determina-

tion. Would you recommend that DGI and DGINDO settle by considering what little is known about the *Unocal* settlement?

14. The *Beanal* decision expands the idea of violations of international law from human rights abuses to environmental damage and "cultural genocide." With regard to the charges of human rights abuses, do the specific charges all constitute human rights violations?

15. Does the court agree that environmental degradation and cultural genocide meet the test of being torts that violate international law? There certainly seems to be some generally recognized environmental rules. The plaintiff refers the court to the 1992 Rio Declaration and a 1995 treatise on the principles of international environmental law. Do they establish international law? The United States has environmental laws; are there not also international environmental laws? The Rio Declaration does say that in exploiting resources the process should not cause "damage to the environment or other states or areas beyond the limits of national jurisdiction."

16. Cultural genocide uses a strong word in "genocide" and one difficult to define in "cultural". Put together what do they mean to the plaintiff? Is the plaintiff any more specific about cultural genocide than about human rights abuses? There is a Convention on the Prevention and Punishment of the Crime of Genocide. Doesn't that apply here? What might be cultural genocide—the destruction of the pyramids, the removal of most of the historical treasures from a nation's national museum in time of war or conflict, e.g., Iraq?

17. The majority opinion in *Kiobel* seems quite simple, all three judges agreed that the plaintiffs failed to plead sufficiently specific facts of human rights abuses to constitute a violation of customary international law. What divided the court was whether there is any customary international law applicable to corporations. Why did the court split over that issue?

18. Why aren't these suits brought against the officials rather than the corporation?

Is it because large sums are sought and corporations have deeper pockets? Why aren't they brought against the clearer perpetrator—the foreign country or its officials? Countries have deep pockets.

19. Would judgments against the foreign country or its officials be upheld in the foreign country?

20. Isn't the scholarship Judge Leval refers to largely aspirational?

21. The long saga of Texaco/Chevron and Ecuador continues, apparently making it the world's biggest dispute, exceeding even the suit against Russia by shareholders of Yukos Oil Company. First filed in the United States (New York) in 1993 and dismissed on *forum non conveniens* grounds, the plaintiffs took the (at the time) unconventional step and filed the suit in Lago Agrio, Ecuador, a small town near the Colombian border. Chevron both defended that suit and took the matter to arbitration. The Ecuadorian court granted a $8.6 billion judgment in early 2011, to be doubled in 15 days unless the oil company publicly apologized. Instead, Chevron went back to the New York federal court and obtained a preliminary injunction against enforcement of the judgment. It further obtained an order from the Permanent Court of

Arbitration in The Hague barring enforcement of the judgment, followed by an award against Ecuador of $96 million. Chevron also filed a RICO civil lawsuit against the trial lawyers and consultants. The case may be followed on numerous websites. See "Chevron and Ecuador."

22. Corporations and the ATCA have set the pens of many to work. See, e.g., Michael D. Ramsey, International Law Limits on Investor Liability in Human Rights Litigation, 50 Harvard Int'l L.J. 271 (2009); Lucien J. Dhooge, A Modest Proposal to Amend the Alien Tort Statute to Provide Guidance to Transnational Corporations, 13 U.C.Davis J. Int'l L. & Pol'y 119 (2007); Joel Slawotsky, The New Global Financial Landscape: Why Egregious International Corporate Fraud Should Be Cognizable Under the Alien Tort Claims Act, 17 Duke J. Comp. & Int'l L. 131 (2006); Tarek F. Maassarani, Four Counts of Corporate Complicity: Alternate Forms of Accomplice Liability Under the Alien Tort Claims Act, 38 N.Y.U.J. Int'l & Pol. 39 (2005–2006).

PROBLEM 10.6 THE TAKING OF AN INVESTMENT BY A THIRD WORLD NATION; OBSTACLES TO RECOVERY; AND LUMP SUM SETTLEMENTS, CLAIMS COMMISSIONS, AND INSURANCE: FISHING RODS IN MARNESIA

SECTION I. THE SETTING

Marnesia is a South East Asian nation that has become an important exporter of assembled products. It is not a member of the WTO but it is a member of the World Bank and adheres to ICSID (International Centre for the Settlement of Investment Disputes). Along with Malaysia, Indonesia, Taiwan, Singapore and the Philippines, Marnesia offers a stable, low cost labor supply for numerous Japanese and U.S. owned investments. Marnesia was formerly a colony of a Western European nation. In the mid–1950s, a revolution overthrew the colonial government, creating a new nation which they named Marnesia. All property of the colonizing power was seized and, under newly adopted Marnesian law, compensation was paid amounting to about one-third of the value assigned by a Marnesian claims review commission. The expropriated companies were mainly extractive, export oriented petroleum and tin companies, plus a number of rubber plantations, and several other agricultural facilities. There was little industry on the island. The Marnesian law provided that because the property belonged to a former colonial power, a two-thirds deduction would be made from the valuation for unfair exploitation. No judicial review was allowed from decisions of the commission. Time heals many wounds, and by the early 1980s, Japanese and U.S. companies began to locate factories in Marnesia to produce products for sale in the United States and Europe.

One of the newer factories is wholly owned by RODCO, Inc., a Delaware chartered corporation with its principal place of business in

Denver. The company manufactures fishing rods and reels of U.S. design, but from parts manufactured in several of RODCO's Asian plants. About 30 percent of the parts are manufactured at the Marnesian plant, from local and imported raw materials.

Several years ago, the Marnesian government enacted mandatory joint venture legislation, requiring all new investment to be at least 51 percent Marnesian owned. The legislation did not provide for retroactive application. Nevertheless, the Marnesian government began to deny import permits, delay moving products through export inspections, and according to RODCO, generally harass foreign investors. Some government officials told RODCO officers that they would receive better treatment if they altered the company to a joint venture with majority local ownership. RODCO refused. Six months ago the government enacted a decree expropriating a list of 24 selected companies. They were all either Japanese or U.S. wholly owned subsidiaries. The only reasons given were in a statement by the Minister of Trade, who said the companies were those most belligerent in refusing to become joint ventures and in slowing the in-flow of technology to Marnesia.

The RODCO Marnesian subsidiary was on the list. Government officials took over physical possession of the plant. RODCO estimates the facility's worth at $5.4 million. RODCO officers were warned that any effort of the U.S. government on behalf of RODCO to pressure the Marnesian government to return the property or make prompt, adequate and effective compensation under what Marnesian officials termed the "U.S. view of international law," would result in the forfeiture of any right to compensation. Marnesian claims that all property owners are to be treated equally, whether domestic or foreign, and that no foreign property owner may have any greater rights, including the pressing of one's claim by its government. Marnesia has refused to participate in any ICSID dispute resolution proceedings. RODCO's Marnesian attorney has indicated that no suits claiming unlawful expropriations have moved beyond the opening of a case file. He has also withdrawn from representing RODCO because of threats from the government. He says it is doubtful that RODCO will find anyone in Marnesia willing to represent RODCO. The attorney believes that the government has placed a hold on the cases. The Marnesian president has spoken out strongly against the companies that have gone to court. He has said repeatedly that the companies will be paid as previously announced, and that the government is "working on" procedures to present claims. As house counsel in Denver, the board has placed you in charge of informing them about what has happened and advising whether RODCO will either get the plant back or be compensated. Unfortunately, the United States has been unable to convince Marnesia to sign a Bilateral Investment Treaty (BIT).

SECTION II. FOCUS OF CONSIDERATION

Although takeovers of foreign investments have nearly always been the product of political upheaval—sometimes partially caused by perceptions of foreign dominance of the means of production and distribution—they have many different characteristics. Some result from conflicts between a host nation government and a particular foreign business or businesses in a single industry. Others are the result of conflicts between two governments with consequences including the taking of foreign owned businesses. Still others are the result of internal conflicts between groups competing for power. Some takeovers result in the property being returned, either soon after intervention, or after a subsequent change in government policy, or, more likely, a change in the government itself. Often the property is never returned. Some takeovers are discriminatory, applying only to the property of certain nations, or to certain industries or specific companies. Some takeovers are retaliatory, usually motivated by an action of the government whose national's property was seized.

Two issues arise. First is the *right* to take property. That right is conceded—it is a long held norm of international law, and in most nations a principle of domestic law. But the right is based on the existence of a public purpose. Should what constitutes a proper public purpose in one nation be measured from abroad. Even if such review is appropriate, there may be differences identifying the applicable norms for the determination of a valid public purpose. It is the second issue which is of primary importance. That is the payment of compensation. The right to some compensation is usually acknowledged, but the appropriate measurement, including deductions, and issues of how much is to be paid, when it is to be paid, and in what form it is to be paid, permeate the conflicts of the taking of foreign property. Add to this the issue of the applicability of international law or domestic law, and if international law is to be applied, what are the rules of international law, and one begins to understand the complexity of the issues. The stakes are high.

Of additional importance is the fact that the issues of taking foreign property are clouded by a conflict of property versus poverty. Developing nations often urge a redistribution of world resources, blaming the industrialized sector for their continued state of lesser development. The taking of foreign property is thus viewed by some to be a part of the larger redistribution of resources. The officers, directors and shareholders of RODCO are mainly concerned with how they may respond so as to minimize their losses. They sympathize with the need to improve living standards in many nations, but they do not believe they have contributed to world poverty. They have paid higher than average wages, have paid all Marnesian taxes and not engaged in transfer pricing, and believe they can establish that their rate of profit in Marnesia was only eight to nine percentage points higher than in the United States.

There have not been any major nationalizations since Iran in the 1970s. But there have been occasional claims against the nationalization of specific enterprises. *Elettronica Sicula S.p.A. (ELSI) Judgment (U.S. v. Italy)* went to the I.C.J. in 1989 on facts occurring in 1968. More recently a number of claims of expropriation have been arbitrated by ICSID at the World Bank, and under the NAFTA Chapter 11 dispute settlement process. In the middle of the first decade of the new century there were some nations with socialist leaders seeking state ownership of foreign owned investment, such as Venezuela's expropriations in 2008 of both several foreign owned (Mexican, French and Swiss) cement industries, and its steel production. Bolivia was also nationalizing foreign owned industries, and Paraguay seemed likely follow. Ecuador has proposed legislation prohibiting use of ICSID for dispute settlement, a position Marnesia is considering, and requiring any arbitration to be in Latin American forums. It is an old view in newer clothing.

The threat of nationalization may have been reduced by an awareness that nationalizations do not seem to have succeeded in raising the level of development, certainly not when the nationalization has been part of a socialist revolution. Other factors may have lessened the risk, such as the increased use of bilateral investment treaties, that often include expropriation compensation provisions. Furthermore, insuring against nationalization under the U.S. OPIC or World Bank MIGA programs, or private insurers, reduces the risk to foreign investors. Nevertheless, there is always the threat that a nation deeply indebted to the large capital exporting nations will succumb to a revolution based on promises to rid the nation of foreign dominance, including taking over foreign investments. The theory of nationalization remains important, including knowing about the defenses of sovereign immunity and act of state in expropriation cases. Additionally useful is knowing how to avoid and insure against expropriation risks.

Parts A and B of the problem consider the act of taking, compensation theory and exhausting local remedies. Parts C, D and E focus on obstacles in obtaining compensation, insurance, claims, commissions, and lump sum settlements.

SECTION III. READINGS, QUESTIONS AND COMMENTS

PART A. THE ACT OF TAKING

Since RODCO has never had its property seized, it would like to know more about the takeover and its consequences to the company. The company also wants you to apply as much pressure as possible on Marnesia through the Department of State. The president of RODCO said something at the last meeting about how "State helped United Fruit in Guatemala when the leftists took over their property back in the 50s, they should help us now. State messed up in Cuba with the Bay of Pigs, but maybe the U.S. could use some unmanned drones in Marnesia to protect our property." Other calmer views prevailed. But there was a strong consensus of hostility to a report presented to the meeting that disclosed that fishing equipment manufactured on RODCO machinery by the Marnesian company since the takeover was being sold in Canada.

The terminology of taking property is often confusing and confused. The initial stage, not always present, is taking physical possession of the facility—called *intervention*—without asserting national ownership. The business could be intervened and run either by government intervenors (management intervention) or run by the owners with supervision by the intervenors (supervision intervention).[a] Under intervention there is hope that the full management will be returned to the owners. If the nation takes title to the properties, the term may be given a more personal flavor, such as Mexicanization or Chileanization. RODCO has been Marnesian-ized. But those terms may also be used to encompass a wider scope of national acquisition of varying levels of the means of production and distribution, such as by a law applying only prospectively that requires host nation majority joint ventures for all new investment. That would not merit the label *expropriation*, and usually not *nationalization*, both of which tend to be used when a taking of currently privately held property is involved. Expropriation often is used to convey a more negative meaning than nationalization, but both are lawful acts if followed by payment under the applicable international law standard, and if they were undertaken for proper purposes. Finally, *confiscation* is usually associated with situations where no compensation is offered, or ultimately forthcoming, in an amount sufficient to "elevate" the taking to a "mere" expropriation or nationalization. Whatever we may wish to call the Marnesian actions, RODCO officials were removed from the plant by gun-carrying soldiers. The officials soon left for Denver. The board is less interested in semantics than what is likely to happen next, and how to get the property back or quickly paid for. We first turn to some UN General Assembly actions that illustrate the developments at the UN as third world member nations in the 1970s began to assert power and attempt to alter the earlier Resolution on Permanent Sovereignty.

RESOLUTION ON PERMANENT SOVEREIGNTY OVER NATURAL RESOURCES

Dec. 14, 1962, U.N.G.A. Res. 1803 (XVII), 17 U.N. GAOR, Supp. (No. 17) 15, U.N. Doc. A/5217 (1963), reprinted in 2 Int'l Legal Mat. 223 (1963).

The General Assembly

Declares that:

1.   The right of peoples and nations to permanent sovereignty over their natural wealth and resources must be exercised in the interest of their national development and of the well-being of the people of the State concerned.* * *

---

a.   Problem 8.1 discussed a French case involving intervention, *Fruehauf Corp. v. Massardy.*

4. Nationalization, expropriation or requisitioning shall be based on grounds or reasons of public utility, security or the national interest which are recognized as overriding purely individual or private interests, both domestic and foreign. In such cases the owner shall be paid appropriate compensation, in accordance with the rules in force in the State taking such measures in the exercise of its sovereignty and in accordance with international law.

DECLARATION ON THE ESTABLISHMENT OF A NEW INTERNATIONAL ECONOMIC ORDER

May 1, 1974, U.N.G.A.Res. 3201 (S–VI), 6 (Special) U.N. GAOR, Supp. (No. 1) 3, U.N.Doc. A/9559 (1974), reprinted in 13 Int'l Legal Mat. 715 (1974).

4. The new international economic order should be founded on full respect for the following principles:* * *

(e) Full permanent sovereignty of every State over its natural resources and all economic activities. In order to safeguard these resources, each State is entitled to exercise effective control over them and their exploitation with means suitable to its own situation, including the right to nationalization or transfer of ownership to its nationals, this right being an expression of the full permanent sovereignty of the State.

(f) The right of all States, territories and peoples under foreign occupation, alien and colonial domination or *apartheid* to restitution and full compensation for the exploitation and depletion of, and damages to, the natural resources and all other resources of those States, territories and peoples;* * *

CHARTER OF ECONOMIC RIGHTS AND DUTIES OF STATES

Dec. 12, 1974, U.N.G.A.Res. 3281 (XXIX), 29 U.N. GAOR, Supp. (No. 31) 50, U.N.Doc. A/9631 (1975), reprinted in 14 Int'l Legal Mat. 251 (1975).

Article 2. (1) Every State has and shall freely exercise full permanent sovereignty, including possession, use and disposal, over all its wealth, natural resources and economic activities.

(2) Each State has the right:* * *

(c) To nationalize, expropriate or transfer ownership of foreign property, in which case appropriate compensation should be paid by the State adopting such measures, taking into account its relevant laws and regulations and all circumstances that the State considers pertinent. In any case where the question of compensation gives rise to a controversy, it shall be settled under the domestic law of the nationalizing State and by its tribunals, unless it is freely and mutually agreed by all States concerned that other peaceful means be sought on the basis of the sovereign equality of States and in accordance with the principle of free choice of means.

QUESTIONS AND COMMENTS

1. The public purpose is difficult to prove and would seem to require substantial proof, perhaps beyond a reasonable doubt. Would any international authority be competent to rule on the issue? Should the public purpose requirement be removed from international standards? What should be considered when evaluating the public purpose? Does the Cuban experience establish that a total nationalization of private property is not in the public interest? Professor Weston states that he could find no "international legal decision, adjudicative or diplomatic, that ever has turned on the public purpose issue alone." Burns Weston, *The New International Economic Order and The Deprivation of Foreign Proprietary Wealth: Reflections Upon the Contemporary International Law Debate,* in Richard Lillich (ed.), International Law of State Responsibility for Injuries to Aliens 94 (1983).

2. Are not all expropriations retaliatory to some degree? There may be a clear case of retaliation against a particular company for certain acts, or a case less clear—possibly RODCO for failing to become a joint venture. But where nationalization occurs, it usually is in retaliation against a domestic system which is viewed not to have worked. Where do you separate a justifiable public purpose "response" to actions by a foreign investor from an unjustifiable discriminatory expropriation?

3. The decree that expropriated RODCO's property accomplished the taking in a single act. But it could have come about by a chipping away at the company's assets and ability to do business—what is sometimes called a "creeping expropriation." At what point such form of taking becomes an expropriation which generates legal requirements of public purpose and compensation is a difficult question. For a discussion of creeping expropriation *see,* Seymour Rubin, Private Foreign Investment 40 (1956); Luis Creel, *"Mexicanization:" A Case of Creeping Expropriation,* 22 Southwestern L.J. 281 (1968); Burns Weston, *"Constructive Takings" Under International Law: A Modest Foray into the Problem of "Creeping Expropriation,"* 16 Virginia J.Int'l L. 103 (1975).

4. If the act of taking was illegal under international law, then RODCO may prefer to ask that the property be returned. But restitution does not always seem to be a very logical solution. Marnesia is unlikely to comply and, if they did, would RODCO officers feel comfortable that they could return and Marnesia would forget the whole thing? With regard to restitution, the Reporters' Notes to the Restatement (Third) of Foreign Relations, state as follows:

> 3. *Forms of reparation.* The essential principle of international law is "that reparation must, as far as possible, wipe out all the consequences of the illegal act and re-establish the situation which would, in all probability, have existed if that act had not been committed." Chorzów Factory (Indemnity) Case (Germany v. Poland), P.C.I.J., ser. A, No. 17, at 47 (1928). The Court added that this result can be accomplished in several ways: through restitution in kind; or, if this is not possible, through "payment of a sum corresponding to the value which a restitu-

tion in kind would bear"; and "the award, if need be, of damages for loss sustained which would not be covered by restitution in kind or payment in place of it." *Ibid.* A few years later, however, in the Central Rhodope Forests Case (Greece v. Bulgaria), 1933, the arbitrator (Undén, Sweden) rejected a request for restitution on the ground that it was hardly likely that the forests were in the same condition in 1933 as when they were seized by Bulgaria in 1918. * * *

In an arbitration between a state and a private company, Texas Overseas Petroleum Co. v. Libyan Arab Republic (1977), 53 Int'l L.Rep. 389, 507–09, 511 (1979), the arbitrator (Dupuy, France) held that restitution is, "under the principles of international law, the normal sanction for non-performance of contractual obligations and that it is inapplicable only to the extent that restoration of the status quo ante is impossible"; called upon Libya "to perform specifically its own obligations"; decided that Libya "is legally bound to perform these contracts and to give them full effect"; and reserved for further proceedings the question what should be done if the award were not implemented. But in the parallel case of B.P. (British Petroleum) v. Libya, the arbitrator (Lagergren, Sweden) rejected the claim that the company be restored to the full enjoyment of its rights, and awarded damages instead (1973), 53 Int'l L.Rep. 297, 356–57. Accord: Libyan American Oil Co. v. Libya (by Mahmassani, Lebanon, 1977), 20 Int'l Leg.Mat. 1, 122–25 (1981) (restitution inconsistent with "respect due for the sovereignty of the nationalizing state"). * * *§ 901 at Vol. 2, pp. 343–44.

What constitutes a taking has been the subject of several NAFTA Chapter 11 arbitrations. Some environmentalists have complained that legitimate environmental regulation has been viewed as a taking. Investors have argued in NAFTA cases that any action that constitutes a deprivation of the investors business must be a taking. Where is the line between legitimate regulation and deprivation?

5. How do the standards for expropriation in the Declaration on the Establishment of a New International Economic Order and in the Charter of Economic Rights and Duties of States differ from the earlier Resolution on Permanent Sovereignty Over Natural Resources? The NIEO declaration was passed with reservations by France, Japan, the United Kingdom, the United States and West Germany, mainly regarding the failure to reaffirm that international law played a role in expropriation. The Charter was passed over the objection to several provisions, including 16 votes against Article 2(2)(c), cast by the major developed nations. But the major concern was not with the right to take, or establishing standards for the public purpose, or even discriminatory or retaliatory nationalizations. It was directed to the use of international law versus the domestic law of the host nation, and particularly to the issue of compensation.

6. Should international law concern itself with an investor from one nation, who without coercion seeks out investment opportunities in another, but then later loses that investment because of an act of expropriation of the host nation? Should the only international standard be that he is entitled to be treated the same as any citizen in the host nation? At least the foreign

investor might be required to exhaust his local remedies. Should it make any difference if RODCO was invited to enter Marnesia, rather than having sought out Marnesia as a plant location? Do you agree with the following statement of Guha–Roy?

> First, a national of one state, going out to another in search of wealth or for any other purpose entirely at his own risk, may well be left to the consequences of his ventures, even in countries known to be dangerous. For international law to concern itself with his protection in a state without that state's consent amounts to an infringement of that state's sovereignty. Secondly, a standard open only to aliens but denied to a state's own citizens inevitably widens the gulf between citizens and aliens and thus hampers, rather than helps, free intercourse among peoples of different states. Thirdly, the standard is rather vague and indefinite. Fourthly, the very introduction of an external yardstick for the internal machinery of justice is apt to be looked upon as an affront to the national system, whether or not it is below the international standard. Fifthly, a different standard of justice for aliens results in a twofold differentiation in a state where the internal standard is below the international standard. Its citizens as aliens in other states are entitled to a higher standard than their fellow citizens at home. Again, the citizens of other states as aliens in it are also entitled to a better standard than its own citizens.

Guha–Roy, *Is the Law of Responsibility of States for Injuries to Aliens a Part of Universal International Law?*, 55 Am.J.Int'l L. 863, 889 (1961).

7. Would the issues of the public purpose, discrimination or retaliation ever arise if the taking nation paid appropriate compensation? Why not move immediately to a discussion of compensation when considering an expropriation? RODCO really doesn't want to go back to Marnesia, at least under the current administration.

PART B.   COMPENSATION

RODCO has received no indication that it might receive back its property in Marnesia. It now appears that the most the company should expect is some form of compensation, not restitution. It would like it *right now,* in U.S. dollars, and it would like $12.4 million. It estimates that figure to represent the value of the plant as a going concern, including expected profits for the next decade. It has been in Marnesia about 15 years, and the current plant and equipment have an expected life of another ten years. The Marnesian government has been talking compensation, but with an emphasis on applying Marnesian law, and deducting from the current tax assessment value of RODCO ($750,000), excess profits which it alleges RODCO earned by paying Marnesian employees only 30 percent of the wages paid in the U.S. plant. It has concluded that the net worth is $130,000 and is willing to pay with Marnesian 35 year government bonds paying two percent interest. The fund to pay the bonds will be created by a complex formula which basically requires the United States to increase trade each year with Marnesia by ten percent over the trade in a base year, 1990, when trade was at its highest between the two nations. RODCO's officers say this is ridiculous and that such fund will never be established because of the current hostility between the two nations. Marnesia claims that hostility is the fault of the United States and Marnesia is ready to trade.

There are very different views regarding compensation. All but a few nations (and a lot more "scholars") believe that some compensation is required for expropriating foreign property. But when one considers the form of compensation offered, the conclusion might well be that the expropriating nation does not intend to pay anything. That is how RODCO officers feel about the offer. They would like to know whether there is a consensus of views. They will soon learn there is not, not on a world basis, nor among the developed nations, nor even within the United States.

SCHACHTER, EDITORIAL COMMENT, "COMPENSATION FOR EXPROPRIATION"

78 Am.J.Int'l L. 121 (1984).*

* * * In the United States especially, the issue ... has centered largely on the requirement of "prompt, adequate and effective compensation," the phrase used by Secretary of State Hull in 1938 in his notes to the Mexican Government claiming compensation for expropriated agrarian lands owned by U.S. nationals. Since that time the U.S. Government has maintained in numerous statements that "prompt, adequate and effective compensation" is required by international law. * * *

The issue has once again emerged in controversy over the formulation of the requirement of compensation in the draft articles of the American Law Institute's *Restatement of the Foreign Relations Law of the United States (Revised)*. The comments * * * acknowledge that the United States has consistently maintained that "just compensation" means prompt, adequate and effective compensation. However, the reporters observe that international practice does not conform to the "ideal" and that there is a wide divergence of views among states as to the international law standard. The implicit conclusion, although not stated in so many words, is that the Hull formula cannot be considered as existing international law applicable to all cases of expropriation of alien property.* * *

It is true that several "traditional" decisions of international tribunals recognize an international obligation to pay compensation when alien property is taken by a state. However, contrary to what is often asserted, these decisions contain no reference to the "prompt, adequate and effective" standard. The *Chorzów* case in the Permanent Court of International Justice in 1928, probably the most frequently cited opinion in this field, refers only to a duty to "payment of fair compensation." The *Norwegian Shipowners Claims* arbitration of 1922 is also often cited. In that decision,

---

* Reprinted with permission of the American Society of International Law.

the tribunal did say that "just compensation" should be determined by "fair actual value at the time and place" "in view of all surrounding circumstances." It is a long stretch from this qualified formula to the assertion that the case supports the "prompt and effective" standard. * * *

It was clear that European state practice showed substantial deviation from what one would ordinarily understand as "full" compensation or as prompt and effective payment. American scholars, by and large, came to share the views of their European counterparts and in the postwar period they increasingly challenged the official U.S. view on the Hull standard. In particular, their examination of state practice in cases of postwar nationalization showed that compensation was less than full value (or fair market value), and that payments were deferred and often made in nonconvertible local currency. * * *

A possible alternative to "just compensation" is the requirement of "appropriate compensation," a standard that received the support of many governments in the United Nations and for which the United States voted. It has also been supported in two important international arbitral decisions and in * * * the Court of Appeals for the Second Circuit * * *. Significantly, none of these decisions described the "prompt, adequate and effective" formula as a rule of law or authoritative standard.

The first international case is the well-known arbitral award by Professor Dupuy in the *TOPCO–Libyan* case of 1977, in which the arbitrator declared that the requirement of "appropriate compensation" was the "opinio juris communis" that reflected "the state of customary law existing in the field."[36] In support of this conclusion, Dupuy cited the acceptance of this standard in UN Resolution 1803, which received support from both the developed and the developing states. He did not mention that the U.S. representative explained his vote for the resolution by stating he was "confident" that "it would be interpreted as meaning prompt, adequate and effective compensation." That very point was controversial in the UN committee debates and a U.S. proposal to include its interpretation was withdrawn. It would be difficult to read into Dupuy's acceptance of the standard of "appropriate compensation" an acceptance of the interpretation the United States hoped would be given to it. It is significant that Dupuy made no mention of the U.S. interpretation in this context.

The second relevant opinion was that of the court of appeals in the *Banco Nacional* case of 1981.[39] * * * [T]he court reviewed much of the literature on the subject. Its conclusion on the standard of compensation merits quotation: "It may well be the consensus of nations that full compensation need not be paid 'in all circumstances,' * * * and that requiring an expropriating state to pay 'appropriate compensation'—even

---

36. *Texas Overseas Petroleum Co./California Asiatic Oil Co. v. Government of the Libyan Arab Republic,* 17 ILM 3, 29 (1978), 53 ILR 389 (1979) (English trans.).

39. *Banco Nacional de Cuba v. Chase Manhattan Bank,* 658 F.2d 875 (2d Cir.1981).

considering the lack of precise definition of that term,—would come closest to reflecting what international law requires." The court did add: "But the adoption of an 'appropriate compensation' requirement would not exclude the possibility that in some cases full compensation would be appropriate."

The third decision was the award in the *Aminoil–Kuwait* arbitration of 1982.[42] The tribunal, which included two of the most respected Western European jurists—Reuter and Fitzmaurice—said that the standard of "appropriate compensation" as set forth in Resolution 1803 "codifies positive principles." The tribunal declared that "the determination of the amount of an award of 'appropriate' compensation is better carried out by means of an enquiry into all the circumstances relevant to the particular concrete case, than through abstract theoretical discussion." The one general notion that the tribunal emphasized was that of "legitimate expectations," a concept invoked by the parties. That concept brought to mind—so the tribunal stated—that "with reference to every long-term contract, especially such as involve an important investment, there must necessarily be economic calculations, and the weighing-up of rights and obligations, of chances and risks, constituting the contractual equilibrium." Nothing was said in the award about the claim that "prompt, adequate and effective" compensation constituted customary international law. In view of these well-considered opinions, a case can be made for considering that just compensation should now be replaced by "appropriate compensation." * * *

On the other hand, the draft *Restatement,* taking a more traditional position, can justify its choice of "just" over "appropriate" by the fact that "just compensation" has been used widely in national constitutions (e.g., the Fifth Amendment), in legislation and in many treaties. It may also be said that "appropriate" would create uncertainty precisely because it would replace "just." It might then be argued * * * that "appropriate" allows for consideration of factors that would not be within the ambit of "just." For example, it might be considered "appropriate" to give weight to the needs and capabilities of the expropriating state. Some would consider this desirable, others unjust. The draft *Restatement* avoids this issue by maintaining the criterion of "just compensation" as the *lex lata.* This still leaves room for considerable flexibility in application. It should enable tribunals to consider such factors as the financial burden of the expropriating state and whether deferred payments and payments in local currency are reasonable in the circumstances.* * *

QUESTIONS AND COMMENTS

1. Do you agree that the norms of Resolution 1803 in Part A of this problem provide a sensible base from which to reestablish some order to the chaos which has been present in the last several decades? The United States

---

42. Arbitration between Kuwait and the American Independent Oil Co. (AMINOIL), 21 ILM 976 (1982).

has focused on creating a just standard in the Restatement, but there was much disagreement among the drafters and considerable concern noted by the Department of State that the United States might alter its traditional view that the only reasonable and just standard is prompt, adequate and effective compensation. Is there really any settled international law in this area? The method of resolution for most claims is by way of claims settlement commissions, where a lump sum is negotiated rather than individual claims heard. Are we not dealing with a dialectical process? Prompt, adequate and effective compensation is the thesis of the developed world. The antithesis of "we can't pay that way" comes in response from the developing world, and we are at a snail's pace moving towards a synthesis—the contents of which are yet unknown. Until that synthesis, ad hoc arrangements will continue to resolve most of the conflicts.

2. What is the *fairest* valuation method? Book value? Adjusted book value? Going concern value? Some weighted mix of several methods? The issue has been thoroughly studied in Richard Lillich (ed. & contrib.), The Valuation of Nationalized Property in International Law (3 vol. 1972, 1973, 1975). Given the task of deciding the RODCO case as an international arbiter, would you choose (1) prompt, adequate and effective, (2) appropriate, or (3) just compensation, were you asked to make your decision on the basis of international law? Or would you use domestic law? Just what is U.S. domestic law regarding compensation? What factors in the RODCO situation would influence your decision? Do the substantive standards differ depending upon which of the above three measurements the forum applies?

3. Arbitration of expropriations is sometimes undertaken by ICSID (International Centre for the Settlement of Investment Disputes), part of the World Bank in Washington. One arbitration panel required Indonesia to pay $4 million for expropriating a Jakarta hotel owned by foreign investors, using as a standard "full" compensation and measuring the enterprise as a going concern. 24 Int'l Leg.Mat. 1022 (1985). The decision was annulled, but not for reasons of the standard of compensation. 25 Int'l Leg. Mat. 1439 (1986). A second award was made by a new panel. ICSID decisions are not always published. Those made public have been published in the ICSID Reports (Cambridge University press), edited by R. Rayfuse and E. Lauterpacht. See http://icsid.worldbank.org/ICSID/FrontServlet?requestType=CasesRH&action Val=ViewPendingCases. See also International Legal Developments in Review—2007, 42 Int'l Law. 359 (2008), and www.investmenttreatynews.org.

4. A specially selected five member Chamber of the International Court of Justice convened at the request of Italy and the United States to hear a claim that the Treaty of Friendship, Commerce and Navigation between the two nations was violated when Italy allegedly prevented Raytheon from controlling and managing its subsidiary and disposing of its assets. *Elettronica Sicula S.p.A. (ELSI), Judgment (U.S. v. Italy)*, 1989 ICJ 15. The issue involved whether Italy had breached the FCN Treaty by allegedly interfering with the liquidation of the foreign company (4–1 in favor of Italy). More an intervention than a takeover, the case is important because it raises the possibility of using specially agreed upon chambers of the ICJ in expropriation cases. The ICJ has not been a very satisfactory source of developments in expropriation theory.

5. The Iran–United States Claims Tribunal, which has been meeting in the Hague since 1981, has not formally applied a "prompt, adequate and effective" standard, but claims approved by the Tribunal generally have been paid promptly from funds established for the purpose, they have been paid in dollars which is surely effective payment, and the Tribunal has used various methods of valuation which seem to satisfy any reasonable adequacy standard. The Tribunal has often used a "just" standard, which is stated in the U.S.–Iran Treaty of Amity, Economic Relations and Consular Rights. Aug. 15, 1955, 8 UST 899, ITAS No. 3853, 284 UNTS 93. The standard is stated as "prompt payment of just compensation." But it goes on to state that it must be paid in "an effectively realizable form" and must be for the "full equivalent of the property taken", thus becoming nearly a prompt, adequate and effective standard. *See,* David Caron, *The Nature of the Iran–United States Claims Tribunal and the Evolving Structure of International Dispute Resolution,* 84 Am.J. Int'l L. 104 (1990). But the law applied by the Tribunal has not been consistent. In one case, *American International Group, Inc. v. Iran*, 4 Iran–U.S. C.T.R. 96 (1983), the Tribunal rejected a suggestion of prompt, adequate and effective as the standard, a view repeated in *Shahin Shaine Ebrahimi v. Iran,* AWD 560–44/46/47–3 (Oct. 12, 1994). But the American Int'l Group Tribunal did conclude that required compensation included goodwill and likely future profits. In *INA Corp. v. Iran,* 8 Iran–U.S. C.T.R. (1985), the Tribunal distinguished large scale nationalizations from isolated takings. For the former, the Tribunal said international law had undergone a reappraisal which may be said to undermine the idea of any full or adequate compensation. But it found the case to be different, and allowed fair market as the standard for compensation. In some ways the Tribunal over the years of its existence offers something for everyone searching for a standard. As of March, 2008, the tribunal had rendered 133 decisions in 140 cases. The last decisions listed as of 2011 are dated 2004, but there remain before the Tribunal several large and complex cases between the two nations. See www.iusct.org.

6. The North American Free Trade Agreement, in Article 1110, requires compensation at the "fair market value" immediately before the expropriation. Valuation is to consider the going concern value. Compensation must be paid "without delay and be fully realizable." Isn't this the equivalent of "prompt, adequate and effective?"

7. Should the U.S. court consider whether RODCO's efforts to seek relief in Marnesia are likely to be successful and refuse to go forward until the company has exhausted its efforts in Marnesia? The idea of exhaustion of local remedies is a long established rule of customary international law. *See* the *Interhandel Case (Switzerland v. United States)* (preliminary objections), 1959 I.C.J. 6. It is also a basic rule of domestic law of most nations. It is an appropriate rule when there are few claimants. One ought not go to an international forum when the courts of the nation in which the claim arose are prepared to consider the claim and, if valid, grant relief. Requiring local exhaustion may be considered a rule of conflicts, or a matter of practical procedure. But when there has been an extensive expropriation of property, the rule is less clearly appropriate. In the area of claims for expropriation, the United States has moved away from requiring local exhaustion. For example, under the Hickenlooper Amendment (which will be referred to below and

which requires the President to withhold aid to any nation which has taken property of U.S. citizens and is not providing means for compensating the claimants), the U.S. investor is not required to have exhausted local remedies before the Amendment is applied. Had RODCO been the only company nationalized, would you be more likely to confront an exhaustion of local remedies rule? Is the rule exclusively based on how many claims are present? Or how large the claim may be? Or whether the claim is to be espoused by the private investor or its government? The exhaustion issue is discussed in F. Dawson & I. Head, International Law, National Tribunals, and the Rights of Aliens (1971); G. Law, The Local Remedies Rule in International Law (1961).

8. An additional concern is that RODCO entered Marnesia having signed an investment agreement which included a provision that RODCO would not seek the assistance of its government, and that if it did the RODCO properties in Marnesia would be forfeited to the government. This is the much disputed Calvo clause, a frequent element of third world investment theory, but consistently rejected by developed nations. Whatever RODCO signed, the U.S. government does not believe that RODCO has the right to prevent the diplomatic efforts of the United States to be initiated when U.S. properties owned abroad are expropriated. There is an interrelationship between the exhaustion and Calvo clause concepts. Both consider that the best method for the resolution of claims is the local forum. Where the Calvo idea parts company, however, is in its exclusiveness. The claimant must *only* seek a remedy in the local court. Neither of these issues seems as fearful as the defenses which must be faced based on sovereign immunity and the act of state, but a few thoughts regarding each are appropriate for you to pass on to the RODCO board. See Shea, The Calvo Clause (1955); Lipstein, The Place of the Calvo Clause in International Law [1945] Brit. Y.B.I.L. 130; Note, The Calvo Clause, 6 Texas J. Int'l L. Forum 289 (1971).

9. The end result of most large scale nationalizations is a settlement agreed to by the two nations with funds distributed through a foreign claims commission in the nation whose citizen's property was taken. The U.S. Foreign Claims Settlement Commission (FCSC) hears claims soon after a nationalization to provide some basis for later discussions with the expropriating nation. The adjudication of claims pertaining to acts occurring in a foreign nation raises obvious problems of proof. When hostilities persist between that nation and the United States, the difficulties are compounded. The documentation most often needed, however, is that left behind in the foreign nation by claimants and beyond the reach of the Commission. The final decisions of the FCSC are usually certified to the Secretary of the Treasury for payment under whatever settlement agreement may be negotiated. The continued viability of the Foreign Claims Settlement Commission is largely dependent upon the success of the Department of State in negotiating sufficiently high percentage settlements with the expropriating nations to justify the continued expense involved. See Richard Lillich & Burns Weston, International Claims: Their Settlement by Lump Sum Agreements (1975).

PART C. LITIGATION: SOVEREIGN IMMUNITY AND THE ACT OF STATE

Marnesian officers and you as house counsel feel better knowing something about expropriation. But you are not very comfortable with the unsettled standards to be applied if the expropriation is taken to court. That is where RODCO is headed. Little success was achieved by being diplomatic. RODCO consequently filed suit in a state court in Denver and the defendant had it removed to the federal district court. The Marnesian Department of Education has an account in a Denver bank, used to pay tuition for Marnesian students attending college in the United States. RODCO wishes to attach that account and funds in other banks, all identifiable with a number of commercial transactions of Marnesia in the United States. One of the accounts has been used during the past year to provide government subsidies to Marnesian industries operating in North America. RODCO has learned that those subsidies included payments for advertising in Canada for the fishing equipment made in the former RODCO plant and now being sold in Canada.

RODCO did not expect two of the defenses, sovereign immunity and the act of state doctrine. The sovereign immunity defense essentially states that, "whatever we did, however wrongful you might imagine it to be, we are the state and your courts may not be used to sue us. The suit must be dismissed solely because as a sovereign nation we are immune to suit." Not a very encouraging position for RODCO to be in. But there are some questions to consider. Are all acts of a nation entitled to the defense of sovereign immunity? It would not seem reasonable for a nation to be able to claim immunity when it engages in activities that are usually performed by the private sector in most of the world. If Marnesia's actions are in violation of international law should it nevertheless be able to argue sovereign immunity?

VERLINDEN B.V. v. CENTRAL BANK OF NIGERIA

Supreme Court of the United States, 1983.
461 U.S. 480, 103 S.Ct. 1962, 1967, 76 L.Ed.2d 81.

CHIEF JUSTICE BURGER delivered the opinion of the Court.

[The case involved a letter of credit. The extraction below outlines the history of sovereign immunity in the United States, leading to the enactment of the Foreign Sovereign Immunities Act of 1976].* * *

For more than a century and a half, the United States generally granted foreign sovereigns complete immunity from suit in the courts of this country. In *The Schooner Exchange v. M'Faddon*, 7 Cranch 116, 3 L.Ed. 287 (1812), Chief Justice Marshall concluded that, while the jurisdiction of a nation within its own territory "is susceptible of no limitation not imposed by itself," * * * the United States had impliedly waived jurisdiction over certain activities of foreign sovereigns. Although the narrow holding of *The Schooner Exchange* was only that the courts of the United States lack jurisdiction over an armed ship of a foreign state found in our port, that opinion came to be regarded as extending virtually absolute immunity to foreign sovereigns.

As *The Schooner Exchange* made clear, however, foreign sovereign immunity is a matter of grace and comity on the part of the United States, and not a restriction imposed by the Constitution. Accordingly, this Court consistently has deferred to the decisions of the political branches—in particular, those of the Executive Branch—on whether to take jurisdiction over actions against foreign sovereigns and their instrumentalities.

Until 1952, the State Department ordinarily requested immunity in all actions against friendly foreign sovereigns. But in the so-called Tate Letter, the State Department announced its adoption of the "restrictive" theory of foreign sovereign immunity. Under this theory, immunity is confined to suits involving the foreign sovereign's public acts, and does not extend to cases arising out of a foreign state's strictly commercial acts.

The restrictive theory was not initially enacted into law, however, and its application proved troublesome. As in the past, initial responsibility for deciding questions of sovereign immunity fell primarily upon the Executive acting through the State Department, and the courts abided by "suggestions of immunity" from the State Department. As a consequence, foreign nations often placed diplomatic pressure on the State Department in seeking immunity. On occasion, political considerations led to suggestions of immunity in cases where immunity would not have been available under the restrictive theory.* * *

In 1976, Congress passed the Foreign Sovereign Immunities Act in order to free the Government from the case-by-case diplomatic pressures, to clarify the governing standards, and to "assur[e] litigants that* * *decisions are made on purely legal grounds and under procedures that insure due process," * * *. To accomplish these objectives, the Act contains a comprehensive set of legal standards governing claims of immunity in every civil action against a foreign state or its political subdivisions, agencies or instrumentalities.

For the most part, the Act codifies, as a matter of federal law, the restrictive theory of sovereign immunity. A foreign state is normally immune from the jurisdiction of federal and state courts, * * * subject to a set of exceptions * * *. Those exceptions include actions in which the foreign state has explicitly or impliedly waived its immunity, * * * and actions based upon commercial activities of the foreign sovereign carried on in the United States or causing a direct effect in the United States * * *. When one of these or the other specified exceptions applies, "the foreign state shall be liable in the same manner and to the same extent as a private individual under like circumstances," * * *.

* * *

VON MEHREN, THE FOREIGN SOVEREIGN IMMUNITIES ACT OF 1976

17 Colum.J.Transnat'l L. 33 (1978).*

* * * Section 1605(a)(2) provides for jurisdiction over a foreign state where the action is based "upon an act outside the territory of the United

---

* Reprinted with permission of the Columbia Journal of Transnational Law.

States in connection with a commercial activity of the foreign state elsewhere and that act causes a direct effect in the United States." The conditions for application of this section would not seem to be met in the first case of expropriation discussed above [foreign investment with no contractual relations with the host government]; there is simply no "commercial activity" of the foreign sovereign upon which jurisdiction can be based. This is not, however, true of the second case [concession contract with the host government]. There the breach of the contract is a commercial activity and, if the United States action were based upon the concession contracts, the first part of the section 1605(a)(2) test would have been met. The plaintiff would still have to show that the "commercial act" (here the breach of contract by the state) caused "a direct effect in the United States." Where the concession holder is an American company, with American shareholders, or a subsidiary of such a company, it should not be difficult to demonstrate that there has been such a direct effect.

Section 1605(a)(3) does not make jurisdiction turn upon the "commercial" or "non-commercial" nature of the initial act of taking. If (a) the taking was "in violation of international law" and (b) the action involves rights in the property taken and "that property or any property exchanged for such property" is (i) present in the United States in connection with a commercial activity carried on in the United States by the expropriating state or (ii) owned or operated by an agency or instrumentality of the expropriating state and that agency or instrumentality is engaged in commercial activity in the United States, the American courts have jurisdiction.

Clearly section 1605(a)(3) would apply, for example, where a foreign state expropriates a fleet of aircraft and uses these aircraft or aircraft exchanged for them to furnish commercial air service to the United States. The section would also apply where the state-owned airline operated these aircraft or aircraft exchanged for them in its air transportation services anywhere, if the state-owned airline were engaged in any commercial operations in the United States: for example, commercial air service to the United States with aircraft entirely unrelated to the expropriated aircraft or substantial solicitation of business in the United States. Thus, section 1605(a)(3) may have a significant effect were the taking of movable property is at issue.

Its impact, however, is likely to be less in the more usual case where the property taken is immovable property (factories, mines) or intangible property (contractual and other rights). Immovable property would ordinarily remain within the territory of the expropriating state. If it were sold, the problem of tracing the proceeds would necessarily be difficult. Section 1605(a)(3) may, nevertheless, be of some significance in cases where the expropriated property is owned or operated by an agency of the foreign state. In such a case, if that agency is engaged "in a commercial activity in the United States," American courts would have jurisdiction even though the property which was taken remained within the territory of the expropriating state.

A significant and perhaps insurmountable barrier to the wide application of section 1605(a)(3) in expropriation cases where the principal claim arises from the abrogation of contractual rights is the limitation that the section applies only in cases involving "rights in property taken in violation of international law." The phrase "rights in property" is not defined in the Immunities Act nor discussed in the legislative history. * * *

The cases interpreting the Hickenlooper Amendment have consistently held that "claim of title or other right to property" does not extend to claims based on contracts. * * *

QUESTIONS AND COMMENTS

1. The act of expropriating property would seem to be a governmental action unrelated to commerce. Property is taken to serve a public purpose, if it is to meet international law standards. Under von Mehren's interpretation of the FSIA, did Marnesia engage in any commercial activity with RODCO, or was the expropriation the first government action? Do you believe it makes a difference? What would be the minimum that the state might do to engage in a commercial activity? What if RODCO had entered the country without having to sign any investment contract with the government, but the government had promoted legislation which provided incentives to foreign investment and allowed that investment to enter without any further approval by the government? Has there been commercial activity under the Act? What if the only "agreement" was entitled "Investment Registration Application" and the only action of the government was to file it automatically as approved as long as the form was filled in properly? Would the process be a commercial activity? And finally, what if the investment proposal had to be submitted to a national commission on foreign investment, where the investor negotiated nearly every aspect of the proposed investment with government officials, and made many modifications to the proposal? Has the government now engaged in a commercial activity?

2. There are several issues which must be considered in bringing suit against a foreign sovereign. First, should the suit be brought in state or federal court? If brought in state court, foreign defendants invariably remove the action to federal court. Second, what types of actions may be taken before the courts? That is governed by the 1976 Foreign Sovereign Immunities Act. That Act essentially affirms sovereign immunity, but then lists exceptions to immunity. Marnesia must come within an exception if it is to succeed. Because the FSIA codified the "restrictive" theory, it is necessary to determine whether an activity of the government was "commercial" and thus not subject to an immunity defense. FSIA § 1605(a)(2). Expropriation is difficult to so classify. Even if the act was a commercial activity, it must come within one of the three-part commercial activity exceptions. But as von Mehren states, jurisdiction does not have to be based on a commercial nature of the activity if the act violated international law and involves rights in property

taken *and also* that property (or property exchanged for it) is in the United States in connection with a commercial activity or owned or operated by an agency of the state which is engaged in commercial activity. FSIA § 1605(a)(3). Can an effective argument for jurisdiction be made on RODCO's behalf under this latter view? What standard of international law should apply? If the property in the United States does not qualify, what about the fishing equipment in Canada, if the Canadian law were to read the same way? Does RODCO have "rights in property" under § 1605(a)(3)? The U.S. Supreme Court ruled that *"forum non conveniens* may justify dismissal of an action though jurisdictional issues remain unresolved," an issue that had divided the lower federal courts. *Sinochem Int'l Co. Ltd. v. Malaysia Int'l Shipping Corp.,* 549 U.S. 422, 127 S.Ct. 1184, 167 L.Ed.2d 15 (2007).

With the complexity of the FSIA, it may be easy to overlook the defendant's rights under the Constitution to due process. The FSIA cannot create jurisdiction precluded by the Constitution. Minimum jurisdictional contacts and adequate notice are required. You cannot forget your knowledge of *International Shoe, McGee* and *World–Wide Volkswagen* just because you are in the lofty strata of international law. *See, e.g., Texas Trading & Milling Corp. v. Federal Republic of Nigeria,* 647 F.2d 300 (2d Cir.1981); *Harris v. VAO Intourist, Moscow,* 481 F.Supp. 1056 (E.D.N.Y.1979); *Bankers Trust Co. v. Worldwide Transportation Services,* 537 F.Supp. 1101 (E.D.Ark.1982).

Remember that success in having a judge rule on the merits does not mean that there will therefore be execution of that judgment. Execution against a foreign state brings into play some additional problems. See FSIA §§ 1609–1611. Would any of these sections allow attachment of the funds in the Denver bank?

A final note: Marnesia is unquestionably a state, which it must be to raise sovereign immunity as a defense. Under the FSIA, a state is "a political subdivision of a foreign state or an agency or instrumentality of a foreign state." FSIA § 1603(a). The FSIA is discussed in *e.g.,* Carl, *Suing Foreign Governments in American Courts: The United States Foreign Sovereign Immunities Act in Practice,* 33 Southwestern L.J. 1009 (1979).

3.   In view of the above, would you recommend any action to RODCO as it considers new direct investment in other nations? Would an express waiver in the investment agreement be satisfactory? *See* Section 1605(a)(1). The FSIA recognizes implied waivers, the U.K. State Immunity Act does not.

4.   The 1976 FSIA has been held to apply to acts involving the expropriation of art during and after World War II. See *Republic of Austria v. Altmann,* 541 U.S. 677, 124 S.Ct. 2240, 159 L.Ed.2d 1 (2004).

———

The act of expropriation is the quintessential state act. Since *Underhill v. Hernandez,* 168 U.S. 250, 18 S.Ct. 83, 42 L.Ed. 456 (1897), when the Court stated that "Every sovereign State is bound to respect the independence of every other sovereign State, and the courts of one country will not sit in judgment on * * * [and determine the legal validity of] * * * the acts of the government of another done within its own territory.", at 252, the United

States has adhered to this act of state doctrine. Other nations also follow the doctrine. Marnesia has requested the court to dismiss the action for act of state reasons as well as sovereign immunity. RODCO officers must be briefed on this concept as well. Unlike the sovereign immunity issue, which is now expressed by statute, the act of state doctrine is embedded in a series of cases. But it is affected by statute. Its application has raised the ire of Congress, which has responded to limit its application.

BANCO NACIONAL DE CUBA v. SABBATINO

Supreme Court of the United States, 1964.
376 U.S. 398, 84 S.Ct. 923, 11 L.Ed.2d 804.

MR. JUSTICE HARLAN delivered the opinion of the Court.

[In retaliation for an American reduction in the import quota for Cuban sugar, the Cuban government nationalized many companies in which Americans held interests, including Compania Azucerera Ver-tientes—Camaguey (CAV). Farr, Whitlock, an American commodities broker had contracted to buy a shipload of CAV sugar. To obtain the now-nationalized sugar, Farr, Whitlock entered into a new agreement to buy the shipload from the Cuban government, which assigned the bills of lading to its shipping agent, Banco Nacional. Farr, Whitlock gained possession of the shipping documents and negotiated them to its customers, but protected by CAV's promise of indemnification, Farr, Whitlock turned the proceeds over to CAV instead of Cuba. Banco Nacional sued Farr, Whitlock for conversion of the bills of lading and also sought to enjoin Sabbatino, the temporary receiver of CAV's New York assets, from disposing of the proceeds. Farr, Whitlock defended on the ground that title to the sugar never passed to Cuba because the expropriation violated international law.]

The classic American statement of the act of state doctrine * * * is found in Underhill v. Hernandez, * * *. None of this Court's subsequent cases in which the act of state doctrine was directly or peripherally involved manifest any retreat from Underhill. * * * On the contrary in two of these cases, *Oetjen* and *Ricaud,* the doctrine as announced in Underhill was reaffirmed in unequivocal terms.[a] * * *

---

a. The Court discussed the *Bernstein* exception but did not pass on it. The exception, named after the decision from which it arose, *Bernstein v. N.V. Nederlandsche–Amerikaansche, Stoom-vaart–Maatschappij,* 210 F.2d 375 (2d Cir.1954), occurs where the court is inclined to apply the act of state doctrine but the Executive requests the court not to apply the doctrine but to proceed to consider the issues which are before the court as a consequence of the actions of the foreign government. The validity of the *Bernstein* exception was discussed in *First National City Bank v. Banco Nacional de Cuba,* 406 U.S. 759, 92 S.Ct. 1808, 32 L.Ed.2d 466 (1972), rehearing denied 409 U.S. 897, 93 S.Ct. 92, 34 L.Ed.2d 155 (1972). Three justices approved the exception (writing as a plurality for the opinion of the court), but two concurring and four dissenting justices disagreed and declined to "relinquish" to the Executive the determination of a political question such as the act of state. Four justices dissenting in *Alfred Dunhill of London, Inc. v. Republic of Cuba,* 425 U.S. 682, 96 S.Ct. 1854, 48 L.Ed.2d 301 (1976), reminded the Court that the First National case had "disapproved finally the so-called *Bernstein* exception", but however tarnished the exception is, a "Bernstein letter" from the Department of State to a court may have a major impact on the disposition of an act of state issue.

We do not believe that this doctrine is compelled either by the inherent nature of sovereign authority, * * * or by some principle of international law. * * * While historic notions of sovereign authority do bear upon the wisdom of employing the act of state doctrine, they do not dictate its existence.* * *

Despite the broad statement in Oetjen that "The conduct of the foreign relations of our government is committed by the Constitution to the executive and legislative * * * departments," * * * it cannot of course be thought that "every case or controversy which touches foreign relations lies beyond judicial cognizance." * * * The text of the Constitution does not require the act of state doctrine; it does not irrevocably remove from the judiciary the capacity to review the validity of foreign acts of state.

The act of state doctrine does, however, have "constitutional" underpinnings. It arises out of the basic relationships between branches of government in a system of separation of powers. It concerns the competency of dissimilar institutions to make and implement particular kinds of decision in the area of international relations. The doctrine as formulated in past decisions expresses the strong sense of the Judicial Branch that its engagement in the task of passing on the validity of foreign acts of state may hinder rather than further this country's pursuit of goals both for itself and for the community of nations as a whole in the international sphere.* * *

If the act of state doctrine is a principle of decision binding on federal and state courts alike but compelled by neither international law nor the Constitution, its continuing vitality depends on its capacity to reflect the proper distribution of functions between the judicial and political branches of the Government on matters bearing upon foreign affairs. It should be apparent that the greater the degree of codification or consensus concerning a particular area of international law, the more appropriate it is for the judiciary to render decisions regarding it, since the courts can then focus on the application of an agreed principle to circumstances of fact rather than on the sensitive task of establishing a principle not inconsistent with the national interest or with international justice. It is also evidence that some aspects of international law touch much more sharply on national nerves than do others; the less important the implications of an issue are for our foreign relations, the weaker the justification for exclusivity in the political branches. The balance of relevant considerations may also be shifted if the government which perpetrated the challenged act of state is no longer in existence, as in the Bernstein case, for the political interest of this country may, as a result, be measurably altered. Therefore, rather than laying down or reaffirming an inflexible and all-encompassing rule in this case, we decide only that the Judicial Branch will not examine the validity of a taking of property within its own territory by a foreign sovereign government, extant and recognized by this country at the time of suit, in the absence of a treaty or other unambiguous agreement regarding controlling legal principles, even if the complaint alleges that the taking violates customary international law.* * *

MR. JUSTICE WHITE, dissenting.

I do not believe that the act of state doctrine, as judicially fashioned in this Court, and the reasons underlying it, require American courts to decide cases in disregard of international law and of the rights of litigants to a full determination on the merits.* * *

I start with what I thought to be unassailable propositions: that our courts are obliged to determine controversies on their merits, in accordance with the applicable law; and that part of the law American courts are bound to administer is international law* * *

The reasons for nonreview, based as they are on traditional concepts of territorial sovereignty, lose much of their force when the foreign act of state is shown to be a violation of international law. All legitimate exercises of sovereign power, whether territorial or otherwise, should be exercised consistently with rules of international law, including those rules which mark the bounds of lawful state action against aliens or their property located within the territorial confines of the foreign state. * * *

Of course, there are many unsettled areas of international law, as there are of domestic law, and these areas present sensitive problems of accommodating the interests of nations that subscribe to divergent economic and political systems. It may be that certain nationalizations of property for a public purpose fall within this area. Also, it may be that domestic courts, as compared to international tribunals, or arbitral commissions, have a different and less active role to play in formulating new rules of international law or in choosing between rules not yet adhered to by any substantial group of nations. Where a clear violation of international law is not demonstrated, I would agree that principles of comity underlying the act of state doctrine warrant recognition and enforcement of the foreign act. But none of these considerations relieve a court of the obligation to make an inquiry into the validity of the foreign act, none of them warrant a flat rule of no inquiry at all. * * *

MICHAEL W. GORDON, THE CUBAN NATIONALIZATIONS: THE DEMISE OF FOREIGN PRIVATE PROPERTY

166 (1976).

The Supreme Court decision was not well received by many U.S. critics. There was little belief in the competence of the executive to obtain adequate redress through diplomatic channels. Legislative curatives were broadly urged to reverse the Supreme Court's unwillingness to find an international law exception to the act of state doctrine. Senator Hickenlooper * * * promoted legislation to reverse *Sabbatino*.[46] There was a

---

46. In 1962 Senator Hickenlooper had sponsored what has since become known as the Hickenlooper Amendment to the Foreign Assistance Act. The amendment purportedly required the President to withhold aid to any foreign country expropriating United States nationals property without "immediate and effective compensation." 108 Cong.Rec. 7893 (1962). The Hickenlooper Amendment contained several restrictions on assistance to Communist countries

sparsity of public involvement in the passage of the amendment. With only minor amendment by the House, the amendment took its place in the stable of foreign investment protective legislation.[a] The essential effect of the amendment was the reversal of the *Sabbatino* presumption,[47] although the amendment also affected the Supreme Court's view of the difficulty of an unsettled international law of compensation following expropriations. The amendment adopts the compensation provisions of Senator Hickenlooper's earlier legislation, commonly referred to as the Hickenlooper Amendment, which had been enacted as an amendment to the Foreign Assistance Act of 1962. That amendment required "speedy" payment in convertible foreign exchange, a standard which has not been accepted as a widely approved rule of customary international law.

The *Sabbatino* decision, having been remanded to the District Court, was quickly disposed of with the application of the amendment which had been designed to reverse the Supreme Court's ruling. With the Sabbatino Amendment applicable to nullify the act of state doctrine, the court on remand felt bound to apply the earlier Circuit Court holding that the Cuban acts had violated international law. * * *

W.S. KIRKPATRICK & CO., INC. v. ENVIRONMENTAL TECTONICS CORP., INT'L

Supreme Court of the United States, 1990.
493 U.S. 400, 110 S.Ct. 701, 107 L.Ed.2d 816.

[Officer of Kirkpatrick & Co., in negotiating a construction and equipment contract with Nigeria, retained a Nigerian citizen to assist in securing the contract. If the contract were obtained, Kirkpatrick would pay two Panamanian entities controlled by the Nigerian a commission amounting to 20 percent of the contract price. That amount would be used

---

with specific prohibitions of aid to Cuba. The intention was to suspend aid to nations which did not comply with United States norms of compensation subsequent to expropriations.

a. This amendment was called the Sabbatino Amendment, or the Second Hickenlooper Amendment. It stated: "Notwithstanding any other provision of law, no court in the United States shall decline on the ground of the federal act of state doctrine to make a determination on the merits giving effect to the principles of international law in a case in which a claim of title or other right [*to property*] is asserted by any party including a foreign state (or a party claiming through such state) based upon (or traced through) a confiscation or other taking after January 1, 1959, by an act of that state in violation of the principles of international law including the principles of compensation and the other standards set out in this subsection: *Provided,* That this subparagraph shall not be applicable (1) in any case in which an act of a foreign state is not contrary to international law or with respect to a claim of title or other right [*to property*] acquired pursuant to an irrevocable letter of credit of not more than 180 days duration issued in good faith prior to the time of the confiscation or other taking, or (2) in any case with respect to which the President determines that application of the act of state doctrine is required in that particular case by the foreign policy interests of the United States and a suggestion to this effect is filed on his behalf in that case with the court." Pub.L. 89–171, 79 Stat. 653. Bracketed language added in 1965.

47. Under the *Sabbatino* decision, the courts would presume that any adjudication as to the lawfulness under international law of the act of a foreign state would embarrass the conduct of foreign policy unless the President says it would not. Under the amendment, the Court would presume that it may proceed with an adjudication on the merits unless the President stated officially that such an adjudication in the particular case would embarrass the conduct of foreign policy. S.Rep. No. 1188, 88th Cong., 2d Sess., pt. 1, at 24 (1964).

to bribe Nigerian officials. The contract was obtained, the commission was paid and was distributed to Nigerian officials. An unsuccessful bidder for the contract learned of the transaction and informed Nigerian and United States authorities. Charges were brought under the Foreign Corrupt Practices Act and the company and officer pleaded guilty. The unsuccessful bidder then brought this civil action and the defendants raised the act of state doctrine as a defense. The federal district court requested a letter from the Department of State on the act of state issue. The Department of State stated that judicial inquiry into the purpose behind the act of a foreign sovereign would not embarrass the Department or interfere with foreign affairs, which may result from a judicial determination that the act of a foreign sovereign is invalid. The district court held that the act of state applied. The circuit court reversed, largely persuaded by the letter from the Department of State. Certiorari was granted.]

JUSTICE SCALIA delivered the opinion of the Court.

The act of state doctrine is not some vague doctrine of abstention but a *"principle of decision* binding on federal and state courts alike." * * * Act of state issues only arise when a court *must decide*—that is, when the outcome of the case turns upon—the effect of official action by a foreign sovereign. When that question is not in the case, neither is the act of state doctrine. That is the situation here. Regardless of what the court's factual findings may suggest as to the legality of the Nigerian contract, its legality is simply not a question to be decided in the present suit, and there is thus no occasion to apply the rule of decision that the act of state doctrine requires. * * *

Petitioners insist * * * that the policies underlying our act of state cases—international comity, respect for the sovereignty of foreign nations on their own territory, and the avoidance of embarrassment to the Executive Branch in its conduct of foreign relations—are implicated in the present case because, as the District Court found, a determination that Nigerian officials demanded and accepted a bribe "would impugn or question the nobility of a foreign nation's motivations," and would "result in embarrassment to the sovereign or constitute interference in the conduct of foreign policy of the United States." * * * The United States, as *amicus curiae,* favors the same approach to the act of state doctrine, though disagreeing with petitioners as to the outcome it produces in the present case. We should not, the United States urges, "attach dispositive significance to the fact that this suit involves only the 'motivation' for, rather than the 'validity' of, a foreign sovereign act," * * * and should eschew "any rigid formula for the resolution of act of state cases generally," * * *. In some future case, perhaps, "litigation * * * based on alleged corruption in the award of contracts or other commercially oriented activities of foreign governments could sufficiently touch on 'national nerves' that the act of state doctrine or related principles of abstention would appropriately be found to bar the suit," * * * and we should therefore resolve this case on the narrowest possible ground, viz., that the letter from the legal advisor to the District Court gives sufficient indication that, "in the setting of this case," the act of state doctrine poses no bar to adjudication, *ibid.**

These urgings are deceptively similar to what we said in *Sabbatino*, where we observed that sometimes, even though the validity of the act of a foreign sovereign within its own territory is called into question, the policies underlying the act of state doctrine may not justify its application. We suggested that a sort of balancing approach could be applied—the balance shifting against application of the doctrine, for example, if the government that committed the "challenged act of state" is no longer in existence. * * * But what is appropriate in order to avoid unquestioning judicial acceptance of the acts of foreign sovereigns is not similarly appropriate for the quite opposite purpose of expanding judicial incapacities where such acts are not directly (or even indirectly) involved. It is one thing to suggest, as we have, that the policies underlying the act of state doctrine should be considered in deciding whether, despite the doctrine's technical availability, it should nonetheless not be invoked; it is something quite different to suggest that those underlying policies are a doctrine unto themselves, justifying expansion of the act of state doctrine (or, as the United States puts it, unspecified "related principles of abstention") into new and uncharted fields.

The short of the matter is this: Courts in the United States have the power, and ordinarily the obligation, to decide cases and controversies properly presented to them. The act of state doctrine does not establish an exception for cases and controversies that may embarrass foreign governments, but merely requires that, in the process of deciding, the acts of foreign sovereigns taken within their own jurisdictions shall be deemed valid. That doctrine has no application to the present case because the validity of no foreign sovereign act is at issue.

COMMENT ON THE ACT OF STATE DOCTRINE AND SOME EXCEPTIONS

As in the case of the application of sovereign immunity, there are exceptions to the act of state doctrine. Those applicable to sovereign immunity are specifically included in the FSIA, but those which limit the act of state doctrine are found, as is the doctrine itself, in the pages of precedent. One exception, where the act violates international law, has been discussed above. Two other actions which are debated as constituting exceptions are waivers and commercial activities. Uncertainty clouds the issue of the existence of a commercial exception to the act of state doctrine. The Supreme Court has stated that:

> [T]he concept of an act of state should not be extended to include the repudiation of a purely commercial obligation owed by a foreign sovereign

---

* Even if we agreed with the Government's fundamental approach, we would question its characterization of the legal advisor's letter as reflecting the absence of any policy objection to the adjudication. The letter * * * did not purport to say whether the State Department would like the suit to proceed, but rather responded (correctly, as we hold today) to the question whether the act of state doctrine was applicable.

or by one of its commercial instrumentalities * * * In their commercial capacities, foreign governments do not exercise powers peculiar to sovereigns * * * Subjecting them in connection with such acts to the same rules of law that apply to private citizens is unlikely to touch very sharply on "national nerves." *Dunhill* at 695, 704.[a]

The *Dunhill* case has become known as the "commercial exception" to the act of state doctrine notwithstanding that only four justices joined in that part of the opinion, and that four other justices wrote that:

[I]t does not follow that there should be a commercial act exception to the act of state doctrine * * * The carving out of broad exceptions to the doctrine is fundamentally at odds with the careful case-by-case approach adopted in *Sabbatino. Dunhill* at 725.

The ambiguity of the court has led to different views expressed in lower federal courts. One court has stated that:

consideration of the commercial nature of a given act is compelled if the doctrine is to be applied correctly. In this connection, attention is owed not to the purpose of the act but to its nature. The goal of the inquiry is to determine if denial of the act of state defense in the case under consideration will thwart the policy concerns in which the doctrine is rooted. *Sage Intern., Ltd. v. Cadillac Gage Co.*, 534 F.Supp. 896, 905 (E.D.Mich.1981).

But another court has observed that:

While purely commercial activity may not rise to the level of an act of state, certain seemingly commercial activities will trigger act of state considerations.... When the state *qua* state acts in the public interest, its sovereignty is asserted. The Courts must proceed cautiously to avoid an affront to that sovereignty * * * [W]e find that the act of state doctrine remains available when such caution is appropriate regardless of any commercial component of the activity involved. *IAM v. OPEC*, 649 F.2d 1354, 1360 (9th Cir.1981).

If a commercial exception is not to be granted, determining that the situs of the activity (commercial or not) is not in the foreign state may cause judicial rejection of the doctrine. This has proven important to the international debt issue. If nonpayment is held to have occurred at the office of the lending bank in the United States, the doctrine may be rejected as a defense. See *Allied Bank Intern. v. Banco Credito Agricola de Cartago*, 757 F.2d 516 (2d Cir.1985), cert. denied 473 U.S. 934, 106 S.Ct. 30, 87 L.Ed.2d 706 (1985).

QUESTIONS AND COMMENTS

1. Were Congress not to have acted after the *Sabbatino* decision, the cause of RODCO would appear quite dim. Was the legislation appropriate—it diminished the scope of a long and carefully worked out concept with sound diplomatic underpinnings? Would you make any alterations to the legislation?

2. The courts have not been receptive to the Sabbatino Amendment. That should not be surprising since it was passed to overrule a judicial

---

a. Alfred Dunhill of London, Inc. v. Republic of Cuba, 425 U.S. 682, 96 S.Ct. 1854, 48 L.Ed.2d 301 (1976).

decision. The amendment has been strictly construed. The act of state doctrine has been preserved except where a case has "precisely" fit the legislation. *See, e.g., Occidental Petroleum Corp. v. Buttes Gas & Oil Co.*, 331 F.Supp. 92 (C.D.Cal.1971), affirmed 461 F.2d 1261 (9th Cir.1972), cert. denied 409 U.S. 950, 93 S.Ct. 272, 34 L.Ed.2d 221 (1972); *Ethiopian Spice Extraction Share Co. v. Kalamazoo Spice Extraction Co.*, 543 F.Supp. 1224 (W.D.Mich. 1982), rev'd 729 F.2d 422 (6th Cir.1984); *French v. Banco Nacional de Cuba*, 23 N.Y.2d 46, 295 N.Y.S.2d 433, 242 N.E.2d 704 (1968). *But see Ramirez de Arellano v. Weinberger*, 745 F.2d 1500 (D.C.Cir.1984), where the court suggested that the Second Hickenlooper Amendment was not intended to be limited only to expropriated personal property which found its way into the United States, but referred to personal property only to diminish fears that the statute might be misread to create a new class of jurisdiction allowing a right to challenge all foreign expropriations in U.S. courts, even when there was *no* attachable property present. 745 F.2d 1500, n. 180 at 1541.

3. Do you expect that RODCO will be adversely affected by the act of state doctrine? What if, rather than being expropriated, Marnesia had enacted exchange controls which prohibited the removal of any funds from the country, and for several years RODCO was unable to repatriate funds on deposit in Marnesian banks? Has an act of state occurred? Would the Sabbatino Amendment apply? We see that while expropriation seems clearly an act of state, many other actions may be taken which are much less clear but nevertheless may seriously harm RODCO. Does the *Kirkpatrick* decision help RODCO? Had RODCO used arbitration, a 1988 amendment to the FSIA might help. It states that a court shall not refuse to enforce for act of state reasons arbitration agreements, confirmation of arbitration awards, or execution of judgments based upon orders confirming awards.

4. The Restatement (Third) of Foreign Relations Law of the United States, Section 443 states, "[C]ourts in the United States will generally refrain from examining the validity of a taking by a foreign state of property within its own territory, or from sitting in judgment on other acts of a government character done by a foreign state within its own territory and applicable there." That is essentially the *Sabbatino* position. Section 444 provides "[T]he act of state doctrine will not be applied in a case involving a claim of title or other right to property, when the claim is based on the assertion that a foreign state confiscated the property in violation of international law." It is a fairly narrow adoption of the Sabbatino Amendment (Hickenlooper #2). *But see* the analysis of the *Ramirez de Arellano* case in comment 2 above. The Restatement discussions were quite controversial, some arguing that the act of state should not be applied where there are challenges that international law was violated, at least if the Executive gives no indication that to decide the issues would harm foreign relations. *See* Halberstam, *Sabbatino Resurrected: The Act of State Doctrine in the Revised Restatement of U.S. Foreign Relations Law*, 79 Am.J.Int'l L. 68 (1985). How would the Restatement affect RODCO if the courts refer to the Restatement?

5. There is debate over whether the act of state ought to be eliminated. When Congress enacted the Cuban Liberty and Democracy Solidarity (Libertad) Act (Helms–Burton) it included as § 302(a)(6) "No court of the United States shall decline, based on the act of state doctrine, to make a determina-

tion on the merits in an action brought under paragraph (1)", which provided civil liability for "trafficking in confiscated property." Congress may well show similar disdain for presidential and judicial discretion in future legislation.

6. What is left of the act of state doctrine? Enough to cause RODCO concern?

PART D.   INSURING THE RISK

RODCO's risks were not insured in Marnesia. Not because the company was not interested, but because Marnesia refused to accept the OPIC program. Because RODCO is searching for a new location to manufacture its products, it wants to explore OPIC and MIGA. The company is evaluating an investment in Jamaica to replace its Marnesian facility. OPIC and MIGA insurance is available in Jamaica and the Caribbean Basin Initiative may offer additional benefits.

There are other insurers. Private companies offer some insurance against expropriation, currency restrictions, revocation of export/import permits, etc. The host government may offer insurance or require that it be obtained from local private companies. But RODCO is not enthusiastic about being insured by any entity within the host nation, and is familiar with the OPIC program. But OPIC is not without some problems. RODCO thus also may wish to consider insurance under MIGA.

COMMENT ON *OPIC* AND *MIGA* INSURANCE

OPIC's mandate is to "mobilize and facilitate the participation of U.S. private capital and skills in the economic and social development of less developed countries and areas, and countries in transition from nonmarket to market economies, thereby complementing the development assistance objectives of the United States." New insurance is halted when foreign relations become embittered with developing nations. When foreign relations with a nation become tenuous, if not hostile, the foreign nation is usually no longer a reasonable risk for investment insurance coverage. OPIC may insure certain risks that private insurers would reject, because U.S. foreign policy is to encourage investment in a certain nation for political reasons. Not long after the USSR and the Eastern European countries shed communist governments, OPIC began to sign agreements with new more market oriented governments for OPIC eligibility. OPIC has also increased its presence in the Middle East and Africa, including financing as well as insurance.

The President has some discretion in designating countries as beneficiaries. Otherwise qualifying countries may be denied OPIC insurance if they do not extend internationally recognized workers' rights to domestic workers, but presidential discretion may result in a waiver of this prohibition on national economic interest grounds. Chile was denied OPIC coverage between 1986 and 1990. In 1990, amid considerable controversy, the President determined that Chile had satisfactorily addressed workers' rights, and restored OPIC coverage.

Initially three principal risks were the reason for the creation of OPIC. They are risk of loss due to (1) inconvertibility, (2) expropriation or confiscation, or (3) war, revolution, insurrection or civil strife. A fourth class has been added called "business interruption" caused by any of the principal three risks. Before insurance against inconvertibility of currency is approved, the investor must obtain assurance from the host country that investor earnings will be convertible into dollars and that repatriation of capital is permitted. If the currency thereafter becomes inconvertible by act of the government, OPIC will accept the foreign currency, or a draft for the amount, and will provide the investor with U.S. dollars.

Expropriation "includes, but is not limited to, any abrogation, repudiation, or impairment by a foreign government of its own contract with an investor with respect to a project, where such abrogation, repudiation, or impairment is not caused by the investor's own fault or misconduct, and materially adversely affects the continued operation of the project." OPIC's standard insurance contract contains a lengthy description of what is considered to be expropriatory action sufficient to require OPIC payment. That definition may help an investor in drafting a contract with the foreign host government, because that government will have to deal with OPIC once OPIC has paid the investor's claim.

Upon payment of the claim, OPIC is subrogated to all rights to the investor's claim against the host government. Because the United States must deal with the foreign government, OPIC will not write any insurance in a foreign country until that country agrees to accept OPIC insurance and thus to negotiate with OPIC after claims have been paid. Some governments have been reluctant to accept OPIC insurance because national leaders have been concerned that acceptance would constitute admission that the nation was susceptible to the various risks covered, particularly revolution and insurrection.

The third form of coverage, "war, revolution, insurrection, or civil strife," (political violence) is not defined by the statute. The usual OPIC contract provides protection against "injury to the physical condition, destruction, disappearance or seizure and retention of Covered Property directly caused by war (whether or not under formal declaration) or by revolution or insurrection and includes injury to the physical condition, destruction, disappearance or seizure and retention of Covered Property as a direct result of actions taken in hindering, combating or defending against a pending or expected hostile act whether in war, revolution, or insurrection." OPIC Contract Article 1.07. Civil strife is politically motivated violence (e.g., civil disturbances, riots, acts of sabotage, terrorism).

Insured investors present claims to OPIC only after exhausting local remedies in the host nations. Claims are then "settled, and disputes arising as a result thereof may be arbitrated with the consent of the parties, on such terms and conditions as the Corporation may determine." OPIC insurance contracts have stated that "any controversy arising out of or relating to this Contract or the breach thereof shall be settled by arbitration in accordance with the then prevailing Commercial Arbitration Rules of the American Arbitration Association." The arbitration process is important; OPIC has challenged a number of claims presented to it by U.S. companies claiming to have lost property through expropriations.

OPIC insurance, which is limited to U.S. investors, led to the establishment of similar insurance on an international level by the World Bank's 1988 creation of the Multilateral Investment Guarantee Agency (MIGA).

Risks covered by MIGA are noncommercial and include inconvertibility, deprivation of ownership or control by government actions, breach of contract by the government where there is no recourse to a judicial or arbitral tribunal or arbitral forum, and loss from military action or civil disturbance. For the most part the coverage is what OPIC covers. Unlike national programs, such as OPIC, MIGA has the force of a large group of nations behind it when it presses a claim. The clear intention of MIGA is to avoid political interference and consider the process solely as creating legal issues. MIGA has yet to face claims experience. If over time the risks MIGA (and other programs such as OPIC) insure substantially diminish, the use of such insurance will decrease. If on the other hand the risks become reality, the effectiveness of the claims procedures will become evident.

Creating MIGA within the World Bank structure offers benefits a separate international organization would lack. MIGA has access to World Bank data on nations' economic and social status, thus helping the assessment of risks. The World Bank has considerable credibility which favors MIGA, and encourages broad participation. It is not certain how MIGA will affect national programs, such as OPIC. A U.S. company, for example, might prefer dealing with OPIC because of greater confidence of claims being paid, of maintaining information confidentiality, and benefiting from legal processes established in bilateral investment treaties. Experience * * * suggests that U.S. investors very much approve the establishment of MIGA, and that MIGA's insurance is compatible with that of OPIC, acting to some degree as a gap filler for U.S. investors when OPIC insurance is not available or inadequate for the project.

QUESTIONS AND COMMENTS

1. The impact of MIGA on OPIC is unclear. The two appear very compatible. A U.S. company may prefer to deal with OPIC because of greater confidence that claims will be paid, that information will remain confidential, and that the legal processes included in bilateral treaties to which the United States is a party will be available. But MIGA offers the voice and pressure of the membership of the World Bank. Investors in nations without an OPIC equivalent are likely to welcome MIGA. MIGA's success ought to be both where it fills gaps and where it competes with a national insurance program. *See* I. Shihata, MIGA and Foreign Investment—Origins, Policies and Basic Documents of the Multilateral Investment Guarantee Agency (1988).

2. When Marnesia refused to accept the OPIC program, the president of Marnesia said, "to do so would admit that my country is unstable, that it is subject to war, revolution or insurrection. It is not. I can assure you of the stability of my country for investments." What might you have said to him about the purpose of the OPIC plan, and how his perception of OPIC is not very sound? Is there any valid reason why a nation might reject the program?

3. Do either OPIC or MIGA conflict with the Calvo doctrine, which states that a person shall not seek the assistance of his own nation, that he is entitled only to the same remedies as host nation citizens? When the OPIC claim has been paid the U.S. government proceeds against the expropriating nation for losses caused by that latter nation's taking of property. Is it an appropriate foreign policy to have the U.S. government pressing claims of private investors?

4. Are there steps RODCO might take to avoid the losses insured against? How predictable are the risks?

5. Would it make any difference were you to learn that OPIC had in force more insurance in one nation than sound risk insurance principles would dictate? Do you really care who pays the loss claims, OPIC or the American taxpayer if the premiums are not sufficient, as long as RODCO's claims are paid?

PROBLEM 10.7 FOREIGN INVESTMENT IN NAFTA: DRILL–BIT OF THE U.S. IN MEXICO AND MUNSON OF CANADA IN THE U.S.

SECTION I. THE SETTING

Drill–Bit, to which we were introduced in Problem 9.4, had been considering in the early 1990s a foreign direct investment in Mexico. Although Drill–Bit has a successful relationship with Productos Petroleos de México, S.A., its licensee, Drill–Bit has decided that an equity investment would allow both greater day-to-day control over the production of oil drilling bits, and greater profits in a growing market by not having to share the benefits with Productos. With an equity investment, Drill–Bit would receive all the profits. Drill–Bit wanted a wholly owned Mexican subsidiary, but it encountered resistance by the Mexican authorities who urged Drill–Bit to create a joint venture with Productos, allowing Productos 51 percent of the equity, and control of management. Although the restrictive Mexican 1973 investment law had been emasculated by the quite liberal 1989 regulations, which seemed to allow Drill–Bit to have a joint venture, the Mexican government made it clear that it preferred a joint venture. Consequently, Drill–Bit continued the licensing arrangement with Productos. Times have now changed, and Drill–Bit has renewed its interest in an equity investment in Mexico. Drill–Bit recently expressed some interest in acquiring Productos, but the Productos management rejected the overture, and Drill–Bit will have to "start from scratch," undertaking a greenfields investment. With the enactment by Mexico of a new quite liberal investment law in December, 1993, and the formation of the North American Free Trade Agreement, Drill–Bit now wishes to explore establishing a wholly owned subsidiary in Mexico, probably in Mexico City. The investment is likely to be about $28 million.

A second company, Munson Ltd. of Ontario, Canada, is also interested in a foreign investment within NAFTA. But its interest is not in Mexico, but in an investment in the United States. Additionally, it is not interested in commencing a greenfields investment, as is Drill–Bit in Mexico. Munson hopes to acquire a U.S. company. Munson Ltd., is partly owned by the Canadian government. It is an importer and exporter of aerotechnology. Munson has had some difficulties with the U.S. Department of Commerce for re-exporting technology purchased from U.S. companies to the People's Republic of China. Munson would like to acquire TECHCO Manufacturing, a U.S. company in St. Louis that manufactures parts for commercial aircraft made by Boeing. Munson is known to have significant contracts with a French military aircraft manufacturer which has sold aircraft to a number of Arab nations.

SECTION II.   FOCUS OF CONSIDERATION

Some of the risks and restrictions confronting the formation and operation of a foreign investment were discussed in Problem 10.0. They raised the kinds of issues faced in commencing a foreign direct investment in developing nations and nonmarket economy nations, including the latter nations in transition to market economies. This problem considers investments in the North American Free Trade Agreement area. In Part A, a U.S. company wishes to invest in Mexico. The problem outlines some of the transition in investment regulation occurring in Mexico from a nation restrictive to foreign investment in the 1970s, becoming more open to investment in the 1980s, and agreeing in the 1990s, as a member of NAFTA, to open the door even wider, at least to NAFTA member nations. The Mexican framework for investment by U.S. and Canadian investors includes the Mexican investment laws, the investment provisions of the NAFTA, and the investment provisions of the World Trade Organization. This investment is by commencing a company rather than by acquisition.

This problem also considers, in Part B, an investment by a Canadian company in the United States. Although the United States is one of the least restrictive nations with regard to control of foreign owned investments, such investments are not free of all control. Many foreign investors consider U.S. antitrust and securities laws to be indirect barriers to entry in the United States. Furthermore, the Omnibus Trade and Competitiveness Act of 1988 included the Exon–Florio provisions which affect foreign acquisitions of U.S. That law was replaced in 2007 by the Foreign Investment and National Security Act (FINSA). The acquisition of the TECHCO Manufacturing company in this problem may be subject to FINSA, since it has technology on the carefully monitored by the Department of Defense. Like the first part dealing with Drill–Bit in Mexico, the investment provisions of NAFTA may affect the proposed Canadian investment.

Part A requires use of provisions of the 1993 Mexican Foreign Investment Law, Chapter 11 of the NAFTA and the Agreement on Trade–

Related Investment Measures (TRIMs) of the WTO. Part B requires use of the U.S. FINSA. All are in the Documents Supplement.

SECTION III. READINGS, QUESTIONS AND COMMENTS

COMMENT ON FOREIGN INVESTMENT IN NAFTA MEMBER STATES

There are two schemes of foreign investment rules which must be addressed. The first are the foreign investment laws and regulations of the individual NAFTA Parties. The current respective foreign investment laws of Canada, Mexico and the United States are not only very different, but have reached their current status by means of quite separate histories. The second scheme is that of NAFTA, which establishes common laws in some areas, and seeks to extend that harmonization to nearly all foreign investment, with minimum exceptions. These are important provisions; the prior Canada–United States Free Trade Agreement (CFTA) included a few very modest provisions governing investment, only one of which addressed dispute settlement. But investment between Canada and the United States was considerably less restricted at the time CFTA was negotiated than between Mexico and the CFTA Parties at the time NAFTA was negotiated. What little groundwork was provided by CFTA for the later development of the NAFTA investment rules was nevertheless a helpful start. The GATT offered no such help, from its beginning it had not been intended to govern investment. Nor did the WTO offer guidelines. The WTO was still in the process of negotiation when the NAFTA was signed in 1992, and the investment provisions finalized in the WTO are of far more limited scope (largely dealing with performance requirements) than those of NAFTA.

CFTA should not be viewed as a harmonization of similar attitudes towards foreign investment, with NAFTA as adding a nation with a restrictive tradition towards such investment. In some respects, Canada and Mexico held similar views towards foreign investment, based on their experience with U.S. investment. Both nations were concerned with dominance by U.S. investment. Both were concerned that they would become the site for foreign (mainly U.S.) investment to extract natural resources for shipment abroad for manufacture. Both were concerned with the impact of dividends returned abroad to the parent corporate owners, and their impact on the nation's balance of payments. And finally, both were concerned that having so many foreign centers of decision-making would lead to few professional managerial positions in Canada and Mexico for host nation citizens, where the best jobs would be the supervision of the extraction of natural resources. This parallel concern of the U.S.'s north and south neighbors is partly why both Canada's and Mexico's foreign investment laws, outlined below, have been quite restrictive. But the Canadian laws have often been more sophisticated, addressing more closely acquisitions than greenfields (starting from scratch in a green field) investment.

There is more to NAFTA, however, than a common scheme of laws governing foreign investment. The Agreement also seeks to assure that a foreign investment is secure, and that treatment accorded foreign investment meets requirements of international law, including national treatment and "fair and equitable treatment." (Arts. 1102, 1105(1).) Because international law has been disappointing in its deficiencies regarding rules governing both the responsibility of the foreign investor towards the host state, and the host state towards the investor, this may be deceptive protection. The nature of international law governing takings of property, for example, has long been a major subject of debate. The NAFTA Parties have addressed this debate, and have included a substantial article governing "Expropriation and Compensation." (Art. 1110.)

The NAFTA Parties were often accused of failing to consider environmental issues in drafting the Agreement. This is certainly true in many areas covered in the Agreement, and the criticism and debate led to the adoption of the environmental side agreement. Chapter 11 contains a provision stating that nothing "shall be construed to prevent a Party from adopting, maintaining, or enforcing any measure otherwise consistent with this Chapter that it considers appropriate to ensure that investment activity in its territory is undertaken in a manner sensitive to environmental concerns." (Article 1114(1)). However, this somewhat circular language would not necessarily preclude a finding by an arbitral panel that an otherwise legal environmental regulation required payment of compensation to a foreign investor whose business was damaged as a result. The fact remains, however, no NAFTA tribunal to date has reached such a conclusion.

The importance of the resolution of investment disputes is evident by the attention given such issue in NAFTA. While the general investment provisions are covered in the first 14 articles of Chapter 11, which comprise Section A, the next 24 articles, which comprise Section B, govern dispute settlement, as do the four annexes to Chapter 11. Chapter 11 was unique in a free trade agreement at the time of the negotiations, as it provides the rules governing foreign investment, the methods to settle disputes involving foreign investment, including the standing of *individual* investors of a Party to challenge the actions of another Party, rather than requiring the government of the investor to bring the claim. In all of these respects, Chapter 11 closely resembles the many bilateral investment treaties ("BITs") concluded by the United States, Canada and many other countries during the past 30 years, more than 1800 as of 2011, 50 by the United States alone (although few with developed nations).

Although Chapter 11 is entitled "Investment", all investment is not necessarily governed by its provisions. As previously discussed, the notable exception is investment in financial services, covered in Chapter 14, which includes rules both governing the investment, and outlining a procedure for the settlement of disputes. The dispute settlement provisions of Chapter 14 (see Art. 1415), however, are integrated with those of Chapter 11.

COMMENT ON THE INVESTMENT LAWS OF CANADA, MEXICO AND THE UNITED STATES

Nations, including the United States, have seldom welcomed *all* foreign investment. Investment which offers the nation something it lacks, such as technology, or significant numbers of jobs, may be so welcome it is offered incentives. But foreign investment which competes with domestic investment may face very complex obstacles, or absolute prohibitions. Thus each nation has its own history of foreign investment rules. The respective histories of Canada, Mexico and the United States in developing each nation's current laws illustrate the struggle with balancing restrictions and incentives.

Canada. Although U.S. persons often view Canada through a mirror and see themselves, thus assuming that Canadians and the Canadian government will be very receptive to foreign investment, the policies of Canada over the years reflect an ambivalent attitude towards investment. Canada has long regulated foreign investment by both federal and provincial laws. Soon after its creation as a federation in 1867, Canada established high tariffs to protect infant industries from exports from the United States. This caused U.S. manufacturers to invest in Canada to surmount the tariff wall. Soon the United States was the principal source of foreign investment, and for U.S. industries Canada was a natural location for the first foreign investment of many U.S. companies.

Most Canadian investment laws have focused on specific sectors, such as financial institutions, transportation, natural resources[1] and, quite importantly, publishing.[2] Canada was always a natural target for investment from the United States, especially since so much of the industrial development of the United States occurred relatively near the Canadian border. Canada's attitude toward foreign investment remained quite receptive until nationalistic forces in the 1960s began to challenge an open investment policy. The first measure of significance was the creation of the Foreign Investment Review Agency (FIRA) in 1974, which allowed the federal government to review proposed foreign investment, especially acquisitions of Canadian companies, and in some cases deny their development. The National Energy Program in 1980 was intended to *reduce* foreign ownership in the oil and gas industry. Most of that foreign ownership was by U.S. companies. A Conservative government elected in 1984 replaced the FIRA with the Investment Canada Act (ICA)(1985), which governs foreign investment in Canada and especially acquisitions. When the CFTA was adopted, it incorporated part of the ICA, providing that a review of an acquisition under the ICA would not be subject to the CFTA dispute settlement provisions. (CFTA Art. 1608(1)). The ICA was to be amended to comply with the CFTA, but considerable definitional language in the ICA was retained by reference. When NAFTA was adopted, excluded from NAFTA dispute settlement provisions were decisions by Canada following a review under the ICA. This, plus the exclusion of "cultural industries" of Canada by incorporation of the CFTA provisions (Art. 2106, Annex 2106.), indicate that Canada has insisted in retaining some domestic control over foreign investment, especially the acquisition of Canadian owned industries, and most especially "cultural" industries.

---

1. Oil and gas acquisitions were prohibited until the *Masse Policy* adopted in 1992 was rescinded, leaving such regulation to the Investment Canada Act, which allowed such investment, but with approval required of some acquisitions. The thresholds before approval was required were quite high, making the law less restrictive than it otherwise appeared.

2. Canada considers publishing to be a cultural industry. Until restrictions in the Canadian *Baie Comeau Policy* on ownership of publishing were relaxed, foreign investment in publishing was very difficult.

Mexico. The U.S. has never viewed Mexico through the same mirror as Canada, seeing itself in the reflection. Despite all the differences between Canada and the United States, Canada usually has been viewed an equal by the United States. Not so with Mexico. The United States has traditionally viewed Mexico as something less than a partner. The United States views Mexico as needing the United States, but the United States had not viewed the United States as needing Mexico, at least until NAFTA raised the prospects of a low wage platform to assist U.S. manufacturers in competing more effectively with their counterparts in the European Union and Japan. Mexico had responded accordingly, with suspicion and deliberation. While Canada never really flirted with socialism by substantially increasing national ownership of the means of production and distribution, Mexico did so in the 1970s. The Mexican investment law, the transfer of technology law, and the trade names and inventions law, all enacted in the 1970s, were models of restrictive laws of developing nations adopted during the tense and often bitter North–South dialogue, when developing nations argued that they were poor because the developed nations were rich, and that there had to be a transfer of wealth from the latter to the former. The 1973 Mexican investment law was such a product.

Several government actions reducing foreign ownership of investment brought considerable industrial production and distribution into government ownership long before the 1973 law. Mexico opened to foreign investment with few restrictions during the *Porfiriato,* the 1876–1911 reign of Porfirio Díaz. But the state assumed a more restrictive role with the new 1917 Constitution, which followed the revolutionary turmoil beginning in 1910. It soon became apparent that the state would begin to intervene in many areas where there was foreign investment already in place in Mexico. After an unsuccessful attempt by Mexico to participate in the foreign owned petroleum industry in 1925, a labor dispute led to the total nationalization of the industry in 1938, reducing in the minds of many Mexicans the apparent conflict with Article 27 of the Mexican Constitution, which decreed all natural resources to be owned by the nation. Two years later, the government severely limited foreign participation in the communications sector. A 1944 Emergency Decree was the first broad attempt to regulate foreign investment, and limited certain investments to joint ventures. The joint venture concept was extended by a Mixed Ministerial Commission established in 1947, although it was of limited effectiveness. The 1950s saw some limited control of specific industries introduced, and electric power was nationalized in 1960. Mining was controlled by an act in 1961, but the next dozen years were relatively free of significant changes.

The 1973 Law to Promote Mexican Investment and Regulate Foreign Investment, to some degree pulled together the policies of encouraging but limiting foreign investment, which had been introduced during the past several decades, and were clearly part of the Echeverrían Administration policy, which began in 1970. A strict 1972 Law for the Registration of the Transfer of Technology and the Use and Exploitation of Patents and Marks, forewarned the coming restrictiveness towards foreign investment. The 1973 Investment Law classified investments, limiting some to state ownership, some to private ownership exclusively by Mexican nationals, and most of the rest where foreign ownership was limited to 49%. The law did not apply retroactively, but if a company expanded into new lines of products or new locations, it was expected to Mexicanize, that is to sell majority ownership to Mexicans. But escape provisions and the operational code in Mexico (the way things really work), resulted in few existing companies converting to Mexican majority ownership. What the laws did accomplish was to curtail significant new investment. A new institution, the National Commission on Foreign Investment, assumed substantial discretionary power to carry out the new rules.

What President Echeverría started, his successor José López Portillo continued when he entered office in 1976. His final year in office in 1982 saw first the amendment of the 1972 Transfer of Technology Law, retaining its restrictiveness and extending its scope, and second, the nationalization of the banking industry. His successor Miguel de la Madrid assumed control of a nation with a defaulted national debt, a plunging currency, and diminished interest by foreign investors. He realized that Mexico must change its policies. De la Madrid issued investment regulations in 1984 which partly relaxed the restrictiveness of the 1970s. Further regulations were issued in the following years, and in 1989, the first year of Carlos Salinas de Gortari's presidency, new Regulations were issued that were so inconsistent with the clear philosophy of the restrictive 1973 law that their Constitutionality was questioned. The direction was turned—Mexico's ascension into the stratosphere of developing nation restrictiveness towards foreign investment had reached its apogee in 1982, and was coming back to earth. Foreign investment was returning. It was further encouraged by Mexico's admission to the GATT in 1985, after years of internal debate. The replacement of the 1973 Investment Law twenty years after its introduction ended an unsettling era of Mexican foreign investment policy.

The 1993 Investment Act was a highlight of the Salinas Administration, an encouragement to the many investors who had made commitments to Mexico during his administration, and a pre-requisite to participation in and compliance with NAFTA. The 1993 law improved access to investment in Mexico, containing investment attracting provisions absent from the earlier law. Abandoned was the mandatory joint venture focus, although that was never successful in stimulating foreign investment, and—over nine years—the elimination of the requirement of government approval for most foreign investments. Moreover, the new law permitted foreign ownership of property in the "prohibited zones"—100 km. from the borders and 50 km. from the seacoasts—for "commercial" purposes. But some significant restrictions remained, including control over natural resources, reservation of some areas for Mexican nationals, and retention of the Calvo Clause doctrine (in likely conflict with the international arbitration obligations of Mexico in NAFTA Chapter 11, Section B), which attempted to limit a foreign investor's use of its own nation's diplomatic efforts in the event of an investment conflict with Mexico. But the law nevertheless was a huge reversal of the policies of the 1970s, and it both established a more efficient National Registry of Foreign Investment, and allowed proposals to be assumed to have been approved if they were not acted upon within the established time-frame. Regulations finally adopted in 1999 are consistent with both the 1993 law and its investment encouraging philosophy. Mexico under NAFTA is not quite as open to foreign investment as are Canada and the United States, but the 1993 law established a sufficiently respectful base from which to participate in NAFTA's foreign investment framework. It was quite a remarkable transformation, and a credit to several of Mexico's leaders.

United States. The United States has no "foreign investment law", or "foreign investment review agency", as have been discussed above with regard to Canada and Mexico, but it is incorrect to suggest that foreign investment is fully and freely admitted in the United States. The United States has restrictions on foreign participation in facilities that produce or use nuclear materials. Domestic airlines are subject to a maximum 25 percent foreign equity (voting shares) ownership. Just as many foreign investment laws of other nations, including those discussed above of Canada and Mexico, have caused consternation in the United States about allegedly ambiguous provisions, the Exon–Florio and FINSA provisions have often proven to be unwelcome abroad. They especially include the absence of any definition of national security; decisions under Exon–Florio, FINSA and similar legislation are excluded from arbitral review under NAFTA Chapters 11 and 20. (Art. 1138.1.) But for the most part the review process has not discouraged acquisition of U.S. businesses, although there have been several instances where proposed acquisitions have been halted, and even reversed.

Comment on Foreign Investment and *NAFTA*

The NAFTA investment provisions in Chapter 11 are included in two major Sections. Section A covers investment rules, and Section B the settlement of investment disputes.

Section A includes several general rules which require each Party to offer specific treatment to each other Party. The most important is "national treatment," requiring treatment to another Party "no less favorable than that it accords" to the Party's own investors. (Art. 1102) This is similar to the provision that follows, that a Party accord investors of another Party treatment no less favorable than that it accords to any other Party or non-Party. (Art. 1103) There is also a requirement that the treatment of investors of another Party meet a minimum standard, incorporating a rule of "international law, including fair and equitable treatment and full protection and security." (Art. 1105) The "fair and equitable treatment" provision has been the subject of enormous debate and at least a half-dozen NAFTA arbitral tribunal decisions. These provisions are a kind of boiler-plate framework, and they have roots in the GATT treatment applicable to the sale of goods and in the bilateral investment treaties ("BITs") concluded by the United States with various developing countries since 1980. The national treatment concept in NAFTA applies equally to goods, services, technology and investment. But foreign investment has some special requirements, and several NAFTA provisions attempt to deal with them.

One ongoing concern of foreign investors has been *performance requirements*, local mandates that a certain percentage of the goods or services be exported, or be of domestic content, or meet a balance between import needs and exports, or link local sales to the volume of exports, or contain certain technology transferred from abroad, or mandate meeting certain exclusive sales targets. Each of these is addressed in NAFTA, with certain exceptions. (Art. 1106) Perhaps the second most disliked domestic restrictions on foreign investment are mandated levels of local equity, the *involuntary joint venture*. A prohibition against a minimum level of domestic equity is included in the national treatment provision. (Art. 1102(4)) There is also a prohibition against a minimum number of local persons being appointed to senior management. (Art. 1107(1)) But there may be a local requirement that a majority of the board of directors (or a board committee) be nationals or residents, as long as the investor is not therefore impaired in controlling the investment. (Art. 1107(2)) A fourth investor concern is free transferability of profits, royalty payments, etc., both during the operation and upon liquidation of the investment. The Agreement attempts to assure this right, with some exceptions dealing with such issues as bankruptcy, securities trading, criminal offenses (money laundering), etc. (Art. 1109).

The above areas of concern deal mostly with the ability to commence and operate an investment free from certain restrictions. There is another time in the life of a corporation which has long been perhaps the most significant risk for foreign investors. That is when the business is nationalized or expropriated. NAFTA includes an eight-part article outlining rules for both the taking, and the compensation. (Art. 1110) Nowhere do the words "prompt, adequate and effective" appear, the standard the United States government has long argued to be the mandate of international law, but constituting a standard specifically rejected by Mexico subsequent to the nationalization of petroleum in 1938. The language of NAFTA addresses each of these areas, however, in detail. Compensation "shall be paid without delay and be fully recognizable." But there have been disputes over whether an expropriation has occurred, particularly where the taking is indirect or "creeping." The adequacy of compensation issue is covered by the NAFTA requirement of "fair market value" appraised "immediately before" the expropriation occurs, and the adequacy by the requirement of payment in a "G7 currency", or one convertible to such currency. The expropriation article has also been the subject of considerable debate during the past ten years, and Article 1110 has been used on a number of occasions to challenge actions which are not traditional nationalizations, but more impediments to effective operation of an investment which significantly reduce its value.

Chapter 11 applies to all investments, as defined in Article 1139. But exempted are financial services investments covered in Chapter 14, and the numerous exemptions contained in Annex III,[3] and where special social services are performed (police, public health, etc.). (Art. 1101) But if the provisions of Chapter 11 conflict with provisions in other chapters, the latter prevails. (Art. 1112)

Section B governs the settlement of investment disputes between a Party and an investor of another Party. This part of Chapter 11 establishes a procedure for claims. It proceeds first by consultation or negotiation (Art. 1118), and then moves directly to arbitration under the ICSID Convention, the latter's Additional Facility Rules, or the UNCITRAL Arbitration Rules.

---

3. The Annex III Mexican reservations do not affect this problem.

Arbitration may be brought under the ICSID Convention where both the disputing Party and the Party of the investor are parties to the Convention; since neither Canada or Mexico are ICSID parties, the standard ICSID mechanism is not available at present for Chapter 11 disputes. However, the ICSID Additional Facility Rules apply if either the disputing Party or the Party of the investor is a party to the Convention, which makes the Additional Facility Rules available for U.S. and Mexico or U.S. and Canada disputes. The UNCITRAL arbitration rules are also available for such disputes, and for disputes between Canada and Mexico. But the matter is not fully shifted to these forms of arbitration; such issues as the selection of arbitrators, the place of arbitration, and enforcement are covered in NAFTA. (Arts. 1123–1124, 1130, 1136.)

The investment provisions of Chapter 11 are a major step in the multilateral agreement process. They are far more developed than those contained in the earlier CFTA, and the more recent WTO Agreement on Trade–Related Investment Measures (TRIMS). As noted above, they follow U.S. practice with BITs, and have served as a model for the investment provisions in such more recent trade agreements as the U.S.–Singapore and U.S.–Chile FTAs, the U.S.–Central American FTA ("CAFTA"), other bilateral FTAs currently being negotiated by the United States, and the 2004 U.S. Model BIT. They will likely be the model for the investment provisions of the FTAA (Free Trade Agreement of the Americas) as well if such an agreement is ever concluded.

However rational the progress in the development of the NAFTA investment rules may appear, these rules are not without their critics. The absence of serious attention to the environment and labor issues led to the adoption of NAFTA-saving environmental and labor side agreements. The negotiations for the FTAA and the various U.S. FTAs are also addressing both of these issues. But that is not enough to satisfy some critics. The rhetoric of the North–South dialogue of the 1960s and 1970s, reflected to some extent in the failure of the "Multilateral Agreement on Investment" at the OECD in 1998, has never really gone away. Turning their attention to NAFTA, some scholars and many NGOs suggest that NAFTA is little more than a way for the United States to further dominate investment in Mexico, by establishing rules which for the most part govern the conduct of Mexico in admitting investment, but omitting any consideration of the responsibilities of the foreign investor. Whether these concerns have some rational basis or are largely misplaced remains to be seen. Few investors have recovered against Mexico under Chapter 11, and expropriation has been found in only one case, *Metalclad*. The concerns about Chapter 11 as a mechanism to dominate Mexico may also have been misplaced. Of the 66 actions filed under Chapter 11 as of late 2010, 19 were against Mexico, 28 against Canada, and 19 against the United States. The more recent activity under Chapter 11 has largely involved claims against Canada. Many early critics have done an about-face, and now complain that Chapter 11 gives foreign investors in the United States greater rights than they would enjoy under U.S. law. The NAFTA jurisprudence, including an excerpt from the tribunal decision in *S.D. Myers v. Government of Canada*, is discussed in this Problem.

PART A. DRILL–BIT IN MEXICO

Drill–Bit would like you, as counsel, to advise the company on the procedures in establishing a direct equity investment in Mexico, preferably a wholly owned entity. They will want to know about the written regulatory scheme of Mexican law which will be applicable. Because Mexico is a member of both NAFTA and the WTO, provisions of those trade agreements which govern foreign investment should be reviewed. Drill–Bit would like to know what restrictions might apply to their investment, and whether the Mexican domestic law is consistent with Mexican obligations under the NAFTA and the WTO. The company would also like to know something about how an investment dispute might be settled.

What is important to Drill–Bit about foreign investment in Mexico is the abrupt reversal from years of restrictive laws and attitudes towards foreign investment in Mexico. Drill–Bit will certainly face the frustrations of dealing with the "Mexican bureaucracy", and receiving timely approval of various filings, but investment in Mexico has become much more like investment in many foreign nations where there are investment laws that are more incentive than restrictive based and interpreted. Drill–Bit may plan its investment with reasonable assurance that compliance with the Investment Law of 1993 and its regulations will allow Drill–Bit to commence business in Mexico. What is also important for Drill–Bit, and is the focus of this part of the problem, is to be aware that in addition to Mexican domestic law regulating investment, the NAFTA in Chapter 11 provides both limitations on what Mexico may undertake regarding regulation of foreign investment, and a process for settling investment disputes. If Mexico were to elect a president in the future who was opposed to foreign investment and began severely restricting Drill–Bit's activities, the dispute resolution provisions of NAFTA would certainly become extremely important to Drill–Bit. Drill–Bit is wise to want to know something about those provisions, and any experience of foreign investors in using Chapter 11 of NAFTA to date.

BRYAN, GONZÁLEZ VARGAS & GONZÁLEZ BAZ, NAFTA VADENMECUM

(1994).*

Under the [1993] provisions, foreign investment is defined simply as participation of foreign investment in Mexican corporations, directly or indirectly, or in activities or acts covered by the law. A foreign investor is defined as anyone other than a Mexican.

Article 5 reserves "the functions determined by the laws" regarding certain strategic areas exclusively to the State. The repealed law reserved the activities in these areas. The difference in phrasing is emphasized by the provisions of Article 7. For example, the functions determined by the

---

* Reprinted with permission of the law firm of Bryan, González Vargas & González Baz, Mexico City.

laws regarding railroads are exclusively reserved to the State, but Article 7(III)(r) permits a number of services relating to railroads to receive up to 49% foreign investment.

Article 6 reserves certain activities to Mexican individuals or Mexican companies, with a Exclusion of Foreigners Clause. The list is quite limited however. . . .

Article 7, sets forth limitations on foreign investment in certain other areas, while Article 8, by implication, lists a number of areas in which foreign investment may participate in up to 49% but providing that if a favorable resolution is granted by the Foreign Investment Commission, foreign investment participation may exceed 49%.

Finally, acquisitions in existing Mexican companies with total asset value over an amount to be established from time to time that directly or indirectly result in foreign participation above 49% require Foreign Investment Commission approval. . . . The new law provisions in effect allow foreign acquisition of an interest in an Mexican corporation in any percentage unless the total asset value exceeds, currently 85 million new pesos (slightly less than 30 million U.S. dollars), assuming, of course, the company is not engaged in one of the still-restricted activities.

In its decision-making process, the only criteria that the Commission [on foreign investment] must examine is the impact on jobs and training of the application, the technological contribution implied, the fulfillment of the environmental regulations, and the general contribution to the competitive position of the Mexican productive plant. While conditions may still be imposed, they may not distort international trade.

During the discussion of the draft proposed by the Administration to the Congress, the . . . main argument was that the law should provide clear and concrete channels for Foreign Investment, not leaving any discretional authority to the National Foreign Investment Commission to decide major percentages of participation in different sectors of our economy. Admission of foreign investment in any percentage is today the rule, not the exception.

MURPHY, ACCESS AND PROTECTION FOR FOREIGN INVESTMENT IN MEXICO UNDER MEXICO'S NEW FOREIGN INVESTMENT LAW AND THE NORTH AMERICAN FREE TRADE AGREEMENT*

When the 1993 Foreign Investment Law so confirmed key openings of the 1989 Regulations, it was an unequivocal repudiation of past Echeverrían economic policies.

In general, the 1993 Law also follows the initiatives of the Regulations in its treatment of the four inner bastions of Article 27.[a] Although

---

* Reprinted with permission of the ICSID Review Foreign Investment Law Journal.

a. Editors Note: The author's "bastions" are a compulsory Calvo Clause, restrictions on foreign ownership of real property, and Mexican state monopolies in hydrocarbons and electric power.

the 1993 Law eliminates the 1973 statute's *ipso facto* application of the Calvo Clause, it adopts the Regulations' requirement that the constitutive documents of a Mexican company must contain either a Calvo Clause or an "exclusion-of-foreigners" clause. Regarding foreign ownership of Mexican real property, the 1993 Law incorporates and broadens the liberalizations of the Regulations. In the Restricted Zone, a Mexican company (with a Calvo Clause) owned by foreigners can acquire real property for non-residential purposes as well as trust rights for residential purposes, and foreign individuals, foreign companies and Mexican companies (with a Calvo Clause) owned by foreigners can be beneficiaries of trusts that hold real property for residential or non-residential purposes.

The 1993 Law guards Article 27's two bastions of state monopoly as zealously as the 1973 statute did. Even their broad statutory identifications ("Petroleum and the other hydrocarbons," "Basic petrochemical," and "Electricity") are undiminished.

Investment Provisions of NAFTA. Although the investment provisions of NAFTA are confusingly labeled and arranged, it is clear that access and protection for investors of the NAFTA Parties are among NAFTA's basic purposes. NAFTA's preamble enunciates the Parties' resolution to "ENSURE a predictable commercial framework for business planning and investment." More categorically, of NAFTA's six listed objectives, one is "to ... increase substantially investment opportunities in the territories of the Parties," and another is to "facilitate the cross-border movement of ... services between the territories of the Parties."

Although some investment "reservations," are negative and others affirmative, the degree to which a NAFTA Party felt obliged to express reservations is a useful measure of that Party's difficulty in adhering to NAFTA's investment obligations. In that regard, Mexico's reservations are conspicuously numerous. For example, in Annex I (Reservations for Existing Measures and Liberalization Commitments), Mexico's reservations occupy eighty-four pages, compared to forty-two for Canada and twenty-three for the United States; and, in Annex II (Reservations for Future Measures) only Mexico lists activities reserved to state monopolies such as Pemex and C.F.E. The residual impression is that NAFTA's objectives of access and protection for foreign investment presented considerably more difficulty for Mexico than they did for Canada or the United States.

Investment Access. NAFTA's basic commitments to access for foreign investment are contained in Section A of Chapter 11. Basically they promise national treatment, most-favored-nation treatment, and the better of the two to investors of another Party.

Investment Protection. For Mexico, the substantive and procedural commitments to investment protection expressed in NAFTA constitute an historic break with the Calvo Doctrine, the "New International Economic Order," and past Echeverrían economic policies. That is particularly true of Mexico's accepting the enforcement mechanism of transnational arbitration. Although for many years Mexico has adhered to multinational treaties that make transnational arbitration agreements and awards enforceable among private parties, even among Latin American nations Mexico has been conspicuous for its unwillingness to adhere to international agreements that require investment-receiving nations to arbitrate foreign investment disputes. As regards investors of other NAFTA Parties, with NAFTA that unwillingness is decisively reversed. As one analyst concluded, NAFTA "represents the first time Mexico has entered into an international agreement providing for investor-state arbitration" and constitutes "a significant departure for Mexico with respect to the role of international law in international economic relations."

GORDON, NAFTA DISPUTE PANELS: STRUCTURES AND PROCEDURES, FROM R. F. FOLSOM, M. W. GORDON AND J. A. SPANOGLE, HANDBOOK ON NAFTA DISPUTE SETTLEMENT

(1998).*

The Settlement of Investment Disputes under Chapter 11

There is no binational panel system for investment disputes. The focus of Chapter 11 is on the use of international arbitration. While nothing prevents an investor and a Party from using arbitration in the event of an investment dispute in the absence of Chapter 11, it provides a procedure calling for consultations and, if unsuccessful, more formal arbitration using a combination of ICSID or UNCITRAL and NAFTA rules.

Mexico's experience with the Calvo Clause long posed some problems when a private investor's government assisted the investor in a dispute with Mexico. [I]t remained as a partial obstacle in the NAFTA negotiations of investment provisions. Mexico agreed to change its view, leading to the structure of Articles 1116 and 1117. Article 1116 allows an investor of one Party (i.e., U.S. corporation) to submit to arbitration a claim that another Party (i.e., Mexican government) has violated the latter's obligations: (1) under the general investment rules of Chapter 11, (2) under provisions applicable to state-owned enterprises of Chapter 15, or (3) under those latter provisions when they involve a monopoly which has acted inconsistent with the general investment rules of Chapter 11. Article 1117 allows any of the same violations to be submitted to arbitration by an investor of one Party (i.e., United States corporation) on behalf of an enterprise of another Party that the investor owns or controls (i.e., Mexican subsidiary of the United States investor corporation). But the investment itself in the other Party (i.e., the Mexican subsidiary which is owned by the United States parent corporation) is not permitted to make the claim on its own behalf.

Chapter 11 has two Parts. Part A is general in scope, and Part B concentrates on the Settlement of Disputes between a Party and an

---

* Reprinted with permission of Transnational Publishers, Inc.

Investor of Another Party. The stated purpose of Part B is to create a "mechanism for the settlement of investment disputes" which assures equal treatment among investors from the Parties following the "principle of international reciprocity", and providing for "due process before an impartial tribunal." The Parties have several choices. One is to ignore the Agreement altogether and decide on how the matter is to be arbitrated under any agreed upon set of rules. Or the Parties could follow Article 1120 of the NAFTA and submit the claim to arbitration under the ICSID Convention, the ICSID Additional Facility Rules, or UNCITRAL.

S.D. MYERS, INC. [SDMI] v. GOVERNMENT OF CANADA

November 12, 2000.*

[**Authors' note:** The *S.D. Myers* decision provides a good example of how NAFTA Chapter 11 tribunals analyze the various issues; it is unusual in that all four major Chapter 11 substantive protections, under Articles 1102, 1105, 1106 and 1110, are addressed. S.D. Myers is an Ohio corporation engaged, inter alia, in remediation of hazardous waste known as PCBs. It entered the Canadian market with the objective of obtaining PCB wastes for treatment in the Ohio facilities, and ultimately established an affiliate, Myers Canada. During the entire period, there was only one Canadian competitor, Chem–Security, located in Alberta. S.D. Myers enjoyed a significant cost advantage because it was cheaper for Ontario PCB producers to ship their waste a few hundred miles to Ohio rather than 1500 miles to Alberta. In 1995, the Canadian Minister of the Environment issued interim and final orders that had the effect of banning PCB exports from Canada. Various documents before the tribunal strongly indicated that the purpose of such ban was to force Canadian companies to have their PCB wastes treated at Chem–Security. However, S.D. Myers' export-import opportunities were only temporary, limited to about 18 months, due to U.S. import restrictions on PCB wastes. On October 30, 1998, S.D. Myers filed its Chapter 11 notice of arbitration against Canada, charging violations of national treatment, fair and equitable treatment, the ban against performance requirements, and expropriation.]

* * *

Article 1102 (National Treatment)

238. SDMI claims that CANADA denied it "national treatment," contrary to Article 1102. Article 1102(1) states:

Each Party shall accord to investors of another Party treatment no less favorable than it accords, in like circumstances, to its own investors, with respect to the establishment, acquisition, expansion, management, conduct, operation, and sale or other disposition of investments.

* * *

* 40 I.L.M. 1408 (2001).

241.   CANADA argues that the Interim Order merely established a uniform regulatory regime under which all were treated equally. No one was permitted to export PCBs, so there was no discrimination. SDMI contends that Article 1102 was breached by a ban on the export of PCBs that was not justified by bona fide health or environmental concerns, but which had the aim and effect of protecting and promoting the market share of producers who were Canadians and who would perform the work in Canada.

250.   The Tribunal considers that the interpretation of the phrase "like circumstances" in Article 1102 must take into account the general principles that emerge from the legal context of the NAFTA, including both its concern with the environment and the need to avoid trade distortions that are not justified by environmental concerns. The assessment of "like circumstances" must also take into account circumstances that would justify governmental regulations that treat them differently in order to protect the public interest. The concept of "like circumstances" invites an examination of whether a non-national investor complaining of less favourable treatment is in the same "sector" as the national investor. The Tribunal takes the view that the word "sector" has a wide connotation that includes the concepts of "economic sector" and "business sector."

251.   From the business perspective, it is clear that SDMI and Myers Canada were in "like circumstances" with Canadian operators such as Chem–Security and Cintec. They all were engaged in providing PCB waste remediation services. SDMI was in a position to attract customers that might otherwise have gone to the Canadian operators because it could offer more favourable prices and because it had extensive experience and credibility. It was precisely because SDMI was in a position to take business away from its Canadian competitors that Chem–Security and Cintec lobbied the Minister of the Environment to ban exports when the U.S. authorities opened the border.

National Treatment and Protectionist Motive or Intent

252.   The Tribunal takes the view that, in assessing whether a measure is contrary to a national treatment norm, the following factors should be taken into account:

— whether the practical effect of the measure is to create a disproportionate benefit for nationals over non-nationals;

— whether the measure, on its face, appears to favour its nationals over non-nationals who are protected by the relevant treaty.

255.   CANADA was concerned to ensure the economic strength of the Canadian industry, in part, because it wanted to maintain the ability to process PCBs within Canada in the future. This was a legitimate goal, consistent with the policy objectives of the Basel Convention. There were a number of legitimate ways by which CANADA could have achieved it, but preventing SDMI from exporting PCBs for processing in the USA by the use of the Interim Order and the Final Order was not one of them. * * *

CANADA's right to source all government requirements and to grant subsidies to the Canadian industry are but two examples of legitimate alternative measures. The fact that the matter was addressed subsequently and the border re-opened also shows that CANADA was not constrained in its ability to deal effectively with the situation.

256. The Tribunal concludes that the issuance of the Interim Order and the Final Order was a breach of Article 1102 of the NAFTA.

* * *

Article 1105

258. SDMI submits that CANADA treated it in a manner that was inconsistent with Article 1105(1) of the NAFTA. Entitled "Minimum Standard of Treatment," it reads as follows:

Each Party shall accord to investments of investors of another Party treatment in accordance with international law, including fair and equitable treatment and full protection and security.

259. * * * The inclusion of a "minimum standard" provision is necessary to avoid what might otherwise be a gap. A government might treat an investor in a harsh, injurious and unjust manner, but do so in a way that is no different than the treatment inflicted on its own nationals. The "minimum standard" is a floor below which treatment of foreign investors must not fall, even if a government were not acting in a discriminatory manner.

263. The Tribunal considers that a breach of Article 1105 occurs only when it is shown that an investor has been treated in such an unjust or arbitrary manner that the treatment rises to the level that is unacceptable from the international perspective. That determination must be made in the light of the high measure of deference that international law generally extends to the right of domestic authorities to regulate matters within their own borders. The determination must also take into account any specific rules of international law that are applicable to the case.

264. In some cases, the breach of a rule of international law by a host Party may not be decisive in determining that a foreign investor has been denied "fair and equitable treatment," but the fact that a host Party has breached a rule of international law that is specifically designed to protect investors will tend to weigh heavily in favour of finding a breach of Article 1105.

265. The breadth of the "minimum standard," including its ability to encompass more particular guarantees, was recognized by Dr. Mann in the following passage:

... it is submitted that the right to fair and equitable treatment goes much further than the right to most-favored-nation and to national treatment ... so general a provision is likely to be almost sufficient to cover all conceivable cases, and it may well be that provisions of the

Agreements affording substantive protection are not more than examples of specific instances of this overriding duty.

266.   Although modern commentators might consider Dr. Mann's statement to be an over-generalisation, and the Tribunal does not rule out the possibility that there could be circumstances in which a denial of the national treatment provisions of the NAFTA would not necessarily offend the minimum standard provisions, a majority of the Tribunal determines that on the facts of this particular case the breach of Article 1102 essentially establishes a breach of Article 1105 as well.

267.   Mr. Chiasson considers that a finding of a violation of Article 1105 must be based on a demonstrated failure to meet the fair and equitable requirements of international law. Breach of another provision of the NAFTA is not a foundation for such a conclusion. The language of the NAFTA does not support the notion espoused by Dr. Mann insofar as it is considered to support a breach of Article 1105 that is based on a violation of another provision of Chapter 11. On the facts of this case, CANADA's actions come close to the line, but on the evidence no breach of Article 1105 is established.

268.   By a majority, the Tribunal determines that the issuance of the Interim and Final Orders was a breach of Article 1105 of the NAFTA. The Tribunal's decision in this respect makes it unnecessary to review SDMI's other submissions in relation to Article 1105.

* * *

Article 1106—Performance Requirements

270.   SDMI contends that CANADA's export ban breached Article 1106 of NAFTA because, in effect, SDMI was required, as a condition of operating in Canada, to carry out a major part of its proposed business, the physical disposal of PCB waste in Canada. In doing so, SDMI effectively would have been required to consume goods and services in Canada.

271.   Article 1106 states:

No party may impose or enforce any of the following requirements, or enforce any commitment or undertaking, in connection with the establishment, acquisition, expansion, management, conduct or operation of an investment of an investor of a Party or a non Party in its territory:

(b) to achieve a given level or percentage of domestic content

(c) to purchase, use or accord a preference to goods produced or services provided in its territory or to purchase goods or services from persons in its territory;

276.   The only part of the definition that might apply to the current situation is ... conduct or operation of an investment ... but in the opinion of the majority of the Tribunal, subparagraph (b) clearly does not apply and, neither does subparagraph (c).

277.   [T]he majority of the Tribunal considers that no "requirements" as defined were imposed on SDMI that fell within Article 1106.

278. By a majority, the Tribunal concludes that this is not a "performance requirements" case.

Article 1110–Expropriation

279. SDMI claims that the Interim Order and the Final Order were "tantamount" to an expropriation and violated Article 1110 of the NAFTA.

280. The term "expropriation" in Article 1110 must be interpreted in light of the whole body of state practice, treaties and judicial interpretations of that term in international law cases.

281. The Tribunal accepts that, in legal theory, rights other than property rights may be "expropriated" and that international law makes it appropriate for tribunals to examine the purpose and effect of governmental measures. The Interim Order and the Final Order were regulatory acts that imposed restrictions on SDMI. The general body of precedent usually does not treat regulatory action as amounting to expropriation. Regulatory conduct by public authorities is unlikely to be the subject of legitimate complaint under Article 1110 of the NAFTA, although the Tribunal does not rule out that possibility.

283. An expropriation usually amounts to a lasting removal of the ability of an owner to make use of its economic rights although it may be that, in some contexts and circumstances, it would be appropriate to view a deprivation as amounting to an expropriation, even if it were partial or temporary.

284. In this case the closure of the border was temporary. SDMI's venture into the Canadian market was postponed for approximately eighteen months. Mr. Dana Myers testified that this delay had the effect of eliminating SDMI's competitive advantage. This may have significance in assessing the compensation to be awarded in relation to CANADA's violations of Articles 1102 and 1105, but it does not support the proposition on the facts of this case that the measure should be characterized as an expropriation within the terms of Article 1110.

285. SDMI relied on the use of the word "tantamount" in Article 1110(1) to extend the meaning of the expression "tantamount to expropriation" beyond the customary scope of the term "expropriation" under international law. The primary meaning of the word "tantamount" given by the Oxford English Dictionary is "equivalent". Both words require a tribunal to look at the substance of what has occurred and not only at form. A tribunal should not be deterred by technical or facial considerations from reaching a conclusion that an expropriation or conduct tantamount to an expropriation has occurred. It must look at the real interests involved and the purpose and effect of the government measure.

286. The Tribunal agrees with the conclusion in the Interim Award of the *Pope & Talbot* Arbitral Tribunal that something that is "equivalent" to something else cannot logically encompass more. In common with the *Pope & Talbot* Tribunal, this Tribunal considers that the drafters of the

NAFTA intended the word "tantamount" to embrace the concept of so-called "creeping expropriation", rather than to expand the internationally accepted scope of the term expropriation.

287.   In this case, the Interim Order and the Final Order were designed to, and did, curb SDMI's initiative, but only for a time. CANADA realized no benefit from the measure. The evidence does not support a transfer of property or benefit directly to others. An opportunity was delayed.

288.   The Tribunal concludes that this is not an "expropriation" case.

* * *

[**Authors' note:** In a separate award dated October 21, 2002, the tribunal ultimately found damages based on the Articles 1102 and 1105 violations in the amount of CDN $6,050,000, plus interest. Canada appealed the award to the courts in Ontario, the situs of the arbitration (under the UNCITRAL Rules); that tribunal rejected the challenge, and Canada and S.D. Myers settled the case.]

QUESTIONS AND COMMENTS

1.   Even though the Mexican attitude towards investment included a restrictive period between 1972 and 1984, it was never inflexible. Even during the most restrictive period, Mexican officials were pragmatic, although not always consistent, in interpreting the legislation. The experience of Gillette in Mexico in forming joint ventures illustrates some of the diversity confronting a company subject to joint venture pressures.

Gillette formed Gillette de México in 1956, to manufacture razors and blades, adding other grooming products and writing pens in the next dozen years. The introduction of the disposable Cricket lighter line in 1973 coincided with the Mexican adoption of the restrictive foreign investment provisions and created a conflict with the manner of Gillette's international expansion of other product lines. The new law required the entire company to either become a majority Mexican owned joint venture or receive permission in order to diversify its product line. After long negotiations with the government, Gillette received permission to produce Cricket lighters without any divestiture of Gillette de México, by making a commitment to export 50 percent of domestic consumption. The company then formed two 51–49 percent (Gillette accepting 49 percent) corporations to produce ball point pens and appliances. One of the joint venture companies would manufacture the Plumibol pen, the second would manufacture Braun appliances (Gillette had recently acquired Braun, a West German company). The original Gillette de México would remain as a wholly foreign owned subsidiary. Critics objected to allowing Gillette to escape Mexicanization, and the decision was not disclosed to the public.

2.   Drill–Bit's planned investment in Mexico must comply with the 1993 Mexican investment law. The 1993 investment law stipulates certain areas left for Mexican state or private ownership, where foreigners may not participate or may not control. How will the 1993 law affect Drill–Bit? Must Drill–Bit obtain approval of its proposed investment from the National Commission

on Foreign Investment? Would your answer be different were Drill–Bit to wish to *acquire* Productos rather than commence a new investment? May any conditions be imposed on the investment, such as jobs or worker training? Must the investment be registered with the National Investment Registry?

3. Professor/practitioner Ewell Murphy, long a perceptive writer on Mexican legal issues, suggests in his piece that Mexico has fundamentally revised Mexican policy towards foreign investment, and in the 1993 law and the NAFTA made significant commitments to access and protection for foreign investment. Do you agree with his conclusions that the four bastions of Mexico's resistance to foreign investment have not fully fallen? How does this bode for Drill–Bit?

4. In the 1970s and 1980s Mexico often gave approval only where a proposed investment agreed to export a specified part of its production. Would such requirement be consistent with the NAFTA?

5. One restriction on foreign investment often used by host nations is a requirement that a certain percentage of the content be local. This might mean that Drill–Bit would have to have at least 60 percent local content, and require it to use Mexican steel even though Swedish steel was less expensive. What does the 1993 Mexican investment law say about local content? Does NAFTA address the issue? Could Mexico give preference to NAFTA area steel over steel from Japan or the European Union, without violating its WTO commitments?

6. Could Mexico prohibit a foreign investment on cultural grounds? For example, assume the prospective foreign investor made an electronic marimba synthesizer, which might make the standard marimba obsolete. Could Mexico prevent the investment because it adversely affected the manufacture and playing of the traditional marimba? Ewell Murphy suggests that to understand Mexico we need to look through three lenses, seeing the "numerical optimism of the lens of economics and the verbal assurance of the lens of law, but also the emotional foreboding of the lens of culture." Proceedings of the Canada–United States Law Institute Conference: NAFTA Revisited: Seeing NAFTA Through Three Lenses, 23 Canada–U.S. L. J. 73 (1997). He wonders whether the "gringo idioms, 'due process' and 'the rule of law,' [are] translatable into the pragmatic vocabulary of Mexican politics" and whether the "Rio Grande [is] too culturally insurmountable for NAFTA to cross." Is there any evidence to date to support his concerns? How does his three lens idea fit with Prof. Gordon's "operational code" in 10.0?

7. Foreign investors have always been concerned with Mexican regulations which "chipped away" at the investment, sometimes called "creeping expropriation". Does NAFTA offer any assurances that that will not happen?

8. Assume Drill–Bit has established a direct foreign investment and that the Mexican government imposes restrictions or makes decisions (such as mandatory joint venture or local content requirements, or a rejection of a proposed acquisition) which Drill–Bit believes are contrary to Mexico's NAFTA obligations. The investment chapter of NAFTA includes specific dispute settlement provisions. What steps must Drill–Bit follow under NAFTA? Is the arbitration process in Chapter 11, Part b, the exclusive remedy? Which arbitration method would be applicable? How would Drill–Bit choose between

two applicable methods? Does Drill–Bit have standing before the NAFTA dispute resolution entity? Would Drill–Bit be able to challenge any such Mexican restrictions under the WTO? Does Drill–Bit have standing before a WTO panel? If the matter could be brought under either the NAFTA or the WTO, how is the choice made?

9. The *S.D. Meyers v. Canada* remains one of the most significant Chapter 11 arbitrations for foreign investors, partly because it addresses the most critical sections of Chapter 11 obligations. Drill–Bit might confront similar issues with its investment in Mexico, especially because it is within, or on the fringe of, the sacred petroleum industry. See also Todd Weiler, Metalclad v. Mexico—A Play in Three Parts, 2 J. World Investment 685 (2001); Patrick G. Foy, Effectiveness of NAFTAs Chapter Eleven Investor–State Arbitration Procedures, 18 ICSID Review—For. Inv. L.J. 44 (2003).

10. Reread the materials in Problem 6.3, Part C, on the maquiladora program. Drill–Bit may wish to establish a maquiladora plant under the November 1, 2006 Decree. Would such as investment be permitted?

PART B. MUNSON OF CANADA IN THE UNITED STATES AND THE FOREIGN INVESTMENT AND NATIONAL SECURITY ACT

Comment on *Exon-Florio* and Its Successor the *Foreign Investment and National Security Act*

The Exon–Florio amendment to the Defense Production Act of 1950, passed as part of the Omnibus Trade and Competitiveness Act of 1988, granted the President the authority to investigate and suspend or prohibit transactions leading to control of American firms by foreign persons based on national security concerns. Exon–Florio was the only U.S. law that broadly regulated foreign investment. The Committee on Foreign Investment in the United States (CFIUS), created prior to the Exon–Florio law as the President's designated center of investigation, is the omnipotent reviewer of foreign acquisitions. CFIUS interpreted national security on a case-by-case basis, leaving other companies, even in similar industries, somewhat baffled about the criteria used to evaluate the transaction. While Exon–Florio included a list of factors to be considered in the evaluation of a transaction's national security implications, there nevertheless remained concern about the potential abuse of the broad language and consequent wide scope of Exon–Florio's national security language.

Before the enactment of Exon–Florio, when concern for wide-spread Arab buyouts of American businesses in the 1970s was perceived as a threat to national security, the U.S. executive, seeking a compromise with the Congress, agreed to create the Committee on Foreign Investment in the United States (CFIUS) as an interagency, interdepartmental group to investigate inward foreign direct investment and recommend policy. There were large inflows of foreign investment in the 1980s, and the administration began to intervene in these inflows more frequently, especially when they constituted planned acquisitions of U.S. companies. The policy of open versus controlled investment seemed most confused when the Japanese electronics conglomerate Fujitsu sought to acquire an 80 percent share in Fairchild Semiconductor. Fairchild had openly solicited the bid. Even though the French concern, Schlumberger, already owned Fairchild, the Commerce, Defense and Justice Departments all joined to oppose the proposed acquisition. The Department of Justice was concerned with antitrust implications, while the Departments of Commerce and Defense appeared to object more to force Japanese markets to open more. Because of this extensive concern, Fujitsu withdrew its proposed acquisition, even though CFIUS at the time lacked the power to block the sale.

By 1988, Congress seemed more intent on creating some mechanism to review proposed foreign investment in the United States. * * * Representative Florio of New Jersey proposed foreign investment control legislation which would allow the President to block the sale of a U.S. owned company to any entity with financing by a potential enemy, to ensure that the U.S. firm's controlled technology would not be acquired by the foreign nation. By 1992, CFIUS had reviewed 650 proposed acquisitions. Twelve detailed investigations led to two withdrawals, but only one presidential order of divestment. Because of its confidentiality requirements, no official reports or summaries of CFIUS investigations under Exon–Florio exist for lawyers or investors to consult. The cases when the President chose not to act, when the parties themselves withdrew, and the one case when the President actually ordered divestment, do present some general patterns of what foreign investors could expect from a CFIUS investigation under Exon–Florio.

British Tire & Rubber (UK)/Norton. A good example of an American firm using political pressure on a foreign buyer through Exon–Florio and other mechanisms is the attempted purchase of the Norton Company of Worcester, Massachusetts, by British Tire and Rubber, PLC (BTR). Norton manufactured ceramic ball bearings used in the space shuttle. More than 100 congressmen urged an investigation, including Senator Kerry of Massachusetts, who noted Norton's role in the Massachusetts economy as justification for an investigation in addition to national security reasons. The Massachusetts state legislature soon enacted a law depriving BTR of control should the purchase succeed, leading BTR to pull out, and a French buyer to make a friendly offer at a much higher price. No security concerns were raised when the friendly French buyer appeared offering a better price, even though Norton had earlier argued that BTR planned to dismember Norton and reduce its research and development budgets to the detriment of national security. Using Exon–Florio, Norton obtained both the buyer and price that it wanted.

China Nat'l Aero Tech./MAMCO. The one transaction that the President decided to reject had already been finalized at the time of the order. The target was MAMCO Manufacturing, Inc., a U.S. company in Seattle that manufactured metal parts for commercial aircraft made by Boeing. MAMCO mainly supplied Boeing, and although some of its products were subject to export controls, MAMCO had no contracts involving classified information. The buyer was China National Aero–Technology Import and Export Corp. (CATIC), owned by the People's Republic of China. During the investigation, it appeared that CATIC had previously violated export control laws concerning aircraft engines purchased from General Electric. But concerns about

CATIC went beyond export control problems with China. Administration sources revealed that CATIC had been trying to obtain technology to build jet fighters capable of refueling during flight. The Executive Order directing CATIC to divest itself of MAMCO contained none of the above concerns or information, but simply stated that the two requirements of Exon–Florio had been satisfied: there existed credible evidence of a threat to national security, and no other provision of law could protect the national security interest. Considering the relatively low level of technology involved, however, the President's action on CFIUS's unanimous recommendation to terminate the investment surprised many observers, leading some to believe that the national security concern was a pretext for other political motives.

Thomson/LTV. By 1992, Congressional dissatisfaction with how the President and CFIUS had interpreted Exon–Florio led to proposals for new and stricter controls. The circumstances that led to the first substantive amendments to the Exon–Florio law involved foreign government participation in a proposed acquisition, the attempted purchase of the missile division of LTV Corp. by Thomson–CSF, a conglomerate owned (58 percent) and financed in part by the French government.

LTV had been operating under bankruptcy protection since 1986. Thomson made a bid for $450 million, outbidding the U.S. defense contractor Martin Marietta by nearly $100 million. LTV favored Martin Marietta because of the prospective problems Thomson would have with CFIUS.

There was immediate adverse Congressional reaction, acknowledging that the United States and France were allies, but noting that French interests have not always been the same as America's. Because the DOD apparently was not intending to object to the sale, it was criticized for failing to consider the questionable record of Thomson and the French government in exporting weapons to countries with which the United States did not have good relations, such as Iran, Libya and Iraq, and also for ignoring a Defense Intelligence Agency warning of extensive technology leakage.

Critics suggested that although an open-door policy makes sense for *private* foreign investors, that policy should be reexamined where foreign *governments* are involved.

It became apparent during the controversy that the CFIUS was almost certain to recommend that the President block the transaction. Consequently, Thomson first withdrew its bid to restructure the deal and ultimately withdrew completely, leading to a suit by LTV for breach of contract.

Congress, not the President or CFIUS, led the effort to gain more information on Thomson, and as a result of its hearings to reconsider the policy of open direct investment involving foreign governments, Thomson's bid was withdrawn. Because of the perception that the administration took up the case only with prompting by Congress, amendments to Exon–Florio soon appeared on Capitol Hill.

Congress identified three factors in the attempted merger of greatest concern. First, LTV was a substantial contractor with the DOD and NASA, and was the largest contractor ever for sale to a foreign firm. Second, as much as 75 percent of the work LTV did for the DOD required access to highly classified information that is generally prohibited for foreign nationals or representatives of foreign interests. Third, the French government owned 58 percent of Thomson's stock.

The first change sought by Congress was to remove any Presidential and CFIUS reticence in carrying out their responsibilities under Exon–Florio. The Byrd Amendment *required* the President or his designee to investigate if the purchasing foreigner was "controlled by or acting on behalf of a foreign government," and if the acquisition "could result in control of a person engaged in interstate commerce in the U.S. that could affect the national security of the U.S."

The second important amendment forbid the sale of some U.S. companies to certain foreign investors, principally those involved with foreign governments. In a separate section to Exon–Florio, entities controlled by a foreign government could not purchase certain Department of Energy or Defense contractors. Such contractors could not be acquired by entities controlled by or acting on behalf of foreign governments if they worked under a national security program that could not be done without access to a "proscribed category of information." Furthermore, any firm awarded at least $500 million in prime DOD contracts or at least $500 million in prime Department of Energy contracts under national security programs could not be acquired.

The Thomson–CSF experience nearly established a process that Congress decided that it did not want followed. The earlier proposed acquisition by CATIC, owned by the Chinese government, also resulted in a failed acquisition attempt, although due to action rather than a somewhat coerced withdrawal. Although the cases involved different national security concerns, the pattern existed that if a foreign government played a role in a foreign investment, CFIUS, or perhaps its apparent watchdog, the Congress, would examine the proposal very carefully.

While most of the prior cases received little public attention, that changed with the attempt by the China National Offshore Oil Corporation (CNOOC) attempt in 2005 to outbid Chevron for shares of Unocal. The strategic characteristic of China seeking ownership of several natural resource companies in various nations ultimately caused CNOOC to withdraw its bid. Shortly thereafter Dubai World Ports 2006 bid to operate several U.S. ports received CFIUS approval and front page coverage, Congress took up the issue of greater control than Exon–Florio had provided.

The result was the enactment of the Foreign Investment and National Security Act (FINSA) in 2007, which essentially amends and updates the Exon–Florio additions to the Defense Production Act of 1950. FINSA codifies changes to CFIUS practice that had evolved after September 11, 2001. The importance of national security is reflected both in the name of the act and the addition of the Director of National Intelligence to CFIUS. Perhaps the most uncertain language in FINSA is what constitutes a proposed investment that would allow foreign control of "critical infrastructure."

FINSA continues the procedure of having CFIUS, acting as the President's designee, investigate the national security impact of mergers, acquisitions, and takeovers by or with foreign persons that could result in control by foreign persons. A government agency that is considered the most appropriate in view of the proposed investment, is designated the lead investigating agency. It has extensive authority to enter the negotiations for the investment, merely monitoring them if appropriate, or demanding modifications and mitigation agreements. FINSA provides for government oversight by requiring an annual CFIUS prepared report and notice to Congress by CFIUS of its decisions. The report is not disclosed to the public under an exemption to the Freedom of Information Act. Congressional action may convince the President to use his authority to suspend or prohibit the acquisition, merger, or takeover, or to seek divestiture for an already completed transaction.

The President must believe that there is "credible evidence" that the foreign interest would exercise "control" which might threaten "national security", and he must believe that other provisions of law, aside from the International Emergency Economic Powers Act, provide inadequate authority to safeguard national security. These findings remain prerequisites to presidential action, but are not subject to judicial review under the statute.

Although considerable debate has occurred, "national security" remains undefined in either the law or regulations. But the provisions suggest that the President consider several factors in evaluating national security concerns. These are mainly directed to the capacity of domestic industry to meet national defense requirements in view of the proposed takeover. Factors for presidential consideration include both the potential for proliferation of missiles, nuclear, and biological weapons, as well as the potential effect of the transaction on U.S. international technological leadership in areas affecting national security.

Critics have charged that CFIUS has abused the confidentiality provisions in some cases, and has left important players out of the investigation process until after CFIUS has made its decisions. The confidentiality provision has made official reports of cases impossible, but has protected both the interests of foreign investors and national security.

The expectation is that FINSA will result in fewer surprises and consequent Congressional and public outrage. This helps reduce concern generated abroad about restrictions on investment in the United States. Foreign nations never viewed the Exon–Florio law very favorably. The 1992 amendments to Exon–Florio were viewed in Canada as a further barrier to investment because they failed to define "defense critical technology." The European Union also objected to Exon–Florio's vagueness of the definition of national security.

QUESTIONS AND COMMENTS

1. Would a proposed acquisition of TECHCO by the Canadian Munson company be likely to be scrutinized under the FINSA? What about an acquisition by a state owned company in Europe? In China? How would the process commence? If TECHCO wanted to reject such an acquisition, could it use the FINSA as an anti-takeover device? Is review a possibility if TECHCO is considering an acquisition of another U.S. company and obtains a loan from a bank, which obtains a security interest in the stock and assets of TECHCO? See generally Manual of Foreign Investment in the United States, 3d (2004).

2.   Most of the trading partners of the United States viewed Exon–Florio as a law used differently by successive administrations to achieve political goals in permitting foreign investment, with little real analysis on the national security implications which are purportedly the foundation of the review process. It is fair to comment that Exon–Florio was not well regarded from abroad. It has allegedly led to diminished foreign investment in U.S. defense contractors. But that was of course intended if such investment would threaten national security. Exon–Florio in its new clothes as FINSA seems unlikely to go away. And the definition of national security seems unlikely to be given certain limits. FINSA updates Exon–Florio as part of the governments "discretionary" power to deal with foreign trade and investment. Once given, it is hard to retrieve. But in focus, nearly all of the proposed acquisitions since 1988 which have been notified under the law were approved without a full investigation.

3.   Could either TECHCO or Munson turn to the NAFTA for help in resisting or assisting the contemplated acquisition? Would your answer be the same were FINSA to allow a rejection of a proposed acquisition for "economic" as opposed to national security reasons, and the requested rejection by TECHCO was for the former rather than the latter reason?

4.   Regulations to Exon–Florio were adopted in 1991, but as expected, they did not provide any clear definition of national security. Nor did FINSA clarify the meaning of national security.

5.   Might Munson wish to consider the U.S. sanctions laws which were considered in Problem 8.2 before it commits to an investment in the United States which might provide the basis for a challenge to Munson's operations in other parts of the world? Total, S.A. of France sold a U.S. operating subsidiary which was an investment of several hundred million dollars. One reason was believed to be fear of sanctions under the Iran–Libya Sanctions Act because of Total's planned investment in Iran.

PART 6

DISPUTE SETTLEMENT

■ ■ ■

CHAPTER 11

THE RESOLUTION OF INTERNATIONAL COMMERCIAL DISPUTES

■ ■ ■

INTRODUCTION 11.0   THE RESOLUTION OF BUSINESS DISPUTES

The preceding chapters primarily focused on the elements of various transactions, such as the sale of goods abroad, the transfer of technology and direct foreign investment, plus government regulation of the import and export process. Many of the conflicts between parties in these problems, such as the effectiveness of an excuse for nonperformance in Problem 4.3, or a claim against a foreign state for expropriation raising defenses of state immunity or act of state as discussed in Problem 10.6, may have to be resolved by some form of dispute resolution, litigation in national or foreign courts, mediation, arbitration, or dispute panels created under various free trade agreements. Many of the problems involved settings where the discussion tried to seek resolution of potential conflicts before they arose by careful planning, so as to avoid a later formal and often expensive process of dispute resolution. But, as every lawyer knows, no one can foresee every potential hazard, and irreconcilable differences and disputes can and do arise—and can and do lead to litigation, mediation, and/or arbitration.

The types of dispute which may arise in the settings which have been addressed throughout this book involve different groups of persons or entities. Some are disputes between two different private parties, such as the U.S. bookseller selling books to the English book buyers. No government entered that dispute. But a government is often involved in international business disputes. The government may be a party to a contract, and breach the contract and claim state immunity from jurisdiction. There are also disputes between private parties and foreign governments, such as the expropriation of the U.S. fishing tackle manufacturer by the government of Marnesia. In that case the government was regulating business conduct, although it might also have breached a contract if it had initially granted a concession. Governments may regulate imports and exports in such a way as to be challenged by private parties in other nations (when they discriminate against foreign goods) or by private parties in their own nation (when they refuse to license certain exports). Domestic administrative agencies and courts may resolve such issues, and multinational trade agreements such as the NAFTA or WTO may provide for special forms of dispute resolution by means of binational or multinational panels.

If a conflict assumes such serious dimensions that the parties are unable to work out their differences together, some form of external dispute resolution is likely to be required. The form might be mediation (voluntary or court ordered), or more formal arbitration, or litigation in the courts. For certain trade issues, such as violations of international trade agreements, there may be an additional alternative, or an exclusive process, in the form of a dispute panel convened under rules included in the trade agreement. Increasingly, investor-state disputes over foreign investment are subject to rules established in trade agreements and bilateral trade agreements.

Not only is the question raised regarding *how* a dispute ought to be resolved, such as arbitration versus litigation, but there are further questions such as *where* the dispute should be resolved, and under *what* rules. These questions may best be addressed well before any dispute arises, and be the subject of provisions in the initial contract or agreement. Such agreements may stipulate that a contract for the sale of goods is to be governed by the ICC INCOTERMS, or the provisions of the applicable state version of the UCC. For substantive contract terms the parties may choose to opt out of the otherwise applicable CISG, instead preferring the UNIDROIT Principles of International Commercial Contracts, or a particular nation's sales law such as the U.S. Uniform Commercial Code, or the Spanish Codigo Comercio. The parties may choose the applicable forum for dispute resolution, although they may not thrust upon a court otherwise inapplicable subject matter jurisdiction. The chosen forum might be the courts of one of the party's nations, or a third nation, or perhaps an international tribunal. There may not be an applicable international court with jurisdiction, but the agreement might provide for international arbitration and further determine how the panel should be selected, or defer that to the procedures of a recognized organization such as the Paris based ICC, or the American Arbitration Association. Investors and the host nation may agree to use the World Bank's generally highly regarded International Centre for the Settlement of Investment Disputes (ICSID) for investment dispute resolution.

While the contracts and agreements concluded in the various problems may not have included any provisions regarding how, where or under what rules any dispute shall be resolved, that may be because the matter was not discussed, or because it was discussed but no agreement was reached. In some previous problems we dealt with torts rather than commercial contracts, such as in Problem 10.5, where a foreign investor was sued for various alleged violations of international law. Such cases do not arise from contracts with choice of forum provisions.

With regard to contracts, hopefully most will be fulfilled and not lead to any dispute. If they do result in a dispute, however, the parties may view the appropriate method of dispute resolution very differently than at the time of planning the contract or agreement, when neither party could foresee the nature of the forthcoming dispute. It is very unlikely that the parties could have predicted every possible form of dispute, and one of the parties may regret having agreed to arbitrate all matters relating to the contract or agreement, and later discover arbitration is demanded by the other party over a matter that does not seem among those areas contemplated to be arbitrable. If one party feels especially strong about their position, they may be disinclined to consider mediation or arbitration, and wish to move directly to litigation. But that view may change when they realize that the litigation may most likely take place in the other party's courts where the court is inclined to apply its own national law.

Each form of dispute resolution has advantages and disadvantages to the parties from their perspectives at the time of drafting the contract or agreement, or in the absence of making the decisions from their perspectives at such later time when a dispute has arisen. A client will expect to be advised as to the most favorable form of dispute resolution for their own individual interests, not some form of resolution based upon some philosophical value judgment of the "fairest" method of dispute resolution or the "best" legal system.

Every form of dispute resolution may not be available to the parties from which to choose. For example, mandatory laws in some nations may prohibit arbitration outside the country. Or one form of resolution may by law be mandatory, such as where the appropriate jurisdiction for litigation has a rule requiring some attempt at mediation before the filed suit may proceed to trial. One form of dispute resolution may be available, but there may be obstacles to its effective use, such as where civil dockets are not addressing many civil cases in order to deal with crowded criminal dockets. The latter is a problem in some U.S. federal courts, where drug related criminal law cases have overwhelmed the courts and effectively forced parties to turn to the arbitration of civil disputes.

The capacity to make decisions and the inclination (or perception of such inclination) to resolve matters on non-legal grounds will influence parties' choice of form of dispute resolution. Mediation is usually by definition a process where the mediator has relatively little power to force conclusions on the parties—the mediator is rather expected to keep the parties negotiating so that they reach their own conclusions and perhaps narrow the issues. But the dispute may require more, it may require someone to step in and make decisions. Arbitration may or may not be the answer. Sometimes arbitrators are perceived as persons who believe that they must find a resolution which satisfies both parties to some degree, the charge of dividing up the pie rather than awarding it all to the party whose legal arguments are correct. However untrue this perception of arbitration may be, it may cause a party who strongly believes that its position is correct, especially after a dispute has occurred and there is no compulsory arbitration, to reject arbitration and turn to litigation. It is to such litigation that we first turn, although the final problem in this chapter will provide an overview of arbitration.

PART A. THE PROCESS OF INTERNATIONAL BUSINESS LITIGATION

Notwithstanding the importance of discussing the use of alternate dispute resolution methods at the time of preparing commercial transaction documents, commercial litigation arises both where parties have made such decisions, such as selecting arbitration or selecting a forum and choice of law, and where they have not. That the documents show no evidence of such choices does not mean that they were not considered. The parties may have discussed the use of arbitration or the selection of a forum or choice of law, but been unable to agree and thus left the matter unaddressed, hoping it would never arise. Furthermore, that they were considered and a choice adopted does not mean that a court will respect such decision, although the likelihood is that a selection of arbitration, or of a particular nation's courts, or of a choice of law, will be respected.

As in the case of Chapters 4 and 10, this introduction progresses through the subject of the following problems. For this introduction that means the various procedural stages of international business litigation, beginning in 11.1–11.3 with issues leading to trial, following in 11.4 with enforcing a trial court's judgment, and ending with 11.5 and the enforcement of arbitral awards. Students will almost certainly have completed civil procedure when they take this course, but they will have been introduced to very few, if any, of the *international* dimensions of the areas that they have studied, whether it is jurisdiction, *forum non conveniens*, choice of law or enforcement of a foreign judgment. Students in this course will probably been introduced to choice of forum and choice of law in the domestic context in the basic civil procedure course, but not where the transaction is international, such as choice of forum (Kansas or Germany) and choice of law (Kansas UCC, German commercial code or CISG) issues as discussed in Problem 4.1.

While there is a natural sequence to most of the topics to be discussed, a few are not so easy to classify within the time frame of an action. For example, personal jurisdiction might be challenged before or after, or at the same time as, subject matter jurisdiction. Personal jurisdiction may also be challenged prior to or after *forum non conveniens*.[1] Choice of law may be part of the *forum non conveniens* argument, or follow a denial of a *forum non conveniens* challenge. But, clearly, service of

---

1. The U.S. Supreme Court in 2007 addressed the issue whether one must challenge jurisdiction before *forum non conveniens*, ruling that there is no mandate to first establish jurisdiction. *Sinochem Int'l Co. Ltd. v. Malaysia Int'l Shipping Corp.*, 549 U.S. 422, 127 S.Ct. 1184, 167 L.Ed.2d 15 (2007).

process should be addressed before choice of law, and jurisdiction before discovery.

One matter needs to be stressed repeatedly. Every one of these areas should be evaluated separately before making decisions regarding any one of them. For example, bringing suit in a nation favorable to the plaintiff with regard to ease of proof and the availability of substantial damages may prove futile if a favorable verdict is gained but the defendant's assets are all located in another nation that does not enforce any foreign judgments, or specifically any judgments of the chosen forum because that nation does not grant reciprocity. Choosing the best forum for a plaintiff means working through each stage for obstacles and solutions, such as whether that forum has the legal authority to and in practice actually does apply foreign law. If it does not, and if the foreign law the plaintiff prefers to have applied is more favorable than the domestic law of the host forum that the court will apply, the plaintiff ought to consider the forum choice carefully—it may be better to initiate the litigation abroad. Maybe the better choice when the plaintiff needs considerable discovery to acquire more evidence about to prove its case is where discovery is most favorable, or maybe the best choice of forum is where the defendant has assets so that a judgment will not have to face enforcement in a foreign nation. The rule should be "Don't take step one without thinking about where that leads with regard to steps two, three and thereafter."

PART B. THE CHOICE OF FORUM

Forum selection clauses. In negotiating a contract, the parties should always at least consider the appropriateness of stipulating a chosen forum. They may not be able to agree and do nothing, but at least they considered the issue. If a choice is made and they submit to a specific forum, accepting jurisdiction, it does not mean that jurisdiction may be thrust upon a court that under the rules of the forum does not have jurisdiction. Nor does it mean that a court that has not been selected, but that under its rules could have jurisdiction, will respect the choice of forum. Such a court would not dismiss the case due to the forum selection clause were the matter to be filed there. While U.S. courts generally respect forum selection clauses, many foreign courts follow rules that require the court to go forward if it has jurisdiction, regardless of the party's choice of a different forum.

One of the most difficult issues for a court is to determine whether a forum selection clause was sufficiently freely negotiated and accepted by both parties, and whether it was the consequence of the use of a standard contract with a forum selection clause chosen by one party and imposed upon the other. In such situation it may be more likely that a court will uphold a forum selection clause that requires a Texas party to submit to a clause selecting another state's courts, such as California, than for that same court to uphold a forum selection clause that requires the Texas party to submit to a foreign court, such as Argentina. The international characteristics of the facts leading to the dispute may be the only difference in the court's decision.

Parties often agree to choice of dispute resolution forms (arbitration versus litigation), choice of court clauses (one nation's courts versus another) and choice of law clauses (one nation's law versus another). The first two are essentially forum selection clauses, and along with the third, attempt to inform and persuade courts as to their appropriateness in being the resolving forum, and applying the selected choice of law rules. The forum before which a particular matter comes, whether it is the forum selected or some other forum, in which one party has initiated an action, will have to determine whether it will accept the choice of forum, and also the choice of law. A forum that was not selected might accept the matter and reject the forum selection clause, or the forum which was selected might reject the forum selection clause and refuse to proceed for any of several reasons such as *forum non conveniens*. The forum that was not selected might be more inclined to apply the selected law than the selected forum, such as where the parties chose a U.S. forum and a foreign law that would be difficult to apply in the chosen U.S. forum. The decision of a court not to accept the matter even when the parties have stipulated it as the proper forum, may well look more like a *forum non conveniens* decision than one of choice of forum.

In many if not most cases the parties do not include a forum selection provision in their commercial agreements. That may be because they did not discuss the matter, or because they did discuss the matter at arm's length but could not agree on a forum. They both expect the contract to be carried out or they would not have agreed to it in the first place. Thus they do not expect the issues of the proper dispute resolution forum or choice of law to arise. But if these issues might arise in the unexpected event that a dispute ensues, the parties may be quite willing to defer to the decision of a court applying the court's proper forum and choice of law rules. That partly may be because the court might not accept even an arm's length and carefully bargained choice of forum and/or choice of law clause agreed to by the parties.

U.S. plaintiff. Where no forum has been chosen by the parties, a U.S. plaintiff will usually assume that a U.S. forum is the best choice. That may not be true. A foreign forum may be the only place where the defendant may be subject to jurisdiction, or where the law is most favorable, or where the defendant has most or all of its assets. If the defendant is also a U.S. party, the dispute is likely to constitute domestic rather than international litigation. But the issue could be the liability of a U.S. hotel operating in a foreign country to a U.S. guest injured while staying in the foreign located hotel. The injured U.S. party has come home to recover and sues the owner of the hotel at home, regardless whether the defendant is only the parent of the foreign subsidiary that operated the hotel abroad. The U.S. plaintiff may assume that the U.S. court will apply U.S. law, but the U.S. defendant may argue successfully in the U.S. court that the law of the place of the injury applies, which would be foreign law. If the defendant is a foreign party, the U.S. plaintiff nevertheless may wish to litigate in the United States, but may have to address complex issues of personal jurisdiction over the foreign defendant in the U.S. court.

Foreign plaintiff. Foreign plaintiffs increasingly seek a favorable U.S. forum to decide matters that often have far more links to their own foreign nation. The reason for such forum shopping, especially where the issue is a tort, is usually the prospect of damages not available in the foreign plaintiff's nation, such as for pain and suffering and punitive damages. But even for commercial litigation the U.S. system may appear the better choice to a foreign plaintiff, with its more extensive discovery, jury system and possible contingent fee arrangement.

Defendant's responses. The response of a defendant may be that the court is an improper forum because it does not have jurisdiction. But it may also be that it is inappropriate to proceed because there is parallel litigation because the defendant has simultaneously sued the plaintiff in the plaintiff's foreign forum on the same facts, and that comity suggests that one of the forums should dismiss or stay the matter in respect of the other. The U.S. court may consider both forums to be proper forums, but the foreign forum to be a more convenient forum, and dismiss the matter under the doctrine known as *forum non conveniens*. That is a doctrine generally limited to common law nations; civil law legal systems usually reject *forum non conveniens* in favor of the position that a court vested of jurisdiction must go forward with the case. A court alternatively may believe it is the *only* appropriate forum, and issue an anti-suit injunction against the defendant, ordering withdrawal from the suit it filed abroad.

The fact that there are international dimensions to these suits makes the resolution of what may be relatively easy issues in domestic litigation quite difficult because the court has before it an international case. One has only to consider what U.S. Supreme Court Justice O'Connor meant in the famous *Asahi*[2] decision, when she noted that the case involved a foreign defendant, thus differing from the most important previous jurisdiction case the Court had dealt with, where the defendant was a U.S. entity—*World-Wide Volkswagen*.[3]

PART C. JURISDICTION

Jurisdiction in U.S. Courts. Personal jurisdiction is the subject of intensive discussion in a first year civil procedure or constitutional law class. U.S. law has a clear division between subject matter and personal jurisdiction. That is not a characteristic of the civil law tradition where the two concepts tend to be fused under the theory of judicial competency of the court. While consideration of personal jurisdiction in the United States turns one's attention to case law and discussions of minimum

---

2. *Asahi Metal Indus. Co. v. Superior Court of California*, 480 U.S. 102, 107 S.Ct. 1026, 94 L.Ed.2d 92 (1987).

3. *World-Wide Volkswagen v. Woodson*, 444 U.S. 286, 100 S.Ct. 580, 62 L.Ed.2d 490 (1980).

contacts and due process, subject matter jurisdiction is found in federal and state constitutions and legislation. Some subject matter jurisdiction provisions may be general and others may address foreign litigation exclusively. For example, the federal Foreign Sovereign Immunities Act is the exclusive means for subject matter jurisdiction over foreign states.

Business torts such as the negligent manufacture of a product may come before U.S. courts because of either a territorial link to the United States, such as negligent manufacture, or a nationality link, such as the incorporation or presence of sufficient doing business in the United States, essentially based on nationality of the parties. There is often a dispute over whether the tort occurred at the place of manufacture or the place of the direct injury. The former is often in the United States where a product was designed and manufactured, while the latter is often abroad where the manufactured product was used and involved in an alleged injury.

Subject matter jurisdiction in the United States may include a question of jurisdiction in federal or state court, or the existence of jurisdiction in either. If brought in state court there may be an effort by the defendant, in some cases an absolute right, to remove the matter to federal court. Diversity, one basis for federal court jurisdiction, becomes complex in international litigation because diversity is based not on citizenship but on domicile, and domicile, defined as residence-in-fact with intent to remain, was not designed to address many international issues, such as a U.S. citizen temporarily residing abroad. There appears to be general agreement that diversity jurisdiction rules are in need of reevaluation in view of the globalization of business, but no serious movement toward revision has taken place.

Personal jurisdiction, in contrast to subject matter jurisdiction, usually focuses on issues of constitutional origin. While the meaning is continually debated the standard is generally recognized to constitute a two-part test, first whether the defendant's presence in the forum satisfies a *minimum contacts* test and, second, whether the exercise of personal jurisdiction over the defendant is reasonable according to notions of *fair play and substantial justice*. When the defendant is foreign, should the reasonableness part of the test involve consideration of the international dimension of the case? The attempts to answer this question confuse many U.S. law students and lawyers, and leave most foreign lawyers and their clients absolutely baffled. The U.S. Supreme Court has not yet provided clear guidance.

Jurisdiction in foreign courts. The first characterization of jurisdiction in many countries, and essential to civil law tradition nations, is that there is no distinction between personal and subject-matter jurisdiction as exists in the United States. The rules of jurisdiction are not contained in due process provisions of foreign constitutions, but in codes of procedure or private international law. But the rules usually seek to achieve much the same result as in the United States, proper links to the court (subject matter) and fairness in bringing the defendant before the court (personal).

In civil law nations there is often a rule that a matter should be decided at the location of the defendant's domicile (general jurisdiction), but may also be decided under an often complex framework addressing the location of the performance of a contract or the place of the commission of a tort (special jurisdiction). These rules place an emphasis on the relationship of the court and the claim, as opposed to the U.S. emphasis of the relationship of the court and the defendant. Unlike the U.S. rules, issues of contract and issues of tort occurring in the same case may have to meet separate special jurisdiction tests.

Some nations have combined the civil law tradition notion of a rules-based jurisdiction with the inclusion of a variant of U.S. due process analysis. In Japan, for example, while the written codes are parallel to those in many civil law tradition nations, there is a theory of *jri* which brings to the jurisdictional analysis a kind of due process consideration.

PART D. SERVICE OF PROCESS

Plaintiffs must select a method of service of process on the defendants that meets the requirements of the law of the forum. If the defendants are in a foreign country, service in accordance with the law of the forum may offend the nation in which the foreign defendant is located. Service by mail, for example, is not recognized in many nations. It may constitute sufficient notice in the selected forum, but any decision in favor of the plaintiff might not be recognized and enforced in the nation of any defendant who was served by mail. Thus, a plaintiff in international litigation must think of complying with the service of process laws of at least two nations, where the plaintiff has filed suit and where each defendant is located.

In most of the areas that we address in international litigation procedure there is little help from international rules. That includes choice of forum,[4] choice of law, *forum non conveniens,* pretrial protective measures and jurisdiction. But in two areas, service of documents abroad and taking evidence abroad, there are conventions that have been adopted in many nations.

The Hague Convention on the Service Abroad of Judicial and Extrajudicial Documents in Civil or Commercial Matters of 1965 addresses service of process. It has been signed by some 64 nations. The United States is a party to this Convention and in compliance with a Convention mandate has designated a private company as the Central Authority to receive requests from other participating states to carry out service in the United States. The Convention provides procedural steps that reasonably assure the plaintiff that such compliance will greatly reduce if not eliminate the possibility of a successful challenge to the service of process or other documents. The Convention allows signatories to take reservations and make declarations to modify or limit obligations under certain provisions

---

4. A Choice of Court Convention was concluded in July, 2005. But it remains to be seen how many nations adopt the Convention. Only Mexico had ratified the Convention as of early 2011, although both the EU and the United States have signed the treaty.

of the Convention. For example, the United States has made a declaration under Article 16 that an application for service will not be entertained under certain time of filing limitations. Several nations, not including the United States, have made Article 10 declarations or reservations prohibiting service by mail in their jurisdictions. This has a significant effect on the use of substituted or constructive service by U.S. plaintiffs, where documents may have to be transmitted abroad to complete the service process.

An important issue with any convention is whether it provides for a mandatory or optional procedure. As we will see later, the Convention governing the taking of evidence abroad has been held to be optional, while it is quite clear that the procedures of the Service Convention are mandatory. Article 1 provides that the Convention "shall apply in all cases, in civil or commercial matters, where there is occasion to transmit a judicial or extrajudicial document for service abroad."

PART E. *FORUM NON CONVENIENS*

When a U.S. court has jurisdiction it does not mean that no other court may have jurisdiction. That other court may be a foreign court, and under its rules be fully competent to hear the matter. In such case, the U.S. court may dismiss the action for reasons of *forum non conveniens*. *Forum non conveniens* has roots in Scottish case law, and has been most favorably received in the United States. That is because of characteristics of U.S. law that many foreign plaintiffs believe favor their causes. That includes contingent fee arrangements, civil trial juries, extensive discovery and, most importantly, pain and suffering damages and even the pot of gold at the end of the international rainbow—punitive damages. The source of *forum non conveniens* is almost exclusively case law, save a few states that have enacted statutes modifying or eliminating its use. It is essentially unknown outside some common law tradition nations. Recently two significant changes to the acceptability of *forum non conveniens* have occurred.

First, English law was modified by judicial decision in 2000 to eliminate the consideration of public interest factors, leaving only private interest factors.[5] But five years later, a decision in the EU court ruled that the UK's use of *forum non conveniens,* even with non-contracting parties (non-EU), was inconsistent with its obligations under the EU jurisdiction regulation.[6] The court believed that *forum non conveniens* use led to needless unpredictability, and that a court vested with jurisdiction under EU rules was obligated to hear the matter if a case were filed. How this will turn out is unclear, especially with regard to those cases involving not the UK and an EU nation, but the UK and a non-EU nation such as the United States. The court did not feel that there should be a distinction.

---

5. *Lubbe v. Cape PLC,* [2000] 2 Lloyd's Rep. 383 (H.L.).

6. *Owusu v. Jackson,* C–281/02 [2005] E.C.R. 0.

The second challenge to *forum non conveniens* has been by movements in some developing Latin American nations to block U.S. courts from making *forum non conveniens* rulings by legislation that removes local jurisdiction if a national first filed suit in the United States. The theory is apparently that the filing in the United States terminates what would otherwise be valid jurisdiction in the home nation, and therefore the U.S. court could not dismiss the case because there was an available foreign forum. How this will turn out is also unclear, but it seems that U.S. courts that understand the issue are not recognizing these foreign attempts to nullify a U.S. legal theory.

A court considering a motion to dismiss based on *forum non conveniens* usually proceeds to consider several matters. One will be whether the plaintiff is foreign or a U.S. national or legal resident. If foreign the choice will be less respected than if United States, because it assumes the foreign plaintiff forum shopped for reasons expressed above such as high damages. A second consideration will be whether the foreign forum is available and adequate. Availability has traditionally been limited to whether the law of the foreign nation provides jurisdiction over the issue and parties. But, as noted above, it is currently also addressing whether any alleged lack of availability is due to the plaintiff's act of making it unavailable. Adequacy, the second related issue, usually considers whether the foreign forum recognizes theories of action that the United States recognizes, such as strict liability, antitrust, class actions or consumer protection. But adequacy also has become enmeshed with considering whether the foreign forum is so corrupt, inefficient, inadequate and/or intimidating, that it would be unjust to transfer the matter abroad only to meet a certain doom. Courts do not like to classify other nations' courts as incapable of providing justice, but the reality is that there are many nations that are so incapable. The third consideration by the court involves what may be a lengthy review of private and public factors. Private factors include where evidence is located and getting it to the forum; the movement and inconvenience of bringing parties, witnesses and experts to the forum; the need to translate documents and testimony; the ability to implead third-party defendants; and implications from fragmenting the suit if it were dismissed in favor of different nations of different plaintiffs, and non-U.S. defendants. Public factors considered include each nation's interest in being the location of the litigation, the burden on the court system and interest of jurors in serving, and sometimes deterring U.S. companies from producing defective products for export.

Often a court will inquire extensively about the substance of the foreign law. If the motion to dismiss is denied, the court may have to apply foreign law. That alone may be a major factor in the court's decision to grant the motion, especially where the foreign law is that of a civil law tradition nation without a highly developed sector dealing with civil litigation. Whether or not the court considers the foreign law in its *forum non conveniens* determination, it will almost assuredly have to address that if the matter remains in the U.S. court.

Courts almost always condition a dismissal subject to some promises from the defendant. The most prevalent is a promise by the defendant to submit to the jurisdiction of the foreign court. Added may be a waiver of any right to use the foreign statute of limitations, but that may not be subject to waiver under foreign law. The next most common is an agreement to pay any judgment rendered in the foreign court, a promise that may be regretted if the foreign nation renders a very large judgment.

In most *forum non conveniens* cases the litigation has been initiated only in the United States. But there are many instances where the same matter is the subject of litigation in the United States and another nation. The plaintiff and defendant in the U.S. court may be, respectively, the defendant and plaintiff in the foreign nation. This is called parallel litigation. A U.S. court could dismiss the case on *forum non conveniens* grounds, but also might stay the matter for reasons of comity, allowing the other court to proceed without each case separately racing for the first judgment.

PART F. DISCOVERY

If the matter is to go forward in the U.S. court, there may be individuals and evidence located abroad that are essential for the trial. In a domestic case, discovery in another state is not significantly different than in the forum state. If the matter is in federal court the differences are essentially eliminated. But when the parties are from two different nations, access to witnesses and evidence in a foreign state may be very difficult. Assuming the matter is in a U.S. court the parties may wish to apply local discovery rules. But if that means discovery in a foreign nation, any request to a witness to appear or to an individual to produce certain documents may clash with the foreign nation's permissible access to evidence. Nations have often used letters rogatory to gain such evidence, essentially constituting a request to the foreign nation's court to assist in obtaining the evidence. Such request will have to be crafted carefully so as not to demand what predictably will not be given. Extensive requests from the United States, made directly to persons or entities that are alleged to be under the jurisdiction of the U.S. court, have led many foreign nations to enact "blocking" laws that prohibit nationals from complying with such requests, or even make it a crime merely to ask for documents to be used in foreign proceedings.

Helpful to the gathering of evidence abroad is the Hague Convention on the Taking of Evidence Abroad in Civil or Commercial Matters of 1968, which has been adopted in some 54 nations. The Convention tries to meet the needs of the forum court to obtain evidence that court considers admissible, while not imposing upon the foreign parties or sources of evidence demands that are overly excessive under the rules of their nation.

An important early question for U.S. courts was whether the Convention procedures were mandatory or an alternative to the rules of the forum. If optional, a second question asked whether the Convention procedures had to be tried first and only if they proved inadequate could the court use discovery rules of the forum. The U.S. Supreme Court ruled that based on the history and language of the Convention use of the Convention was optional and there was no need to use the Convention first.[7]

One problem faced by the United States is reflected in Article 23 of the Convention. This article allows signatories to restrict pretrial production of documents, which many in the United States believe reflects a lack of understanding by civil law tradition nations of common law trial procedure. Article 23 is often cited as a reason given by foreign nations for rejecting requests for discovery.

PART G. CHOICE OF LAW

Most international cases involve the presence of at least two different sets of substantive rules. The approaches to deciding a choice of law question may differ depending upon whether the issue is contract or tort. It is an important decision for a court, because a ruling that a foreign law applies that offers very nominal damages is tantamount to a victory for the defendant.

Contract. A sales contract negotiated across borders might reasonably be decided in the nation of the seller or the buyer. Fortunately, international sales of goods rules have been partly harmonized by the United Nations Convention on Contracts for the International Sale of Goods (CISG) of 1980, which has been enacted by more than 60 nations. But different nations may reach different interpretations of the same article, just as may different states in interpreting the Uniform Commercial Code.

A choice of law provision is often included in a contract, and such choices are respected in many nations. Where there is no such choice made in the contract, rules tend to determine the nation most closely connected to the transaction or at least having a significant relationship to the transaction.

Tort. Torts usually occur outside of the framework of a contract that might have an applicable choice of law provision. But there are some such provisions, for example where a person signs an agreement for a stay at a resort or to take a cruise, and the contract has a choice of law (and quite possibly a choice of forum) provision in the event of any injury. But in many tort cases, such as the numerous cases brought against companies for injuries allegedly caused by the company's practices abroad, there is no contract and therefore no choice of law provision. In such case the courts tend to use the long held theory that the law of the place where the injury occurred is the proper choice. But the injury that occurs in one country

---

7. *Societe Nationale Industrielle Aerospatiale v. United States District Court*, 482 U.S. 522, 107 S.Ct. 2542, 96 L.Ed.2d 461 (1987).

may be attributable to negligence in another, such as where a product is negligently made in the United States and an injury occurs in a foreign nation after the product is exported. The consequence of the decision may be very important, because damages under U.S. law are likely to be much higher than under the foreign law.

Proving Foreign Law. Part of the analysis of what law should apply may include the problems associated with proving foreign law. While a U.S. court is deemed to know U.S. law, it is not deemed to know foreign law. It must be proved. That means an understanding of Rule 44.1 of the Federal Rules of Civil Procedure, assuming the matter is before a federal court. Rule 44.1 requires a party who plans to request the application of foreign law to give reasonable notice. It also allows the court wide latitude in determining foreign law. That usually includes the use of experts to explain both the nature of the foreign legal system, such as how case law fits into the hierarchy of law, and the substantive characteristics of the applicable law. Experts usually provide affidavits that include translations of the applicable legal provisions.

PART H. RECOGNITION AND ENFORCEMENT OF FOREIGN JUDGMENTS

U.S. courts are not required to give full faith and credit to foreign judgments. But comity and an important 1895 foundation decision of the U.S. Supreme court suggest that foreign judgments should in many instances be recognized and enforced.[8] Not all nations agree. Many foreign nations have no statutory process to enforce foreign judgments, although most of the more developed civil law nations have a process of *exaquator* that allows enforcement, although only by bringing an enforcement action in the foreign nation that may appear to be little different than a new action on the merits. But some decisions of the foreign court may be respected under a theory comparable to *res judicata*. The European Union has harmonized the enforcement process in the Brussels Regulation of 2000. That Regulation governs jurisdiction as well as judgment recognition and enforcement, and mandates recognition unless one of the Article 34 defenses is proven. Those defenses are not unlike the defenses available in many states in the United States that have adopted the Uniform Foreign–Money Judgments Recognition Act or its successor, the Uniform Foreign–Country Money Judgments Recognition Act.

The UFMJRA and UFCMJRA, enacted in nearly 30 states, provide for recognition unless one of the listed defenses is met. They are classified under two headings, situations where foreign judgments should not be recognized and situations where they need not be recognized. The fact that enforcement in the United States remains state law creates problems for foreign nations, especially where they have adopted reciprocity as a norm for enforcement. For example, Spain requires reciprocity. Will a Spanish court enforce a Texas judgment if (a) Texas has enforced Spanish

---

8. *Hilton v. Guyot,* 159 U.S. 113, 16 S.Ct. 139, 40 L.Ed. 95 (1895).

judgments, (b) Texas has never either enforced or rejected a Spanish judgment, but has a record of enforcing judgments from other civil law tradition nations, or (c) Texas has never enforced any foreign judgments but other states have? It is likely that only in (a) might Spain enforce the Texas judgment. Thus, Spain and other foreign nations may tend to view enforcement of judgments from the United States as though it were dealing with 50 different nations.

U.S. recognition law has never been federalized. It remains the determination of each state. But for years negotiations have been ongoing for the creation of an international convention governing enforcement. If it is ever completed, and if the United States adopts the convention, a major shift will have been made from state law to treaty-based federal law. Until then, the recognition and enforcement of U.S. court decisions is very uncertain.[9]

Some foreign nations have very clear rules allowing recognition and follow those rules, some foreign nations have very clear rules allowing recognition but never recognize foreign judgments, and some foreign nations remain without any methods for recognition of foreign judgments. It is important to know the position of any foreign nation when bringing suit in one country that will have to be recognized and enforced in another because the latter is where the assets are located.

Courts sometimes speak of positive and negative reciprocity. It has to do with which party argues what. The party attempting to enforce a foreign judgment in the United States will try to "positively" establish that the United States would enforce a judgment of the foreign nation if the tables were turned. The party against whom the judgment was rendered will attempt to establish "negative" reciprocity by proving that the United States would not enforce such a foreign judgment.

PART I. WHEN THINGS GO WRONG—THE PROBLEMS IN 11.1–11.5

The above briefly introduces some of the characteristics of litigation when it crosses borders. The problems that follow offer a further introduction to these issues, including the essential cases and ideas of each area. The problems are principally devoted to litigation, but the last addresses the enforcement of arbitral awards. We have chosen what we hope will offer an introduction to some of the principle issues that face lawyers as they confront civil conflicts with cross border characteristics. The subject of international civil dispute resolution has become a separate course at many institutions for students interested in pursuing the matter more thoroughly.

Problem 11.1 focuses on the choice of forum and jurisdiction. It assumes the contract or agreement is silent regarding choices of the form of dispute resolution, and considers which courts might entertain personal

---

9. See Yoav Oestreicher, *"We're on a Road to Nowhere"—Reasons for the Continuing Failure to Regulate Recognition and Enforcement of Foreign Judgments*, 42 Int'l Law. 59 (2008).

jurisdiction. Subject matter jurisdiction is also briefly discussed. It has already been addressed in several problems, such as jurisdiction over a foreign state under the Foreign Sovereign Immunities Act in Problem 10.6, jurisdiction under the Alien Tort Claims Act and Torture Victims Protection Act in Problem 10.5, and jurisdiction to resolve contract issues such as in Problem 4.1, the sale of insulation to Germany.

Problem 11.2 considers service of process, *forum non conveniens* and choice of law. We were introduced to some issues of the choice of law in Problem 4.1, where the sale of insulation to Germany could be governed by the German Commercial Code, the U.S. (Kansas) UCC, or the Convention on Contracts for the International Sale of Goods. (CISG).

Problem 11.3 explores two issues, discovery abroad and extraterritoriality—conflicts when one nation legislates and/or adjudicates on matters which principally or partly occur outside its territory. The problem explores the limits of extraterritoriality, and the actions other nations may take when they believe such extraterritoriality has exceeded fair limits and unduly affected their interests. The response from abroad may be in the form of "blocking" or "clawback" laws. Blocking laws, which usually prohibit persons from complying with foreign court orders, strongly affect the process of discovery abroad. Clawback laws attempt to allow parties subject to judgments abroad which are perceived to be unfair, illegal or inappropriate, to take back the judgment from assets of the plaintiff located in the country which has enacted the clawback law.

Problem 11.4 assumes that a judgment has been entered in one jurisdiction and the successful party wishes to have the judgment recognized and enforced in another nation. If the judgment is enforced, there may be an issue whether the judgment will be enforced in the currency of the nation issuing the decision, or will be converted to the currency of the enforcing nation. If there is a conversion, the law may stipulate or the court may have discretion to determine the appropriate date of conversion, such as the date of the wrong, the date of the judgment, the date of the enforcement, or the date of the payment.

Problem 11.5 assumes that an arbitral decision has been rendered and considers some of the issues of enforcing that decision. The decision might have been rendered in the same nation where enforcement is attempted, or in a different nation. The nations may be parties to enforcement conventions. Without enforcement the process of arbitration is threatened as an institution.

PART J. ALTERNATIVES TO LITIGATION

The use of alternatives to litigation to resolve international disputes merits some comment. Many nations may perceive that litigation is the primary means of dispute resolution, but there are other forms that one might wish to consider. That might be viewed as a kind of hub and spoke arrangement, with litigation the hub, and spokes leading to arbitration, mediation and trade agreement dispute panels. But other nations may give more equal status to these latter methods, and view litigation on a more horizontal plane along with the other methods. Japan, China and some other countries tend to share this view. But some nations, including Germany and the United Kingdom, seem to view litigation at the apex of a pyramid that leaves other forms at a very distant bottom, if they are part of the pyramid at all. Perhaps that fairly leads to a sense that the former group is at one end and the latter at the other, with the United States somewhere in between.

Litigation versus arbitration may be viewed by different institutions dealing with specific issues, such as banks dealing with letters of credit. It is important for U.S. lawyers representing clients engaged in a dispute with a foreign party to be able to understand not only the characteristics of the various choices of dispute resolution, but how opposing foreign counsel may view the alternatives.

Arbitration is considered to have many of the same problems as litigation. However, in litigation, a major problem arises with the extensive use of pretrial discovery; on the other hand, a major problem with arbitration is that the limited discovery permitted may hinder fact development. Thus, one major criterion for choosing litigation or arbitration will be the relative need for this type of fact development in your client's case, and in your opponent's case. As a theoretical matter, you may have a mechanism which you inherently prefer (unrelated to the specific dispute, parties, etc.)? Part of your choice will depend upon the attitudes and style of the individual advocate. Are you more comfortable with a formal setting or an informal setting? If "objective criteria" are ambivalent in selecting a mechanism, "subjective criteria" (e.g., in what setting are you as an individual more effective) should not be ignored. On the other hand, there are some disputes in which "objective criteria" should be determinative.

Perhaps we ought not to view alternative forms as associated with different nations, but as associated with different uses by different institutions in different nations. Why is arbitration preferable to banks for the resolution of letter of credit issues? The securities industry has long used arbitration, as Thomas H. Oehmke notes:

> In 1897 the United States Supreme Court upheld the arbitration process as a fair, equitable and efficient method for settling disputes in the securities industry.* * * Today, nearly all disputes in the securities industry are arbitrated, rather than litigated. This is due to the federal judiciary's recognition of the FAA's preemptive effect in the field of arbitration and to the industry's pervasive effort to have all public customers, member and associated persons sign arbitration contracts. Arbitration, 89 AmJur Trials 55 (2008).

Remember that both parties must agree if litigation is not to be used and another mechanism substituted. The reception of a suggestion to use an agreed-upon forum will depend upon what the parties believe the most likely forum will be if no agreement is reached. Only a determination as to what court or courts have jurisdiction in the absence of agreement will allow the parties to make a comparison between that forum and other mechanisms and courts located elsewhere. What might be an interesting exercise would be to go back through the problems asking what would be the likely forum in the event of litigation and the absence of a forum selection clause. An additional inquiry might be considering when arbitration should be called for, either in advance of the problem, or as a means of resolving a conflict after it has arisen.

PROBLEM 11.1   RESOLUTION OF INTERNATIONAL DISPUTES: TELEVISIONS EVERYWHERE: CHOICE OF FORUM AND JURISDICTION

SECTION I.   THE SETTING

Camelot, plc., is a Canadian manufacturer of televisions sold in Canada and abroad and largely made from Japanese components purchased by Camelot from Mitsuey, a Tokyo, Japan, TV parts manufacturer. Camelot's international sales are administered through a wholly owned subsidiary, Lancelot Sales, Inc., a Delaware corporation with its only U.S. place of business in Boston, Massachusetts, where it leases a one room office, several word processors, some furniture, and some space in a warehouse. Foreign origin orders are shipped to the buyer usually from the Boston warehouse (where goods are sometimes stored for two or three days awaiting shipment). Sometimes, however, they are shipped directly from Camelot's manufacturing plant in Quebec, even though the contract is between the buyer and Lancelot.

SECTION II.   FOCUS OF CONSIDERATION

This problem focuses on two important pretrial procedural issues. First is the range of possible actions and courts that might be involved in litigation arising from the sale by Lancelot to Pellinore, S.A., a Spanish corporation, including the use of choice of forum provisions in contracts to limit the scope of possible forums. Choice of forum is the focus of Part A. Where a choice of forum provision is included in a contract there is often also a choice of law provision. Choice of law will be part of Problem 11.2.

In Part B we briefly consider the 2005 Hague Convention on Choice of Court Agreements, a convention which attempts to harmonize the legitimacy and acceptance of choice of court provisions. We then turn to jurisdiction. The availability of a particular court depends primarily on its jurisdiction—both over the parties and over the claim or subject-matter. In Part C we consider personal jurisdiction over foreign defendants in U.S. courts, and in Part D discuss parallel issues of jurisdiction before courts in the European Union and Asia, specifically in Spain and Japan. (We will not delve into the mysteries of subject-matter jurisdiction of U.S. courts, which has been discussed in detail in other problems, such as 4.1. But we will consider what is effectively subject-matter jurisdiction in the European Union and Japan, where it is part of a general consideration of what in the United States we separately call subject-matter and personal jurisdiction.)

There is an EU Regulation in the Documents Supplement that must be consulted in order to analyze this problem. It is properly entitled the EU Regulation on Jurisdiction and the Recognition and Enforcement of Judgments in Civil and Commercial Matters, and addresses choice of forum or forum selection clauses, as well as its principal focus, jurisdiction and enforcement. It is more commonly called the Brussels Regulation (sometimes called Brussels II because it essentially superceded the 1968 EU "Brussels" Convention that earlier addressed the same issues). The Hague Convention on Choice of Court Agreements is also included in the Documents Supplement.

SECTION III. READINGS, QUESTIONS AND COMMENTS

PART A. CHOICE OF FORUM

Before attorneys choose a forum or a dispute resolution mechanism, they should first know what options are available to each party and whether any of these options may have been foreclosed by a choice of forum provision in the contract. Our hypothetical continues with additional facts where a choice of forum and law provision has been included in the contract, although not as a result of negotiation. Choice of forum provisions are frequently used in contracts. They may also affect some torts, where the tort is related to the contract. Contracts for travel, such as shipboard cruises, group travel tours and stays at resorts, increasingly include provisions designating a "choice" of forum and law.

There are limits on party autonomy. There are some issues that a nation may want decided by its own courts under its own law. Criminal law is an archetypical example of this principle, but it may be illustrated in other types of regulatory law. Where does that become involved in a commercial transaction? Note that arbitration by the American Arbitration Association or the International Chamber of Commerce may result in appearance before a tribunal which is located in a nation having no relation to the transaction. Finally, if the parties cannot agree on the law of any particular jurisdiction, may the parties simply choose to have "international law" govern the transaction, whatever that means? For example is there an international law governing letters of credit? There is the ICC UCP, but they are recommended rules and not law except in the few jurisdictions that have incorporated them into domestic law.

Assume that after three months of negotiations between Boston and Madrid, including telephone calls, e-mail, faxes, letters and visits to each others offices, Lancelot sold a large quantity of Camelot televisions to Pellinore, S.A., for shipment to Madrid directly from Quebec. Lancelot wanted to break into the Spanish market, and agreed without objection to a contract provision that appeared for the first time in Pellinore's final offer to purchase, that also contained all the various agreements discussed and worked out during the negotiations. The new provision stated as follows:

> All claims and disputes arising under and in relation to this contract shall be litigated before the courts of Madrid, Spain. This contract shall be governed by the laws of Spain.

Choice of forum and/or law were never specifically discussed during the negotiations. Lancelot was not pleased with the added provision but felt it might lose an order it needed to enter the Spanish market. It signed the agreement and shipped the goods. A letter of credit was not used. When Lancelot forwarded the documents to Spain for payment, Pellinore refused to pay alleging that the television sets were nonconforming. Pellinore stated that the TV sets that arrived are all in silver metal cabinets, while it expected them to be in black metal cabinets. Apparently, the Spanish market considers the silver metal cabinets to be used for low cost electronics equipment and black metal cabinets for the high cost electronics, including the Camelot products. Pellinore notes that the contract referred to "blk" in the description of the goods. Pellinore says "blk" means *black*. Camelot's TVs had never been sold to Spain before this sale. Lancelot believes Pellinore is simply trying to get the television sets at a reduced price and that the "blk" description referred to a *bulk* sale, not to the color black. At least we may assume that there is a legitimate contract law issue regarding whether or the goods are conforming. Pellinore has also stated that Lancelot must perform its obligation to supply the TVs in black cabinets because the holiday season is approaching when Pellinore does most of its sales.

You are advising Lancelot. You would like Lancelot to sue Pellinore in a U.S. court notwithstanding the choice of forum provision. You want payment for the goods or at least their return. And you do not want to have to supply black cabinet TVs, which would cost sufficiently more to cause a loss on the sale. After talking with your client, your first research is to determine whether a U.S. court will enforce the choice of forum provision.

An alternative that Lancelot and Pellinore might have chosen is arbitration. The readings below also address some issues when the choice has been arbitration, but it is challenged, usually by one of the parties filing suit in a court and the defendant requesting dismissal because of the choice of arbitration clause in the contract.

M/S BREMEN v. ZAPATA OFF–SHORE CO.

Supreme Court of the United States, 1972.
407 U.S. 1, 92 S.Ct. 1907, 32 L.Ed.2d 513.

MR. CHIEF JUSTICE BURGER delivered the opinion of the Court.

We granted certiorari to review a judgment of the * * * Fifth Circuit declining to enforce a forum-selection clause governing disputes arising under an international towage contract between petitioners and respondent. The circuits have differed in their approach to such clauses. * * * [W]e vacate the judgment of the Court of Appeals.

In November 1967, respondent Zapata, a Houston-based American corporation, contracted with petitioner Unterweser, a German corporation, to tow Zapata's * * * drilling rig *Chaparral* from Louisiana to a point off Ravenna, Italy, in the Adriatic Sea, where Zapata had agreed to drill certain wells.

Zapata had solicited bids for the towage, and several companies including Unterweser had responded. Unterweser was the low bidder and Zapata requested it to submit a contract, which it did. The contract submitted by Unterweser contained the following provision, which is at issue in this case:

"Any dispute arising must be treated before the London Court of Justice."

In addition the contract contained two clauses purporting to exculpate Unterweser from liability for damages to the towed barge.

* * *

On January 5, 1968, Unterweser's deep sea tug *Bremen* departed Venice, Louisiana, with the *Chaparral* in tow bound for Italy. On January 9, while the flotilla was in international waters in the middle of the Gulf of Mexico, a severe storm arose. The sharp roll of the *Chaparral* in Gulf waters caused its elevator legs, which had been raised for the voyage, to break off and fall into the sea, seriously damaging the *Chaparral*. In this emergency situation Zapata instructed the *Bremen* to tow its damaged rig to Tampa, Florida, the nearest port of refuge.

On January 12, Zapata, ignoring its contract promise to litigate "any dispute arising" in the English courts, commenced a suit in admiralty in the [U.S.] District Court at Tampa, seeking $3,500,000 damages against Unterweser *in personam* and the *Bremen in rem,* alleging negligent towage and breach of contract. Unterweser responded by invoking the forum clause of the towage contract, and moved to dismiss for lack of jurisdiction or on *forum non conveniens* grounds, or in the alternative to stay the action pending submission of the dispute to the "London Court of Justice". Shortly thereafter, * * * before the District Court had ruled on its motion to stay or dismiss the [U.S.] action, Unterweser commenced an action against Zapata seeking damages for breach of the towage contract in the High Court of Justice in London, as the contract provided. Zapata appeared in that court to contest jurisdiction, but its challenge was rejected, the English courts holding that the contractual forum provision conferred jurisdiction.

* * * [T]he District Court denied Unterweser's * * * motion to dismiss or stay Zapata's initial [action, relying] on the prior decision of the Court of Appeals in Carbon Black Export, Inc. v. The Monrosa. In that case the Court of Appeals had held a forum-selection clause unenforceable,

reiterating the traditional view of many American courts that "agreements in advance of controversy whose object is to oust the jurisdiction of the courts are contrary to public policy and will not be enforced." * * *

On appeal, a divided panel of the Court of Appeals affirmed, and on rehearing *en banc* the panel opinion was adopted, with six of the 14 * * * dissenting. As had the District Court, the majority rested on the *Carbon Black* decision, concluding that " 'at the very least' " that case stood for the proposition that a forum-selection clause " 'will not be enforced unless the selected state would provide a more convenient forum than the state in which suit is brought.' " From that premise the Court of Appeals proceeded to conclude that, apart from the forum-selection clause, the District Court did not abuse its discretion in refusing to decline jurisdiction on the basis of *forum non conveniens*. It noted that (1) the flotilla never "escaped the Fifth Circuit's mare nostrum, and the casualty occurred in close proximity to the district court"; (2) a considerable number of potential witnesses, including Zapata crewmen, resided in the Gulf Coast area; (3) preparation for the voyage and inspection and repair work had been performed in the Gulf area; (4) the testimony of the *Bremen* crew was available by way of deposition; (5) England had no interest in or contact with the controversy other than the forum-selection clause. The Court of Appeals majority further noted that Zapata was a United States citizen and "[t]he discretion of the district court to remand the case to a foreign forum was consequently limited"—especially since it appeared likely that the English courts would enforce the exculpatory clauses. In the Court of Appeals' view, enforcement of such clauses would be contrary to public policy in American courts under Bisso v. Inland Waterways Corp. Therefore, "[t]he district court was entitled to consider that remanding Zapata to a foreign forum, with no practical contact with the controversy, could raise a bar to recovery by a United States citizen which its own convenient courts would not countenance."

We hold, with the six dissenting members of the Court of Appeals, that far too little weight and effect were given to the forum clause in resolving this controversy. For at least two decades we have witnessed an expansion of overseas commercial activities by business enterprises based in the United States. The barrier of distance that once tended to confine a business concern to a modest territory no longer does so. Here we see an American company with special expertise contracting with a foreign company to tow a complex machine thousands of miles across seas and oceans. The expansion of American business and industry will hardly be encouraged if, notwithstanding solemn contracts, we insist on a parochial concept that all disputes must be resolved under our laws and in our courts. Absent a contract forum, the considerations relied on by the Court of Appeals would be persuasive reasons for holding an American forum convenient in the traditional sense, but in an era of expanding world trade and commerce, the absolute aspects of the doctrine of the *Carbon Black* case have little place and would be a heavy hand indeed on the future development of international commercial dealings by Americans. We cannot have trade and commerce in world markets and international waters exclusively on our terms, governed by our laws, and resolved in our courts.

Forum-selection clauses have historically not been favored by American courts. Many courts, federal and state, have declined to enforce such clauses on the ground that they were "contrary to public policy," or that their effect was to "oust the jurisdiction" of the court. Although this view apparently still has considerable acceptance, other courts are tending to adopt a more hospitable attitude toward forum-selection clauses. This view, advanced in the well-reasoned dissenting opinion in the instant case, is that such clauses are prima facie valid and should be enforced unless enforcement is shown by the resisting party to be "unreasonable" under the circumstances. We believe this is the correct doctrine to be followed by federal district courts sitting in admiralty. * * * Not surprisingly, foreign businessmen prefer, as do we, to have disputes resolved in their own courts, but if that choice is not available, then in a neutral forum with expertise in the subject matter. Plainly, the courts of England meet the standards of neutrality and long experience in admiralty litigation. The choice of that forum was made in an arm's-length negotiation by experienced and sophisticated businessmen, and absent some compelling and countervailing reason it should be honored by the parties and enforced by the courts.

The argument that such clauses are improper because they tend to "oust" a court of jurisdiction is hardly more than a vestigial legal fiction. It appears to rest at core on historical judicial resistance to any attempt to reduce the power and business of a particular court and has little place in an era when all courts are overloaded and when businesses once essentially local now operate in world markets. It reflects something of a provincial attitude regarding the fairness of other tribunals. No one seriously contends in this case that the forum-selection clause "ousted" the District Court of jurisdiction over Zapata's action. The threshold question is whether that court should have exercised its jurisdiction to do more than give effect to the legitimate expectations of the parties, manifested in their freely negotiated agreement, by specifically enforcing the forum clause.

There are compelling reasons why a freely negotiated private international agreement, unaffected by fraud, undue influence, or overweening bargaining power, such as that involved here, should be given full effect. In this case, for example, we are concerned with a far from routine transaction between companies of two different nations contemplating the tow of a extremely costly piece of equipment from Louisiana across the Gulf of Mexico and the Atlantic Ocean, through the Mediterranean Sea to its final destination in the Adriatic Sea. In the course of its voyage, it was to traverse the waters of many jurisdictions. * * *

* * * The correct approach would have been to enforce the forum clause specifically unless Zapata could clearly show that enforcement would be unreasonable and unjust, or that the clause was invalid for such

reasons as fraud or overreaching. Accordingly, the case must be remanded for reconsideration.

We note, however, that there is nothing in the record presently before us that would support a refusal to enforce the forum clause. The Court of Appeals suggested that enforcement would be contrary to the public policy of the forum because of the prospect that the English courts would enforce the clauses of the towage contract purporting to exculpate Unterweser from liability for damages to the *Chaparral*. A contractual choice-of-forum clause should be held unenforceable if enforcement would contravene a strong public policy of the forum in which suit is brought, whether declared by statute or by judicial decision. * * *

Courts have also suggested that a forum clause, even though it is freely bargained for and contravenes no important public policy of the forum, may nevertheless be "unreasonable" and unenforceable if the chosen forum is *seriously* inconvenient for the trial of the action. Of course, where it can be said with reasonable assurance that at the time they entered the contract, the parties to a freely negotiated private international commercial agreement contemplated the claimed inconvenience, it is difficult to see why any such claim of inconvenience should be heard to render the forum clause unenforceable. We are not here dealing with an agreement between two Americans to resolve their essentially local disputes in a remote alien forum. In such a case, the serious inconvenience of the contractual forum to one or both of the parties might carry greater weight in determining the reasonableness of the forum clause. The remoteness of the forum might suggest that the agreement was an adhesive one, or that the parties did not have the particular controversy in mind when they made their agreement; yet even there the party claiming should bear a heavy burden of proof. Similarly, selection of a remote forum to apply differing foreign law to an essentially American controversy might contravene an important public policy of the forum. * * *

This case, however, involves a freely negotiated international commercial transaction between a German and an American corporation for towage of a vessel from the Gulf of Mexico to the Adriatic Sea. As noted, selection of a London forum was clearly a reasonable effort to bring vital certainty to this international transaction and to provide a neutral forum experienced and capable in the resolution of admiralty litigation. * * *

The judgment of the Court of Appeals is vacated and the case is remanded for further proceedings consistent with this opinion.

Vacated and remanded.

MR. JUSTICE DOUGLAS, dissenting.

* * *

Respondent is a citizen of this country. Moreover, if it were remitted to the English court, its substantive rights would be adversely affected. Exculpatory provisions in the towage control provide (1) that petitioners, the masters and the crews "are not responsible for defaults and/or errors in the navigation of the tow" and (2) that "[d]amages suffered by the towed object are in any case for account of its Owners."

Under our decision in Dixilyn Drilling Corp. v. Crescent Towing & Salvage Co., "a contract which exempts the tower from liability for its own negligence" is not enforceable, though there is evidence in the present record that it is enforceable in England. * * *

I would affirm the judgment below.

QUESTIONS AND COMMENTS

1. In *The Bremen v. Zapata Off-Shore Co.,* the Court upheld a clause selecting the London Court of Justice in a contract between an American corporation and a German corporation, as "a freely negotiated private international agreement, unaffected by fraud, undue influence, or overweening bargaining power, such as that involved here [which] should be given effect."

The Bremen decision seems to put to rest the idea that forum selection clauses should not be respected. But it sets conditions. Does it establish workable legal standards, or merely tell business to be reasonable in using forum selection clauses?

2. *Bremen* is the foundation pronouncement by the Court on the subject of choice of forum clauses in international transactions. The dissent presents fully the arguments of the rig-owner: that use of an English forum determines this outcome of the case because English courts under English law would allow a tug by contract to disclaim its own negligence, while a U.S. court under U.S. law would not allow it to do so. Thus, the rig owner is losing substantive rights that it would otherwise have under U.S. law. The majority does not accept this argument. At what analytical level does the majority confront this argument and respond to it?

3. What is "freely negotiated" language of *The Bremen* decision? In *Carnival Cruise Lines, Inc. v. Shute,* 499 U.S. 585, 111 S.Ct. 1522, 113 L.Ed.2d 622 (1991), the Supreme Court upheld a forum-selection clause between two American contracting parties. Mrs. Shute had purchased a ticket for a Carnival Cruise Lines tour from Los Angeles down the Mexican coast and back. She purchased the ticket from a travel agent in Arlington, Washington, where she lived, and paid in advance. When the ticket arrived, it included a Contract with 25 numbered paragraphs, all in type much smaller than in this casebook. Paragraph 8 required any disputes arising under the Contract to be litigated before Florida courts, to the exclusion of all others. When Mrs. Shute was injured on board ship in international waters, she attempted to sue Carnival in the State of Washington. The Court of Appeals refused to enforce the forum-selection clause for two reasons: (1) because it "was not freely bargained for", and (2) because "the Shutes are physically and financially incapable of pursuing the litigation in Florida," and the clause should not be used to deprive parties of their day in court.

The U.S. Supreme Court reversed. It recognized that there would be no negotiations, and no "bargaining parity" in such a form contract; but stated that "a reasonable forum clause in a form contract could be upheld." The cruise line's clause was found reasonable. Since the line otherwise could be subject to suit "in several different fora," the clause created certainty for the parties, "conserv[ed] judicial resources," and saved money for the line—which might result in reduced fares. As to the second ground, the Court found that the Shutes had "not satisfied the heavy burden of proof required to set aside the clause on grounds of inconvenience," especially since "Florida is not a remote alien forum."

Does this line of analysis apply to forum-selection clauses adopting alien fora? Florida was considered a reasonable forum because Carnival's principal place of business was there. The dissent notes that Carnival is incorporated in Panama, and wonders whether a clause on the ticket selecting Panamanian courts would be upheld. How would you analyze that issue?

4. What if a person in South Florida, using the internet, purchased a vacation for her family that included lodging at a hotel in the Bahamas owned by a Bahamas corporation, but only when they arrived at the desk of the hotel in the Bahamas to check in were they asked to sign an agreement that any litigation that might arise out of their stay would be litigated in the Bahamas under Bahamian law? Does this differ from *Carnival Cruise Lines?* The federal district court in Florida held that it did differ, essentially because of the unreasonableness of the time at which the choice of forum and law clause was presented. In *Carnival Cruise Lines*, the party was informed of the forum selection when her ticket arrived *before* departure on the trip. In *Sun Trust Bank* the persons were not informed until they were at the front desk waiting for their room key. See *Sun Trust Bank v. Sun Int'l Hotels, Ltd.*, 184 F.Supp.2d 1246 (S.D.Fla. 2001).

5. In *Bremen,* the parties chose a neutral forum, that of London. The U.S. Supreme Court upheld this choice stating that "in the light of present day commercial realities and expanding international trade we conclude that the forum clause should control absent a strong showing that it should be set aside." *Bremen* has now been supplemented by *Carnival Cruise Lines. Bremen* and *Carnival Cruise Lines* both involve *services* contracts. However, the Lancelot–Pellinore contract involved a sale of *goods*. That should not affect the choice of forum provision.

This language seems to uphold the choice of forum clauses, including that with Lancelot. What if the choice of forum stated London, is London at all related to the transaction? What if a London solicitor drafted the contract, the official version was in English (with British spelling style), and the parties signed the final agreement in London because they were there to see the Spain–England futball (soccer) final in the World Cup? Is London any less related than it was in *Bremen?* Does it need to be related to the transaction? Does your analysis change if the parties chose the courts of Rotterdam, The Netherlands? Tokyo, Japan? Lagos, Nigeria?

6. As to the EU and choice of forum, the Brussels Regulation has superceded the Brussels Convention. The Brussels Regulation is the foundation for EU forum selection. Article 23 would place jurisdiction upon the Spanish court as a result of the written provision in the contract. But have the parties "agreed" on the forum? Has there been an agreement in accor-

dance "with a usage of which the parties are or ought to have been aware and which in such trade or commerce is widely known to, and regularly observed by, parties to contracts of the type involved in the particular trade or commerce concerned."? Isn't the Lancelot–Pellinore contract a kind of contract that commonly includes a choice of forum provision, whether for a specific nation's courts or for arbitration? Article 23 seems to sanctify the Lancelot–Pellinore choice of Madrid courts, but there is no discussion of the affect of an adhesion contract in the EU Regulation. Does that mean that an adhesion contract is not an "agreement" that is governed by the Regulation. Are we any better off using the Regulation than the reasoning of U.S. courts such as in *Bremen, Carnival Cruise Lines* and others?

7. Assuming Lancelot shipped the goods by sea to Madrid. Note the difference between legal issues concerning the sales contract performance and those concerning COGSA. We have previously seen that COGSA is regarded as "mandatory law." (See Problem 4.2) Would U.S. courts hold that a choice of forum clause could oust them of jurisdiction over the case if COGSA is the governing law? *Indussa Corp. v. S.S. Ranborg*, 377 F.2d 200 (2d Cir. 1967), provided the traditional answer that since there was no party ability to select any law but COGSA, there was also no party ability to select any forum but U.S. courts. The Supreme Court's decision in *Bremen* did not overturn this line of cases, although later decisions shifted the rationale to include the absence of bargaining in the bill of lading transaction, a rationale that was weakened by *Carnival Cruise Lines.*

8. In *Fireman's Fund Ins. Co. v. M.V. DSR Atlantic*, 131 F.3d 1336 (9th Cir. 1997), the court stated that *Vimar Seguros y Reaseguros, S.A. v. M/V Sky Reefer*, 515 U.S. 528, 115 S.Ct. 2322, 132 L.Ed.2d 462 (1995), overrules *Indusa* and allows the parties to choose any forum (foreign court as well as arbitral tribunal) for any issue. If "mandatory law" governing international contracts can now be determined by arbitration tribunals under an arbitration clause, it can also be determined by foreign courts under a forum selection clause. In other words, the *Indusa* rule requiring COGSA issues to be decided by U.S. courts, and not foreign courts, is no longer valid.

9. The new battleground in this area is represented by *Central National–Gottesman, Inc. v. M.V. "Gertrude Oldendorff,"* 204 F.Supp.2d 675 (S.D.N.Y. 2002), and asks whether the forum selection clause was "unreasonable." The bill of lading chose both English law (not COGSA) and the English courts. The court declined enforcement of the forum selection clause because of the "pragmatic goal of ensuring that no party, subject to COGSA coverage, enjoys protection short of that guaranteed by the Act," and because of *Sky Reefer's* comfort with there being "a subsequent opportunity for the district court to review the foreign court's decision to ensure that it comported with the interest in enforcement of the laws in the United States." In *Central National–Gottesman* the clause chose English law, which meant that it was not a case where the foreign court was to apply COGSA, and the fear was that it would apply COGSA differently than a U.S. court. COGSA would simply be inapplicable. That was going too far. Are these the same issues as were raised in *Bremen* and *Carnival Cruise Lines*? Can those cases be distinguished?

10. *Bonny v. Society of Lloyd's*, 3 F.3d 156 (7th Cir. 1993), cert. denied, 510 U.S. 945, 114 S.Ct. 385, 126 L.Ed.2d 333 (1993), is representative of many cases involving Lloyd's "Names" initiated in the United States. *Bonny* and most of the decisions upheld the forum selection of England. See also *Richards v. Lloyd's of London*, 135 F.3d 1289 (9th Cir. 1998); *Allen v. Lloyd's of London*, 94 F.3d 923 (4th Cir. 1996); *Roby v. Corporation of Lloyd's*, 996 F.2d 1353 (2d. Cir.), cert. denied, 510 U.S. 945, 114 S.Ct. 385, 126 L.Ed.2d 333 (1993). The saga of Lloyd's is discussed in James Gange, *Richards v. Lloyd's of London: The Ninth Circuit Denies Access to the Securities Laws to American Investors,* 24 Brook. J. Int'l L. 625 (1998).

11. Care must be used in drafting choice of forum clauses. Many courts are still hostile to such attempts to oust them of jurisdiction. Thus, if a court can construe such a clause as merely permissive, rather than as exclusive and mandatory, it will do so. See, e.g., Albemarle Corp. v. AstraZeneca UK Ltd., 2009 WL 902348 (D.S.C. Mar. 31, 2009) (Federal Dist. of South Carolina). Might any of the forum selection clauses in this Problem be construed as merely permissive?

12. The ultimate choice of forum clause is one which chooses no court at all, but an alternative dispute resolution mechanism, such as an arbitration tribunal. The courts for a long period of time resisted validating such clauses (e.g., as depriving a party of due process of law), a reaction one might expect toward a competitor. However, legislatures were far more sympathetic to this device, and the issue seems to be settled. But not in all countries, Germany is arguably less inclined to favor arbitration than is Japan.

13. Can parties take issues concerning "mandatory law" to arbitrators for decision, rather than having such issues decided by U.S. courts? Another way of asking the same question is: Can the courts be ousted of jurisdiction over "mandatory law" through contrary agreement of the private parties? *Bonny* (and *Scherk v. Alberto–Culver Co.,* 417 U.S. 506, 94 S.Ct. 2449, 41 L.Ed.2d 270 (1974) (discussed in *Mitsubishi* in Problem 11.5)) allow enforcement of arbitration clauses in international contracts to determine rights under the Securities Exchange Acts of 1933 and 1934. *Mitsubishi Motors Corp. v. Soler Chrysler–Plymouth,* discussed in Problem 11.5 allows enforcement of the arbitration clause in an international contract to determine rights under U.S. antitrust laws and the Automobile Dealers Day in Court Act. For differing analysis of this problem, compare Andreas Lowenfeld, *The Mitsubishi Case: Another View,* 2 Arbitration J. 178 (1986) with William Park, *Private Adjudicators and the Public Interest: The Expanding Scope of International Arbitration,* 3 Brooklyn J. Int'l L. 629 (1986).

14. How does this affect disputes under COGSA? If Lancelot has a dispute with the carrier, and COGSA was applicable, would a mandatory arbitration clause in the bill of lading be enforceable? In *Sky Reefer,* the Supreme Court reasoned that *Scherk* and its progeny had decided that there was no longer any mandatory law exception to the parties ability to choose an arbitration forum for any issue. Does it make any difference if the bill of lading contract uses the first or second alternative immediately following?

First: All actions under this bill of lading shall be brought before the courts of Monrovia, Liberia (where the ship is registered), and the laws of the Republic of Liberia shall apply.

Second: All actions under this bill of lading shall be brought before the courts of London, and all rights and liabilities of any party to this bill shall be governed by the Hague–Visby Rules and the laws of England. (Assume the carrier was owned by a Liberian corporation and the ship was registered in Liberia).

15.   Is there good reason not to uphold the Madrid choice of forum in our hypothetical? In 2005, a Florida appellate court upheld a choice of Madrid provision in a franchising agreement. *Corsec, S.L. v. VMC Int'l Franchising, LLC*, 909 So.2d 945 (Fla.App. 3d DCA 2005). The court concluded that: "It should be incumbent on the party seeking to escape his contract to show that trial in the contractual forum will be so gravely difficult and inconvenient that he will for all practical purposes be deprived of his day in court. Absent that, there is no basis for concluding that it would be unfair, unjust, or unreasonable to hold that party to his bargain."

PART B.   ENTER INTERNATIONAL LAW: THE CONVENTION ON CHOICE OF COURT AGREEMENTS

Negotiations for more than a dozen years to achieve a jurisdiction and recognition of foreign judgments convention were not successful. Although the European Union nations have long had such a convention (now Regulation), the United States did not appear prepared to accept many of the proposals for an international convention. Instead of totally abandoning the effort, however the Hague Conference on Private International Law reduced its scope of aspirations considerably and in June of 2005 signed the Hague Convention on Choice of Court Agreements. How well the Convention will ultimately be received is yet to be determined, but the ratification to date after six years by only one nation, Mexico, is not encouraging. The Convention is not yet in force. This brief part considers the applicability of the Convention to our Lancelot/Pellinore hypothetical assuming the Convention becomes law in Spain and the United States.

HAGUE CONVENTION ON CHOICE OF COURT AGREEMENTS

Signed June 30, 2005.

The New Hague Convention on Choice of Court Agreements

By Ronald A. Brand

Introduction

* * * This new Hague Convention is perhaps most easily understood as the litigation counterpart to the New York Arbitration Convention. Like the New York Convention, it will establish rules for enforcing private party agreements regarding the forum for the resolution of disputes, and rules for recognizing and enforcing the decisions issued by the chosen forum.

The Convention on Choice of Court Agreements concludes more than a decade of negotiations that began in 1992 with a request from the United States for the negotiation of a convention on jurisdiction and the recognition and enforcement of foreign court judgments. * * * It became clear that some countries, particularly the United States, could not agree to the convention being considered, and efforts were redirected at a convention of more limited focus.

The Scope: International Business-to-Business Agreements

Designed to "promote international trade and investment through enhanced judicial co-operation," the new Convention will govern international business-to-business agreements that designate a single court, or the courts of a single country, for resolution of disputes ("exclusive choice of court agreements"). It will not apply to agreements that include a consumer as a party. Nor will it apply to purely domestic agreements in which "the parties are resident in the same Contracting State and . . . all other elements relevant to the dispute . . . are connected only with that State."

The Basic Rules

The Convention sets out three basic rules:

1) the court chosen by the parties in an exclusive choice of court agreement has jurisdiction;

2) if an exclusive choice of court agreement exists, a court not chosen by the parties does not have jurisdiction, and must decline to hear the case; and

3) a judgment resulting from jurisdiction exercised in accordance with an exclusive choice of court agreement must be recognized and enforced in the courts of other Contracting States (other countries that are parties to the Convention).

Through a declaration process, the Convention offers an optional fourth rule. Contracting States may declare that their courts will recognize and enforce judgments given by courts of other Contracting States designated in a non-exclusive choice of court agreement. This provision recognizes that, once the parties have agreed that a tribunal is acceptable, there is value in the free movement of its judgment. It is a response to discussions during the negotiations indicating that a significant number of industries rely on non-exclusive choice of court clauses. If Contracting States exercise this declaration option, it will substantially expand the recognition and enforcement benefits of the Convention.

* * * If ratified by the United States, this will be the first U.S. treaty that has the recognition and enforcement of judgments as a principal focus. While the New York Arbitration Convention provides for recognition and enforcement of arbitration agreements and the resulting awards in over 130 Contracting States, no such global convention exists for the recognition and enforcement of judgments. If the Hague Convention

becomes as widely accepted as the New York Convention, parties entering into international trade contracts should have a more balanced choice between selecting arbitration or litigation as the method for settling disputes.

Special Issues

The Convention includes safeguards acknowledging governmental interests that might otherwise be frustrated by the parties' choice of court. Thus, in addition to the exclusion of consumer transactions, it excludes application to employment relationships, family law matters, insolvency proceedings, nuclear damage, and personal injury claims, among others. It also allows courts not chosen to ignore choice of court agreements and courts asked to recognize judgments to refuse recognition and enforcement under limited circumstances that are consistent with traditional rules found in national and regional law. Thus, for example, recognition or enforcement of a judgment may be refused if it "would be manifestly incompatible with the public policy of the requested State."

Of particular concern during the negotiations was the application of the Convention to matters of intellectual property rights. Patent, trademark, and other such rights are often considered to be within the exclusive jurisdiction of the courts of the state granting the right, particularly where registration is involved. At the same time, many international transactions include the transfer of intellectual property rights in some manner. Thus, full exclusion of intellectual property rights matters from the Convention would have left it with limited value. The solution chosen was to exclude most issues of validity and infringement of intellectual property rights (other than copyright and related rights) from the scope of the Convention, but to make clear that the exclusion does not apply when those issues arise only as preliminary matters in reaching the main object of the proceedings.

An additional safeguard is found in Article 11 of the Convention, which allows refusal of recognition and enforcement of a judgment "if, and only to the extent that, the judgment awards damages, including exemplary or punitive damages, that do not compensate a party for actual loss or harm suffered." This provision recognizes existing practice in the use of public policy defenses to refuse recognition and enforcement of punitive damage awards, and responds to concerns about judgments that may be considered excessive in amount.

QUESTIONS AND COMMENTS

1. Is the choice of forum clause in our hypothetical in Part A a proper choice of court provision under the Convention? Doesn't the provision have to use language that clearly makes the choice the *exclusive* court?

2. Do any of the exceptions of the Convention apply? Intellectual property exemption? Consumer contract exemption? The Convention does not address the issue of the validity of choosing a foreign forum where a mandatory

law, such as COGSA, would not be the applicable law, or might not be the applicable law, or might be the applicable law but might not be applied in the same way as in a U.S. court.

3. The Convention includes obligations of participants' courts to enforce judgments of the exclusive court, nevertheless reserving the traditional rights to refuse recognition for such reasons as public policy. Consideration of those rights is part of Problem 11.4.

PART C. PERSONAL JURISDICTION IN U.S. COURTS AGAINST FOREIGN DEFENDANTS

In prior courses, you have already discussed some problems concerning jurisdiction of courts over parties in litigation within the United States, both as to state courts and as to federal courts. We are not going to revisit the intricacies of *International Shoe* to *World-Wide Volkswagen*, but we do look briefly again at *Asahi*, because it offers a very brief thought on whether personal jurisdiction should be viewed differently when the defendant is foreign, as in the case of *Asahi*, as well as the earlier *Helicopteros* decision that made no such distinction. Are the problems arising out of international transactions merely an extrapolation of those problems from domestic transactions as studied in prior courses, or are they a unique category that require courts to consider the international dimensions central to proper resolution of the problems? What is clearly added to domestic cases by international transactions is an expanded range of courts to be considered, including international tribunals and courts of other nations not regulated by U.S. laws. The starting point for analysis of jurisdictional issues is the statute that grants jurisdictional powers to the particular court. Most such statutes have ambiguities which must be interpreted. Broad claims of jurisdiction in a statute, or broad interpretations of statutes, may be subject to the limiting principles of due process. Note that some of the claims which concern Lancelot (and that we turn to later) arise out of *tort* claims while others arise out of *contract* claims. Should such differences create distinctions in the application of jurisdictional concepts? Some of the claims which concern Lancelot arise out of international trading of goods and others arise out of foreign investments. Should such differences create distinctions in the reach of a court, or should it be able to "pierce the corporate veil"?

The questions of jurisdiction in this problem include:

1. Will a U.S. court have personal jurisdiction in a suit by Lancelot (U.S.) versus Pellinore (Spain)?

2. Will a U.S. court assert personal jurisdiction over Camelot (Canada) if Pellinore sues Lancelot and Camelot? Might the U.S. court obtain jurisdiction over Camelot by veil piercing?

MALTZ, UNRAVELING THE CONUNDRUM OF THE LAW OF PERSONAL JURISDICTION: A COMMENT ON ASAHI METAL INDUSTRY CO. v. SUPERIOR COURT OF CALIFORNIA

1987 Duke Law Journal 669.*

As virtually every law student knows, the modern law of personal jurisdiction began with the case of *International Shoe Co. v. Washington.* *International Shoe* discarded the legal fiction of "presence" as the test for asserting jurisdiction and established the rule that a state may assert jurisdiction only over those defendants who "have certain minimum contacts with [the forum state] such that the maintenance of the suit does not offend 'traditional notions of fair play and substantial justice.' "

* * *

[P]urposeful availment analysis has come to dominate the Court's approach to personal jurisdiction problems. Prior to *Asahi*, the parameters of the doctrine in the *specific* personal jurisdiction context were largely defined by three cases: *World–Wide Volkswagen Corp. v. Woodson, Keeton v. Hustler Magazine, Inc.* and *Burger King Corp. v. Rudzewicz.*

In *World–Wide Volkswagen,* two New York residents brought a products liability suit in Oklahoma state court against numerous defendants, including a New York auto retailer who sold the plaintiffs an allegedly defective car. The suit arose following an automobile collision on an Oklahoma highway while plaintiffs were en route to their new home in Arizona.

Plaintiffs based their jurisdictional argument on the theory of actual foreseeability. Because of the nature of the highly mobile product, plaintiffs argued, the defendants should have foreseen the possibility that it would be used in another state and cause injury there. Notwithstanding the fact that the relevant defendants had no other contacts with the forum state, plaintiffs contended that the assumption of jurisdiction was constitutionally permissible.

Justice White, speaking for a six-member majority, rejected the plaintiffs' actual foreseeability argument. He asserted that although foreseeability is [not] wholly irrelevant ... the foreseeability that is critical to due process analysis is not the mere likelihood that a product will find its way into the forum State. Rather, it is that the defendant's conduct and connection with the forum State are such that he should reasonably anticipate being haled into court there.

The Court contended that absent some "purposeful availment" by the defendant corporation of the " 'privilege[s] of conducting activities within the forum State,' " due process does not permit the assertion of personal jurisdiction over nonresident defendants based on the "unilateral activity"

---

* Reprinted with permission.

of plaintiffs over which defendants exercise no control. Finding a "total absence of those affiliating circumstances that are a necessary predicate to any exercise of state-court jurisdiction." Justice White concluded that the minimum contacts requirement had not been met.

* * *

Taken together, *World–Wide Volkswagen, Keeton and Burger King* clearly establish the primacy of the concept of purposeful availment in personal jurisdiction analysis. In *World–Wide Volkswagen,* jurisdiction was barred because the defendant's only contact with the forum state was created by the " 'unilateral activity of those who claim some relationship with a nonresident defendant.' " In contrast, when the defendants created the relationship with the forum state—as in *Keeton* and *Burger King*—the assertion of jurisdiction was held constitutional. While leaving some cases at the margins unclear, these principles provide clear guidance in most situations involving domestic defendants. None of the three decisions, however, addressed the problem of jurisdiction over aliens.

Several commentators have suggested that different standards should be applied when dealing with alien defendants. Prior to *Asahi,* the Supreme Court never explicitly addressed the question. The issue had, however, been potentially relevant in two earlier decisions—*Perkins v. Benguet Consolidated Mining Co.* and *Helicopteros Nacionales de Colombia, S.A. v. Hall (Helicol).*

The defendant in *Perkins* was a corporation operating under Filipino charter. While the Japanese occupied the Philippine Islands during World War II, the corporation carried on "a continuous and systematic, but limited, part of its general business" in the state of Ohio. The Ohio activities of the corporation included directors' meetings, business correspondence, banking, stock transfers, payment of salaries and purchasing of machinery for mining operations. The Supreme Court held that the due process clause neither compelled nor prevented the Ohio courts from asserting postwar jurisdiction over the corporation in an action that did not relate to or arise out of its Ohio activities.

Helicol involved a Texas tort action arising from a helicopter crash in Peru. The defendant, Helicol, was a Colombian corporation that had contracted to provide helicopter transportation for a Peruvian consortium that in turn was the alter ego of a joint venture headquartered in Houston. The defendant had sent its chief executive officer to Houston to negotiate the transportation contract; accepted checks drawn on a Texas bank; purchased helicopters, equipment and training sessions from a Texas manufacturer; and sent personnel to that manufacturer's facilities for training. The defendant had no other contacts with the forum state. Treating the issue solely as one of general jurisdiction, the Supreme Court held that the Texas courts had no jurisdiction over the defendant.

Neither *Perkins* nor *Helicol* suggest that alien defendants, at least for jurisdictional purposes, should be treated differently than American citizens or corporations. Both cases, however, dealt only with issues of *general* jurisdiction—jurisdiction based on claims unrelated to the defendant's contact with the forum. Neither addressed the standards to be applied to assertions of *specific* jurisdiction—jurisdiction over actions arising from or related to the defendant's connections to the forum state. A defendant subject to general jurisdiction would in any event have substantial connections with the forum; under these circumstances the significance of any potential distinction between aliens and American citizens would be reduced. Thus, it is not surprising that it was in a specific jurisdiction case—*Asahi*—that the defendant's alien status emerged for the first time as an important factor in the Court's personal jurisdiction analysis.

Asahi involved a products liability action arising from a motorcycle accident in California. The cause of the accident was a rear tire blowout. The rider of the motorcycle sued, among others, Cheng Shin Rubber Industrial Co., Ltd., the Taiwanese manufacturer that had produced the motorcycle inner tube and made twenty percent of its total United States sales in California. Cheng Shin in turn filed a cross-complaint seeking indemnity from Asahi, the manufacturer of the tube's valve assembly. Asahi, a Japanese corporation, sold 1,350,000 valve assemblies to Cheng Shin in the period from 1978 to 1982; in addition, Asahi valve assemblies were incorporated into the tubes of numerous other manufacturers selling their product in California. Asahi itself, however, had no offices, property or agents in California and neither solicited business nor made any direct sales in that state.

The Supreme Court unanimously held that the due process clause prevented California from asserting jurisdiction over Asahi. Eight Justices agreed that, regardless of whether Asahi had "purposefully availed" itself of the benefits and burdens of doing business in the forum state, "the facts of [the] case [did] not establish minimum contacts such that the exercise of personal jurisdiction [would be] consistent with fair play and substantial justice." The Court was deeply divided, however, on the question of whether the Japanese manufacturer could be said to have purposefully availed itself of the privilege of doing business in California.

Justice O'Connor, Chief Justice Rehnquist, and Justices Powell and Scalia (the O'Connor Group) argued that Asahi's position was analogous to that of the defendant in *World–Wide Volkswagen*. The O'Connor Group contended that "awareness that the stream of commerce may or will sweep the product into the forum State does not convert the mere act of placing the product into the stream into an act purposefully directed toward the forum State." Instead, "[t]he 'substantial connection' between the defendant and the forum State necessary for a finding of minimum contacts must come about by *an action of the defendant purposefully directed toward the forum State.*" Because Cheng Shin, and not Asahi itself, had made the choice to send Asahi's products to California, there was no purposeful availment and the assertion of jurisdiction was unconstitutional. The O'Connor Group, however, did not address the question of whether purposeful availment alone would *always* provide a sufficient predicate to subject a defendant to jurisdiction.

In contrast, Justices Brennan, White, Marshall and Blackmun (the Brennan Group) argued that the purposeful availment requirement is satisfied once a manufacturer inserts its product into the stream of commerce with knowledge that the product will eventually be used in the forum state. Justice Stevens would have declined to reach the purposeful availment issue; instead, he would have adopted an intermediate approach, basing the constitutional analysis on "the volume, the value and the hazardous character of the components" at issue. Stevens suggested that "[i]n most circumstances" he would have found jurisdiction over a manufacturer such as Asahi constitutionally permissible.

Because five members of the Court—Justices Brennan, White, Marshall, Blackmun and Stevens—appear to believe that Asahi purposely availed itself of the benefits and burdens of doing business in California, the decision *not* to grant the California courts jurisdiction over Asahi turned on other factors. Of paramount importance in ascertaining these factors is the portion of Justice O'Connor's opinion supported by all the Justices except Justice Scalia. In that part of her opinion, Justice O'Connor concluded that the assertion of jurisdiction, regardless of one's view of the purposeful availment issue, would offend traditional notions of fair play and substantial justice and therefore was unconstitutional. The opinion recited the familiar litany of factors used by the Court in earlier personal jurisdiction cases: "the burden on the defendant, the interests of the forum state, ... the plaintiff's interest in obtaining relief, ... 'the interstate judicial system's interest in obtaining the most efficient resolution of controversies; and the shared interest of the several States in furthering fundamental substantive social policies.' "

In finding the assertion of jurisdiction improper, Justice O'Connor relied heavily on two factors derived from the international scope of the jurisdictional problem: "The unique burdens placed upon one who must defend oneself in a foreign legal system" and the potential implications for United States foreign policy. She also focused on the distance that the defendant would be forced to travel to defend itself, and the fact that the plaintiff's claim against Cheng Shin had been settled, leaving only the indemnity issue to be adjudicated. Justice O'Connor argued that because no California resident was a party to the cross-claim, the interest of the state in the resolution of the claim was "slight," and thus insufficient to justify the imposition of the "serious burdens" on Asahi. In short, in *Asahi,* the Court for the first time since its adoption of the purposeful availment analysis denied jurisdiction over a defendant that had purposefully availed itself of the benefits and burdens of doing business in the forum.

On a purely theoretical level, the treatment of the concept of minimum contacts is one of *Asahi's* most significant developments. Until quite recently, the Court consistently held that the existence of minimum contacts is both a *necessary* and *sufficient* condition for the constitutional assertion of jurisdictional authority. While the rhetoric of purposeful availment had come to dominate modern opinions, that concept seemed to be a simple gloss on the minimum contacts test itself. Thus, as late as 1984, Justice Rehnquist was able to state confidently for a unanimous Court in *Calder v. Jones* that "[t]he Due Process Clause ... permits personal jurisdiction over a defendant in any State with which the defendant has 'certain minimum contacts ... such that the maintenance of the suit does not offend "traditional notions of fair play and substantial justice." ' "

The first hint of a change in the role of minimum contacts came in Justice Brennan's majority opinion in *Burger King*. While noting that "the constitutional touchstone remains whether the defendant purposefully established 'minimum contacts' in the forum State," he also stated that "[o]nce it has been decided that a defendant purposefully established minimum contacts within the forum State, these contacts may be considered in light of other factors to determine whether the assertion of personal jurisdiction would comport with 'fair play and substantial justice.' " The precise import of this language was not entirely clear; it seemed, however, to imply that in some circumstances the assumption of jurisdiction would be unconstitutional even if the defendant had minimum contacts with the forum state.

Asahi confirms this interpretation. The opinion for the Court states that "[w]hen minimum contacts have been established, *often* the interests of the plaintiff and the forum in the exercise of jurisdiction will justify even the serious burdens placed on the alien defendant," but that the imposition of these burdens was not justified in *Asahi*. The clear implication is that assertion of personal jurisdiction over Asahi would have been unconstitutional *regardless* of the existence of Asahi's contacts with the forum state. * * * *Asahi* thus clearly establishes that the existence of minimum contacts is a necessary but not sufficient condition to satisfy the constitutional requirements for personal jurisdiction. In all cases, the courts must also test the facts against equitable notions of "fair play and substantial justice." * * *

JUENGER, A SHOE UNFIT FOR GLOBETROTTING
28 Univ. Calif., Davis L.J. 1027 (1995).*

There is no longer any doubt: American jurisdictional law is a mess. Split opinions, loaded footnotes, and convoluted opinions larded with a fanciful vocabulary that attempts to give half-baked concepts an aura of reality by dressing them up as political science or presenting them in the garb of folksy similes, signal the Justices' inability to devise a satisfactory approach to the simple question of where a civil action may be brought. While scholars—unlike practitioners—revel in uncertainty, even in aca-

---

* Reprinted with permission of the University of California (Davis) Law Journal.

demic circles the applause and admiration for the Court's forays into the field of jurisdiction have long ago given way to a distinct disenchantment. * * *

* * *

Much of this criticism is familiar, but the deficiencies of the Court's jurisdictional case law bear reiteration before one ponders the implications of the Court's jurisprudence as it relates to international jurisdictional and recognition problems. First of all, it stands to reason that if the Court's work product is unsatisfactory in the domestic context, it can hardly serve as a model for international cooperation. Secondly, while Justice Field—however misguided his *Pennoyer* opinion may have been— still professed to deal with jurisdiction from an international point of view, the Court now—with the exception of Justice O'Connor's opinion in *Asahi*—tends to treat transnational cases as if they were interstate in nature. Thirdly, the assumed interrelationship between due process and state sovereignty is bound to distract the Court's attention from what is going on in the rest of the world at a time when "globalization" has become a cliché.

Our Supreme Court's preoccupation with domestic constitutional puzzles is especially regrettable considering that more than two decades of experience gathered in the European Common Market demonstrate the possibility of a global approach to jurisdiction and judgments recognition. Since its inception, the Convention on Jurisdiction and the Recognition of Judgments in Civil and Commercial Matters has streamlined the recognition and enforcement of judgments within Europe. It has done so despite the fact that the European Union's member nations—unlike the states of our Union—are truly sovereign, that they lack a shared common legal heritage, that their procedural and substantive laws differ widely from one country to another, and that a different language is spoken every few hundred miles.

* * *

Clearly, in many respects the Brussels Convention offers sounder practical solutions and greater fairness than our Supreme Court case law. In marked contrast to *Carnival Cruise Lines, Inc. v. Shute*,[76] the Convention bars powerful enterprises from imposing forum-selection clauses on weaker ones, such as consumers. Common sense and fairness also inform the resolution of multiparty litigation, which the Convention allows to proceed in a single forum. Moreover, the Convention's jurisdictional bases are reasonably clear and cogent, and the Court of Justice's case law is not marred by such nebulous notions as "state interests" and "purposeful availing," or weasel words such as "haling" and "stream of commerce."

* * *

---

76. 499 U.S. 585 (1991).

The difficulty of presenting our confused jurisdictional law to the outside world is bound to impede the negotiation of recognition treaties and conventions with foreign nations. Worse yet is the fact that our highest Court insists on its prerogative as the ultimate arbiter of jurisdictional propriety. Foreign nations can hardly be expected to accept, for instance, such American idiosyncracies as the notion of "doing business" a relic of pre-*Shoe* days, as a basis for general jurisdiction. Even if they were ready to swallow such exorbitance, how could they be assured that our Supreme Court will not tomorrow alter the definition and import of this term? The predictability for which international compacts aim will remain illusory if jurisdictional bases can change with each change in the Court's membership. Accordingly, the United States Supreme Court has not only created an unsatisfactory body of jurisdictional law, it has tied the hands of the Executive. Frustrating efforts to reach an accommodation with foreign nations in the field of judgments recognition, the Court unduly limits this nation's treaty-making power.

* * *

[T]he fact that we are saddled with a chaotic law inhibits us from pursuing a transnational jurisdictional and recognition compact. This is too bad, not only for us, but for our potential treaty partner. Though the European Union's jurisdictional and enforcement scheme is superior to ours, it is by no means free from flaws. The Brussels Convention is marred, above all, by xenophobia. Its article 4 specifically authorizes suits against nonresidents on the exorbitant jurisdictional grounds listed in article 3, which may not be invoked against individuals and enterprises domiciled within the Union. However misguided the Supreme Court's *Asahi* decision may have been otherwise, it at least did not discriminate against outsiders. (In fact, the Court counted alienage as a factor militating against the exercise of jurisdiction.) Nor is discrimination the Brussels Convention's only flaw. Some of its jurisdictional bases are of questionable wisdom, so that negotiating with the United States could also serve the ends of reforming the law within the European Union.

But, as matters stand, such hopes seem vain. Beyond the internal havoc they have caused, *International Shoe* and its progeny present formidable obstacles to international harmonization. Because our own house is in disarray, we are unable to render a contribution to the world at large. Only if the Supreme Court would countenance a change of jurisdictional bases by treaty—which it might well be prepared to do, considering that some of the Justices seem to be fully aware of the practical shortcomings of the Court's jurisprudence—could there be progress internationally. But as long as our highest court persists in its misguided attempt to derive jurisdictional law from two incongruent sources—due process and state sovereignty—we cannot effectively deal with other nations, however interested they and we may be in securing worldwide faith and credit.

QUESTIONS AND COMMENTS

1. Lancelot's obtaining personal jurisdiction over the Spanish entity Pellinore in a U.S. court requires an analysis probably commencing with *International Shoe* and including *World-Wide Volkswagen*, both cases without a foreign element, and proceeding to *Helicopteros* and *Asahi*, cases with foreign defendants. How do you explain to Lancelot's management the current rules of personal jurisdiction? Are you comfortable in predicting the outcome? Will Lancelot be willing to take the matter to the U.S. Supreme Court for a favorable ruling? Is such a ruling assured? Might the matter be such a crap shoot that it is better for Pellinore to pass on challenging jurisdiction and head for another game of chance, probably *forum non conveniens*?

2. Is it enough that Pellinore benefitted from purchasing goods from Lancelot? In most cases the defendant has been selling to the United States, not buying from the United States. The minimum contacts in the latter scenario are likely to be fewer. Pellinore never placed products in the "stream of commerce" which flowed into the United States. But what if Pellinore was searching for a supplier of TVs and set up a purchasing office in the United States staffed with several Pellinore employees who traveled throughout the United States searching for and obtaining the best products for Pellinore? What if Pellinore had purchased many millions of dollars of electronic products in the United States over the past decade, in addition to those bought from Lancelot? When does "minimum contacts" kick-in? And when does due process kick-in?

3. *Anderson v. Dassault Aviation*, 361 F.3d 449 (8th Cir. 2004), cert. denied, 543 U.S. 1015, 125 S.Ct. 606, 160 L.Ed.2d 484, held jurisdiction to be present applying principles of "fairness and reasonableness" rather than "rigid rules." The defendant was the French manufacturer of a jet that during a turbulent descent into Michigan from Oregon, allegedly caused injuries to a flight attendant who sued Dassault first in federal court in Michigan, where the case was dismissed for lack of personal jurisdiction, and subsequently in Arkansas, where jurisdiction was also found lacking, but with a focus more on veil piercing. The Eighth Circuit reversed, suggesting that the lower court placed too much reliance on veil piercing for jurisdiction. The Circuit Court found sufficient contacts on a traditional analysis. If a plaintiff can pierce the veil of a subsidiary/parent relationship, jurisdiction may be obtained over an otherwise non-reachable potential defendant. If Pellinore sues Lancelot in the United States, it might also sue Camelot, the Canadian parent. The facts do not show very much presence by Camelot in the United States, but if the veil is pierced it adds all the activities of Lancelot. Veil piercing for jurisdiction is not well developed in the United States. Should the same requirements for veil piercing for substantive liability be required for veil piercing for jurisdiction, or is there some lesser standard? See *Clark v. Matsushita Electric Industrial Company Ltd.*, 811 F.Supp. 1061 (M.D. Pa. 1993); *Color Systems, Inc. v. Meteor Photo Reprographic Systems, Inc.*, 1987 WL 11085 (D.C.D.C. 1987); *Hargrave v. Fibreboard Corp.*, 710 F.2d 1154 (5th

Cir. 1983); *Bulova Watch Company, Inc. v. K. Hattori & Co., Ltd.*, 508 F.Supp. 1322 (E.D.N.Y. 1981).

4. Note that most cases seem to deal with tort issues about products sold in the United States where injury occurred, such as *Asahi*. Our case involves a contract issue, nonconforming goods. Does it really make any difference for the jurisdiction analysis?

PART D. JURISDICTION IN EUROPEAN UNION AND JAPANESE COURTS

This part introduces us to different concepts of jurisdiction in both a European Union and Asian nation. Assuming Pellinore sues Lancelot in Madrid and the choice of forum provision does not constitute a submission to jurisdiction, the Madrid court will have to find jurisdiction in the EU Regulation on Jurisdiction and the Recognition and Enforcement of Judgments in Civil and Commercial Matters, adopted in 2000 and essentially replacing the 1968 EU Convention that also covered jurisdiction and judgment enforcement. The agreement between Mitsuey of Japan and Camelot might be the subject of litigation. Assuming Mitsuey sues Camelot and Lancelot in a Tokyo court, it will have to consider jurisdiction under Japanese norms. This part introduces us to some very different approaches to jurisdiction.

RONALD A. BRAND, CURRENT PROBLEMS, COMMON GROUND, AND FIRST PRINCIPLES: RESTRUCTURING THE PRELIMINARY DRAFT CONVENTION TEXT

A Global Law of Jurisdiction and Judgments: Lessons from the Hague Convention 75, 89–91 (John J. Barcelo III and Kevin M. Clermont, eds., 2002).*

Article 2 of the Brussels Regulation provides for jurisdiction in the courts of the state in which the defendant is domiciled. In the Brussels context, Article 2 jurisdiction is referred to as the rule of "general" jurisdiction, with other rules (including the tort provision of Article 5(3)), referred to as rules of "special" jurisdiction.

Pursuant to Article 2 of the Convention, persons domiciled in a Contracting State are, subject to the provisions of the Convention, 'whatever their nationality, to be sued in the courts of that State'. Section 2 of Title II of the Convention, however, provides for 'special jurisdictions', by virtue of which a defendant domiciled in a Contracting State may be sued in another Contracting State . . . . . [4]

The principle laid down in the Convention is that jurisdiction is vested in the courts of the State of the defendant's domicile and that the jurisdiction provided for in [the "special jurisdiction" articles are] exception[s] to that principle.

---

* Copyright 2002 Kluwar Law International. Reproduced with permission.

4. Case 189/87, Kalfelis v. Schröder, 1988 E.C.R. 5565, 5583, ¶ 7.

[T]he 'special jurisdictions' enumerated in Articles 5 and 6 of the Convention constitute derogations from the principle that jurisdiction is vested in the courts of the State where the defendant is domiciled and as such must be interpreted restrictively.

Thus, in *Kalfelis v. Schröder*, the European Court held that, in an action in both tort (Article 5(3)), and contract (Article 5(1)), "a court which has jurisdiction under Article 5(3) over an action in so far as it is based on tort or delict does not have jurisdiction over that action in so far as it is not so based." The existence of tort jurisdiction in the German courts over a Luxembourg defendant did not bring with it the existence of contract jurisdiction over the same defendant resulting from the same set of facts.

The restrictive interpretation of special jurisdiction provisions of the Brussels Convention was also a part of the decision in the *Shevill* case, when the Court stated that the Article 5(3) tort rule of jurisdiction, as interpreted in *Bier* to provide a two-pronged choice to the plaintiff,

is based on the existence of a particularly close connecting factor between the dispute and the courts other than those of the State of the defendant's domicile which justifies the attribution of jurisdiction to those courts for reasons relating to the sound administration of justice and the efficacious conduct of the proceedings.[7]

Thus, the Court emphasized the court/claim nexus that is the foundation of the "special" jurisdiction rules of the Brussels Convention.

Three rules of interpretation under the Brussels Convention are thus clearly established:

(1) Article 2 jurisdiction is more "general" than the rules of special jurisdiction;

(2) the special jurisdiction rules (Articles 5–16) are to be narrowly interpreted; and

(3) the rules of special jurisdiction are based on a "close connecting factor between the dispute and the courts."

These rules generate several observations about a convention that mixes jurisdictional rules based on different relationships to the court. First, it is instructive that the "general" rule of jurisdiction focuses on the court/defendant nexus, but that so many problems have arisen from the court/claim nexus that underlies the subsidiary "special" rules of jurisdiction. The *Bier-Dumez-Shevill* line of cases indicates the difficulties the European Court has had with the interpretation of the Article 5(3) rule that provides jurisdiction in the "place where the harmful event occurred." Even more difficult problems have resulted from the court/claim nexus found in the Article 5(1) Brussels Convention rule that jurisdiction in a contract case lies in the courts of the "place of performance of the obligation in question."

---

7. Case C–68/93, *Shevill v. Presse Alliance*, S.A., 1995 E.C.R. I–415, I–459, ¶ 19.

Two other results of the European Court's jurisprudence under Article 5(3) add to the problems created by a focus on a court/claim connection. The first is "the hostility of the Convention towards the attribution of jurisdiction to the courts of the plaintiff's domicile." The second is the assumption that the "scheme and objectives of the Convention" (including (1) the structure of Article 2 jurisdiction in the courts of the state of the defendant's domicile and (2) the special jurisdiction rules based on a court/claim nexus), result in a presumption against a proliferation of forums.

In the *Dumez* case, the European Court acknowledged concerns with rules that lead to jurisdiction in the plaintiff's home state:

> [T]he hostility of the Convention towards the attribution of jurisdiction to the courts of the plaintiff's domicile was demonstrated by the fact that the second paragraph of article 3 precluded the application of national provisions attributing jurisdiction to such courts for proceedings against defendants domiciled in the territory of a contracting state.[12]

PETER F. SCHLOSSER, LECTURES ON CIVIL-LAW LITIGATION SYSTEMS AND AMERICAN COOPERATION WITH THOSE SYSTEMS

45 U. Kan. L. Rev. 9, 19–20, 22–23 (1996).*

* * *

. . . [T]he distinction between jurisdiction and venue is little developed in Europe. Justice Holmes' "power concept" as the basis for jurisdiction, is foreign to civil-law systems. Except for Switzerland, uniform codes of civil procedure are in force in all European states. These uniform codes are not like the United States Uniform Commercial Code. European states are either unitarian, with uniform law over all the territory, or they are federal. Civil procedure is a matter of federal law everywhere except Switzerland. All the codes include provisions on what is called "territorial competence." If, in an international case, no court is found to be competent by reason of territory, that is because international competency is lacking. Territorial competence is mostly derived from the fact that the courts of the state in question also have international competency. In some states, as for example in Austria, there is an additional requirement that the case must be related to the state of the court addressed. Only in very few respects is international competence dealt with in a different way than local competence. In Germany, for example, decisions on local competence cannot be appealed. In contrast, decisions on the issue of whether any competence can be found in Germany can be appealed.

The lack of distinction between jurisdiction and venue has some very important and characteristic implications. Jurisdiction and service of

---

12. *Dumez*, 1990 E.C.R. I-79, ¶ 16.

* Reprinted with permission.

process are totally disassociated from each other in civil-law countries. It is inconceivable to base jurisdiction on the mere fact that a document is served upon the defendant. It is true that in civil-law countries it is possible to serve process upon the defendant at any place where he may be found. But this event is without any significance for the jurisdiction of the court.

* * *

But, however service is accomplished, it has nothing to do with establishing jurisdiction. If the defendant does not enter any appearance, the court has to verify, on its own motion, whether or not it has jurisdiction. The plaintiff must provide sufficient evidence for the facts on which he wants to base the jurisdiction of the court. On the other hand, a court having jurisdiction is not prevented from exercising it by the mere fact that service of process may turn out to be impossible. In Germany, as a last resort, service of process may be realized by publishing the document initiating proceedings in a newspaper and simultaneously putting it on the court's official board. In France, and in many other countries, service may be made with an official whose normal function is public prosecution ("signification au parquet").

Because there is no civil-law concept of jurisdiction fundamentally distinct from venue, nothing exists in civil-law countries which could properly be called a long-arm statute. A European court has jurisdiction over categories of lawsuits and other kinds of proceedings instituted against categories of persons as defined by the respective provisions in the state's code of civil procedure.

A German court, for example, must enforce a judgment of any other German court by garnishments if the debtor has his residence within the court's district. If enforcement is to be made by an entry into the land register, any German judgment must be enforced by the court in the district of which the respective piece of land is located. No registration for enforcement is required.

As far as jurisdiction for normal lawsuits is concerned, a long-lasting tradition distinguishes between specific jurisdiction and general jurisdiction. Today, this distinction is also known in the United States, but this is only due to a recent development. The Supreme Court of the United States did not adopt this distinction before its well-known decision in *Shaffer v. Heitner.*

In civil-law countries this distinction is as old as the codes of civil procedure. General jurisdiction is based only on the defendant's permanent residence. As far as specific jurisdiction is concerned, there are many particularities in the numerous codes of civil procedure of the various civil-law countries. Where a tort occurs is recognized almost everywhere as a good venue for lawsuits arising out of it. Very often there is also a basis for specific jurisdiction for matters relating to a contract. Doing business in a particular jurisdiction does not figure among the bases for specific jurisdiction, let alone of general jurisdiction. There must be an actual branch or other establishment of the foreign debtor in the respective country. Only recently have consumers and employees very often enjoyed the privilege of a basis for specific jurisdiction at their own permanent residence.

On the European continent, no rule against ousting the jurisdiction of the court has ever existed. The liberal European tradition allowed practically unlimited freedom to agree upon which court or courts would have jurisdiction. But for two decades there has been a strong movement in Europe to invalidate such agreements in contracts to which a consumer is a party.

No doctrine of forum non conveniens has ever been developed in civil-law countries. A court having jurisdiction is committed to exercise it, because it is a public service entrusted to it by statute. A German or French judge would find it very awkward if he had any discretionary power to decline jurisdiction. When the United Kingdom negotiated for accession to the Brussels Convention, it was made clear to them by express terms that they ought to be under an obligation to exercise all jurisdiction they would have under the Convention.

* * *

All civil-law systems have provisions creating jurisdiction over defendants neither residing within the jurisdiction nor having sufficient contact with the court's district that would normally allow specific jurisdiction to be exercised. All these provisions may be characterized as provisions discriminating against foreigners. Only very recently have Europeans started to discuss whether these provisions conform to due process standards. Switzerland, however, has a longer tradition in this respect. Pursuant to article 59 of the Swiss constitution, a Swiss national can only be sued in the courts of his own canton. Put into American legal terms, the Swiss constitution prohibits long-arm statutes. Yet, this constitutional provision is protective only of Swiss nationals. The Swiss are very distrustful of persons residing abroad. Considering the time when the Swiss constitution came into force, this is very understandable. To be compelled to sue somebody abroad was very cumbersome and often useless. Hence, they have developed a kind of quasi-in-rem jurisdiction, which, however, will be restricted by 1997 to claims with a sufficient relationship to Switzerland.

French law provides that every Frenchman can sue his opponent in France if the underlying legal relationship has a contractual nature. In Germany, Austria, and some Scandinavian countries, any person not residing within the court's jurisdiction can be sued in that court if his or her assets are located in that jurisdiction. The lawsuit need not be related to these assets. According to case law, minimal assets may be sufficient. For example, in Sweden, a hotel guest forgot his umbrella in the room he had rented. This was found to be a sufficient ground to assume jurisdiction over him. Since that time, such provisions have been called umbrella provisions.

The most ridiculous case in this respect was decided in Germany. In previous legal proceedings, a German plaintiff had lost a case instituted against a foreigner. The consequence was, under the German system allocating the cost of the proceedings, that the foreigner had a claim against the German plaintiff to be reimbursed for his expenses, including lawyer's fees. The foreigner's claim was held to be located at the residence of the German plaintiff in Germany. The foreign defendant thus had assets in Germany. This was found to constitute sufficient grounds to assume jurisdiction over the foreigner in a second lawsuit, which was entirely unrelated to the first one. The German provision does not only protect German nationals or people residing in Germany. In the aftermath of the Iranian Revolution, United States and British banks were able to sue the Iranian National Oil Company in Germany for more than $100,000,000 because both banks had bank accounts in Germany.

In 1992, the German Federal Court decided that due process considerations were a compelling reason to restrict the scope of this provision. This had been proposed for a decade by legal theorists. According to the German Federal Court, jurisdiction is lacking if the case is not in any way related to Germany. Regrettably, the court seems to be in favor of the proposition that the lawsuit is related to Germany if the plaintiff is a resident of Germany. I am convinced, however, that the court will go further and decide that the underlying legal relationship must also be related to Germany.

Case law discussing other aspects of due process and jurisdiction is lacking in civil-law countries.

GOTO v. MALAYSIA AIRLINE

35 Minshü (No. 7) 1224 (Supreme Court, Oct. 16, 1981).
translated in 26 Japanese Annual of International Law 122 (1983).*

STATUTORY REFERENCES

Code of Civil Procedure:

Article 4

(1) The general forum of a juridical person or any other association or foundation shall be determined by the place of its principal office or principal place of business, or in case there is no office or place of business, by the domicile of the principal person in charge of its affairs.

. . .

(3) In regard to the general forum of a foreign association or foundation, the provisions of paragraph 1 shall apply to the office, place of business or person in charge of its affairs in Japan.

---

* Reprinted here as amended by John O. Haley with permission.

Hōrei (Law Concerning the Application of laws in General):

Article 7

(1) As regards the formation and effect of a juristic act, the question as to the law of which country is to govern shall be determined by the intention of the parties.

(2) In case the intention of the parties is uncertain, the law of the place where the act is done shall govern.

DECREE

1. The appeal is dismissed [Decision below affirmed.]
2. The cost of appeal shall be borne by the appellant.

REASONS

In their Grounds for Appeal Nos. 1 and 2(1) and (2), Yasuomi Hayashida and Toshihiko Kashiwagi, counsel for the appellant, argue as follows: the court below reversed the judgement of the court of the first instance which dismissed the lawsuit on the ground that it was not subject to Japanese jurisdiction; however, in doing so, the court below erred in the interpretation and application of Article 4, paragraph 3 and Article 5 of the Code of Civil Procedure and, accordingly, the court below did not provide sufficient reasons for its judgement.

This case involves claims for damages by Japanese nationals against a foreign corporation. The appellees allege as follows: on December 4, 1977, Tomio Goto made a contract of air transport with the appellant in the Federation of Malaysia; in accordance with the contract, he boarded a plane operated by the appellant from Penang to Kuala Lumpur; the plane crashed in Johore Bahrn in Malaysia on the same day and he died in that accident; therefore, the appellant shall be liable for payment of 40,454,442 Yen to Tomio Goto as compensation for damages caused by the crash of the plane which constitutes the appellant's breach of the air transport contract; the appellees Michiko Goto (his wife), Yukiko Goto and Takayuki Goto (his children) succeeded to his rights in proportion to their shares in the succession, which are one-third each; accordingly, each appellee demands the appellant to pay 13,330,000 Yen for the above damages.

In general, adjudicatory jurisdiction (*saiban kankatsuken*) is exercised as an effect of the national sovereignty, and the scope of adjudicatory jurisdiction is in principle co-extensive with the scope of the national sovereignty. Consequently, if a defendant is a foreign corporation with a main office abroad, it is ordinarily beyond the adjudicatory jurisdiction of Japan, unless it is willing to subject itself to Japanese jurisdiction. Nevertheless, as an exception, a defendant can be subjected to the adjudicatory jurisdiction of Japan, whatever its nationality may be or wherever it may be located, if the case relates to Japan or if the defendant has some legal nexus with Japan. With respect to the limits of such an exception, we have no statutes expressly prescribing international adjudicatory jurisdiction, no treaties that apply, nor any well-defined, generally recognized rules of international law. Under these circumstances, it is reasonable to determine international adjudicatory jurisdiction in accordance with the principles of *jōri*, which require that fairness between parties be maintained and an appropriate and speedy trial be secured. In accordance with these principles of *jōri*, a defendant may be appropriately subjected to the jurisdiction of Japan when the requirements of the provisions for domestic territorial jurisdiction (*tochi kankatsuken*) set out in the Code of Civil Procedure are satisfied, for example, when the defendant's domicile (article 2), if a juridical person or other association, office or place of business (article 4), the place of performance (article 5), the location of the defendant's property (article 8), the place of tort (article 15), or such other place for trial (*saiban-seki*) as set forth in the Code of Civil Procedure is located in Japan.

In accordance with the findings of the court below, the appellant is a Malaysian corporation which is established under the Company Law of the Federation of Malaysia and has its head office in that country. The appellant has appointed Gyokusho Cho as its representative in Japan and has established a place of business in Tokyo. On these premises, the appellant shall be reasonably subjected to the jurisdiction of Japan, even though it is a foreign corporation that has its head office abroad. Therefore, we affirm the decision of the court below which held that a Japanese court has jurisdiction over this case. The judgment of the court below is not erroneous as the appellant argues. We cannot accept the appellant's argument which criticizes the judgement below from a point of view different from our above-stated view.

In their Grounds for Appeal No.2 (3), counsel for the appellant argue as follows: the court below did not transfer this case to the Tokyo District Court, which is located in the place where the general forum of the appellant exists, but sent it back to the Nagoya District Court, the court of the first instance; in doing so, the court below erred in the interpretation of Article 4, paragraph 3 and Article 5 of the Code of Civil Procedure.

However, the parties may not appeal to the Supreme Court on the ground that the court below erred in the application of the rules for domestic, non-exclusive jurisdiction (See articles 381, 396 and 395, paragraph 1, item 3 of the Code of Civil Procedure). We cannot accept this point raised by the appellant, because such is not a ground for appeal to the Supreme Court.

Thus, in accordance with articles 401, 95 and 89 of the Code of Civil Procedure, this Court unanimously renders the judgment as stated in the Decree.

Presiding Justice Tadayoshi Kinoshita

Justice Kazuo Kurimoto

Justice Yasuyoshi Shiono

Justice Goichi Miyazaki

QUESTIONS AND COMMENTS

1.   The Brussels Regulation has essentially replaced the Brussels Convention. But this case involves a non-EU defendant. Does that mean the Brussels Regulation still applies, or do jurisdictional provisions in the Spanish Code of Civil Procedure apply? Assuming the Regulation applies, where do we start? Article 2 seems to be the first focus. But this rule of general jurisdiction, the domicile of the defendant, does not work for a suit against Lancelot (or Camelot) by Pellinore in a Spanish court. Thus we move on to the rules of special jurisdiction in Article 5.

2.   The issue is one of contract. What if there were also a tort issue present? Would jurisdiction under the contract provision extend to the tort issue as well as the contract claims? Jurisdiction in civil law countries tends to be a relationship between the court and the claim, rather than between the court and the defendant, as in the United States.

3.   This brief part illustrates some concern within Europe about extraordinary jurisdiction. Extraordinary jurisdiction in the United States is exemplified by "tag" jurisdiction, which is not recognized in most civil law tradition nations. German asset based jurisdiction and French jurisdiction based on the domicile of the plaintiff are other forms of extraordinary jurisdiction, as discussed in the Schlosser extract. If Pellinore were French rather than Spanish, it could initiate suit in a French court because it (Pellinore) is French and the matter arose from a contract, without concern about the reach of French law to a foreign party with no real contacts in France. At least the German asset based jurisdiction requires the presence of some assets in Germany, although as Schlosser notes they are sometimes quite illusory, or were before the German federal Court acted to introduce a little due process in the discussion.

4.   Japan's post WWII code of civil procedure was influenced by that of Germany. But the Japanese courts have introduced fairness into the discussion under the concept of jōri. The 1981 *Goto v. Malaysia Airline* decision was the first to do so, and the subsequent adoption in 1996 of the revised civil procedure code has not affected that theory, which has been supported in recent decisions. See John O. Haley, The Adjudicatory Jurisdiction of Japanese Courts in Transnational Litigation, in Law and Justice in a Multistate World (Nafziger and Symeonides eds. 2002).

PROBLEM 11.2   SERVICE OF PROCESS, *FORUM NON CONVENIENS* AND CHOICE OF LAW: ORCHID FERTILIZER TO VENEZUELA

SECTION I.   THE SETTING

Mott, Inc., is a U.S. corporation incorporated in Texas and with its principal manufacturing and office facilities in Houston. Mott manufactures Suregrow™ which is a slow release fertilizer long used on such plants as ornamentals (e.g., azaleas, camellias, rhododendrons, palms, firs, and ferns). Extensive tests showed that it could be used on orchids and Mott began to advertise and sell Suregrow™ for that purpose. Epiphytes, S.A., the largest orchid grower in Venezuela, bought large quantities of Suregrow™ and has been applying it to its orchids for over a year. Mott discovered that Epiphytes has a practice of withholding payment for goods purchased without using a letter of credit. Mott did not insist on a letter of credit, believing that its product was so outstanding that it would build a long term relationship with Epiphytes over the coming years. It now regrets that action. Epiphytes continued to refuse to pay for a large purchase ($104,000) of Suregrow™. The contract between Mott and Epiphytes had no choice of forum provision. Mott discovered that Epiphytes does extensive business in the United States, some 80% of its orchid production is sold throughout the United States using a Miami marketing subsidiary. The Suregrow™ contract was negotiated by communications between Venezuela and Houston, with several trips by Epiphyte officials to Houston, and, after the contract was signed, several Mott technicians traveled to Venezuela to provide instruction in the application of Suregrow™.

Mott's outside law firm in Houston was involved in the preparation and execution of the contract. But that firm does not deal with litigation and has retained you because your speciality is international civil and commercial litigation. They did, however, suggest suing in federal court in Houston and, following Texas law, serving Epiphytes by registered mail to its Panama office. Your young associate wonders whether service might instead be made on the Miami subsidiary of Epiphytes as agent for Epiphytes, S.A. in Panama.

SECTION II. FOCUS OF CONSIDERATION

Part A of this problem explores some issues of service of process, including the basic U.S. federal rules and the Hague Service Convention. Parts B and C will consider different litigation between the same parties, specifically the issues of *forum non conveniens* and choice and proof of foreign law.

The Hague Service Convention is included in the Documents Supplement.

SECTION III. READINGS, QUESTIONS AND COMMENTS

PART A. SERVICE OF PROCESS

Service of process must comply with the law of the forum. The party seeking service may have various options for serving the defendants in the home forum or serving outside the state. Service outside the state may mean service in a different state or in a different nation. If the latter there will be rules of the foreign forum for service of process that may be very different in comparison to those of a U.S. forum. Additionally, there may be international rules that are applicable. We must determine the best method of providing effective service on the defendants, wherever they may be. If we do not we may not be able to have a judgment obtained against a foreign party enforced in the defendant's own nation's courts, or in *any* other nations'.

The cost of service abroad may be considerably higher than in the United States, especially if documents have to be translated. Plaintiff's lawyers must be cautious when deciding to minimize costs by using such methods as substituted or constructive service. Serving one of the defendants while on a business trip to the United States may not be recognized as proper service by that person's nation. That may not matter with respect to effective service for an action in a U.S. court, but it may cause a judgment to be rejected when taken to the defendant's home nation for recognition and enforcement.

Because we look to the state laws governing service of process, we should look for provisions governing service "outside the state". But a warning is needed—that provision may have been drafted thinking solely of *outside* the state but *within* another state in the United States. When the service is outside the United States other rules may govern. This is where the Hague Service Convention and/or Inter–American Convention on Letters Rogatory and Additional Protocol may apply. The United States and Venezuela are parties to both.

Rule 4 of the Federal Rules of Civil Procedure outlines methods of service and procedural requirements to establish jurisdiction over foreign parties to litigation in U.S. courts. In establishing the proper source of federal jurisdiction Rule 4(k) authorizes for federal question jurisdiction the use of federal long-arm jurisdiction where the defendants cannot be served under any state law but can be constitutionally subjected to jurisdiction of the federal courts. For diversity based jurisdiction Rules 4(e) and (h) provide that state law service rules apply to service upon individuals and corporations, whether foreign or domestic, within a judicial district of the United States. Rule 4(f) provides alternative means of service upon individuals in a foreign country. Nothing in Rule 4 requires specific state or federal statutory authorization for the method of service of process used abroad. That is where the Hague and Inter–American conventions become important. Nevertheless, effective use of the conventions does not eliminate the need to acquire valid personal jurisdiction over persons "doing business" in the United States, including adherence to state "long arm" jurisdiction requirements. Use of domestic statutes may implicate the conventions, such as Rule 4(f) that provides for the alternative means of service on individuals in foreign countries "by any internationally agreed means" that would include the Hague Service Convention. Rule 4(f)(3) allows service "by other means not prohibited by international agreements, as the court orders." This has given rise to substantial litigation.

VOLKSWAGENWERK A.G. v. SCHLUNK

Supreme Court of the United States, 1988.
486 U.S. 694, 108 S.Ct. 2104, 100 L.Ed.2d 722.

JUSTICE O'CONNOR delivered the opinion of the Court.

This case involves an attempt to serve process on a foreign corporation by serving its domestic subsidiary which, under state law, is the foreign corporation's involuntary agent for service of process. We must decide whether such service is compatible with the [Hague Service Convention].

I

The parents of respondent Schlunk were killed in an automobile accident in 1983. Schlunk filed a wrongful death action on their behalf in the Circuit Court of Cook County, Illinois. Schlunk alleged that Volkswagen of America, Inc. (VWoA), had designed and sold the automobile that his parents were driving, and that defects in the automobile caused or contributed to their deaths ... Schlunk successfully served his complaint on VwoA ... Schlunk then amended the complaint to add as a defendant Volkswagen Aktiengesellschaft (VWAG), which is the petitioner here. VWAG, a corporation established under the laws of the Federal Republic of Germany, has its place of business in that country. VWoA is a wholly owned [U.S.] subsidiary of VWAG. Schlunk attempted to serve his amended complaint on VWAG by serving VWoA as VWAG's agent.

VWAG asserted that it could be served only in accordance with the Hague Service Convention, and that Schlunk had not complied with the Convention's requirements. The Circuit Court denied VWAG's motion. The court ... reasoned that VWoA and VWAG are so closely related that VWoA is VWAG's agent for service of process as a matter of law, notwithstanding VWAG's failure or refusal to appoint VWoA formally as an agent. The court relied on the facts that VWoA is a wholly owned subsidiary of VWAG, that a majority of the members of the board of directors of VWoA are members of the board of VWAG, and that VWoA is by contract the exclusive importer and distributor of VWAG products sold in the United States. The court concluded that, because service was accomplished within the United States, the Hague Service Convention did not apply.

The Circuit Court certified two questions to the Appellate Court of Illinois. For reasons similar to those given by the Circuit Court, the Appellate Court determined that VWoA is VWAG's agent for service of process under Illinois law, and that the service of process in this case did not violate the Hague Service Convention. After the Supreme Court of Illinois denied VWAG leave to appeal, [we granted] certiorari to review the Appellate Court's interpretation of the Hague Service Convention, ... which has given rise to disagreement among the lower courts.

The Hague Service Convention is a multilateral treaty that was formulated by the . . . Hague Conference of Private International Law . . . intended to provide a simpler way to serve process abroad, to assure that defendants sued in foreign jurisdictions would receive actual and timely notice of suit, and to facilitate proof of service abroad.

The primary innovation of the Convention is that it requires each state to establish a central authority to receive requests for service of documents from other countries. Once a central authority receives a request in the proper form, it must serve the documents by a method prescribed by the internal law of the receiving state or by a method designated by the requester and compatible with that law. The central authority must then provide a certificate of service that conforms to a specified model. A state also may consent to methods of service within its boundaries other than a request to its central authority . . .

Article 1 defines the scope of the Convention, which is the subject of controversy in this case. It says: "The present Convention shall apply in all cases, in civil or commercial matters, where there is occasion to transmit a judicial or extrajudicial document for service abroad." Schlunk does not purport to have served his complaint on VWAG in accordance with the Convention. Therefore, if service of process in this case falls within Article 1 of the Convention, the trial court should have granted VWAG's motion to quash.

The Convention does not specify the circumstances in which there is "occasion to transmit" a complaint "for service abroad." But at least the term "service of process" has a well-established technical meaning. Service of process refers to a formal delivery of documents that is legally sufficient to charge the defendant with notice of a pending action. The legal sufficiency of a formal delivery of documents must be measured against some standard. The Convention does not prescribe a standard, so we almost necessarily must refer to the internal law of the forum state. If the internal law of the forum state defines the applicable method of serving process as requiring the transmittal of documents abroad, then the Hague Service Convention applies.

. . . The preliminary draft of Article 1 said that the present Convention shall apply in all cases in which there are grounds *to transmit or to give formal notice of* a judicial or extrajudicial document in a civil or commercial matter to a person staying abroad. . . . The delegates . . . criticized the language of the preliminary draft because it suggested that the Convention could apply to transmissions abroad that do not culminate in service. The final text of Article 1 eliminates this possibility and applies only to documents transmitted for service abroad. The final report confirms that the Convention does not use more general terms, such as delivery or transmission, to define its scope because it applies only when there is both transmission of a document from the requesting state to the receiving state, and service upon the person for whom it is intended.

The negotiating history of the Convention also indicates that whether there is service abroad must be determined by reference to the law of the forum state. The preliminary draft said that the Convention would apply "where there are grounds" to transmit a judicial document to a person staying abroad. The committee that prepared the preliminary draft realized that this implied that the forum's internal law would govern whether service implicated the Convention. The reporter expressed regret about this solution because it would decrease the obligatory force of the Convention. Nevertheless, the delegates did not change the meaning of Article 1 in this respect.

The drafting committee then composed the version of Article 1 that ultimately was adopted, which says that the Convention applies "where there is occasion" to transmit a judicial document for service abroad. After this revision, the reporter again explained that one must leave to the requesting state the task of defining when a document must be served abroad; that this solution was a consequence of the unavailability of an objective test; and that while it decreases the obligatory force of the Convention, it does provide clarity. The inference we draw from this history is that ... "service abroad" has the same meaning in the final version of the Convention as it had in the preliminary draft.

VWAG protests that it is inconsistent with the purpose of the Convention to interpret it as applying only when the internal law of the forum requires service abroad. One of the two stated objectives of the Convention is "to create appropriate means to ensure that judicial and extrajudicial documents to be served abroad shall be brought to the notice of the addressee in sufficient time." The Convention cannot assure adequate notice, VWAG argues, if the forum's internal law determines whether it applies. VWAG warns that countries could circumvent the Convention by defining methods of service of process that do not require transmission of documents abroad. . . .

. . . VWAG argues that, if this determination is made according to the internal law of the forum state, the Convention will fail to eliminate variants . . . that do not expressly require transmittal of documents to foreign defendants. Yet such methods of service of process are the least likely to provide a defendant with actual notice.

. . . [T]here is no...evidence in the negotiating history that the Convention was meant to apply to substituted service on a subsidiary like VWoA, which clearly does not require service abroad under the forum's internal law. Hence neither the language of the Convention nor the negotiating history contradicts our interpretation of the Convention, according to which the internal law of the forum is presumed to determine whether there is occasion for service abroad.

Nor are we persuaded that the general purposes of the Convention require a different conclusion. One important objective of the Convention is to provide means to facilitate service of process abroad. Thus the first stated purpose of the Convention is "to create" appropriate means for service abroad, and the second stated purpose is "to improve the organization of mutual judicial assistance for that purpose by simplifying and expediting the procedure." By requiring each state to establish a central authority to assist in the service of process, the Convention implements this enabling function. Nothing in our decision today interferes with this requirement.

VWAG correctly maintains that the Convention also aims to ensure that there will be adequate notice in cases in which there is occasion to serve process abroad. Thus compliance with the Convention is mandatory in all cases to which it applies, Articles 15 and 16 provide an indirect sanction against those who ignore it. Our interpretation of the Convention does not necessarily advance this particular objective, inasmuch as it makes recourse to the Convention's means of service dependent on the forum's internal law. But we do not think that this country, or any other country, will draft its internal laws deliberately so as to circumvent the Convention in cases in which it would be appropriate to transmit judicial documents for service abroad. For example, there has been no question in this country of excepting foreign nationals from the protection of our Due Process Clause. Under that Clause, foreign nationals are assured of either personal service, which typically will require service abroad and trigger the Convention, or substituted service that provides "notice reasonably calculated, under all the circumstances, to apprise interested parties of the pendency of the action and afford them an opportunity to present their objections." *Mullane v. Central Hanover Bank & Trust Co.,* 339 U.S. 306, 314 (1950).

Furthermore, nothing that we say today prevents compliance with the Convention even when the internal law of the forum does not so require. The Convention provides simple and certain means by which to serve process on a foreign national. Those who eschew its procedures risk discovering that the forum's internal law required transmittal of documents for service abroad, and that the Convention therefore provided the exclusive means of valid service. In addition, parties that comply with the Convention ultimately may find it easier to enforce their judgments abroad. For these reasons, we anticipate that parties may resort to the Convention voluntarily, even in cases that fall outside the scope of its mandatory application.

In this case, the Illinois long-arm statute authorized Schlunk to serve VWAG by substituted service on VWoA, without sending documents to Germany.... VWAG contends ... that service on VWAG was not complete until VWoA transmitted the complaint to VWAG in Germany ...

VWAG explains that, as a practical matter, VWoA was certain to transmit the complaint to Germany to notify VWAG of the litigation. Indeed, as a legal matter, the Due Process Clause requires every method of service to provide "notice reasonably calculated, under all the circumstances, to apprise interested parties of the pendency of the action and afford them an opportunity to present their objections." VWAG argues that, because of this notice requirement, every case involving service on a foreign national will present an "occasion to transmit a judicial ... document for service abroad" within the meaning of Article 1. VWAG emphasizes that in this case, the Appellate Court upheld service only after determining that "the relationship between VWAG and VWoA is so close that it is certain that VWAG 'was fully apprised of the pendency of the action' by delivery of the summons to VWoA."

We reject this argument. Where service on a domestic agent is valid and complete under both state law and the Due Process Clause, our inquiry ends and the Convention has no further implications. Whatever internal, private communications take place between the agent and a foreign principal are beyond the concerns of this case. The only transmittal to which the Convention applies is a transmittal abroad that is required as a necessary part of service. And, contrary to VWAG's assertion, the Due Process Clause does not require an official transmittal of documents abroad every time there is service on a foreign national. Applying this analysis, we conclude that this case does not present an occasion to transmit a judicial document for service abroad within the meaning of Article 1. Therefore the Hague Service Convention does not apply, and service was proper. The judgment of the Appellate Court is *Affirmed*.

———

Article 10 of the Hague Service Convention allows service by mail. But many member states have made reservations or declarations prohibiting service by mail within their nations. Does the word "send" in Article 10 mean "service"? This has created a problem, especially with Japan. The following case shows one view—that Article 10 was not intended to authorize mail as an effective means of service. But other courts have interpreted "send" in Article 10 to mean "service". Courts continue to be divided, thus making a decision to use mail especially uncertain.

BANKSTON v. TOYOTA MOTOR CORP.

United States Court of Appeals, Eight Circuit, 1989.
889 F.2d 172.

The appellants ... attempted to serve process upon Toyota by sending a summons and complaint by registered mail, return receipt requested, to Tokyo, Japan. The documents were in English and did not include a translation into Japanese. The receipt of service was signed and returned to appellants. Toyota renewed its motion to dismiss, arguing that the appellants' proposed method of service still did not comply with the Hague Convention. The district court concluded that Article 10(a) of the Hague Convention does not permit service of process upon a Japanese corporation by registered mail....

[T]his court entered an order granting appellants leave to take an interlocutory appeal.

The crucial article for this discussion is Article 10, under which appellants herein purportedly attempted to serve process upon Toyota by registered mail. Article 10 provides in relevant part:

Provided the State of destination does not object, the present Convention shall not interfere with—

(a) the freedom to send judicial documents, by postal channels, directly to persons abroad,

(b) the freedom of judicial officers, officials or other competent persons of the State of origin to effect service of judicial documents directly through the judicial officers, officials or other competent persons of the State of destination,

(c) the freedom of any person interested in a judicial proceeding to effect service of judicial documents directly through the judicial officers, officials or other competent persons of the State of destination.

Japan has objected to subparagraphs (b) and (c), but not to subparagraph (a). The issue before this court is whether subparagraph (a) permits service on a Japanese defendant by direct mail.

In recent years, two distinct lines of Article 10(a) interpretation have arisen. Some courts have ruled that Article 10(a) permits service of process by mail directly to the defendant without the necessity of resorting to the central authority, and without the necessity of translating the documents into the official language of the nation where the documents are to be served.

In general, these courts reason that since the purported purpose of the Hague Convention is to facilitate service abroad, the reference to " 'the freedom to send judicial documents by postal channels, directly to persons abroad' would be superfluous unless it was related to the sending of such documents for the purpose of service." These courts have further found that the use of the "send" rather than "service" in Article 10(a) "must be attributed to careless drafting."

The second line of interpretation, advocated by Toyota, is that the word "send" in Article 10(a) is not the equivalent of "service of process." The word "service" is specifically used in other sections of the Convention, including subsections (b) and (c) of Article 10. If the drafters of the Convention had meant for subparagraph (a) to provide an additional manner of service of judicial documents, they would have used the word "service." Subscribers to this interpretation maintain that Article 10(a) merely provides a method for sending subsequent documents after service of process has been obtained by means of the central authority.

We find this second line of authority to be more persuasive. It is a "familiar canon of statutory construction that the starting point for interpreting a statute is the language of the statute itself. Absent a clearly expressed legislative intention to the contrary, that language must ordinarily be regarded as conclusive." In addition, where a legislative body "includes particular language in one section of a statute but omits it in another section of the same Act, it is generally presumed that [the legislative body] acts intentionally and purposely in the disparate inclusion or exclusion." In *Suzuki Motor Co. v. Superior Court*, 249 Cal.Rptr. at 379, the court found that because service of process by registered mail was not permitted under Japanese law, it was "extremely unlikely" that Japan's failure to object to Article 10(a) was intended to authorize the use of registered mail as an effective mode of service of process, particularly in light of the fact that Japan had specifically objected to the much more formal modes of service by Japanese officials which were available in Article 10(b) and (c).

We conclude that sending a copy of a summons and complaint by registered mail to a defendant in a foreign country is not a method of service of process permitted by the Hague Convention. We affirm the judgment of the district court and remand this case with directions that appellants be given a reasonable time from the date of this Order in which to effectuate service of process over appellee Toyota Motor Corporation in compliance with the terms of the Hague Convention.

GIBSON, CIRCUIT JUDGE, concurring.

I concur ... in every respect.... I ... only express nagging concerns I have about the practical effect of our opinion. Automobiles are subject to a plethora of regulations requiring particular equipment and detailed warnings. Should an automobile manufactured in Japan carry a disclosure that, if litigation ensues from its purchase and use, service of process on the Japanese manufacturer can only be obtained under the Hague Convention? Should the purchaser also be informed that this special service of process will cost $800 to $900, as we are told, and must include a translation of the suit papers in Japanese? These decisions we must leave to others. I write only to express my discomfort with the practical effect of Toyota's insistence on strict compliance with the letter of the Hague Convention.

QUESTIONS AND COMMENTS

1. Serving a business official of Epiphytes while on a trip to the United States, what we call "tag" jurisdiction, is not welcomed in most locations abroad. But it does provide adequate jurisdiction for the case in the United States, if not for a judgment that would be enforced in Epiphytes' nation, Venezuela. There is debate about whether such service is effective on *foreign* corporations. *See MBM Fisheries, Inc. v. Bollinger Mach. Shop and Shipyard, Inc.*, 60 Wash.App. 414, 804 P.2d 627 (1991). *But see, American–European Art Assoc., Inc. v. Moquay*, 1995 WL 317321 (S.D.N.Y. 1995). Do you recommend gambling on its effectiveness?

2. When the Hague Convention is applicable, we should look for any reservations taken by the particular nation. If we find that an Article 10 reservation has been taken by Venezuela, and we will, we would be unwise to use service by mail.

3. Might Mott consider using the "waiver of summons" provisions of Rule 4(d)? The Advisory Committee Notes to the 1993 Amendment to Rule 4(d) comment as follows:

> The aims of the provision are to eliminate the costs of service of summons on many parties and to foster cooperation among adversaries and counsel. The rule operates to impose upon the defendant those costs that could have been avoided if the defendant had cooperated reasonably in the manner prescribed. This device is useful in dealing with defendants who are furtive, who resided in places not easily reached be process servers, or who are outside the United States and can be served only at substantial and unnecessary expense. Illustratively, there is no useful purpose achieved by requiring a plaintiff to comply with all formalities of service in a foreign country, including costs of translation, when suing a defendant manufacturer, fluent in English, whose products are widely distributed in the United States.

What if Epiphytes refused to acknowledge service under the Rule 4(d) procedures. Does "waiver of summons" under Rule 4(d) constitute effective service on foreign parties? Where "waiver" procedures are used, does Epiphytes have a good defense if enforcement of the U.S. judgment is sought abroad?

4. Is it ever advisable to bypass Hague Service Convention procedures to save costs and avoid delays? Are there situations where abbreviated or questionable methods might be justified? Suppose the U.S. court is anxious to move the case forward and the certificate of service has not yet been returned by the foreign central authority? Is Epiphytes justified in seeking dismissal of the case for lack of personal jurisdiction?

5. In *Schlunk* the Supreme Court affirmed the mandatory nature of the Hague Service Convention "when it applies." Mott has sought to serve Epiphytes through the latter's subsidiary marketing agent. Is *Schlunk* applicable?

6. Does the *Bankston* decision help Mott's arguments if *Schlunk* does not?

7. Rule 4(f)(3) has generated considerable litigation, especially the meaning of "as the court orders" in the sentence that allows for service "by other means not prohibited by international agreements, as the court orders." Prior court approval is clearly needed before trying an alternative means under Rule 4(f)(3). See, e.g., *International Raelian Movement v. Hashem,* 2009 WL 2136958, at *3–5 (E.D.Cal. July 15, 2009). Approved service might be that using the defendant's U.S. counsel or electronic means such as e-mail. *United States v. Machat,* 2009 WL 3029303, at *3–4 (S.D.N.Y. Sept. 21, 2009); But see *Mapping Your Future, Inc. v. Mapping Your Future Services,* Ltd., 2009 WL 3105565 (D.S.D. Sept. 23, 2009).

PART B. *FORUM NON CONVENIENS*

Epiphytes was concerned with the disruption of its orchid sales in the United States caused by the litigation in Part A above. Before any rulings on service of process were issued in the case, Epiphytes settled the matter by paying the bill.

Prior to dealing with Mott, Epiphytes had been having trouble with trying methods to induce rapid growth and control seasonal blooming in its orchids. It had abandoned a previously used fertilizer purchased from a small Venezuelan manufacturer (with little ability to pay for any damages its product caused) when the fertilizer seemed to cause some deadly viruses to spread through Epiphytes' orchid houses. It never identified the viruses or their cause. After the introduction of Suregrow™, the virus seemed to disappear (partly the reason for the above settlement), but soon the orchids again began to die and Epiphytes states that it has now lost half of its orchid stock. Mott believes its Suregrow™ is perfectly safe to use with orchids and that Epiphytes has used unsanitary growing practices that have caused the new losses, which Mott attributes to another virus.

Epiphytes considered suing Mott in Venezuela, but its Venezuelan lawyers recommended retaining a Texas law firm to sue in a South Texas state court, where juries are perceived as being unsympathetic towards large companies and judgments are high. A suit subsequently was filed in South Texas by Epiphytes against Mott, alleging both breach of contract and tort claims. Mott responded by filing a motion to dismiss based on *forum non conveniens.* Venezuela was alleged to be the more convenient forum. You have been retained again by the law firm for Mott to help with the *forum non conveniens* based motion to dismiss. What is your advice?

L. W. NEWMAN AND D. ZASLOWSKY, LITIGATING INTERNATIONAL COMMERCIAL DISPUTES

85 (West 1996).*

Initially, in determining whether to dismiss a case on the basis of *forum non conveniens,* a district court must find that there exists an adequate alternative forum for the litigation. If the court so finds, it will then consider the various factors set forth by the Supreme Court in *Gulf Oil Corp. v. Gilbert* and *Koster v. (American) Lumbermens Mutual Casualty Co.,* and more recently recapitulated in *Piper Aircraft v. Reyno.* Beginning with the general presumption that a plaintiff's choice of forum should be respected, the court will weigh both private and public interests to determine whether this choice should be respected in the case before it. Although the Supreme Court in *Gilbert* stated that, "[w]isely, it has not been attempted to catalogue the circumstances which will justify or require" dismissal on *forum non conveniens* grounds, the court went on to list the following private interests of the litigant as factors to be considered:

(1) The relative ease of access to sources of proof;

(2) The availability of a compulsory process for securing the attendance of uncooperative witnesses;

(3) The costs of obtaining the attendance of witnesses;

(4) The possibility of viewing the relevant premises;

---

* Reprinted with permission of West Publishing Co.

(5) Other practical problems which will allow the trial to be easy, expeditious, and inexpensive; and

(6) The enforceability of a judgment if obtained.

In addition, there are public interests to be weighed including the following:

(1) The administrative difficulties that arise when litigation is piled up in congested centers instead of being handled at the origin;

(2) Imposing jury duty on the people of a community that has no relation to the litigation;

(3) The desire to have localized controversies decided at home; and

(4) Not burdening courts with complex conflicts of law problems and with applying a law that is foreign to them.

The courts weigh these and other factors to determine which available forum is the most appropriate for trial and resolution of the issues. In *Piper,* the Supreme Court reaffirmed the broad discretion given to the trial courts to determine the *forum non conveniens* issue and only if there is an abuse of that discretion will a district court's decision be disturbed.

* * *

PIPER AIRCRAFT CO. v. REYNO

Supreme Court of the United States, 1981.
454 U.S. 235, 102 S.Ct. 252, 70 L.Ed.2d 419.

[Respondent, as representative of the estates of several citizens and residents of Scotland who were killed in an airplane crash in Scotland during a charter flight, instituted wrongful-death litigation in a California state court against petitioners, which are the company that manufactured the plane in Pennsylvania and the company that manufactured the plane's propellers in Ohio. At the time of the crash the plane was registered in Great Britain and was owned and operated by companies organized in the United Kingdom. The pilot and all of the decedents' heirs and next of kin were Scottish subjects and citizens, and the investigation of the accident was conducted by British authorities. Respondent sought to recover from petitioners on the basis of negligence or strict liability (not recognized by Scottish law), and admitted that the action was filed in the United States because its laws regarding liability, capacity to sue, and damages are more favorable to respondent's position than those of Scotland. The action was removed to a Federal District Court in California and then transferred to the United States District Court for the Middle District of Pennsylvania. The District Court granted petitioners' motion to dismiss the action on the ground of *forum non conveniens.* However, the Court of Appeals reversed, holding that the District Court had abused its discretion in conducting the *Gilbert* analysis and that, in any event, dismissal is automatically barred where the law of the alternative forum is less favorable to the plaintiff than the law of the forum chosen by the plaintiff.]

JUSTICE MARSHALL delivered the opinion of the Court.

The Court of Appeals erred in holding that plaintiffs may defeat a motion to dismiss on the ground of *forum non conveniens* merely by showing that the substantive law that would be applied in the alternative forum is less favorable to the plaintiffs than that of the present forum. The possibility of a change in substantive law should ordinarily not be given conclusive or even substantial weight in the *forum non conveniens* inquiry.

Gilbert implicitly recognized that dismissal may not be barred solely because of the possibility of an unfavorable change in law. Under *Gilbert*, dismissal will ordinarily be appropriate where trial in the plaintiff's chosen forum imposes a heavy burden on the defendant or the court, and where the plaintiff is unable to offer any specific reasons of convenience supporting his choice.

[I]f conclusive or substantial weight were given to the possibility of a change in law, . . . dismissal would rarely be proper.

The Court of Appeals' approach is not only inconsistent with the purpose of the *forum non conveniens* doctrine, but also poses substantial practical problems. If the possibility of a change in law were given substantial weight, deciding motions to dismiss on the ground of *forum non conveniens* would become quite difficult. Choice-of-law analysis would become extremely important, and the courts would frequently be required to interpret the law of foreign jurisdictions.

The American courts, which are already extremely attractive to foreign plaintiffs, would become even more attractive. The flow of litigation into the United States would increase and further congest already crowded courts.

We do not hold that the possibility of an unfavorable change in law should *never* be a relevant consideration in a *forum non conveniens* inquiry. Of course, if the remedy provided by the alternative forum is so clearly inadequate or unsatisfactory that it is no remedy at all, the unfavorable change in law may be given substantial weight; the district court may conclude that dismissal would not be in the interests of justice. In these cases, however, the remedies that would be provided by the Scottish courts do not fall within this category.

The Court of Appeals also erred in rejecting the District Court's *Gilbert* analysis. The Court of Appeals stated that more weight should have been given to the plaintiff's choice of forum, and criticized the District Court's analysis of the private and public interests.

The District Court acknowledged that there is ordinarily a strong presumption in favor of the plaintiff's choice of forum, which may be overcome only when the private and public interest factors clearly point towards trial in the alternative forum. It held, however, that the presumption applies with less force when the plaintiff or real parties in interest are foreign. . . . The District Court's distinction between resident or citizen plaintiffs and foreign plaintiffs is fully justified.

[T]he deference accorded a plaintiff's choice of forum has never been intended to guarantee that the plaintiff will be able to select the law that will govern the case.

In analyzing the private interest factors, the District Court stated that the connections with Scotland are "overwhelming." . . . Particularly with respect to the question of relative ease of access to sources of proof, the private interests point in both directions. [R]ecords concerning the design, manufacture, and testing of the propeller and plane are located in the United States. She would have greater access to sources of proof relevant to her strict liability and negligence theories if trial were held here. However, the District Court did not act unreasonably in concluding that fewer evidentiary problems would be posed if the trial were held in Scotland. A large proportion of the relevant evidence is located in Great Britain.

The District Court correctly concluded that the problems posed by the inability to implead potential third-party defendants clearly supported holding the trial in Scotland. Joinder of the pilot's estate, Air Navigation, and McDonald is crucial to the presentation of petitioners' defense. If Piper and Hartzell can show that the accident was caused not by a design defect, but rather by the negligence of the pilot, the plane's owners, or the charter company, they will be relieved of all liability.

The District Court's review of the factors relating to the public interest was also reasonable. [I]t concluded that if the case were tried in the Middle District of Pennsylvania, Pennsylvania law would apply to Piper and Scottish law to Hartzell. It stated that a trial involving two sets of laws would be confusing to the jury. It also noted its own lack of familiarity with Scottish law. Consideration of these problems was clearly appropriate under *Gilbert*; in that case we explicitly held that the need to apply foreign law pointed towards dismissal.

Scotland has a very strong interest in this litigation. The accident occurred in its airspace. All of the decedents were Scottish. Apart from Piper and Hartzell, all potential plaintiffs and defendants are either Scottish or English. As we stated in *Gilbert*, there is "a local interest in having localized controversies decided at home." Respondent argues that American citizens have an interest in ensuring that American manufacturers are deterred from producing defective products, and that additional deterrence might be obtained if Piper and Hartzell were tried in the United States, where they could be sued on the basis of both negligence and strict liability. However, the incremental deterrence that would be gained if this trial were held in an American court is likely to be insignificant. The American interest in this accident is simply not sufficient to justify the enormous commitment of judicial time and resources that would inevitably be required if the case were to be tried here. [T]he judgment of the Court of Appeals is *Reversed*.

REPUBLIC OF BOLIVIA v. PHILIP MORRIS COMPANIES, INC.

United States District Court, S.D. Texas, 1999.
39 F.Supp.2d 1008.

Kent, J. Plaintiff, the Republic of Bolivia, brings this action to recover from numerous tobacco companies various health care costs it allegedly incurred in treating illnesses its residents suffered as a result of tobacco use. This action was originally filed in the District Court of Brazoria County, Texas, and removed to this Court.... The governments of Guatemala, Panama, Nicaragua, Thailand, Venezuela, and Bolivia have filed suit in the geographically diverse locales of Washington, D.C., Puerto Rico, Texas, Louisiana, and Florida, in both state and federal courts. Why none of these countries seems to have a court system their own governments have confidence in is a mystery to this Court. Moreover, given the tremendous number of United States jurisdictions encompassing fascinating and exotic places, the Court can hardly imagine why the Republic of Bolivia elected to file suit in the veritable hinterlands of Brazoria County, Texas. The Court seriously doubts whether Brazoria County has ever seen a live Bolivian ... even on the Discovery Channel. Though only here by removal, this humble Court by the sea is certainly flattered by what must be the worldwide renown of rural Texas courts for dispensing justice with unparalleled fairness and alacrity, apparently in common discussion even on the mountain peaks of Bolivia! Still, the Court would be remiss in accepting an obligation for which it truly does not have the necessary resources. Only one judge presides in the Galveston Division-which currently has before it over seven hundred cases ... And, while Galveston is indeed an international seaport, the capacity of this Court to address the complex and sophisticated issues of international law and foreign relations presented by this case is dwarfed by that of its esteemed colleagues in the District of Columbia who deftly address such awesome tasks as a matter of course. ...Such a Bench, well-populated with genuinely renowned intellects, can certainly better bear and share the burden of multidistrict litigation than this single judge division, where the judge moves his lips when he reads.

[I]t is the Court's opinion that the District of Columbia ... is a much more logical venue for the parties and witnesses in this action because, among other things, Plaintiff has an embassy in Washington, D.C., and thus a physical presence and governmental representatives there, whereas there isn't even a Bolivian restaurant anywhere near here! Although the jurisdiction of this Court boasts no similar foreign offices, a somewhat dated globe is within its possession. While the Court does not therefrom profess to understand all of the political subtleties of the geographical transmogrifications ongoing in Eastern Europe, the Court is virtually certain that Bolivia is not within the four counties over which this Court presides, even though the words Bolivia and Brazoria are a lot alike and caused some real, initial confusion until the Court conferred with its law clerks. Thus, it is readily apparent, even from an outdated globe such as that possessed by this Court, that Bolivia, a hemisphere away, ain't in south-central Texas, and that, at the very least, the District of Columbia is a more appropriate venue (though Bolivia isn't located there either). [T]his case is hereby TRANSFERRED to the United States District Court for the District of Columbia.

COMMENT ON THE *BRIDGESTONE/FIRESTONE* AND *FORD* CASES BROUGHT BY PLAINTIFFS FROM VENEZUELA IN INDIANA AND TEXAS COURTS.

Accidents involving Ford Explorers equipped with Bridgestone/Firestone (B/F) tires occurred in a number of Latin American countries. Suits were filed in the United States, in both state and federal courts, and most of the latter were consolidated in Indiana. See *In re Bridgestone/Firestone, Inc., Tires Products Liability Litigation*, 190 F.Supp.2d 1125 (S.D.Ind. 2002). Defendants sought dismissal of the 121 Venezuelan and Colombian plaintiff cases before the court on *forum non conveniens* grounds. The Venezuelan and Colombian cases were addressed separately, the Venezuelan plaintiffs arguing that Venezuelan law foreclosed the Venezuelan courts from asserting jurisdiction when a Venezuelan citizen chose to initiate the suit abroad rather than in Venezuela, and the foreign court dismissed the suit on *forum non conveniens* grounds. Indiana federal district court judge Barker thus ruled that the Venezuelan courts were not available because they did not have jurisdiction.

What the court did not address was why Venezuela might enact a law that seemed to deprive its citizens of access to Venezuelan courts. The law in question is Venezuela's Statute on Private International Law. Plaintiffs' expert noted that Article 39 provided that "the first forum for bringing suit against a non-domiciliary defendant is the country where the defendant is domiciled." Because such a law could not create jurisdiction in the United States, the Venezuelan law includes exceptions. One, in Article 40(4), provides that "Venezuelan courts shall have jurisdiction to hear trials resulting from the actions in property when the parties should expressly or tacitly submit to their jurisdiction." That reads very much like a fairly common provision in the law of many nations that allows parties to choose a forum in a contract. It is an affirmation of the use of a forum selection clause by providing that the courts shall recognize such provisions. But plaintiff's expert responded that 40(4) requires *both* of the parties to provide an express submission to the Venezuelan courts subsequent to a *forum non conveniens* dismissal. The defendants would of course agree to such submission. But the plaintiffs would not because refusal held out hope of returning to the land of large damages. Unfortunately, Judge Barker was unaware of any of the background that would have illustrated the recent attempts in Latin America to nullify U.S. *forum non conveniens* based motions to dismiss that were the core of the plaintiffs' arguments.

The origin of that attempt in part of Latin America is unclear. Arguments regarding the lack of availability of the courts of Panama, Costa Rica,

Guatemala and Ecuador, based on the absence of jurisdiction of the foreign plaintiffs' domestic forum, if a U.S. court dismissed a case brought by the foreign plaintiff on *forum non conveniens* grounds, arose in *Patrickson v. Dole Food Company, Inc.*, Civil No. 97–01516 (Haw. 1998). The court considered each of the four nation's laws and dismissed the case on *forum non conveniens*, finding that the plaintiffs had the right to file the action in their home courts, notwithstanding varying degrees of attempts to remove local jurisdiction following a U.S. dismissal on *forum non conveniens* grounds. The Ecuadorian attempt also was raised in another case, *In re Ecuadorian Shrimp Litigation*, Case No. 94–10138–27 (1999), in a Florida state court. The court dismissed the action on *forum non conveniens* grounds and the plaintiffs returned to Ecuador first to seek the enactment of Law 55, which stated that if an Ecuadorian chose first to initiate a suit outside Ecuador and it was dismissed, Ecuadorian jurisdiction was terminated. With that law in place the plaintiffs took the unusual step of filing suit solely to then seek its dismissal. With the dismissals in hand, the plaintiffs were soon back in the Florida court asking for reassertion of jurisdiction. The court rejected Ecuador's attempt to "force" the Florida court "to expend scarce and valuable resources on cases that have no connection with the state's interests," suggesting that "if Ecuador refuses to provide a forum to its own citizens to litigate claims arising from acts occurring in Ecuador, that is its prerogative."

Ecuador's passage of Law 55 was consistent with a movement in a few Latin American nations to assist their nationals in responding to *forum non conveniens* dismissals in U.S. courts. The Latin American Parliament (Parlatino), is little known in the United States. It is an organization of a few members of some of the Latin American legislatures apparently organized after a U.S. federal district court in Texas dismissed a case on *forum non conveniens* grounds involving plaintiffs from twelve nations, including Costa Rica, Ecuador, Guatemala, Honduras, Nicaragua and Panama, *Delgado v. Shell Oil Co.*, 890 F.Supp. 1324 (S.D.Tex. 1995), for injuries allegedly from use of a nemotocide on their farms. Some of the rejected plaintiffs returned to their nations not to initiate suit but to find some way back to the U.S. court. In 1998 Parlatino challenged *forum non conveniens* by drafting a brief Model Law on International Jurisdiction and Applicable Law to Tort Liability. The law reads:

> Art. 1. National and international jurisdiction. The petition that is validly filed, according to both legal systems, in the defendant's domiciliary court, extinguishes national jurisdiction. The latter is only reborn if the plaintiff desists of his foreign petition and files a new petition in the country, in a completely free and spontaneous way.
>
> Art. 2. International tort liability. Damages. In cases of international tort liability, the national court may, at the plaintiff's request, apply to damages and to the pecuniary sanctions related to such damages, the relevant standards and amounts of the pertinent foreign law.

Parlatino suggested that its proposed law would allow a plaintiff to choose a foreign forum that met the norms of the Bustamante Code and that the foreign "judge will not be able to close the doors of the [foreign] court on him as, for instance, has been happening with the theory of forum non conveniens." Since none of the Parlatino nations recognizes the doctrine of *forum non conveniens*, the reference of foreclosure can only refer to the United States, or other foreign courts recognizing that theory. But it is not the parliaments of other nations that open or close the doors to the U.S. courts. U.S. judges have discretion to decide *forum non conveniens* based motions to dismiss that civil law system judges do not share. But failure to possess such discretion is hardly a justifiable reason to attempt to abolish it from abroad. Parlatino has been careful not to fully extinguish jurisdiction of a plaintiff from a member state when it files abroad. Each plaintiff is presented with an escape valve. The model law allows one of its citizens who has been dismissed abroad, presumably for any reason, whether it be lack of subject matter or personal jurisdiction, statute of limitations or *forum non conveniens*, to file an action in the home court, as long as it is done in a "completely free and spontaneous way." If a suit has been dismissed in the U.S. court, the foreign plaintiff is "completely free" to decide what to do next. That may be to propose settlement negotiations with the other parties who were the defendants in the dismissed suits, to appeal the dismissal to the appropriate appellate court in the United States, to file a suit in any other country including but not necessarily that of the plaintiff, or to do absolutely nothing.

Two years after the Indiana decision the federal district court for the South District of Texas analyzed and rejected the reasoning of the Indiana court on the issue of availability, and found Venezuela to be an available forum. *Morales v. Ford Motor Co.,* 313 F.Supp.2d 672 (S.D.Tex. 2004). The Texas court viewed the Venezuelan plaintiffs' argument as being based on "unwillingness" rather than unavailability. The plaintiffs were unwilling to file suit in Venezuela, whether before or after the action filed in the United States, a motivation that the court would not find justifying characterizing Venezuela as an unavailable forum.

Perhaps the most curious feature of the movement of Parlatino is its members' apparent belief that there is no hope of reforming Latin American legal systems so that they might be able to deal effectively with complex tort litigation. Some nations have or prefer to develop that ability and have consequently rejected the Parlatino theory (e.g., Mexico, Chile), some have that ability but seem not to believe in their systems (e.g., Costa Rica), and some have very good reason to believe that their systems are currently incapable of providing due process in any such action (e.g., Guatemala, Bolivia, Nicaragua, etc.). In some cases the laws on the books provide a very effective system for the resolution of such disputes, but the system functions so corruptly, inefficiently, or subject to intimidation or political influence that its plaintiffs are justified in being litigation immigrants. The question facing U.S. courts is whether they are legal or illegal litigation immigrants.

COMMENT ON THE CHANGES TO THE ENGLISH THEORY AND USE OF FORUM NON CONVENIENS

The theory of *forum non conveniens* has its origins in Scottish and later English law. But the future of the theory is uncertain. Two cases, one in the House of Lords and the other in the European Court of Justice, cast a shadow on the future of the theory in the United Kingdom. In *Lubbe and Others v.*

Cape PLC, [2000] 2 Lloyd's Rep. 383 (H.L.), Lord Bingham stated that "public interest considerations not related to the private interests of the parties and the ends of justice have no bearing on the decision which the Court has to make." Lord Hope added "I would decline to follow those judges in the United States who would decide issues as to where a case ought to be tried on broad grounds of public policy: see Union Carbide Corporation Gas plant Disaster at Bhopal, and Piper Aircraft Co. v. Reyno.... [T]he Court is not equipped to conduct the kind of inquiry and assessment of the international as well as domestic implications that would be needed if it were to follow that approach." While this case limited the scope of *forum non conveniens*, the 2005 European Union Court decision in *Owusu v. Jackson*, C–281/02 [2005] E.C.R. 0, affects it use much more extensively. The EU Court found the use of the theory to be inconsistent with the U.K.'s obligations under the EU Regulation on Jurisdiction and the Recognition and Enforcement of Judgments in Civil and Commercial Matters (essentially superceding but often still referred to as the Brussels Convention) because the doctrine of *forum non conveniens* is incompatible with the legal certainty provided by the Brussels Convention that allows a defendant to foresee which courts in which he may be sued, other than the courts of his domicile. The Brussels Convention prohibits a court of a Contracting State from declining jurisdiction on the ground that a non-contracting state would be the more appropriate forum. The case involved a British national and domiciliary (Owusu) against another British domiciliary (Jackson) and other Jamaican defendants for an accident occurring at a Jamaican villa rented by Jackson to Owusu. The decision suggests that a U.K. court could not dismiss a matter brought by a U.S. plaintiff in a U.K. court on *forum non conveniens* grounds, a theory that is an important part of the law in both nations. The EU Court said that jurisdiction could not be declined "even if the jurisdiction of no other Contracting State is in issue or the proceedings have no connecting factors to any other Contracting State."

IN RE UNION CARBIDE CORPORATION GAS PLANT DISASTER AT BHOPAL, INDIA IN DECEMBER, 1984

United States Court of Appeals, Second Circuit, 1987.
809 F.2d 195.

Defendant in personal injury and wrongful death actions arising out of release of gas from chemical plant in Bhopal, India, sought to dismiss on grounds of forum non conveniens. The United States District Court for the Southern District of New York, granted the motion subject to certain conditions, and appeals were taken. [The conditions were: (1) consent to the jurisdiction of the courts of India and continue to waive defenses based on the statute of limitations, (2) agree to satisfy any judgment rendered by an Indian court against it and upheld on appeal, provided the judgment and affirmance "comport with the minimal requirements of due process," and (3) be subject to discovery under the Federal Rules of Civil Procedure of the United States.]

MANSFIELD, CIRCUIT JUDGE:

Judge Keenan dismissed the actions against UCC on grounds of *forum non conveniens* upon the conditions indicated above, after obtaining UCC's consent to those conditions subject to its right to appeal the order.

The first condition, that UCC consent to the Indian court's personal jurisdiction over it and waive the statute of limitations as a defense, are not unusual and have been imposed in numerous cases where the foreign court would not provide an adequate alternative in the absence of such a condition. The remaining two conditions, however, pose problems.

In requiring that UCC consent to enforceability of an Indian judgment against it, the district court proceeded at least in part on the erroneous assumption that, absent such a requirement, the plaintiffs, if they should succeed in obtaining an Indian judgment against UCC, might not be able to enforce it against UCC in the United States.

UCC contends that Indian courts, while providing an adequate alternative forum, do not observe due process standards that would be required as a matter of course in this country. As evidence of this apprehension it points to the haste with which the Indian court in Bhopal issued a temporary order freezing its assets throughout the world and the possibility of serious prejudice to it if the UOI is permitted to have the double and conflicting status of both plaintiff and co-defendant in the Indian court proceedings. It argues that we should protect it against such denial of due process by authorizing Judge Keenan to retain the authority, after *forum non conveniens* dismissal of the cases here, to monitor the Indian court proceedings and be available on call to rectify in some undefined way any abuses of UCC's right to due process as they might occur in India.

UCC's proposed remedy is not only impractical but evidences an abysmal ignorance of basic jurisdictional principles, so much so that it borders on the frivolous. The district court's jurisdiction is limited to proceedings before it in this country. Once it dismisses those proceedings on grounds of *forum non conveniens* it ceases to have any further jurisdiction over the matter unless and until a proceeding may some day be brought to enforce here a final and conclusive Indian money judgment. Nor could we, even if we attempted to retain some sort of supervisory jurisdiction, impose our due process requirements upon Indian courts, which are governed by their laws, not ours. The concept of shared jurisdictions is both illusory and unrealistic. The parties cannot simultaneously submit to both jurisdictions the resolution of the pre-trial and trial issues when there is only one consolidated case pending in one court. Any denial by the Indian courts of due process can be raised by UCC as a defense to the plaintiffs' later attempt to enforce a resulting judgment against UCC in this country.

We are concerned, however, that as it is written the district court's requirement that UCC consent to the enforcement of a final Indian judgment, which was imposed on the erroneous assumption that such a judgment might not otherwise be enforceable in the United States, may create misunderstandings and problems of construction. Although the

order's provision that the judgment "comport with the *minimal* requirements of due process" (emphasis supplied) probably is intended to refer to
"due process" as used in the New York Foreign Country Money Judgments Law and others like it, there is the risk that it may also be
interpreted as providing for a lesser standard than we would otherwise
require. Since the court's condition with respect to enforceability of any
final Indian judgment is predicated on an erroneous legal assumption and
its "due process" language is ambiguous, and since the district court's
purpose is fully served by New York's statute providing for recognition of
foreign-country money judgments, it was error to impose this condition
upon the parties.

We also believe that the district court erred in requiring UCC to
consent (which UCC did under protest and subject to its right of appeal) to
broad discovery of it by the plaintiffs under the Federal Rules of Civil
Procedure when UCC is confined to the more limited discovery authorized
under Indian law. We recognize that under some circumstances, such as
when a moving defendant unconditionally consents thereto or no undis-
covered evidence of consequence is believed to be under the control of a
plaintiff or co-defendant, it may be appropriate to condition a *forum non
conveniens* dismissal on the moving defendant's submission to discovery
under the Federal Rules without requiring reciprocal discovery by it of the
plaintiff. Basic justice dictates that both sides be treated equally, with
each having equal access to the evidence in the possession or under the
control of the other. Application of this fundamental principle in the
present case is especially appropriate since the UOI, as the sovereign
government of India, is expected to be a party to the Indian litigation,
possibly on both sides.

For these reasons we direct that the condition with respect to the
discovery of UCC under the Federal Rules of Civil Procedure be deleted
without prejudice to the right of the parties to have reciprocal discovery of
each other on equal terms under the Federal Rules, subject to such
approval as may be required of the Indian court in which the case will be
pending. If, for instance, Indian authorities will permit mutual discovery
pursuant to the Federal Rules, the district court's order, as modified in
accordance with this opinion, should not be construed to bar such procedure. In the absence of such a court-sanctioned agreement, however, the
parties will be limited by the applicable discovery rules of the Indian court
in which the claims will be pending.

As so modified the district court's order is affirmed.

QUESTIONS AND COMMENTS

1. Epiphytes is a foreign plaintiff coming to the United States to sue.
Would a U.S. plaintiff be entitled to any greater deference in choosing a U.S.
forum? Is the reasoning in *Piper* sound? Might it violate U.S. obligations
under Friendship, Commerce and Navigation treaties? What if there were
both Venezuelan and U.S. plaintiffs? Might the court dismiss the case as to
the Venezuelan plaintiffs but retain it as to the U.S. plaintiffs?

2. Is Venezuela an adequate and available forum under the test in *Piper*? Just what does adequate and available include? Should adequacy include whether the Venezuelan legal system is corrupt, inefficient and its judges subject to intimidation?

3. How might a court evaluate private and public interest factors? Is it clear which are private and which are public? Might a U.K. court after *Lubbe* characterize what might be prohibited public factors as private factors? It is too soon to determine the outcome in the United Kingdom from the *Owusu* decision. Should the EU Court have extended its dislike for *forum non conveniens* to cases between the United Kingdom and non-contracting parties?

4. Are there any conditions other than the ones mentioned in the *Bhopal* case that might be appropriate and pass appellate review? What about posting a bond to assure payment of a judgment? Or to agree that U.S. damages law shall apply in the foreign court? Or perhaps that it shall not be applied by the foreign court?

5. The *Republic of Bolivia* case is as serious as it is amusing. It reflects the concern of many U.S. courts about forum shopping in the United States by foreign plaintiffs. But wasn't Philip Morris in that case reverse forum shopping by trying to move it first to federal court in Texas, then to federal court in Washington, D.C., and probably subsequently trying to move it to Bolivia?

6. Does the theory of *forum non conveniens* make any sense in a globalized world? Does its use constitute judicial abdication of jurisdiction that had been conferred by Congress?

PART C. CHOICE OF LAW

The choice of law question may arise as part of the consideration of a *forum non conveniens* based motion to dismiss, because the court may feel the foreign forum is a more appropriate forum if the law of that foreign forum is the proper law. It may also arise if the case is not dismissed under *forum non conveniens* and the question then arises as to the proper law. Assume that the court denied the motion to dismiss based on *forum non conveniens*. The defendant Mott must now consider which law is more favorable to its case in each of the contract and tort claims. Problem 4.1 considered choice of law in the context of a Kansas seller and German buyer of insulation, first without considering the Convention on the International Sale of Goods (CISG), and then with the CISG applicable. In this problem the analysis would be similar. A U.S. court, considering the contract claims, will look to the UCC § 1–105. choice of law provisions, perhaps with the help of the Restatement, Conflicts of Law (Second) §§ 6 and 188. The revised UCC Article 1 replaces § 1–105 with § 1–301, eleven states have adopted the Revised Article 1, but no state has yet adopted the revision in § 1–301. A Venezuelan court addressing the contract issues would look to its own choice of law rules, found in its rules of private international law. Each such source allows the parties to make a choice, and each has guidance in the absence of a choice. As in problem 4.1, both parties are signatories to the CISG. Thus the contract issues would be governed by the CISG in the absence of an opting out of the CISG. This problem does not repeat the analysis of problem 4.1.

There is also a tort claim against Mott. The U.S. court will likely be asked by Mott to apply Venezuelan law because that is where the injury occurred. That is the application of *lex loci delicti*. Epiphytes is likely to counter with a request that U.S. law apply, based on allegations that the tort actually occurred in the United States, because that is where the Suregrow™ was designed, formulated, manufactured, processed and packaged. There may be allegations that insufficient instructions were written in the United States. Epiphytes needs to be successful on this issue if it hopes to have more favorable U.S. substantive law provisions apply, such as strict liability and punitive damages.

Thus, the first question for the court will be what is the proper law. If it is determined to be Venezuelan law, a second task is addressed—how is Venezuelan law to be determined by the court.

Rule 44.1 of the Federal Rules of Civil Procedure

A party who intends to raise an issue concerning the law of a foreign country shall give notice in his pleadings or other reasonable written notice. The court, in determining foreign law, may consider any relevant material or source, including testimony, whether or not submitted by a party or admissible under the federal Rules of Evidence. The court's determination shall be treated as a ruling on a question of law.

DAVID EPSTEIN, JEFFREY L. SNYDER & CHARLES S. BALDWIN, IV, INTERNATIONAL LITIGATION

§§ 9.01–9.06 (3d ed. 2002).*

Rule 44.1 is an endeavor to furnish the federal courts with a uniform and effective procedure for raising and determining an issue concerning the law of a foreign country. Prior to 1966, foreign law questions were regarded as questions of fact which had to be proved as such. Treating foreign law considerations as a question of fact meant that foreign law issues had to be raised in the pleadings and proven in accordance with the rules of evidence. It further encouraged courts to regard juries as the appropriate body to ascertain questions of foreign law, thus limiting appellate review of determinations of foreign law. . . .

Rule 44.1 provides that a "party who intends to raise an issue concerning the law of a foreign country shall give notice in his pleadings or other reasonable written notice."

The notes of the Advisory Committee on Rules state:

In some situations the pertinence of foreign law is apparent from the outset; accordingly the necessary investigation of that law will have been accomplished by the party at the pleading stage, and the notice can be given conveniently in the pleadings.

---

* Reprinted with the permission of Transnational Publishers, Inc.

The pleader, however, does not have to commit to the application of foreign law before pretrial discovery.

Any form of notice is sufficient provided there is no issue of "unfair surprise." Although foreign law materials may be considered at any time, a party should submit such evidence as early in the proceeding as possible, preferably in the district court and not at the appellate stage. In this connection it has been held that plaintiffs waived their right to rely on foreign law because the issue was not raised for the first time until the plaintiffs' motion for reconsideration.[10] Some courts have held that if a party fails to give reasonable written notice in the district court, it is precluded from raising the issue of foreign law on appeal.[11] Other courts have held that, absent special circumstances, the parties should present issues of foreign law in their appellate briefs at the latest.[12] Similarly, where a party fails to raise a foreign law issue prior to the issuance of a final order, it may have waived the foreign law issue on remand of the case to the trial court.[13]

Rule 44.1 permits the court, in determining foreign law, to consider any relevant material or source, including testimony, without regard to whether the material considered would be admissible under the rules of evidence. This liberal standard of proof is intended to make the process of determining foreign law identical, to the extent possible, with the methods of ascertaining domestic law. Thus, the court is free to accept any material presented by the parties, including extracts from foreign written sources and written or oral expert testimony, and to give whatever probative value, in the court's opinion, is deserved.

* * *

In considering "any relevant material or source ... whether or not submitted by a party" under Rule 44.1, a court has the choice of conducting its own research or insisting that counsel fully engage in this task.

Expert testimony is not a necessity in establishing foreign law, and a court may reach different conclusions based on an individual examination of foreign legal authorities. * * *

The use of affidavits or other written statements to present expert testimony on foreign law is more common than oral testimony in federal courts. Generally, translated copies of the relevant foreign law upon which the expert relies are attached to the affidavit?

The best method of proving foreign law (i.e, by documents or foreign law experts) undoubtedly depends on the availability of foreign law sources and the nature of the foreign law issue to be addressed. Although the assistance of foreign law experts is often essential, the need to use

---

10. Frietsch v. Refco, Inc., 56 F.3d 825, 828 (7th Cir.1995).

11. *See* Ruff v. St. Paul Mercury Ins. Co., 393 F.2d 500, 502 (2d Cir.1968).

12. *See* Stuart v. United States, 813 F.2d 243, 251 (9th Cir.1987), *revd on other grounds,* 489 U.S. 353 (1989).

13. Thyssen Steel Co. v. M/V Kavo Yerakas, 911 F.Supp. 263, 267–268 (S.D.Tex.1996).

them in every case has been questioned. As such, experts are not required to meet any special qualifications, and federal courts are not bound by their testimony and may reject their conclusions.

What are the consequences of a party's failure to provide evidence of foreign law where local choice of law rules provide that the case is governed by foreign law? * * * [W]hile under Rule 44.1 a court is still permitted to apply foreign law even if not requested to do so by a party, Rule 44.1 would allow the application of the law of the forum, where the parties had not asserted at trial that the foreign law applied with respect to underlying obligations involved on the part of the defendant. * * *

TWOHY v. FIRST NATIONAL BANK OF CHICAGO

United States Court of Appeals, Seventh Circuit, 1985.
758 F.2d 1185.

Stockholder in Spanish corporation brought action against bank for breach of contract, fraud, misrepresentation, and libel arising out of bank's failure to provide agreed-upon financing to corporation.

Cummings, Chief Judge.

Twohy, the majority shareholder and principal of Bevco Baleares, S.A. (hereinafter "Bevco"), a Spanish corporation, brought suit ... against the defendant, First National Bank of Chicago (hereinafter "First Chicago" or "the Bank"), a national banking association with its principal place of business in Chicago, Illinois. Plaintiff's claims arise out of a series of events involving an alleged loan transaction with the defendant that was to facilitate an expansion of Bevco's business in Spain to Mallorca and the Canary Islands.... Twohy charged breach of contract and counts of fraud, misrepresentation and libel.

First Chicago filed a "Motion for Judgment on the Pleaded Defenses" ... In support of the motion, the Bank attached the affidavits of Rolf K. Zion, an Assistant Vice–President of First Chicago stationed in Spain, and of James A. Baker, an attorney licensed to practice law in Illinois and Spain and an expert in Spanish law. ... The Baker affidavit opined that under Spanish conflict of law rules, Spanish law would govern the action and that under Spanish law ... "a shareholder, such as the plaintiff, has no right to proceed in contract, tort or libel on the alleged contract and alleged transaction of the corporation of which he is a shareholder", or in other words Twohy "has no standing to bring this complaint for the remedies alleged as a matter of law" The Baker affidavit contains no citations to authority of any kind to support the opinions contained therein.

[After the court denied the motion] First Chicago filed a motion for reconsideration. The motion ... took issue with Judge Leighton's claim that unresolved questions of fact remained in the case. As to the court's assertion that plaintiff could prove he personally contracted with defendant, First Chicago responded that plaintiff in his individual capacity only could assert an action for recovery of a broker's or finder's fee (but had not done so) and that plaintiff as a shareholder simply could not recover under Spanish law for injury and damages asserted in the complaint-injury to and harm suffered by the shareholder's corporation. In support of the motion for reconsideration, defendant filed a supplemental affidavit of Mr. Baker which stated that under Spanish law, Twohy, acting in his individual capacity, could not enter into a contract on behalf of Bevco and that even if Twohy had established an agency relationship with Bevco, any action arising out of the contract would belong solely to the corporation.

Plaintiff responded to the motion for reconsideration by filing the joint counter-affidavits of Antonio de Fortuny y Maynés and Valentín Molins Altarriba, licensed Spanish attorneys. The affidavits discussed issues of jurisdiction, venue, nationality, and citizenship of the parties and asserted that plaintiff Twohy had in fact stated a valid "personal action" ("acción personal") under Spanish law. The affidavits conceded that "between Mr. Twohy and the First National Bank of Chicago there was no contract" and asserted that plaintiff's claims were based on Spanish civil law, Article 1902 of Chapter 2cd, which states: "The person that by action or omission causes damages to another party with fault or negligence, is obliged to repair the damage". The affidavits also pointed out that under Spanish Civil Law, Article 1903 of the same Chapter, the acts of representatives of a person, such as directors and employees, may give rise to liability for that person under Article 1902. No authority apart from the statutes was cited in the affidavits to serve as a basis for Twohy's suit.

Defendant filed further supplemental affidavits of Mr. Baker and of Mr. Francisco J. Iglesias, another Spanish law expert, with its reply memorandum in support of the motion to reconsider. The memorandum and affidavits pointed out that the plaintiff's affidavits of Fortuny y Maynés and Molins focused solely on the liability of defendant and failed to address the so-called "standing" issue of whether Twohy was a proper plaintiff to bring the suit. . . . Finally, plaintiff filed further counter-affidavits of Fortuny y Maynés and Molins and reasserted that Twohy had commenced a valid personal claim under Article 1902 of Spanish civil law.

The trial court reconsidered its order and granted defendant's motion for judgment on the pleaded defenses. [T]he district court found: [t]hat the Pleaded Defenses raise only questions of law on this record; considering those questions of law in light of the applicable law, the Complaint does not state any claim which the Plaintiff has a right to bring in his personal capacity, nor is he personally entitled to any relief . . . . .

Plaintiff filed a . . . motion to amend the judgment to allow the filing of an amended complaint. The trial court entered an order denying the motion to amend. Plaintiff appeals both the dismissal of the case and the denial of his motion to amend the judgment.

II

The district court was correct in determining that the substantive law of Spain governed the action and that, as a matter of Spanish law, plaintiff failed to state a claim upon which relief could be granted.

CHOICE OF LAW

The district court did not specifically utilize the Illinois conflict of law principles to determine which law would govern the substantive issues of the case because the parties had expressly stipulated that the law of Spain would apply. We agree with the district court that the plaintiff did so stipulate, although Twohy later hedged his position.

Judge Leighton in his Judgment found that "all parties agree that the law of Spain controls [the action]." At a hearing he stated that "[e]vidently everybody agrees that the law of Spain controls," and asked both parties' counsel, "Is that correct?" Plaintiff's counsel replied affirmatively. Furthermore, plaintiff acted at all times consistently with the position taken at the hearing. Twohy filed counter-affidavits of Spanish law experts pursuant to seeking to contradict defendant's memorandum of law and the affidavits of its foreign law experts. Plaintiff also failed to contend at any time prior to judgment that Spanish law was inapplicable or that any other law governed the alleged contract dispute and injury arising out of it.

In plaintiff's motion to amend, Twohy asserted that his counsel's stipulation that Spanish law governed the case was incorrect and inadvertent, that plaintiff intended to bring the action at all times under the laws of the United States and that the attorney making the stipulation was acting only as his local counsel at the time and was unfamiliar with the legal issues of the case. Judge Leighton correctly rejected these arguments. The court characterized Twohy's use of the term "local counsel" ... as "misleading" and noted both the firm's status as plaintiff's only counsel of record and the absence of any indication that its authority was limited in any way during the early stages of litigation. The court further observed that plaintiff litigated the Spanish law questions raised by defendant and "never so much as suggested that any other law might apply."

... Here, the law of Spain bears a reasonable relationship to the alleged transaction and injury in question[2] and does not violate public policy nor call into question the court's subject matter jurisdiction.

... [I]t would be a waste of the court's resources and an inequity to allow plaintiff to return to the district court and attempt to show that some other law should govern this action and perhaps escape his stipulation.

DETERMINATION OF SPANISH LAW

The district court correctly determined the substance of Spanish law and held that it required dismissal of plaintiff's complaint. In his decision to dismiss, Judge Leighton focused on an inadequacy of the complaint

---

2. The law of Spain bears a significant relationship to or has significant contacts with the parties and alleged transaction and injury in this suit. The relationship of the parties was centered in Spain, the alleged injury occurred in Spain, and the alleged loan agreement was both negotiated in Spain and intended to be performed in Spain.

raised several times by defendant and its foreign law experts. The court ruled that Twohy was not entitled to sue in his individual capacity for injury to a corporation of which he was a shareholder, where plaintiff's sole relation with the corporation was as shareholder and principal. Judge Leighton found that the complaint alleged no injury to Twohy in his individual or personal capacity and, consequently, held that no question of fact was involved in the case and that plaintiff was not entitled to relief. . . . Plaintiff alleges injury in contract and tort to the Bevco business arising out of the defendant's alleged failure to provide agreed-upon financing. Although the pleading states that the defendant "destroyed plaintiff's ability to operate and expand his business" and "impaired plaintiff's ability to obtain financing from other banks," it alleges no injury apart from that suffered by the corporation. Indeed, in measuring his damages, Twohy describes the requested $1.125 million dollars as representing "profits that Bevco could reasonably have expected to realize had promised financing been provided". . . . The only charge that conceivably could be characterized as alleging harm to Twohy personally, apart from his shareholder's interest, is that First Chicago's conduct constituted libel and caused "injury to the business reputation of plaintiff" . . . Yet plaintiff asserted no harm to his ability to conduct business in Spain or elsewhere regarding activities apart from Bevco's business.

The question which remains is whether the district court was correct in determining that under Spanish law plaintiff could not maintain an action for injury to a corporation solely on the basis of his status as shareholder of the corporation. Our review under the appropriate standard convinces us that the lower court's determination was correct, although we cannot fully endorse the court's method of reaching its conclusion.

As noted previously, both parties submitted a series of affidavits of foreign law experts concerning issues of Spanish law relevant to the case, including the issue of a shareholder's right to sue. Plaintiff's experts, however, never directly responded to the defendant's challenge to Twohy's individual right to maintain an action. The Fortuny y Maynés and Molins affidavits, stating that an action exists under Spanish civil law providing that "The person that by action or omission causes damages to another party with fault or negligence, is obliged to repair the damage * * *", merely beg the question, as does the citation to Spanish law providing that acts of representatives of a person may subject that person to liability. . . .

Distinguished commentators have noted the benefits, and at times necessity, of independent research and analysis by courts on questions of foreign law. . . . The inadequacy in research . . . unfortunately is present in the instant case. Defendant's experts, attorneys practicing in Spain, opined from their personal knowledge that plaintiff's action is barred under Spanish law because, as is the rule in common law, shareholders of Spanish corporations may not sue for third party harms to the corporation in which they hold stock. Something more concrete might have been expected of defendant, and plaintiff has been quick to point out the lack of discussion of substantive law within and the conclusory nature of defendant's affidavits. Plaintiff's experts have fared no better in this matter, however, in view of their above-noted failure even to address the issue. Nor are we convinced that the district court fully met its duty to ascertain foreign law under Rule 44.1, although we recognize that investigating Spanish law on the relevant issue presents no simple task. Nothing in Rule 44.1 strictly requires a district judge to engage in private research. Under these circumstances, however, it would have been appropriate for the court to demand a more "complete presentation by counsel" on the issue.

The lower court's investigation of foreign law appears to have been limited to the district judge's understanding that Spanish law did not differ from the law of Illinois on the question of a shareholder's right to sue for a third party breach of a corporate contract: "And it is amazing when you look at it, how similar are the laws of the various countries— that is the civilized countries—of the world. . . . It is fundamental. The law of Spain, the civil law, the common law—one person cannot sue for injury to another person."

The court was correct in not dismissing plaintiff's claim merely because Twohy had failed to establish relevant controlling Spanish law . . . Under the circumstances, if the district court had decided not to request a more detailed presentation by counsel, before plaintiff's complaint properly could be dismissed, Rule 44.1 required a deeper inquiry into the law of Spain than that undertaken by the court below. Nevertheless, we are convinced that Spanish law does not permit plaintiff Twohy's action against First Chicago.

Under general principles of United States corporate law, as well as under Illinois law, a stockholder of a corporation has no personal or individual right of action against third persons for damages that result indirectly to the stockholder because of an injury to the corporation. Certain "often overlapping" exceptions to the general rule have been recognized such as where a special contractual duty exists between the wrongdoer and shareholder or where the shareholder suffers an injury separate and distinct from that suffered by other shareholders. Our inquiry . . . must focus on whether, as defendant's experts suggest, the law of Spain utilizes the same general rule regarding stockholder actions and whether similar or broader exceptions to the rule exist under Spanish law.

Comparative law studies of shareholder rights and shareholder suits indicate that the American rule barring shareholder damages actions arising out of corporate transactions with third parties has universal application among Western nations. . . . A major comparative law treatise describes the "non-interference rule" as follows: "The shareholder normally can only sue for damages other than that incurred by him because of the fact that the corporation has been hurt. The decrease in value in his shares is normally no[t a] sufficient basis for an individual cause of action." XIII International Encyclopedia of Comparative Law–Business and Private Organizations 4–256 (A. Conard ed. 1973). Spain is not cited as an exception to this general rule ... The law of the United States is singled out as allowing the most significant encroachment upon the general "non-interference rule." The Spanish system of civil law, in contrast, appears to follow the "non-interference rule" quite strictly.

The Spanish corporation, or "sociedad anónima" (S.A.) (more correctly referred to in English as a "joint stock company"), is "similar in all major respects to a United States corporation." Translations of the Spanish Code of Commerce and the Law for Joint Stock Companies confirm this point and indicate that shareholders in a joint stock company enjoy very limited rights regarding management of the company. Article 116 of the Code of Commerce provides that each commercial company "will have juridical personality in all its acts and contracts."

Plaintiff's suit does not fall within ... exceptions to the non-interference rule. More importantly, the description of these special standing situations as departures from the normal rule strongly indicates that Spanish law does not recognize a suit of the type plaintiff brought before the district court. Plaintiff failed to state a cognizable claim under Spanish law.

The judgment of the district court is AFFIRMED.

QUESTIONS AND COMMENTS

1. To what nation's law do the conflicts rules point for any contract issues in our case? For the tort claims? Is *lex loci delicti* the most appropriate basis for the choice of tort law?

2. Is the judge deemed to know foreign law as a U.S. judge is deemed to know U.S. law? Does proof of foreign law as a question of law differ significantly from proof of U.S. law as a question of law? Just how is foreign law proven?

3. In our hypothetical, would there be any justification for applying any law other than that of Venezuela or the United States? For the contract issue we are back to Problem 4.1, insulation from Kansas to Germany. Both Venezuela and the United States are parties to the CISG, which would be the substantive contract law in the absence of a decision to opt out of its application, probably in favor of either Venezuelan or U.S. law, as the agreement would state.

4. How important is the use of experts in proving foreign law? How would you select an expert on Venezuelan law? Would you want someone who can explain something about the civil law, and how many of its provisions seek to achieve the same goal, such as responsibility for breach of contract or negligent conduct?

5. The *Twohy* case involves a common problem in failing to distinguish between derivative and direct actions. If Twohy suffered injury distinct from that alleged to the corporation, Spanish law allows a number of causes of

action, including that mentioned under Article 1902, the basic provision for extracontractual (tort) liability in Spanish law. There might also have been actions based on unjust enrichment or deceit (simulación). The complaint should have been amended much sooner than after the judgment was rendered. Courts tend to be patient in allowing amendments in such cases when the direct causes arise out of the same facts as a possible derivative action.

6. Is there an international law of tort that might apply? Most nations place responsibility on a party for injury caused to another by way of negligence or fault. What about a tort that continued across borders, such as a kidnaping? Is there any customary international tort law to be applied? With regard to the contract issues we have some international law, the CISG. Furthermore, there are the UNIDROIT Principles of International Commercial Contracts. They have not been adopted as law but are often used in arbitration proceedings. Can there be a Lex Mercatoria when two different legal systems each has a legitimate claim?

PROBLEM 11.3　EXTRATERRITORIAL JURISDICTION AND DISCOVERY: ANTITRUST, AIR TRAVEL AND THE NORTH ATLANTIC

SECTION I.　THE SETTING

Skylow Airways is a Delaware corporation headquartered at Newark Airport which was formed to take advantage of the United States—European Union Open-Skies Aviation Agreement (effective March 2008) by operating transatlantic flights between New York and London. Skylow has obtained all United States and United Kingdom permits necessary to operate daily flights between those cities. Skylow has pursued a low-price, high volume marketing strategy. In its initial year of operation, Skylow averaged 80 percent seat utilization on its New York-London flights and earned an eight percent profit on gross revenues. Many of Skylow's passengers have been students and retired persons.

Skylow desires to expand its transatlantic services to include daily flights from Los Angeles direct to London. Executives from Skylow's principal and long established competitors, two British corporations and two United States corporations, met in London and decided:

(1) To match any price Skylow offered. The competitors believed this necessary to preserve their market share, even though in some cases it meant setting a price below cost. There were a considerable number of hostile comments against Skylow and some executives thought such action would "teach this new price cutter a lesson."

(2) To contact Skylow's bankers and plane manufacturers. The executives agreed that they would point out the precarious financial position of new airlines in general and that because they were willing to match Skylow's prices, it was unlikely that Skylow would be able to survive for very long. They further agreed to suggest that bankers

would be wise to consider carefully and even oppose Skylow's requests for loans for acquiring new planes or for refinancing previous loans. Several executives suggested that they would tactfully remind the bankers and plane manufacturers that they (the two British and two United States airlines) were important clients.

These decisions have been consistently carried out for the past several months.

Skylow filed a private action in federal district court against the four competitors for treble damages under the antitrust laws of the United States. Skylow alleges that its competitors' actions constitute restraints of trade and conspiracies to monopolize the New York—London and New York—Los Angeles air passenger markets in violation of the Sherman Act (15 U.S.C.A. §§ 1, 2).

One British defendant has announced that the complaint is yet another "arrogant example of United States extraterritorial jurisdiction in violation of international law." That defendant did not answer Skylow's complaint and a default judgment for $1,000,000, trebled to $3,000,000, has been rendered against it. The other defendants have denied Skylow's allegations and seek to forestall discovery of documents relating to their executives' meeting in London and any depositions of those executives. The remaining British defendant has asked for protection under the United Kingdom Protection of Trading Interests Act of 1980.

SECTION II. FOCUS OF CONSIDERATION

The application of United States antitrust laws to foreign-based corporations, and activities undertaken outside the territorial limits of the United States, is but one example of the "extraterritorial" reach of many types of national or supranational laws. Despite a general presumption against extraterritoriality (see EEOC v. Arabian American Oil Co., 499 U.S. 244, 111 S.Ct. 1227, 113 L.Ed.2d 274 (1991)), other examples could be drawn from U.S. criminal, securities, labor, tax or trademark law. And there is growing body of European Union extraterritorial competition law. We previously looked at similar issues concerning United States export controls, boycott law, and conservation laws.

This problem focuses on the differing perspectives of the United States and the United Kingdom on issues of extraterritoriality, the practical difficulties of successfully asserting jurisdiction and obtaining discovery from foreign defendants to United States antitrust actions in the face of foreign "blocking statutes" like the U.K. Protection of Trading Interest Act of 1980, and the risk of multiple antitrust liabilities in international business activities are also central to this problem. The readings include a discussion of possible solutions to extraterritorial discovery and antitrust law disputes, notably the European Union–United States cooperation agreements.

Reference generally on U.S. and European antitrust law to R. Folsom, M. Gordon and J.A. Spanogle, *Principles of International Business Trans-*

actions 2d (West Concise Hornbook Series, 2010), Chapter 20, is recommended. Web resources for further study include international antitrust coverage at *www.usdoj.gov.* and competition law coverage at *www.europa. eu.*

SECTION III. READINGS, QUESTIONS AND COMMENTS

SHERMAN ACT (1890)

15 U.S.C.A. § 1, 2 and 7.

An act to protect trade and commerce against unlawful restraints and monopolies.

Sec. 1.   Every contract, combination in the form of trust or otherwise, or conspiracy, in restraint of trade or commerce among the several States, or with foreign nations, is declared to be illegal. Every person who shall make any contract or engage in any combination or conspiracy hereby declared to be illegal shall be deemed guilty of a felony and, on conviction thereof, shall be punished by fine not exceeding $10,000,000 if a corporation, or, if any other person, $350,000, or by imprisonment not exceeding three years, or by both said punishments, in the discretion of the court.

Sec. 2.   Every person who shall monopolize, or attempt to monopolize, or combine or conspire with any other person or persons, to monopolize any part of the trade or commerce among the several States, or with foreign nations, shall be deemed guilty of a felony, and, on conviction thereof, shall be punished by fine not exceeding $10,000,000 if a corporation, or, if any other person, $350,000, or by imprisonment not exceeding three years, or by both said punishments, in the discretion of the court.

* * *

Sec. 7.   [FTAIA*] This Act shall not apply to conduct involving trade or commerce (other than import trade or import commerce) with foreign nations unless—

(1) such conduct has a direct, substantial, and reasonably foreseeable effect—

(A) on trade or commerce which is not trade or commerce with foreign nations, or on import trade or import commerce with foreign nations; or

(B) on export trade or export commerce with foreign nations, of a person engaged in such trade or commerce in the United States; and

(2) such effect gives rise to a claim under the provisions of this Act, other than this section.

---

* Foreign Trade Antitrust Improvements Act of 1982.

If this Act applies to such conduct only because of the operation of paragraph (1)(B), then this Act shall apply to such conduct only for injury to export business in the United States.

FOX, EXTRATERRITORIALITY IN THE AGE OF GLOBALIZATION; CONFLICT AND COMITY IN THE AGE OF *EMPAGRAN*

4 Matthew Bender Antitrust Report 3 (2005).*

We must "help[] the potentially conflicting laws of different nations work together in harmony—a harmony particularly needed in today's highly interdependent commercial world."

Justice Breyer, *F. Hoffmann-La Roche v. Empagran S.A.*[1]

Empagran was a road mark in antitrust jurisprudence. In *Empagran*, the Court construed broadly the scope of a statutory cutback of Sherman Act jurisdiction over trade involving foreign commerce, on grounds of not treading on trading partners' toes. Extolling the virtues of restraint in an interdependent world, *Empagran* seems to have given new life to the doctrine of negative comity.

Negative comity (retreat and restraint) complements a twin pillar—convergence of law. Convergence of law reduces conflict substantively. Negative comity reduces conflict by withdrawal. It may be argued that negative comity and convergence are the principal answers to the multitudinous discontinuities in the application of antitrust laws by the nearly 100 antitrust jurisdictions of the world.

* * *

ALCOA TO THE FTAIA

Alcoa, decided in 1945,[9] gave birth to the effects doctrine. It fell at the cusp of the era in which the United States recognized the need to control offshore cartels to protect Americans. The problem was that competition was not widely embraced as the rule of trade, and cartels were legal abroad. The home nations of the cartelists complained. The United States held its ground, and was exonerated only some forty years later when most of the world accepted the paradigm of markets and realized that they too, in a globalized world, needed effects jurisdiction to protect themselves. From the vantage of the twenty-first century, the utility of the effects doctrine is clear. Were there not an effects doctrine, either the whole world would now be cartelized or we would long since have adopted an international law against cartels.

---

1. F. Hoffmann-LaRoche Ltd. v. Empagran S.A., 124 S.Ct. 2359, 2366 (2004).

9. United States v. Aluminum Co. of America, 148 F.2d 416 (2d Cir. 1945).

The 1960s and 1970s brought other efforts and concerns. On the one hand, antitrust was seen as a moral imperative and U.S. courts were not reluctant to require American firms to behave abroad as they had to behave at home. Some courts decreed that the U.S. antitrust laws followed U.S. firms in foreign markets. *Industria Siciliana Asfalti*[10] was a case in point. On the other hand, as for in-bound commerce, there was continued resistance by trading partners to the application of U.S. law to condemn acts done on their home territories that were lawful where done. The voices of resistance, often led by the United Kingdom, produced U.S. court decisions that seemed to soften the unbending U.S. position that U.S. law applies to foreigners that directly, substantially, and foreseeably hurt the American market. *Timberlane*[11] and *Mannington Mills*[12] heralded negative comity: if the foreign concerns outbalanced the U.S. interests, the court might either declare that it had no jurisdiction or exercise discretion to dismiss the case. The softening, however, was almost entirely rhetorical. In not one instance in which there was in fact antitrust harm in the United States did a court dismiss a case on grounds of comity or lack of subject matter jurisdiction.

The line of cases eventually led to *Hartford Fire* (1993),[13] in which Lloyds of London reinsurance firms were accused of conspiring to cut back reinsurance coverage in the United States and of using a boycott to pressure the cutback. The U.K. defendants moved for dismissal on the basis of comity, noting that the United Kingdom gave the power of self regulation to Lloyds of London to assure the financial soundness of the "London market," that U.K./Lloyds of London maintained a pervasive system of regulation, that the challenged acts of the U.K. firms were legal in the United Kingdom, and that, therefore, there was a conflict between U.S. and UK law that required dismissal. The Supreme Court disagreed, stating simply that the defendants intended to affect and did affect the U.S. market, and there was no cognizable conflict warranting dismissal because the U.K. firms could follow the Sherman Act without violating U.K. law.

Meanwhile, the famous statute intervened. Largely to answer the complaints of American business that U.S. antitrust law should not follow them into foreign markets, for it was handicapping them at a time (the early 1980s) when they particularly needed to enhance their efficiencies and become more competitive in world markets, Congress enacted the Foreign Trade Antitrust Improvements Act of 1982 ("FTAIA"). The FTAIA, no model of clarity, accomplished one thing clearly: to the extent that the U.S. law held American firms accountable for their harms in, into and to foreign markets, it no longer did so. When in Rome, or when selling

---

10. Industria Siciliana Asfalti, Bitumi, S.p.A. v. Exxon Research & Eng'g Co., 1977 WL 1353 (S.D.N.Y. Jan. 18, 1977).

11. Timberlane Lumber Co. v. Bank of America, 549 F.2d 597 (9th Cir. 1976).

12. Mannington Mills, Inc. v. Congoleum Corp., 595 F.2d 1287 (3d Cir. 1979).

13. Hartford Fire Ins. Co. v. California, 509 U.S. 764 (1993).

into Rome, it was fine to do what the Romans did (to Romans). It was not necessary to follow, also, the U.S. law.

The U.S. legislators, however, had a hard time drafting this legislation, and decided to parse the problem in the following way. They would be clear that conduct involving imports was not affected by the cutback. It was outside of the statute. Conduct involving imports would continue to be analyzed under existing principles, which were normally understood to recognize jurisdiction where the U.S. effect was direct, substantial, and reasonably foreseeable. Then Congress tackled "all other conduct" involving trade with foreign nations. "All other conduct" was conceived and debated largely in terms of exports, not world cartels, which usually involve imports. The main point was to make clear that export conduct was beyond the reach of the Sherman Act if it hurt only foreigners; that is, if export associations' foreign restraints did not unreasonably and anticompetitively exclude other Americans, as in the *Alkalai* case, and if export cartels did not have a ratchet-back effect into the United States, hurting American consumers. Therefore, "all other conduct" was placed beyond the reach of the Sherman Act unless it had a direct, substantial, and reasonably foreseeable effect on U.S. commerce.

During the drafting and debate, a concern was raised that the FTAIA might be used as a hook for expanded extraterritorial jurisdiction. One might launch a Sherman Act challenge against non-import conduct that had an anticompetitive effect only abroad but that did have an effect of some unrelated sort on U.S. commerce such as saving or destroying jobs. Moreover, U.S. exporters blocked from foreign markets by U.S. export association restraints (the *Alkali* case) might claim that the FTAIA gave them a cause of action (because the FTAIA excluded from the cutback actions by exporters injured in their export business), even while, under the case law, the substantive merits of this claim was becoming increasingly doubtful. To make clear that no jurisdictional hook or bootstrap was intended, Congress added to the FTAIA what is now paragraph (2): "such effect [the direct, substantial and reasonably foreseeable effect on domestic commerce or export trade] [must] give[] rise to a claim under the provisions of [the Sherman Act], other than this section." Thus, the jurisdictional effect must be an anticompetitive effect proscribed by Section 1 or 2 of the Sherman Act. No one challenged this meaning for many years.

Meanwhile, on another tack, globalization produced a global imperative rising above the narrower horizontal (nation-to-nation) perspective. This meant looking outward and appreciating a more nearly borderless world. Nations began to understand that proper antitrust enforcement in global markets would naturally and legitimately involve multiple enforcers (in the absence of law at a higher level); and it required vision beyond borders, and cooperation to achieve common and synergistic goals. Beginning in 1991 with the U.S./EU Cooperation Agreement and then numerous bilateral agreements following this model, nations pledged not only to inform their trading partners of proceedings that may affect their partners' interests and to exercise restraint in proper cases, but also to come to the aid of one another especially when the requested agency was better placed to challenge a violation that harmed a cross-jurisdictional marketplace. The positive comity (coming to the aid) aspects were enshrined in the U.S./EU 1998 Cooperation Agreement, in which voluntary procedures were put into place to require that each party notify its partner of suspected violations occurring principally on its soil, provide information concerning the violation, and withhold its own enforcement during such time as the requested party was proceeding apace to challenge and remedy the violation.

Beginning at least in this period, from the mid-1980s, antitrust agencies began to wear "cosmopolitan" hats. They understood the dangers of a narrow nationalistic vision. They (but not their politicians) accepted the perspective that firms do not "belong" to countries; that national industrial policy (e.g., facilitating market power of national champions) undermines world economic welfare and is bad for the world. The idea that one nation should exercise restraint and not attack a cartel because the home nation of the cartelists championed their behavior as good for the home country was now seen as anti-antitrust rather than welcome good citizenship. Negative comity, which often entails retreat by one nation in the face of nationalism by another, seemed to be giving way to positive comity and cosmopolitanism.

EMPAGRAN

The *Empagran* story begins several years before the case itself came before the Supreme Court. The days of antitrust were heady. On the cusp of the millennium, the antitrust community united to condemn world cartels, which were identified as the number one enemy to consumer welfare. On podiums from New York to London to Fiesoli to Berlin to Tokyo to Jakarta, the antitrust enforcers of the world agreed: cartels are hurtful, cartels are wrong. Collaborative initiatives were organized to track them down and stamp them out.

This new or at least tighter consensus gave inspiration to plaintiffs and their lawyers. Several actions were brought in the courts of the United States (home of treble damages, class actions, broad discovery, and the Alien Torts Claims Act), alleging that cartels violate the human rights of consumers; that, in view of the world consensus, customary international law condemns cartels, and that the U.S. Alien Torts Claims Act provides a jurisdictional vehicle for suits against cartelists wherever in the world they work their harm. These allegations appeared in complaints on behalf of alleged classes of cartel victims who made their purchases abroad, e.g., in tobacco cases, in the auction houses cases, in cases against Microsoft, and in the case of the worldwide vitamins conspiracy. The plaintiffs simultaneously sued under the Sherman Act. All of the customary international law claims were dismissed. This was an argument before its time. But the Sherman Act claims remained to be contested. By the time the price-fixers of vitamins sought certiorari in the U.S. Supreme

Court to review the D.C. Court of Appeals' holding that the FTAIA did not deprive the courts of subject matter jurisdiction over the foreign plaintiffs' suits, there was a conflict of circuits on the point. The Supreme Court stepped in to resolve the question.

The *Empagran* plaintiffs were direct purchasers of price-fixed vitamins. They were companies from Australia, Ecuador, Panama, and the Ukraine. They bought their vitamins at sites outside of the United States. Defendants moved to dismiss their case on the basis of subject matter jurisdiction. * * *

The future of negative comity

The second set of issues emanating from *Empagran* relates to comity. *Empagran* takes a strong position in favor of the use of comity. The Supreme Court said:

> We conclude that principles of prescriptive comity counsel against the Court of Appeals' interpretation of the FTAIA. Where foreign anticompetitive conduct plays a significant role and where foreign injury is independent of domestic effects, Congress might have hoped that America's antitrust laws, so fundamental a component of our own economic system, would commend themselves to other nations as well. But, if America's antitrust policies could not win their own way in the international marketplace for such ideas, Congress, we must assume, would not have tried to impose them, in an act of legal imperialism, through legislative fiat.

These are strong words, and they are curious words. America's cartel policies have, 98 percent, won their way in the international marketplace. Cartel deterrence as a goal is accepted in the world. We are quibbling about how to deter cartels. If applied literally and retrospectively, the quoted passage would require reversals in a long line of cases in which U.S. principles had much more clearly failed to win their way into the international marketplace of the time, including *Alcoa*, the uranium cartel cases, and *Hartford Fire*. Indeed, as applied to *Hartford,* the quoted passage would not tolerate either of the two statutory interpretations that the *Hartford* Court endorsed—the embrace of Sherman Act jurisdiction in the face of conflicting U.K. regulation and the refusal to apply to the London reinsurers a reciprocal McCarran-Ferguson Act (insurance) antitrust exemption such as that enjoyed by the London firms' American partners.

The *Empagran* Court applied prescriptive comity—asking what Congress proscribed, rather than judicial comity—asking whether a court should exercise discretion to withhold jurisdiction. One might, however, understand the spirit of the opinion to embrace comity wherever appropriate in order to "take account of the legitimate sovereign interests of other nations" and thereby help the multitudinous and often overlapping laws "work together in harmony." The sentiment is admirable. In practice, however, the embrace of comity as articulated in *Empagran* has limits.

First, in *Empagran,* the rhetoric is stronger than the delivery. The case purports to restrict the scope of U.S. law in order to accommodate the interests of our trading partners. It conveys a sense of moving away from American unilateralism and toward accommodation. However pleasing to European and other friends, this suggestion is an illusion. The Court obviously believed that it gave up nothing of value to America. While plaintiffs argued that the sword-of-Damocles of worldwide treble damages would be an important deterrent of world cartels that harmed Americans, the U.S. Justice Department made the opposite argument—that hosting worldwide treble damage suits would deter whistle-blowers from coming forward, undermine detection, and undermine deterrence. As noted, the Supreme Court did not decide the empirical question, but it called resolution of the question unimportant and clearly did not believe that its ruling undermined deterrence and hurt Americans.

The telling case would have been one in which experts were of one voice in concluding that worldwide treble damages would contribute significantly to deterrence of cartels that hurt Americans, but nonetheless the U.S. courts rejected a more robust and at least equally plausible reading of the FTAIA so as not to undermine our neighbors' choice of single damage remedies. But American courts have never made the choice to withhold application of our antitrust laws when America's ox would be gored.

Second, comity is a doctrine of reciprocity; of mutual restraint. It implies: I will refrain from hurting you if you will refrain from hurting me. Like equity, it is a doctrine of unpredictable dimensions, and, therefore, may lessen the clarity and certainty of the law.

Third, and most important, restraint is often likely to be a retreat from doing what is right in the interests of competition and consumer welfare, both globally and nationally. If Judge Learned Hand had restrained himself from legally condemning the aluminum cartel, this would not have been good for the world. The global perspective would not ask what bargain might be struck between the United States and (e.g.) the United Kingdom or Japan. It would ask what set of arrangements is likely to enhance world economic or consumer welfare by deterring cartels. If inclusive jurisdiction better deters world cartels than narrow jurisdiction, this fact should influence the choice between alternative statutory constructions, and indeed is a much more appropriate factor than is the mere fact of opposition to jurisdiction by another sovereign. Japan, for example, opposed jurisdiction for fear that the Japanese cartelists would be saddled with too much liability for their crimes. Other countries, likewise, may plead on behalf of their producers, not their consumers. In a world in which markets customarily extend beyond borders, the primary motivating concept should not rightly be negative comity (retreat) but a higher-level inquiry: how do the pieces fit together to improve economic welfare? The word "extraterritoriality," with its connotation of illegitimate intrusion, should be replaced by a concept that conveys a common enterprise to expand vision at least as far as the true boundaries of any market and thereby to maximize the common interest.

* * *

KAHN, THE PROTECTION OF TRADING INTERESTS ACT OF 1980: BRITAIN'S RESPONSE TO U.S EXTRATERRITORIAL ANTITRUST ENFORCEMENT

2 Northwestern J. Int'l Law & Bus. 476 (1980).*

The impetus for the British Protection of Trading Interests Act is directly traceable to the protracted *Westinghouse* uranium cartel litigation which began in 1975.[36] This litigation provoked Britain and the other countries whose nationals were defendants. The disputed issues are best understood through a brief summary of the litigation.

In 1975, twenty-seven separate suits were brought against the Westinghouse Electric Corporation for breaching contracts to supply uranium to electric utility companies. Westinghouse responded *inter alia* with a defense of commercial impracticability arising from an international uranium producers cartel, consisting of corporations from Canada, Britain, South Africa and Australia. This cartel allegedly denied Westinghouse access to supplies and conspired to raise the market price of uranium, which had increased eightfold. To sustain its commercial impracticability defense, Westinghouse sought to produce thousands of documents located abroad by utilizing the letters rogatory procedure. Both the Canadian and Australian courts refused to honor the letters of request, referring to the discretionary nature of this procedure and the existence of domestic laws and policies which conflicted with disclosure.

Unlike its Australian and Canadian counterparts, however, the High Court of England gave effect to the letters rogatory, pursuant to the Hague Convention on the Taking of Evidence Abroad in Civil and Commercial Matters, to which both Britain and the United States are signatories. The parties and corporations named in the letters refused to testify, claiming privilege under the fifth amendment to the U.S. Constitution and comparable E.E.C. and British safeguards. In an unusual step, the U.S. Department of Justice assured the presiding U.S. district court judge that since the evidence requested by the letters rogatory might be indispensable to a grand jury investigation of the uranium cartel underway in Washington, the witnesses' testimony would be immunized from use in criminal prosecution in the United States. The British defendants appealed to the House of Lords, both as to the appellate court's order that the letters be effectuated and as to their entitlement to immunity from testifying under the fifth amendment privilege. On several grounds, the House of Lords denied effect to the letters. That decision discouraged any

---

* Reprinted by special permission of the Northwestern Journal of International Law and Business, © by Northwestern University School of Law, Vol. 2, No. 2.

36. *In re Westinghouse Elec. Corp. Uranium Contracts Litigation*, 405 F.Supp. 316 (J.P.M.D.L. 1975). *See Westinghouse Elec. Corp. v. Rio Algom Ltd.*, 617 F.2d 1248 (7th Cir.1980); * * *.

further attempts by Westinghouse to obtain documents in the breach of contract action.

The activities of the international uranium cartel also formed the basis of a separate antitrust action lodged by Westinghouse in October 1976 against twelve foreign and seventeen domestic uranium producers. In this case, nine of the twelve foreign defendants rejected outright the personal jurisdiction of the U.S. district court by failing to appear or otherwise reply to Westinghouse's complaint. Final default judgments were entered against these firms in January 1979 and temporary restraining orders were imposed on their wholly owned U.S. subsidiaries that required the firms to give notice to the court twenty days before assets exceeding $10,000 could be transferred out of the country. Upon appeal, the Seventh Circuit Court of Appeals upheld the default judgments and the temporary restraining orders. The court stayed a determination of damages against the defaulters pending judgment as to the non-defaulting defendants, unless Westinghouse decided to drop claims against the answering defendants.

Of the active defendants, ten were ordered to produce documents situated abroad. Upon their refusal to comply, the district judge ordered the disclosure of these documents, despite the existence of foreign statutes imposing criminal penalties for disclosing the information. Rejecting a balancing approach advocated by several defendants, the court maintained that "[i]t is simply impossible to judicially 'balance' [the] total contradictory and mutually negating actions" of the United States and the foreign countries to determine which interest predominates. Additionally, by demonstrating to the defendants that they were not immune from sanctions for noncompliance, the court hoped to induce the defendants to take affirmative steps towards securing the documents.

The *Westinghouse* litigation * * * has already provoked widespread controversy and resulted in the modification or enactment of five foreign statutes, the most important of which is the British Protection of Trading Interests Act. The *Westinghouse* case is not the first extraterritorial antitrust suit against multinational defendants to arouse foreign antipathy. There are three reasons, however, for *Westinghouse's* extraordinary effect.

First, Westinghouse threatens the survival of industries critical to the well-being of foreign nations. The plaintiffs are seeking treble damages under the Clayton Act, which could amount to six billion dollars. This award would devastate Australia's uranium industry and injure that of Britain, Canada, and South Africa. By providing for treble damages, Congress intended the antitrust laws to be prophylactic and sought to encourage private attorneys general to prosecute violations. Foreign governments, however, have long protested that such damages, which are uniquely American, are penal and hence, should not be available to private plaintiffs.

Second, each of the foreign courts which received letters rogatory suggested that the substance of the requests and possibly the purpose for which they were intended as well, constituted an attempt to abuse this procedure. Extensive use of pretrial discovery in the United States has no foreign counterpart. Even in a noncontroversial case, a foreign court will deny the release of information that would not be similarly available to litigants in that country. Additionally, in the *Westinghouse* suit, national security considerations have made foreign governments particularly unwilling to allow the disclosure of documents or information on uranium production and marketing arrangements. Furthermore, the British courts, which initially were amenable to the letters of request, ultimately refused to compel either the required testimony or production of the documents because the Justice Department's intervention to immunize the parties' testimony was deemed to have transformed the private civil proceedings into a criminal proceeding. The House of Lords concluded its opinion by finding "that the attempt to extend the grand jury investigation extraterritorially into the activities of the [British] companies was an infringement of United Kingdom sovereignty." [83]

Third, the defaulting foreign defendants may be held liable for satisfying all of Westinghouse's alleged damages, since antitrust defendants are jointly and severally liable, and their failure to contest the complaint is construed as an admission. The appeal of the active defendants to the Seventh Circuit prevented the district court from holding an immediate hearing to set damages, but the district court's judgment as to the defaulters was upheld. Thus, regardless of the outcome on the merits for the active defendants, the defaulters will remain liable. Moreover, the temporary restraining order imposed on their American subsidiaries to impede the transfer of certain assets outside the country, ensures that execution on a future damage award will not be totally frustrated. * * *

THE PROTECTION OF TRADING INTERESTS ACT 1980 [U.K.]

Ch. 11.

An Act to provide protection from requirements, prohibitions and judgments imposed or given under the laws of countries outside the United Kingdom and affecting the trading or other interests of persons in the United Kingdom

1. Overseas Measures Affecting United Kingdom Trading Interests

(1) If it appears to the Secretary of State—

(a) that measures have been or are proposed to be taken by or under the law of any overseas country for regulating or controlling international trade; and

---

83. [1978] 2 W.L.R. at 93.

(*b*) that those measures, in so far as they apply or would apply to things done or to be done outside the territorial jurisdiction of that country by persons carrying on business in the United Kingdom, are damaging or threaten to damage the trading interests of the United Kingdom,

the Secretary of State may by order direct that this section shall apply to those measures either generally or in their application to such cases as may be specified in the order.

(2) The Secretary of State may by order make provision for requiring, or enabling the Secretary of State to require, a person in the United Kingdom who carries on business there to give notice to the Secretary of State of any requirement or prohibition imposed or threatened to be imposed on that person pursuant to any measures in so far as this section applies to them by virtue of an order under subsection (I) above.

(3) The Secretary of State may give to any person in the United Kingdom who carries on business there such directions for prohibiting compliance with any such requirement or prohibition as aforesaid as he considers appropriate for avoiding damage to the trading interests of the United Kingdom.

(4) The power of the Secretary of State to make orders under subsection (I) or (2) above shall be exercisable by statutory instrument subject to annulment in pursuance of a resolution of either House of Parliament.

(5) Directions under subsection (3) above may be either general or special and may prohibit compliance with any requirement or prohibition either absolutely or in such cases or subject to such conditions as to consent or otherwise as may be specified in the directions; and general directions under that subsection shall be published in such manner as appears to the Secretary of State to be appropriate.

(6) In this section "trade" includes any activity carried on in the course of a business of any description and "trading interests" shall be construed accordingly.

2. Documents and Information Required by Overseas Courts and Authorities

(1) If it appears to the Secretary of State—

(*a*) that a requirement has been or may be imposed on a person or persons in the United Kingdom to produce to any court, tribunal or authority of an overseas country any commercial document which is not within the territorial jurisdiction of that country or to furnish any commercial information to any such court, tribunal or authority; or

(*b*) that any such authority has imposed or may impose a requirement on a person or persons in the United Kingdom to publish any such document or information, the Secretary of State may, if it appears to him that the requirement is inadmissible by virtue of subsection (2) or (3) below, give directions for prohibiting compliance with the requirement.

(2) A requirement such as is mentioned in subsection (I)(*a*) or (*b*) above is inadmissible—

(*a*) if it infringes the jurisdiction of the United Kingdom or is otherwise prejudicial to the sovereignty of the United Kingdom; or

(*b*) if compliance with the requirement would be prejudicial to the security of the United Kingdom or to the relations of the government of the United Kingdom with the government of any other country.

(3) A requirement such as is mentioned in subsection (I)(*a*) above is also inadmissible—

(*a*) if it is made otherwise than for the purposes of civil or criminal proceedings which have been instituted in the overseas country; or

(*b*) if it requires a person to state what documents relevant to any such proceedings are or have been in his possession, custody or power or to produce for the purposes of any such proceedings any documents other than particular documents specified in the requirement.

(4) Directions under subsection (I) above may be either general or special and may prohibit compliance with any requirement either absolutely or in such cases or subject to such conditions as to consent or otherwise as may be specified in the directions; and general directions under that subsection shall be published in such manner as appears to the Secretary of State to be appropriate.

(5) For the purposes of this section the making of a request or demand shall be treated as the imposition of a requirement if it is made in circumstances in which a requirement to the same effect could be or could have been imposed; and

(*a*) any request or demand for the supply of a document or information which, pursuant to the requirement of any court, tribunal or authority of an overseas country, is addressed to a person in the United Kingdom; or

(*b*) any requirement imposed by such a court, tribunal or authority to produce or furnish any document or information to a person specified in the requirement,

shall be treated as a requirement to produce or furnish that document or information to that court, tribunal or authority.

(6) In this section "commercial document" and "commercial information" mean respectively a document or information relating to a business of any description and "document" includes any record or device by means of which material is recorded or stored.

3. Offences Under ss. 1 and 2

(1) Subject to subsection (2) below, any person who without reasonable excuse fails to comply with any requirement imposed under subsection (2) of section I above or knowingly contravenes any directions given under subsection (3) of that section or section 2(I) above shall be guilty of an offence and liable—

(*a*) on conviction on indictment, to a fine;

(*b*) on summary conviction, to a fine not exceeding the statutory maximum.

(2) A person who is neither a citizen of the United Kingdom and Colonies nor a body corporate incorporated in the United Kingdom shall not be guilty of an offence under subsection (I) above by reason of anything done or omitted outside the United Kingdom in contravention of directions under section I(3) or 2(I) above.

(3) No proceedings for an offence under subsection (I) above shall be instituted in England, Wales or Northern Ireland except by the Secretary of State or with the consent of the Attorney General or, as the case may be, the Attorney General for Northern Ireland.

(4) Proceedings against any person for an offence under this section may be taken before the appropriate court in the United Kingdom having jurisdiction in the place where that person is for the time being.

* * *

4. Restriction of Evidence (Proceedings in Other Jurisdictions) Act 1975

A court in the United Kingdom shall not make an order under section 2 of the Evidence (Proceedings in Other Jurisdictions) Act 1975 for giving effect to a request issued by or on behalf of a court or tribunal of an overseas country if it is shown that the request infringes the jurisdiction of the United Kingdom or is otherwise prejudicial to the sovereignty of the United Kingdom; and a certificate signed by or on behalf of the Secretary of State to the effect that it infringes that jurisdiction or is so prejudicial shall be conclusive evidence of that fact.

5. Restriction on Enforcement of Certain Overseas Judgments

(1) A judgment to which this section applies shall not be registered under Part II of the Administration of Justice Act 1920 or Part I of the Foreign Judgments (Reciprocal Enforcement) Act 1933 and no court in the United Kingdom shall entertain proceedings at common law for the recovery of any sum payable under such a judgment.

(2) This section applies to any judgment given by a court of an overseas country, being—

(*a*) a judgment for multiple damages within the meaning of subsection (3) below;

(b) a judgment based on a provision or rule of law specified or described in an order under subsection (4) below and given after the coming into force of the order; or

(c) a judgment on a claim for contribution in respect of damages awarded by a judgment falling within paragraph (a) or (b) above.

(3) In subsection (2)(a) above a judgment for multiple damages means a judgment for an amount arrived at by doubling, trebling or otherwise multiplying a sum assessed as compensation for the loss or damage sustained by the person in whose favour the judgment is given.

(4) The Secretary of State may for the purposes of subsection (2)(b) above make an order in respect of any provision or rule of law which appears to him to be concerned with the prohibition or regulation of agreements, arrangements or practices designed to restrain, distort or restrict competition in the carrying on of business of any description or to be otherwise concerned with the promotion of such competition as aforesaid.

(5) The power of the Secretary of State to make orders under subsection (4) above shall be exercisable by statutory instrument subject to annulment in pursuance of a resolution of either House of Parliament.

(6) Subsection (2)(a) above applies to a judgment given before the date of the passing of this Act as well as to a judgment given on or after that date but this section does not affect any judgment which has been registered before that date under the provisions mentioned in subsection (I) above or in respect of which such proceedings as are there mentioned have been finally determined before that date.

6. Recovery of Awards of Multiple Damages

(1) This section applies where a court of an overseas country has given a judgment for multiple damages within the meaning of section 5(3) above against—

(a) a citizen of the United Kingdom and Colonies; or

(b) a body corporate incorporated in the United Kingdom or in a territory outside the United Kingdom for whose international relations Her Majesty's Government in the United Kingdom are responsible; or

(c) a person carrying on business in the United Kingdom,

(in this section referred to as a "qualifying defendant") and an amount on account of the damages has been paid by the qualifying defendant either to the party in whose favour the judgment was given or to another party who is entitled as against the qualifying defendant to contribution in respect of the damages.

(2) Subject to subsections (3) and (4) below, the qualifying defendant shall be entitled to recover from the party in whose favour the judgment was given so much of the amount referred to in subsection (I) above as

exceeds the part attributable to compensation; and that part shall be taken to be such part of the amount as bears to the whole of it the same proportion as the sum assessed by the court that gave the judgment as compensation for the loss or damage sustained by that party bears to the whole of the damages awarded to that party.

(3) Subsection (2) above does not apply where the qualifying defendant is an individual who was ordinarily resident in the overseas country at the time when the proceedings in which the judgment was given were instituted or a body corporate which had its principal place of business there at that time.

(4) Subsection (2) above does not apply where the qualifying defendant carried on business in the overseas country and the proceedings in which the judgment was given were concerned with activities exclusively carried on in that country.

(5) A court in the United Kingdom may entertain proceedings on a claim under this section notwithstanding that the person against whom the proceedings are brought is not within the jurisdiction of the court.

(6) The reference in subsection (I) above to an amount paid by the qualifying defendant includes a reference to an amount obtained by execution against his property or against the property of a company which (directly or indirectly) is wholly owned by him; and references in that subsection and subsection (2) above to the party in whose favour the judgment was given or to a party entitled to contribution include references to any person in whom the rights of any such party have become vested by succession or assignment or otherwise.

(7) This section shall, with the necessary modifications, apply also in relation to any order which is made by a tribunal or authority of an overseas country and would, if that tribunal or authority were a court, be a judgment for multiple damages within the meaning of section 5(3) above.

(8) This section does not apply to any judgment given or order made before the passing of this Act.

7. Enforcement of Overseas Judgment Under Provision Corresponding to s. 6

(1) If it appears to Her Majesty that the law of an overseas country provides or will provide for the enforcement in that country of judgments given under section 6 above, Her Majesty may by Order in Council provide for the enforcement in the United Kingdom of judgments given under any provision of the law of that country corresponding to that section.

(2) An Order under this section may apply, with or without modification, any of the provisions of the Foreign Judgments (Reciprocal Enforcement) Act 1933.

* * *

B. HAWK, UNITED STATES, COMMON MARKET AND INTERNATIONAL ANTITRUST: A COMPARATIVE GUIDE

315 (1st ed. 1979).*

Foreign discovery in antitrust cases is generally governed by the same rules applicable to foreign discovery in any federal court action. There are a number of issues, however, which are particularly troublesome in antitrust cases. * * *

One issue which has frequently arisen in antitrust cases is the extent to which documents located outside the United States must be produced. The general rule is that a United States court has the power to order such foreign production where it has in personam jurisdiction over the custodian, stated conversely, it is an insufficient objection to a request for production that the documents are located abroad. Thus, the courts are unanimous that a United States-based company must produce its own records whether or not those documents are located within the United States or abroad. As the district court stated in *In re Grand Jury Subpoena Duces Tecum addressed to Canadian Int'l Paper Co.,*[6] "The test is control—not location of the records." The standard is the same with respect to documents located abroad of a foreign subsidiary of a United States parent; that is, the documents must be produced where the parent exercises control over the foreign subsidiary. Foreign corporations are subject to the same general rule and they have been compelled to produce documents located abroad where the court has in personam jurisdiction over the corporation:

> That part of a corporation's records and documents are physically located beyond the confines of the United States does not excuse it from producing them if they are in its possession and the court has jurisdiction of the corporation.

* * *

A more difficult situation is where an order is directed to the United States subsidiary of a foreign corporation to produce documents from the parent's head office abroad. This situation was recently discussed in *In re Uranium Antitrust Litigation*[8-1] where the court held that a U.S. subsidiary must produce documents located in Canada in the possession, custody and control of its Canadian parent. Evidence existed that both subsidiary and parent operated as a single functional unit in all aspects of their uranium business; that they shared an interlocking structure of corporate directors, officers, and executive and administrative personnel; that numerous officers of the U.S. subsidiary had held dual positions with the parent, enabling them to perform identical uranium-related functions for

---

* © Law and Business, Inc. Reprinted with permission.

6. 72 F.Supp. 1013, 1020 (S.D.N.Y.1947).

8-1. [1980–1] Trade Cas. ¶ 63,124 (N.D.Ill.1980).

each corporation; and that both had been treated as a single uranium business not only by themselves but by other members of the uranium industry and by their ultimate parent in the United Kingdom. The court concluded that there was a strong likelihood that the U.S. subsidiary was withholding responsive documents in the files of its parent's personnel who have had and/or continue to have responsibility for the subsidiary's mining and marketing of uranium. The court distinguished between the test for discovery of documents and the test for liability for a subsidiary's acts. The court stated that while the latter may require actual control, the former does not and it is sufficient that the foreign corporation have or once had control over its directors, officers, or employees who manage the uranium-related activity of the U.S. corporation alone or of both corporations. Accordingly, the court ordered the U.S. subsidiary to produce all responsive documents held by those employees or former employees, even if those documents found their way into the foreign parent's files.

* * *

A second issue in foreign discovery concerns the conditions under which a subpoena may direct a *non-party* alien (for example, a witness) to produce documents which are not located within the United States or to appear personally to give testimony. Section 13 of the Clayton Act, providing that a witness subpoena may run from the forum judicial district to any other judicial district, permits subpoenas directed only to persons who can be found within a judicial district of the United States. Rule 45 of the Federal Rules of Civil Procedure provides for service of a subpoena on a witness located in a foreign country only as permitted under section 1783 of the Judicial Code, which in turn authorizes extraterritorial service only upon a citizen or resident of the United States. Thus, it appears that a witness subpoena may be properly issued to a foreign non-resident corporation or individual only if the corporation or individual can be served with process in a judicial district of the United States. The few decisions which have addressed the issue of service upon a non-party foreign *corporation* have adopted a *Scophony* approach,[11] that is, a factual determination of the extent of the foreign corporation's business activities within a judicial district.

As the issuance of a subpoena is within the court's discretion, it can impose conditions upon such issuance. For example, a deposition abroad can be ordered rather than a personal appearance within the United States if the court determines that justice can better be served. As a practical matter, however, depositions outside the United States are often feasible only if the witness voluntarily appears and testifies or if the foreign jurisdiction is willing to compel his testimony or document production. As seen below, this permission has not always been forthcoming in antitrust actions. Moreover, in several foreign countries permission to depose even a voluntary witness must be obtained from local authorities.

* * *

---

11. *United States v. Scophony Corp.,* 333 U.S. 795, 68 S.Ct. 855, 92 L.Ed. 1091 (1948).

The major discovery issue in antitrust cases today concerns foreign nondisclosure laws or limitations on discovery. Resolution of this issue is made difficult by the conflicting policies or principles involved. The principle of *lex fori* holds that the forum court applies its own procedure, while international comity holds that the forum court should not take action that may cause violation of another nation's laws. An increasing number of countries have enacted "blocking statutes" which prohibit under varying circumstances production of documents and other discovery methods in connection with foreign proceedings. * * *

While the conflicts engendered by these statutes are not new, they have become aggravated recently as a result of private and government attempts to obtain information concerning alleged anticompetitive activities involving foreign governments. The most recent example is the alleged uranium cartel where the Canadian government moved to prevent United States authorities from acquiring information in Canada about alleged international price fixing of uranium. A grand jury issued subpoenas to several United States subsidiaries of foreign uranium producers and to two Canadian parents. The Canadian reaction came in the form of federal government approval of a regulation under the Canadian Atomic Energy Control Act to prevent the removal from Canada of information relating to uranium marketing activities during the 1972–1975 period. The Canadian Minister of Energy, Mines and Resources stated that the action was taken in light of the "sweeping demand" of U.S. subpoenas which called for information in the possession of subsidiary or affiliated companies of United States enterprises "wherever located." The Minister stated further that the subpoenas sought information on activities approved and supported by the Canadian government: "Clearly this must be regarded as an issue of sovereignty." Australia and South Africa have passed similar prohibitions also in response to the same uranium cartel investigation. The Canadian legislation has also been the subject of several decisions in private actions involving the alleged uranium cartel.

This increasingly hostile foreign reaction prompted the Justice Department to announce a new policy in November 1977, to wit, that the Department would notify a foreign government whenever an Antitrust Division official wishes to conduct investigative interviews or other official business within its territory. And in November 1978 a Justice Department official announced that the Antitrust Division would first proceed by requests for voluntary submissions (rather than by compulsory process) where there is no serious threat of document destruction.

This strong foreign reaction may also be having an effect on United States courts, some of which are manifesting a greater sensitivity to foreign law prohibitions on United States discovery than was evident in the past. The general rule has developed that failure to produce documents is excused where there is a good faith inability to comply with the discovery order, as opposed to willfulness, bad faith or fault. Where that inability is based on foreign law prohibitions, two conditions are usually required to satisfy the good faith inability test. First, the party or witness must not itself encourage or induce the foreign law prohibition. This condition is based upon language in *Société Internationale,* the only Supreme Court decision to address the issue of foreign law prohibitions on discovery, where the Court stated that if plaintiff had "courted legal impediments" to production of the Swiss records, the district court might have been justified in dismissing the action.[37] Second, the party or witness must make a "good faith" effort to have the foreign authorities modify or waive the prohibition.

* * *

An excellent example of a pragmatic, albeit temporary, resolution of the foreign blocking statute problem is the district court's decision in Compagnie Francaise d'Assurance pour le Commerce Extérieur v. Phillips Petroleum Co., No. 81–4463, slip op. (S.D.N.Y. Jan. 24, 1983). Plaintiffs were two French corporations—Coface, a national company and an agency of the French government which insures French companies against the risk of non-payment on export contracts, and CNIM, which builds ocean-going vessels. Briefly, plaintiffs brought a diversity action against the American Phillips for damages arising out of a breach of contract on the part of a joint venture which purchased but never paid for ships. Plaintiffs objected to defendant's request for documents on the ground, among others, that the French blocking statute prevented disclosure by defendants. The court first found that the requested document did fall within the prohibition of the French statute. The court continued that the United States court has the power to order production regardless of a foreign blocking statute to the contrary. The court also held that neither the Hague Convention nor the principles of international comity require the court to defer to the French statute. * * * The court stated further that while restraint in ordering compliance might be advisable under certain circumstances (such as where the requested information is available from other sources or is sought from a non-party witness), it would hardly be appropriate in the present case where plaintiffs are domiciliaries of the country whose nondisclosure law they seek to invoke. In effect, the court then ordered plaintiffs to make a good faith effort to obtain a waiver from the French government, and, very interestingly, suggested that in the interim the following procedures should be followed:

> Plaintiffs are directed to make a good faith effort to seek and obtain from the appropriate authorities of the French government, a waiver of so much of Article I of French Law No. 80–538 as may be required to permit them to produce the requested documents. It would seem obvious from the broad generic description of the items sought that many of them in truth and in fact are non-confidential, and their limited disclosure under a protective order will not affect any legitimate interest of French sovereignty. If a blanket waiver cannot be obtained, then individual waivers should be sought as to each of those

---

37. *Société Internationale Pour Participations Industrielles et Commerciales, S.A. v. Rogers,* 357 U.S. 197, 78 S.Ct. 1087, 2 L.Ed.2d 1255 (1958).

documents which appear to be within the terms of the French statute, but are not within its historical purposes.

Simultaneously, counsel for the parties are directed to meet and confer, and to attempt to agree upon the preparation of a separate list of those documents which are or reasonably should be available by discovery from a third-party non-French source. With respect to such documents and information which can be obtained elsewhere, there is simply no purpose in forcing the issue of the interface of the French statute with the Federal Rules of Civil Procedure.

Plaintiffs are also directed to provide a list specifying those documents, if any, not otherwise accessible and for which a waiver cannot be obtained. This will enable the court to evaluate both defendant's need for any particular document and the applicability, if any, of the French statute thereto.

This "discovery compromise" ordered by Justice Brieant provides an excellent model for disputes of this sort.

SOCIÉTÉ NATIONALE INDUSTRIELLE AÉROSPATIALE v. UNITED STATES DISTRICT COURT

United States Supreme Court, 1987.
482 U.S. 522, 107 S.Ct. 2542, 96 L.Ed.2d 461.

Jᴜsᴛɪᴄᴇ Sᴛᴇᴠᴇɴs delivered the opinion of the Court.

The United States, the Republic of France, and 15 other Nations have acceded to the Hague Convention on the Taking of Evidence Abroad in Civil or Commercial Matters, opened for signature, Mar. 18, 1970, 23 U.S.T. 2555, T.I.A.S. No. 7444.[1] This Convention—sometimes referred to as the "Hague Convention" or the "Evidence Convention"—prescribes certain procedures by which a judicial authority in one contracting state may request evidence located in another contracting state. The question presented in this case concerns the extent to which a Federal District Court must employ the procedures set forth in the Convention when litigants seek answers to interrogatories, the production of documents, and admissions from a French adversary over whom the court has personal jurisdiction.

The two petitioners are corporations owned by the Republic of France. They are engaged in the business of designing, manufacturing, and marketing aircraft. One of their planes, the "Rallye," was allegedly advertised in American aviation publications as "the World's safest and most economical STOL plane." On August 19, 1980, a Rallye crashed in Iowa, injuring the pilot and a passenger. Dennis Jones, John George, and Rosa George brought separate suits based upon this accident in the United

---

1. The Hague Convention entered into force between the United States and France on October 6, 1974. The Convention is also in force in Barbados, Cyprus, Czechoslovakia, Denmark, Finland, the Federal Republic of Germany, Israel, Italy, Luxembourg, the Netherlands, Norway, Portugal, Singapore, Sweden, and the United Kingdom. Office of the Legal Adviser, United States Dept. of State, Treaties in Force 261–262 (1986).

States District Court for the Southern District of Iowa, alleging that petitioners had manufactured and sold a defective plane and that they were guilty of negligence and breach of warranty. Petitioners answered the complaints, apparently without questioning the jurisdiction of the District Court.

* * *

Initial discovery was conducted by both sides pursuant to the Federal Rules of Civil Procedure without objection. When plaintiffs served a second request for the production of documents pursuant to Rule 34, a set of interrogatories pursuant to Rule 33, and requests for admission pursuant to Rule 36, however, petitioners filed a motion for a protective order. App. 27–37. The motion alleged that because petitioners are "French corporations, and the discovery sought can only be found in a foreign state, namely France," the Hague Convention dictated the exclusive procedures that must be followed for pretrial discovery. App. 2. In addition, the motion stated that under French penal law, the petitioners could not respond to discovery requests that did not comply with the Convention. Ibid.[6]

* * *

In arguing their entitlement to a protective order, petitioners correctly assert that both the discovery rules set forth in the Federal Rules of Civil Procedure and the Hague Convention are the law of the United States. Brief for Petitioners 31. This observation, however, does not dispose of the question before us; we must analyze the interaction between these two bodies of federal law. Initially, we note that at least four different interpretations of the relationship between the federal discovery rules and the Hague Convention are possible. Two of these interpretations assume that the Hague Convention by its terms dictates the extent to which it supplants normal discovery rules. First, the Hague Convention might be read as requiring its use to the exclusion of any other discovery procedures whenever evidence located abroad is sought for use in an American court. Second, the Hague Convention might be interpreted to require first, but not exclusive, use of its procedures. Two other interpretations assume that international comity, rather than the obligations created by the treaty, should guide judicial resort to the Hague Conven-

---

6. Article 1A of the French "blocking statute," French Penal Code Law No. 80–538, provides:

"Subject to treaties or international agreements and applicable laws and regulations, it is prohibited for any party to request, seek or disclose, in writing, orally or otherwise, economic, commercial, industrial, financial or technical documents or information leading to the constitution of evidence with a view to foreign judicial or administrative proceedings or in connection therewith."

* * *

Article 2 provides:

"The parties mentioned in [Article 1A] shall forthwith inform the competent minister if they receive any request concerning such disclosures."

* * *

tion. Third, then, the Convention might be viewed as establishing a supplemental set of discovery procedures, strictly optional under treaty law, to which concerns of comity nevertheless require first resort by American courts in all cases. Fourth, the treaty may be viewed as an undertaking among sovereigns to facilitate discovery to which an American court should resort when it deems that course of action appropriate, after considering the situations of the parties before it as well as the interests of the concerned foreign state.

* * *

We reject the first two of the possible interpretations as inconsistent with the language and negotiating history of the Hague Convention. The preamble of the Convention specifies its purpose "to facilitate the transmission and execution of Letters of Request" and to "improve mutual judicial co-operation in civil or commercial matters." 23 U.S.T., at 2557, T.I.A.S. No. 7444. The preamble does not speak in mandatory terms which would purport to describe the procedures for all permissible transnational discovery and exclude all other existing practices. The text of the Evidence Convention itself does not modify the law of any contracting state, require any contracting State to use the Convention procedures, either in requesting evidence or in responding to such requests, or compel any contracting state to change its own evidence-gathering procedures.

The Convention contains three chapters. Chapter I, entitled "Letters of Requests," and chapter II, entitled "Taking of Evidence by Diplomatic Officers, Consular Agents and Commissioners," both use permissive rather than mandatory language. Thus, Article 1 provides that a judicial authority in one contracting state "may" forward a letter of request to the competent authority in another contracting state for the purpose of obtaining evidence. Similarly, Articles 15, 16, and 17 provide that diplomatic officers, consular agents, and commissioners "may . . . without compulsion," take evidence under certain conditions. The absence of any command that a contracting state must use Convention procedures when they are not needed is conspicuous.

Two of the Articles in chapter III, entitled "General Clauses," buttress our conclusion that the Convention was intended as a permissive supplement, not a preemptive replacement, for other means of obtaining evidence located abroad. Article 23 expressly authorizes a contracting state to declare that it will not execute any letter of request in aid of pretrial discovery of documents in a common-law country. Surely, if the Convention had been intended to replace completely the broad discovery powers that the common-law courts in the United States previously exercised over foreign litigants subject to their jurisdiction, it would have been most anomalous for the common-law contracting parties to agree to Article 23, which enables a contracting party to revoke its consent to the treaty's procedures for pretrial discovery. In the absence of explicit textual support, we are unable to accept the hypothesis that the common-law contracting states abjured recourse to all pre-existing discovery procedures at the same time that they accepted the possibility that a contracting party could unilaterally abrogate even the Convention's procedures. Moreover, Article 27 plainly states that the Convention does not prevent a contracting state from using more liberal methods of rendering evidence than those authorized by the Convention. Thus, the text of the Evidence Convention, as well as the history of its proposal and ratification by the United States, unambiguously supports the conclusion that it was intended to establish optional procedures that would facilitate the taking of evidence abroad. * * *

An interpretation of the Hague Convention as the exclusive means for obtaining evidence located abroad would effectively subject every American court hearing a case involving a national of a contracting state to the internal laws of that state. Interrogatories and document requests are staples of international commercial litigation, no less than of other suits, yet a rule of exclusivity would subordinate the court's supervision of even the most routine of these pretrial proceedings to the actions or, equally, to the inactions of foreign judicial authorities. * * *

While the Hague Convention does not divest the District Court of jurisdiction to order discovery under the Federal Rules of Civil Procedure, the optional character of the Convention procedures sheds light on one aspect of the Court of Appeals' opinion that we consider erroneous. That court concluded that the Convention simply "does not apply" to discovery sought from a foreign litigant that is subject to the jurisdiction of an American court. 782 F.2d, at 124. Plaintiffs argue that this conclusion is supported by two considerations. First, the Federal Rules of Civil Procedure provide ample means for obtaining discovery from parties who are subject to the court's jurisdiction, while before the Convention was ratified it was often extremely difficult, if not impossible, to obtain evidence from nonparty witnesses abroad. Plaintiffs contend that it is appropriate to construe the Convention as applying only in the area in which improvement was badly needed. Second, when a litigant is subject to the jurisdiction of the district court, arguably the evidence it is required to produce is not "abroad" within the meaning of the Convention, even though it is in fact located in a foreign country at the time of the discovery request and even though it will have to be gathered or otherwise prepared abroad.

* * *

Nevertheless, the text of the Convention draws no distinction between evidence obtained from third parties and that obtained from the litigants themselves; nor does it purport to draw any sharp line between evidence that is "abroad" and evidence that is within the control of a party subject to the jurisdiction of the requesting court. Thus, it appears clear to us that the optional Convention procedures are available whenever they will facilitate the gathering of evidence by the means authorized in the Convention. Although these procedures are not mandatory, the Hague Convention does "apply" to the production of evidence in a litigant's possession in the sense that it is one method of seeking evidence that a court may elect to employ. * * *

Petitioners contend that even if the Hague Convention's procedures are not mandatory, this Court should adopt a rule requiring that American litigants first resort to those procedures before initiating any discovery pursuant to the normal methods of the Federal Rules of Civil Procedure. See, e.g., Laker Airways, Ltd. v. Pan American World Airways, 103 F.R.D. 42 (DC 1984) * * *.

The Court of Appeals rejected this argument because it was convinced that an American court's order ultimately requiring discovery that a foreign court had refused under Convention procedures would constitute "the greatest insult" to the sovereignty of that tribunal. 782 F.2d, at 125–126. We disagree with the Court of Appeals' view. It is well known that the scope of American discovery is often significantly broader than is permitted in other jurisdictions, and we are satisfied that foreign tribunals will recognize that the final decision on the evidence to be used in litigation conducted in American courts must be made by those courts. We therefore do not believe that an American court should refuse to make use of Convention procedures because of a concern that it may ultimately find it necessary to order the production of evidence that a foreign tribunal permitted a party to withhold.

Nevertheless, we cannot accept petitioners' invitation to announce a new rule of law that would require first resort to Convention procedures whenever discovery is sought from a foreign litigant. Assuming, without deciding, that we have the lawmaking power to do so, we are convinced that such a general rule would be unwise. In many situations the Letter of Request procedure authorized by the Convention would be unduly time-consuming and expensive, as well as less certain to produce needed evidence than direct use of the Federal Rules. A rule of first resort in all cases would therefore be inconsistent with the overriding interest in the "just, speedy, and inexpensive determination" of litigation in our courts. See Fed.Rule Civ.Proc. 1.

Petitioners argue that a rule of first resort is necessary to accord respect to the sovereignty of states in which evidence is located. It is true that the process of obtaining evidence in a civil-law jurisdiction is normally conducted by a judicial officer rather than by private attorneys. Petitioners contend that if performed on French soil, for example, by an unauthorized person, such evidence-gathering might violate the "judicial sovereignty" of the host nation. Because it is only through the Convention that civil-law nations have given their consent to evidence-gathering activities within their borders, petitioners argue, we have a duty to employ those procedures whenever they are available. Brief for Petitioners 27–28. We find that argument unpersuasive. If such a duty were to be inferred from the adoption of the Convention itself, we believe it would have been described in the text of that document. Moreover, the concept of international comity requires in this context a more particularized analysis of the respective interests of the foreign nation and the requesting nation than petitioners' proposed general rule would generate. We therefore decline to hold as a blanket matter that comity requires resort to Hague Evidence Convention procedures without prior scrutiny in each case of the particular facts, sovereign interests, and likelihood that resort to those procedures will prove effective.[29]

Some discovery procedures are much more "intrusive" than others. In this case, for example, an interrogatory asking petitioners to identify the pilots who flew flight tests in the Rallye before it was certified for flight by the Federal Aviation Administration, or a request to admit that petitioners authorized certain advertising in a particular magazine, is certainly less intrusive than a request to produce all of the "design specifications, line drawings and engineering plans and all engineering change orders and plans and all drawings concerning the leading edge slats for the Rallye type aircraft manufactured by the Defendants." App. 29. Even if a court might be persuaded that a particular document request was too burdensome or too "intrusive" to be granted in full, with or without an appropriate protective order, it might well refuse to insist upon the use of Convention procedures before requiring responses to simple interrogatories or requests for admissions. The exact line between reasonableness and unreasonableness in each case must be drawn by the trial court, based on its knowledge of the case and of the claims and interests of the parties and the governments whose statutes and policies they invoke.

---

29. The French "blocking statute," n. 6, supra, does not alter our conclusion. It is well settled that such statutes do not deprive an American court of the power to order a party subject to its jurisdiction to produce evidence even though the act of production may violate that statute. See Societe Internationale Pour Participations Industrielles et Commerciales, S.A. v. Rogers, 357 U.S. 197, 204–206, 2 L.Ed.2d 1255, 78 S.Ct. 1087 (1958). Nor can the enactment of such a statute by a foreign nation require American courts to engraft a rule of first resort onto the Hague Convention, or otherwise to provide the nationals of such a country with a preferred status in our courts. It is clear that American courts are not required to adhere blindly to the directives of such a statute. Indeed, the language of the statute, if taken literally, would appear to represent an extraordinary exercise of legislative jurisdiction by the Republic of France over a United States district judge, forbidding him or her from ordering any discovery from a party of French nationality, even simple requests for admissions or interrogatories that the party could respond to on the basis of personal knowledge. It would be particularly incongruous to recognize such a preference for corporations that are wholly owned by the enacting nation. Extraterritorial assertions of jurisdiction are not one-sided. While the District Court's discovery orders arguably have some impact in France, the French blocking statute asserts similar authority over acts to take place in this country. The lesson of comity is that neither the discovery order nor the blocking statute can have the same omnipresent effect that it would have in a world of only one sovereign. The blocking statute thus is relevant to the court's particularized comity analysis only to the extent that its terms and its enforcement identify the nature of the sovereign interests in nondisclosure of specific kinds of material.

The American Law Institute has summarized this interplay of blocking statutes and discovery orders: "[W]hen a state has jurisdiction to prescribe and its courts have jurisdiction to adjudicate, adjudication should (subject to generally applicable rules of evidence) take place on the basis of the best information available.... [Blocking] statutes that frustrate this goal need not be given the same deference by courts of the United States as substantive rules of law at variance with the law of the United States." See Restatement § 437, Reporter's Note 5, pp. 41, 42. "On the other hand, the degree of friction created by discovery requests ... and the differing perceptions of the acceptability of American-style discovery under national and international law, suggest some efforts to moderate the application abroad of U.S. procedural techniques, consistent with the overall principle of reasonableness in the exercise of jurisdiction." Id., at 42.

American courts, in supervising pretrial proceedings, should exercise special vigilance to protect foreign litigants from the danger that unnecessary, or unduly burdensome, discovery may place them in a disadvantageous position. Judicial supervision of discovery should always seek to minimize its costs and inconvenience and to prevent improper uses of discovery requests. When it is necessary to seek evidence abroad, however, the district court must supervise pretrial proceedings particularly closely to prevent discovery abuses. For example, the additional cost of transportation of documents or witnesses to or from foreign locations may increase the danger that discovery may be sought for the improper purpose of motivating settlement, rather than finding relevant and probative evidence. Objections to "abusive" discovery that foreign litigants advance should therefore receive the most careful consideration. In addition, we have long recognized the demands of comity in suits involving foreign states, either as parties or as sovereigns with a coordinate interest in the litigation. See Hilton v. Guyot, 159 U.S. 113, 40 L.Ed. 95, 16 S.Ct. 139 (1895). American courts should therefore take care to demonstrate due respect for any special problem confronted by the foreign litigant on account of its nationality or the location of its operations, and for any sovereign interest expressed by a foreign state. We do not articulate specific rules to guide this delicate task of adjudication.

JUSTICE BLACKMUN, with whom JUSTICE BRENNAN, JUSTICE MARSHALL, and JUSTICE O'CONNOR join, concurring in part and dissenting in part.

Some might well regard the Court's decision in this case as an affront to the nations that have joined the United States in ratifying the Hague Convention on the Taking of Evidence Abroad in Civil or Commercial Matters, opened for signature, Mar. 18, 1970, 23 U.S.T. 2555, T.I.A.S. No. 7444. The Court ignores the importance of the Convention by relegating it to an "optional" status, without acknowledging the significant achievement in accommodating divergent interests that the Convention represents. Experience to date indicates that there is a large risk that the case-by-case comity analysis now to be permitted by the Court will be performed inadequately and that the somewhat unfamiliar procedures of the Convention will be invoked infrequently. I fear the Court's decision means that courts will resort unnecessarily to issuing discovery orders under the Federal Rules of Civil Procedure in a raw exercise of their jurisdictional power to the detriment of the United States' national and international interests. The Court's view of this country's international obligations is particularly unfortunate in a world in which regular commercial and legal channels loom ever more crucial.

I do agree with the Court's repudiation of the positions at both extremes of the spectrum with regard to the use of the Convention. Its rejection of the view that the Convention is not "applicable" at all to this case is surely correct: the Convention clearly applies to litigants as well as to third parties, and to requests for evidence located abroad, no matter where that evidence is actually "produced." The Court also correctly rejects the far opposite position that the Convention provides the exclusive means for discovery involving signatory countries. I dissent, however, because I cannot endorse the Court's case-by-case inquiry for determining whether to use Convention procedures and its failure to provide lower courts with any meaningful guidance for carrying out that inquiry. In my view, the Convention provides effective discovery procedures that largely eliminate the conflicts between United States and foreign law on evidence gathering. I therefore would apply a general presumption that, in most cases, courts should resort first to the Convention procedures. An individualized analysis of the circumstances of a particular case is appropriate only when it appears that it would be futile to employ the Convention or when its procedures prove to be unhelpful.

R. FOLSOM, PRACTITIONER TREATISE ON INTERNATIONAL BUSINESS TRANSACTIONS

§§ 20.27 and 20.29 (2011–12).

The extraterritorial reach of Articles 101 and 102

There is a question about the extent to which the competition rules of Europe extend to activity anywhere in the world, including activity occurring entirely or partly within the territorial limits of the United States, Mexico or Canada. Decisions by the Commission and the Court of Justice suggest that the territorial reach of Articles 101 and 102 TFEU* is expanding and may extend to almost any international business transaction.

For an agreement to be incompatible with the Common Market and prohibited under Article 81(1), it must be "likely to affect trade between Member States" and have the object or effect of impairing "competition within the Common Market." Taken together, these requirements amount to an "effects test" for extraterritorial application of Article 81. This test is similar to that which operates under the Sherman Act of the United States.

The Court has repeatedly held that the fact that one of the parties to an agreement is domiciled in a third country does not preclude the applicability of Article 81(1). Swiss and British chemical companies, for example, argued that the Commission was not competent to impose competition law fines for acts committed in Switzerland and Britain (before joining the EU) by enterprises domiciled outside its scope even if the acts had effects within the Common Market. Nevertheless, the Court held those companies in violation of Article 81 because they owned subsidiary companies within the Union and controlled their behavior. The foreign parent and its subsidiaries were treated as a "single enterprise" for purposes of service of process, judgment, and collection of fines and penalties. In doing so, the Court observed that the fact that a subsidiary

---

* Treaty on the Functioning of the European Union (2009).

company has its own legal personality does not rule out the possibility that its conduct is attributable to the parent company.

The Court has extended its reasoning to the extraterritorial application of Article 82. A United States parent company, for example, was held potentially liable for acquisitions by its subsidiary which affected market conditions within the Common Market. In another decision, the Court held that a Maryland company's refusal to sell its product to a competitor of its affiliate company was a result of united "single enterprise" action. It proceeded to state that extraterritorial conduct merely having "repercussions on competitive structures" in the Common Market fell within the parameters of Article 82. The Court ordered Commercial Solvents, through its Italian affiliate, to supply the competitor at reasonable prices.

In 1988, the Court of Justice widened the extraterritorial reach of Article 81 in a case where wood pulp producers from the U.S., Canada, Sweden and Finland were fined for price fixing activities affecting Union trade and competition. These firms did not have substantial operations within Common Market; they were primarily exporters to it. This decision's utilization of a place of implementation "effects test" is quite similar to that used under the Sherman Act. And the reliance by the U.S. exporters upon a traditional Webb-Pomerene export cartel exemption from United States antitrust law carried no weight in European law. The Court has also affirmed the extraterritorial reach of Articles 81 and 82 to airfares in and out of Europe.[5]

* * *

United States-European antitrust cooperation

In 1991 the European Community (of which Britain is still a member) and the United States reached an antitrust cooperation agreement. This accord commits the parties to notify each other of imminent enforcement action, to share relevant information and consult on potential policy changes. It was prominently used in 1994 to jointly settle charges of restrictive trade practices with the Microsoft Corporation. An innovative feature is the inclusion of "comity" principles, each side promising to take the other's interests into account when considering antitrust prosecutions. Since the Commission has traditionally permitted U.S. lawyers to appear before it on competition law matters, the FTC announced on the same day as the signing of the antitrust cooperation agreement that European lawyers would be permitted to appear before it on a reciprocal basis.

The agreement has had a significant effect on mergers of firms doing business in North America and Europe. Each side has agreed to notify and consult with the other regarding antitrust matters, including mergers and acquisitions, that "may affect important interests." In its first six months of operation, about 45 notifications were exchanged between the Commission, the U.S. Federal Trade Commission, and the Antitrust Division of

---

5. Ahmed Saeed Flugreisen v. Zentrale zur Bekämpfung unlauteren Wettbewerbs (1989) Eur.Comm.Rep. 838.

the U.S. Justice Department. A large portion of these notifications concerned international mergers and acquisitions. Since both Europe and the U.S. have pre-merger notification systems, the exchange of such information has increased rapidly. In the first year after the cooperation agreement, U.S. antitrust enforcers sent 37 such notifications to the European Commission and received 15 in return. About 20 percent of all the mergers reviewed by the Commission under its competition law were simultaneously being reviewed by U.S. antitrust authorities.

In April of 1997 the Justice Department made its first "positive comity" request to the European Commission under the U.S.-E.U. Antitrust Cooperation Agreement. The Justice Department has asked the Commission to investigate alleged anticompetitive conduct by European airlines regarding U.S.-based airline computer reservation systems (CRS). In 1998, the European Union and the United States signed a "Positive Comity Agreement." This agreement reinforces the 1991 Cooperation Agreement by establishing procedures for positive comity requests and responses, including parallel investigations against Microsoft. The Agreement can be found at www.usdoj.gov.

In 2007, the European Court of First Instance (CFI) strongly affirmed the Commission's decision that Microsoft had abused its dominant position by bundling a media player with its Windows operating system, and denying competitors information needed to make their computers work with Microsoft software. Microsoft was fined over 2 billion Euros. The CFI decision, contrasted with the comparatively docile settlement of Microsoft's prosecution in the United States, illustrates that transatlantic antitrust cooperation does not necessarily result in similar legal outcomes. By 2008, the Commission was investigating Microsoft's bundling of its web browser with Windows, and the compatibility of its Office Software with rival programs. Other U.S. technology firms are also under the EU competition law microscope: Qualcomm, Intel, Google and Apple included. In 2009, the Commission fined Intel a massive 1.06 billion Euros for abusing its dominant position in microprocessors for PCs. Intel's price discounts and loyalty rebates are the center of this judgment, now on appeal. In 2010, Microsoft agreed *not* to bundle its web browser with windows.

QUESTIONS AND COMMENTS

1. The excerpt by Fox concerning limitations on the application of the United States antitrust laws to foreign commerce suggests that the extraterritorial reach of the Sherman Act has been tempered by judicial decisions and considerations of comity. Do the activities of Skylow and the four defendants give rise to Sherman Act jurisdiction under this case law? How would you argue against comity on behalf of Skylow in these circumstances? What opposing arguments would you expect?

2. Should *any* extraterritorial antitrust jurisdiction be retained? Why? Would diplomatic channels provide a workable alternative?

3.   As noted by Fox, the Sherman Act was amended in 1982 by the Foreign Trade Antitrust Improvements Act. Comparable amendments were made to the Federal Trade Commission Act (15 U.S.C.A. § 45(a)(3)). Do the activities of Skylow and the four defendants give rise to subject matter jurisdiction under the 1982 Act? Does this provision alter the existing state of the law?

Is Skylow's airline business domestic, import or export commerce? Does it matter? Suppose Skylow carries almost exclusively United States passengers to Britain and back. Might that fact make a difference?

4.   Hawk suggests that obtaining discovery in extraterritorial cases is complicated not only by "blocking statutes," but also by judicial decisions under the Federal Rules of Civil or Criminal Procedure and decisions of foreign courts concerning disclosure of documents or the taking of depositions. Suppose the United States defendants have United Kingdom offices or subsidiaries where documents relevant to the Skylow litigation are located. Must they be produced? Suppose the British defendants have United States offices or subsidiaries, but most documents relevant to the litigation are kept in Britain. Must these documents be produced? In the Skylow litigation, when may testimony or document production be compelled of third-party witnesses (U.S., British and foreign) who reside abroad?

5.   What evidence would be relevant to the question of whether the British defendants can show a "good faith inability to comply" with Skylow's discovery requests? How does the Protection of Trading Interests Act of 1980 affect your conclusions?

Should considerations of comity be entertained in extraterritorial discovery disputes? Should the comity analysis used to assess subject matter jurisdiction be used in discovery disputes?

6.   Would applications for letters rogatory under the Hague convention be likely to assist Skylow in its discovery efforts? Should such requests always be made as a matter of comity? Must they be made? See the *Aérospatiale* decision.

7.   A number of nations have enacted "blocking statutes" designed to deal with assertions of extraterritorial jurisdiction over their citizens. Other nations possess blocking laws which apply to particular industries, *e.g.,* Canada on uranium. Why?

The United Kingdom Protection of Trading Interests Act of 1980 is a prime example of a "blocking statute." Does that Act encourage other nations to enact reciprocal blocking laws? What protection might each of Skylow's British competitors be seeking under the Act? Can Skylow influence the outcome in any way?

8.   Suppose that protective action is taken under the Protection of Trading Interests Act which bars further extraterritorial discovery in Skylow's litigation and prohibits enforcement in Britain of the outstanding $3,000,000 judgment. Has Skylow been "blocked"? Suppose Skylow successfully recovered on its $3,000,000 judgment. What remedy might the British defendant pursue?

9. What if Skylow were a British corporation seeking antitrust relief in a federal district court. Would Skylow be "blocked" from pursuing such an action under the Protection of Trading Interests Act? Is Skylow, because it is a British corporation, blocked from pursuing federal antitrust relief by the Foreign Trade Antitrust Improvements Act?

10. The British have a convenient way of ignoring the fact that they are now members of the Common Market, which under Articles 101 and 102 TFEU has an ever expanding extraterritorial branch of its competition law. Should the United States adopt its own blocking statute?

No jurisdiction in Europe provides for private treble damages relief. Should Skylow file a complaint with the Commission in hopes of persuading it to prosecute? Does Skylow need to rely upon *Wood Pulp* as a basis for asserting jurisdiction? See the Folsom excerpt. How about a complaint to the Antitrust Division of the Justice Department?

In 1998, the European Union and the United States signed a "Positive Comity Agreement." This agreement reinforces the 1991 Cooperation Agreement by establishing procedures for positive comity requests and responses, including parallel investigations such as those against Microsoft. What kind of "cooperation" can the Commission expect from United States law enforcement officials if it decides to take up Skylow's complaint? And vice-versa? How does "positive comity" differ from the "negative comity" analyses found in *Timberlane* or *Empagran*?

11. Congressional support for cooperative international antitrust investigations can be found in the 1994 Antitrust Enforcement Assistance Act. This Act authorizes aid in obtaining antitrust evidence pursuant to mutual assistance agreements. In other words, the DOJ and FTC may at the request (say) of the European Commission seek a court order to compel testimony or document production to assist the Commission in determining whether European competition law has been violated. And vice-versa when the U.S. authorities ask the Commission for assistance. Think of this Act as "positive comity" for discovery, an alternative to the Hague Convention deemed optional in *Aerospatielle*. Might it help Skylow?

12. The labyrinthine Laker Airways antitrust litigation, upon which this problem is modeled, is summarized by the Court of Appeals for the District of Columbia Circuit in a March 7, 1984 decision containing a lengthy discussion of international comity and upholding an injunction forbidding Sabena and KLM from joining the United Kingdom proceedings brought by British Airways and British Caledonian Airways to enjoin Laker's liquidator from pursuing American antitrust relief. *See Laker Airways Limited v. Sabena, Belgian World Airlines*, 731 F.2d 909 (D.C.Cir.1984). On July 19, 1984, the House of Lords unanimously held that Laker's antitrust suit in a U.S. federal district court was not unconscionable and allowed Laker's appeals against the injunction of the English Court of Appeal restraining Laker from pursuing such a remedy. *British Airways Board v. Laker Airways*, 3 W.L.R. 413 (1984). The House of Lords upheld the dismissal of Laker's application for judicial review of British Secretary of State's order under the Protection of Trading Interests Act. Thus, that order remains intact and no person carrying on business in the United Kingdom (other than American air carriers) may

comply with "United States antitrust measures" arising out of the Laker litigation. In the Fall of 1984, the United Kingdom Department of Transport blocked plans by major United States and British air carriers to discount transatlantic fares after Virgin Atlantic Airways (a small British carrier) alleged that such discounts would be "predatory." The Department sought guarantees that British carriers participating in the discounted fares would not be subject to public and private antitrust complaints. The Justice Department issued an assurance that no public prosecutions would be undertaken. The Justice Department also terminated a grand jury investigation of possible antitrust violations by British carriers which paralleled the *Laker* litigation. The grand jury investigation was terminated at the request of President Reagan, who cited "foreign policy" reasons. In October of 1984, District Judge Greene issued a preliminary injunction prohibiting British Airways and British Caledonian from asking Parliament or British authorities to take action that would frustrate the ability of United States courts to continue the *Laker* lawsuit. In March of 1985 the Southern District of New York District Court vacated deposition subpoenas duces tecum served by Laker's liquidator on non-party witnesses. In July of 1985 a settlement was reached which provided for significant payments to Laker's creditors, attorneys and Sir Freddie and his wife.

PROBLEM 11.4 ENFORCEMENT OF FOREIGN JUDGMENTS

SECTION I. THE SETTING

Roger Cough is an English national who moved to British Columbia in Canada. There he engaged in several business activities. Cough borrowed $700,000 in U.S. dollars from the Bank of Montreal branch in Vancouver, British Columbia, which he used to make some very unwise investments in property in Seattle, all of which have failed. The loans were secured by Cough's leaving shares of IBM with the bank worth at the time of the loan $700,000 U.S. The loan agreement (which used the $ sign throughout, never noted specifically whether it meant U.S. or Canadian dollars) included the following provision:

> This contract shall be construed in accordance with the laws of British Columbia. For the purpose of legal proceedings, this contract shall be deemed to have been made in British Columbia and to be performed there. Courts of British Columbia shall have jurisdiction over all disputes which may arise under the contract, but nothing in this contract shall prevent the Bank at its option from proceeding against the borrower in the courts of any other Province or country.

The stock market fell lowering the value of the IBM stock. Cough defaulted on the loan and moved to California. The bank sold the stock for $400,000 U.S. and then sought a deficiency judgment against Cough for the balance of $300,000. Process was served by the Canadian court by certified mail from Canada which reached Cough in California. The process was in French and English. Seeing the French part first, and both not knowing French and incorrectly assuming the entire set of papers were in French, Cough threw them out. Cough did not appear in the Canadian proceedings. The bank obtained a default judgment for the uncollected loan principal. The award was rendered in Canadian dollars in the amount of $461,538 Canadian, being the equivalent of $300,000 U.S. and the Canadian bank seeks to enforce that Canadian judgment in the state in which Cough now lives.

SECTION II. FOCUS OF CONSIDERATION

If you represent a client whose activities are solely within the United States, you might be inclined to feel "safe" if the client is sued in a court in some foreign nation, especially where jurisdiction was based on some principal not known in the United States. If a judgment has been rendered in that foreign court, it cannot move directly against your client's U.S. assets. Only a domestic court in this country can do so. However, if that foreign judgment might be given effect by U.S. domestic courts, then the time has come to worry about foreign litigation. But the time to begin to worry is when the suit commences—or earlier. Your client may feel that foreign judgments should not reach into the United States, but that view may not be shared by our courts for any one of several reasons. We will explore some of them below.

This problem deals with *money* judgments; the enforcement of non-money judgments, such as specific performance, meets considerably more difficulty. That is to be expected. The nation may not recognize the *form* of judgment, an issue which is not a problem with a money judgment in general, but may be a problem when parts of the judgment include what may clearly or even possibly be punitive in nature. Part A's hypothetical is a fairly common transaction, reflected in the case considered. In Part B we shift to cases involving many foreign plaintiffs who have sued first in the United States where they were dismissed under *forum non conveniens*. But unlike many *fnc* cases the matter did not end, the plaintiffs filed in their home nation where they quickly received a very large judgment in a procedure that on its face may have raised issues of corruption, fraud and the presence of a system lacking the level of due process required for enforcement. However reasonable some of the plaintiffs' claims may have been, they did not have the benefit of a judicial system oriented to rendering a fair, impartial decision after proof presented in a trial. It may have looked good from their viewpoint when they received a quick and most favorable judgment, but it was not viewed by the defendants as one rendered with due process, one of the arguments raised that when the judgments were brought to the United States for recognition and enforcement. In Part C we return to the Part A facts and considered a related issue–what currency should the judgment be given in and when should any necessary currency conversion be measured. The date of the wrong complained of? The date the case was filed? The date of the judgment? The date of payment?

The 2005 Uniform Foreign–Country Money Judgments Recognition Act (successor to the 1962 Uniform Foreign–Money Judgments Recognition Act) and the Uniform Foreign–Money Claims Act are essential to an analysis of this problem. They appear in the Documents Supplement.

SECTION III. READINGS, QUESTIONS AND COMMENTS

PART A. RECOGNITION AND ENFORCEMENT OF FOREIGN JUDGMENTS

We know that judgments from one state in the United States are enforceable in all other states under the "full faith and credit" clause of the U.S. Constitution. That clause does not apply to judgments of foreign courts. Nor is there a rule that U.S. courts must not enforce foreign judgments. Thus, the courts have been left to their own analyses in developing policies and doctrines.

What might a court do faced with the judgment of a foreign court? The court might accept the foreign judgment as a judgment of its own and enforce it in the same manner as a domestic judgment. Or, the court might enforce the foreign judgment without accepting it as its own, thus avoiding giving it an imprimatur of the same legitimacy as one of its own decisions. Then why would the court enforce it? Perhaps for reasons of international comity, or reciprocity—the decision depending on whether the courts of the rendering nation would enforce a judgment of the court asked to enforce the present one. Another choice would be to absolutely reject the judgment, with the implication that if a judgment is to be enforced against one subject to the domestic court's jurisdiction, then the suit should be brought in that court, not elsewhere. Finally, the court could follow some in between practice. It could examine the judgment to determine whether it was rendered under concepts of due process acceptable to the court. All of this power may be removed from the court, however, if the nation enters into international agreements for the recognition and enforcement of foreign judgments. The E.U. has such a convention (the Brussels Regulation we considered in Problem 11.1). The United States has not entered into any international convention for the enforcement of foreign judgments. See Yoav Oestreicher, *"We're on a Road to Nowhere"—Reasons for the Continuing Failure to Regulate Recognition and Enforcement of Foreign Judgments*, 42 Int'l Law. 59 (2008).

The common law rule in England was that a judgment for money rendered by a court in a foreign country was only prima facie evidence of the subject matter it purported to decide, and was subject to impeachment before the English courts. Thus, foreign judgments were not conclusive on the merits of the dispute, and could act as neither res judicata nor collateral estoppel to actions in English courts by the loser in the foreign court. The U.S. Supreme Court did not follow the English approach. The leading case remains *Hilton v. Guyot,* 159 U.S. 113, 16 S.Ct. 139, 40 L.Ed.

95 (1895). The Court denied enforcement of a French judgment, announcing that,

> where there has been an opportunity for a full and fair trial abroad before a court of competent jurisdiction, conducting the trial upon regular proceedings, after due citation or voluntary appearance of the defendant, and under a system of jurisprudence likely to secure an impartial administration of justice between the citizens of its own country and those of other countries, and there is nothing to show either prejudice * * * or fraud * * *, the merits of the case should not, in an action brought in this country upon the judgment, be tried afresh. * * *

The Court did not find any prejudice, fraud or lack of due process in the French courts, but it did find that the defendants had alleged that French courts would not give conclusive effect to judgments of U.S. courts. Since "mutuality and reciprocity" were not available for U.S. judgments in France, the Court refused to hold that the French judgment was conclusive in the United States.

Hilton may remain the leading case on the subject, but it is seldom controlling. Even actions brought in federal court are dependent, under the doctrine of *Erie v. Tompkins,* upon state law—and *Hilton* is not Constitutional doctrine. State courts have felt free to pursue other analyses and doctrines. For example, the New York Court of Appeals, with Pound on the bench, did give conclusive effect to the judgment of a French court, despite the known lack of reciprocity and comity, in *Johnston v. Compagnie Générale Transatlantique,* 242 N.Y. 381, 152 N.E. 121 (1926). The court deliberately stated that it was not bound by the *Hilton* decision or doctrine.

Inconsistent and sparse state law ultimately led to the National Conference of Commissioners on Uniform State Laws (NCCUSL—the same people who brought you the UCC and who have more recently approved the Uniform Foreign Money Claims Act, discussed in Part C of this problem) to produce the 1962 Uniform Foreign Money–Judgments Recognition Act.[1]

The purpose of the Act was to attempt to bring uniformity of result to such cases, and to furnish many states with a coherent and consistent set of rules on the problem involved. But even with the significant adoption of the UFMJRA, many states adopted variations, including the requirement of reciprocity in a few states. Consider the perplexed state of the foreign possessor of a judgment against a person or corporation in the United States, the foreigner trying to understand how foreign judgments are recognized and enforced in a multi-state system. Should the suit be

---

1. Thirty states plus the District of Columbia and the Virgin Islands adopted the Act prior to its replacement in 2005. Alaska, California, Colorado, Connecticut, Delaware, Florida, Georgia, Hawaii, Idaho, Illinois, Iowa, Maryland, Massachusetts, Michigan, Minnesota, Missouri, Montana, New Jersey, New Mexico, New York, North Carolina, Ohio, Oklahoma, Oregon, Pennsylvania, Texas, Virginia and Washington. Factsheet, ULC, at www.nccusl.org/Update/uniformact_factsheets/uniformacts-fs-ufmjra.asp.

brought in a federal court or state court? Is the judgment debtor in a state which has adopted the Uniform Act, or one which has not? The Uniform Act was not based on the *Hilton* doctrine, but upon an independent analysis of the problems conducted by the National Conference. The Commissioners in 2005 promulgated a new revision of the 1962 Act. The new Uniform Foreign–Country Money Judgments Recognition Act is very similar to the 1962 version, with five primary differences. They are (1) clarification that judgments entitled to full faith and credit are not enforceable under the new Act, (2) party seeking recognition has the burden of proving the judgment is subject to the new Act, (3) party objecting to recognition and raising specific grounds has the burden of proving those grounds, (4) establishment of procedures for seeking enforcement depending on whether it is an original action or part of a pending action, and (5) prohibition of the action if the judgment may no longer be enforced in the country of the judgment, with a maximum of 15 years from its date of effectiveness. As of mid-2011 the UFCMJRA was the preferred form and was replacing the UFMJRA.[2] The NCCUSL provides a very useful commentary on the new Act in www.nccusl.org.

Before turning to the cases, it should be noted that courts may give one of two effects to a foreign decision. The court may recognize the judgment, or it may additionally enforce it. If it limits its action to recognition, it decides that there is an issue, or issues, which do not need to be relitigated. If it enforces the judgment, it goes further and grants to the successful party some part or all of the judgment decreed by the foreign court. In trying to predict what a court will do, one should consider that (1) the governing law is for the most part state rather than federal, (2) enforcement first requires recognition, (3) direct enforcement is unusual—the process to expect is reduction of the foreign judgment to a judgment of the enforcing court in the United States, and (4) there is little statutory law on the subject—one ought to look to the cases.[3] Once in the United States court, success is dependent upon whether (1) the foreign court had jurisdiction over the person or subject matter, (2) adequate notice was given, (3) there was no fraud in obtaining the judgment, and (4) the public policy of the United States was not harmed. And finally, the issue of reciprocity may be raised.

SOCIETY OF LLOYD'S v. TURNER

United States Court of Appeals, Fifth Circuit, 2002.
303 F.3d 325.

DENNIS, CIRCUIT JUDGE:

The Names' [Lloyd's syndicate investors] claims for fraud were brought all together in the Jaffray action. Despite notice of this action from Lloyd's, neither Webb nor Turner joined in the Jaffray litigation.

---

2. As of early 2011 it had been adopted in 15 states and been introduced in five more plus the District of Columbia.

3. Courts will almost never enforce the revenue or criminal laws of a foreign nation.

The English court * * * entered summary judgment against Turner in England on March 11, 1998, holding him liable to Lloyd's for approximately £71,000. * * * In May 2000, Lloyd's sought recognition of the English monetary judgments against Turner and Webb in separate divisions of the Northern District of Texas. In both cases, the Names sought summary judgment, asking for non-recognition of the English judgments, and, in both cases, Lloyd's filed cross motions for summary judgment, seeking recognition of the judgments. Both district courts granted summary judgment in favor of Lloyd's, holding that the English judgments were enforceable under the Texas Foreign Country Money–Judgment Recognition Act. Webb and Turner have both separately appealed and, because of the similarity of the cases, we consolidated them for review.

Foreign Judgment Recognition

The Uniform Foreign Country Money–Judgment Recognition Act has been adopted by Texas and governs whether a judgment entered by a foreign nation will be recognized in this country. * * * A court may refuse to enforce a foreign judgment if certain provisions * * *are applicable. Relevant here, "[a] foreign country judgment is not conclusive if . . . the judgment was rendered under a system that does not provide impartial tribunals or procedures compatible with the requirements of due process of law." Texas statutory law also provides a court with the discretion not to enforce a foreign country judgment if "the cause of action on which the judgment is based is repugnant to the public policy of this state."

As with all matters of statutory construction, we begin our analysis of the Texas Recognition Act by considering the plain language of the statute. In that vein, we observe that the Texas Recognition Act requires that the foreign judgment be "rendered [only] under a system" that provides impartial tribunals and procedures compatible with "due process of law."[15] Moreover, as the statute requires only the use of "procedures compatible with the requirements of due process," the foreign proceedings need not comply with the traditional rigors of American due process to meet the requirements of enforceability under the statute.[16] This provision has been "interpreted . . . to mean that the foreign procedures [must only be] 'fundamentally fair' and . . . not offend against 'basic fairness.' "

"The origins of our concept of due process are English, . . . [and] United States courts which have inherited major portions of their judicial tradi-

---

15. Bridgeway Corp. v. Citibank, 201 F.3d 134, 137–138, 142–44 (2d Cir.2000) (refusing to enforce a Liberian judgment because of "Liberia's judicial system was in a state of disarray and the provisions of the Constitution concerning the judiciary were no longer followed"); Bank Melli Iran v. Pahlavi, 58 F.3d 1406, 1410–13 (9th Cir.1995) (concluding that after the Shah of Iran was deposed, the Iranian judicial system did not afford protections compatible with due process); Kam–Tech Syst. Ltd. v. Yardeni, 340 N.J.Super. 414, 774 A.2d 644, 649–52 (2001) (concluding that the defendant "has provided us with no basis for concluding that the civil justice system of the State of Israel can in any way be considered lacking the attributes of due process.").

16. Hilton v. Guyot, 159 U.S. 113, 16 S.Ct. 139, 40 L.Ed. 95 (1895) ("[W]e are not prepared to hold that the fact that the [foreign] procedure . . . differed from that of our own courts is, of itself, a sufficient ground for impeaching the foreign judgment.")* * * Uniform Foreign–Money Judgments Recognition Act § 4, U.L.A. (1986) ("[A] mere difference in the procedural system is not a sufficient basis for non-recognition. A case of serious injustice must be involved.").

tions and procedure from the United Kingdom are hardly in a position to call the Queen's Bench a kangaroo court." This court, in particular, has noted that "England [is] a forum that American courts repeatedly have recognized to be fair and impartial." In short, "[a]ny suggestion that th[e] [English] system of courts does not provide impartial tribunals or procedures compatible with the requirements of due process of law borders on the risible." Because "the courts of England are fair and neutral forums," the district courts did not err in recognizing the judgments that Lloyd's obtained there.

Turner and Webb also argue that the district courts erred in enforcing the English judgments because they contravene the public policy of Texas. Under the Uniform Foreign Money–Judgments Recognition Act, "[a] foreign country judgment need not be recognized if . . . the cause of action on which the judgment was based is repugnant to the public policy of the state."[23] To deny enforcement of a foreign judgment based on a public policy argument, the "level of contravention of Texas law has to be high. . . . "

In conducting our analysis, we again begin with the "the plain language of the Texas Recognition Act" and note that it is "the cause of action on which the judgment is based" which must be contrary to Texas public policy before non-recognition is allowed. In Southwest Livestock & Trucking Co., Inc. v. Ramon, we stated that "[t]his subsection of the Texas Recognition Act does not refer to the judgment itself, but specifically to the 'cause of action on which the judgment is based.' Thus, the fact that a judgment offends Texas public policy does not, in and of itself, permit the district court to refuse recognition of that judgment." Ramon involved a "Mexican judgment [that] was based on an action for collection of a promissory note" with a 48% interest rate. The Mexican court ruled in favor of the creditor and ordered the debtor to satisfy the debt and the 48% interest rate in full. The district court, however, refused to recognize the judgment because it violated Texas public policy. This court reversed, concluding that the district court erred in failing to recognize the Mexican judgment because the cause of action for collection on a promissory note did not offend Texas public policy.

Lloyd's sued Webb and Turner for breach of contract and obtained a judgment in England on that cause of action. In presenting their challenge here, Webb and Turner do not argue that a cause of action for breach of contract is contrary to Texas public policy, but instead claim that their particular judgments are contrary to Texas's breach of contract law because Lloyd's needed only to assert the existence of a contract and the amount owed, while Texas requires four elements to be established for a

---

23. Tex. Civ. Prac. & Rem. § 36.005. While the Appellants' due process argument for non-enforcement of the English judgment is a "mandatory" grounds for non-enforcement under subsection (a) of the statute, the public policy argument offered here falls under subsection (b) of the statute, which grants the district judge the "discretion" not to enforce the judgment if he finds that one of the enumerated conditions are met. Although such a requirement seems to mandate an abuse of discretion standard, see, Banque Libanaise Pour Le Commerce v. Khreich, 915 F.2d 1000, 1004 (5th Cir.1990), we have previously employed a de novo review in this context.

breach of contract claim (i.e., (i) the existence of a contract, (ii) proof of the plaintiff's performance, (iii) evidence of the defendant's breach, and (iv) damages). In short, the Appellants argue that the English judgments should not be enforced because the legal standards applied by the English courts are different from the standards that the Texas courts would have applied, had Lloyd's brought its claim there.

Accepting the Appellants' characterization of English breach of contract law as true, the standard for non-recognition of a foreign judgment under the Texas Act is whether the "cause of action" is repugnant to state public policy, not whether the standards for evaluating that cause of action are the same or similar in the foreign country. In other words, [e]nforcement of a judgment of a foreign court based on the law of the foreign jurisdiction does not offend the public policy of the forum simply because the body of foreign law upon which the judgment is based is different from the law of the forum or because the foreign law is more favorable to the judgment creditor than the law of the forum would have been had the original suit been brought at the forum. The very idea of a law of conflicts of law presupposes differences in the laws of various jurisdictions and that different initial results may be obtained depending upon whether one body of law is applied or another.

Because a breach-of-contract cause of action is not contrary to Texas public policy, the district courts did not err in rejecting the claims of Webb and Turner and in recognizing the English judgments. Despite the clear language of the statute and this court's precedent, Webb and Turner also argue that the judgments in their particular cases violate the Texas public policy on cognovit judgments and on the non-waivable protections of consumers from fraud and noncompliance with Texas securities laws. These arguments are without merit, as "[u]nder the Texas Recognition Act, it is irrelevant that the [foreign] judgment itself contravened Texas's public policy...." Ramon, 169 F.3d at 321.

For the foregoing reasons, the judgments of the district courts are AFFIRMED.

Questions and Comments

1. *Hilton* made no commitment to use or discard reciprocity. The truth is that many nations require reciprocity. Why not a position that is perhaps closer to the French, as discussed in *Hilton*, that is not to recognize judgments from nations that do not recognize them from any other nations? That is not reciprocity. Although reciprocity remains an important factor in some states, the Uniform Act does not make reciprocity a precondition for enforcement. But in adopting the Act some states have added a reciprocity requirement. Reciprocity has been criticized in that it conflicts with the desired goal of bringing to an end litigation, that the holder of a judgment has no control over the acts of the country in which the judgment was obtained, and that it probably does not measurably protect Americans abroad or encourage foreign nations to give effect to U.S. judgments.

2. Is comity, as suggested in *Hilton v. Guyot,* actually based on mutuality and reciprocity? Or is it based rather on the merits and persuasiveness of the foreign judgment itself, and on the policy of resolving disputes by litigation which is nonrepetitious?

3. The federal district court applying Texas law in *Hunt I* (a 1980 decision decided prior to the Texas adoption of the UFMJRA, and thus to the *Lloyd's* decision), seemed to classify other legal systems as "favored" or "nonfavored". What criteria are to be used to place a system in one or the other? What is the danger of such a test? Would it measure favored v. unfavored on political grounds? Would you thus place all socialist systems in nonfavored status? And all proceedings in English courts in the favored category—the *Lloyd's* case seems to favor the English system. *Hunt I* had said that "Because this was an English judgment, in the absence of proof to the contrary, it was not necessary, for example, to gauge the fairness of the initial trial." Isn't the court really trying to say we want to separate systems where there is due process and fairness from systems where there is not? But is that distinction based on whether the system is common or civil law? Certainly not. How would you feel if another nation, perhaps the Netherlands or Italy, used the same classification and found the U.S. legal process to lack due process because it was considered to be excessively costly, to provide inadequate aid to the poor, or to be too adversarial in nature? Should we be measuring how "good" a system is, or trying to avoid enforcing judgments where there are elements suggesting serious deficiencies in a legal system? Should the standard be that the system is in the nonfavored class when it to any degree provides less due process than in the United States? How would you classify the Canadian legal system for purposes of this problem? Favored or nonfavored? Would the *Hunt I* court's classification of "favored" give that label to the Mexican legal system in view of its references to *Southwest Livestock & Trucking Co., Inc. v. Ramon*? Much earlier Texas decisions did not seem to favor Mexico. See Comment, Foreign Judgments in American and English Courts: A Comparative Analysis, 26 Seattle U.L.Rev. 591 (2003).

4. Application of a test of whether the foreign proceeding was fair under American concepts of fairness thrusts the court into a difficult and complex task. Much must be known about the foreign legal process. In the *Lloyd's* case, the court considers whether the defendant's staying on for a hearing on the merits after unsuccessfully challenging jurisdiction is a waiver of any right to challenge the decision, whether a counterclaim constitutes a waiver, whether the form of service of process was reasonable, the comparative convenience of the suit in England or Texas, whether enforcement would violate public policy of Texas and whether it would conflict with international law. Would you prefer to opt for an easier test? Is public policy a judicial reservation to achieving fairness in unusual circumstances, or a definable defense? Is a definition of injury to public health, public morals, public confidence in the legal system, or individual rights adequate? Is *Lloyd's,* decided under the UFMJRA, clearer than prior to that Act's adoption in Texas?

5. Cough threw the notice out because he could not read French. *Julen v. Larson,* 25 Cal.App.3d 325, 101 Cal.Rptr. 796 (1972), held under the California UFMJRA that service of Swiss process in German was not reason-

ably calculated to give the defendant notice of the action which resulted in the Swiss judgment. Does that reasoning apply to Cough?

6. Would it be better to have a federal common law governing the recognition and enforcement of foreign judgments? Do you doubt that a federal statute could preempt the area? The United States could by a multilateral or bilateral treaty preempt the area. No such treaty or federal statute has been established, long treaty negotiations were unsuccessful other than concluding the Choice of Court Convention. There have been proposals, also unsuccessful, for a United States–United Kingdom Convention. *See* Smit, *The Proposed United States–United Kingdom Convention on Recognition and Enforcement of Judgments: A Prototype for the Future?,* 17 Va.J.Int'l L. 443 (1977). The Uniform Act has been held not to be preempted by federal law implementing the Convention on Recognition and Enforcement of Arbitral Awards, 9 U.S.C.A. § 201 *et seq. Island Territory of Curacao v. Solitron Devices, Inc.,* 489 F.2d 1313 (2d Cir.1973), cert. denied 416 U.S. 986, 94 S.Ct. 2389, 40 L.Ed.2d 763 (1974). The court held the federal statutes only applied to arbitration awards, not foreign money judgments or enforcement of foreign judgments confirming foreign arbitral awards.

7. We have dealt solely with money judgments above. The Canadian court might have also, or solely, issued an order for specific performance. The Uniform Act is limited to money judgments, so that does not help. Article 28 of the CISG would allow the California court to avoid enforcing specific performance. But are specific performance orders really used in commercial transactions? The party who did not receive goods has probably had to obtain them from other sources to meet contract or production demands. Money damages are by far the reality of breached international commercial transactions.

8. The European Union adopted the Convention on Jurisdiction and the Enforcement of Judgments, which entered into force in 1973. The Convention has been superceded by the Brussels Regulation. The Brussels Regulation's principles are thus in effect, or likely to become so, in a very substantial part of Europe. This has an impact on the United States because its rules are discriminatory as to litigation between signatory states of the Regulation and nonsignatory states such as the United States. Thus, a French judgment entertained solely because of the French citizenship of the plaintiff could be enforced in the United Kingdom against a U.S. defendant. However, article 59 allows a treaty between a signatory state and a nonsignatory state to include a provision that the signatory state will not recognize the judgments of other signatory states against domiciliaries of the nonsignatory state in a jurisdictionally improper forum. Such a provision was included in the proposed treaty noted above between the United States and the United Kingdom.

COMMENTARY ON THE RECOGNITION AND ENFORCEMENT OF FOREIGN JUDGMENTS IN THE COURTS OF OTHER NATIONS

Canada. Anyone seeking the recognition of a foreign money judgment will have to seek its enforcement before a competent provincial court. In 1990 the Canadian Supreme Court ruled that one province must enforce the judgment of another province if the basis for personal jurisdiction was sufficient for obtaining personal jurisdiction in the recognizing province. *De Savoye v. Morguard Investments Ltd.*, 76 D.L.R.4th 256 (Can. 1990). But Quebec, following the French customs established by the Code Michaud of 1629, denies conclusive effect to foreign judgments as a matter of law. Nadelman, *Enforcement of Foreign Judgments in Canada*, 38 Can.Bar.Rev. 68 (1960).

General Canadian practice calls for the recognition of foreign money judgments on "comity" principles similar to those used by the U.S. Supreme Court in *Hilton v. Guyot*, that a foreign judgment ought to be treated as equally binding as a domestic judgment if rendered by a competent court having proper jurisdiction over the defendant. But the understanding of jurisdiction used in the recognition of foreign judgments is different from the standards used by Canadian courts to determine their own jurisdiction. For example, Ontario does not project its jurisdictional rules onto the foreign court. The courts will instead use an "international" standard which limits recognized jurisdiction to five bases: 1) where defendant is a subject of the country in which the judgment is rendered, 2) where he was a resident of the country when the action began, 3) where the defendant, in the character of plaintiff, selected the forum in which he was sued, 4) where he voluntarily appeared, 5) where he has contracted to submit himself to the judgment of the foreign court. *Rousillon v. Rousillon*, 14 Ch.D. 351, 371 (1880); *Ontario Power Co. v. Niagara etc. Power Co.*, 52 Ont.L.R. 168, 173 (C.A.1922); *Metropolitan Trust & Savings Co. v. Osborne*, 14 Ont.W.R. 135, 140, affd., 16 L.W.R. 226 (C.A.1909); *Curtis v. Curtis*, [1943] Ont.W.N. 382. Thus, Canadian courts are not as likely to recognize foreign judgments as would be expected, since concepts of jurisdiction exercised by U.S. courts may not be recognized by Canadian courts. However, contractual specifications of submission to U.S. courts in contracts entered into with Canadians seems to be recognized.

A Canadian court will sometimes recognize a U.S. decision enforcing a legal obligation voluntarily undertaken even when there is no jurisdiction based strictly on the above principles. In *Allen v. Standard Trusts Company*, [1920] 57 D.L.R. 105, a Manitoba court recognized a U.S. judgment (in this case a double liability upon stock assessed by a Minnesota court against the executors of a British subject resident in Manitoba) that arose from a legal obligation assumed by the defendant on purchase of the stock. But generally there will be a distinct imbalance between the extent of the recognition given to Canadian judgments in U.S. courts and U.S. judgments in Canadian courts. For example, in *Gyonyo v. Sanjenki*, 23 D.L.R.3d 695 (Alta.S.C.1971), a default judgment obtained in a Montana court against a resident of Alberta was not recognized in that province. The court held that the U.S. tribunal lacked the required *in personam* jurisdiction over the defendant under the "international" rules discussed above. It made no reference to the Montana statutes that allowed the state court jurisdiction in the case (in this instance, the action arose from a traffic action in Montana involving the Alberta defendant) despite considerable similarity between the Montana and Alberta jurisdictional statutes. Further, the defendant's promise to return to Montana was held not to be a contract to submit to the Montana courts. Such a contractual agreement could not be implied absent a written undertaking.

Thus, only written agreements to be subject to the jurisdiction of U.S. courts will subject a Canadian resident to their jurisdiction.

France. "Absent an international agreement to the contrary, a foreign judgment, in order to have res judicata effect or to be enforceable in France, needs a so-called *exequatur.*" P. Herzog, Civil Procedure in France, at 586 (1967).

Hence, a foreign judgment that has not received the *exequatur* may be used as evidence in a French proceeding involving the same subject matter. However, since it does not have *res judicata* effect, it is not binding and conclusive evidence. Furthermore, a foreign judgment without *exequatur* may be considered sufficient evidence of a claim to entitle its holder to obtain an appropriate provisional remedy, such as an attachment, in France. An *exequatur* must, however, be obtained before the actual execution takes place. *Id.,* at 588.

Five requirements must be met for a foreign judgment to be given an *exequatur.* First, the judgment must have been rendered by a court having jurisdiction under pertinent French rules. If the French courts had jurisdiction to adjudicate the original dispute, and that jurisdiction was not waived by the party against whom enforcement is sought, the foreign judgment will not receive an *exequatur.* "Similarly, if the parties had agreed to give exclusive competence to a French court, a foreign judgment rendered in disregard of that agreement will not be granted an *exequatur.*" *Id.,* at 589. Where no French court is competent, the law is unsettled. Logic has guided some courts to rely on the foreign court's findings of jurisdiction under foreign law. But in cases of migratory divorce, some judgments are denied effect if the defendant were French.

The second requirement is that the foreign judgment comply with the minimum standards of procedural fairness prescribed by *ordre public.* The defendant must have been given actual notice. "French courts will not enforce a foreign judgment in an action in which the defendant was served only by publication, if the plaintiff knew the defendant's address and could have used a method of service better calculated to give the defendant actual notice. *Cie Naviera Baracaldesa v. Lloyd de France,* Trib. Seine, Jan. 18, 1929, 56 Clunet 1056 (1929)." *Id.,* at 590. "If the defendant actually receives timely notice * * * it is not too important what method of service is used, provided it complies with the laws applicable where the action is pending. *E.g., S.A. Wouters et Cie. v. Robert–Berin,* Trib.Gde Inst. Seine Dec. 12, 1961, 89 Clunet 1032 (1962)." *Id.* The defendant must also have been given adequate time to appear and to prepare his defense.

Third, the foreign court must have applied the "correct" law. That is, the foreign court must have applied that law which would have been applicable in a French court under the French choice of law rules. Some more "liberal" decisions have given effect to foreign judgments if the law actually applied and the law applicable under French choice of law rules lead to the same result. For example, a judgment in New York granting a divorce to a French couple under New York law, because of a finding of adulterous acts, will be given force in France, if under French law those same acts are adulterous and adultery is a ground for divorce. *Dame Cureau v. Cureau*, Trib.Seine, May 14, 1956, 8 Clunet 146 (1957).

Fourth, even where French choice of law rules are satisfied, a judgment that violates public policy will not be given effect. An example of this might be where a party temporarily changes his residence, or even nationality, to effect a decision other than that which would have followed under the applicable law before the change.

Finally, a foreign judgment need not be final, but "the judgment must be *executoire*—in other words * * * it must be capable of immediate enforcement in the place of its origin." *Id.*, at 593. Neither the possibility, nor the actual solicitation, of an appeal prevents an *exequatur*, but, in practical effect, it might stay it.

Questions and Comments

Would Cough be less subject to enforcement of the Canadian judgment against him were he in France? What more do you need to know?

PART B. ENFORCING MASS TORT JUDGMENTS FROM QUESTIONABLE LEGAL SYSTEMS

Perhaps two decades ago, when large multinationals began to be sued in U.S. courts by groups of plaintiffs who were almost all from another country and complained about use of U.S. designed or manufactured products allegedly causing injury in their country, the strategy appeared initially to be to defend the suit in the same manner as a totally domestic case—that was to at most seek to remove the case from a state to federal court and go forth applying U.S. law. When lawyers for the defendants learned more about other legal systems and discovered that most foreign nations allowed quite limited damages, and permitted neither contingent fees nor punitive damages, they began to argue that the choice of law pointed to the law of the foreign country where the acts occurred. *Lex loci delicti* helped. But that meant there would be a trial in the United States. Perhaps that trial could be avoided altogether by moving to dismiss on *forum non conveniens* grounds. When many of the cases were so dismissed, and especially when that effectively ended the matter, *forum non conveniens* became the motion of choice. In response, about a decade ago Ecuador enacted a law that attempted to govern the U.S. courts *forum non conveniens* argument, by disallowing any Ecuadorian who had first sued abroad (read—in the United States) from being able to bring the suit in Ecuador if the suit were dismissed abroad. The law attempted to remove local jurisdiction, although there were usually escape holes that would allow such a suit if it benefitted the local party. Because of the relatively minimal development of tort law theory in most of the plaintiffs' nations, the existence of few lawyers who were "tort attorneys," the lack of punitive damages and the prohibition of contingent fees, few cases were taken home for trial. Winning the *forum non conveniens* motion to dismiss essentially meant ending the litigation. Some nominal settlement often was the last nail in the coffin. But lawyers are creative beings and it was only a matter of time before they worked out the fee problems. As for punitive damages, why couldn't the foreign nation allow punitive damages, or some variant thereof, only where the defendant was a large foreign multinational. As to the actual trial, that could be abbreviated by presumptions of injury and overlooking causation. And one further characteristic of many of these nations didn't hurt, a corrupt and nationalistic judiciary. Thus, not very long ago, a few of these cases began to be brought abroad, ending with large judgments against the U.S. defendants. But the putatively successful plaintiffs faced one serious obstacle. Since the defendants were usually careful not to have significant assets in the foreign country, the foreign judgment would have to be taken abroad for recognition and enforcement—usually to the United States.

How would U.S. courts deal with these cases? Many of the states had recently adopted the UFMJRA or UFCMJRA and were thus apparently prepared to enforce foreign judgments. But, as we will see with the materials below, that was not to be.

OSORIO v. DOLE FOOD CO.

United States District Court, Southern District of Florida, 2009.
665 F.Supp.2d 1307, aff'd 635 F.3d 1277 (11th Cir. 2011).

This is an action to enforce a $97 million Nicaraguan judgment under the Florida Uniform Out-of-country Foreign Money–Judgments Recognition Act (Florida Recognition Act). Plaintiffs are 150 Nicaraguan citizens alleged to have worked on banana plantations in Nicaragua between 1970 and 1982, during which time they were exposed to the chemical compound dibromochloropropane (DBCP). DBCP is an agricultural pesticide that was banned in the United States after it was linked to sterility in factory workers in 1977. Nicaragua banned DBCP in 1993. Defendants are Dole Food Company and The Dow Chemical Company, both Delaware corporations. Dow manufactured DBCP from 1957 until 1977, and Dole used DBCP on its banana farms in Nicaragua until the farms were expropriated by the Sandinista regime that came to power in 1979.

The judgment in this case was rendered by a trial court in Chinandega, Nicaragua. The trial court awarded Plaintiffs approximately $97 million under "Special Law 364," enacted by the Nicaraguan legislature in 2000 specifically to handle DBCP claims. The average award was approximately $647,000 per plaintiff. According to the Nicaraguan trial court, these sums were awarded to compensate Plaintiffs for DBCP-induced infertility and its accompanying adverse psychological effects. Defendants have appealed the judgment to an intermediate appellate court in Nicaragua. That appeal is still pending.

Defendants raise several objections to domesticating the judgment. They contend that under the Florida Recognition Act this Court cannot enforce the judgment because (1) the Nicaraguan trial court lacked personal and/or subject matter jurisdiction under Special Law 364, (2) the judgment was rendered under a system which does not provide procedures compatible with due process of law, (3) enforcing the judgment would violate Florida public policy, and (4) the judgment was rendered under a judicial system that lacks impartial tribunals.[1] For the reasons set forth below, the Court holds that Defendants have clearly established their entitlement to non-recognition on each of these independent grounds.

The first DBCP lawsuits were brought in the mid–1990s * * * in Texas against various defendants. Those cases were consolidated and the defendants, who included Dole and Dow, won dismissal on forum non conveniens grounds after arguing that the plaintiffs' various home countries provided adequate alternative forums. See Delgado v. Shell Oil Co., 890 F.Supp. 1324, 1362 (S.D.Tex.1995). None of the plaintiffs in Delgado are plaintiffs in this action.

In response to Delgado, which resulted in plaintiffs filing numerous DBCP claims in Nicaragua, the Nicaraguan National Assembly passed the "Special Law for the Conduct of Lawsuits Filed By Persons Affected By the Use of Pesticides Manufactured with a DBCP Base," commonly referred to as "Special Law 364." Since the passage of Special Law 364 in October 2000, over 10,000 plaintiffs have filed approximately 200 DBCP lawsuits in Nicaragua, most of which are still pending. To date, however, Nicaraguan courts have awarded over $2 billion in judgments, including the $97 million judgment that is the subject of this case. In a sister case tried after this one, Herrera Ríos v. Standard Fruit Co., the same trial judge awarded 1248 plaintiffs over $800 million, an average recovery of approximately $648,000 per plaintiff.

Nicaraguan claimants have made one previous attempt to enforce a DBCP judgment in the United States. In 2003, more than 450 Nicaraguan plaintiffs attempted to enforce a $489 million judgment in California, but their complaint was dismissed on technical and jurisdictional grounds without reaching the merits of the defendants' substantive objections.

* * * Special Law 364 is unique in that its provisions apply only to DBCP litigation, and only against specific defendants such as Dole and Dow. Nicaragua has no comparable law that only applies to a specific type of litigation and a narrowly defined class of defendants. * * * Special Law 364's stated purpose is to regulate procedures for DBCP lawsuits "with regard to compensation" of persons injured by the pesticide. Article 1. To accomplish this goal, the law contains some notable provisions which to a great extent are the crux of this litigation. Article 2 states that DBCP defendants, defined as companies that manufactured, imported, distributed, marketed, or applied the pesticide, acted with full knowledge of DBCP's harmful effects, which the law says include sterility and kidney, liver, and spleen damage. * * * Article 9 provides that plaintiffs who prove that (1) they were exposed to DBCP and (2) are now sterile, are

---

1. Defendants also contend that the judgment is the offspring of a conspiracy by American and Nicaraguan plaintiffs' attorneys to manufacture fraudulent DBCP claims in Nicaragua and the United States. The Court bifurcated the fraud issue from the rest of this case, and provided that it would be addressed only in the event Defendants fail to prevail on their other defenses.

entitled to an "irrefutable presumption" that DBCP exposure caused their sterility. * * * Each prevailing plaintiff is entitled to minimum damages of $125,000 ($100,000 under Article 3 and $25,000 under Article 11), but the law permits the trial court to award sums in excess of the mandatory minimums that it finds are comparable to similar personal injury verdicts obtained by plaintiffs in foreign countries such as the United States. * * * With regards to litigation costs, Special Law 364 presumes that the plaintiffs are indigent and provides that the Nicaraguan government will cover their costs. In contrast, the law imposes several burdens on the defendants' right to participate in the proceedings. For example, defendants are required to post a $100,000 bond "as a procedural prerequisite for being able to take part in the lawsuit." Article 4. The law provides that the bond will be used to cover court costs and provide compensation to the plaintiffs. Defendants are also required to deposit 300,000,000 córdobas, approximately $15 million, within 90 days after receiving notice of the complaints, "to guarantee payment of the possible compensation to the workers and other costs of the lawsuit." Article 8.

Article 12 requires the presiding trial judge to enforce a "3–8–3" summary proceeding upon pain of punishment. In a 3–8–3 proceeding, "defendants have three days to answer the complaint, the parties have eight days to present their evidence, and the court has three days to issue a verdict." Special Law 364 also eliminates any relevant statutes of limitations, retroactively applies to pending cases, and provides that judgments are immediately executable notwithstanding the pendency of an appeal. * * * Another notable provision, Article 7, appears to give the defendants the right to select their venue and opt out of Special Law 364 by agreeing to defend themselves in the United States:

Companies that, within ninety (90) days of being given notice of this Law by the plaintiff and service of process through the corresponding channel, have not deposited the sum established in Article 4 hereof, must subject themselves unconditionally to the jurisdiction of the courts of the United States of America for the final judgment of the case in question, expressly waiving the defense of forum non conveniens invoked in those courts. In the event that the defendants decide that the proceedings are to continue in the Nicaraguan courts, they are to deposit the amount established in Article 4 of this Law.

Because they elected not to make the Article 4 deposits, Dole and Dow argue that the Nicaraguan trial court improperly exercised jurisdiction over them in clear contravention of Article 7. Moreover, they contend that Special Law 364's other provisions, which apply only to them—the bond and deposit requirements, minimum damages, irrefutable presumptions of knowledge and causation, 3–8–3 summary proceedings, abolition of statutes of limitations, and effective curtailment of appellate review—are incompatible with due process of law and violate Florida public policy. Defendants also assert that Special Law 364 impermissibly targets a narrowly defined group of foreign companies for disparate treatment.

After the passage of Special Law 364, the Nicaraguan Attorney General rendered a legal opinion that the law violated Nicaragua's constitution. The Attorney General sent his opinion to the Supreme Court of Justice of Nicaragua and asked the court to forward his opinion to all civil judges in Nicaragua so that when rendering judgments they would be guided by his analysis of Special Law 364's constitutional infirmities. First, the Attorney General argued that it was inappropriate to try a complex lawsuit that could potentially produce large damage awards under a 3–8–3 summary proceeding. * * * Second, [he] found that Special Law 364 was unconstitutional because it does not allow an appeal to the Supreme Court. * * * Third, the Attorney General found that the law was unconstitutional because it treats plaintiffs and defendants unequally, which "violates the Constitutional right of equality of conditions of parties in proceedings or actions." Under Special Law 364, the plaintiffs enjoy all the rights of indigent parties while the defendants are required to make deposits as a prerequisite for being able to participate in the proceedings. * * * Under the Attorney General's reading of Special Law 364, the law assumes that the plaintiffs will automatically prevail and does not even contemplate the possibility that DBCP defendants might succeed in defeating plaintiffs' claims. * * * As the Court explains below in its analysis of Special Law 364, this crucial provision operates to establish legal liability without any reliable proof that the defendants actually caused the plaintiffs' injuries. Following the Attorney General's opinion challenging Special Law 364's constitutionality, the Nicaraguan Supreme Court issued an advisory opinion upholding the law.

Unlike the Attorney General's opinion, which described the constitutional right of equality as a principle that ensures an even playing field between plaintiffs and defendants in the same action, the Supreme Court equated the "Principle of Equality" with an affirmative duty to discriminate in favor of a socioeconomically disadvantaged party. According to the Supreme Court, "the Principle of Equality is based on the social reality of [Nicaragua]" and is designed to ameliorate inequality in the political, social, and economic life of Nicaragua by providing procedural advantages to putatively disadvantaged elements of society. * * * In effect, the Nicaraguan Supreme Court acknowledged that Special Law 364 provides unequal treatment to DBCP defendants because Special Law 364 is an attempt to level the litigation playing field by giving the DBCP plaintiffs, termed "peasants" by the court, disproportionate advantages which are not available in other Nicaraguan litigation.

Defendants' Jurisdictional Challenge and Appeal. The Nicaraguan trial court ordered Defendants to appear and deposit the bond and guarantee monies required by Articles 4 and 8 of Special Law 364. Dole and Dow declined to make the deposits. Instead, they consented to jurisdiction in the United States and waived their defenses under the forum non conveniens doctrine. Their initial pleadings contested the trial court's jurisdiction and attempted to exercise their opt-out rights under Article 7. * * * [T]he trial court denied Dole and Dow's jurisdictional challenges. * * * Apparently, the court interpreted Article 7 to provide plaintiffs with a choice of venue, but permit defendants to argue forum non conveniens in the United States only if they first comply with the deposit requirements of Article 4. * * * After failing in its jurisdictional argument before the trial court, Dow declined to participate further in the trial proceedings because it did not want its continued participation to be interpreted as a waiver of its jurisdictional objections. Dole remained in Nicaragua and defended itself under protest.

During the evidentiary period, the trial court heard oral testimony from ten out of 201 plaintiffs. * * * All of the medical evidence, including the evaluations by the specialized doctors, was examined by * * * the court appointed medical examiner. . . . The trial court denied Dole's request for an independent doctor to examine individual plaintiffs, as well as Dole's request to depose the laboratory technicians who took the spermograms.

The trial court awarded the 150 prevailing plaintiffs a total of $97.4 million. The average award was approximately $650,000 and the minimum award was $188,500. * * * [T]he trial court, by its own admission, had no evidence before it demonstrating a causal relationship between DBCP exposure and the individual plaintiffs' injuries.

Defendants contend that each mandatory ground, as well as the discretionary public policy and fraud grounds, bar enforcement of the judgment.

The Florida Recognition Act requires that the rendering court possess both subject matter jurisdiction and personal jurisdiction over the defendants. Defendants argue that because they opted out of Nicaragua's jurisdiction under Section 7 of Special Law 364, the Nicaraguan trial court lacked jurisdiction over them. Plaintiffs * * * argue that Section 7 does not allow defendants to opt out of Nicaragua's jurisdiction, but merely provides plaintiffs with a choice of venue. The issue the Court must decide is whether Defendants were subject to jurisdiction in Nicaragua under Section 7 of Special Law 364.

In light of the onerous conditions imposed on DBCP defendants by Special Law 364, the history of the DBCP litigation, the Nicaraguan legislature's reaction to the dismissal of DBCP claims in Delgado, and the acknowledged discriminatory treatment of DBCP defendants in Nicaragua, it is not undue speculation to infer that Special Law 364 may not have been primarily intended for the actual litigation of cases in Nicaragua, but instead to provide Nicaraguan plaintiffs with a forum in the United States. The law accomplishes this by effectively eliminating forum non conveniens defenses in the United States in DBCP litigation because it makes the foreign forum so unattractive from a defendant's perspective. * * * Special Law 364 appears to be somewhat unique among blocking statutes in that it operates by establishing onerous conditions under which defendants would litigate and then providing the defendants with the right to opt out of Nicaragua's jurisdiction.

It is beyond dispute that Special Law 364 provides ample incentives for the defendants to exercise their opt-out rights by * * * effectively depriving them of due process in their effort to mount a defense. As the Nicaraguan Supreme Court rationalized * * * the constitutionality of Special Law 364 rests in large part on the defendants' right to choose to litigate in the jurisdiction most convenient to them. In other words, either DBCP defendants have a right to opt out of Nicaragua's jurisdiction, which requires that the Court deny recognition under Fla. Stat. 55.605 § (1)(b)–(c), or they are subject to a legal regime that does not provide due process, which requires denying recognition under Fla. Stat. 55.605 § (1)(a). In practical terms, it does not matter which of these is actually the case because either circumstance constitutes a mandatory ground for refusing to recognize this judgment under the Florida Recognition Act. This is Plaintiffs' "Catch–22."

The Court finds that Article 7 is a jurisdictional provision because it affects the courts' power to resolve the issues before it. * * * Ultimately, it does not matter whether the impact of Article 7 is stated in terms of subject matter or personal jurisdiction because either interpretation results in a mandatory ground for non-recognition under the Florida Recognition Act. * * * Accordingly, the Court finds that Defendants effectively invoked their opt-out rights under Article 7 of Special Law 364. This act divested the Nicaraguan trial court of jurisdiction. Therefore, the Florida Recognition Act does not permit the Court to enforce this judgment because the foreign court lacked subject matter and/or personal jurisdiction over Defendants.

A foreign judgment cannot be recognized in Florida if it was "rendered under a system which does not provide ... procedures compatible with the requirements of due process of law." The term "due process" in this context does not refer to the "latest twist and turn of our courts" regarding procedural due process norms, * * * Rather, it is meant to embody an "international concept of due process," defined as "a concept of fair procedures simple and basic enough to describe the judicial processes of civilized nations, our peers."

Defendants argue that the procedures under which this case was tried are incompatible with the requirements of due process because numerous provisions of Special Law 364 fail to provide "basic fairness" to the DBCP defendants subject to its provisions. The Court takes up this issue as follows: First, it examines the scientific basis for the irrefutable presumption of causation afforded to plaintiffs who establish DBCP exposure and sperm damage, and evaluates whether the presumption constitutes a procedure consistent with due process in light of the medical testimony in this case. * * * The Court does not hesitate to conclude that awarding damages without regard for fault is the antithesis of basic fairness both in domestic and international litigation. The Florida Recognition Act contains enumerated, mandatory grounds for non-recognition of foreign judgments precisely to prevent courts in this state from becoming a party to such legal caprice.

Defendants and similarly situated United States companies constitute the limited targets of Special Law 364. The evidence in this case, and the terms of Special Law 364 itself, demonstrate that the law was meant to apply, and does apply, to the specific DBCP defendants who were parties in Delgado. This alone, of course, does not mean that Special Law 364 denies the covered defendants due process. It is the combination of Special Law 364's limited applicability along with its unique discriminatory provisions that together amount to a denial of due process.

In an effort to justify the statutorily mandated minimum damages in Special Law 364, Plaintiffs argue that damages established by statute are not rare in Nicaragua. * * * There is no evidence whatsoever that any other defendants in the Nicaraguan legal system are subject to minimum damages of the magnitude required by Special Law 364.

Another example of Special Law 364's unfair, discriminatory nature is its procedure for appellate review. In Article 14, Special Law 364 provides for an appeal only to the intermediate appellate court, not to the Supreme Court. * * * The Court also notes that in this case, Defendants have not yet enjoyed any appellate process in Nicaragua. The Court heard expert testimony that appeals in Nicaragua normally take six to twelve months, but the Nicaraguan court of appeals has not acted on any of Defendants' multiple appeals, one of which has been ripe for adjudication for four and a half years.

Defendants also contend that Special Law 364 discriminates against DBCP defendants by requiring a 3–8–3 summary proceeding for medically complex cases involving hundreds of plaintiffs and circumstances going back almost thirty years. * * * The application of the 3–8–3 summary procedure is particularly inequitable here because the events giving rise to the plaintiffs' claims took place over thirty years ago and were followed by political upheaval which resulted in the loss of most, if not all, documents relevant to the employment of banana farms workers and the use of DBCP at those farms.

In sum, Special Law 364 contains numerous unique provisions that apply only to a narrow class of foreign defendants, and operate to their distinct disadvantage in a pronounced discriminatory fashion. The Court also finds that Special Law 364's disparate treatment of defendants is fatally unfair and discriminatory, fails to provide the minimum level of due process to which all foreign defendants are entitled, and is, therefore, incompatible with the requirements of due process of law under the Florida Recognition Act.

The Court, therefore, finds that Defendants have met their burden of proving that the legal regime set up by Special Law 364 and applied in this case does not comport with the "basic fairness" that the "international concept of due process" requires. It does not even come close. "Civilized nations" do not typically require defendants to pay out millions of dollars without proof that they are responsible for the alleged injuries. Basic fairness requires proof of a connection between a plaintiff's injury and a defendant's conduct (i.e., causation) before awarding millions of dollars in damages. Civilized nations do not target and discriminate against a handful of foreign companies and subject them to minimum damages so dramatically out of proportion with damage awards against resident defendants. In summary, civilized nations simply do not subject foreign defendants to the type of discriminatory laws and procedures mandated by Special Law 364, and the Court cannot enforce the judgment because it was rendered under a legal system that did not provide "procedures compatible with the requirements of due process of law."

The Florida Recognition Act provides that the enforcing court need not recognize a judgment if it is based on a cause of action or claim of relief that is repugnant to Florida public policy. Defendants have identified thirteen different ways in which, they contend, enforcing the $97 million judgment would violate public policy. The Court, however, limits its analysis to Defendants' challenges to the portions of Special Law 364 which the Court has already concluded are inconsistent with the international concept of due process embodied in the Florida Recognition Act, because they discriminate against a narrowly defined group of United States companies and target them for legal rules and procedures unique to Special Law 364.

A judgment should not be enforced on public policy grounds when enforcement would clearly undermine public confidence in the administration of the law or in the security of individual rights.

Defendants argue that the irrefutable presumption of causation relied upon in the Judgment is repugnant to Florida public policy because it deprived them of their basic right to defend themselves. The Court agrees. * * * As the Court has explained, the presumption of causation in Special Law 364 contradicts known scientific fact and affords no opportunity for rebuttal. It creates liability by legislative fiat and mandates large damage awards without determining whether the defendants actually injured the plaintiffs. Special Law 364's presumption of causation would, therefore, be unconstitutional in Florida.

The Court must now determine whether the difference between Florida law, which requires plaintiffs to prove causation in accordance with medical science and provides defendants with an opportunity to rebut the plaintiffs' allegations, and Nicaraguan law, which exempts the plaintiffs from offering medically sufficient proof of causation and denies the defendants an opportunity for rebuttal, is sufficient to warrant non-recognition based on public policy grounds. The Court does not find this to be a difficult question, and holds that the irrefutable presumption of causation applied in this case is a sufficiently consequential departure from Florida law to warrant non-recognition on public policy grounds. * * * The Court finds that enforcing this judgment would undermine public confidence in the tribunals of this state, in the rule of law, in the administration of justice, and in the security of individuals' rights to a fair judicial process. As such, the Court declines to recognize this judgment because the "cause of action or claim for relief on which the judgment is based is repugnant to the public policy of this state."

Finally, the Court reaches the issue of whether Nicaragua has impartial tribunals, as required for recognition by Fla. Stat. § 55.605(1)(a). The Court admits that it is not entirely comfortable sitting in judgment of another nation's judicial system, but does so in deference to the Florida Recognition Act, which includes the absence of impartial tribunals as a mandatory basis for non-recognition. After reviewing the evidence and assessing the credibility of live testimony, the Court concludes that the evidence is compelling that Nicaragua lacks impartial tribunals. This conclusion is based on the credible evidence that, while on paper and in theory Nicaragua has all the trappings of an independent judiciary, in practice the judiciary does not act impartially. * * * [I]t appears to the Court that the unanimous view among United States government organizations and officials (including United States ambassadors to Nicaragua), foreign governments, international organizations, and credible Nicaraguan authorities, is that the judicial branch in Nicaragua is dominated by political forces and, in general, does not dispense impartial justice. * * * Plaintiffs have not cited a single report or independent authority, other than their own experts, that claims Nicaragua possessed an impartial judiciary during or after the pendency of the Osorio action. * * * [T]he Court is compelled to find that the judgment in this case cannot be recognized under the Florida Recognition Act because it "was rendered under a system which does not provide impartial tribunals[.]" Fla. Stat. § 55.605(1)(a).

This court holds that Defendants have established multiple, independent grounds under the Florida Recognition Act that compel non-recognition of the $97 million Nicaraguan judgment. Because the judgment was "rendered under a system which does not provide impartial tribunal or procedures compatible with the requirements of due process of law," and the rendering court did not have jurisdiction over Defendants, the judgment is not considered conclusive, and cannot be enforced under the Florida Recognition Act. Fla. Stat. § 55.605(1)(a)-(c). Additionally, the judgment will not be enforced because "the cause of action or claim for relief on which the judgment is based is repugnant to the public policy of this state." Fla. Stat. § 55.605(2)(c). The Court, therefore, orders that Plaintiffs' judgment shall be neither recognized nor enforced.

[**Author's note:** This decision was upheld in a brief decision that focused exclusively on the issue of jurisdiction of the Nicaraguan courts. See 635 F.3d 1277 (11th Cir. 2011).]

QUESTIONS AND COMMENTS

1. Why would the appellate court not at the very minimum explore the issues of due process and public policy that were discussed at length by the district court?

2. One might compare Special Law 364 of Nicaragua with Law 55 of Ecuador, discussed in Part B of Problem 11.2. Are these sound responses to

the frustration of developing nations' citizens in not having legal systems capable of dealing with mass tort litigation?

3. What do you consider the most damaging feature of Special Law 364 with regard to the due process aspect? Indeed, how many due process concerns are there?

4. Is the consideration of conflicts with Florida's notions of public policy dependent upon the due process argument?

5. The *Osorio* court stated that in an "action to enforce a judgment, the general proposition that it is inappropriate for United States courts to sit in judgment of foreign judicial systems in the forum non conveniens context," citing *Warter v. Boston Sec., S.A.*, 380 F. Supp. 2d 1299 (S.D. Fla. 2004)(Argentina adequate forum). *Osorio* shows that it is possible using experts to establish that a foreign legal system is inappropriate in either the context of a *forum non conveniens* or enforcement consideration. Then why are courts reluctant? What would your list of inadequate systems be?

6. Does the Osorio decision raise a broader question—should courts enforce judgments rendered in nations with corrupt or fundamentally impaired legal systems? Does fundamentally impaired include fraud? See 44 Int'l Lawyer 902–912 (2010)(discussing three Mexican cases).

PART C. RENDERING JUDGMENTS—THE CHOICE OF CURRENCY

When the Canadian court rendered its judgment against Roger Cough, it was given in the currency of the nation of the court, Canada. But the loan was in U.S. dollars and Cough expected to repay it in U.S. dollars. He certainly also must have expected to pay any judgment related to the loan in U.S. dollars. The Canadian court gave judgment in Canadian dollars ($461,538), which were equivalent to $300,000 U.S. at the time of the judgment. But some time has passed since the judgment was rendered in Canada and, being unpaid, is now the subject of the enforcement proceeding in the United States. Assume the U.S. dollar began to drop soon after the judgment and the U.S. and Canadian dollars are again at parity. We may assume that at the time a judgment is given in any state in the United States enforcing the Canadian judgment (if a U.S. court is willing to enforce the judgment), the $461,538 (Canadian) is likely to be worth $461,538 (U.S.). Cough probably believes that if he has to pay up, it will be the $300,000 and perhaps interest. But if the judgment is enforced in Canadian currency, or in U.S. dollars measured at the time of the enforcement determination, he may have to pay much more. Isn't the bank only entitled to be made whole, that is receiving $300,000 U.S.? That is the currency of the debt. What would be the impact were the judgment court to adopt (1) the date of the breach, (2) the date of the Canadian judgment, (3) the date of the enforcement decision, or (4) the date of the payment?

Choice of time for establishing a judgment in another currency is a separate question than enforcement of a foreign judgment. But it might affect a court asked to recognize and enforce a judgment. We have some guidance in the Uniform Foreign Money Claims Act, which has been adopted in California.[4]

MANCHES & CO. v. GILBEY

419 Mass. 414, 646 N.E.2d 86 (1995).

WILKINS, JUSTICE.

On August 20, 1992, the Queen's Bench Division of the High Court of Justice in London entered a default judgment in favor of Manches & Co. (Manches), a London firm of solicitors, against Suzanne Gilbey and Peter Thornton totaling £30,138.35. On November 9, 1992, Manches commenced this action in the Superior Court in Barnstable County to enforce the foreign judgment pursuant to [the Massachusetts version of] the Uniform Foreign Money–Judgments Recognition Act. Manches's underlying claim was that the defendants were liable for legal services rendered to Gilbey in England following the death of her father.

The principal issue in this appeal concerns the amount of the judgment that should have been entered in Massachusetts in view of changes in the exchange rate between the British pound and the American dollar. It appears that on August 20, 1992, the date that judgment was entered in London, approximately $58,450 equaled the amount stated in pounds in the English judgment (£30,138.35). On December 13, 1993, the date on which summary judgment was granted in favor of Manches in Barnstable Superior Court, approximately $45,130 would have purchased £30,138.35. Thus, because of the decline in the British pound in relation to the American dollar, the defendants could satisfy their obligation to Manches, expressed in pounds, by paying out considerably fewer dollars in late 1993 than they could have sixteen months earlier when the English default judgment was entered.

Because the motion judge entered judgment in dollars using the latter exchange rate (the one more beneficial to the defendants), Manches has appealed. Because the motion judge entered judgment in favor of Manches, the defendants have appealed, arguing that, for various reasons, the English judgment is not worthy of enforcement in Massachusetts.* * * If the defendants are correct in their claim that the English judgment is unenforceable, the question of the proper amount of any judgment that should be entered in favor of Manches in Massachusetts is unimportant. Therefore, we shall discuss the defendants' appeal first. We conclude that the English judgment is enforceable in Massachusetts. . . .

The obligation to pay pounds, expressed in the English judgment, should be enforced by a judgment that orders the defendants at their option either (a) to pay £30,138.35 (with interest) or (b) to pay the equivalent in dollars of £ 30,138.35 (with interest), determined by the exchange rate in effect on the day of payment (or the day before payment).

---

4. The UFMCA has been adopted in the District of Columbia, the U.S. Virgin Islands, and in 20 states.

Manches is entitled to be restored to the position in which it would have been if the defendants had paid their obligations, but it is not entitled to more. The so-called payment day rule achieves this result. In re Oil Spill by the Amoco Cadiz, 954 F.2d 1279, 1328 (7th Cir.1992).

There is no guiding Massachusetts law on this point. The decided cases in this country have adopted various positions. Some have followed the breach day rule, the one Manches advocates, in which the conversion of foreign obligations is made as of the date of breach of the obligation. See, e.g., Gathercrest, Ltd. v. First Am. Bank & Trust, 805 F.2d 995, 997 (11th Cir.1986). Others have used the judgment day rule, converting the foreign obligation into dollars based on the exchange rate on the date the judgment is entered. See, e.g., Agfa–Gevaert, A.G. v. A.B. Dick Co., 879 F.2d 1518, 1524 (7th Cir.1989) (applying New York statute). The latter is the rule that the defendants prefer and that the motion judge adopted. We prefer a third option, the payment day rule.

The Restatement (Third) of Foreign Relations Law § 823 (1987) advises that the conversion to dollars should be "made at such rate as to make the creditor whole and to avoid rewarding a debtor who has delayed in carrying out the obligation." In comment c of § 823, the Restatement becomes more specific and tentatively adopts the breach day rule if, as here, the foreign currency has depreciated since the breach, and, if the foreign currency has appreciated since the breach, it adopts the exchange rate on the date of judgment or the date of payment. "The court is free, however, to depart from those guidelines when the interests of justice require it."

The Uniform Foreign–Money Claims Act, which has been enacted in eighteen American jurisdictions (but not in Massachusetts), adopts the payment day rule. It is this rule that, for the circumstances of this case, we apply as a matter of common law. That rule will award Manches in pounds (or the equivalent in dollars on or near the day of payment) the amount it would have recovered had it been able to collect on the judgment in Great Britain. Satisfaction of the judgment in present day pounds will make Manches whole. In entering judgments, courts do not normally reflect changes in the purchasing power of local currency between the date of a breach and the date of the award of judgment. As the prefatory note to the Uniform Act states: "The principle of the Act is to restore the aggrieved party to the economic position it would have been in had the wrong not occurred.... Courts should enter judgments in the money customarily used by the injured person." Manches incurred its expenses in England, expected to be compensated in pounds, and sustained its loss in pounds. The payment day rule is fair in this case because its application meets the reasonable expectations of the parties in this case.

It is said that the payment day rule is the one used in "most of the major civilized countries of the world." If the circumstances were reversed, courts in England would apply it or use the nearest practicable date. See Miliangos v. George Frank (Textiles) Ltd., [1976] App.Cas. 443 (favoring payment date rule because "[t]his date gets nearest to securing to the creditor exactly what he bargained for," where payment date was understood as the date execution of judgment would be authorized). See also Owners of M.V. Eleftherotria v. Owners of M.V. Despina R, [1979] App.Cas. 685 (where the contract provides no answer to the currency question, "the damage should be calculated currency in which the loss was felt by the plaintiff or 'which most truly expresses his loss' ").[8]

Judgment shall be entered ordering that Manches & Co. shall recover from the defendants, at the defendants' option, either (a) the amount of the English judgment (£30,138.35) or (b) the equivalent in dollars of the English judgment determined at the exchange rate in effect on the day of or the day before payment, with interest on that amount (in each instance), payable in pounds or dollars, at the Massachusetts rate of interest from the date of entry of the action until the date of payment.[9]

FREEMAN, JUDGMENTS IN FOREIGN CURRENCY— A LITTLE KNOWN CHANGE IN NEW YORK LAW
23 Int'l Law. 737 (1989).*

With little if any fanfare or public attention, the New York State Legislature recently amended New York law to provide expressly that for the first time judgments may be rendered in currencies other than United States dollars. The amendment specifically provides that in a case where a cause of action is based on an obligation denominated in a currency other than U.S. dollars, a New York court must render its judgment in the foreign currency at a rate of exchange prevailing on the date of entry of judgment. The amendment takes an innovative step toward resolving complex and potentially inequitable results stemming from transnational, cross-currency transactions, which often involve disparate conversion choices and volatile exchange rates. Neither courts nor commentators, nor presumably even many practitioners, however, appear to be aware of the amendment.

I. Foreign Currency Judgment Law Before the Amendment

Until the recent New York amendment, it was generally assumed that New York and other American courts did not have the power, or at least

---

8. There has been no claim that, on conflict of laws principles, the conversion date question should be determined by the law of Great Britain where the contract for services was made and the default judgment was entered. We assume, without deciding, that the internal substantive law of Massachusetts governs the conversion date question.

9. If there is action taken to execute on the judgment, it is likely that only option (b) of the judgment will be practicable. The parties did not raise the question in the Superior Court of how interest should be expressed in the Massachusetts judgment or whether English or Massachusetts law should determine interest questions. The judge awarded interest from the time of entry of this action at the rate of interest payable under Massachusetts law. No challenge was made on appeal to that ruling, although Manches states that English law would call for interest at an annual rate of 15% from the date of the English judgment, payable on the base amount due (i.e., not including interest) expressed in the English judgment.

* Reprinted with permission of the American Bar Association and the author. Copyright © 1989 American Bar Association.

the precedent, under which to render judgments in foreign currency. As the Restatement (Third) of the Foreign Relations Law of the United States (the Restatement) explained: "The traditional United States rule has been that courts in the United States are required to render money judgments payable in United States dollars only, regardless of the currency of obligation or loss." No decision has been located, either before or after the foreign currency judgment amendment, in which a judgment was awarded by an American court in a foreign currency. Nor has any other state statute been located authorizing foreign currency judgments. Curiously, at least one decision and article dated after the amendment do not even mention the amendment.

A. Legal Rationales

The basis for this general rule against the rendering of judgments in foreign currencies has not been clearly or consistently articulated. Some courts have referred to a common law principle that a judgment in a foreign currency was not enforceable. Although the common law notion was rejected in 1976 in Great Britain, other courts have relied on principles of sovereignty and the impracticality of obtaining other currencies.

B. Conversion of Foreign Currency Claims to U.S. Dollars

To provide recovery to litigants in U.S. currency, courts have generally selected one of two dates on which to exchange foreign currency into U.S. dollars—the date of the judgment or the date of the breach.

The judgment day conversion rule has been used by federal courts in suits based on obligations existing under foreign law where the debt is payable in the foreign currency. As the Supreme Court has explained, the judgment day rule has been utilized on the theory that "[a]n obligation in terms of the currency of a [foreign] country takes the risk of currency fluctuations...."[25] Thus, conversion as of the judgment day includes any appreciation or depreciation of the foreign currency as against the U.S. dollar up through the date of judgment. Such a rule, it is argued, avoids inconsistent results as between an action in the United States and an action in the foreign court; the foreign court generally would give judgment in its currency without regard to currency fluctuations, which would be equivalent to a U.S. dollar judgment converted as of the day of judgment. It is also argued, however, that the judgment day rule may unduly reward a dilatory defendant during a time of depreciation of the foreign currency.[27]

---

25. Deutsche Bank v. Humphrey, 272 U.S. 517 (1926); *see* Zimmermann v. Sutherland, 274 U.S. 253, 255–56 (1927); Vishipco Line v. Chase Manhattan Bank (*Vishipco I*), 660 F.2d 854, 865 (2d Cir.1981) ("It is true that federal courts sitting in *non*-diversity cases have rather consistently adopted the judgment-day rule."), *cert. denied,* 459 U.S. 976 (1982); Vishipco Line v. Chase Manhattan Bank (*Vishipco II*), 754 F.2d 452, 454 (2d Cir.1985) (noting the "currency-conversion rule employed by New York courts, pursuant to which recovery in United States currency is to be measured by the dollar value of the [foreign currency] on the date of breach.") * * *.

27. * * * *see also* Deutsche Bank v. Humphrey, 272 U.S. at 520, 525 (Sutherland, J., dissenting) (criticizing the majority's adoption of the judgment day rule: "The amount of the

As to New York and certain other state law claims, courts have generally converted the foreign currency to dollars as of the date of the breach or injury. Courts generally characterize the choice of conversion dates as substantive rather than procedural, which invokes the *Erie* doctrine and subjects the issue to state law determination. Use of the breach day rule has been justified on the theory that a plaintiff is best made whole by putting him back in the position he would have been in, but for the breach.

The breach day conversion rule has also been subject to question. According to the Second Circuit: "[T]he breach-day rule is favorable to a plaintiff only when the foreign currency in which the obligation was originally measured has depreciated with respect to the defendant's currency ... during the period since the breach. If it has appreciated, the judgment rule will be more favorable." Recently, in *Teca–Print,* a New York trial court carefully reviewed New York case law, concluding that there was no "strict rule" requiring the use of the breach day for currency conversion and questioning the "continued viability" of the breach day rule. In that case, a Swiss plaintiff sought recovery in New York for the sale of certain goods billed in Swiss francs. The sole issue before the court was the applicable conversion date, either the traditional breach day or the federal, "more modern," judgment day. Apparently unaware of the foreign currency judgment amendment, the court assumed (incorrectly) that it lacked the authority to render a foreign currency judgment. Instead, because of the continuing fluctuation of the U.S. dollar against the Swiss franc, the court chose the date of conversion that provided a "fair and equitable result"—not the breach day, but the judgment day.

Of course, there is a third alternative date of conversion—the date of payment—but American courts have generally not adopted such a rule. Nonetheless, the Restatement has endorsed the use of the date of payment as the proper date of conversion whether it would "serve the ends of justice in the circumstances." In addition, English courts at present generally award a prevailing party an amount expressed in foreign currency or its sterling equivalent at the time of payment. This appears to change the prior British rule whereby courts required conversion of the foreign currency to sterling at the date of breach.

C.   Impetus for Change

In recent years, American courts have faced complex questions and potentially inequitable results in awarding judgments solely in U.S. dollars even though the underlying cause of action arose out of matters regarding non-U.S. currency. Several factors seemed to suggest the need for re-examination of the foreign currency judgment assumptions. These factors included the move away from fixed exchange rates and the change in the

---

recovery will depend upon whether suit is promptly brought or promptly prosecuted; whether the defendant interposes dilatory measures; whether the call of the docket is largely in arrears or is up-to-date; and, perhaps, upon whether there is a successful appeal and a new trial with the consequent annulment of the old judgment and the rendition of a new one.").

law by the British courts. In addition, the Restatement * * * examined the applicable law and context of foreign currency judgments, and concluded that a change in the law was desirable.

1. Exchange Rate Volatility

In the 1970s, the system of exchange rates was subject to serious disturbances and underwent basic revision. Previously, as established by the Bretton Woods agreement, fixed par values of Member State currencies were denominated in terms of gold or another currency pegged to gold, generally the U.S. dollar. Over time, however, with mounting pressure on the dollar, and declining confidence in it, the United States suspended its commitment to convert dollars into gold. A new system of floating exchange rates was adopted under which no major currency issuer any longer undertook to maintain a specific exchange rate in terms of other currencies or of gold. Following this revision, exchange rates have been subject to considerable volatility.

2. Decisions by the British Courts

Beginning in 1976, the British courts have changed their law as to the rendering of judgments in foreign currencies. In *Miliangos v. George Frank (Textiles) Ltd.*,[46] the Swiss seller of certain goods to an English buyer sought to recover the purchase price of the goods. The contract was governed by Swiss law, and the money of account (or currency in which the contract obligation was expressed) and payment were denominated in Swiss francs.

The trial judge was faced with a difficult choice between following an earlier decision of the House of Lords, the *Havana Railways* case,[47] which held that judgment could be given only in sterling on a foreign currency claim, or a recent decision of the Court of Appeal, *Schorsch Meier G.m.b.H. v. Hennin*,[48] in which the court declined to follow *Havana Railways* and issued a foreign currency judgment. The lower court followed the House of Lords case, holding that British courts could express their judgments only in sterling.[49] The Court of Appeal, however, saw its own *Schorsch* decision as binding, and reversed.[50] Payment was ordered in Swiss francs or the equivalent in sterling at the time of payment.

The House of Lords affirmed the decision of the Court of Appeal. In a lengthy opinion, the high court ruled that British courts can in fact render judgments in foreign currency.[52] The court abandoned the "common law" rule, which had "nothing but precedent to commend it." To provide the

---

46. [1976] App.Cas. 443.

47. *In re* United Rys. of Havana & Regla Warehouses Ltd., [1961] App.Cas. 1007.

48. [1975] Q.B. 416.

49. Miliangos v. George Frank (Textile) Ltd., Feb. 10, 1974 (Bristow, J.).

50. [1975] Q.B. 487.

52. [1976] App.Cas. 443.

seller "neither more nor less than he bargained for," the seller was permitted to recover in Swiss francs.

PREFATORY NOTE TO UNIFORM FOREIGN–MONEY CLAIMS ACT

13 Unif. Laws Annotated 23 (1990 Supp.).*

This Act facilitates uniform judicial determination of claims expressed in the money of foreign countries. It requires judgments and arbitration awards in these cases to be entered in the foreign money rather than in United States dollars. The debtor may pay the judgment in dollars on the basis of the rate of exchange prevailing at the time of payment.

A Uniform Act governing foreign-money claims has become desirable because:

These claims have increased greatly as a result of the growth in international trade.

Values of foreign moneys as compared to the United States dollar fluctuate more over shorter periods of time than was formerly the case.

United States jurisdictions treat recoveries on foreign-money claims differently than most of our major trading partners.

A lack of uniformity among the states in resolving foreign-money claims stimulates forum shopping and creates a lack of certainty in the law.

American courts historically follow one of two different rules in selecting a time during litigation for converting foreign money into United States dollars. These are called the "breach day rule"—the date the money should have been paid—and the "judgment date rule"—when judgment is entered. Many other countries use the "payment day rule"— when the judgment is paid. See *Miliangos v. George Frank (Textiles) Ltd.* (1976) A.C. 1007. The merits of this approach have begun to be recognized in this country. The payment day rule is endorsed by this Act.

The three rules produce wildly disparate results in terms of making an injured person whole. This is illustrated by the following example:

An American citizen (A) owes 18,790 pounds sterling to a British corporation (BCo) suing in New York, and the pound is falling against the dollar. Due to the declining value of the pound, the three rules worked out as follows:

Date	Rate of Exchange	BCo Gets
Breach day	Pound = $2.20	$41,338
Judgment day	Pound = $1.50	$28,185
Payment day	Pound = $1.20	$22,548

---

* Reprinted with permission of the National Conference of Commissioners on Uniform State Laws.

A judgment of $41,338 may be entered based on the breach day rule. However, the payment in dollars was worth 34,449 pounds ($41,338 divided by $1.20) when eventually received, an excess of L15,659 over the actual loss.

This example is adapted from an actual case. See *Competex v. Labow,* 783 F.2d 333 (2d Cir.1986). The facts are simplified.

If conversion is delayed until the date of actual payment, the creditor is recompensed with its own money or the financial equivalent in United States dollars; the debtor bears the risk of a fall in the debtor's money or reaps the benefit of a rise therein. If conversion is made at breach or judgment date, the risk of fluctuation in value of a money not of its selection falls on the creditor.

The real issue is where the risk of exchange rate fluctuation should be placed. This Act recognizes the right of the parties to agree upon the money that governs their relationship. In the absence of an agreement, the Act adopts the rule of giving the aggrieved party the amount to which it is entitled in its own money or the money in which the loss was suffered.

The principle of the Act is to restore the aggrieved party to the economic position it would have been in had the wrong not occurred. Thus, for example, if oil is spilled on the coast of France by an American ship, the loss is felt by the French in francs and a judgment of an American court for damages should reflect this fact. Courts should enter judgments in the money customarily used by the injured person.

The payment day rule, on which the Act is based, meets the reasonable expectations of the parties involved. It places the aggrieved party in the position it would have been in financially but for the wrong that gave rise to the claim. States which adopt it will align themselves with most of the major civilized countries of the world.

The Act also covers other issues that may arise in connection with foreign-money claims. These include revalorization and interest. In order to determine aliquot shares for distributions from funds created in insolvency and estate proceedings, the Act specifies use of the date the distribution proceeding was initiated for conversion of foreign money into United States dollars.

QUESTIONS AND COMMENTS

1. The Canadian court followed the traditional rule, that is to render judgments only in the currency of the court's nation, regardless of the currency of the obligation or the loss. Which party was favored by this decision, Cough or the Bank of Montreal? Did the Bank of Montreal expect to be paid in Canadian currency had Cough repaid the loan? Had there been some settlement? By court judgment? Did the Bank receive an unjust windfall?

2. When a court gives judgment in a foreign currency, it should note the time of the conversion. That would be the time of the breach, judgment or payment. Consider each time and the impact on Cough and the Bank. What if the court did not mention the time of conversion—what time should it be?

3. In addition to the major shift from the above stated rule limiting judgments to the currency of the nation of the court, much time has been devoted to deciding when the judgment amount should be converted. The Restatement, § 823 discussed in the Freeman article, has avoided designating the specific date, but adopts the view that the rate of conversion should "make the creditor whole" and should not reward a debtor who delayed in carrying out the obligation. Does the Cough–Bank of Montreal situation fit nicely into that provision? What if Cough did not know the IBM shares had dropped in value? And what if he moved to the United States not to escape any obligation, but to accept a new employment opportunity? What if the bank absolutely refused to sit down and discuss a settlement, rejecting numerous requests for such a discussion by Cough?

In contrast to the Restatement, the Uniform Foreign–Money Claims Act, approved by the National Conference of Commissioners on Uniform State Laws in 1989, and as of 2011 adopted by 20 states, California, Colorado, Connecticut, Delaware, Hawaii, Idaho, Illinois, Minnesota, Montana, Nevada, New Jersey, New Mexico, North Carolina, North Dakota, Ohio, Oklahoma, Oregon, Utah, Virginia, Washington and Wisconsin,(plus the District of Columbia and the Virgin Islands) adopts the payment date as the rule. But its intention is similar to the Restatement. The UFMCA tries to give the aggrieved party the amount it is entitled to in its own money or in the currency of its loss. Does the Cough–Bank of Montreal case come out the same way under the Restatement and the UFMCA?

4. The UFMCA recognizes that the parties should be able to choose the currency for any payment. Is that not the case with Cough and the bank?

5. The UFMCA address the enforcement issue, stating in section 10 that an enforceable foreign judgment expressed in a foreign currency should be entered as provided in section 7 whether or not the foreign judgment confers an option to pay an equivalent amount in United States dollars. Does that mean the judgment against Cough, if enforceable, will be entered in Canadian or United States dollars?

PROBLEM 11.5   INTERNATIONAL ENFORCEMENT OF FOREIGN ARBITRAL AWARDS: CARS FROM MALAYSIA

SECTION I.   THE SETTING

Pluto Motors is a Malaysia corporation, which is a joint venture between General Motors, Inc., a Delaware corporation, and Pluto Manufacturing, a Malaysia corporation. Pluto Motors manufactures in Malaysia, and sells on a world-wide basis, small automobiles which are jointly designed by GM and Pluto Manufacturing. Pluto Motors has a network of dealerships in the United States, and this network is separate from any GM dealership network.

Mickey's Motors is a Pluto dealership located in Buffalo, New York. Mickey's also owns a small Canadian Ford dealership in Niagara Falls,

Canada, across the border to which it ships an increasing number of Pluto autos for sale in a small area in that Canadian city. Mickey's and Pluto Motors signed a Distribution Agreement, which was to govern all sales by Pluto to Mickey's for a five year period. The Distribution Agreement, and all other Pluto Motors contracts with its dealers in the United States, contained the following clauses:

"Dealer [Mickey's] promises to resell all new cars bought from Pluto Motors only at the full retail price (the list price) specified for that automobile by Pluto."

"Dealer promises to resell all new cars bought from Pluto only within the geographic area allocated to Dealer by Pluto Motors, and to refuse to sell to any potential buyer who resides outside the geographic area so designated." [The geographic area so designated by Pluto for Mickey's was "the City of Buffalo"]

"Dealer agrees that this contract may be cancelled by Pluto Motors at any time, with or without cause, and without any prior notice."

"All disputes between Dealer and Pluto Motors arising out of this Distribution Agreement shall be finally settled by arbitration in Japan, in accordance with the rules of the Japanese Commercial Arbitration Association."

"Dealer agrees that this Distribution Agreement shall be governed by Malaysian law, and no law of the United States or Japan shall be applicable to it."

During the first year of this Agreement Mickey's made all its sales only at Pluto's "list price," and only to buyers who resided within the Buffalo city limits. Sales were brisk because Plutos were a "hot, new item", and everybody was happy. During the second year of the Agreement, however, Pluto sales collapsed. It seems that there were some quality control problems in the manufacture and assembly of Pluto; and that fact was reported by Consumer Reports and spread by "the grapevine". Jay Leno started making jokes about the defects of Plutos, and Mickey's suddenly was stuck with a large inventory of Plutos that no one wanted to buy.

Mickey's first response to this situation was to reduce its sales price from Pluto's "list price"—sometimes by 35%. That produced some sales in Buffalo, but not enough. So, Mickey's second response was to begin to sell outside the city of Buffalo—and to cut prices on such sales. Pluto began to get complaints about these sales from its other dealers in Rochester, New York, and Erie, Pennsylvania. Finally, when Pluto began to receive complaints from its Canadian dealers in Hamilton and Toronto and also to receive demands for compensation for lost sales by all of these dealers, Pluto decided to act. It sent a letter to Mickey's, informing it that the Distribution Agreement was cancelled immediately and demanded that Mickey's turn over to Pluto all proceeds of any sale that has been made either at less than "list price" or to any person who resided outside of

Mickey's geographic area. Pluto planned to use those funds to compensate the aggrieved dealers, and then return any balance of the funds to Mickey's.

Mickey's refused Pluto's demands for the proceeds. Pluto then began an arbitration process under the rules of the Japanese Commercial Arbitration Association. After reading *Mitsubishi Motors v. Soler Chrysler–Plymouth* (reproduced in the Reading Materials), Mickey's decided not to seek judicial proceedings in U.S. federal courts, but instead to participate in the arbitral proceedings. The arbitration tribunal consisted of a U.S.-educated Japanese practicing attorney, a Malaysian professor of comparative law, and an experienced retired Malaysian judge. At the end of the proceedings, the tribunal awarded Pluto Motors $1 million as compensation for lost profits to other U.S. and Canadian dealers, for termination of the sales to the Niagara Falls dealership, and for "harm to Pluto's reputation due to sales below Pluto's list price."

Although Mickey's had based most of its defense upon asserted violations of U.S. federal antitrust statutes and the U.S. Automobile Dealers Day in Court Act, 15 U.S.C. § 1221 *et seq.*, those defenses did not prevail. (You may assume that it is at least arguable that U.S. courts would find the contract to be in violation of such statutes.) The tribunal in its decision dealt with these defenses in two sentences: "Mickey's alleges that the contract violates certain United States laws; but, under the contract and Malaysian doctrines of conflicts of law, no laws of the United States can be applicable to this contract or any dispute arising under it. Even if U.S. laws were applicable to this contract, we find that the Distribution Agreement does not violate U.S. antitrust statutes or the Automobile Dealers Day in Court Act."

Pluto Motors has located assets owned by Mickey's and has petitioned for recognition and enforcement of its arbitral award in the local U.S. District Court. Mickey's has entered its opposition to this petition. You are the law clerk for the U.S. District Judge of that court, and she has asked you to do the necessary research to advise her on whether to grant this petition.

Mickey's challenged the petition on several grounds. It first argued that the enforcement of the award would be contrary to U.S. public policy, because the Distribution Agreement was canceled partly because of Mickey's action after it learned that the reason the sales from the small Canadian unit were so successful was that the manager of that unit was selling the Plutos to Cuba, where there was a market for almost any new car. Fearful of violating U.S. boycott rules, Mickey's had closed the Canadian unit, ending those sales. Pluto Motors was furious with the termination and demanded that Mickey's continue those sales, which were very profitable, and were to a country with which both Canada and Malaysia maintained diplomatic and trade relations.

Mickey's next argued that the award ought not be enforced because the matter was not capable of settlement by arbitration under the law of

Malaysia because Malaysia had no antitrust laws and indeed encouraged various business activities such as territorial allocations, price fixing, and other practices the United States prohibits. The reason for allowing these practices is that Malaysia believes they ought to be permitted while the nation is developing (they help to gain market share, etc.), and that when it has achieved a level of development similar to the United States, it can think of restraining such practices.

Finally, Mickey's argued that the decision of the arbitrators was so brief and conclusional, and lacking in sufficient substance and reasoning, that Mickey's is unable to adequately prepare a defense to the enforcement proceeding. Mickey's also thought that the award constituted a manifest disregard of the law.

SECTION II. FOCUS OF CONSIDERATION

Unlike the enforcement of judgments of foreign courts, the enforcement of the awards of foreign arbitral tribunals is completely a matter of federal law. It is the subject of both a treaty ratified by the United States—the Convention on the Recognition and Enforcement of Foreign Arbitral Awards (the New York Convention) set forth in the Documents Supplement—and a federal statute—the Federal Arbitration Act (FAA). The latter even provides for the removal of such cases from state courts to federal courts "at any time before the trial." (Section 205).

Although the Convention and the FAA provide for recognition and enforcement of foreign arbitral awards, they also provide exceptions and conditions on their coverage. Jurisdictional limitations stated within the Convention include that the award must be made by a foreign arbitral tribunal, and cannot be "considered as [a] domestic award." In addition, the United States declared two jurisdictional reservations: one requires that the award be "made only in the territory of a Contracting State"; the other requires that the dispute arise out of a relationship considered to be "commercial" under U.S. law. New York Convention, Article I(3).

The Convention also provides in Article V a short list of express defenses available to a party which opposes recognition or enforcement. They include incapacity of a party to the arbitration agreement, lack of fair opportunity to be heard, an award which is outside the scope of the submission to arbitration, improper procedure or composition of the tribunal, and non-finality of the award due to a stay or suspension. However, three other express defenses are of more precise interest to our law clerk's analysis: (1) the agreement providing for arbitration is invalid under the law to which the parties have subjected it (Article V 1(a)); (2) the subject matter of the dispute cannot be arbitrated under the law of the recognizing or enforcing nation (Article V 2(a)); and recognition or enforcement of the award would be contrary to the public policy of the recognizing or enforcing nation (Article V 2(b)).

Much of the litigation about "non-arbitrability" has related to expropriation by a foreign sovereign, the Foreign Sovereign Immunities Act and the Act of State Doctrine. See, e.g., *Ipitrade Intern., S.A. v. Federal Republic of Nigeria, 465 F.Supp. 824 (D.D.C.1978); Libyan American Oil Co. v. Socialist People's Libyan Arab Jamahirya (LIAMCO), 482 F.Supp. 1175 (D.D.C.1980),* vacated without opinion and following settlement 684 F.2d 1032 (D.C.Cir.1981). Thus, these decisions are more related to the issues raised in Problem 10.6, Part C, and are not particularly relevant to Pluto's award.

Articles I through V of the Convention on the Recognition and Enforcement of Foreign Arbitral Awards (1958) are essential to an understanding of this Problem. They are set out in the Documents Supplement.

SECTION III. READINGS, QUESTIONS AND COMMENTS

The *Parsons & Whittemore* decision is one of the first U.S. cases to interpret the Convention. It remains an important precedent. Comments of the U.S. Supreme Court in *Mitsubishi Motors* are also important, although Mickey's is aware that its conclusion effectively precludes any successful challenge to the arbitration process on the grounds that U.S. antitrust issues are the exclusive territory of the judicial process, not arbitration. *Mitsubishi Motors,* which has a fact setting much like Mickey's (except that in *Mitsubishi Motors* arbitration has not yet taken place) has other comments which may be dictum, but nevertheless may be helpful. The U.S. Supreme Court seems to indicate that there may be a later opportunity to consider whether the arbitration clause effectively waived a party's rights under the U.S. statute, when Mitsubishi seeks to enforce the arbitral award. That enforcement action would be brought under the New York Convention, and the readings following *Mitsubishi* set forth the available precedent under the "contrary to public policy" and other defenses available under Article V of that Convention.

I. MACNEIL, R. SPEIDEL, & T. STIPANOWICH, FEDERAL ARBITRATION LAW: AGREEMENTS, AWARDS AND REMEDIES UNDER THE FAA*

§ 44.40.2.10 (Supp.1997).

Public policy defense interpreted narrowly. The lower courts have interpreted the public policy defense narrowly when the question is enforcement of arbitration agreements. They have done the same thing both before and after *Mitsubishi* respecting enforcement of awards, using such phrases as "would violate our 'most basic notions of morality and justice' " and "should be construed narrowly."

The courts have been as good as their word, severely limiting the availability of the public policy defense in reviewing international FAA awards. [See] Parsons & Whittemore Overseas Company v. Societe Generale de L'Industrie du Papier (RAKTA) (2d Cir.1974).

Grounds not raising issues of the public policy defense. As already mentioned, the courts have excluded from the public policy defense various concerns about American international affairs and arbitrability of antitrust issues. In *Waterside Ocean Navigation Co. v. International Navigation Ltd.* (2d Cir.1984) the court excluded from the defense a claim that "directly inconsistent testimony was given in different proceedings," there having been no claim that the party seeking to uphold the award knowingly presented perjured testimony or even that the testimony was in fact perjury. Similarly, in *Geotech Lizenz A.G. v. Evergreen Systems, Inc.* (E.D.N.Y.1988) the court held that a rehash of previously rejected arguments relating to consent, scope of submission, and notice did not rise to the level of violations of "this nation's most basic notions of justice."

Grounds raising issues of the public policy defense. The courts have treated the following grounds as raising issues of public policy within the meaning of Article V(2)(b): alleged arbitrator partiality under the principles of *Commonwealth Coatings Corp. v. Continental Casualty Co.* (U.S.1968); award of interest the court deemed to be penal; award giving purchase price for breach of contract alleged to violate antitrust laws; and arbitration allegedly in conflict with the United States Vessel Owner's Limitation of Liability Act. In *Ministry of Defense of the Islamic Republic of Iran v. Gould Inc.* (9th Cir.1989) the court held, with no mention of Article V(2), that an award in violation of United States export regulations or Treasury Department regulations would be unenforceable. In *Northrop Corp. v. Triad Financial Establishment* (C.D.Cal.1984) the court, without deciding whether the Convention or the domestic FAA applied, held that, applying California substantive law, an award upholding any agreement illegal under Saudi Arabian law was unenforceable.

Comment on the manifest disregard of the law defense. Manifest disregard of the law is separate from public policy. Violating public policy does not mean there has been a manifest disregard of the law. But the opposite is less clear–does manifest disregard of the law constitute a violation of public policy under FAA Article V(2)(b)?

In 2008 the Supreme Court, in Hall St. Assoc., L.L.C. v. Mattel, Inc., 552 U.S. 576 (2008), held that the exclusive regimes for review under the FAA are in Sections 10 and 11. That raised the question whether manifest disregard of the law, which was a judicially created defense, remained a ground for vacatur under the FAA. The federal circuit decisions since have not been decisive. See, e.g., Ramos–Santiago v. United Parcel Serv., 524 F.3d 120 (1st Cir. 2009); Comedy Club, Inc. v. Improv West Assoc., 553 F.3d 1277 (9th Cir. 2009), cert. denied, 130 S.Ct. 145 (2009); Citigroup Global Mkt., Inc. v. Bacon, 562 F.3d 349 (5th Cir. 2009).

PARSONS AND WHITTEMORE OVERSEAS CO.
v. SOCIETE GENERALE DE L'INDUSTRIE
DU PAPIER (RAKTA)

United States Court of Appeals, Second Circuit, 1974.
508 F.2d 969.

[RAKTA, an Egyptian corporation, contracted with Overseas, for Overseas to construct and manage a paperboard mill in Egypt. The Agency for International Development (AID) was to provide financing by providing RAKTA with funds to obtain letters of credit in Overseas' favor. The contract included an arbitration clause to settle differences arising in the course of performance. There was also a force majeure clause which excused Overseas' performance due to circumstances beyond its control. While construction was in progress it was halted by the Arab–Israel Six Day War and Overseas employees fled the hostile environment. They would have had to leave anyway, because Egypt broke diplomatic relations with the United States. Some Americans could stay, with a special visa. RAKTA rejected the force majeure claim and, after no settlement was reached, initiated arbitration. An ICC arbitral tribunal recognized Overseas' force majeure defense as valid only for a brief 34 days period. The panel found that Overseas made no serious attempt to obtain the special visas and continue work. The AID withdrawal of financing did not justify Overseas' unilateral abandonment of the project. The tribunal made an award to RAKTA, which sought to obtain the amount from a letter of credit issued at Overseas' request in favor of RAKTA by the Bank of America. The purpose of the letter had been to satisfy any penalties an arbitral tribunal might impose upon Overseas for a future breach of contract. Overseas sought a declaratory judgment in the federal district court to prevent payment under the letter of credit, using the arguments reviewed in this decision. The federal district court granted RAKTA summary judgment, leading to this appeal.]

I.   Overseas' Defenses Against Enforcement

The 1958 Convention's basic thrust was to liberalize procedures for enforcing foreign arbitral awards: While the [superceded] Geneva Convention [of 1927] placed the burden of proof on the party seeking enforcement of a foreign arbitral award and did not circumscribe the range of available defenses to those enumerated in the convention, the 1958 Convention clearly shifted the burden of proof to the party defending against enforcement and limited his defenses to seven set forth in Article V. ... Not a signatory to any prior multilateral agreement on enforcement of arbitral awards, the United States declined to sign the 1958 Convention at the outset. The United States ultimately acceded to the Convention, however, in 1970, and implemented its accession with the existing Federal Arbitration Act, [which] applies to the enforcement of foreign awards except to the extent to which the latter may conflict with the Convention.

A. Public Policy

Article V(2)(b) of the Convention allows the court in which enforcement of a foreign arbitral award is sought to refuse enforcement, on the defendant's motion or *sua sponte*, if "enforcement of the award would be contrary to the public policy of (the forum) country." The legislative history of the provision offers no certain guidelines to its construction. Its precursors in the Geneva Convention and the 1958 Convention's ad hoc committee draft extended the public policy exception to, respectively, awards contrary to "principles of the law" and awards violative of "fundamental principles of the law." In one commentator's view, the Convention's failure to include similar language signifies a narrowing of the defense.... On the other hand, another noted authority in the field has seized upon this omission as indicative of an intention to broaden the defense....

Perhaps more probative, however, are the inferences to be drawn from the history of the Convention as a whole. The general proenforcement bias informing the Convention and explaining its supersession of the Geneva Convention points toward a narrow reading of the public policy defense. An expansive construction of this defense would vitiate the Convention's basic effort to remove preexisting obstacles to enforcement.... Additionally, considerations of reciprocity—considerations given express recognition in the Convention itself—counsel courts to invoke the public policy defense with caution lest foreign courts frequently accept it as a defense to enforcement of arbitral awards rendered in the United States.

We conclude, therefore, that the Convention's public policy defense should be construed narrowly. Enforcement of foreign arbitral awards may be denied on this basis only where enforcement would violate the forum state's most basic notions of morality and justice....

Under this view of the public policy provision in the Convention, Overseas' public policy defense may easily be dismissed. Overseas argues that various actions by United States officials subsequent to the severance of American–Egyptian relations—most particularly, AID's withdrawal of financial support for the Overseas–RAKTA contract—required Overseas, as a loyal American citizen, to abandon the project. Enforcement of an award predicated on the feasibility of Overseas' returning to work in defiance of these expressions of national policy would therefore allegedly contravene United States public policy. In equating "national" policy with United States "public" policy, the appellant quite plainly misses the mark. To read the public policy defense as a parochial device protective of national political interests would seriously undermine the Convention's utility. This provision was not meant to enshrine the vagaries of international politics under the rubric of "public policy." Rather, a circumscribed public policy doctrine was contemplated by the Convention's framers and every indication is that the United States, in acceding to the Convention, meant to subscribe to this supranational emphasis. *Cf. Scherk v. Alberto-Culver Co.*, 417 U.S. 506, 94 S.Ct. 2449, 41 L.Ed.2d 270 (1974).

To deny enforcement of this award largely because of the United States' falling out with Egypt in recent years would mean converting a defense intended to be of narrow scope into a major loophole in the Convention's mechanism for enforcement. We have little hesitation, therefore, in disallowing Overseas' proposed public policy defense.

B. Non–Arbitrability

Article V(2)(a) authorizes a court to deny enforcement, on a defendant's or its own motion, of a foreign arbitral award when "the subject matter of the difference is not capable of settlement by arbitration under the law of that (the forum) country."

Resolution of Overseas' non-arbitrability argument, however, does not require us to reach such difficult distinctions between domestic and foreign awards. For Overseas' argument, that "United States foreign policy issues can hardly be placed at the mercy of foreign arbitrators 'who are charged with the execution of no public trust' and whose loyalties are to foreign interests," ... plainly fails to raise so substantial an issue of arbitrability. The mere fact that an issue of national interest may incidentally figure into the resolution of a breach of contract claim does not make the dispute not arbitrable. Rather, certain *categories* of claims may be non-arbitrable because of the special national interest vested in their resolution.... Furthermore, even were the test for non-arbitrability of an ad hoc nature, Overseas' situation would almost certainly not meet the standard, for Overseas grossly exaggerates the magnitude of the national interest involved in the resolution of its particular claim. Simply because acts of the United States are somehow implicated in a case one cannot conclude that the United States is vitally interested in its outcome. Finally, the Supreme Court's decision in favor of arbitrability in a case far more prominently displaying public features than the instant one, *Scherk v. Alberto–Culver Co., supra*, compels by analogy the conclusion that the foreign award against Overseas dealt with a subject arbitrable under United States law.

The court below was correct in denying relief to Overseas under the Convention's non-arbitrability defense to enforcement of foreign arbitral awards. There is no special national interest in judicial, rather than arbitral, resolution of the breach of contract claim underlying the award in this case.

C. Inadequate Opportunity to Present Defense

Under Article V(1)(b) of the Convention, enforcement of a foreign arbitral award may be denied if the defendant can prove that he was "not given proper notice ... or was otherwise unable to present his case." This provision essentially sanctions the application of the forum state's standards of due process.

Overseas seeks relief under this provision for the arbitration court's refusal to delay proceedings in order to accommodate the speaking schedule of one of Overseas' witnesses, David Nes, the United States Charge d'Affaires in Egypt at the time of the Six Day War. This attempt to state a due process claim fails for several reasons. First, inability to produce one's witnesses before an arbitral tribunal is a risk inherent in an agreement to submit to arbitration. By agreeing to submit disputes to arbitration, a party relinquishes his courtroom rights—including that to subpoena witnesses—in favor of arbitration "with all of its well known advantages and drawbacks." ... Secondly, the logistical problems of scheduling hearing dates convenient to parties, counsel and arbitrators scattered about the globe argues against deviating from an initially mutually agreeable time plan unless a scheduling change is truly unavoidable.

The arbitration tribunal acted within its discretion in declining to reschedule a hearing for the convenience of an Overseas witness. Overseas' due process rights under American law, rights entitled to full force under the Convention as a defense to enforcement, were in no way infringed by the tribunal's decision.

D. Arbitration in Excess of Jurisdiction

Under Article V(1)(c), one defending against enforcement of an arbitral award may prevail by proving that:

> The award deals with a difference not contemplated by or not falling within the terms of the submission to arbitration, or it contains decisions on matters beyond the scope of the submission to arbitration. . . .

This provision tracks in more detailed form 10(d) of the Federal Arbitration Act, which authorizes vacating an award "where the arbitrators exceeded their powers." Both provisions basically allow a party to attack an award predicated upon arbitration of a subject matter not within the agreement to submit to arbitration. This defense to enforcement of a foreign award, like the others already discussed, should be construed narrowly. Once again a narrow construction would comport with the enforcement-facilitating thrust of the Convention. In addition, the case law under the similar provision of the Federal Arbitration Act strongly supports a strict reading.

In making this defense as to three components of the award, Overseas must therefore overcome a powerful presumption that the arbitral body acted within its powers. Overseas principally directs its challenge at the $185,000 awarded for loss of production. Its jurisdictional claim focuses on the provision of the contract reciting that "neither party shall have any liability for loss of production." The tribunal cannot properly be charged, however, with simply ignoring this alleged limitation on the subject matter over which its decision-making powers extended. Rather, the arbitration court interpreted the provision not to preclude jurisdiction on this matter. As in United *Steelworkers of America v. Enterprise Wheel &*

Car Corp., *supra*, the court may be satisfied that the arbitrator premised the award on a construction of the contract and that it is "not apparent," 363 U.S. 593 at 598, 80 S.Ct. 1358, that the scope of the submission to arbitration has been exceeded.

Although the Convention recognizes that an award may not be enforced where predicated on a subject matter outside the arbitrator's jurisdiction, it does not sanction second-guessing the arbitrator's construction of the parties' agreement. The appellant's attempt to invoke this defense, however, calls upon the court to ignore this limitation on its decision-making powers and usurp the arbitrator's role. The district court took a proper view of its own jurisdiction in refusing to grant relief on this ground.

E. Award in "Manifest Disregard" of Law

Both the legislative history of Article V, see supra, and the statute enacted to implement the United States' accession to the Convention are strong authority for treating as exclusive the bases set forth in the Convention for vacating [sic] an award. On the other hand, the Federal Arbitration Act, specifically 9 U.S.C. 10, has been read to include an implied defense to enforcement where the award is in "manifest disregard" of the law. * * *

[E]ven assuming that the "manifest disregard" defense applies under the Convention, we would have no difficulty rejecting the appellant's contention that such "manifest disregard" is in evidence here. Overseas in effect asks this court to read this defense as a license to review the record of arbitral proceedings for errors of fact or law—a role which we have emphatically declined to assume in the past and reject once again. "Extensive judicial review frustrates the basic purpose of arbitration, which is to dispose of disputes quickly and avoid the expense and delay of extended court proceedings." * * *

Insofar as this defense to enforcement of awards in "manifest disregard" of law may be cognizable under the Convention, it, like the other defenses raised by the appellant, fails to provide a sound basis for vacating [sic] the foreign arbitral award. We therefore affirm the district court's confirmation of award.

* * *

Affirmed.

MITSUBISHI MOTORS v. SOLER CHRYSLER–PLYMOUTH

United States Supreme Court, 1985.
473 U.S. 614, 105 S.Ct. 3346, 87 L.Ed.2d 444.

JUSTICE BLACKMUN delivered the opinion of the Court.

The principal question presented by these cases is the arbitrability, pursuant to the Federal Arbitration Act, * * *, and the Convention on the

Recognition and Enforcement of Foreign Arbitral Awards * * * of claims arising under the Sherman Act, and encompassed within a valid arbitration clause in an agreement embodying an international commercial transaction.

I

Petitioner-cross-respondent Mitsubishi Motors Corporation (Mitsubishi) is a Japanese corporation which manufactures automobiles and has its principal place of business in Tokyo, Japan. Mitsubishi is the product of a joint venture between * * * Chrysler International, S.A. (CISA), a Swiss corporation registered in Geneva and wholly owned by Chrysler Corporation, and * * * Mitsubishi Heavy Industries, Inc., * * * The aim of the joint venture was the distribution through Chrysler dealers outside the continental United States of vehicles manufactured by Mitsubishi and bearing Chrysler and Mitsubishi trademarks. Respondent-cross-petitioner Soler Chrysler–Plymouth, Inc. (Soler), is a Puerto Rico corporation with its principal place of business in * * * Puerto Rico.

On October 31, 1979, Soler entered into a Distributor Agreement with CISA which provided for the sale by Soler of Mitsubishi-manufactured vehicles within a designated area, including metropolitan San Juan. On the same date, CISA, Soler, and Mitsubishi entered into a Sales Procedure Agreement (Sales Agreement) which, referring to the Distributor Agreement, provided for the direct sale of Mitsubishi products to Soler and governed the terms and conditions of such sales. Paragraph VI of the Sales Agreement, labeled "Arbitration of Certain Matters," provides:

> "All disputes, controversies or differences which may arise between [Mitsubishi] and [Soler] out of or in relation to Articles I–B through V of this Agreement or for the breach thereof, shall be finally settled by arbitration in Japan in accordance with the rules and regulations of the Japan Commercial Arbitration Association."

* * * In early 1981, however, the new-car market slackened. Soler ran into serious difficulties in meeting the expected sales volume, and by the spring of 1981 it felt itself compelled to request that Mitsubishi delay or cancel shipment of several orders. About the same time, Soler attempted to arrange for the transshipment of a quantity of its vehicles for sale in the continental United States and Latin America. Mitsubishi and CISA, however, refused permission for any such diversion, citing a variety of reasons, and no vehicles were transshipped. Attempts to work out these difficulties failed. Mitsubishi eventually withheld shipment of 966 vehicles, apparently representing orders placed for May, June, and July 1981 production, responsibility for which Soler disclaimed in February 1982.

The following month, Mitsubishi brought an action against Soler in the United States District Court for the District of Puerto Rico under the Federal Arbitration Act and the Convention. Mitsubishi sought an order to compel arbitration in accord with ¶ VI of the Sales Agreement. Shortly after filing the complaint, Mitsubishi filed a request for arbitration before the Japan Commercial Arbitration Association.

Soler denied the allegations and counterclaimed against both Mitsubishi and CISA. It alleged numerous breaches by Mitsubishi of the Sales Agreement, raised a pair of defamation claims, and asserted causes of action under the Sherman Act; the federal Automobile Dealers' Day in Court Act; the Puerto Rico competition statute; and the Puerto Rico Dealers' Contracts Act, P.R.Laws Ann. In the counterclaim premised on the Sherman Act, Soler alleged that Mitsubishi and CISA had conspired to divide markets in restraint of trade. To effectuate the plan, according to Soler, Mitsubishi had refused to permit Soler to resell to buyers in North, Central, or South America vehicles it had obligated itself to purchase from Mitsubishi; had refused to ship ordered vehicles or the parts, such as heaters and defoggers, that would be necessary to permit Soler to make its vehicles suitable for resale outside Puerto Rico; and had coercively attempted to replace Soler and its other Puerto Rico distributors with a wholly owned subsidiary which would serve as the exclusive Mitsubishi distributor in Puerto Rico.

After a hearing, the District Court ordered Mitsubishi and Soler to arbitrate each of the issues raised in the complaint and in all the counterclaims save two and a portion of a third. * * * The District Court held * * * that the international character of the Mitsubishi–Soler undertaking required enforcement of the agreement to arbitrate even as to the antitrust claims.

* * * The United States Court of Appeals for the First Circuit affirmed in part and reversed in part. * * * [I]t reversed the judgment of the District Court insofar as it had ordered submission of "Soler's antitrust claims" to arbitration. * * *

We granted certiorari primarily to consider whether an American court should enforce an agreement to resolve antitrust claims by arbitration when that agreement arises from an international transaction.

III

We now turn to consider whether Soler's antitrust claims are nonarbitrable even though it has agreed to arbitrate them. * * * As in *Scherk v. Alberto–Culver Co.*, we conclude that concerns of international comity, respect for the capacities of foreign and transnational tribunals, and sensitivity to the need of the international commercial system for predictability in the resolution of disputes require that we enforce the parties' agreement, even assuming that a contrary result would be forthcoming in a domestic context.

Even before *Scherk*, this Court had recognized the utility of forum-selection clauses in international transactions. In *The Bremen* an American oil company, seeking to evade a contractual choice of an English forum and, by implication, English law, filed a suit in admiralty in a United States District Court against the German corporation which had contracted to tow its rig to a location in the Adriatic Sea. Notwithstanding the possibility that the English court would enforce provisions in the towage contract exculpating the German party which an American court would refuse to enforce, this Court gave effect to the choice-of-forum clause. It observed:

> "The expansion of American business and industry will hardly be encouraged if, notwithstanding solemn contracts, we insist on a parochial concept that all disputes must be resolved under our laws and in our courts. * * * We cannot have trade and commerce in world markets and international waters exclusively on our terms, governed by our laws, and resolved in our courts."

Recognizing that "agreeing in advance on a forum acceptable to both parties is an indispensable element in international trade, commerce, and contracting," the decision in *The Bremen* clearly eschewed a provincial solicitude for the jurisdiction of domestic forums.

Identical considerations governed the Court's decision in *Scherk,* which categorized "[a]n agreement to arbitrate before a specified tribunal [as], in effect, a specialized kind of forum-selection clause that posits not only the situs of suit but also the procedure to be used in resolving the dispute." 417 U.S., at 519. * * * Accordingly, the Court held Alberto–Culver to its bargain, sending it to the international arbitral tribunal before which it had agreed to seek its remedies.

The Bremen and *Scherk* establish a strong presumption in favor of enforcement of freely negotiated contractual choice-of-forum provisions. Here, as in *Scherk,* that presumption is reinforced by the emphatic federal policy in favor of arbitral dispute resolution. And at least since this Nation's accession in 1970 to the Convention, and the implementation of the Convention in the same year by amendment of the Federal Arbitration Act, that federal policy applies with special force in the field of international commerce. * * *

* * *

We are left, then, with the core of the *American Safety* doctrine—the fundamental importance to American democratic capitalism of the regime of the antitrust laws. Without doubt, the private cause of action plays a central role in enforcing this regime. As the Court of Appeals pointed out:

> " 'A claim under the antitrust laws is not merely a private matter. The Sherman Act is designed to promote the national interest in a competitive economy; thus, the plaintiff asserting his rights under the Act has been likened to a private attorney-general who protects the public's interest.' " 723 F.2d, at 168, quoting *American Safety,* 391 F.2d, at 826.

The treble-damages provision wielded by the private litigant is a chief tool in the antitrust enforcement scheme, posing a crucial deterrent to potential violators.

The importance of the private damages remedy, however, does not compel the conclusion that it may not be sought outside an American court. Notwithstanding its important incidental policing function, the treble-damages cause of action conferred on private parties by § 4 of the Clayton Act, and pursued by Soler here by way of its third counterclaim, seeks primarily to enable an injured competitor to gain compensation for that injury.

* * * And, of course, the antitrust cause of action remains at all times under the control of the individual litigant: no citizen is under an obligation to bring an antitrust suit, and the private antitrust plaintiff needs no executive or judicial approval before settling one. It follows that, at least where the international cast of a transaction would otherwise add an element of uncertainty to dispute resolution, the prospective litigant may provide in advance for a mutually agreeable procedure whereby he would seek his antitrust recovery as well as settle other controversies.

There is no reason to assume at the outset of the dispute that international arbitration will not provide an adequate mechanism. To be sure, the international arbitral tribunal owes no prior allegiance to the legal norms of particular states; hence, it has no direct obligation to vindicate their statutory dictates. The tribunal, however, is bound to effectuate the intentions of the parties. Where the parties have agreed that the arbitral body is to decide a defined set of claims which includes, as in these cases, those arising from the application of American antitrust law, the tribunal therefore should be bound to decide that dispute in accord with the national law giving rise to the claim.[19] And so long as the prospective litigant effectively may vindicate its statutory cause of action in the arbitral forum, the statute will continue to serve both its remedial and deterrent function.

Having permitted the arbitration to go forward, the national courts of the United States will have the opportunity at the award-enforcement stage to ensure that the legitimate interest in the enforcement of the

---

19. In addition to the clause providing for arbitration before the Japan Commercial Arbitration Association, the Sales Agreement includes a choice-of-law clause which reads: "This Agreement is made in, and will be governed by and construed in all respects according to the laws of the Swiss Confederation as if entirely performed therein." The United States raises the possibility that the arbitral panel will read this provision not simply to govern interpretation of the contract terms, but wholly to displace American law even where it otherwise would apply. The International Chamber of Commerce opines that it is "[c]onceivabl[e], although we believe it unlikely, [that] the arbitrators could consider Soler's affirmative claim of anti-competitive conduct by CISA and Mitsubishi to fall within the purview of this choice-of-law provision, with the result that it would be decided under Swiss law rather than the U.S. Sherman Act." At oral argument, however, counsel for Mitsubishi conceded that American law applied to the antitrust claims and represented that the claims had been submitted to the arbitration panel in Japan on that basis. The record confirms that before the decision of the Court of Appeals the arbitral panel had taken these claims under submission.

We therefore have no occasion to speculate on this matter at this stage in the proceedings, when Mitsubishi seeks to enforce the agreement to arbitrate, not to enforce an award. Nor need we consider now the effect of an arbitral tribunal's failure to take cognizance of the statutory cause of action on the claimant's capacity to reinitiate suit in federal court. We merely note that in the event the choice-of-forum and choice-of-law clauses operated in tandem as a prospective waiver of a party's right to pursue statutory remedies for antitrust violations, we would have little hesitation in condemning the agreement as against public policy.

antitrust laws has been addressed. The Convention reserves to each signatory country the right to refuse enforcement of an award where the "recognition or enforcement of the award would be contrary to the public policy of that country." While the efficacy of the arbitral process requires that substantive review at the award-enforcement stage remain minimal, it would not require intrusive inquiry to ascertain that the tribunal took cognizance of the antitrust claims and actually decided them.

As international trade has expanded in recent decades, so too has the use of international arbitration to resolve disputes arising in the course of that trade. The controversies that international arbitral institutions are called upon to resolve have increased in diversity as well as in complexity. Yet the potential of these tribunals for efficient disposition of legal disagreements arising from commercial relations has not yet been tested. If they are to take a central place in the international legal order, national courts will need to "shake off the old judicial hostility to arbitration," *Kulukundis Shipping Co. v. Amtorg Trading Corp.* and also their customary and understandable unwillingness to cede jurisdiction of a claim arising under domestic law to a foreign or transnational tribunal. To this extent, at least, it will be necessary for national courts to subordinate domestic notions of arbitrability to the international policy favoring commercial arbitration.

Accordingly, we "require this representative of the American business community to honor its bargain," by holding this agreement to arbitrate "enforce[able] * * * in accord with the explicit provisions of the Arbitration Act." *Scherk,* 417 U.S., at 520.

The judgment of the Court of Appeals is affirmed in part and reversed in part, and the cases are remanded for further proceedings consistent with this opinion.

It is so ordered.

JUSTICE STEVENS, with whom JUSTICE BRENNAN joins, and with whom JUSTICE MARSHALL joins except as to Part II, dissenting.

* * *

* * * This Court's holding rests almost exclusively on the federal policy favoring arbitration of commercial disputes and vague notions of international comity arising from the fact that the automobiles involved here were manufactured in Japan. * * *

I

The federal policy favoring arbitration cannot sustain the weight that the Court assigns to it. A clause requiring arbitration of all claims "relating to" a contract surely could not encompass a claim that the arbitration clause was itself part of a contract in restraint of trade. Nor in my judgment should it be read to encompass a claim that relies, not on a failure to perform the contract, but on an independent violation of federal law. The matters asserted by way of defense do not control the character, or the source, of the claim that Soler has asserted. Accordingly, simply as a matter of ordinary contract interpretation, I would hold that Soler's antitrust claim is not arbitrable.

II

Until today all of our cases enforcing agreements to arbitrate under the Arbitration Act have involved contract claims. * * * But this is the first time the Court has considered the question whether a standard arbitration clause referring to claims arising out of or relating to a contract should be construed to cover statutory claims that have only an indirect relationship to the contract. * * *

In view of the Court's repeated recognition of the distinction between federal statutory rights and contractual rights, together with the undisputed historical fact that arbitration has functioned almost entirely in either the area of labor disputes or in "ordinary disputes between merchants as to questions of fact," it is reasonable to assume that most lawyers and executives would not expect the language in the standard arbitration clause to cover federal statutory claims. Thus, in my opinion, both a fair respect for the importance of the interests that Congress has identified as worthy of federal statutory protection, and a fair appraisal of the most likely understanding of the parties who sign agreements containing standard arbitration clauses, support a presumption that such clauses do not apply to federal statutory claims.

III

The Sherman and Clayton Acts reflect Congress' appraisal of the value of economic freedom; they guarantee the vitality of the entrepreneurial spirit. Questions arising under these Acts are among the most important in public law.

The provision for mandatory treble damages—unique in federal law when the statute was enacted—provides a special incentive to the private enforcement of the statute, as well as an especially powerful deterrent to violators. What we have described as "the public interest in vigilant enforcement of the antitrust laws through the instrumentality of the private treble-damage action," * * *, is buttressed by the statutory mandate that the injured party also recover costs, "including a reasonable attorney's fee." * * *

* * *

* * * Arbitration awards are only reviewable for manifest disregard of the law, * * * and the rudimentary procedures which make arbitration so desirable in the context of a private dispute often mean that the record is so inadequate that the arbitrator's decision is virtually unreviewable.[31]

---

31. The arbitration procedure in this case does not provide any right to evidentiary discovery or a written decision, and requires that all proceedings be closed to the public. Moreover, Japanese arbitrators do not have the power of compulsory process to secure witnesses and

Despotic decisionmaking of this kind is fine for parties who are willing to agree in advance to settle for a best approximation of the correct result in order to resolve quickly and inexpensively any contractual dispute that may arise in an ongoing commercial relationship. Such informality, however, is simply unacceptable when every error may have devastating consequences for important businesses in our national economy and may undermine their ability to compete in world markets. Instead of "muffling a grievance in the cloakroom of arbitration," the public interest in free competitive markets would be better served by having the issues resolved "in the light of impartial public court adjudication."

IV

It may be that the subject-matter exception to the Convention ought to be reserved—as a matter of domestic law—for matters of the greatest public interest which involve concerns that are shared by other nations. The Sherman Act's commitment to free competitive markets is among our most important civil policies. This commitment, shared by other nations which are signatory to the Convention, is hardly the sort of parochial concern that we should decline to enforce in the interest of international comity. Indeed, the branch of Government entrusted with the conduct of political relations with foreign governments has informed us that the "United States' determination that federal antitrust claims are nonarbitrable under the Convention * * * is not likely to result in either surprise or recrimination on the part of other signatories to the Convention." * * *

V

The Court's repeated incantation of the high ideals of "international arbitration" creates the impression that this case involves the fate of an institution designed to implement a formula for world peace. But just as it is improper to subordinate the public interest in enforcement of antitrust policy to the private interest in resolving commercial disputes, so is it equally unwise to allow a vision of world unity to distort the importance of the selection of the proper forum for resolving this dispute. Like any other mechanism for resolving controversies, international arbitration will only succeed if it is realistically limited to tasks it is capable of performing well—the prompt and inexpensive resolution of essentially contractual disputes between commercial partners. As for matters involving the political passions and the fundamental interests of nations, even the multilateral convention adopted under the auspices of the United Nations recognizes that private international arbitration is incapable of achieving satisfactory results.

In my opinion, the elected representatives of the American people would not have us dispatch an American citizen to a foreign land in search of an uncertain remedy for the violation of a public right that is protected

---

documents, nor do witnesses who are available testify under oath. Cf. 9 U.S.C. § 7 (arbitrators may summon witnesses to attend proceedings and seek enforcement in a district court).

by the Sherman Act. This is especially so when there has been no genuine bargaining over the terms of the submission, and the arbitration remedy provided has not even the most elementary guarantees of fair process. Consideration of a fully developed record by a jury, instructed in the law by a federal judge, and subject to appellate review, is a surer guide to the competitive character of a commercial practice than the practically unreviewable judgment of a private arbitrator.

NATIONAL OIL CORP. v. LIBYAN SUN OIL CO.

United States District Court, D.Delaware, 1990.
733 F.Supp. 800.

NOC is a corporation organized under the laws of the Socialist People's Libyan Arab Jamahiriya ("Libya"), and wholly owned by the Libyan Government. Sun Oil is a Delaware corporation and a subsidiary of Sun Company, Inc. The dispute currently before the Court stems from an Exploration and Production Sharing Agreement ("EPSA") entered into by the parties on November 20, 1980. The EPSA provided, *inter alia,* that Sun Oil was to carry out and fund an oil exploration program in Libya.

Sun Oil began exploration activities in the first half of 1981. On December 18, 1981, Sun Oil invoked the *force majeure* provision contained in the EPSA and suspended performance. Sun Oil claimed that a State Department order prohibiting the use of United States passports for travel to Libya prevented its personnel, all of whom were U.S. citizens, from going to Libya. Thus, Sun Oil believed it could not carry out the EPSA "in accordance with the intentions of the parties to the contract." NOC disputed Sun Oil's claim of *force majeure* and called for continued performance.

In March of 1982, the U.S. Government banned the importation into the United States of any oil from Libya and severely restricted exports from the United States to Libya. Export regulations issued by the U.S. Department of Commerce required a license for the export of most goods, including all technical information. Because it "had planned to export substantial quantities of technical data and oil technology to Libya in connection with the exploration program," Sun Oil claims that it filed for such an export license "so as to be prepared to resume operations in Libya promptly in the event the U.S. Government lifted the passport prohibition." The application for a license was denied. Thereafter, in late June of 1982, Sun Oil notified NOC that it was claiming the export regulations as an additional event of *force majeure.*

On July 19, 1982, NOC filed a request for arbitration with the Court of Arbitration of the International Chamber of Commerce ("the ICC") in Paris, France, pursuant to the arbitration provision contained in the EPSA. * * *

The arbitration proceedings were held in Paris, France. In May and June of 1984, the Arbitral Tribunal held hearings on the issue of *force majeure.* It issued an initial award on May 31, 1985, that stated there had been no *force majeure* within the meaning of the EPSA. The Arbitral Tribunal later held further hearings, and on February 23, 1987, it rendered a second and final award in favor of NOC and against Sun Oil in the amount of twenty million U.S. dollars. NOC has since been unable to collect payment from Sun Oil.

NOC filed this petition for confirmation of the Tribunal's award on July 24, 1989. On September 15, 1989, Sun Oil moved to dismiss the petition. The Court heard oral argument on November 29, 1989 and January 26, 1990. * * *

Therefore, having found all of its arguments without merit, the Court will deny Sun Oil's motion to dismiss NOC's petition.

The Convention on the Recognition and Enforcement of Foreign Arbitral Awards attempts "to *encourage* the recognition and enforcement of commercial arbitration agreements in international contracts and to unify the standards by which agreements to arbitrate are observed and arbitral awards are enforced in the signatory countries." This Court must recognize the award rendered by the ICC Arbitral Tribunal in NOC's favor unless Sun Oil can successfully assert one of the seven defenses enumerated in Article V of the Convention. Sun Oil has invoked three of the seven defenses against recognition. It bears the burden of proving that any of these defenses is applicable.

After considering the evidence and arguments of the parties, this Court, for the reasons outlined below, rejects Sun Oil's defenses and concludes that the arbitral award is entitled to recognition and enforcement under the Convention. * * *

Sun Oil's final challenge to confirmation of the award rests solely on the public policy exception contained in article V, section 2(b), of the Convention. Both parties in this case agree that the public policy defense "should be construed narrowly," and that confirmation of a foreign award should be denied on the basis of public policy "only where enforcement would violate the forum state's most basic notions of morality and justice." Not too surprisingly, however, the parties do not agree as to whether this particular case fits within such a definition of the public policy defense.

Sun Oil argues that confirmation of the award in this case would violate the public policy of the United States for three reasons. First, Sun Oil contends that because confirmation would "penalize Sun for obeying and supporting the directives and foreign policy objectives of its government," other companies and individuals would be less likely to support U.S. sanctions programs, thereby diminishing "[t]he ability of the U.S. government to make and enforce policies with economic costs to U.S. citizens and corporations...." Secondly, Sun Oil contends that confirming the award would simply be "inconsistent with the substance of United States antiterrorism policy", and thirdly, that it would also "undermine the internationally-supported antiterrorism policy ... by sending a contradictory signal concerning U.S. commitment to this policy and by making possible the transfer to ... Libya ... funds which could be employed to finance its continuing terrorist activities." Sun Oil also presents much statistical and historical information designed to demonstrate the character of the Qadhafi Government.

The problem with Sun Oil's arguments is that "public policy" and "foreign policy" are not synonymous. For example, in *Parsons & Whittemore Overseas Company,* the Second Circuit addressed this very issue, saying: "To read the public policy defense as a parochial device protective of national political interests would seriously undermine the Convention's utility. This provision was not meant to enshrine the vagaries of international politics under the rubric of 'public policy.' " * * *

The United States has not declared war on Libya, and President Bush has not derecognized the Qadhafi Government. In fact, the current Administration has specifically given Libya *permission* to bring this action in this Court. Given these facts and actions by our Executive Branch, this Court simply cannot conclude that to confirm a validly obtained, foreign arbitral award in favor of the Libyan Government would violate the United States' "most basic notions of morality and justice."

Although Sun Oil argues that confirmation of this award would mean that U.S. dollars would end up financing Qadhafi's terrorist exploits, the Court has already pointed out that the President is empowered to prevent any such transfer through the Libyan Sanctions Regulations. Furthermore, Sun Oil's argument that U.S. companies will be less likely to support sanctions if this award is confirmed *assumes* that Sun Oil is correct on the central issue in the arbitration underlying this petition for confirmation: that is, that Sun Oil was justified in suspending performance under the EPSA. The Arbitral Tribunal, however, concluded that Sun Oil was *not* justified in suspending performance because of U.S. actions at that time. Because Sun Oil was able to present all of these arguments, regarding *force majeure* and Sun's attempts to support U.S. policy, before the Arbitral Tribunal, this Court will not reexamine that issue here. * * *

* * *

The Court will recognize and enforce the Tribunal's award in favor of NOC and against Sun Oil in the amount of 20 million U.S. dollars, with prejudgment and postjudgment interest as described above.

A final judgment will be entered in accordance with this opinion; but execution on the judgment will be stayed, and the judgment may not be registered and transferred in accordance with 28 U.S.C. § 1963 unless the Libyan Sanctions Regulations are complied with. * * *

SPIER v. CALZATURIFICIO TECNICA, S.p.A.

United States District Court, Southern District of New York, 1999.
71 F.Supp.2d 279.

HAIGHT, SENIOR DISTRICT JUDGE.

Martin I. Spier renews his petition to enforce an arbitration award rendered in Italy by Italian arbitrators against respondent Calzaturificio Tecnica S.p.A ("Tecnica").

The verb "renew" reflects the fact that Spier has previously moved for that relief. In the circumstances then obtaining, and for the reasons stated in *Spier v. Calzaturificio Tecnica S.p.A.,*663 F.Supp. 871 (S.D.N.Y. 1987) ("*Spier I*"), familiarity with which is assumed, I deferred the enforcement proceedings until the ultimate outcome of Tecnica's then pending challenge to the validity of the award in the Italian courts. That ultimate outcome has now been achieved. Specifically, the Italian court of first instance, the Treviso Tribunal, entered judgment nullifying the award in Spier's favor. The Court of Appeals of Venice affirmed that judgment, and was in turn affirmed by the Supreme Court of Cassation, Italy's highest court.

Nothing daunted, Spier renews his petition in this Court to enforce the award. He argues that this Court should confirm the award and enter judgment thereon, notwithstanding the decisions of the Italian courts. Predictably enough, Tecnica contends that the decisions of the Italian courts require that Spier's petition be denied.

In 1969 Spier, an engineer resident in New York and an American citizen, entered into a contract with Tecnica, an Italian corporation, calling for Spier to furnish Tecnica with expertise for the manufacture by Tecnica in Italy of plastic footwear and ski boots, in exchange for the payment of certain fees by Tecnica. * * *

While the intricacies of the Italian courts' reasoning may be partially lost in translation, it seems entirely clear that all three courts nullified the award because they concluded that the arbitrators, casting off all restraints imposed by the contract between Spier and Tecnica, conferred upon Spier a "bonus" or a "pay-off" in a manner and an amount that exceeded the arbitrators' powers. In these seemingly inauspicious circumstances, Spier renews his petition to this Court to enforce the Italian arbitration award.

Spier's petition to enforce the Italian arbitrators' award falls under the Convention on the Recognition and Enforcement of Foreign Arbitral Awards. * * * Tecnica defended against Spier's petition in this Court, and cross-petitioned to deny enforcement of the award, by invoking Articles V and VI of the Convention, quoted in pertinent part in *Spier I,* 663 F.Supp. at 873. To summarize, Article V provides that "[r]ecognition and enforcement of the award may be refused, at the request of the party against whom it is invoked, only if that party" proves to the authority where enforcement is sought (here, this Court) that, *inter alia,* the underlying contract was not valid under the law of the country where the award was made (here, Italy), Art. V(1)(a); or the arbitral award contained decisions on matters beyond the scope of the submission to arbitration, Art. V(1)(c);

or governing law provides that the award is not binding on the parties, Art. V(1)(e).[1]

Notwithstanding that distinction, [*Yusuf Ahmed Alganim & Sons, W.L.L. v. Toys "R" Us*, 126 F.2d 15 (2d. Cir. 1997)] is instructive in the case at bar because of what the Second Circuit says about the available grounds for resisting enforcement of an award when enforcement is sought in a United States district court.

In *Yusuf,* the arbitration was held and the award issued in the United States, and enforcement was sought in the United States. Those circumstances, the Second Circuit held, were sufficient to entitle Toys "R" Us, the party against whom the award was made, to invoke the FAA's implied grounds for refusing to enforce to the award, in addition to the limited statutory grounds found in the FAA for vacating an award, *see* 9 U.S.C. § 10, or modifying it, *see id.* § 11. The implied grounds for *vacatur* recognized by the FAA are found "where the arbitrator's award is in manifest disregard of the terms of the agreement, or where the award is in manifest disregard of the law." *Yusuf,* 126 F.3d at 23 (citations and internal quotation marks omitted). And in those particular circumstances, the principles of domestic American law for *refusing to enforce* an award apply, notwithstanding the fact that a petition to *enforce* the award falls under the Convention.

However, where (as in the case at bar) an arbitral award is made in one State adhering to the Convention and sought to be enforced in another adhering State, the grounds for resisting the award are limited to those found in Article V of the Convention. In *Yusuf* the Second Circuit explains the difference:

> In sum, we conclude that the Convention mandates very different regimes for the review of arbitral awards (1) in the state in which, or under the law of which, the award was made, and (2) in other states where recognition and enforcement are sought. The Convention specifically contemplates that the state in which, or under the law of which, the award is made, will be free to set aside or modify an award in accordance with its domestic arbitral law and its full panoply of express and implied grounds for relief. See Convention art. V(1)(e). However, the Convention is equally clear that when an action for enforcement is brought in a foreign state, the state may refuse to enforce the award only on the grounds explicitly set forth in Article V of the Convention. 126 F.3d at 23.

The Second Circuit's more recent decision in [*Baker Marine (Nig.) Ltd. V. Chevron (Nig.) Ltd.,* 199 WL 781594 (2d. Cir. Oct. 1, 1999)("Baker Marine")]* illustrates the "very different regime[ ] for the review of arbitral awards" when the award is rendered in one State and sought to

---

1. As more fully stated *infra,* Article V(1)(e) also provides, as a ground for refusing to enforce an award, proof that the award "has been set aside or suspended by a competent authority of the country in which, or under the law of which, that award was made." In view of the decisions of the Italian courts, all post *Spier I,* that Convention provision now lies at the heart of the case.

be enforced in another. Nigerian and American companies entered into two contracts to provide barges for use in servicing Nigeria's oil industry. The contracts provided for arbitration in Nigeria. Two panels of arbitrators made monetary awards in favor of Baker Marine. Baker Marine sought enforcement of both awards in the Nigerian Federal High Court. The losing parties appealed to the same court to vacate the awards. In that effort they succeeded; the Nigerian court set aside both arbitration awards.

Invoking the Convention, Baker Marine then petitioned the Northern District of New York to enforce the awards. Judge McAvoy denied those petitions, reasoning that "under the Convention and principles of comity, it would not be proper to enforce a foreign arbitral award when such an award has been set aside by the Nigerian courts." The Second Circuit affirmed. It cited *Yusef* for the proposition that where enforcement of an arbitral award is sought in a State other than that where the award was made, "Article V [of the Convention] provides exclusive grounds for setting aside" the award .. The Nigerian court having set aside the Nigerian arbitration awards, Article V(1)(e) furnished the ground for a United States district court to refuse to enforce them. The court of appeals said:

> Article V(1)(e) provides that a court may refuse enforcement of an award that "has been set aside or suspended by a competent authority of the country in which, or under the law of which, the award was made." Convention, art. V(1)(e). Baker Marine does not contest that the Nigerian High Court is a competent authority in the country in which, and under the law of which, the award was made. The district court relied on the decision of the Nigerian court and Article V(1)(e) in declining to enforce the award.

In an effort to preserve the awards, Baker Marine made a number of arguments which the Second Circuit rejected. It is instructive to consider the court of appeals' rejections of those arguments, since Spier also makes them in the case at bar.

First, Baker Marine argued that the Nigerian court set aside the awards for reasons that would not be recognized under domestic United States law as valid grounds for vacating the awards. In aid of that contention, Baker Marine criticized the district court for disregarding Article VII(1) of the Convention, which provides that the Convention shall not "deprive any interested party of any right he may have to avail himself of an arbitral award in the manner and to the extent allowed by the law or the treaties of the country where such award is sought to be relied upon." That language, Baker Marine contended, served to incorporate into the Convention the domestic law of the United States as grounds for resuscitating Nigerian awards nullified by a Nigerian court.

The Second Circuit rejected the argument. It reasoned that "the parties contracted in Nigeria that their disputes would be arbitrated under the laws of Nigeria." Moreover, "[t]he governing agreements make no reference whatever to United States law," and "[n]othing suggests that the parties intended United States domestic arbitral law to govern their disputes." Indeed, the intrusion of United States law on the scene would frustrate that law's public policy, since "[t]he primary purpose of the FAA in ensuring that private agreements to arbitrate are enforced according to their terms." *Id.* (citations and internal quotation marks omitted). Nor did Baker Marine contend "that the Nigerian courts acted contrary to Nigerian law." The Second Circuit's opinion in *Baker Marine* reminds the reader of its prior holding in *Yusuf* that domestic arbitral law may be applied only by "a court under whose law the arbitration was conducted," *id.* at 3, citing and quoting *Yusuf.* Lastly, the *Baker Marine* court cites approvingly a commentator's observation that "mechanical application of domestic arbitral law to foreign awards under the Convention would seriously undermine finality and regularly produce conflicting judgments," the foreseeable consequence of such application being that "a losing party will have every reason to pursue its adversary 'with enforcement actions from country to country until a court is found, if any, which grants the enforcement.'"

Second, Baker Marine argued that because Article V(1) of the Convention begins with the permissive phrase that "[r]ecognition and enforcement of an award *may* be refused" if one of the subsequently enumerated grounds for doing so is proved (emphasis added), rather than a mandatory term, the district court "might have enforced the awards, notwithstanding the Nigerian judgments vacating them." Rejecting that contention, the Second Circuit's pointed response was that "Baker Marine has shown no adequate reason for refusing to recognize the judgments of the Nigerian court."

It is also instructive to note that at that point in the *Baker Marine* text, the Second Circuit dropped footnote 3, which distinguishes a case upon which Spier places primary reliance: *In re Chromalloy Aeroservices,* 939 F.Supp. 907 (D.D.C.1996). In *Chromalloy,* an American company bearing that name entered into a military procurement contract with the Egyptian Air Force (hereinafter "Egypt"). The contract required arbitration of all disputes, recited that "both parties have irrevocably agreed to apply Egypt [sic] Laws and to choose Cairo as seat of the court of arbitration," and further provided that "[t]he decision of the said court shall be final and binding and cannot be made subject to any appeal or other recourse." Disputes having arisen, the arbitrators issued an award which Chromalloy petitioned the District Court for the District of Columbia to enforce. Egypt responded by seeking and obtaining from the Egyptian Court of Appeal a judgment nullifying the award, which Egypt then pleaded in bar to Chromalloy's petition in the district court to enforce the award.

In these particular circumstances, the district court held that Chromalloy could invoke Article VII of the Convention in order to take advantage of the FAA, and enforced the award. The court regarded as central to its decision the fact that Egypt, by appealing the arbitration award to the Egyptian court, "seeks to repudiate its solemn promise to abide by the results of the arbitration," in breach of the contractual agreement that "the arbitration ends with the decision of the arbitral panel." Because the FAA and its amendment to implement the Convention "demonstrate that there is an emphatic federal policy in favor of arbitral dispute resolution, particularly in the field of international commerce, [a] decision by this Court to recognize the decision of the Egyptian court would violate this clear U.S. public policy."

On the facts presented in *Baker Marine,* the Second Circuit distinguished *Chromalloy,* writing in footnote 3:

> The district court [in *Chromalloy*] concluded that Egypt was "seeking to repudiate its solemn promise to abide by the results of the arbitration," and that recognizing the Egyptian judgment would be contrary to the United States policy favoring arbitration. Unlike the petitioner in *Chromalloy,* Baker Marine is not a United States citizen, and it did not initially seek confirmation of the award in the United States. Furthermore, Chevron and Danos did not violate any promise in appealing the arbitration award with Nigeria. Recognition of the Nigerian judgment in this case does not conflict with United States public policy.

In some respects *Chromalloy* bears a superficial resemblance to the case at bar, since Spier is a United States citizen and seeks confirmation of the award in the United States. But I read this footnote in *Baker Marine* to identify as the decisive circumstance Egypt's repudiation of its contractual promise not to appeal an arbitral award. Only that circumstance is singled out as violating American public policy articulated in the FAA, thereby justifying the district court's enforcement of the Egyptian award.

In the light of these recent Second Circuit cases, I consider Spier's several arguments in favor of enforcement by this Court of the award against Tecnica.

First, Spier argues that "[t]he threshold issue . . . is whether or not the award would be set aside under American law," and collects American cases to support the proposition that it should be. But the Second Circuit's holdings in *Yusuf* and *Baker Marine* preclude this Court from reaching that threshold, let alone crossing it. Spier seeks to apply domestic United States arbitral law in order to escape the Italian courts' nullification of an Italian award. That effort cannot survive the court of appeals' observation in *Yusuf* that under the Convention "the state in which, or under the laws of which, the award is made, will be free to set aside or modify an award in accordance with its domestic arbitral law and its full panoply of express and implied grounds for relief." The award at bar was set aside by that state's highest tribunal, the Supreme Court of Cassation of Italy; no American court or statute may be cited to the contrary. In other words, Spier cannot be heard to argue that the Italian courts' decisions should not be recognized on the ground that an American court would reach a different result with respect to the award if it had been rendered in the United States.

Nor may Spier introduce domestic United States law, statutory or decisional, into the case at bar through the vehicle of Article VII of the Convention. *Baker Marine* precludes that effort. There is no basis for applying American law to the rights and obligations of the parties, including dispute resolution by arbitration. Just as did the parties in *Baker Marine,* Spier and Tecnica contracted in a foreign state that their disputes would be arbitrated in that foreign state; the governing agreements make no reference to United States law; and nothing suggests that the parties intended United States domestic arbitral law to govern their disputes.

Spier's reference to the permissive "may" in Article V(1) of the Convention does not assist him since, as in *Baker Marine,* Speir has shown no adequate reason for refusing to recognize the judgments of the Italian courts.

Finally, the *Chromalloy* district court's reliance upon the FAA to disregard an Egyptian court's decision nullifying an Egyptian award was prompted by a particular circumstance not present in the case at bar: Egypt's blatant disregard of its contractual promise not to appeal an award. Spier points to no comparable provision in his contract with Tecnica; and, while Spier deplores the Italian courts' decisions, he does not suggest that Italian domestic law, made applicable to this Italian award by the Convention as construed by the Second Circuit in *Yusuf,* did not entitle Tecnica to challenge the award in the Italian courts.

It remains only to say that even if, contrary to my conclusions previously stated, Spier is entitled to test this award by the measures of domestic United States law, it avails him nothing. That is because all three Italian courts nullified the award on the ground that in making it the arbitrators had exceeded their powers, a ground for vacatur under the FAA. See 9 U.S.C. § 10(a)(4).[6]

For the foregoing reasons, Spier's renewed petition to enforce the arbitral award is denied.

QUESTIONS AND COMMENTS

1. Does the federal district court have jurisdiction under the Convention? Consider Article I.1. Should this award be considered a "domestic

---

6. In his Reply Brief Spier makes the alternative argument that even under the Italian courts' decisions, certain sums awarded by the arbitrators to him survive, and "[i]t would take little effort for this Court to extract from the arbitrators' decision amounts which are clearly due" to Spier. Reply Brief at 7. Whether that exercise would be easy or onerous, I decline to undertake it. As a practical matter, the exercise would involve amending or modifying the arbitrators' award or the judgments of three Italian courts or all of the above. Those functions lie well beyond the limited subject matter jurisdiction conferred upon this Court by the Convention and its implementing domestic legislation which, in respect of an arbitral award rendered in a foreign contracting State, empower me to do enter one of only two judgments: enforcing the award, or refusing to do so upon proof of one of the grounds specified in Article V(1) of the Convention.

award" or not? After all, the dispute is between a joint venture, which is one-half owned by a U.S. corporation, and one of its dealerships, another U.S. corporation. Further, the real parties in interest may be primarily a group of U.S. dealerships (who did abide by their contract's geographical restrictions on sales) and another U.S. dealership which did not. Finally, the dispute between the parties involves an analysis of the effect of U.S. antitrust laws on the contracts. In what sense is this dispute "international" and not "domestic"? Cf., *Bergesen v. Joseph Muller Corp.*, 548 F.Supp. 650 (S.D.N.Y.1982), affirmed 710 F.2d 928 (2d Cir.1983).

2. Does the federal district court have jurisdiction under the Convention? Consult Article I.3. The United States did declare that it would apply the Convention only on the basis of reciprocity and only to awards made in the territory of another Contracting State. Japan and the United States are both Contracting States, but suppose that Malaysia is not. Would recognition and enforcement of this arbitral award to Pluto (a Malaysian corporation) provide reciprocity? Why would the United States, when ratifying this Convention, declare that reciprocity was required—what goals would it be seeking to accomplish by such a declaration—and, would those goals be served by recognizing this award to Pluto? There are two non-U.S. locations involved: the site of the arbitral tribunal (Japan) and the situs of the non-U.S. party (Malaysia). Which is more important to reciprocity in enforcement of an award? Cf., *La Societe Nationale v. Shaheen Natural Resources*, 585 F.Supp. 57 (S.D.N.Y.1983).

If the goal is that both parties to an arbitration proceeding should have equal ability to marshall assets to pay any award, then the location of the parties is important. If the goal is that both parties want certainty of world-wide recognition of the award, then locating the tribunal in a Contracting State is important, regardless of the present or future location of the offices of the parties.

Much of this analysis goes back to the original drafting of the contract clauses. It is at that time that each attorney should consider whether to choose a tribunal located in a Contracting State, and also where the assets of the other party are most likely to be found, and whether that location is in a Contracting State—as well as the competence, impartiality, etc., of the proposed tribunal.[a]

3. Does Mickey's have a defense that the contract is invalid under the U.S. antitrust laws? Consult Article V.1(a). What is "the law to which the parties have subjected" the agreement? According to the choice of law clause of the contract, *Malaysian* law is the applicable law. But, as we discovered in Problem 4.2, there are substantive areas which are governed by "mandatory law," and the parties are not free to choose the applicable law in those areas. Illustrations in prior problems of "mandatory law" range from COGSA (Carriage of Goods by Sea Act) to import and export restrictions. Antitrust law is regulatory and provides criminal sanctions for violations, two of the typical attributes of "mandatory law" of a State. Can the parties be said to have "subjected" the contract to U.S. antitrust law by choosing to do business

---

a. It should be noted that Malaysia is, in fact, a Contracting State to the New York Convention.

in the United States? Or, can the Article V invalidity defense arise only out of a law selected by the contract—giving the parties complete control over defenses assertable under the Convention? Compare *Mitsubishi* and *ACME* (American Construction Machinery), above. Is your analysis assisted by using grammatical construction techniques to determine whether "the law to which the parties have subjected" the agreement includes only laws expressly chosen, or also includes law chosen by implication? Consider footnote 19 to the majority opinion in *Mitsubishi.*

4. Does Mickey's have a defense, under Convention Article V.2(a), that antitrust disputes cannot be settled by arbitration under U.S. law? Consult *Mitsubishi,* and especially its interpretation of *Scherk v. Alberto–Culver* as it applies to "the *American Safety* doctrine." The Court seems to be saying that antitrust issues are arbitrable in international disputes, *even though* they may not be arbitrable in domestic disputes. Is that result required by the Convention, or by "international comity," etc.?

Since the Court places emphasis on its recognition of "forum selection clauses in international transactions" and on choice (by implication) of law, its analysis may have implications concerning whether U.S. antitrust law is now "mandatory law," at least in international disputes. At the least, it may be inconsistent both to consider U.S. antitrust to be mandatory law, enforceable by the State and with criminal penalties, and also to allow the parties to determine the applicability of those laws through use of choice of forum and choice of law clauses. Should the analysis of Comment 3 be reconsidered?

Several authors have indicated that the different parts of the Court's analysis do not fit together very well. See, Thomas Carbonneau, *The Exuberant Pathway to Quixotic Internationalism: Assessing the Folly of Mitsubishi,* 19 Vand. J. Transnat'l L. 265 (1986); William Park, *Private Adjudicators and the Public Interest: The Expanding Scope of International Arbitration,* 3 Brook. J. Int'l L. 629 (1986). The contrary view is presented in Andreas Lowenfeld, *The Mitsubishi Case: Another View,* 2 Arbitration J. 178 (1986). That is fine to authors, but what should your district judge do?

5. Does Mickey's have a defense, under Convention Article V.2(b), that recognition and enforcement of this award would violate U.S. "public policy"? Note the Court's language in *Mitsubishi:* " . . . it would not require intrusive inquiry to ascertain that the tribunal took cognizance of antitrust claims and actually decided them." That, together with the earlier reference to "public policy," seems to indicate that the Court believes all the analytical problems described in prior comments are solved by allowing district courts to review the tribunal's decision for antitrust misinterpretations which are also violations of U.S. "public policy." There are at least two problems with this approach.

First, what does the Court's language mean? The tribunal making Pluto's award said it took such cognizance and decided that there was no violation. Is that formal recital sufficient? Many arbitration tribunals traditionally do no more than announce their result. Should the awards of such tribunals be made uncertain because of this tradition? Certainly, it would be difficult for the court to review the tribunal's analysis without exploring the legal issues *de novo.*

But, would the award be more enforceable if the tribunal had spelled out its rationale? Such a review illustrates the second problem: What standard of review should the district court use? Should the court review the tribunal's reasoning in the same way an appellate court would normally review its own decisions on questions of law? However, the usual standard applied by lower federal courts under the Convention's "public policy" defense has concerned a "manifest disregard" of the law.

The Macneil, Speidel, & Stipanowich treatise excerpt considers the "public policy" defense under the Convention at some length, and analyzes most of the U.S. cases arising under it. The authors determine that the public policy provision of V(2)(b) does not confer upon the courts a license to review arbitral proceedings for errors of law. The results in the cases discussed would certainly indicate that it will be difficult for your district judge to refuse recognition or enforcement of an arbitral award as violations of "this nation's most basic notions of justice" or for "manifest disregard" of U.S. antitrust law, if the tribunal states a rationale and she disagrees with that rationale. However, Pluto's award is not based on any detailed rationale. Is this the type of situation which allows the district court to raise "manifest disregard" to a public policy defense?

6.   The *Sun Oil* court clearly distinguishes the "national interest" of the U.S. Government from "public policy." Are our concepts of antitrust law and promotion of a market economy any stronger than our interests in blocking terrorism? If the *Sun Oil* court states what "public policy" is not, does it help us determine what public policy *is,* or how it can be identified? Alternatively, would the court have used the same analysis if all Libyan accounts had not been already blocked by the Libyan Sanctions Regulations? One prior decision, and the only one involving possibly successful assertion of the "public policy" defense under the Convention, is *Laminoirs–Trefileries–Cableries de Lens, S.A. v. Southwire Company,* 484 F.Supp. 1063 (N.D.Ga. 1980).

7.   Considering the public policy discussions in *Parsons and Whittemore,* in *Sun Oil,* as well as in the Macneil et al extract, what is the best public policy argument Mickey's might make? Is it advisable for Mickey's to combine the public policy argument with a manifest disregard of the law argument? Assume Mickey's can establish that when Mickey's first began to comment on the antitrust laws during the arbitral proceedings, planning to establish how their application would not incompatible with Malaysian concepts of trade restraints, the arbitrators cut off Mickey's attorneys with a terse comment that they knew what the U.S. laws stated and they were not applicable, and thereafter neither made not allowed any further comment regarding the antitrust laws, other than the statements in the facts contained in the arbitral decision.

8.   Suppose Pluto petitions the district court for pre-judgment attachment of Mickey's assets, so that they will not be dissipated. This petition can be granted in enforcement of domestic arbitral awards, but the Convention contains no express provisions on this issue. Does such a petition contravene one purpose of the Convention, which is to obtain settlement of disputes solely through arbitration proceedings? Or, does the Convention's silence mean that all locally available procedures for domestic awards are also

available for foreign awards? *Compare McCreary Tire & Rubber Co. v. CEAT S.p.A.*, 501 F.2d 1032 (3d Cir.1974), with *Carolina Power & Light Co. v. Uranex*, 451 F.Supp. 1044 (N.D.Cal.1977).

9. There is one other assistance which Mickey's might seek from the district court—a deferral or delay in enforcement under Article VI of the Convention. Adjournments of enforcement may be made during appeal of the award in the courts of State in which the tribunal is located. That is discussed in *Spier v. Calzaturificio Tecnica S.p.A. (Spier I)*, 663 F.Supp. 871 (S.D.N.Y. 1987). And adjournment will be denied in such a situation only if the defendant's litigation position is "transparently frivolous." Adjournment is available, however, only for appeals to the courts in the country of origin of the award. However, if the court does adjourn the enforcement decision, it may also order Mickey's to "give suitable security" to protect Pluto's interests. Article VI. In further proceedings in the *Spier* case (an extract of *Spier II* is in the readings), the court ordered the defendant to post security in the form of an irrevocable letter of credit issued by a New York bank or a bond which conformed to Civil Rule 37(b) of the Rules of the Court. Why did the court reject the defendant's offer of a bank guarantee issued by its Italian bank?

10. May a litigant seek to enforce a foreign arbitral award in the U.S. court where that award has been previously annulled by a court in the country of arbitration? There is an interplay between New York Convention Article V(1)(e) (court *may* decline to enforce such awards) and Article VII (convention *shall* not deprive any party of rights to award to extent allowed under the laws of the country where enforcement is sought). The Second Circuit declined to enforce an award previously annulled by a Nigerian court in *Baker Marine (Nig.) Ltd. v. Chevron (Nig.) Ltd.*, 191 F.3d 194 (2d Cir. 1999), but the D.C. district court enforced an award previously annulled by an Egyptian court in *Chromalloy Aeroservices v. Arab Republic of Egypt*, 939 F.Supp. 907 (D.D.C. 1996).

11. Considering *Spier* what if the foreign court in annulling the award based its decision on grounds outside the exceptions to enforcement contained in the New York Convention? See the citation in *Spier* to the *Yusuf* decision. Which is the better view, using the "full panoply of express or implied grounds" or restricting non-enforcement to "explicit grounds" in the Convention?

12. Does *Spier* allow an arbitration clause that prohibits any award or its enforcement from being contested?

13. Does Mickey's have any argument that the award constituted a manifest disregard of the law? In view of the Supreme Court *Hall* decision noted in the Comment, Mickey's has two questions. First, whether Hall remains a ground for vacatur and, second, whether it may fit into Article V(2)(b) as an issue of public policy.

APPENDIX

THE EUROPEAN UNION *

■ ■ ■

INTRODUCTION TO THE EU LEGAL SYSTEM
A Timeline of European Integration

1948—Benelux Customs Union Treaty
1949—COMECON Treaty (Eastern Europe, Soviet Union)
1950—European Convention on Human Rights
1951—European Coal and Steel Community ("Treaty of Paris")
1957—European Economic Community (EEC) ("Treaty of Rome"), European Atomic Energy Community Treaty (EURATOM)
1959—European Free Trade Area Treaty (EFTA)
1968—EEC Customs Union fully operative
1973—Britain and Denmark switch from EFTA to EEC; Ireland joins EEC; Norway rejects membership; remaining EFTA states sign industrial free trade treaties with EEC
1979—Direct elections to European Parliament
1981—Greece joins EEC
1983—Greenland "withdraws" from EEC
1986—Spain and Portugal join EEC, Portugal leaves EFTA
1987—Single European Act amends Treaty of Rome to initiate campaign for a Community without internal frontiers by 1993
1990—East Germany merged into Community via reunification process
1991—COMECON defunct; trade relations with Central Europe develop rapidly
1993—Maastricht Treaty on European Union (TEU), EEC officially becomes EC
1994—European Monetary Institute established
1995—Austria, Finland, and Sweden join EU, Norway votes no again
1999—Amsterdam Treaty
1999—Common currency (EURO) managed by European Central Bank commences with 11 members
2003—Treaty of Nice, EU Charter of Fundamental Rights "declared," draft Constitution for Europe released
2004—Cyprus, Estonia, Slovenia, Poland, Hungary, the Czech Republic, Slovakia, Latvia, Lithuania, Malta join EU

---

* See generally R. Folsom, *Principles of European Union Law* (2011) and *European Union Law in a Nutshell* (2011).

1308

2005—Constitution for Europe overwhelmingly defeated in France, Netherlands

2007—Accession of Bulgaria and Romania, Reform Treaty of Lisbon proposed

2008—Irish voters reject Reform Treaty

2009—Reform Treaty approved in Ireland ... takes effect Dec. 1, 2009, EU Charter of Fundamental Rights becomes binding law, EU accedes to European Convention on Human Rights, Treaty of Rome becomes Treaty on the Functioning of the European Union (TFEU)

2010—Greece and Ireland bailed out, 1 trillion EURO safety net created for financial crises

2011—Portugal bailed out, Italy and Spain under pressure, EURO in crisis

SECTION I. THE SETTING

Functioning as a lawyer with clients participating in trade, licensing or investment in the European Union nations mandates some knowledge of its law and how its legal system works. Your client may buy and sell products and discover that attempts to allocate distributors' territories by nation are unacceptable. It may license intellectual property to Europeans, an area heavily covered by regional law. The client may decide to produce in an EU nation and wish to establish a subsidiary, only to discover that it is not only national law, but European law as well, that regulates companies. Or your client may be involved in agriculture and come into conflict with the Common Agricultural Policy (CAP), which makes it very difficult to plan sales.

The European Union is a huge market; you simply cannot ignore it. How else might your clients come into contact with its law? What are the enforcement powers of its institutions? What if there is a Commission investigation of your client's activities? How must you respond? When and how can you litigate legal issues in the national courts? And how do you get those issues before the European Court of Justice? Just exactly what is a "directive"? What happens when regional and national law conflict? Can you influence the development of European law, especially the onslaught of new legislation adopted for the single market campaign? All of these questions are frequently posed. Thus, regardless of the particular circumstances and needs of a client, counsel should initially seek to understand some basic attributes of the legal system of the European Union.

SECTION II. FOCUS OF CONSIDERATION

Before considering special fact situations and hypothetical problems, this introduction examines several aspects of the operation of the European Union. We will consider a few important institutional structures and legal process in a general manner focused upon law-making and judicial review. The readings should serve to introduce the expansive scope of the EU treaties. We should note that the EU is not the only common market. There are other unions of varying levels of economic integration, including the European Free Trade Area (EFTA) and the North American Free Trade Area (NAFTA). But most involve developing nations and few have had any success with the development of viable legal and legislative systems. So we consider with particular interest the role of the European Court of Justice in developing the law of economic integration.

Extensive Web resources for further study are available at *www. europa.eu.*

SECTION III. READINGS, QUESTIONS AND COMMENTS

PART A.   LAW–MAKING

R. FOLSOM, EUROPEAN UNION LAW IN A NUTSHELL
Chapters 3 and 4 (2011).

The Europeans have been creating law at dazzling though sometimes irregular speed. The focus in this chapter is on law-making institutions and procedures. Without an understanding of these areas, it is almost impossible to function as a lawyer on EU matters.

Primary and Secondary Law

The two founding treaties of the European Union, the Treaty on the Functioning of the European Union (TFEU) and the Maastricht Treaty on European Union (TEU), are the "primary" sources of regional law. They are, in this author's opinion "quasi-constitutional." The treaties have a common set of core institutions. These are the Council, the Commission, the Parliament and the Court of Justice. These institutions, supplemented by the European Council, European Central Bank and other EU bodies, and by national legislatures, courts and tribunals, have been busy generating a remarkably vast and complex body of "secondary" law.

Some law is adopted directly at the regional level, but much of it is enacted by national governments under regional "direction." Similarly, some (and the most important) of the case law is created by decisions in the European Court of Justice, and its companion General Court, but much development also occurs in the national courts, acting in many instances with "advisory rulings" from the Court of Justice. European secondary law also includes international obligations, sometimes undertaken through "mixed" regional and national negotiations and ratifications.

There are two primary types of legislative acts, directives and regulations (see below). These acts should be distinguished from declarations, resolutions, guidelines, notices, policy statements, guidelines, recommendations, opinions and individual decisions, all of which rarely involve legislative acts and are sometimes referred to as "soft law." For example, the 1981 European Council resolution on the adoption of EU passports with uniform characteristics fits this mold. This symbolic resolution has been fully implemented, adding significantly to the consciousness of the European Union among its citizens. Another example is the Council's Declaration on Democracy (1977) which "codifies" the longstanding tradition that no European state can join or remain associated with the EU without a pluralistic democratic form of government. A third example is the formulation of foreign policy resolutions by the European Council (Chapter 2).

THE POWER TO LEGISLATE

The starting point for a basic understanding of European law-making is, as always, the founding treaties. The TFEU is premised upon the idea of a regional government of limited or conferred powers (compétence d'attribution). That is to say, the TFEU does not convey a general power to create EU law. European law-making is either specifically authorized or dependent upon the terms of Article 352. That article permits action if "necessary to attain, in the course of the operation of the common market, one of the objectives of the Union and this Treaty has not provided the necessary powers."

Article 352 has been used repeatedly, and in ways which suggest that there are relatively few limits upon what the region can legislate, or negotiate by way of international agreements, once a unanimous consensus to move forward has been reached in the Council and the Parliament consents. For example, Article 352 was widely used as the legal basis for environmental programs well prior to Single European Act amendments that specifically authorize action in this field. However, the Court of Justice has been retreating from a doctrine of *implied* treaty powers, most notably concerning external relations.

The Reform Treaty of 2009, in new TFEU provisions, enumerates categories and areas of exclusive, shared and supportive EU competences or powers. These enumerations determine when and to what degree the EU and/or the member states may legislate. Exclusive EU competences (Article 3 TFEU) include the customs union, internal market competition rules, EURO zone monetary policy, marine conservation, and the Common Commercial Policy (external trade relations). The Union also has exclusive competence over international agreements provided for EU legislative acts, necessary to enable the exercise of its internal powers, or those agreements whose conclusion may affect common rules or alter their scope. In all these areas, member states may legislate only if empowered by the Union to do so, or to implement EU acts.

When the TFEU enumerates a shared competence (Article 4), the Union may legislate. Member states may legislate only to the extent the EU has not done so or ceased to exercise a shared competence. Shared competences include the internal market, social policy, cohesion, agriculture and fisheries, the environment, consumer protection, transport, trans-European networks, energy, the area of freedom, security and justice, and common public health safety concerns. Special more permissive rules allow member states greater latitude in the areas of research, technology development, space, third world development and humanitarian aid.

Lastly, the Union is authorized to legislate in support of, to coordinate with, or to supplement (but not supersede) member state competence in areas designated in Article 6 TFEU. These include human health, industry, culture, tourism, education and training, youth, sport, civil protection and administrative cooperation. EU acts in these areas may not entail harmonization of member state laws or regulations.

Article 5 TFEU reserves to the member states all competences not conferred upon the Union under its founding treaties.

THE PRINCIPLE OF SUBSIDIARITY

The Treaty on European Union (Maastricht 1993) and to a lesser extent the Single European Act (1987) formalized "subsidiarity" and "proportionality" principles. The Amsterdam Treaty of 1999 added a Protocol on the application of the principles of subsidiarity and proportionality. These much debated principles hold that the region can act in areas where it does not *exclusively* have power only if the member states cannot sufficiently achieve the objectives, i.e., "by reason of scale or effects [the] proposed action [can] be better achieved by the Union" (subsidiarity principle). In all cases, European action must not go beyond what is necessary to achieve the objectives of the TFEU (proportionality principle).

Subsidiarity is a kind of "states' rights" amendment intended to limit the growth of regional government in Europe. An inter-institutional agreement by the Council, Commission and European Parliament on the application of subsidiarity principles by all institutions was quickly negotiated. Subsidiarity guidelines were adopted by the European Council in 1992 and a Protocol implemented in 1999 with the Amsterdam Treaty. Moreover, the Commission regularly reviews proposed and existing legislation in light of the subsidiarity principle. This has caused a number of legislative proposals and acts to be withdrawn or amended. Under the Subsidiarity Protocol, if a third or more of the *national* Parliaments gave reasoned opinions that a proposal breached the subsidiarity principle, the Commission must reconsider. Since the Reform Treaty of 2009, national parliaments get notice early in the EU legislative process, and can force the Commission and even the Council and Parliament to review proposed laws in terms of subsidiarity. National parliaments may also file suit before the European Court of Justice to seek annulment of EU legislative acts on subsidiarity grounds. The Committee of the Regions can do likewise.

The European Council takes the position that subsidiarity principles do not have direct effect in member state legal systems. If this is correct, subsidiarity issues cannot be raised in litigation before member state courts and tribunals. However, interpretation of these principles and review of compliance by European institutions are subject to judicial review before the Court of Justice through challenges initiated by a member state or another regional institution. It is the Court, therefore, that will ultimately determine whether and to what degree subsidiarity will limit regional governance. To date, its opinions relating to subsidiarity have been studiously opaque though generally deferential to EU legislative powers and recitals of need. Should subsidiarity preclude action, member states are still required to ensure fulfillment of their Treaty obligations and abstain from measures that could jeopardize their objectives.

LEGISLATION—DIRECTIVES AND REGULATIONS

Article 288 of the TFEU clarifies the powers of the Council and the Commission to make regulations and issue directives. EU regulations are similar in form to administrative regulations commonly found in North America. EU directives, on the other hand, have no obvious parallel. The Court of Justice has repeatedly affirmed that both regulations and directives must state the "reasons" on which they are based.

A directive establishes regional policy. It is then left to the member states to implement the directive in whatever way is appropriate to their national legal system. This may require a new statute, a Presidential decree, an administrative act or even a constitutional amendment. Sometimes it may require no action at all. As Article 288 indicates, a directive is "binding as to the result to be achieved" but "leave[s] to the national authorities the choice of form and methods." The vast majority of the legislative acts of the single market campaign were directives. All directives contain time limits for national implementation. The more controversial the policy, the longer the likely allotment of time. The Reform Treaty of 2009 makes it clear member states must adopt all measures necessary to implement legally binding Union acts.

The Commission's civil servants initiate the process of legislation by drafting proposals which the Council (comprised of ministers from the governments of the member states) has the power to adopt into law. Although the Council and Parliaments may request the Commission to submit legislative proposals, neither can force the Commission to do so except by way of litigation before the Court of Justice. Only the Commission can draft legislative proposals. This makes the Commission the focal point of lobbying activities. Readers will immediately note that the European Parliament does not have the power to propose legislation!

The Commission's legislative proposals are always influenced by what it believes the Council will accept. The Council, however, has the right to amend legislative proposals by unanimous vote. Parliament's role was traditionally consultative. Over time, it became and remains the source of *proposed* amendments. Note that Parliament does not have the power to enact law! This absence of legislative power is so fundamental that many observers decry a "democratic deficit" in Europe. This deficit has been partially "remedied" by conveying "co-decision" powers to Parliament.

These powers amount to a Parliamentary right, in the absence of conciliation with the Council, to veto selected legislative proposals.

* * *

WHICH COUNCIL?

Council

The foregoing analysis of legislative process illustrates the dominant role of the Council in regional affairs. The Council, also known since 1993 as the Council of the European Union (EU Council), is a bit of a moving target. The Council consists of representatives of the governments of the member states. Thus there are presently 27 Council members since the accession of Bulgaria and Romania in 2007. However, the people who comprise the Council change according to the topic at hand. The national ministers of foreign affairs, agriculture, economy and finance (ecofin), social affairs, environment, etc. are sent to Brussels to confer and vote on matters within their competence. Some refer to the Ecofin Council, the Environment Council, the Agriculture Council and so forth in order to differentiate the various Councils. Several different Council meetings can take place at once. It is from all these meetings that the European legislation of the pours forth.

* * *

European Council

Then there is the "European Council." With growth, legislative and other decisions have inevitably become more political and thus more difficult. A new institution emerged to keep Europe moving, mostly forward but arguably (at times) backward. The "European Council" consists of the heads of the state or government of the member nations, a kind of ultimate Council. The heads of state have met twice a year since 1974 to formulate broad policy guidelines or initiatives for the Union. For example, the European Council has shown leadership on direct elections to Parliament, the European Monetary System, new memberships and innovative legislative agendas. Its meetings are sometimes called "summits," and Article 2 of the Single European Act of 1987 formally recognized their existence. The Reform Treaty of 2009 established an elected President of the European Council, a post that lasts 2.5 years. Despite this development, the traditional 6–month Rotating Council Presidency was retained. It is unclear exactly how these two Presidencies will interact.

* * *

Qualified Majority Voting

Most of the voting in the Council now takes place on a qualified majority basis. The rules that define this procedure are given in Article 238 TFEU. Prior to Nov. 1, 2014, and thereafter upon request by a member state until March 31, 2017, pre-Lisbon Treaty rules continue to apply. That means, under the Nice Treaty Enlargement Protocol, there are a total of 345 votes. Germany, France, Italy and Britain have 29 qualified majority votes each, Spain and Poland have 27 votes, Romania 14 votes, the Netherlands 13 votes, and Belgium, Greece, Portugal, the Czech Republic and Hungary 12 votes. Austria, Sweden and Bulgaria have 10 votes, Denmark, Ireland, Finland, Slovakia and Lithuania 7 votes, Luxembourg, Latvia, Slovenia, Estonia and Cyprus 4 votes, and Malta has 3 qualified majority votes.

To adopt legislation prior to 2014, under the allocations noted above, 255 votes must be cast in favor by a majority of the member states (for measures requiring a proposal from the Commission) *or* two-thirds of the members (for all other measures). In addition, the qualified majority must when challenged by a member state constitute 62 percent of the total EU population. Thus, compared with the law prior to the Treaty of Nice Enlargement Protocol, two demanding rules were added: (1) The majority or two-thirds member state requirement; and (2) the percentage of population challenge requirement. The third requirement, the qualified majority vote count, was tightened by slightly raising the percentage of votes needed to pass legislation. Byzantine hardly seems adequate to describe these "triple majority" rules on qualified majority voting.

After Nov. 1, 2014, a qualified majority is defined as at least 55% of the members of the Council (with a minimum number of 15) who represent member states comprising 65% of the population of the Union. Any blocking minority must include at least 4 Council members. Thus a simplified "double majority" voting system will be undertaken in 2014.

* * *

THE COMMISSION AS AN INSTITUTION AND LAW–MAKER

The pivotal role of the European Commission in the law-making process should be evident. Apart from administrative cooperation on criminal and police matters, where a quarter of the member states can initiate EU acts, the Commission alone drafts legislative proposals. As the GSP litigation makes clear, the Commission can also prosecute when proper legislative procedures are not followed. Furthermore, in certain areas (notably agricultural and competition law) the Commission has been delegated by the Council the authority to issue implementing regulations and decisions that establish law. These acts detail administrative rules rather than create new or broad policies. Thus the Council establishes the "target prices" for agriculture, but the Commission issues thousands of regulations aimed at actually realizing these goals.

The Commission has also promulgated an important series of "group exemption" regulations for business competition law. These cover franchising, technology transfers, distribution and a variety of other business agreements. Lastly, the Commission is authorized by Article 106 TFEU to issue (on its own initiative) *directives* addressed to member states regarding public enterprises. This authority avoids the usual legislative process. The Reform Treaty of 2009 added a citizen's initiative procedure. One million EU citizens from a significant number of member states may "invite" the Commission to submit proposals in areas of regional concern.

When exercising law-making powers conferred upon it by the Council, the Commission must first consult various committees. These requirements are known as the "comitology" rules of the Council. These rules, in essence, allow the Council to actively monitor the Commission as a lawmaker. In most cases, they vest a power of reversal or modification in the Council.

The Commissioners and Their Tasks

Who and what is the European Commission? Under the Nice Treaty Enlargement Protocol, there are 27 Commissioners, one from each member state. Germany, France, Italy, Britain and Spain gave up their second Commissioners. The Reform Treaty sought to reduce the number of Commissioners to two-thirds the number of member states starting in November 2014, but negotiations with Ireland caused this change to be dropped. Commissioners are appointed by a qualified majority of the Council subject to Parliament's approval for five-year renewable terms. The President of the Commission is similarly appointed by the European Council and Parliament. Great pains are taken to ensure the independence of Commissioners from their home governments. Article 245 stipulates that Commissioners must be chosen on the basis of competence and their independence must be "beyond doubt." Any breach of this trust by Commissioners could lead to compulsory retirement, or since the Nice Treaty, dismissal by the President of the Commission.

Unlike the ministers of the Council, Commissioners are not supposed to function as representatives of their nations. Over the years, in large measure, this has been true. Indeed, Prime Minister Thatcher once failed to renew a British Commissioner's appointment because he had "gone native." Sent over to Brussels in a stormy period when the Prime Minister was quite hostile to developments, this Commissioner proceeded to act independently, too independently as it turned out. His non-renewal, however, broke with a longstanding tradition of regular reappointments for competent Commissioners. Renewal decisions have thus become more politicized in recent years and Commissioners no doubt look over their shoulders towards home as their five-year terms begin to expire.

The TFEU also establishes voting rules for the European Commission. Simple majority votes prevail. As a matter of custom, considerable deference is usually given to the Commissioner in charge when legislative or other proposals are being reviewed by the Commission as a whole. This is sometimes achieved by circulating files with proposed actions which are implemented unless objections are shortly received. Individual Commissioners can be delegated authority to act for the body on routine matters. For example, when the Commissioner on Agriculture adopts new regulations, these are likely to involve such delegation.

The Commission performs a number of functions in addition to those concerning law-making. The most important of these include its prosecutorial powers against individuals and enterprises for breach of selected laws, and against member states for failure to adhere to their treaty obligations. The Commission negotiates international trade and other agreements. It also administers the EU budget and publishes a general and a series of specific annual reports (e.g., on competition policy), all of which are a good way to survey regional affairs.

* * *

DIRECT EFFECTS DOCTRINE

The right to commence litigation in national forums must be given to the plaintiff by national law. In other words, European law has not (as yet) been interpreted to create national causes of action. What it does do, according to the "direct effects doctrine," is give litigants the right to raise many issues ("Euro-defenses" and "Euro-offenses") in national courts and tribunals. In doing so, individuals often function as guardians (like the Commission) of the founding treaties. Americans might analogize this role to that of "private attorneys general," a law enforcement technique adopted in a number of United States statutes. The Court of Justice has noted that the vigilance of private litigants enforcing their rights is an important element in the European legal system.

The direct effects doctrine is, to a very large degree, a product of the jurisprudence of the European Court of Justice. It can apply to treaties, directives, regulations, decisions and international agreements. When any of these measures are of direct effect, this impact generally commences from the date of its entry into force. But the direct effects doctrine is not automatically applied. For example, although the General Agreement on Tariffs and Trade (GATT) and the WTO Agreements are binding upon the Union and its member states, they have been construed by the Court not to have direct legal effects. Both the Council of ministers and the European Council tend to issue resolutions or declarations when there is a political consensus but no desire to adopt legislation. For the most part, the Court of Justice has held such acts incapable of creating direct legal effects in the member states.

Regulations

The legal effects of regulations are the easiest to understand. Article 288 TFEU provides that regulations are "directly applicable in all member states." In other words, regulations have immediate unconditional legal effect without any need for national implementation. They are law in the member states from the moment of issuance, binding upon all individuals, business organizations and governments. For litigants, when regulations are applicable, they control the outcome. This is true under the supremacy doctrine even in the face of contrary national law. See Chapter 3.

Directives

Directives are more difficult to understand. Article 288 does *not* specify that they shall have "direct applicability." In part, their design prohibits this. Directives are addressed to member states, instructing them to implement (in whatever way required) certain regional policies within a fixed timetable. These policies do not become law in the member states until implemented or, if timely implementation does not follow, until the European Court rules that the directive is of "direct effect." Some national courts, notably in France, have opposed this judge-made doctrine.

Not all directives have direct effect. The Court of Justice has selectively ruled that only those directives that establish clear and unconditional legal norms and do not leave normative discretion to the member states are of direct effect. Most "framework" directives will not meet these criteria. Once the ECJ has decided that a European directive has direct effect, litigants can rely on it to the full extent of its application to member states, public service entities and local governments. Litigants can challenge contrary national law, including defective implementing measures.

Interpretative Duties

Unlike regulations, directives cannot be used to challenge private activities. Thus it is said that directives are incapable of "horizontal" direct effects. Even so, the Court of Justice has held that in applying national law the member state courts and tribunals are required by Article 4 (3) TEU to interpret their law in light of the wording and purposes of all directives. National law must be interpreted in the light of regional directives even if the directive has not yet been implemented. Some commentators have characterized these duties, derived from the *Marleasing* case, as involving the "indirect effect" of directives.

The obligation to interpret national law in view of directives is limited by general principles of law and in particular the principles of legal certainty and non-retroactivity. Even so, in considerable private litigation before the tribunals and courts of member states, European directives will be given effect through judicial interpretations of national law. This is likely to have the same practical impact as would adoption of a "horizontal" direct effects doctrine at the regional level. Moreover, it has been argued that Article 4 (3) TEU mandates that *all* provisions of national law (not just those touched by directives) must be interpreted in conformity with *all* European law (not just directives). If this argument becomes binding law, the doctrine of direct effects will reach a zenith which few would have ever dreamed.

DIRECTLY EFFECTIVE TREATY PROVISIONS

The third major category of directly effective law originates in the founding treaties. The Court of Justice has ruled that parts of these treaties are capable of having immediate, binding legal effect in the member states. Here again the Court has been selective, sorting out which treaty provisions establish clear, unconditional and nondiscretionary legal norms. Those many articles of the treaties that are largely aspirational, procedural or written as guidelines for the exercise of member state discretion are unlikely to have direct effect.

The Court of Justice has consistently refused to view the treaties as merely creating obligations among the contracting states. Citing Article 267, the Court found acknowledgment that the Treaty of Rome (now TFEU) was intended to have effect in national legal regimes.

> "The conclusion to be drawn ... is that the Community [Union] constitutes a new legal order of international law for the benefit of which the States have limited their sovereign rights, albeit within limited fields, and the subjects of which comprise not only Member States but also their nationals. Independently of the legislation of Member States, Community law therefore not only imposes obligations on individuals but is also intended to confer upon them rights which become part of their legal heritage. These rights arise not only where they are expressly granted by the Treaty, but also by reason of obligations which the Treaty imposes in a clearly defined way upon individuals as well as upon the Member States and the institutions of the Community." *Van Gend en Loos v. Nederlandse Administratie der Belastingen* (1963) Eur.Comm.Rep. 1.

Once the Court has held a Treaty term directly effective in the member states, litigants before national courts and tribunals can rely fully upon it. They can, under the supremacy doctrine, use it to set aside contradictory national law. Like regulations, directly effective Treaty provisions apply horizontally to private parties. This follows, in the court's view, because national courts are an arm of the states that signed the Treaty and therefore bound to apply its law in all cases.

PESCATORE, THE DOCTRINE OF "DIRECT EFFECT: AN INFANT DISEASE OF COMMUNITY LAW"

8 Eur.L.Rev. 155 (1983).*

This is no doubt a topic of great importance for both legal practice and legal theory. But I am wondering whether those who chose to invite me have not been mistaken because I must confess, * * * that I have written recently that the discussion on direct effect has been a sort of "infant disease" of Community law. This should not scare anyone. Infant diseases are happily in most of the cases mild diseases and they have one advantage: once one has gone through them they leave immunity for a lifetime.

May I, before unfolding the many facets of the problem, say just a word on the cure I am proposing. My cure is a matter of philosophy rather than of legal technique; not just my personal philosophy, but a reflection on the legal approach which has been practised by the European Court in this matter throughout the years, a way of thinking which pervades the

---

* © Sweet & Maxwell, Ltd. Reprinted with permission.

many decisions taken in relation to the problem of what we are accustomed to call "direct effect" or "direct applicability" of Community law.

This philosophy is very simple indeed. It means that legal rules, by their very nature, have a practical purpose. Any legal rule is devised so as to operate effectively (we are accustomed, in French) to speak here about *effet utile*. If it is not operative, it is not a rule of law. The task of lawyers is therefore not to thwart effects of legal rules, but to help in putting them into operation. In other words, practical operation for all concerned, which is nothing else than "direct effect," must be considered as being the normal condition of any rule of law. The non-operation of a rule of law appears thus to be not an ordinary phenomenon, but a real antinomy in the legal system. In other words, "direct effect" must be presumed, it has not to be established *a priori*. * * *

I would say that "direct effect" is the normal state of health of the law: it is only the absence of direct effect which causes concern and calls for the attention of legal doctors.

* * *

These final considerations on goodwill and the "art du possible" bring me back to my introductory remarks. The exploration of the relevant case law shows that the dominant preoccupation of the European Court is to ensure in all the circumstances the operative character of the rules of Community law. Doing this, the Court has tried to go to the extreme limits of the operability of the provisions of Community law by a detailed analysis of the provisions which were at stake in varying circumstances. This has led the Court to discover elements of effectiveness even within provisions which at first sight would seem to be too vague or to imply too wide a margin of discretion. It is the same inspiration which has prompted the Court, while respecting the discretion reserved to Member States in the choice of the means best adapted to the implementation of directives, to make sure that those acts of "indirect legislation" had at least a minimal effect in the event of Member States disregarding their obligations.

I think that this persistent attitude can be best explained by the sort of philosophy I ventured to explain at the beginning of this text. The purpose of any legal rule * * * is to achieve some practical aim and it would be running counter to its essential purpose if one handled it in such a way as to render it practically meaningless. Effectiveness is the very soul of legal rules and therefore I think that it is not excessive to say that any legal rule must be at first sight presumed to be operative in view of its object and purpose.

So my last conclusion is: why do you ask questions about the "direct effect" of Community law? You had better try to apply it, just to find out that "direct effect" is nothing but the ordinary state of the law. Questions will therefore arise only in those exceptional cases where the implementation of a given Community rule, whatever its source and whatever its form, meets some obstacle in law or in fact which even the best-intentioned lawyer feels it difficult to overcome. Then you will be faced with a genuine problem about "direct effect" which is worthwhile analyzing.

QUESTIONS AND COMMENTS

1.   The Treaty on the Functioning of the European Union (TFEU) (2009) is the primary source of European law. How does the Treaty allocate law-making power among the Council, the Commission and the European Parliament? When may the EU legislate exclusively? Jointly with member states? In support of member states? See the Folsom excerpt on EU "competences."

The development of regional law is not without internal institutional conflict and struggle for power. Is there an effective system of checks and balances in EU governance? How does the "principle of subsidiarity" affect your conclusions?

2.   Is the independence of the members of the Commission from their home governments protected? What functions does the Commission perform?

3.   Article 288 TFEU concerns "secondary" sources of law: regulations, directives, decisions, recommendations and opinions. Do you understand the differences among these sources of law? How would you establish the authority of the EU to promulgate a regulation or directive?

4.   What procedures must be followed to adopt secondary law? Who drafts the regulations and directives? May the Council amend a directive proposed by the Commission?

5.   Would you advise a client to lobby before the European Parliament concerning proposed legislation? Before the Commission?

Why does the Parliament *not* possess the power to initiate and enact legislation? What is the significance of Parliament's "co-decisional" role?

6.   How does the doctrine of direct effect establish individual rights and obligations? Who ultimately decides whether a Treaty provision is directly effective?

Not all provisions of the TFEU are directly effective. When are treaty provisions likely to be held to be directly effective law? What is the significance to member states of directly effective regional law?

7.   What is the significance of the fact that all regulations are directly applicable? Is there any authority in the Treaty for the argument that directives can be directly effective? When should they be held directly effective law? See the provocative comments of Judge Pescatore of the European Court of Justice.

PART B.   THE EUROPEAN COURT OF JUSTICE

TREATY ON THE FUNCTIONING OF THE EUROPEAN UNION (TFEU) (2009)

Article 258

If the Commission considers that a Member State has failed to fulfil an obligation under this Treaty, it shall deliver a reasoned opinion on the matter after giving the State concerned the opportunity to submit its observations.

If the State concerned does not comply with the opinion within the period laid down by the Commission, the latter may bring the matter before the Court of Justice.

* * *

Article 263

The Court of Justice shall review the legality of acts adopted jointly by the European Parliament and the Council, of acts of the Council, of the Commission and of the ECB, other than recommendations and opinions, and of acts of the European Parliament intended to produce legal effects vis-à-vis third parties.

It shall for this purpose have jurisdiction in actions brought by a Member State, the Council or the Commission on grounds of lack of competence, infringement of an essential procedural requirement, infringement of this Treaty or of any rule of law relating to its application, or misuse of powers.

The Court shall have jurisdiction under the same conditions in actions brought by the European Parliament and by the ECB for the purpose of protecting their prerogatives.

Any natural or legal person may, under the same conditions, institute proceedings against a decision addressed to that person or against a decision which, although in the form of a regulation or a decision addressed to another person, is of direct and individual concern to the former.

The proceedings provided for in this Article shall be instituted within two months of the publication of the measure, or of its notification to the plaintiff, or, in the absence thereof, of the day on which it came to the knowledge of the latter, as the case may be.

Article 264

If the action is well founded, the Court of Justice shall declare the act concerned to be void.

In the case of a regulation, however, the Court of Justice shall, if it considers this necessary, state which of the effects of the regulation which it has declared void shall be considered as definitive.

* * *

Article 267

The Court of Justice shall have jurisdiction to give preliminary rulings concerning:

(a) the interpretation of this Treaty;

(b) the validity and interpretation of acts of the institutions of the Community and of the ECB;

(c) the interpretation of the statutes of bodies established by an act of the Council, where those statutes so provide.

Where such a question is raised before any court or tribunal of a Member State, that court or tribunal may, if it considers that a decision on the question is necessary to enable it to give judgment, request the Court of Justice to give a ruling thereon.

Where any such question is raised in a case pending before a court or tribunal of a Member State against whose decisions there is no judicial remedy under national law, that court or tribunal shall bring the matter before the Court of Justice.

COMMISSION v. UNITED KINGDOM

European Court of Justice, 1982.
1982 Eur.Comm.Rep. 2601.

OPINION OF MR. ADVOCATE GENERAL VERLOREN VAN THEMAAT

Mr. President,
Members of the Court,

The Commission asks the Court to declare that, by failing to adopt the laws, regulations or administrative provisions needed to comply with Council Directive 75/117/EEC of 10 February 1975 on the approximation of the laws of the Member States relating to the application of the principle of equal pay for men and women, the United Kingdom has failed to fulfil its obligations under that directive as regards the abolition of discrimination in respect of "work to which equal value is attributed".

* * *

According to the Commission the legislation of the United Kingdom concerning the principle of equal pay does not meet the requirements of Community law as regards "work to which equal value is attributed". The legislation in point is the Equal Pay Act 1970, as amended by the Sex Discrimination Act 1975. Under the Equal Pay Act any contract of employment is deemed to include an equality clause where a woman is employed on "like work" or "work rated as equivalent". Those two terms are defined in Section 1(4) and 1(5). According to Section 1(4) a woman is employed on like work with men "if her work and theirs is of the same or a broadly similar nature".

According to Section 1(5) a woman is employed on work rated as equivalent if the jobs have been given an equal value in terms of certain criteria (for instance, effort, skill, decision) on the basis of a system of evaluating work in an undertaking. The entire concepts of both "equal work or work to which equal value is attributed" are summed up in that manner. The proceedings concern, with regard to the United Kingdom legislation, jobs which are not equal or nearly equal in nature but which may nevertheless be said to be of equal value despite their differences.

The effect of the United Kingdom legislation is that in the case of work which is not equal or nearly equal in nature an equality clause is incorporated only if the work has been judged to be of equal value on the basis of a job classification system. According to the case-file, a job classification system can be applied in an undertaking only with the consent of those concerned, that is to say on a voluntary basis. In my opinion the fact that the implementation of such an evaluation system is dependent on the employer's agreement is particularly important in this case.

* * *

I believe that in order to decide this case it is necessary to start with the aims of Article 119 [renumbered Article 157, TFEU], as construed in the Court's judgment in *Defrenne No 2* and amplified in Directive 75/117. According to that judgment, all discrimination, both direct and indirect, must be abolished. An individual employee has a subjective right to this which not only concerns direct reliance on Article 119 but must also apply to those situations which are shown to constitute indirect discrimination. As regards that kind of discrimination Article 119 and the directive, particularly Articles 2 and 6 thereof, require Member States to take the measures necessary to ensure that the principle of equal pay is applied.

An examination of the United Kingdom legislation regarding the term "work of equal value" in relation to that aim gives the following picture. The fact that under the United Kingdom legislation the evaluation of different jobs has to be done on the basis of a job classification system can but win approval. For the documents on the file show that in the state of current knowledge this method of evaluating work provides the most objective method and is often based on scientifically established criteria. As I said earlier, there is still no universally accepted system of evaluation so that different methods are used in each of the different Member States.

As a result of that method's being required coupled with the fact that its application in an undertaking is voluntary or dependent on the employer's consent, the aim of Article 119, namely the total abolition of wage discrimination, for work of equal value too, is not achieved. In that situation it is conceivable, particularly because of the consent required from the employer, that different wages continue to be paid for work of (supposedly) equal value. Without his employer's consent an employee cannot himself take steps to have the value of different jobs determined, a situation which was confirmed at the hearing by Counsel for the United Kingdom.

The Netherlands legislation, for instance, also requires that a system of evaluating jobs should first be used for evaluating work. In the absence of such a system, however, the Netherlands legislation states that work must be evaluated "fairly". I do not believe that any useful purpose is served by examining what is "fair". It is important to note, however, that the Netherlands legislation makes provision for the situation in which there is no system of evaluating work, which is not the case with the United Kingdom legislation.

It is not for the Court to indicate how the United Kingdom should adapt its legislation in order to ensure that the principle of equal pay for work of equal value is actually applied in every case. It is important to note that in this matter the Member States must moreover take account of their "national circumstances and legal systems" as stated in Article 6 of the directive. It is precisely in this area that the practice of Member States differs greatly owing to the greater or lesser amount of freedom enjoyed by the two sides of industry. Be that as it may, in my opinion the result, which the Member States must ensure is achieved pursuant to Article 119 and the directive and which I again summarize below, is clear. They are required to take the measures necessary to achieve that result.

* * *

I. FACTS AND WRITTEN PROCEDURE

(a) The Relevant Community Law

Article 119, first paragraph, of the EEC Treaty provides as follows:

Each Member State shall during the first stage ensure and subsequently maintain the application of the principle that men and women should receive equal pay for equal work.

Article 1 of Directive No. 75/117 provides as follows:

The principle of equal pay for men and women outlined in Article 119 of the Treaty, hereinafter called "principle of equal pay" means, for the same work or for work to which equal value is attributed, the elimination of all discrimination on grounds of sex with regard to all aspects and conditions of remuneration.

In particular, where a job classification system is used for determining pay, it must be based on some criteria for both men and women and so drawn up as to exclude any discrimination on grounds of sex.

(b) The Relevant National Legislation

In the United Kingdom, the Equal Pay Act 1970, as amended by the Sex Discrimination Act 1975, is the legislation that was adopted in the field governed by Directive No. 75/117.

Section 1(1) of the Act states the principle that any contract under which a woman is employed at an establishment in Great Britain is to be deemed to include a clause requiring equal pay for men and women. Paragraph (2) of that section distinguishes between the case of a woman employed on like work with a man in the same employment and that of a woman employed on work "rated as equivalent" with that of a man in the same employment. Section 1(4) defines "like work" as work which is of "the same" or "a broadly similar" nature when the differences, if any, between the work done by the woman and that done by the man are not of practical importance in relation to the terms and conditions of employment.

As to work which is rated as equivalent, paragraph (5) provides that

A woman is to be regarded as employed on work rated as equivalent with that of any men if, but only if, her job and their job have been given an equal value, in terms of the demand made on a worker under various headings (for instance, effort, skill, decision), on a study undertaken with a view to evaluating in those terms the jobs to be done by all or any of the employees in an undertaking or group of undertakings. * * *

(c) Procedure

On April 3, 1979, the Commission sent the United Kingdom Government a letter initiating the procedure provided for in Article 169, first paragraph, of the EEC Treaty. Since the Commission was not satisfied with the observations submitted on June 19, 1979, by the government in question it delivered to the United Kingdom on May 19, 1980, a reasoned opinion, dated May 8, 1980, in accordance with the above-mentioned provision. After stating that in its opinion Article 1 of Directive No. 75/117 had been incorrectly applied in the United Kingdom legislation, the Commission invited the United Kingdom to adopt, within a period of two months, the measures needed to comply with the reasoned opinion.

In reply to the reasoned opinion, the United Kingdom stated in a letter dated November 3, 1980, that it considered the United Kingdom legislation to be wholly in conformity with the relevant Community provisions and that in the circumstances no measures whatsoever were necessary in order to comply with Article 119 of the Treaty and with Directive No. 75/117.

Considering that the United Kingdom had failed to comply with the reasoned opinion, the Commission decided to make this application, which was received at the Court Registry on March 18, 1981.

Upon hearing the report of the Reporting Judge and the views of the Advocate General, the Court of Justice decided to open the oral procedure without any preparatory inquiry. However, it requested the Commission to reply in writing before January 31, 1982, to the following questions:

1. How have the Member States complied with the obligation resulting from Directive No. 75/117 in respect of work to which equal value is attributed? What are the national provisions adopted? Do those provisions, in the Commission's view, constitute a correct application of the directive?

2. Has the Commission any information on the actual application of the directive, in particular by the courts?

3. Could the Commission give the Court details of the other methods, apart from the introduction of the system of compulsory evaluation to which it refers in point 14 of its reply, making it possible to ascertain or determine whether work is of equal value?

The Commission's replies to the questions are dealt with at the end of this report.

* * *

II. CONCLUSIONS OF THE PARTIES

The *Commission* asks that the Court:

1. Declare that, by failing to adopt the laws, regulations or administrative provisions needed to comply with Council Directive No. 75/117/EEC, of February 10, 1975, on the approximation of the laws of the Member States relating to the application of the principle of equal pay for men and women, as regards work to which equal value is attributed, the United Kingdom has failed to fulfill its obligations under that directive;

* * *

IV. WRITTEN REPLIES SUBMITTED BY THE COMMISSION IN RESPONSE TO THE QUESTIONS ASKED BY THE COURT

1. Reply to the First Question

As to the principal national provisions which have been adopted by the various Member States on the subject, the Commission refers in the main to the Commission Report to the Council of January 16, 1979, on the Application of the Principle of Equal Pay for Men and Women of February 12, 1978. However, it adds the following points:

Belgium: In the Belgian Loi de Réorientation [Reorientation Law] of August 4, 1978 (Moniteur Belge, August 17, 1978, pages 8, 411), Title V of which concerns equal treatment for men and women, Article 128 specifies that working conditions means the provisions and practices relating in particular "to remuneration and its protection."

Denmark: There is no provision concerning work of equal value; the Commission therefore sent a formal letter of complaint to Denmark on March 30, 1979. In its reply of June 22, 1979, that country argued that the expression "samme arbejde" used in its legislation had a much broader significance than the words "same work" and, in fact, extended to "work of equal value."

Nevertheless, the Commission decided that a reasoned opinion should be issued but delayed its transmission pending a report by a legal expert as to whether there was a substantive or purely linguistic problem. Since, notwithstanding the report, a number of points remained unclear, the Commission decided on December 10, 1980, to leave this matter "in cold storage."

Federal Republic of Germany: A law concerning, *inter alia,* equal treatment for men and women at work was adopted on August 13, 1980 (Bundesgesetzblatt 1980, I, pages 1308 et seq.). Article 1 of that law incorporated into the German Civil Code the principle of equal pay for men and women in respect of equal work or work of equal value.

Greece: Article 22 of the 1975 Constitution states that "all workers, irrespective of sex or other discriminations, shall be entitled to equal pay for work of equal value." A law implementing the directives on equal treatment is being prepared.

The Commission concludes that eight of the Member States have correctly applied the principle of equal pay for work of equal value. In none of those countries is the operation of the principle as restricted as in the United Kingdom. As regards Denmark, the position remains under constant review by the Commission in order to establish whether the directive is being correctly applied there.

2. *Reply to the Second Question*

As to the actual application of the directive by the national courts, the Commission refers once again to its report for the main points. It adds that the cases before the courts, which are in any case relatively few in number, are based not on the directive itself but on the national implementing legislation.

3. *Reply to the Third Question*

In the first place, the Commission observes that "in order to be able to determine whether two (different) jobs have an equal value, they must be compared one with the other or evaluated against a common standard." That being so, the Member States have a duty to set up a system whereby employees are able to obtain, if necessary by recourse to the courts, equal pay for work of equal value. This means that it is not necessary to oblige all employers to adopt job evaluation schemes, but that at the same time enabling employers to choose whether or not to introduce such schemes without making any provision for equal pay in respect of jobs of equal value where they do not, is inadequate.

Hence, in many cases work of equal value will be compared within the framework of a collective agreement, or under a job evaluation scheme, or even more informally, without any detailed study having been undertaken. The State may also set up a system of official surveillance or less formal conciliation.

What is essential, in the view of the Commission, is that, in the final count, individuals should have the possibility of succeeding in the argument that the two jobs in question are of equal value.

The Commission then reviews the different systems adopted by the Member States, relying for the most part on its report. In Belgium, France, Italy and Luxembourg, as also in the Federal Republic of Germany, many problems are resolved by works inspectorates, and where a question falls to be resolved by the courts, the latter are not necessarily bound by the results of job evaluation schemes. In The Netherlands the question of whether work is of equal value is assessed on the basis of a reliable system of job evaluation. Under the Irish legislation—which the Commission believes to be an example of how the United Kingdom could comply with its obligations under Directive No. 75/117—any dispute on the subject of equal pay may be referred to one of the three Equality Officers who, after investigating the matter, will issue a recommendation. Since such recommendations are not legally binding, it is ultimately for the courts to decide the matters referred to them.

The Commission concludes from the foregoing that, on a technical level, there are several possible ways in which the Equal Pay Act might be amended in order to make it comply with Community law. In this respect it emphasizes that in the United Kingdom itself the Equal Opportunities Commission and the Trades Union Congress have drafted proposals along those lines. As to which system, or combination of systems, would be preferable, the Commission refers the Court of Justice to its report * * *.

OPINION

In an application lodged at the Court Registry on March 18, 1981, the Commission of the European Communities brought an action pursuant to Article 169 of the EEC Treaty [Article 258, TFEU] for a declaration that the United Kingdom had failed to fulfill its obligations under the Treaty by failing to adopt the laws, regulations or administrative provisions needed to comply with Council Directive No. 75/117/EEC of February 10, 1975, on the approximation of the laws of the Member States relating to the application of the principle of equal pay for men and women (Official Journal No. L 45, page 19), as regards the elimination of discrimination for work to which equal value is attributed.

* * *

The reference to "work to which equal value is attributed" is used in the United Kingdom in the Equal Pay Act 1970, as amended by the Sex Discrimination Act 1975. Section 1(5) of the Act provides:

A woman is to be regarded as employed on work rated as equivalent with that of any men if, but only if, her job and their job have been given an equal value, in terms of the demand made on the worker under various headings (for instance, effort, skill, decision), on a study undertaken with a view to evaluating in those terms the jobs to be done by all or any of the employees in an undertaking or group of undertakings, or would have been given an equal value but for the evaluation being made on a system setting different values for men and women on the same demand under any heading.

Comparison of those provisions reveals that the job classification system is, under the directive, merely one of several methods for determining pay for work to which equal value is attributed, whereas under the provision in the Equal Pay Act quoted above the introduction of such a system is the sole method of achieving such a result.

It is also noteworthy that, as the United Kingdom concedes, British legislation does not permit the introduction of a job classification system without the employer's consent. Workers in the United Kingdom are therefore unable to have their work rated as being of equal value with comparable work if their employer refuses to introduce a classification system.

The United Kingdom attempts to justify this state of affairs by pointing out that Article 1 of the directive says nothing about the right of an employee to insist on having pay determined by a job classification system. On that basis, it concludes that the worker may not insist on a comparative evaluation of different work by the job classification method, the introduction of which is at the employer's discretion.

The United Kingdom's interpretation amounts to a denial of the very existence of a right to equal pay for work of equal value where no classification has been made. Such a position is not consonant with the general scheme and provisions of Directive No. 75/117. The recitals in the preamble to that directive indicate that its essential purpose is to implement the principle that men and women should receive equal pay contained in Article 119 of the Treaty and that it is primarily the responsibility of the Member States to ensure the application of this principle by means of appropriate laws, regulations and administrative provisions in such a way that all employees in the Community can be protected in these matters.

To achieve that end, the principle is defined in the first paragraph of Article 1 so as to include under the term "the same work" the case of "work to which equal value is attributed," and the second paragraph emphasizes merely that where a job classification system is used for determining pay it is necessary to ensure that it is based on the same criteria for both men and women and so drawn up as to exclude any discrimination on grounds of sex.

It follows that where there is disagreement as to the application of that concept a worker must be entitled to claim before an appropriate authority that his work has the same value as other work and, if this is found to be the case, to have his rights under the Treaty and the directive acknowledged by a binding decision. Any method that excludes this option prevents the aims of the directive from being achieved.

This is borne out by the terms of Article 6 of the directive, which provides that the Member States are, in accordance with their national circumstances and legal systems, to take the measures necessary to ensure that the principle of equal pay is applied. They are to see that effective means are available to take care that this principle is observed.

In this instance, however, the United Kingdom has not adopted the necessary measures and there is at present no means whereby a worker who considers that his post is of equal value to another may pursue his claims if the employer refuses to introduce a job classification system.

The United Kingdom has emphasized (particularly in its letter to the Commission dated June 19, 1979) the practical difficulties that would stand in the way of implementing the concept of work to which equal value has been attributed if the use of a system laid down by consensus were abandoned. The United Kingdom believes that the criterion of work of equal value is too abstract to be applied by the courts.

The Court of Justice cannot endorse that view. The implementation of the directive implies that the assessment of the "equal value" to be "attributed" to particular work may be effected notwithstanding the employer's wishes, if necessary in the context of adversary proceedings. The Member States must endow an authority with the requisite jurisdiction to decide whether work has the same value as other work, after obtaining such information as may be required.

Accordingly, by failing to introduce into its national legal system in implementation of the provisions of Council Directive No. 75/117/EEC of February 10, 1975, such measures as are necessary to enable all employees who consider themselves wronged by a failure to apply the principle of equal pay for men and women for work to which equal value is attributed and for which no system of job classification exists to obtain recognition of such equivalence, the United Kingdom has failed to fulfill its obligations under the Treaty.

L. NEVILLE BROWN AND FRANCIS G. JACOBS, THE COURT OF JUSTICE OF THE EUROPEAN COMMUNITIES

233 (2d ed. 1983).*

[T]he Court's decisions constitute a source of Community [Union] law in a number of ways. First, in relation to the Treaties and legislation made thereunder, decisions of the Court provide authoritative interpretations, explaining and developing the texts by reference to concrete cases: as such they supply an essential gloss upon the *corpus* of Community *lex scripta*,

---

* © L. Neville Brown and Francis G. Jacobs. Reprinted with permission.

which must always be read in the light of the Court's rulings, much as the English statute book (or the French Civil Code) is incomplete unless annotated with references to the relevant case-law. The Court of Justice has evolved its own style of interpretation * * *.

Secondly, the Treaties refer to the general principles of law common to the Member States as a source of Community law. The elucidation of these principles is an important function of the Court and amounts * * * to a creative act of judicial legislation. For whatever the fiction, the legal reality is that the Court largely invents, and does not merely declare, these general principles. Inevitably, a common lawyer will be reminded of the Blackstonian theory of the King's judges declaring the immemorial customs of the realm as the common law of England.

Thirdly, in fulfilling its two previous functions, the Court has had to come to terms with the principle of *stare decisis*. Like any court, the Court of Justice seeks to be consistent, and to the extent that consistency prevails over the competing pressure to adjust Community law to ever-changing circumstances, the Court's decisions are "precedents" in the English sense—or (better) in the American sense, being at most persuasive and never binding upon the Court for the future.

* * *

Undoubtedly, the great advantage of the single judgment is to enhance its authority. Whatever the hidden reservations or concealed dissents, the judgment moves, syllogistically, to its logical conclusion, to which the appearance of singlemindedness then attaches greater legal certainty. * * * [T]he need to prolong deliberation to secure, if at all possible, a collegiate judgment without recourse to a vote helps to produce an agreement (or compromise) which is truly *communautaire,* that is, one in which the judges, with their differing viewpoints, bring forward and blend together in the eventual judgment various elements from all the national legal systems. In this way, as Professor Schermers points out, the inability openly to dissent "aids the amalgamation of rules from all the national legal orders and their assimilation into Community law" (*Judicial Protection in the European Communities,* 1976, 368).

* * *

In addition, the single judgment is seen as a means of strengthening judicial independence. The twin principles—of secrecy of deliberation and singleness of judgment—provide together an effective shield for the individual judge against pressure from his Government or from public opinion in his own country.

* * *

The methods of interpretation employed by the Court have added importance for British lawyers since they constitute the "European way" which Lord Denning recognised the courts of England (and Scotland) should follow when called upon themselves to interpret Community law. In *Bulmer v. Bollinger* [1974] Ch. 401, at p. 425 Lord Denning declared:

> The (EEC) treaty is quite unlike any of the enactments to which we have become accustomed * * * It lays down general principles. It expresses its aims and purposes. All in sentences of moderate length and commendable style. But it lacks precision. It uses words and phrases without defining what they mean. An English lawyer would look for an interpretation clause, but he would look in vain. There is none. All the way through the treaty there are gaps and lacunae. These have to be filled in by the judges, or by regulations or directives. It is the European way * * * Seeing these differences, what are the English courts to do when they are faced with a problem of interpretation? They must follow the European pattern. No longer must they argue about the precise grammatical sense. They must look to the purpose and intent * * * They must divine the spirit of the treaty and gain inspiration from it. If they find a gap, they must fill it as best they can * * * These are the principles, as I understand it, on which the European Court acts.

* * *

LORD MacKENZIE STUART, THE COURT OF JUSTICE OF THE EUROPEAN COMMUNITIES: THE SCOPE OF ITS JURISDICTION AND THE EVOLUTION OF ITS CASE LAW UNDER THE EEC TREATY

3 Northwestern J.Int'l Law & Bus. 415 (1981).*

In order to ensure uniformity in the interpretation and application of Community law, Article 177 [now Article 267, TFEU] provides that the Court of Justice shall have jurisdiction to give preliminary rulings concerning the interpretation of the Treaty and the validity and interpretation of "acts" (which effectively means regulations, decisions and directives) of the Community institutions. Article 177, thus, constitutes a vehicle for judicial cooperation between the Court of Justice and the national courts and tribunals for the purpose of ensuring, as far as possible, the uniform interpretation of Community law throughout the ten Member States.

The importance of Article 177 lies not only in the fact that it constitutes a mechanism for achieving the uniform interpretation of Community law within the limits of judicial cooperation, but also in the fact that the Court of Justice frequently decides points of law arising in disputes between private persons and between private persons and national authorities charged with the implementation of Community regulations. * * * It is frequently open to the private person to contest before his

* Reprinted by special permission of the Northwestern Journal of International Law and Business, © by Northwestern University School of Law, Vol. 3, No. 2.

national court the validity of a Community regulation and to ask that court to refer the question of validity to the Court of Justice under Article 177. If the Court rules that the regulation in question is not valid, the plaintiff will have achieved indirectly what he probably could not have achieved by means of a direct action for annulment under Article 173 [now Article 263, TFEU] against the institution that issued the regulation.

* * *

Furthermore, the Court, as a result of cases brought before it under Article 177 has been able to expressly formulate two fundamental principles of Community law which have given a powerful impulse towards "European integration." First, the Court has developed the doctrine that provisions of the Treaty and of acts by the Community institutions can have *direct effect,* that is to say, they can create rights for private persons which that person can invoke before their national courts and which those courts are bound to protect. Secondly, the Court developed a doctrine of the primacy of Community law over national law. In other words, a provision of Community law will prevail over a conflicting provision in the national law of the Member States.

* * *

The second doctrine developed by the Court involves rare cases in which direct conflicts arise between a provision of national law and a provision of Community law and gives rise to an issue in litigation before national courts. As Judge Pescatore stated:

> as regards the *solution of such conflicts,* from the point of view of Community law the position is simple and clear-cut: Community law cannot fulfill its function if it is incapable of prevailing purely and simply, in case of conflict, over provisions of national law. In other words, for Community law primacy over national law is a genuinely "existential" requirement, and for this reason absolute and imperative, on which it cannot yield on pain of ceasing to be itself.

The doctrine that Community law prevails over conflicting national law was clearly expressed in the Court's judgment in *Costa v. ENEL.*[39] This reference for a preliminary ruling arose out of a dispute before a Milan court on the compatibility of an Italian law which nationalized the production and distribution of electrical energy, with certain provisions of the Treaty. The Italian government intervened in the proceedings before the Court of Justice and argued that the reference was inadmissible because the sole function of the national judge was to apply domestic law. In reply to this objection, the Court defined the primacy of Community law in terms which have become classic. It said *inter alia:*

> * * * The executive force of Community law cannot vary from one State to another in deference to subsequent domestic laws, without jeopardizing the attainment of the objectives of the Treaty * * *.

---

39. [1964] E.Comm.Ct.J.Rep. 585 [1964] Comm.Mkt.L.R. 425 (reference for preliminary ruling).

The obligations undertaken under the Treaty establishing the Community would not be unconditional, but merely contingent, if they could be called in question by subsequent legislative acts of the signatories * * *.

* * * the law stemming from the Treaty, an independent source of law, could not, because of its special and original nature, be overridden by domestic legal provisions, however framed, without being deprived of its character as Community law and without the legal basis of the Community itself being called into question.

The transfer by the States from their domestic legal system to the Community legal system of the rights and obligations arising under the Treaty carries with it a permanent limitation of their sovereign rights, against which a subsequent unilateral act incompatible with the concept of the Community cannot prevail. Consequently, Article 177 is to be applied regardless of any domestic law, whenever questions relating to the interpretation of the Treaty arise.

Subsequent Court decisions demonstrate that the doctrines of *direct effect* and of the primacy of Community law over a conflicting provision of national law constitute the keystones of the Court's "integrationalist" jurisprudence. The re-affirmation of these doctrines often occurs in the context of preliminary rulings by the Court on questions referred to it by national courts under Article 177.

C.I.L.F.I.T. SRL v. MINISTRO DELLA SANITA

European Court of Justice, 1982.
1982 Eur.Comm.Rep. 3415.

OPINION

In an order of March 27, 1981, which was received at the Court of Justice on October 31, 1981, the Corte Suprema di Cassazione [Supreme Court of Cassation] referred to the Court of Justice for a preliminary ruling pursuant to Article 177 [now Article 267, TFEU] of the EEC Treaty a question on the interpretation of the third paragraph of Article 177 of the EEC Treaty.

That question was raised in connection with a dispute between wool importers and the Italian Ministry of Health concerning the payment of a fixed health inspection levy in respect of wool imported from outside the Community. The firms concerned relied on Regulation (EEC) No. 827/68 of June 28, 1968, on the common organization of the market in certain products listed in Annex II to the Treaty (Official Journal, English Special Edition 1968 (I), page 209). Article 2(2) of that regulation prohibits the Member States from levying any charge having an effect equivalent to a customs duty on imported "animal products," not specified or included elsewhere, classified under heading 05.15 of the Common Customs Tariff. Against that argument the Ministry of Health contended that wool is not included in Annex II to the Treaty and is therefore not subject to a common organization of agricultural markets.

The Ministry of Health infers from those circumstances that the answer to the question concerning the interpretation of the measure adopted by the Community institutions is so obvious as to rule out the possibility of there being any interpretative doubt and thus obviates the need to refer the matter to the Court of Justice for a preliminary ruling. However, the companies concerned maintain that since a question concerning the interpretation of a regulation has been raised before the Corte Suprema di Cassazione, against whose decisions there is no judicial remedy under national law, that court cannot, according to the terms of the third paragraph of Article 177, escape the obligation to bring the matter before the Court of Justice.

Faced with those conflicting arguments, the Corte Suprema di Cassazione referred to the Court the following question for a preliminary ruling:

> Does the third paragraph of Article 177 of the EEC Treaty, which provides that where any question of the same kind as those listed in the first paragraph of that article is raised in a case pending before a national court or tribunal against whose decisions there is no judicial remedy under national law that court or tribunal must bring the matter before the Court of Justice, lay down an obligation so to submit the case which precludes the national court from determining whether the question raised is justified, or does it, and if so within what limits, make that obligation conditional on the prior finding of a reasonable interpretative doubt?

* * *

The question submitted by the Corte Suprema di Cassazione seeks to ascertain whether, in certain circumstances, the obligation laid down in the third paragraph of Article 177 might nonetheless be subject to certain restrictions.

It must be remembered in this connection that in its judgment of March 27, 1963, in Joined Cases Nos. 28 to 30/62 (Da Costa v. Nederlandse Belastingadministratie [1963] E.C.R. 31 [¶ 8010]), the Court ruled that "Although the third paragraph of Article 177 unreservedly requires the courts or tribunals of a Member State against whose decisions there is no judicial remedy under national law * * * to refer to the Court every question of interpretation raised before them, the authority of an interpretation under Article 177 already given by the Court may deprive the obligation of its purpose and thus empty it of its substance. Such is the case especially when the question raised is materially identical to a question that has already been the subject of a preliminary ruling in a similar case."

The same effect, as regards the limits set to the obligation laid down in the third paragraph of Article 177, may be produced where previous decisions of the Court of Justice have already dealt with the point of law in question, irrespective of the nature of the proceedings that led to those decisions, even though the questions at issue are not strictly identical.

However, it must not be forgotten that in all such circumstances the national courts and tribunals, including those referred to in the third paragraph of Article 177, remain entirely at liberty to bring a matter before the Court of Justice if they consider it appropriate to do so.

* * *

Finally, the correct application of Community law may be so obvious as to leave no scope for any reasonable doubt as to the manner in which the question raised is to be resolved. Before it comes to the conclusion that such is the case, the national court or tribunal must be convinced that the matter is equally obvious to the courts of the other Member States and to the Court of Justice. Only if those conditions are satisfied may the national court or tribunal refrain from submitting the question to the Court of Justice and take upon itself the responsibility for resolving it.

However, the existence of such a possibility must be assessed on the basis of the characteristic features of Community law and the particular difficulties to which its interpretation gives rise.

To begin with, it must be borne in mind that Community legislation is drafted in several languages and that the different language versions are all equally authentic. An interpretation of a provision of Community law thus involves a comparison of the different language versions.

It must also be borne in mind, even where the different language versions are entirely in accord with one another, that Community law uses terminology which is peculiar to it. Furthermore, it must be emphasized that legal concepts do not necessarily have the same meaning in Community law and in the law of the various Member States.

Finally, every provision of Community law must be placed in its context and interpreted in light of the provisions of Community law as a whole, regard being had to the objectives thereof and to its state of evolution at the date on which the provision in question is to be applied.

In light of all those considerations, the answer to the question submitted by the Corte Suprema di Cassazione must be that the third paragraph of Article 177 of the EEC Treaty is to be interpreted as meaning that a court or tribunal against whose decisions there is no judicial remedy under national law is required, where a question of Community law is raised before it, to comply with its obligation to bring the matter before the Court of Justice, unless it has established that the question raised is irrelevant or that the Community provision in question has already been interpreted by the Court of Justice or that the correct application of Community law is so obvious as to leave no scope for any reasonable doubt. The existence of such a possibility must be assessed in light of the specific characteristics of Community law, the particular difficulties to which its interpretation gives rise, and the risk of divergences in judicial decisions within the Community.

QUESTIONS AND COMMENTS

1. Why did the Commission bring suit against the United Kingdom concerning its equal pay law? Were you satisfied with the Commission's answers to the court's questions regarding Directive 75/117?

What must the United Kingdom do to bring its law into conformity with the decision of the Court of Justice? Suppose it does nothing. What result?

2. How should a United States investor be counseled on equal pay law? Does it require payment according to "comparable worth"?

3. What is the function of the Advocate General before the European Court of Justice? Is he or she as important as a judge?

4. Read Article 263, TFEU. Is the power of the Court of Justice to review the legality of the acts of the Council or Commission unlimited?

The grounds for Article 263 actions are principally derived from French administrative law, which must always be consulted to obtain a proper understanding of their meaning. For example, an action under French administrative law for "détournement de pouvoir" is relatively narrow compared to British actions for "misuse of powers" (the official English translation) or "abuse of powers" under United States law.

5. There are over 20 working EU languages. Which would you use to determine the authoritative text of the TFEU? Of a directive or regulation? Of a European Court of Justice opinion?

6. How does Article 267 serve as a lynchpin between the European Court and national legal systems? When are Article 267 references of European law issues from national courts and tribunals to the Court of Justice mandatory? Discretionary?

7. The Court's decision in *C.I.L.F.I.T.* reflects the French administrative law doctrine of "acte clair." What does that mean? Does the Court consider and decide the merits of national cases which raise issues of law referenced under Article 267?

8. Assume that your client wishes to challenge the legality of a national rule of law under the Treaty or a secondary source of law. How and when might this be done? See Articles 263 and 267, TFEU.

9. Suppose that regional law and a national law are in clear conflict. Does the Treaty provide an answer to the question of which will prevail? Consider the *Costa* case discussed in the readings by Lord MacKenzie Stuart, a former judge on the European Court of Justice. Should it matter whether the conflicting national law is of constitutional origin?

10. Brown and Jacobs state that the European Court of Justice has functioned as a "law-maker." Do you agree? How may the Court ascertain "general principles" of law?

Most of the judges of the Court have been trained in the civil law tradition. What is the significance of this training on the Court's treatment of precedent and the drafting of opinions?

11. The 1987 Single European Act authorized the creation of the Court of First Instance (First Appeals) attached to the European Court. The TFEU of 2009 renamed the CFI the General Court. It most commonly deals with competition law and international trade remedy cases, along with torts, EU trademarks, contracts and employment disputes. Appeals from the General Court can be made to the European Court of Justice on grounds of lack of competence, infringement of regional law and breach of procedure.

INDEX

References are to Chapter, Section and Problem Numbers

†